GW01143790

This is the 25th anniversary edition of **The World of Professional Golf.** We began publishing in the heyday of Arnold Palmer, Gary Player, and Jack Nicklaus, and have since chronicled the entire careers of present-day stars such as Greg Norman.

Introduction

Those four names - Palmer, Player, Nicklaus and Norman - linked in golf history will soon be brought together at Desaru International Resorts, now under construction in Malaysia.

Four championship golf courses are being designed, one by each of those greats. This is the first time that all four will have been involved on a single resort project, and it may never happen again. We at International Management Group are very excited about managing all the sports facilities at Desaru.

Desaru is a truly visionary undertaking in many respects, and I congratulate the Kajima Corporation, Japan, K & S International Inc., U.S.A., Inver Venture, Malaysia, T Thangathurai and Bill Richards, in particular, on their endeavours and also offer my thanks for their support of this golf annual.

Mark H. McCormack

*D*esaru *I*nternational *R*esort
Johor, Malaysia

1994 will witness the opening of a unique resort situated on the south east coast of Malaysia, in the State of Johor. A resort which combines more world-class sports and leisure facilities than any other single destination resort in the world. To be known as Desaru International Resort, it will enjoy 17 kilometres of some of the South China Seas' most beautiful coastline.

Preservation and enhancement of the area's rich environment is key to the Desaru philosophy. Top priority is being given to minimising the disruption to the local ecosystem and to the maintenance of environmental care and conservation.

Desaru is less than an hour's journey by high speed catamarans from Singapore's Changi International Airport. It will offer a choice of nine hotels, located in prime positions around 4,300 acres of beachside, wilderness and rich tropical rainforest. Guests will be able to experience and enjoy the diversity of Malay, Chinese, Indian, Moorish, Portuguese, Mediterranean and British architectural styles and settings.

Sports enthusiasts will be able to enjoy an unparalleled variety of leisure pursuits. These will range from four golf courses designed by four of the world's leading professional golfers to top-class centres for tennis, yachting and equestrian pursuits designed by Nick Bollettieri, John Bertrand and Mark Phillips respectively.

With these outstanding, world-class sporting facilities, coupled with its care for the environment, Desaru is set to become not only the world's first New Age resort but also an important centre for local and international sporting events. At the same time, Desaru will maintain its commitment to cater for everyone, from the family who want a beach site for a picnic to international visitors looking for world-class golfing and six-star luxury.

Mr T. Thangathurai
Chairman & Chief Executive Officer
Desaru International Resorts Sdn Bhd

PROJECT LOCATION MAP

N

- KOTA TINGGI
- JOHOR BAHRU
- SINGAPORE
- TG. RELUNGKOR
- DESARU INTERNATIONAL RESORT

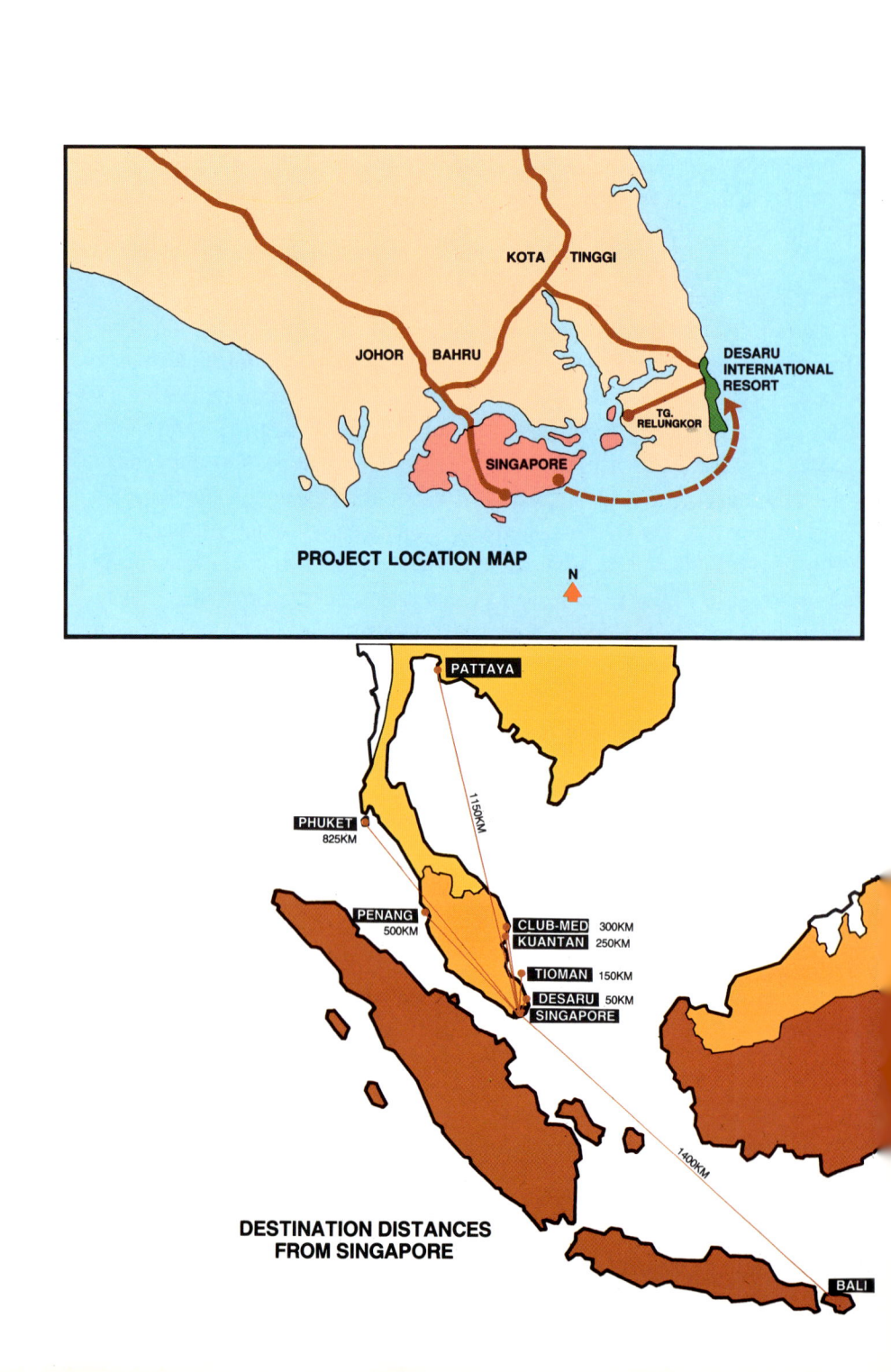

DESTINATION DISTANCES FROM SINGAPORE

- PATTAYA — 1150KM
- PHUKET — 825KM
- PENANG — 500KM
- CLUB-MED — 300KM
- KUANTAN — 250KM
- TIOMAN — 150KM
- DESARU — 50KM
- SINGAPORE
- BALI — 1400KM

❝ *I am tremendously excited about being involved with this outstanding project. For the first time ever, golfers will be given the chance to play on four signature golf courses, all located at the one resort. It is also my aim that golfers visiting Desaru will have the world's finest Arnold Palmer Golf Academy which will offer outstanding facilities to enable golfers of all levels to improve their games.* **❞**

Arnold Palmer

❝ *Being a part of the world's first single destination, New Age resort, offering four signature golf courses, is extremely exciting. I believe Desaru will offer golfers a once-in-a-lifetime opportunity to experience the very best of golf in a spectacular tropical resort setting. I look forward to designing a unique course at Desaru that will provide a challenging and enjoyable game to golfers from around the world.* ❞

Gary Player

> *I am delighted to be designing one of the four 18-hole signature golf courses at Desaru International Resorts. I believe Desaru should become one of the foremost golfing venues in the Asia Pacific region and it has the commitment to provide top class facilities for both the competitive and daily resort players.*

Jack Nicklaus

❝ *Desaru's jungle golf course will enjoy a spectacular setting in the lush tropical rainforest of South East Malaysia. The design of my course will follow Desaru's philosophy of preserving and enhancing the resort's rich environment. I feel honoured and excited about this opportunity to be involved in the development of the world's most outstanding golfing venue.* ❞

SCORECARD FROM BACK TEES

HOLE	PAR	LENGTH (YDS)	HOLE	PAR	LENGTH (YDS)
1	5	549	10	4	428
2	4	390	11	3	149
3	4	309	12	4	416
4	3	145	13	5	533
5	4	342	14	4	390
6	5	507	15	4	344
7	3	168	16	3	197
8	4	402	17	4	384
9	4	400	18	5	536
TOTAL	36	3462	TOTAL	36	3387
			TOTAL	72	6849

Greg Norman

Marina

Desaru's marina area, a delightful Malaccan blend of Portuguese, Dutch and Mediterranean styles, will look out over an impressive 34 acre boat harbour. Guests will be able to enjoy the pleasant open air atmosphere of a lively waterfront village or take a leisurely stroll along the glorious marina promenades. For the more active, the John Bertrand world-class yachting club will offer unparalleled yachting and training facilities.

World-class conference facilities will be available at Desaru's five star conference hotel. Located in Desaru's largest luxury accommodation with 700 rooms and facilities for conference groups of up to 2500 guests. No other resort in the world can claim to offer such outstanding

Conference Hotel

services for the businessman, with the setting of a tropical paradise and the finest sporting and leisure facilities for relaxation.

Golf Club House

After an enjoyable round of golf, players will be able to relax in the luxury and comfort of this stylish Ultra Country Club, with its glorious British Colonial setting overlooking the Palmer and Nicklaus Golf Courses. The Club's first class facilities will include two restaurants, a health club and a professional golf shop and guests will have the unique opportunity of improving their game at the finest golf academy in the world, designed by Arnold Palmer.

Desaru

PRESENTS

Mark H. McCormack's The World of Professional Golf 1991

Photographs by Lawrence Levy

An IMG PUBLISHING Book

An IMG PUBLISHING Book

All rights reserved
First published 1991
© International Merchandising Corp. 1991

Designed and produced by Davis Design

ISBN 1-878843-01-X

Printed and bound in the United States of America.

Contents

1	The Sony Ranking	1
2	The Year In Retrospect	12
3	The Masters Tournament	35
4	The U.S. Open	55
5	The British Open	80
6	The PGA Championship	98
7	The Dunhill Cup	114
8	The World Match Play Championship	122
9	The U.S. Tour	133
10	The U.S. Senior Tour	175
11	The European Tour	207
12	The African Tours	246
13	The Australasian Tour	264
14	The Asia/Japan Tour	275
15	The Women's Tours	302

APPENDIXES

World Money List	336
The Sony Ranking	340
World's Winners of 1990	344
Multiple Winners of 1990	349
Career World Money List	350
World Senior Money List	351
LPGA Money List	352
The U.S. Tour	354
The U.S. Senior Tour	411
The European Tour	447
The African Tours	491
The Australasian Tour	504
The Asia/Japan Tour	514
The Women's Tours	553

1. The Sony Ranking

It could be said that the rivalry which has developed between Nick Faldo and Greg Norman is the first of the computer age in professional golf. In years past, we would just argue about who was the best: Byron Nelson, Ben Hogan or Sam Snead; Arnold Palmer, Jack Nicklaus or Gary Player. We may not argue any less these days, but we have had an authoritative reference source since the Sony Ranking was launched five years ago.

This weekly, computer-generated listing has no emotion, and is not stirred to make impulsive judgements, like so many of our golf writers. How often have you read—usually after a major championship or after a couple of victories within a short span—that Order O'Merit must be the best golfer in the world. Then O'Merit misses the 36-hole cut, U.S. Moneylist wins by six strokes, and suddenly Moneylist is being proclaimed as No. 1.

So there was an outcry in the press in 1990 when Faldo won the Masters, tied for third place in the U.S. Open, then won the British Open—and Norman was still No. 1 on the Sony Ranking. Faldo later took the top position for six weeks, but Norman finished the year with a narrow advantage.

The Sony Ranking was not saying that Norman was absolutely a better golfer than Faldo, but that there was very little between them, and they were definitely the two best golfers in the world. That is an accurate assessment, far too bland for most golf writers.

Golf must be viewed with a broader perspective than most of our games. Performances over a few weeks or months mean little, and even a year is insufficient time to evaluate a player.

This year, rookie Robert Gamez won two tournaments in the United States in the first three months. According to the newspapers, Gamez was a star; the Sony Ranking put him no higher than No. 48 in the world. We didn't read about Gamez again, because his best finish after that was 12th place. The Sony Ranking had to downgrade Gamez only slightly, to No. 53.

Also this year, Wayne Levi, who had won eight tournaments in the previous 13 years, won four events on the U.S. PGA Tour. He was No. 2 on the money list, and Player of the Year by most accounts. He advanced from No. 67 to only No. 20 on the Sony Ranking.

In the spring of 1986, the Sony Corporation announced the launch of this world ranking system for professional golf. The Sony Ranking is sanctioned by the Championship Committee of the Royal and Ancient Golf Club of St. Andrews, and is endorsed by the major professional tours. It is a specially developed computerized system to evaluate the relative performances of the world's leading players.

Some of the most respected people in golf worldwide bring their opinions to bear on the workings of the system. The Sony Ranking Advisory Committee meets at St. Andrews each October, and its recommendations are passed on to the R&A for approval. In addition to myself, the Sony Ranking Advisory Committee consists of:

Brenda Blumberg (advisor to South African PGA), Peter Dobereiner (Association of Golf Writers), Tim Finchem (U.S. PGA Tour), Taizo Kawata (Japan Golf Association), Graham Marsh (PGA Tour of Australia), Colin Phillips (Australian Golf Union), Richard Rahusen (European Golf Association), Pat Rielly (PGA of America), Ken Schofield (PGA European Tour), Frank Tatum (past president, United States Golf Association) and Peter Townsend (PGA European Tour Policy Board).

All tournaments from the world's golf tours are taken into account and points are awarded according to the quality of the players participating in each event. The number of points distributed to each player is dependent upon his finishing position. The four major championships and The Players Championship are weighted separately to reflect the greater prestige of the events and the strong fields participating.

The Sony Ranking is based on a three-year "rolling" period, weighted in favor of more recent results, and a divisor is used to take into account the number of tournaments played by each golfer. Points accumulated over the current 52-week period are multiplied by four, points earned over the previous 52-week period are doubled, and points from the first 52-week period are simply added to the total.

Each golfer is then ranked according to his point average, which is determined by dividing his total number of points by the number of starts he has made over the three-year period. A golfer must, however, play in at least 60 tournaments over the three-year period. Should he play in fewer, his divisor is still 60.

Fifty points are awarded to the winner of a major championship, then 30 points for second place, 20 for third, 15 for fourth, 12 for fifth and down to at least one point for every golfer competing in the final round. The winner of The Players Championship is awarded 40 points, then down to one point for 50th place. All other events have a points system based upon the number and rank of the top-100 ranked players participating in that event.

For this purpose, each top-100 ranked player is assigned ratings points, ranging from 65 for the No. 1 player to one for the No. 100 player, and the total of the points is then used to adjust the Sony Ranking points to reflect the quality of the field. The points vary from a maximum of 40 for the winner down to one point for 50th place in a high-quality tournament, to two points for the winner and one point to the player finishing fourth in a minor tournament.

Minimum points safeguards for winners of official tour events have been set at four points for events in Asia and Africa, six points for Australia, New Zealand and Japan, and eight points for Europe and the United States. In addition, the Volvo PGA Championship in Europe has a minimum points level of 32 for the winner.

The Sony Ranking is compiled and released to the press and to the governing bodies of professional golf each Monday from London.

The final Sony Ranking of 1990 is listed at the end of this chapter, along with a table of the system for determining the Sony Ranking points to be distributed at each event. A more detailed listing of the Sony Ranking may be found in the Appendixes of this annual.

For our discussion here, following were the Sony Ranking leaders:

Pos.	Player	Average	Pos.	Player	Average
1	Greg Norman	18.95	11	Fred Couples	9.69
2	Nick Faldo	18.54	12	Curtis Strange	9.58
3	Jose Maria Olazabal	17.22	13	Larry Mize	8.86
4	Ian Woosnam	15.47	14	Bernhard Langer	8.78
5	Payne Stewart	12.75	15	Chip Beck	8.58
6	Paul Azinger	11.63	16	Hale Irwin	8.36
7	Seve Ballesteros	10.15	17	Masashi Ozaki	8.16
8	Tom Kite	10.10	18	Tim Simpson	7.78
9	Mark McNulty	10.06	19	Ronan Rafferty	7.71
10	Mark Calcavecchia	9.96	20	Wayne Levi	7.69

If the Sony Ranking were based on just one year, or only on the major championships, Faldo would be the leader. He was dominant in the major events of 1990, and accumulated 848 ranking points in 22 starts for a 38.54 average. Norman was second with 788 points in 23 events for a 34.26 average, Ian Woosnam had 816 points in 25 starts for a 34.00 average, and Jose Maria Olazabal had the most points, 932 in 29 events for a 32.14 average.

The current year should be and is the most important in the calculations and, almost without question, those are the four best golfers in the world—Norman from Australia, Faldo from England, Olazabal from Spain and Woosnam from Wales—while Payne Stewart leads the United States in the tightly grouped lower portion of the top 10 players.

The most impressive gains within the top 10 on the Sony Ranking during 1990 were by Olazabal and Woosnam, who each won five tournaments, and Mark McNulty, who won twice and was second five times, including the British Open and Suntory World Match Play Championship. Olazabal, only 24 years old, advanced from No. 7 to No. 3, Woosnam climbed from No. 9 to No. 4, and McNulty went all the way from No. 31 to No. 9. Curtis Strange dropped from the top 10 in a winless year, falling from No. 4 to No. 12, and Seve Ballesteros, who had one European victory, slipped from No. 3 to No. 7, changing places with his countryman, Olazabal.

U.S. Open champion Hale Irwin, who also won the Buick Classic, jumped from No. 98 to No. 16, and PGA Championship winner Wayne Grady climbed from No. 42 to No. 27. As noted earlier, Levi moved up 47 places to No. 20 with his four victories. Gil Morgan climbed from No. 61 to No. 26, winning the Kemper Open and placing third in the PGA Championship. Mike Harwood, with three wins in Europe and Australia, went from No. 68 to No. 32.

As a rookie, Gamez started from the bottom of the computer list, No. 742, and finished as No. 53 with his two victories. Second-year player Billy Mayfair went from No. 231 to No. 67 with his two runner-up finishes and seven top-10 placings. John Morse, whose two victories included the Australian Open, advanced from No. 493 to No. 72. Others coming into the top 100 of the Sony Ranking included No. 57 John Bland, No. 59 Loren Roberts, No. 62 Steve Elkington, No. 65 John Huston, No. 74 Jim Gallagher, Jr., No. 81 Colin Montgomerie, No. 93 Billy Ray Brown, No. 95 Mark Brooks and No. 99 Brian Tennyson.

These and other changes on the Sony Ranking are detailed in charts which follow.

1990 Sony Ranking Review

Major Movements Within Top 50

Upward

Name	Net Points Gained	Position 1989	Position 1990
Jose Maria Olazabal	479	7	3
Mark McNulty	322	31	9
Ian Woosnam	259	9	4
Rodger Davis	249	43	23
Tim Simpson	202	35	18
Jodie Mudd	196	49	25
Wayne Grady	154	42	27
Peter Jacobsen	145	46	29

Downward

Name	Net Points Lost	Position 1989	Position 1990
Curtis Strange	415	4	12
Sandy Lyle	406	14	41
Seve Ballesteros	346	3	7
Mark McCumber	236	18	40
Tom Kite	205	6	8
David Frost	205	13	24
Ben Crenshaw	180	17	28
Larry Nelson	170	23	47

Major Movements Into Top 50

Name	Net Points Gained	Position 1989	Position 1990
Hale Irwin	423	98	16
Wayne Levi	303	67	20
Mike Harwood	269	68	32
Gil Morgan	205	61	26
Ian Baker-Finch	189	59	36
Eduardo Romero	155	53	35
David Feherty	149	79	46
Davis Love III	136	65	44
Ray Floyd	88	74	48
Sam Torrance	54	60	50

Major Movements Out of Top 50

Name	Net Points Lost	Position 1989	Position 1990
Dan Pohl	205	46	134
Isao Aoki	188	34	63
Blaine McCallister	155	45	84
Scott Simpson	132	36	54
Dan Pooley	128	39	75
Ken Green	125	33	56
Bill Glasson	109	50	85
Fuzzy Zoeller	52	47	64
Bob Tway	30	40	51
Naomichi Ozaki	16	48	58

Other Major Movements

Upward

Name	Net Points Gained	Position 1989	Position 1990
Robert Gamez	308	742T	53
Billy Mayfair	242	231	67
John Morse	188	493	72
Steve Elkington	188	142	62
Colin Montgomerie	175	162	81
Billy Ray Brown	170	226	93
John Huston	168	128	65
John Bland	163	113	57
Jim Gallagher, Jr.	160	158	74
Ryoken Kawagishi	154	432	116
Loren Roberts	154	105	59
Brian Tennyson	149	181	99
David Peoples	140	285	120
Mark Brooks	134	172	95
Stephen McAllister	134	387	129
Steven Richardson	132	742T	130

Downward

Name	Net Points Lost	Position 1989	Position 1990
Clarence Rose	132	96	221
Dave Rummells	119	73	125
Tateo Ozaki	111	83	154
Howard Clark	109	58	98
Hal Sutton	103	57	96
Jim Carter	102	100	185
Gordon Brand, Jr.	101	52	78
Jay Haas	90	63	93
Mark Wiebe	85	78	112
Robbie Black	85	126	260
Joey Sindelar	84	51	68
Gary Koch	82	103	181
Mike Sullivan	81	93	180
Denis Durnian	73	122	195
Hajime Meshiai	73	140	245
Ken Brown	72	164	318

Highest Points Earners in 1990

Name	1990 Sony Points	Sony Rank at end of 1990	Name	1990 Sony Points	Sony Rank at end of 1990
Jose Maria Olazabal	932	3	Fred Couples	496	11
Nick Faldo	848	2	Bernhard Langer	468	14
Ian Woosnam	816	4	Tim Simpson	468	18
Greg Norman	788	1	Mark Calcavecchia	456	10
Mark McNulty	624	9	Wayne Levi	452	20
Payne Stewart	612	5	Mike Harwood	440	32
Paul Azinger	580	6	Ronan Rafferty	428	19
Hale Irwin	512	16	Ian Baker-Finch	416	36
Larry Mize	504	13	Mark O'Meara	412	22
Rodger Davis	500	23	Jodie Mudd	404	25

In examining the question of Faldo versus Norman more closely, we find that they have gone head-to-head 32 times in the past three years. Norman has come out in front 19 times; Faldo, 11 times, and twice they were tied. Norman's advantage has come from ordinary tournaments, and Faldo has led only three of 21 meetings, with one tied. In the major championships, Faldo has led eight of 11 meetings, with one tied. Each has won three times when the other was in the field; all of Faldo's were in major events. In 1990, Norman led seven of 11 meetings and one was tied, but Faldo led in three major events, plus their tie in the PGA Championship. Following is the table:

Year	Norman Led	Faldo Led	Tied
1988	6	2	1
1989	6	6	0
1990	7	3	1
Total	19	11	2
Majors	2	8	1
Others	17	3	1

In that three-year period, Norman has won 14 tournaments (no major titles) to Faldo's 10 victories, including two Masters and one British Open. They each won three tournaments in 1990. Faldo has placed second 12 times to Norman's eight, and Norman has more top-five and top-10 finishes, and has missed the 36-hole cut fewer times. The summary of those finishes, with head-to-head matches in **bold** type:

GREG NORMAN

Year	Wins	Seconds	Top-5	Top-10	MC/WD/DQ	Total
1988	6	3	13	19	2	26
1989	5	3	13	13	1	25
1990	3	2	11	15	2	23
Total	14	8	37	47	5	74

NICK FALDO

Year	Wins	Seconds	Top-5	Top-10	MC/WD/DQ	Total
1988	2	8	14	17	2	28
1989	5	1	8	10	2	29
1990	3	3	11	12	2	22
Total	10	12	33	39	6	79

6 / THE SONY RANKING

1988

GREG NORMAN

Tournament	Finish
Palm Meadows Cup	1
Pebble Beach Pro-Am	3
Australian Masters	T-4
ESP Open	1
Australian TPC	1
Bay Hill Classic	T-11
Players Championship	T-11
Masters Tournament	T-5
Heritage Classic	1
Independent Ins. Agents	2
Las Vegas Invitational	T-23
Italian Open	1
Memorial Tournament	T-6
Westchester Classic	T-2
U.S. Open	WD
PGA Championship	T-9
World Series	12
Canadian Open	MC
Lancome Trophy	T-3
Jun Classic	T-7
New South Wales Open	1
Australian PGA	2
Nabisco Championship	30
Australian Open	T-6
Bicentennial Classic	T-6
Daikyo Open	T-8

NICK FALDO

Tournament	Finish
Sanctuary Cove	T-18
Tournament of Champions	T-3
Palm Meadows Cup	T-32
Australian Masters	T-4
Los Angeles Open	MC
Barcelona Open	T-2
Players Championship	MC
Greensboro Open	81
Masters Tournament	T-30
Heritage Classic	T-29
Epson Match Play	T-17
Spanish Open	2
Volvo PGA Championship	10
Dunhill Masters	T-2
Westchester Classic	T-54
U.S. Open	2
French Open	1
Monte Carlo Open	6
British Open	3
Benson & Hedges Int'l	2
PGA Championship	T-4
Irish Open	T-2
European Masters	T-7
European Open	2
Lancome Trophy	T-28
German Masters	T-12
World Match Play	2
Volvo Masters	1

1989

GREG NORMAN

Tournament	Finish
Tournament of Champions	4
Palm Meadows Cup	T-19
Australian Masters	1
Australian TPC	1
Nestle Invitational	T-13
Players Championship	T-4
USF&G Classic	T-2
Masters Tournament	T-3
Heritage Classic	MC
Greensboro Open	T-5
Chunichi Crowns	1

NICK FALDO

Tournament	Finish
Phoenix Open	T-35
Pebble Beach Pro-Am	MC
Los Angeles Open	T-22
Doral Ryder Open	MC
Honda Classic	T-27
Nestle Invitational	T-66
Independent Ins. Agent	T-42
Masters Tournament	1
Heritage Classic	T-11
Byron Nelson Classic	T-24

THE SONY RANKING / 7

GREG NORMAN		NICK FALDO	
Tournament	Finish	Tournament	Finish
Memorial Tournament	**T-12**	**Memorial Tournament**	**T-55**
Westchester Classic	T-23	Colonial Invitational	T-23
		Volvo PGA Championship	1
		Dunhill Masters	1
U.S. Open	T-33	U.S. Open	T-18
Canadian Open	T-26	Canadian Open	T-18
Western Open	T-20	French Open	1
		Scottish Open	T-20
British Open	**T-2**	**British Open**	**T-11**
PGA Championship	**T-12**	**PGA Championship**	**T-9**
International	1		
World Series	**4**	**World Series**	**T-20**
Milwaukee Open	1	European Open	T-20
Lancome Trophy	**T-16**	**Lancome Trophy**	**T-29**
Nabisco Championship	T-11	German Masters	T-7
		World Match Play	1
		Volvo Masters	2
		Dunlop Phoenix	T-31
Australian Open	**T-30**	**Australian Open**	**5**
Johnnie Walker Classic	**2**	**Johnnie Walker Classic**	**T-4**

1990

GREG NORMAN		NICK FALDO	
Tournament	Finish	Tournament	Finish
Tournament of Champions	T-5		
Palm Meadows Cup	DQ		
Australian Masters	**1**	**Australian Masters**	**T-2**
Doral Ryder Open	1	Desert Classic	T-9
Players Championship	T-16		
Nestle Invitational	**2**	**Nestle Invitational**	**T-13**
		Independent Ins. Agent	T-15
Masters Tournament	**MC**	**Masters Tournament**	**1**
Heritage Classic	**T-4**	**Heritage Classic**	**T-16**
USF&G Classic	2	Spanish Open	T-2
Byron Nelson Classic	T-7	Benson & Hedges Int'l	T-12
Memorial Tournament	1	Volvo PGA Championship	T-2
		Dunhill Masters	T-54
Western Open	**T-5**	**Western Open**	**T-32**
U.S. Open	**T-5**	**U.S. Open**	**T-3**
Anheuser-Busch Classic	T-23	French Open	T-4
		Scottish Open	T-5
British Open	**T-6**	**British Open**	**1**
PGA Championship	**T-19**	**PGA Championship**	**T-19**
International	T-66	European Open	T-4
World Series	T-6		
Milwaukee Open	T-16		
World Match Play	**T-3**	**World Match Play**	**T-5**
Nabisco Championship	T-7	Taiheiyo Masters	MC
Australian Open	**T-3**	**Australian Open**	**T-11**
Johnnie Walker-Australia	**T-16**	**Johnnie Walker-Australia**	**WD**
		Johnnie Walker-Hong Kong	1

The Sony Ranking
(as of December 31, 1990)

POS.	PLAYER, CIRCUIT	POINTS AVERAGE
1	Greg Norman, ANZ 1	18.95
2	Nick Faldo, Eur 1	18.54
3	Jose Maria Olazabal, Eur 2	17.22
4	Ian Woosnam, Eur 3	15.47
5	Payne Stewart, USA 1	12.75
6	Paul Azinger, USA 2	11.63
7	Seve Ballesteros, Eur 4	10.15
8	Tom Kite, USA 3	10.10
9	Mark McNulty, Afr 1	10.06
10	Mark Calcavecchia, USA 4	9.96
11	Fred Couples, USA 5	9.69
12	Curtis Strange, USA 6	9.58
13	Larry Mize, USA 7	8.86
14	Bernhard Langer, Eur 5	8.78
15	Chip Beck, USA 8	8.58
16	Hale Irwin, USA 9	8.36
17	Masashi Ozaki, Jpn 1	8.16
18	Tim Simpson, USA 10	7.78
19	Ronan Raffert, Eur 6	7.71
20	Wayne Levi, USA 11	7.69
21	Lanny Wadkins, USA 12	7.49
22	Mark O'Meara, USA 13	7.39
23	Rodger Davis, ANZ 2	7.08
24	David Frost, Afr 2	7.01
25	Jodie Mudd, USA 14	6.64
26	Gil Morgan, USA 15	6.35
27	Wayne Grady, ANZ 3	6.32
28	Ben Crenshaw, USA 16	6.32
29	Peter Jacobsen, USA 17	6.27
30	Steve Jones, USA 18	6.18
31	Mark James, Eur 7	6.05
32	Mike Harwood, ANZ 4	5.88
33	Mike Reid, USA 19	5.81
34	Craig Stadler, USA 20	5.74
35	Eduardo Romero, SAm 1	5.68
36	Ian Baker-Finch, ANZ 5	5.65
37	Craig Parry, ANZ 6	5.30
38	Nick Price, Afr 3	5.28
39	Scott Hoch, USA 21	5.24
40	Mark McCumber, USA 22	5.18
41	Sandy Lyle, Eur 8	5.12
42	Bruce Lietzke, USA 23	5.05
43	Tom Watson, USA 24	5.03
44	Davis Love III, USA 25	4.91
45	Peter Senior, ANZ 7	4.67
46	David Feherty, Eur 9	4.62
47	Larry Nelson, USA 26	4.61
48	Ray Floyd, USA 27	4.56
49	Steve Pate, USA 28	4.53
50	Sam Torrance, Eur 10	4.41
51	Bob Tway, USA 29	4.33
52	Brett Ogle, ANZ 8	4.27
53	Robert Gamez, USA 30	4.22
54	Corey Pavin, USA 31	4.09
55	Scott Simpson, USA 3	4.07
56	Ken Green, USA 33	4.04
57	John Bland, Afr 4	4.04
58	Naomichi Ozaki, Jpn 2	3.99
59	Loren Roberts, USA 34	3.95
60	Peter Fowler, ANZ 9	3.93
61	Gene Sauers, USA 35	3.83
62	Steve Elkington, ANZ 10	3.73
63	Isao Aoki, Jpn 3	3.55
64	Fuzzy Zoeller, USA 36	3.52
65	John Huston, USA 37	3.51
66	Tsuneyuki Nakajima, Jpn 4	3.49
67	Billy Mayfair, USA 38	3.47
68	Joey Sindelar, USA 39	3.41
69	Jeff Sluman, USA 40	3.37
70	Tom Purtzer, USA 41	3.32
71	John Mahaffey, USA 42	3.32
72	John Morse, USA 43	3.27
73	Graham Marsh, ANZ 11	3.26
74	Jim Gallagher, Jr., USA 44	3.24
75	Don Pooley, USA 45	3.19
76	Vijay Singh, Asa 1	3.18
77	Jose Maria Canizares, Eur 11	3.18
78	Gordon Brand, Jr., Eur 12	3.16
79	Jose Rivero, Eur 13	3.13
80	Donnie Hammond, USA 46	3.12
81	Colin Montgomerie, Eur 14	3.07
82	Eamonn Darcy, Eur 15	3.04
83	Mike Donald, USA 47	2.98
84	Blaine McCallister, USA 48	2.97
85	Bill Glasson, USA 49	2.96
86	Tony Johnstone, Afr 5	2.93
87	Christy O'Connor, Jr. Eur 16	2.84
88	Philip Walton, Eur 17	2.81
89	David Ishii, USA 50	2.79
90	Kenny Perry, USA 51	2.73
91	Peter O'Malley, ANZ 12	2.68
92	Brian Jones, ANZ 13	2.66

THE SONY RANKING / 9

POS.	PLAYER, CIRCUIT	POINTS AVERAGE	POS.	PLAYER, CIRCUIT	POINTS AVERAGE
93T	Billy Ray Brown, USA 52T	2.63	147	Toru Nakamura Jpn 9	1.69
93T	Jay Haas, USA 52T	2.63	148	Michael Allen USA 82	1.69
95	Mark Brooks, USA 54	2.61	149T	Andrew Magee, USA 83	1.67
96	Hal Sutton, USA 55	2.55	149T	Jeff Hawkes, Afr 7	1.67
97	John Cook, USA 56	2.54	151	Hideki Kase, Jpn 10	1.65
98	Howard Clark, Eur 18	2.52	152	Nobuo Serizawa, Jpn 11	1.64
99	Brian Tennyson, USA 57	2.50	153	Frankie Minoza, Asa 3	1.63
100	Frank Nobilo, ANZ 14	2.43	154	Tateo Ozaki, Jpn 12	1.62
101	Tommy Armour III, USA 58	2.41	155	Yoshinori Kaneko, Jpn 13	1.61
102	Roger Mackay, ANZ 15	2.41	156	Kenny Knox, USA 84	1.61
103	Fulton Allem, Afr 6	2.39	157	Teruo Sugihara, Jpn 14	1.60
104	Dan Forsman, USA 59	2.37	158	Mark Roe, Eur 31	1.60
105	Des Smyth, Eur 19	2.35	159	Vicente Fernandez, SAm 2	1.60
106	Scott Verplank, USA 60	2.34	160	Andrew Murray, Eur 32	1.59
107	Mike Hulbert, USA 61	2.34	161	David Graham, ANZ 18	1.57
108	Miguel Angel Martin, Eur 20	2.32	162	Jeff Maggert, USA 85	1.57
109	Roger Chapman, Eur 21	2.30	163	Gordon J. Brand, Eur 33	1.55
110	Richard Boxall, Eur 22	2.28	164	Tony Sills, USA 86	1.55
111	David Edwards, USA 62	2.27	165	Robert Wrenn, USA 87	1.53
112	Mark Wiebe, USA 63	2.25	166	Kirk Triplett, USA 88	1.52
113	Andy Bean, USA 64	2.24	167	Richard Zokol, Can 2	1.51
114	Bill Britton, USA 65	2.18	168	Peter McWhinney, ANZ 19	1.49
115	Ted Schulz, USA 66	2.17	169	Doug Tewell, USA 89	1.48
116	Ryoken Kawagishi, Jpn 5	2.16	170	Russ Cochran, USA 90	1.46
117	Bob Gilder, USA 67	2.16	171	Phil Blackmar, USA 91	1.45
118	Ove Sellberg, Eur 23	2.12	172	Bob Lohr, USA 92	1.45
119	Mike Clayton, ANZ 16	2.11	173	Mark Mouland, Eur 34	1.45
120	David Peoples, USA 68	2.10	174	Paul Broadhurst, Eur 35	1.44
121	Brad Faxon, USA 69	2.09	175	Jay Don Blake, USA 93	1.43
122	Russell Claydon, Eur 24	2.08	176	Bobby Wadkins, USA 94	1.41
123	Dave Barr, Can 1	2.06	177	Tom Sieckmann, USA 95	1.41
124	Mats Lanner, Eur 25	1.99	178	Bob Estes, USA 96	1.40
125	David Rummells, USA 70	1.97	179	Jim Thorpe, USA 97	1.40
126	Morris Hatalsky, USA 71	1.96	180	Mike Sullivan, USA 98	1.35
127	Greg Turner, ANZ 17	1.94	181	Gary Koch, USA 99	1.32
128	Masahiro Kuramoto, Jpn 6	1.94	182	Trevor Dodds, Afr 8	1.32
129	Stephen McAllister, Eur 26	1.89	183	Ken Trimble, ANZ 20	1.30
130	Steven Richardson, Eur 27	1.89	184	Hubert Green, USA 100	1.29
131	Mark Lye, USA 72	1.83	185	Jim Carter, USA 101	1.29
132	Saburo Fujiki, Jpn 7	1.82	186	Bill Sander, USA 102	1.28
133	Chris Perry, USA 73	1.82	187	Rick Hartmann, USA 103	1.28
134	D.A. Weibring, USA 74	1.79	188	Brad Bryant, USA 104	1.26
135	Dan Pohl, USA 75	1.79	189	Anders Sorensen, Eur 36	1.25
136	Billy Andrade, USA 76	1.78	190	Mike Smith, USA 105	1.24
137	Derrick Cooper, Eur 28	1.75	191	Jay Delsing, USA 106	1.23
138	Rocco Mediate, USA 77	1.74	192	Danny Mijovic, Can 3	1.23
139	Jack Nicklaus, USA 78	1.73	193	Magnus Persson, Eur 37	1.23
140	Brian Claar, USA 79	1.71	194	Jim Benepe, USA 107	1.22
141	Noboru Sugai, Jpn 8	1.71	195	Denis Durnian, Eur 38	1.21
142	Tom Byrum, USA 80	1.70	196	Curt Byrum, USA 108	1.21
143	Nolan Henke, USA 81	1.70	197	Larry Rinker, USA 109	1.20
144	Chen Tze Chung, Asa 2	1.70	198	David Williams, Eur 39	1.19
145	Barry Lane, Eur 29	1.69	199	Terry Gale, ANZ 21	1.18
146	Malcolm Mackenzie, Eur 30	1.69	200	Carl Mason, Eur 40	1.17

Detailed Structure For Allocation of Sony Ranking Points

Pos.	0-5 SAm, Can & Regional Minimum	6-10	11-15 Asa, SAf & Safari Minimum	16-20	21-25 Austr/NZ & Japan Minimum	26-30	31-40 Europe & USA Minimum	41-50	51-60	61-70	71-80	81-90	91-100	101-110	111-120	121-130	131-140	141-150	151-175	176-200	201-225	226-250	251-275	276-300	301-325	326-350	351-375	376-400	401-425	426-450	451-475 Europe PGA Champ. Minimum	476-500	501-525	526-575	576-625	626-675	676-725	726-775	776-825	Players Championship	MAJOR CHAMPIONSHIPS
1st	2	3	4	5	6	7	8	9	10	11	12	13	14	15	16	17	18	19	20	21	22	23	24	25	26	27	28	29	30	31	32	33	34	35	36	37	38	39	40	40	50
2nd	1	2	2	3	4	4	5	5	6	7	7	8	8	9	10	10	11	11	12	13	13	14	14	15	16	16	17	17	18	19	19	20	20	21	22	22	23	23	24	24	30
3rd	1	1	2	2	2	3	3	4	4	4	5	5	6	6	6	7	7	8	8	8	9	9	10	10	10	11	11	12	12	12	13	13	14	14	14	15	15	16	16	16	20
4th		1	2	2	2	2	2	3	3	3	4	4	4	5	5	5	5	6	6	6	7	7	7	8	8	8	8	9	9	9	10	10	10	11	11	11	11	12	12	12	15
5th		1	1	1	2	2	2	2	2	3	3	3	3	4	4	4	4	4	5	5	5	6	6	6	6	7	7	7	7	8	8	8	8	9	9	9	9	10	10	10	12
6th			1	1	1	2	2	2	2	2	2	3	3	3	3	3	3	3	4	4	4	4	4	4	5	5	5	5	5	6	6	6	6	6	7	7	7	8	8	8	10
7th			1	1	1	1	1	1	1	2	2	2	2	2	2	2	3	3	3	3	3	3	4	4	4	4	4	4	5	5	5	5	5	5	6	6	6	6	7	7	9
8th				1	1	1	1	1	1	1	1	1	2	2	2	2	2	2	2	2	3	3	3	3	3	3	3	4	4	4	4	4	5	5	5	5	5	6	6	6	8
9th					1	1	1	1	1	1	1	1	1	1	1	1	2	2	2	2	2	2	2	2	3	3	3	3	3	3	3	3	4	4	4	4	4	4	5	5	7
10th						1	1	1	1	1	1	1	1	1	1	1	1	2	2	2	2	2	2	2	2	2	2	2	3	3	3	3	3	3	3	3	4	4	4	5	7
11th								1	1	1	2	2	2	2	2	2	2	2	2	2	2	2	2	3	3	3	3	3	3	3	3	3	3	3	4	4	4	4	4	5	6
12th										1	1	2	2	2	2	2	2	2	2	2	2	2	2	2	2	2	3	3	3	3	3	3	3	3	3	3	3	4	4	4	6
13th										1	1	1	1	2	2	2	2	2	2	2	2	2	2	2	2	2	2	3	3	3	3	3	3	3	3	3	3	3	3	4	5
14th											1	1	1	1	2	2	2	2	2	2	2	2	2	2	2	2	2	2	3	3	3	3	3	3	3	3	3	3	3	4	5
15th											1	1	1	1	1	1	2	2	2	2	2	2	2	2	2	2	2	2	3	3	3	3	3	3	3	3	3	3	3	3	5
16th												1	1	1	1	1	1	2	2	2	2	2	2	2	2	2	2	2	2	3	3	3	3	3	3	3	3	3	3	3	4
17th													1	1	1	1	1	1	1	2	2	2	2	2	2	2	2	2	2	2	3	3	3	3	3	3	3	3	3	3	4
18th													1	1	1	1	1	1	1	2	2	2	2	2	2	2	2	2	2	2	2	3	3	3	3	3	3	3	3	3	4
19th														1	1	1	1	1	1	2	2	2	2	2	2	2	2	2	2	2	2	2	3	3	3	3	3	3	3	3	4

RATING POINTS

Current Rank of Players	Rating Points
1st	65
2nd	60
3rd	55
4th	50
5th	45
6th	40
7th	35
8th	30
9th	25
10th	20
11th to 15th	5 x 15
16th to 25th	10 x 10
26th to 50th	25 x 6
51st to 75th	25 x 2
76th to 100th	25 x 1

51st plus all making 36-hole cut in major championships

2. The Year In Retrospect

When the year of 1990 began, the most publicized issues in professional golf were U-grooved irons and the impending cutback of RJR Nabisco's sponsorship on the PGA Tour in the United States. Nick Faldo's name was not being spoken in the same sentence with Ben Hogan's, but Curtis Strange's name was. Robert Gamez had not yet made an impression, and Hale Irwin was all but forgotten. Jose Maria Olazabal was well-known in Europe, unheard of in America.

Shoal Creek Country Club was preparing to host the PGA Championship in the suburbs of Birmingham, Alabama. In the months before the championship, there was a storm of controversy that put Shoal Creek in the civil rights lexicon and forced an examination of the membership policies of clubs that would host future tournaments.

The result was some of the most significant changes in golf in this century.

By saying that Shoal Creek would not be pressured into accepting blacks as members, Hall Thompson, the founder of the club, assured that not only would Shoal Creek do just that, but that most other clubs would be changing their policies as well. Every organization that conducts golf tournaments was put under immense pressure to take their events only to clubs that demonstrate they do not discriminate because of race, creed, sex or national origin.

Pressure to end discrimination also was felt by clubs with no interest in hosting tournaments, accompanied by varying degrees of publicity, most notably the Kansas City Country Club, which was stung by the withdrawal of its best-known member, Tom Watson, when the club's membership committee denied the application of a proposed member who was Jewish, Henry Bloch, founder of the H&R Block tax return preparation service. Watson is not Jewish, but his wife and children are. The decision on Bloch's membership was soon reversed but, as of this writing, Watson had not re-applied.

The Shoal Creek controversy began innocently enough when William Bell, a black member of the Birmingham City Council, questioned whether the city should buy a $1,500 advertisement in the program for a PGA Championship played at a course where blacks would not be accepted as members. It seemed such a reasonable objection that the *Birmingham Times-Herald* sent Joan Mazzolini, one of its general assignment reporters, to interview Thompson, a round-faced, balding, retired tractor dealer, who was also among Birmingham's most prominent citizens. Thompson not only founded Shoal Creek, he was also its chairman and principal spokesman.

Mazzolini was working on a three-part series examining restrictive membership practices in Birmingham clubs. During the interview, lasting an hour and a half, Thompson said the Shoal Creek membership included women, Jews, Italians and Lebanese, and added, "I think we've said we don't discriminate in any other area except blacks." He said furthermore, "Bringing up this issue will just polarize the community ... but it can't pressure us ... We have the right to associate or not to associate with whomever we choose. The country club is our home, and we pick and choose who we want."

Thompson added, "If our members feel comfortable bringing blacks out here, they're welcome to," but when asked if any have ever invited blacks, he answered, "No; that's just not done in Birmingham."

Thompson's comments touched off a series of protests. Among the milder demands, civil rights groups insisted that the PGA of America move the championship from Shoal Creek. Taking a wider view of discrimination, Dr. Benjamin Hooks, the executive director of the National Association for the Advancement of Colored People, called discriminatory practices "repugnant, immoral, and un-American." Looking at Shoal Creek, he said the situation there was "but the tip of the iceberg." The Reverend Joseph Lowery, however, called for direct action. The president of the Southern Christian Leadership Conference, Lowery called for a demonstration.

As the controversy raged, friends of both races rushed to defend Thompson. Jesse J. Lewis, Sr., the founder of the *Birmingham Times*, a black weekly newspaper, said, "Hall Thompson is not a racist. He is a man of integrity who made the wrong statement at the wrong time ... To continue to judge a man by this one incident is unfair."

John Harbert, a friend, backed up Lewis by saying, "Hall is the most active and generous man in the state when it comes to worthwhile causes and charities." Speaking of Thompson's civic involvement and contributions, Harbert added, "He has taught other people how to give. He has forced them to think bigger about giving money where it's needed."

Harbert's comments drew support from Joe Dickson, editor of the *Birmingham World*, the country's second oldest black daily newspaper, who said, "Hall Thompson is probably the most generous person in Alabama. I think he has given more than anybody else for the betterment of the people here. As a person, I don't believe Hall Thompson is a bigot. He is a good man who has provided a lot of money and a lot of jobs for the black community."

Some said Thompson was uniquely blunt, not uniquely biased. Dickson seemed to agree.

"Hall told it like it is," he said. "He's right; you can't force people on people. Many of our readers have written to say Hall has the right to invite whomsoever he likes to join his club. Where there is a problem is where you use taxpayers' money to exclude people. That's my only problem with the whole situation."

Others argued differently. The Reverend Abraham Woods, president of the Birmingham chapter of the SCLC, said, "The impression I have always had of Hall Thompson is that he was an out-and-out racist."

Angus McEachran, the editor of the *Pittsburgh Press*, who came to the paper from the *Birmingham Post-Herald*, claimed Thompson was a key member of a committee that fought to keep blacks out of the Birmingham Rotary Club.

None of this mattered at this stage; the rhetoric, claims and counter claims had no effect at all, and the PGA Championship was going ahead as scheduled at Shoal Creek. Nothing would change.

Then corporate America spoke. Within a short period, the ABC television network writhed as sponsors pulled $2 million worth of advertising out of the PGA Championship telecast. The American Honda Motor Company, IBM, Anheuser-Busch, Toyota Motor Corporation, and Lincoln Mercury withdrew their advertising, and Delta, official airline of the PGA, said it would limit its level of participation.

IBM became the first to withdraw, stating, "Supporting, even indirectly, exclusionary activities is against IBM's practices and policies."

Toyota sponsors a number of players, including Lee Trevino, who had won the PGA Championship when it was played at Shoal Creek six years earlier. The company recommended they avoid wearing Toyota logos on their shirts, caps and other equipment. Speaking for the Japanese auto maker, Mindy Geler said the company had no choice but to cancel its advertising, because of Toyota's support of minority groups. "To do otherwise," she said, "would go against everything we're trying to accomplish in work with minorities."

Jim Awtrey, the executive director of the PGA of America, expressed understandable dismay. "It was disappointing to see the corporate sponsors distance themselves from us so fast," he said. "We thought it would have been nice if they had given us a little time to resolve the issue before they pulled out."

Thompson acted then. First he apologized. Then he extended an honorary membership to Louis J. Willie, the 66-year-old president of the Booker T. Washington Insurance Company. Thompson had known Willie for some years. He had been the first black Kiwanis Club member, and the first black in the Downtown Club and The Club, both Birmingham dining organizations.

Although Willie could have afforded it—his insurance agency operates two radio stations, two cemeteries, and real estate and construction companies—he wasn't asked to pay the club's $35,000 initiation fee.

While the advertisers didn't come back, Shoal Creek's concessions, along with encouragement from Richard Arrington, Birmingham's first black mayor, defused the situation enough to call off the demonstrations.

Perhaps they would have gone ahead had the SCLC heard the comments of some players as they arrived at Shoal Creek early in the week of the championship. Hardly a diplomat, Payne Stewart said, "I think it's been blown way out of proportion. Discrimination is all over the world. It didn't start here at Shoal Creek. The players have probably made more jokes about it than anything else."

Hubert Green wouldn't be drawn into the dispute. "I'm here to play golf," he said. "It's the PGA; it's a major championship. I'm not going to talk about it. I'm going to play golf."

Fuzzy Zoeller said, "I think our job is to go down there and play golf. I don't have anything to do with politics."

Jim Thorpe, the only black golfer who qualified for the PGA Championship, intended to play, saying, "Hopefully it will all blow over now. I'll stand with the minority leaders because I'm a minority. But I also make my living on the PGA Tour. I feel people are right to speak out against Hall Thompson, but that's no reason for me to boycott the tournament."

Lanny Wadkins and Dave Stockton, two former PGA champions, responded with thoughtful comments.

"I don't think anything has ever been intentional," Wadkins said. "I don't think the players feel they have slighted minorities. It wasn't callousness. We didn't check the membership lists. Nobody did. Maybe it was wrong that tournaments have been held here, and organizations condoned it. But it was not intentional."

Stockton said, "Just because we play golf doesn't make us smarter. I think a lot of us didn't realize there was a problem. We're golfers, not politicians. I mean, if I influence one nine- or 10-year-old, black or white, by the way

I play, then I've had a great week. You don't do it with words."

Still, the pressure continued building, and the PGA felt it. Something clearly had to be done. Early in the week of the championship, the organization met and revised its guidelines for selecting future sites for its championships. The key element stated:

"The PGA requires that prospective host courses have demonstrably open membership policies and practices prohibiting discrimination on the basis of race, creed, color, national origin or gender, and that the maintenance of such open membership policies be contractually guaranteed."

The PGA Tour fell into line quickly, writing a new provision that organizers of its tournaments "shall require that the practices and policies of any and all clubs proposed as tournament sites do not discriminate on the basis of race, religion, sex or national origins. Additionally, the PGA Tour staff shall be empowered to terminate any such agreement without penalty for breach of such representation."

The Tour said also that it would inquire into the membership practices of all its clubs, and where "questionable" practices were found, would demand that the club "take appropriate action to encourage minority membership. Consequently, no new contracts will be extended unless the PGA Tour is satisfied that its non-discriminatory policies are being enforced."

With the Tour conducting 118 tournaments on the regular PGA Tour, Senior PGA Tour and Ben Hogan Tour, the policy obviously would be difficult to enforce. Lowery, however, continued his pressure, saying he believed at least five tournaments were scheduled at clubs with no black members. Lowery pointed toward the television contract, and suggested that sponsors would be wary of more controversy. "If they aren't," he said, "I want to know if this applies. The case is, if they don't have black members, are they going to hold the tournament? I think sponsors would be interested in whether those clubs are going to desegregate."

Speaking for the PGA Tour, Sid Wilson, the director of public relations, said the Tour would take each case individually. "Just because a club doesn't have a black member doesn't mean it's exclusionary," he said. "The club may have had one previously, or no one has applied. But we are going to make sure every effort is being made."

No one expected every club to accept the mandate and change its membership. Predictably, some dropped out. "We lost six clubs (two on each circuit)," said Tim Finchem, deputy commissioner of the PGA Tour, "but we've been encouraged by the support of the majority."

Perhaps the most damaging to the Tour, Cypress Point Golf Club, that glorious course on the shores of the Pacific Ocean, in Pebble Beach, California, said it wouldn't continue as one of the three courses of the AT&T Pebble Beach National Pro-Am. "We have a waiting list of approved applicants of several years, and we couldn't bypass them" to conform, said a spokesman for Cypress Point.

(Vice President Dan Quayle was a victim of the changing attitudes when, during the Christmas holidays, he played a round at Cypress Point and was severely criticized. "His playing at a race-exclusive club is a source of humiliation for the troops in the Persian Gulf," said the Reverend Jesse Jackson. "For him to play at a club where more than half of those soldiers cannot play because of race or class is a moral disgrace." A day later, a statement from Quayle's office said he had been unaware of the controversy.)

Aronimink Golf Club, an outstanding Donald Ross course on the outskirts of Philadelphia, withdrew from the 1993 PGA Championship. With a seven-year waiting list, it could not accommodate a black member by the time of the championship without risking legal action by those already accepted but waiting for an opening. Butler National, set in the outskirts of Chicago, withdrew from the Centel Western Open, but within days the Western Golf Association agreed to hold the 1991 tournament at Cog Hill, a daily-fee complex in Lemont, another Chicago suburb.

Old Warson Country Club in St. Louis, an old-line club that had been the site of the 1971 Ryder Cup Match, withdrew as the host club of the 1991 Southwestern Bell Classic, a part of the Senior PGA Tour. Explaining Old Warson's position, Greg Mooney, the club's president, said, "We don't feel we can guarantee any proposed time schedule" in bringing a black member into the club. Old Warson evidently was given legal advice that if it brought in minority applicants before those who had already been in the membership process, the club could face a suit.

As those prominent and highly visible clubs chose to withdraw from participating in tournaments rather than upset their normal membership procedures, the PGA Tour, PGA of America and, of course, the United States Golf Association waited to see if they would lose more. (The Ladies Professional Golf Association has always required proof of non-discrimination in its contracts with host clubs.) Most chose to comply with the new guidelines calling for minority memberships wherever these practices were possible. Most organizations recognized that demographics would have some effect; clubs in some geographic areas might not be able to find black members.

Augusta National Golf Club, one of the nation's most exclusive clubs and home of the Masters Tournament in Augusta, Georgia, was among the frontrunners in the effort to integrate club memberships. Augusta National admitted its first black, 48-year-old Ron Townsend, president of the Gannett Television Group. Townsend said he felt a certain nervousness when he stepped on the tee there for the first time in October, but he boomed a drive to the middle of the fairway, and straight into history. "Now," said Townsend, "you can dream about being a member of any club."

As a result of Shoal Creek, the direction of golf was irreversibly changed and the consciousness of all of sport was raised. "The golf industry was lurking in the corner, undisturbed as elitist and a white enclave," Lowery said. "Shoal Creek put a floodlight on the industry and compelled it to move into the world of racial inclusiveness. But the issue is bigger than Shoal Creek and membership in country clubs."

The PGA and USGA expanded their junior golf and intern programs, and planned to aggressively encourage minority participation. Looking beyond golf, Lowery formed the National Task Force for Justice in Sports. "We've got to have equality in management and in the front office," he said. "We haven't matched what's happening on the playing field with what's happening on the paying field." An early result was that the National Football League agreed to award minority contracts for the Super Bowl to be held in January.

"Shoal Creek," said Lowery, "put the matter of economic justice on the agenda, but not just for golf, for all sports." In the aftermath, Lowery, one of Shoal Creek's harshest critics, was invited by a member to play the course. "And," he said, "I will accept."

The issue of U-grooved irons faded into the background in January when, less than an hour before the annual meeting of the United States Golf Association, a settlement was agreed between the USGA and Karsten Manufacturing Corporation, maker of the Ping Eye-2 irons, which the USGA had banned because the grooves did not conform to the Rules of Golf. Principals in the settlement were the USGA president whose term was about to expire, William C. Battle; USGA executive director David Fay, and John Solheim, son of Karsten Solheim, founder of the golf equipment company. Following were the terms:
- "Affirmation (by Karsten Manufacturing) of the USGA as the sole rulemaking body in the U.S."
- "Conversion of Karsten Manufacturing's plant to manufacture golf clubs that comply with USGA specifications. This will be achieved as near to March 31, 1990, as possible."
- "Inasmuch as the dispute has been strictly of a technical nature and there was no competitive advantage to a user of the clubs, it was the desire of both parties to work out a plan that would protect those many golfers who had bought the clubs. To do that, the Ping Eye-2 will be treated as complying with USGA specifications." In other words, existing Ping Eye-2 irons were made legal by this "grandfather" clause, but no more would be manufactured after the agreed date.

Karsten Manufacturing had sued the USGA—and the Royal and Ancient Golf Club of St. Andrews, Scotland—for $100 million. Before the settlement, the R&A had been dropped from the suit for lack of jurisdiction. Karsten also sued the U.S. PGA Tour which had banned not only the Ping Eye-2, but all U-grooved irons. Without reciting all the details, generally speaking, those governing organizations believed the irons provided excessive backspin and control over shots, especially when used by skilled professionals and particularly shots out of high grass. Karsten argued that the Rules of Golf were not being developed or applied in a fair and rational manner. The ban was to have taken effect on January 1, 1990 for national competitions and on January 1, 1996 for the general public.

Reaction to the USGA settlement was mixed. Battle received a sustained ovation when he made the announcement at the annual meeting, but there was rumored to be a large minority who opposed the settlement. Some were said to consider it a "grandstand" ploy by Battle, who was literally in his final hour as president of the organization. The R&A did not concur with the settlement—the ban went into effect for the British Open and other R&A competitions—and the PGA Tour maintained its suit. Karsten obtained an injunction to block implementation of the PGA Tour ban.

Other professional tours worldwide followed the R&A in banning the irons, but U-grooves were out of the news.

Another early-year development was RJR Nabisco's cutback on the U.S. PGA Tour. In headier days, under former chairman F. Ross Johnson, RJR Nabisco had signed a 10-year contract with the Tour. Two years into the agreement, following the record $25 billion buyout of RJR Nabisco by Kohlberg, Kravis Roberts & Co.—which resulted in a reported annual debt of $2.3 billion a year—the company wanted out. The settlement was estimated to be for $8 million.

RJR Nabisco had been spending $5.75 million a year in direct sponsorship and millions more indirectly. Included were the $2.5 million Nabisco Championship, $1 million bonus program, $2 million team charity competition and $250,000 statistical program. The company would continue its sponsorship of electronic scoreboards, which began in 1981, and of the Senior PGA Tour under its Vantage cigarettes banner, as well as the Dinah Shore event on the LPGA Tour.

T. Wayne Robertson, RJR Nabisco's senior vice president of sports marketing, downplayed the significance of the move. "Of the 2,400 events we run every year," Robertson said, "this decision effects only 60." He compared it to routine changes in their print advertising schedule, except "when we make a change in sports marketing, it is more evident to the public." RJR Nabisco's total advertising expenditures are over $800 million a year, according to *Advertising Age*.

The PGA Tour announced plans to continue the Nabisco (now called Tour) Championship, with a $500,000 reduction in the purse, and the team charity competition, but dropped the individual bonus scheme.

A harsher economic climate in 1990 was creating problems for other tournaments, as well, with a higher than usual attrition rate for sponsors. Total purses on the American circuit were expected to rise in 1991 by $1.5 million to $46.5 million after $5 million average annual increases in each of the previous four years. The Boston events on both the PGA Tour and LPGA Tour were without sponsors entering 1991, while the PGA Tour's New Orleans and San Diego stops were looking for new sponsors starting in 1992. It appeared that more tournaments might be seeking new sponsors in the short term.

At the same time, however, the PGA Tour launched the Ben Hogan Tour, a minor league with 30 events offering $100,000 purses. It gave more golfers an opportunity to play and opened more markets to tournaments, with a $20 million investment over five years by the Ben Hogan Company. By all accounts, it was a success. The top five money winners for the year—Jeff Maggert, Jim McGovern, Dick Mast, Mike Springer and Ed Humenik—earned their player's cards for the 1991 PGA Tour, plus a lot of competitive experience. As one of the players put it, "The Hogan Tour has been great, but nobody wants to play on it. You want to move ahead."

Our company, International Management Group, provided a significant new landmark on the 1991 calendar with the announcement of the Johnnie Walker World Championship, to be held on December 19-22, at Tryall Golf Club in Jamaica. There will be a $2.5 million purse—$525,000 to the champion—for the 26 players who qualify. The participants will include the winners of the four major championships and other designated events worldwide, as selected by the International Advisory Committee, and other leading players chosen off the World Money List.

We are confident of having all the best players for this tournament, which will fill an obvious void in the schedule. With golf becoming more international, no longer dominated by the American players, the time has come for a true world championship.

On that note, let's consider what took place in 1990.

Accolades were poured upon Nick Faldo including Player of the Year awards from nearly every organization and publication, following his major championship victories in the Masters and British Open, plus a late-season win in Hong Kong. Faldo was even Player of the Year on the points system of the PGA of America, although he played only seven times in the United States.

Faldo was not honored by the U.S. PGA Tour, but the recognition he received elsewhere led to the creation of a new Tour Player of the Year award which, by vote of the players, went to Wayne Levi, the winner of four Tour events.

Faldo did not win probably for good reason—he was not a member of the Tour in 1990—but the choice of Levi over Greg Norman was debatable, since Norman won twice in the U.S. (three times worldwide), won the Vardon Trophy for low scoring average and led the American circuit with winnings of $1,165,477 despite playing only 17 U.S. events.

Levi, who was second on the official money list with $1,024,647, missed the cut nine times in his 23 starts, and only one of his victories, the Centel Western Open, came against top-notch opposition. Norman missed the cut once, at the Masters, and his victories were over strong fields in the Doral Ryder Open and Memorial Tournament. He lost twice when an opponent holed out.

The vote of the PGA Tour players was understandable. The vast majority could relate more easily to a journeyman, Levi, than to a star, Norman, and if Levi were ever to win such an award, this would be the year. The vote came as no surprise, and anyone might have done the same if in their place.

However, there was no denying Faldo's accomplishments on the worldwide stage, even if Norman remained No. 1 on the Sony Ranking by a small margin over Faldo on the basis of three years' play.

Faldo became the second man ever to win the Masters back-to-back (Jack Nicklaus was the first in 1965-66), and he became the first since Tom Watson in 1982 to win two major titles in the same year. It just as easily could have been three. He missed a playoff for the U.S. Open when his putt on the 72nd green rolled over the lip of the hole. Instead, Hale Irwin, whose 45-foot birdie putt there was the Shot of the Year, went on to win the title over Mike Donald. An injury to Faldo's left wrist, and an 80 in the third round, left him tied for 19th place in the PGA Championship, won by Wayne Grady.

A perfectionist who has stirred comparisons to Ben Hogan, Faldo has devoted himself to winning major championships. He now has four: 1989-90 Masters and 1987-90 British Open. "My goals are always the same," he says, "to keep adding the majors. That's what you prepare for and play for every year." At age 33, he would appear to have another decade to win more, realistically one every year or two.

"But he won't be satisfied with that," said his teacher, David Leadbetter. "His goal is to win the Grand Slam (all four major titles in one year). He believes it can be done, and he believes he can do it."

Faldo has been characterized as being rude or impersonal, but those who know him well draw a different picture. "His mind is so focused on what he's doing that it's almost as if he's oblivious to everyone else," Leadbetter said. "Sometimes people think he's being brusque, but it's not intentional. It doesn't bother me anymore because I know how he is.

"Nick is not a totally cold guy. He can be a fun guy to spend time with away from the course, but he has a very businesslike approach to his golf game. He's so involved, it's almost like he's in a daydream."

The Faldo saga began in 1971 when, while watching the Masters on television, 14-year-old Nick announced that golf was a game he wanted to play. His parents had tried to interest him in various activities, including acting, modeling and piano. He had an affinity for sports, especially individual sports such as cycling and swimming. "My parents were very much of the mind, 'Let's keep giving him the opportunity to do things,'" he said. "And then it came off. We found the right one."

He took on golf with that characteristic single-minded determination, and within four years was an amateur star in Britain. He made a brief detour at the University of Houston, but after a few weeks he found he did not have the time he wanted for practice, and returned home. He became a professional golfer in 1976 and the next year was undefeated in the Ryder Cup. Through 1984, Faldo had 13 victories (his current total is 25), including three British PGA titles and the Heritage Classic in America. He wasn't satisfied. Enter Leadbetter, who rebuilt Faldo's swing and built reputations for both of them.

They met at the Memorial Tournament in 1985. Faldo had just missed the cut and asked Leadbetter to "throw the book at me." Leadbetter did just that.

"My swing was all wrong," Faldo said. "Perhaps the only good thing was its tempo. The rest—grip, posture and plane—were all inadequate. I hit the ball on a very high trajectory and so I struggled in anything more than a stiff breeze. In short, I needed to change if I was ever to fulfill my dream of winning a major championship, the British Open in particular."

With Faldo's success to that point, his decision to change his swing was criticized in the press. But Leadbetter had an obsessive pupil, and they ignored everyone else. Said Faldo, "The biggest thing David did for me was to put the enjoyment back into playing golf. Suddenly, in 1987, I went out and started hitting the ball the way I wanted."

He had what he needed to win the 1987 British Open in the wind and cold of Muirfield. He lost a playoff to Curtis Strange in the U.S. Open the next year, but won the Masters in a playoff with Scott Hoch in 1989 and again in 1990 in a playoff with Raymond Floyd.

Of the currently active players, only two have more major titles than Faldo's four—Tom Watson with eight and Seve Ballesteros with five. Faldo says, "I've been very close in a couple of U.S. Opens and a couple of our Opens that I haven't won, but then my first three majors were very close and I snuck through. So you don't know what to feel. The bottom line is that you feel very lucky every time you get one."

Faldo took different routes to his two major victories of 1990. At the Masters, he was four strokes behind Floyd with six holes to play; at the British Open, he virtually wrapped up the title and a five-stroke triumph with his 67 in the third round. That was the day Norman shot 76 in the same pairing after they had tied for the lead through 36 holes.

Floyd, attempting to become the oldest Masters champion at age 47, was struggling with his game despite the lead he held on the closing holes, and chose not to gamble on the par-five holes. Birdies on two of those, Nos. 13 and 15, enabled Faldo to reduce the margin to two strokes. Nick birdied the

16th from 15 feet, Raymond bogeyed the 17th, and they were tied. Floyd got to the playoff only after recovering from two bunkers for a par on No. 18.

In the playoff, Faldo made par from a bunker at No. 10 while Floyd left a 15-foot birdie putt short of the cup. Then, at the fateful 11th, where Faldo also won in 1989, Raymond pulled his seven-iron approach into the pond guarding the green, and Faldo needed only a safe par for the victory.

Thrilling though the victory was for Faldo, it was painful for Floyd, who said he was "as devastated as I've ever been in my life ... This would have meant so much to me, you can't imagine. To be the oldest, to win another major. Nothing has ever affected me like this. At this stage of my life, how many more chances am I going to have? If you're 25 and you lose one, you still believe in yourself, you still believe you're going to get a lot more chances."

After missing that putt from 12 or 15 feet for the U.S. Open playoff, Faldo said to himself, "Okay, I'm going to win the (British) Open." And Faldo dominated the championship at St. Andrews from the third round onwards. He and Norman equalled the 36-hole record with 132 totals, 12 under par, then Faldo crushed his rival by nine strokes in the third round, and eventually won by five shots over Payne Stewart and Mark McNulty.

With the now-familiar sight of his female caddy, Fanny Sunesson, at his side, Faldo shot the lowest score ever for an Open at St. Andrews, and the lowest in relation to par ever in the championship. He was 18 under par,

1990 World Money List

Jose Maria Olazabal was the leading money winner in professional golf worldwide for 1990 with $1,633,640. Ian Woosnam was second on the World Money List with $1,512,060, and Greg Norman was third with $1,457,378. Norman is the only golfer to win $1 million or more for three years (also 1986 and 1989), and Woosnam holds the record of $1,793,268, which he won in 1987. Fourteen golfers won $1 million or more in 1990, bringing the all-time total to 30 golfers. The complete 1990 World Money List appears in the Appendixes of this annual.

The leading money winners of 1990 were:

Pos.	Name	Money	Pos.	Name	Money
1	Jose Maria Olazabal	$1,633,640	11	Jodie Mudd	1,055,746
2	Ian Woosnam	1,512,060	12	Larry Mize	1,051,672
3	Greg Norman	1,457,378	13	Mark Calcavecchia	1,042,097
4	David Frost	1,456,393	14	Tim Simpson	1,026,176
5	Payne Stewart	1,283,333	15	Hale Irwin	964,890
6	Wayne Levi	1,151,306	16	Masashi Ozaki	956,726
7	Fred Couples	1,145,669	17	Ian Baker-Finch	950,988
8	Bernhard Langer	1,134,452	18	Ronan Rafferty	946,643
9	Paul Azinger	1,106,009	19	Nick Faldo	871,916
10	Mark McNulty	1,084,326	20	Mark O'Meara	837,387

while the previous record-holder, Watson, was 13 under when he won at Muirfield in 1980. He made only four bogeys all week, and three were on the infamous Road Hole, the par-four 17th, which he played cautiously each day.

Any doubts about Faldo's stature in the game were erased. He was proclaimed the best British sportsman since Roger Bannister, and as a golfer, the equal of Sir Henry Cotton, and perhaps the best since Harry Vardon. He was on the threshold of becoming the best ever from the Isles where the game was born.

And what about Greg Norman? He had a typical Norman year which ended with another bout of Great White Shark-bashing because he did not win a major championship. It's something he's had to live with as a man with immense fame and fortune and one major title, the 1986 British Open. There's only one way for Norman to answer his critics, and that is to win the big ones. Meanwhile, Norman's overall accomplishments tend to be overshadowed by the absence of major victories.

Norman won three times in 1990, as previously noted, twice in the United States and another in the Australian Masters, where he beat Faldo. He shot a final-round 62 then chipped in for an eagle in a playoff to win the Doral Ryder Open, and his victory in the Memorial Tournament was after a rain-out of the fourth round, but he lost twice when others holed out.

In The Nestle Invitational at Bay Hill, Robert Gamez holed a seven-iron shot from 176 yards—the longest shot ever holed from the fairway on the last hole to win a PGA Tour event—and in the USF&G Classic in New Orleans, David Frost holed a bunker shot in a playoff.

Perhaps Norman seems to lose more often than other players because he's in contention more often, but Norman also seems to inspire his opponents. "He's been built up so much, I think when other guys get a chance to beat him, they just play that much harder," Hal Sutton says. "Don't get me wrong. I'm a great admirer of his ability. But he's Greg Norman, and that makes other guys play harder, whether they know it or not."

Norman's most disappointing rounds of the year were his opening 78 in the Masters and then that 76 on the third day of the British Open, on a series of missed shots and three-putt greens. "After that," Norman said of the British Open, "I just sort of lost interest. I really didn't want to get out and play."

At year's end, Norman sought the help of his old friend and teacher, Australian club pro Charlie Earp. "Charlie has known me for 18 years, from when I was a 27-handicapper until now," Greg said. "If anybody could straighten me out, he could."

He would be 35 years old early in 1991, which is one year younger than Hogan was before he won his first major championship. There's still time for him to earn a place among the all-time great golfers.

Wayne Levi won eight times in his first eight years on the PGA Tour, but had not won since 1985. With his four 1990 victories—BellSouth Atlanta Classic, Centel Western Open, Canon Greater Hartford Open and Canadian Open—Levi earned more than twice his previous-best money winnings on the circuit. Levi advanced 47 places to No. 20 on the Sony Ranking. He said the difference was in his putting, as "I came off a horrendous five years of putting."

With a simple and efficient swing, Levi had been regarded as an underachiever and, at age 37, unlikely to change. He was known to prefer staying at home, near Utica, New York, with his wife and four children, to watch sports on television and dabble in investments, than to endure the grind of professional golf. "My philosophy is to make things as easy on myself as possible," Levi has said. "I have no problem admitting I'm out there for the money."

Still, Levi savored the attention and Player of the Year honors he received, while acknowledging that his 1990 performance was not without flaws. The four victories aside, he was among the top-25 finishers only two other times. "I played erratically," he said. "Other than four wins, I had a lousy year."

Levi's record in the major championships came under scrutiny. This year, he missed the cut in the Masters and U.S. Open, withdrew from the PGA Championship and did not play in the British Open, an event he has never entered. For his career, Levi has never been among the top-10 finishers in a major event, and of the 27 which he has entered, he has missed the cut or withdrawn from 11. "I can't be missing the cut anymore," Levi said. "I've got to show up at majors now and perform."

Levi explained his lack of success in the majors this way: "There's always a million people around at the majors, the pace of play is always slow, and there are so many distractions. I just always let things get to me." He said he has become more determined, and "I'm going to win the U.S. Open before I'm done."

The only thing for sure is that Levi is a paradox.

Probably the most enduring image of 1990 will be Hale Irwin's 45-foot putt on the 72nd green of the U.S. Open at Medinah Country Club, near Chicago, and his reaction—a high-stepping, high-fiving trot around the green as the crowd roared.

This was a putt Irwin ordinarily would have been pleased to get close enough to avoid three-putting. But Irwin was trying to make it, because "I figured I had to get to eight under to have a chance. I told myself I was due." It had a left-to-right break of seven or eight feet, and crossed a hump about 20 feet short of the cup. Taking the downslope on line with the hole, the ball found the center of the cup "as sweet as a baby's kiss," Irwin said. "In my 22 years of pro golf I've never made a putt like that to win, or to give me a chance to win, a tournament."

The leaders entering the final round were 34-year-old journeyman Mike Donald, who had one career victory, and a colorful young Texan right off the pages of a Dan Jenkins novel, Billy Ray Brown. Their staying power surprised everyone, especially since Donald had started the Masters with a 64 then followed with an 82. Faldo and Norman, who was paired with Irwin, were also in with a chance, Greg having one of his blazing Sundays until midway of the last nine. Donald, Brown and Faldo all bogeyed No. 16, Medinah's toughest hole, and none could birdie No. 18, which meant that Donald went into a playoff at eight-under-par 280, and the other two went home.

The playoff the next day was not decided until the 19th hole, when Irwin birdied with an eight-foot putt after they had tied with 74s for the regulation 18 holes. Hale was two strokes down with three holes to play, and the key shot was his sensational two iron at No. 16, which he had to draw around the trees. He put it six feet from the hole for a birdie. Donald bogeyed the 18th after hitting his tee shot into the gallery, his second shot into a greenside bunker and then missing a 15-foot putt.

So Irwin, at age 45, became the oldest man ever to win the U.S. Open as he took the championship for the third time, having previously won in 1974 and 1979. Irwin won again the next week in the Buick Classic at Westchester Country Club in New York, gaining his 19th career victory after going winless for over five years. He went to No. 16 on the Sony Ranking after starting the year as No. 98.

All the talk before the U.S. Open had been focused on a third victory—a third consecutive by Curtis Strange, who sought to duplicate the feat of Willie Anderson in 1903-05. Strange had devoted his year to being prepared for this one week. "The odds are very much against me, but whether I play good or bad, you'll know I'll give it my best," he said.

Strange missed only five of 56 fairways—he was the most accurate driver in the field—but he finished tied for 21st at two under par. He had all he ever asked for—a chance to win in the final round, starting out two strokes behind the leaders, and he hung on for six holes. He then bogeyed the par-five seventh and bogeyed again at the ninth. He couldn't muster the shots he needed, the birdies simply wouldn't come. The large gallery stayed with him, though, and he received a marvelously warm reception at the final hole.

The challenge took its toll on Strange. After winning 16 PGA Tour events in the 1980s, he won only an unofficial tournament in Pittsburgh in 1990, his official Tour earnings put him in 53rd place with $277,171, and he fell from fourth to 12th on the Sony Ranking. No one doubted, however, that Strange would be back among the game's best players, and a victory at the Skins Game (worth $220,000) over the Thanksgiving weekend brightened his spirits before he began a six-week layoff. "This was the first time I've had trouble getting enthusiastic about playing," Curtis said then. "When you don't have enthusiasm to do your job, you're not going to do it well."

The Skins Game meant that Strange would "have something positive to go back to the off-season with. This was great therapy this week."

Whether trend or coincidence, the average age of winners on the U.S. PGA Tour continued to rise in 1990. Notable exceptions were 22-year-old Robert Gamez, who was Rookie of the Year with his two victories in the Northern Telecom Tucson Open and The Nestle Invitational, and the best young player in the world, Jose Maria Olazabal, age 24, who stormed to a 12-stroke victory in the NEC World Series of Golf in one of his only eight American appearances. Olazabal had five triumphs worldwide.

The average age of winners was 33.07 years, over two years higher than the 31.05 figure in 1980. As *Golf World* noted, there was one stretch of 10 weeks when every winner was 35 or older, which was part of a 16-week streak when every winner was 30 or older. Nine winners were in their 20s, down from 20 in 1986 and the 10-year average of 16.3 a year. Five winners were 40 or older, including Irwin's two victories. Others were Kite, Lanny Wadkins and Gil Morgan. "I think you'll see that trend continue," said Larry Nelson, age 43, a former U.S. Open and PGA champion.

"Sometimes, I wonder if the competition is greater out here. You always hear that. I'm not so sure the competition is greater above a certain level. That's the reason we saw some older guys winning this year. A lot of people are capable of making cuts and making a lot of money on the Tour, but there aren't as many capable of winning as there were five or 10 years ago. We're really strong on guys making cuts and money and handling the general pressure of the Tour, but we're very thin in people who can consistently win."

"Certainly, a lot has to do with improved physical fitness awareness, and the Senior Tour has a lot to do with that," said Tom Kite, age 41, who won the Federal Express St. Jude Classic for his 14th career victory. "Players in their 40s now say, 'I'm not at the end of my career. I've got another 15 or 20 years of golf.' So players today take better care of themselves. Hale Irwin did that. You get in better shape. It doesn't always produce wins, but it doesn't hurt."

Youth was also served, including 16-year-old Chris Couch, who shot a 65 in the qualifying round of the Honda Classic. Couch missed the cut, but later shot a 63 while winning the PGA Junior Championship.

In addition to Norman, Levi and Irwin, the year's big winners included Payne Stewart, who won twice and was second twice (all in the space of six events), and was third on the money list. Stewart also was a runner-up in the British Open, the low individual in the World Cup, and the leading American player on the Sony Ranking as No. 5 in the world. Paul Azinger, No. 6 on the Sony Ranking, won the season-opening Tournament of Champions, but nothing else, while finishing second three times and was a top-10 finisher 12 times. He was fourth on the money list, just ahead of Jodie Mudd, whose two victories were in significant events, The Players Championship and the Nabisco Championship. Mudd did not have an exceptional year otherwise, with only two more top-10 placings.

The U.S. Public Links champion twice before turning professional in 1982, Mudd took nine years to live up to his potential. In the 1983 Masters, Mudd was two strokes off the lead entering the last round, then shot an 86. "Those scars lasted a long time," he said. He won his first tournament in 1988 and another in 1989. At lunch before the final round of The Players, Mudd told his brother and caddy, Tommy, "Today is the day we take it up one more level." He did it with a closing 69 to beat Mark Calcavecchia by one stroke. In another stellar finish, with birdies on the last three holes, Mudd shot a final-round 68 and defeated Billy Mayfair in a playoff for the Nabisco Championship. Mudd advanced from No. 49 to No. 25 on the Sony Ranking.

Calcavecchia placed seventh on the money list without winning. He had five second-place finishes, four in his first nine tournaments, and also was runner-up in the Carrolls Irish Open. The defending British Open champion had disappointing showings in the major championships. He tied for 20th in the Masters, and missed the cut in the other three. After placing second at Hartford in late June, Calcavecchia didn't have another top-10 finish. He dropped from No. 8 to No. 10 on the Sony Ranking.

Rounding out the top 10 of the money list were Tim Simpson and Fred Couples, who each won once, and Mark O'Meara, who had two victories, including a repeat at Pebble Beach with his father as his partner in the AT&T National Pro-Am. Simpson had 12 finishes in the top 10, and Couples had a second place in the PGA Championship among his nine top-10 finishes. On the Sony Ranking, Couples placed No. 11; Simpson, No. 18, and O'Meara, No. 22.

The controversy at Shoal Creek rendered the name of the winner of the PGA Championship as a footnote to history, but it was no insignificant accomplishment as far as the champion, Wayne Grady, was concerned. "I know one thing," Grady said. "These things go with you to your grave. No matter how hard you scratch it, you're not going to get my name off that trophy, and I'm just happy to have it there."

The victory was the fifth of Grady's career and his second in America, raising his position on the Sony Ranking from No. 42 to No. 27. He finished 21st on the money list and as the fourth Australian behind Norman, Ian Baker-Finch and Steve Elkington, winner of the K-mart Greater Greensboro Open. Grady, who lost a playoff for the 1989 British Open title, won at Shoal Creek with a six-under-par 282 total, beating Couples by three strokes after Couples bogeyed four consecutive holes late in the final round. "It happened so quickly, it was kind of sickening," said Couples, who missed three putts in a row from four feet. "They're not gimmes. They don't look very far, but when you need to make 'em, they're pretty tough."

The severe rough drew complaints from many players, and the scores included an 80 by Faldo, 79 by Strange, 77 by Norman and 83 by Seve Ballesteros. "I'm glad it's over," Faldo said Sunday night. "It was the most frustrating week ever."

The most notable newcomer to the American circuit was Gamez, the youngster from Las Vegas who left the University of Arizona after three years and won twice in his rookie season. He had a four-stroke victory in the Northern Telecom Tucson Open, then came the real eye-opener, Gamez's seven-iron shot into the hole from 176 yards for an eagle-two to win The Nestle Invitational. However, Gamez did not have another top-10 finish, and he missed the cut nine times while earning $461,406 for 27th place on the money list. He was No. 53 on the Sony Ranking.

Second-year player Billy Mayfair, the 1987 U.S. Amateur champion, had a better year than Gamez in many respects. He made the biggest improvement on the PGA Tour, soaring from 116th on the money list as a rookie to 12th this year. He went from No. 231 to No. 67 on the Sony Ranking. He placed in the top 10 seven times and lost twice in playoffs—to Jim Gallagher, Jr., in Milwaukee, when Mayfair bogeyed both the 72nd and the playoff holes, and in the Nabisco Championship, when Mudd needed those three birdies to beat him. He had every right to be pleased. "I'm going to hold my head high," Mayfair said. "I'm going to work hard in the off-season, and come back next year and kick some butt."

On the downside, Mark McCumber had a curious year, dropping to 97th on the money list after being 13th and 14th for the two previous years, and from No. 18 to No. 40 on the Sony Ranking. Usually, that sort of decline is punctuated by a series of missed cuts, but McCumber was in the money in 20 of 24 tournaments. His best finishes, however, were two ties for ninth and another for 10th place.

Popular Peter Jacobsen won an official event for the first time since 1984—he also won the 1989 Kapalua International—when he claimed the Bob Hope Chrysler Classic. He placed 19th on the money list ... David Ishii, a regular on the Japan Tour, scored a home-state victory in the Hawaiian Open ... Tommy Armour III joined his famous grandfather on the victory rolls by winning the Phoenix Open ... John Huston's Weight-Rite shoes were declared illegal by the USGA, so Huston changed to a conventional pair and won the Honda Classic ... Steve Elkington, the Greensboro winner, got more notice after placing 21st in the USF&G Classic, when he read the newspaper the next day, realized that he had turned in the wrong score, and gave back his $10,000 check ... Jim Gallagher, Jr., and Steve Pate made double eagles in the same round of the same tournament, The International ... Recovering from wrist surgery, John Cook placed 28th on the money list and lost twice in playoffs ... Dan Pohl, a 12-year veteran with two victories, sat out the entire year after undergoing back surgery ... Former U.S. Open champion Jerry Pate, whose career was sidetracked by a shoulder injury in 1982, was in the money eight times in 17 tournaments between his duties as a television commentator. With a new swing that takes the pressure off his shoulder, Pate planned to try the Tour full-time in 1991.

Willie Wood played the 1990 season with a special exemption, granted after his wife, Holly, died of cancer. For much of the fourth round of the Hardee's Classic, it appeared that Wood would complete his long road back from tragedy. Joey Sindelar defeated Wood in a playoff, but Willie still finished 90th on the money list and earned his Tour card for 1991.

The PGA European Tour was home to three of the world's four top golfers, none of whom were Seve Ballesteros, according to the Sony Ranking— No. 2 Nick Faldo, No. 3 Jose Maria Olazabal and No. 4 Ian Woosnam. Faldo's accomplishments were recited earlier; Olazabal and Woosnam each won five tournaments. While Olazabal's stunning victory in the NEC World Series of Golf put him squarely in the limelight, and he won another event in Japan, Woosnam was the Tour's leading player with all five of his victories there. He also was second four times and third twice worldwide. He led the European Order of Merit with £574,166, plus unofficial earnings of £100,000 for winning his second Suntory World Match Play Championship. And Ballesteros won just once.

The final 1990 Sony Ranking listed 16 regulars on the European Tour among the top 50 players in the world, including 10 European natives. Among the top 25 on the Sony Ranking were No. 7 Ballesteros (he and Olazabal changed places during the year), No. 9 Mark McNulty, No. 14 Bernhard Langer, No. 19 Ronan Rafferty and No. 23 Rodger Davis.

Following Woosnam on the 1990 Order of Merit were McNulty, Olazabal, Langer and Rafferty, all earning more than £300,000 on the European circuit.

These are all players who might have divided their time between the European and American Tours, if not for the controversial rule requiring a minimum of 15 tournament appearances for U.S. PGA Tour membership. Faldo and Langer both withdrew from the American circuit late in 1989, and the sole remaining European, Sandy Lyle, resigned after the 1990 season.

This wasn't Woosnam's best year; in 1987, he won eight tournaments and led the World Money List with a record of $1,793,268, and at age 32 he has 22 career victories. In addition to the World Match Play, this year Woosnam won the American Express Mediterranean Open, Torras Monte Carlo Open, Bell's Scottish Open and Epson Grand Prix of Europe. He was a co-favorite with Faldo in the British Open, entering the championship with two consecutive victories, and placed fourth.

All that's lacking on Woosnam's record is a major title. He and Olazabal are the two best golfers in the world who have never won a major. "I've got a second, third and fourth in the majors, so I've been knocking on the door," Woosnam says. "I just need a bit of luck now.

"In terms of my status as a golfer, I don't think a major is all that important. I know how good I am, and I know that on my day I can beat anyone in the world. But as far as the public perception of me goes, I do need a major and that is something which I am realizing more and more. It's not simply for myself and my family, it's for that seal of approval from everyone out there."

A farmer's son from Wales, Woosnam turned professional at age 18 and struggled for three years—he won only £1,049 in his first year—before winning his first tournament, the Swiss Open in 1982. He has been among Europe's top-10 money winners ever since. In 1987, among his eight wins, he was the first Briton ever to take the World Match Play title.

Galleries marvel at his strength and size. He can hit the ball as far as anyone, but he stands just five feet, four inches tall. He gained his muscles while working on a 700-acre farm with his father, Harold, and now spends equally long hours working on his golf game, his ambition being to replace Norman and Faldo at the top of the world rankings. "I want to knock them off that perch," he said after one of his victories this year.

Olazabal has similar thoughts, having already taken No. 1 among Spanish golfers from Ballesteros. "I wouldn't like to depart this world without winning at least one," Olazabal says, and it would be a shock if this 24-year-old won only one.

He could be a factor in professional golf for the next 20 years or more, and so there are two things which should be remembered: His name is pronounced Ola-THA-bal, and he does not like comparisons to Ballesteros. "I have to beat him if I am to be the best," he says, "but my position with Seve is a bit special. He was not my hero, because even when I was 14, I had never heard of him. I did not know he had won the British Open. He lives two hours from me, but the Spanish papers, they have no time for golf.

"I do not want to be the second Ballesteros. I want to be the first Olazabal. My motivation is to win, to play good, to be No. 1, to beat all the other guys."

Like Woosnam, Olazabal comes from a farming family, in the Basque region. A few years before Olazabal was born, the Royal San Sebastian golf course was moved to his town, Fuentarrabia, to avoid the attentions of the Basque separatists who were busy on that stretch of coast at the time. The club bought the Olazabal family land. Olazabal's grandfather, and then his father, became greenskeepers. On the day before he was born, Jose Maria's mother was setting pins for the opening day of the season.

He grew up on the golf course and, before he became a professional late in 1985, he had won the British Boys, Youths and Amateur trophies, a trio of victories that had eluded everyone before him. His first year on the European Tour, 1986, he won two tournaments and was second on the Order of Merit. He now has 12 career victories.

His five wins this year were in the Benson & Hedges International, Carrolls Irish Open, NEC World Series of Golf, Lancome Trophy and Visa Taiheiyo Masters in Japan. In 29 starts worldwide, he was out of the top 10 only nine times, and five of those were in his first six tournaments.

Olazabal tied for eighth in the 1989 Masters and tied for ninth in the U.S. Open. This year, only Faldo had a better record in the major championships: Olazabal was 13th in the Masters, tied for eighth in the U.S. Open, tied for 16th in the British Open, and tied for 14th in the PGA Championship.

"They say you can't put an old head on young shoulders," says commentator Peter Alliss, "but this young man is the exception to that rule."

Of Ballesteros, Alliss has this to say: "He came in with a great deal of ammunition, but it's possible he may not have any left. With as much globe-hopping as he's done, and as hard as he plays, he may have put into 14 or 15 years what someone else put into 25. It's too early to tell, but if he hasn't come roaring back by 1992, I would daresay that it's probably come to an end for Seve."

When Ballesteros won the 1988 British Open, he seemed sure to continue the assault that had yielded 56 worldwide victories since 1976. But Seve has won only four tournaments since, all in Europe, and only one in 1990, the Open Renault de Baleares in Majorca. He did have 13 finishes in the top 10, including four third places, but he missed the cut in both the British Open and PGA Championship.

And this was the year his first child was born, an eight-pound boy, Baldomero, named after Seve's late father. Has the addition of a wife and child lessened Ballesteros' drive to be the best?

"Nothing has changed," Ballesteros said in an interview with Jaime Diaz of *Golf Digest*. "I will have more demands on my time, but everything else will continue in the same direction. I think it will help my golf, because I will get more rest when I come home."

Ballesteros saw 1990 as an inevitable slump, finally arriving when he was 33 years old. "I got in trouble by pushing myself," he said. "After not much success in 1989, I was anxious to pick up the form, and I was trying too many things—the grip, the ball position, the takeaway. Too many things. I got to the point where I was confused. Also, I was tired mentally. For some reason, my concentration was not very good this year."

He insists he will win major titles again. "I think I deserve more majors," he said. "And I think I will get them. How long it will take, I don't know. But I know it will happen."

Mark McNulty, the 37-year-old Zimbabwean, had a year that was almost the equal of, or better than, Woosnam's and Olazabal's. While earning £507,540 to be No. 2 in Europe, McNulty was a top-10 finisher in 20 of his 28 tournaments. He won twice in the Credit Lyonnais Cannes Open and Volvo German Open, and was second or tied for second five times, including the British Open, World Match Play and Bell's Scottish Open. He now has 32 career victories and has been in the top 10 of the Order of Merit for five consecutive years.

Former Masters champion Bernhard Langer, now age 33, was not far off McNulty's pace as he placed fourth on the Order of Merit with £320,449 and demonstrated again that his recurring problems with the putter cannot keep him down for long. Langer won twice—Cespa Madrid Open and Austrian Open—and was second four times and in the top 10 for half of his 28 starts. Then, in one of the big surprises of the year, Langer and little-known teammate Torsten Giedeon won the World Cup for Germany.

The leader of the Order of Merit in 1989, Northern Ireland's Ronan Rafferty further established himself among the world's best golfers at age 26. Rafferty placed fifth on the money list this time with £309,851. He won three tournaments for the second year in a row, raising his career total to 12. His victories were in the Coca-Cola Classic in Australia, PLM Open in Sweden and Ebel European Masters. He also was a member of the Irish team, along with David Feherty and Philip Walton, that won the Dunhill Cup for the second time at St. Andrews. Walton also won the Peugeot French Open, and Feherty was a runner-up four times.

Other notable accomplishments on the European Tour included Australian Mike Harwood snaring a double that was the equivalent of Jodie Mudd's in America. Harwood won both the Volvo PGA Championship and Volvo Masters, plus one tournament in Australia ... Another Aussie, Rodger Davis, also won twice in Europe and once in their home country ... Mark James triumphed in both the Dunhill British Masters and NM English Open ... Two Argentinians, Eduardo Romero and Vicente Fernandez, won European tournaments. Romero also was a runner-up in America at The International, and Fernandez won their national championship ... Stephen McAllister won twice and was among the five first-time winners ... Sam Torrance wielded his long putter to a late-year win in the Mercedes German Masters, his first in Europe since 1987, and was runner-up in the Volvo Masters ... Sandy Lyle became the latest European to give up his U.S. Tour card. Lyle has not won since his great 1988 campaign, when he had five victories, including the Masters. This year Lyle had only four top-10 finishes, none in America.

In 1991, the Europeans will be gearing to retain the Ryder Cup for the fourth consecutive time against the United States at Kiawah Island, South Carolina, in what will undoubtedly be one of the highlights of the year. Bernard Gallacher will be the European captain, replacing Tony Jacklin, who led the three successful efforts, while Dave Stockton will take over the American team from Raymond Floyd.

Before the players began accumulating points for the team, the Europeans were already quarreling over control of the Match between the Tour and the British PGA, and over the venue for the next contest on their side of the Atlantic in 1993. They reached a compromise over the control, and The Belfrey was selected as the site for the third successive time.

The Belfrey was chosen after the Tour, yielding to Seve Ballesteros' strong wishes, proposed Club de Campo in Spain and the British PGA renominated their home course in the English Midlands. Lord Derby, president of both organizations, cast the deciding vote for The Belfrey, then resigned from the Tour, because he could "no longer be thought of as impartial."

In other matters, a plan was drafted in the autumn to eliminate appearance fees on the European Tour by 1992, the Tour launched a feasibility study for a senior circuit, and a 1991 schedule was announced with over 40 tournaments in 17 countries, between mid-February and mid-November. The Tour was continuing to prosper, despite a troublesome economy. "The recent rapid growth of the Tour is running parallel with the outstanding international success of leading Tour members and Volvo's outstanding support as our overall sponsor," said executive director Ken Schofield, who added that prize money would again rise substantially when all negotiations were completed. Prize money in 1990 was £16 million, an 18 percent increase over the previous year.

While economic difficulties held back growth on the Australasian Tour, Aussie golfers had a sensational year. With Wayne Grady's major title, the PGA Championship, as the crowning achievement, a total of 14 Australian players won tournaments around the world, accumulating 22 victories, eight in Australia and New Zealand, six in Europe and four each in America and Japan.

The winners were Greg Norman (3), Rodger Davis (3), Mike Harwood (3), Brian Jones (2), Brett Ogle (2) and these players with one victory each—Grady, Ian Baker-Finch, Steve Elkington, Peter Senior, Roger Mackay, David Smith, Graham Marsh, Ken Trimble and Wayne Riley. Not included among the victors were three players from the top 100 of the Sony Ranking—Craig Parry, Peter Fowler and Peter O'Malley.

The listing of that impressive lineup begs the question: What if there were a Ryder Cup-type competition between Australia and the United States or Europe?

Despite the Australians' success, the only person to win twice on the home circuit was a little-known American, John Morse, who had failed five times to qualify in the United States. Morse won a small event in Perth, the Nedlands Masters, then one of the biggest events on the circuit, the Australian Open, taking a playoff over Parry.

Just as surprising in this outstanding year, Australia lost in the first round of the Dunhill Cup for the second time in a row. Norman, Grady and Davis lost to New Zealand on the same day that France, which beat the Aussies in 1989, caused another upset by defeating the United States team of Curtis Strange, Mark Calcavecchia and Tom Kite.

Strange and Nick Faldo were among the overseas contenders in the most important events, but neither won there. Davis eagled the second playoff hole to deny Strange back-to-back victories in the Daikyo Palm Meadows Cup, and Norman out-dueled Faldo in the Australian Masters, as the Great White Shark took that title for the sixth time. Two more victories later on in the United States raised Norman's career total to 61 triumphs.

Davis was the Order of Merit winner, as he was out of the top 10 only once in eight Australasian events, won once and tied for second twice. With a 33-event schedule, the popular 39-year-old Sydney native had 16 top-10 finishes, including European victories in the Peugeot Spanish Open and Wang Four Stars National Pro-Celebrity. While Davis advanced 20 places to No. 23 on the Sony Ranking, he missed the cut in the only two major championships for which he qualified or was invited, the British Open and PGA Championship. He is good enough to win a major title, but there are not many chances left for him.

On the Japan PGA Tour, Masashi (Jumbo) Ozaki led the money list again, but did not play well outside the country. Internationally, Ozaki's greatest impact was his Bridgestone-made driver, called J's Professional Weapon, which became a sensation in the spring after golfers visiting Japan had seen it in action. Players with that club were on the leaderboards across the world, but not Jumbo himself. In 10 overseas appearances, Ozaki missed the cut four times and his best finish was 23rd in the Masters, resulting in his drop from 12th to 17th in the Sony Ranking.

Since the second highest-ranking Japanese player in the world was his brother, No. 58 Naomichi (Joe) Ozaki, Jumbo's hold on professional golf there was not seriously threatened. Jumbo won four times—Fuji Sankei Open, Yonex Hiroshima Open, Maruman Open and Daiwa KBC Augusta Open—and was second six times, including five of his last seven tournaments, while winning ¥129,060,500. But those were sub-standard results for Ozaki, age 42, who had won six times in 1988 and seven times in 1989.

Frankie Minoza of the Philippines won twice in Asia and once in Japan, in the Dunlop International tournament. After going without a victory in 1989, Tsuneyuki (Tommy) Nakajima reestablished his position in Japan by placing second on the money list with ¥96,979,100 and winning three tournaments, including the Japan Open. Third place with ¥87,350,200 went to rookie Ryoken (Ricky) Kawagishi, who had great amateur success in Japan and America before winning three tournaments in his first professional season. Just behind Kawagishi, earning ¥85,060,727, was Joe Ozaki, who also had three wins, the most important of which was the Japan Series. A senior-age player, Teruo Sugihara, also had three victories. Other multiple winners were Noboru Sugai with three, and Saburo Fujiki, Tadao Nakamura and Toru Nakamura with two each. Veterans Isao Aoki and Masahiro Kuramoto were among the one-time winners.

As noted earlier, Japan Tour regular David Ishii won the Hawaiian Open, but Ishii did not win in Japan. As usual, overseas visitors won some of the important Japanese and Asian tournaments. Four of the winners were Australians—Brian Jones (twice), Roger Mackay and Graham Marsh. Jose Maria Olazabal won the Visa Taiheiyo Masters for his fifth triumph of the year, and Nick Faldo won the Johnnie Walker Classic in Hong Kong for his third. American winners were Ken Green in the Martell Hong Kong Open, Bob Gilder in the Acom Stableford, Larry Mize in the Dunlop Phoenix Open and Mike Reid in the Casio World Open.

Short tours were again conducted in Africa (one in South Africa and another in the black-ruled nations) and South America. There were national championships in Zimbabwe, Zambia, Nigeria and the Ivory Coast featuring lower-echelon European Tour players, with Gordon J. Brand of England and David Llewellyn of Wales among the winners.

The feature of the South African, or Sunshine, circuit once more was the Sun City Million Dollar Challenge in the tribal homeland of Bophuthatswana, which attracted a good field of American, European and Australian golfers for the 10-man tournament. For the second year in a row, David Frost kept the $1 million check at home, winning by one stroke over Olazabal and by two over Bernhard Langer and Steve Elkington. Frost was the second repeat champion; Seve Ballesteros won in 1983 and 1984. On the regular South African circuit, natives John Bland and Fulton Allem, who both honed their games there before advancing to the European and American Tours, returned to win three tournaments each.

Three tournaments were held in South America. European Tour regular Vicente Fernandez won his national title, the Argentina Open, to go with his victory in the Tenerife Open. Angel Franco of Paraguay won the Los Leones Open in Chile, and Bruce Fleisher of the United States won the Sao Pablo Open in Brazil.

The U.S. Senior Tour was dominated by first-year player Lee Trevino, which came as no surprise. Trevino had seven victories and $1,190,518 in earnings—more even than Greg Norman won to lead the regular Tour, although Norman was far ahead of Trevino in worldwide earnings. There were 11 players who won two or more tournaments, although Frank Beard offered this assessment of Trevino: "He's a better player than any of us, in every area. It's not inconceivable that someday he could win a tournament by 15 shots."

Trevino was a top-10 finisher in 26 of his 28 tournaments and won these: U.S. Senior Open, Royal Caribbean Classic, Aetna Challenge, Vintage Chrysler Invitational, Doug Sanders Kingwood Celebrity Classic, NYNEX Golf Digest Commemorative and Transamerica Senior Championship.

Another Senior rookie, Jack Nicklaus, came out for only four events and won twice, a sort of schedule he is likely to maintain for the next several years, although he may play more when he reaches age 53 or 54. Nicklaus infuriated the over-50 set when he was quoted in *Golf Digest* as saying that "playing pro-ams on short courses with no rough doesn't motivate me" and that he would be competing against "the same guys I have beaten for 30 years" and that many players winning on the Senior Tour "were good players but marginal. They weren't exceptional."

There has never been any mistaking Dave Hill's annoyance, and he was really angry about Nicklaus' comments. "I used to have a lot of respect for Jack," Hill said. "I thought he was the greatest I had ever seen play. But he forgot what humility was like. He couldn't have been No. 1 without the competition. What he said made a lot of guys angry. We didn't think he felt we were mediocre players. His game may have deteriorated more than ours.

"He has nothing to gain out here now. If we beat up on him—and some weeks we will—he is going to have to take some heat."

For *Golf World*, Nicklaus then tried to put his remarks in perspective: "I never intended to demean or diminish the Senior Tour or the players. They are old friends of mine. As for the statement of not getting excited about going out there against players I have been beating for 30 years, hey, they beat me too, more often than not, and now there are more with which to contend.

"That's what I was referring to in discussing the new life given many former players who may not have had great careers before but certainly are now. They seem to be in their prime, and I think it is wonderful. But I guess I've got to convince myself first that I can't compete on the regular Tour."

Arnold Palmer said that he understood that adjustment. "I told Jack that it will come around and he will be happy he can continue with something that has been very rewarding," Palmer said. "Nothing has changed in life. He's just moving on. As time passes, I suspect he will be out here even more than he thinks."

Palmer did not win in 1990; the highlight of his year was in his farewell to the British Open at St. Andrews, where he had first played in that championship 30 years ago. Arnold missed the cut by one stroke, and only because a record leading score for 36 holes put him more than 10 strokes behind the front-runners.

One of Nicklaus' victories was in a Senior major, the Mazda Senior TPC Championship. Gary Player won the other two, which were his only victories of the year, the PGA Seniors Championship and Volvo Seniors British Open. Other multiple winners were Hill and George Archer with five victories each, Jim Dent with four, Chi Chi Rodriguez and Bob Charles with three each, and these players with two each: Charles Coody, Bruce Crampton, Dale Douglass and Rives McBee. One of Coody's victories included the rich Vantage Championship.

On the LPGA Tour, Beth Daniel exerted a Trevino-like presence, winning seven tournaments and a record $863,578. She then added an eighth victory in the mixed team event, the J.C. Penney Classic, with Davis Love III. Daniel was second in two other tournaments and had 16 top-10 finishes in 23 starts. She won her first major title, the Mazda LPGA Championship, and swept both of the Tour's first $1 million events, adding the Centel Classic to her LPGA titles.

But Daniel was not the only star. Betsy King won two major championships, the Nabisco Dinah Shore and U.S. Women's Open, among her four victories. Patty Sheehan won five times, but suffered a distressing collapse in the U.S. Women's Open. Sheehan led by 11 strokes after three holes of the third round, but lost to King by one shot. The other LPGA major event, the du Maurier Classic, was won by Cathy Johnson. Other standouts, with three triumphs each, were Cathy Gerring and Pat Bradley; for Gerring, those were the first victories of her career. Among the other winners was crowd favorite Nancy Lopez, who had one victory.

The WPG European Tour had only two multiple winners. Trish Johnson had four victories and Florence Descampe won three times. Such star attractions as Marie Laure de Lorenzi and Laura Davies had one victory each. Europe's major championship, the Weetabix Women's British Open, was won by Helen Alfredsson.

For the first time, the American and European circuits met in a Ryder Cup-type format. This first Solheim Cup, sponsored by the Karsten Manufacturing Corp., was won by the United States in Orlando, Florida.

But Daniel was the story in women's golf in 1990. Her success marked a return from a dismal slump for the 34-year-old South Carolinian, who was once hailed as one of the best players of her era. For five years, she was hindered by illness (mononucleosis), injury, poor putting and a confused outlook. She finally decided that she had become lazy, and set out to do something about it.

As Daniel told *Golf World*, "(in 1989) I had something to prove. I had to show people, and myself, that I wasn't going to quit, that I could still play this game." That year, she won four tournaments and $504,851, and "this year, the momentum just carried over."

Bill Blue's tenure as LPGA commissioner was short-lived and he was replaced by former television executive Charles Mechem.

Before turning to the 1990 season in detail, we recall the passing of ... Lew Worsham, 73, winner of the 1947 U.S. Open and five PGA Tour events. Hitting one of the most famous shots in golf history, Worsham holed out to win the 1953 World Championship at Tam O'Shanter Country Club in Chicago ... Fred Daly, 79, winner of the 1947 British Open and the only Irishman to win that championship ... Keith Mackenzie, 69, secretary of the Royal and Ancient Golf Club of St. Andrews from 1967 to 1983.

3. The Masters Tournament

The 1990 golf season had begun in a strange sort of way. The PGA Tour had settled into a sort of malaise. By the time of the Masters, the Tour had been in action for 13 weeks, and aside from Robert Gamez's having won twice in his rookie year and Greg Norman's chipping into the cup for an eagle-three on the first extra hole at Doral and winning a playoff for a change, nothing much had happened. Except for Sandy Lyle, the leading European players—Nick Faldo, Seve Ballesteros, Ian Woosnam, Jose Maria Olazabal, Ronan Rafferty—had stayed at home, and Curtis Strange, then the best of the Americans, had been playing abroad as well, until four weeks before the Masters.

The game thrives on confrontations among the great players, but we were seeing very little of it. Until 1990 we would see them come together occasionally in the early tournaments, but then the leading European golfers dropped off the American circuit because they refused to play 15 tournaments each year, as the PGA Tour demanded. With most of the leading players scattered, the early events had been won by the likes of Tommy Armour III, David Ishii, Dan Forsman, John Huston, and Jodie Mudd, good players indeed, but not names that make the blood boil.

We have always looked to the major tournaments to establish who are the game's best players. All of those who mattered would be at each other's throat for the first time at Augusta. For most of the world, then, the golf season would begin with the first full week in April.

It turned out to be quite a beginning, as usual full of surprises, first with Mike Donald, a player of shaky credentials, coming within one stroke of the tournament's 18-hole record, then 50-year-old Jack Nicklaus stirring the gallery by hanging close to the lead through three rounds, then Raymond Floyd nearly becoming the oldest Masters winner ever, taking a four-stroke lead into the last six holes, and finally Nick Faldo winning the two-hole playoff from Floyd, and becoming the second man to win two successive Masters (Nicklaus had been the first, in 1965 and 1966).

What a difference in the careers of Faldo and Norman. Greg's career has been filled with tournaments snatched from him by lucky shots. First Bob Tway holed from a bunker on the 72nd hole of the 1986 PGA Championship, beating him by a stroke, then Larry Mize holed a pitch-and-run on the second playoff hole in the 1987 Masters, and in 1990 alone Robert Gamez holed a full seven iron on the last hole at Bay Hill, and David Frost holed out from a bunker on the 72nd at New Orleans.

Contrast that record with Faldo's. Nick had won two Masters and one British Open by then, each because of others' mistakes. Paul Azinger held the 1987 British Open in his hands with only two holes to play, but he bogeyed them both, and Faldo won by a stroke. Nick then won the 1989 Masters when Scott Hoch missed a short downhill putt that would have ended the playoff on the first extra hole, and he won the 1990 Masters when Floyd first three-putted the 71st hole, causing the playoff, and then pulled his approach into the pond before the 11th green on the second playoff hole.

No matter how it came about, though, Faldo won them.

Curiously though, he wasn't given much attention as the Masters approached, even though he had been playing reasonably well throughout the year. He had tied for second in the Australian Masters. He had played only once on the European Tour, placing ninth in the Desert Classic played in Dubai, in the United Arab Emirates, bordering the Persian Gulf. He came over to the United States toward the end of March in time to finish 13th in The Nestle Invitational at Bay Hill, in Orlando, Florida, and then shot 64 in the last round of the Independent Insurance Agents Open at The Woodlands, in Houston, climbing to 15th place. He had played only four tournaments on either the Australian, European or the American Tours.

Assessing the state of his game, Faldo said he was feeling "pretty good. I've played very well from tee to green, and I've sorted out my putting, so that's a good boost."

While Faldo took a low-key approach, Norman brimmed with the confidence befitting a man who hadn't finished lower than fifth in his last four Masters. He felt the tournament owed him a victory, since he had come so close in the past. He suffered through his first disappointment in 1986, when he came to the last hole with a chance to tie Jack Nicklaus but pushed his approach into the crowd and bogeyed, falling into a tie for second with Tom Kite. The following year Mize beat him with his improbable shot, and then in 1989 a par on the 18th would have earned him a place in the playoff, but he underclubbed his approach, bogeyed, and dropped to third.

"I don't believe in jinxes," Norman said. "You control your own ability, and what other people do is beyond your control."

He had won the Australian Masters and played in four American tournaments leading up to Augusta, winning at Doral, finishing second at Bay Hill, fifth at the Tournament of Champions, the first event of the season, and 16th at The Players Championship.

Looking at his record, Nicklaus said, "Every tournament he's played in he's played well. The Greg Norman of 1990 is not the Greg Norman of 1989. Last year his swing was not good. He was not confident. This year he's confident. He's swinging well, and he believes he's going to win."

Curtis Strange was even more emphatic.

"Greg's going to win."

While Norman had indeed played well, so had Mark Calcavecchia, although he hadn't won a tournament. Instead, he had placed second in four events, including his last three. He had lost the playoff at Doral when Norman holed his chip, fell two strokes short of John Huston at the Honda Classic, and lost The Players Championship by one stroke when Mudd birdied the 17th hole.

With this record Calcavecchia felt at least as confident as Norman.

"There is no part of my game I don't think is ready to go," he said as he left the locker room after a practice round.

There is a certain similarity between Calcavecchia's Masters record and Norman's. Mark felt he had won the 1988 tournament when Sandy Lyle drove into the fairway bunker on the 18th, but like Norman with Mize, Mark could only watch while Sandy played a stunning seven iron, nipping his ball clean and flying it onto the green within holing distance for the birdie that beat Calcavecchia by a stroke.

Looking back, Calcavecchia said, "It's hard to describe the feeling. One minute you're thinking about winning, and then next you're numb with disappointment."

Hoch, too, knows the feeling. He had just gone through a difficult year. Because he had missed that short putt a year earlier, he had been the victim of a series of thoughtless and cruel remarks. As an example, he was sitting at a poker table in a Las Vegas casino a month later when a stranger recognized him and asked, "Aren't you the guy who screwed up the Masters?"

Scott gritted his teeth and kept on playing. Later in the week, he won the Las Vegas Invitational.

As the 1990 Masters approached, Hoch was invited to an interview in the Brobdingnagian press palace, a new building replacing a Quonset hut that had been in place since the early 1950s. The new building seats reporters in tiers overlooking the big scoreboard. From the floor the arrangement looks like a meeting of the Politburo. Nevertheless, it is the best in the game, the Taj Mahal of press facilities.

Knowing what he was in for, Hoch accepted the invitation nevertheless, but before he began he warned the reporters, "Okay, fellas, take your shots, but when this is over, the 1989 Masters is history. Please don't ask me one more question about it."

Scott admitted, however, his mistake with that short putt will never be forgotten.

"If I win a bunch of tournaments, people will always remember me as the guy who blew the Masters. But I did the best I could with it. There were 72 other guys who screwed up earlier than I did. I played pretty damn good to be there in the end."

To recount the story. Faldo had roared home in 65, and Hoch, playing later, had bogeyed the 17th after a poor drive, shot 69, and matched Nick's 283. Masters playoffs begin at the 10th hole, a formidable par-four that stretches 480 yards, most of it downhill but the last 175 yards or so upward to an elevated green. Nick had played it badly, driving to the right side of the fairway, dropping his approach into the right greenside bunker, and bogeying. Scott, meanwhile played it perfectly: a well-placed drive, and a solid iron that left him about 15 feet under the hole. Scott's first putt glided about two feet or so past the hole, leaving him one putt to win the playoff.

He took his time lining it up, figuring a slight right-to-left break, set himself over the ball, and then stepped away. Satisfied he had read the line properly, Hoch set himself again, stroked his putt, then turned away as it ghosted past the left edge of the cup.

He had halved a hole he figured to win, and Faldo won the Masters with a birdie on the 11th, one of Augusta National's more terrifying holes.

Had Scott choked?

"I would have been choking if I'd gone ahead and hit it. I went to stand over the ball and I thought, 'Hey, I don't even know how I want to hit this putt. That's why I thought the tournament was mine." We do know, however, that he was indeed charged with the crime. Scott claims his treatment by the press was downright cruel.

"I got cut down pretty hard," he said.

"People constantly reminding me how much that putt cost me in fame and money made it tough. The more you look at it that way, the more it hurts, but after a while you develop a thick skin."

He also recalled the comment of a retired player sitting behind him in the dining room of his hotel at the U.S. Open a few months later. Not aware of Hoch during a discussion of the Masters, the former player said, "Nobody's ever screwed up as bad as that guy."

Hoch insists, however, he didn't yip the putt.

"I can honestly say I wasn't nervous at any time. I didn't line it up properly. I saw that when I watched a tape the other day. I had it read correctly; I just didn't have the putter lined up. I know it felt fine when I stroked it. It had a left to right break, and I was trying to putt it inside the left edge of the cup. Some people said I hit it too hard. No; if you baby it, it can really break.

"Anyway, that's not where I lost the tournament; I lost it with my drive on the 17th." Scott pulled his tee shot onto the side of a hill, overshot the green with his approach, played a wonderful little chip that almost hit the flagstick, but missed the putt, dropping him into the tie.

Hoch bounced back from his Masters disappointment and won the 90-hole Las Vegas Invitational the following month, defeating Robert Wrenn by birdieing the fifth hole of a playoff.

"I don't think I'd have won if I'd won at Augusta. The things that cost me at the Masters I made sure didn't happen at Vegas. I concentrated that much more so it wouldn't happen again."

His victory at Las Vegas was his fourth in a 10-year career, but his first since 1984. After he had won, he and his wife stood before the crowd and cried as he donated $100,000 of his $225,000 in prize money to the Arnold Palmer Children's Hospital in Orlando, where the Hochs' young son, Cameron, had been treated for a rare bone infection in his right leg. It had been a frightening experience for them, and had helped put the Masters loss into a different perspective.

Despite the public's attitude, Hoch drew a large gallery as he played the 10th hole in his practice rounds.

"I guess they all wanted to see if I was going to chop that green to pieces."

Even though he had been suffering with tendinitis in his hand, Hoch had placed fourth at Bay Hill, and had come into the Masters in fairly good shape.

At this stage, however, Robert Gamez seemed like the young player of hope, even though he was invited to his first Masters. He was the only man to have won two 1990 American tournaments, and he seemed to be playing with confidence.

A rather short and stocky young man of Mexican ancestry, Gamez stands 5-foot-9 and weighs 170 pounds. With a nut brown complexion, black wavy hair, and dark eyes set in an oval face, Gamez was only 21. The number one player with the University of Arizona, he had left school at the end of his junior year to join the Tour, and had been wildly successful so far, winning at both Tucson, the second tournament of the year and his first as a Tour player (he wasn't eligible for the first, the Tournament of Champions), then holing his seven iron to nip Norman at Bay Hill. He had also missed three cuts, however, and had finished in such ignoble positions as 19th, 38th, and 46th. Life hadn't been all success.

Nevertheless, Gamez's failures had had no noticeable affect, for Gamez was driven by the thirst to do more than simply earn a comfortable living. "I know what I want to do and what I can do, and I know I can win major golf tournaments, maybe this year. I want to be known as one of the better players in the world, right up there on a level with Greg Norman, Mark Calcavecchia, and Curtis Strange." Lofty goals, but the timid seldom climb that high.

Gamez had played a few practice rounds with Ben Crenshaw, the 1984 winner, and had been listening to his advice.

"I've been learning the course a little bit, and I feel I have a chance to win," he said. "I'm not nervous; it's just another tournament, on a larger scale, of course, but the object is just the same—to shoot the lowest score."

Standing in the Bay Hill locker room after Gamez had won, Paul Azinger asked a group of reporters, "You guys looking for the next superstar? It's that little sucker over there," he said, pointing to Robert.

Fuzzy Zoeller, so far the only man since Gene Sarazen 55 years earlier to have won the first Masters he entered, also showed confidence in Gamez, saying, "There's a guy who can win here."

Still, Zoeller is aware of the emotional tides that sweep over the leaders during the late holes.

"It may not hit him right away, but if he's in contention on Saturday or Sunday it will hit him. You can't be a golfer all your life and not have this place hit you."

With Gamez the youngest of those attracting attention, at 50, Nicklaus was the oldest. Even though he hadn't won a tournament since the 1986 Masters until he joined the Senior Tour early in the year and won The Tradition, in Arizona, Jack felt he could win at Augusta.

"I don't care where you're playing," Nicklaus maintained, "winning breeds winning. I hadn't been in contention in five years (actually four), but now I feel good and solid. If you had asked me two weeks ago if I thought I could win the Masters, I'm not sure I could have said yes, but if I play the same way I did in Arizona, I'll be in contention. This is the best golf I've played since the 1970s," he continued, overlooking 1980, when he won both the U.S. Open and the PGA.

Furthermore, among the many qualities that set Nicklaus above the general run of players, he probably hit more greens from the rough than any man who ever played the game. "Augusta National doesn't accent what I've lost in my golf game—the ability to play out of the rough."

As the week began, two developments emphasized how the popularity of the Masters had grown. Within living memory, this has been the toughest ticket in sports. The waiting list was cut off some years ago when someone estimated the last person added to the list would have to wait 50 years. Some relief was added though; tickets for the practice rounds have always been on sale at the gates, but that policy was in danger after the massive crowd that showed up on the eve of the tournament proper to watch the par-three tournament. Tickets actually ran out, but still the crowds came, and substitute tickets had to be found.

No one had ever seen such crowds at Augusta as those that swarmed over the course on Wednesday. It was certainly the largest ever to walk the grounds. This was a different kind of spectator from those who attend the Masters proper. They behaved differently, neither so quiet nor so informed as we see once the tournament begins. The size and demeanor of the crowd not only made the entertaining par-three event difficult to watch, it prompted Hord Hardin, the chairman of the Masters, to reconsider the policy of ticket sales at the gate. He indicated that tickets to future practice rounds might have to be more tightly controlled.

At the same time as those immense crowds streamed onto the course, word leaked that counterfeit tickets to the Masters proper had been circulated, and that every badge would be examined through the four days of the tournament. Gates were opened earlier than normal, and 20 or more counterfeit tickets were seized, including two from a pair of California businessmen who claimed they bought them from a ticket broker for $2,300.

These matters seemed of little consequence, though, once Thursday morning arrived. As usual, the field was relatively small, just 85 players while the normal Tour event draws 144 and the U.S. Open 156, but these 85 make up the cream of international golf.

The normal smaller, more sedate gallery was on hand, those who come regularly and know what is expected of them, some taking their places at favorite locations and remaining stationary throughout the day, others following some favorite golfer, and still others hopping from one hole to another, trying to follow developments, which is more difficult to do.

The air was cool after a night when the temperature had dropped into the 30s, and a soft spring breeze drifted through the tall Georgia pines. Under a bright, cloudless blue sky, the temperature climbed throughout the day, but it remained comfortable under the shade of the loblollies.

The course was immaculate, as always, the grass a deep green, and the bunkers faced with clean, white sand. One change had been effected. Fairways are commonly mowed in two directions, a mower running, for example from tee to green along one side, then turning and running from green to tee on the other, leaving patterns in the grass showing the trail left by the big mowers. As they cut, however, the mowers also flatten the grass so that those blades running away from the tee look shiny, and those facing the tee appear dull. This method has other effects as well. Players had commented that a ball runs farther on the side of the fairway where the mowers ran toward the green than on the other: a drive along the left side of one fairway might run farther than a drive hit along the right.

Augusta solved the problem by lining up a series of mowers all facing the same direction and mowing each fairway in one sweep. No more patterns in the grass, and no more excuses.

Something else was missing as well. Because of the unusually mild winter and warm early spring, the show of bright spring colors from flowering trees and bushes that so often peak at Masters time had passed, and the red azaleas that line the bank behind the 13th green, the blossoms of the yellow jasmine along the eighth, and the pink dogwood were missing, lost to unpredictable weather.

The loss was felt only momentarily, however, when Gene Sarazen and Sam Snead played their ceremonial nine holes at the head of the field. The gallery had come to see the players, not the flowers. Teeing off at 9:33, Ray Floyd and South African David Frost carried the first sizable gallery of the day, just ahead of Tom Watson and Australian Ian Baker-Finch, who had shot to prominence in the early rounds of the 1984 British Open at St. Andrews.

Floyd hadn't been a factor in a tournament in some years. He hadn't won since 1986, when he took both the U.S. Open and the Walt Disney Classic, and he had just gone through his worst year since 1973, wining only $74,699 at a time when the leading money winners hover over $1 million. His indifferent year could be explained and ignored because of the the distraction of having served as captain of the American Ryder Cup team, which had tied the European team in England the previous September, but no one could ignore the effects of age. By the spring of 1990, Floyd had reached 47.

None of this seemed to matter to Raymond, though. He had birdied the ninth hole to break a seven-man tie and win the par-three tournament with a score of 23, four under par, and then began the first round by birdieing the opening hole. After reeling off seven consecutive pars, Floyd birdied the ninth to dip two under, then played an erratic home nine, scoring three pars, three birdies, and three bogeys. He stood at four under par with only the last three holes to play, but he missed the 16th green and three-putted the 18th, bogeyed both, and shot 70.

Floyd's was a good, solid score, and it would have lasting effects on the tournament, but by the time he lost his stroke at the 18th, he had fallen four strokes off the lead, and eventually would lag farther behind. Three groups earlier, John Huston had come in with a 66.

A 27-year-old native of Illinois of medium height and slight build, and wearing a dark mustache, Huston had attracted attention first by wearing shoes that violated the rules of golf. The outer edges of the soles were raised, creating a better stance and weight distribution, the manufacturer claimed. The USGA evidently agreed, banned the shoe, and the manufacturer entered the great American sport of litigation, and sued.

Huston, meantime, changed shoes and won the Honda Classic, and a week or so later was forced off a Florida road and into a ditch at 40 miles an hour. The crash flung him against the windshield, where he cut his head so badly doctors needed 11 stitches to close the wound.

By winning the Honda, he earned a place in the Masters for the first time, and he made the most of it. Paired with Hubert Green and teeing off a little after 9 o'clock, Huston hit every green and played a bogey-free round.

Before Huston teed off, Mark McCumber had warned him, "Whatever happens, don't let it surprise you too much." Worthwhile advice, for some of Huston's shots had the element of surprise. He salvaged his par four on the ninth after driving into the woods along the left, and the 15th after his drive caromed off a spectator's chair, then birdied the 18th even though he drove into the woods again.

Even so, Huston could have scored better, because he played some wonderful irons—a six iron to 12 feet on the first, a five iron to eight feet on the sixth, a wedge to 15 feet on the seventh, and a seven iron to six feet on the 10th, and missed the putts, settling for pars. Huston made only two putts outside gimme range—a 10-footer after a crisp nine iron on the 14th, and from 15 feet on the 18th after a six iron through the trees.

He birdied four other holes, three of them par-fives, and he played only one indifferent shot, hitting a poor chip after his three-iron second missed the green of the 15th, a 500-yard par-five over water.

Huston was just finishing when Mike Donald started out, paired with Dan Forsman, the winner of the Shearson Lehman Hutton Open in San Diego in mid-February.

As far as anyone could remember, Donald hadn't done anything in the big tournaments since he led the first round of the 1984 U.S. Open, but on this day he played the round of his life, birdieing five holes on the first nine and three on the second, and shooting 64, which matched the opening round record that had stood for 50 years, since Lloyd Mangrum had opened with 64 in 1940. Donald's score fell just one stroke shy of the Masters record 63 Nick Price had shot in the third round in 1986.

Donald played an unusual round for a score so low. Even though he broke Augusta's par of 72 by eight strokes, he missed five greens. They cost him nothing; he saved par on four, and birdied the other, chipping in from 40 feet on the ninth.

His putting had never been better. He holed one putt from 35 feet, two from 20, and another from 15 feet, but at the same time he missed one putt from seven feet on the seventh, and two others from 15 feet on the first and second.

Donald made his first birdie on the fourth, at 205 yards the longest of Augusta's four par-three holes. A two iron left him 35 feet from the hole, but he ran the putt home.

"I felt like I had won the tournament," he said later.

A streaky player, Donald was off to a wonderful run of holes, birdieing six of the next eight and taking command of the first round. A 15-footer fell on the fifth, a particularly strong par-four of 435 yards with a rolling green, and a 20-footer dropped on the sixth. Three under now, and in a groove. A sand wedge to eight feet on the seventh, but the putt slipped past the cup, then after two big shots and a sand wedge, he holed a 20-footer on the eighth, a par-five then holed a chip on the ninth after pushing his approach wide of the green.

Now he stood at five under par and the gallery rushed after him, hoping to catch a glimpse of what was turning into a great round of golf.

A big drive on the 10th and an eight iron to six feet. Six under, but a shaky 11th, saving his par by holing an eight-footer after flying his approach into a greenside bunker.

Now for the 12th, the devilish little par-three across a pond to a wide but frighteningly shallow green, where the ground rises beyond into a shrub-infested slope. No problem for Donald, though; a solid seven iron left him only a foot and a half from the cup, and he ran it in.

Donald stood at seven under par then, on a pace to shoot 65, but with the 13th and 15th, two reachable par-fives, coming up, he could realistically look for two more birdies. It didn't work out quite that way. He pulled his second to the 13th, leaving his ball on the bank rising to the left of the green, just outside a bunker and almost among the azaleas above. He pitched on, but not close enough.

No birdie there, but another on the 15th, where he laid up short of the pond and pitched to within four feet.

Eight under par; one more and Donald would match the Masters record. But he didn't have another birdie in him. Sound pars on the 16th and 17th, and then a five iron pulled about 10 or 15 feet left of the 18th green. It was not an automatic par.

Applause began building as Donald walked up the hill to the green, and swelled as he walked toward his ball. Without hesitation he drew a lofted club, strode to the hole, then back to his ball, took two little practice swings, and played a little pitch. The ball rolled toward the hole, and for one heartstopping moment looked as if it might fall. No; it eased past the left edge of the cup and stopped within inches. A par four and 64.

Sensational as it was, Donald's round was not a reckless bid for birdies. He played somewhat carefully, explaining, "You were better off on some holes playing away from the pins. That's not necessarily playing safe; but it was playing smart."

When the day ended Donald held a two-stroke lead over Huston, and three over Peter Jacobsen, who breezed around Augusta National in 33-34—67.

Altogether, 19 men broke Augusta's par of 72, and 13 others matched it—32 men at par or better, four of them under 70 (Bill Britton shot 68). At this stage, it looked as if the 72-hole record might be in danger.

Not from Donald, though; he had no such ideas. Nor would he admit he had thoughts about winning, saying, "To be honest, I was just hoping I wouldn't play a real bad round and shoot myself out of contention. I just want to make the top 24 and come back next year."

Not a very lofty goal for someone who had just shot 64, but he was in much better shape than some others who had come to Augusta. Among those you might expect to see at the top, Robert Gamez shot 73, Jodie Mudd, the TPC winner, Mark Calcavecchia, Fred Couples, and Seve Ballesteros, with a four-putt green at the 16th, shot 74; Mark O'Meara, who had won at Pebble Beach, and Tom Kite shot 75; Sandy Lyle, still locked in a slump, had 77, and Greg Norman a dismal 78.

Norman played some shoddy golf, particularly surprising considering his earlier form. For example, he three-putted the eighth after reaching the green with his second, settling for a par five, drove the ball perfectly on the 13th, so long and so well placed he had only a six iron to the green, then dumped the approach into the creek and took a bogey six, rolled his second shot over the 15th green and chipped so badly he settled for another unsatisfactory par. On these three holes alone, he played one over par golf where he might reasonably have expected to have played them in three under. Four shots lost.

What had gone wrong?

"A bad day. Bad concentration, bad everything. And I felt great coming here this morning."

The first round leaders:

Mike Donald	64
John Huston	66
Peter Jacobsen	67
Bill Britton	68
George Archer	70
Raymond Floyd	70
Curtis Strange	70
Larry Mize	70
Bernhard Langer	70
Bill Glasson	70
Masashi Ozaki	70

Other scores of interest:

Scott Hoch	71
Nick Faldo	71
*Chris Patton	71
Jack Nicklaus	72
Lee Trevino	78
Paul Azinger	80

None of those who had shot in the 60s played anywhere near his first-round form the next day. Huston and Britton shot 74, and Jacobsen 75.

Donald played worse; he shot 82, three-putting four of the first six greens. Twenty-four men passed him, and he dropped from first place into a tie for 25th. He was terrible; no Masters leader had ever fallen so far. The difference of 18 strokes between the two rounds—a stroke a hole—topped Raymond Floyd's 14-stroke drop in 1965, when he followed an opening 69 with 83 in the second round. Like Donald's, that was Floyd's first Masters. Now Donald was in danger of failing to qualify automatically for the 1991 tournament.

His turnaround wasn't exactly a new experience. He had led the first round of the 1984 U.S. Open, but began the second with four bogeys and dropped like a stone.

Donald might have broken 80 except for bad luck at the 18th. When he pulled his drive, his ball hit one of the trees along the left and disappeared into a drain. (His caddy said, "The water carried the ball to Savannah.") Donald argued the drain should be considered an obstruction, giving him relief without a penalty, but the rules officials said the drain had always been marked as a hazard but by mistake hadn't been marked this year. Their view carried the day, and Donald made seven, losing three strokes on this one hole.

Through it all, he held onto his sense of humor, saying, "I went down the drain in more ways than one."

Trying to analyze what had happened to him, he pointed out, "I had 40 putts today to 21 yesterday; that tells you quite a bit right there. I had five three-putt greens."

Asked if he were heartbroken at the disappointing round, Donald replied, "Are you kidding? I've had the chance to do what 30 million other people would love to do—play in the Masters."

While the first-round leaders fell, others rose to take their places. Floyd was the best of those, shooting 68 to go with his opening 70 and climbing into first place, with 138. Hoch matched Floyd's 68 and moved into second place, at 139, a stroke ahead of Huston, at 140. Masashi (Jumbo) Ozaki, the long-hitting Japanese, shot 71, moving up a notch to fourth place, at 141, a stroke ahead of Jacobsen, Craig Stadler, Mike Hulbert, Bill Britton, and Jack Nicklaus, who followed his opening 72 with 70.

Curtis Strange made his move early. With birdies on the first and the very difficult fourth, he dipped four under par for the 22 holes he had played, but Curtis couldn't keep a rally going. He lost a chance to birdie the eighth by pulling his drive into the trees and leaving himself no opportunity to play his second close to the green. Then he began going bad at the ninth. He overshot the green, chipped all the way down the green's slippery incline and off the front, and made six, a double bogey. Both strokes he had picked up on the early holes were gone.

Another stroke lost at the 10th, where his approach rolled off the green, and he had to struggle for a bogey on the 12th, where he bunkered his tee shot and failed to recover with his first attempt. Where once he had seemed to be closing in, now he was trying to hold on. One over par for the day now, he finished with 73 to go with his opening 70, and had 143 for the 36 holes.

As Strange struggled, Hoch grew hot, turning what started out as an unpromising round into a very good one. A birdie on the second was lost to a bogey-five on the relatively easy third, where Scott bunkered his drive. Another stroke lost at the third, where he followed a short tee shot with a chip that ran well past the hole.

That was his last mistake. Hoch scored his second birdie of the round at the eighth, reaching the green with a three-wood second and two-putting, then holed a 30-footer on the ninth. Out in 35, he birdied three more holes coming in, dropping a seven iron within 10 feet on the 12th and holing the putt, reaching the 13th green with a four-iron second and two-putting, and two-putting the 15th from 50 feet after a two-iron second.

Hoch stood at five under for the day then, six under for the tournament, and had taken the lead.

The day had begun under bright sunshine, but clouds had rolled in throughout the afternoon, and now a light rain began to fall as Hoch faced those last three demanding holes. Needing three more pars to shoot 67, he made the first two, but pulled his drive into the bunkers bordering the left side of the 18th fairway and dropped a stroke, finishing with 68.

"It's nice to come back here and play well," Hoch said when the round ended. "As little practice and as little competitive golf as I've played, I'm thrilled to be in the position I'm in."

Because of injured tendons in his hand, Hoch hadn't played tournament golf for seven weeks before he entered Bay Hill two weeks earlier, and he said his hand no longer bothered him.

"I'm hitting the ball a lot more solid now. I'm able to hit my long irons with no pain; I couldn't do it two weeks ago. If I wasn't able to hit long irons now, I wouldn't be here."

Hoch had been playing about two and a half holes ahead of Floyd, who had come into the Masters with little support. He hadn't won a tournament in nearly four years, not since the fall of 1986, a few months after winning the U.S. Open at Shinnecock Hills, and he had given no indication he was about to break through. He had spent most of the previous year and a half preparing for his role at captain of the Ryder Cup team, and he ranked 61st on the money list, with third place in the Honda his best finish of the year.

Like Hoch's, Floyd's round had had a shaky beginning, but it turned around quickly. He stood at one over par after two bogeys and a birdie through the first seven holes, but he rifled a big drive far down the center of the eighth fairway, then followed up with a screaming three wood that covered 260 yards, much of it uphill, and rolled onto the green within 12 feet of the hole. From his recognizable stiffly upright stance, Floyd rammed the putt home for an eagle-three dropping to one under par for the round, three under for the tournament.

With that shot, Floyd turned into a different player. Now he stalked the lead. Four straight two-putt pars, one saved from eight feet, and then he reeled off three consecutive birdies, reaching both the 13th and 15th with iron clubs and making two-putt birdies. Another on the 14th, rolling in an 18-footer after reaching the green with a three wood and eight iron. But that was all; he had only one reasonable birdie opportunity on the three home holes, but he missed from eight feet on the 17th and played the home nine in 33.

Floyd seemed especially pleased with his eagle on the eighth, saying, "I hadn't reached that green in a couple of years.

"I'm tickled pink with the way I'm playing," he went on. "I'm having a lot of fun. After being non-competitive for a couple of years, you always wonder if you can come back. It's tough to lay down your clubs when you're 45, but that's what I did. I concentrated all my time on the Ryder Cup. I started back working and practicing in December to see if I could in fact play."

As for his round, "It was like old times on the par-fives. It brought back some fond old memories."

When Floyd won the 1976 Masters, he played Augusta's four par-five holes in 15 under par. He had played them in two under par in the first round, and in five under in the second, close to the pace he had set 14 years earlier when he matched the Masters record of 271 Nicklaus had set in 1965.

Nicklaus, meanwhile, played as if he had been reborn, pounding his drives farther than he had in years. He gave credit to two sources—to Jim Flick, a prominent teacher who offered Jack some advice when Nicklaus played in The Tradition, his first senior tournament, and to a new metal-headed graphite-shafted driver given to him by Jumbo Ozaki after an exhibition match in Japan. Noticing how far Ozaki drove the ball, Nicklaus commented he would like to have one of those drivers for himself, and Ozaki obliged. It was the same model, by the way, that Floyd was using as well.

"I'm hitting some drives I haven't hit at this place in a long, long time," Jack said.

Looking at his position after paring two strokes from par with a four-birdie round—ruined, incidentally, by a double-bogey five on the 12th, where he missed the green, then three-putted—Nicklaus said, "If you'd told me two weeks ago that I'd be sitting here just four shots out of the lead after two rounds, I'd have said you've got to be crazy. It shows what playing well one week does to your frame of mind. I had the opportunity to shoot a really low score, but I didn't put many putts in the hole. Most of the putts I had were easy, from under the hole, but I left a good half of them short."

Scoring had become more difficult from the first to the second round, where 32 men had played Augusta in par or better on Thursday, only 19 had shot 72 or under on Friday, and where six men had broken 70 in the first round, only four had made it in the second. On the other hand, where five men had gone over 80 Thursday, seven had shot 80 or more on Friday.

Among those, Arnold Palmer shot an even 80, missing the 36-hole cut for the seventh consecutive year, but vowing nevertheless he would return in 1991. Ken Green matched him, with two costly holes on the home nine. After going out in 36, Green hit two balls into the pond in front of the 12th green, making six, then drove into the woods on the 13th, took a couple of shots to reach the fairway, hit into the water again, and took 10 strokes.

He was gone then, missing the cut along with Palmer, Greg Norman, whose 72 wasn't good enough, and Sandy Lyle, who left a trail of blood behind his two rounds of 77 and 74. During the opening round, Lyle had sent a drive screaming into the gallery on the eighth, stunning a spectator, and on Friday Sandy played three wild shots into the galleries, the first the most serious.

Playing the second hole, Lyle's four iron overshot the green and smashed into the face of a woman spectator, shattering her glasses and cutting her face below the eyes badly enough to call for an overnight stay in a hospital. The ball, incidentally, fell into the pocket of her jacket. Three holes later Lyle hit a man on the leg off the fifth tee, and scattered spectators lining the sixth green with another wild shot. That explains why the British press called him the Tartan Terror.

The second round leaders:

Raymond Floyd	138
Scott Hoch	139
John Huston	140
Jumbo Ozaki	141
Jack Nicklaus	142
Craig Stadler	142
Mike Hulbert	142
Bill Britton	142
Peter Jacobsen	142

Other scores of interest:

Nick Faldo	143
Bernhard Langer	143
Curtis Strange	143
*Chris Patton	144
Ben Crenshaw	146
Lee Trevino	147
Seve Ballesteros	147
Mark Calcavecchia	147

Missed the cut:

Robert Gamez	148
Greg Norman	150
Sandy Lyle	151
Hal Sutton	152
Arnold Palmer	156
Paul Azinger	156
Ken Green	158

While Floyd was rushing to the lead, a good share of attention focused on Chris Patton, who had developed an enthusiastic following of his own. Patton had been invited as the U.S. Amateur champion, and while amateurs had indeed made the cut in the past, very few had been among the leaders at this stage. Patton was among the exceptions. One of only five amateurs in the field, Patton had shot 65 in a practice round on Monday, but hadn't let the score go to his head, saying, "I just want to be here on Saturday." Indeed, he made the cut handily, shooting 71 in the first round and 73 in the second, and with a score of 144, even par, went into the third round tied for 15th place, six strokes out of the lead.

Blessed with a lovely, fluid, repeating swing, an outstanding short game, and immense power, Patton's appeal lay as much in himself as it did in his golf game. He was the biggest man in the field. At 6-foot-1, with big, broad shoulders, Chris said he weighed 300 pounds. He had been heavier. When he won the Amateur, at Merion the previous August, he said he had just lost 50 pounds.

With reddish gold hair and a ruddy complexion, he had a round, chubby face with puffy cheeks, as one might expect, wore a mustache so light it might be missed from a distance, had a big chest and a wide midsection that bulged and hung over his beltline, and strong, powerful arms. He swung with a rhythmic motion, and chipped and putted like a dream.

Watching him hit some of his big drives, Gary Player said, "It's the first time I saw a man hit a ball and seen a spark on green grass."

With it all he was the nicest kid you'd want to meet. And he had a lively sense of humor. Asked if he were related to George Patton, the bold, aggressive World War II general, or to Billy Joe Patton, the amateur from Morganton, North Carolina, who had nearly won the 1954 Masters, Chris said he didn't think so.

"I've never seen them at family reunions."

A senior at Clemson University, Patton grew up in Fountain Inn, near Greenville and Clemson in western South Carolina, within a couple of hours' drive of Augusta.

A sensitive young man, who speaks in a soft voice tinged with the inflections of the South, Chris has been hurt by comments on his build.

"I want to be respected as a golfer," he said, "but some of the things people do make you feel like a freak."

Before he left home for the trip to Augusta, Patton told a reporter, "With all those big names there, I don't expect anyone to pay attention to me. Not unless I'm leading, and the headlines say, 'Fat Ass Leads Masters.'" Obviously he doesn't have to be reminded he's overweight. "I look in the mirror every day."

Patton was wrong in believing no one would pay attention to him. He had a big following that included a fair number of younger spectators wearing shirts imprinted with an orange tiger's paw, a symbol of Clemson. His appeal, however, reached into every element of the gallery. As he climbed the long hill leading to the 18th green on Friday, the gallery rose and applauded his courage in fighting off the pressures and playing better than most of the game's leading players.

His performance had been courageous indeed, for he looked as if he had lost control of his game when he double-bogeyed the 12th, taking four from the edge of the green. He had been one stroke over par for the day then, going out in 37, but as he walked off the green, his caddy said, "Just hang in there. Don't force it; you're playing good."

He won those strokes back by holing long, curling birdie putts at both the 14th and 16th and finished the round in 73.

Those last few holes convinced Patton he can play championship golf.

"When you play at a different level," he said, "you have to think the way the others think. I'm adjusting to that pretty well. I feel I belong here."

He convinced himself even more the next day when he continued to hang around the fringes of the leading group by shooting 74, two over par, but at 218 for 54 holes, he had left himself in 22nd place. That was his high point, though. Struggling to play well enough to earn an invitation to the following year's tournament, Patton finally gave in to the strain, shot 40 on the first nine of the last round, finished with 78 and 296, dropping him to 39th place with two others. He beat eight men.

The Masters began taking its final shape on Saturday, the day of the third round. With the field down to 49 men, 12 shot in the 60s, two more than in the first two rounds combined, and 10 others shot par or better. Clearly, scoring had improved.

Both Faldo and Kite shot 66, and Tom Watson suddenly recovered his old touch and came in with 67. Only Faldo's score mattered, though. Kite and Watson had fallen too far behind over the first two rounds, and had very little hope by then. With 214, Kite climbed into a tie for 10th place with Strange, and Watson had tied for 15th place, one stroke further behind.

Floyd hung onto the lead at 206, following another 68, and John Huston caused mild surprise by climbing into second place at 208, with a 68 of his own. More ominous noise came from behind them, though. Faldo had played two solid but uninspiring rounds of 71 and 72 until he roared to life with his 66, leaping into third place and making the first move in the drive to his second consecutive Masters.

Faldo stood at 209, just three strokes behind Floyd, and two ahead of Nicklaus, who clung to fourth place, at 211, with 69. Hoch held fifth, another stroke behind Nicklaus after a dull 73, and in a tie with Bernhard Langer, who shot 68. We were down to the final make-up of the coming battle.

For a time though, Floyd looked as if he might not last. Off to a strong start with a very good birdie on the 555-yard second, where he drove so far his ball rolled to the bottom of the hill, leaving him only a 165-yard shot to the green. With an overhanging tree limb partially blocking the direct line to the flag, Floyd punched a low five iron between two bunkers and onto the far side of the green, an estimated 110 feet from the hole—definitely three-putt range. Floyd played a superb lag, coaxing his first putt within four feet of the cup, then holed it for his birdie.

His luck changed then, and he bogeyed three of the next four holes, missing both the third and fifth green, and three-putting the sixth, the par-three, from 35 feet. A birdie on the seventh, where he pitched to within five feet, and he made the turn in 37, one over par.

Floyd had been playing some loose golf through the first nine, and while his game didn't improve much coming home, he had better luck. A six iron to 12 feet, one of his better irons, and a birdie on the 10th, and then he dropped a 35-footer from off the green on the 12th. One under par for the round then, Floyd picked up another birdie at the 14th, where he holed a sand wedge after his approach ran six feet or so off the green.

Laying up short of the pond on the 15th, Floyd pitched within 15 feet and holed it, and then made his third consecutive birdie by holing a roller-coaster 35-footer.

Struggling pars on both the 17th and 18th, where indifferent irons left him 55 and 45 feet from the cup, and Floyd was back in 31, turning what had been an unpromising round into a solid four-under-par score, which held the lead for him.

By the time Floyd was making his final run for home, Faldo had already finished. He had gone into the round with the idea of somehow projecting himself into the fight, and he succeeded by playing some exceptional irons, birdieing three holes on the outward nine, and three more coming back.

The sky was clear and bright as Faldo started out, and although the wind had a chilly bite, it blew with less force from a different direction. Paired with Langer, Faldo opened with a stunning five iron that settled within a foot of the hole. That shot not only set up a birdie on the first hole, but also set the tone of the day.

Nick followed his opening birdie with five routine pars, then played the short par-four seventh with a three iron and a wedge to four feet, and came back with another wedge to within a foot on the eighth for his third birdie of the first nine.

A seven iron to eight feet and another birdie on the 10th, a par saved on the 12th, two putts for a birdie, after a one-iron second reached the 13th green, and then another superb wedge to eight feet on the 14th and Nick's last birdie of the day.

Faldo almost lost one of his strokes when he left a 12-footer for a par on the 18th, but he holed it for his 66, finally in the hunt for a second consecutive Masters.

Nicklaus, meanwhile, kept himself in contention with a scrambling 69, holding him in fourth place and leaving him in better position than in 1986, when he passed six men and won his sixth Masters.

"I only have three guys ahead of me now," he said, while admitting he'd have to play better than he had so far.

How the leaders stood after three rounds:

Raymond Floyd	206
John Huston	208
Nick Faldo	209
Jack Nicklaus	211
Bernhard Langer	212
Scott Hoch	212

A bright sun rode high in the azure sky as the last round began, and the barest hint of a breeze ruffled the upper branches of the tall pines. The day was perfect for scoring. Except for those spectators who preferred to follow particular players, fans who had flocked through the gates early in the day had settled around the greens and tees from the first hole through the 18th. As the leader, Floyd played in the last pairing, with Huston. Faldo and Nicklaus played just ahead, a group behind Langer and Hoch. Much of the big crowd followed Nicklaus, who had played so much thrilling golf here for nearly 30 years. If they could be said to have a favorite, he was their man. But hard work lay ahead of him.

Floyd, of course, looked like his main problem. He is a tough front-runner who rarely gives up a lead. He would be hard to catch, and yet he had problems as well. Huston stood only two strokes behind him, showing no signs of caving in to the emotional strain of the Masters, but even more menacing, Faldo, the most dangerous player of the last few years, lurked only three strokes behind him. Still, if either Huston, Faldo, or even Nicklaus, another two strokes behind Faldo, were to overtake Floyd, they would have to play sub-par golf.

Or so it seemed. We were to find out, though, that not even a strong front-runner such as Floyd could be immune to the pressure.

Nor was Faldo, who had been a factor in nearly every U.S. Open, British Open and Masters since he won the 1987 British Open. He realized that to catch Floyd, he would have to play an exceptional round, but he was in trouble from the start. His opening drive drifted right and settled in the bunker at the crest of the hill, and from there he had made poor contact with the ball, leaving it well short of the green. Compounding this error, he three-putted, taking a double-bogey six. Now he stood five strokes behind before Floyd had played a single hole.

Moments later, from the top of the hill on the second hole, Faldo played a less than crisp iron that fell far short of the green. On a day when he would need his best game to make up ground on such an unyielding spirit as Floyd's, he didn't look sharp.

Faldo, though, had some steel in him as well. He pitched onto the green and holed his putt for the birdie. Now he stood four strokes back, and off to another classic finish to the Masters.

While Faldo had begun with some shaky golf, Floyd wasn't on top of his game, either. The second hole indicated how his day would go. A decent enough drive rolled onto a level patch of ground over the brow of the hill leading downward to the green, but he hit a terrible shot from there, pulling his ball into the pines bordering the fairway. Luckily, the ball thunked into a tree and fell into a clearing in the pine straw, leaving him an opening to the green. Unlike Faldo, though, Floyd missed his birdie. A stroke lost.

Even after failing to birdie a hole he might have counted on, and even though he had dropped a stroke, Floyd was in an even stronger position than when he had begun, because Huston, meantime, was unraveling, opening with two bogeys. With 16 holes to play, Floyd held a four-stroke lead over the field, for while he stood 10 strokes under par, Nicklaus, Faldo, and Huston stood six under, Langer four under, and Hoch and Kite three under.

Paired with Faldo, Nicklaus had birdied the second hole with a nice pitch below the hole, followed by a solid putt, and had picked up his pars on the third and fourth holes. The fifth is the best unknown hole at Augusta, a 435-yard par-four whose fairway swings gently left, and whose undulating green is dominated by a depression at the front left resembling the swale at the front right of the better-known 14th green.

Nicklaus had his first setback here. Still four strokes behind, Jack would have to make a move soon if he were to catch up. He played a good drive that left him within easy range of the flagstick, but with the green falling away sharply at the rear, it is better to be short than long. Jack and Nick both left their approaches short, just at the base of the depression and only a few inches off the actual putting surface. With his son Jackie, his caddy, attending the flagstick, Nicklaus studied the line, then struck the putt. The ball rolled up the grade directly on line, and as it approached the hole, Jackie pulled the flagstick, thrust a clenched fist high overhead, and danced away from the hole, signaling the putt would fall.

Jackie had guessed wrong. Struck with a little too much force, the ball caught the right lip of the cup, spun 180 degrees, and scooted three or four feet left. It had been a terrific putt, but not quite good enough. His second putt didn't even touch the hole, and he bogeyed. Back to even par for the day, five under for the tournament, and five strokes behind Floyd.

On to the sixth, the par-three. Once again Jack missed a short putt for a par, and even though he birdied the seventh by holing out from a bunker, those two bogeys ended his threat. He played the first nine in 36, even par, but shot 38 coming in, with an unusually weak finish of three bogeys on the last five holes.

Meanwhile, Floyd had been playing indifferent golf through the early holes. Besides the loose shot at the second, he had pulled his drive into the woods bordering the fifth fairway, and with no opening to the green had pitched safely out, costing him one stroke of his lead.

Another loose shot to the sixth left him the width of the green from the hole, set in the back right, and he overshot the seventh green after pulling another drive. Still, he saved his pars on both, then played two wonderful shots to reach the eighth green once again, and scored another birdie. Once again, though, he pulled his drive on the ninth, overshot another green, but again saved his par with a lovely flip that rolled dead about two feet above the hole on a dangerously canted green.

Up ahead Faldo had birdied the seventh after a lovely pitch, and followed with another stunning iron to the ninth, holing another short birdie putt. After his miserable start on the first hole, Nick had played the next eight holes in three under par, and had turned for home in 35, eight under par for the distance. More importantly, though, he had closed to within two strokes of Floyd.

Quickly one of those strokes was lost, for Faldo skied his drive and bogeyed the 10th just as Raymond saved his par on the ninth. Now Floyd looked safe once more; only that dangerous swing through the early holes of the second nine could make much difference, for Floyd led Faldo by three strokes. Only the two of them mattered by now, and they were playing a hole apart.

Into Amen Corner they went, both men making their fours on the 11th, the best hole Floyd had played since the eighth, and then Faldo looked as if he had faltered. Overshooting the 12th green and finding his ball embedded in the rear bunker, Faldo faced a dangerous shot, heading directly toward the pond crossing the front of the green. Digging his feet into the sand and waggling the clubhead longer than usual, Nick swung into the ball about as gently as he dared, dug it out, and ran the ball past the hole. For a breathless moment it looked as if it might run far enough to tumble into the pond, but it stopped just a foot or so beyond the putting surface. Now for the putt that could hold him within range of the lead.

He crouched over the ball while the silent gallery strained against the ropes holding its breath. After what seemed an age, Nick drew his club back and tapped the ball. At first Nick felt he had struck the putt too softly. As it ghosted toward the hole, it gradually lost pace, and Nick squatted low, urging the ball onward toward the hole. For an instant he gave up on it, but the ball inched forward, and on its last roll it fell. A three where he might have made anything.

Still, it looked academic, because Floyd came up next, overshot the green as well, but from the grassy patch behind the green he rolled in an 18-footer for a birdie.

Eleven under par now, he had increased his lead to four strokes over Faldo. The tournament looked as if it were over. It wasn't; instead, Faldo was about to play an inspired stretch of golf.

Two big shots, the second from 200 yards, left Nick just outside 20 feet on the 13th, and when he birdied, he had picked up one stroke on Floyd, for Raymond made only a par five. Now Faldo had closed to within three strokes, but with only five holes to play, he still faced a difficult climb.

Now the great crowd massed behind the last two groups, picking up those who had seated themselves at the early holes to watch the field play through. With every shot they scrambled ahead, straining to catch a glimpse of the players.

Floyd still looked like the winner, but he was 47 years old, and tough though he was through years of competing at the highest level, his nerves might not hold up.

They looked strong enough on the 14th, where he turned his drive around the corner of the gentle dogleg, then played a hard seven iron that barely rolled off the back edge of the green. Huston had played his approach inside Floyd's, and had marked his ball with a penny. The coin lay almost on Floyd's line, and Huston asked if Raymond wanted it moved. Floyd said no, then chipped with his wedge. As it rolled toward the hole, the ball nipped the penny and caromed toward the cup. Floyd had judged the pace just right, but the ball sat on the right edge of the cup. A par, and still three strokes ahead.

Still battling, Faldo pecked away. A 230-yard two iron rolled off the back of the 15th, and a pitch stopped four feet short of the hole. Faldo rolled it in for another birdie. Moments later, after another pulled drive, Floyd parred, his birdie putt barely slipping past the low edge of the cup. Two strokes ahead with three holes to play. Faldo was closing in.

As Floyd walked toward the 15th green, Faldo played a six iron onto the 16th green, cut near the left edge, close to the pond that threatens the slightly pulled shot, and left of the flag. Faldo's ball pulled up short of the flag, and he rolled it in from about 25 feet. Another birdie, his third in the last four holes.

Minutes later Floyd steered his tee shot well right of the pond, leaving himself 30 feet from the cup with a putt breaking so severely left he stood with his back toward the hole at about a 45-degree angle. Nevertheless, he nearly holed if for a matching birdie. The ball barely slipped past the hole, and he settled for a par three. One stroke ahead with two holes to play.

Up ahead, Faldo nearly holed his birdie putt on the 17th, then drove up the 18th fairway. With the hole cut in the rear, Nick made sure he had enough club, and rolled his ball off the back edge.

As he climbed the grade toward the green, word flashed that Floyd had three-putted the 17th from 70 feet or more. Just then the big crowd roared as Floyd's score went up on the big board close by the 18th green. Uncertain of what the noise meant, Nick turned and watched the number 10 replace the 11 beside Floyd's name. Faldo had gained four strokes within five holes, and now he and Floyd were tied.

As Floyd's second putt had glided past the hole on the 17th, some of the gallery broke and raced toward the 10th hole, expecting a playoff, and stacked themselves five and six deep around the green.

Just before Faldo putted on the 18th, word raced through the gallery that Floyd had driven into the fairway bunker, his ball buried in the sand. First to play, Faldo putted down the slope, but his ball broke away from the hole, settling about three feet away. As Floyd watched from the bunker, Faldo holed it. He had played the last nine holes in 34 and shot 69. He was in with 278 for the 72 holes, and Floyd faced a struggle to catch him now.

To reach the green, Raymond would have to play a shot from a buried lie that would have to rise quickly to clear the front lip of the bunker and fly far enough to reach the green. Instead, Floyd's ball shot off to the right and dropped into a greenside bunker. He might not even make the playoff. Needing a par now, Raymond played a nerveless recovery and saved his four. He had shot 72, even par, and matched Faldo's 278, forcing another playoff.

The crowd was enormous, ringing the 10th fairway from the tee to the green as both men drove the fairway. From the top of the hill, Faldo played an indifferent approach that fell short and into the right greenside bunker, just where he had been a year earlier in his playoff with Hoch. There was a difference, however; where he had bogeyed in 1989, he made his par here.

Floyd, meanwhile, played a superb approach, flying his ball directly at the flagstick and leaving it about 15 feet short of the cup. His putt, though, was hit a bit too timidly; it stopped five or six inches short of the hole. He tapped it in for the matching four, and they moved on to the 11th.

The sun was riding low now, giving the high branches a golden cast, and shadows covered the ground. Again both men drove the fairway, but now Floyd was away, for Faldo had flown his ball at least 30 yards past him. Raymond's ball had found an awkward lie as well; he would have to play a medium iron from a hanging lie, but he had a clear line to the flagstick, right of the pond that shoulders into the front left of the green.

Somehow, though, Floyd pulled his approach; the ball soared left and dropped into the pond bordering the green. It was all over.

Relaxed now, Faldo played an easy eight iron, then nearly holed his first putt, leaving it sitting on the edge of the cup.

For the second consecutive year, Faldo had won the Masters when someone else had let it slip away, first Hoch by missing a holeable putt on the first playoff hole in 1989, then Floyd by three-putting the 17th and then misplaying his approach into the water on the second playoff hole.

Still, Faldo had played those last six holes as well as any winner had, except for Art Wall back in 1959, when he birdied five of the last six. Nick hadn't done that well, but he had played the shots he had to play, and no one can do better than that.

4. The U.S. Open

Early in the week of the U.S. Open, I was struck with the thought that, more than any generation before us, we've become obsessed with records. What had been accepted as normal progression in earlier days had become subjects of intense study by the late years of the century. Interviewed on his 86th birthday, Mark Koenig, the shortstop for the powerful 1927 New York Yankees, remembered that no one gave much thought to Babe Ruth's 60th home run that year. After all, he had hit 59 once before, and a 60th seemed routine. Koenig, who hit second in the lineup, just ahead of Ruth, had been on base when the Babe connected; he said he simply trotted onto the dugout without thinking much about it. Thirty-four years later, in 1961, when Roger Maris hit 61 homers, he was given barely a moment's peace. Later, when Hank Aaron passed Ruth's 714 career home runs, all of American sport focused on that moment.

We have had the same phenomenon in golf. As far as we know, no one thought much about Willie Anderson's winning three consecutive U.S. Opens, in 1903, 1904, and 1905, or about Harry Vardon's winning six British Opens. No one thought much about Bobby Jones' giving up the opportunity to win three consecutive U.S. Opens because of his retirement after the 1930 season. Ben Hogan's going for a third consecutive U.S. Open generated interest in 1952, but hardly the intense year-long ordeal Curtis Strange lived through leading up to the 1990 Open. It hadn't seemed significant then, and as far as we can remember, no one resurrected Anderson's ghost.

But the world moves on. From the time Strange holed his final putt at Oak Hill, in 1989, winning his second Open, Willie Anderson became mildly popular. A mysterious figure who came to this country late in the last century and turned into the best of our immigrant professionals, Anderson had nearly won the 1897 Open when he was just 17. Only a miraculous three by Joe Lloyd on the Chicago Golf Club's 18th, a 465-yard hole, held him off. (To digress, Lloyd's three may have been the best finish ever by an Open champion. Par wasn't to come into popular use until 1911, but when it did, holes of 450 yards or more were designated par fives. Under those standards, then, Lloyd closed with an eagle. It would be interesting to know if he finished before or after Anderson, but the few records we have don't give us the pairings.)

It took Anderson another four years to win his first, in 1901, and then he added three more.

He dominated the game in the United States as no one had. From 1901 through 1905 he was nearly unbeatable. In addition to his four Opens, he won the Western Open twice, and lost a playoff to Alex Smith, his great rival, in the first Metropolitan (New York) Open, in 1905. In 14 Opens from 1897 through 1910, he finished lower than fifth in only three, placed second once, third once, fourth twice, and fifth three times. In the others, he placed 11th twice, and 15th once. Anderson is the only man to have won the Open with both the gutta-percha ball and the rubber ball.

Those who played against him and watched the great golfers of later years said he was as good as anyone who ever played. He had a full, flowing, although somewhat flat, swing and he moved into the ball with a smooth, rhythmic stroke. He was probably at his best with the mashie, the equivalent of the modern five iron, and it was his favorite club.

Sadly, his career was as brief as it was brilliant. He died at the age of 30, it was said from arteriosclerosis, normally a disease of the elderly, but more likely from alcohol; like many golf professionals of the period, he drank heavily.

Except for establishing him as the best American golfer of his time, Anderson's four Opens meant very little in those times, but as the years passed and only Bob Jones, Ben Hogan, and later Jack Nicklaus had the skill to win four, its significance grew.

The significance of other achievements grew as well. A number of men won two consecutive Opens—Johnny McDermott in 1911 and 1912, Jones in 1929 and 1930, Ralph Guldahl, a burly Texan, in 1937 and 1938, and Hogan in 1950 and 1951. No one since then, though, until Strange won in 1988 and 1989, a period of 38 years. Those who couldn't include some of the best golfers the game has known: Cary Middlecoff couldn't, although he came close, nor could Arnold Palmer, Tom Watson, Lee Trevino, or even Jack Nicklaus, the only man who has won four Opens without winning in consecutive years. These were the best golfers of their times; their failures indicate the difficulty of winning consecutive Opens.

Strange understood that winning three is obviously much more difficult. Facing a large group of reporters on the Tuesday before the Open began, he said, "The odds are very much against me, but whether I play good or bad, you'll know I'll give it my best.

"I've been thinking about this week for a year. Not a day has gone by when it hasn't been on my mind. It has consumed me for the last couple of months—since the end of the Masters. There's a knot in my stomach right now, but my preparation has been the same as always. I don't want to overdo it. Trying to peak for four days out of the year is tough, but this is a great position to be in. Win, lose, or draw, I'll look back on it as fun.

"I want to tee it up and say, 'Let's go,' yet I think I'll leave here Sunday without the trophy. There'll be an empty feeling Sunday night. I've felt like there's been this fictitious person beside me the last two years. I don't know exactly what I mean when I say that, except that if I don't win this week, it will be like losing my best buddy."

Greg Norman claimed he rooted for Strange to repeat, saying, "If he doesn't do it this week, it could be another hundred years before someone does. I'd like to see it."

While public attention centered around Strange, the specter of Norman hung over every tournament he entered. Statistics from the PGA Tour help explain why. He ranked first in money-winning with $799,438 through the Western Open; led average scoring with 68.78 strokes per round; led driving distance with an average of 276.5 yards on the two holes the Tour tests in each round; birdied (or better) 23 percent of the holes he played; led final round scoring with an average of 68.89; ranked among the leading five players in putting; and stood on top of the Sony Ranking.

Statistics explain only part of the reason why Norman has been such a power on the Tour. He not only hits the ball a long way, he also hits it straight; there is little doubt he is the longest straight driver of his time, and that he is not reluctant to use his driver where others might back off. Furthermore, he had won the Australian Masters and two Tour tournaments already in 1990, at the Doral early in the year, where he holed a chip to win a playoff, and again at the Memorial, shortened to 54 holes because of bad weather.

Although Norman had been a powerful force in tournament golf, he hadn't been particularly effective in the Open. He had, of course, tied Fuzzy Zoeller at Winged Foot in 1984, but he had lost the playoff. In eight other Opens, his best showings had been 12th in 1986, and 15th in 1985. He had placed 51st in 1987, withdrew because he injured his wrist in 1988, and placed 33rd in 1989. He had finished well only once, shooting 69 in the last round at Winged Foot, but never again scoring lower than 72. Leading the 1986 championship after three rounds, he closed with 75 at Shinnecock Hills and dropped to 12th.

Some of the leading players of the time ignored those failures. Mark Calcavecchia, who beat him in a playoff in the 1989 British Open, said, "When Norman is on one of his streaks, he is more awesome than anyone." Using a term generally used in boxing, Curtis Strange said, "Pound for pound I think he's the best player going right now."

Perhaps Strange used the pound-for-pound reference to exclude Nick Faldo, who some others accepted as the game's best player, the winner of two consecutive Masters along with the 1987 British Open, and who had lost to Strange in the U.S. Open playoff two years earlier.

Possibly the best British golfer since Harry Vardon, whose career spanned the late 19th and early 20th centuries, and certainly the best since Henry Cotton, who was at his best in the 1930s and 1940s, Faldo is the most robotic of the modern golfers, with none of the flair of Norman or Seve Ballesteros, and even less dash than Ben Hogan, who did breathe fire when shots misbehaved.

Through disciplined, dedicated work, Faldo had built a sound, reliable, repeating swing that behaved precisely the same every time. When he reached the top of his backswing, the club was set in the same position shot after shot. As a result, the ball seemed to go wherever he wanted it to go.

At that stage of his career, he was sound in every part of his game. He rarely missed a fairway with his long, unwavering drives, his iron play was exceptional, crisp and dead on line, and he putted extremely well, seldom missing from inside six feet. Still, he didn't hole everything, and in the end, two missed putts from holeable distance cost him the U.S. Open.

Nevertheless, he remained the most reliable big occasion player in the game. Beginning with the 1987 British Open, he had placed no worse than fourth in six of the eight majors he had played, and he had won three of them. Something about them seemed untidy, however; he won all three because someone else had thrown them away—Paul Azinger bogeyed the last two holes at Muirfield when he shouldn't have, costing him the 1987 British Open, Scott Hoch had missed a two- or three-foot putt he shouldn't have, costing him the 1989 Masters playoff, and Ray Floyd not only three-putted the 17th at Augusta, in 1990, but also tossed away the playoff with a bad approach to the second playoff hole. None of this really mattered, though, because Faldo's name had already gone into the record book as the winner.

By the time of the Open, Faldo had played in 11 tournaments in 1990, one on the Australasian Tour, five on the European Tour, five in the United States, including the Western, a week before the Open, at the Butler National Golf Club, another Chicago course, where he tied for 32nd place. Although he had won nothing other than the Masters, he had placed second in the Australian Masters, Spanish Open and Volvo PGA Championship. He was having a very good, although not exceptional, year.

A month short of his 33rd birthday, Faldo nevertheless had been around for quite some time. He surfaced as a player of international stature by representing England in the 1977 World Cup, in Manila, when he was just 20 years old. Strangely enough, though, he had played in only three previous U.S. Opens, even though he had followed the American Tour for a time. He had tied for 55th place at Winged Foot four years before tying Strange at The Country Club, in Brookline, Massachusetts, and then placed 18th at Oak Hill, in 1989. He would be a factor at Medinah until the end.

While Faldo, Strange, and Norman were drawing unqualified support, Jack Nicklaus' following seemed a bit more tentative, which could only be expected. After all, Jack had turned 50 in January, and only Harry Vardon had been a serious Open threat at that age. Vardon had nearly won the 1920 Open, at Inverness, in Toledo, Ohio, but gale-strength winds off Lake Erie cost him strokes on the late holes, and he fell one stroke short of matching Ted Ray, his countryman.

Nevertheless, it is never wise to underestimate Nicklaus. He had begun playing the Senior Tour early in the year, which seemed to revive his game. Then, while the regular Tour labored around long and hard Butler National, Nicklaus demoralized the rest of the field at the Dearborn, Michigan, Country Club by shooting 65-68-64-64—261, beating par by 27 strokes, and finishing six strokes ahead of Lee Trevino, like Jack a rookie on the Senior Tour. Nicklaus had scored 28 birdies and two eagles, and had bogeyed only five holes.

By winning, Jack earned $150,000, the most he had ever won in one tournament. Furthermore, he had won $295,000 in three senior events, more prize money than he had ever won in a full season.

Shaking his head, Nicklaus said, "I amazed myself. Making that many birdies isn't my style." In the four days, Jack needed only 111 putts. "I don't think I've ever putted like this for four days," he said. "Hopefully, Medinah's greens will be exactly the same. I don't expect them to be much different."

No one, of course, gave a thought to Hale Irwin, with good cause. He was 45 at the time, past the age when anyone other than the truly exceptional golfer can compete at the game's highest levels, and even though he had won two U.S. Opens, 11 years had passed since he won his last, at Inverness in 1979. Is it any wonder, then, that his winning—indeed his even competing—caught so many of us by surprise?

Perhaps it shouldn't have, because Irwin owns a competitive spirit that upon occasion leads him to play golf at an inspired level. Obviously off his game through the early holes of the playoff, driving poorly, and occasionally using what seemed to be bad judgement, Irwin refused to yield, and in the end, when he stood two strokes behind Mike Donald with six holes of the playoff left, he played them in three under fours, sending the playoff to extra holes. Then he birdied the 19th. Seven holes in four under fours; only one man within memory had finished an Open better. Scott Simpson played the last six holes at Olympic in four under fours in winning the 1987 championship. Irwin's extraordinary run followed an exceptional 31 on the second nine of the fourth round, lifting him into the tie for first place.

Irwin's winning ranks among the more unexpected results of recent years, perhaps even more unexpected than Jack Nicklaus' winning the 1986 Masters, or Raymond Floyd's coming so close in the Masters earlier in 1990. While at 45 Irwin had a one-year advantage in age over Nicklaus, who had been 46 in 1986, Nicklaus is, after all, Nicklaus, and it is never safe to assume he can't win again simply because of his age.

On the other hand, Irwin seemed finished in big-time golf. He hadn't won a tournament of any kind since the 1985 Memorial, and in his last four Opens he had missed the 36-hole cut twice, then placed 17th in 1988 and 54th in 1989. He had no better record in Tour tournaments. While he had placed as high as third and fifth in two of the 10 he had played earlier in 1990, he had also placed 25th, 31st, 46th, and 52nd, and had missed the cut in the Bob Hope Classic, his first event of 1990, and in New Orleans. Furthermore, he had shot 290, six over par, at the Heritage Classic, played on the Harbour Town Golf Links, in Hilton Head, South Carolina, a course he had always played well.

Then, when it wasn't expected, Irwin had shown signs of regaining his form by shooting 276 and finishing third at the Kemper, two weeks before the Open, then taking a week off.

And then he won the Open, the game's biggest prize, when other men with greater reputations and higher expectations couldn't find the answer to Medinah, the site of previous Opens in 1949 and again in 1975. Where others had failed, Irwin played Medinah in 69-70-74-67—280, tying Donald's 67-70-72-71, then winning the playoff the next day.

For him to have won the Open, especially after playing not only a loose third round but rather indifferent golf through the first nine holes of the last round, should tell us never to be surprised at what might happen in golf, because we must remember too that Irwin won the Open only after beating Donald. Based on his record, who would have believed Donald could have hung so close for so long? This is the same man who had opened the Masters with 64, then threw away strokes as fast as he could swing a club, slipping to 82 the next day. Remember, too, that in the 1984 Open, Donald had followed an opening 68 with 78, and earlier in 1990 had shot successive rounds of 69-84 at Pebble Beach.

He had settled down somewhat in the few weeks leading up to the Open, though, and played rather consistently: 70-73-68-71 in the Colonial, 68-72-68-70 in Atlanta, and 71-71-71-72 at the Kemper. Unfortunately, while he placed fifth in Atlanta, the other consistent scores brought him very little—29th at the Colonial and 31st at the Kemper. It is also well to remember that Donald had played the Tour for 11 years, and had won only the 1989 Anheuser Busch Classic, in Williamsburg, Virginia.

On the other hand, Irwin had been successful throughout his career. Through the 1985 Memorial, he had won 17 tournaments, including two Opens, and he had nearly caught Tom Watson in the 1983 British Open, but in a careless moment had tapped at a ball hanging on the lip of the cup, hit the ground instead, and missed tying Watson by one stroke.

That had been seven years earlier. Irwin had fallen from the ranks of the leading players in the interim, and as a matter of fact, would have had to qualify for a place in the Open field if the USGA hadn't awarded him one of its few special exemptions, and added him to the starting field of 156. His 10-year exemption from having won the 1979 Open had run out.

His was the 21st such exemption given since the USGA began the practice in 1966. The first, by the way, was given to Ben Hogan. He placed 12th. Until Irwin came along, this was the best finish by anyone awarded these exemptions.

Irwin had won his two previous Opens over severe and demanding courses where par stood as the standard of excellence. He won his first at the Winged Foot Golf Club, in Mamaroneck, New York, perhaps the most severe test of the game we have seen since 1955, at the Olympic Club, in San Francisco, and only marginally easier than Oakland Hills, near Detroit, the course Hogan called a monster after he had won the 1951 championship there. Irwin won with a score of 287, seven strokes above par.

He won again five years later at Inverness, another demanding examination of the game.

Irwin had made a career of winning at difficult golf courses. Over the years he had won at Harbour Town, Butler National, Pebble Beach, and now at Medinah. They all called for accurate driving, and precise iron play. Above all, they demanded perseverance.

As the Open approached, Medinah seemed as if it would ask for all of that. At 7,195 yards it stretched farther from the first tee to the 18th green than any Open course ever, although not significantly so. (Bellerive Country Club, near St. Louis, had measured 7,191 yards in 1965.) It had also been redesigned to a degree following the 1975 Open.

Although Medinah had been the site of two previous championships, the USGA had never been happy with the 18th hole, a par four of 411 yards that doglegged right. It was a dull sort of hole, because in this age of orbiting drives, the players laid up by playing irons from the tee to avoid hitting through the bend of the fairway. The USGA felt that since the Open is the national championship, the final hole should stand as a severe challenge. When Medinah asked for another Open, the USGA told the club that it must change the closing hole before its invitation would be considered.

Medinah did more than alter the 18th. It built three new holes, one a par three across a lake that, unfortunately, is nearly a duplicate of two others. The other two new holes, however, turned out to be worthwhile additions. The 15th hole had been a mild little par four of 325 yards or so that ran away from the lake. The club moved the tee to the far side of the lake and turned it into a par five of 545 yards. In the rerouting caused by the new holes, it became the 14th. The architects moved the 18th to a new location, and turned it into a 440-yard par four, whose tee sat on a man-made peninsula jutting into the lake, and whose fairway wove through a somewhat narrow avenue of oaks.

The design changes proved worthwhile, because both the 14th and the 18th changed the thrust of the tournament.

I have never been impressed with Medinah; I've always found it dull. On my first visit I felt it was overrated. After watching two Opens there, I've seen nothing to change my mind, even though two of the three men who won there rank among the best of their times. Cary Middlecoff, the 1949 and 1956 champion, ranks among the best golfers of the middle years of the century, and Hale Irwin is certainly among the more enduring, with Open championships spanning 16 years, a period exceeded only by Nicklaus, whose first, in 1962, and fourth, in 1980, cover 18 years. Lou Graham won the other Medinah Open, in 1975, but he won only one other tournament in his Tour career.

Nevertheless, Medinah does nothing for me. After one round of the Open, it did nothing—or very little—for the players.

In the week leading up to the championship, P.J. Boatwright, the man who sets up Open courses for the USGA, couldn't help being pleased when he surveyed the course. Medinah was long, in keeping with the distance modern golfers generate, its fairways and greens firm, and the greens especially fast, approaching 11 feet on the Stimpmeter, the device invented by Edward Stimpson, a Massachusetts golf fanatic, to establish a standard measurement of how far a ball rolls.

Even so, a day before the Open began, Boatwright commented to Tim Simpson, who was playing a practice round, "I'd like to have these greens a little firmer."

Amazed, Simpson asked, "How do you make rocks harder?"

They had met early in the day. A storm broke Wednesday night, the evening before the Open was to begin, and poured an inch and a half of rain on the golf course, changing the nature of the Open. Rain continued to fall when the early starters turned out Thursday morning, and the USGA delayed the start while the grounds crew pumped water from the bunkers, and generally put the course back in shape. When play began, Medinah had lost much of its sting.

Designated the club's No. 3 course, it had been conceived in the early 1920s as a course for women, a sporty little thing where families of Medinah members could play without interfering with the men, who had their No. 1 and No. 2 courses.

Tom Bendelow had been the architect. An able golfer and religious zealot, Bendelow, a Scottish immigrant, had been a typographer with the *New York Herald*. Hired by the A.G. Spalding Company, he had come out of the composing room to become one of our more prolific golf course designers, laying out an estimated 650, many of them in one morning. He established the routing and the length of the holes, and left the actual construction to others. Obviously, he spent more time doing Medinah No. 3, because once the men saw it, they decided it was too good for women and children, and kept it for themselves. The women and children inherited the No. 2 course.

Proud of their golf course, the members had been stunned when Lighthorse Harry Cooper tore No. 3 apart, shooting 63 in a tournament. Obviously it wasn't as strong as the members had imagined. It would have to be revised. Half the holes were redesigned, and the remodeling added 800 yards to its length. A member wrote in the club's magazine, "Let Mr. Harry Cooper try to shoot 63 over this new course." Neither Cooper nor anyone else had approached 63 since then.

For a time early in 1975 it looked as if it might give up record scores when Tom Watson opened with 67-68, but Watson's game collapsed in the late rounds, and Graham and Mahaffey tied at 286, two strokes over par.

As the players began arriving early in the week, a score of 286 looked as if it might be good enough to win, because for one thing, the latest revisions had added a stroke to Medinah's par, raising it to 72, or 288 for 72 holes. Where early in the week a par round seemed a good score, once play began it earned only a tie for 40th place. When the day ended, 39 men had broken par, and another 21 had matched it.

The scoring astounded the galleries and stunned the members. They complained the USGA had set up the course to play too easily. They grumbled they played tougher pin positions themselves. A committee of members met with Boatwright pleading their case and asking him to make the course play harder.

Boatwright listened politely, then went ahead with the USGA's original plans. When the Open ended, Medinah had given up 124 sub-par rounds, nearly double the record 64 The Country Club had yielded in 1988.

Medinah's vulnerability had been exposed early in the first round. Playing in the 10th group off the tee, starting out about nine o'clock, Scott Hoch began by birdieing the first three holes, adding two more on the par fives, and heading for home in 31—five under par. The word was out: Medinah could be had. Not by Hoch, though; he bogeyed three of the last six holes, came back in 39, shot 70, and dropped out of the picture. When the day ended, Scott Simpson, the 1987 Open champion, Tim Simpson, one of the game's better ball-strikers, and Jeff Sluman, the undersized 1988 PGA champion, shared first place at 66, one stroke ahead of Mike Donald and Steve Jones, at 67. Two others shot 68, four more 69, 12 shot 70, and 16 more 71. The record had been broken after only one year; 21 men had broken par at Oak Hill, in 1989.

While some had taken advantage of the conditions, others hadn't. The victim of poor putting, Curtis Strange had shot 73, Nick Faldo and Greg Norman 72, Mark Calcavecchia and Jose Maria Olazabal 73, Tom Watson and Fred Couples 74, and Tom Kite 75.

While Tim Simpson and Jeff Sluman surprised much of the gallery, we might have expected to see Scott Simpson shoot a good score. He had played exceptionally well in the previous three Opens, winning in 1987, and placing sixth in both 1988 and 1989. He might have done even better than sixth in 1989, but locked in a close battle with Strange and Tom Kite, he double-bogeyed the eighth hole, which seemed to upset him, and then lost more strokes on the second nine, shot 75, and finished with 281, three strokes behind Strange.

A pleasant, apparently mild-mannered man, tall and lanky at 6-foot-2 and 180 pounds, wearing a thick, dark mustache and seeming to hide inside a visor pulled low over his eyes, Simpson started off badly. Medinah's first hole is about the easiest on the course. A par four of 385 yards, it asks for nothing more than a pitch, depending on the drive, the fairway is wide and straight, one bunker borders the left side of the fairway, and two more crowd the opening to the two-level green. Simpson's eight-iron approach dropped into a greenside bunker, and he bogeyed.

He made no more mistakes and played no more loose shots, running off seven birdies over the next 17 holes, principally because of well-played irons. He birdied both the second, the first of the three par threes that cross the lake, and the sixth from 30 feet, then followed with some first-class irons—a nine iron to three feet on the seventh, a long par five of 581 yards, a wedge to 15 feet on the 10th, another par five of 577 yards with a narrow fairway weaving among nests of fairway bunkers, an eight iron to four feet on the 11th, a 411-yard par four that bends sharply left, a sand wedge to four feet on the 14th, the par five that had been converted from a par four by moving the tee behind the lake, and another wedge to six inches on the 15th, another short par four of 384 yards.

He had another birdie opportunity chance on the 17th, where his tee shot braked within 10 feet of the cup, but his putt slipped past, and then he two-putted from 20 feet on the 18th.

While Scott Simpson's round had a little bit of adventure—the bogey and a par saved when he missed the green of the 12th—Tim Simpson played perhaps the best round of the week. He hit every fairway, and while he wasn't on the actual putting surface of every green with the appropriate stroke, he was on the collar of the two he missed, and he putted from both of them. His round was surely as precise as David Graham's closing 67 at Merion, when he won the 1981 Open.

Simpson went out in 33 and came back in 33, birdied six holes, bogeyed none, and had only one five on his scorecard, a par on the seventh. Never known as a good putter, Tim holed two long ones, running in 25-footers on the 10th and 17th. He began his string of birdies with an eight iron to four inches on the fifth, then a wedge to one foot on the fifth, the first of the par fives. A five iron to eight feet on the sixth brought him his third birdie.

After a par on the ninth by nursing his ball down in two from 60 feet, Simpson birdied the 10th from 25 feet, the 14th from four feet, and the 17th, a par three across the lake, from 25 feet. A 66, matching the best round he'd ever shot in an Open.

Reflecting on his round, Simpson admitted the rain had caused some of the low scoring, saying, "The course definitely played a couple of shots easier. The greens were awfully hard on Tuesday. We hoped they'd soften them up, but we knew the USGA wouldn't. God did."

Simpson had come to the Open early in the week with only a few hours sleep after an unusual training regimen. While most of the Open field had labored around Butler National in the Western Open, Simpson had spent a week fishing for salmon in Alaska.

"We stood in a boat 10 hours a day and fished," Simpson said. "Got 10 king salmon, 110 pounds of fillet. I'll go back home and cook up a bunch of it."

In explaining why he flew off to Alaska, Simpson pointed to his Open record—he had missed the 36-hole cut in both 1988 and 1989, and had never placed better than 10th.

"I think there's a tendency to over-prepare for the Open," he said. "You think of all those things to do, hitting all those balls and so many putts, and then you go out and shoot about a million because you have no energy left."

Jeff Sluman had an energy problem of his own. After winning the PGA Championship and more than $500,000 in 1988, Jeff had an emergency appendectomy, and then injured his shoulder. From 18th among money-winners in 1988, he dropped to 89th in 1989. Among the most active of Tour players, Sluman had played in 32 tournaments in 1988, but because of his disorders, he cut back to 23 in 1989, still a considerable number, and where he had placed among the low 10 scorers in six 1988 events, he finished among the leaders in four 1989 tournaments.

Discussing the differences between 1988 and 1989, Sluman claimed, "The appendectomy was no big thing, I played Westchester 18 days later and made the cut. The biggest thing was trying to change my swing after 1988 to hit the ball higher. That was a mistake; it took me three months to make the change, and a lot longer to get the old swing back."

His shoulder had the most lasting effects.

"It's been nagging me for months, but I can play so long as I'm careful."

So far 1990 had not been a successful year, either. Jeff had played 17 tournaments through the Western Open, and had placed higher than 27th only once, tying for second place at Greensboro. He had missed the cut in five, and had placed in such ignoble positions as 54th, 50th, and had dropped to 66th in the Western Open.

His 66 was his lowest round of the year, but he began as if he might be lucky to break 80, missing the first three greens and holing 15-footers to save pars on the first and third, and chipping to two feet and saving another on the second. He began rolling after that, dropping another 15 footer and birdieing the fourth, and pitching to two feet for another birdie on the fifth—five consecutive one-putt greens.

Another birdie on the eighth, the only par three that doesn't cross the lake, and Sluman was out in 33 with only two two-putt greens (he had saved another par from off the ninth green).

Birdies on the 10th and 11th, then two more saved pars, and he had one-putted six consecutive greens. A four wood and nine iron to four feet set up his last birdie of the day, and brought him home with another 33.

Sluman had had a remarkable scrambling round. He had one-putted 13 greens, seven of them for pars, six for birdies. Where Tim Simpson could have come in several strokes lower than he had, Sluman could have shot several strokes higher, but Jeff claimed that except for the first three holes, he really hadn't played scrambling golf, saying, "The scrambling I did was at the first and third holes. After that, when I didn't get to the green it was because I had hit my drive through a dogleg with a pretty good shot."

Perhaps he saw it that way, but both the second and 13th are par threes, and they don't dogleg, and the ninth and 12th bend so slightly they hardly qualify. The 16th, a 426-yard par four that would play the major role in Irwin's victory, does bend radically, turning left nearly 90 degrees at the drive zone. Sluman left his approach short, chipped to within two feet, and rolled the putt into the cup.

While Sluman saved his round with exceptional putting, Strange couldn't hole anything. He put the prospect of his winning a third consecutive Open at risk from the start.

Thinking back over the previous two years, I have the vision of Strange holing putt after putt from the 10-foot range. He was absolutely deadly; he never seemed to miss. Those who were there will never forget those last few holes at Oak Hill, where Strange holed a putt from at least six feet to save his par on the 15th, a delicate par three, or the birdie he holed at the 16th, the stroke that gave him the cushion he needed over those last two trying holes.

Now, a year later, Strange had lost that touch. The putts that once dove into the hole skimmed past, or worse, stopped short. The smooth stroke had become a little jerky. His troubles began at the first hole, where he three-putted, missing from four feet, the kind he usually holed without thinking. He missed from six feet at the second, missed another six-foot birdie chance at the seventh, and finished the first nine by three-putting the ninth, missing another four-footer. Out in 37, he struggled home in 36, again three-putting the 16th from 50 feet. When he finally holed out, he flung his putter, then fidgeted with his clubs as he stood on the 17th tee.

He stood two over par then, but he won back a stroke at the 18th, where he holed a 20-footer. When the putt fell, he stopped short, his jaw dropped, and he broke into that disarming grin.

"If I lose this thing by a couple of strokes," Curtis said, "I'll look back at today. I missed four putts that might stretch out to 16 feet if they were strung together."

Oddly enough, Curtis knew he was drawing back his putter outside his line and pulling the ball left of the hole, but he couldn't cure it, no matter what he tried. Nevertheless, Curtis hung in the chase until the end.

The first-round leaders:

Tim Simpson	66	John Huston	68
Scott Simpson	66	Mark Brooks	68
Jeff Sluman	66	Billy Ray Brown	69
Mike Donald	67	Emlyn Aubrey	69
Steve Jones	67	Hale Irwin	69

With bright, sunny skies and a breeze that barely rustled the upper branches of the oaks, the field tore into Medinah again the next day. Where 39 men had broken par in the first round, 47 broke 72 in the second. Mike Hulbert shot 66, the lowest round of the day, and Larry Nelson and Jeff Wilson shot 67s. Nelson's round kept him on the fringes, with 141, but Hulbert had opened with 76, leaving him at 142, and Wilson, with an opening 80, didn't even make the cut, which fell at 145, the lowest ever.

Tim Simpson continued to play superb golf, adding 69 to his opening 66, and moving into the lead at 135, one stroke off the Open's 36-hole record, and one stroke ahead of Sluman, who by then had played 36 holes without a bogey. Scott Simpson, meanwhile, slipped to 73 and dropped into a tie for fifth, behind Donald, at 137, and Mark Brooks, at 138. Scott Simpson and Irwin also broke 140 for the 36 holes, and 30 others stood under the 36-hole par of 144.

Where Tim Simpson had hit every green in the first round, he missed four in the second, but still saved his pars on each of them. He did bogey a hole, though, three-putting the second from 18 feet, but right away he rolled in a 40-footer from off the front edge of the third, pulling back to even par for the round. He still stood at even par through the 12th, and then he began his stirring run for home, dropping a six iron within 15 feet on the 13th for one birdie, playing a two iron and then a four iron to the 16th and holing from 18 feet, then hitting a six iron within four feet on the 18th and birdieing again, his fourth of the day.

All day long Simpson had struggled to reach nine under par. Until this day only two men had ever reached nine under par in the Open, the oldest championship on the North American continent. Predictably, they were Ben Hogan and Jack Nicklaus. Hogan had birdied the 10th at the Riviera Country Club in the last round of the 1948 Open, the first of the four he had won, and Nicklaus had gone nine under on the third hole at Baltusrol during the second round of the 1980 Open. Neither man held his position, though. Hogan had held on through the 14th, but he bogeyed the 15th, a strong par four of 440 yards, three-putting from about 75 feet, and Nicklaus had bogeyed the sixth, another long and demanding par four that stretched to 470 yards. Both Hogan and Nicklaus had won those Opens with scores eight under par, Hogan with 276, and Nicklaus with 272.

Simpson, on the other hand, had finished the round at nine under par, which no one else had ever done.

Once again Sluman labored to save his pars, and fought through the day without bogeying a hole, once more saving himself with his putter. Bunkered on the first, he came out to five feet and saved his four, and holed another putt from five feet on the sixth. His magic reached its climax on the 11th and 12th, where he holed a 15-footer after he had driven into the rough and had no option except waste a shot chopping back to the fairway, then holed still another from 20 feet on the 12th.

He couldn't hole everything, though; he missed two putts from 12 feet and another from 20 on the next three holes. Still even par for the day, Sluman began making up ground on the 16th, where he positioned a four wood at the bend of the fairway, then ripped a three iron straight at the flagstick. The ball bit and braked three feet from the cup for his first birdie.

Jeff had run off 15 consecutive pars, but then he made his first birdie, rifling a three iron to three feet on the 16th and a seven iron to three feet on the 17th. He finished off the round as it began, holing a six-footer to save still another par on the 18th.

Understating his performance, Sluman said, "My putter was a pretty good friend today. When you make 15- and 20-foot putts on two straight holes, pars like that make you feel better than going birdie-bogey-birdie-bogey."

Meanwhile, Mike Donald surprised much of the gallery by shooting 70 and hanging close to the lead, only two strokes behind Simpson. Along with his history of bad rounds following sensational rounds, he owned a dismal record in the Open. The 1984 championship, where he had shot 68-78, had been his first; he had played in two others, at Olympic in 1987, and at Oak Hill in 1989. He didn't make the cut in either.

A bachelor, Donald seldom missed a tournament. He had entered 18 by the time of the Open, and had finished higher than 18th only once, placing fifth in Atlanta two weeks before he came to Medinah. He would have played the Western, but he had forgotten to enter. Now he had played 36 holes of the game's most demanding tournament and had hung close to the lead. Still, he was haunted by the memory of his collapse at Augusta.

"I got a telegram from a man in Boston," he told some friends. "He said 'Forget about the Masters. You can do it.' Now how am I supposed to forget it, if it's the first thing he mentions?"

As he played Medinah in five under par the first day, someone asked him if he had learned anything from the Masters.

"We'll have to wait until tomorrow to find out."

He began the second round as he had begun so often in the past, playing loose shots on both the first and second holes, but where he might have gone into terminal collapse, he fought back, playing a crisp seven iron to 10 feet on the third, and then running the putt home. Four routine pars seemed to settle him down, but once again his game threatened to cave in when he three-putted the eighth from three feet, then bunkered his approach to the ninth. Two straight bogeys and he had gone out in 37, one over par.

Those were his last mistakes of the round. Where he might have snapped in the past, he dug in now, birdied the 11th by holing a 20-footer, struggled to get down in two from 80 feet on the 12th, and then ran off five consecutive pars, missing one birdie chance from eight feet on the 15th. Even par now, with two hard holes to play, Donald had shown he could at least play reasonably well under pressure. Then he proved he could play at his best. A six iron bit and drew back to 10 feet on the 17th, and he coaxed the putt home, and then he drilled a four iron inside 10 feet on the 18th. Once again the putt toppled into the cup—a second consecutive birdie. Two birdies where a few months ago he might have made anything. Back in 33, and with 70 for the round, Donald had shown himself he could indeed play at his best when it mattered most. He realized as well, though, that he would have to do it all over again the next two days.

While Donald was proving to the galleries that he was indeed a first-class player, Hale Irwin was proving to himself that he deserved the special invitation by shooting a 70 of his own. Tied with Scott Simpson, at 139, Irwin sat in fifth place with 36 tiring holes ahead of him.

Reflecting on those first 36 holes, Irwin said, "I've played very few U.S. Open courses as well as I've played Medinah these last two rounds. The more I play well, the more I remember what it takes."

Like Donald, Irwin had a strong finish. One over par after 13 holes, he had pulled back to two under by birdieing the 14th, a par five, then the 16th, a par four, and the 17th, a par three, by playing three superb irons to 15 feet, five feet, and 12 feet.

Irwin had indeed played quality golf, and he had been clearly outstanding at the finish. Where he had birdied three of the last five holes of the second round, he had birdied two in the first, closing with birdies on the 17th and 18th. He stood at five under par for 36 holes, and five under on the last five holes of the course.

Where Irwin fought to stay within reach of the leaders, Curtis Strange and Seve Ballesteros strained to survive the 36-hole cut. Midway through the second round, Strange stood at two over par, and by then it seemed clear this wouldn't be good enough. He needed some birdies, but try as he might, the putts that once fell into the hole rolled past.

He had changed putters after his dismal opening round, and now used a zebra, a mallet-headed club with black and white stripes running perpendicular to the line of play, designed to help the player set the clubhead on line. The change looked like a waste when he opened by missing a four-footer on the first, but he holed two 20-footers for birdies on the first nine, then lofted a sand wedge to four feet and birdied the 14th. Safe from the cut now, if he made no mistakes, Strange tore into a three iron on the 18th and ran in a 40-footer for his fourth birdie of the day. He had finished with 70, and at 143 had at least made the cut.

Ballesteros, too, had been struggling. but a miracle birdie on the 10th turned him around and led to a round of 69. Seve had opened with 73, and had been going nowhere through the first nine. A bogey at the ninth and he had gone out in 37, another stroke over par, and now he was in danger of missing the cut.

His position looked grim when he hooked his drive into a fairway bunker on the 10th, a solid par five with a fairway that threads through a series of bunkers to a slightly elevated green. Ballesteros, however, was accustomed to finding his ball in out-of-the-way places. He tried to turn a five iron around a stand of trees, but he hooked the shot too much, and rather than flying around the trees, it landed among them.

Now he lay about 130 yards from the green with no opening. He would have to play under the low-hanging branches. Perhaps the most ingenious golfer of his generation, Ballesteros had manufactured all kinds of shots that those with less imagination couldn't dream of. Here he punched a six iron that rose no more than waist high, carried just short of the green, skipped between a pair of bunkers, scaled the slope onto the green, and pulled up eight inches from the cup. It was such a good shot, he was unlucky he hadn't holed it.

Inspired, Seve took the second nine apart, rushing home in 32, and saving himself for another day.

A number of other first-class players didn't, caught by the exceptionally low 36-hole cut. Although the score of 145 had been matched in the past, most recently at Oak Hill in 1989, with Medinah's par at 72, the cut was the lowest ever in relation to par. The 36-hole leaders:

Tim Simpson	135
Jeff Sluman	136
Mike Donald	137
Mark Brooks	138
Hale Irwin	139
Jim Gallagher	140
John Huston	140
Ian Woosnam	140
Billy Ray Brown	140

Saturday, the day of the third round, turned out to be a spectacular afternoon. Both Tim and Scott Simpson reached nine under par and toyed with 10 under, but neither made it, and both of them, in fact, dropped from the race. Billy Ray Brown, a big, round-faced Texan, shot 69 and climbed into a tie for first with Donald, who continued to confound the gallery by refusing to collapse.

With the field down to 68 players, the wind beginning to blow, and the finish of the Open drawing closer, Medinah played a bit tougher. Only 15 men broke 70, with 68 the lowest score (by seven men), but nine others broke 72, and 11 more matched it. The field grew tightly bunched as well. While Donald and Brown shared first place, 25 others ranged within four strokes of them.

Still, the day belonged to Curtis Strange.

Curtis had played spotty golf throughout the early rounds, wallowing in 27th place. He could blame his putting, because he ranked at the top in every other phase of his game. He had hit 24 of the 28 fairways on driving holes, more than any other player, and he had hit 28 of the 36 greens, only three fewer than Hale Irwin and Gil Morgan, who had hit the most.

Solid as he had played from tee to green, on Saturday he played even better. Strange hit every fairway and every green, shot 68, and climbed into threatening position, tied for seventh place, only two strokes behind Donald and Brown. By then he led in both fairways and greens hit, and those unnerving five- and six-footers had finally begun to fall. He played a round of easy tap-ins and narrowly missed birdies. Like any good round, it could have been a few strokes better.

A par at the first, the easiest of the par fours, gave him some hope, since he had bogeyed it the first two rounds, and then he picked up his first birdie on the fourth, a 434-yard par four with the fairway rising to an elevated green. Curtis played a string-straight four iron within five feet of the flagstick, and for once the ball found the cup. One under now, but for the longest time it looked as if this would be all. From the fifth through the 12th he played a frustrating series of two-putt pars, watching his ball skim past the edges of cups.

Still he struggled on. Strange's game is built around steady, patient golf: Hit the fairways, hit the greens, and something will happen. It had worked for him at The Country Club and at Oak Hill, and if he kept up this level of play, he would have to be rewarded.

He was. A five iron dug into the 13th green 15 feet from the cup, and he holed it. Two under now. Two more standard pars at the 14th and 15th, then to the 16th, the challenging dogleg with the wide but shallow green. After a drive placed in just the right spot on the fairway, Strange rifled a four iron directly at the flagstick, set about 20 feet from the right edge of the green and perhaps 25 feet from the front, just behind a deep and threatening bunker. It was a daring shot, unusual from a man who avoids risk and plays to the center of greens.

It paid off. The ball shot off the face of the club, climbed into the brilliant sky, and sped dead at the stick. It hit short, bounced, then slammed into the flagstick, caromed off softly, and settled four feet from the cup. The crowd thundered a cheer, and Curtis grinned as he climbed the hill and saw his ball resting only a few feet from the hole. He holed it.

Three under. On to the 17th, the last of the par threes, across the lake one more time. Curtis played a seven iron, and pulled it just a touch. The ball stopped hole-high, about 20 feet left of the cup, but he had left himself with a wicked line. Sizing it up, Curtis saw he had to play the putt about seven or eight feet left and let the ball drift down the slope.

He had another problem. He would have to focus all his concentration on this shot, but throughout the afternoon pickets had patrolled outside the perimeter fence, only a few yards off, and had chanted slogans of the International Ladies Garment Workers Union, which was striking against La Mode du Golf, a maker of shirts and other accessories, and against the USGA, which sold them. Their cat-calls had annoyed other golfers, but when Curtis strode onto the green, it was as if the strikers understood he was attempting to do what only one man had ever done, and they stood as silently as the gallery while Curtis studied the line.

Finally ready, he stroked his ball then watched it, his face creased with a deep frown. The ball rolled up the slope, then down, caught a corner of the hole, and for a heart-stopping moment looked as if it might run down the grade of that slick green. Instead it spun all the way around the cup, then dropped. Another birdie. Four under now with only the 18th to play. A solid four there, and Curtis not only had his 68, he had played like the Curtis of old. Now he stood squarely back in the race, at 211; he would have his chance to win a third straight Open.

He would have to beat Donald, though, and Mike had given no hint he might fail, although he did waver, shooting even-par 72. Off fast with a birdie at the first, Donald gave the stroke away by missing the fourth green. Even then, he birdied the seventh, a par five, with a sound pitch, but then lost the stroke with another bogey on the 12th, a very difficult par four. Donald closed out with a series of pars, then looked around and saw he still held a share of the lead.

"The rest of the field reacted like it's a U.S. Open," he said. "A lot of guys backed up, and it turned out my pars were pretty good."

They were indeed. Consider how some of the other leaders had played. Tim Simpson hadn't bogeyed a hole through the first 36 holes, but he started with two on the first three holes, turned for home in 38, and closed with 37. With 75, he fell from sight.

Scott Simpson lasted longer. As Strange studied the leaderboard following the second round, he had said Scott Simpson frightened him. Scott had won the 1987 Open, and had played a significant part the following year. One stroke off the lead after 54 holes, he played the first nine badly, shooting 39, closed with 74 and dropped to sixth place. Once again he had held second place after 54 holes of the 1989 Open, and again he played shoddy golf through the last round, shot 75, and fell to sixth once again.

Here, though, he opened by birdieing the first two holes, then dropped a stroke at the third, parred the fourth, then ran off three straight birdies. Five birdies in seven holes, and Simpson had become the fourth man to reach nine under par in an Open. He was hot, and he might make 10 under. It turned into a struggle; hole after hole Simpson putted for the birdie that would do it for him, and hole after hole the putts teased the cup but wouldn't fall. He had gone out in 32; par in and he would shoot 207 and hold a two-stroke lead with one round to play. Then it would be up to him to hold himself together where he had failed the last two years.

The holes flew past as Simpson played flawless golf, never quite making the birdie that would drop him to 10 under par. His tense run ended at the 16th, where he drove into the woods and bogeyed. Now he was back to eight under par. Worse lay ahead.

Simpson stepped onto the 17th tee and found the wind at his back. Still, he chose a seven iron for his shot across the lake. He had made the wrong choice; his ball cleared the green, plunged into the rear bunker, and settled on the rear upslope, giving him a downhill lie to a green that fell away toward the lake. He had been left with a nightmare shot. Blade the ball and it would skip into the pond; play too timidly and he could leave it in the fringe above the green, or even worse, still in the bunker.

Studying the shot, Scott felt he could not play directly at the cup because of the risk; instead, he set himself to play safely to the right of the hole, toward the widest part of the green. Digging his feet into the sand, Scott swung into the shot. The ball popped up, but he had played too cautiously and left it in the sand. One more inch and he might have saved himself. He played out cleanly with his third, but the ball rolled across the green and into the rough. A chip short, then a missed putt, and Simpson had taken six.

He had slipped to four over par on the second nine, and had fallen behind. Shaken, he drove into the left fairway bunker on the 18th and bogeyed once again. He had played the second nine in 41, shot 73, and dropped into a 13th-place tie. He was through.

The Simpsons weren't alone. Huston played the 15th through the 17th with two bogeys and a double bogey; Mark Brooks three-putted the 17th from no more than 10 feet; Ian Woosnam missed the 17th green, stubbed his chip and left it short, then three-putted for a six; and Jeff Sluman bogeyed six holes from the second through the 12th, and shot 74, with six pars, seven bogeys, and five birdies.

Medinah had become more difficult as the day wore on. By the time the field had come down to the last five pairings, only the leaders were left, but even they weren't up to the rising difficulty. Of those 10 men, the players who had gone into the third round at 140, four under par, only one broke par. Billy Ray Brown shot 69 and climbed into a tie for first place.

Brown was as shocked as anyone. Climbing the gentle grade to the 18th green, he saw the red number "7" at the top of the leaderboard. He knew he stood at seven under, so he must be tied for the lead.

Did it affect him?

"To tell you the truth," he said, "when I got to the 18th green, I couldn't breathe."

The 54-hole leaders:

Mike Donald	209
Billy Ray Brown	209
Mark Brooks	210
Jeff Sluman	210
Tim Simpson	210
Larry Nelson	210

Now the stage had been set for the final round. Two players of uncertain quality at the top, with Larry Nelson the only proven big-event player within a stroke of them. But the principal threat seemed poised a stroke farther back, where Mike Reid, Fuzzy Zoeller, Larry Mize, Jose Maria Olazabal, and above all Curtis Strange sat poised at 211.

With the leaders beginning to play the second nine on Saturday, Strange had said he would have to be within four strokes of first to become a force in the championship. He did better than that; he lay in ambush only two strokes behind Donald and Brown.

"The game is on," he said.

Strange, however, had no more to give. His game didn't approach his game of the third round, where crisp and accurate irons left him a series of birdie opportunities. With a third Open within reach, Curtis struggled throughout the day. The irons that had flown at the flagsticks on Saturday, missed the greens on Sunday.

Leading an enthusiastic gallery as he teed off at 12:23, in the fourth pairing from the end, Curtis played a routine first hole. The ball safely in the cup, the gallery broke ranks and raced across the footbridge that links the second tee to the second green and waited.

Now Strange gave us the first indication that this would not be his day. Still holding the honor, he hit his shot a little fat. For a sickening moment the ball looked as if it might fall into the lake. It barely cleared the far bank and stopped short of the green. A weak chip and a missed putt and Strange had bogeyed.

Two holes later he hit another iron fat and although the ball reached the green, it came to rest far short of the hole. He saved his par there, and birdied the fifth to pull back to even par, but a three-putt green at the seventh and he had bogeyed a par-five hole. One over par then, when Strange bogeyed again at the ninth, he stood at two over par for the round, and only three under par for 63 holes. He knew he was in serious trouble, and when he played an iron short of the 12th green and saw it roll off the green and onto the apron on the right, he knew it was over. He had somehow lost his ability to concentrate on the shots he had to play, and the birdies simply wouldn't come.

The gallery stayed with him, though. Grim and tight-lipped as he strode onto the 17th green, Strange hardly acknowledged cheers from the good-natured and slightly rowdy gallery, but when the volume amplified, he broke into a grin and mouthed the words, "Thank you."

Par there, and another on the 18th, and Strange finished with 75 for the day, and 286 for the championship, two over par, with no hope, for by then Greg Norman had ripped the first nine to shreds.

The most exciting fourth-round player of the time, Norman began the round at 214, two under par, but he closed in on the leaders by playing the first nine in 33. After four rather routine pars, he played two massive shots to the fifth, a par five, and scored his first birdie, then played a spectacular shot onto the sixth, hooking an iron from the rough, under tree branches, and onto the green for another. A 40-footer fell at the eighth, and then he stood at five under par for 63 holes. Another 33 coming in, and Norman might win.

He began the second nine as he began the first. Another birdie at the 10th, and still another at the 12th and he stood at seven under par. One more, or maybe two, and Norman would have passed the field. The 14th, a par five he could reach with two solid shots, and the 15th, a shortish par four of 384 yards, offered birdie opportunities. Of course he also faced the 16th and 18th, two severe holes, but he had birdied the 16th on Saturday, and he had parred the 18th every day.

He didn't have the chance to find out. After another par three at the 13th, he played a good, solid drive down the 14th fairway that left him in position to go for the green, but he found a glob of mud clinging to his ball. The mud changed everything.

With the hole measuring 545 yards, he figured he had about 275 yards to the front of the green. At first he thought he would play his driver and go for the front bunker, but he decided against it because of the mud. Then he felt he might play a one iron to the bottom of the hill short of the front bunker, but finally determined to play a three iron.

Whenever Norman is in a tight spot and hits a bad shot, it usually flies out of control to the right. He did it on the 72nd hole at Winged Foot in 1974, and again on the 72nd at Augusta in 1986. He did it here. Trying to steer the ball straight down the fairway, Greg pushed the shot into the woods to the right. He made six, dropping back to six under, and he was finished. Another bogey at the 17th, and he shot 69 for the day when 66 would have won a place in the playoff.

Paired with Irwin, Norman had teed off at 10:53, two hours ahead of Donald and Billy Ray Brown, the last men to play, and they had finished the first nine by the time Donald and Brown had finished the first hole. While Norman had made up ground, Irwin had done nothing. At 213 for 54 holes, he had fallen four strokes behind Donald and Brown.

A 36 out while Norman shot 33 didn't help at all, but suddenly Irwin began a stretch of first-class golf that would move him into contention and lead to his third Open championship.

He had begun the day playing the same loose golf he had played on Saturday, driving into the rough at the first and fighting to get down in two from 65 feet, then missing the second green and dropping a stroke. Five behind. An eight-footer fell on the seventh, though, bringing him back to even for the day, but he could make no headway through the next three holes. Out in 36, and with a routine five on the 10th where he should have been thinking of a birdie, and he seemed headed nowhere, still five strokes behind. Maybe everybody was right; at 45 he might be too old to win at this level. Still, he fought on.

Suddenly the indecisiveness was gone, and he played a series of glorious irons that wrung cheers from the gallery and sent them racing after him as he reeled off four consecutive birdies: A seven iron to six feet on the 11th; a five iron to four feet on the hard 12th; a four iron that danced around the hole of the 13th and stopped just three feet away; and then a wedge to 12 feet on the 14th. Every putt found the center of the hole, and now Irwin stood seven under par.

Seven under wouldn't do it; he needed another birdie, because Donald had slipped to nine under on the early holes. A struggling par on the 15th, where his putt ran seven feet past, and then a three iron to eight feet on the tough 16th. A birdie chance there, but, no; again the putt missed.

Only two holes left. Another birdie chance on the 17th, where a good iron stopped 12 feet away, but again the putt wouldn't fall. Only the 18th left now, and birdies were hard to find there. Irwin moved into the drive with his quick motion, then played an indifferent seven iron that settled on the right front of the green, leaving him a putt of 40 or 50 feet over a rolling, tumbling green.

He needed this putt if he were to have a chance at a playoff; he never considered winning the Open here; he looked only for the chance at a playoff.

He had to play a right-to-left break of seven or eight feet and roll his ball over a hump about 20 feet short of the cup. It was the kind of putt he would ordinarily hope to coax close enough to the hole to avoid three-putting.

After studying the line, Irwin stroked his putt. The ball rolled up the hump and down the other side, began taking the break, and with Irwin crouching down as he saw it follow the line, it kept turning as it lost speed, and dived into the hole. A birdie-three, and he had played the second nine in 31, five under par. He had shot a closing round of 67, and had finished at 280, eight under par. Now it was up to Donald and Brown to see if they could hang on.

As that last glorious putt fell, the shot of the year in professional golf, Irwin raced off the green and galloped toward the gallery standing behind the ropes cheering and waving their arms. Trotting past them, Irwin reached out and slapped hands on a victory lap.

As Irwin celebrated at the 18th, Donald and Brown had just finished nine holes, Donald in 34 and Brown in 36. Donald held the clear lead by then after dropping a 12-foot putt on the first hole, and then playing a stunning five iron within three feet of the cup on the second. Nine under now, Donald had moved two strokes ahead of Brown, and Billy Ray fell three strokes behind with a double-bogey seven on the seventh.

As they turned for home and the final nine holes, Nick Faldo closed in too. Off an hour before the co-leaders, Nick had played the first nine in 34, two under par, and had moved to within three strokes of Donald. One of the two best players in the game at that time, Faldo wasn't out of it yet. He had won the last two Masters Tournaments, and had lost a playoff to Strange in the 1988 Open.

Another birdie on the 11th, and now Faldo had closed to within two strokes. Solid pars on the next two, and then another birdie on the 14th. Eight under, one stroke back now, and certainly within range. Another birdie or a mistake by Donald and he would be tied. Donald, though, was making no mistakes, picking up par after par, thriving on the pressure of his biggest day in golf. Nick would have to birdie another hole.

A missed opportunity at the 15th, and now Faldo stood on the tee of the 16th, three holes to play, and one stroke down.

Nick had fought an erratic driver throughout the week, and by then had been driving with his one iron. He drew it from his bag here and placed his ball at the bend of the fairway, leaving himself a straight shot to the green. While he had an open line to the flag, the green lay 220 yards away. Distance, though, means very little to players of this quality. Faldo played a three iron, but pulled it a little, leaving his ball perhaps 60 feet left of the hole, set on the right of the green.

A steady putter, Faldo misread the green's pace and left his first putt perhaps eight feet short. Then he missed, leaving a downhill putt an inch or so short. Back to seven under par. A sound par on the 17th, and then a perfectly placed drive on the 18th and a stunning approach that settled 12 or 15 feet from the cup. He would have to hole this to stand a chance. He stroked the putt nicely, but the ball skimmed past the edge. A par four, a round of 69, and a 72-hole score of 281. One too many.

Donald, meanwhile, had played a series of frustrating holes. From the third through the 11th, he hit every green, and every putt seemed to have touched the edge of the hole. None fell. He stood nine under par; if he could hold on he would beat Irwin by one stroke.

A bad hole at the 12th, though, and Donald struggled to hole a 25-foot putt for his four, then another shaky hole at the 14th, where he drove into the rough, punched out to the fairway, and overshot the green with his third. A chip to 15 feet and another good putt for the par five.

Brown, meanwhile, had gained a stroke with a birdie at the 11th, and now stood two strokes behind Donald.

Now they stood on the 16th tee, Medinah's toughest hole, with the Open at stake. Both men drove decently, but then both made mistakes, Donald letting his three iron slide off to the right and into a deep bunker at the right front of the green, and Brown following with a five iron into another bunker. Donald came out within 12 feet of the cup, and Brown to eight feet. Both men missed.

With the bogey, Donald had fallen into a tie with Irwin. Unless he birdied one of the last two holes, the Open would be settled by a playoff, and unless Brown birdied both of the last two holes, he would be finished.

Here Billy Ray played the kind of shot a golfer dreams about. With the Open hinging on it, Brown played a nine iron that hit beyond the flagstick and drew back within two feet of the cup. An easy birdie. Now for another at the 18th.

As the players climbed the slope leading to the tee, Donald told his brother, Pete, who caddied for him, "Man, this is what I've been practicing 20 years for."

Both men drove into the fairway, and both men reached the green with their approaches. Brown, though, had played a much better shot than Donald, who debated between an eight and a nine iron, chose the eight, and then played a loose shot that stopped about 40 feet right of the cup, on about the same line as Irwin's two hours earlier.

Away, Donald stroked his putt nicely, and for an instant it looked as if it might fall, but once again the ball slid past the cup, and he faced a three-footer coming back.

Meantime, Brown needed his putt to match Irwin's 280. As he stood behind his ball studying his line, he drew a deep breath, then glanced over at Donald. Mike looked him squarely in the eye and said, "Make it."

Brown didn't make it. The ball ran up to the hole, and ran past the edge. A par and 281. As the ball slid past the hole, Billy Ray slumped over his putter, and his visor tumbled to the ground. He had fought hard, but he hadn't played well enough. Still, for a player who had failed to qualify the four previous times he had entered, he had played a sensational Open.

Donald's turn once more. His first putt had glided three feet past the cup; he stepped up and rolled the ball into the center of the cup. Back in 37, one stroke over par, he had shot 71 for the round, and had matched Irwin's 280.

The final standing:

Hale Irwin	280
Mike Donald	280
Billy Ray Brown	281
Nick Faldo	281
Mark Brooks	283
Tim Simpson	283
Greg Norman	283

From July of 1989 through June of 1990, the U.S. Open, the British Open, and the Masters Tournament had been settled by playoffs, an uncommon situation in itself that had become even more complex because each playoff followed a different formula. Taking them in chronological order, Mark

Calcavecchia had beaten Greg Norman and Wayne Grady on the last hole of a planned four-hole playoff at Royal Troon in July of 1989 because the Royal and Ancient Golf Club of St. Andrews schedules British Open playoffs over four or five holes, depending on the configuration of the course, always ending on the 18th. Then Nick Faldo had won the Masters on the second hole of sudden death, beginning at the 10th, when Raymond Floyd pulled his approach to the 11th into a pond.

Now Donald and Irwin would play 18 holes for the United States Open championship. The question of why the different events follow different methods arose quite naturally. Hord Hardin, the chairman of the Masters Tournament, remembered 18-hole playoffs of the past, but, reflecting on them, he said, "None were very exciting. One of the players was usually well ahead, like Fuzzy Zoeller and Greg Norman in the playoff for the 1984 Open." (Zoeller opened a sizable lead on the early holes, and won by eight strokes, shooting 67 against Norman's 75). Hardin made a further unusual observation, saying, "When you analyze it, the guys are playing sudden death from about the 70th hole in. Nothing is more exciting than sudden death on Sunday evening. People expect the tournament to be over then; they don't want to come back Monday for another round."

Speaking for the R&A, George Wilson, the deputy secretary, said the four- or five-hole had been adopted principally because the club wanted to end the British Open on the scheduled day, but found sudden death too sudden.

"For example," Wilson said, "take the man who comes in with a low score and then is tied by another man who comes in two hours later. The advantage is to the man who finishes late. His adrenalin is flowing, while it's all gone from the man who finished earlier."

This was exactly the case with Irwin, who completed his round two hours ahead of Donald, and who felt drained and emotionally flat by the time Donald holed out on the 18th.

The R&A had other reasons for adopting its playoff formula. The pressures on players to move on to the next tournament, and, Wilson went on in a rueful tone, "We have to admit regretfully to the pressures of television."

Before converting from 18 holes, the R&A asked for opinions from the players. Some of them urged the club not to be swayed by television's influence. Wilson told of an impassioned plea from Isao Aoki, the Japanese golfer who finished second to Jack Nicklaus in the 1980 U.S. Open. He wrote: "Please do not let the demands of television transcend the interests of golf."

Impressed by the players' comments, Wilson said, "Having examined their replies and insisting we wanted to finish on the scheduled day, we came upon this scheme. I assure you it was not done lightly." After a pause, Wilson sighed, "You know there is no finite answer to this."

The USGA had struggled with many playoff formats, first playing 18 holes, then 36, and back to 18 again. The USGA prefers a full round rather than a hole or two, or even a larger number. Furthermore, the players seem to prefer it for the national championship. Asked if he would have preferred to meet Donald in sudden death, Irwin said he would not; he felt it wouldn't have been fair to him, since he had completed his round so much earlier than Donald had.

Donald objected to a hole-by-hole playoff as well. He said the Open is too important to risk on one hole that could be decided by a fluke shot.

Asked to defend the USGA's position, which stands in contrast to playoff formats of the British Open, the Masters, and the PGA Championship, which follows the sudden-death method, Grant Spaeth, the USGA president, said, "The USGA maintains there is something special about a round of 18 holes. It is the traditional form of the game, and it's fair. I am not comforted that one particularly good or bad shot, or one particularly good or bad break would decide the championship then and there.

"Furthermore, it would not have been fair to drag Hale Irwin out of the clubhouse after he had been sitting around for nearly two hours and ask him to play sudden death against a man who had finished his round only minutes ago.

"We have to remember that we've been in the business of maintaining traditions for nearly 100 years, and we've been having playoffs of at least 18 holes throughout that time."

Had he felt the need, Spaeth might have called on the words of Harry Vardon for support—but then Vardon went beyond the USGA's position. In his book, *My Golfing Life*, Vardon wrote of his playoff with Francis Ouimet and Ted Ray for the 1913 U.S. Open that one round wasn't enough to establish the better player, that luck played too much a part. He preferred 36 holes.

For the moment, 18 holes it would be, so at one o'clock on Monday afternoon of June 18, Irwin and Donald strode onto Medinah's first tee and began their struggle. It was a struggle indeed, for the wind had come up, the ground had dried, and Medinah had become the test everyone had expected before the championship had begun. Add to that the understandable nervousness both men felt, and the result was somewhat lesser golf than either had played throughout the week.

After an opening birdie, Donald bogeyed three of the next five holes, and had to birdie the ninth to save 37, one over par. Even so, he had a stroke on Irwin, who shot 38, once trying somewhat foolishly to play a four wood from a rut in heavy grass bordering the right side of the fifth fairway and moving his ball barely 10 feet. He also missed both the eighth and ninth greens, and his rather loose approaches had left him only one reasonable birdie opening, and he missed that 15-footer on the sixth.

Donald was no better, and in fact, had missed three greens himself, and other than the first hole, where he had played a nice wedge five feet from the hole, had been in birdie range only once again, missing a 12-foot putt at the seventh. Otherwise, he had played such indifferent approaches he had had to putt from 50 feet on both the second and third, and 25 feet on the fifth and ninth. He had been bunkered on the sixth, and had missed a saving putt from five feet.

Both men continued to struggle through the early holes of the second nine. Donald had a chance to open a three-stroke lead when Irwin butchered the 11th and 12th, but he three-putted the 11th, and led by two strokes with six holes to play.

Their games seemed to turn around then. Both men played the next three holes with two pars and a birdie, and Donald still clung to his two-stroke lead, but now Irwin had only three holes left to catch up, and those are three of Medinah's most severe tests.

Irwin needed a birdie, but the 16th hardly seemed the logical hole; it had given up only 37 birdies through four rounds, and it had claimed 134 bogeys. The field had averaged 4.31 strokes, the highest in relation to par.

Irwin's drive split the fairway and settled at the bend, but branches from one of the trees hung over the fairway and blocked his direct line to the flagstick, and his ball lay 210 yards from the hole, leaving him little choice of club selection.

Irwin barely hesitated; he drew his two iron, the club he had used to work such wonders in the past.

Hale had always played the long irons especially well, sometimes playing shots that would take your breath away. Looking back 16 years, he had approached the 72nd hole at Winged Foot believing he needed a par four to save the 1974 Open. After a fair drive—Irwin is not a long driver—he rifled a two iron into the heart of the green, and eventually won by two strokes over Forrest Fezler. Five years later he stood in mid-fairway of the 13th hole at Inverness and watched Tom Weiskopf hole an eagle putt after playing a glorious four iron within eight feet of the cup. His competitive juices flowing, Irwin said something to his caddy about making an eagle of his own, drew out his two iron, and drilled a shot that nearly knocked the flagstick from the cup. The shot carried 225 yards and settled three feet from the hole. He made his eagle, and went on to win his second Open.

A few years later, in a playoff for the AT&T National Pro-Am, he drove into a fairway bunker at the 16th hole at Pebble Beach, and even from the sand he felt confident enough in his swing to play the two iron once again. The ball cleared the lip of the bunker, carried onto the green, and expired nine feet from the hole. Irwin won the playoff.

Now he faced another important shot with the two iron in his hand. This, however, was different; normally a left-to-right player, he would have to draw the ball right-to-left around the overhanging branches. He moved into the shot with his usual quick motion and met the ball crisply. It soared off straight enough at first, climbing high above the green, then turned only slightly, dropped left of the hole, and braked no more than six feet from the cup. He holed the putt, and now Donald's lead was down to one stroke.

A slight mistake at the 17th, where Irwin's six iron pulled up on the front fringe of the green, but he nearly chipped in, and Donald's putt from 10 feet curled around the cup but missed. Still one stroke separated them as they climbed onto the 18th tee.

Up first, Irwin drove down the center of the fairway and stepped aside as Donald teed his ball. One more good drive and the Open probably would be his, and Donald had been driving especially well. In 13 driving holes, he had missed only the fourth fairway. Here, though, he made a serious mistake. He said he didn't feel nervous, but he drew his drive to the left, into the gallery, where it hit a spectator and dropped into shaggy grass. From where his ball lay he had no clear shot to the flag; the hole was cut to the left, behind a greenside bunker with a high lip. Aiming for the opening to the left, Donald played a five iron that flew farther left than he had hoped and dropped into the bunker. Irwin, meanwhile, dropped a five iron onto the green perhaps 25 feet from the cup.

Needing a par four to win the Open, Donald played only a fair recovery;

his ball rolled 15 feet from the cup, and he missed the putt. Irwin had parred, and they had tied, at 74.

Dating back to its beginning, in 1895, the Open had seen 29 playoffs; only five had been tied, calling for additional rounds (the 1931 playoff had been scheduled for 36 holes, and when Billy Burke and George Von Elm each shot 144, they played 36 additional holes, with Burke winning by one stroke). The USGA decided in 1953, however, that ties in future playoffs would continue hole-by-hole. The 1990 Open would be the first sudden-death finish.

It finished quickly. As they stood on the first tee, Donald seemed to have the clear edge. He had played the first hole five times by then, and had three birdies and two pars. Irwin, on the other hand, had played the hole with three fours, a five, and a three.

Still first on the tee, Irwin played a three wood over the rise in the fairway to a level lie at the base of the slope beyond, leaving him only a sand wedge to the green. Donald's tee shot pulled up short of Irwin's, but still only a wedge away.

The first green has two levels, the lower at the back. Away, Donald played what looked to be a timid shot short of the dip, leaving him a difficult putt, because the hole was cut close to the base of the downslope. Irwin's turn now. Here he played the bolder shot. His ball cleared the downslope and settled on the lower level within birdie distance, eight or 10 feet left of the cup.

First to putt, Donald missed, then stood by while Irwin studied his line, then stroked his putt. Hale's ball ran true to the hole and tumbled into the cup. A birdie, and Irwin had won.

Seeing his ball dive into the hole, Irwin turned away from the green, leaped twice, then raced toward his wife, Sally, who had broken through the crowd and run toward him. As they stood by the green hugging one another, their 18-year-old daughter ran to them, and they stood there holding on while tears rolled down their cheeks. Then, as they climbed into a golf cart for a short drive to the presentation ceremony, Sally sat on Hale's lap, and he buried his face in her back.

At 45, Irwin had become the oldest man ever to win the U.S. Open, although not the oldest to have won one of the game's four most important competitions. Julius Boros won the 1968 PGA Championship at 48. Still, Irwin had two years on both Raymond Floyd, who won at Shinnecock in 1986, and Ted Ray, the Englishman who won the 1920 U.S. Open at Inverness.

Reflecting on his victory a short time later, Irwin looked over a sea of reporters and said, "I've always felt I had a certain kind of tenacity and never-give-up attitude. You can call it guts, confidence, experience, any number of things, and I think they're all appropriate when you talk about winning a U.S. Open."

Should the USGA's exemption policies continue as they are, Irwin will be eligible to play through the year 2000, when the Open celebrates its 100th playing. He will be 55 then, and will have had the opportunity to fulfill a tradition that had held up throughout the championship's history:

No one has won three Opens without winning a fourth.

5. The British Open

When a brawny young American came to play in the 1960 British Open, he was such a force in golf that, as historic moments go, this was nothing less than the rebirth of the British Open. This was Arnold Palmer, who resurrected the championship in 1960, and who won it twice, in 1961 and 1962. Now, in 1990, he would be taking his last bow where he took his first—at the shrine of the game, the Old Course at St. Andrews. Back in 1960, Palmer was the undisputed king of golf, the man with the bold, brash, muscular game. In 1990, he was 60, still brawny, still beefy-armed, and still electric when he strode the fairways. But now his hair was gray and so was his putting. In golf, most of the magic is in the putting, and his magic had been gone for years. He had said he would play tournament golf as long as he thought he could be competitive. Now he was winding down. Some years earlier, he gave up playing regularly on the PGA Tour to concentrate on the Senior PGA Tour. He also quit playing in the U.S. Open. And now he and his wife, Winnie, had come to St. Andrews, and they would be saying goodbye to the British Open.

"It's time," Palmer said. "I'm getting older."

He was leaving this stage to men who were toddlers, or not much more, back when he first came to St. Andrews. Nick Faldo, who would win this 119th Open, the 24th at St. Andrews, was only three years old in 1960, as was Seve Ballesteros. Greg Norman and Curtis Strange were five, Ian Woosnam was two, and Mark Calcavecchia, the defending champion in 1990, was only a month old. They no longer feared Palmer on the golf course, but they recognized their debt to him. Norman said it most eloquently, "We owe everything to this man. He shaped the boundaries of modern golf. Whatever we achieve now is only because Arnie was there to make it happen. I think he's a little sad, this being his last Open. But when you have set the highest standards, you must do what you think is right. I'm going to miss Arnie a lot."

Whatever else modern golf owes to Palmer, it certainly has him to thank for the British Open as we know it. The oldest championship in the world, dating to 1860, was pretty much dying of indifference, especially where the American golfers were concerned. The Americans had become the dominant golfers in the 1920s and 1930s. And except for the one-time visits and victories of Sam Snead in 1946, and Ben Hogan in 1953, they ignored the Open. Their own Tour was growing fast. Besides, overseas travel then was expensive and time-consuming. Everything changed in 1960. Palmer put the seal of the king on the Open merely by entering. Suddenly, everyone who wanted to be someone in golf wanted to play in the British Open. The Royal and Ancient Golf Club has never ceased to recognize Palmer's contribution, and some years ago the Club paid tribute by keeping the door open for him. The R&A did this by establishing a rule which grants an automatic berth in the Open to all former champions under age 65.

Americans have been coming in force since 1960. The turnout was heavier than usual this time, probably because of the attraction of St. Andrews. Of the 156 in the starting field, 51 were Americans.

The popular belief, by the way, is that Palmer entered the 1960 Open because it was the next leg of what became known as the Grand Slam, golf's four major events. He already had won the first two, the Masters and the U.S. Open. If he could take the British Open, then the American PGA Championship, that would be the Slam, and nobody had ever won it. And that's why Palmer went to St. Andrews in 1960? "Not true," Palmer said. "It wouldn't have mattered whether I had won the Masters and the U.S. Open or not. I had committed to the British Open long before I won those two. It was a commitment I had made to my dad. Very simply, I just never felt you were a total success in the game until you won the British Open. It's part of the tradition of the game."

In a nutshell, that was the breath of new life for the British Open in 1960. It had come back to St. Andrews, site of the richest history in the game. Here, Kel Nagle beat Palmer by a stroke in 1960. Tommy Nakajima took his infamous nine at No. 17, the Road Hole, in 1978. And most recently, in 1984, Tom Watson crashed at No. 17, and Seve Ballesteros parred it, birdied No. 18, and won his second Open. But for all of the 24 Opens at the Old Course, and for all the old town has seen over the years, there's always something new. Take, for example, the case of the favorites.

What's an Open without that delicious pre-tournament speculation? Well, an odd thing happened this time. For a defending champion, Mark Calcavecchia was getting precious little respect. Hardly anybody seemed to think he had a chance to repeat. The bookmakers established Faldo as the favorite, and offered Calcavecchia at somewhat distant odds. And the press and other observers also paid him little attention. For example, *The Guardian* listed six favorites—Norman, Ballesteros, Strange, Faldo, Woosnam, and Jose Maria Olazabal. It put Calcavecchia down among the "six challengers who might pull off a major coup." *The Independent* didn't even give him that much consideration. Its six "outsiders who could upset the odds" were Fred Couples, David Feherty, Eduardo Romero, Mark James, Lanny Wadkins, and Rodger Davis.

Whatever became of Mark Calcavecchia? He hadn't won since taking the 1989 British Open at Royal Troon. He was outstanding in his first visit to the Old Course, in the autumn of 1989, leading the American team to victory in the Dunhill Cup, and by mid-July was third on the American money list with $717,754, just a good payday behind No. 1 Greg Norman. He had five second-place finishes.

There was the matter of the broken little toe on his left foot. Just about a month earlier, he played in the Irish Open—his sixth runner-up finish—with the top of his left shoe cut away. "It's fine now, though," Calcavecchia said at St. Andrews. "After more aches and pains this year than I've ever had, nothing hurts now. But I'm 30 now," he added, with a grin, "and maybe I'm losing it."

It wasn't likely that a man of only 30, and who had come to the top only four years ago, would lose his game so soon. Some thought it might be attitude. Perhaps too casual. Most golfers want to arrive as early as possible on Open week. By that standard, Calcavecchia came late. "It's kind of tough to fly over here on a Tuesday and have one day to regroup," he said. "But I knew one practice round would be enough. I have charts and yardages from the Dunhill last fall, and nothing has changed from then."

Greg Norman, co-runner-up with Wayne Grady at Troon a year earlier, had won the Australian Masters and won twice on the American Tour already—the Doral Ryder Open on a chip shot in a playoff, and the Memorial Tournament, shortened to 54 holes by rain. But that old lightning had also struck again—twice. First, Robert Gamez, rookie sensation on the American Tour, holed out a 176-yard seven-iron approach for an eagle to beat him in The Nestle Invitational. Then David Frost holed out from a bunker on the final hole in the USF&G Classic. Norman shrugged. "If other guys hole their shots and beat me, I have no control over that," he said. "But when they do it to me, it's a sign that I'm in contention more than anyone else."

Don't forget the 1989 British Open at Royal Troon. Norman shot a final-round 64 to tie with Wayne Grady and Calcavecchia. Then the four-hole aggregate playoff, the first in Open history, turned into a Calcavecchia-Norman duel. Norman went birdie-birdie-bogey, and Calcavecchia par-birdie-par, and they were tied going to the final hole, Troon's 18th. Norman hit a tremendous drive, but ended up in a fairway bunker. His second shot went into another bunker, and from there he hit over the green and out of bounds. Calcavecchia hit a brilliant approach to within six feet, below the hole. Norman—lying four and not yet on the green—picked up. Calcavecchia closed out like a champion. He holed the putt for a birdie.

The biggest thing Curtis Strange had to recommend him in this Open was that he owned the record at the Old Course, the breathtaking 62 he shot in the 1987 Dunhill Cup. Strange was not himself so far in 1990. He carried the pressure of the world on him going into the U.S. Open. He had won it in 1988 and 1989, and now the big question was, would he become only the second man in history to win three in succession? The answer was no. He came to St. Andrews without a victory of any kind. "I've played well, but I haven't putted well," Strange said. "And that's what I'm struggling with now."

Seve Ballesteros, who won the second of his three Opens at St. Andrews in 1984, had switched caddies in hopes of finding a spark for his game. This time, he went back to his brother, Vicente. He did have other things on his mind, though. He and his wife, Carmen, were expecting their first child in October. Did the prospect of parenthood affect him? Who knows? But aside from his victory in the Renault de Baleares Open in March, this was not the Ballesteros everyone knew.

If Ballesteros was puzzled, his countryman, the dynamic young Jose Maria Olazabal, was baffled. A two-time winner this year, his game was gone. "After the Irish Open (which he won five weeks earlier), I rated my chances of winning here very high," he said. "But not now. I can't see that I have a realistic chance here. I don't know what's going on."

Ian Woosnam came to the Open as the hottest golfer. He had just won the Scottish Open, and the Monte Carlo Open the week before that, which gave him three victories for the year. But his chronic bad back had acted up. "I'm used to it, but this time it's a little bit more sore than usual," he said. "But I'll play if I have to play on one leg. Winning the Open is what I've wanted to do all my life." Still, he wasn't exactly grief-stricken at the prospect that he might not win this Open. "If you had known me 12 years ago, I think you would have said I've done myself justice," Woosnam said. "You want to make enough money to live on for the rest of your life, and that was my goal. I definitely want to win a major, but if it never happens, it is not the end of the world. I have achieved what I wanted to in life, really."

Nick Faldo, with three majors already to his credit, struck a different note. "I thrive on majors," he said. "When you get into position to win one, it's nerve-wracking. You say this is what it's all about." He won the 1987 British Open at Muirfield. And in April, he had won his second consecutive Masters. He might have had the 1990 U.S. Open to his credit, too. In June, at Medinah, he came within one more turn of the ball from joining the playoff with Mike Donald and eventual winner Hale Irwin. That's how close his birdie putt came on the final hole. In seven European events, he had two seconds, a fourth, a fifth, and a ninth. He closed strong to tie for fifth in the Scottish Open the week before the British Open. "In the last round, I worked on a few things, and I had a chance to shoot a hell of a round," Faldo said. Most would consider a 65 at Gleneagles just that. "But that's always encouraging," he said. "It's always nice to play well and be putting better, reading the greens better. Any time you do that, it's good for the confidence."

The Open week began uneventfully, but it had its interesting moments. Among them was the arrival of the U.S. Amateur champion, Chris Patton, the most imposing golf figure in years—at least 300 pounds. He planned to turn professional soon after the Open. Then there was the former British Amateur champion, Russell Claydon, who was not impressed by the Old Course. "It's a pretty silly course," Claydon said. "It's almost sacrilege, but I don't like it. You can stand on the tee and hit it anywhere you want, as hard as you want." Maurice Flitcroft, the now-legendary hacker-impostor, surfaced again, despite the R&A's efforts with new entry rules. This time, Flitcroft, now age 60, called himself James Beau Jolley, and dyed his hair and moustache. He couldn't disguise his game, though. He lasted two holes in the qualifier. And all this after he had promised the last time that he wouldn't do it again. "I'm tempted to go and ask for my entry fee back," Flitcroft said. But he didn't.

Add this as something to watch for in 25 years: According to *The Guardian*, a Bob Hamlet, of West Bromwich, bet £10 at 10,000-to-1 odds that his son Jack, now age four, will win the British Open by the year 2015. And while that story was making the rounds, two Scots from Glasgow were making the rounds, playing the 18 watering holes of St. Andrews. This would hardly delight the temperance workers, but a "course" of pubs was laid out in *Golf World* magazine, and these two set out with their own scoring system on Wednesday of Open week—a pint of beer and a whiskey, or a half-pint and a large whiskey were worth an eagle; a half-pint and a whiskey were a birdie; a small whiskey or a pint, a par; a half-pint, a bogey; and a soft drink or a coffee, a double bogey. They teed off at Chariots, a pitch shot from the R&A clubhouse. They were last heard from at No. 10, the Jigger Inn, along the fairway of the real 17th.

Nick Faldo, by the way, turned 33 on Wednesday, July 18, the day before the Open was to begin. He was about to give himself a terrific birthday present.

Indifferent to the history that was unfolding on the golf course just a short distance inland from them, some natives of St. Andrews took to the beach that Thursday, the first day of the 1990 British Open. They walked the kids and ran the dogs in the foamy edge of the North Sea on that great sweep of peaceful, beige sand stretching away almost as far as the eye can see. Experienced observers of the British Open will notice the significance of the natives at play there: if it's beach weather at St. Andrews, then it really isn't British Open weather. Remember the Scottish admonition: "If it's nae wind and nae rain, it's nae golf." There had been some rain a few days earlier, but not enough to break the prolonged drought that had plagued the area. To save wear and tear, public play on the Old Course had been cut back earlier in the season. For this first day of the Open, there was sun, balmy temperatures, and no rain. There were occasional brisk breezes, helping golfers to drive some greens, but not the flag-rippers the Open is famous for. "The flags are very difficult, and rightly so," said Lee Trevino, after shooting 69. "The R&A knew it wasn't going to blow."

The 119th Open began with a mass assault on the 600-year-old course. By day's end, 50 of the 156 starters broke the par of 72. Greg Norman, happily driving par-four greens, and little-known American Michael Allen, handling transcontinental putts, shared a one-stroke lead on 66. Nick Faldo was at 67, eight men were at 68, five at 69, 14 at 70, and 20 at 71. Anyone who wasn't near par must have been making travel plans for Friday night.

The signs of this attack came early in a pair of body blows by American rookie Robert Gamez. He won his PGA Tour debut, the Tucson Open, the second week of January, then added The Nestle Invitational late in March. This was Gamez's first trip to Europe, and at the start, it showed. For his first shot, he nervously topped his two-iron drive so badly that he needed a four iron to reach the green. Even Trevino, a short hitter, needed only a sand wedge second to set up his birdie. Gamez quickly pulled himself together and got his par. Then came the fireworks. At No. 3, he holed out a sand wedge from 84 yards for an eagle-two, and at No. 5, he hit a four wood to 65 feet and holed the putt for an eagle-three. Two eagles in the span of three holes, and he was on the leaderboard at four under par through five holes. The Old Course does not gracefully suffer such indignities from a rookie. Gamez was sobered by two quick bogeys, three-putting from 25 feet at the seventh, and three-putting from 60 feet at the eighth. His hot start ended up a two-under-par 70, four strokes off the lead. But he refused to let this spoil his introduction to the Open and St. Andrews. "I love it!" he said. "This is the way golf should be played. You have options on shots—real golf. Not just another tournament, not this week!"

Hot as Gamez's start was, he wasn't alone. Australian Craig Parry, known as "Popeye" on the European Tour because of his big forearms, ran off four consecutive birdies from No. 2 and joined Gamez on the leaderboard at four under through five holes. He would have been no worse than co-leader except for No. 17, the Road Hole. Balmy weather or not, the 17th once again would be the pivotal point of the Open. Parry had got to seven under through the 15th, and was within three holes of holding the lead by himself. But he gave one stroke back with a bogey at the 16th. That left him six under. Now he could at least tie for the first-round lead. But the 17th knocked him back into the pack. Getting a double bogey at the 17th is easy from anywhere. Parry got his from the grass strip across the road, near the wall. His pitch didn't clear the three-foot high bank of the green. He settled for a 68, two off the lead.

Also at 68 was Peter Jacobsen, who also suffered at No. 17. He shrugged it off. "There's a true innocence to this golf course," Jacobsen explained, with poetry and forgiveness in his heart, right after a crippling error knocked him out of a share of the lead. "When the wind is down, you can get your red numbers in a hurry." Which he did—five consecutive birdies from No. 2, then another at No. 10. He was six under par and tied for the lead with Norman and Allen, who had already finished. He had eight holes to play. The lead was his for the taking. "Of course," Jacobsen added, "she'll take 'em away, too." Which she also did. He bogeyed the par-three 11th, three-putting from about 120 feet, which didn't upset him, but missed a two-foot par putt at the 13th, which did. The bogeys cancelled out birdies at the 10th and 12th, and a birdie at the 14th put him back at six under and tied for the lead.

Then came the killer, the 17th. Many golfers don't like a left-to-right wind there, blowing toward the Old Course Hotel and the out-of-bounds, but Jacobsen does. It's the reverse he doesn't like, the right-to-left toward the rough, and that's what he got. He hit his drive into the gorse, chopped the ball out, and put his third into the Road Bunker. A blast and two putts left him with a double bogey-six and a sheepish grin. "That was my second double bogey in a row at No. 17," Jacobsen said. He got some odd looks from the press corps. After all, this was the first round. "I double-bogeyed it in the last round in 1984," Jacobsen explained. But the 17th hadn't heard the last from him. Unfortunately, he hadn't heard the last from it, either.

Norman drove the 316-yard 12th green. Imagine the surprise of Scott Simpson. He was putting when a ball came rolling up. "I hit it right of the bunker, and the wind drifted it left and rolled it up," Norman said. "Then it rolled down again." He two-putted from 40 feet. He also drove pin-high at the 354-yard 18th—and this time imagine the roar from the crowd in the grandstands at the green. He used his putter. His first putt was 12 feet short. He holed the second for his sixth birdie in a bogey-free 66, his best first round in the Open.

Norman's lead seemed safe enough, benign conditions or not. Then along came Michael Allen, playing about an hour and a half behind him, in his first competitive round on the Old Course. Allen was the day's most-unlikely-to-succeed. He's an interesting mix. He likes wine-tasting, snow skiing, the San Francisco 49ers, and he went to college for horticulture. As for golf, it took him three tries in the qualifying school to make it to the American PGA Tour, and he also qualified for the European Tour. "And here, I was able to play with some of the best in the world and make good money," Allen said. But until he won the Scottish Open in 1989, with a final-round 63 at Gleneagles, he was pretty much dead in the water.

Allen played in the 1988 Open at Royal Lytham and St. Annes, and started with an 82. He had come around 180 degrees this time. Only a bogey at the 18th, where he missed a five-foot par putt, kept him from taking the lead by himself. It was a strong seven-birdie round, three going out and four coming home. He two-putted from 80 feet for a birdie at No. 14, and two-putted for a par from 100 feet at No. 15. The jewel of the round, however, was the cross-country putt for a birdie that dropped at No. 13. "At least 100 feet," he said. "Maybe 150, I don't know." He said it broke a little, from left to right, and he hit it as hard as he could. "It bounced up in the air, about a foot," he said. "Peter Jacobsen was on the other hole (No. 5) and bowed to me, and I was thanking the gods." Someone asked him whether he'd ever made a putt that long before. "Make one that long?" he said. "I've never even had one that long."

If Norman drew a roar from the grandstands at the 18th, think of the reception Nick Faldo got. Norman drove to the left of the green, and two-putted for a birdie. Faldo drove short, by design, then holed a 40-yard pitch for an eagle-two.

The shot erased a big regret. Helped by a tailwind, some golfers were almost driving the 18th green. Faldo drove with his two wood, which he had put into his bag especially for St. Andrews and its winds. He used it at five holes. "But as I stood in the middle of the 18th fairway, I'm three back of Greg Norman already," Faldo said. "I left myself too close to the green. I hit the two wood to try to stay farther back and leave myself a full wedge shot. Then I wished I had hit the driver. If I had, it would have gone into the Valley of Sin and 20 yards farther up." He lay about 40 yards off the green, and pulled out his eight iron. "A genuine Scottish bump-and-run," he said, with a big grin. "I got the break right—right-to-left first, and then left-to-right."

Faldo had a nearly trouble-free round. He birdied No. 5 from 12 feet for an outward 35, then he got hot coming in. He hit a three iron off No. 10 tee to leave himself a full shot in, and the strategy worked beautifully. He dabbed a sand wedge pitch to four feet and holed for the birdie. He birdied the 12th from 10 feet, the 13th from eight, and four holes later had his only real difficulty at No. 17. His two iron was long, his pitch good, to eight feet, but he two-putted for the bogey. Then came the eagle at the 18th, and a 67 and third place all alone.

Ian Woosnam, en route to a 68, hit 18 greens in regulation, but a balky putter kept him from finishing them off. Over the first 15 holes, he was inside Craig Parry, his playing partner, 10 times. But Parry was seven under par, and Woosnam only three under. Also at 68 were Payne Stewart, who matched Norman on two holes. Stewart drove the green at No. 12 and two-putted from 80 feet for a birdie, and came even closer to driving the 18th green, stopping just short of the green, from where he two-putted for another birdie.

Ian Baker-Finch was an unknown Australian who became known in a hurry in the 1984 Open at St. Andrews, when he started with a 68, just one stroke off the lead. He shot 68 again this time, two strokes off the lead. "I have lots of fond memories of 1984," Baker-Finch said. And one bad memory. "That last round was unkind and hard to live with," he said. He led through the second round, shared the lead through the third, and in the fourth, went out in a crippling 41. He finished with a 79, and dropped into a tie for ninth.

Defending champion Mark Calcavecchia shot a listless 71. He even found himself on the wrong green at the 11th, after shanking a seven iron. "I played a bunch of rotten golf," he said.

Among the more sympathetic characters of the first round was Russell Weir, a Briton from the Isle of Butte. At No. 17, he drove into the rough on the left, and didn't escape with his second shot. His third flew the green, the road, and the wall, and ended up out of bounds in the crowd. He took a penalty drop, and then hit it onto the road. He finally got on the green in six, and two-putted for a quadruple bogey-eight, the highest score of the day there. Just a stroke behind was David Jones, of Northern Ireland. Jones ended up in the Road Bunker. "Against my better judgement, I decided the ball was playable," Jones said. "I didn't get it out, and left it completely unplayable. At that point, I began to think of all the poor souls whose bones are buried there." Jones finally got out—playing backwards.

The real heroes of the day were Arnold Palmer, for pleasing the crowd with a 73 to start his final Open, and Craig Stadler, just for finishing the first round. He shot 82. This was not a Stadler-like round. It was that infected ingrown toenail on his left big toe, he said. The pain caused him to jerk his foot away when he hit the ball. Everything else went wrong, too. He said he wanted to crawl into one of the many bunkers he visited. "And not come out." Things got so silly, he was able to grin about it. At the par-four sixth, he five-putted from 100 feet for a seven. He even had a one-incher for his six. "I put a 'Hale Irwin' on it," Stadler said, referring to Irwin's whiff of a one-incher in the 1983 British Open. All told, Stadler had one triple bogey, three doubles, three singles, and two pars—all going out. That was a 48, 12 over par. "I never quit in my life, but the temptation was very strong," Stadler said. Coming in, he not only was bogey-free, he made two birdies and even parred the 17th. He came home in 34. He started to laugh. "That's going to look bad in the papers," he said. "People are going to wonder what the hell happened—on the back nine."

The first round leaders:

Greg Norman	66
Michael Allen	66
Nick Faldo	67
Martin Poxon	68
Christy O'Connor, Jr.	68
Ian Baker-Finch	68
Craig Parry	68
Ian Woosnam	68
Payne Stewart	68
Peter Jacobsen	68
Sam Torrance	68

Friday was another sunny, agreeable, un-British Open day on the Old Course. But it was "Sunday" for Greg Norman, a holiday for Nick Faldo, and Doomsday for Mark Calcavecchia and Curtis Strange. Norman had become known for some electrifying rallies in the last round of tournaments. Some called them "Norman Sundays." This time, his Sunday fell on Friday, the second round, another six-under-par 66 for 12-under-par 132 total and a share of the lead after 36 holes. Faldo frolicked around the Old Course in 65, matching Norman. The two led by four strokes over Payne Stewart (68) and Craig Parry (68). And Peter Jacobsen enjoyed a "magical moment" at the Road Hole. That is, he got away with murder. Meanwhile, things weren't so magical for some. Michael Allen, the obscure American who shared the first-round lead on 66, ballooned to a 75. But at least he made the cut. You wouldn't believe who didn't.

The cut came in at 143, one under par, the lowest in British Open history.

Among the victims: Tom Kite, at 73—144; at 145, five-time winner Tom Watson (73), Lanny Wadkins (74), Howard Clark (72), Curtis Strange (71), and three-time champion Seve Ballesteros (74), his first miss since he was an 18-year-old lad in his British Open debut in 1975. At 146, there were Bob Tway (73), and at 147, Gordon Brand, Jr. (70) and 1989 co-runner-up Wayne Grady (74).

Perhaps the most surprising victim of all was defending champion Mark Calcavecchia (75—146). "I didn't think about missing the cut until I realized it was possible at No. 14," he said. He bogeyed there, right after a double bogey-six at the 13th, where he missed a one-foot putt for a single bogey. Calcavecchia was quietly steaming. "Golf is just a game—an idiotic game most of the time," he said later.

The toll also included all four amateurs in the field. England's Tony Nash bowed out on 72—145, Japan's Yasunobu Kuramoto on 72—149, U.S. Amateur champion Chris Patton on 75—149, and British Amateur champion Rolf Muntz, of Holland, on 74—152.

The unkindest cut of all fell on Arnold Palmer, who wanted nothing more than to make that last walk up the 18th fairway on the last day. He had played his best golf in a long time, especially at the last two holes, where he turned on the will-power of Young Arnie. He had birdied No. 1 from 10 feet, three-putted No. 3 from 20 feet for a bogey. He parred the eighth from 10 feet, and three-putted No. 9 from 30 feet for a bogey. He started parring from the 10th, but he knew that wouldn't be enough. So, figuratively speaking, he hitched up his pants.

"At No. 13, I knew I had to finish level par to have any chance to play in the last two rounds," Palmer said. He needed a birdie, and he got it at No. 15, on a 10-foot putt. Another would be nice, but he dare not bogey coming in. He parred No. 16 routinely. Then you could hear the thunder at the 17th all over the course. Palmer had hit a so-so tee shot, and his four-wood second left on the front, about 80 feet from the cup. His birdie putt ran over the edge of the hole. He parred. At the 18th, his approach ended up in the Valley of Sin, a good 60 feet from the cup. You could feel the tension in the crowd. They knew what he needed as much as he did, and a 60-footer from down in that valley was an "iffy" proposition at best. The ball sped up the smooth slope of the valley, bent, and headed right for the cup. The crowd erupted again. But the ball stopped about three inches short. Palmer tapped in the par. And those three inches were to cost him his hero's finale. The tap-in gave him a one-under-par 71, for his even-par 144.

Then came the wait. The whole golf course waited with him. Palmer had finished about 1:15 p.m. Norman didn't tee off till 2:50, and Faldo not till 3:20. It was generally believed that Palmer was safe at par. In any other Open, he would have been. But the Old Course was playing so meekly. It would be some six hours after he finished before he really knew. As Norman and Faldo proceeded to light up the course with fireworks, Palmer's chances grew slimmer and slimmer with each passing hole. He knew it and the fans knew it. The low 70 scorers and ties, and anyone within 10 strokes of the lead, would make the cut. All Norman and Faldo had to do was falter, just a little. But they didn't. Arnold Palmer had already made that last walk up the 18th. He would have good memories. "I could feel the vibrations from the gallery as I walked up the fairways," Palmer said. "I think they were as nervous as me, and didn't know whether I could still shoot a 71. I was pleased that I managed that, at least," Palmer missed the cut by one stroke.

Shortly before Palmer made his final triumphal march up the 18th fairway, an unknown Englishman had made his first. This was Jamie Spence, 27, who left his mark in the finest tradition of the obscure who rise to the heroic moment. It took Spence five tries in the qualifying school to make it to the European Tour where, this year, his best finish was a tie for ninth and his winnings were a modest £20,000-plus. He had to go through the qualifiers to get into the Open. He was still weak from food poisoning he had contracted the previous Saturday. And now here he was, marching up the 18th to the cheers of thousands, about to complete a seven-under-par 65 that would tie Neil Coles' 1970 record, the best ever in 24 Opens on the Old Course. The 65 also put him right on the leaderboard. "God," he thought, "if Dad switches on the TV and sees this, he could drop dead." Spence wasn't being flip. His dad, James, had suffered a heart attack back on Christmas Day.

The only blot on Spence's card was a bogey-six at No. 5, where he got caught in a fairway bunker. Otherwise, the Old Course was his—three birdies over the last four outward holes, and coming in, four over a five-hole stretch from the 13th. He even birdied No. 17, where his 188-yard five-iron approach hit the flagstick and stopped eight feet away. This—to complete the drama—was his first British Open, his first visit to the Old Course, and he was the first man off the tee, at 7:15 a.m. "It will all sink in when I go back and sit in my bedroom," he said. "I'll switch on the TV, and see my name up there, and think, 'Gee, have I really done that?'"

Yes, he had, on a day that dwarfed the first round for damage to the Old Course's reputation. Where 50 broke par in the first round, 86 did it this time, and 25 of them didn't even make the cut.

The way Craig Parry saw it, the big lead Faldo and Norman had taken was a blessing, not a curse. "There's not too much pressure, being four behind the lead," said Parry, who matched Payne Stewart with a second 68 for 136 and a share of third place. "I'm in a good position." His four-birdie start put him in even stronger position, but he tailed off coming in. He got two more birdies, but he cancelled them out with two bogeys. The first came at No. 13, where he missed a four-foot par putt, and the other came at No. 17. But at least he was gaining on the 17th. He had double-bogeyed it in the first round. He made just a bogey this time, two-putting from 15 feet.

Parry shoulders the burden of all Australian golfers—the inevitable comparison with Greg Norman. Can he beat Norman here? "The only way I could beat him at the moment," Parry said, "would be to hole more putts." Stewart had no such burden. A lack of confidence has never been his problem. "I'm not saying I'm going to win the Open," Stewart said, "but I'm capable of winning it." His 68 consisted of one bogey, a two-putt from 15 feet at the 12th, and five birdies.

The travails of Craig Stadler continued, and mercifully they ended. Like Spence, Stadler might also wonder, "Gee, have I really done that?" Stadler would be asking for a different reason, though. The infected toe that cost him an 82 in the first round was no better. In fact, he accidentally made it worse. Convinced he would miss the cut, he had packed his bags that morning. He was carrying a suitcase down to the hotel lobby, and he dropped it on his sore foot. Rodger Davis, who also had an 82 playing with Stadler in the first round—surely both were tempted to withdraw—went out looking for their third, Davis Love III. He found him at the practice tee, warming up. "I thought I'd turn up," Davis said, "in case you had no one to play with." To the surprise of both, Stadler also showed up, to see the thing through. He and Davis had 71s, and Love 75, and they all missed the cut.

Among others who kept the pot bubbling in the second round:

American Steve Pate, playing in his third Open, but his first visit to St. Andrews, added a 68 for 138, a tie for ninth place. He would have one memento for sure—he birdied the 17th. He hit a four iron to about 30 inches. Also in that group at 138 was Sam Torrance (70), who rode that long putter to a burst of four consecutive birdies from No. 3. What perplexed him was the drive at the par-five 14th, with the wind changed, forcing him to go far to the left. "When they were putting up the grandstand there, you would never think it was in the line of anything, but it is," he said. "You have to hit over it." Which he did—over the spectators' heads. He ended up in the Beardies, but scrambled a par.

Anders Sorensen, also at 138, the first Dane to be exempt into the Open, had two bright marks in his 68. One was an eagle, the other a bogey. He eagled the fifth with a 75-foot putt. The bogey came at No. 17, where his tee shot ended up on the road by the hotel, just two yards from the out-of-bounds. He hit a two iron fat, and coming down some 50 yards short of the green. Then he pitched on and two-putted.

Nick Price, two-time Open runner-up (to Tom Watson in 1982, to Seve Ballesteros in 1989), surprised everyone, especially himself, by playing so well. He had broken a finger pulling the starting cord on an outboard motor in the Caribbean. He missed 19 days and two tournaments on the American Tour, including the U.S. Open. The long layoff showed when he returned. He was putting abysmally, he said. So what kind of chance would he have at St. Andrews? But his touch suddenly returned, and a bogey-free 67, highlighted by a number of two-putt pars from 50 and 60 feet, put him at 137, seven under par and five strokes off the lead.

Mike Reid also authored a 67—137, and pondered the relentless give-and-take of the game. He eagled No. 5 with a four wood to three feet, birdied No. 6, and ran off three consecutive birdies from the 13th. "I wanted to play a strong game today," Reid said, "to make up for the double bogey at No. 17 yesterday."

Just a stroke behind lurked Jose Maria Olazabal, gathering steam. Two full rounds now, and he had yet to miss a green in regulation. Jack Nicklaus, his playing partner, was one impressed golfer. "For two days, Ollie just knocked the flagsticks out of the holes," Nicklaus said. Four of Olazabal's five birdies were from inside 10 feet. But aside from those, he couldn't buy a putt. He stood a 71-67—138, six strokes off the lead. "The last few years, I putted good for a couple of days, and then suddenly it all goes," he said. "And that's what happened again." He three-putted twice, had 37 putts overall, and 32 putts in the first round.

Jodie Mudd, The Players Championship winner, finished with 66—138, and could have been at least a stroke lower. Did he curse his luck? No. He looked on the bright side of things. It could have been worse. "I was a bit lucky at No. 17," he said. "I could've made seven or eight." He escaped with a bogey-five. He was trying to get a six iron second from the left rough to the front of the green. "But the high grass turned the club in my hands," he said. "The ball went 10 or 15 yards." He put his next on the road, 70 feet from the flag, chipped to six feet, and holed the putt. "I've hit it in the left rough for two days," Mudd said. "I can't get it into my head to hit it to the right." He'd had a different kind of communications problem earlier. It was his Scottish caddy. "It took me a couple of days to figure out what he was saying," Mudd said.

Meanwhile, the adventures of Peter Jacobsen at the Road Hole rolled on. When last seen, Jacobsen was racking up an ungainly double bogey in the first round. Not this time. He hit a perfect drive, then a four iron short. He was on the front of the green, at least 75 feet from the hole, with the shoulder of the Road Bunker between him and the hole—the classic Tommy Nakajima position from the 1978 Open. All he could think of was how Nakajima made nine after his putt was sucked down off the shoulder and into the bunker. "I thought, what if I do putt it into the bunker?" Jacobsen said. "What will my mom and dad think? I'm supposed to be good. If I get this putt wrong, I could be making 12." Then a strange thing happened. A quiet confidence swept over him, as though some part of him could see the future. "It was one of those magical moments, when you know it's going in," he said. "I told the caddy to go get the ball out of the hole when it goes in, and he's thinking—'I hope he keeps it on the green!'" Jacobsen said the putt broke 12 feet to the right, 20 feet left, then eight feet back to the right, and dropped. He finished at 70—138, and was walking on air when he left the course. "When I'm 80 and sitting in my armchair," he said, "I can say I've had the best of times and the worst of times on the Road Hole."

While all this was going on, Greg Norman and Nick Faldo were turning the British Open into a two-man show. There was a familiar look to it. It seemed, at the moment, that the script came from the same fine hand that wrote the great Tom Watson-Jack Nicklaus shootout at Turnberry in 1977. It's doubtful that anything could ever match that one's symmetry. Watson and Nicklaus matched scores through the first three rounds, 70-68-65. In the final round, Watson shot 65, Nicklaus 66.

This one lacked that round-for-round match-up, but the rising tension was identical. Norman started off at 2:50 p.m., Faldo a half-hour later. Norman's 66 included two bogeys, a burst of four consecutive birdies, and an eagle. Faldo's 65 was spotless. No one else in the field was even close.

Ian Woosnam, who started at 3:10 p.m.—two groups after Norman and one ahead of Faldo—gave them both something to think about. He birdied six of the first 11 holes. He was on his way to the top. But the 17th stopped him in his tracks. He put his approach into the Road Bunker and had to come out sideways, and finally he faced a putt of about two feet for a bogey. He missed it. The double bogey handed Woosnam 69, which put him at 137, five off the leaders.

"When you're playing well, you want to birdie every hole," Norman said. "When you're not, you hope you make par. Right now, I'm playing well and putting well. When I get the ball on the green, I feel I'm going to make the putt." That feeling hit him sometime shortly after he three-putted from 40 feet for a bogey at No. 1. He dropped a 14-footer for a birdie at No. 4, then caught fire. Starting at No. 7, he ran off four consecutive birdies—one-putts of 12, 14, and 28 feet, and at No. 10, with a favorable wind, a two-putt from 40 feet after he drove the green. A poor approach cost him a bogey at the 13th, but he got that back and more when he holed an 80-yard pitch for an eagle-three at the tough 14th. "I didn't see the ball go in," Norman said. "I saw it bounce and screw back, but I couldn't see the bottom of the hole." The gallery told him all he needed to know. Then a birdie at the 16th, from 18 feet, and two closing pars gave him another 66 and a 132 total.

Faldo came in about a half-hour later and caught Norman. Actually, all he had to do was par the last two holes for his 65. This meant, of course, he had to handle the 17th. It was one of the better pars of his career, a two-putt from 90 feet at the old heartbreaker. "Tied at 12 under—that's a good position for both of us to be in," Faldo said. "You have a long way to go, and you play as hard as you can." He certainly fit his own bill. He went the entire day without a bogey. He was out in 32. A 15-foot putt got him his first birdie, at No. 2. After two pars, then came three birdies in succession: a two-putt from 90 feet at No. 5, then a five-footer, then an 18-footer. He came home in 33, getting birdies at the 10th from 18 feet, the 15th from two, and the 16th from four. Add that long-range par at the 17th, and a neat two-putt par from 35 feet at No. 18, and you have a strong round.

"On Wednesday, I didn't think that anybody would be 12 under by today," Faldo said. "We've had the weather relatively easy. When it blows here, it does blow. The seagulls walk."

"Do you relish a shootout with Faldo?" came the question to Norman.

"I wouldn't relish it, because it doesn't matter who I'm playing," Norman said. "I just want to win the British Open." His meaning was perfectly clear. But sure enough, his words would be lifted out of context just far enough to make him sound as though he feared going head-to-head with Faldo. Faldo was more experienced with the press. He had already been burned once this Open week, so when the same question came to him, he dismissed the subject. "I can't comment...," he said. "It's too dangerous, the way the stories have been coming out this week."

The 36-hole leaderboard:

Nick Faldo	132	Ian Woosnam	137
Greg Norman	132	Jose Maria Olazabal	138
Payne Stewart	136	Jodie Mudd	138
Craig Parry	136	Peter Jacobsen	138
Jamie Spence	137	Sam Torrance	138
Nick Price	137	Steve Pate	138
Mike Reid	137	Anders Sorensen	138

Of all the stunning moments in British Open history, and there were many in the previous 118 years, the one in the 1970 Open at St. Andrews is up there with the most memorable. This was Doug Sanders, needing a three-foot putt on the final hole to win. He missed it, and lost to Jack Nicklaus the next day in an 18-hole playoff. And who should turn up now at the scene of his most bitter disappointment but Sanders himself, 56, but still flamboyant, still fun-loving. He decided abruptly to come to St. Andrews. He withdrew from the American Senior Tour event of that week, went home to Houston to get some warm clothes—he had not forgotten Scottish weather—and zipped right over. "I felt I owed it to myself to see these great stars play on one of the greatest courses a person ever has the opportunity to play," Sanders said.

He re-created that woeful moment of 20 years earlier: Of how he had 76 yards to the green; of how, fearing the Valley of Sin, he put his approach 30 feet from the flag; of how his first putt was three feet short; and of how that last putt was a formality. "As I looked at that second putt," he said, "I was thinking about what I was going to do—throw the ball or the club in the air, and bow to the gallery. And try to be a humble winner." He got set to putt. But he thought he saw a brown spot in his line, and bent down to look at it. There was nothing there. "I was told later that Ben Hogan was watching on television, and he was saying, 'Walk away from it, walk away from it!'" Sanders said. "I didn't." And he missed the putt. It's been 20 years. Does it still bother him? "I don't think about it much," Sanders said, with that familiar grin. "Sometimes I go five minutes without it crossing my mind."

It was early, 10 a.m., and the crowd was just building to its one-day record of 45,587. But the fourth twosome off would draw its own huge following in a hurry. A young Englishman was in the process of creating a memorable moment of his own.

Paul Broadhurst, 24, 1989 Rookie of the Year on the European Tour, who only just made the 36-hole cut on 74-69—143, caught fire in the third round for a 63 that tied the Open record and put him on the leaderboard. "I couldn't believe the figures I was shooting," said Broadhurst, whose lone Tour victory was in the 1989 Cannes Open. "It just kept getting better and better." He got a little chuckle from his playing partner, David Graham. "I'll write down birdies on every hole, if you like," Graham said.

Broadhurst must have had that in mind. He birdied eight of the first 10 holes—No. 1 from 10 feet, No. 3 from 12, then five in succession to complete an outward 29. He two-putted the par-five fifth, then one-putted to the turn, with taps of from a foot at No. 7 to 15 feet at No. 8. At the 10th, he drove the green and two-putted from 40 feet for his sixth consecutive birdie. He wrapped up his bogey-free day with a par at No. 17, and then his ninth and final birdie from a foot at No. 18. The 63 put him at 206, 10 under par and seven strokes off the lead. But he'd played enough golf to know that today's fire can become tomorrow's fizzle. "A lot of those who have shot low rounds have gone on to shoot 80," Broadhurst said. "But I don't think I will."

The Open came within an eyelash of having two 63s on the same day. In fact, within about three hours of one another. Only a bogey at the 17th kept Ian Baker-Finch from getting the other. The Australian also went out in 29, and was on course for the 63 until his four-wood approach to No. 17 came up a bit short and rolled back down into the swale at the front of the long green. He three-putted from there, suffering his only bogey of the day, and settled for a 64 and a 12-under-par total of 204.

"The 1984 Open has been constantly on my mind for the last 12 months," Baker-Finch said. "I thought I could make amends for the last time and shoot a good enough score today to get into contention." He was an unknown at the 1984 Open, and he made a big splash. Mercifully, the Ballesteros-Watson finish put down enough of a smoke screen to cover his final-round collapse. He had opened with a 68, one stroke off the lead. A 66 gave him a three-stroke lead through 36 holes. A third-round 71 left him tied for the lead with Watson after 54 holes.

"I was happy to be where I was," Baker-Finch said. "I was 23 then, and totally inexperienced." It showed that final day. His pitch at No. 1 hit the green, then spun back into Swilcan Burn. He bogeyed, and the fall was on, to 79, and a tie for ninth place. Not this time, he vowed. "I said to my caddy, 'A 64 is what I need today,'" he said. "And I said we are going for everything, going for a birdie on every hole." He birdied the first two, then went birdie-eagle-birdie from No. 4. The eagle, at the 564-yard fifth, came on a four wood to 15 feet. "I'll be going to bed basically thinking of what I have to do to win," he said. "Whatever that is."

A comparison with past scores would show you how Faldo was dominating this Open. Going into the final round in 1984, Baker-Finch was at 205 and shared a one-stroke lead. This time, he was a stroke better, at 204, but he was tied for second and trailing by five shots.

Or, as Payne Stewart put it: "Can you believe you could shoot three 68s and be five shots behind?" He had done just that and found himself no better than tied for second with Baker-Finch at 204. "I played well, but I could have been a lot better," Stewart said. He missed from 10 feet at No. 1, for example, and drove the green at No. 10, but three-putted for a par. "I hit every green in regulation," he said, "but I wouldn't consider that one at No. 13 close." In fact, it was about 100 feet from the hole. But he made a great two-putt save for his par. He was playing well, but his work was cut out for him. "At the start, if someone had said would I accept 12 under par to win, I would have taken it," he said. "But the way Nick has played the first three days, if he goes on, no one will catch him. His game is so good that he doesn't make many mistakes."

Craig Parry stayed in the chase with a 67—205, 11 under par and alone in fourth place. Some awesome putting got him there. Of his four birdies, the shortest was an 18-footer, at No. 15. He holed a 60-footer at No. 2, two-putted from 30 feet at No. 5, and dropped a 90-footer at No. 8. Nobody can hope to keep that up for long. "We can only go out and play the course," he said. "When Nick is in the lead, he's always hard to catch."

Ian Woosnam also was beginning to feel futile. "The game isn't over," he said, "but obviously, I've got to shoot seven or eight under tomorrow to at least have a chance." His 70—207 left him eight strokes out of the lead. His driver turned cranky coming in. His putter was balky. "I've had seven three-putts in the three rounds," he said. Including the one at the 10th for one of his two bogeys in the third round. And his back was still sore. "It may have made me tired," he said, "I don't know—maybe winning in Monte Carlo, and then in the Scottish Open. I can't seem to keep my concentration, so maybe I'm tired."

A familiar figure reappeared—Sandy Lyle, the 1985 Open champion and the victim of a long and mysterious slump. Was he breaking out? He started 72-70, then added a 67. This is one of the strongest stretches of golf he had played in about two years. "My self-confidence is building up slowly," Lyle said. "It's doing wonders for me after a year of missed cuts." Lyle was trying to get some swing repairs to work. "The problem," he said, "is that the old swing feels comfortable while the new one doesn't. But I'm on the right track." He had no delusions about this Open, however. At 209, he was 10 strokes behind. "It's great to be scoring well," he said, "but to be honest, a top-six finish is my target."

It's fair to say that Broadhurst was only half of the surprise of the third round. The other half was Greg Norman, but for the opposite reason. He shot 76. A Watson-Nicklaus rematch with Nick Faldo, his playing partner in the final twosome, was now dead. Norman said, "I just putted terribly. I had a couple of bad breaks on the 12th and 13th, and that was the end of my day." He was out in 36, with two birdies and two bogeys. Coming in, he bogeyed the 12th, 13th, 15th, and 16th for a 40. He would go into the final round at 208, tied for eighth and nine strokes off the lead.

Which was to say that—to anyone who knew anything about the game and about Nick Faldo—this Open was over. The bookmakers put their imprimatur on that notion. They quit taking bets on Faldo. This was a battle for second place, and they would take bets on that. There was at least one soul who didn't subscribe to this idea—Faldo himself. He intended to play the last round as though the devil were after him.

"I won't be content to make pars tomorrow," Faldo said. "I want birdies." And who missed that barb? It was an echo of the 1987 Open, his first Open victory, his first major. Critics said he won it by default, that he was content to grind out 18 consecutive pars and hope for the best. Which he got in spades when Paul Azinger, the leader, bogeyed the last two holes. Faldo protested. He was trying to make birdies, but they just refused to happen. So this time he was vowing there would be no room for criticism. He wasn't going to sit on that five-stroke cushion. He had just shot a 67, his third consecutive round under 70, to become the first man in Open history to break 200 for 54 holes. He was at 199, and led by five over Baker-Finch and Stewart.

"I only hit a couple of bad shots coming in," Faldo said. "I hit a lot of good iron shots, and that's been the key. And my putting obviously has been great. I just have to keep it going one more day."

Faldo balanced his third round neatly, with three birdies on each side. And his putting was great. He birdied No. 1 from 18 feet, No. 5 from 40 (two putts), and No. 9 from 15. He dropped a 15-footer at the 11th, a 20-footer at the 16th and, with a theatrical finish, he nearly eagled the 18th again, but settled for a birdie from two feet. The lone bogey came at the 17th. Faldo didn't mind admitting that he prefers to tiptoe past that hole.

Someone asked Faldo whether he was beginning to look invincible as a golfer. He fielded the unanswerable question with a grin and the only possible answer. "Not yet," he said. Truth was, though, that the distorted scoreboard was beginning to suggest otherwise.

The third-round leaderboard:

Nick Faldo	199	Corey Pavin	208
Ian Baker-Finch	204	Tim Simpson	208
Payne Stewart	204	Vicente Fernandez	208
Craig Parry	205	Peter Jacobsen	208
Paul Broadhurst	206	Nick Price	208
Frank Nobilo	207	Greg Norman	208
Ian Woosnam	207		

Sunday, the day of the final round of the British Open, would be no different. Nick Faldo got up early, as usual. But there was nothing routine about the way he felt. "With a five-shot lead, everybody expects to win," he said. "If I lose, it's a major blow-out. I was getting very nervous." He went to practice for an hour with the man who rebuilt his swing, David Leadbetter, then went back home. He still had time for about an hour's sleep. He snoozed for about a half-hour. He spent the other half getting jittery. "I was just praying to get on the course," he said. "I went to the practice ground and the putting green. And then, at the first, I hit two really good shots, and I felt great."

True to his word, Faldo was going to go after birdies in the final round. He wasn't going to sit back on that five-stroke cushion. He wasted no time. He launched his attack on the very first hole—a disciplined two iron off the tee, a meticulous sand wedge pitch to four feet, and a true putt. He was barely out of the starting gate, and he had already picked up a stroke on his nearest competition, Payne Stewart and Ian Baker-Finch. They parred No. 1. Now Faldo led by six. The bookies were right. This Open was over.

The final round was hardly a mere formality, though. Stewart mounted a charge shortly after the turn, and came within two strokes of Faldo. "It was pretty scary," Faldo said. The picture looked like this: Faldo, paired with Baker-Finch in the final twosome, lost a stroke to a two-putt bogey at No. 4, but got it right back with a two-putt birdie from 60 feet at No. 5. Stewart, paired with Craig Parry in the group just ahead, had already birdied No. 5, so they were five strokes apart. Faldo settled into a run of pars. "I wasn't trying to be defensive," he said. "I was trying to hit the right shot at the right time." So was Stewart, and he was getting results. He birdied the fifth and sixth, and was four strokes behind. He birdied the 10th, and was three behind—15 under to 18 under. Then he made a fine recovery shot at the 12th and holed a seven-foot putt and went to 16 under. A minute later, Faldo parred the 11th behind him. His lead was now two strokes. "My heart was racing," Faldo said. "When it got down to two, I was battling with my mind. Not until it went back to three did I feel comfortable."

That was when Stewart bogeyed the 13th after bunkering his tee shot. "I drove into one bunker all week," Stewart said. "I was aiming left at 13, but I blocked it out and hung it out to the right." A half-hour later, Faldo birdied No. 15 on an eight-foot putt to drop to 19 under par, and that about locked things up. He was leading by four strokes. He bogeyed the 17th, but it was practically a conceded bogey. Cautiously, he three-putted, giving the old devil its due rather than risk greater damage. He could afford to. Nobody was threatening now. The Open was a battle for second place. Stewart bogeyed the 17th up ahead of him, then bogeyed the 18th as well, taking three putts from the Valley of Sin. He had let sole possession of second place slip out of his hands. He finished with a 71 and a 275 total, 13 under par, falling into a tie with Mark McNulty, who had finished about an hour and a half earlier with a bogey-free 65, the best round of the day. Faldo, meanwhile, two-putted the 18th from 25 feet for a 71, and a five-stroke victory at 18-under-par 270, by six strokes lower than the previous Open low at St. Andrews.

And the other challengers? Baker-Finch, playing with Faldo, couldn't get anything going. He shot 73 and tied for sixth at 277 with Greg Norman, who posted a 69. But Craig Parry, who began the day in fourth place, stumbled to a 42 coming in and finished with a 77 and a tie for 22nd at 282. Jodie Mudd and Ian Woosnam came on to tie for fourth at 276. Mudd closed with a rush for a nine-birdie 66, and if he could learn to play the 17th, he might have finished second. A par would have put him there. But after three bogeys, this time he double-bogeyed. ("Now that I think about it," Mudd said, "I should have played for a bogey.") And Woosnam recovered enough from his aches and pains for a six-birdie 69. Paul Broadhurst, author of the 63 in the third round, who felt sure he wouldn't blow to an 80, didn't. He shot a 74 and tied for 12th.

There were regrets enough to go around, but, ironically enough, maybe the sharpest belonged to none other than Nick Faldo himself. If his putt at the final hole of the U.S. Open had taken just one more turn, Hale Irwin and Mike Donald would have had company in that playoff. And then he might have added the U.S. Open to the Masters, and this British Open would have given him three legs of golf's Grand Slam. Then it would be on to the U.S. PGA Championship, and who would have bet against Faldo's becoming the first ever to take all four legs? But there are too many ifs in there. Reality wasn't all that bad, to tell the truth.

"I've been very fortunate to win a green jacket at Augusta," Faldo said, "but you want to win at St. Andrews on a day like this, with the atmosphere of this fabulous town. It's a golfer's dream."

Faldo had won the British Open in 1987, the Masters in both 1989 and 1990, and now the British Open in 1990. That's four majors overall in a span of just 36 months. More to the point, three in 16 months. And he was the first since Tom Watson in 1982 (U.S. and British Opens) to win two in the same year. He's also had a second, two thirds, and a fourth in the majors.

Faldo turned pro in 1976, but he didn't really blossom until he decided to change his swing in the mid-1980s. Golfers are always tinkering, but starting over the way he did is playing Russian roulette for a golfer. However, Faldo knew something nobody else knew.

"I wanted a swing that would hold up under pressure," Faldo said.

He was getting amazing efficiency out of that swing. Heading into this British Open, he had played in only seven of the 22 European events. He finished second twice, then fourth, fifth, ninth, 12th, and 54th. His visit to the U.S. Tour in 1990 was brief but profitable. He played in seven events, won the Masters, finished third in the U.S. Open, and won $345,262. He was among the overseas golfers who quit the U.S. Tour in 1990 when Commissioner Deane Beman refused to relax the 15-tournament requirement.

All of this was forgotten on that late Sunday afternoon in St. Andrews. Now was a time for basking in the glow of victory. Faldo spoke of the almost metaphysical state he went through on his way to the championship.

"You see yourself doing things, and your body tells you you are happy and not scared of the situation," he said. "And you can cope with it. At my first Open, I can remember walking across the tented village and looking at the leaderboard. I remembered what Gary Player told me—visualize your name up there. And I visualized my name at the top of the board and I said, 'I can handle that.'"

Now his name is on the old silver claret jug again. He can handle that, too.

6. The PGA Championship

The 1990 PGA Championship became one of the more significant golf tournaments ever played, not because it was won by Wayne Grady, but because of how developments in the months leading up to the championship effected club membership policies throughout the country. By saying the Shoal Creek Country Club, located in the suburbs of Birmingham, Alabama, would not be pressured into accepting blacks as members, Hall Thompson, the founder of the club, assured that not only would Shoal Creek do just that, but that many other clubs would be forced to change their policies as well.

Because of a few honest but unfortunate remarks, every organization that conducts golf tournaments was put under immense pressure to take their events only to clubs that demonstrate they do not discriminate because of race, creed, sex, or national origin.

Those matters lay in the future. Everything seemed possible in early August, particularly another golf tournament for Nick Faldo to win. The tall Englishman had by then won the Masters, narrowly missed either winning outright or at least tying for first place in the U.S. Open (he three-putted the 16th, and his birdie putt on the 18th caught a piece of the hole), and he overwhelmed the field in the British Open, playing the Old Course in 270 and winning by five strokes over Payne Stewart and Mark McNulty. He came into the PGA as arguably the best player in the game, and certainly the best British golfer since Henry Cotton, who ruled British golf from the mid-1930s until the 1950s.

By the time of the PGA, Faldo had played in six American tournaments and had missed placing among the leading 16 scorers only once, falling into a tie for 32nd place at the Western Open. Back home on the European Tour, Nick had played in eight events, placing second in both the Spanish Open and the Volvo PGA, fourth in the French Open, and fifth in the Scottish.

He had also played in eight PGA Championships, beginning in 1982, and had not made much of an impression in his early appearances, missing the cut at Riviera, in Los Angeles, when Hal Sutton won, in 1983, and again at Inverness, in Toledo, where Bob Tway pitched into the final hole from a bunker, nipping Greg Norman by a stroke.

Later, though, he had become a threat, placing fifth at Oak Tree, in Oklahoma, where Jeff Sluman won the 1988 championship, and tying for ninth at Kemper Lakes, near Chicaco, behind Payne Stewart, in 1989.

After winning the Masters, Faldo began the yearly quest for the Grand Slam. It ended when he failed to win the U.S. Open, but after taking the British, he could win three of the four major tournaments. No one had won all four in one year, and only Ben Hogan had won three, taking the Masters, and the U.S. and British Opens of 1953. Twenty-seven years had passed since Hogan had been at his peak, but no one had equaled his record.

Four men had had the opportunity—Arnold Palmer, Jack Nicklaus, and Tom Watson twice each, and Lee Trevino once. Each of those men had come to the PGA Championship, usually the last of the four majors (the 1971 Championship was played in February) with victories in hand. None of them won the third:

Palmer	1960	Masters, U.S. Open
	1962	Masters, British Open
Nicklaus	1966	Masters, British Open
	1972	Masters, U.S. Open
Watson	1977	Masters, British Open
	1982	U.S. Open, British Open
Trevino	1971	U.S. Open, British Open
Faldo	1990	Masters, British Open

The British Open had ended on July 22, and the PGA was scheduled to begin August 9, a period of less than three weeks. As he began the slow descent from his emotional high following his British Open victory, Faldo said he would skip the next two tournaments.

"By then," he said, "I will have recovered emotionally, and I'll be ready to go again."

Naturally he regretted losing the chance to win all four in the same year, an opportunity Hogan didn't have. The PGA and the British Open overlapped, in those days, the PGA, at match-play, ending on Tuesday, and British Open qualifying taking place on the same Monday and Tuesday, with the first round on Wednesday (it ended with a double round on Friday).

Reflecting on his final putt of the U.S. Open that looked so good but caught the right lip of the cup and slipped past the hole, Faldo said, "Who knows what would have happened if that putt had gone in."

Hale Irwin, however, had made the putts he had had to make, and won the U.S. Open. Since that June afternoon in Chicago, he had more success, winning the Buick Classic the following week at Westchester, New York, and placing second in the Buick Open, played in Grand Blanc, Michigan, four weeks later. He had played in the British Open, too, without showing the spark that had won two consecutive events back home. While he was among those from whom great things had been expected in the PGA, Irwin didn't make a ripple in Shoal Creek. He opened with 77, shot 293, and finished 11 strokes behind Grady.

Stewart came into Birmingham as the defending champion. He had won at Kemper Lakes, near Chicago, the previous year when Mike Reid had butchered the last few holes. Stewart, however, seemed to do everything he could to make himself controversial. First of all, he made his rather insensitive and frankly stupid comments about the racial issue, and then, following a practice round, he condemned the PGA, claiming the high bermuda-grass rough made the course nearly unplayable.

"If you don't play the ball from the fairway," he said, "you can just pack your bags and go home. They should draw red lines down both sides of the fairways and call the rough a hazard. There's a one-shot penalty every time you miss the fairway, because you're not going to get it to the green. If the PGA thought Shoal Creek was too easy, they should have gone to another golf course."

The rough had indeed been allowed to grow high, perhaps higher than it should have been. The PGA claimed it had been cut to three and a half inches, but it looked longer. Bermuda-grass rough has always been a problem, principally because, unlike most other kinds of golf course grasses, the stems won't support the weight of a golf ball. Instead, the ball sinks almost to ground level, and in most cases a player is left with nothing but a pitch back to safety.

Shoal Creek was hard enough without those conditions. To begin with it was long, measuring 7,145 yards. Laid out over gently rolling ground, it was carved through thickets of mature trees, and some holes follow the course of streams that feed into a number of lakes. Water, in fact, influences play on eight of its 18 holes.

With a balanced par of 36-36—72, it has 10 par-four holes, only one of them under 405 yards, and the shortest of its par threes, the eighth, plays 173 yards, with its green sitting against one of the ponds. Three of its four par-five holes can be reached in two only at great risk, because, again, their greens sit hard against either one of the streams or, in the case of the 11th, behind an arm of a pond.

Its finish had been carefully planned to add both variety and difficulty. A round at Shoal Creek closes with, in order, a 216-yard par three, a 530-yard par five whose green is guarded by a rocky stream bed, and a 446-yard par four with a pond crowding the left side of the green.

While the fairways and roughs were planted with bermuda grass, its greens were of bent grass, a northern strain quite difficult to maintain in the hot, steamy climate of the deep South. Shaved down to championship height, the greens indeed showed stress; some were rather spotty, with bare patches around the edges, and although they seemed relatively flat, they weren't easy.

The players complained as well that the greens were too hard. Stewart again led the complaints.

"You can hear the ball hit the green all the way from the fairway." Slapping a table with his open palm, he said, "It sounds like this."

Nicklaus, whose organization laid out the course, agreed, saying, "Right now the greens sound hollow."

Still, the rough became the overriding issue.

Nicklaus seemed perplexed.

"They told me the rough is supposed to be three and a half inches, but it looks like five to me," he claimed. "Maybe the mowers are dull. The golf course is not set up the way it was designed. It should have more fairway area. I like to see options in playing the game, but the PGA felt it would be more difficult like this."

Tom Kite, who ranks among the straightest drivers in the game, claimed, "This is some of the most difficult rough we've seen in many years. If you don't put it in the fairway, it's just going to kill you."

Irwin, another straight driver, added, "You'll be lucky to find your ball much less play it."

Continuing his assault, Stewart approached Mickey Powell, a former PGA president, and railed, "I thought you guys would learn. You've taken the shots out of the golf course."

Perhaps, but while some of the better golfers agreed the rough seemed high, they felt the conditions might be justified. Kite seemed to approve.

"This is very typical of what major championships used to be," he recalled. "I think we've seen some easing up in major championships recently. In my opinion, this is one of the toughest majors we've seen in many years."

Irwin said, "I happen to like the course. It seems to eliminate those of us who are playing poorly and give an advantage to those who are playing well. You feel like par here is a good score."

While agreeing the rough had been allowed to grow higher than he would like, Nicklaus showed little sympathy toward Stewart's complaints.

Asked if a golf course was supposed to offer some chance of reaching the greens from the rough, Nicklaus snapped, "Where does it say that? I personally feel that in the majors you're supposed to drive the ball into the fairways, hit the greens, make the putts, and shoot as low as you can on a course that is as difficult as it can be."

We saw just how difficult Shoal Creek could be in the first round. Irwin, who had played so well over the last two months, shot 77; Kite, who had won at Memphis a week earlier, shot 79; Nicklaus, hitting only three fairways, shot 78; and Arnold Palmer, 81. Curtis Strange couldn't hole a putt, shot 79, and left the grounds seething; both Lee Trevino and Larry Nelson shot 77, along with Greg Norman, Mark Calcavecchia, Seve Ballesteros, and Jim Thorpe.

Irwin had been paired with Stewart and Faldo, who both shot 71s. The round over, Stewart continued his assault on the course setup, claiming, "The PGA wants to see the winning score somewhere around par. I played with a pretty good group. Any time we put it in the rough, it was automatic: You jerked out the sand wedge and chopped it back to the fairway."

Faldo expressed sympathy for the gallery, adding, "This can't be exciting golf for the fans. You absolutely have to keep the ball in the fairway. It's a driving contest."

Tim Simpson, though, another 71 shooter, seemed more concerned with the greens.

"I've been on the Tour for 14 years," he said, "and I've never seen harder greens than these. A 16-pound shot wouldn't dent them. It's unfortunate to have greens like these."

With its high rough and hard greens, Shoal Creek gave up strokes only grudgingly. Of the 152 men who played that day, only 15 shot under par, 13 others matched it, and 28 shot 80 or higher. The field averaged 75 strokes.

The high, punishing grass intimidated the game's best players. Both Stewart and Irwin stood in the rough just 80 yards short of the 17th green. Under normal conditions they would probably have gone for the green. Instead, they pitched back to the fairway. Both men made six. Faldo bogeyed the ninth after driving into the rough. To reach the green, the second shot had to carry a pond, but the ball seemed to be sitting up, and so Nick drew an eight iron from his bag, figuring he had half a chance of getting there. As he addressed his ball, a tuft of grass sprang up behind the clubhead, and the odds climbed favoring a disaster. Nick stepped away, and chose instead to play back to safer ground; he would give up one stroke rather than risk losing more.

The day ended with an improbable leader. Complaining bitterly about the choking rough, Bobby Wadkins, without a victory in 16 years on the Tour, shot an erratic round of 68, going out in 37 with a double bogey on the fourth, a straightaway, bunkerless par four of 456 yards that claimed five other sixes through the day and yielded only 11 birdies.

Wadkins led by a stroke over Mark O'Meara and Fred Couples, a pair of veteran players, and by two over Billy Mayfair and Scott Verplank. Ten men shot 71.

Aside from his double bogey on the fourth, Wadkins bogeyed two other holes on the first nine, but he birdied three, parred two, and went out in 37. He was headed nowhere, but he turned his game around suddenly and raced home in 31, reeling off five birdies on the second nine.

Wadkins began quickly enough, playing a soft eight iron within 10 feet of the first hole and then holing the putt, but he missed an opportunity for another birdie at the third, a par five of 516 yards, where he reached the green with his second, then three-putted from 45 feet.

One under after three holes, Wadkins made another mistake at the fourth. Trying to play cautious golf and avoid the rough, he drove with his one iron, but the ball veered off the fairway and nestled deep in the grass. Wadkins tried to play out safely with a seven iron, but the grass smothered the shot, and his ball streaked across the fairway into the left rough. From there he chopped out with a pitching wedge and finally reached the green with his sand wedge. Two putts and he had his six. Birdies on the next two holes dropped him back to one under par again, but he closed out the first nine with two more bogeys.

The 11th green sits on a peninsula that juts into one of the ponds. After a drive of about 270 yards, Wadkins hit a three wood he estimated at 245 yards. The ball cleared the pond, then ran over the back of the green. A pitch to four feet, and Bobby had his fourth birdie of the round. It seemed as if he had just begun. A 20-footer fell on the 12th, a solid par four of 451 yards cut through the woods, then he rolled in another putt from 25 feet on the 15th, a dogleg left of 405 yards that plays shorter than its yardage.

Two under now, Wadkins made his par on the 16th, then went for the green on the 17th, another par five. Once again his three wood cleared the water hazard guarding the front, and rolled over. A chip to six feet, and Wadkins had another birdie.

Only the 18th was left now. A three wood from the tee, and then his best iron shot of the day, an eight iron six feet from the cup. The putt curled into the hole, and Wadkins had his eighth birdie of the day.

Not a grammarian, Wadkins said, "I played as good as I could play. The last nine holes were probably as good as I can play on any golf course. I missed one fairway and hit every green."

There were other unusual rounds. Extremely long, Couples doesn't always hit the ball where he aims, but on this day he played an unusual round as well. On 14 driving holes, he hit 14 fairways; nobody could remember when he drove so well. Of course he used his driver only on three of the four par-five holes, and drove mostly with his three wood, along with an occasional iron.

He might have shared the lead except for a lapse on the final hole. Out in 34 with three birdies and a bogey, Couples started back with a bogey on the 10th, where he bunkered his six-iron approach, but he won that stroke back by pitching to within 10 feet on the 11th and holed the putt. Back to two under par.

Two more pars, and then Couples birdied three of the next four holes, reaching the 17th with a four-iron second.

Four under par, he overshot the 18th with a seven-iron approach, played a loose pitch that left him 15 feet from the cup, then missed the putt, his fourth bogey of the round.

Happy over his round, Couples couldn't constrain himself about his driving.

"I probably couldn't go out there with a seven iron and hit every fairway," he joked. "For me to do that is like Michael Jordan not missing a free throw for a year. To be honest, I wasn't looking forward to this week because of the heavy rough, but I like tree-lined courses. It's a lot easier to visualize a shot coming out of a chute of trees."

O'Meara played an even more erratic round than Wadkins and Couples. Through the first 12 holes he had only three pars, and he struggled for one of those, driving into the rough on the 11th, chopping out, then drilling a two iron into a greenside bunker. He saved his five by holing a 10-foot putt.

O'Meara stood four under par then. He had opened with a bogey, birdied five of the next six holes, and closed out the first nine with two birdies and a bogey from the seventh through the ninth. He holed only one putt as long as 20 feet through that stretch. After saving the par, O'Meara bogeyed the 12th, then closed by running off six consecutive pars.

"You have to drive the ball well, because no one can get out of this rough," O'Meara said. "I thought if I could swing the way I did in the practice rounds, I'd do well."

Where Wadkins, O'Meara, and Couples played erratic rounds, Mike Reid played the steadiest of all in shooting 71. Although he had to struggle, he made his pars on 17 of the 18 holes, and birdied only the 10th, where he played a seven iron within a foot of the hole.

Faldo could thank a spectacular shot for his 71. He missed the second fairway with his drive and could only pitch back to the fairway, but from 120 yards out, Nick pitched his ball into the cup for a birdie-three. A great roar rose over the pines when Faldo's ball banged against the flagstick and dived into the hole. It was the only crowd noise of the day; the demands of the course stifled the enthusiasm of both fans and players alike, and the gallery stood by nearly mute.

In Mayfair and Verplank we had two former U.S. Amateur champions trying to find their way in professional golf. While Mayfair was in only his second year as a professional, Verplank had played the Tour since 1986 with only occasional success. After he had won the 1985 Western Open as an amateur, he came into professional golf hailed as a superb prospect, but in five years he had won only the 1988 Buick Open. A diabetic, he had struggled to find a method that would help him keep up his strength throughout a complete round. He had lost 15 pounds in less than a month during the winter, but he seemed to be recovering. Scott had finished among the low 10 scorers in his previous eight tournaments.

No one had a better start at Shoal Creek. Playing a series of stunning irons, Verplank pitched to within three feet on the first, 10 feet on the second, and after reaching a greenside bunker with his second shot at the third, played out to within five feet. Three under after three holes.

Another birdie on the sixth, again pitching from the sand within 12 feet, and Verplank stood at four under par. Out in 32, he played a bit more erratically on the home nine, birdieing two and bogeying two through the 16th. Then he lost two strokes on the 17th, where he made a bad swing and pushed his ball into the trees. Then the horrors began. An eight iron clipped a tree and dropped back among the trees; a nine iron ran to the lip of a bunker; a shanked nine iron that ran into the bunker; a sand wedge back to the fairway, and then a seven iron onto the green and one putt. A seven, and Verplank finished with 70.

Verplank was playing ahead of Faldo, Irwin and Stewart. Talking about it later, they said they had to wait five minutes before they teed off, and had no idea what Scott was doing.

"I was confused," Faldo said. "We could see balls flying everywhere."

Like almost everyone else, Mayfair had a rather erratic round. Starting off with two birdies, he played the next 16 holes with two more birdies and two bogeys. He holed nothing of great length, his longest putt from 12 feet on the sixth, a 540-yard par five with its green guarded by one of the streams.

The leaders:

Bobby Wadkins	68	Chip Beck	71
Fred Couples	69	Tim Simpson	71
Mark O'Meara	69	Robert Gamez	71
Billy Mayfair	70	Steve Pate	71
Scott Verplank	70	Brian Tennyson	71
Mike Reid	71	Stan Utley	71
Nick Faldo	71	Mike Hulbert	71
Payne Stewart	71		

A day later, Bobby Wadkins drew back his driver on the 17th tee and suddenly stopped in mid-swing. His driver, though, kept going. It fell to the ground 10 yards behind him.

Perplexed, and somewhat amused once the round had ended, Wadkins said, "The shaft just broke on my backswing. I had to drive with my three wood."

Because the club had broken before he had begun his downswing, he escaped without a penalty stroke. That was about his best news of the day. He bogeyed the 18th, three-putting once he reached the green, and shot 75. From first place he dropped into a tie for sixth, with 143, four strokes behind Wayne Grady, a 33-year-old Australian, who had been playing professional golf since 1978. Grady was perhaps best known for having lost a playoff to Mark Calcavecchia in the 1989 British Open. After opening with 72, Grady shaved five strokes from Shoal Creek's par with 67, and led with a 36-hole score of 139.

Some of the first-round leaders cracked, but others hung close. Couples shot 71 and tied Larry Mize for second, at 140; Mayfair stood a further stroke back, at 141, after shooting 71, and Payne Stewart had 143 after posting 72.

Faldo, though, slipped to 75, the first step toward a shattering experience, and O'Meara and Verplank fell out of the race, with 76s, dropping O'Meara into a tie for 15th place, Verplank into a tie for 18th, along with Faldo. Worse lay ahead.

With 68, Larry Mize had climbed to a second-place tie, and Chip Beck, with 70, had jumped to a tie for fourth, at 141, with Mayfair. Wadkins dropped into a tie with Stewart, Fuzzy Zoeller, and Stan Utley, at 143.

Shoal Creek continued to frustrate the players, demonstrating all over again that to miss the fairway led to an almost certain bogey. Where three men had broken 70 in the first round, four shot 69 or better in the second, but where 15 had broken par after 18 holes, the total had dropped to nine after 36 holes. Furthermore, the average score soared to 76—152.

Tim Simpson suffered through a wild turn. Three under par after 13 holes, he had a promising round in hand until he missed the 14th fairway and triple-bogeyed. Instead of a possible 69, he shot 73.

Some of the players turned their emotions loose. Stewart had played the first 10 holes in one over par and had only a pitch left to the 11th, a par five. When he pulled his shot into a greenside bunker, he threw back his head, raised his wedge heavenward, then slammed it to the ground, raising a carpet-sized divot with his third angry swing, and sent it flying at least 10 feet skyward.

The gallery crowded around the green growled a low chorus of boos as Stewart flung his club at his bag and walked toward the green.

Faldo went through much the same experience. After hacking his way out of a particularly bad patch of rough on the same hole, he took a vicious swipe at the grass, as if in revenge, then said to the gallery, "This must be very exciting for you."

Faldo hadn't shot a round that high in one of the four major competitions since the rain-interrupted third round of the 1989 Masters, where he finished badly on Sunday morning, before beginning the fourth round later in the day. It was also his first round over par in one of those events since the PGA later that year, when he shot 73 in the second round at Kemper Lakes.

Faldo had always been a patient player, not forcing shots, and taking his bogeys calmly, but he lost that patience at Shoal Creek.

"This was my most frustrating 18 holes," he admitted.

Stewart also spoke of his moment of rage.

"I felt much better after I did that," he said. "I know it isn't nice for the fans to see, but you just have to release your frustrations."

Even though he shot 71 and moved into a contending position, Zoeller didn't feel any better toward Shoal Creek, saying, "This is the hardest damned golf course I've ever played. I have a lot of patience, but this place can get on your nerves."

Grady, of course, had very little frustration to release. A consistent although not especially exciting player to watch, Grady had won four tournaments during his 12 years as a professional, including one in Australia in 1978, his first year, but he had also placed second in 29 others. Three of his victories had been abroad, he had won only the 1989 Westchester Classic in the United States.

Not particularly long, Grady is a first-class iron player. His 67 was based on his accuracy. He hit all but two fairways, and missed just one green, costing him his only bogey of the day. He birdied four holes on the first nine, consistently hitting his approaches within holing distance—a nine iron to 10 feet on the second, another nine iron to six feet on the sixth, and a seven iron to 10 feet on the ninth. In addition to those three birdies, Grady also holed a 30-footer on the fourth, but missed from 10 feet on the third.

Out in 32, he dropped a stroke at the 12th, the long par four through the woods, where he drove into the rough and couldn't reach the green. Three under then, Grady played a three iron to the 215-yard 16th that flew arrow-straight at the hole, slammed into the flagstick, and rolled eight feet away. He holed the putt, then birdied the 17th, rifling a three wood into a greenside bunker and recovering to six feet.

Mize stood among the minority after shooting his 68 and jumping into a tie with Couples. He confessed he liked Shoal Creek, but he also admitted, "I could have bit into the ball a couple of times." He had parred only seven holes, and had to struggle for two of those, saving himself from a bunker on the fifth, and driving into the rough on the 18th.

Although he drove rather well, using his driver on all the driving holes, and hitting 10 of the 14 fairways, Mize played only moderately good golf through the first 14 holes. He scored four birdies, but he gave all but one of those strokes away with three bogeys.

Starting with the 15th, though, he suddenly began stringing his approaches directly at the hole. He floated an eight iron to 10 feet there, then a three iron inside three feet on the 16th, and a sand wedge to 12 feet on the 17th. Those three birdies made the difference; from one under par, he dropped to four under, and leaped from a tie for 16th place into a tie for second.

Couples, meantime, played more like the Couples we all know. Using his driver on only three holes, and his three wood and one iron on the others, he missed three fairways in the second round where he had missed only one in the first. He still managed a 71, which kept him in the thick of the fight. Three under par as the round began, Fred dropped to four under with a birdie at the fourth, but he lost all those strokes over a stretch of six holes. He bogeyed both the seventh, where he was bunkered and had to hole a 35-footer to save his five, and the 11th, where he drove into a creek. He double-bogeyed the 12th, driving into a bunker and three-putting.

Even par now, Couples suddenly turned his game around and closed out his round by birdieing four of the last six holes. Rather than 144, he finished at 140, matching Mize.

Mayfair had to scramble for his 71 as well, playing an unusual round for him. Where Billy normally might expect three or four birdies on a good day, mixed in with two or three bogeys, he birdied seven holes, bogeyed six, and played only five in regulation figures. He had parred only three of the first 13 holes, and stood even par at that point, but after parring the 14th, he missed the 15th green and bogeyed, then birdied both the 16th and 17th. His birdie on the 17th involved a bit of luck. After a good drive, Mayfair gambled with a four wood for his second, hoping to reach the green, but he pushed his ball into a stand of bleachers. Under the rules, he was allowed to drop his ball clear of the grandstand without a penalty stroke, pitched onto the green, and holed out from 10 feet.

One under par then, he closed with a par on the 18th, shot 70, and clung to a tie for fourth place with Beck, who had five birdies of his own.

Meantime, the 36-hole cut to the low 70 and ties fell at 151, catching a surprising number of prominent players. Seldom had a player of such stature gone out of a championship as gloriously as Ballesteros. After shooting 77 in the opening round, Seve played even worse in the second, staggering in with 83, his worst score since the 1979 French Open. His 160 missed the cut by nine strokes, the sixth cut he had missed during the season, four of them in the United States. He hadn't missed so many since 1976, the year he shot into prominence by leading the early rounds of the British Open when he was just 19. (Ballesteros, by the way, had also missed the cut in the British Open.)

Nicklaus joined him on the road home, although he had beaten Seve by eight strokes. His 152 missed by a stroke.

Calcavecchia was gone, too, with two 77s, his fifth cut in seven tournaments. Strange improved from 79 to 76, but still not good enough, and Trevino left as well, with 152.

Irwin nearly joined them. Eight over par after the first nine holes, Hale birdied the next three, and saved himself with a par round of 72 and 149. Kite turned his game around, too, going from 79 in the first round to 71 in the second, and with an eagle-three on the second, Norman shot 69, passing 72 players, and rising from the brink of elimination into a tie for eighth place.

The 36-hole leaders:

Wayne Grady	139
Fred Couples	140
Larry Mize	140
Billy Mayfair	141
Chip Beck	141
Payne Stewart	143
Fuzzy Zoeller	143
Bobby Wadkins	143
Stan Utley	143

With the field down to a more manageable 74 players, the leaders were bunched at the end of the field, and spectators tended to delay arriving until later in the day. Predictably the narrow, two-lane roads leading into the secluded enclave of Shoal Creek clogged with traffic. By mid-morning long lines of cars crept through the wooded avenues, eventually backing up almost to the broad limited-access highway that fed traffic toward the golf course.

While the drivers fumed at the traffic's sloth-like crawl, the golfers seethed about the golf course. It wouldn't let up, humiliating the best players in the game, leading them to believe they had finally taken control, then snatching strokes away like the vanishing dew. It turned promising rounds into disasters, and yet it relented occasionally and allowed others to avoid punishment for ill-played shots. Some of the day's events were laughable, some trod the line between tragic (in a golfing sense) and comic.

Wayne Grady went into the third round leading by one stroke, and played a struggling round of even-par 72. In almost any other tournament, par would have won him nothing, and possibly cost him first place. Here he increased his lead to two strokes.

Nick Faldo, on the other hand, suffered through possibly his most embarrassing moment since he began playing championship golf. Before teeing off that morning, he said, "I'll need two rounds under 70 to have a chance now." Instead, he shot 80. He couldn't remember the last time he played that badly.

After a 69 in the second round, Norman played the first eight holes of the third in two under par, then double-bogeyed both the 10th and 11th and shot 76. Mize stood one over par for the day and three under for the distance after the 17th hole, then hooked a six-iron approach into the pond, triple-bogeyed, and shot 76, too.

Shoal Creek gave, and it took away. With seven birdies offset by six bogeys on Friday, Mayfair birdied five more holes on Saturday, but again gave away almost as many strokes as he had saved, with four bogeys. Hitting only five greens, Fred Couples birdied four and bogeyed five, one-putting the 10th through the 17th for two birdies, two bogeys, and four pars, and shot 73.

At the same time, Gil Morgan, who had opened with a shaky 77 and followed with 72, ripped through Shoal Creek in 65. More puzzling, on a course where mistakes nearly always cost a stroke, he birdied every hole where he missed either a fairway or a green.

Only 12 men broke par, and only Morgan, and David Frost, with 69, broke 70. With the scoring generally high, the field spread out. Where 14 men had stood within five strokes of the lead after 36 holes, only seven remained within five strokes of Grady after 54. Chip Beck had been within two strokes of the lead after 36 holes, but he fell like a stone, shooting 78 in the third round and dropping eight strokes back. Fuzzy Zoeller shot 76, and Bobby Wadkins, the first-round leader, and Stan Utley each staggered in with 80s. Ben Crenshaw crippled his chances with 78, and Mark O'Meara went into terminal arrest with 79.

When the carnage ended and the wounds were bandaged if not healed, Grady stood atop the field at 211, followed by Payne Stewart and Couples, at 213, then Morgan and Loren Roberts, at 215, and Mayfair and Mize, at 216.

By tearing into Shoal Creek as he had, Morgan had passed 48 men. He had gone into the third round in a 49th-place tie, and now stood behind only Grady. His sudden rise caught everyone by surprise, perhaps even himself, because he hadn't played competitive golf in five weeks. Morgan had had the rotator cuff of his left shoulder repaired five years earlier, and now he had a painful right shoulder. Under the advice of his doctor, he hadn't even practiced.

Morgan began by steering a three wood into a fairway bunker, but followed with a superb eight iron that settled six feet from the cup. The putt fell, and Morgan was off to the best round of the championship. Two holes later he reached the green of the third with a driver and four wood, and two-putted for another birdie. He saved his par after bunkering his approach to the fourth, then birdied the sixth when he looked as if he was about to drop a stroke.

His third shot, a pitch across a creek, rolled off the green and hung on the edge of a bunker. Rushing to play the shot before the ball dropped into the sand, Morgan pitched a sand wedge into the hole for the birdie-four. He had made two mistakes, and had birdied both holes.

A five iron to 10 feet and another birdie on the seventh, then a six iron to 12 feet on the eighth, but a missed putt. Four under then, Morgan three-putted the ninth from 35 feet and turned for home in 32.

Another birdie on the 11th after a pitching wedge from 100 yards braked within five feet of the hole, and then another drive into a bunker at the 14th. Another eight iron out, and he rolled home a 15-footer for his sixth birdie. He was five under then, and needed only four pars to match Grady's 67.

A missed opportunity on the 15th, where a 15-footer slid past the cup, and then two putts on the 16th, where he ripped a two iron within 20 feet of the cup. A big drive on the 17th left him within two-iron range of the 17th green, but his shot rolled dead at least 50 feet from the cup. Two putts, though, and he had his seventh birdie of the day.

Another solid drive on the 18th, and then a five iron to 12 feet. The putt fell, and Morgan had shot 65.

Until the Kemper Open, in early June, Morgan hadn't won a tournament in seven years, not since the 1983 Los Angeles Open, but now he had thrust himself into position to win his second of 1990.

At about the time Morgan finished his first nine, Faldo stepped onto the first tee. He began the day determined to improve on his first two rounds, and indeed picked up one stroke by birdieing the third, but he double-bogeyed the fourth, driving into the rough, chopping out 80 yards farther, pitched to 25 feet, then three-putted.

"After that my concentration was zero," he said. "I was just hitting it and enjoying the view."

Three more bogeys on the sixth through the eighth, and he had gone out in 40.

Faldo lost whatever dim hope he may have held with a triple-bogey seven on the 10th hole, a par four of 421 yards whose green perches close to ground that plunges downward to a rock-strewn creek. With the hole set 18 feet from the right edge of the green, Faldo went for the pin, lost his five-iron shot to the right, and hit it into the stream. Instead of taking a penalty stroke and dropping outside the hazard, Nick played the ball, splattered himself with mud, but didn't reach the green. He finally staggered off with a seven.

After another bogey at the 12th, Nick played the last six holes in even par, shot 40 coming home, and posted his 80.

He said he couldn't remember his last 80, except maybe "when I went from nappies to shorts." He had been scheduled to play in The International, in Denver, the following week, but after his debacle at Shoal Creek, he canceled, saying, "I've had enough brain damage for August."

Norman, too, felt damaged. He had worked his way from two over par to even through the eighth hole, but then he misjudged his approaches to both the ninth and 10th, double-bogeyed both, then bogeyed the 13th through the 15th, like Faldo struggling home in 40 for his 76.

Looking back, he said, "I thought I had a chance until the ninth, and then I go double, double. I'm just going to shrug this week off."

Grady was just beginning his round when Faldo muddled home. He had to battle to save his par on the first, where his nine iron bounced over the green, and from there on he birdied three holes and bogeyed three. Making fours on two of the par fives, chipping within two feet on both the third and the 11th, and his third on the 16th, where he played a lovely three iron within eight feet. He offset those with bogeys on the fifth, the first of the par-three holes, where he missed the green and two-putted from 30 feet; the seventh, where he found himself in both the rough and a bunker, and the 18th, again driving into the rough, wedging out, and two-putting from 30 feet.

Still, his 37-35—72 kept him ahead of the field, although Stewart had played exceptionally steady golf, opening with 71, then shooting 72 in the second round, and 70 in the third. He had birdied 13 of the 54 holes he had played, nearly one in four, which should have won him more than he had, but Shoal Creek's draconian demands claimed 10 bogeys, leaving him just three strokes under par, at 213.

Where Stewart had returned consistent scores, Couples had shot progressively higher, opening with 69, adding 71, and then climbing to 73. Nevertheless, he clung to a second-place tie, only two strokes behind Grady.

With four birdies in the third round, Couples had birdied 16 of the 54 holes, about 30 percent, a higher percentage than Stewart. Again, however, Shoal Creek claimed a high percentage of bogeys as well, close to one in four from Couples.

Fred had played the first nine in 37, birdieing two holes and bogeying three. Coming in he lost a stroke on the 10th, pushing his approach into the same creek Faldo had found, but Fred escaped with a five where Nick had made seven.

Two over then, Couples pulled back to even, rolling in a 30-foot putt at the 13th, and followed by lofting a nine iron within 10 feet on the 14th and holing the putt. It didn't last. He overshot the 15th hole and missed from eight feet, losing the opportunity to hold second place alone.

The 54-hole leaders:

Wayne Grady	211
Payne Stewart	213
Fred Couples	213
Gil Morgan	214
Loren Roberts	214
Billy Mayfair	216
Larry Mize	216

Crowds had flocked to Shoal Creek throughout the championship, and when 35,097 fans, the largest crowd of the week, poured in on Sunday, the total climbed to 197,788, the most ever to have seen the PGA.

Shoal Creek continued to bedevil the players. Only Nick Faldo broke 70, with a meaningless 69, and only five others shot 71. No one shot 70. Eight others shot 80 or more.

Grady had been paired with Couples on Saturday, but on Sunday he played with Stewart, beginning at 12:30. He had come to the course with very little sleep. After leaving the course Saturday afternoon, he had called Australia to talk about his day, had a few beers with friends, and cooked some steaks on the barbecue. Restless during the night, he had climbed out of bed at five in the morning, turned on the television, and watched Theirry Boutsen win the Hungarian Grand Prix. It seemed like a good omen, because Boutsen "won from beginning to end," Grady said, and Wayne had led the PGA through two rounds.

Then, as he strode onto the first tee he saw Stewart dressed in the green and gold colors of the Green Bay Packers.

Smiling, Grady teased, "Green and gold—the colors of Australia." Then he threaded a driver down the middle of the first fairway, played an indifferent eight iron to the front of the green, and holed a 60-foot putt for an opening birdie. With that the final round was off to a dramatic start. The day would end with Couples throwing the championship away, Stewart losing his opportunity to become the first man since Denny Shute, in the late 1930s, to win consecutive PGA Championships, and Gil Morgan not having enough ammunition left to head off Grady.

Paired with Morgan, Couples had begun eight minutes before Grady and Stewart, and just behind Mize and Loren Roberts. Both Mize and Roberts dropped from the race, Roberts by shooting 76, and Mize 77.

With a birdie at the first, Morgan had remained three strokes behind Grady, but he cut his margin to two strokes when Grady bogeyed the second, pushing his drive into the trees, and taking a five. Recovering quickly, Wayne birdied the third, an eminently reachable par five that was perhaps the easiest hole Shoal Creek could offer, and the fourth, dropping to two under par for the day. Another mis-directed tee shot at the ninth cost him another stroke, and he turned for home in 35.

By then, with 34s on the first nine, Couples had closed to within one stroke of Grady, and Morgan remained within two. Stewart, with 38, meanwhile, was on his way out. Four strokes behind Grady as he stood on the 10th tee, Payne played the 10th in par-four, and remembering he had shot 31 on the second nine at Kemper Lakes a year earlier, when he won the PGA, he felt he still had a chance. Then he pulled his drive into the rough along the 11th fairway, pitched out, and faced an approach of a little under 160 yards. With the light wind at his back, Stewart drew an eight iron and hit the ball crisply. He thought he had played the ball perfectly, judged to clear the front of the green, where it is shorn up from the water by pilings. He hadn't; the ball fell yards short, and plunged into the pond.

Stewart was shocked. Looking back later, he said, "I thought I hit it good. I still can't believe it."

He scored an eight, bogeyed two more holes, played the home nine in 41, and shot 79. Rather than win his second championship, he fell into a tie for eighth place.

Couples, meanwhile, had been playing steady golf. He had birdied both par-five holes on the first nine, and parred every other hole. Only one stroke behind Grady then, he was putting on the pressure. The question seemed to be whether or not Grady could stand up to it.

Playing a hole behind, Grady could watch both of them, and always knew how they stood.

He watched as Morgan holed a 35-foot putt on 10th, catching Couples, who had parred, then he floated a nine iron within six feet of the hole and rammed it home. Still two strokes ahead of Morgan, and two clear of Couples as well.

The race tightened over the next two holes. Both Grady and Morgan made routine fives on the 11th, but with his enormous length, Couples reached the green with a drive and a five iron, two-putted, and climbed within one stroke of Grady once again. One hole later he moved in front.

Grady had seen Couples birdie the 11th, but he had driven into the left rough and had no chance to reach the green with his second. He pitched on with his third, but missed from eight feet. As he watched from the 12th tee, Couples, up ahead, dropped a six iron 15 feet from the cup and rolled in another putt, his fourth birdie of the day. Moments later, Grady pulled his drive into the left rough and missed the green with his second. A bogey, a two-stroke swing, and he had fallen a stroke behind Couples.

"Here we go again," Grady said to himself, remembering the 1989 British Open, where Calcavecchia had beaten him in a playoff.

Just when his world appeared bleakest, the championship turned around again on the 13th, a 195-yard par three played across a deep chasm. Couples carried his five iron just a bit too far, running it off the back edge. No worry, an approach putt left him four feet from the hole, the kind he had gobbled up throughout the week. He hadn't hit a bad putt all day, and he stepped up fully confident he would roll it in.

He didn't; the ball caught the left edge of the cup and spun away. A bogey four, and back into a tie with Grady.

While Couples had gone ahead at the 12th, Morgan had closed within a stroke of Grady, but while Fred was bogeying the 12th, Gil was doing worse. His four iron had slipped in his hand as he had swung into the tee shot, and his ball squirted off to the right, crashing down among the trees. His second pulled up short, and after chipping on, he took two putts to get down. A double-bogey five, and Morgan was finished.

Now it was between Grady and Couples, neither of whom had won anything of real meaning. They had five hard holes to play, and they had to know that one of them would leave Shoal Creek that night as the champion.

It wouldn't be Couples. His bogey on the 12th opened a flood of misplayed shots. His approach to the 14th strayed into the rough off the edge of the green, he pitched to four feet, and faced a fast putt that would break right. It broke off as soon as he tapped the ball, and he missed another. A stroke behind now. On to the 15th.

His approach spun off the green, leaving him a delicate downhill chip that stopped four or five feet away. He lipped it out. Another stroke gone. Two strokes behind with three holes to play. Now for the 16th, a 215-yard par three played from an elevated tee to a green canted right-to-left, with the pin behind a deep bunker. Here Couples hit a bad shot. He had wanted to go at the flag, but his ball pulled up 10 yards short. A four, his fourth consecutive bogey.

Watching Couples throw strokes away, Grady, meanwhile, had played reliable, steady golf, reaching the greens and two-putting: a five iron to 25 feet on the 12th, a three wood and nine iron to 15 feet on the 13th, three wood and five iron to 30 feet on the 15th, and after Couples had bogeyed the 16th, Wayne played a four iron to 25 feet and two-putted once again.

By then Grady had opened a three-stroke lead over Couples, with Morgan a further stroke behind. It was over.

Routine pars on the 17th and 18th, and Grady came in with 71, a score beaten by only Faldo on this day, and 282 for the 72 holes, six strokes under Shoal Creek's par. Both Couples and Morgan had finished by parring the 17th and 18th, and shot 285 and 286. Only they, among the 74 men who had survived the 36-hole cut, had beaten par. With a closing 71, Bill Britton had climbed to fourth place, at 289, one stroke over par. Beginning with such hopes for a second consecutive PGA Championship, Stewart had shot 79, finishing at 292.

Looking back at the carnage this terribly difficult course had caused, statisticians pointed out that:

—The average score soared to 75.758.

—Over the four days Shoal Creek claimed nearly twice as many bogeys (2,053) as it yielded birdies (1,036). The course also claimed 285 double bogeys, and 41 players gave up more than two strokes on single holes.

—Even though its par stood at 72, usually a vulnerable figure, Shoal Creek gave up only 49 rounds under par.

Couples felt despondent, of course, saying, "I'm past the stage of saying this is a learning experience. When the touch had to be there, I didn't have it. The bogeys happened so fast it was sickening. This was a day when I let myself down, because I hit the ball great."

While Couples fought off depression—10 years on the PGA Tour with only three victories to show for it, the most important the 1984 TPC—Grady rode high.

Seeing Grady after he had won, Stewart told him, "This will change your life."

It certainly changed his stature in the game. In addition to the prize money of $225,000, Grady won a lifetime exemption into the PGA Championship, a 10-year exemption into Tour events, five years into the U.S. Open and the Masters, and three years into the British Open.

Add as well the immense satisfaction of having played his best when he needed his best. Facing the press corps, Grady began by saying, "If I don't seem too excited, believe me I am. Winning here shows me I can play under very tough circumstances. Hopefully, it will give me the confidence to win other tournaments."

Grinning, he also implied the PGA should be worried about its championship.

"I've won two tournaments they don't play anymore," he said, referring to some Australian events, "and now I win one that will be remembered for the controversy. Well, I won't remember it for that."

Then, pointing to the Wanamaker Trophy, named for the department store merchant who helped organize the PGA itself, back in 1916, he said, "No matter how hard you scratch that thing, you aren't going to take my name off it."

7. The Dunhill Cup

They came full of expectation, but they did not conquer. From the moment the United States and Australia, joint favorites for the Dunhill Cup at St. Andrews, were beaten in the first round by France and New Zealand, respectively, it was a tournament of first surprise, then confusion and finally high drama as, for the second time in three years, Ireland emerged as the champion. Over four days Ireland defeated Korea, Spain, New Zealand and then England. For Ronan Rafferty, it was a double triumph. He had been on the side which won in 1988, but now David Feherty and Philip Walton were his teammates, not Eamonn Darcy and Des Smyth.

It revealed once again how strong, for a relatively small country, the Irish are and indeed have always been. Only a few weeks before, their amateurs won the Home Internationals at Conwy and a year earlier Christy O'Connor, Jr., had been the toast not only of Ireland, but many other countries besides, as he played one of the great strokes of 1989, a two iron to the 18th green on the final day that helped Europe to tie the Ryder Cup.

Christy is the nephew of perhaps the greatest Irish golfer of them all, Christy, Sr., or "Yer Man" as he is known in the Emerald Isle. There have been others, too, like Harry Bradshaw, who nearly won the British Open Championship in 1948 and might have done but for his shining honesty in playing the ball as it lay and doing so out of a broken bottle; Fred Daly, who did win the Open; Joe Carr, one of the great amateurs; Cecil Ewing and, not least, Jimmy Bruen, who, but for the war years, might have done anything, so strong was he with a swing that defied every textbook ever written.

There is a joyousness about Irish golf that cannot be found anywhere else in the world, and they also have a humor that is as engaging as it is refreshing. Feherty, who was the captain at St. Andrews, looked back on one particular match that took Ireland into the final and said that he and his opponent, Miguel Jiminez of Spain, were so nervous that "we were almost biting each other's fingernails."

There were other occasions when anxiety hung thick in the air over the Kingdom of Fife, and never more so than on that extraordinary first day when those two golfing superpowers, the United States and Australia, were both beaten. They were rated by the bookmakers as the first and second favorites. The seeding committee put them at opposite ends of the draw, scheduled to meet in the final. For both to go out as early as the first day was unprecedented.

This was the same American team that had won 12 months earlier: Mark Calcavecchia, Tom Kite and Curtis Strange, who made only the briefest of visits to St. Andrews. Strange's Concorde flight from America had to turn back, he did not arrive until Wednesday morning and was gone by Thursday afternoon.

Once it would have been unthinkable for a country like France, which has hardly produced an outstanding player since Jean Garailde in the 1960s and '70s, to have a chance of beating a country like America. It still was, bearing in mind that between them Calcavecchia, Kite and Strange had won more than $15 million compared to the combined earnings of Marc Farry, Jean Van de Velde and Emmanuel Dussart, which amounted to £350,000.

Against this might, France nevertheless came within a touch of beating them 3-0, the final score being 2-0 with the remaining match halved. Farry beat Calcavecchia with 70 against 73—the format being medal matchplay—Dussart defeated Kite with 73 against 74, and Van de Velde halved with Strange, both having 69s. With the result decided, there was no need for the final match to go into extra holes.

Farry benefited from some slack play by Calcavecchia over the first nine holes and led by three at the turn with an outward half of 35. The American's putting was poor and he never got into the game at all. The picture was much the same behind them, particularly so with Van de Velde three ahead of Strange with four holes to play and Dussart two ahead of Kite with two to play. But, as so often happens at St. Andrews, the scales tipped.

First Strange, in the second match, made a good birdie at the 16th and then Van de Velde, still two ahead, played a rash second stroke to the formidable Road Hole, the 17th. He could have laid up but pulled his second low and into the Road Bunker on the left.

From there, Van de Velde had to play to the front of the green and away from the flag, far enough for him to take three putts for a six. With Strange making a solid four, they were even, but Strange could not summon the birdie at the 18th that would have made the score 1-1, and all was left to Kite in the last match.

The advantage was with the Frenchman, Dussart, until he took fives at the 13th and 15th, but he regained his two-stroke lead at the 16th, which Kite three-putted. Dussart then chipped beautifully to save his four at the 17th. If all looked secure for Dussart as he came to the last hole, it was far from it.

Faced with a seemingly simple second shot to the 18th over the Valley of Sin, Dussart found himself in two minds over the sort of shot he should play. He promptly duffed his lofted pitch halfway to the green. Left with a pitch and run, he hit it much too hard. Worse was to follow, as the Frenchman left his approach putt six feet short, and the awful prospect was that he could now take six against Kite's four. It would have meant another tied game and extra holes, but fortunately for the French and much to the relief of Dussart, he holed out for a five and the victory was achieved.

New Zealand's defeat of their Australian neighbors came from different circumstances. For much of the time, New Zealand seemed to be fighting a lost cause. It all hinged on the middle match, between Simon Owen and Wayne Grady, who earlier in the year had won the PGA Championship. In the first match, Frank Nobilo had a runaway victory over Greg Norman to draw first blood for New Zealand and in the last match, Rodger Davis of Australia swamped Greg Turner.

Norman, having arrived from Tokyo, where he had been lobbying Australia's unsuccessful bid to stage the 1994 Olympic Games, was short of practice and form. His timing was off, his putting rusty and there was not much of merit that could be said of his 76. Perhaps Norman's worst moment was at the 12th, where he had the chance of a birdie, missed it, went to drag the ball in for his four and then missed that, as well. Certainly it made life easier for Nobilo, and he played well for 67. Davis, on the other hand, was never threatened by Turner, the Australian having 66, also to win by nine strokes.

It was always the match between Owen and Grady on which everything hung. Grady was having the better of things when he went through the turn one ahead. His lead became three strokes when the New Zealander went through the back of the par-three 11th green with his tee shot and took five. Grady drove into a bunker to drop a shot, but he was still two ahead with five to play. It was at the 14th that disaster struck. Like many before him, the Australian drove into the Beardies, under the lip of the bunker. He tried to come out backwards and caught the lip. Then he tried to come out frontwards and caught the lip again. A third attempt also failed, and it all led to a horrible nine. From two ahead, Grady went two behind in the space of one hole. Very nearly the same thing happened to him as well at the 16th, where he took two to get out of the Principal's Nose bunker.

One way or another, Grady took 43 to come home for 78 and Owen's 74 was comfortably good enough. It was a satisfying moment for the New Zealander, for it was here in 1978 that he had looked as if he was going to win the British Open, only to be overtaken by Jack Nicklaus. The five he took at the 16th against Nicklaus' birdie-three was something he had never forgotten.

The rest of this first day was uneventful, all the other seeded teams coming through relatively unscathed. Japan beat Argentina 2-1 with Satoshi Higashi playing the best golf, shooting 68, although winning by only a couple of strokes over Miguel Guzman. Spain put away Sweden in an impressive manner, Miguel Jiminez, Jose Rivero and Jose Maria Canizares all being under par in a 2-1 victory, Jiminez the best with 67.

England had a 3-0 win over Thailand, Howard Clark being the leader with 68, and this brought them through to a quarter-final against Scotland, who got the better of Mexico by 2-0 with the other match halved. It was Sandy Lyle's 68 against Rafael Alarcon that gave Scotland their impetus. It was a shame these old enemies had to meet so soon, for the departure of either was bound to take some of the local interest out of the tournament.

Ireland had a 3-0 win over Korea, although only David Feherty succeeded in breaking 70, his 69 giving him a 12-stroke victory over Choi Yoon Soo. The fourth of the home countries, Wales, also survived, beating Taipei 2-1, it all hanging on Philip Parkin's birdie putt at the 18th to beat Kuo Chie Hsiung.

While Thursday had been grey and chilly, Friday was bright, warm and windy. It was the perfect golfing day for St. Andrews. Howard Clark declared that he had never known the course to be so difficult, particularly with the positions of some of the flags. It was just a pity that it had not been like this during the British Open, when only gentle breezes ruffled the flagsticks and the scoring was predictably low.

The big match of the day was won by England as they eliminated Scotland by 2-1. It was a familiar story, the fourth successive year that they had beaten Scotland. Somehow the Scots never seem to give their best on these occasions and this was no exception. Only Mark James managed to match par of 72 and his was the decisive point as he got home by a stroke over Sam Torrance. Richard Boxall found 73 was good enough to beat Stephen McAllister by a couple of strokes, and it was left to Sandy Lyle to retrieve what little Scottish pride there was, although Lyle's 75 to Clark's 78 was hardly scintillating.

It gave England a semi-final place against Japan, which played the best golf of the day, although the wind was lighter in the morning. Japan had little difficulty in disposing of France, which understandably perhaps suffered some reaction from the defeat of the United States. The score was 3-0 and each of the Japanese was under par, Hajime Meshiai the best with 70 as he beat Jean Van de Velde by two strokes. Satoshi Higashi and Yoshinoro Kaneko both shot 71s, Higashi the winner by nine strokes over Marc Farry and Kaneko four better than Emmanuel Dussart.

Ireland took a place in the semi-finals with a 2-1 defeat of Spain. Philip Walton, with 70, came up trumps with a 12-stroke margin over Jose Rivero. The crucial point was gained by their captain, David Feherty, with 76 to Miguel Jiminez's 77. The one Spanish point was gained by Jose Maria Canizares with 70 against 71 by Ronan Rafferty.

New Zealand also won by 2-1 against Wales, for whom Ian Woosnam again did his stuff, though to no avail. He was the only man all day to break 70, his 67 being too good for Frank Nobilo, well though he also played for 70. It was always clear that Wales was likely to be a one-man team and the defeats of Mark Mouland, with 83 to 72 by Simon Owen, and of Philip Parkin, with a 76 to Greg Turner's 72, proved it.

Much of the afternoon was almost a comedy of errors as England defeated Scotland. In the first match, for instance, Boxall had a three-stroke lead over McAllister with five holes to play and then let his advantage slip by taking six at the 14th and five at the 15th. There was still one stroke between them as they stood on the 17th tee but McAllister promptly drove out of bounds into the hotel and although Boxall took six, with three putts, he still won the hole for a two-stroke lead he preserved at the 18th hole.

In the second match, Lyle enjoyed a four-stroke lead with five to play and was further assisted when Clark drove out of bounds at the 17th. He was so wide that he missed the hotel on the right, of all places. Lyle, having found the fairway, then fired his second shot over the stone wall and out of bounds as well. It did not matter because his six, like that of Boxall, still won the hole.

Everything thus depended on the match between James and Torrance. It was close for a long time but James, with birdies at the 11th and 15th, gained a two-stroke advantage that was not cut until Torrance made an unlikely four via the Road Bunker at the 17th. To take the match into extra holes, Torrance needed a birdie-three at the 18th but he never gave himself much of a chance with a misjudged pitch some way from the flag, and England went through to the semi-finals.

Ireland's defeat of Spain was the most gripping, and it was also bizarre, hinging on Feherty's 76 against Jiminez's 77. Walton, playing in the last match, was in immediate control against Rivero, who obliged him by going into the burn twice at the first hole en route to a seven, 42 out and a deficit of eight strokes. Canizares consistently had the upper hand against Rafferty, and for most of the time was two strokes ahead. Only at the 18th did the Irishman cut the margin to a single stroke.

Meanwhile, Feherty found himself four strokes clear of Jiminez after only six holes. He was by then three under par and going great guns. However, at the seventh he took four putts. The wind was then very strong and, when

Feherty left his approach putt three feet short from above the hole, his next caught the rim and spun six feet away from where he missed again. With three putts again at the eighth, Feherty's lead had dwindled to only one and by the 11th they were tied. These were desperate times and Feherty remarked later than they were both so edgy that "we were almost biting one another's nails." They halved with bogeys at the 14th, 15th and 16th, Feherty going out of bounds at the 14th, but both played the 17th well, halving it in perfectly played fours.

Tied with one hole to play, Feherty won almost unintentionally. Jiminez left a longish approach putt six feet short and the Irishman had thoughts only of laying his putt from 10 feet close, in the slight hope that his opponent would three-putt. Instead, Feherty's putt went in the hole for a three.

Woosnam's golf for Wales was outstanding from the beginning. He started birdie, birdie and was out in 33 despite dropping a shot at the seventh, where he took three putts. Nobilo was no slouch either, with 35 to the turn, but he could do nothing about the excellent golf by the Welshman that, unfortunately, did not rub off on the rest of his team. Mouland had one of his very "off" days and failed to give Owen much of a game.

Parkin made a better scrap of it against Turner, both out in 35. The neat pitch Turner played to the 10th for birdie-three gave him a lead he never again lost, although with three holes to play there was still only one stroke between them. However, at the 16th the Welshman missed the green with a three-iron second—which gives some indication of the strength of the wind, for normally it is a much shorter club—and then buried his chances at the 17th, where he drove out of bounds. What a merciless hole the 17th was again proving to be.

There was every indication that France had gone off the boil as soon as Farry, in the first match, started four, seven, five, five against Higashi's three, four, four, four. There was no way back from there but Dussart kept his end up for 11 holes against Kaneko, both of them then even par. The difference came over the last seven holes, as Kaneko played them in even par against the Frenchman's three over. The final match was of no consequence, Van de Velde, having led at the turn with 35, being overtaken by the superior golf of Meshiai, who came back in 34 for a round of 70.

If the defeats of the United States and Australia on the first day and of Scotland on the second had taken something out of the tournament, a great deal more was put back into it by the events on Saturday. England, by dint of some heroic play from Mark James and Howard Clark and the assistance of the rules of the competition, won a semi-final a large number of people present thought had already been secured by Japan. Some indeed had left the course, believing it was all over, after Yoshinoro Kaneko had beaten Richard Boxall with 69 to 70, the other two matches having earlier been halved, Satoshi Higashi and Clark both completing rounds of 70, as did Hajime Meshiai and James.

To many, including BBC television, who were not quite sure what was going on, this read like a 1-0 win to Japan with the other two matches halved. However, the rules of the competition, which too few had bothered to read, stated quite clearly that if two matches were halved they had to be played to a conclusion over extra holes, just as would also have been the case if the score was 1-1 and the other tied.

The confusion arose because Clark and Higashi, playing the first match, stopped by the 18th green to await the end of the other two matches in case extra holes were superfluous. The sight of them sitting down and spectating was nevertheless a strong suggestion that they had finished, and some spectators left the course believing that it was all over. It was not and England, having already gained one reprieve from the birdies both Clark and James made at the 18th to tie their matches, went on to win them both in extra holes.

Ireland reached the final by beating New Zealand by 2-0, with the third game halved. Again it was David Feherty, their captain, who shouldered the ultimate responsibility after Philip Walton had defeated Simon Owen with 70 to 71, Ronan Rafferty and Frank Nobilo meanwhile finishing even at 68 apiece. In this instance extra holes were unnecessary, for it would have made no difference to the overall result.

With the wind having dropped, the scoring improved considerably and every one of the 12 players from the four teams was under par. It was a terrific match between England and Japan from the beginning, Clark inching his way back after trailing Higashi by two strokes as early as the fifth hole. When Higashi took three putts at the eighth, there was only one stroke between them and there it stayed until the 18th, where Clark finally drew even, hitting a wedge to four feet and safely sinking the putt for a birdie.

Both were in with 70s, and Kaneko and Boxall had just as tight a match, the Japanese with the advantage through the first nine holes, out in 33 and one up. However Boxall, having drawn even with a fine two at the 11th, was two ahead with four holes to play. Safe though this seemed, it was not enough. Boxall dropped a shot at the 15th, could not match Kaneko's birdie at the next, nor his four at the 17th. It was a three-stroke swing that proved decisive.

All four players now anxiously awaited the last match. James was one ahead at the turn after going out in 34 but then two strokes behind as Meshiai reeled off three successive birdies from the 12th. It was back to only one at the 16th, where the Japanese took three putts. It was seemingly a disaster for England when James then drove out of bounds at the 17th, but he still got a half in six, Meshiai finding the Road Bunker with his second and then taking three putts from 30 feet. It was not until the 18th that James drew even, pitching to 10 feet and holing a wonderful putt under the circumstances for a birdie and a halved game.

After all the confusion that followed, the Japanese thinking they had won when they had not, the two undecided matches embarked on extra holes, Japan having to win one of them, England both. It was Clark who drew first blood straightaway, holing from around six feet for a birdie at the first hole to beat Higashi. Next came James and Meshiai, the latter having the better chances at the first and second holes but failing to take them. It was then that James became a hero. From the front of the 17th, the third extra hole, he putted woefully short but miraculously got the next one in from probably 20 feet, credit nevertheless going to Meshiai as well, as he followed him in from six feet.

The odds were very much on a Japanese victory when Meshiai pitched to four feet at the 18th, but James did even better, a pitch to 18 inches. When his opponent missed for his birdie, James tapped his ball safely home.

Ireland's victory was not quite as fraught, but there was precious little difference in it even so. What first gave Ireland concern was Walton's uncertain play after the turn. Walton, after playing the first 10 holes in 35 for a six-stroke lead over Owen, saw his margin dwindle to only one with five holes to play. Owen made three successive birdies from the 11th, which was a two-stroke swing in the cases of the 12th and 13th, where Walton each time took five. Some Irish breathing space came at the 14th, where Owen was bunkered in the Beardies and took six. That was cancelled out by Walton's five at the 16th, with three putts. With one stroke between them, both made fours at the 17th and they halved the 18th as well. First blood to Ireland.

Rafferty also led Nobilo at the turn, 32 against 33. They then halved the 10th in birdie-threes, but the five the Irishman took at the 11th put a different slant on things. Rafferty did not let it worry him and, with a birdie-four at the long 14th, where he pitched close, drew even again. Birdies were matched at the 16th, as were fives at the 17th, and with two pars at the 18th, both were in with 68s.

Everything rested once again on Feherty, who was two strokes down at the turn as Turner went out in 32. He was still two behind with six holes to play. At the 13th the Irishman holed from 15 feet for a birdie. Quickly he drew even, Turner hitting his second in Hell bunker, having to play out backwards and taking six at the 14th. There was quick recovery by the New Zealander at the next, as he wedged to six feet for a birdie, but Feherty responded at the 16th, holing from 15 feet for a three to draw even again. It was the 17th that decided it. Feherty made a four; Owen, after a huge drive that left him with a comfortable pitch to the green, underclubbed with a nine iron and three-putted from 90 feet. Feherty was in front again and, with a safe par under the shadow of the clubhouse, he had brought his team safely home.

Sympathy was with Ireland in the final, perhaps because the Scots, who make up most of the gallery, felt that England got into the final on false pretences. However, even the most impartial observers could not fail but to have been stirred by the grand climax of the Dunhill Cup, another gripping match as, for the second time in three years, the Irish took the title by the narrowest margin yet, 3-1/2 to 2-1/2 with all depending on the last match, as Feherty beat Mark James over extra holes with the two teams tied.

The final is played in two sessions, three points in the morning and three in the afternoon, six points in all being at stake. At lunch everything was still delicately poised at 1-1/2 to 1-1/2 — no extra holes in this instance — and England was thankful for having very much got out of jail, substantially down in all three matches at various stages. They particularly had to thank James, who, after a bad start, found himself four strokes behind Walton after six holes, even though the Irishman was no better than even par. It was not until the 11th that James cut his deficit with a birdie, then he birdied again at the 12th. With a third at the 14th, where Walton took six, they were even and though Walton quickly regained the lead with a birdie at the 15th, he could not match James's four at the 17th and the match was halved, both in with 72s.

Behind them, Boxall trailed Rafferty nearly all the way. He was two down at the turn, though unexpectedly drawing even at the 13th, where Rafferty took six. Two holes later, the Irishman was back in the lead again with a birdie, and a four at the 17th extended his lead, so he got home by two strokes with 71 to 73. Feherty, meanwhile, was having the better of things against Clark in the last match, three clear at the turn as he went out in 35. But Clark came back in 35 with birdies at the 11th and 13th and only one dropped shot at the 17th, which cost him nothing since Feherty took five there as well. Clark was therefore in with 73 and won by a stroke.

If Feherty felt he had let his side down, he certainly did not in the afternoon. Indeed, he was to play a captain's role when all depended on him, beating Clark at the third extra hole with the two teams tied. It was a windy afternoon and James drew first blood for England, albeit not very gloriously with 76 to 77 by Walton. But Rafferty, who was under par in all his rounds over the Old Course and played a key role in this second Irish success in three years, brought the two teams even again when he outplayed Boxall with 71 to the Englishman's 76.

All therefore rested on Feherty, who seemed to be shouldering much of the responsibility all week. He had lost to Clark in the morning and must have been further shaken when he saw a three-stroke lead at the turn dwindle to nothing over the next four holes, dropping shots at both the 11th and 13th, Clark further punishing the first of these mistakes with a birdie. Feherty's birdie-four at the 14th, with a six iron to three feet, looked like reviving him at just the right moment but his shoulders sagged again when, at the 17th, having flirted dangerously with the Road Bunker, he laid an approach putt only three feet from the hole, only to miss the next and take five.

Clark, from a much more difficult position short and left of the Road Bunker, had meanwhile played a gorgeous chip and run through all the steep humps and hollows to 12 feet and capped it by holing the putt for his par. So there they were even again, and England could have won it outright at the 18th, had Clark not putted feebly from about eight feet for his birdie. He left it, of all things, short when he had that for game, set and match. Both were in with modest 75s.

As on Saturday, England went into extra holes and, in mounting excitement, there was still nothing to separate Feherty and Clark for two holes, although both had to sink teasing putts at the second. It was the 17th, as always seemed likely, that settled it. Clark, with a three-iron second, again dragged his shot wide and left, while Feherty, summoning every ounce of his courage, struck the most perfect four iron to the heart of the green. This time there was hardly a shot for Clark. Although he nearly holed a long putt for his four, it stopped just short, leaving Feherty with two for the Dunhill Cup, which he safely negotiated. It had been quite a match, and quite a tournament for that matter, as well.

8. The World Match Play Championship

In the autumn of 1986, it looked as if no British golfer would ever be destined to win the Suntory World Match Play Championship. For 23 years, it had gone unfailingly to overseas players, Gary Player taking the title five times, Severiano Ballesteros on four occasions, Greg Norman three, and Arnold Palmer and Hale Irwin twice each.

The British breakthrough came at last in 1987, when Ian Woosnam defeated Sandy Lyle. It opened the floodgates, for 12 months later Lyle was triumphant, then Nick Faldo in 1989 and now again it was Woosnam, who became the first double British winner. With a scintillating performance in the morning and a more dogged one in the afternoon, Woosnam defeated Mark McNulty of Zimbabwe by 4 and 2. It was his second triumph in only five appearances and, 12 months earlier, he had also been beaten in the final.

Woosnam brought his total victories for the year to four, the others being in the Mediterranean, Monte Carlo and Scottish Opens, and there was still more to come in what was an Indian summer, not only in terms of weather after many golden months of sunshine, but also for Woosnam as he played some of the finest golf of his life. Each of his three wins, by 5 and 4 against Ronan Rafferty, 5 and 3 against Chip Beck and 4 and 2 against McNulty, were all very comfortably gained, which was surprising.

Only two weeks earlier in the European Open at Sunningdale, Woosnam decided that he should alter his grip. It had been on his mind for some time but for someone who had enjoyed so many fruitful years, it took courage for him to actually do it.

In theory Woosnam's is a slightly weak grip, across the base of the fingers of his left hand, rather than across his palm, but it has added strength to his game, enabling him to swing the club with greater freedom and hit the ball further. "It is just going miles," he said, and illustrated the point by talking of a one iron at the 18th he had hit 320 yards. Another ally was a new driver which he had acquired for a lower and more penetrating flight into the wind. Not that it exactly blew at Wentworth.

Against such a fusillade, McNulty, a much quieter swinger of the club but an extremely well organized player who was at the time at the head of the European Tour's Order of Merit, was always up against it, often conceding 30 or 40 yards from the tee and consequently having to play two or even three clubs more to the green.

It was something the modest Zimbabwean, who in a 12-month period in 1986-87 won 13 tournaments worldwide, generously admitted. "Ian played much the better golf," he said afterwards, though when pressed on the matter he still put Faldo, Norman and Jose Maria Olazabal ahead on "technical points," which were confirmed by the Sony Ranking. McNulty was thinking of Woosnam's occasional fallibility with his putter, though it was not evident this week.

Another factor in Woosnam's favor was that, as one of the four seeded players—Faldo, Norman and Irwin were the others—he had only three days of 36-hole golf whereas McNulty went through four. It did make a difference, and by the 27th hole of the final, McNulty admitted to his caddy that his legs were "going." His progress had not been unduly difficult, 4 and 2 against Billy Ray Brown, 6 and 4 against Irwin and 3 and 2 against Norman, but it did take its toll.

Not that there had been any sign of that in the morning's play. There had been nothing between them for 15 holes, Woosnam 1-up with a birdie at the first, McNulty 1-up by the third with a par and then a birdie. Then Woosnam squared the match with an eagle at the fourth, home in two with a one iron and two iron before holing from 10 feet. Three holes later he was 2-up with a birdie at the sixth, and took the seventh as well, when McNulty missed the two-tier green from the bottom of the hill. Out in 32, three under par, the Welshman was still 2-up but it was not to last.

McNulty came back with a birdie at the 11th hole after an accurate pitch to four feet and drew even when Woosnam took three putts at the 14th, a par three with another two-tier green, the tee shot uphill. It was a crucial moment for Woosnam and particularly so when McNulty hit a great second to the 15th, only six feet from the hole. But the Welshman followed him, and they halved the hole in birdie-threes. It was the beginning of an inspired period for Woosnam, who played those last four holes before lunch in birdie, birdie, birdie, eagle for a three-hole lead.

At the 16th, a seemingly innocuous short par four, Woosnam pitched to three feet; at the 571-yard 17th he was home with a one iron from the tee and then a two iron for a two-putt four; and the same two clubs did the business as well at the 18th before he thrust home a putt from 36 feet for his eagle and a round of 64. McNulty was two under par for those last four holes but he lost three of them and, despite his 67, was 3-down.

It was a chastening experience, but McNulty is a very patient player, always down the middle, invariably on the green and consequently one against whom it is dangerous to take any liberties. For another six holes in the afternoon, the two of them matched one another, shot for shot, all pars with the exception of the fourth, where birdies were customary on the still fast-running fairways.

At the seventh, McNulty got a new lease on life. With a seven iron to six feet, he holed the marginally shorter putt for a three and immediately struck again. Once more it was his seven iron which paved the way, though this time it was a putt of 15 feet which found its mark. Suddenly he was back to only 1-down though it was as he was walking down the ninth fairway that he remarked to his caddy that his legs were "going." It had to be pure physical fatigue, for to have won two holes in succession, as he had just done, should have got the adrenalin flowing.

Tiredness nevertheless may have had something to do with the three-iron second shot he then pulled into the trees. McNulty was lucky to find a reasonable lie, chipped through the foliage and then holed a putt of 30 feet for his par to win the hole. Woosnam, bunkered in two, took five and they were tied again.

The next hole over the West course at Wentworth, the 10th, is a par-three and it was here that McNulty made his cardinal mistake. It could have cost him the match. Having drawn even and still with the honor, it was paramount for him to hit the green and keep the pressure up. Instead he missed, down the slope on the right, failed to negotiate it the first time and Woosnam, safely on the green with a six iron, was not in the end required to putt. The advantage was Woosnam's again and the strength seemed slowly to ebb from McNulty's game.

Woosnam went 2-up on the long 12th hole, when McNulty hit two hooks and Woosnam unerringly found the green with a drive and four iron. With a five iron to 10 feet for another birdie at the 15th, Woosnam was 3-up and in a virtually unassailable position. The end came at the 16th, so close was Woosnam to the flag, no more than five feet, that McNulty conceded when he had failed to make his birdie putt.

Woosnam was 12 under par for the 34 holes but he admitted that he had still been nervous. "It may not show," he said, "but it keeps eating away at my insides. I try to keep control with deep breathing and thinking positively. The main thing is to take my time and relax. The nervousness is at its worst at the start, for the first two or three holes or so. Then it leaves me until it comes back again over the last few holes when you don't want to make a mistake. At the same time I think you have to be nervous to play good golf."

His tactics are always the same in match play. "I just go out and play the course," he explained. "I keep thinking that if I can shoot four or five under par in every round, my opponent has to play some extra special golf to beat me. I am naturally aggressive and don't have to change my game at all. It helps to play a course you like and I am always comfortable here."

McNulty was full of praise for his opponent. "I was always struggling to find a shot to compete with Ian's down-the-middle shots and then rifling it into the green. I have always felt in the last three years that Ian has been one of the best iron strikers I have seen. I never played with Nicklaus at his best, but I cannot think that he was a much better. When those iron shots are rippling into the green and the putts are going in, it is a hard act to follow."

Yet there had been some doubt on the Friday evening that Woosnam would be able to play at all. When he beat Rafferty in the quarter-finals by 5 and 4, he pulled a small muscle in his groin and spent the last few holes limping badly. He said that if it did not improve overnight, there was no way he could walk two rounds. Some heatwave treatment and a good night's rest worked like magic.

There had been some controversy at the beginning of the week when it was announced that Severiano Ballesteros, who has won the championship four times and is only one short of Gary Player's record of five victories, had not been seeded. However, Ballesteros had been playing poorly for most of the year and it would have been difficult to justify seeding him instead of Woosnam, Greg Norman, the leader of the American money list, Nick Faldo, not only the holder but also the winner this year of both the Masters and the British Open, and Hale Irwin, the U.S. Open champion.

Not even Wayne Grady, the popular Australian winner of the American PGA, got a seeding spot, and the field was among the strongest to have been assembled in the championship's 27 years. Grady was making his first appearance in the World Match Play and was drawn against Bernhard Langer, a finalist in both 1984 and 1985, when each time he lost to Ballesteros, as indeed he did in earlier rounds in 1982 and 1983.

Chip Beck, who had the best American record in the 1989 Ryder Cup match, was back for a second time and faced Royoken Kawagishi, the former Japanese Amateur champion, who had made a most promising start to his professional career and is regarded very much as a player for the future. McNulty was up against Billy Ray Brown, the "wild card" in that his chief claim to fame was that he tied with Faldo for third place in the U.S. Open at Medinah, likewise getting to within a putt of the playoff Irwin won at the 19th hole against Mike Donald.

There was no doubt as to where most of the interest lay on this opening day and that was in the match between Ballesteros and Ronan Rafferty, now one of the stars of the European Tour and the leading money winner in 1989. There had been a feeling beforehand that this could be the week when Ballesteros, faced now with only one man at a time, might rediscover his lost form. Far from it. He lost by 8 and 6, and that was the worst drubbing he had received in his 15 consecutive appearances at Wentworth. In 1986 he had lost by 7 and 6 to Rodger Davis of Australia, and by the same margin to Sandy Lyle in 1988.

One can only say that Rafferty was blessed with a touch of Irish magic. In the morning he completed the formidable West course in an approximate 62 strokes to stand 6-up. The approximation is necessary because there was a putt of 10 feet at the 13th that he was not required to hole for his birdie-three, since Ballesteros had already taken five. However there was every reason to suppose that the young Irishman would have sunk it, for he was unerring on the greens, with 10 one-putts, three from at least 20 feet.

His longest was one of 30 feet for an eagle-three at the 17th as he followed Ballesteros in for a half to remain 7-up. That he was cut back to six was due to Ballesteros making another eagle at the 18th. When the Spaniard started the afternoon with a birdie-three to become 5-down, there seemed to be a chance that he was not dead yet. Nor might he have been had he holed a short putt for a two at the 20th, nor wasted another opportunity at the 21st, where he followed Rafferty into a bunker.

Only once had Ballesteros been in the lead, with a four at the first hole in the morning. That it was not to be his day seemed clear at the second hole of the day where, admittedly from a difficult spot, he putted into a bunker, his ball catching the always dangerous slope. Rafferty promptly took the third and fourth holes with a par and an eagle to lead by 2-up and with more birdies at the sixth and seventh and then a par at the ninth, where Ballesteros was deep in the trees, advanced to 5-up.

There was a brief flicker from the Spaniard, when he made a two at the 10th, holing from five feet, but Rafferty took the 12th with a four and then the 13th, where Ballesteros was bunkered beside the green. A remarkable Spanish recovery from the trees to the left of the 15th fairway somehow salvaged a four, but he was soon 7-down as Rafferty pitched to nine feet and holed the putt.

It was great stuff when Ballesteros, from the edge of the green, holed for an eagle-three at the 17th only for Rafferty to follow him in and it is hard to remember anyone making successive eagle-threes as the Spaniard did when he sank another putt, this time of 50 feet or so, for a three at the last to go into lunch at 6-down. The spark was still there when a three-iron second shot to the first hole in the afternoon reduced his deficit to 5-down, but the next two holes were decisive. To say that Rafferty had escaped would be an exaggeration and, in any case, Ballesteros was soon back to his bad old ways.

Having lost the sixth to a birdie to go 6-down again, Ballesteros then lost the seventh and eighth as well, though this time to pars, bunkered at the former and taking three putts from 50 feet at the latter. Now 8-down, his time was running out fast and though he did make one more birdie, at the 11th, the Irish tide finally engulfed him at the 12th, the 30th hole of the match, where Rafferty made an eagle-three. Even at his best, Ballesteros would have been pressed to stand up to the sort of golf Rafferty threw at him. The Spaniard had shown glimpses of his best all too rarely.

The comeback of the day belonged to Grady, who was 4-down after 12 holes in the morning, but beat Langer by 2-up. Langer has again overcome his putting troubles with a unique grip whereby, with his left hand far down the shaft, he jams the handle between his right hand and his left forearm. By and large, it works well enough.

It was for a time the Langer of old, as he raced to the turn in the morning in 29, with a birdie at the second, an eagle-three at the fourth and then more birdies at the fifth, seventh and ninth. Only at the short fifth did Grady match him.

Other than at the 10th, which he lost to a three, Langer did not make a mistake until the 16th, hitting a three wood into the trees on the left. That brought him back to 3-up, but it was the 17th which probably began to turn the match. Here Grady was in all manner of trouble left and right and scraped out a five only by virtue of a one-putt. Langer was on the green in two shots less with a drive and one iron, only to three-putt to let him off with a half. Then at the 18th, Grady gave himself genuine hope with a drive and one iron a long way from the flag, but still holing the putt for an eagle-three. Langer's four was no match for that and 2-up at lunch was far removed from the 4-up he had been only three holes earlier.

For all that, Langer began the afternoon round with a birdie-three to go 3-up again. He missed the green at the short second, did the same at the third and lost both to pars. The same could have happened at the fifth, but Grady missed what seemed a golden opportunity by three-putting. Langer did the same at the sixth to go back to even, and he was overtaken at the eighth, where once again his putter failed him with another three putts.

Grady had played the first nine holes of the afternoon in 33 to Langer's rather ragged 38, and now that the Australian had got himself off the hook, there was no way he was going to be caught again. He was not asked to putt at the 10th, where Langer again missed the green, and though a series of halves followed, Grady took the match with birdie-threes at both the 15th and 16th.

Beck was always in control against Kawagishi, 1-up straightaway and only caught once when he conceded the Japanese the fourth hole after taking four shots and had still only reached the greenside bunker. Kawagishi, on the green in two, did not have to putt. However, it was a brief respite, for Beck was quickly 2-up with a two at the fifth, and though he lost the eighth, birdies at the 10th and 11th took him to 3-up. By lunch it had become 4-up as he won the 16th with a four, the 17th with a birdie but lost the 18th, where Kawagishi got down in two and Beck took three putts.

There were a couple of occasions in the afternoon when Kawagishi got to within striking distance again, though it was more Beck's doing than his own. The American took three putts at the sixth and made a real nonsense of the ninth to go back to only 2-up. The 10th and 11th were exchanged, but Beck finally took hold at the 12th, where the Japanese took three putts, and then wound things up with a birdie at the 15th. Experience had been the factor, as much as anything, and Beck was full of praise for his young opponent and predicted Kawagishi was a player on whom to keep a careful eye in the future.

For a long time the closest match was that between McNulty and Brown, who was playing match play golf for the first time since his college days in 1984. He nevertheless made a fair game of it and was even at lunch, both having 69. There had been little between them, McNulty 1-up at the second, Brown 1-up by the fifth, McNulty ahead again by the seventh and not caught again until the 13th, where Brown hit a seven iron to five feet and holed for his three.

McNulty made a two at the 14th, but still he could not shake his man off. The American pitched and one-putted to draw even at the 16th, lost the 17th to a four but won back the 18th, where he was on the green with two big hits, a drive and three iron for a four. After two holes in the afternoon, Brown was ahead, McNulty making rather a mess of things, but the young American could not hold it. McNulty took the fourth with a birdie to draw even, and then the sixth and eighth with two more birdies.

It was not yet over, because McNulty was down the bank to the right of the 10th green and in the end conceded, took the 11th with a birdie but then lost the 12th to a birdie. With only one hole still between them, all the signs were for a tight finish. It was not to be, because McNulty at last moved into top gear with four threes in a row from the 13th, three of them birdies and was home by 4 and 3. It had been a lot closer than the score indicated.

The big guns moved in on the Friday and two of them promptly moved out again, Faldo going down by 2 and 1 to Beck, and Irwin suffering a mauling from McNulty, who beat him by 6 and 4. Even Norman had his work cut out, only getting the better of his fellow Australian, Grady, at the second extra hole. The only seed who enjoyed a comfortable day was Woosnam, a 5-and-4 winner over Rafferty, who was nothing like he had been when he removed Ballesteros 24 hours earlier.

As the fifth British golfer to win both the Masters and British Open in the same year, Faldo had a surprising defeat at the hands of Beck. He did not go down without a fight and, indeed, at one stage he really had the crowds in hot pursuit as he came back from 5-down after 19 holes to draw even with eight to play. As so often is the case after such recoveries, however, the man who had been down seemed to run out of steam, and instead it was Beck who drew away over the closing holes.

Though he made no excuses, Faldo had decided that he would take a five-week rest. Ever since the U.S. Open in June he had been suffering on and off from strained wrists and forearms as a result either of playing on hard ground earlier in the year, or through just the wear and tear of the new swing he had developed. He had more than once withdrawn from tournaments at a late hour—notably the Irish Open at Portmarnock and The International at Denver, Colorado—and now at the end of the season, he had the opportunity to take a prolonged break, "in the interests of the next 10 years," as he put it.

There was no doubt that Faldo was far below his form of Augusta and St. Andrews, and he was 4-down at lunch to Beck. Those first 18 holes took him an approximate 75 strokes. Most of that was taken on the inward half when he took 40 to go from 1-up to 4-down. Faldo enjoyed an encouraging start: a drive and one iron at the first before holing from eight feet for a three, and then he went 2-up at the second, where Beck was bunkered. The American clipped his deficit to one at the fifth, where he holed from 15 feet for a two and drew even at the seventh, as Faldo bunkered his second shot.

The defending champion also erred at the ninth, losing it to a par, and had further mistakes at the 10th, 12th and 15th, where each time he dropped shots, left him 4-down. Even iron clubs from the tee got Faldo into trouble and, though he had brief encouragement at the 17th, with a chip-and-putt birdie, he conceded the 18th after taking five with Beck only four feet from the flag in two.

When Faldo hit into a bunker at the first hole in the afternoon, he went 5-down and was fast losing his grip. He then began a stirring recovery that for a time suggested he could yet win the match. Beck failed to get down in two from the edge of both the third and fourth greens, and then took three putts at the short fifth. In three holes Faldo had gone from 5-down to 2-down and when he pitched to 10 feet for a birdie at the seventh, only a single hole separated them.

Beck's morale was boosted when, after much the shorter tee shot down the eighth, he played much the longer but superior second shot to four feet for a birdie. His lead of 2-up was short-lived. Faldo got up and down from sand for a winning four at the ninth, and though he missed the green at the short 10th, so did Beck. The American had to take a penalty drop out of a ditch and the match was even.

Beck quickly gathered himself again, making a splendid three with the longer putt at the 11th and went 2-up when, for the second time, Faldo hooked his tee shot down the 12th and could not get a matching birdie-four. The British Open champion made up for it with a three at the next, playing a brilliantly daring shot to catch the bank to the left of the 13th green and holing quite a long putt for his three.

Faldo was still in with a chance, halved the next three holes and had to summon himself for one last effort at the 17th and 18th, where he undoubtedly had the advantage in length. It was not there, his one iron to the 17th drifting right and down the slope from where he would get down in two more. Beck, though short in two, chipped well, sank his putt and was through to the semi-finals.

There he was due to meet Woosnam, and one has to write "due" because Woosnam suggested that there was some doubt as to whether he would be able to play. Just as he was cruising to victory over Rafferty he made what he felt was a bad swing on the ninth tee in the afternoon and it left him with a pulled muscle in his groin. For the remaining holes he was limping quite badly, and said that if there was no improvement he could not possibly walk two rounds the following day. He would have some heat treatment, because it was an injury he had had before, but he would not make the decision until the morning.

Woosnam had a more comfortable victory than had been expected. Rafferty completely lost his game, especially over the last nine holes of the morning, when he went from 1-up to 5-down. Having won the second hole with a three, Rafferty increased his lead to two at the eighth, where Woosnam three-putted. Rafferty, however, drove into thick rough at the ninth and then lost the 10th as well, missing the green.

Suddenly the game turned right around. Rafferty was bunkered at the 11th, in the trees with his second shot to the 12th and missed the green at the 14th. Nor could he match the Welshman's birdies at the 17th and 18th and, with Woosnam home in 33 against 40, some of the fire went out of their games. Nor did the embers come to life again, Woosnam going 6-up straightaway after lunch, although he lost the next two holes to pars.

Rafferty was allowed no further encouragement, Woosnam going 5-up again with a two at the fifth, losing the ninth to a par but settling matters once and for all when he holed from 30 feet for an eagle at the 12th. After losing the 13th to a birdie, Woosnam knocked a five iron to five feet for a two at the 14th. He was only one under par for the afternoon's 14 holes but it was quite adequate. "It was a pretty scrappy game," remarked Woosnam afterwards. "Neither of us played very well, but Ronan seemed to lose his game after that bad drive to the ninth in the morning. He was not the same player again."

Probably the best match of the day was that in which Norman beat Grady at the 38th hole, and he had to produce some very gutsy golf to do it, since he did not get in front until the 27th hole and even then his lead was short-lived.

It was seven holes before Grady drew first blood and then he went 2-up as Norman took three putts at the eighth. Two bad holes by Grady at the 10th and 11th swiftly made the match even again. There was a brief moment of brilliance at the 12th, which they halved in eagle-threes, then Grady won both the 15th and 17th to go into lunch two ahead. Norman was bunkered by the green at the 15th, neither reached the 17th in two but Grady played much the better chip, to about three feet.

There was an early flurry in the afternoon, Norman getting a hole back after both were bunkered, but Grady took the second and third to go back to 3-up. The big swing came at the sixth, seventh, eighth and ninth holes, all of which Norman won, though with nothing better than pars. Twice this was due to Grady three-putting. Then the errors were on Norman's side, as he lost the 13th and 14th holes to pars to go 1-down again. It was that sort of match, and sure enough, Grady managed to miss the 16th green with his pitch to even the match.

It was only then that in many ways the "real" game began. Neither reached the 17th green in two but both chipped well, Norman holing from 10 feet for his birdie-four and Grady following him in from perhaps three feet closer. Tied and one hole to play, both played the 18th perfectly, Grady a three wood and two iron to 10 feet, Norman a three wood and four iron to 40 feet. Here was a great chance for Grady, but he missed the putt for an eagle-three and victory and off they had to go into extra holes. Grady succeeded in saving his neck at the 37th with a bunker shot to eight feet but Norman, having also got down in two from off the green, nailed his man at the next with an eight iron to six feet and a putt safely holed for a two.

The best golf was played by McNulty against Irwin, and hardly surprisingly so since McNulty was approximately eight under par for their 32 holes. At no stage did Irwin, who was making his eighth appearance in the championship and had won it twice, get ahead. It was an even contest for nine holes, both out in 33. McNulty had been 2-up as early as the third hole, where he made a memorable three with a five wood to eight feet and holed the putt.

Irwin won back the fifth hole with a two, sinking a very long putt, and also won the eighth with another birdie, this time from shorter range but still 20 feet or so. It was on the inward half that the pendulum swung McNulty's way. Irwin three-putted the 10th, lost the 11th to a birdie, rallied with an eagle-three at the 12th with a stunning one iron to within inches of the flag, but quickly lost his touch.

He lost three holes in a row from the 15th, first to a par and then to two birdies and largely had to blame himself. He was in all manner of trouble down the 15th, could not do too much about McNulty's three at the 16th, but damagingly ran up three putts at the 17th.

The same thing happened at the 18th, and there was not the slightest chink in McNulty's game in the afternoon. He took two of the first three holes, both in pars, to go 6-up and though Irwin got back the fifth and seventh holes with birdies, that signalled the end of his recovery. Birdies by McNulty at the eighth and 11th made him 6-up again and on the 14th green, Irwin decided that he had had enough.

Now on the crest of a wave, McNulty went on to cause a major surprise in the semi-finals when he beat Norman by 3 and 2, meeting in the final Woosnam, who got the better of Beck by 5 and 3. It was, as has already been stated, Woosnam's third final in his five appearances but McNulty's first. In 1987 the Zimbabwean got to the semi-finals, where he lost at the third extra hole to Lyle, and 12 months later he had been beaten in the first round by Mark McCumber. At 37, McNulty was proving to be at the height of his golfing powers, playing with more consistency than ever. He had also made a swift recovery from a rib injury, when he fell getting out of his bath, forcing him to withdraw from the European Open only two weeks earlier at Sunningdale.

This was the better of the two semi-finals. Whereas Woosnam was never behind against Beck, McNulty found Norman in much sharper form with a round of 68 in the morning which left the Australian 1-up. It was not until the fifth hole in the afternoon that McNulty regained a lead he had lost at the 10th hole in the morning. He then surged home over the last nine holes.

Norman had drawn first blood with a birdie at the second, hitting an eight iron to eight feet and knocking in the putt for a birdie-two. It was a short-lived lead as McNulty took the third with a fine birdie-three, holing from 20 feet after a two-iron second to this modified green, there no longer being quite such a slope to the second tier. Then he took the fourth as well with a birdie-four, Norman failing to get up in two or, for that matter, down in two.

When Norman took three putts from the bottom tier of the seventh green, the difference between became two holes but the Australian struck back with a vengeance when he took four holes in a row from the 10th to go from 2-down to 2-up. A par three was good enough at the 10th but then came two birdies, a wedge to nine feet at the 11th, a two-putt four at the 12th after which he was presented with the 13th, when McNulty hit his second into the ditch and had to drop under penalty.

This was a bad time for McNulty, but he got back the 15th hole with a six-iron second shot to six feet for a three. The key to his victory could well have come at the 17th and 18th holes. With Norman on the green in two at the 17th, McNulty had to get down in two to avoid going 2-down, and sure enough, he played a deft chip to four feet. Even better was his recovery at the last for again Norman was on in two while McNulty was bunkered left. It was one of those awkward medium-length bunker shots, so easy to hit too strong or not strong enough. McNulty judged it perfectly to four feet, and sank the putt.

Equally important were the fourth and fifth holes in the afternoon. With Norman on the green in two at the par five and McNulty short, there was a fair chance that the Australian would go two ahead again. Instead he became even, taking three putts while McNulty got up and down in two. Then at the short fifth hole, Norman hit a brilliant five iron to five feet, only for McNulty to hole a putt of three times that length for a two, his opponent then missing for the half.

Though Norman chipped-in for a three at the sixth, McNulty sank a 15-foot putt for a half and, having gone out in 32, he went 2-up at the 10th, Norman conceding after missing the green on the right. Then the screw was turned even tighter when McNulty holed from off the green at the 12th for an eagle-three. Although Norman won back the 14th with a two, the end came at the 16th, when he went through the 16th green and failed to get down in two more.

"It was always going to be a tough match," said McNulty afterwards. "Greg is a hell of a competitor. It doesn't matter how much you are ahead, you know he'll come back. I know he drives the ball 40 yards past me, but I kept playing my own game and as long as I made few mistakes I knew I had a chance. I have been putting well all week and I putted well again today. That was the difference."

Woosnam's victory over Beck was always in the cards, it taking him only 12 holes to shake his man off. Twice early on he was brought back to even, the American holing a big putt for a two at the fifth after falling behind to a par at the third, which he three-putted. Both were out in 34 and birdies were exchanged at the 10th and 11th, first Woosnam being conceded a tiny putt for a two and then Beck responding with an eight-footer at the next.

Beck went out of bounds with his second to the 12th, and also made a bad slip at the 13th. Having hit a wonderful second shot with a five iron over the trees to three feet, he missed the putt which would have brought him back to even for the third time. It was over the last three holes of the morning round that Beck began to lose his touch. Woosnam holed from 25 feet for a birdie at the 16th, chipped close to the 17th and then went 3-up at the 18th with two fine shots to the green whereas Beck, who bunkered his second shot, could not get up and down in two more.

Even so, Beck won the first two holes of the afternoon, each in birdies, although it was not long before Woosnam reasserted himself with a putt of 14 feet for a two at the fifth. It was after that that Beck completely lost his touch on the greens. He took three putts at both the seventh and ninth to go 4-down, checked his downward spiral by winning back the 10th with a birdie and the 11th with a par, where it was Woosnam's turn to three-putt.

Beck had a putt of 20 feet or so at the par-five 12th while Woosnam was bunkered beside the green. Not only did the American miss it, but he missed the one back as well, Woosnam having meanwhile come out of the sand to eight feet, from where he holed out for his four. It was a classic case of the two-hole swing. Three up again, Woosnam was soon to take the 14th, where yet again Beck three-putted, and with the American bunkered by the green at the 15th and unable to salvage his four, he conceded Woosnam's very holeable putt for the three he did not need.

"I can't remember a day when I putted so badly," Beck said later. "It was like cutting your wrists." Woosnam has had days like that, too. But not this week, and 24 hours later he was champion again.

9. The U.S. Tour

Who won the most tournaments on the United States PGA Tour in 1990? If you said Wayne Levi, it shows you've been paying attention. If you didn't, consider yourself among the countless number of people who probably failed the test. And if you asked, "Who is Wayne Levi?" Well, that's understandable, too.

Levi joined the PGA Tour in 1977 and scored his first victory with Bob Mann in the National Team tournament in 1978. Levi has been a steady player ever since, although he has not devoted all of his time to the Tour. He preferred to allot time to his growing family—three daughters, one son—instead of chasing glory and money. Nevertheless, he won tournaments every year from 1979 through 1985, with the exception of 1981, and had his best year in 1989, when he placed 16th in money winnings with $499,292. But hardly anyone knew he was out there. The trouble was Levi failed to win one of the four majors, and rarely was in contention. Mike Donald got more notice from losing to Hale Irwin in a playoff for the 1990 U.S. Open than Levi did from winning four tournaments.

However, it must be admitted that Levi had a great year. He won the BellSouth Atlanta Classic, Centel Western Open, Greater Hartford Open and Canadian Open and placed second in money winnings with $1,024,647 behind Greg Norman's $1,165,477. The only players who have won as many as four American tournaments in a year since Tom Watson won six in 1980 are Craig Stadler (1982), Calvin Peete (1982), Bob Tway (1986) and Curtis Strange (1988).

Strange had an off year. The leading tournament winner for the preceding five years with 13 victories, Strange failed to win for the first time since 1982. He plunged from seventh to 53rd in money winnings with $277,172. He didn't have a finish in the top three of any tournament. Strange's best showing came in an unofficial event in Pittsburgh, which he won while nursing an aching back. A number of theories have been discussed as reasons for Strange's poor year, the most prominent being his concentration on winning a third straight U.S. Open. When he failed at Medinah, the disappointment was long-felt. But Strange was still only 35 years old, his prime far from over.

The Player of the Year? Nick Faldo by the PGA's point system, even though he played a limited schedule in the United States. Faldo won the Masters for the second consecutive year in a playoff—this time with Raymond Floyd—and won the British Open for the second time in four years. He competed in only seven U.S. events, yet placed 37th with $345,262. But he spent most of his time on the European Tour.

Another overseas player who made a big impression on the U.S. Tour was Jose Maria Olazabal of Spain. Olazabal came out of the shadow of Seve Ballesteros with an astounding performance in the World Series of Golf. Olazabal broke a number of records at Firestone Country Club in Akron, Ohio, with a nine-under-par 61 in the first round and an 18-under-par 262 total for 72 holes and a 12-stroke victory, the most decisive of the year.

Olazabal played in one more U.S. tournament than Faldo and placed a notch behind him with $337,837.

It was a year for foreign-born players and aging stars. In addition to Faldo and Olazabal, Norman (Australia) led the money winners with $1,165,477—second only to the $1,395,278 Tom Kite won in 1989—and captured the Vardon Trophy with his scoring average of 69.10 and Wayne Grady, another Australian, won the PGA Championship. The money championship was the second for Norman; he led with $653,296 in 1986. Norman won twice—the Doral Ryder Open and the rain-shortened Memorial Tournament—and placed second twice. He was also the victim in several notable moments, the most amazing one Robert Gamez's eagle at the final hole of The Nestle Invitational at Arnold Palmer's Bay Hill Club in Orlando, Florida.

That was the second victory of the year for Gamez and cemented his position as rookie of the year. Gamez earned his Tour card by placing 42nd in the qualifying tournament and won the first event he entered, the Northern Telecom Tucson Open at the TPC at StarPass, where he had played many of his college matches for the University of Arizona. In his first year on the Tour, Gamez won more than $461,000 and marked himself as a possible star of the future.

The Tour is undergoing a number of changes, some spawned by the controversy surrounding the PGA Championship at Shoal Creek Country Club in Birmingham, Alabama, others by economic conditions. But some things change slowly, such as the leading money winners. Norman went from fourth in 1989 to first in 1990, Payne Stewart from second to third and Paul Azinger from third to fourth. The biggest jump was John Cook from 172nd to 28th.

Irwin's victory in the U.S. Open moved him from 93rd to sixth and was one of four triumphs by the 40-and-over set. Gil Morgan, 43, won the Kemper Open; Lanny Wadkins, 40, won the Anheuser-Busch Classic, and Tom Kite, 40, placed first in the Federal Express St. Jude Classic. Floyd, 47, nearly made it five until he was overtaken by Faldo in the Masters. But Floyd did win an unofficial tournament at the end of the year, the RMCC Invitational in partnership with Fred Couples.

MONY Tournament of Champions—$750,000
Winner: Paul Azinger

Paul Azinger was constantly in contention but won only one tournament, the Greater Hartford Open, in 1989. His performance left him asking himself, "Why didn't I win more? It was probably impatience. I got irritated a couple times." Patience and a little luck helped Azinger win the first PGA Tour event of 1990, the MONY Tournament of Champions.

A six-under-par 66 tied Azinger with Baker-Finch and Greg Norman for the first-round lead. Baker-Finch outshot Azinger, 67-68, in the second round to take a one-stroke lead as Norman slipped behind with a 72. Azinger moved into a two-stroke lead over Baker-Finch with a 69 on his 30th birthday as Baker-Finch turned in a 72. Mark Calcavecchia was another stroke behind Baker-Finch and Mark O'Meara was another stroke behind him. The tournament had just begun.

After starting the final round with a bogey, Azinger appeared headed for at least another bogey when his attempt to reach the par-five second hole in two ran across the green toward a lake beyond it. The ball hit a rake and stopped short of the water. Azinger parred with a seven-foot putt. He struggled for a par at the third hole, and after he hit his tee shot into the rough at the fourth, he asked his caddy for advice. Azinger slowed down his swing and played well the rest of the way.

After a warning for slow play, Baker-Finch rushed his second shot at the fifth hole and hit into a pond, costing him a double bogey. But he birdied seven of the next 11 holes. Baker-Finch finally caught Azinger with a 12-foot birdie putt at the 15th hole. Still tied with one hole left, Baker-Finch hit his tee shot into a fairway bunker at No. 18. He laid up short of the green as Azinger put his second shot 18 feet from the hole. Baker-Finch's chip ran 20 feet past the hole and he missed his par putt. Azinger had no difficulty two-putting for the victory.

Northern Telecom Tucson Open—$900,000
Winner: Robert Gamez

Every so often a golfer comes along who makes a sudden impression on the PGA Tour. Some go on to greatness or near greatness; others burn out. In what category Robert Gamez belongs may be left to history, but he had an impressive victory in the Northern Telecom Tucson Open. Gamez, 21, became the first to win a tournament in his PGA Tour debut since Ben Crenshaw began his career with a victory in the San Antonio Open in 1973. Gamez did it impressively, winning by four strokes over Mark Calcavecchia and Jay Haas with an 18-under-par 270 total.

Gamez was an All-America at the University of Arizona who had placed 42nd in the PGA Tour qualifying tournament in 1989. It helped that his home course in college was the TPC at StarPass, one of two courses used in the Tucson Open. The other was Randolph Park North, an easier public course. The familiarity with the course and the cheers of his college teammates served as inspiration. In the second round, he shot a 66 at StarPass, his best ever from the back tees. That round got him back in contention at 131, a stroke behind David Frost and Jay Haas.

Pat McGowan opened the tournament with a 62 at Randolph Park, but he failed to break par in the next three rounds. Haas started 66-64. Frost followed a 70 with a 12-under 60, one shot off Al Geiberger's PGA Tour record. It was the eighth 60 in Tour history, the first since Sam Snead's at Dallas in 1957, and it included a bogey. Frost started the round on the back nine and began making almost everything after parring his first two holes. Included in his round were eagles at No. 13 and No. 3. He used only 22 putts.

Paired with the leaders on the third round of his first pro tournament, Gamez shot a 69, aided by a 60-foot bunker shot at the seventh hole and a 15-foot eagle putt at No. 8, and took the lead as Frost shot a 71 and Haas a 72. Gamez was 16 under par, and Haas and Frost were the only ones within five strokes of him.

Gamez had won a number of big tournaments in college and he was on a familiar course. He never let anybody get close in the final round. The decisive holes were Nos. 6 and 7. He sank a three-footer to go 18 under par at No. 6. After a 15-minute wait on the tee—the last two rounds each took five hours to play—he hit a six iron to within 10 feet of a difficult pin position at No. 7. Haas and Frost, both desperate for birdies, gambled and lost, and Gamez widened the margin by sinking his birdie putt. He went to 20 under par with a birdie at No. 10 and the chase was over. He was even afforded the luxury of a three-putt double bogey at the final hole.

Bob Hope Chrysler Classic—$1,000,000
Winner: Peter Jacobsen

Peter Jacobsen had a reputation for impersonating winners rather than being a winner. He ruptured a disc in his lower back in 1985 and the rehabilitation, coupled with some heart-breaking defeats—two in the Western Open—had extended his victory drought since 1984. Jacobsen had, however, won the unofficial Kapalua International late in 1989. His famine in official events would end in the Bob Hope Chrysler Classic, a five-day, 90-hole tournament over four courses.

John Cook, Don Pooley, Fred Funk and Dave Stockton tied for the first-round lead with 65s. Cook and Stockton came back with 68s and Jacobsen, with 67-66, tied them. Cook and Funk failed to survive the 72-hole cut; Stockton tied for second-last among those who played 90 holes. Pooley took over the lead by himself at 201 with a 66 in the third round and Jacobsen, with a 69, and Steve Elkington, with a 65, were one stroke behind.

Jacobsen planned his strategy: "Get a bunch under par" at Bermuda Dunes in the fourth round, then "Go back to a more conservative style of play" in the final round at the Palmer course of PGA West. His planning worked to perfection. A 66 at Bermuda Dunes gave him a 20-under-par 268 for 72 holes and a two-stroke lead over Mike Reid, who had lurked near the lead every round. Reid plunged to a 77 and was not a factor in the final round.

Jacobsen's opposition came from Scott Simpson, Brian Tennyson, Tim Simpson, Tom Kite and Ted Schulz. Kite birdied No. 18 for a 69 that tied him at 341 with Tim Simpson and Schulz.

No. 18 is 520 yards with a lake on the left. A good drive made it reachable in two, setting up the possibility that the tournament could be won by a birdie or an eagle. Tennyson birdied Nos. 14, 15 and 16 to get to 20 under par and tied for the lead with Jacobsen. A birdie at No. 18 seemed likely, even after his second shot found a bunker 25 yards short of the green.

Tennyson's blast caught the edge of the cup and spun four feet away. The birdie putt missed, giving Tennyson a 66 and a tie at 340 with Scott Simpson, who birdied the hole.

So long as he didn't hit a big hook off the tee at the 18th hole, it figured that Jacobsen would birdie the hole and break out of the tie with Tennyson and Simpson. Jacobsen took out some of the suspense with a 290-yard drive, then reached the green, 30 feet from the hole, with a three iron. He knocked his first putt close enough to ensure the birdie.

Phoenix Open—$900,000
Winner: Tommy Armour III

At age 30, Tommy Armour had a prominent name in golf and years of experience. He inherited the name from a grandfather whom he hardly remembers—the Hall of Famer died when he was nine—and his experience came from tournaments outside the United States. The name has helped to open doors, he admits, but it probably was the experience he earned on the European and Asian tours that helped him score his first PGA Tour victory in the Phoenix Open.

Armour shared the first-round lead with three others, then led by himself the rest of the way as he won by five strokes over Jim Thorpe with a 17-under-par 267.

Armour got his Tour card for the first time in 1981 and lost it after one year. He failed on four attempts to win it back. Between qualifying tournaments, he tried to make a living on the overseas tours. He qualified again in the fall of 1987 and his game seemed to come together. The $162,000 he earned for winning at Phoenix was about $23,000 less than he collected in all of 1989.

It seemed surprising that victory would come so easily for someone who had struggled for so long. But no one gave him a hard time at Phoenix. After his opening 65, he shot a 67 that left him one stroke ahead of Tom Purtzer, then he matched that score on Saturday for a 199 total that left him three strokes ahead of Brian Tennyson. "I told my caddy Saturday afternoon I'd win the tournament with my driver," Armour said.

Armour hit his driver with unerring accuracy in the final round, missing only one fairway. He went out in 31 in the final round, much to the dismay of Thorpe. "I got to the turn at four under and hadn't gained a shot," Thorpe said. "It was pretty much a case of holding on to what I had then."

Armour bogeyed the 17th hole, but it didn't mean a thing. It was only his third bogey of the week and by then the only question was whether Thorpe could hold onto second place. He did, by two strokes over Billy Ray Brown and Fred Couples. The latter played the final 54 holes in 14 under par after an opening 75.

AT&T Pebble Beach National Pro-Am—$1,000,000
Winner: Mark O'Meara

Mark O'Meara has had a love affair with the Monterey Peninsula ever since he attended Long Beach State. O'Meara's two-stroke victory in the AT&T Pebble Beach National Pro-Am was his third in the tournament and his second in succession. This triumph had an extra sweet touch. His father, Bob, was his partner in the pro-am, and was able to walk every step of the way. Bob said the thrill got to him on the 16th hole of the final round. "I told my caddy, 'It can't be true. This has got to be a dream. This can't be happening. I'm out here playing with my son.'"

O'Meara finished with an even-par 72 for a seven-under-par 281, two strokes ahead of Kenny Perry. For two rounds, O'Meara marked time although his opening 67 left him only a stroke behind Payne Stewart. A 73 in the second round dropped him three strokes behind Stewart, Rocco Mediate and Bob Gilder, and the best was yet to come. O'Meara might have been a part of the deadlock except for a drive out of bounds at Pebble Beach's 15th hole that cost him a triple bogey. He followed that with a birdie as if to show he hadn't lost his grip.

Then came Saturday and with it the weather that made the tournament famous. The wind blew at a steady 40 miles an hour. It elicited many horror stories. "When it's bad weather here, you want to be at Cypress or Spyglass," said Gilder. Gilder played Cypress Point and shot an 85 that caused him to miss the cut by a stroke. Bernhard Langer, three under par after 36 holes, shot an 83 and missed the cut; Jim Thorpe, in contention at six under, fell out with an 83; Lon Hinkle took a 13 at the 17th hole at Cypress Point; Ed Dougherty took a 14 at one hole after eleven-putting. Mediate played the last four holes at Cypress Point in three over par, sinking a 25-foot putt for par at the 15th, and called them "the hardest four holes I've ever played." At the 17th hole, the wind blew him off balance and he topped his ball. From 107 yards, he hit a low five iron that stopped pin high and watched in astonishment as the wind blew his ball into the cup for a bogey-five. Mediate managed a 73 that left him only a stroke behind O'Meara.

The wind-blown third round won it for O'Meara. While almost everyone else was struggling just to keep from getting blown over, O'Meara was shooting a 69, and moving into the lead. It was a position from which he was not to be moved, although Stewart gave it a try. Stewart opened the round with a bogey, then birdied five of the next eight holes, his birdie at No. 9 tying O'Meara for the lead. O'Meara went a stroke ahead with a birdie at No. 11 with a seven iron to within five feet, then watched from the 12th tee as Stewart bogeyed the hole in front of him, giving O'Meara a two-stroke lead. Stewart never recovered, limping in with a 40 for a 73 that tied him for third place with Tom Kite.

It wouldn't be complete to write a report about Pebble Beach without mentioning the exploits of actor Jack Lemmon, who had failed to make the cut in 26 previous Pebble Beach Pro-Ams. His streak went to 27. He and partner Peter Jacobsen missed the cut by eight strokes.

Hawaiian Open—$1,000,000
Winner: David Ishii

Every PGA Tour professional wants to win in his home town, a dream that seldom comes true. It came true for David Ishii in the Hawaiian Open at Waialae Country Club in Honolulu. Ishii won by one stroke with a nine-under-par 279, the tournament's highest winning score since 1967 and the third highest in its history.

Paul Azinger, Craig Stadler, Clark Dennis and Hubert Green had their chances before Ishii won his first Tour event with a somewhat routine par-72 in the final round. Azinger placed second, a stroke behind; Stadler and Dennis tied with Jodie Mudd for third place, another stroke back.

"I thought about winning the Hawaiian Open for a long time. I can't believe it's true," said Ishii, who plays Waialae often on breaks from the Japanese Tour. He had won nine times in Japan and was their leading money winner in 1987, but the 67 he shot in the second round of the Hawaiian Open was his best round ever on the course.

Azinger took advantage of the par fives to birdie two and eagle one for an opening 68 that tied him for the lead with Mike Smith. Wind is usually a factor at Waialae, and it was a positive factor for Azinger. At the 18th, he reached the green with a five iron from 250 yards. Stadler bemoaned the way he played the par-fives in the second round even though he took the lead with a 67—138. Azinger, Ishii and Grant Waite trailed by one stroke. "I had a lot of chances out there," Stadler said, which could have been his lament after the 72nd hole.

Green eagled the 18th in the third round for a 66 on the heels of a 67 that gave him a one-stroke lead over Ishii, who had a 68. Azinger, with a 71, and Stadler, with a 72, were tied at 210, four strokes behind Green.

The trade winds were relatively calm for the final round, and it appeared Green couldn't handle the unexpected conditions. He hit two balls out of bounds, turning the lead over to Ishii at the ninth hole as Ishii birdied. Green never recovered, limping in with a 77, and Ishii never gave up the lead.

Dennis never got closer than one stroke en route to a 70. Azinger eagled the 18th with a 40-foot putt, then watched as Ishii made a necessary par to win with 279. The hole that secured the victory for Ishii was the par-three 17th, where he missed the green with his tee shot, then saved par.

Shearson Lehman Hutton Open—$900,000
Winner: Dan Forsman

The reason the PGA Tour opens the season in places such as California and Arizona is because of the supposedly mild weather. By the third round of the Shearson Lehman Hutton Open, in San Diego, it seemed that the tournament had been transported east. The third round was played in cold and windy weather, and the fourth round was played on a Torrey Pines course dampened by a morning rain that caused a 15-minute delay in play.

Dan Forsman won by two strokes over Tommy Armour by shooting even-par 72 on each of the last two rounds for a 13-under-par 275. The weather was a factor; the 18th at Torrey Pines is 499 yards, a par-five usually reachable in two shots. Armour needed a birdie to put pressure on Forsman, but was unable to go for the green in two because there was too much mud on his ball.

When the tournament began, even-par rounds cost players dearly. Bob Eastwood and Rick Fehr opened with 65s at the North course, which is nearly 400 yards shorter than the South, and Forsman was back in the pack with a 68. Forsman shot a 63 on the North course in the second round, a score that was almost overlooked. Mark Brooks, who opened with a 75 at the South course, turned in a tournament-record 61 at the North, twice stringing together three birdies and going birdie-eagle-birdie at the 13th, 14th and 15th holes. Eastwood moved in front with a 65 on the South course for a tournament-record 130 for 36 holes for a one-stroke lead over Forsman.

Then the weather turned nasty, and many couldn't handle it. Eastwood shot 76-76 the final two rounds; Brooks followed his 61 with a 75, and Armour shot a 73. Forsman shot a 72 and took first place at 203, two strokes ahead of Armour. Only two rounds under 70 were turned in Saturday, the best a 67 by Mark O'Meara, who had won under blustery conditions at Pebble Beach the week before. The round moved O'Meara to within four strokes of the lead.

The final round was almost anticlimactic. The best rounds came from those out of contention; those in contention managed only par or so. The play was so slow—playing in threesomes, it took five hours, 15 minutes for a round—and that might have contributed to the lack of excitement. It also nearly contributed to the excitement. Forsman was warned about playing slow at the 13th hole and played the remainder of the round under the threat of a penalty. "I just had to get to No. 18 on guts and determination," he said.

Nissan Los Angeles Open—$1,000,000
Winner: Fred Couples

After almost three years without a victory, Fred Couples brought his game together to win the Nissan Los Angeles Open at Riviera Country Club, aided in part by his own play and partly because this time others had the bad luck. Couples shot a course record-tying nine-under-par 62 in the third round and rode that to a three-stroke victory over Gil Morgan with a 266 total.

Michael Allen, a 31-year-old Tour rookie who won the Scottish Open in 1989, led through the first 36 holes with 63-68, but failed to break par on the last two rounds. Rocco Mediate, with 65-67, was a stroke behind after 36 holes and Couples trailed by four. Morgan (67-67) was three behind.

Peter Jacobsen shot a 66 and tied for third place with Mediate at 270, but Sunday was mostly a three-man race involving Couples, Morgan and Mediate. Morgan kept coming up with birdie putts, but couldn't make them. Couples kept hitting irons with unerring accuracy. After he set a tournament 54-hole record of 197 with his 62, Couples said, "Every time I looked up, the ball was going in the hole."

It didn't go in as often on Sunday, and eventually Morgan caught him. But at the 13th hole, Morgan tried to draw a drive around the trees, hit a tree and went out of bounds. The penalty put Morgan two strokes behind. Two holes later, Mediate hit a small tree while trying to come out of the rough and he, too, fell two strokes behind Couples.

At the par-three 16th, Couples sank a 10-foot putt for birdie, building his lead to three strokes. At the 18th hole, he curled in another birdie putt for good measure.

Doral Ryder Open—$1,400,000
Winner: Greg Norman

Greg Norman has been the victim of some of the most spectacular shots in golf history, but Norman came up with one of those breaks in the Doral Ryder Open, winning a four-man playoff on the first hole with a chip-in for an eagle. But that was merely the final act. The acts preceding it were just as amazing.

First Norman had to come from seven strokes behind to have a chance for a playoff. He did that with a 10-under-par 62 over Doral's Blue Monster that set tournament and course records. Then he had to wait for Paul Azinger and Calcavecchia to falter. And after his chip-in eagle, Norman had to wait out an eagle attempt by Tim Simpson that threatened to prolong the playoff.

It was Norman's second victory in eight playoffs on the U.S. Tour. "I don't live in the past," he said. "I just keep working and believing in my ability."

That belief was tested in the first three rounds. An opening 68 left him three strokes behind Jim Gallagher and a 73 left him seven strokes behind Azinger and Fred Couples after 36 holes. Azinger and Couples both shot 70 in the third round, and so did Norman, leaving him seemingly playing for only a high finish.

Norman has become known for low scores in final rounds, and this was one of his best. "Why do I do it on Sundays? I don't know. Maybe it's the challenge of coming back," he said.

Between Norman and Azinger and Couples were Mike Reid, Tom Purtzer, Bob Tway and Simpson as the final round began. Norman reached the par-five No. 1 hole in two with a one iron and two-putted for birdie. At the eighth hole, he sank a 93-yard wedge shot for an eagle. He went out in six-under-par 30 and the chase was on. He birdied Nos. 12, 14, 15 and 17, but it looked like he still needed a birdie at the final hole to even make a playoff. His approach at the difficult par-four hole missed the green to the left and he chipped 30 feet past the hole. He saved par and the wait was on.

Couples was the first of the contenders to exit. He took the lead with a birdie at the first hole, but he drove into a lake at the third hole, bogeyed the fourth, three-putted the 12th and lost his steam. It came down to Azinger, Calcavecchia and Simpson. Simpson got into contention with a 66 on Saturday and was to shoot another 66 on Sunday with birdies on three of the last five holes, capped by a 12-footer at the final green.

Calcavecchia hit a poor drive at No. 17, but salvaged par. He was not so lucky at No. 18. He sliced his tee shot into the trees, caught a limb coming out and eventually two-putted for bogey and a 65 for 273. That left Azinger one shot ahead as he teed off at No. 18. After a drive in the rough, Azinger attempted to reach the green with a six iron, to set up a winning par. His shot stopped in front of the green, about 30 feet from the hole. He chipped six feet past, giving himself a makeable putt for par. The putt broke off at the last moment, and his 69 made him join the crowd at 273.

At the first hole of the playoff, a 514-yard par-five, Simpson hit a two iron that rolled to the back fringe, Azinger hit a three iron to within 30 feet of the hole, Norman smacked a four iron that rolled off the back fringe, about 30 feet from the hole, and Calcavecchia hit a four iron to within 28 feet of the hole. Azinger left his eagle putt two feet short, and Calcavecchia got six inches closer. It looked as if all four might make birdies. Norman's caddy, Bruce Edwards, said to him, "Chip it in; you're due," and Norman did just that. Simpson still had a shot from the fringe to continue the playoff, and instead of chipping he decided to putt. The ball hit the rim of the cup and stayed out. "I hit a great putt and it didn't go in," he said.

Norman had eight birdies and two eagles in the final 19 holes. Simpson called Norman's eagle in the playoff a "one in one thousand shot," but Norman had an answer for that, "I've seen one in a thousands happen."

Honda Classic—$1,000,000
Winner: John Huston

Before he hit his first shot in the Honda Classic, John Huston had to plunk down $160 for a new pair of golf shoes, which can be a considerable expense for a young man who has won only $3,900 going into the 10th tournament of the year. The $180,000 he earned for winning his first PGA Tour event in his third year on the circuit made the outlay and aggravation worthwhile.

For nearly two years, almost from the time he joined the Tour, Huston had worn Weight-Rite golf shoes, which have weighted wedges on the outside edge. The company says they provide better balance. The day before the Honda Classic, the United States Golf Association said the shoes do not conform to the rules of golf.

Huston bought a conforming pair in the pro shop, then went on to prove it is the man, not his apparel, that makes the difference. Huston opened with a four-under-par 68—the only round under 70 on a day when the course was raked by high winds—and won by two strokes over Mark Calcavecchia with a six-under-par 282. The outcome was in doubt until the last two holes.

Joel Edwards, with 71-69, took over the lead by one stroke over Huston, who had a 73 in the second round, after 36 holes. Huston regained his lead with a 70 in the third round, putting him one ahead of Mark Brooks, who had a steady 71-71-70. Edwards dropped out of contention with a 77 and Calcavecchia, who had a 76 in the second round, bounced back into contention, four behind Huston, with a 69.

Huston began the final round by hitting his approach to within one foot of the hole at the first green, and from there he kept building on his advantage, at one time getting his lead to five strokes, as he played the first 10 holes masterfully. Tom Watson and Raymond Floyd made threatening gestures, but their threats died amid the waters of Eagle Trace.

Then Huston's only hurdle was Calcavecchia, who moved to within one shot of him with birdies at the 10th, 11th, 14th and 15th holes. Huston helped keep it close by missing an eight-foot birdie putt at the 15th hole, a par-five rated a birdie hole. Calcavecchia was playing directly in front of Huston, so Huston was able to keep an eye on him. He saw Calcavecchia miss a three-foot par putt at No. 16. Moments later, Huston sank a 12-foot putt for par at the same hole and said, "That was a big putt." Indeed. At No. 17, Huston three-putted for a bogey, trimming his lead to one stroke.

Calcavecchia figured he had to birdie the last hole to have a chance and, with 180 yards to the green, he hit a seven iron over it. As he surveyed his chip shot, he noticed Huston's drive in the middle of the fairway, setting up an almost certain par. "I thought I had to chip in," said Calcavecchia, whose attempt rolled three feet past. Then he missed the putt and a relieved Huston won with a routine par.

The Players Championship—$1,500,000
Winner: Jodie Mudd

You knew there were many who were not contenders in The Players Championship because they don't like the TPC at Sawgrass and its devilish island 17th green. A number joined them when they found the greens below the standard that might be expected. Poor conditions can put a struggling player in a poor frame of mind.

Many found reasons why Jodie Mudd won. Mudd, a 29-year-old with two victories in his first eight years on the Tour, was raised on public courses, where greens can play like corrugated paper and it's difficult to distinguish the fairways from the rough. Mudd hasn't played many courses such as that in recent years, but he remembers how it was. And he put memory to good use to beat Mark Calcavecchia by one stroke with a 10-under-par 278 total.

The greens at Sawgrass had been ravaged by rains the previous fall and a freeze and snow around Christmas. Compounding the problem was that resort guests played as late as a week before the tournament. The greens were bumpy, many lacked grass and they spiked easily. Mudd agreed the first and second greens were bad, but said that maybe some players are spoiled. "I know what it's like to play under conditions that are bad. These guys play under great conditions every week," he said.

Mudd began the final day in the midst of his third round. A heavy rain Saturday afternoon stopped play with 48 players on the course, and they completed that round before starting the fourth round. One victim of the continuation was Tom Watson, who went from contender to also-ran with eights at the 16th and 17th holes. Mudd also suffered when his tee shot at the island 17th bounced over the green and into the water for a double bogey, cutting his lead to one stroke over Calcavecchia and Ken Green after 54 holes.

Mudd's putting kept him at the forefront all week, and he maintained his putting touch in the final round as Calcavecchia applied the pressure. Mudd used only 26 putts in his closing 69 and averaged 27.5 for the week. The green at the par-five second hole, the one so much maligned, proved friendly to Mudd. He eagled it in the third round and two-putted it for birdie in the final round. He sank a 10-footer for birdie at the third hole, 15-footers to save par at the sixth and seventh holes, and an eight-footer for birdie at No. 14.

Meanwhile, Calcavecchia birdied three of the first seven holes on the second nine, a four-footer at No. 15 and an 18-footer at No. 16 pulling him to within one stroke of Mudd. After Calcavecchia put his tee shot on the green at No. 17, he broke into a broad smile. "I was real nervous," Mudd said about his tee shot. He hit a gutsy shot that stopped 10 feet away from the cup. "I looked at him and said, 'Tell me you pushed that,'" said Calcavecchia. "He's good but he ain't that good." Mudd confessed, "I kind of pushed it a bit."

Mudd holed his putt for birdie, giving him a two-stroke lead over Calcavecchia with one hole remaining, a par-four bordered on the left by a lake. Mudd drove into the right rough, and had his approach to the green obstructed by a small tree. Calcavecchia, in an attempt for a birdie, walloped a long drive down the left side of the fairway. Mudd sliced a five iron around the tree and short of the green. Calcavecchia hit a nine iron 20 feet below the hole. After Mudd chipped to within 15 feet, Calcavecchia figured he had to sink his birdie putt to give him a chance for a playoff, but he missed and Mudd two-putted for a bogey.

Mudd and Calcavecchia had waged a battle all week. Mudd shot a 31 on the back nine for a 67 that tied him with Calcavecchia for the lead after 18 holes. With wind making conditions difficult, Hale Irwin took over the lead by one stroke over Mudd and Rocco Mediate in the second round with a 68 for 138. Mudd shot a 72 and Mediate a 67. Calcavecchia fell four strokes behind with a 75. The rain-interrupted third round ended with Mudd on top, as Calcavecchia pulled to within a stroke of him with a 68.

It was the third straight week Calcavecchia finished in second place, the fourth time in the season. One consolation: The $162,000 he earned from the second-largest purse on the schedule moved him into first place among the money winners with $551,040.

The Nestle Invitational—$900,000
Winner: Robert Gamez

In the third round of The Players Championship the week before, Robert Gamez was closing in on the leaders until he came to the island-green 17th hole. Then he hit four balls into the water and took an 11. "He could've won if not for that 11," said his brother, Randy, who caddied for him. "That deflated him. After that, he went down like the Titanic. But I knew after last week he was ready to win again."

Gamez, 21, had won at Tucson in his debut on the PGA Tour. And his brother was right, he was ready to win again in The Nestle Invitational at Arnold Palmer's Bay Hill Club in Orlando, Florida. He had to pull off one of golf's more dramatic shots of the year to do it, sinking a 176-yard seven-iron approach for an eagle-two at the 441-yard 18th hole, ranked as the toughest hole on the Tour in 1989.

Larry Mize had birdied the par-three 17th and Greg Norman two-putted the par-five 16th for a birdie to tie them for the lead, a stroke ahead of Gamez, who was paired with Mize. Mize hit his approach at No. 18 and the spectators around the green cheered, even though it went into a bunker. Gamez thought he needed a birdie, to get to 13 under par, to have a chance at a playoff. "I had a six iron in my hand and after Larry hit, everybody was cheering and I was pumped up, so I pulled out a seven iron. I hit it flush. It just went in. I was relieved I didn't have to putt." Gamez's ball took one bounce, then hopped sideways into the hole for an eagle two. "I went nuts," Randy said.

"I knew exactly what happened. A roar like that, you know somebody holed out," said Norman. He needed a birdie on one of the last two holes to tie, but he was thinking birdie-birdie. At No. 17, his five-iron shot stopped 12 feet from the hole and his birdie putt shaved the left side of the hole. At No. 18, he hit a six iron to within 18 feet, but missed the putt. Gamez had finished with a 66, Norman a 68 that left him at 275, one stroke behind. "What can you say? A guy holes a shot, God bless him," Norman said. Mize failed to get his bunker shot close and bogeyed, placing third at 276.

Tom Byrum ran off a superlative 64 in the first round, but wasn't excited about it. "The first-round leaders are usually down the line on Sunday," he said. Byrum was down on Friday after an 81. Scott Hoch, who withdrew the previous week because of tendinitis in his left hand, took the lead after 36 holes with 69-68. Jay Don Blake was one stroke behind, but was rushed to a hospital before the third round began to undergo an emergency appendectomy. Norman shot a 65, Curtis Strange a 68 and Hoch a 70 to tie for the third-round lead at 207. Gamez, improving every day, was at 208 along with Mize, Craig Parry and Fulton Allem, who had a 65.

Gamez tied for the lead with an eagle at the sixth hole and a birdie at the seventh in the final round. Mize went two strokes ahead with birdies at the eighth, ninth and 10th holes, then took a double bogey at No. 11 with a ball in the water. Gamez took the lead with a birdie at No. 11. Strange dropped out of the picture with a double bogey at the eighth hole, and Paul Azinger moved in with birdies at the 13th and 14th holes. After Azinger bogeyed the 16th hole and Hoch bogeyed the 14th, there were only three players left, and Gamez disposed of the others with his miraculous shot at No. 18.

Independent Insurance Agent Open—$1,000,000
Winner: Tony Sills

It's possible that if the Independent Insurance Agents Open had gone the scheduled 72 holes, Tony Sills might not have won it. But don't bet on it. After years of overcoming disappointments and physical problems, Sills is not the type to give up, even in the face of Seve Ballesteros, Gil Morgan, Larry Mize and Scott Simpson.

Rain interrupted play Thursday and Friday and caused the tournament to be reduced to 54 holes. Sills trailed by six strokes after 36 holes and had a gang of players between him and co-leaders Hal Sutton and David Peoples. But Sills combined some magnificent play with a few breaks—at the seventh hole his approach somehow avoided going into the lake, and after flubbing a putt from the fringe he sank a 10-footer for par—for a seven-under-par 65 that tied him at 204 with Morgan, who turned in a 67.

"I know I was in the right place at the right time," Sills said after his first Tour victory. "There were a lot of good players clustered on the leaderboard, but nobody seemed to be able to get anything going down the stretch. You know, it's unusual to win at 12 under when the leaders start at 11 under."

P.H. Horgan III jumped off to a six-under 66 Thursday morning, but he had to wait until Friday night to learn if it would lead. Only half the field had completed their rounds when thunderstorms stopped play. Play resumed Friday morning, but rain intervened again two hours after the restart, halting play until 3:30 p.m. By then the only hope was to get the first round completed and reduce the tournament to 54 holes. Sills and Morgan were in a group at 67.

With the lift-and-clean rule in effect, par at the TPC course at The Woodlands in Houston, Texas, took a beating. Sills' even-par 72 was one of the higher scores of the day and dropped him six strokes behind. Hal Sutton, who hadn't won since the 1986 Memorial, shot an eight-under 64 and jumped into the lead with Peoples, who had 69, at 133. Sutton hit the pin twice with approach shots on the first four holes and finished with birdies at Nos. 14, 16 and 18 in what he called "my best putting round in a long time. My confidence is building." Peoples was medalist in the Tour qualifier at The Woodlands the previous winter and attributed familiarity with the course for his 67-66 start.

Sutton's confidence shattered amid a bogey-marked 74 in the final round. Peoples got to 12 under par, then bogeyed the par-five 15th with a ball out of bounds and added a bogey at No. 17 as he finished in an eight-man tie for third, one stroke behind Sills and Morgan. Ballesteros also got to 12 under, but he also bogeyed No. 17. So that left it to Sills and Morgan.

Morgan, playing steady golf, got to 12 under with a birdie at No. 17. Sills got hot on the back nine, birdieing Nos. 14, 15 and 16. On the first playoff hole, Sills hit his approach just over the back of the green. Morgan knocked his to within 45 feet of the hole. Using his putter, Sills hit his third shot to within 18 inches of the hole, a tap-in. Morgan rammed his six feet past and missed the comebacker.

Sills' triumph was another warm chapter on the Tour of a player overcoming adversity. Sills had a colostomy that reduced his weight to 100 pounds at one time and he had to compete numerous times in the qualifying tournament. His best previous finish was a tie for second in the 1986 Phoenix Open and the next year he lost his card. He had to requalify in 1988 and 1989. The $180,000 he won in the IIA was almost as much as he won ($216,881) in his best year, 1986.

Deposit Guaranty Classic—$300,000
Winner: Gene Sauers

With the cream of the Tour competing in the Masters, Gene Sauers was obviously the premier player in the Deposit Guaranty Classic, played the same weekend in Hattiesburg, Mississippi. Sauers proved it, even though he used new clubs that he said were too heavy. But Sauers might have been playing in Augusta, if not for a penchant for coming up with one bad round a week.

So Sauers went to Hattiesburg to break in some new clubs, a putter, driver and irons. He felt the driver was too heavy, so he had his wife send his old driver before the tournament began. The irons felt heavy, too, but he stuck with them and they helped him to avoid that one bad round as he shot a 12-under-par 67-65-68-68—268 and won by two strokes over an ecstatic Jack Ferenz. Ferenz had won his card back after losing it following the 1984 season and said the $32,400 he earned for second place, "was the biggest check I've ever earned. It takes a lot of money pressures off me."

Doug Weaver, with his wife Patricia carrying his bag, took the first round lead with a 64, then slipped out of the race with a 74 the second day. Lennie Clements, with 67-64, moved into first place at the halfway point, a stroke ahead of Sauers. Clements' 131 tied the tournament record for 36 holes; he finished 73-73. The cool, windy conditions thinned out the contenders in the fourth round as Sauers took a three-stroke lead over Ferenz (68 after a second-round 64) and Lance Ten Broeck (69). Nobody got closer than two strokes of Sauers in the final round.

MCI Heritage Classic—$1,000,000
Winner: Payne Stewart

Payne Stewart was zero-for-five in playoffs before the MCI Heritage Classic began, his most recent playoff loss coming at the hands of Tom Kite at this same Harbour Town Links on Hilton Head Island, South Carolina, in the Nabisco Championships six months earlier. But Harbour Town was becoming Stewart's favorite course.

When Stewart tied Larry Mize and Steve Jones at eight-under-par 276 after 72 holes, there was a good chance Stewart would win in extra holes. He had won the tournament the previous year, and then there was that playoff loss to Kite. This time Stewart was not to be denied. He birdied the first playoff hole, No. 17, with a one-foot putt. After Mize forced the playoff to another hole with a 10-foot birdie putt, Stewart wrapped it up with a 25-foot putt for birdie at No. 18 as Mize's attempt from 10 feet failed.

It was odd that Stewart had such success at Harbour Town—he won $594,000 in a 12-month period there—because at one time he had it on his "don't-return" list of tournaments. At the 1984 Heritage, the thin greens were top-dressed the morning of the final round, a move Stewart thought was unprofessional. He did not enter the tournament the next four years. He returned in 1989 only because the Nabisco tournament was scheduled there the following October. He also came back to a revitalized course, one with four rebuilt greens, a course that had been restored to its old grandeur by its new owners, the Sea Pines Homeowners Association.

The Heritage fell the week after the Masters and included the Masters champion, Nick Faldo, who did well for three rounds, trailing by only two strokes after 54 holes. Gene Sauers, who had won the Deposit Guaranty Classic, also came into the tournament on a high and carried it through the first round, as he tied Billy Ray Brown for the lead with a five-under 66. His letdown came as he shot 72-72 the next two rounds.

Calvin Peete, recovering from a back problem and a non-winner since 1986, showed some of his old ability in the first two rounds, missing only one fairway each day and tying Steve Pate for the lead at the halfway point at 136. Then Peete shot 72s in the last two rounds. "I'm trying to find a swing that will take me to the Senior Tour," he said.

Stewart, after shooting 70, 69 on the first two days, took over in the third round, jumping two strokes in front with a 66 for 205. Two strokes behind were Greg Norman, another former Heritage winner; Faldo and Jones. Norman moved into a tie for the lead in the final round with birdies at the fourth and fifth holes before stalling with a bogey at the eighth hole. It became a three-man battle among Stewart, Mize and Jones.

Mize went out in three-under 33 and caught Stewart with birdies at the 10th and 12th holes. He followed that outburst with a bogey at No. 13 and a double bogey at the par-three No. 14, and that seemed to signal his exit. But Mize wasn't finished. He birdied Nos. 15, 17 and 18 for a 66 and 276. Stewart was only able to match his total with pars as Jones threatened to overtake both of them. He birdied No. 16, hit a seven iron to within six inches for a tap-in birdie at No. 17, and had an eight-foot birdie putt at No. 18 that would have won. The putt broke off and Jones never got another chance, as he missed the green at the first playoff hole and quickly exited.

K-mart Greater Greensboro Open—$1,250,000
Winner: Steve Elkington

For three rounds of the K-mart Greater Greensboro Open, Australian Steve Elkington was like everyone else in the field, just trying to make pars. After a mild winter, Forest Oaks Country Club was in great condition, with swift greens and tenacious rough. The conditions were reflected in the scores. Only one player broke 70 in the first round, only three in the second round and just two the third day.

When Elkington shot a six-under-par 66 in the final round, it almost assured him of his first victory in his fourth year on the PGA Tour. The 66 enabled Elkington to come from seven strokes behind in the final round—to be more precise, from seven strokes behind with nine holes to play—and post a six-under-par 282. Mike Reid, Jeff Sluman, Fred Couples and Paul Azinger all took a crack at it without success. Reid, with a final 75, and Sluman, with a 71, tied for second place, two strokes behind Elkington.

The difficult course and wind combined to keep the scoring high in the first round, as only Lennie Clements, with a 69, broke 70. Clements faded to 74-75 in the middle rounds, but under conditions that didn't drop him very far behind, and a closing 69 let him tie for 10th place at 287.

Jim Gallagher shot a second consecutive 70 in the second round, giving him a one-stroke lead at the halfway point. Reid, one of the Tour's most accurate drivers—a necessity at Forest Oaks—turned in a 67 in the third round that gave him a three-stroke lead over Couples (71). Elkington, meanwhile, had moved along with 74-71-71.

Elkington went out in a one-under 35 in the final round, which didn't conjure up thoughts of a victory. He still trailed by seven strokes. Then he birdied Nos. 11, 12 and 13 with putts of 10, eight and six feet and "winning became more realistic." He made a 15-foot birdie putt at No. 17 and hit a nine iron to within six inches of the hole for a birdie at No. 18 to cap a back-nine 31 that gave him a 66, then waited to see if anyone would match or beat his total.

Couples faded first, staggered by a 38 on the front nine. Reid waded through a field of bogeys before birdieing the 15th hole and could do no more. Sluman pulled into a tie for the lead before bogeying two of the last four holes. The greatest threat proved to be Azinger. He had torn up the front nine and was torn up by the back nine for the first three rounds, and once again he was on a front-nine tear. Azinger came from nine strokes behind to grab a share of the lead after 11 holes, the comeback launched by a 30-foot putt for eagle at the second hole. Then the back nine caught him again. He played the last seven holes in three over par.

USF&G Classic—$1,000,000
Winner: David Frost

David Frost snatched victory out of the jaws of The Shark in the USF&G Classic at English Turn in New Orleans, Louisiana.

Greg Norman's charge began late in the third round. He sank a 25-foot chip shot to save par at the 15th hole after hitting his second shot into the water, then birdied the 17th and 18th holes. That 71 left Norman five strokes behind Frost and got his game in gear for the final round. After six holes on Sunday, Norman was tied for the lead with Frost and Russ Cochran, then took the lead by himself with a chip-in birdie from 35 feet at the eighth hole.

Norman dropped back into a tie for the lead with Cochran with a bogey at the ninth hole. He missed a 15-foot putt for par at the 14th hole and slipped two strokes behind Frost and Cochran. The 15th hole is a peninsula green, a 524-yard par-five that tempts the brave. Norman three-putted it the year before in a vain attempt to beat Tim Simpson. This time, he hit a five iron eight feet from the hole and his eagle putt was unerring. He hit a wedge almost into the hole at No. 16 and, when Cochran faded, only Norman and Frost were left.

Frost birdied No. 15 as Norman bogeyed No. 17, giving Frost the lead. Norman needed a birdie at the 18th hole, which had yielded only one birdie to the earlier players. Norman hit a spectacular two iron, the kind that is supposed to win tournaments, to within six inches of the hole. That put it to Frost—par for a tie, birdie for a win, bogey and lose.

Frost's tee shot caught a fairway bunker, dismissing his thoughts of going for the green. He aimed for a bunker to the left front of the green with a three iron and came up with a good lie, about 50 feet from the hole. "I just knew it would go in the hole," he said afterward about the bunker shot that did indeed go into the hole. Norman had shot a 65, but he was one short of the 69, and 276 total, by Frost.

A 65 seemed impossible early in the tournament. Wind kept the first-round scores high, with four players tying for the lead at 69. Gary Koch took the halfway lead with 70-67—137, but played most of his round after a two-hour rain suspension softened the course. Frost and Norman trailed by four strokes.

Frost, who had missed the cut in eight previous tournaments while trying out a new set of clubs following a 60 at Tucson, shot a 66 in the third round that gave him a one-stroke lead over Brian Tennyson and five over Norman and Cochran.

GTE Byron Nelson Classic—$1,000,000
Winner: Payne Stewart

Payne Stewart attended Southern Methodist University and used to make his home in Dallas, so he was overjoyed when he won the rain-abbreviated GTE Byron Nelson Classic at the TPC at Las Colinas. "Besides Bay Hill (1987), this is probably the most emotional win I've ever had," he said. "I really wanted to win in Dallas. To have a trophy with Byron Nelson's name on it..."

Stewart had come close in the past, but this tournament had become a jinx for him. He had placed among the top 10 in four of the previous six, and some of his losses had been bizarre.

This time only the weather was bizarre. A storm Tuesday night dropped four inches of rain on the course, and a storm Wednesday night added another four inches. The first round on Thursday was delayed as workers tried to make the course playable, then was called off and the tournament was shortened to 54 holes. There was enough daylight Sunday to play 36 holes, but the telecast was scheduled for 3 to 5 p.m., so much of the daylight went to waste.

Steve Lamontagne, a Tour rookie, emerged with the first-round lead at four-under-par 66, one stroke ahead of Stewart. Lamontagne disappeared in the second round with bogeys at the first four holes. Stewart, starting at the No. 10 tee, birdied the last four holes on the back nine and finished with a 68 for 135 and a two-stroke lead over four others. Lanny Wadkins, with a 65 that would earn him second place, put the heat on Stewart briefly, but Stewart responded by hitting a wedge to within two feet of the cup at the 11th hole and the birdie took the suspense out of the outcome.

Memorial Tournament—$1,000,000
Winner: Greg Norman

This isn't the way tournaments are supposed to end, with Greg Norman on the practice range, but that's the way it was at Muirfield Village Golf Club in Dublin, Ohio, as Norman collected his third victory of the year, and his second on the PGA Tour, in the Memorial Tournament.

Norman saved par from a buried lie in a bunker beside the 18th green Saturday, but never figured the 15-foot putt he sank would be the tournament winner. It turned out it was when the fourth round was canceled because of rain. Norman was on top with an even-par 216 total, while Payne Stewart, Fred Couples and Don Pooley mulled over what might have been.

The Memorial had been moved up two weeks to the second weekend in May, and the scheduling hardly could have been worse. Wind gusts of 40 miles an hour combined with temperatures near 50 degrees to give conditions a wintry feel. Muirfield Village can be difficult in good weather, never mind adding wind and numbing temperatures.

The conditions produced some bizarre scores and led to an exodus of players. Mark Calcavecchia shot an 88 and departed. Tim Simpson and Jeff Sluman picked up after nine holes. Ken Green and Larry Nelson had 82s, and Gene Sauers an 83 and they, too, left. Mark McCumber shot an 88, didn't sign his scorecard and was disqualified. Host Jack Nicklaus shot a 78 and said, "That's as good as I've ever struck it."

Amid this, Couples shot a three-under-par 69 that gave him a four-stroke lead and the admiration of the other survivors. Norman and Pooley were among seven tied at 73. Stewart shot a 74 despite eagling two of his first five holes.

The wind slacked off and the temperature rose Friday, and Couples managed a 74, which was nearly five strokes under the average of the first round. Pooley, who won here in 1987, shot a 71 and moved to within a stroke of the lead, one ahead of Jay Delsing, who had a 72. Norman and Stewart matched Couples' score and trailed by four and five strokes, respectively.

Saturday's weather took another turn for the worse. The temperature dropped and there was rain. Despite that, Stewart and Norman both shot 69s, a score matched by only two others. Stewart played nearly flawless golf, hitting 17 greens. Norman wasn't nearly as accurate, but scrambled well, especially at No. 18.

"At that time, Freddy was on No. 15 and was one under par and I figured he'd pick up a birdie or two," said Norman, who thought he was in contention only for a final run. "I saw Norman made the putt at No. 18, but I couldn't have cared less," Couples said. "Whether I came in with 71 or 78, I figured there's always Sunday." Couples bogeyed No. 16 after putting his tee shot into a bunker, and double-bogeyed No. 18 after he drove into a creek to the left of the fairway. The 75 dropped him into a four-man tie for third, two strokes behind Norman.

Tomorrow never came for Couples, Stewart and Pooley. The start of play was suspended until 11:15 a.m. because of rain. It was rescheduled for 1:15 p.m., only to be called off at 1:10 p.m., when the course became unplayable and would not recover in time to end the tournament that day. Norman learned he was the winner as he hit irons on the practice tee in the rain. "I don't know what to say," he said. "Yes, this is one back, but it doesn't work that way. I feel more sorry for Freddy. He's probably the one who feels the hardest done by the whole deal."

Southwestern Bell Colonial—$1,000,000
Winner: Ben Crenshaw

Ben Crenshaw had his putter working in the Southwestern Bell Colonial in Fort Worth, Texas, as he won the tournament for the second time. For a native Texan, what could be better than to win on the course Ben Hogan calls home?

Crenshaw won by three strokes over John Mahaffey, Corey Pavin and Nick Price with 69-65-72-66—272 total, eight under par. He finished with a flourish, making just about every putt inside 15 feet. "Nobody could have caught Ben today," Price said.

Russ Cochran was the first-round leader with a 65, and stayed in contention until the 13th hole of the third round. A 69 in the second round tied Cochran with Crenshaw for the lead. Crenshaw shot a 65, but he hit the ball only 63 times. At No. 12, the ball moved three inches after he soled his club, costing him a stroke. Then he hit a seven iron into a bunker near the green and holed a 50-foot blast for what he though was "the best par I ever made." Wrong. The PGA Tour staff informed him he had to add another penalty stroke because he hadn't replaced his ball to its original spot after it had moved.

Curtis Strange, with his third straight under-par round (69), moved into a tie for the lead with Crenshaw after 54 holes as Crenshaw shot a 72 in the windy conditions. Price, Cochran and Pavin trailed by one stroke. Strange began the final round with a birdie that gave him the lead, but three-putted the next two holes and watched the gang pass by. A birdie from 15 feet at the second hole gave Crenshaw the lead for good and, after he sank a 30-foot birdie putt at the ninth hole, his lead was up to three strokes over Pavin and Price. When they bogeyed No. 10, it went to four strokes.

Crenshaw hadn't won in more that two years and in that time he had turned in some poor final rounds. That was on his mind after he hit his approach into a buried lie in a bunker at the 12th hole. He blasted to within 12 feet and sank the par putt. "That was probably the most important putt

I made all week," he said. At the 17th hole, Crenshaw faded his drive into a cement drainage canal. "I can make anything from there. A six, seven, anything," he said. He hit a high fade over the trees to within 15 feet of the hole and two-putted for bogey. Price, his closest competitor, also bogeyed the hole, making the walk to the 18th green a victory march for Crenshaw.

BellSouth Atlanta Classic—$1,000,000
Winner: Wayne Levi

Wayne Levi has the distinction of being the first player to win on the PGA Tour playing a non-white ball. He won the 1982 Hawaiian Open while using an orange ball. When he won the BellSouth Atlanta Golf Classic he could have used one of those balls that light up for night play.

Levi won at Atlanta Country Club with a 42-inch birdie putt on the final green in the last rays of daylight, putting an end to a long day and avoiding a return later for one hole or so. Levi shot 72-66-68-69—275 and won by one stroke over Larry Mize, Keith Clearwater and Nick Price. Hours before Levi collected his first victory since 1985, it looked as if the $180,000 first prize would go to Clearwater.

Clearwater's 66 in the third round gave him a 54-hole score of 204 and a two-stroke lead over Levi, Mize and Price. He still led by that margin when play was halted by a thunderstorm at 12:05 p.m. As the storm passed, play was scheduled to resume at 3:45 p.m., but another storm at 3:30 delayed the restart. Play finally resumed at 6:05 p.m. with the possibility that the round might have to be completed on Monday. The last group of Mize, Clearwater and Levi had 11 holes to play.

Mize made birdies at the 10th, 11th, 12th and 14th holes to take a one-stroke lead, then dropped back into a tie with a bogey at No. 15. Levi made it a threesome with birdies at Nos. 14 and 15.

The leaders could have asked for play to be stopped because of darkness before they played their final two holes, but none wanted to return the next day, except for a possible playoff. All four had a chance to win or tie at the final green. Clearwater missed a birdie putt from 35 feet at the par-five hole, Mize hit his approach over the green and Price missed an eagle putt by a foot.

Levi could only see the flag on the green, but he knew he was 103 yards away on his second shot and he swung a wedge. "I knew I hit it perfect, but I couldn't see where it ended up because of the dark and fog," he said. "But I knew it was pretty good when I heard the gallery." There was just enough daylight to see his way to the hole from just over three feet, and victory.

The first three rounds were played in good weather and raised the possibility that maybe 20 under par, instead of 13 under, would win. Mize, Wayne Grady and Steve Lowery took the first-round lead with 66s and Mize took over with a 69 for 135 at the halfway point. Clearwater, improving by two strokes a day, fired a 66 in the third round for 204 and a two-stroke lead.

Kemper Open—$1,000,000
Winner: Gil Morgan

His victory in the Kemper Open at the TPC at Avenel in Potomac, Maryland, eased Gil Morgan's mind. "I let two get away this year, so I questioned my ability to win again," he said.

Morgan underwent rotator cuff surgery in September, 1986, a not uncommon operation for baseball players, but one that could spell the end for a pro golfer. He had won twice in 1983, but he hadn't won since.

He placed second in the Los Angeles Open and lost a playoff to Tony Sills in the Independent Insurance Agent Open. The third time was the charm in the Kemper Open, as Morgan won by one stroke over Ian Baker-Finch with a gutsy performance down the stretch.

Baker-Finch was a master from bunkers as he charged in with a five-under-par 66 for 275 about an hour before Morgan was to finish. Baker-Finch had finished with a bogey, so when Morgan teed off at No. 14 he was in a tie for the lead and knew he had to play the final five holes in one under par to win. His best bet for birdie, he thought, was No. 14, a short par-four. The birdie came instead at the 467-yard, par-four No. 15, where he sank a 15-foot putt.

He now had to hold the lead. At the par-three No. 17, he two-putted from 70 feet for par. Morgan's tee shot at the 18th hole left him with 187 yards to the green. He didn't want to be in the bunker left of the green, from where Baker-Finch had bogeyed earlier. The pin was cut in 15 feet from that side, making a recovery shot difficult. "I aimed about 20 feet to the right of the hole," said Morgan, who hit a cut shot that stopped off the right side of the green. It left him with a delicate 60-foot chip shot over a rise, but he hit it well, putting his ball four feet from the hole. This time he grabbed the opportunity, ending his seven-year drought.

Morgan, nearing 44 years of age, opened with a 68 that had him three strokes behind Ted Schulz and Pat McGowan. He came back with a 67 for a 36-hole 135 total that left him a stroke in front of Scott Hoch. Steve Jones, bidding for his first victory of the year after a three-win season in 1989, took a three-stroke lead over Morgan, Hoch, Joel Edwards and Clark Burroughs.

The big pickup for Jones was a hole-in-one at the ninth hole. Morgan matched Jones' birdie at the first hole Sunday. It was Jones' last hurrah. He bogeyed Nos. 5, 6 and 7 and double-bogeyed No. 9, as Baker-Finch and Hoch took over the lead. Hoch tripped and fell with a double bogey at the 12th hole, leaving Baker-Finch in the lead until Morgan eventually overtook him.

Centel Western Open—$1,000,000
Winner: Wayne Levi

With the likes of Payne Stewart, Tom Watson, Greg Norman and Paul Azinger chasing him into the final round of the Centel Western Open, Wayne Levi shot a three-under-par 69 at Butler National Golf Club, one of the more demanding courses on the PGA Tour, and won going away. By four strokes, to be exact. It was his second victory in three weeks and the 10th victory of his career.

Two weeks earlier, Levi won the BellSouth Atlanta Classic in virtual darkness with a birdie putt at the final green. At Butler, he shook off most of his pursuers with a four-under 32 on the front nine, then played even par as the others self-destructed. His 70-66-70-69—275 total tied the tournament record for Butler set by Mark McCumber a year earlier. Stewart took second place with a 279 total, and Peter Jacobsen came in with a 68 to tie Loren Roberts for third place at 280.

Levi's third-round 70 gave him a one-stroke lead over Stewart. "Guys were coming at me from the left and right," said Levi. Instead of playing for pars, as many leaders would do on a tough course, Levi went for birdies— and got them. He birdied four of the first six holes. After he chipped in for a birdie at No. 11, his margin was six strokes.

Tom Watson got life when he birdied the 15th hole as Levi took a double bogey at the 14th, pulling Watson within three strokes of the lead. Watson bogeyed after hitting bunkers at the 16th and 17th holes, and finished with a triple bogey at No. 18 after hitting two shots into the water.

The others went sooner than Watson. Stewart dropped out of contention with bogeys at the seventh, eighth and ninth holes, although he did rally to claim second with an eagle at No. 12 and a birdie at No. 17. Azinger took double bogeys at the fifth and seventh holes and Mark Brooks, who matched Levi's 32 on the front nine, played the final nine in 40. Jacobsen, six under for the day and in second place, double-bogeyed the 18th hole, giving Stewart second place to himself.

Another Stewart, Ray, took a three-stroke lead with a 65 in the first round, but failed to break par in the last three rounds. Payne Stewart started 68-67 to give him a one-stroke lead on Levi and Brooks after 36 holes. Levi and Payne Stewart exchanged positions as Levi shot a 70 and Stewart a 72 in the third round, as wind held the under-70 rounds to four.

Buick Classic—$1,000,000
Winner: Hale Irwin

Hale Irwin unveiled the Irwin Trot when he won the U.S. Open for the third time—a run around the 18th green, high-fiving the fans near the ropes and blowing kisses to those beyond. It was grand for a 45-year-old man savoring perhaps the greatest moment of his career. But the music didn't stop when he left Medinah. Irwin did an encore after he made a hole-in-one at No. 6 during the first round of the Buick Open at Westchester Country Club in Rye, New York, and he returned for a curtain call at the 72nd hole after he had won his second tournament in a row.

He was the first to win the week after winning the U.S. Open since Billy Casper did it in 1966. "These two weeks would at least tie with anything I've ever done," said Irwin. "Actually, three weeks. I was third at the Kemper Open (two weeks before the U.S. Open). I'm not surprised. I always felt, always believed, I could still play well."

Irwin pleaded fatigue when the tournament began, but his ace washed away much of that. He opened with a five-under-par 66 that tied him for second place, a stroke behind Kirk Triplett, who had qualified for the Tour six months earlier. Blaine McCallister followed a 66 with a 67 to take the lead, and Triplett slipped to a 74 that was to be the difference between winning and placing third. He followed with 67-66 and finished in third place, three stroke behind Irwin. Jay Haas birdied the last four holes and moved into second place, one stroke behind McCallister.

McCallister sank a 22-foot birdie putt at the final hole and Irwin finished bogey-bogey-birdie-birdie as they tied for the lead at 203 after 54 holes, three strokes ahead of six others, including Azinger.

Irwin played the front nine in four-under in the final round as McCallister bogeyed the third hole and double-bogeyed the fifth. That finished him, but Azinger was just getting started. Azinger got to within a stroke of Irwin by sinking a 15-foot birdie putt at the 15th hole. He needed another birdie and No. 18, a benevolent par-five, looked like the hole to get it. But Azinger drove into the rough near some trees and had to lay up on the second shot. He hit his approach to within eight feet, but the birdie putt failed to drop. Irwin went to No. 18 needing a par to win. Instead of laying up, he went for the green with a three wood and hit his ball to the back fringe. He two-putted for birdie and a 66 for 269, 15 under par.

After his run around the green, he said he wouldn't try to run his winning streak to three weeks in a row. He was too tired. "I'm going to step off the merry-go-round before I get dizzy."

Canon Greater Hartford Open—$1,000,000
Winner: Wayne Levi

"This is for everyone who thinks I can't play," said Wayne Levi, after he scampered past a fallen Mark Calcavecchia to win the Canon Greater Hartford Open for his third victory of the year.

Levi can play, he knows how to take advantage of other's mistakes, and he has confidence in himself. When he entered the final round one stroke out of the lead, he felt he was in good position to win. Ahead of him were Brad Fabel and Nolan Henke and immediately behind were such as Chris Perry, John Cook, Paul Trittler, Jim Booros, Loren Roberts and Steve Jones.

None could be viewed as imposing figures. "Those guys aren't particularly used to this," Levi said. He was correct. As the field averaged 69.08 the final round, the only ones among those to break par of 70 at the TPC of Connecticut course were Perry and Roberts. The real struggle came from a more noted player, Calcavecchia, who trailed Levi by two strokes going into the final round.

Levi birdied the first hole to gain a share of the lead and went one stroke in front with a birdie at the fourth hole. Fabel and Henke bogeyed themselves out of the chase in the middle of the back nine, but as the scores went down on the leaderboard, Levi noticed the red numbers behind the name of Calcavecchia, who made three birdies in a row on the back nine to take the lead. Calcavecchia drove the green on the 299-yard par-four 13th and two-putted for birdie. Levi bogeyed the par-three No. 11 and the gap between them was two strokes.

Then came the fateful No. 17. Calcavecchia's drive into the left rough stopped near a cart path, and he was given a free drop. Calcavecchia hit his next shot into the lake in front of the green, and walked off with a double bogey. He wouldn't talk about the shot later.

Levi had just birdied the 13th hole and was faced with a birdie putt of 13 feet at No. 14 when he learned about Calcavecchia's mistake. "I thought, 'If I make this putt, I've got it,'" Levi said. He made it, but he really didn't have it. Not until Calcavecchia played the 18th hole.

Calcavecchia made a strong bid to sink a 12-foot birdie putt at the final green and knocked it past the hole. Then he missed again. That gave some room to Levi, who had bogeyed the 16th hole. When he reached the 18th hole in two, he raised his arms, his victory assured.

Some of the lesser lights looked like genuine contenders in the early rounds. Perry opened with a seven-under-par 63 for a one-stroke lead over Jones, and Bob Eastwood followed a 67 with a 64 to take the 36-hole lead. Then Fabel and Henke, with 67s, grabbed a one-stroke lead over Levi, Cook and Perry after 54 holes. Levi had been in the position before. In 1987, Paul Azinger beat him with a great putt at the final hole and in 1989 Azinger did it again with a chip-in at the final hole. This time Azinger shot four consecutive 68s and Levi was able to take care of the other guys.

Westinghouse-Family House Invitational—$674,000
Winner: Curtis Strange

Curtis Strange's back hurt so much that he called sponsor Frank Fuhrer and told Fuhrer not to expect much if he played. Fuhrer said never mind what you shoot, come on. The Westinghouse-Family House Invitational is an unofficial tournament that raises money to house the families of patients with serious illnesses at Pittsburgh hospitals, and Strange was one of the biggest gate attractions.

So Strange strapped on a back brace and, of course, he won by two strokes with a 10-under-par 134, on rounds of 65 and 69 at St. Clair Country Club. His two-day ordeal earned him $125,000 from the $674,000 purse, the largest for a non-Tour event.

Strange said his back problem began shortly after the U.S. Open, when he reached down to pick up a ball on the putting green. He took a strange stance to read putts at St. Clair, but he read them well enough to shoot a course-record 65 in the first round, giving him a two-stroke lead on Mike Hulbert and Mike Donald.

David Frost was one who thought Strange might not be able to play nearly as well in the second round, but not just because of his back, but because, "He hasn't played in two weeks." Strange didn't play nearly as well, but the only one who gave him problems in the second round was Frost. Frost got to within a stroke of Strange with a birdie at the 17th hole, but he missed a birdie at the par-five finishing hole. Just for emphasis, Strange hit a nine iron to within seven feet of the hole and sank the birdie putt.

Anheuser-Busch Classic—$1,000,000
Winner: Lanny Wadkins

Natives of Virginia, Lanny Wadkins and Curtis Strange had never been paired together as professionals until the final round of the Anheuser-Busch Classic. The last time they had been paired was in the semifinals of the 1970 Virginia State Amateur, and Wadkins won that match.

When Scott Verplank missed a six-foot par putt at the 18th hole, Strange moved into second place after 54 holes of the Anheuser-Busch Classic and set up a last-round pairing with Wadkins, who led him by three strokes.

The anticipated shootout never developed at Kingsmill Golf Club in Williamsburg, Virginia. Wadkins is a great front-runner—"I've only lost two tournaments when I was ahead going into the last round"—and after Strange staggered through the front nine, Wadkins polished off Larry Mize on the back nine to win by five strokes with an 18-under-par 266 total.

Wadkins hadn't played in the tournament since 1987 because it had been scheduled the week before the British Open. The tournament was two weeks earlier and Wadkins played, along with a number of the leading money winners. Mark O'Meara and Greg Hickman opened with 64s that gave them a one-stroke lead over Wadkins and Brian Claar. O'Meara had the lead to himself until the 36th hole. He pulled his tee shot into the water there and the double bogey handed the lead to Wadkins, who had added a 66 to his opening 65.

Wadkins shot a 67 in the third round to increase his margin from one stroke to three, but he might have had no margin at all if not for a strategically placed bunker at the 17th hole and a hot putter. Wadkins' tee shot at the 177-yard par-three hit the right side of the elevated green and bounded down the hill. It might have ended up in the James River, if not for the bunker. Wadkins had to place his right foot on a retaining plank to play the shot and he hit it to the fringe on the opposite side of the green, about 40 feet from the cup. Then he sank the par putt.

Strange, using a putter he had pulled out of his locker five minutes before the round, sank four birdie putts between 10 and 30 feet and chipped in for a birdie at the final hole for a 68 and set up the all-Virginia confrontation.

Strange double-bogeyed the eighth hole and bogeyed the ninth in the final round and Wadkins extended his lead to five strokes. Mize picked up two strokes by going out in 33 and got to within two strokes with a birdie at No. 12. Wadkins bogeyed No. 12, but he followed that with a five iron to within 10 feet of the hole at the 179-yard No. 13 and after he sank the birdie putt he felt the tournament was over. "After that putt went down, I felt I was in control."

Bank of Boston Classic—$900,000
Winner: Morris Hatalsky

At age 38 and in his 15th year on the PGA Tour, Morris Hatalsky said he had entertained thoughts of retiring. Since he scored his third victory in the Kemper Open in 1988, his career had gone downhill. "I lost my game. I lost my mental edge. I was 149th (in money winnings) last year and 179th this year. That is plummeting."

When Hatalsky won the Bank of Boston Classic, the emotion of the moment left him near tears. Then he waited out the last few groups, all with the opportunity to overtake him. That no one did could be attributed to the quality of the field and the difficulty of the golf course.

Only one of the top 25 money winners, Mark Calcavecchia, was in the field; and the course, softened by all-day rain Thursday, had dried out by Sunday. The wind made it hard to keep approach shots on the greens.

Hatalsky had turned in steady rounds of 70, 68 and 69, and trailed Scott Verplank by four strokes entering the final day. He was struggling when he bogeyed the 14th hole in the final round. Stung by the bogey, Hatalsky figured he would just try to play the final four holes as well as he could, never mind about winning.

The thought of winning came after he birdied the 15th hole from eight feet, saved par at No. 16 after missing the green, then birdied the last two holes from 15 and 10 feet. That gave him a 68 for a nine-under-par 275 total. "I felt confident if I got nine under, I would win, and that putt (at No. 18) went in," he said.

But he had to sweat out the victory. Mike Smith, who led the first round with a 65, followed a bogey at No. 15 with a birdie at No. 16 to pull to within a stroke of Hatalsky. Then, taking no chance on hitting the water, Smith overclubbed at No. 17 and bogeyed. Verplank, who shot 67-68-68 in the first three rounds and led after 36 and 54 holes, and Brian Tennyson saw their chances dwindle on the last few holes. Verplank bogeyed Nos. 10, 11 and 13 and Tennyson missed four-foot putts at the fourth and fifth holes. Nevertheless, both had chances to tie at the 583-yard finishing hole. Each needed an eagle. Tennyson hit his approach shot into the crowd and walked off with a bogey. Verplank's approach left him 30 yards from the hole, but the best he could do was pitch to two feet and make birdie, giving him second place at 276.

Buick Open—$1,000,000
Winner: Chip Beck

After the way he finished the 1989 season, Chip Beck was expecting to have a brilliant year in 1990. He won 3-1/2 out of a maximum four points in the Ryder Cup match and had placed ninth among money winners with almost $700,000 without winning a tournament. At age 33 and in his 12th year on the PGA Tour, this looked like his year. By the end of July, however, Beck had had only two finishes in the top 10 and had earned only about $130,000.

"Over the last three years I had worked myself into some bad habits," Beck said. "I had just a few swing thoughts and I overworked those." All the good thoughts came together in the final round of the Buick Open, as Beck came from eight strokes behind with a seven-under-par 65 to beat out Hale Irwin, Fuzzy Zoeller and Mike Donald by one stroke with a 16-under-par 272 total.

Until Beck's charge, it appeared Irwin might score an unusual double—victories in the Buick Classic and Buick Open. Irwin won the Buick Classic at Westchester the week after winning the U.S. Open. The Buick Open at

Warwick Hills Golf and Country Club in Grand Blanc, Michigan, was his first on American soil since the other Buick event. The previous week, Irwin had competed in the British Open. Beck was there, too, but he missed the cut, and decided to enter the Buick Open for the first time since 1984 because "I played well but scored terrible" at St. Andrews.

Warwick Hills is a 7,014-yard course that usually takes a beating from the pros. This year was no different until the final round, when Beck took advantage of the conditions to muscle his way past the leaders. Beck was then eight strokes behind Irwin, whose 54-hole total of 199 included a 63 in the second round.

The course had been soft and yielding through the first three rounds, thanks to rain the week before the tournament. Wind made the course play hard and fast in the final round, and the effect on the leaders was startling. Of the final 18 players in the final round, only Beck, with a 65, broke 70. Fred Funk, even further back than Beck after 54 holes, also shot a 65, giving him fifth place.

Beck picked up his birdies in flocks in the final round—at the first, second, third, seventh, eighth, 10th, 12th, 13th and 14th—and when the others looked up, they saw they had a job to do. Zoeller kept coming close with putts, but few dropped. Donald lipped out a birdie putt at No. 18.

Irwin had an up-and-down round with birdies at the 13th and 14th holes followed by a bogey at No. 15. He reached the par-five 16th with two drivers and two-putted for birdie, gaining a tie with Beck at 16 under par. With a chance to take the lead, Irwin left a 10-foot downhill birdie putt short at the 17th green. Then, as Beck warmed up for a possible playoff, Irwin bogeyed No. 18 for a disappointing 74 that left him tied for second.

Irwin didn't make a bogey in the first three rounds. He took control by two strokes with his second-round 63 and followed that with a 67 that left him one stroke ahead of Billy Andrade. Then Irwin made six bogeys in a final round that he described as "a woeful performance."

Federal Express St. Jude Classic—$1,000,000
Winner: Tom Kite

Of the top 10 all-time money winners on the PGA Tour, only one has never won one of the four major championships. The lone exception is the all-time leading money winner, Tom Kite. Kite became the first to top $6 million in PGA Tour earnings when he raised his total to $6,144,890 with his victory in the Federal Express St. Jude Classic at the TPC at Southwind course in Memphis, Tennessee.

Four shots stood out in Kite's 14th career victory. John Cook missed a four-foot birdie putt at the 16th hole, leaving the door open for Kite. Then Kite hit a three-iron shot at the 17th hole that rolled to within a foot of the cup, setting up the birdie that tied him with Cook at 15 under par, and ultimately put them in a playoff after they tied at 269. The third was Kite's seven iron to the first playoff hole, the 430-yard No. 13, that stopped within 12 feet of the hole. The fourth was Kite's putt after Cook blasted out of a bunker and appeared in position to send the playoff to another hole.

Both shot 67s in the final round with Kite seemingly in command, then with Cook taking over and setting sail for what seemed to be his first victory in three years. Kite came from seven strokes behind to tie with Cook after 54 holes by tying a two-day-old record of 62. Kite continued on his hot streak by making an eagle and two birdies in the first five holes in the final round. "At one point I was six shots behind and was playing with the guy who had the lead," Cook said.

David Canipe, playing a hole ahead of the Kite-Cook pairing, moved into second place, three strokes behind. But Cook regrouped, birdieing the fifth and sixth holes. "After the fifth hole and all the way through the 12th and 13th holes, I thought everything was in control," Kite said. Then it got out of control. Cook birdied the 12th, 13th, 14th and 15th holes. The big swing came at the 14th, a 231-yard par-three that was rated the sixth toughest on the Tour in 1989. Cook hit the green with a three iron and sank an 18-foot putt for birdie. Kite missed the green and bogeyed. That tied Cook with Kite, and when Cook birdied No. 16 and Kite missed birdie putts at Nos. 15 and 16, Cook had a one-stroke lead. Then came the fateful four strokes.

Larry Silveira, in his second year on the Tour, set a course record for the TPC at Southwind course with a 62 in the first round. He followed that with a 71 that kept him one stroke ahead after 36 holes. Cook, with 69-67, trailed by three strokes and Kite, with 72-68, was another four strokes behind him. Cook improved by another stroke with a 66, and Kite carved out his 62 in the third round, putting them in a deadlock for the lead, a stroke in front of Canipe, who climbed into contention with a 64. Silveira, meanwhile, moved aside with a 75. Then Canipe and everybody else moved aside as Kite and Cook staged their two-man battle down the stretch.

The International—$1,000,000
Winner: Davis Love III

It would figure Davis Love III at some time in his career would win The International. The modified Stableford scoring system tournament is held at Castle Pines Golf Club in Castle Rock, Colorado, and a golf ball in the Rocky Mountains is supposed to travel about 10 percent farther than one at sea level.

If a man could routinely drive a ball 300 yards, shouldn't he be able to reach par-five holes in two and even drive some par-fours in the Rockies? Love used that ability for a three-point victory after watching Eduardo Romero of Argentina nearly force a playoff at the 18th hole.

The triumph concluded a difficult period for Love, whose father, Davis, Jr., a famous teacher in North Carolina, died in an airplane crash in 1988. No one knew the son's game better than the father, who had fashioned it. Davis scored his first PGA Tour victory in the 1987 Heritage Classic, his second year as a touring pro. The next year, his father was killed. Davis lost some desire, and his game took another setback when he broke a bone in his left hand while practicing for the 1989 British Open.

By the summer of 1990, Love was looking at The International as a tournament he could win. The format seemed to fit his style: five points for an eagle, two points for a birdie, no points for a par, minus one for a bogey and minus three for a double bogey or worse. "The tournament favors inconsistency," Love said. "You can just blow by people with one aggressive round."

In its fifth year, The International had undergone changes every year. The biggest change for 1990 was that the scoring would be on a cumulative basis through the first three rounds. Previously, cuts were made after each round and points were not carried over to the next round.

Prize money would be awarded to the players with the best scores after 36 holes, and to those with the best scores in the third round. Only in the final round would the players again start with zero points. Mark Calcavecchia, with nine points in the first round and 14 points in the second round, took the top money for the first 36 holes; Love, with 15 points, earned the third round's top money. Romero and Jose Maria Olazabal were the leaders after 54 holes with 26 points, one more than Steve Elkington. Love, who scored eight points in the first round, recovered from a pointless second round with a brilliant third round to land safely among the 24 qualifiers for the final round with 23 points.

None of the tournament's previous winners—Ken Green, John Cook, Joey Sindelar, Greg Norman—or the course designer, Jack Nicklaus, qualified for the final round.

Tom Purtzer made two eagles on his first eight holes en route to a 14-point day that gave him the first-round lead, but he went minus-two and plus-four the next two days and barely qualified for the final round. Calcavecchia and Stan Utley had the best days on Friday with 14 points each.

In the final round, Steve Pate made a double-eagle-two at the eighth hole with a 238-yard two iron. With 11 points, Pate led the field by six. Love, playing behind Pate, was closing in. He birdied Nos. 11, 13, 14, 17 and 18 to reach 14 points. Fifteen players were still on the course, including Romero, who had 11 points after 14 holes, and Peter Senior, who was making a move after scoring six points on the front nine.

Senior reached 10 points with birdies at the 11th and 14th holes, but bogeyed the 16th and birdied the 17th to tie for second place with 11 points. Romero eagled No. 14 with a 15-foot putt after a 213-yard three iron. He had 11 points and the par-five 17th was still ahead. Then he missed an 18-inch putt at No. 16. A birdie at No. 17 made it 12 points. He needed another birdie at No. 18 to force a playoff.

Romero's approach shot went into a bunker, but he had a good lie and thought he would make the next shot. The ball hit the cup, lipped out and he missed the remaining eight-foot putt for par, settling for a second-place tie with Pate and Senior.

Fred Meyer Challenge—$700,000
Winners: Lanny Wadkins and Bobby Wadkins

Lanny Wadkins has been on the PGA Tour since 1971 and his younger brother, Bobby, since 1975, but the Fred Meyer Challenge in Portland, Oregon, marked the first time they had played as partners in a professional event. "We've been wanting to do this for a couple of years," Lanny said, after they won by three strokes over the teams of Fred Couples and Lee Trevino, and Greg Norman and Curtis Strange, with a better-ball score of 122 for 36 holes, 22 under par.

Lanny made six birdies and Bobby, four, in the final round. Bobby's three birdies at the 15th, 16th and 17th holes were the big ones as they shook off Couples and Trevino for a 62 in the second round. In the two rounds, they had 20 birdies and an eagle. Couples and Trevino matched the Wadkins' opening 60 in the second round, and Norman and Strange played consistently for a 62-63.

NEC World Series of Golf—$1,100,000
Winner: Jose Maria Olazabal

In the NEC World Series of Golf, Jose Maria Olazabal not only demolished the famed Firestone South course in Akron, Ohio, but left the field so far behind, it seemed they were playing a different course.

"He was in another zone. He went to a different level," said Paul Azinger, after Olazabal shot 61-67-67-67 for an 18-under-par 262 total and a 12-stroke victory over Lanny Wadkins. Hale Irwin placed third, 15 strokes behind. Olazabal set tournament and course records for 18, 36, 54 and 72 holes. Only three golfers—Bobby Locke, Ben Hogan and Byron Nelson—have won by a greater margin in PGA Tour history. Olazabal's margin might have been wider if Wadkins, who held the previous 72-hole record, had not shot 31 on the final nine.

Winning for the third time in 1990, Olazabal was blazing from the start. He began with five threes—birdie, eagle, birdie, birdie, par. He missed his only fairway and green at No. 7 for his only bogey, recovered for a birdie at No. 8, then began a four-birdie streak at the 11th hole. He came this close to matching Al Geiberger's all-time low score of 59: At the 15th hole he missed a three-foot birdie putt, and at the 17th he missed another birdie from six feet. "You're not going to hole every putt," he said, but at that time everybody thought he would.

There were the usual remarks that the tournament wasn't over after Olazabal's 61 gave him a four-stroke lead. Even Geiberger had to struggle to win after he shot 59. But Olazabal hits the ball straight and long, is a good putter, has international experience, and plays well beyond his 24 years.

Olazabal followed his 61 with a 67, and the only round better than that on Friday was a 65 by Donnie Hammond, who opened with a 73. That gave Olazabal a 36-hole total of 128, and a nine-stroke lead over Irwin and Larry Mize. "It's a fairly competitive tournament except for one man," Irwin said. Irwin followed his second-round 67 with a 66, and all he gained on Olazabal was one stroke. Olazabal began the final round with two birdies, and Irwin three-putted both holes for bogeys, leaving little doubt about the outcome.

"What can I say?" remarked Olazabal afterwards. "I've never had that kind of lead before. I've played this well, tee to green, but I've never putted like this before. When you see only three other guys under par, and I'm 12 strokes ahead, that tells you I played great golf all week."

Chattanooga Classic—$500,000

Winner: Peter Persons

Peter Persons shot 64-64-65-67—260 — 20 under par for the relatively short (6,641 yards) Valleybrook Golf and Country Club course in Chattanooga, Tennessee—and set a record for the Chattanooga Classic while turning in the lowest 72-hole score so far in the year. He won by two strokes over Richard Zokol.

His 17-under-par 193 total was the lowest 54-hole score of the year and his 36-hole 128 total tied the low fashioned by Jose Maria Olazabal in Akron. Kenny Knox got in on the record-setting with a course-record 61 in the third round. Dave Rummells, far behind after 54 holes, matched Knox's 61 in the final round.

Persons, who placed 14th in the 1989 qualifying tournament, was pessimistic early on about his chances of winning. After Persons jumped past Steve Lowery, who opened with a 62, into a two-stroke lead after 36 holes, he said, "There is no way I'm going to win this tournament." His last victory had come in the 1984 Georgia Amateur.

Persons chipped in five times during the tournament, three times for eagles, and, after taking a three-stroke lead into the final round, he wasn't seriously threatened. Zokol birdied the second hole to move to within two strokes, but Zokol bogeyed the third hole and Persons birdied the fourth. Persons was particularly devastating on the par-five holes, 13 under par for the tournament. His margin of victory might have been greater, but he bogeyed the last hole and Zokol birdied.

Greater Milwaukee Open—$900,000

Winner: Jim Gallagher, Jr.

Jim Gallagher, Jr., will always have a warm spot in his heart for the Greater Milwaukee Open, but his first PGA Tour victory could well have been snatched from him by Billy Mayfair or Ed Dougherty. In the final round at Tuckaway Country Club in Franklin, Wisconsin, Mayfair had a 15-foot eagle putt at the 16th hole rim the cup and stay out, hit a four iron to within two inches of a hole-in-one at the 17th hole, and had a 10-foot par putt that would have given him the victory stop short of the hole at the 18th. That gave Mayfair a 68 and a 72-hole total of 271, and a tie with Gallagher and Dougherty.

After finishing with a 66, Dougherty went to the practice range in anticipation of a playoff. He thought it would start at the par-four No. 10, which was near the clubhouse, not the par-three No. 17. "I never even hit a five iron," he said. In the playoff, Dougherty hit his tee shot into a bunker in front of the green.

Gallagher who, like Dougherty, had shot a 66 to come from five strokes behind, pulled his five iron to the left-center of the green, 45 feet from the hole. Mayfair, who had nearly aced the hole a short time before, let his shot get away from him into the rough beyond the green. Mayfair hit a good chip, but once again the fates frowned on him. It hit the cup and went eight feet past. Dougherty hit a recovery shot about five feet above the pin. Gallagher ran his putt seven feet past the hole.

Gallagher asked an official who was away and the official, forgetting Mayfair, said Gallagher was. He sank the putt for a par. Mayfair and Dougherty missed. "Things went my way. Maybe that was something that was supposed to happen," said Gallagher about the official's error.

Things did indeed go Gallagher's way. Jim Thorpe and Ray Stewart opened with 63s that left Gallagher six strokes behind. Stewart, with a 70, led by one stroke over Ken Green after 36 holes and still was in front after 54 holes, by three over Scott Verplank, Morris Hatalsky and Mayfair.

Stewart's putter went cold in the final round, and after he birdied the 16th hole he went to the 18th needing a birdie to win, a par to join the playoff. He hit a bunker with his tee shot, another bunker with his approach and bogeyed. Verplank, who at one time shared the lead, faded with bogeys at the 14th and 15th holes. Steve Lowery had a chance to put pressure on the leaders, but a bogey at No. 18 left him with a 65 and 272 total, tied with Stewart and Scott Hoch, who played the first six holes in five under par, then bogeyed the 18th hole for a 67.

It almost seemed that Gallagher was destined to win. In 1988, Gallagher had lost his playing card and had to turn down a sponsor's exemption to the tournament because he had used his allotted five invitations. He won a place in the Monday qualifier and nearly won the tournament, finishing in a tie for second. That earned him a temporary playing card, and he went on to finish the year among the top 125 players, earning an exemption. In 1989, he placed 50th with more than $265,000.

Hardee's Golf Classic—$1,000,000
Winner: Joey Sindelar

Almost everyone was pulling for Willie Wood to win the Hardee's Golf Classic in Coal Valley, Illinois. Bob Tway, who shared the lead with Wood after three rounds, said, "If I can't win, I hope Willie does." Wood almost did, but Joey Sindelar, like Wood, also had some reasons for wanting a victory. In 1988, Sindelar placed third among the money winners. Going into the Hardee's tournament he was 131st on the money list, six below the cutoff position.

Sindelar didn't need to place among the top 125 to keep his playing card. His standing among the top 50 all-time money winners would have been enough. But when he hit the green at the final hole, he told his caddy, "That's our Tour card for next year." Sindelar figured he would win about $30,000 or $40,000, which would lift him comfortably above 125th place. Instead, he won $180,000 with his first victory in two years.

Wood bogeyed the 17th hole, and was tied at 12 under par with Sindelar. Jim Gallagher, Jr., was 12 under when he bogeyed No. 17 and finished a stroke behind, tied at 269 with Ian Baker-Finch, Dave Barr, Bill Britton and Jay Delsing. With a 66, Sindelar had picked up three strokes on Wood. Tway, meanwhile, faded to a 71.

Sindelar said he understood why the fans were for Wood in the playoff. It was a year earlier at this tournament that Wood had learned that his wife, Holly, had died of cancer. Because his wife's illness had virtually curtailed his 1989 season, Wood had received a special exemption to play the Tour in 1990. "I can't say I was rooting for Willie, but Willie is everybody's buddy out here," Sindelar said. "He has been through a rough time."

Sindelar wasn't going to let compassion affect the way he played. At the 72nd hole, he hit a 140-yard nine iron to within four feet of the hole, setting up a birdie that gave him a 268 total. In the playoff, he hit a sand wedge out of the rough at the first hole to within six inches of the cup for a certain birdie. He won after Wood's chip shot from the same vicinity hit a sprinkler head and went 10 feet past the hole, from where he missed.

Wood's 63 in the second round got him to within a stroke of Billy Mayfair, who opened with successive 65s. A 68 by Wood and a 67 by Tway in the third round gave them a two-stroke lead over four others and put Wood in position to score his first victory in his seventh year on the Tour. The $108,000 second-place money was a great consolation. "Now I'm exempt for next year and that's where I wanted to be," Wood said.

Canadian Open—$900,000
Winner: Wayne Levi

It seems that Wayne Levi always is proving himself, but after Levi won the Canadian Open at Glen Abbey Golf Club in Oakville, Ontario, even he was surprised. "I never thought I could win four in a year. This is beyond my wildest dreams," he said.

In his early years on the Tour, Levi usually played long enough to accumulate enough money to assure a place on the Tour the following year, then spent most of the rest of the time with his family. From 1978, his second year on the Tour, through 1985, he won at least one tournament a year. Although his earnings were good from 1986 through 1989, he didn't win a tournament.

He won the BellSouth Atlanta Classic in May and followed that with victories in the Centel Western Open and Greater Hartford Open. Given his history, it was surprising that Levi was still playing in mid-September.

Levi had played only twice in eight weeks, and figured he wasn't ready to win when he teed off at Glen Abbey. He had spent some time with instructor Rick Christie in Tampa, Florida, and Christie had convinced him he could win "half a dozen tournaments a year if I set loftier goals and practiced harder. I would just laugh." He's not laughing anymore, at least not at that idea.

Levi slipped a stroke behind Buddy Gardner with a 72 on a cold and windy Saturday. The weather was the same in the final round, which meant it would not take a low score to win. Levi shot a two-under-par 70 for a 278 total, although not without some dramatics at the end. A bogey at the 17th hole reduced his lead to one stroke. It didn't shake his confidence. The 18th at Glen Abbey is a par-five and on this day it was playing downwind.

"If you can't hold a one-stroke lead on a par-five, you ought to be shot," Levi said. He hit his third shot, a nine iron, to within 15 feet of the hole and had no problem two-putting. The problems were left to those who earlier tried to catch him. Gardner extended his lead by chipping for a birdie at the first hole, but took a double bogey at the sixth and disappeared with bogeys at the 11th, 12th and 13th holes. Nick Price played well with every club except his putter. When he three-putted the 10th hole he was gone. Canadian Dave Barr was still in contention until he hit the water at the ninth hole, and took a triple bogey.

The last to go were Ian Baker-Finch and Jim Woodward. Baker-Finch finished with birdies on the last two holes, but fell one stroke short, just as he had in the Hardee's Classic a week earlier. Woodward played the back nine in 32, giving him a 66 that tied for second place with Baker-Finch. The $88,000 check boosted Woodward to 116th in money winnings. Levi's $180,000 lifted him to $772,397, but he still trailed Greg Norman and Payne Stewart among the money leaders despite his four victories.

B.C. Open—$700,000
Winner: Nolan Henke

By late September, with the PGA Tour season drawing near a close, the focus was on placing among the top 125 money winners, assuring a place on the exempt list for 1991. At the B.C. Open at En-Joie Golf Club in Endicott, New York, only one of the season's top 10 money winners, Wayne Levi, was in the field, and he missed the cut.

The tournament developed into a battle among those trying to avoid a return to the qualifying tournament. Nolan Henke led Barry Jaeckel by three strokes with one round to play, but the thought in the minds of many was, "would he hold up?" "I was thinking the same way," Henke said. "When am I going to fall apart?" He never did, winning by three strokes over Mark Wiebe with a 16-under-par 268 total. Doug Tewell, who tied Jim Benepe, Brian Tennyson and Jaeckel for third place, also assured himself a place among the top 125, jumping from 130th to 114th, and Jim Hallet clinched a spot, as well, after tying for ninth place.

Henke, who was second in the 1987 NCAA Championship in his final year at Florida State, had missed the cut in four of his previous six tournaments. He played like a determined young man at En-Joie. A 66 gave him a share of the first-round lead and he moved two strokes in front of Hallet with a 64 in the second round. A 70 in the third round maintained his lead, but now the man behind him was Jaeckel, who had a 65.

Jaeckel cut the difference to one stroke by playing the first 11 holes of the final round in four under par. Henke hit a marvelous wedge shot to within five feet of the hole for a birdie at No. 12. Jaeckel bogeyed Nos. 14 and 15, and Wiebe went past him with a 64, capped by a birdie at the final hole. Henke, playing behind Wiebe, birdied the par-three 16th for a four-stroke lead with two holes to play. "My heart was pounding," he said. "I just didn't want to do anything stupid. Somehow I got it in the hole."

Buick Southern Open—$600,000
Winner: Kenny Knox

Kenny Knox has yet to win a major championship, but after he won the Buick Southern Open in Columbus, Georgia, he said, "Next to the majors, I would rather win this tournament than any other. I've never wanted anything more than this. This is special."

Knox was born in Columbus, and spent his first 16 years there. Many of those with whom he grew up were there to cheer as he shot 69-62-68-66— 265 and beat Jim Hallet on the second playoff hole. Maybe the surroundings, the extra incentive played a part in Knox's third victory on the PGA Tour. It could be, considering his play on the final seven holes in regulation and the two playoff holes.

At the 12th hole, Hallet tapped in a 15-inch putt for birdie. Knox faced an eight-foot birdie putt; miss it and he's three strokes behind. He made it. "That was the turning point," Knox said. At No. 13, Knox hit his tee shot into the woods. He then hit a seven iron through the trees to the green, and parred. At No. 14, he sank a big breaking 25-foot birdie putt and got to within a stroke of the lead. He caught Hallet with a 10-footer at No. 17. At the 18th, Hallet had a 10-footer to win, but missed the putt.

Knox's magic continued in the playoff. Hallet sank a 12-foot birdie putt at the first hole, and Knox matched it with a five-footer. Then Knox won with a 12-foot birdie putt at the next hole.

Howard Twitty took the first-round lead with a 62, then fell back. David Peoples and Knox shot 62s in the second round, giving Peoples a two-stroke lead over Knox and Jeff Wilson, who had a 64. Knox shot a 68 in the third round and was tied at 199 with Hallet, who followed a 66 with a 65. "This is the most nervous I've been in a tournament in a long time," Knox said. "It's so important to me." When it counted, Knox showed he had the ability to keep his nerves under control.

H.E.B. Texas Open—$700,000
Winner: Mark O'Meara

The year had not been a good one for Gary Hallberg. He was in 180th place in money winnings and it had been a long time since he was in the chase for a victory. Here was Hallberg, on the final hole of the Texas Open, his ball 30 feet from the cup. Two putts for par and a playoff with Mark O'Meara, who earlier had bogeyed the par-three hole after a sensational string of birdies.

Hallberg's first putt was seven feet wide of the hole. "Maybe he fell asleep," said Nick Price, who was paired with him. Hallberg had putted well all day, and when he hit the green with his tee shot, O'Meara was on the practice range, preparing for a playoff. O'Meara had missed a par putt from seven feet on the hole minutes earlier, and had finished with a seven-under-par 63 for a 261 total. He didn't expect Hallberg to miss, too.

But Hallberg's putt for par was off-line by a couple inches, and O'Meara and Hallberg both felt good, despite Hallberg's initial disappointment. O'Meara had his second victory of the year, and the $86,400 Hallberg earned moved him to 112th among the money winners, virtually assuring him of a Tour card for 1991.

With Hallberg shooting 63-69 and O'Meara 64-68, they were tied after 36 holes. Hallberg's opening 63 gave him a share of the lead with Emlyn Aubrey, then Hallberg, Aubrey and O'Meara all slipped behind in the second round as Steve Jones took the lead with a 63 for a 128 total, and Duffy Waldorf moved into second place with a 63. John Dowdall, who had opened with a 72, broke the Oak Hills Country Club course record with a 61, but failed to break par in the final two rounds. Price, with 65-66-63, moved into the lead by two strokes over Hallberg after three rounds. O'Meara trailed by four strokes.

Price stumbled with bogeys at three of the first seven holes in the final round and watched the parade go by. O'Meara led with birdies at Nos. 1, 5, 7, 8, 9 and 10. The sixth birdie put him three strokes ahead of Price. Birdies at Nos. 13 and 17 by O'Meara shook off everyone except Hallberg. Then O'Meara missed the green at No. 18, giving Hallberg a chance for his first victory in seven years. Hallberg also had bogeyed early, but hit a wedge to within five feet at No. 17, made the birdie putt, and was even with O'Meara at 20 under par. Then he hit his tee shot at the 198-yard No. 18. "The adrenaline started flowing and I just hit the putt too hard," he said. "I put the 'make' stroke on it instead of the lag."

Las Vegas Invitational—$1,300,000
Winner: Bob Tway

If you play the PGA Tour, it helps to be a fatalist. There's a time to win and there's a time to lose. For Bob Tway, the Las Vegas Invitational was apparently a time to win, and for John Cook to lose. Luck played a big role in Tway's first victory since the 1989 Memorial Tournament, but he gave it a nudge with some skill that others might view as luck.

Cook had to come from behind to take the lead on the final nine holes. He three-putted the 16th green, putting them in a deadlock for the lead. At the par-five 18th, Cook reached the green, about 40 feet from the hole, with his second shot and Tway barely cleared the lake, his ball landing on a cart path. Tway chipped to four feet and Cook left his eagle putt a foot short, leaving them tied with 334 totals for the 90 holes, Cook with a 67 and Tway with a 70.

At the first playoff hole, Tway drove into a fairway bunker and Cook pulled his drive left, behind a tree. All Cook could do was chip out to the fairway. After Tway blasted from the sand to the green, Cook hit an accurate 95-yard wedge shot to the green—too accurate. The ball landed in the cup and ricocheted out, stopping on the fringe, about 15 feet from the hole. Normally a shot of that sort will hit the pin, at least, and maybe stop within a few feet of the hole. Tway two-putted for par, and won when Cook's 15-footer to tie stayed out.

Cook was disappointed, but he was happy, too, not just because he earned $140,400 for second place. After enduring pain for several years, Cook had surgery on his right wrist in May, 1989, and received a special exemption to play in 1990. His runner-up finish moved him into 28th place among the money winners with $387,612. "I've come a long way, for sure," he said. It was his second second-place finish of the year; he lost to Tom Kite in a playoff for the Memphis title two months earlier.

The Las Vegas Invitational is played on three courses—Las Vegas CC, Desert Inn CC and Spanish Trail. Tway and Cook were in contention all the way. Cook opened with an eight-under-par 64 that tied him for the lead with

David Frost. Mark O'Meara took the lead by two strokes with a 64 in the second round. Tway moved to within a stroke of O'Meara after 54 holes with a 65, as O'Meara shot a 67. Cook, with a 66, trailed Tway by one stroke. Tway took the lead by himself with another 65 in the fourth round. Cook's bandaged wrist was holding up as he shot a 67, but O'Meara began to show signs of weakening as he took a 69 that tied him with Cook, three strokes behind Tway.

Tway failed to birdie any of the first three par-fives in the final round, which could have been fatal. At the seventh hole, Tway had to sink a 10-foot putt for par to maintain a one-stroke lead after Cook sank a 15-footer for birdie. Cook tied for the lead with a birdie at the eighth hole, after Tway made a six-footer for par. It could have been worse. Tway's tee shot seemed headed out of bounds when it hit a tree and dropped straight down, staying inbounds by about six feet.

Cook moved one stroke ahead with a birdie at No. 10, and once again Tway could have been further behind. He drove into the water, but managed to save a par with a 15-foot putt. At No. 12, Tway drove into a fairway bunker—just as he was to do in the playoff—and made par from 10 feet. Then Tway and Cook stopped making putts, and once again Tway was fortunate as Cook's three-putt green at No. 16 caused another deadlock that was to be broken some time later with a fateful fairway shot that wouldn't stay in.

Walt Disney World/Oldsmobile Classic—$1,000,000
Winner: Tim Simpson

In a season of records, Tim Simpson seemed on the verge of breaking another with 18 holes to play in the Walt Disney World/Oldsmobile Classic in Lake Buena Vista, Florida. After rounds of 64, 64 and 65, Simpson was 23 under par and had a six-stroke lead on Davis Love III. He needed only a five-under-par 67 to break the PGA Tour record for most strokes under par, set by Ben Hogan in 1945 and tied by Mike Souchak in 1955. He didn't get the record, and he didn't win in a runaway, because the weather played a profound role.

The Walt Disney Classic is played on three courses, and for the first three rounds it's a pro-amateur. As a result, pin positions were in easier places in the first three rounds and the pros took advantage. In the final round, approaches had to be played with a greater degree of accuracy. A storm that hit in the middle of the round, combined with Simpson's nerves, produced a 71 and a one-stroke victory over John Mahaffey. "The rains made the greens slower," Simpson said. "The speed changed pretty dramatically. I left putts short at Nos. 12, 13, 14 and 15. I made it tougher on myself than I would've liked."

Simpson's first victory of the year was one of those rarities—wire to wire. Simpson had taken a six-week vacation to go deer hunting before returning to action in the Las Vegas Invitational a week earlier, and the layoff showed at Las Vegas. On Monday before the Disney tournament, Simpson spent three hours on the practice putting green with Morris Hatalsky, who, Simpson said, made a vast change in his setup. In the first round he shot an eight-under-par 64 and led by two strokes. Another 64 in the second round put him four strokes in front of Paul Azinger.

Everyone was shooting low scores, but not as low as Simpson's. A 65 in the third round put him six strokes in front of Love and with the feeling that birdies were routine. "If you slip up and make a par, it's almost like a double bogey," he said. The wind and rain took the steam out of his run in the final round. Even before the rain hit, the birdies had come to a virtual end, and Love and Mahaffey began to make things closer. Mahaffey, playing in front of Simpson, shot a 64 for 265, then waited to see what Simpson would do. Simpson, paired with Love, bogeyed No. 13 and, when Love birdied the hole, Love trailed by one stroke. Sniffing victory, the long-hitting Love attempted to reach the green at the 595-yard No. 14 in two, but hit his three wood fat and the ball went into the lake. Love finished with a 67 that relegated him to third place at 266. The relieved Simpson was able to maintain his one-stroke edge on Mahaffey over the finishing holes.

Nabisco Championship—$2,500,000
Winner: Jodie Mudd

The final official PGA Tour event of the year was also the richest, with 30 players shooting for a first prize of $450,000. Jodie Mudd had won the second richest event, The Players Championship, which paid $270,000 to the winner, and his goal at Champions Golf Club in Houston was to win enough to put a down payment on a 200-acre farm back home in Kentucky. With last place earning $40,000, he was almost guaranteed of all he needed.

Then Mudd went out and won enough to almost pay for the farm in cash, as he beat Billy Mayfair with a dazzling display of putting down the stretch. Mudd shot 68, 69, 68, 68 for an 11-under-par 273 total.

He saved the best for last. Wayne Levi was already in with a sparkling 63 for a 276 total, and Mudd trailed Mayfair by one stroke as they came to the 17th hole. Mayfair hit a good approach to the green, but Mudd hit his a little closer. Then Mayfair rolled in a putt of about 15 feet for birdie, putting the pressure on Mudd to sink a 10-footer to stay one behind. He sank it. At No. 18, Mudd putted first and knocked a 20-foot birdie putt into the heart of the hole. Mayfair faced an 18-footer that would have won, but his attempt grazed the edge of the cup.

The first playoff hole was the 431-yard No. 14 and you must know this: In the four rounds of the tournament, the only players who had birdied Nos. 14, 17 and 18 were Mark O'Meara and Mudd, who had already birdied the three holes this day. Mayfair pushed his tee shot into the woods and was forced to chip out to the fairway. Mudd's drive was true and his approach with a nine iron left him with a 15-footer for birdie. Mayfair recovered well, hitting a wedge within five feet of the hole. Unless Mudd had one more magic putt left, it appeared they would go another extra hole. Mudd had that one more putt left, almost a duplicate of the one he rolled in at No. 18.

"The putts on the last three holes were all straight and I hit them on line," Mudd said. "To go the limit and birdie the last two holes and the playoff hole ... It's nice to know all my hard work was paying off." Mayfair, a second-year pro without a victory, had lost to Jim Gallagher, Jr., in a playoff at Milwaukee the month before after bogeying the 72nd hole. This was different. Mudd had won it; Mayfair hadn't lost, and the $270,000 for second place was a great consolation.

Greg Norman, the year's leading money winner and stroke average leader, and Tim Simpson, who had won the week before at Walt Disney World, took the first-round lead with 66s on a day in which only eight players broke par. Mudd trailed by two strokes, and Mayfair, by three. Norman got a boost when he sank a 40-foot bunker shot at the fifth hole for an eagle. But Norman had no more shots like that in his bag. He settled to shoot three consecutive 71s and place seventh at 279. A 73 in the second round took Simpson out of the picture, as Mayfair took over the lead by a stroke over Nick Price with a 66. Mudd, Norman and Chip Beck were another stroke in back of Price.

Mudd and Mayfair both found their games on Saturday, and for Mayfair it was almost disastrous. Hitting the ball more solidly, he went over the green on four of the first five holes. Mudd had scrambled in the first round and had walked off the practice tee before the third round with a glum outlook, but he gathered his game for 68s both days. When Mayfair shot a 70 on Saturday, he was deadlocked with Mudd after 54 holes, but Price was only two strokes behind and Ian Baker-Finch, who was to be a factor in the race for a time the final day, was one of three who trailed by three strokes.

Baker-Finch and Mudd both birdied the seventh hole, and were tied for the lead with Mayfair. Then Baker-Finch stepped aside, as Mayfair and Mudd made it a two-man race for the title. Mudd hit his drive out of bounds at No. 10, and Mayfair grabbed the lead with birdies at the ninth and 10th holes. Mudd pulled within one stroke with a birdie at No. 14. Up ahead, Levi was finishing with his course-record 63 with birdies at three of the last four holes, but Mudd and Mayfair seemed oblivious to his score. There was just the two of them, and when Mudd sank his birdie putt on top of Mayfair's birdie putt at No. 17, it should have been a tip-off of what was to come.

Mexican Open—$600,000
Winner: Bob Lohr

Bob Lohr nearly matched his winnings on the PGA Tour with his four-stroke victory in the Mexican Open at La Hacienda Golf Club in Mexico City. Lohr earned $100,000 with rounds of 69, 66, 67, 67 for a 19-under-par 269. Lohr, whose last victory in the U.S. came in the 1988 Walt Disney World Classic, finished 109th on the 1990 Tour with winnings of $141,260.

Blaine McAllister led the first round with a 66 and Steve Elkington took over after 36 holes with 68 and 66 for a 134 total. Lohr had moved into position with his second-round 66, then took over with successive 67s in the final two rounds. Carlos Espinoza of Mexico finished with 65-69 and placed second, four strokes behind Lohr. Kenny Knox placed third, another three strokes behind Espinoza.

Isuzu Kapalua International—$700,000
Winner: David Peoples

A good year got even better for David Peoples in the Kapalua International at the Kapalua Resort in Maui, Hawaii. Peoples, 30, had gained his PGA Tour card for the sixth time by finishing first in the qualifying tournament in December, 1989, and early on he gave indications that this time his stay on the Tour would be lengthier. He placed 57th among money winners with $259,367—nearly as much as he had earned in his six previous forays on the Tour—with his highest finish a tie for third in the Independent Insurance Agent Open. And at Kapalua Peoples gave signs that 1991 might be even better for him as he led from start to finish, scoring an impressive five-stroke victory over Davis Love III.

The trade winds were not nearly as fierce as they have been in the past, but strong enough for some players to launch drives of more than 350 yards. Peoples opened with an eight-under-par 63 for a one-stroke lead over Ben Crenshaw. Crenshaw followed his 64 with a 73 and didn't recover. Peoples, meanwhile, came back with a 69, his 132 total giving him a three-stroke edge on Tom Purtzer (67-68). Love, who trailed by six strokes after 36 holes, matched Peoples' opening 63 in the third round, but gained only three strokes on Peoples, whose 66—198 total gave him a good working edge to take into the final round.

Peoples said he feared the long-hitting Love might come back with another 63 in the final round and that he might become nervous trying to hold onto his lead. But Love managed only a 68 and Peoples shot a 66 for a 264 total and a five-stroke triumph. His victory was worth $150,000.

RMCC Invitational Hosted by Greg Norman—$1,000,000
Winners: Fred Couples and Raymond Floyd

The Ronald McDonald Childrens Charities Invitational at Sherwood Country Club in Thousand Oaks, California, had a field of 10 two-man teams. The 54-hole tournament was played with a different format each day: best-ball in the first round, alternate shot in the second round, and scramble in the third round. Fred Couples and Raymond Floyd proved the most adept in the three competitions, as they won by five strokes over Arnold Palmer and Peter Jacobsen with a 64, 57, 61—182 total.

Curtis Strange and Mark O'Meara led the best-ball play with a 59, two strokes better than Palmer and Jacobsen. Couples and Floyd took command in the second round, thanks to Couples' awesome driving. They gained 12 strokes on Strange and O'Meara with their 57, and took a six-stroke lead over Palmer and Jacobsen, and Mark Calcavecchia and Ian Baker-Finch into the final round.

The closest any team got to them in the final round was five strokes, that when Jacobsen sank an 89-yard wedge shot for an eagle at the 10th hole. Floyd set up a three-foot eagle putt with a three-iron shot at the 11th hole. "After that, it was come on home," Floyd said. In the three rounds, Floyd and Couples had 26 birdies and four eagles.

World Cup—$1,100,000
Winner: Germany

The World Cup victory by Bernhard Langer and Torsten Giedeon not only underscored the fact that golf is spreading worldwide but that another country, Germany, may be about to join the wave.

Langer, a former Masters champion, had competed previously in the tournament that brings together two-man teams from most of the world's golf-playing countries. He was unable to find a countryman who would provide a bonafide shot at the title, so he declined to play after 1980. The 1990 tournament was at the Grand Cypress Resort in Orlando, Florida, and Langer, who has a second home in Boca Raton, planned to be in Florida anyway. So he teamed with Giedeon and won the first team event in any sport for the newly unified Germany.

Langer said he had been watching Giedeon and "he's a much better player than he thinks he is." Giedeon turned in a seven-under-par 65 in the third round. He and Langer used that as a springboard to win by three strokes over England (Mark James and Richard Boxall) and Ireland (David Feherty and Ronan Rafferty) with a combined score of 556. Wales (Ian Woosnam and Mark Mouland) placed fourth with 561, one stroke in front of the favored American team of Payne Stewart and Jodie Mudd.

Other countries were also heard from. Saneh Sanqsui of Thailand opened with a 65. Anders Sorensen of Denmark shot 67-67-70-69—273 and placed second in the individual competition to Stewart, who shot 69-68-68-66—271. The Americans' attempt to win from four strokes back fizzled out when Mudd slipped to a 77 in the final round.

James and Boxall put England in front with 68s in the first round and they still led by a stroke after three rounds. Giedeon's 65 had put Germany in position to win, and Germany and England were paired for the final round. England increased its lead from one stroke to three after two holes, then the team began to slip. James bogeyed the fourth and fifth holes and Boxall bogeyed the seventh. Langer and Giedeon, who each played the first four holes in one under par, moved in front. When Boxall and James both bogeyed the 15th hole, that left an opening for Ireland to catch them. Feherty shot a 63—a competitive record at Grand Cypress and one stroke off Gary Player's World Cup record set in Marbella, Spain, in 1973—and Rafferty a 72, as the Irish picked up 10 strokes on the English.

Sazale Classic—$1,000,000
Winners: Fred Couples and Mike Donald

Fred Couples showed a distinct preference for best-ball play when he teamed with Mike Donald to win his second consecutive tournament in the Sazale Classic at the Binks Forest Country Club in Wellington, Florida. Their 254 total provided a four-stroke victory over Curt and Tom Byrum.

In the first round, Couples and Donald were in the middle of the pack with a 65 as the teams of Rocco Mediate and Jim Carter, and Greg Bruckner and Kirk Triplett, tied for the lead with 12-under-par 60s. But Couples and Donald added a 60 to pull into a tie with three other teams after 36 holes. As a stiff wind thinned out the competitors, Couples and Donald climbed into the lead with a 63 in the third round, giving them a four-stroke lead over the Byrum brothers. "The course couldn't have played any longer," Couples said. "Discipline did it."

Couples and Donald continued their bogey-free play in the final round and their 66 was enough to maintain their four-stroke advantage. The Byrums also shot a 66 for a 258 total, which was one stroke better than three teams tied for third place. Couples earned $90,000 for his share of first place, giving him $215,000 in two weeks of team play.

10. The U.S. Senior Tour

Lee Trevino sounded an ominous note at the end of his spectacular "rookie" season on the Senior PGA Tour, shunting aside somebody's observation that his intensity level would be down and with it his degree of success in 1991. "It will be better," he said. "I really think I can play better and win more." This from a man who may or may not have stated, as reported in the late months of 1989 before he turned 50, that he would win eight, 10, 12, maybe even 15 tournaments in 1990. This from a man who just about delivered on that promise with seven official victories, another in a sortie to Japan and a lead role in the U.S. victory in the annual Chrysler Cup matches. This from a man who won $1,190,518 on the Senior Tour.

The 51-year-old Trevino exploded onto the Senior Tour scene by winning three of his first four 1990 tournaments; scattered four more through the schedule, highlighted by his victory in the U.S. Senior Open at Ridgewood, and was out of the top 10 in just two of his 28 starts. He placed second eight times, including a playoff defeat in the year-ending New York Life Champions.

LEE TREVINO IN 1990 ON SENIOR PGA TOUR

Tournament	Finish	Money
Royal Caribbean	1	$60,000
GTE Suncoast	2	40,000
Aetna Challenge	1	60,000
Vintage Chrysler	1	60,000
Tradition	T24	7,700
PGA Seniors	T3	25,000
Las Vegas	T4	22,433
Sanders Kingwood	1	45,000
Bell Atlantic	6	20,000
NYNEX Commemorative	1	52,500
Mazda Senior TPC	2	88,000
Digital Classic	2	28,000
U.S. Senior Open	1	90,000
Northville	T16	7,500
Kroger Classic	T4	24,600
Newport Cup	T4	15,000
PaineWebber	T9	13,500
Showdown Classic	T2	25,500
GTE Northwest	T9	8,775
Vantage Bank One	T6	9,335
Greater Grand Rapids	T7	9,258
Crestar Classic	2	28,000
Vantage Championship	T4	81,750
Gatlin Southwest	2	25,500
Transamerica	1	75,000
Security Pacific	T4	24,667
GTE Kaanapali	T2	36,000
New York Life	T2	95,000

Throw in Trevino's other winnings in unofficial and team events on and off the circuit and the bottom line grows to an enormous $1,377,698.

One can only wonder how different the impact would have been had Jack Nicklaus approached the Senior PGA Tour with the same enthusiasm and full commitment when he reached his 50th birthday in January as Trevino did. Nicklaus said all along that he would play sparingly on the 1990 Senior Tour—and that's what he did. Jack continued to compete in some regular events at home and abroad, limiting his senior play to four major events—winning the Tradition at Scottsdale in his first outing and later the Mazda Senior TPC in a rout, finishing second to Trevino in the U.S. Senior Open and third behind winner Gary Player in the PGA Seniors Championship, banking $340,000 for those efforts.

The season-long glare on Trevino and the occasional spotlight on Nicklaus overshadowed the career year of Mike Hill, a journeyman pro in the past who won five times and was rarely out of contention throughout his second senior season. The victories, two more than he won in some two decades on the PGA Tour, and 16 other top-10 finishes boosted Hill to an $895,678 season, which would have been a new Senior Tour record in itself had it not been for Trevino's phenomenal year. Four of Hill's wins came during the final three months of the season, climaxed by his $150,000 playoff victory in the rich New York Life Champions tournament that concluded the season.

The 1990 season was also the first in senior golf for big George Archer, whose exploits may have not received proper recognition as well. Archer followed a 1989 victory in his first start on the circuit with four triumphs in 1990, including the opening Tournament of Champions, with a fifth win in the late-season Seniors Challenge in Hawaii as an added attraction. Charles Coody landed the biggest check of the year—$202,500—in the Vantage Championship to finish third on the money list, just ahead of Archer. He also teamed with Dale Douglass to capture the Legends of Golf.

Jim Dent, a second-year man; Chi Chi Rodriguez, Bob Charles, the leading money winner in 1989, and Gary Player were the most successful of the other nine winners during the season. Dent collared four titles, Rodriguez and Charles three each, while Player landed two important ones—the PGA Seniors and the Seniors British Open at Turnberry. Rives McBee followed his surprise 1989 victory in the Bank One Classic with two more wins in 1990, while Frank Beard, Don Massengale and Jimmy Powell scored their first victories as seniors during a year when the 42-tournament schedule carried some $20 million in prize money.

MONY Senior Tournament of Champions—$250,000
Winner: George Archer

George Archer made it two for six as a neophyte senior when he ran away with the MONY Senior Tournament of Champions, the opening stop on the 1990 Senior PGA Tour. The towering Archer, who marked his debut on the circuit the previous October by winning the Gatlin Brothers Southwest Classic and finishing in the top 10 in three of the other four 1989 events, had an easy time of it at La Costa Country Club in Southern California the first weekend of January in contrast to his playoff victory back in October. He rode a seven-stroke margin into the final round and, despite a closing 74, finished with the same cushion. He was five under par at 283.

The best indications of Archer's dominance were his rounds of 67 and 69. Nobody else shot better than 71 as the seniors, winning their argument of the previous year, played the course from the same tees as the regular tour pros in action in the year's only concurrent event involving both circuits. The 69 came in the second round and moved him past first-round leaders Bruce Crampton and Bobby Nichols (71s) into a two-stroke lead over Chi Chi Rodriguez with a 142 total. When George followed with the 67 Saturday, playing partner Rodriguez declared, "You can engrave his name on the trophy now." The thankless task of trying to win from second place had then fallen to Al Geiberger, who was at 216, seven behind the leader. Of the 67, Archer said afterward, "I didn't have a hole today that even looked like I was going to make a bogey." Actually, he missed a 30-inch par putt for one at the sixth hole to go with four birdies on the front nine and two on the back.

Entering the final round, Archer was just six strokes behind Paul Azinger, who was leading the main event, and thinking about how his Sunday finish would stack up against the regular tour wind-up. However, he put that out of his mind early on when he double-bogeyed the fourth hole with a ball in the water. He went on to the 74 to finish seven ahead of Crampton and Nichols, who closed with 72 and 71 respectively.

Royal Caribbean Classic—$400,000
Winner: Lee Trevino

When Lee Trevino joined the Senior PGA Tour at the end of the 1989 season, he was confident he would do some extensive winning. But, he never expected victories to fall into his lap as the first one did in the Royal Caribbean Classic, the retitled tournament with a new sponsor at Key Biscayne, Florida.

Trevino put his first senior title onto his record in just his second start, thanks to the unwilling generosity of Jim Dent. Coasting home with a five-stroke lead on Trevino, Dent lost his wheels on the last three holes. He finished bogey, bogey, double bogey while Lee was scoring birdies from three feet at the 16th and 30 feet at the 17th and parring the 18th for 68 and 206. Dent, who "went to sleep" in slumping to 73, dropped into a second-place tie with Butch Baird, who closed with 67.

A two-time winner in 1989, his first Senior Tour season, big Jim took charge in the second round at Key Biscayne as the circuit moved into the meat of its schedule a month after the limited-field Tournament of Champions started it off. He and Arnold Palmer sat two shots off the lead Friday night after 66s as Bruce Devlin, who has been a struggling senior, came up with a seven-under-par 64. Then, Dent surged three strokes in front with 68 Saturday for 134. Frank Beard was at 137 with 69-68 rounds, as Devlin slumped to 74 and Palmer took a 73.

Trevino gave off no victory sparks early Sunday, taking bogeys at the second and third holes and falling eight shots off the lead as Dent birdied the first and fourth. A bogey and a birdie later, Jim made the turn with a five-stroke lead over Baird, Beard and Jim Ferree, seven over Trevino, who then birdied No. 10 and No. 11. Lee was still five back when they reached the 16th tee. Dent, perhaps unwisely, used a driver there, hooked into the woods and took bogey. He three-putted the 17th green and drove badly again at the 18th, that time into the water. He ultimately missed a 15-foot bogey putt as Trevino two-putted from 30 feet to capture the surprise victory.

GTE Suncoast Classic—$450,000
Winner: Mike Hill

Mike Hill accumulated more than $400,000, a rookie record, in his first season on the Senior PGA Tour in 1989, but the year had its shortcoming— no victories. Still, the younger of the talented Hill brothers remained confident that "my time would come." That "time" ensued in early February, 1990, in the GTE Suncoast Classic at Tampa, where he fought off a late pair of bogeys and scored a two-stroke win with a nine-under-par 207 at Tampa Palms Golf and Country Club.

Hill, who had won the 1989-ending Mazda Champions with partner Patty Rizzo but no individual title since the 1977 Kings Island Open on the regular tour, had 20 top-10 finishes in his winless 1989 campaign prior to the Mazda and another at Key Biscayne before arriving at Tampa. Mike, with 68, was among 23 par-breakers in the first round and just a shot off the lead, shared by Larry Mowry and J.C. Goosie. The field remained bunched after Saturday's second round as Hill moved into the lead with 69—137. Mowry, with 72, and Dale Douglass, with 69-70, trailed by two, Lee Trevino by three with 69-71—140.

With three birdies on the first seven holes Sunday, Hill widened his margin to four shots, saved pars from a variety of troubles on the next three holes and still had that edge after a birdie and three pars on the next four. The closest pursuer then was Trevino, who had a run of five birdies in the middle of the round. The week before when in the same position, Trevino had been the beneficiary of Jim Dent's collapse in the stretch and Hill showed similar signs at Tampa when he overshot the 15th and drove into the trees at the 16th, taking bogeys on both holes. However, Mike steadied with two rock-solid pars finishing up, posting a 70 for the 207. Trevino was already in with 69 and 209, two in front of Mowry and Ben Smith. It was a calm finish, in contrast to 1989, when brother Dave blew a sizable lead amid a flurry of birdies and Bob Charles won a four-man, three-hole playoff.

Aetna Challenge—$400,000
Winner: Lee Trevino

Lee Trevino had expected to enrich his bank account in major proportions when he went to work on the Senior PGA Tour, figuring that he had the talent to be in serious contention most of the time. He was a little surprised, though, when he had two victories in his pocket four starts after joining the circuit. The second in three February weeks came in the Aetna Challenge at Naples, Florida, the two surrounding a second-place finish in Tampa.

Trevino outfought Bruce Crampton in an exciting duel down the stretch Sunday, his 16-under-par 200 at The Club at Pelican Bay nipping the Australian by a stroke. Lee's rounds of 66-67-67 earned him the $60,000 winner's check and hiked his 1990 Tour income to $160,000. In mounting the only challenge to Trevino, Crampton shot rounds of 70-65-66.

Trevino never trailed after his opening 66, which staked him to a two-stroke lead over Mike Hill, the Suncoast winner the previous Sunday. Lee still led by two after Saturday's round, thanks to five birdies on the last six holes, but Crampton then was the runner-up. The stage was set for the head-to-head battle Sunday. After nine holes, the two men were both two under for the day and nobody else was in sight. Then Crampton ran off three straight birdies and was even with Trevino at 14 under at the 14th tee. Bruce took a costly and unlikely bogey on that hole when he overshot the green with a wedge. Both men birdied the 15th and Lee went two shots ahead with another at the 16th. Crampton kept his hopes alive with a brave birdie at No. 17, then both missed the 18th green with their approaches. Lee was bunkered with a peculiar lie, Bruce was over the green. Trevino blasted to three feet and, after Crampton sank his five-foot par putt, dropped his short one for the victory.

Chrysler Cup—$600,000
Winner: United States

The Chrysler Cup continues to show that, until recent years, the bulk of the finest players in the world hailed from the United States. Unlike the Ryder Cup, which during the 1980s became highly competitive and unpredictable, the Chrysler Cup, its senior counterpart, has been dominated by the Americans in all except one year of its existence. The U.S. team made it four out of five at Sarasota's TPC at Prestancia the last weekend of February, winning or tying all except one of Sunday's concluding singles matches to post a 53-1/2 to 30-1/2 decision over the International team.

The point allocations for each of the four different types of competition that comprise the Chrysler Cup insured that the winning team wouldn't be decided before Sunday's telecast, particularly when heavy rains washed out 16 points worth of singles at match play Friday. The Americans had jumped off to a 12-4 lead in the opening four-ball team match play. Lee Trevino, making his Chrysler Cup debut, and Chi Chi Rodriguez began their all-winning week by beating the strong International team of Bob Charles and Bruce Crampton in the first match, 4 and 2. Arnold Palmer/Orville Moody and Al Geiberger/Dave Hill scored the other U.S. victories, Gary Player and Harold Henning averted a shutout by defeating Miller Barber and Don Bies, 2 and 1.

Saturday's 28 points were split as Trevino/Rodriguez tripped Player/Crampton, 66-68, but Charles/Bruce Devlin and Roberto De Vicenzo/Harold Henning kept the Internationals alive with victories. Barber/Geiberger scored the other U.S. win. Any doubt about the final outcome faded early Sunday when Captain Palmer put pointless Bies out first and he responded with a 69-72 victory over De Vicenzo. Hill followed with a key win, too, clipping Charles, 70-72. With Trevino on the way to a rout of Peter Thomson, the Americans had the title in the bag. Rodriguez also won against Billy Dunk, three other matches were halved and Henning defeated Palmer, his team's only victory.

What a bleak outlook the Internationals have with Jack Nicklaus and George Archer in particular eligible for the 1991 competition and no apparent strong additions available for the opposition.

Vintage Chrysler Invitational—$400,000
Winner: Lee Trevino

Chi Chi Rodriguez was the first to say it a couple of weeks earlier—"Lee Trevino is in a league by himself." But, by the end of play in the Vintage Chrysler Invitational, most of the rest of the regulars on the Senior PGA Tour were in vocal agreement. Trevino had just completed annexation of his third title in four 1990 outings, the fastest start by any player in the circuit's existence. Even though his run of 11 straight sub-par rounds ended that Sunday with a (horrors!) par-72, Lee snared a one-stroke victory in the Vintage, the pioneer big-money event on the Senior PGA Tour at the plush Vintage Club in Indian Wells, California. He was 11 under par at 205.

Although he struggled a bit and showed some signs of fatigue from his no-breaks schedule in the final round, Trevino was clearly heading for another victory the first two days. He crafted a smooth 66 Friday, running off eight pars for starters and scoring birdies on six of the remaining 10 holes. That gave him a one-stroke lead over Don Massengale, the consistent Mike Hill and John Brodie which he expanded to three with another battering of the Mountain Course's back nine. He birdied five holes and bogeyed the 17th coming in for 67 and 133. The lead was particularly comfortable for Lee, since Massengale was the only man within five strokes of him going into the final round. Don had shot 69, finishing with a wet tee shot at the 16th and a birdie on the 18th.

Trevino had his hands full with Massengale in the early going Sunday. In fact, after seven holes, Don had chalked up three birdies after three-putting the first green and had overtaken the leader. They remained deadlocked until they played the par-three 11th, where Lee dropped his six-iron tee shot three feet from the cup and Massengale missed the green. The two-shot swing there gave Trevino the lead for keeps, Don edging within a stroke when he birdied the 17th but missing a tough 20-foot birdie putt on the final green. Hill and Dale Douglass tied Massengale at 206. Hill shot 66 and Douglass 67, but they had too much ground to make up. Mike needed four birdies on the last five holes for 205 and Douglass birdied the last three holes to finish in the runners-up deadlock.

Vantage at the Dominion—$300,000
Winner: Jim Dent

Jim Dent was in no mood for an instant replay when the Senior PGA Tour's Vantage at the Dominion tournament reached its closing stages. Dent had positioned himself in much the same leading situation in that final round as he had at Key Biscayne where he muddled away the victory. Fortified by his resolve not to let it happen again, he put on a finish that was as strong as the Miami closing was weak and rolled to a three-stroke victory at San Antonio's Dominion Country Club. He closed with 66 for his 11-under-par 205.

With chatterbox Lee Trevino skipping the tournament, another "talker"—Ken Still—enjoyed a rare couple of days in the sun. The popular Still, going the entire 18 holes with the same ball, a rarity among the pros, opened with 66, dropping birdie putts on five of the last six holes. He shared the lead with Dale Douglass, who had just 24 putts in his round. Dent shot 69, then followed with 70 for 139, sitting two strokes behind Still and one behind Douglass and Harold Henning. Still had a 71 in leading a PGA Senior Tour event going into the final round for the first time since 1985.

Just as happened in the Quadel Classic that year, Still, a non-winner as a senior, couldn't hang on in the final round. He was out of it early on his way to 75. Dent started Sunday's round poorly with his third straight bogey at No. 1 and just got back to even par with a 15-foot birdie putt at the fifth hole. He was explosive from there in. He reached the par-five seventh in two with a huge downwind drive on the breezy afternoon and a nine iron to two feet for a tap-in eagle. Jim followed with birdies at the ninth, 10th and 11th, at the 10th chipping in from 40 feet, to go 10 under par and added two more at the 13th and 15th to secure a five-shot lead. A bogey at the 17th only reduced his final margin to three over Harold Henning, who birdied the 18th for 70 and 208. Mike Hill had another good tournament, tying for third at 210 with Lou Graham.

Fuji Electric Grand Slam—$400,000
Winner: Bob Charles

One has to think that Bob Charles can hardly wait for the Fuji Electric Grand Slam tournament in Japan to come up on the schedule. Case in point: Charles had not seriously challenged in any of the early 1990 tournaments on the Senior PGA Tour when he and a sizable group of American tour seniors made the annual trek to Tokyo for the Grand Slam, a lucrative event that highlights Japan's senior season. Charles won the tournament for the third year in a row, handling rugged, windy conditions the last two days to post a two-under-par 214 and a two-stroke victory over Taiwan's Hsu Chi San.

The weather was no problem the first day at Oak Hills Country Club at Kurimotomachi as Larry Mowry jumped off with a one-stroke lead over Hsu, one of the more successful players on the Asia circuit in his earlier years. Four other players in the 60s were in front of Charles at that point. Powerful winds played havoc Saturday, particularly with the late finishers. Only two players broke par as wind gusts up to 50 miles an hour in the area forced a halt to operations at Japan's major airport at nearby Narita. Topsoil from adjacent sweet potato fields blew through the air, darkening the atmosphere. Mowry soared to 79. Orville Moody shot 80. Hsieh Min Nan, another Taiwanese star of the past, had a 70, the day's best round, and moved into a tie for the lead at 143 with Hsu (76) and Dave Hill (69-74). Charles shot 75 and was two back at 145.

Temperatures dropped Sunday, the winds didn't, and the scores were again high, except for that of Charles, who, explaining why, said that, "I spent most of my life playing in cool, windy conditions at home in New Zealand." He shot a near-flawless 69, scoring two birdies on each side and taking a harmless bogey on the last hole. Hsu rallied on the back nine for 73 and his 216. Hill slumped to 76 and Hsieh to 77, Hill dropping into a three-way tie for third at 219 with Lee Trevino and Miller Barber, a former Fuji winner.

The Tradition at Desert Mountain—$800,000
Winner: Jack Nicklaus

Jack Nicklaus had two achievements in mind for his limited 1990 tournament schedule—wins on both the Senior and regular PGA Tours. Although he didn't accomplish the tougher feat, Nicklaus took care of the other order of business with great dispatch, winning in his first appearance as a senior in the Tradition at Desert Mountain. Playing the Cochise course as if he owned it—he just designed it—Nicklaus set himself in good position when the Tradition got underway Friday after a Thursday rain-out, surged in front Saturday and pulled away to a four-stroke victory at 10-under-par 206. Thus, he joined Arnold Palmer, Gary Player and George Archer as a winner in his first senior start.

Thursday was a miserable day—wind, heavy rain, hail—in Scottsdale, Arizona, forcing a cancellation of the round in what is one of the few 72-hole events on the senior circuit. Four players—Bruce Crampton, Mike Hill, Al Geiberger and Phil Rodgers—shot 69s Friday to lead the prime field, but only Crampton was a factor by week's end. Nicklaus made his move Saturday, perhaps getting his winning spark when he chipped in from heavy grass behind the 18th green for an eagle, 67 and a two-stroke lead at 138 over Crampton, Rodgers and Player. Rodgers bogeyed the last hole, the victim of a three-shot swing.

Crampton took an early run at Jack with birdies on the first two holes and gained a tie when Nicklaus bogeyed the par-five fourth hole. Bruce promptly fell out of contention with a double bogey at the sixth. Player got within two shots with a birdie at No. 8, but no closer. Nicklaus bogeyed the 12th hole in the face of an approaching thunderstorm that delayed play for more than an hour, but came back with birdies at the 14th and 15th when play resumed and coasted home. Player fashioned a 70 Sunday to take second place, two shots ahead of Crampton and Charles Coody. It was far from equalling his fee for designing the course, but the $120,000 first prize made a nice initial entry into the Nicklaus record as a senior.

PGA Seniors Championship—$450,000
Winner: Gary Player

Like most players at the top level of ability, Gary Player particularly relishes victories in the premier tournaments. During his younger years, Player won nine major titles, his own national championship 13 times and many other events of special significance. In his first four full seasons on the Senior PGA Tour, Gary bagged the PGA Seniors and U.S. Senior Open twice each along with the Senior TPC in 1987. So, it was not the least bit surprising that Player made the 1990 PGA Seniors his first victory of the season in its new April slot on the Senior PGA Tour schedule.

As expected, the championship at PGA National Golf Club in Palm Beach Gardens, Florida, drew a blue-ribbon field, including Jack Nicklaus and Lee Trevino in their first PGA Seniors appearances. By the time the tournament reached its final round, the situation seemed as though it had been scripted. There were Player, Nicklaus and Trevino in the final threesome, set to battle for the important title. One problem, though. Player had a five-stroke lead on Nicklaus, six on Trevino, thanks to a sensational third-round 65 that included a double bogey, and he wasn't about to relinquish it. Neither of his fellow superstars could do anything about it, either, Jack encountering a failed putting stroke and Lee doing such damaging things as whiffing a two-inch tap-in.

Actually, Player's only threats were Chi Chi Rodriguez, who closed with 66 to vault into second place, and two rain delays totalling more than an hour wait in the round. When play resumed on a puddled course with darkness fast approaching, Gary found the permanent water and double-bogeyed No. 16. But he steadied and parred in for 73, seven-under-par 281 and a two-shot victory over Rodriguez. Nicklaus (72) and Trevino (71) tied for third at 285. Nicklaus had jumped off with a three-stroke lead with a 68 the first day, but followed with 78 Friday as Trevino got into the act with 67—144 to trail Player and Harold Henning (74-69s) by a stroke. Then came Player's 65 round, in which he played the front nine in 29 with an eagle and five birdies. He made sure it wasn't a wasted effort Sunday.

Liberty Mutual Legends of Golf—$750,000
Winners: Charles Coody and Dale Douglass

One of the ideas in moving the Liberty Mutual Legends of Golf from its long-time home at Onion Creek across Austin, Texas, to the new Barton Creek Club was to make things a bit tougher for these select, two-man teams of seniors. In the last three Legends (no longer an apt tournament title, by the way), the winning pairs were a record 29, 26 and a record-tying 29 under par for the 72 holes. Bad idea. Charles Coody and Dale Douglass were 33 under par after just 54 holes en route to their runaway victory in the 13th playing of the television-oriented event that spawned the Senior PGA Tour. They finished 39 under at 249, breezing in with a seven-stroke victory.

Good friends off the course, Coody and Douglass proved a masterful pairing. Douglass rode Coody's coattails in the opening round. After shooting 63 in the pro-amateur, Charles made a hole-in-one at No. 3, followed with seven birdies and concluded the round with an eagle. With Dale's lesser contributions, the team posted a 59 and took a five-stroke lead over Chi Chi Rodriguez/ Dave Hill and Tom Shaw/Miller Barber. The eventual winners were off and running. Each pitched in five birdies for 62 Friday, widening the margin to six strokes over Al Geiberger/Harold Henning. They dispelled all doubts with another 62 Saturday to reach that astonishing 33-under-par score and go eight ahead of Geiberger/Henning and Rodriguez/Hill.

Even though their birdie production geared down, Coody and Douglass still managed a closing 66, saving each other from serious trouble on several occasions. Geiberger and Henning chipped only one shot off the margin with their 65—256. Larry Mowry and Frank Beard were third at 258 and those two teams also bettered the old record of Onion Creek vintage. Rodriguez and Hill slipped to 259 with their closing 68. Coody and Douglass each collected $70,000 for the victory, Coody's second and Douglass' sixth on the Senior Tour.

Murata Reunion Pro-Am—$400,000
Winner: Frank Beard

After a fistful of near-misses during his first 12 months of senior golf, Frank Beard seemed to have his first PGA Senior Tour victory in the palm of his hand as he teed off in the final round of the Murata Reunion Pro-Am. The winner of 11 tournaments during his career on the regular PGA Tour, Beard was tagged as a sure victor as a senior, too, although most allowed for rust from his decade of inactivity as a tournament contestant. Now, there he was, carrying a six-stroke lead into Sunday's Reunion finale at Stonebriar Country Club near Dallas. What figured to be a walk in the park turned into a shaky stagger through a minefield before Frank got home with a two-stroke victory.

Beard led from the start in the "Crosby-style" tournament, opening with a six-under-par 66 on the rain-soaked course that gave him a two-shot margin on Walt Zembriski and Bobby Nichols. A 7:50 start helped Frank Saturday. He got in a near-flawless 67—five birdies ("All except one were kick-ins") and 13 pars—before gusty winds came up and had the six-shot advantage when the day's play had ended.

Dale Douglass was closest at 139, but it was Zembriski, then at 141, who almost and certainly could have spoiled Beard's day. Frank's putting stroke virtually disappeared on the opening holes. He three-putted four of the first six holes and made putts of five and 10 feet on the other two for pars as his lead melted steadily. First, Rocky Thompson challenged from far back (144) with an outgoing 30 before Zembriski came to the fore. Beard had steadied with birdies at the seventh and ninth, but found himself out of the lead for the first time when he overshot the green into the water at the par-three 15th and made a tough bogey while Zembriski was two-putting the par-five 17th for his fourth straight birdie (eighth in 12 holes) and going nine under. However, Walt, using his driver instead of a safe iron, duck-hooked his tee shot into the water at the 18th and took a double bogey for 68 and 209. Beard birdied the 17th and finished with 74 and 207, winning for the first time since the 1971 New Orleans Open. The $60,000 prize was his biggest tournament check ever.

Las Vegas Classic—$450,000
Winner: Chi Chi Rodriguez

Chi Chi Rodriguez, an emotional sort, had gotten down on himself, his game in such a state that he was considering a severe cutback in his play on the Senior PGA Tour. A seven-tournament winner and top man on the money list in 1987, Rodriguez hadn't won since the Crestar Classic in September of 1989 when he came to the Las Vegas Classic, sustained by improved performances with a new set of clubs during the preceding month. At week's end at Desert Inn Country Club, he had outfought Charles Coody and George Archer in the final round and owned his 14th Senior PGA Tour title.

The last-round battle set up this way: Lee Trevino, already a three-time winner but troubled by a sore knee, joined a leading 67 first-place tie with Bob Charles and Coody, who had beaten Rodriguez in a two-hole playoff at Las Vegas the previous November for his first senior victory. Rodriguez (touch of food poisoning) and Archer (flu symptoms) came off the sick list to share the second-round lead at 135, Chi Chi with 68-67 and George with 69-66. Coody was then three back and Trevino had slipped to 72 and 139.

Rodriguez never trailed after nailing a birdie on the first hole Sunday, but the issue came down to the final hole. By the 12th hole, he had established a three-stroke lead, but it dropped to one when he bogeyed the 13th and Archer almost holed his wedge approach and birdied there. Coody, playing ahead of them, was in the process of shooting a five-birdie 67. Chi Chi regained his two-shot edge with a 12-foot birdie putt at No. 14, but tightened the finish when he pushed his two-iron tee shot under a tree at the 17th and bogeyed. Undaunted, he parred the 18th routinely for 69 and the victory after watching Archer just miss a chip shot for birdie after driving under a tree. Coody had two-putted from 20 feet at the 18th, not knowing that, if he had made the 20-footer, he probably would have wound up in another playoff against Rodriguez. In nipping Archer and Coody by a stroke, Chi Chi was 12 under par at 204 and observed: "This is the first time a 12 beats an 11 at Las Vegas."

Southwestern Bell Classic—$450,000
Winner: Jimmy Powell

The unlikeliest winner of the Senior PGA Tour season surfaced in the Southwestern Bell Classic in the person of Jimmy Powell. This is not to say that Powell is not a competent player, even though he had never won on either PGA Tour, regular or senior, since he first appeared as a tour player in 1959. He had made occasional strong showings over those years. But, it was what had transpired since the last one—his playoff loss to George Archer in the Gatlin Brothers Southwest Classic late in 1989—that made Powell's victory at Quail Creek Golf and Country Club in Oklahoma City so surprising.

Immediately after that November near-miss in Abilene, Texas, Jimmy contracted a back ailment that had disastrous consequences on his game. He fell to the lower regions of the tournament standings in the remaining events of 1989 and the early tournaments of 1990. He shot 90 in missing the cut in the PGA Seniors and reached the nadir when he had a 93 in the Murata Reunion. On the verge of quitting the circuit, Powell went on to Las Vegas, where cod liver oil pills recommended by long-time tournament scorekeeper Ken Everett did the trick. Without back pain and with his swing re-grooved, Jimmy broke par for the first time all year and tied for ninth before heading for Oklahoma City.

Charley Owens and Terry Dill attracted the headlines the first two rounds at Quail Creek. The admirable Owens limped through the wind and rain Friday to shoot 67 and take a three-shot lead over Dill, who took over Saturday when Owens dropped to 75. Dill, also a non-winner on both Tours who practiced and taught law in the interim, posted 69 for 139 and a two-stroke lead over Mike Hill. Powell was at 143.

Jimmy started his charge Sunday when he birdied four times in a five-hole stretch in the middle of the round to close within a stroke of Dill, who managed only one birdie on the front nine. The 14th hole was the turning point. Powell birdied there, but it later cost Terry a bogey. Another birdie at No. 16 gave Jimmy a two-shot lead and his par at the tough 17th and a final birdie at the 18th secured his three-stroke victory. His closing-round 65 gave him an eight-under 208. Dill, Hill, Rives McBee and Jim Dent tied for second at 211.

Doug Sanders Kingwood Celebrity Classic—$300,000
Winner: Lee Trevino

Lee Trevino appropriately resumed his merry-making in the "fun tournament" of the Senior PGA Tour—the Doug Sanders Kingwood Celebrity Classic—and did so in the most decisive fashion of his new senior career. Trevino broke the tournament's 36 and 54-hole records on the way to his fourth victory of the season, putting together rounds of 67-67-69 for a 13-under-par 203 at the Deerwood Club at Kingwood in suburban Houston, Texas. Gary Player made a late charge but all it did was move him up into second place six strokes behind the winner.

Trevino led from the start. Gusty winds affected most of the players, but didn't bother Lee in Friday's opening round. He shot 32 on the front nine despite a ninth-hole bogey and 35 on the tougher back side for the first 67 and a one-stroke lead over Jim Ferree. George Lanning, the only other player in the 60s, was two back and Player, Bob Charles and Dave Hill all started with 70s.

Despite the second 67, Trevino found himself upstaged Saturday when President George Bush took time out from other activities of a Texas visit and played with son George, Tour Commissioner Deane Beman and host Sanders, who had invited the Chief Executive. Amid the hubbub, Trevino mustered an eagle at the 16th hole, four birdies and a bogey, though maintaining that, "I wasn't paying any attention to what I was doing. I was trying to watch the President play." The 134 broke the tournament record by three strokes and staked him to a four-shot lead over Charles and six over Lanning and Orville Moody, who had a hole-in-one on his way to a 66.

Lee was never threatened Sunday. Player created a stir with his 65, but it never worried Trevino because a 74 Saturday had set Gary 10 strokes back. After a bogey at the 15th dropped him back to even par for the day, Lee insured his victory by birdieing the last three holes. His check for $45,000 reminded him that, at another Houston area course, Sharpstown, he had won the Texas State Open, his first victory as a pro, and carried off first money of $1,000.

Bell Atlantic Classic—$500,000
Winner: Dale Douglass

One of the great success stories of the Senior PGA Tour gained another chapter at Philadelphia. Dale Douglass, one of several players who have enjoyed far greater success on that circuit than they did in their years on the regular PGA Tour, picked up his sixth individual win in the over-50 competition with a playoff victory over Gary Player in the Bell Atlantic Classic's last stand at Chester Valley Golf Club in suburban Malvern. It came five weeks after he and Charles Coody had run away with the Legends of Golf. Douglass won only three times in more than two decades of full-time play on the PGA Tour.

Lee Trevino carried over his brilliant play from his win in the Sanders Classic in Houston and joined a three-way tie for the lead with defending champion Dave and Mike Hill at three-under-par 67 over the rolling Chester Valley course. They were a shot up on George Archer, Terry Dill and 67-year-old Charley Sifford. Douglass opened with 70, then seized the lead Saturday, when early-morning rain delayed the start of play for two hours. Dale shot 66 and inched a stroke ahead of Player and Coody as Trevino shot 71 for 138 and the Hill brothers fell out of serious contention. Ken Still, one of only four players to break par Saturday, had 67 and joined Trevino at 138.

Coody and Charles were in the fight much of the way Sunday and wound up missing the playoff by a stroke, Coody shooting 70 and Charles 67. Bob was tied with Douglass and Player until he blew an 18-inch par putt at the 17th hole. Player exhibited his unmatched mastery of sand play at the 18th, saving par for 69 to Dale's routine par and 70 for his four-under-par 206. Player parred again from a greenside trap at the first extra hole in the tournament's third consecutive playoff, but lost his bid for a second 1990 victory when he drove into the trees at the next hole and eventually took a double bogey. Douglass, who also had tree trouble on the hole, one-putted for par and the victory, his first individual one on the Senior PGA Tour since February of 1988, when he won the GTE Suncoast Classic in Florida.

NYNEX Commemorative—$350,000
Winner: Lee Trevino

Strange things were happening on the Senior PGA Tour in the late spring. Three weeks after Jimmy Powell, a guy who had never won on any PGA circuit, went from a 93 to a victory in 15 days, a 67-year-old pro fired a final-round 64 and carried the year's overwhelming star five overtime holes before yielding a title. The latter remarkable happening came about in the NYNEX Commemorative the first of June when stolid Mike Fetchick took part in the Senior Tour's longest playoff ever before bowing to Lee Trevino, the year's leading everything.

Low scores are common at Sleepy Hollow Country Club, a par-70, 6,545-yard course up the Hudson River from New York City, where it has always taken at least 200 to win the tournament, and so it was again in 1990 from start to finish. Dick Rhyan opened with 63 and had only a one-stroke lead on the aforementioned Powell. Then Bob Charles, the 1988 and 1989 champion, shot 64 Saturday for 131, yet he just had a stroke on Trevino (66-66) and two on Powell, Chi Chi Rodriguez and Walt Zembriski. Hardly noticed at 135 was Fetchick, who was the oldest PGA Tour winner ever when he won the Hilton Head Seniors in the fall of 1985 at age 63.

Charles led by as much as three strokes early Sunday, but a parade of players caught up later on. At one point with the contenders well along on the back nine, six of them were tied for the lead at 11 under. Fetchick, who didn't make a bogey on his last 33 holes, was first in with his 64—199, 45 minutes ahead of the final threesome, and he was joined at that score by Powell, then Trevino and Rodriguez from the last group, Chi Chi making par from a bunker at the 18th for 66. Trevino shot 67. Charles missed the playoff because he double-bogeyed No. 16, and Player, totally out of character, flubbed a sand shot, his eternal specialty, at the last green to finish one back. Trevino topped Fetchick's 18-foot birdie putt on the first extra hole, eliminating Powell and Rodriguez. Then Mike doggedly matched pars with Trevino until Lee dropped a winning 10-footer on the fifth overtime hole to cage his fifth victory in 10 starts in 1990.

Mazda Senior TPC Championship—$1,000,000
Winner: Jack Nicklaus

Jack Nicklaus changed his mind about the Mazda Senior TPC Championship and the rest of the players in the field probably wished that he would have stuck to his guns and stayed at home. It would have given somebody else a shot at the prestigious title and the season's biggest first prize of $150,000. Nicklaus, who had hit balls only once in 10 days before arriving at Dearborn Country Club in Michigan for the championship, made a shambles of the competition, allowing only Lee Trevino to get within 11 strokes of his Senior PGA Tour record score of 27-under-par 261. Lee was six back at the end.

Deciding to enter under the influence of his ties with ABC-TV and son Gary's failure to qualify for his Ohio State team's trip to the NCAA Championship that week, Nicklaus found Dearborn's easy par-fives and excellent greens to his liking. "I made a lot of 20-footers this week," Jack observed afterward. "I don't think I have ever putted this well for four days."

The destruction started Thursday when Nicklaus opened with a seven-under-par 65 in his first competitive round in almost a month. He took only 25 putts, 10 with a chip-in on the back nine, and shared the lead for the first and last time all week—with Ben Smith. On Friday Jack shot 68 and took sole possession of the lead, a shot ahead of Trevino and Terry Dill. Nicklaus and Trevino began to outdistance the others when they began with birdies Saturday. Jack went on to tie the course record with 64 for 197, Lee had 66 for 200 and nobody else was closer than 204 at day's end. Even Trevino knew his chances were gone fairly early Sunday as Nicklaus went eagle-birdie-birdie, starting at the third hole. He went on to another 64 for the 261 that gave him his second Senior PGA Tour victory in three starts and the biggest winner's check of his storied career.

It did nothing to cement his interest in that circuit, though. He talked, instead, about the U.S. Open coming up later that week in Chicago. "I still can't get it out of my system that I'm not competitive on the other tour," he concluded.

The Masters

Nick Faldo overcame Augusta, and Raymond Floyd, to win his second consecutive Masters in another playoff.

The Masters was Floyd's until Faldo's inspired finishing stretch.

Starting with 74, Fred Couples rallied for fourth in the Masters.

Lanny Wadkins (left) finished well to tie John Huston for third place.

U.S. Open

Hale Irwin secured his third U.S. Open title with four consecutive birdies on the last nine, a stirring 45-foot putt at No. 18, and then a 19-hole playoff.

Tenacious Mike Donald hung on longer than anyone expected in the U.S. Open—all the way to extra holes in the playoff.

Billy Ray Brown (left) and Nick Faldo were one stroke away from the playoff.

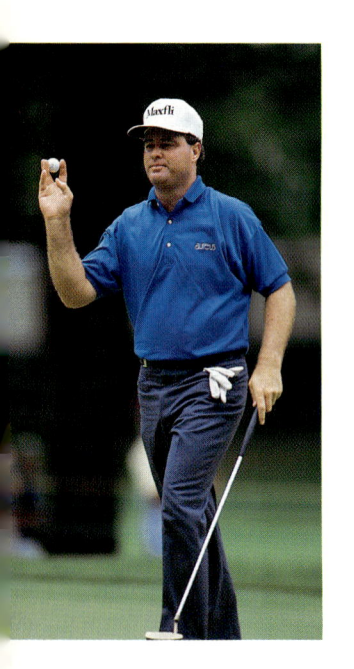

Tim Simpson (left) led after 36 holes, and tied for fifth place. Curtis Strange made a great bid for three in a row.

British Open

Nick Faldo basked in the applause for his five-stroke victory in the British Open.

As Faldo lifted the silver cup, wife Gill (left) and caddy Fanny Sunneson were at his side, with the Faldo children.

Payne Stewart (left) and Mark McNulty shared runner-up honors.

On a hot streak, with two consecutive wins, Ian Woosnam tied for fourth place.

Greg Norman kept pace with Faldo for two rounds, but a 76 on the third day left the Shark in sixth place.

Perhaps the greatest scene in golf—the 72nd hole at St. Andrews.

PGA Championship

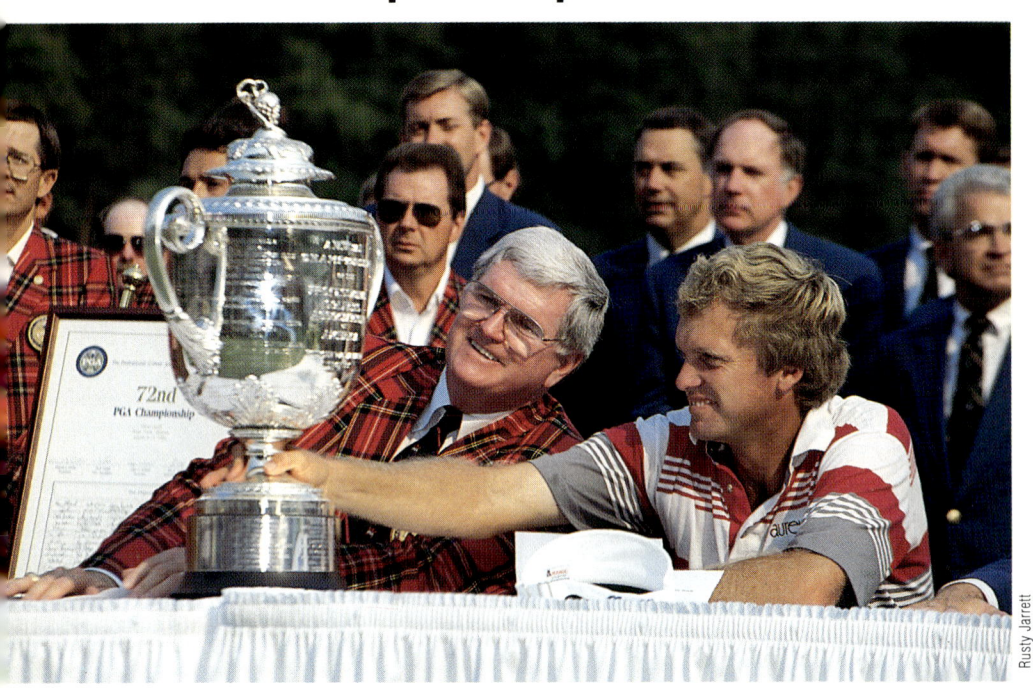

Australia's Wayne Grady (with PGA president Pat Rielly, above left) saw his name etched on the famous trophy, after winning by three strokes in the PGA Championship.

Many were frustrated at Shoal Creek, including Fred Couples (above), who placed second.

Despite an opening 77, Gil Morgan took third place in the PGA Championship.

Golf Isn't Their Only Sport

Water skiing is among Ian Woosnam's pasttimes.

David Feherty enjoys a game of cricket.

Seve Ballesteros is a trick-shot artist in snooker, as well as golf.

Photographer Lawrence Levy switched places and made a birdie for the cameras in the RMCC Invitational Pro-Am.

On the end of Greg Norman's line is — what else? — a Great White Shark, off the Australian coast.

World Match Play

The Woosnam clan celebrated Ian's second World Match Play title.

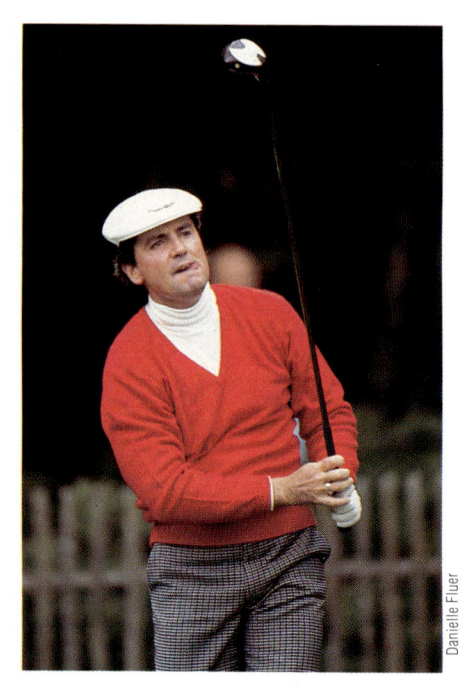

Woosnam's opponent in the final was Mark McNulty (right), who fell by a 4-and-2 margin.

In deep trouble at the World Match Play were McNulty (above) and Greg Norman (below), whom McNulty beat in the semi-finals.

Dunhill Cup

The winning Irish team: Ronan Rafferty, David Feherty and Philip Walton.

Captain Feherty led Ireland to a second Dunhill Cup title.

MONY Syracuse Classic—$300,000
Winner: Jim Dent

It had not been a good year for defending champions on the Senior PGA Tour. In fact, when the diluted field teed off in the MONY Syracuse Classic in mid-June, no 1989 winner had repeated in a circuit event and few had even come close. Jim Dent put an end to that at Lafayette Country Club, finishing on top in the tournament in which he had scored his first Senior PGA Tour victory just one month into his first season on the over-50 circuit in 1989.

Many of the better-known names were missing at Syracuse, one of the oldest events on the Senior Tour and one that usually has field problems. With events every week, many of those who bypassed Syracuse probably did so because of the minimum $300,000 purse in the aftermath of the rich Mazda Senior TPC. Even if all of the big guns had been present, though, it may not have made any difference in the outcome. Dent, the big hitter who has worked hard on his short game as a senior, won the tournament with a 199, equalling the low 54-hole score of the season shot by the four playoff protagonists in the NYNEX Commemorative two weeks earlier.

Dent began his trail to victory with a 66 Friday, joining Mike Hill and two other pros in second place, a stroke behind leader Dick Hendrickson. Then, he and Hill grabbed shares of the lead Saturday with 67s for 133, a shot better than Larry Mowry and two in front of George Archer and ageless Charley Sifford. Hill's erratic round included two double bogeys created by wild tee shots as he went for a day with a 45-inch driver. Dent had a double bogey, too, on Sunday when the ranks of the contenders narrowed to him and Archer. He double-bogeyed the fifth hole, but rebounded with a birdie-eagle-birdie stretch to turn in 33 and lead Archer by a stroke. Dent yielded the lead briefly on the back nine, but Archer's only bogey of the weekend put Jim back into a one-stroke lead and he carried it to the finish, preserving it with a spectacular birdie after a wild tee shot at the 17th, the last of Lafayette's five par-fives. Dent shot 66 Sunday in capturing his fourth Senior PGA Tour victory.

Digital Classic—$350,000
Winner: Bob Charles

Talk about "reading putts!" Bob Charles perused a chapter in a book he had written about golf in 1964, when he was considered perhaps the finest putter in the game, and turned the quick review of his comments about that phase of the game into his first Senior PGA Tour victory of the 1990 season. After the remedial reading suggested by his wife, Verity, prior to the second round of the Digital Classic in Massachusetts, Charles put together a pair of 67s and posted his second straight Digital victory, winning by two strokes with his 13-under 203.

The lefthander from New Zealand, who had won 13 times in his four seasons on the PGA Senior Tour and led the circuit's money list in 1988 and 1989, had won in 1990 only in Japan's Fuji Electric Grand Slam in March before arriving at Nashawtuc Country Club in Concord to defend one of his five 1989 titles. His opening 69 wasn't bad, but he was five shots behind Chi Chi Rodriguez, whose three-year string of victories he had ended in 1989. Verity brought out photocopies of the old book and insisted Bob read the putting chapter. In doing so, he realized that he wasn't squaring his putting stance. With that adjustment, Bob moved within a stroke of leaders Rodriguez and Mike Hill Saturday and went on to the victory Sunday, remarking afterward, "I don't think I missed a putt under six feet the last two days."

Charles set up his final-round move with a back-nine 31 for the 67. Nobody asserted himself on the front nine Sunday, although Lee Trevino climbed from four strokes off the pace into a first-place tie at 10 under par with Charles and Rodriguez. Bob then birdied the next two holes and held the lead until Lee made his sixth and last birdie at the 15th. Charles regained first place when he, too, birdied the short 15th, as Rodriguez fell back toward his eventual third-place finish with a bogey. Trevino missed birdie chances on each of the last three holes and settled for 66—205. Charles parred in for 67—203, three strokes higher than his winning score at Nashawtuc in 1989.

U.S. Senior Open—$500,000
Winner: Lee Trevino

Three weeks earlier in the Senior TPC Championship, Jack Nicklaus and Lee Trevino left the rest of the classy field in the dust. They did it again in the U.S. Senior Open at the end of June, but there was one distinct difference in the final outcome. Nicklaus won the Senior TPC. Trevino got even at Ridgewood Country Club, though not quite as decisively as was the six-stroke margin of Nicklaus at Dearborn. Trevino brought home a 67 the last day for a two-shot win at 13-under 275, his sixth victory of the year.

Others were in the picture in the early rounds at the Paramus, New Jersey, club, but Trevino was in front for two days. He opened with 67, taking a one-stroke lead over Walt Zembriski, Jim Dent, John Paul Cain, Charles Coody and Ken Still. His 68 Friday left him a shot ahead of Dent and at least three in front of everybody else. Nicklaus was five back after his 71-69 start, mainly because he had failed to convert a goodly number of birdie putts.

It was a different story Saturday. Jack birdied the second from 23 feet and eagled the par-five fifth with a 45-footer from the front fringe. He made four more birdies on the way to a 67 and 207, which gave him a one-stroke lead over Trevino, Dent and Gary Player, who had started with 75 and came back with 65-68. Trevino didn't lose the lead until he bogeyed the last hole from the sand after trading birdies and bogeys all afternoon. Dent shot 72 (and a final-round 76) with 15 stitches in a finger he gashed closing his car door.

Player faltered with four back-nine bogeys Sunday for 73, finishing in a third-place tie at 281 with Chi Chi Rodriguez, who closed with 66, and Mike Hill, who posted his eighth top-four finish of the season. Trevino gained the upper hand on Nicklaus on the front nine with three birdies on the first six holes and, when he birdied again at the 10th, he had a four-shot lead over Nicklaus, who was one over on the front. Lee made 15-foot birdie putts at

Nos. 15 and 16 and finished with 67. Jack birdied the same two holes, but lost his chance to catch Trevino, already finished, when he bogeyed the par-five 17th after mishitting an eight-iron third shot. He shot 70 for 277.

Northville Long Island Classic—$450,000
Winner: George Archer

George Archer had won twice in his first six starts as a senior and said, "I really thought this tour was going to be a piece of cake." Instead, it turned out to be a painful experience as back trouble that has plagued him through much of his career reared up again. While the tall Californian didn't exactly sink into a deep funk, he went six months before winning again. It happened in the Northville Long Island Classic at Jericho's Meadow Brook Club and the victory did not come easily.

In fact, Archer almost withdrew before play even began. He struggled through the Thursday pro-am with backaches he had endured since mid-February at Naples, Florida, in the Aetna Challenge and aggravated when he walked the four rounds of the U.S. Senior Open the previous weekend. He stuck it out, though, and opened the tournament Friday with a respectable 69, two strokes behind Gary Player, the leader and a former Northville winner when it was an unofficial event. Player backed up to 74 Saturday and Archer jumped into first place with 67—136, two strokes in front of Frank Beard, Homero Blancas and Charles Coody.

No winner of 1990 had been as erratic as Archer was Sunday. He made his first of four bogeys at No. 1, Beard eagled the par-five third as George was making a birdie and they were tied. They traded the lead three times on the next nine holes, then carried a tie to the par-three 15th, where Beard holed a 40-foot birdie putt. Archer made a 40-footer himself at the next hole, but it was just for a par after he hooked his tee shot into deep trouble. Beard had tee-shot difficulties at the 17th and it cost him the tournament. He buried his drive in a bunker, blasted out, found the woods and a greenside trap and two-putted for a double bogey. Archer made his par there and at the 18th, gaining a one-stroke victory with his par-72 finish when Beard just missed a 10-foot birdie putt for the tie and a playoff. Frank had 71 as did Coody and they shared the runner-up spot.

Kroger Classic—$600,000
Winner: Jim Dent

Things didn't go very well for the new kid on the block, although Jim Dent had no complaints about his shopping in the inaugural Kroger Classic at the end of a waterlogged weekend in Cincinnati. The new event, sporting a $600,000 purse, one of the season's biggest, lost its Thursday pro-amateur and Saturday's second round to heavy rains. The pros slogged over soaked fairways of Kings Island's Grizzly Course in the two rounds that went into the books and established Dent as the winner of the $90,000 first-place check, by far the biggest of his long career.

Almost half the players in the field had a legitimate shot at the Kroger title going into Sunday's final round. Lee Trevino, gunning for his seventh victory of the season, and Dave Hill, seeking his first, shared the first-round lead with 65s. Trevino had a string of four birdies on the back nine en route to his 65. At day's end, Joe Jimenez, Walt Zembriski and John Paul Cain were just a stroke behind and Dent was in a five-player group at 67. Forty-two pros in the field of 78 shot par or better.

The additional overnight rain that ran the week's total to seven inches and washed out Saturday's round—the Senior PGA Tour does not double up rounds on a single day nor carry tournaments over to Mondays—left a soggy course that enabled all of the players to "shoot darts" at the pins but drastically cut down on the roll of the tee shots. Big-hitter Dent, with his extra carry off the tee, took that advantage and rolled to victory, his third of the season, a total exceeded only by Trevino. Jim birdied the first four holes to race past an ineffective Trevino and had first place to himself when Hill, after two early birdies, bogeyed the fourth and fifth holes.

Harold Henning mounted the only serious challenge. Out in 32, the South African birdied the 15th to go eight under and was just a stroke behind the leader when Dent took his last bogey at No. 14. Henning missed a birdie putt for 63 on the final green and finished second at 134 when Jim parred the 18th from a fairway bunker for 66 and 133.

Ameritech Open—$500,000
Winner: Chi Chi Rodriguez

Chi Chi Rodriguez declared himself King for the week on the Senior PGA Tour—Jack Nicklaus and Lee Trevino were playing in the British Open and "I go from Crown Prince to King when they're not here"—and the flippant Puerto Rican performed in regal fashion in the Ameritech Open with a runaway victory. In winning by seven strokes, matching the season's biggest margin, Rodriguez became the fifth multiple winner on the 1990 Senior PGA Tour and put victory No. 15 on his senior career record. He was 13 under par at 203.

The tournament, which was played in Cleveland in 1989 and moves to Chicago in 1991, was staged on the Bear course of the Grand Traverse Resort in Northern Michigan, but it didn't live up to its fearsome billing, thanks to softening rains and moderate set-up. In the first round, Jim O'Hern tied the competitive record with 66, a shot better than the starts of Rodriguez and Don January, one of the circuit's dominating players through much of the 1980s. Twenty-eight men were at par or better.

As O'Hern faded Saturday, January and Rodriguez took over. January, now past his 60th birthday, birdied four of his last five holes Saturday for 69—136 and a one-shot lead over Rodriguez. But January's bid for his first win since 1987 went away with a 76 Sunday. Nobody was going to stop Rodriguez that day, not when the man makes two eagles on the first six holes. Chi Chi hit the green on the par-five third with a three-wood second shot and dropped the 10-foot eagle putt, birdied the fourth and knocked a six iron four feet from the cup on the 480-yard sixth hole, which was playing downwind, and eagled it for the second day in a row. A lull set in, and Rodriguez lost a stroke over the next six holes, giving Dave Hill a chance to advance to within three strokes. That threat ended for Chi Chi when he birdied the par-three 13th and Hill put a ball in the water and double-bogeyed the 15th. Rodriguez established his final margin with one last birdie at the 16th. George Archer and Al Kelley, a Monday qualifier, were the distant runners-up at 210, Kelley picking up by far the biggest check of his unproductive career—$40,000.

Newport Cup—$300,000
Winner: Al Kelley

"You always think you are better than you are. You just haven't proved it yet." Al Kelley made this pungent observation in the joyous aura of his first-ever victory in a tour event of any denomination. How well he described the feelings of so many hundreds of aspiring tournament players who never made it to the winner's circle. "But, I guess I proved it today," said Kelley of his two-stroke victory at the end of July in the Newport Cup, one of the Senior PGA Tour's longest-running events. He was 10 under par at 134 in the year's second rain-shortened tournament.

Determined to break through, the 55-year-old Kelley had been participating in the tough Monday qualifiers for three years, encouraged in 1989 by better showings and the tournament victories of two Monday qualifiers—Rives McBee and John Paul Cain. He hinted that he was ready to win when he tied for second in the Ameritech Open the previous week, his highest finish ever on the senior circuit or during his four seasons on the regular PGA Tour in the 1960s.

Al was just a stroke off the lead after the rain-delaying opening round was played at fabled Newport Country Club in Rhode Island. But the attention was on Lee Trevino, just back from the British Open and off and running in quest of his seventh senior title of the season. Lee began with 65 as Kelley shared second place at 66 with Terry Dill. That meant Kelley was grouped with Trevino on Sunday and who would have expected the soft-spoken non-winner to outplay the superstar? It happened, basically on the greens. Kelley took just 27 putts to Trevino's 32, four times one-putting for saves from traps. With birdie putts of 20 feet at the 13th and a slippery five feet at the 15th, Al took a two-stroke lead after earlier bids of Jim Dent and George Lanning had dissipated. He met another challenge with another five-footer out of the sand at the 16th and wrapped up the victory with solid pars on the last two holes, finishing two shots in front of Cain and Dent with his 68 and 134. Trevino three-putted the final green to drop into a tie for fourth with McBee and Joe Jimenez.

Volvo Seniors British Open—£150,000
Winner: Gary Player

It couldn't last. The benign weather that had carried through the British Open at St. Andrews continued the following week on the other coast of Scotland when the Seniors British Open was staged for the fourth year on the noted Ailsa course of the Turnberry Hotel. It didn't. On Sunday, with increasing ferocity as the day progressed, the skies unleashed the type of golfing weather for which Scotland is notorious and it became a matter of who would be the best survivor. As it turned out, Gary Player was. Even though he struggled to shoot 75 and double-bogeyed the last hole in doing so, Player captured the championship with an even-par, 72-hole score of 280, becoming the tournament's first two-time winner.

Until the very end, the story at Turnberry had been Deane Beman. The Commissioner of the U.S. PGA Tour, wrapping up a tournament-studded, six-week vacation in Scotland that had included an unsuccessful attempt to qualify for the British Open at St. Andrews, seized the lead by a stroke over Player and Arnold Palmer the second day and held it until the horrendous weather did him in on the final holes Sunday.

As was the case with the British Open prior to the 1960s, the Seniors British Open attracts only a handful of the better Americans. But, what was lacking in quantity was present in quality. Palmer, shaking off the disappointment of missing the cut in the British Open, opened with 66 and shared the first-round lead with Brian Waites before Beman added a 66 to his first-day 67 and moved a shot ahead of Palmer (68) and Player (65). Deane widened the gap to three over Palmer and five over Player Saturday before the weather turned sour. Even then, Beman, who hadn't been in such a position since he left the PGA Tour in the early 1970s to become an administrator, maintained his lead amid the gales until the final holes, where it all unraveled. He double-bogeyed the 15th and 16th and bogeyed the 17th, opening the door to Player, who was only three over par for the day until he took a double bogey himself at the 18th, missing the green and three-putting. Palmer almost chipped in there to forge a tie and moments later Beman missed from eight feet for another bogey, giving Player the victory. Beman and Waites tied for second, a shot ahead of Palmer.

PaineWebber Invitational—$450,000
Winner: Bruce Crampton

When a professional golfer has won 15 tournaments during the previous four seasons, you would hardly expect another victory to be considered a surprise. Yet, in the case of Bruce Crampton's triumph in the PaineWebber Invitational at Charlotte, North Carolina, that tag was appropriate. The intense, driven Australian had dropped off the Senior PGA Tour back in May and was gone for 11 weeks, the victim, doctors told him, of depression. He called it a stress-related illness. Whatever, his game was shot when he returned and he did nothing in his first two starts. No hint of what was to happen the first week of August when the PaineWebber Invitational set up shop at its new site—the TPC at Piper Glen—after its first decade at Quail Hollow Country Club.

Encouraged and helped by several of his friends on the circuit, Crampton shot 68, his first sub-par round since April, to establish himself as a contender from the start. He was just two shots off the first-round lead as Bob Charles posted a 66. Harold Henning and DeWitt Weaver had 67s, three others shared the 68 slot with Crampton and, in all, 32 of the 72 starters were under par the first day. Charles clung to his one-stroke lead Saturday, but it remained anybody's victory with 19 players, including six 1990 winners, within five shots of the top. Crampton fashioned a 67 and joined the remarkable Joe Jimenez and Tom Shaw in the runner-up slot.

Charles, Shaw and Crampton fought it out Sunday in the North Carolina heat. Shaw frittered away a birdie-eagle start with two three-putt greens, Crampton worked out a 33 on the front nine and was tied for the lead with Charles at 10 under when Bob birdied the 11th hole. However, the lefthander fell back when he buried his tee shot in a bunker at the par-three 12th (where Palmer made a hole-in-one earlier in the final round). Crampton, who numbers the 1986 PaineWebber among his PGA Senior Tour victories, birdied from the woods at the par-five 16th and finished with 68—205, 11 under. Shaw shot 69 for 206, finishing a shot in front of Charles and Larry Mowry.

Sunwest Bank/Charley Pride Classic—$350,000
Winner: Chi Chi Rodriguez

Chi Chi Rodriguez passed another milestone in his exceptional career in the Sunwest Bank/Charley Pride Classic. With his hard-fought victory at Four Hills Country Club in Albuquerque, New Mexico, Rodriguez boosted his overall PGA Tour earnings over the $3 million mark. What makes the total more impressive is that almost two-thirds of it was compiled during his five seasons on the Senior PGA Tour.

Rodriguez started fast at Four Hills, posing a four-under-par 66 to take a one-stroke lead over Jim Dent, three over Gay Brewer, Billy Casper and Joe Jimenez, then yielded the top spot Saturday to Jimenez (69-67—136) and Charles Coody (70-66—136). Chi Chi was one back after his second-round 71.

Coody, Dent and Jim Ferree battled Rodriguez for the title Sunday. Chi Chi built a two-stroke lead over the first 11 holes, making five birdies and three-putting the ninth for an outgoing 32, then adding a sixth birdie at the 11th to go 12 under par. However, he double-bogeyed the 12th, missing the green and three-putting, and dropped into a first-place tie with Dent, who had just run off four birdies in a five-hole stretch. Rodriguez bounced back with his final birdies of the round at the next two holes with putts of 15 and six feet. Dent had shot his wad and played the final six holes in one over par. The weather intervened as the final group reached the 15th green. A violent thunderstorm lashed the course, forcing a 2-1/2 hour delay. Chi Chi missed an eight-foot birdie try before heading for cover and Coody made his when play resumed to get within two of the lead. But, nobody got closer.

Coody and Rodriguez both bogeyed the 16th in the windy aftermath of the storm and parred the final two holes, although Chi Chi had to make a breaking 15-footer at No. 17 and a nine-footer at No. 18 to finalize his 16th PGA Senior Tour victory and third of 1990. He shot 68 for 205. Coody, Dent and Ferree tied for second at 207. Well down the standings at 214 was Bob Charles, who had won the Sunwest tournament the three previous seasons.

Showdown Classic—$350,000
Winner: Rives McBee

How things changed between the visits Rives McBee made to Salt Lake City in 1989 and 1990. The first time, McBee arrived in the Utah city in a discouraged mood, on the verge of giving up his fling on the Senior PGA Tour. His wife, Kay, had persuaded him to stick it out a little longer, despite his series of failures in the circuit's Monday qualifiers. He made the field of the Showdown Classic there that week and began such a successful surge that, by the time he returned to the Jeremy Ranch Golf Club in Park City in 1990, he had a tournament victory under his belt and close to $500,000 in the bank. As if in celebration at the site of the turnaround, the husky Texan scored his second senior win and collected another $52,500 as records fell right and left.

It wasn't an easy victory as McBee was up against Lee Trevino, the Tour's leading money and title winner, and the steady Don Bies in the final round. In fact, he rolled in a five-foot par putt on the 18th green for 68—202 to eke out a one-shot win over Trevino and Bies.

Rives was in the middle of contention from the start as he smashed the competitive course record Friday with an eight-under-par 64. Even that was only good enough for a two-stroke lead over Bies and Mike Hill with Trevino lurking another shot behind. Bies, a five-time winner on the Senior PGA Tour, repeated his 66 Saturday and that, too, was a tournament record. It gave him two strokes on McBee and Hill and Trevino was still three behind going into the final round.

Hill fell back with a 72 and Bies dropped from contention when he four-putted the sixth green for a triple bogey. Thus, Trevino, a Texas friend and traveling companion for a time during McBee's brief, unsuccessful run on the PGA Tour in the late 1960s, became the ominous threat for Rives. The turning point came at the par-five ninth where, after Trevino had birdied it to catch McBee at 12 under, Rives eagled it with a huge drive, a 123-yard wedge shot and 30-inch putt. When he later bogeyed the 17th, he gave both Trevino and Bies a chance at No. 18, but neither could convert birdies and his tense par secured the win.

GTE Northwest Classic—$350,000
Winner: George Archer

It was a particularly inappropriate time for Don Bies to repeat a near-miss. Bies was trying to score his first 1990 victory on the Senior PGA Tour before his family and friends in hometown Seattle in the GTE Northwest Classic the last week of August. The week before in Salt Lake City, he had opened with a pair of 66s and carried a two-shot lead into the final round only to finish second by a stroke. At Seattle's Inglewood Country Club, Bies virtually duplicated the performance. This time, he doubled 67s for a two-stroke lead going into Sunday's concluding 18 and once again came up short, three strokes short of George Archer's winning 11-under-par 205.

A bad stretch of holes in the middle of the final round ruined the chances of Bies. He ultimately finished third behind Archer, who scored his third

1990 triumph and fourth since his circuit debut the previous October, and Bruce Crampton, a two-time Northwest Classic winner, who closed strongly with 67 for 207. Bies had 74 for 208.

Bob Brue, the fast-talking trick-shot artist, had a day in the sun Friday when he opened with 66 to lead Bies by a shot. Don then took over Saturday with the second 67, one better than Archer and his 69-66—135 score. Chi Chi Rodriguez was next at 138. Bies started birdie-eagle-birdie and followed with three more birdies and two bogeys. Archer also had an eagle, but felt the critical hole was the 15th, where he sank an eight-footer for a bogey.

Archer and Bies swapped the lead in the early going Sunday, George going in front for good when he birdied the eighth from 30 feet and Don bogeyed from a trap. Inches separated the two balls after both men pulled their tee shots at the ninth, but Bies was out of bounds and he took a double bogey. Archer scrambled to a bogey and added two more strokes to his lead with a birdie to a Bies bogey at the 10th hole. Now the challenge came from Crampton, who started the day six strokes off the pace and, when he holed a 25-foot birdie putt at the 15th, had pulled within two shots of Archer. But, both men bogeyed the 16th and birdied the 18th to conclude the Showdown.

GTE North Classic—$450,000
Winner: Mike Hill

So what if Mike Hill had never been in a playoff during his many years on the PGA Tour. He didn't have any trouble figuring out what to do on the first extra hole after opponent Bruce Crampton had overshot the 16th green. Pull out a sand wedge and knock it six inches from the cup. The victory, Mike's second in a season in which he had several excellent chances late in other tournaments, was his after Crampton missed his desperate pitch to keep the playoff alive.

Hill's first Senior PGA Tour win came in another GTE-sponsored tournament—the Suncoast Classic—in February. In the interim, he had 14 top-10 finishes in 20 starts and, with the $67,500 first-place check for the GTE North Classic victory in Indianapolis, pushed his fifth-ranking earnings close to $500,000. It was the second week in a row in which a late charge fell just short for the resurgent Crampton.

Dale Douglass, Terry Dill and Rocky Thompson tied the tournament record with first-round 65s at Broadmoor Country Club. They were a shot in front of Hill, Rives McBee and Agim Bardha. Douglass moved from that deadlock into sole possession of the lead Saturday. His 67 for 132 put him a stroke in front of Hill (66-67) and three ahead of Crampton (68-67), setting up the final grouping for Sunday's climax round. Nobody else got into the act.

Douglass held the lead until he bogeyed to Hill's birdie at the fifth hole. Mike added another at the sixth and remained in front until the 11th hole as Crampton caught fire with a five-birdie string starting at the ninth hole. Bruce went ahead with the fourth birdie at No. 12, where Hill missed the green from the rough and took his only bogey. Both birdied the 13th and followed with pars until Mike deadlocked it with his third straight birdie at the par-five 17th. They went to the playoff hole after Bruce's chip for the win at the 18th stopped an inch short of the cup. It was just the third playoff of the 1990 season and the first since a four-man exercise the first of June. Douglass finished with 71—203 to place two behind Hill (68) and Crampton (66).

Vantage Bank One Classic—$300,000
Winner: Rives McBee

Three weeks earlier, Rives McBee won the Showdown Classic, the tournament at which his Senior PGA Tour fortunes had begun to turn around the year before. They climaxed in 1989 with his victory in the Vantage Bank One Classic in Lexington, Kentucky. The pattern established, McBee repeated that triumph when the circuit returned to the Kentucky city in early September of 1990, becoming the sixth multiple winner of the season.

That the tournament moved from Griffin Gate, its original home, to the new Kearney Hill Links for the 1990 event didn't faze McBee, the latest of a small group of players who have found success as seniors that they never experienced in their younger days on the regular PGA Tour. The 55-year-old Texan was solid from his opening tee shot. He fired a first-round 66, jumping off to a two-stroke lead that he never relinquished over the weekend. He strung together four birdies, starting at the second hole, and added two more on the back nine's par-fives for his two-shot margin over Quinton Gray, Orville Moody, Dave Hill and Terry Dill.

On Saturday, he eagled the 531-yard 18th for 67 to maintain his two-stroke margin over Gray with the 133. The major threats to McBee at that point appeared to be Lee Trevino and Harold Henning at 137. As seemed likely, Gray faded to 75 Sunday, but neither Trevino nor Henning mounted a challenge. Instead, the only noise came from Mike Hill, who had so rarely been out of contention all season. This time, Hill shot 64, but he had started the final round too far back at 141, so it really wasn't a threat to McBee. It just enabled Hill to leapfrog everybody else and pick up runner-up money of $25,500 for his 205. Meanwhile, McBee was putting together a steady 68 to finish 15 under par at 201. Henning closed with 70 and tied for third with George Archer and Tommy Aaron at 207. Trevino's 72 lodged him at 209 with four other players. The $45,000 first prize jumped McBee's 1990 earnings over $300,000, quite impressive for a man who had been a nearly broke Monday qualifier when he arrived in Lexington in 1989.

Greater Grand Rapids Open—$300,000
Winner: Don Massengale

Lightening often strikes when and where it is least expected, which is an apt allusion to Don Massengale's victory in the rain-abbreviated Greater Grand Rapids Open, the mid-September stop on the Senior PGA Tour. Massengale had been trying for his first senior victory since joining the circuit in the spring of 1987. Two seconds and a playoff loss in 1988 were the closest he had come and it didn't appear that it was going to happen that week at The Highlands course at Grand Rapids, Michigan.

When local favorite Dave Hill opened with a stirring 64 on the par-71

Highlands course, a new venue for the tournament, Massengale found himself far back in the field with his 69. The situation seemed even more futile for Massengale because the Friday round had been washed out and cancelled. So, Massengale had five strokes to make up on one of the Tour's better players in just 18 holes.

His personal lightening struck in the middle of the Sunday round. At the ninth green, Massengale rolled in a 50-foot birdie putt, followed with a 34-footer at No. 10 and a 15-footer at No. 11. "That got things going," the 53-year-old Texan observed later. Still, he was just tied for first with Hill after an easy (two-foot) birdie putt at No. 17. Hill saved par there a short time later, then elected to gamble for the win at the final hole. Trying to slide a tee shot around a dogleg right, Hill watched the drive sail too far right and out of bounds. The bogey for 71 dropped Dave into a second-place tie at 135 with Terry Dill and Larry Laoretti. Massengale had 65 for his 134 Sunday. It was his first PGA Tour victory since 1966, when he won the Bing Crosby and the Canadian Open. Don had left the PGA Tour in 1970 and worked for 17 years as a club professional in New York and Texas before returning to action on the Senior PGA Tour in 1987 when he turned 50.

It was a second straight runner-up finish at Grand Rapids for Michigan-native Hill, who good-naturedly chided brother Mike: "I should kill Mike. He's been giving him (Massengale) lessons."

Crestar Classic—$350,000
Winner: Jim Dent

The last time Jim Dent had played the final round of a tournament in the company of Lee Trevino, disaster struck. Dent blew a five-stroke lead and the title to Trevino in the Royal Caribbean Classic back in February, starting Lee on the way to his record-breaking season. Although Dent recovered quickly from that shock and won three tournaments over the next six months, he had to get special satisfaction from his fourth 1990 victory in the final Crestar Classic in Richmond, Virginia, at the end of that head-to-head confrontation with Trevino.

Actually, it came down to Dent and Trevino only at the very end at the Hermitage Country Club. Gary Player had carried the lead into the final round after a tournament-record start of 67-64—131 and was five ahead of Trevino and six in front of Dent, both playing in the threesome ahead of him Sunday. Dent had started the tournament with a one-over 73, seven back of leader Rives McBee, and closed the gap by just a shot Saturday despite a 64, since Player posted the same score in taking over first place.

A 31 on the outgoing nine with birdies at the fourth, fifth, sixth, seventh and ninth and another birdie at the 12th put Dent in serious contention and Trevino was only slightly less successful over that stretch. Still, Player remained in front until his game unraveled on the back nine. He bogeyed the 13th and 14th to yield first place to Dent and suffered fatal damage when he dumped a shot in the water and bogeyed the par-five 16th. At that point as both stood on the 17th tee, Trevino a stroke behind, he said to Dent, "It's just you and me, baby." Forgetting Key Biscayne, Dent put on a solid finish with two regulation pars for 65 and 202. Trevino hit poor approaches at both holes and left his 25-foot putt for a tie at the 18th a foot short. He finished with 67 for 203, a shot in front of Player, who took 73. Dent's 202 tied the tournament record, set by Arnold Palmer in 1988. With the $28,000 second-place check, Trevino broke Bob Charles' 1989 single-season earnings record. It gave Lee a total of $740,102.

Fairfield Barnett Space Coast Classic—$300,000
Winner: Mike Hill

All Mike Hill was thinking about when he teed off Sunday in the final round of the Space Coast Classic was shooting "low numbers." That he did with a 64. But he got more than he bargained for with that score—the tournament title—when Bob Charles blew "the biggest lead of my life" and Hill scored his second playoff victory in a month.

Defending his championship in the Senior PGA Tour's oldest regular tournament at Melbourne, Florida, Charles seemed headed for a wire-to-wire repeat for 45 holes. He opened with 65 for a one-stroke lead over Hill, Dale Douglass and Bob Rawlins, and widened it to two over Douglass Saturday with 66 for 131. Douglass was at 67—133, Homero Blancas at 135 and Hill at 136 after his second-round 70. Even though Hill began to fulfill his plan by scoring birdies on the first three holes at Suntree Country Club Sunday, it seemed likely only to be heading him for another in a long list of high finishes. Charles was still blazing. He shot a five-under 31 on the front nine to go 18 under and carry a six-stroke lead over Douglass at the turn.

The start of Charles' demise was not of his own doing. Douglass holed a 140-yard, seven-iron shot for an eagle at the 10th and it admittedly rattled Charles, even though he still led by four. They both drove into the water at the 11th, but Dale escaped with just a bogey while Charles was taking a double bogey. Hill had birdied the 10th and 11th ahead of them and was then in the picture, tied with Douglass and three behind Charles. When Charles three-putted at the 15th, he dropped into a three-way tie, then fell a stroke behind as Hill and Douglass both birdied the 17th. All three parred the 18th, Charles for 39, 70 and 201, Hill for 64 and Douglass for 67 for the 200s that forced the playoff.

Hill, who defeated Bruce Crampton in his first-ever playoff in the GTE North Classic, made it 2-0 when he parred the first extra hole—the 18th—and Douglass three-putted from 40 feet. It was Hill's third win of the season.

Vantage Championship—$1,500,000
Winner: Charles Coody

It was the old case of being "not how, but how many." Charles Coody's "how many" was 202 and that was easily good enough to give him the title in the Vantage Championship, the richest tournament on the Senior PGA Tour, and its $202,500 first-place check, by far the biggest of his long career.

Coody's three-stroke victory and his closing-round 70 really don't hint at the rather shabby finish he and Al Geiberger managed at Winston-Salem's Tanglewood Park golf course in the $1.5 million event, a finish that prompted

Bob Charles to delay his departure from the course after closing with 64 and putting 205 on the scoreboard, a finish that led Coody to remark afterward: "Wasn't that pathetic?"

The reference was to the final four holes played by Coody and Geiberger, who won the first Vantage in 1987. Coody was sailing along with a four-stroke lead when the trouble began with a hooked two iron off the 15th tee. He trapped his approach, left his first bunker shot in the sand and wound up with a double bogey. Geiberger missed a seven-foot birdie putt, but still cut Coody's lead in half. The 17th was a comedy of errors for both men, in the course of which Charles decided to stick around. Both butchered second shots on the par-five hole, then Coody muffed a pitch shot halfway to the green and Geiberger went from one trap to another. They only reached the fringe with their fourth shots, but, after Geiberger chipped close, Coody chipped in from 25 feet for an ugly par. It was all he needed to regain his composure and he parred the 18th routinely to sew up the victory. By then, Charles was on his way to the airport. Geiberger salvaged a tie for second with Charles after nearly driving out of bounds at No. 18, getting a helpful ruling involving a permanent bird feeder and making par from a trap behind the green. It was a lucrative save as he and Charles each collected $126,000.

Coody had led up to his "exciting" finish by taking the lead the second day with a five-birdie streak on the front nine on his way to a tournament-record 132 (67-65) after Rives McBee continued his fine play with an opening 66. Charles followed with a front-nine 32 Sunday to establish the cushion that made the shaky finish less traumatic.

Gatlin Brothers Southwest Classic—$300,000
Winner: Bruce Crampton

Bruce Crampton continued his resurgence from a disconcerting period of discontent that left a void in the middle of his 1990 season on the Senior PGA Tour when he breezed to an easy victory in the Gatlin Brothers Southwest Classic. And breezy it was at Fairway Oaks Country Club in Abilene, Texas, as the circuit headed west for its final regular events of 1990.

The Australian has lived in Dallas for some 20 years and is familiar with the winds off the Texas plains. Over the last two rounds, when the winds kicked up, he was the only man to break 70 both days. With his rounds of 68 and 69 and his 12-under-par score of 204, he posted a four-stroke victory over Lee Trevino and Terry Dill, his second in the latter half of 1990. He won in early August in the PaineWebber Invitational. It was Trevino's sixth runner-up finish of the season, matching his victory total for the year.

Crampton shared the first-round lead at 67 with two unlikely contenders—Bob Gaona and Bob Betley, two qualifiers who left positions of junior college golf coach and Idaho policeman to try the Senior PGA Tour. One shot back were Al Kelley, J.C. Goosie and Dill, a frequent early contender during the season, while Trevino started with 71. Crampton surged three strokes in front in the gales that came up Saturday, shooting the 68 despite a ball in the water and a double bogey at the par-three 16th. Gaona kept his chances alive with 71—138 and Trevino lost ground with his 70—141.

With birdies on the first two holes Sunday, Crampton left little room for a serious challenge. Chi Chi Rodriguez had a strong front nine on his way to a 68 and Gaona got back to a three-stroke deficit when he birdied the fifth hole, but fell back at the seventh when Crampton birdied and he bogeyed. Trevino also closed to three en route to a final-round 67, but he bogeyed the 17th to kill his chances of catching Crampton. The victory was the 17th for Bruce in his five-plus seasons on the Senior PGA Tour.

Transamerica Championship—$500,000
Winner: Lee Trevino

You just knew that it had to happen. It was just a matter of when Lee Trevino would add another victory to his brilliant 1990 record on the Senior PGA Tour. After nearly four months of major money-winning, but no additional titles, Trevino bagged his seventh win in the Transamerica Championship at Silverado Country Club in Napa, California, finishing two shots in front of the ever-present Mike Hill with his 11-under-par 205.

Trevino came out of a six-player logjam in Sunday's final round, when his major challenges came from Hill and Miller Barber, one of the Senior PGA Tour's biggest stars in its early years in the 1980s. Jim Dent had opened with 67 and taken a two-stroke lead over Don January before the massive deadlock developed Saturday. The 140-shooters were Trevino and Dent along with Lou Graham, Gary Player, Rives McBee and Orville Moody. As it turned out, though, none of them were close at the finish. Moody and Dent shot 71s, Graham a 72 and Player a surprising 76. McBee hung tough through the front nine, eventually settling for fourth place off his 69—209.

Ahead of him, Trevino knew that Barber and Hill were firing hot rounds and that he couldn't afford to lose any more ground after he bogeyed the 11th hole. So, he proceeded to birdie the next three holes and felt he was home free when he dropped a 12-foot birdie putt on the 17th. He made the margin two strokes when he wedged to four feet at the final hole. Barber's performance was his finest in some time and brought him his highest finish of 1990. His closing 64, with seven birdies on the last 10 holes, matched the competitive course-record scores shot by Richard Crawford (1969) and Al Geiberger (1973) in Kaiser International tournaments on the regular PGA Tour. Hill followed Barber to the 18th, where he wrested second place away from Miller with a two-putt birdie for 65 and 207.

The victory, Trevino's first since he won the U.S. Senior Open on July 1, and its $75,000 first-place check moved him within striking distance of $1 million in official money for his splendid "rookie" senior season.

Gold Rush at Rancho Murieta—$350,000
Winner: George Archer

Just when it appeared that George Archer might be running out of gas at the end of a long season, the towering 51-year-old struck again on the Senior PGA Tour. During a 10-tournament run starting with his victory on Long Island in early July and ending in late September, Archer won again in Seattle and was never worse than sixth. Three mediocre performances followed, then George came to life and outdueled Dale Douglass for the title at the Gold Rush at Rancho Murieta, near Sacramento, California, at the end of October.

Archer raced from far behind in the final round to annex the one-stroke victory, his fourth of the season and fifth as a senior. It all hinged on a string of four birdies in the middle of the final round and a good luck/bad luck situation at the 13th hole. Trailing by four with 10 holes to play, George birdied the eighth through the 11th and trailed by a shot. Then, at the tough 13th, he hit a wild tee shot right that bounced off a cart path and a post on an out-of-bounds fence and stayed in play. He bogeyed the hole. Moments later, Douglass came to the same hole and pulled his drive badly. It hit a tree and a house and stayed out of bounds. He dropped into a tie with Archer with that double bogey and fell behind by a stroke when George birdied the 14th hole. Archer birdied again at the 15th, but Dale reduced the margin to one with a birdie at the 16th. However, he couldn't get another on the last two holes to catch the big man. Archer's 66 gave him a 12-under 204 while Douglass had 68 for 205. Charles Coody finished third at 209.

Bob Charles, who ultimately finished fourth at 210, was the first-round leader, opening with a 68 as Dick Hendrickson shot 69 and Archer and new senior J.C. Snead had 70s. The scoring improved on a calm Saturday as Douglass surged into the lead with 66 for 137. Bob Betley also shot 66 and shared second place at 138 with Archer (68) and Charles (70). Douglass remained hot on the early holes Sunday, making five birdies on the first eight holes before Archer began his closing rush.

Security Pacific Classic—$500,000
Winner: Mike Hill

One thing about the Senior PGA Tour: The season's stars are still around at the end of the season, not globe-trotting or resting on their laurels at home, as is usually the case with the top guns on the regular circuit, leaving the spoils to the lesser lights. Not only are the year's leading seniors still in action, they are still winning. When Mike Hill captured his fourth victory of the season in the Security Pacific Classic, the then-second-ranking money winner followed No. 4 George Archer (Rancho Murieta) and No. 1 Lee Trevino (Transamerica) to the winner's circle in that late-fall stretch.

Hill produced a sensational final round to win the Security Pacific at venerable Rancho Park, the municipal course in Los Angeles that was the scene of many exciting finishes over the many years it hosted the Los Angeles Open on the PGA Tour. He fired an eight-under-par 63 for 201 to nose out Gary Player by a stroke.

Player got off to a fast start at Rancho Park Friday, shooting a 66 to share the first-round lead with John Schlee. Joe Jimenez, George Lanning and Dave Hill were at 67 and five men were at 68, including Arnold Palmer, who won the Los Angeles Open three times at Rancho. He wasn't to land a fourth, though, as Player continued his strong play Saturday with 68 for 134 and a one-shot lead over Chi Chi Rodriguez, Orville Moody and Jimenez. With rounds of 70 and 68, Hill trailed by four and considered it unlikely that he could beat Player Sunday.

Player, whose only 1990 victory had come in April in the PGA Seniors, didn't exactly open the door for Hill, either. He shot his third straight round in the 60s—a 68—but could only remark afterward: "What can I say? I shoot 66-68-68 and don't win." Hill had eight birdies, including a streak of four beginning at the eighth hole. The seventh came at the par-three 17th and put him in a tie for the lead when Player bogeyed at the 14th at about the same time. Mike followed with a 15-foot birdie putt on the 18th for the 63 and Gary could do no better than par on his last four holes. The $75,000 first prize jumped Hill's earnings to $680,861, not bad for a man who had targeted $250,000 as his goal for the season.

Du Pont Cup—$550,000
Winner: United States

They changed the format, but the result—a United States victory—was the same as in the initial Du Pont Cup seniors competition in Japan in 1989. For the second year of the event, a variation on the Ryder Cup program was adopted and, as is often the case with American pros, the U.S. fell behind in the opening round of alternate-shot play. However, the Americans recovered with a sweep of the better-ball matches Saturday and wrapped up a 20-12 triumph Sunday with five wins and a tie in the singles.

Only the tie of George Archer and Gene Littler with Tetsuhiro Ueda and Yoshimasa Fujii, 70-70, prevented an American blanking Friday. Kesahiko Uchida and Seiichi Kanai routed Jim Dent and Rives McBee, 66-73; Hisashi Suzumura and Shozo Miyamoto beat Dale Douglass and Charles Coody, 70-72, and Teruo Suzumura and Shigeru Uchida nipped Dave and Mike Hill, 71-72.

Neither team changed lineups Saturday, but the U.S. pros flourished in the better-ball format, winning all four matches to take a 9-7 lead. Douglass/Coody, the victorious Legends of Golf pairing earlier in the year, shot 61 for a five-stroke victory over Hisashi Suzumura/Miyamoto. The Hills bumped Teruo Suzumura/Shigeru Uchida, 64-67; Archer/Little clipped Ueda/Fujii, 65-70, and Dent/McBee nipped Kanai/Kesahiko Uchida, 66-67.

The Americans clinched things early in the Sunday singles, winning the first five matches. Mike Hill took Kesahiko Uchida, 68-72; Dent handled Hisashi Suzumura, 72-77; Dave Hill trimmed Miyamoto, 70-73; Archer, the top point-maker on the team, trimmed Ueda, 71-78, and Coody defeated Shigeru Uchida, 73-73. The Japanese salvaged the next two matches, Fujii defeating Littler, 69-71, and Kanai beating Douglass, 69-74. McBee and Teruo Suzumura halved the final match with 74s. The U.S. players each received $45,000, the Japanese $23,750. Site of the event was the TPC at Batoh course.

Seniors Challenge—$300,000
Winner: George Archer

George Archer added a final extracurricular touch to his excellent first full season on the Senior PGA Tour on the front end of a two-week visit to

Hawaii the first of December. The winner of four regular 1990 events, Archer acquired a fifth title in the non-Tour Seniors Challenge at Princeville Golf Club on the island of Kauai, posting a one-stroke victory over Bob Brue with his five-under-par 211 total.

The rangy Californian never trailed. He shared the first-round lead at 70 with Dale Douglass, the defending champion, and Tommy Aaron, then moved in front Saturday with 69—139. That turned out to be the only round in the 60s during the tournament with the trade winds up. Douglass shot another 70 for 140 and Brue took over third place with 70—141. George opened the final round with a bogey, picked up two birdies and a bogey on the next seven holes, then parred the last 10 holes for an even-par round. Brue, a non-winner on the senior circuit, caught Archer with a birdie at the 11th hole, but fell back when a poor chip at the 17th cost him a bogey. He parred the 18th for 71—212, finishing far ahead of Douglass, who struggled to a 76 and third place at 216.

GTE Kaanapali Classic—$450,000
Winner: Bob Charles

Two breaks, one from the Tour and the other from the golfing gods, helped Bob Charles to capture his third title of the 1990 season in the wind-blown GTE Kaanapali Classic, the final full-field event on the year's schedule. Fresh from a three-week spell back home in New Zealand, Charles positioned himself on, then just off the lead through the first two rounds at Royal Kaanapali and managed a splendid par-70 in fierce weather conditions the final day to put up a 206 total for a four-stroke victory.

Refreshed by the time off the tournament trails, Charles began with a five-under 65 and jumped off to a one-stroke lead over Arnold Palmer, who made his best start of the season with his 66, the product of a putting revival. Twenty-one others among the 78 in the field broke par in ideal weather Friday, a total contrast to what was to come Sunday. Among them was Lee Trevino, who shot 69 despite a triple bogey with a ball in water at the par-three 17th.

Harold Henning, winless on the Senior PGA Tour since 1988, inched into the lead with a 68—135 Saturday, as Charles shot 71 and Trevino 67 for 136s for shares of the runner-up position. A double-bogey start headed Palmer out of contention to a 73-79 finish. The later starters Saturday got a taste of the weather to come as the scores went up. By starting time Sunday, it was raining so hard and blowing horizontally at some 40 miles an hour that the first tee time was delayed for an hour. (In the later view of Henning, it should have been delayed permanently, as was the final round of the 1989 Classic.)

Then came Bob Charles' other break. His opening tee shot, slicing out of bounds, struck a tree and remained barely in play. With the reprieve, the lefthander worked out a par in the ferocious weather. Bob's experience in such windy conditions served him in good stead the rest of the day as he played for the first time without glasses in the driving rain. Henning took himself out of contention with bogeys on the first three holes, leaving the battle to Charles and Trevino. The two played the front nine in two over par, then Lee fell a stroke behind with another bogey at the 10th. Bob moved two in front with a birdie at the 13th, both birdied the par-five 15th and the final margin went to four when Trevino bogeyed the last two holes to fall into a tie for second place with George Archer at 210. Archer shot one of the day's four 73s. The winner's 70 was the only better score in the field and an admiring Trevino remarked afterwards that, "It would have been a 62 under normal conditions."

New York Life Champions—$1,000,000
Winner: Mike Hill

Under most circumstances, Mike Hill's victory in the season-ending New York Life Champions tournament in Puerto Rico would have drawn the full focus of attention. After all, it was Hill's fifth victory of the year on the Senior PGA Tour and the $150,000 first prize inflated his seasonal winnings to nearly $900,000, well above the previous record earnings year of Bob Charles in 1989. Yet, Hill found himself sharing the stage with Lee Trevino, one of his two victims in the tournament's concluding playoff at the Hyatt Dorado Beach's East course, because Trevino won a battle even though he lost the "war." The $95,000 runner-up money Lee received enabled him to surpass by $25,041 the earnings total of Greg Norman, No. 1 on the PGA Tour.

Hot rounds abounded among the three playoff participants—Hill, Trevino and Dale Douglass—as they wound up in the deadlock over the 54-hole distance in the successor event to the Mazda Champions, in which for five year-end appearances in the Caribbean the top seniors and LPGA pros teamed up and played for big purses. All three men shot 15-under-par 201s to force the overtime. It ended at the first hole when Hill rolled in a 40-foot birdie putt, achieving victory on the same course on which he and Patty Rizzo won the final Mazda Champions in 1989.

Douglass and Al Geiberger were the big par-breakers Friday, shooting 65s to lead Chi Chi Rodriguez and Don Massengale by a stroke. Hill went them one better Saturday, storming into a first-place tie with Douglass with 64—133 as Dale carded 68. Trevino trailed by three at that point after a pair of 68s. Then Sunday was his day for the hot round. He rang up eight birdies, four on the incoming nine, and took a bogey in recording his 65—201. Mike made his sixth and tying birdie at the 17th with a 12-foot putt for 68 and Dale nailed his 68 with a 12-footer on the 18th green. Both Douglass and Trevino were well inside Hill with their approaches on the playoff hole, but failed to convert their putts after Mike, "just trying to lay up for a two-putt," holed his 40-footer.

11. The European Tour

There was a certain fairy tale flavor to the 1990 European Tour. It opened with a bang—rookie Stephen McAllister breaking through in his and the Tour's debut, the Vinho Verde Atlantic Open, and in the first six-way playoff in Tour history. And the year ended with a bang—Nick Faldo winning the Player of the Year Award from the PGA of America. This award is not an honorary award. It's made from a point system based on performance, and Faldo ran away with it for winning two majors in the same year, the Masters (his second in succession) and the British Open. What made this seem awkward was that Faldo had quit the American Tour (separate from the PGA) because of the rule requiring golfers to play at least 15 tournaments in order to be members. Special invitations were available, and so Faldo played in seven American events, wining $345,262, 37th on the U.S. money list. Bernhard Langer also quit the American Tour for the same reason. Sandy Lyle remained the only European who also was a member of the American Tour. Lyle showed signs of pulling out of that long, mysterious slump, and Faldo, riding the top of his game, ended the season nursing an injured wrist that kept him out of some events.

The 1990 European Tour enjoyed some of the most significant advances in its history. Four tournaments were added—the Vinho Verde Atlantic Open, American Express Mediterranean Open, Murphy's Cup, and Austrian Open. They boosted the overall schedule to a record 47 events, and lifted prize money by 18 percent, to £16 million. The average purse was £340,000, more than five times greater than the average at the start of the European Tour in 1980, when prize money for the entire season totalled £1.3 million.

McAllister was just two days past his 28th birthday when he won the Atlantic Open in Portugal. He was the 36th first-timer in the five years of the Tour's all-exempt system. And he was the first of five first-timers. Brett Ogle won the AGF Open; Richard Boxall, Italian Open; Philip Walton, French Open; and Michael McLean, Portuguese Open.

And the stars still shone. Ian Woosnam outran Mark McNulty in a race for the top of the Volvo Order of Merit. Woosnam won four tournaments (plus the unofficial Suntory World Match Play Championship) and a record £574,166. McNulty was second with two victories and £507,540, and Jose Maria Olazabal third with three wins (five worldwide) and £434,765. For two of the year's surprises, take the continued comeback of Bernhard Langer (two wins, fourth on the Order of Merit with £320,449), and the slide of Seve Ballesteros. The volatile Spaniard won early, the Open Renault de Baleares in March, and slipped right into the doldrums. Ballesteros was only 33, turning that age in April. Could that mighty game be gone already? Or was he distracted by the wait and then birth of his and Carmen's first child?

The two major issues on the tour in 1990 were slow play and that nagging case of the square-grooved irons. The European Tour hit both immediately. Trying to eliminate the five-hour round of golf, the Tour established time guidelines for play. This program was similar to the American Tour's, and, critics argued, just as toothless. A £250 fine meant nothing to golf's multimillionaires. Critics called for a two-stroke penalty.

At any rate, as if showing fast play could be good play, Eamonn Darcy opened the year with a first-round 66 in the first tournament, the Atlantic Open. He played in less than four hours. The new rules took their first bite in the Emirates Airline Desert Classic, the second tournament of the season. Magnus Persson, Ken Brown, and Jean Van de Velde, a third-year pro from France, all were timed and found wanting, and fined £250 each. Warnings were issued later in the year. Ballesteros was not happy to be among the targets.

And the grooves: The Royal and Ancient Golf Club of St. Andrews and the U.S. Golf Association ruled that it wasn't the shape of the grooves—square vs. vee—but the distance between them that made the difference. The matter became confused when the American Tour ignored the measurement issue and focused on the shape: It banned all square-grooved clubs. (Which action, of course, was followed by the Tour's being sued by Karsten Manufacturing Co. of Phoenix, Arizona, which makes the popular Ping Eye 2 irons. The suit settled down in court for a long appeals process.) The European Tour, on the other hand, adopted the R&A position on the measurement factor. Accordingly, the 1990 season dawned at the Atlantic Open with players having their irons measured.

That point being settled, they got on with the golf.

Vinho Verde Atlantic Open—£200,000
Winner: Stephen McAllister

Call it poetic justice, or golf's equivalent thereof, but what you had in mid-February was the start of a new PGA European Tour season, a new tournament and a first-time winner. And one other thing—the first six-way playoff in European Tour history.

This was the Vinho Verde Atlantic Open, at the Estela Golf Club near Oporto, Portugal. Who should break through but Stephen McAllister, a fourth-year pro from Scotland, becoming the 36th first-time winner in the last five years under the Tour's all-exempt system. You could also call it his birthday present to himself. McAllister turned 28 two days before his victory.

McAllister had to win the hard way. Playoffs are tough on everybody, and especially on golfers who haven't felt the heat of the lead under pressure. In brutal wind and rain, McAllister came from six strokes off the lead in the final round, played the last 13 holes in a remarkable even par, and posted a two-over-par that tied him with five others at even-par 288.

The playoff started at No. 10, a not-intimidating par four of 404 yards, and ended there on McAllister's par. That seemed a modest finish, until one considered the weather. McAllister sank a 12-foot par putt for the victory. But playing into the near-gale wind and the whipping rain, he needed a drive, a three wood, and a pitch to get there. His five victims: Ronan Rafferty, No. 1 on the Order of Merit and a three-time winner in 1989, who bunkered his approach, Richard Boxall, who three-putted after being the only one to reach the green in two, David Williams, in trouble off the tee, and Stephen Hamill and Anders Sorensen, who both two-putted for bogeys.

Off rounds of 71-71-72-74, McAllister was never closer to the lead than four strokes until the end. Eamonn Darcy, who hadn't played competitively in four months, launched the new season with a 66 for the first-round lead. While Darcy followed that with a 76, Hamill found out what it felt like to lead a Tour event for the first time in his eight-year career with a 67 that included two eagles. ("Just getting through the cuts is important," Hamill said. "I'm buying a house and my bank account is down to about, £2,000.") Hamill, at 138, led by one over American Ronald Stelten, who was to become the unhappiest victim of them all. Stelten had his first career victory dead in his sights. He was leading by two strokes going into the final round. Then he shot 80 in the fierce weather. "Nothing prepared us for a day like this," Stelten said. "I just couldn't get the ball on the green."

McAllister turned pro in 1983, after winning the Lytham Trophy as an amateur, and failed to qualify that year. He tried again in 1987, and made it. Late in 1988, he seemed headed back to the qualifying school, but he pulled himself together just in time and kept his spot on the Tour with a fifth place in the English Open—his best until this victory.

Emirates Airline Desert Classic—£275,000
Winner: Eamonn Darcy

Life has had its stumbling blocks for Eamonn Darcy. He once wanted to be a jockey. but before long he had to change his mind. There aren't many 6-foot-1, 190-pound jockeys. Back in 1989, he thought of quitting the European Tour and becoming the pro at Delgany Club back in his home, Wicklow, Ireland. But it would have cost too much. The hard-bargaining members wanted a full handicap plus one stroke for their little frolics. "I shoot 62 and 63s," Darcy said, "and they take the money."

So, at only age 37, he decided to take another crack at the Tour. Good timing. Despite the presence of Seve Ballesteros, Nick Faldo, Ronan Rafferty, and Mark James, Darcy led untouched from start to finish for a four-stroke victory in the Emirates Airline Desert Classic. He started with an eight-under-par 64 for a three-stroke lead, then added 68-75-69 for a 12-under-par 276 total and a four-stroke victory over David Feherty. Ballesteros tied for third at 282, Faldo had 286, Rafferty 287, and James 288.

The first round of this Desert Classic was known for two things. One was the show of teeth by the Tour in its campaign against slow play. Fines of £250 each were levied against Jean Van de Velde, of France, and Sweden's Magnus Persson. The other was Darcy's opening charge. Darcy is famed for his 1987 Ryder Cup singles victory over Ben Crenshaw. It guaranteed that the Cup would remain in European hands. A crucial putt did the job then, and a collection of them did the job this time. He needed only 22 putts in the round. Five birdies came on putts ranging from six to 30 feet. He chipped in for the other. That gave him his second first-round record of the young season. He had started with a record 66 in the Atlantic Open the week before. He faded to 25th there. He didn't fade this time.

Darcy was threatening to turn the tournament into a shambles in the second round. He started with a pair of birdies, from 15 and 10 feet, had an eagle, then proved he was human by three-putting from five feet for his only bogey so far. He was nine strokes ahead at one point, but settled back for a 68—

132, and a six-stroke lead on Australian Peter O'Malley, who was at 70—138.

Darcy was bound to cool off, but it took some swirling desert winds in the third round to do it. He couldn't find the fairways, and admitted, "I panicked a bit." He shot 75—207, but lost only one stroke of his lead. O'Malley soared to a 77, and second place, at 212, was shared by Denis Durnian (73), David Gilford (69), Feherty (70), and the ever-dangerous Ballesteros (71).

In the final round, Darcy's lead twice was down to two. But he steadied himself and held Feherty off coming home. Feherty, playing ahead of Darcy, birdied the par-five 10th. Darcy birdied it behind him. Both bogeyed the 12th, and both birdied the 13th. Then Feherty simply ran out of holes. He birdied the 18th for a 68—280, but so did Darcy, for 69—276 and the fourth victory of his career and the first since the 1987 Belgian Open.

American Express Mediterranean Open—£400,000
Winner: Ian Woosnam

The American Express Mediterranean Open was making its debut on the European Tour, at Las Brisas on Spain's Costa del Sol the first week of March. It was also the season debut for Jose Maria Olazabal, Bernhard Langer, and Ian Woosnam. Of the bunch, the man who had reason to celebrate was Woosnam, who marked his 32nd birthday on Friday and his 13th victory on Sunday.

Langer had come back a renewed man, with an adjustment in his swing. He began to suspect that in a subconscious attempt to protect his delicate back, he was dipping his pelvis on the takeaway. He hoped he had corrected that by using a more lateral turn of the hips. Woosnam also was back after a spell in drydock. Putting was his problem. "When I lost to Curtis Strange in the Ryder Cup last year," he said, "I was reading the greens perfectly, but I started missing putts when I became nervous. Over the past couple of seasons, I feel I've been giving Seve, Nick and the rest a shot a round starting on the greens." His solution (he hoped): Put the hands closer together to prevent the right hand from taking control.

The first-round figures suggested he was on the right track. Woosnam, bumped into second place with a 68 by two late bogeys, rang up seven birdies, matching leader Mark James, who got seven in a 67. Woosnam got his seven in the first 12 holes, three of them on par-three holes. In an outward four-under-par 33, his longest putt was a 20-footer to save par at No. 2.

Woosnam would have had the lead, but he bunkered his tee shot at the 16th and his pitch to the 17th hit three feet from the hole and bounced off the green. He bogeyed both. James birdied five of the first eight holes, off a brilliant approach game. His only putt of any distance was a 30-footer for a birdie-two at No. 7. The other four birdies were from three feet and less.

A hint of things to come hit in the second round. A good breeze came up off the nearby Sierra Blanca and turned the fast greens into near-demons. Woosnam got the best of the weather, posting his second four-under-par 68 for an eight-under 136 that held up for a two-stroke lead over James (71) and Miguel Martin (69), tied at 138. Among those stung by the winds were

Ballesteros (74) and Eamonn Darcy (74). Woosnam made only one bogey, that on a three putt at No. 18 (his ninth). When the wind came up, he had only five holes to play, and four of those were with the wind. He needed only a five iron to get home at the 490-yard eighth, and he dropped a 10-foot putt for an eagle-three.

The winds of the second round promised trouble, and it arrived in the third on Saturday in the form of rain and howling gales that washed out play and cut the tournament to 54 holes. That was almost one round too many for Woosnam. He ran into trouble fast in the finale. A bogey at No. 2, and a double-bogey seven at No. 3, and the tournament had a new leader. Miguel Martin, who opened the day two strokes behind, and who parred the first three holes, was ahead by one. Woosnam caught him at the turn, then went ahead with an eagle-three at the 12th. Martin (74) and Eduardo Romero, who eagled two holes going out en route to a 71, tied for second. Good tries, but Woosnam—68-68-74—210, six under par and a winner by two strokes—was busy having a birthday party.

Open Renault de Baleares—£275,000
Winner: Seve Ballesteros

Maybe they should make Seve Ballesteros play one-handed.

You won't get an argument from Magnus Persson, who was so close to his first victory he could taste it. But he just happened to get in the way when Ballesteros was feeling his worst.

Persson, 24, one of the bright hopes of Swedish golf, was playing possibly the best of his eight-year career in the Renault Open de Baleares at Son Vida, Majorca. He had his first title right at his fingertips. Ballesteros should have been the last player he would have to worry about. Ballesteros was battling not only the distractions of being the tournament organizer and a player at the same time, but also a heavy flu and a fever of over 100 degrees. He felt obliged to play, but he wasn't even sure he could finish. If all this didn't brighten Persson's world, how about a five-stroke lead with 10 holes to play?

But none of it was Ballesteros-proof. Ballesteros shook off all of his difficulties, caught Persson in a wild finish, then beat him in a playoff. It was Ballesteros' second Open de Baleares win in three years, his 46th European Tour title, and it made him the first to top £2 million in European winnings. It was also his 60th title worldwide.

Ballesteros shot 66-65-70-68, Persson 65-65-66-73, and they tied at 19-under-par 269. Son Vida, a shortish par 72 at 6,239 yards, was not the most testing of courses. More than 60 players broke par on opening day, but the show was stolen by little-known American Bill Malley. He had played only nine holes in practice, walked the other nine, then shot a 63 for a two-stroke lead. But he couldn't keep pace with the Persson-Ballesteros show.

Persson, former Swedish boy wonder, took the halfway lead at 130 with his second 65. It included a run of four birdies on his first nine, the inward half, then a set of three coming home. Ballesteros left a sick bed, endured a 101-degree fever, and stayed a stroke behind Persson with a 65 of his own. He three-putted the 16th, but back at the turn he had dropped putts of 10 to 15 feet for three successive birdies.

If Persson was feeling the heat, he didn't show it in the third round. He slipped once, a bogey at the par-three 12th, which Ballesteros birdied. Persson rebounded, birdied the next two holes, and added another at the 17th for a 66. He not only kept his lead, he padded it—from one shot to five, against Ballesteros' 70.

And that's where things stood when they reached the ninth tee of the final round—Persson leading by five with 10 holes to play. Then he made an error at the dogleg ninth, hooking his tee shot into the water. It cost him a double-bogey six and three strokes of his lead, because Ballesteros birdied the hole. Persson regrouped and birdied the 10th, then gave that back at the 12th. Ballesteros kept the pressure on with a birdie at the 16th, where two huge shots got him home. At the 510-yard 18th, he slugged another big drive, birdied, and caught Persson, 68-73. Persson made one more error. In the playoff, which started at No. 18, he used his four wood off the tee, and hooked it into the water.

"I think that was his big mistake of the tournament," Ballesteros said. "He had been using an iron before."

So Ballesteros won with a routine par-five, and found some hope despite his illness. "My game is back," he said. "It was the best I've felt on the golf course in six or seven months."

Tenerife Open—£200,000
Winner: Vicente Fernandez

For Jose Maria Olazabal, it was like following a birdie with a double bogey. He came to defend his Tenerife Open title feeling the best he had felt in weeks. Those impacted wisdom teeth were gone. They were at least partly to blame for his missing the cut in the Mediterranean Open two weeks earlier—his first miss after making it 65 consecutive times over three years. "I don't like to blame my teeth," he said, "but they did disturb my concentration." And so he was off to a winning start, a 68, just two strokes off the first-round lead. A 69 in the second round left him one stroke out of the 36-hole lead. And then it was discovered he had signed an incorrect scorecard. He was disqualified.

That was merely one of the week's surprises. For openers, there was German Garrido, brother of the veteran Antonio Garrido, taking the first-round lead by a stroke with a bogey-free, six-under-par 66. And for closers, there was the Argentine veteran, Vicente Fernandez, 43, shaking off a four-putt crash to beat Mark Mouland on the third hole of a playoff, the third in five weeks. It was Fernandez' fourth European victory and his first since the 1979 PGA Championship. They had tied at six-under-par 282, on the 6,590-yard, par-72 Amarilla course, Fernandez shooting 67-74-72-69, and Mouland 70-73-71-68.

Neither man topped the leaderboard until the final round. And it was another surprise that the tournament went to a playoff. It seemed Fernandez had thrown it away. Awful putting was supposed to have been Mouland's specialty in this tournament—he brought four putters, and he three-putted eight times in the first three rounds—but Fernandez suffered his own version at the 10th. He four-putted for a double-bogey seven. Mouland closed with a 68. Fernandez caught him with birdies at two of the last three holes. Christy O'Connor, Jr., needed to eagle the par-five 18th to join the playoff, but his approach went over the green, and he was out.

The playoff began on the 157-yard, par-three 17th. Both parred. At the 18th, Mouland missed the green with his second, and put his chip shot 20 feet from the hole. Fernandez hit his second just off the green, and putted up to three feet. They both two-putted, and it was back to the par-three 17th.

Mouland put his tee shot next to a bush, and Fernandez put his on the fringe. Mouland, finding his ball in an awkward position, had to invent a left-handed shot, and chipped to five feet. The shot was so splendid that even Fernandez applauded. Fernandez then putted up to about 10 inches. Mouland missed his five-footer, and it was over.

"I misread the short putt completely," Fernandez said, looking back at the three-footer that could have ended it at the second playoff hole. "But all week," he added, grinning hugely, "I knew something must go right for me."

Volvo Open—£200,000
Winner: Eduardo Romero

Back in Argentina, fellow professionals call Eduardo Romero "The Cat," for the way he comes sneaking in from nowhere to pick off victories. The European Tour found out what they meant in the 1989 Lancome Trophy, when he slipped through one of the strongest fields of the year—including Greg Norman, Curtis Strange, and 11 of the 12 European Ryder Cuppers. Romero, 35, was up to his old tricks in the Volvo Open at Florence. Russell Claydon and Colin Montgomerie locked up in a wonderful slugfest. And Romero birdied four of the last five holes, giving Argentina its second European Tour winner in eight days.

Romero, who never led until the finish, shot 68-66-64-67—265, a whopping 23 under par, for a one-stroke victory over the astonished Colin Montgomerie and Russell Claydon. Thus ended one of the worst beatings a European Tour course ever suffered. All told, on the 6,280-yard, par-72 Ugolino course, the field shot 662 under par and piled up 1,353 birdies and 22 eagles. There were three 63s, the first by Claydon for the first-round lead, followed by two in the second round, by Rodger Davis and Mats Hallberg. You had to go down to 20th place to find the first man to go over par for a single round, and that was David Feherty, with a one-over 73 in the third. Par meant nothing in this tournament. It took two-under 142 just to make the 36-hole cut.

Claydon, who turned pro in 1989 after helping the European Walker Cup team to its first victory ever in the United States, set the pace in the first round with the 63, for a two-stroke lead over Montgomerie. Romero was back in the pack with his 68. Montgomerie leap-frogged into the lead in the second round with a 64 for a 15-under-par 129, two strokes ahead of Claydon (68), Roger Chapman (66), and Peter O'Malley (64), all at 131. Romero, with a 66, was five off the lead, at 134.

Romero didn't join the hunt until the third round, and he did it with a flourishing stretch drive. At the par-four 12th, he holed out his pitch for an eagle, and followed that up with four consecutive birdies that brought him home in 30 for a 64 and an 18-under-par total of 198. That lifted him into third place behind Montgomerie (196) and Claydon (197). The real battle came in the final round, and he wasn't really a part of it. It was the Claydon-Montgomerie shootout.

Claydon jumped into the lead at No. 3, sinking a 15-yard chip shot for an eagle-three, and he went two strokes ahead with a birdie from 10 feet at No. 5. Montgomerie missed 10-foot birdie putts at the fifth and seventh, then picked up two strokes with only one putt over the next three holes. How can that be? Simple: The putt was a 12-footer for a birdie at No. 8. Then he chipped in from 50 feet to save par at No. 9, and holed out from a bunker for a birdie at No. 10.

And so the shootout went. And while it was going on, The Cat was stalking both of them. Going out, Romero birdied both par-fives, No. 5 and No. 8, to get to 20 under par. But why would anyone notice? He was still five strokes out of the lead with only seven holes to play. A man in that kind of hole hardly bears watching. While no one was looking, Romero birdied four of the last five holes for a 67, leaving Montgomerie (70), Claydon (69), and the gallery stunned.

AGF Open—£200,000
Winner: Brett Ogle

It's been said a million times that golf is a funny game, and so it is. For the next episode in this continuing story, try the 1990 AGF Open at Montpellier, France: Australian Wayne Riley holed out a nine-iron shot at the 151-yard 16th in the third round, which won him a £20,000 Volvo. The problem was, he had just been suspended for a year from driving back in Britain, "after having one beer too many at a dinner party with friends," he explained.

Aside from that, there wasn't much to laugh at. Brett Ogle, the long-hitting Australian, who had seven top-10 finishes in 1989, his second year on the Tour, took all the fun out of the AGF. He simply grabbed the lead in the second round and raced home for a comfortable, breakthrough victory. Ogle, becoming the second first-time winner of the season, covered the 6,704-yard, par-72 La Grande Motte course in 72-66-70-70 for a 10-under-par 278 total. He beat Paul Curry and Bill Longmuir by three strokes.

"When my driving is good, the rest of my game falls into place," Ogle said. Des Smyth, who played with Ogle in the third round, described his driving: "Awesome," Smyth said. The slender 6-foot-3 third-year man has that in common with another Australian. "My swing was measured by a computer recently," Ogle said, "and the clubhead speed at impact was found to be 119 miles per hour. I guess it's due to a very wide arc and strong hands. I doubt if many other professionals, including Greg Norman, are faster."

Ogle shot 72 in the first round and trailed leader Miguel Martin by four strokes. After that, it was all Ogle. He barged into the 36-hole lead with a second-round 66 to go three strokes clear.

And where others might have criticized the Robert Trent Jones course, he found it to his liking. "It's a very testing course, and that's bringing out the best of me," he said, after the second round. In part, that meant an outward 32 that included three long birdie putts on the fast greens. In the third round, Ogle suffered perhaps his worst error, a watered tee shot that cost him a double bogey at the par-four ninth. But he shook it off and posted a 70 for a 208 and a two-stroke lead on Curry (69—210).

It was a question of poise again in the final round, when the victory threatened to slip through his hands. Ogle birdied No. 3, then bogeyed the next two holes after overshooting the greens, allowing Curry to slip into the lead with birdies at No. 3 and No. 7. Then Curry three-putted the eighth, and Bill Longmuir, who birdied five of the first 10 holes, took the lead.

But Longmuir couldn't hold it, either. At the 18th, he drove into a fairway bunker and bogeyed the hole for a 69—281, and Curry (71) caught him with a birdie-birdie finish. Ogle birdied the 14th from three feet and the 16th from 12 feet, and at No.18—where he could make five and still win—he holed from the fringe for yet another birdie, and the cushy win.

El Bosque Open—£200,000
Winner: Vijay Singh

It was a new tournament at a new course, and it couldn't have come at a better time for Vijay Singh. He was reaching top form, and he made a prophet out of Jose Maria Canizares. Asked who would win this new El Bosque Open, Canizares, though hoping to break a seven-year victory drought, plucked the names Jose Rivero and Vijay Singh out of the air. Rivero never was in the running—he tied for 10th—but Singh, the big Fiji Islander, rolled from start to finish for the second victory in his three years on the European Tour.

The tournament, running opposite the Masters, replaced the Jersey Open. The El Bosque Golf and Country Club course, in the rolling countryside near Valencia, was designed by Robert Trent Jones, Jr. The course, which opened in October, 1989, is a par 72 of 6,965 yards, running around lakes that come into play on six holes.

Singh played it like an old friend. He shot 66-69-74-69—278, 10 under par, and won by two strokes over Chris Williams (68-71-70-71) and Richard Boxall (70-69-70-71). Singh's only real danger was in the third round, where it took a bolt of luck and a blazing finish to save him a share of the lead with Williams, Boxall, and Paul Carrigill, all at seven-under-par 209.

Strong winds had come up and left much of the field baffled. "I'm not a great wind player," Carrigill admitted. "And I hate putting in the wind on fast greens." So he was pleased with his 73. Boxall was the opposite. He made five birdies but also took three bogeys for his 70. Williams made an even more scrambled 70—six birdies, two bogeys, and a double bogey. And then there was Singh.

He was one puzzled man. He couldn't remember any grievous errors in his outward nine, yet the damage came to a 42, six over par. But he got a big boost—off a spectator's head—at the 490-yard 11th. Singh's tee shot seemed headed for the trees. Instead, it hit a spectator squarely on the head and bounced back into the fairway. "I'm glad he wasn't hurt," Singh said. "It was a header Pele would have been proud of." From there, after checking on the man, Singh went on to birdie the hole. He closed with three birdies over the last four holes for a 74 and a share of the lead.

There was some of the other luck, too. Carrigill got some of it. Coming out of a bunker at the first hole of the final round, he hit the ball twice. He called the penalty on himself, and took a triple bogey seven. He was on his way to a 76 and a tie for 15th. Then Australian Mike Clayton had two strokes of bad luck. On No. 13 green in the third round, his ball moved as he addressed it. He shot 70, and was one stroke off the lead. Then in the final round, at No. 15, the ball moved again. Clayton shot 73—283, and tied for 10th.

It was the same 15th hole where Singh pretty well locked up the title. He had to punch his tee ball back into the fairway, and then he fired a great eight-iron approach over the fronting lake to just two feet from the cup. The putt gave him a two-stroke lead. All he had to do was see it safely home, and he did.

Credit Lyonnais Cannes Open—£300,000
Winner: Mark McNulty

To paraphrase a worn-out travelers' joke: "If this is the south of France, the winner must be Mark McNulty."

You can play a variation on that theme, to wit:

"If is the first hole at Cannes Mougins, that crash must have been Ronan Rafferty."

Or ...

"If that's Ian Woosnam playing through, this must be the Twilight Zone."

In fact, all three were true.

This was the south of France, and the Credit Lyonnais Cannes Open at Cannes Mougins Country Club, and McNulty racked up his third career victory in the Cote d'Azur. The Sunningdale-based Zimbabwean won the Cannes Open in 1988 and the Monte Carlo Open in 1989. And this time, he added another Cannes Open with 69-71-69-71—280, eight under par, to beat Rafferty by a stroke.

Rafferty would have won if he hadn't had to play his nemesis, the first hole. Let Rafferty muse over his 73-67-72-69—281, and he's bound to go back to the first hole in the first round. He hooked his drive under a tree on the narrow 441-yarder, played out left-handed, shanked his third shot into a lake, and staggered off the green with a triple-bogey seven. "The toughest opening hole on the European circuit," Rafferty insists. In four visits to the Cannes Open, he has four sevens and an eight there.

Now, all things being equal, Woosnam would have won instead of tying for eighth (69-72-67-77—285) if he hadn't strayed into the Twilight Zone, that place of the unreal popularized by the American television series. First, he had to play the second and third rounds on the day of the third round, Sunday, after rain washed out part of the second-round field. Woosnam, who won the rain-shortened Mediterranean Open just six weeks earlier, shot 72-67 for those rounds and took a one-stroke lead into the final round. It would have been a two-stroke lead, but ...

Woosnam was at his eighth hole (No. 17) in the third round, about to tap a par putt, when an official started up his golf cart nearby. Woosnam missed. He finished the day one ahead of McNulty (69) and Mark Roe (66), both at 209. This was, by the way, the closest McNulty had come to the lead so far. He would finally pull ahead when the fates had finished with Woosnam. At No. 4 in the final round, Woosnam's approach shot hit a woman spectator on the head and bounced out of bounds. The woman ended up in the hospital, and Woosnam ended up with a double-bogey six. He added sixes at No. 7 and No. 10, on his way to an inward 40 and a 77. "I was naturally unhappy at what happened to the lady," Woosnam said, "but I still feel I should have won. I simply didn't play well enough."

This was a perfect set-up for McNulty. "Both Mougins and Mont Agel in Monte Carlo are tricky, patient golfer's courses," he said, "and that's exactly what I am. I usually get a lot of birdies when I win, but this week it was pure consistency that paid off."

If McNulty didn't get a lot of birdies, he got his share. In the third round, in what he called the key to his victory, he chipped from 10 yards behind the green for a birdie at No. 4, his 13th hole. Then he birdied three of the last five holes for a 69 to move to within a stroke of Woosnam. Then, talk about consistency—in the final round, he had only two birdies, but suffered only one bogey, and the 71 got him home. McNulty pocketed the £50,000 check that lifted him to the top of the Order of Merit, said his thanks, and you could almost read his mind, checking the calendar for the next stop in the south of France. It would be the Monte Carlo Open in the first week of July, twelve weeks away.

Cepsa Madrid Open—£275,000
Winner: Bernhard Langer

For devotees of weird happenings, the Cepsa Madrid Open was the place to be. Not so much for Seve Ballesteros missing the 36-hole cut in front of the home fans. That was merely embarrassing. But how about someone missing a putt because of snow? Or a leader picking up his ball on the green before he marked it? Or shooting 61 in the final round and coming up short because your caddy stepped on your ball.

Only a surprise winner could top this kind of stuff, and that's what the Madrid Open got—Bernhard Langer, a man practically given up for dead not long ago. Why the rejuvenation? There seemed to be two best guesses: The awkward putting style had calmed the dreadful yips, and his back problems were gone, or at least quiet. There certainly was no limp in his 70-67-66-67—270, an 18-under-par performance at the 6,941-yard, par-72 Puerta de Hierro course. He won by a stroke over Rodger Davis.

To clear up the assortment of mysteries:

The man who lifted his ball without marking it was Mariano Aparicio, 34, a little-known Spaniard. What a time to draw a blank. Aparicio was just three strokes out of the lead after the third round. Then on the first hole of the final round, he picked up his ball without putting down a marker. The penalty cost him a double bogey and a 74. He finished tied for 12th at 280.

Next, consider the sad case of Brett Ogle, who scored his first victory in the AGF Open three weeks earlier. Ogle shot a Puerta de Hierro-record 61 in the final round, and finished third, two strokes behind Langer. The penalty back in the first round now looked bigger and uglier. How often does your own caddy step on your ball?

In the first round, 57 of the 144 starters broke par, led by a traffic jam of five at 67. American Rick Hartmann eagled the par-five 18th and joined M.A. Jimenez, Michael Harwood, Jose Rivero, and Rodger Davis. The traffic improved a bit in the second round. Four tied at 137—Davis (70), Langer (67), John Hawksworth (63), and a little-known Swede, Magnus Sunesson (65), who had regained his tour card in December, in his fifth visit to the qualifying school. Sunesson, 25, was an unexpected force. He had missed the cut in his last three tournaments.

In the third round, Langer birdied three of the last four holes to match Sunesson in the lead at 66—203, a two-stroke edge on Davis (68). Langer also tripped on a strange hazard. When he was on the 13th green, a brief snow hit. "All I could see was lots of small white dots," Langer said. He was trying to make a three-foot putt. He missed.

There was no stopping him in the final round, though. Sharp iron play got him four birdies in the first eight holes, but a missed five-footer at No. 9, his only bogey of the day, put him briefly into a tie with Sunesson (who would finish fourth on 70—273). And at this point, at No. 9, Ogle's electrifying 61 went up on the leaderboards. Now they were battling not only each other, but also a man who was safely in the clubhouse.

Davis, playing ahead of them, was out in 32 and trailed by just a stroke. Langer got a birdie at the 11th, and when he came to No. 15, he needed another badly because Davis had eagled the hole moments earlier and tied him. Langer got that birdie, retook the lead, and stayed there, keeping his career record intact. He had won at least one European tournament each year in the 1980s, and now he had his first for the 1990s. It was the 21st European victory of his career.

Peugeot Spanish Open—£300,000
Winner: Rodger Davis

When it came to getting a long-range bet down, Rodger Davis had it all figured out. At the start of the season, he wanted to bet a London bookmaker £1,000 that he would lead the Order of Merit at the end of the year. After some hard bargaining with a bookie who was offering 20-to-1, the mustachioed Australian and some friends got the bet at 33-1. Davis had an edge the bookie didn't know about. "I don't think he realized that I came over early and planned to play in about 25 events," Davis said, "compared with the 12 or so of guys like Faldo and Langer."

It must have dawned on the bookie, eventually, that a golfer who plays 25 tournaments a year has a far better chance of topping the Order of Merit than one who plays only 12. So it would have been interesting to see that bookie's face when Davis won the Peugeot Spanish Open. Best of all was the way he did it—with a wild finish right out of Arnold Palmer's primer.

For three rounds at the 6,966-yard, par-72 Club de Campo, near Madrid, Davis was just one of the pack. He shot 74-69-68, and was seven strokes behind after each of the first two rounds, and two behind after the third round. Then he outran the field with a final-round 66, highlighted by an eagle. His 11-under-par total of 277 gave him a one-stroke victory over Nick Faldo, Peter Fowler, and Bernhard Langer. That was an interesting twist, by the way. In the Madrid Open a week earlier, Langer beat Davis by a stroke.

Davis was chasing a mixed cast in this Spanish Open. Colin Montgomerie, the man who beat him in the Portuguese Open in 1989, led the first round on a 67 that included an eagle-three and four consecutive birdies from the 12th. "I played just as well at the Madrid Open last week, but I missed the cut," he said. "I couldn't make a putt then, but today, I made a few, and here I am in the lead."

Montgomerie's big moment was upstaged by a flap over whether the 1993 Ryder Cup ought to be played at the Club de Campo. The condensed debate: "I don't think you could fit the Ryder Cup in here," Nick Faldo said, arguing that the holes are too narrow to handle the galleries. Said Seve Ballesteros, who was promoting the course as the site: "I disagree with everything he said. The Ryder Cup has to come to Spain in 1993, not 1997."

Roger Chapman (67—136) took the lead after 36 holes, and the third round ended up in a scramble, with three men tied at 209—Jose Maria Olazabal (71), Peter Fowler (69), and little-known American Stephen Bowman (68). Bowman, 32, had to overcome a bad case of nerves brought on by playing with Nick Faldo and by being in an unfamiliar position—the lead. He made six birdies, and said the key was rebounding from a double bogey at No. 1 with a birdie at No. 2. "I bounced right back from the disaster, and it made me feel real good," he said.

In the final round, Bowman kept his nerve and shot 72, but it was good only for a tie for sixth, with Davis charging home for a 66. Faldo was the hottest challenger, shooting the 65, even knowing it probably wouldn't be enough. He was four under par for the outward nine, and figured five under par on the back would win. "Then all of a sudden I looked up at the scoreboard, and Davis was 11 under," Faldo said. He closed with three consecutive birdies. Davis was on No. 17 tee when Faldo's last dropped at No. 18 and set off a roar.

"I knew Nick had gone to 10 under," Davis said, "but I was more worried about Langer and Fowler catching me."

But nobody could catch him. The main reason, he said, was the way he played the par-five holes. "Three birdies and an eagle isn't bad," he said, a big smile wrenching at his mustache. The best of that bunch—an eagle at No. 7, off a one iron to 15 feet. He also ran off birdies at the 12th, 13th, and 14th.

"I played very solidly today," Davis said. The £50,000 first prize took him to the top of the Order of Merit. His idea of solid play could cost some bookie a nice figure.

Benson and Hedges International Open—£350,000
Winner: Jose Maria Olazabal

Two separate duels were going on in this Benson and Hedges International Open. One came at the end, a dogfight between Jose Maria Olazabal, 24, the brilliant Basque, and Ian Woosnam, winner of the Mediterranean Open nine weeks earlier. Olazabal won, scoring not only his first victory of the season but his first as a professional on British soil. (As an amateur, he had won the British Amateur, Boys, and Youths titles.) The other battle was raging between Andrew Oldcorn and himself—if raging was the word. Oldcorn was a quietly heroic story. He had to drag himself around St. Mellion, one of Britain's more demanding courses. It wasn't a question of whether he could win, but whether he could even play.

This was an intense personal drama, hidden from golf fans. Oldcorn was suffering from something called myalgic encephalomyelitis, also know as "Yuppie flu," an affliction that leaves the victim listless and cramped. Oldcorn had it for more than a year. Golf generally is not uppermost in the mind of the victims. He kept his European Tour playing card only through a special exemption. He played in only four events in 1989, and in only three through early May in 1990. But in the second round of the Benson and Hedges, he somehow managed a course-record 65—bettering the 66 shot earlier in the day by Brian Marchbank—and went on to finish tied for eighth, his best in a long time.

Beyond that, this was a rather strange tournament. Some of golf's finest were kicked around pretty hard by the 7,054-yard, par-72 course. For example, Ronan Rafferty, Europe's No. 1 player in 1989, and Richard Boxall shared the first-round lead on 67. Then they faded. Rafferty closed with 74-74, and Boxall with 77-74. Nick Faldo opened with a 78, and Seve Ballesteros shot 77 in the second round and 76 in the last. Of golf's other big guns, the only real move came from Bernhard Langer, he of the recovering game. Langer, who won the Madrid Open two weeks earlier and tied for second in the Spanish Open the week before the Benson and Hedges, closed with a 70 for third place at six-under-par 282. And so it was an Olazabal-Woosnam show to the end.

Olazabal shot 69-68-69-73 for a nine-under-par 279 and a one-stroke victory, but not until they had gone through a wild fourth round. Olazabal opened with a one-stroke lead and lost it immediately when Woosnam birdied No. 1. Then Woosnam took the lead when Olazabal bogeyed the third and fourth. But Woosnam couldn't hold it. At No. 5, he plunked a nine iron into the water and rang up a double bogey. And so it went until they reached the stretch drive.

Olazabal birdied No. 10 from six feet, and at No. 11 he saved his par against Woosnam's bogey. At the par-five 12th, Woosnam had to take a penalty drop from a ditch, then smacked a three wood to the green and saved par brilliantly, but he still lost ground because Olazabal birdied the hole, two-putting from 15 feet. Olazabal was now three ahead with three to play. But it still wasn't over.

Woosnam picked up one valuable stroke with a birdie at No. 16. Then the tournament was settled at No. 17. Olazabal bogeyed—there went another stroke—and Woosnam now was just three feet from a birdie and a tie. But he missed the putt. Olazabal held his ground on the final hole and rang up the seventh victory of his five-year career.

Peugeot-Trends Belgian Open—£250,000
Winner: Ove Sellberg

Two men with nearly the same problem: Ian Woosnam was wondering—what do you have to do to win? Ove Sellberg was wondering pretty much the same thing. Actually, his predicament was broader: What do you have to do to make the cut?

Sellberg, tabbed years ago by Tony Jacklin as the most likely to become the first Swede on the European Ryder Cup team, had fallen on hard times. Sellberg won the Epson Grand Prix Match Play in 1986 and the Open de Baleares in 1989, but lately had fallen on very hard times. So far this season, through mid-May, he had made only three cuts in nine starts. Confidence was his problem. When he found some after a few shaky moments in the final round, he was on his way. Sellberg made the Peugeot-Trends Belgian Open his third career victory, shooting 68-66-67-71, a 16-under-par 272 at the par-72 Royal Waterloo Golf Club near Brussels.

And if the victory ended Sellberg's frustration, it only deepened Woosnam's. It was his second successive second-place finish. He was runner-up to Jose Maria Olazabal in the Benson and Hedges International just the week before. But he lost by only a stroke in the Belgian Open, he shot 66-70-70-70, and lost by four.

It didn't matter to Woosnam that he now had one victory (Mediterranean Open), two seconds, and an eighth in just five starts. "I'm sick of finishing second," the scrappy Welshman said. "I did it a lot last year as well." Four times, in fact.

Sellberg's surge was surprising. Given his poor record coming into the Belgian Open, nobody expected much from him. Himself included. He shot 68 in the first round, and was one of a crowd sharing second place, two strokes behind Woosnam (66). The most it could mean for Sellberg was that he had a good chance of making his fourth 36-hole cut of the season. And that he did—in spades. Sellberg bolted to the front at the halfway point, shooting a second-round 66 for a 10-under-par 134 total and a two-stroke lead on Woosnam (70—136). Now the third round: Was it time to fold yet? On the contrary. Sellberg hammered out a 67—201, powering his way to a five-stroke lead on Woosnam (70—206).

The shakes finally arrived in the last round. "I played very badly to start with," Sellberg said. "I hit the ball all over the place. I kept losing my concentration. I came to a point where I didn't know what was going to happen. I'd lost control."

He'd started hooking off the tee, and his five-stroke lead was down to two over the first five holes, after he bogeyed No. 1 and No. 5, and Woosnam birdied No. 4. But suddenly calm returned to Sellberg, and he birdied the seventh, ninth, and 11th. The final boost came at the 387-yard 13th. Sellberg, clinging to a two-stroke lead, drove off the fairway to the right, but put his approach 20 feet from the flag. Woosnam drove into the fairway, then misfired on an eight iron. The wind carried it to the right, where it bounced off the edge of the green and into a water hazard. The damage was two-fold: Woosnam bogeyed, and Sellberg's spirits got a big lift.

"I started to think better, then I really started to play pretty well," Sellberg said. But one tournament does not a recovery make. "I still don't feel too confident," he said. "And if I had felt like this a few years ago, there would have been no chance."

Lancia-Martini Italian Open—£300,000
Winner: Richard Boxall

The way Richard Boxall tells it, he finally figured out that a golf tournament is not a 100-meter dash. "I've tried to slow myself down, and not charge up the fairway as though the tournament were a race," he said. Once that sank in, along with that fundamental swing change, Boxall—29, English, a non-winner, and in his eighth year on the European Tour—was ready to go. He picked a good spot. The Italian Open was where Ronan Rafferty broke through a year earlier. Maybe it's the cooking. At any rate, Boxall, in becoming the third first-time winner on the European Tour this season, left nothing to the imagination. This was a wire-to-wire victory, and one of the most decisive performances in years. Boxall led by as many as seven strokes, and won by five. He shot 65-64-70-68—267, 21 under par at the 7,043-yard, par-72 Milan Golf Club.

If it seems he wasn't challenged, note that Jose Maria Olazabal had to settle for second, five strokes behind, after breaking 70 for four consecutive rounds (67-69-68-68). Note also that Eduardo Romero was third, John Bland fourth, and Seve Ballesteros fifth, 11 strokes off the lead. This, by the way, was another Ballesteros miracle—of sorts. Ballesteros, whose prodigious game was sputtering, opened with a 75 and seemed doomed to miss the 36-hole cut. He was three over par with five holes to play in the second round. And then, in those last five holes, he holed a bunker shot for an eagle and birdied two other holes for the 68, and made the cut with two strokes to spare.

Boxall's previous career highlight was in the 1985 Portuguese Open. He had better finishes, but in this one he tied Ballesteros for sixth and moved to 121st on the Order of Merit, and this enabled him to keep his Tour card. That is a precious milestone in any hopeful's career. Then it took a fundamental change in thinking to get Boxall to the next point.

"I finally realized you don't win anything when you keep knocking the ball into the rough," Boxall said, explaining why he made his big change. He had been a right-to-left player—the draw, which gives greater distance but is more difficult to control. So he switched to the fade, the left-to-right game. He sacrificed about 20 yards off the tee for greater accuracy.

Boxall led off with a course-record 65, which was good for a one-stroke lead on Andres Sorensen. The record lasted about 24 hours. He broke it the next day with a 64, for a 15-under-par 129 total, seven strokes ahead of Olazabal (69) and Craig Stadler (68). If you can call it a slip, Boxall did it in the third round, shooting a 70 for a 199 total, which lopped two strokes from his lead and left him five strokes ahead of Olazabal.

In the final round, Olazabal birdied the first two holes, but Boxall matched him, sinking putts of 10 and 60 feet. Olazabal, ever dangerous, made a late move. But Boxall snuffed it out with birdies at the 13th and 15th, both from 25 feet. All told, Boxall carded 24 birdies and an eagle. And thus he ended a lot of doubts on a key point. "A lot of people were starting to think I might never win," Boxall said. "Including me."

Volvo PGA Championship—£400,000
Winner: Mike Harwood

Golfers often speak of having a "good ball-striking round," sometimes as though the score were incidental to it all. Maybe the function of striking the ball is somehow separate from the game itself. Obviously there's a great deal of satisfaction in good ball-striking, but if that's the peak of the golfer's day, what makes up for poor ball-striking? Can a victory do it?

That was the question facing Mike Harwood after he won the Volvo PGA Championship at the Wentworth Club outside London late in May. All he did was come from behind to outdistance Jose Maria Olazabal and hold off a charge by Nick Faldo, to say nothing of brushing off John Bland and Rodger Davis. Reminded of the magnitude of his accomplishment, Harwood only nodded and said, "Oh, sure, I putted exceptionally well, but my ball-striking was still poor."

Harwood, 31, certainly qualified as a surprise winner. When he fought his way into contention, he found himself in the company of Olazabal, Faldo, and much of the cream of the European Tour. He seemed out of place. His best finish in the PGA Championship was a tie for 44th in 1986. He had played rather well on the European Tour in recent years, and in 1989 he finished 14th on the Order of Merit after winning the PLM Open. There was nothing modest about his performance this time, though. He entered the final round trailing Olazabal by a stroke. He erased that deficit on the first hole, took the lead at the fourth, and fought off all comers the rest of the way. Wentworth's famed West Course—6,945 yards, par 72, home to the Suntory World Match Play Championship—is not a stroll in the park. But Harwood beat it with a 17-under-par 271, shooting 69-68-67-67, to become the third Australian to win on the European Tour this season.

Faldo, who won his second consecutive Masters about six weeks earlier, shot 67-71-69-65, falling a stroke short at 272. He tied for second with John Bland (67-67-71-67). Olazabal, who had to settle for a tie for fourth with Davis, very nearly was the hero of the piece, however. He was playing under the miseries of the flu—"very bad," he said—but was on the top of the leaderboard most of the way. He shared the first-round lead on 66 with Eduardo Romero, Tony Johnstone, and Paul Curry. He shot 68 in the second round for a 10-under-par 134, tying for the lead with Bland (67). And in the third round, a 69 left Olazabal all alone at the top at 13-under-par 203, a stroke ahead of Harwood, two ahead of Johnstone and Bland, and four ahead of Faldo, who never led but who was never out of reach or out of mind.

The final round was more of a stampede than a battle. Harwood got a grip on the championship when he came out of the turn with two birdies and an eagle from the 10th. He needed them. Faldo was on a rampage up ahead, making seven birdies over the last nine holes for a 31 and a 65, the best round of the week. Davis, who won this title in 1986, came home in 30 for a 66. All told, seven men were within reach of Harwood, five of them finishing between 65 and 68. Only two were out of the 60s—Olazabal, at 70, and Johnstone, 71.

Harwood would have been forgiven had he cracked under this heat, but he remained calm and calculating. He knew, finally, that a par at the par-five 18th would win. So that's what he played for, and that's what he got.

Dunhill British Masters—£300,000
Winner: Mark James

Mark James' formula for winning the Dunhill British Masters was simple enough. He went without a bogey for the last 43 holes, he missed only one green in the final 18, and he hit one pair of binoculars. Despite crazy weather— a mix of heat, lightning, winds, and heavy rain—James was wonderfully consistent in notching his 13th European Tour victory. He posted 70-67-66-67, an 18-under-par total of 270 at the par-72 Woburn Golf and Country Club for a two-stroke victory over David Feherty.

It was the third round, the 66, that finally put James atop the leaderboard. It gave him a 13-under-par 203, tying him with Feherty, who was at or near the top in the first two rounds, and long-hitting Brett Ogle. Feherty finished at 65-70-68-69—272, two ahead of Carl Mason (67—274). Ogle (73) tied for fourth at 276 with Mark McNulty (66), and Jeff Hawkes (66).

James' victory again stamped him as a strong front-runner. "I do tend to win more often than I should when I'm in contention," James said. "Maybe I'll run out of luck any time now."

Sometimes you get a break, and sometimes you make your own. James had a little of each. In the third round, at the 16th hole, he fired his tee shot into the gallery. The ball bounced off a spectator's binoculars and back into the fairway. So much for luck. Now for skill. Also at the 16th—this time in the final round, while he was trying to hold a two-stroke lead over Feherty— he drove behind a tree to the right. He had two choices. He could chip back out to the fairway, or he could try to maneuver his way around that tree, with the green 190 yards away. "With Feherty only two behind, I had to go for it," James said. "It was not a difficult shot—a low, punch-draw." The roar from the gallery at the green told him he had made it.

The 16th also was a crucial hole for Feherty. In the second round, his approach was headed for trouble until it hit a spectator square in the forehead and bounced back onto the green, 15 feet from the flag. "It was a sickening blow," Feherty said. "I could hear it from where I was standing, and it was going so fast, it would have gone to Newport Pagnell." Golfer and spectator survived.

Feherty shared the first-round lead on 65 with Australian Peter O'Malley, who blew to a 79 in the second round. Sam Torrance (66) and Bill Longmuir (67) held the second-round lead at 10-under 134, a stroke ahead of Feherty (70), Ogle (65), Colin Montgomerie (67), and Andrew Murray, who shot a tournament-best 64.

James still hadn't climbed the leaderboard. He trailed by five in the first round, and by three in the second. The third-round 66, thanks in part to the binoculars shot, got him a share of the 54-hole lead with Feherty (68) and Ogle (68). In the final round, Ogle left the party when he bogeyed two of the first five holes. James moved to the front and stayed there.

Nick Faldo was the man in a side drama. He was bidding for a two-year sweep of Masters titles. In 1989, he won both the U.S. Masters and the Dunhill British Masters. And now in 1990, just about two months earlier, he won his second consecutive U.S. Masters. But his bid for a second British Masters went sour early, and he found himself fighting just to avoid missing his first cut in Europe in four years. A birdie-eagle finish in the second round saved him. He hit from 20 feet for the birdie at No. 17, and dropped an 18-footer for an eagle-three at No. 18 for 71 that just made the cut at 144. He finished tied for 59th at 289.

"I played lousy, I putted lousy, and the weather's lousy," Faldo said.

Scandinavian Enterprise Open—£400,000
Winner: Craig Stadler

Craig Stadler had said that the Scandinavian Enterprise Open is a "special tournament" to him. Maybe years of frustration tend to lift some events above the pain level. Stadler had played there six times before the 1990 event, and twice the title was snatched right out of his hands. In 1983, Sam Torrance beat him on the last hole, and three years later, Greg Turner beat him on the first hole of a playoff. Stadler was beginning to wonder what a guy had to do to win. This time, he found out.

It took a monumental effort, though. Going into the final round, Stadler was four strokes off the lead. Then he exploded for an 11-under-par 61, a course record, and won by four strokes over Craig Parry. The classic round smashed the old record by three strokes on the 6,747-yard, par-72 Drottningholm Golf Club course near Stockholm. Stadler birdied the first four holes, had nine birdies in all, and an eagle on the par-five 18th. And with rounds of 68-72-67-61, he also tied the tournament record set by Ronan Rafferty in 1989.

"It's very nice to win here for the first time because I'd been so close a couple of times before," Stadler said. "This is a special tournament for me."

For one thing, it marked the end of a long drought. Stadler was a sensation in 1982, with four victories on the American Tour, including the Masters. Then he lost his edge. His last victory on the American Tour was the 1984 Byron Nelson Classic, and his last victory of any kind was the 1987 Dunlop Phoenix in Japan.

For three rounds in the Scandinavian Open, Stadler gave no indication that he was about to break out of that prison. His first-round 68 looked good, but it was three off the pace set by Howard Clark and Sweden's Johan Rystrom. They both shot 65s, just a stroke shy of the record 64 set by American Bill Garrett in 1976.

Rystrom gave the home fans something to cheer about for three rounds, then made an awkward exit. He shared second place after a third-round 68, then discovered he had signed an incorrect scorecard. He was disqualified. Gordon Brand, Jr., meanwhile, moved into a two-stroke lead with a 68 of his own for a 13-under-par total of 203. Tied for second at 205 were Brian Marchbank (65), Roger Chapman (65), and Parry (69). Rafferty, the defending champion, also shot 65, and was among seven players at 206. So it was not surprising that Stadler, with a 67—207, was hardly noticed. Then came his grand finale, the 61. Along with a severe case of understatement. How do you explain a 61?

Stadler barely twitched his mustache. "I was hitting the ball very well," he said. "And my putting was also very good."

Wang Four Stars National Pro-Celebrity—£225,000
Winner: Rodger Davis

Maybe a 39-year-old man who wears plus-twos and autographed socks these days has to do things the hard way to keep the giggling down. Anyway, Rodger Davis—who didn't merely vow to top the Order of Merit at the end of this season, he bet he would—not only came from back in the pack, he went through a seven-hole playoff to take the Wang Four Stars National Pro-Celebrity at Moor Park.

That's one way to make a bet pay off. Davis had put £1,000 on himself at 33-1 that he would head the Order of Merit. "That looks very good right now," the heavily mustachioed Australian said. "And there is still half the season left." In fact, the victory did lift him to the top for now. But he wasn't counting his money from the bookies yet. This was only mid-June, and Europe's big guns would be back soon from the U.S. Open, which was being played this week.

Reducing things to their simplest terms, Davis beat countryman Mike Clayton on the seventh extra hole of what started as a four-man playoff. It made Davis, who won the Peugeot Spanish Open seven weeks earlier, the first double-winner of the season. It was also his fifth European victory and 19th worldwide.

This was American Bill Malley's tournament to win. Malley, 35, an ex-truck driver from California, who joined the European Tour in 1985, was about to score his first European victory. He had carded 68-66-67, and all he needed was a par four at the final hole. But he couldn't get up and down from a bunker, and the bogey left him at 70 and 17-under-par 271. Mark McNulty joined the party with a 65, Clayton with a 67, and Davis most dramatically of all, with a birdie from 10 feet on the last hole for 67. Before that, you could hardly find Davis.

In the first round, he was only a stroke off the lead, one of four at 67. But he was tied for fifth. Four were tied for the lead on 66—Rick Hartmann, Peter Mitchell, Andrew Sherborne, and Sam Torrance. Davis was worse off after 36 holes. Hartmann and Mitchell each put up another 66 and tied through the second round at 12-under-par 132. Davis was seven strokes back on 72—139. In the third round, a tournament-low 65 (matched by others) brought him back to within three, at 204, behind the 201 posted by Mitchell (69) and Malley (67). That bookie was not exactly mopping his brow.

But along came Davis, with the birdie on the 72nd hole, and the rush was on. The playoff was held on the 17th and 18th holes, and what tournament director could expect a playoff to last more than, oh, three holes? McNulty and Malley dropped out on the first extra hole, and Davis and Clayton battled on. Forever, it seemed.

They halved the 17th and 18th three times. Then they returned to the par-five 17th for the fourth time. Clayton's drive ended up to the right, behind a tree. He punched back out into the fairway, then hit the green. Davis hit the green in two. Clayton two-putted for a par, and Davis two-putted for the winning birdie.

Which ought to set up another bet for him some day. This was his sixth victory in seven playoffs.

Carrolls Irish Open—£347,390
Winner: Jose Maria Olazabal

Could there be something to the tales of the "Little People" of Ireland? Maybe Mark Calcavecchia, the 1989 British Open champion, is beginning to think so. He had been struggling this year. He had a number of second-place finishes but couldn't quite find that last little burst to get over the hill. And now it was late in June, and he was laboring.

He came to the Carrolls Irish Open, and in the first round it felt like the good old days again. He returned a six-under-par 66 and took a one-stroke lead. Portmarnock, that crusty campaigner, all 7,102 yards of it, didn't seem so tough after all. "This is an easy course when the wind doesn't blow," Calcavecchia announced. And that was just about the end of him.

His putter suddenly had a mind of its own. He shot 75 in the second round, and that threw the door wide open.

Jose Maria Olazabal, the 24-year-old Spanish whiz, who needs no invitations to begin with, jumped through and led the rest of the way for his second victory of the year. Olazabal, winner of the Benson and Hedges International seven weeks earlier, toured Portmarnock in 67-72-71-72—282, six under par. He was the only man in the starting field of 144 not to go over par in any round. He won by two over Calcavecchia and Frank Nobilo, both at 285.

Another example of how golf is flexing its muscle in Europe popped up in the person of Marc Farry, 30-year-old Frenchman and a professional since 1979. Farry also shot 67 in the first round and tied Olazabal for second behind Calcavecchia. It was a modest showing, but like the French victory over Greg Norman and his Australian team in the 1989 Dunhill Cup, it certainly was a departure. Farry actually was in the running until the end. He was tied for the lead with Olazabal at 210 going into the final round. Then an 80 dropped him to a tie for 11th.

Olazabal took over the lead in the second round with a par 72 for a five-under-par total of 139, a stroke ahead of John Bland (69), Eamonn Darcy (70), and Farry (73). Nobilo, who owned one victory in his six years on the European Tour, scrambled into the chase in the third round with a 69—212. He was in third place, two behind Olazabal and Farry.

But nothing and nobody could dislodge Olazabal. "I said to myself on the first tee—'I am ready to win. I want to win,'" he said. And so he did. Only five years on the European Tour, and he already had his eighth victory.

The tournament was hardly a hallmark for some others. Ian Woosnam, for example, went to Portmarnock hoping to take his third successive Irish Open. But nothing was farther out of his reach. Woosnam, the Mediterranean Open winner in March, had a weird tournament—69-75-70-77. That roller-coaster ride left him at 291 and tied for 14th.

And two well-known American names didn't even make the cut. PGA Tour Commissioner Deane Beman shot 74-75—149 and missed by a stroke, and Gary Nicklaus, Jack's youngest son, and an amateur, shot 78-80—158.

Peugeot French Open—£350,000
Winner: Philip Walton

"I'll only really believe this in a few hours," Philip Walton was saying, the Peugeot French Open trophy safely beside him. "It's so hard to win on this circuit, but somebody up there took care of me today. After the hole-in-one, this had to be my week."

It was nothing if not Walton's week. The 28-year-old Irishman was seven strokes off the lead in the first round. He was six behind in the second, and it took a hole-in-one to get him that close. He was only one behind going into the final round, but the crowd in front of him, tied for the lead, included nobody less formidable to a non-winner than Mark McNulty and Masters champion Nick Faldo. But suddenly, there he was. He birdied the 72nd hole to force a tie with another intimidating figure, Bernhard Langer, winner of the Madrid Open in April. His prospects weren't promising, though. His best finish was a second in the 1989 Carrolls Irish Open, and that was a playoff loss to Ian Woosnam. Now he faced another shootout against a tested opponent. But it was his turn this time. He beat Langer on the second extra hole, and thus became the fourth first-time winner on the European Tour of the season. Walton shot 73-66-67-69—275, five under par on the 6,983-yard, par-70 Chantilly course outside Paris. Langer, who also rallied in the final round, shot 71-65-72-67.

Faldo's bid for a third successive French Open title fizzled in a two-over-par 72 final round. He finished fourth, a stroke behind Eduardo Romero (70—276). McNulty closed with a 73—278, tied for sixth, but who knows what might have happened if he hadn't forgotten that extra putter in his bag. He shot 63 in the second round, but it turned into a 65 with the two-stroke penalty—too many clubs—which knocked him from one stroke to three strokes off the lead after 36 holes. The most prominent crashes: Peter Teravainen, tied for the lead going into the final round, blew to a 78 for a 283 total, plunging to a tie for 21st. Steve Bowman, first-round leader with a 66 and just a stroke off the lead going into the final round, also shot 78. He plummeted to a tie for 27th on 284. Other prominent victims: American amateur Gary Nicklaus, son of Jack Nicklaus, shot 68-76—144, and American PGA Tour Commissioner Deane Beman shot 75-71—146, both missing the 36-hole cut.

Walton, a European Tour pro since 1983, had shown a lot of promise. He missed only two cuts in 29 starts in 1989, and had seven top-10 finishes. There was no indication that this French Open would be anything more than another top-10. He was just one of the bunch until he scored the hole-in-one at No. 16 in the second round. That won him a car, but didn't appreciably improve his position. With 66—139, he was six strokes behind Rick Hartmann (65—133), another non-winner. The breakthrough came in the final round.

Faldo, McNulty, Teravainen, and Richard Boxall were all locked up at 205. They slid, and Walton held on. He birdied the first hole, bogeyed the 12th, then birdied the 18th for a 69, catching Langer, who had finished with a 67, best round of the day. They halved the first playoff hole, then Langer made the fatal error on the second. He bunkered his approach shot, and failed to get up-and-down, and Walton two-putted for his par and his first victory.

Torras Monte Carlo Open—£354,970
Winner: Ian Woosnam

Someone ought to check with David Skelton, to see whether Ian Woosnam has paid for that putter yet. Woosnam dropped in at Skelton's shop near his home in Wales, and picked up a new Zebra putter. This one was a women's model, an inch shorter than standard. "I've been having terrible troubles, as everybody knows," Woosnam explained. "But the new putter has given me back my confidence."

Indeed. Woosnam shot 60 with it. That was in the final round of the Torras Monte Carlo Open, and he won going away.

"I haven't paid David for it yet," Woosnam said. "I expect the price will have gone up now."

Woosnam came within a whisker of shooting the first 59 in a European Tour event, and also tying the American record set by Al Geiberger in 1977. Woosnam had two holes left, and he needed a birdie-birdie or eagle-par finish for the 59. He came within a heartbeat at the par-five 17th. He hit a drive and a seven iron to 12 feet, but the eagle putt grazed the hole and stayed out. So now he needed a birdie at the 18th. His drive left him at point-blank range, just 74 yards from the flag. But his pitch didn't bite, and the ball went 30 feet past the cup. He two-putted for his par and the 60, and felt let down. The 59 had been right at his fingertips.

"I'll probably never get that close again," he said.

Woosnam shot 66-67-65-60—258, 18 under par on the 6,198-yard, par-69 Mont Agel course, for a five-stroke victory over Italy's Costantino Rocca. Rocca vaulted into second place, his best finish ever, when he birdied the last two holes for 63—263.

Woosnam's 60 included 10 birdies and one bogey. He needed just six putts in the first seven holes, and 25 over all.

If Woosnam earned some sympathy, what of Mark Mouland, his fellow Welshman? Mouland found Mont Agel completely to his liking. Returning 63-67-65, he led the first three rounds—by one over Hugh Baiocchi and Jose Maria Canizares in the first, by two over Wayne Riley in the second, and by three over Woosnam through the third. He shot no worse than an even-par 69 in the final round, and that dropped him to a tie for third. Woosnam simply overran the field.

Ironically, it was a tip from Mouland that got Woosnam going. Woosnam had been troubled by his grip. He asked Mouland to check it. Mouland told him it was too open, and Woosnam made an adjustment. "All of a sudden, everything was coming off the club much more solid," Woosnam said.

Woosnam started his historic round with five consecutive birdies. He holed from four feet at No. 1 (after escaping from two bunkers). At No. 2, he holed from 25 feet for his two, then from three feet at the third, and from 12 at No. 4. A 15-footer wrapped up the streak at No. 5. The only flaw in the gem was a bogey at the par-three eighth, where he bunkered his tee shot. He brushed that off and birdied the 11th, 12th, 15th, 16th, and 17th.

Woosnam missed the record 59, but he tied three others—low round (60), low two rounds (125), and low 72 holes (258).

There was one final irony. Five years earlier, before Mont Agel had a sprinkler system installed, Woosnam complained that the fairways were too hard and bouncy, and he left without hitting a shot.

Not that it needed saying, but Woosnam said it anyway: "I'm glad I came back."

Bell's Scottish Open—£400,000
Winner: Ian Woosnam

Since it falls the week before the British Open, the Bell's Scottish Open is regarded as the crucial barometer of who's hot and who's not. That being the case then, the first surprise in the Scottish Open occurred at the halfway point. This was the 36-hole cut, and look who missed it—Jose Maria Olazabal, a two-time winner already this season, and Bernhard Langer, Sandy Lyle, David Frost, Mark James, and Wayne Grady, who lost in a playoff in the 1989 British Open. It would take some doing to upstage a casualty list like that one, but that's exactly what Ian Woosnam did.

Woosnam shot a course-record 62 over the Gleneagles King's Course in the second round, and ran away with the championship by four strokes. This was his third victory of the season, and the second in succession. He won the Torras Monte Carlo Open the week before, shooting another course record in the process, a 60. If the question is, who's hot, then the answer definitely is Ian Woosnam. He shot 72-62-67-68—269, 15 under par, and won by four strokes over Mark McNulty (73-67-64-69—273).

Not only did Woosnam run away with the tournament, he even spotted the field a seven-stroke head start. Gordon Brand, Jr., took a two-stroke lead in the first round, getting revenge on Gleneagles with a six-under-par 65. It must have been a great feeling. He led the 1989 Scottish Open going into the final round, then collapsed to a 78. His 65 this time was more than revenge, it was remarkable. In those winds, it was difficult enough to walk, much less play golf.

Brand held firm with a 67 for a 10-under-par 132 in the second round. He led by two over Woosnam, who blasted his way toward the front with the 62—two eagles, six birdies, and one bogey. Then a third-round 67 lifted Woosnam to the top, at 12-under 201 for a three-stroke lead on Brand Jr. (72).

Then came a dark cloud. The morning of the final round, Woosnam woke with a very sore back. Many golfers know the sensation. Most play on, but with limited results. "I went to the practice ground to try to loosen it," Woosnam said, "but I was struggling. I took tablets on the way around, and they seem to have got me through." His start was shaky. He missed the green on three of the first four holes, but got down in two each time. Then he loosened up, and when McNulty bogeyed No. 3 after a poor chip, Woosnam was on his way.

As to who's hot and who's not, Nick Faldo was the man to watch. He opened with 72-73, and that left him no chance to win. He was 13 strokes off the lead. In fact, he made the cut with only one stroke to spare. But his closing 67-65 were a bright sign for the British Open at St. Andrews, just an hour away. Faldo started that 65 with five successive birdies, beginning at No. 4, for an outward 30. The only blot was a double bogey at the par-three 11th, where he was nearly unplayable in a bush. "Touch wood," Faldo said, "all is now in order."

KLM Dutch Open—£350,000
Winner: Stephen McAllister

It's an article of faith in golf—keep your head down and your eye on the ball. You also "play them one at a time." Stephen McAllister wasn't even close to keeping these commandments in the KLM Dutch Open. Coming down the stretch, he kept one eye on the leaderboard. But if ever a golfer didn't have to look over his shoulder, it was McAllister. It's not often that a man has the kind of cushion McAllister enjoyed. Maybe he was thinking of another commandment: You can't be too careful. It wasn't until he stepped off the 18th green with a four-stroke victory that he finally relaxed. Suddenly, 1990 had turned into a big year for McAllister. Winless since joining the European Tour in 1987, he now had two victories for 1990. He won the season opener, the Vinho Verde Atlantic Open, back in February. That one couldn't have been tighter. He won it in a six-way playoff. This one couldn't have been looser. Even so ...

"I watched the leaderboards the last five, six holes," McAllister said. And he felt progressively more secure. "At the 16th, I felt comfortable," he said. "I knew I had a very good chance to win. And when Chapman bogeyed the 17th, then I knew. There wasn't much pressure." Actually, McAllister, who failed to qualify for the British Open, played the week before, seemed to be playing this one all alone. And he must have been weatherproof.

Even though it was the end of July, some really nasty weather hit near Zandvoort, in The Netherlands, and McAllister was the only one able to calm the 6,597-yard, par-70 Kennemer Golf and Country Club. Leading wire-to-wire—he shared the lead in the first round—McAllister shot 69-67-68-70—274, six under par. That may not seem like much in these days when par gets embarrassed every week, but par more than held its own this time. The cut figure was the highest of the season so far, eight over par. Among those who missed: Christy O'Connor, Jr. (73-76) and Mark Calcavecchia (75-79). Out of 144 starters, only three broke the par of 280—McAllister, at six under; Roger Chapman, who finished second at two-under 278, and Jose Maria Olazabal, at 279. And only two, Colin Montgomerie and Danny Mijovic, matched par.

The tournament opened like a rush-hour traffic jam. Seven tied for the lead on one-under-par 69—McAllister, Anders Forsbrand, Andrew Murray, Peter Baker, Antonio Garrido, Andrew Hare, and Tortsen Giedeon.

Then McAllister pulled away in the second round, a 67—136 putting him three strokes ahead of Montgomerie (68—139). The gap remained the same, but the faces changed in the third round. Montgomerie faltered (73—212), and up popped Roger Chapman, seemingly from nowhere, shooting a 66 for a 207 total, three behind McAllister (68—204). Chapman gave him a thrill in the final round, scoring birdies at the first, third and 16th. McAllister could almost feel the breath down his neck. But then things got away from Chapman for an instant. He bogeyed the 17th. McAllister could draw a breath again. Moments later, he had the second title of his four-year career.

PLM Open—£350,000
Winner: Ronan Rafferty

By the first week of August, 1989, Ronan Rafferty was pretty much sitting on top of the golf world. He not only had won his first European Tour event, he added a second, and also had nine other top-10 finishes. Compared to that performance, it seemed in 1990 that Rafferty had disappeared—until the first week of August. Maybe there's something about Sweden that brings out the best in him. In 1989, the first week of August, he won the Scandinavian Enterprise Open, his second win of a three-win year that put him atop the Order of Merit. This time, it was the PLM Open at Bokskogen. It wasn't even a contest. Rafferty simply ran away with it.

It wasn't cool weather, though. A record-breaking heat wave was punishing Britain, and it had spread up to the Nordic countries, pushing temperatures into the upper-80s. But not hotter than Rafferty. He raced through Bokskogen, a 6,889-yard, par-72 course near Malmo, with 64-67-70-69—270, 18 under par, and won by four strokes over Vijay Singh, who shot 69-71-69-65—274.

Actually, Rafferty took all the fun out of the tournament. That opening 64 not only tied the course record, it gave him a three-stroke lead on Frank Nobilo, Ian Mosey, Michael McLean, and Danny Mijovic, all at 67. Of this foursome, only Nobilo would stay within sight of the top. He tied for ninth, 10 strokes behind Rafferty. Mosey and McLean, the latter a struggling 27-year-old Englishman, soared by 10 strokes and shot 77s in the second round. Mosey tied for 47th, McLean for 61st. Mijovic, a Canadian who was on the leaderboard at the British Open briefly, closed with a 77 and tied for 70th.

Rafferty still led by three through the second round, over Ove Sellberg, and then by five through the third round, over Sellberg and Jean Van de Velde, a 24-year-old Frenchman. Rafferty gave his chasers a flicker of hope early in the final round, when he bogeyed No. 3 and No. 4. His lead was down to two strokes. But not for long. He birdied two of the next three holes, and the PLM Open was closed once again. It was back to a race for second place. Singh won that battle by a stroke over Bernhard Langer, 274-275. They were 14 and 15 under par, respectively, which is enough to win many tournaments. But the sizzling Rafferty took the PLM out of that category.

Rafferty drew nothing but praise from Fred Couples, the siege gun of the American Tour. Couples was in that crowd of futile chasers. He played some strong golf, 70-72-69-65—276. But that only got him a tie for fourth with Sellberg. "The way Ronan played against Mats Lanner and me the first two days here," Couples said, "you would have thought he was playing against a couple of 10-year-olds." (Lanner shot 73-73—146, missing the cut by two strokes.) "We weren't playing badly at all," Couples said, "but he was streets in front. I think he's ready for the American Tour."

Murphy's Cup—£250,000
Winner: Tony Johnstone

When Tony Johnstone, former scourge of South Africa's Sunshine Tour, got finished with the Murphy's Cup, some shuddered to think what he might do if, say, the British Open were played under the same modified Stableford scoring system. This scoring system awards points for birdies and eagles, and takes them away for bogeys, double bogeys, and worse. So this is where the bold step forth. The golfer who doesn't attack the course has no real chance. Whoever isn't making a birdie is losing ground.

The Murphy's Cup is the European Tour's version of The International, which has become famous in its few years on the American Tour schedule, even though most fans—and most of the golfers, for that matter—are puzzled by the scoring. The International was the first Tour event to abandon the conventional stroke play and use a modified Stableford system.

Johnstone took to it instantly, and rang up his second victory in 11 years on the European Tour, and his first since the 1984 Portuguese Open. Johnstone got a total of 50 points, two better than England's Malcolm Mackenzie. Johnstone got his teeth into it with a spectacular second round. In stroke play, it would have been a 61, 11 under par on the 6,807-yard, par-72 Fulford Golf Club in England. Under the modified Stableford, it was a 23-point day, by far the best single round in the tournament. (England's Glyn Krause was next-best with 17, also in the second round.) Here's the other way to look at Johnstone's round: He made 10 birdies overall—eight of them in succession—and an eagle.

It was far from a lock, however, and Johnstone knew that better than anyone. Especially in the final round, when he flirted with disaster and came away mopping his brow. He was even par through eight holes, and there seemed little sign of the fire that touched off his second round. Then things got even worse. At the par-five ninth, his tee shot took a bad bounce and ended up in the heather. "I was moaning and swearing to myself," Johnstone admitted. "But the lie wasn't too bad, and I managed to hook a three iron 216 yards around a tree and onto the green." He made the putt for an eagle, worth four points, then eagled the 11th and birdied the 13th, and he was on his way. Mackenzie took second with 48 points, and Russell Claydon third with 44.

The Murphy's Cup was also good news for Sandy Lyle fans. He finished fourth with 40 points, but more important to him, he had four consecutive solid rounds—68-68-69-67. He made 21 birdies and two eagles in the four days, for his best outing since he finished fourth in the 1989 Volvo Masters. "It's certainly an uplift," Lyle said. "At one stage, I thought I might win here. And now I think I can win again."

NM English Open—£400,000
Winner: Mark James

If Sam Torrance thought a sore back was the worst of his problems, he was badly mistaken. The biggest pain was a case of bad timing. It cost him the NM English Open.

And so Mark James prevailed at The Belfry, taking his second consecutive English Open, and his second victory of the season (after the Dunhill British Masters early in June). He birdied the first hole of a playoff to beat Torrance. Before that, the decisive factor was an eagle putt that wouldn't drop. It cost Torrance a penalty and the tournament. Without the penalty, he would have won outright. Not that this mathematical proposition in any way diminishes James' performance. He had to come from well back in the field even to get close to the lead.

Heavy winds whipped The Belfry in the first round. Steven Richardson, Gordon Brand, Jr., and Sandy Stephen shared the lead on 71, just one under par. James started shakily but rebounded beautifully for 76-68-65-75 and tied Torrance (75-67-69-73) at four-under-par 284.

The back trouble had taken Torrance by surprise. "I never had back problems before in my life," he said. "It's fine now." He took some treatment just before the tournament, and for two weeks he had been on a strict diet and exercise program. A good score is something else that can do wonders for pain. Torrance had opened with a 75, but in the second round he shot a five-under-par 67 for a 142 total and the lead through 36 holes. He was one ahead of Antonio Garrido (67—143), and two ahead of Seve Ballesteros (72) and James (68), both at par-144. Garrido, who started on the inward nine, finished in a blaze—five birdies over the last eight holes. Garrido and Torrance were the only two players out of 153 to break the par of 144 for two rounds in the battering winds. But now Ballesteros seemed to be stirring.

"I'm not worried about Seve or anybody else," said Torrance, who was looking for his first victory in Europe in three years. "I'm only concerned about me."

James broke through in the third round. He started off at even par, birdied four holes going out, then raced past Torrance with birdies on three of the last four holes for a 65 and a three-round total of 209. Torrance shot 69—211, Ballesteros 68—212.

Then, in the third round, came the putt that wouldn't fall. It happened at the 301-yard 10th, so popular with big, bold hitters who can reach it, if they're willing to risk the water in front. Torrance not only reached it, he was a mere 12 feet from an eagle. But his eagle putt hung on the lip. He decided to wait. He waited too long.

"I timed it at 25 seconds," said tournament director Andy McFee, who studied the episode on a television replay. He handed Torrance the penalty. "Sam accepted it without argument," he said.

The next day, the penalty loomed larger. Playing conditions had become difficult. Rains had soaked the 7,202-yard course and delayed the start of the final round for more than three hours. It came down to the 18th, where Torrance had won the 1985 Ryder Cup for Europe. James birdied from 30 feet. Torrance followed him in from 15.

The first playoff hole, ironically, was the 10th, where Torrance had waited too long. This time, Torrance pitched across the water and got his par, but James rolled in a treacherous 15-foot, downhiller for the birdie and the win. It was the 14th of his 15-year career on the European Tour.

Volvo German Open—£467,445
Winner: Mark McNulty

Mark McNulty must have been hurting something awful, judging from the way he ran off with the Volvo German Open.

Nobody asked after McNulty's health, but it would have been of academic interest, at least, to know how he was feeling. The state of McNulty's health, Fulton Allem contends, is always crucial to the outcome of any tournament. It was Allem, during their great battles on the Sunshine Tour in South Africa, who used to say, "If Mark said he was feeling fine before a tournament, then maybe I could win. But if he'd say, 'Oh, my knee hurts,' or 'Oh, I've got a terrible upset stomach,' or something like that, then I didn't stand a chance."

McNulty won the German Open in 1980 and in 1987, but he seemed destined to be nothing more than a tag-along in this late-August outing. Oh, he was playing well enough. But everybody else was tearing up the 6,756-yard, par-72 Hubbelrath Golf Club course, near Dusseldorf. There was Anders Forsbrand, in particular, a pleasant Swede who must be wondering what a soul has to do to win. Actually, it's what he had better not do. And that is, he'd better not slip, not even a little bit. Forsbrand owns just one European Tour victory, the 1987 European Masters-Swiss Open, and he seemed well on his way to his second. He started by tying the course record with a 10-birdie 64, and that gave him a two-stroke lead. Then came a lurch in the third round. It was a mere one-over-par 73, but down he went.

Then there was defending champion Craig Parry (he beat Mark James in a playoff in 1989), catching Forsbrand in the third round at 13-under-par 203. But he also got run over by McNulty in the fourth round, and finished second. American Rick Hartmann was just a stroke off the lead going into the final round, but he took himself out with a 75, his only round over par, and dropped to a tie for 19th. Eamonn Darcy never did go above par, a pair of 70s being his highest, but even that was too much against the charging McNulty. Darcy tied Forsbrand for third.

McNulty kept the leaders within range in the first three rounds with 67-68-70. Then he sprinted home in 65 for a 270 total, 18 under par, a three-stroke victory over Parry. It was McNulty's second victory of the season— he won the Cannes Open in April—and he also had three seconds, one of them in the British Open, behind Nick Faldo. The £77,896 first prize at Hubbelrath put him on top of the Volvo Order of Merit with £362,783.

McNulty left the field in the dust with a brilliant spurt over the final nine. It started at the par-five 12th, where he fired a seven-iron approach to within four feet, and holed the putt for an eagle-three. He followed that up with three successive birdies. Not a bad comeback for a man who missed the 36-hole cut in the English Open at The Belfry just the week before. It was, by the way, his first miss after making 40 in succession.

Ebel European Masters-Swiss Open—£460,000
Winner: Ronan Rafferty

You'd think a man who had just shot 21 under par and won his second consecutive start would be feeling pretty perky. Not Ronan Rafferty. Grateful, yes. But not perky. "I was more than a shade lucky," he insisted. He shot 70-65-66-66—267, and won the Ebel European Masters-Swiss Open by two over John Bland (70-66-66-67—269).

Rafferty, who won the PLM Open in his previous European start four weeks earlier, didn't lead in this one until he was in the last round. "I was fortunate no one challenged me on the final day," he said. Consider the case of Ove Sellberg, he said. Sellberg had shot 66-67-67 and was leading by a stroke going into the final round. Then he shot 77. "That's surprising," Rafferty said, "because 64s are usually two-a-penny on Sundays here." The 6,745-yard, par-72 Crans-Sur-Sierre course, for all of its breathtaking Alpine beauty, is easy picking for the pros. Note that the 36-hole cut came in at three-under-par 141. Also note that of the 63 finishers, all but the last three broke par for the tournament. American Steve Bowman, who finished 60th, was at two-under-par 286.

Starting out, Rafferty looked like anything but a winner. He opened with a two-under-par 70, but that was rather high for the day. Of those 63 finishers, only 14 shot higher, and 73 was the highest of the day—including, surprisingly, defending champion Seve Ballesteros. Howard Clark, one of Europe's big guns just a few years earlier, showed signs that he was coming back. He shot 64 in the first round, and led by one over Mark McNulty. Clark built his lead to three through the rain-interrupted second round with 66—130. He led over a mixed trio—Sellberg (67), the rising Swede; Sandy Lyle (66), another former power starting to stir again, and Jamie Spence (67), who rose from the depths of the unknown with a 65 in the British Open only some two months earlier.

In the third round, Clark slipped to a 72, Sellberg took the lead (67—200), and some heat was generated in another quarter. Ballesteros was just getting to be happy. His game was coming around. Then he, Swede Jasper Parnevik, and Frenchman Jean Van de Velde were warned by an official about slow play—not once, but twice. "I said, 'You've got to be kidding,'" Ballesteros said. "It's the first time I've been officially warned in my life. The warnings broke my concentration and affected my score." He managed a 69, but was eight strokes behind Sellberg, who led by one. Like Rafferty, Sellberg considered himself a luck man, and he wasn't talking about holing that bunker shot for an eagle-two at No. 7. "I hardly hit a fairway," he said. "It's lucky this is a forgiving course."

Not everybody was lucky at Crans, however. England's Mark Davis and South Africa's Chris Williams forgot to exchange scorecards and sign one another's card, and both were disqualified. So was Portugal's Daniel Silva. He was on the verge of perhaps the best payday of his career after a 69-68 start. But he misread his starting time for the third round.

Rafferty, it developed, did enjoy some luck. But it was Sellberg's bad luck. Sellberg had already shot 66-67-67, so it was clear that the 60s were easily within his reach. But he exploded to a final-round 77 (tying for 21st on 277). The door was wide open, and it was Rafferty, with a six-birdie 66, who tramped through for a two-stroke victory.

Panasonic European Open—£400,000
Winner: Peter Senior

The Panasonic European Open was a tournament of questions: Would Ian Woosnam score his fourth victory of the European season? Would Nick Faldo survive his sore wrist, to say nothing of the Rules of Golf? Would Tim Simpson break the course record? Would Peter Senior quit the game?

The answer to the last question, by the end of the tournament, was a rousing no. Why quit when you're ahead? But things had looked grim for a while. Senior, the mustachioed and good-natured Australian, had come within a whisker of quitting, if you can believe a golfer speaking from the depths of despair. He missed four consecutive cuts up to the British Open. "I lost my confidence," he said. "I was hitting some of the worst shots you've ever seen." So after some time off, some soul-searching, and some practice, he got well in a hurry in the European Open the first week of September, his first European Tour event in the eight weeks since the British Open. Fate teased him to the end, though. He didn't have the lead until he was well into the final round. Playing some of the finest golf of his career, he finished at 13-under-par 267, shooting 67-68-66-66 on the 6,607-yard, par-70 Sunningdale Old Course.

Which meant that no, Woosnam would not win his fourth here. Woosnam, the 36-hole leader, played beautifully—65-68-68-67—but fell short by a stroke, taking second place on 268.

A bomb hoax—a sign of the times—delayed play in the first round for more than three hours, leaving 42 golfers to complete the round the next day. Aside from that, Faldo, the Masters and British Open champion, was the center of attention for a number of reasons. First, he was nursing an injured wrist. "I've just got to make sure I don't stress it too much," said Faldo, after opening with a 68, four strokes off Hugh Baiocchi's hot start (64). Faldo said he would withdraw if the wrist problem flared up. "I won't be playing through any pain barrier," he said. "That would be the dumbest thing to do."

Then there was the rules episodes. He had two of them. In the second round, his blast from a bunker hit the lip in front of him and caromed back over his head, and he hit the ball again, on his follow-through. He added a penalty stroke for hitting the ball twice. The next problem came from a television viewer, who thought Faldo hit the sand—grounded his club—on his final recovery shot at that same bunker. The viewer called a Royal and Ancient official, who in turn called a tournament official at Sunningdale, who then investigated and reported that whatever Faldo had hit was outside the bunker. Faldo tied for fourth place at 270, three strokes behind Senior.

Tim Simpson, who came close in the U.S. Open and the U.S. PGA Championship, was bearing down on Faldo's record 62 in the third round. He was eight under par for the day coming to No. 17. Then he had to play one-handed and back-handed from against a tree, ran into other trouble, and took a double bogey-six. He settled for a 64—203.

Senior hung close to the lead during all this, but couldn't break through until the final round. He locked it up at the 16th with a magnificent blast from a greenside bunker that ended up just three inches from the cup. Two solid pars, and the tournament was his. And just in time. "My brother and I have a pawn-brokering business back home," Senior said. "I suppose I could have pawned my clubs. Trouble is, the way I'd been playing, they wouldn't have fetched much."

Lancome Trophy—£420,000
Winner: Jose Maria Olazabal

"It looks like the only way I'll ever beat this guy," Colin Montgomerie was saying, "is if he's taken ill."

That was frustration plus admiration talking at the Lancome Trophy. Montgomerie, the European Tour's 1988 Rookie of the Year, had been within a whisker of the second victory of his career. He led the Lancome through the middle rounds, he led by two in the final round, and he shot 67. But the victory was plucked right out of his hands.

Jose Marie Olazabal, the brilliant young Spaniard, launched a five-birdie charge in the final round, vaulting over Montgomerie to a one-stroke victory, his third win of the year in Europe, his fourth overall. Olazabal shot 68-66-70-65—269, 11 under par on the 6,756-yard, par-70 St. Nom-La-Breteche course, outside Paris. Montgomerie shot 69-63-71-67—270. Plucked is the right word. Olazabal had just blown two strokes of a three-stroke lead coming down the final stretch, and then he was about to bogey the par-three 18th as well. His tee shot went hooking into the grandstand. But it caromed back out into the fairway, some 35 yards short of the flag. His chip nicked the flagstick and stopped about three feet away. A disaster had turned into a par—and a victory.

"Colin must be sick of me," Olazabal said, chuckling. "I had a hole-in-one and beat him in the European Amateur." And how about the 1984 British Amateur Championship, Montgomerie said. He was two up, and lost to Olazabal, 5 and 4. "He holed a full eight iron, two bunker shots, and two chips to beat me," Montgomerie said. Once again, Montgomerie played well, but Olazabal played a bit better.

Two sudden disappearances marked the start of the tournament. Ian Woosnam and Peter Senior—the latter fresh from winning the European Open—took the first-round lead on 67s. Then neither was a factor after that. Woosnam had five three-putt greens in a second-round 75. U.S. Open champion Hale Irwin figured he could become the first American since Lee Trevino in 1980 to take the Lancome. "Once I eliminate the jetlag and the lapses, I can win this," Irwin said. He shot 68 in the first round, but then a 72 dashed his chances. Also at 68 was Olazabal, who almost holed a chip shot at the final hole for a share of the lead.

Montgomerie exploded in the second round. He was out in two-under-par 33, then starting on No. 11, he birdied five of the next six holes, holing a cluster of putts between 10 and 35 feet. The streak gave him a 63—132, and a two-stroke lead over Olazabal (66—134). In the third round, Olazabal was almost standing still. He dropped three strokes to par, then charged to four birdies in five holes. After a dazzling birdie at the 16th—he chipped in from 25 feet—he made a dazzling bogey at the 17th. His five-iron approach ended up under a bush beyond the green. He had two choices, both bad. He could take a penalty drop and go beyond the bush some 20 yards, or "I could try to hit the ball through a gap in the branches—about five inches—a yard in front of me," he said. "I went for the gap and made the green. I was very lucky." He shot 70, and trailed Montgomerie (71—203) by only one stroke through 54 holes.

In the final round, Olazabal trailed Montgomerie by two strokes after five holes. Then he erupted for a barrage of five birdies in eight holes to vault over the frustrated Montgomerie.

"Olazabal is now third in the world rankings," Montgomerie said. "But if there are two guys better than he is, they must be bloody good."

BMW International Open—£400,000
Winner: Paul Azinger

A bunch of memories were revived when Paul Azinger beat David Feherty in the BMW International Open. The ones that hit the hardest—Azinger in the 1987 British Open, in the 1988 U.S. PGA Championship, and in the 1989 Ryder Cup Matches.

Remember that great, daring three wood Azinger smacked over two lakes at the final hole at The Belfry to beat Seve Ballesteros in the 1989 Ryder Cup Matches? He hit a similar shot this time, caught Feherty, then beat him in a playoff. Then commiserated with him. "I know how he feels," Azinger said. "David deserved it as much as I did. After all, he led all the way, and he took all the pressure until I got to him at the very end." The memories still gnaw at Azinger—how he led the 1987 British Open through the 70th hole, then bogeyed the last two, letting Nick Faldo walk over him; how he led the 1988 PGA Championship in the final round until Jeff Sluman sank that dazzling wedge shot for an eagle.

Feherty felt no such sting when he was winning the 1989 BMW International, the inaugural edition. He started out with a course-record 62 then, and he swept to a five-stroke victory on 19-under-par 269. "I guess I had to get caught sometime," Feherty said. For a number of reasons—a fierce storm was one of them—things didn't go as smoothly this time at the 6,910-yard, par-72 Golfplatz Munchen Nord-Eichenried, near Munich. Amazingly enough, Feherty opened with a 62 again. The gods of golf know how to run a golf tournament, by the way. In the 1989 BMW International, the 63 was worth a three-stroke lead. All Feherty had this time was a one-stroke lead. Azinger had shot 63, and one of the hottest duels of the season was on. Feherty shot 62-72-71-72—277, 11 under par. Azinger (63-73-73-68) caught him with that birdie on the final hole, then won with another.

Feherty launched his first-round rampage by chipping in from 40 feet at No. 2. Then he birdied four of the next seven holes. Coming in, he had five threes in the first seven holes, and four of them were birdies. He bogeyed the par-three 17th after missing the green, but an eagle-three at the 18th, on a five-foot putt, gave him 62. Azinger matched Feherty's outward 31, the keys being a birdie from 25 feet at No. 1, and an eagle-three at No. 6. He also bogeyed the 17th, after bunkering his four-iron tee shot.

Given the storm that hit the second day, it was even-money that the tournament would even be finished. A gale hit at mid-morning of the second round. Winds topping 50 miles an hour knocked over the leaderboard at the 16th, then the main scoreboard, and then a big tree behind No. 3 green. Wayne Riley and Ignacio Gervas were about to hit their second shots when a big tree started giving off loud cracking sounds. They broke and ran as the tree came crashing down. "I was really scared that it was going to come down on top of me," Riley said. That was close enough for Riley. He withdrew, and so did some six others. The storm delayed play, forcing some players to complete their round on Saturday morning. When the 36-hole cut was finally made, it sent the 149s and higher on their way.

Feherty led by four strokes going into the final round. Azinger and Russell Claydon were tied for second at 209. Then Azinger pulled away, and closed in on Feherty, who was shooting a par 72. Azinger finally came to the 565-yard, par-five 18th needing a birdie to tie. Shades of the Ryder Cup. Azinger had an iffy lie, weighed the dangers against the prize, then decided to go for it. He crushed his second shot some 250 yards to the edge of the green, chipped to five feet, and sank the birdie putt for his 68 and a tie at 277. The playoff began at the par-four 16th, and ended there. Azinger put his approach to 15 feet, and putting first, dropped the putt for a birdie. Feherty needed a 10-footer to tie. He missed.

Epson Grand Prix of Europe—£400,000
Winner: Ian Woosnam

One day it was a hot temper, the next a cold putter, but nothing was going to turn Ian Woosnam away from his second consecutive victory and his fifth of the season. He closed September with a flourish. He had just won the Suntory World Match Play the week before, beating Mark McNulty in the final, and now it was his time again. But it was beginning to look like a two-man show. The man he beat this time was McNulty—again. McNulty couldn't keep up, and Jose Maria Olazabal couldn't catch up, and that was that, much to the delight of Woosnam's fellow countrymen at Chepstow, Wales.

Woosnam's most doubtful moments came in the first round, if you can call a tie for the lead doubtful. He was all alone the rest of the way, leading by two through the second round, by three through the third, and then winning by three strokes. He would have won by four, but his 10-foot putt for a par at the final hole grazed the cup and stayed out. He dominated the par-71, 6,883-yard St. Pierre course, covering it in 65-67-67-72—271, 13 under par. McNulty, who dogged him all the way, also closed with a one-over-par 72, and Olazabal finished with a two-under 69. They tied for second at 274.

"I think I was very lucky to win," Woosnam said. "I didn't play very well. But Mark and Ollie couldn't hole a putt. I've never seen three worse men on the greens."

The tournament opened with a scramble. Woosnam, who hadn't played since winning the World Match Play, arrived just some three hours before his first round. He proceeded to shoot the 65 and tie Colin Montgomerie for the lead. A stroke behind came Jose Maria Canizares and Brett Ogle at 66. Then came Seve Ballesteros, with a 67, enjoying his strongest start since March. He was all set to join that tie for the lead, but he bogeyed the final two holes and tied McNulty. Ballesteros didn't return worse than a par 71, that in the second round, but he couldn't generate one of his famous whirlwinds, and he had to settle for a tie for seventh at 276, eight under par.

What had the makings of a fine battle evaporated in the second round, when Montgomerie shot 72, Canizares blew to a 75, and Ogle couldn't do better than a 70. Olazabal and McNulty rushed in to fill the vacuum with 67s, but they couldn't close the gap on Woosnam.

It was an angry Woosnam in the third round, despite a four-under-par 67 and a three-stroke lead on McNulty, 199-202. It took Woosnam more than five hours to play the third round. A steady rain that finally turned into a downpour slowed play, but Woosnam said the real villains were the golfers themselves. "We took four hours and 15 minutes for the first 15 holes, which I think was disgraceful," he said. "I know it was wet, but there are obviously some very slow players out there. It's time the PGA did something about it, and not just a fine but a two-stroke penalty." It would prove fortunate for him that the PGA did not take his advice.

The course record was threatened in the third round. The diminutive Miguel Angel Martin came to the 18th needing a birdie for a 62. But it's a forbidding hole, a par three of 237 yards. Martin had to settle for the par and a record-tying 63. American Rick Hartmann would gladly have settled for a par the day before. He came to No. 18 just a par away from a 68, which would have put him eight strokes behind the leaders. But he hooked his tee shot out of bounds, pulled his next one near a wall at the green, dubbed the next, and then found a bunker. He staggered off with an eight and a 73.

The final round was held up for four hours because an overnight rain had flooded the course. By then, Woosnam's temper had cooled, and so did his putter, but was his face red. Daylight was failing, and he and his threesome were seven minutes behind the group ahead. They were told to speed up. "It was quite a shock," Woosnam said. "That's the first time I've ever been told to get a move on."

Mercedes German Masters—£450,000
Winner: Sam Torrance

Sam Torrance was just about awe-struck. "This," he said, after winning the Mercedes German Masters, "is the best golf I've produced, tee-to-green, in my whole life."

That was saying a lot, considering the popular, 37-year-old Scot goes back a ways. He turned pro in 1970, and was the Rookie of the Year in 1972. This victory came along at the right time. It was the 13th of his career, but the first since the 1987 Italian Open. And it wasn't a late charge that did it. It was a pair of inspired middle rounds that sent Torrance barreling past local favorite Bernhard Langer and on his way to as easy a victory as anyone could hope for. It took a 62 by Ian Woosnam in the final round just to make him feel a little heat. Torrance shot the 6,839-yard, par-72 Stuttgarter Golf Club course in 70-65-64-73—272, 16 under par, to win by three strokes over Langer and Woosnam (275).

The tournament opened with a heavy rain, that first week of October, but it didn't seem to bother anybody—there were 31 sub-par scores—and especially not Langer. "It didn't affect my performance," he said. That was clear enough from the six-under-par 66 and the first-round lead. Langer, who won the Madrid Open in April, birdied the second, fifth, and eighth going out, and the 11th, 13th, and 15th coming in. Paul Broadhurst was second, a stroke back at 67, and a good international mix tied for third at 68—New Zealand's Frank Nobilo, France's Emmanuel Dussart, and Britain's Grant Turner. Dussart blew to a 79 in the second round and just made the 36-hole cut on three-over-par 147. The other three slipped into the low 70s and drifted out of contention.

Langer shot 67 in the second round for a 133 total, and now Torrance made his grand entrance, tying the course record with a 65 that left him alone in second place, two strokes back at 135. "It took me completely by surprise," Torrance said. "I thought the record was 62. Now I'll just have to go out and do it tomorrow."

And that's exactly what he did. He birdied five holes going out, then rode the roller coaster coming in. He made two breathtaking par-savers, a 10-footer at No. 10 and a six-footer at No. 11. Then he birdied Nos. 12, 13, and 15. He bogeyed No. 17, and so he needed a birdie at the par-five 18th for the record. And the record hung, finally, on an eight-foot putt. He made it for the record 64, a three-round total of 199, and an intimidating eight-stroke lead on Langer, who struggled to a 74—207. "I think I played the best round of my life today," Torrance said. "But Sunday, I'll have to play just as well. You can see from Bernhard how fast you can drop out of the lead."

Torrance kept the lead, but he had some tense moments in the final round. He was still leading by six strokes with 10 holes to play, but Woosnam was on a tear. Torrance's record 64 was just a day old, and Woosnam smashed it with a 10-birdie, 10-under-par 62. Think where he might be if he hadn't opened with a 75. At any rate, he cut Torrance's lead to only two strokes with five holes to play. But Torrance responded to the pressure, birdied the par-five 14th, and finished three strokes to the good. But that pressure was nothing compared to the pincers that gripped him on the final putt of the third round, for the then-record 64.

"The pressure I felt over that putt," Torrance said, "was the greatest I've felt since I holed the winner in the 1985 Ryder Cup at The Belfry. It gave me a hell of a kick when it went in."

Austrian Open—£250,000
Winner: Bernhard Langer

Sometimes familiarity can have a neutral effect. It may not breed contempt, or love, or even familiarity, for that matter. Take the observation from Jack Nicklaus, playing in his first-ever European Tour event. He had just shot 71 in the first round of the Austrian Open, at the 6,806-yard, par-72 Gut Altentann course near Salzburg. "Just because I designed it, doesn't mean I know how to read the greens," Nicklaus said. (It has become his practice to play in tournaments held at courses he designs.) He knew the question would be raised the moment he complained about his putting. "And the annoying thing," Nicklaus added, "was that I haven't played better this season, tee-to-green."

It was an academic point, however. The rejuvenated Bernhard Langer, winner of the Madrid Open in April, was rolling again. Langer started hot, got caught by Lanny Wadkins, then staged a furious comeback to tie him and beat him in a playoff. This was stale news for Wadkins. Langer had beaten him four times in Ryder Cup matches in the 1980s.

Almost overlooked in the exciting finish was Des Smyth's course-record 62, his best in a 16-year pro career. Smyth raced through the course with eight birdies and an eagle, and there was Nicklaus to congratulate him when he stepped off the course. The streak lifted Smyth to a solo third finish at 273, two strokes off the lead. Nicklaus shot 71-72-70-69—282, a tie for 14th.

Langer shot 65-66-72-68, and Wadkins 67-68-68-68, to tie at 17-under-par 271. But it looked like a Langer runaway at the start. In the first round, the man with the most celebrated case of the yips in golf made four birdies on putts of from 12 to 18 feet, and needed only 28 putts overall in a 65 (a course record that would be broken by Smyth only three days later) for a two-stroke lead. Wadkins would have tied, but he three-putted the 16th from 15 feet for a bogey, then bogeyed the 17th, missing a three-footer. In the second round, Langer three-putted twice, but made six birdies from inside seven feet, and added an eagle-three at the 18th on a 15-foot putt.

The third round changed things completely. Langer seemed doomed when he suffered three consecutive bogeys going out. But he pulled himself together and birdied the ninth, 12th, and 16th. A watery bogey at the 17th left him with a par 72. Wadkins, meanwhile, was on a tear. He birdied the 13th and 15th from 10 feet, the 17th from 15, then eagled the 18th after a four wood to 25 feet for a 68. They were tied at 13-under-par 203. Then things turned sour for Langer in a hurry. In the final round, he found himself four strokes behind Wadkins with only eight holes to play. "I told my caddy I needed four birdies to catch Lanny, because he wasn't making any mistakes," Langer said. "He was hitting the flag with every shot." Then, as though on cue, came the mistakes.

At No. 11, Wadkins hooked his tee shot into a bunker. He said a spectator clicked a camera just as he was hitting. But that was just the start of his problems. "I couldn't see green from there," Wadkins said. "And then my caddy gave me the wrong yardage. The ball landed in another bunker."

Langer put on a furious charge, getting the four birdies he needed, including a dramatic finish. At the 18th, he pulled his drive into the trees, dangerously close to the water, and had to hit from long grass through a gap three yards wide. He got through, then pitched on and holed a three-foot putt for the tying birdie, forcing the playoff. At the third extra hole—No. 18, again—Langer bunkered his approach, but blasted out to three feet and holed the putt for a birdie and the victory.

Portuguese Open-TPC—£275,000
Winner: Mike McLean

It's a familiar story in golf: First despair, then success. "My nerve went," Mike McLean was saying, "and I began asking myself whether I had the ability to be a professional golfer, let alone a champion." The years had been long and cruel, but McLean, an unknown Englishman, finally answered a lot of questions about himself—and more important, to himself—when he came from nowhere to take the Portuguese Open-Tournament Players Championship. He was the fifth first-time winner on the European Tour of the year. And just in time. This was late in October, and it was the next-to-last tournament of the season. All of a sudden, McLean's future was brighter.

McLean, a baby-faced 27-year-old, didn't figure to have much of a chance to begin with. He was in the depths of the Order of Merit—83rd to be exact. And after 36 holes, he was seven big strokes off the lead. And his name would hardly strike fear into the hearts of those in front of him. But the 7,095-yard, par-72 Quinta do Lago course held no fear for him. He toured it in 69-69-65-71—274, 14 under par for a one-stroke victory over Gordon Brand, Jr., the veteran Scot, and Volvo PGA champion Mike Harwood.

One man's breakthrough is another man's heartbreak. Magnus Persson had come close enough to victory in his eight years to know how sharp disappointment can be. He had lost twice in playoffs—just months ago, in May, to Seve Ballesteros in the Majorca Open, and in 1987 to Gordon Brand, Jr. in the Scandinavian Enterprise Open. But now he was well on the way to his own first victory. He opened with a tournament-best 64 for a three-stroke lead (McLean was five back, at 69). Persson added a 67 in the second round for a 131 total and a four-stroke lead (McLean was now seven behind, at 69—138). Then came a dramatic 10-stroke swing. In the third round, Persson soared to a 75, and McLean countered with an eight-birdie 65 for 203, and just that fast he was leading the tournament. He was two up on Ove Sellberg (70—205) and three up on Persson and Brand (68) at 206 in a very tight race. In fact, only six strokes separated the top 13 players, a group that also included—for McLean's contemplation—Harwood, Mark James, and Mark McNulty. Could McLean hold on?

"I did get a bit twitchy on the course in the closing stages," McLean confessed. He had to call on the only real pressure-proofing he had available—the mental callouses of nine years of struggle and three passes through the qualifying school.

Harwood launched a hot charge in the final round, with seven birdies in the first 16 holes. But he crashed at No. 17, where a poor approach from 60 yards out left him 20 feet above the flag. His first putt raced downhill, six feet past, and he missed coming back. The bogey-six gave him a 66, best of the day, but took him out of a possible playoff. Now it was between McLean and Brand, and it soon looked like Brand's title. Brand picked up three strokes over the first nine holes, and then a birdie at No. 14 put him 15 under and two ahead of McLean. But that lead evaporated in a hurry. Brand three-putted the 16th from 30 feet for a bogey. McLean, from 100 yards out, flipped his approach to a foot from the hole at No. 17. He tied Brand with the tap-in birdie. It came down to the dogleg 18th.

Brand was in trouble instantly. He hit a tree with his drive, then put his approach 30 feet above the hole. His first putt went five feet past, and when he missed coming back, his fate was sealed. McLean had driven perfectly, then fired his approach to 15 feet. Two putts gave him a 71, a 274, and at long last, the first victory of his career.

"I had thought of quitting many times," McLean said. "But I always had a feeling that my name might be on the trophy, and I just hung in there."

Volvo Masters—£450,000
Winner: Mike Harwood

What a way to finish the year ...

The 1990 European Tour came to an end in the last week of October with the Volvo Masters at Valderrama, at Sotogrande, Spain, and that's what so many were saying—what a way to finish the year.

Four players were disqualified. Brett Ogle and Roger Chapman departed over a misinterpretation of the rules dealing with, of all things, spike marks on the green. And Russell Claydon and Derrick Cooper signed incorrect scorecards. Jose Maria Olazabal ran afoul of a tree. He was beating Valderrama, a brute of a par 71, 6,951 yards. In the third round, he was leading by two strokes coming to No. 18. But he drove next to a tree, and tried to hit out left-handed with an upside-down seven iron. He took a triple-bogey seven. There went the lead, for good.

Then there was Mike Harwood, 31, winner of three tournaments in his five years on the Tour, including the Volvo PGA Championship back in May. When Harwood came to the 17th tee, he figured he had two chances of winning—slim and none. Sam Torrance, winner of the German Masters just four weeks earlier, and Steven Richardson, an ambitious rookie, were leading a stroke ahead of him. "I thought to myself, if I could par the last two holes, I'd have a very slim chance," Harwood said. When he reached the 17th green, he got a jolt. "Suddenly, I saw my name at the top of the leaderboard," he said. Torrance and Richardson, playing behind him, had run into trouble. The door was open.

The fourth round had ended like a morning rush hour. Four men were tied for the lead at one-over-par 214—Torrance, Richardson, David Feherty, and Colin Montgomerie. Four others were a stroke behind—Anders Forsbrand, Bernhard Langer, Olazabal, and Harwood. In the final round, Montgomerie and Feherty left the hunt with 75s. Langer, Forsbrand, and Olazabal slipped with 73s. The race was between Torrance, the German Masters champion, and Richardson, the rookie. Suddenly, Harwood was part of it when Richardson missed the 13th green and bogeyed, and Torrance three-putted the 15th.

Harwood nearly took himself out at the 18th. He drove into the light rough, near a tree, then put his approach into a bunker. Things were looking grim again. Then came the crucial bunker shot. "I thought I'd got it a bit fat," he said. "But luckily, it rolled a few more feet than I expected." In fact, to about a foot from the hole. Harwood was home free with a 71—286, two over par. Now came the longest 45 minutes of his life.

Out on the course, his victory was taking shape. Torrance bogeyed the 16th after driving into a fairway bunker. At No. 18, he needed a 20-foot putt to tie, but he missed. Richardson also could catch Harwood, but he bogeyed the 16th and 17th after errant drives, and that did him in. He finished with a flair, though. He played the 18th up the 10th fairway and sank a 30-foot putt for a birdie to tie Torrance for second at 287. Richardson shot 71-73-70-73, and Torrance 69-73-72-73.

When the last putt dropped, Harwood, already in with 70-72-73-71, a two-over-par 286, was the champion. It was the highest winning total in a long time, certainly the highest of the year, two strokes over Stephen McAllister's even-par total in the season-opening Atlantic Open. This finale also settled the Order of Merit race. Mark McNulty could have been No. 1 if he had won, and if Woosnam had finished lower than third. Woosnam tied for 21st, but a tie for fourth was the best McNulty could do. So it was Woosnam locking up the top spot with £574,166, and McNulty taking second with £507,540.

12. The African Tours

If you were to put a title on South Africa's Sunshine Tour in 1990, it would have to be "The Man Who Found His Touch." Sounds like something from the pen of John Le Carre, the famous British spy novelist. It may lack the ominous zip of, say, "The Spy Who Came in from the Cold," but it does have a little tang to it.

But this was no spy novel, just a bit of a golf thriller: Of how that mysterious thing called "touch" came to John Bland at precisely the right time, and this 46-year-old veteran practically torched the Sunshine Tour. He had the best season of his 16 years as a touring pro—three victories and three seconds. He might have mopped up completely except for Fulton Allem, John Daly, and Tony Johnstone. Daly, a long-hitting young American, and Johnstone, the veteran African campaigner, robbed him with a couple of miracle finishes. Allem, that smiling bulldozer of a golfer, won three tournaments himself, stopping Bland in one of them. Bland took the Dewar's White Label Trophy, the Minolta Copiers Match Play, and the Bloemfontein Spoornet Classic. Allem won the Lexington PGA Championship (shooting a dazzling 61 in the first round), the Twee Jongegzellen Masters, and the year-ending Goodyear Classic. (That was the second of two Goodyear Classics in 1990, by the way. Philip Jonas won the first, in February. Allem's came late in December.)

While not matching Allem and Bland, some others enjoyed standout years. Trevor Dodds broke through for the Protea Assurance South African Open—which also put him into the World Series of Golf—and the Trust Bank Tournament of Champions later. Daly came through in the clutch twice, winning the AECI Charity Classic and the Hollard Insurance Royal Swazi Sun Classic.

At the start, Bland's year not only didn't look special, it was fast shaping up as a year of misfires and frustration. In February, the Swazi title was just at his fingertips when Daly snatched it away at the 71st hole. The next week, Johnstone closed with a 66 to pluck the Palabora Classic out of his hands. The reversals seemed to make Bland more determined. The very next week he won the Dewar's White Label Trophy. That was one victory and two seconds in the early segment of the Sunshine Tour. Things got even better when it resumed in November. Bland started things off by rolling over everybody in the Minolta Match Play. His toughest match was against Hugh Baiocchi in the final, and he won that one by five strokes. Then he won the Bloemfontein Spoornet Classic by six strokes, and made a good run before falling just short of Allem in the second Goodyear event. It was his third runner-up finish and the end of a great year.

"It was good," Bland said, "to find my touch."

It was a far different story on the Safari Tour: Five tournaments, five winners, including an old crowd favorite, Christy O'Connor, Jr., and a first-timer, Wayne Stephens.

Grant Turner, struggling on the European Tour since 1983, found the secret in the Safari's season-opening Zimbabwe Open. He also got a huge round of applause from Mother Nature. A stunning bunker shot at the final hole left him within inches of the cup, and when he tapped in for a one-stroke victory, a thunderclap rocked the land.

Two veterans stepped to the front next. Gordon J. Brand ran off with the Zambian Open by four strokes, and O'Connor, although he had hardly touched his clubs for months, took the Kenya Open late in January before everybody packed up and headed for the European Tour. The action resumed early in December with an oddity. The Nigerian Open was cut to three rounds, but not by rain or fog. By local politics. An election was being held. That was fine with Wayne Stephens, former club pro. After a year of near-despair—he had missed the 36-hole cut in 12 of his 15 tournaments—he ran away with the tournament by six strokes. David Llewellyn, again flowering in Africa, took the Ivory Coast Open to close out the year.

Zimbabwe Open—£46,431
Winner: Grant Turner

With the Zimbabwe Open, the new golf year was dawning, and maybe a career was, too. Grant Turner knew frustration and disappointment as few would know it. He had won Rookie of the Year honors on the European Tour in 1983. After that tantalizing start, little happened. The years dragged on, still offering promise, but almost nothing more. Then came mid-January and the start of the 1990 Safari Tour at the Chapman Club at Harare, and Turner, 32, made it all worthwhile.

It came down to a two-man battle between Turner and another struggler, England's Lee Jones, who was just days from his 27th birthday. At the most critical of times—the final hole, that is—Turner put his approach into a greenside bunker. For a man who had known such discouraging times over the years, this was a time ripe for folding. But he refused to. Instead, he popped the ball out of that bunker and right to the cup, where it teetered on the edge. Turner went up and tapped it in for the birdie and the victory.

Turner shot 68-71-71-71—281, seven under par, for a one-stroke win over Jones. Stephen Richardson, the 1989 English Amateur champion, was third at 286.

One possible challenge to Turner never got a chance to materialize. That was the pre-tournament favorite, Gordon J. Brand. He was hampered by a very sore toe, which helped cost him a 75 in the first round. Brand bounced back for a 69 in the second, and a 144 total, five strokes behind Turner's 139 lead. Brand immediately went in search of medical help for the toe. He tied for fourth at 287, six strokes behind Turner.

Meanwhile, it was all part of the learning process—a painful learning process—for Andrew Hare, one of the victorious 1989 British Walker Cup team. Somehow, the game didn't used to seem this nerve-racking. Hare opened with a 78, then followed with a 77. His 155 total missed one of the plumpest of 36-hole cuts, 154, and he was baffled. "I don't think I've ever hit so many wild shots," he said. "First to the right, then to the left. And when I did recover, I three-putted. It's been an embarrassment."

Turner knew the feeling. At the outset, failure and frustration simply didn't seem to be in the cards for him. He was a young flash, winning British Boys and Youths international honors and also the 1977 Belgian Open Amateur

Championship. He played college golf on a scholarship in the United States. He was the top qualifier on the 1982 European Tour. Then the struggles began. He had to go back through the qualifying in 1984, and finally things started to brighten in 1989. His best finish was a tie for fourth in the AGF Open, and he won £42,467 for the year, his best in seven seasons to that time. It seemed he was earning his wings. Then came the start of the 1990 Safari Tour.

Zambia Open—£75,000
Winner: Gordon J. Brand

Gordon J. Brand was informed on the final hole of the Zambia Open—a championship that had eluded him for years—that only a complete disaster could keep him from finally winning it.

Almost as if to prove a point, what should Brand do but flirt with disaster. He righted himself, kept the damage down to a bogey-six, and still won by four strokes. That left him just one championship shy of sweeping all the Safari Tour titles. He previously won the Nigerian, Ivory Coast, and Zimbabwe events. The Kenya Open would complete his set. But it would have to wait for another year. The Zambia Open ended his Safari trip for the year.

Brand shot 70-74-68-72—284, eight under par on the 7,216-yard Lusaka Golf Club, which carries a par of 73. Despite the double-bogey finish, he won by four over Phil Golding and defending champion Craig Maltman. But the outcome was in doubt early on.

Brand was tied with Welshman John Price for the first-round lead with a 70. Price blew himself out of the picture with an 80 in the second round. Stephen Richardson took the 36-hole lead at 142, with a tournament-low 67. There was just one other 67, and it was in the final round, lifting Paul Carman—who had opened with a 78—into a tie for fourth with Richardson and Paul Carrigill. There were only seven rounds in the 60s, and no one had more than one.

Brand got his, a 68, in the third round, and it boosted him back to the top. At seven-under 212, he led by two strokes over Golding going into the last round. Then the rout was on. Or the retreat, depending on how one looks at it.

Going out, Brand was just so-so. He dropped a shot, and Maltman tied him for the lead. That sobering development seemed to get him charged up. He birdied the treacherous 13th and 14th, both par fives and both water holes, and nearly chipped in at the 15th. At the same time, Maltman was stumbling to bogeys at the 14th and 16th.

Brand was home free, and then for some reason changed his game plan for a flourishing gamble at the finish. That was his driver he hit into the trees at the 18th.

"I suppose I shouldn't have finished by taking out the driver," Brand said. "It was the one club which got me into trouble during the week. Generally, I drove well when I used the three wood. Lusaka's a very tight course, and you need accuracy."

That crucial and fundamental point, he noted, was either missed or ignored by some young pros, and so they spent more time in the trees than they could afford. Maybe they would learn, as he had. He had chased the Zambia Open many times. This time, he wouldn't let it slip away.

Kenya Open—£75,205
Winner: Christy O'Connor, Jr.

It's said that youth must be served, and Christy O'Connor, Jr., age 41, couldn't agree more. But what he served to youth in the heat of this weekend at the Kenya Open was a winning smile. And on that pleasant Irish face, that's considerable.

O'Connor shared the lead in the first round, but after that, all he showed to a clutch of young pursuers were his smile and his heels. O'Connor cruised through the heat at Muthaiga, Nairobi, in 66-67-67-71—271, 13 under par, for a comfortable two-stroke victory over Chris Platts (67-68-67-71—273). It was the sixth victory in his 21 years as a touring pro. Platts, 26, struggling in his 10 years on the European Tour, and winner of the 1988 Kenya Open, thought he had O'Connor a couple of times. In the third round, for example. "I thought I had no chance when he went five up on me," Platts said. "But I putted well on the back nine, and now I've given myself every chance." Platts had matched O'Connor's 67 and stayed just two strokes behind going into the last round. But then O'Connor, a crusty veteran, broke free for good just after rounding the final turn.

It may have looked like an easy win, but the pressure was heavy on O'Connor. For one thing, he was rusty. He had all but left his clubs hanging since November. "But I was pleased with my game, tee to green," he said. And second, the pressure was intense, some of it coming from the youths, some from the strength-sapping heat. And then the putting. "I had great difficulty reading the lines and guessing the speed of the greens," he said. His local caddy was his salvation, and he thanked him.

O'Connor was the crowd favorite when the tournament opened. Fans wanted to see that two iron in action, the one he used for the brilliant shot to three feet on the final hole to close out Fred Couples in the 1989 Ryder Cup. But that club had already been sold for charity, so the fans had to settle for a new model. And the old O'Connor didn't disappoint them. His first round, over the baked-out course, included three birdies and an eagle for a 66 and a share of the lead with Andrew Hare and Mark Litton. A stroke back, in a group at 67, were Platts and defending champion David Jones.

It was the second round that shaped the outcome. Cashing in some strong recoveries and escaping some shaky putting, O'Connor shot a 67—133, for a two-stroke lead after 36 holes. "If I could have putted," O'Connor said, "then goodness knows what I might have posted." Platts took sole possession of second place with 68—135. Lytham assistant pro Paul Eales was well back at 72—141, but that included a crash at the final hole that he would remember with some pain two days later. He suffered a triple bogey-eight. (He was to close with 66-67 and finish a solo third at 274—precisely a triple bogey behind O'Connor's winning 271.)

O'Connor felt even more heat in the final round, the heat of pursuit. Platts wouldn't be put off. Then they passed the turn, and the crack came. O'Connor birdied the 10th to go a stroke up, and Platts three-putted the 11th for a bogey, and now it was O'Connor who wouldn't be budged, not even when he missed a tap-in at the 15th. But it was a good chase. Eales' charge sputtered on the inward nine. Mark Mouland started to roll, then broke down when he ran afoul of a bush at No. 4 and took a double bogey. And Platts, of course. O'Connor, praising the youth, nonetheless beat them.

Platts offered a kind of philosophy on the matter. "To play well and only lose in the end to a player like Christy O'Connor," he said, "can't be bad."

ICL International—R250,000
Winner: Gavin Levenson

The ICL International may be starting to feel like home to Gavin Levenson. If only he didn't have to wait so long between stops.

Levenson, the 36-year-old from Johannesburg, outraced the field in the final round and took the tournament by two strokes over Wayne Westner at Zwartkop Country Club. The victory ended a three-year drought for Levenson. Before this, the last time he won was in 1986—in the ICL International.

This time, Levenson left nothing to chance. He entered the final round with a one-stroke lead on Jeff Hawkes and a three-stroke lead on the threesome of Westner, Hugh Baiocchi and Jimmy Johnson. He proceeded to make short work of things. He scored four birdies on the front nine and moved three strokes ahead, then birdied the 12th and 13th and was up by four. He got home without mishap and wrapped up a week in the 60s—67-68-66-68—269. Westner birdied the last three holes to edge out Johnson for second place, 271-272.

It was not a walk in the park for Levenson, however. His opening 67 left him two behind Baiocchi and David Feherty, both with 65s. Both were to drift away, but Feherty did it with some fireworks. First, with all the challengers in the 60s in the second round, he stumbled with a 73. In the third round, he closed to within four of Levenson, thanks to a burst of birdies on the last three holes. Then he tripped over his putter in the final round—three three-putts in the span of four holes. Thus ended possibly the oddest performance in the ICL. Feherty finished 11th, at 276.

For Levenson, the victory was more than that. It was an encouraging sign. He endured four years of frustration on the American Tour early in the 1980s, then returned home and enjoyed some real success, with two victories in 1984, including the Lexington PGA Championship, then the South African Open in 1985, and the ICL in 1986. Then his game went cold. Maybe the ICL would warm it up again.

Lexington PGA Championship—R250,000
Winner: Fulton Allem

Sometimes a golfer knows when it's his day. The fates send a sign. In the Lexington PGA Championship, Fulton Allem would have to admit that if what happened to him in the last round wasn't a sign, nothing was.

Allem, veteran South African star, was cruising home at the Wanderers Golf Club, Johannesburg, all set to pick off his second PGA, when for a fleeting instant things got away from him. At the par-three 15th, his heart sank. He didn't merely miss the green with his tee shot, he missed to the left. From there, he said later, it would be very easy to make double bogey. The errant ball was on its way down the slope.

"But fortunately—for me," Allem said, "it hit a women on the backside, and it stopped where I was able to chip on and save my par."

Allem got his par, and the women got a quick token of his gratitude.

"I did the only thing I could think of," he said. "I gave the woman my ball."

If this was a week for signs, Allem had already sent one of his own. He opened the tournament with a course-record, nine-under-par 61 that smashed the previous record by two strokes. He added 71-67-67 for a 14-under-par 266 and won by two strokes over British rookie Chris Davison.

This was also the week for turning the par-70 Wanderers into a shooting gallery. Note that Allem was out of the lead only once, and that was after he followed his opening 61 with nothing worse than a 71 in the second, and that dropped him three strokes off the lead. South African Wayne Bradley took over with 65—129 after 36 holes. Allem regained the lead after 54 holes with a 67 that included a double bogey at the 15th, where he was to get the luckiest break of the tournament the next day—by bouncing his tee shot off that spectator.

That wasn't his only narrow escape in the final round. He also had to reach for help at the par-five fifth. He hooked his drive into the trees and seemed to be stone dead. He was looking at bogey or worse. But he slashed a low three iron that left him just short of the green, from where he saved his par. That helped him to a 67, which didn't seem all that great on a course that had been whipped soundly all week. He made just three birdies. But then, he didn't make any bogeys. The championship was his.

The PGA is an especially coveted title on the Sunshine Tour, not only in its own right but because it opens a door to the American Tour. Which is exactly how Allem got there. The PGA title gives the winner an automatic berth in the World Series of Golf in Akron, Ohio. Allem won the PGA in 1987, and finished second in the World Series. That was worth $86,400, which not only qualified him for the American Tour but put him into the top 125 all-exempt category (he was 105th) for 1988. He's stayed up there ever since. His next goal is the World Series title itself. That's worth a 10-year exemption.

Protea Assurance South African Open—R325,000
Winner: Trevor Dodds

Sometimes the race goes to the steady, not the quick, as Trevor Dodds proved in the Protea Assurance South African Open. Despite some heavy winds, there was plenty of "quick" in the tournament at the tough Cape Royal course at Cape Town. Des Terblanche shot a course-record 66 in the second round, and Mark James matched it in the third. Then there was a 67 by John Bland, a 68 by Wayne Player, and 69s by Hugh Royer and Simon Hobday.

Dodds, on the other hand, never got out of the 70s. And the victory came just in time. "I needed a win like this one to get my mind right," said Dodds, who was trying to regroup after losing his American Tour card in 1989. This was a good start. For one thing, winning the South African Open got him into the World Series of Golf, which a few years earlier was the stepping stone to the American Tour for Fulton Allem, an outstanding South African. Allem, who won the Lexington PGA just a week ago, would be heading back to the United States for the 1990 season.

Dodds shot 72-71-72-70—285, three under par, for a one-stroke victory. It probably seemed a pretty modest performance to anyone who hadn't witnessed those ripping late-January winds. And then there were those sharpshooters, each one taking a turn at making a rush at the lead. Dodds was merely hanging on at the fringes all the way.

Ian Palmer solved the battering winds to take the first-round lead with a two-under-par 70. Dodds was two behind with a par 72. Terblanche grabbed the 36-hole lead with that course-record 66 for a 141 total. Dodds (71) was still two strokes back, tied for second at 143. The group included a big-hitting young American, John Daly (67), and Wayne Player (68), son of Gary. Then Player took the lead in the third round with a 70 for a 213 total, and Dodds (72) was still two behind, at 215.

In the final round, a new threat was heard from. This was Mark James, as tough and crusty a competitor as anyone would want. James is always dangerous. Just consider his situation: He had opened with a whopping 79 in the gale-force winds in the first round, and now here he was, making a move on the lead. Fate decided otherwise, however. James was just starting to close in on the lead when he stumbled at the par-five fifth. A stray iron shot and three putts cost him a double bogey-seven that killed his bid. He rallied to make five birdies the rest of the way, but he also suffered two bogeys. He finished with a one-under-par 71 and a 288 total, good for solo third place, three strokes behind Dodds (70—285). American Hugh Royer took second with 71—286.

AECI Charity Classic—R250,000
Winner: John Daly

The AECI Charity Classic, at Rand Park, Johannesburg, ended up with one of golf's classic questions: What does a guy have to do to win? David Feherty must have been muttering under his breath. Consider this: Feherty opened with a course-record, 10-under-par 62; he had only one round out of the 60s, and that was a 70; he led by four strokes with nine holes to play, and he closed with a 67 for a 23-under-par 265 total, which broke the old tournament record. But he didn't win.

It's fitting at this point for someone to note, again, that golf is a game of how much. True. But somehow, that rings hollow here. It seems a guy who shoots 23 under par ought to win. But then, what about a guy who shoots 24 under? Which, of course, is what sank Feherty. And the end came, cruelly enough, on the 72nd hole.

The author of a winning, last-hole birdie and the tournament-record 264 total was John Daly, 23-year-old American who just a month earlier, in the first week of January, led the qualifying school for the new Ben Hogan Tour in the United States. Daly is possibly the tops of the next generation of power hitters. Some say he may be longer than anyone on the PGA Tour, including Greg Norman and Davis Love III. Though Daly stands only 5-feet, 11-inches, and weighs 175 pounds, he consistently drives over 300 yards.

But a golfer needs more than sheer power, and Daly had everything at Rand Park. Most of all, he had nerves. He came to the final hole facing a putt of about 12 feet for a birdie. He could feel the apprehension sweep through him. "I kept thinking about the 18th in the Swaziland last year," Daly said. "I needed a putt of about the same length to tie with Jeff Hawkes. But that one I hit too hard, and it bounced back in the cup, and then out." He tied for second, a stroke back. Now he was facing the same situation. "I thought I had missed this one, too," said Daly. "But it sneaked in the side door."

In fact, Daly—who shot 70-67-62-65—had more or less "sneaked in" himself. He was just another face way back in the crowd until the third round. Feherty was making this one his tournament from the outset, starting with an intimidating course-record 62 for a three-stroke lead in the first round. Daly was eight strokes back, at 70. Then Chris Williams, a two-time winner on the Sunshine circuit in 1989, shot 65—130 for a two-stroke lead on Feherty (70) in the second round. Daly was still tagging along, seven strokes back with 67—137. He finally surfaced in the third round, when he matched Feherty's fresh course-record 62 to jump to second place, a stroke behind Feherty, who regained the lead with 66—198.

In the final round, Feherty took off like a jet, with a 29 on the outward nine (including seven birdies) for a four-stroke lead on Daly. Then the cracks started to show, the worst of them at No. 14, where he hooked his drive into a river and took a double bogey-six. Daly, meanwhile, his wits firmly in hand, crept closer and closer, and finally it came down to that 12-foot putt on the last hole.

Goodyear Classic—R250,000
Winner: Philip Jonas

It's said gold is where you find it. You can add "victory" to that old saw, Philip Jonas will tell you. He has the 1990 Goodyear Classic championship, his first victory as a professional, to prove it. "I expected to win on the Sunshine Tour, but this was the last course where I thought it would happen," said Jonas, 27, a tall South African living in Canada. "I've never played well here, and I'm not a great wind player."

This was at Humewood, at Port Elizabeth. Jonas took the lead in the second round and was sitting pretty for a while, but things got dangerously iffy toward the end. He had squandered a three-stroke lead, and then the tournament hung on the final hole. Jonas, who fights the yips by turning around and putting left-handed, steadied himself and finished with a clutch par to take his first victory when challenger Steve van Vuuren stumbled to a bogey. And how did that first win feel?

Sorry, golf fans. No whistles and bells here. Said the understating Jonas: "It's good to win a tournament, at last."

Jones shot Humewood in 72-71-70-74—287, a one-under-par total for a one-stroke victory over van Vuuren, who enjoyed the distinction of being the only player to break par in each of the last three rounds. In fact, van Vuuren needed an inspired performance just to survive the 36-hole cut. He staggered through the first round, then made a great recovery: 79-69-70-70—288.

Jonas trailed only in the first round, when Wayne Bradley solved the stiff early-February winds better than anyone else and took the lead with a one-under-par 71. Jonas was in a small group right on his heels, at 72. And this on a day of winds so severe that officials considered suspending play. In the second round, a 76 knocked the unfortunate Bradley off the leaderboard and pretty much out of the chase. Jonas, one of only 12 players to break par that day, took the lead with a 71 that included three birdies and an eagle. That gave him a 143 total and a two-stroke lead over Sunshine circuit veteran Tony Johnstone, who snapped back from a wind-driven 78 in the first round for a day's-best 67 for 145.

Then in the third round, with the wind threatening play again, the tournament was turning into a race for second place. Jonas solved the elements for a 70—213, boosting his lead to three strokes over Johnstone (71) and the man who caught him, John Mashego (69) in a tie for second at 216. But in the final round, Jonas' three-stroke lead evaporated in the span of two holes. He dropped two strokes of his own, with bogeys at the 16th and 17th, and van Vuuren picked up the other with a birdie at No. 17. Now they were tied.

That had to be a tense moment for Jonas, when he mounted the 18th tee. His first victory had been right on his fingertips, and the elusive thing danced away with those bogeys on the past two holes. Could his nerves hold together? Van Vuuren helped him. It was the approach shots that made the difference. Van Vuuren pulled his into a bunker, then came out too strong and two-putted for his bogey-five. Jonas, on the other hand, planted his eight-iron approach on the green. Two putts gave him a par—and his first victory.

Hollard Royal Swazi Sun Classic—R250,000
Winner: John Daly

John Daly, the big-hitting young American, was beginning to make a habit of it. Once again, as he had in the AECI Charity Classic two weeks earlier, he picked off a victory at the last minute. Well, not the very last minute. Daly wasn't quite so dramatic this time. He didn't win this one on the last hole, the way he won the AECI. He won this one on the next-to-last hole. That was hardly a consolation to South African veteran John Bland, 44, who led through the second and third rounds and who had come within two holes of scoring the 17th victory of his 19-year career. Daly shot 66-71-64-66—267, for a comparatively luxurious two-stroke victory over Bland (67-66-65-71—269). Like the AECI, this wound up as a two-man race. Tony Johnstone was a distant third at 273.

Daly's finish, a three-stroke swing at the 71st hole, was just the right dramatic touch for a tournament born in drama. Hugh Baiocchi opened with a 65, but he'd have to wait for a day to see whether he was the leader. That was because shortly after he finished, a fierce hail storm ripped across the

Royal Swazi Golf Club at Mbabane, Swaziland, stopping play and leaving 48 of the 120 starters to finish their rounds the next morning. And yes, Baiocchi's 65 did stand up. He held a one-stroke lead on Daly and two others. But Baiocchi was a marked man. The fates obviously figured they owed him one after delaying the hail till he got that 65. They would get him this time, but not with hail.

Baiocchi, a late starter in the second round, was even later, thanks to play behind delayed by the hail the day before. And so he was finishing the second round as dusk was falling. "Somehow, I sank a 12-foot birdie putt in the half-dark at the 17th," he said, "and then I sank a very shaky three-footer in total darkness at the last." That gave him a 68 and a share of the 36-hole lead at 133 with Bland, who had finished off a 66 earlier, in broad daylight. Trevor Dodds, the South African Open winner three weeks earlier, shot an eight-birdie 64 to sit at 134, just a stroke off the lead. Dodds had not missed a fairway in 36 holes, and that included his hail-interrupted first round, whose last five holes he had to complete early on the morning of the second round. (A closing 73 would put him back in the pack.)

Then the tournament shook out into a two-man chase. Bland shot 65 in the third round and held a three-stroke lead over Daly (64) going into the final round, 198-201. In the AECI, it was the leader, David Feherty, who was hot going out in the final round. This time it was Daly. He blistered the outward nine for five birdies, and by the time he and Bland reached the 17th, they were tied. Then came Bland's fatal error. His tee shot got away from him, and went out of bounds to the right. It cost him a double bogey. The tournament was all but in Daly's bag. And he did his part. He might have nursed this big opportunity home safely, but instead he attacked the hole, and birdied it. Now he was three strokes ahead with one hole to play. Moments later, he had his second Sunshine trophy in three weeks.

Palabora Classic—R250,000
Winner: Tony Johnstone

Ordinarily, finishing second in back-to-back tournaments would be something to brag about. Not as good as finishing first, of course, but still quite an accomplishment. Don't bother trying to convince John Bland of that, though. This was getting to be old news to the South African veteran. First John Daly, outrunning him in the Swazi Sun Classic the week before, and now Tony Johnstone, in the baking heat of the Palabora Classic. Johnstone, launching his attack from a course-record 65 in the third round, came from behind in the final round, passing both Bland and Wayne Westner to score his first victory since the 1989 Lexington PGA Championship. Johnstone shot 73-70-65-66—274, 14 under par at Hans Merensky Country Club in Phalaborwa, to win going away. Three strokes back in a tie for second at 277 were Bland (67-71-68-71) and Westner (67-71-69-70). It was a spread-eagled field. Tied for fourth, three strokes further back at 280, were Justin Hobday and American Jim Johnson.

Johnstone, who led the Sunshine Order of Merit in 1989, credited this victory to Scottish teaching pro Bob Torrance, father of European Tour player Sam Torrance. "I had a session with him during the PGA last month, and he gave me a few pointers," Johnstone said. "My game started coming right almost immediately, and only my putting has prevented me from winning in the past two weeks." He finished third in the Swazi Sun the week before, and third in the Goodyear Classic the week before that.

Johnstone opened the Palabora far astern of the leaders, shooting a one-over-par 73 in the 100-degree-plus heat that lifted scores later in the day. In the relatively cool earlier, Bland, Westner, and Ian Palmer all shot five-under-par 67s and led by a stroke. The heat eased a bit in the second round, but the competition didn't. The lead was still a three-way dogfight, but with one new face. Des Terblanche (67) tied at 138 with Bland (71) and Westner (71), while a 72 dropped Palmer into a tie with Wayne Player (69) at 139. Johnstone (70) was five strokes off the pace, at 143. He would need a heroic round to get back into the race. And that's exactly what he got in the third round—a course-record 65. He announced his arrival by sinking an eight-iron second shot from 142 yards out for an eagle at No. 1. Then he added five birdies. The 65 lifted him to third place at 208, two strokes behind Bland, the leader with 68—206, and one behind Westner, 69—207.

Strong as that 65 was, however, it was Johnstone's bogey-free 66 in the final round, in brutal 110-degree heat, that brought down the house—and Bland with it. "I don't think I've ever hit the ball better over 18 holes," Johnstone said. "I just didn't feel it was possible for me to hit a bad shot. It's a great feeling to win again."

Suddenly, the future looked bright for Johnstone. He would be heading for the European Tour soon, where he had just one victory, the 1984 Portuguese Open. He had reason to believe he could add to it. "If I continue striking the ball like this," Johnstone said, "then I can do really well in Europe this year."

Dewar's White Label Trophy—R250,000
Winner: John Bland

Maybe getting turned back two weeks in succession was a bit too much for John Bland. Here it was, the third week of that stretch, and the Sunshine Tour found itself at Durban Country Club for the Dewar's White Label Trophy, where Bland was the defending champion. He arrived with more than just that credential. He was getting to be known as Mr. No. 2, and that's not the sort of thing that sits well with a golfer. Just the week before, he was about to win the Palabora Classic, but Tony Johnstone came from behind to beat him. The week before that, he was even closer to winning the Swazi Sun Classic, and young John Daly, the long-hitting American, overran him with two holes to play. Now Bland, age 44 and a veteran in his 16th year of golf's wars, arrives at the Dewar's. What's that he's saying? "Enough's enough!?"

Well, if he didn't actually say that, he must have been thinking it, because he played like a lion guarding its young. Bland had claimed this Dewar's as his own. Now all he had to do was go out on the golf course and make it official. Which he did, with a performance that read 64-70-71-69—274, 14 under par. And in the process, he had to turn back three hard-charging Americans. Jay Townsend finished second, a stroke back at 275. And tied for third at 276 were Tommy Tolles and Daly, a two-time winner already this season.

Not that anyone conceded this one to Bland. For example, he shot 64 in the first round, just a stroke off the course record. That had to be an inspired and inspiring performance, but all it got him was the solo lead. Bruce Vaughan, another American, was right on his heels with a 65. Then it seemed Mr. No. 2 was going to get beat out of this one early. Vaughan caught him with a 69 to a 70 in the second round and grabbed a share of the 36-hole lead on 134. It didn't last, though. Vaughan left the party with a third-round 74. But the other Americans took up the chase, and it must have been a familiar feeling to Bland. When he was winning the 1989 Dewar's, there were 42 Americans in the starting field. But this time, there were only three or four who concerned him—the ones breathing down his neck, such as Townsend and Tolles, tightening the screws in the third round. Townsend shot a 67, Tolles a 68, and they were tied for second at 207, just two strokes behind Bland's lead (71—205).

Things got hotter in the fourth round. Townsend finished with a 68 and was in with a 275. And the dangerous Daly was closing in, but he fell short with a 67 for 276. Bland, meanwhile, was jealously guarding his lead, and with 11 holes to play, he had to walk a tightrope. He couldn't afford so much as one mistake. Nor did he make one. He finished with a flourish—a birdie on the final hole for a 69 that clinched the victory. The win was sweet in its own right, but it was sweeter still for two good reasons. First, it was his first of 1990, and second, it ended his reluctant reign as Mr. No. 2.

Trustbank Tournament of Champions—R250,000
Winner: Trevor Dodds

When last seen, Trevor Dodds was wondering where his next victory was coming from. That was in those tentative days of the Protea Assurance South African Open, back in late January, when he had no real reason to think that his time had come. But then, after winds that would have made Scotland proud, and after a host of challengers fired and fell back—Des Terblanche, John Bland, Wayne Player and Mark James all took their shots—there stood Dodds with the victory. He didn't have one round in the 60s, but he had nothing above 72, either, for a rock-steady, three-under-par 285. Then six weeks later, early in March, he found himself in similar circumstances. It was the Trustbank Tournament of Champions, a showdown of the top 100 money leaders on the Sunshine Tour. And of all the golfers at the Kensington course in Johannesburg, Dodds could hardly be described as the most likely to succeed.

Especially in the first round, when he trailed by four strokes. The leader was Francis Quinn, 24, an American who had lost his European Tour card, and what a terrific irony this was going to be. Because Dodds, 30, a Namibian, had also lost his playing card on the American Tour. At any rate, Quinn was the surprise leader in the first round with a 66. Then at 67 was the ever-present American, John Daly, along with Wayne Westner, a two-time runner-up. Mark Carnevale was in at 68, and Jeff Hawkes and Alan Henning at 69. Dodds had shot 70, but he couldn't be written off. He had already shown that he can make up ground in a hurry. In the South African Open, he trailed by three in the first round, and then by two going into the fourth.

In was Dodds' turn to get caught this time. He stood at 203 going into the final round, and Quinn was at 206. By the time they reached the final hole, Dodds' three-stroke lead had evaporated. He had to sink a 35-foot putt for a birdie at No. 18 to beat the charging Quinn. Dodds finished at 69—272, and Quinn was second at 67—273.

Minolta Copiers Match Play—R280,000
Winner: John Bland

It all depended on how you looked at it. On the one hand, John Bland said he hadn't played very well, especially on the outward nine. On the other hand, Hugh Baiocchi, his opponent, figured it was like getting run over.

This was the wrap-up of the Minolta Copiers Match Play Championship. A look at the scoreboard in this battle of the veterans—Bland was 45 now, and Baiocchi 44—would be the easiest way to settle the debate. The final score in the championship match: Bland, 70; Baiocchi, 75. Here, in the second week of November, it was a great way for Bland to resume the Sunshine Tour. He was picking up where he left off. Some eight months earlier, in the next-to-last week of the winter segment in March, Bland had broken through for 1990 in the Dewar's White Label Trophy, after finishing second in the previous two weeks. It was proving to be a very good year.

And odd as it may seem, the Minolta finale was as much a tribute to Baiocchi, the loser, as it was to Bland, the winner. That may sound like a silly thing to say about such a decisive loss. But Bland was playing so well that that was his closest call, if you can call five strokes close. Bland was simply handling the long, tough Gary Player Country Club course at Sun City very nicely and the others weren't handling it at all. Including a 74 in his first match, Bland totalled 11 under par in running off five victories, an all-around performance that more than justified his pre-tournament top seeding. No one was surprised. Bland plays some of his best golf in head-to-head competition. He was the runner-up in the 1989 Minolta. He lost to Fulton Allem in a playoff after beating, among others, Allan Henning and American Tour standout David Frost.

If the 1990 edition wasn't a cakewalk, it was a good imitation. Bland shot 74, 69, 69, 67, and the 70 in the final. He beat, in order, John Fourie by six strokes, Ferdie Van Der Merwe by nine, Greg Reid by seven, Michael Green by eight, and then Baiocchi by five.

Here's another way of looking at how Bland dominated the event. He won his first four matches by a total of 30 strokes, an average of 7.5 per match. Still, he wasn't confident early in the finale against Baiocchi.

"I just didn't do very well in the first seven holes," he said. But as the saying goes, he got well in a hurry. He birdied No. 8 from about 24 feet, added another at the ninth, and he was on his way. "He played great golf all week," Baiocchi said. "In this mood, he's a real tough customer."

Twee Jongegzellen Masters—R350,000
Winner: Fulton Allem

It's gotten to be a cliche, borrowing the "I can't get no respect" theme of American comedian Rodney Dangerfield. But it seems to fit Fulton Allem perfectly. Two years ago, there was something of an outcry when Allem was named to play in the Million Dollar Challenge. Critics said he didn't belong in the field. Allem ignored the critics and went ahead and won it. That ought to have proved something, but apparently it didn't. Now, late in November, 1990, he was hearing that two-year-old chorus again when he arrived at the Twee Jongegzellen Masters. He had been named to play in the Million Dollar Challenge again, and once again the cry of the critic was heard in the land.

It was a question of credentials. The big complaint was that Allem should not have been nominated ahead of John Bland, whose two victories and two seconds put him atop the Sunshine Tour's Order of Merit. Allem had one Sunshine victory this year, the Lexington PGA back in January. That was before he headed for the American Tour, where he plays most of his golf. Bland, a full-time Sunshine player, had won the Minolta Copiers Match Play Championship (his second win of the year) just the week before. Such stuff makes for good debates at the 19th Hole. Allem, an amiable, easy-smiling man in a weightlifter's body, just shrugged it off. The Million Dollar Challenge was set for early December. That was days away. He had another fish to fry first—the Masters at Stellenbosch Golf Club, Cape Winelands.

By the time Allem had finished, there was no more carping about whether he belonged or where he belonged. He silenced his critics by running off with the Masters. He moved to the top in the third round, and then there was no stopping him. He shot 69-69-68-70—276, and won by two strokes over Ian Palmer (278), another Free Stater who occasionally plays the European Tour. And nobody could accuse Bland of tarnishing his credentials. He started 71-70, and trailed Allem by three through the second round, then matched him with a 68-70 finish for a 279 total, three strokes off the winning score.

Million Dollar Challenge—$2,500,000
Winner: David Frost

You could call the 10th Sun City Million Dollar Challenge a club-throwing exhibition. Of course, that's stretching a point, but the key to understanding this tournament was knowing who was throwing which club, and why.

The man throwing an iron in the second round was Bernhard Langer. He definitely wasn't a happy man. He had led the first round, and would still be leading in the second except that he had bogeyed the 16th, and now, at the 17th, his tee shot had strayed into the rough and come to rest behind a large rock. It blocked his line to the green. That's enough to inspire any would-be leader to fling a club, which he did. It wasn't a hot-tempered slam, though. He just threw it to the ground. The message was clear. Maybe that rock didn't cost him the title, but it sure didn't help him. Langer ended up tying for third, four strokes behind the winner.

And that was David Frost throwing his putter on the final green, so you knew who the winner was. Actually, this throw was a toss—up into the air, followed by pumping arms and a huge smile. This was one happy man. Frost had just become the second player—Seve Ballesteros was the first—to win two consecutive Million Dollar Challenges. Frost shot four 71s for a four-under-par total of 284 and a one-stroke victory over Jose Maria Olazabal (69—285). It was worth $1 million to him. Langer and Steve Elkington closed with 75s and tied for third at 288, ending one of the tightest of all Challenges. All four were still in the chase at the final turn.

The rest of the 10-man field: Fulton Allem, the 1988 Challenge winner, was fifth at 290; Robert Gamez and Ken Green tied for sixth at 293; struggling Sandy Lyle, who opened with an 80 and closed with a 76, was eighth at 297; Tommy Armour III, ninth at 300, and Tim Simpson, 10th at 303.

Langer got off to a hot start with a three-under-par 69, good for a four-stroke lead on Frost (71). Frost, with another 71, took the second-round lead when Langer's driving acted up and cost him bogeys on the last two holes. His tee shot caught a bunker at No. 16, and at the 17th, he ended up behind that rock. A 74 dropped him into a tie for second with Olazabal (70).

Meanwhile, Elkington, all but counted out after an opening 77, was making up ground with giant steps. He celebrated his 28th birthday on Saturday, December 8, the day of the third round, with his second consecutive 68. And that hauled him into a tie with Frost (71) and Langer (70) for the lead at three-under-par 213. "I've found my rhythm after that terrible first round," Elkington said.

The real drama emerged in the final round. Olazabal started the day three strokes off that three-way tie. But the young Spaniard, known for an unshakeable game and a fierce determination, made up that deficit in a hurry. Suddenly, it was a four-man race. Then Elkington and Langer broke out in a rash of bogeys and stumbled down the final stretch, on their way to 75s. Now it was a two-man race.

Olazabal was about to take it to the next and irreducible level—a one-man race. Olazabal was leading by one coming to No. 17. Frost needed a small miracle. He got two. First, a birdie at the 17th pulled him even. Then came the decisive final hole. Both men hit the middle of the fairway with their drives. Then both hit the green, both to within about eight feet of the cup. Olazabal was just slightly away, and he was putting first—with a cool million at stake. Something distracted him, and he backed off the ball. He backed off again. Then finally, he putted. The ball stopped just short. Now it was Frost's turn. His putt wasn't short, but was a tad wide, to the left. But it caught the edge of the hole, then dropped. Now it was Frost's turn to throw a club. Up went that putter.

"I don't think anyone could have dreamed a finish like this, let alone me," Frost said. "I didn't have any miracles this week, just a lot of steady golf."

Bloemfontein Spoornet Classic—R280,000
Winner: John Bland

John Bland was having a Mark McNulty-kind of year. Not quite the same crushing command, but certainly a reasonable facsimile thereof. It reminded you a lot of those McNulty rampages of 1986 and 1987, and the Tony Johnstone blitzes of 1987 and 1988. Bland was hot, and anyone waiting for him to cool off was doomed to disappointment and a distant finish. This by way of saying that Bland made the Bloemfontein Spoornet Classic, in mid-December, the latest scalp at his belt.

Bland showed up at Schoeman Park Golf Club, stuck his tee into the ground, and it was all over—his third victory of 1990. He already had two second-place finishes, too, and so already had his best year ever in 16 years as a pro.

Bland led the Bloemfontein from start to finish, and in the process of building up a lopsided victory, he set the stage for one of the hotter battles for second place, that being the only thing left to shoot for. And the winner of the "other tournament" (as Hubert Green once called the fight for second in a runaway) was none other than Hugh Baiocchi—again. Baiocchi finished second to Bland for the second time in 1990, and in fact, for the second time in a month. Bland beat him by five strokes for the Minolta Match Play Championship in mid-November. A month later, Baiocchi was looking up at him again.

Bland roared around Schoeman Park in 65-67-73-68—273. He led the first round by two strokes, the second by three, and the third by two (after his only over-par round, a 73). When Fulton Allem skied to a 74 in the final round, Bland was home free with a huge six-stroke victory.

"I played really solidly," Bland said. "And it was good to find my touch…"

When was it lost? the others were wearily wondering. Precisely when he found his touch seemed open to debate. Some thought he had already found it back in March, when he broke through for the Dewar's White Label Trophy, his first victory since 1989. If not then, then certainly when the Tour resumed in the autumn and he ran off and hid in the Minolta Match Play.

In the runner-up chase at Bloemfontein, only five strokes separated second place from 10th. Baiocchi won the "other tournament" with 71—279, Ernie Els was third on 67—280, and Wayne Westner (71) and Allem (74) tied for fourth on 282.

Goodyear Classic—R280,000
Winner: Fulton Allem

There was something familiar about this tournament: It was the second Goodyear Classic of 1990 on the Sunshine Tour. There was something familiar about the winner, too. Fulton Allem, the burly South African native, had once again overstayed his welcome. Home from the American PGA Tour, Allem dropped in at Humewood Golf Club at Port Elizabeth, and came from behind to win the Goodyear title. He toured the par-72 course in 72-69-68-68—277, 11 under par, to slip in ahead of—fittingly enough—John Bland.

"Fittingly" is the appropriate word in this case. This Goodyear Classic, falling late in December, was the final tournament on the Sunshine Tour for 1990, and here were the Tour's two dominant figures at the head of the class.

The victory was Allem's third in an abbreviated appearance on the 1990 Sunshine circuit. In mid-January, he won the Lexington PGA Championship. Then he joined the American Tour, which was just getting under way, and when it ended in the autumn, he returned home and took the Twee Jongegzellen Masters late in November, and then the Goodyear Classic, which ended just three days before Christmas.

(The first Goodyear Classic of 1990 was played in February, also at Humewood. It was won by Philip Jonas.)

Allem had to come from behind to get this one. Hendrik Buhrmann and Ian Palmer each shot 69 to share the first-round lead, and Allem was three behind, on par 72. In the second round, Buhrmann inched ahead with another 69 for a 138 total, six under par, while Palmer, runner-up to Allem in the Masters, faded by a stroke, with 70—139. Allem (69—141) held third place, three strokes off the lead. Then he took command. In the third round, when Buhrmann went to a 73 and Palmer to a 72, Allem jumped at his chance and grabbed a two-stroke lead on them with a 68—209.

So far, Bland was scrambling to stay in the hunt, but he hardly rated a second glance. He trailed by six strokes after the second round, and a 69 in the third round ate up some ground but still left him four big strokes (209-213) behind Allem going into the final round. Now, Allem is hardly the type to squander that kind of lead. Still, Bland had him sweating a bit. And while Bland was closing out with a 66, the pressure-tested Allem stood his ground and authored a 68 that held up for a comfortable two-stroke victory, his third win of the year. As for Bland—well, they may remember who finished second this time. This was his third runner-up finish of the year. He also won three times. Put it all together and there was a man with his best year ever.

Nigerian Open—£78,863
Winner: Wayne Stephens

Earlier in 1990, it seemed Wayne Stephens was an odds-on favorite not to finish the year. It certainly wasn't shaping up as the year he would win his first tournament. In the first half of the season, he played in 15 tournaments and missed the 36-hole cut in 12 of them. In the three tournaments he completed, his best finish was a tie for 34th in the Cepsa Madrid Open. This is not exactly an encouraging performance. But Stephens stuck to his guns, and it paid off in the Nigerian Open early in December.

Stephens was two strokes off the lead in the first round, then charged to the front on a course-record 64 and waltzed the rest of the way for his first victory as a professional, a six-stroke romp. Stephens toured the 6,389-yard, par-71 Ikoyi Golf Club, at Lagos, in 68-64-66—198, 15 under par. (The tournament was cut to three rounds because of local government elections.) Chris Platts, the first-round leader, finished second on 66-70-68—204. Tied for third at 206 were Roger Winchester, David R. Jones, and Sunday Okpe, a local golfer.

Stephens, 29, a former assistant to Tommy Hortan at Royal Jersey, had missed his tour card by a single stroke at Montpellier, but he looked every bit the winner at Ikoyi. The second-round 64 had catapulted him from a two-stroke deficit into a four-stroke lead over Platts (70), Jones (69), and Paul Lyons (66).

Then Stephens started to wilt. In the third and final round, his four-stroke lead had slipped to two over the first seven holes. He still had a long way to go, and his immediate future looked anything but bright. But he staged a furious comeback after the turn. He birdied the 11th, 12th, and 13th, then the 15th and 17th. The birdie at No. 17 not only put the championship out of reach, it was the stuff fiction is made of. Stephens hit an out-of-bounds wall behind the green—then holed the pitch shot. The way his putter was working, though, he would probably have holed the putt if he had hit the green. He needed just 19 putts in the round, including two from 10 feet for a par at the 18th.

Ivory Coast Open—£82,547
Winner: David Llewellyn

David Llewellyn's theme song must be a variation off that folksy old American charmer, "Back Home Again in Indiana." With Llewellyn, it's "Back Home Again in Africa." It may not have the same lilt to it, but it means more than a sentimental homecoming for Llewellyn. It means success. Africa brings out the best in his game, for some reason. Witness his victory in the Ivory Coast Open, the finale for 1990. It was the seventh victory of his career, and four of them had come in Africa, including the 1985 Ivory Coast Open.

Wrapping up an excellent Christmas gift to himself that mid-December week at Yamoussoukro, Llewellyn shot the President Golf Club in 67-66-71-71—275, 13 under par, for a two-stroke victory over Jeff Pinsent (69-70-68-70—277). It's not that Llewellyn coasted to this victory, but once past the first round, he didn't exactly feel any really hot breath on his neck.

His opening 67 gave him a one-stroke lead over Gordon J. Brand, Stephane Hales, and Stephen Keenan. Then the 66 in the second round gave him some real breathing room. It put him five ahead of Brand (70—138) and six ahead of Pinsent (70) and Adam Hunter (67), who were tied at 139. Not that he could relax, however. A 68 brought Pinsent to within three through the third round, 204-207. It was just a matter of holding on, and Llewellyn knows how to do that.

This victory brought back pleasant memories of his "rebirth." Go back 18 years: He was in his third year as a touring pro in 1972, when he scored his first victory in the Kenya Open. And then his game dried up. Bedeviled by frustration—"I was going nuts," he'd said—he left the tour and stayed away for two years. Then he was going nuts from staying away, and he rejoined the tour in 1980. He made the painful climb back, and finally reached the top in the 1985 Ivory Coast, leading from wire-to-wire to win by one.

13. The Australasian Tour

The stars turned out for the Australasian Tour, but the only one able to have his name engraved on two trophies was a little-known American player, John Morse. Morse won the Nedlands Masters in Perth, a small event and a victory which gave no indication of his next triumph, which was in the jewel of the circuit, the Australian Open. His demeanor is the same as his golf, solid, consistent and dependable, and if excitement is not the word which describes his play, there is no doubt about his ability, nor about his character.

Greg Norman won the Australian Masters at Huntingdale in a battle with Nick Faldo, who finished tied for second place with Morse and Mike Clayton. Norman produced the shot of the year in Australia immediately following a double bogey, an eagle at the par-five seventh, holing out from a bunker in Bob Tway style. Norman seemed at odds with himself in the Australian Open, and then at Royal Melbourne during the Johnnie Walker Classic, he never seemed to have his game under control, although it might be more accurate to say he seemed at odds with his putter. The holeable ones from 10 to 15 feet just wouldn't fall for him, and though he was challenging in the Open and, to a lesser extent in Melbourne, he could never quite catch the leaders.

In the Daikyo Cup at Palm Meadows early in the year, Norman disqualified himself after accidentally making an incorrect penalty drop alongside a water hazard, the right decision as he would have been disqualified by officials, but a tough one, coming as it did after he had established a course-record 63 on the previous day.

Norman still commanded the biggest galleries and the most media attention, slightly ahead of Faldo, whose Australian visits could hardly be said to have run smoothly. First, in the early part of the circuit, he was beaten by Norman in the Masters event after the Shark holed his sand shot, then, while flying to Australia later in the year, he contracted food poisoning, the airline lost his clubs and he was shunted to Melbourne instead of Sydney, where the Open was to be played at the Australian Club. Because of a recurrence of a wrist problem, Faldo pulled out of the final round of the Johnnie Walker Classic at Royal Melbourne. He bounced back to win the other Johnnie Walker Classic in Hong Kong a week later.

Rodger Davis' very consistent year was rewarded, almost on the last putt, by winning the Australasian Order of Merit. It was the first time Davis had achieved this, and he showed genuine pleasure at Royal Melbourne when it was announced. He earned no additional money for winning the Order of Merit, but gained even more respect from his peers. As might be imagined, Davis had a consistent year, not only in Australia but in Europe as well, his only problem being that he played so well on the European Tour he was tempted to play more than he should, and his game suffered a lapse. He won the Daikyo Palm Meadows Cup in a shoot-out with Curtis Strange.

There was triumph and tragedy for both Brett Ogle and Ian Baker-Finch. Ogle won the PGA title at Riverside Oaks and then the following week, in the Australian Open, suffered a hairline fracture of the knee when his ball smashed back from a tree and struck him. A two-stroke penalty and a fractured bone seemed a harsh double penalty. Baker-Finch looked the likely winner of the Johnnie Walker Classic until the last day, when Greg Turner outgunned him but, more disastrous, was that Baker-Finch's game fell away under the pressure. It had happened before but, hopefully, the experience would produce benefits, although it might have been difficult to convince him of that at the time.

In fact, he bounced back the following week in the Hyatt Regency Coolum Classic, winning by five shots at 17 under par, a wonderful effort in the light of what had happened only seven days previously.

Mike Harwood had a fine year and steadily is becoming one of Australia's outstanding golfers. Victories for David Iwasaki-Smith in the Mercedes-Benz Match Play, Ken Trimble in the New South Wales Open and Wayne Riley in the Air New Zealand Shell Open made sure the headlines were shared.

Ronan Rafferty took the Coca Cola Classic, played at Royal Melbourne, and over in Perth Jeff Maggert won the inaugural Vines Classic on his way to an outstanding series of tournaments on the Ben Hogan Tour in the U.S. John Morse won the Nedlands Masters two months later and, for him to follow that up with the Australian Open victory, was a marvellous effort from one of the most likeable American players to visit Australia in many years.

Daikyo Palm Meadows Cup—A$800,000
Winner: Rodger Davis

It was the stuff of which the very best sports films are made, a golf tournament which had the hero disqualifying himself two days after an inadvertent breach of the rules, allegations that others had made the same error but remained in the event, and the winner needing to go to the second hole of a sudden-death playoff to collect the money and the kudos.

Greg Norman was the short-time hero, Rodger Davis the one who stayed the distance, fighting off Curtis Strange, who was seeking back-to-back victories in the Daikyo Palm Meadows Cup. Davis, with a great 69 in the last round, was playing ahead of Strange, who needed a 12-foot putt on the 72nd hole to win outright, but the ball just slid past the edge of the hole. They were tied at 271, 13 under par at the Palm Meadows Golf Club in Queensland.

Even though Mike Harwood's challenge fell away, he still finished only two strokes behind those two leaders with his last-round 71, and there were four others, including the very promising Japanese player Ryoken Kawagishi, a further two strokes back and 13 under par for the four rounds.

By the time Davis sank the winning putt, the large and very exciting crowd had all but forgotten Norman was not still in the field. The Shark had actually led after two rounds, playing sensational golf to shoot 66 and 63, the latter a course record and, at that stage, he was 15 under par. Even though the course was at its most benign, this was a stunning performance, but it was during the first-round 66 that Norman inadvertently broke Rule 26.

Norman's 10th hole as he played the course, the first hole of the layout, has a lateral water hazard running down the left-hand side, and when Norman's drive trickled into it, he took relief with a one-stroke penalty. The ball rolled back into the hazard on being dropped and, to play his next shot, Norman's heels were still within the hazard line. He was of the opinion he was entitled to "total" relief, as would have been the case if dropping under the rule relating to ground under repair. Not so. He should have played the ball after the first drop, rather than dropping twice and then playing.

Everything had seemed set for a classic Norman-Strange confrontation but, instead, Norman spent the last two days of the event doing television commentary while Davis took his place on the leaderboard as Australia's representative against Strange. Ironically, the Australian PGA Tour, some months earlier, had asked the New South Wales Golf Association to write to the Royal and Ancient Golf Club of St. Andrews for clarification of this aspect of Rule 26, because of what they regarded as ambiguity.

On the third day Peter Lonard, a promising New South Wales professional, returned a 63 to take over as course-record holder from Norman, whose second-round score had been automatically removed with his disqualification. Strange, after rounds of 66 and 64, began the third day one shot ahead of Davis and his 69, against Davis's 71, increased the lead to three, with Mike Harwood challenging after an excellent third-day 69.

Then came the splendid confrontation between Davis and Strange on the final day. Strange began by racing to a three-stroke lead after four holes but then double-bogeyed the fifth and Davis came back at him with three birdies on the front nine. Suddenly Davis got the lead on the 13th where he birdied from 25 feet. This was followed by bogeys on Nos. 16 and 17 and, when they finished tied after the 72 holes, Strange sank a wonderful curling putt to stay in the match at the first playoff hole. On the second hole, the 18th, which Davis had played well all week, he again elected to hit across the water while Strange opted for the safer one-iron lay-up. Davis grabbed his eagle and the title, in one of the most exciting and controversial tournaments of recent years.

Coca Cola Classic—A$700,000
Winner: Ronan Rafferty

Ronan Rafferty took to Royal Melbourne what he described as a "very, very rusty swing and 16 pounds of extra bodyweight" owing to the excesses of Christmas and New Year, and then walked away with a check for $126,000 after shooting a well-controlled 69 on the final day for a 10-under-par 278 total. He was assisted by overnight leader Peter Fowler, who was in front most of the last day until double-bogeying the 16th hole to finish with 73 and 281, an error of judgement that was to cost him $90,000.

Even a four-putt at the fifth hole had not severely dented Fowler's chances earlier in the day, with no one making a real charge at him, but the 16th hole was shattering. Bryan Watts, an American on his first tour of Australia, grabbed second place with a 280 total and his biggest-ever check for $75,600, while his more experienced compatriot, Donnie Hammond, was one of four players who finished three behind the winner.

Britain's Russell Claydon made a reappearance at Royal Melbourne, but this time as a professional. In 1989 Claydon played in Australia as an amateur, finishing second to Greg Norman in the Masters at Huntingdale, and he remained in the amateur ranks to be on the winning Walker Cup team against the United States. This was to be no fairy-tale return. Claydon missed the cut by three strokes.

Rafferty was in no doubt about the reason for his success. "This course is like St. Andrews," he said. "You need a lot of patience and you can get into a great deal of trouble if you try for something really extravagant. It's necessary to keep the ball below the hole for your first putt and that's what I tried to do."

When Fowler hit his tee shot at the short 16th into the right-hand bunker, and took four more to get down, he had underlined his own statement at the end of the third day when he was co-leader and had been asked about his chances in the last round. "Never feel over-confident here," he said. "Just when you think you have Royal Melbourne conquered, the course jumps up and kicks you in the teeth."

Rafferty shut everyone out with a fine birdie at No. 17 for a two-stroke cushion and, after the prize-giving, said he was hoping to be the first player ever to win $2,000,000 in a year, and that A$126,000 was a very promising beginning.

Vines Classic—A$700,000
Winner: Jeff Maggert

There have been a number of young Americans who have established themselves as promising professionals in Australia, and Jeff Maggert's name could be added to that list after his fine performance under difficult conditions in the inaugural Vines Classic in Perth. Maggert was never out of the top two during the event and hung on wonderfully well on the final day to win by one stroke with a 281 total, seven under par.

His last-round 73, played in rain squalls and a fierce easterly wind, stamped him as a player with skill and an excellent temperament. Brett Ogle fought hard on the back nine and was second by one stroke with a 74, and another young American player, John Morse, who finished in third place, two behind, underlined his outstanding potential. Maggert ran away to a three-stroke lead on the field with a first-round 64, three ahead of Bryan Watts, who reduced the deficit to two in the second round, where Mike Harwood, with a brilliant 67, joined him in second place. On the third day, Morse slipped into the lead and played some very consistent golf, shooting a 68.

It was no fun out there on the fourth day. Craig Stadler said he had encountered more difficult conditions just once, and that was in the British Amateur back in the mid-70s. Ogle reckoned there was only the Australian Open at Royal Melbourne in 1985 to compare with the wind, rain and toughness of the golf course.

Ogle who, under the conditions, did well to play the first 15 holes in even par, thought he had caught Maggert at the 16th hole when the American's third shot bounced through the green and he was faced with a very difficult 10-foot putt for par. Maggert made it though and then, on the next hole, had a long second shot from an awkward stance and still managed to hit the ball to the apron of the green. He left himself a tricky six-footer for par which he made, and Ogle three-putted.

Maggert, who was preparing himself for his fifth attempt at gaining a player's card on the U.S. PGA Tour, was full of praise for the Marsh-Watson course which was only a year old. "The weather made it a real test of survival on the last day though," he said. "But this win, on this course, is the most important thing that has happened to me in my career."

Mercedes-Benz Australian Match Play—A$200,000
Winner: David Smith

Match play is one of the more unpredictable aspects of golf, and this year's Mercedes-Benz Australian Match Play Championship provided a fairy-tale ending for one of Australia's battling professionals, David Smith, who beat Peter Fowler 4 and 2 in the final. It was his first win in four years on the professional circuit and it came just a few weeks before he was due to be married.

Prior to the win, Smith was racking his brains working out how he could pay for the wedding and whether his car, a 1975 Ford Falcon affectionately known as "George," would hold together long enough to get him to the church on time. The omens weren't good as "George" and the power steering had failed the night before this event when he was driving out of Kingston Heath.

Three day later, he was $36,000 richer after beating Fowler and, as a bonus, he had the use of a Mercedes for a year and Mercedes added that they would provide cars for the wedding day. All very exciting particularly as, in addition to the other prizes, he won two Australia-Europe tickets from Lufthansa and an exemption for the German Open in August.

On his way through to the final, Smith defeated Tim Elliott, Mike Harwood, John Clifford, Bob Shearer and Mike Clayton and he was full of confidence, having made it to the semi-final the previous year before Fowler knocked him out. He liked the course and played it well, at least in match play. After a shaky start, Smith never relaxed the pressure on Fowler in the 36-hole final, nor for that matter did he relax the pressure on himself.

At the halfway mark, while Fowler was having a shower and lunch, Smith grabbed a sandwich and listened to his motivator, Adrian Davies, as he gave him a run-through of what had to be done to win in the afternoon. "Real Rocky stuff, eye of the tiger, that kind of thing," Smith said later. Whatever it was, it did the trick and there was no shortage of tears of joy after the stunning and most timely victory provided Smith and his future wife with the $36,000 check.

Australian Masters—A$500,000
Winner: Greg Norman

It was a tough assignment, but Greg Norman won the Australian Masters as a champion should, overcoming disaster and then overwhelming the opposition that included Nick Faldo. They had a wonderful battle on the final day.

The Huntingdale course was in perfect condition, and Mike Clayton's first-round 64 was an indication that something like the existing record of 19 under par might be needed as a winning score. Norman was only four shots off the pace on the opening day, and he was at the top of the leaderboard after the second day with rounds of 68 and 67, as others fell away. Faldo shared the lead with him at that stage and the brilliant Englishman (68) was two strokes ahead of the Shark (70) when they began the fourth round. It was a measure of the skills shown that Faldo did nothing wrong in his one-under-par 72, other than consistently shave the hole with his putts instead of having them drop in.

In the end Faldo had to be content with a share of second place with Mike Clayton and John Morse, each of whom played brilliantly over the last 18 holes. Norman's final-round 68 and 19-under-par 273 score included 21 birdies and an eagle over the four rounds, and it was the eagle which turned the tournament around. It happened on the par-five seventh hole of 515 yards, only minutes after he had a numbing double bogey at the previous hole, a monster 563-yard par-five.

At the seventh his drive was long and straight, but he slightly pulled his second into the left-hand bunker guarding the green. The lie was good and those watching at the course and on television knew Norman desperately needed at least a par and preferably a birdie. He played the perfect sand shot from 30 yards for the ball to check on the green and then gently roll into the hole. Norman said later, "I knew that, realistically, I had to have no worse than birdie from that bunker and, even at that stage, I was looking ahead. As well as the birdie it was essential to play the last 12 holes in seven under par. As it turned out, I was only six under par for that stretch, but it was enough."

That was the plan, and Norman began the chase with a great birdie on the eighth hole to get to within a single stroke of Faldo. He had chances for birdies on the 12th, 13th and 14th but missed the putts, then a 25-footer on the par-three 15th gave him the one-stroke break on Faldo, who was still having problems on the greens.

Faldo now was faced with a putt he had to make on the 17th, and missed, and Norman needed only to make certain of hitting the fairway on No. 18 for the victory. He later classed the drive as his best shot of the day, knowing that to be off the narrow final fairway is to court disaster. Faldo was a picture of disappointment at the end, saying, "I played better today than on the third day, but I certainly didn't putt better." Norman's last words could be pasted on the golf bag of every golfing enthusiast in the world. "It just shows, you should never give up on the golf course, no matter what happens to you. To have a victory this way against a competitor like Nick, who you know also never gives up and gives nothing away, is the very best way to win."

Monro Interiors Nedlands Masters—A$150,000
Winner: John Morse

John Morse will recall the 1990 golf circuit in Australia with a great deal of pleasure after adding the Nedlands Masters title to some excellent finishes he made in other tournaments early in the year. He was never off the leaderboard at Nedlands and it was the experience of being in contention at the Vines Classic and the Masters at Huntingdale which allowed him to control his game and his temperament in Perth when Terry Price and Ray Picker were challenging him. Morse had rounds of 67, 69, 70 and 69 for a 275 total, 13 under par, to win by one stroke over Price and by two over Picker.

It was not a tournament without incident. American player Paul Hiskey became the first competitor disqualified because of the ban on square-groove Ping clubs since the Australian PGA Tour ruling was brought into effect on January 1, 1990. The Tour operations manager, Trevor Herden, disqualified Hiskey, who claimed the clubs had been certified by the manufacturers as being legal after their code number had been checked with factory records. Later in the tournament, a Western Australian club pro, John Fowler, was also disqualified for having in his bag a non-conforming Ping wedge.

None of this affected Morse, who played steadily, and at times brilliantly throughout the four days, and accumulated $75,000 from the two Perth events in which he played during the Australasian circuit.

On the final day only Terry Gale briefly threatened the leaders, but the ninth and 10th holes provided for his undoing. He bogeyed No. 9 and then, on the 10th, a short par-four, drove the green but three-putted for a disappointing par.

For Morse it was a special tournament and a special win because he had to make the trip to Perth to ensure he retained his Order of Merit status under new rules requiring participation in a minimum of five tournaments. Morse, Price and Picker made up the final group on the course on the last day and Morse broke away to a one-shot lead on the 17th when he hit a marvellous eight iron seven feet from the pin and sank the putt for birdie. He then closed with a safe par and it was left to Price to edge out Picker from second place with a 15-foot putt for birdie and a one-under-par 71.

Air New Zealand Shell Open—NZ$250,000
Winner: Wayne Riley

Three years ago Wayne Riley needed a relatively simple 18-inch putt to win the New South Wales Open over a stumbling Craig Parry. Riley's putt didn't touch the hole, Parry won the tournament, and their careers took different paths. Parry was successful on the European Tour, while Riley languished.

It all changed for Riley in the Air New Zealand Shell Open, when the 28-year-old Australian broke through to win by a massive seven-stroke margin over New Zealander Frank Nobilo. The victory was not entirely unexpected. The previous week Riley had played solid golf in the New South Wales Open, an unofficial tournament with only $50,000 in prize money.

Riley led every round except the first, when he was two strokes off the pace set by Wayne Smith, Kenny Cross and Olivier Edmond. Scores of 65 and 66 took Riley to a four-stroke lead entering the fourth day, as Nobilo and Craig Warren were his main challengers.

The main interest on the final day was whether Riley could withstand whatever pressure was applied. In difficult conditions, with a cold and blustery wind blowing across the course, he shot par-70 for a 268 total, and only

Bob Charles was able to better that score with his one-under-par 69. Nobilo shot 73 for his runner-up 275 total.

There were moments on the last day when it looked as though Nobilo's challenge would provide a tight finish. He birdied the second hole, Riley took three to get down from the fringe, and suddenly the margin was three. On the par-five sixth, Nobilo's one-iron second shot finished three feet from the pin. He missed the eagle putt and had to settle for birdie, but he was within two strokes of Riley.

At the par-three seventh, Riley bogeyed and just one shot separated the pair. From that moment, however, Riley played with great confidence and ended with the biggest winning margin in the event since 1981, when Bob Shearer defeated Graham Marsh by eight strokes.

Charles won the concurrent Seniors event and finished third overall at 279, but spectators were captivated on the third day by the performance of Kel Nagle, about to celebrate his 70th birthday, who, with only 22 putts, played the course in 67 strokes despite recently having undergone back surgery.

West End South Australian Open—A$150,000
Winner: Mike Harwood

When Mike Harwood flew in for the West End South Australian Open, he was returning from European Tour victories in the Volvo PGA Championship and Volvo Masters. When he left Adelaide a week later, he had added another win to his record on the delightful Alistair Mackenzie-designed Royal Adelaide course. He did it decisively, winning by five strokes with a 12-under-par 278 total, after a stiff contest over the first three days with Simon Owen. When Owen could do no better than par in the last round, rookie Paul Maloney came in to tie Owen for second place at 283.

Owen is semi-retired from golf, a farmer in New Zealand who, in 1978 at St. Andrews, made a great charge at Jack Nicklaus in the British Open, eventually losing by two strokes. These days Owen is a far more relaxed competitor who thoroughly enjoys golf as a pastime rather than a profession. On the third day he slipped into a tie for the lead with Harwood by virtue of some lovely iron play and nerveless putting for a 69 to set up the final challenging 18 holes.

No one could catch Harwood, who shot 68 on the last day. He played steadily over the first eight holes, birdied the long par-five ninth, the difficult par-four 10th and spreadeagled his challengers with a fine shot into the elevated 11th green where he sank the putt for another birdie. Just when it seemed he had completely broken away from Owen, Wayne Smith, Rodger Davis and Peter O'Malley, he was faced with a tricky 15-footer for par on the 12th and one from around the same distance on the 13th. He holed both putts.

Craig Mann, from Western Australia, had finished with 66 for a 286 total to tie Smith for fourth place.

Australian PGA Championship—A$500,000
Winner: Brett Ogle

When Brett Ogle won the Australian PGA Championship, he was grateful for Lyndsay Stephen's advice on the practice tee. "Lyndsay told me I was standing much too far away from the ball and that was why I was having difficulty keeping the ball on line," Ogle said after winning by five strokes over Wayne Grady and Rodger Davis. "I instantly started to hit it gun-barrel straight and from that moment I played really well."

Ogle started with a blistering 65, one shot off the lead set by Sandy Armour, and then was the leader after the second and third rounds with scores of 70 and 69. A final-round 69 provided a 273 total, 11 under par. Grady threatened to stay with him, then shot 75 on the third day. In the last round, Grady equalled the best score of the day, 67, to tie Davis for second place.

Davis had something of a reprieve on the fourth day. An incorrect ruling was given when everyone believed he had hit his ball into the water hazard on the 14th. Davis took a drop and played towards the green. His original ball was then found but, when a second ruling was given, the facts were not correctly passed from the first official to the second, and Davis was instructed to play the original ball. The whole thing thoroughly confused the officials, as well as Ogle and Davis, but there was no penalty where, with a correct ruling, it would have been two shots.

Armour, grandson of the legendary Tommy, hit his second shot into the 17th hole for a double eagle (or albatross) on his way to an opening-round 64, then fell back with 73, 80 and 76. Fellow American Lee Carter, who started with 69 and faded with a second-round 74, came back to shoot 64 and 72 in the last two rounds and finished in fourth place. Carter was in second place going into the final 18 holes, three shots behind Ogle, but Ogle's 69 prevented anyone from getting closer.

Australian Open Championship—A$600,000
Winner: John Morse

John Morse was so short of money that he could not afford $10,000 to try to qualify for the U.S. PGA Tour for the seventh time. Instead, Morse played once again in Australasia and collected $108,000 for winning the Australian Open.

It was one of the most sensational Australian Opens of the past 50 years, a true rags-to-riches story of a golfer who had faith in himself and his game, and who now has his name on the famous trophy alongside Arnold Palmer, Gary Player, Jack Nicklaus, David Graham, Tom Watson, Peter Thomson, Kel Nagle, Norman Von Nida, Jack Newton and Greg Norman.

Morse won over Craig Parry at the first playoff hole, the 17th, at the Australian Golf Club at Kensington, Sydney, a Nicklaus-redesigned course which provided a stern test of golf, occasional frustration on the subtly contoured greens and some extraordinary happenings.

Norman had a double eagle on the par-five fifth hole on the second day. He hit a three wood on to the collar of the green, and the ball ran straight into the hole, a 276-yard shot.

On the final day, Brett Ogle was one stroke behind Morse and Parry, playing the 17th, when he hit his tee shot into the trees. He needed to fade a two iron around one of the trees, two yards in front of him but, instead, the ball smashed off the tree trunk into his left kneecap.

Ogle collapsed and momentarily blacked out, and play was held up while he had medical attention. Because Ogle had been hit by his own ball, he was penalized two strokes, carded a nine on the hole and finished limping down the 18th for a 76. X-rays subsequently revealed a hairline fracture.

Parry was then the only one with a possibility to tie Morse, who had equalled the low round of the day, 68, to be leader in the clubhouse at 283. Parry knew an eagle at the 18th would win the event and a birdie would take Morse into a playoff. He hit a drive down the left-hand side of the fairway. For his second shot, he decided on a brave attempt over the greenside lake, and was unlucky as the ball checked as it did, leaving him with a 20-foot putt for eagle. He had to be satisfied with a birdie for an even-par 72 and the playoff.

At the playoff hole, Morse hit a great drive and a beautiful iron to the back of the green, then putted to six inches for his par. Parry found a fairway bunker and then another bunker beside the green. He played a great sand shot to four feet, but his putt caught the edge of the hole and stayed out, giving Morse his victory.

It was billed as a clash between Norman and Nick Faldo, but that never took place. First, young Chris Gray fired a 69, as did Vijay Singh. Gray, a former winner of the Australian Amateur title, was in his fourth professional event. Norman had a 70, and Faldo had a 74. In the second round, Norman shot 68, and Faldo had a 70. Gray crashed with a 78, and another rookie, Don Fardon from Queensland, made the cut by firing a 65 to go with his first-round 80. It was that kind of week.

Continuing with the topsy-turvy third round, Parry shot a 69 to go into the final day two shots ahead of Ian Baker-Finch. Norman slumped with a 76, Faldo struck the ball well but couldn't make a putt all day and shot 74, and Gray was back with a 70. Perhaps ignored, just one stroke behind Norman, was Morse, who shot 73 to go with his earlier rounds of 72, 70.

No one yet had approached the stage of asking, "John Who?" When they finally did, they found a quietly spoken, 32-year-old American, saying modestly he felt he had concentrated well, hit the ball solidly, putted consistently and was excited at the thought of winning a trophy which had been won previously by such great players.

Johnnie Walker Classic—A$1,000,000
Winner: Greg Turner

David Leadbetter has become well-known in golf because of his successful teaching methods, with Nick Faldo as his star pupil. There are others, however. When Faldo was forced because of a wrist injury to withdraw from the final round of the Johnnie Walker Classic, Greg Turner, another of Leadbetter's students, won the tournament by four shots.

The Faldo-Turner stories do not run along similar lines. Faldo was a fine golfer before he made the decision completely to remodel his swing under Leadbetter. Turner had been a promising golfer but his swing was letting him down, and he went through some tough times before, in a sense of desperation, he too went to Leadbetter. "It was a big gamble for me," Turner said. "I went through a tremendous amount of heartache and doubt wondering if it would ever be right. I persevered, and it has worked out. This is the reward and it justifies all the work I've done and the risks I've taken."

Turner won the 1986 Scandinavian Open and his next win was in the 1989 New Zealand Open, but even then he was saying he felt, with Leadbetter's methods, he could see a real change for the future. To win at Royal Melbourne, Turner needed to come from two strokes behind Ian Baker-Finch, and the whole field had to combat miserably cold conditions and heavy showers on the final day.

Turner was right up with the leaders throughout the four days, sporting an environmental Greenpeace logo on his shirt and golf bag. He was two strokes behind the leaders with 69 on the opening day. A 68 in the second round gave him a one-stroke lead over 19-year-old Swede Gabriel Hjertstedt, and then a one-under-par 70 was enough to keep him only two strokes behind Baker-Finch going into the last day, despite Baker-Finch's third-round 63.

Baker-Finch never recovered from a bogey to Turner's birdie on the second hole in the final round, and Turner's new swing not only held together but his 69 equalled the best of the day in the testing conditions. It gave Turner a 276 total and victory by four shots over Davis, with Baker-Finch and Peter McWhinney one stroke further back.

Hyatt Regency Coolum Classic—A$150,000
Winner: Ian Baker-Finch

Twenty-seven thousand dollars is a handy prize, but this was one of the times when the victory meant more than the winner's check presented to Ian Baker-Finch. He had been beaten the previous week at Royal Melbourne by Greg Turner, but he had also contributed to his own downfall.

At Coolum, Baker-Finch fired a 66 in the opening round despite a recurrence of back problems. He finished in pain, but was only one stroke off the lead. He then shot consecutive 67s, which allowed him to go into the final round with a four-shot lead, reminiscent of the previous week. This time, however, Baker-Finch's closing 71 provided a five-stroke victory over Rodger Davis with a 271 total, 17 under par.

The Trent Jones-designed course at Coolum takes full toll of wayward shots off the tees, as well as into greens closely guarded by attractive lagoons, but the good players on the third day seemed oblivious both to the difficulties and some torrid pin positions. There were many high scores and the cut had been at 149, but there was exciting golf played as well, including Wayne Riley's hole-in-one at the 176-yard sixth hole and Craig Parry's eagle on the 600-yard par-five 15th, a 40-foot putt completing the three.

Davis, the resident touring professional, played steadily throughout the event and closed with a 69 to join Englishman Stephen Bennett in second place, but the pressure of trying to pick up four strokes on Baker-Finch proved too much for the field.

14. The Asia/Japan Tour

Most of the important things that happened during the 1990 season in Asia were anything but surprising.

On the Japan Tour, Masashi (Jumbo) Ozaki continued his dominance for a third straight year. He remained the No. 1 man in victories and prize money, leading the money list with almost $1 million and the victory list with four titles. Ozaki placed second six other times, among them runner-up finishes in the Japan Open and Taiheiyo Club Masters, as he made a runaway of the money race and boosted his all-time-high victory total to 68.

At season's end, he was more than $200,000 ahead of No. 2 Tsuneyuki Nakajima, whose re-emergence at the top level seemed almost a foregone conclusion. Nakajima ended a two-year-plus absence from the winners' circle with three victories, including his third Japan Open championship. Nor was the brilliant professional debut season of Ryoken Kawagishi much of a shocker, considering his excellent record in collegiate and other amateur golf. The 23-year-old had run out of amateur titles to win when he turned pro prior to the 1990 season, so he started collecting a new batch in his third start in the Shizuoka Open. Kawagishi won two other events, most notably the Lark Cup in the rich fall stretch of tournaments, and was otherwise in frequent contention.

Frankie Minoza finally fulfilled his promise on the Asia Circuit, winning three of the last five events and losing another in a playoff. The third victory came against a powerful field in the season-ending Dunlop Open, which is also an important early stop on the Japan Tour. The 30-year-old's finest season by far brought him the circuit's overall Order of Merit championship, the first for a pro from the Philippines, something not even the legendary Ben Arda accomplished in his heyday. It was the first three-victory performance on the Asia Circuit since Hsu Sheng San of Taiwan did it in 1982 and Minoza added a fourth win in the non-Tour Malaysian Masters later in the year.

On the other hand, the Japan Tour was the setting for a truly incredible show of untarnished skill. Teruo Sugihara, a winner in Japanese golf since the 1960s who in 1990 was 52 years old, stunned his younger fellow competitors and the followers of the game in that country by capturing three victories during the season and missing a fourth when he lost to Minoza in a playoff for the Dunlop Open title. Sugihara won the Bridgestone Aso early, the Kansai Open for the ninth time in the late summer and the Daikyo Open on Okinawa at the end of the year.

Two other Japanese pros scored three victories during the season. Naomichi Ozaki, Jumbo's younger of two Tour-playing brothers, landed two prestigious titles—the Japan Match Play and the Japan Series—along with the Jun Classic, while lesser-known Noboru Sugai highlighted his three-win season with victory in the Chunichi Crowns in the early season. Four others, including Australian Brian Jones, were double winners in 1990, while the big fall events fell, as is so often the case, to outsiders, in this case top world money winner Jose Maria Olazabal (Taiheiyo Club Masters), Larry Mize (Dunlop Phoenix), Mike Reid (Casio World) and Bob Gilder (Acom P.T.)

Australians Roger Mackay and Graham Marsh, who rarely goes a year without winning in Japan, had 1990 victories there and the season ended on a high note in Hong Kong when Nick Faldo, the Masters and British Open champion, won the inaugural Johnnie Walker Asian Classic.

It was a big year for the Philippines. Besides the sparkling play of Minoza, Robert Pactolerin (Philippine Open) and Antolin Fernando (Singapore) posted victories on the Asia Circuit, the most ever for pros from that nation. On the other hand, the usual dominance of Taiwan was missing, Lu Wen Ter scoring the only victory at Thailand. Native son Lee Kang Sun won the Korea Open and the other events went to Americans. Ken Green dropped in from the U.S. PGA Tour and picked up the Hong Kong Open title, Andrew Debusk won in India and Glen Day in Malaysia.

San Miguel Beer/Coca Cola Philippine Open—US$140,000
Winner: Robert Pactolerin

For the first time in more than a decade, the Philippine Open title remained in the country when the travelers on the Asia Circuit completed their first 1990 stop and moved on to Hong Kong. Not since the popular Ben Arda won his third Philippine Open in 1979 had a native son captured the national title until Robert Pactolerin scored a two-stroke victory in mid-February in the San Miguel Beer/Coca Cola-sponsored tournament.

Pactolerin birdied two of his last four holes in tough playing conditions at the venerable Wack Wack Golf and Country Club outside of Manila for a par-72 and a one-under-par 287, two ahead of American qualifier Lee Porter and Taiwan's Lai Chung Jen and Chen Liang Hsi. The Filipino pro hovered around the lead throughout the tournament and took over the national colors when the more experienced Frankie Minoza, the second-round leader, faltered to 79 on the windy Saturday. Another U.S. qualifier, Russell Biersdorf, shot the week's best round—67—Thursday to take the early lead by a stroke over Pactolerin, who had six birdies in a row on the front nine before slipping back to 68.

Minoza, a two-time winner on the Asia Circuit, carded his second 70 to take a one-shot lead over Antolin Fernando, as Biersdorf skied to 78 and Pactolerin skidded to 75 and was three back at 143 with Porter, Lai and Chen. When Minoza incurred a surprising 79 in the third round, Lai jumped a stroke in front with 71 for 214 as Pactolerin, Chen and Porter each shot 72s, while Fernando was taking 77. Pactolerin jumped to his first win from that leading pack Sunday.

Martell Hong Kong Open—US$200,000
Winner: Ken Green

Hong Kong was a particularly hospitable spot in the 1980s for Americans playing on the Asia Circuit and Ken Green kept it that way as the 1990s began. Unlike the four U.S. winners of the last decade who were full-timers on the circuit, Green just took a week off from the U.S. PGA Tour and flew in for the Martell Hong Kong Open. It was a wise move, even though the

$33,320 first prize was a far cry from the victory payoffs in America.

Green, a five-time winner in the U.S., led from start to finish at Royal Hong Kong Golf Club's Fanling Course, as heavy weekend rains washed out the Saturday round and delayed play on Sunday. With some solid help from his putter, Ken shot a five-under-par 66 Thursday, sharing first place with Korea's Choi Kwang Soo. Then, the American moved three shots in front of Yau Sui Ming, an unheralded Hong Kong pro, with 67 for 133 on the soggy Fanling course. Yau had 69 for his 136 and was followed by Choi at 137, Lee Porter at 138 and Bernhard Langer, the other international star in the field, at 139.

After waiting several hours to tee off Sunday because of the wet weather, Green bogeyed the first hole, but was never in trouble after that. Three birdies and a bogey on the next 11 holes staked him to a six-stroke lead and his two closing bogeys merely pushed the day's round to one-over-par 72 and his total to eight-under 205. He won by three over fellow American Brian Watts and Canadian Danny Mijovic, who both shot closing 67s for their 209s.

Thai International Thailand Open—US$150,000
Winner: Lu Wen Ter

A new Taiwanese star emerged at the Thai International Thailand Open when Lu Wen Ter, playing in his first tournament on the Asia Circuit, claimed the title with a 12-under-par 276, hanging on with a final-round 73 for a one-stroke victory. The rookie established his position with a 64 in the second round and outlasted Canadian Danny Mijovic and Korean Park Nam Sin, who tied for second at 277.

Mijovic led the first day at the Royal Thai Army Golf Club with a 66, then yielded first place Friday to Lu, who joined a distinguished list of eight countrymen who have won the Thailand Open over its 25-year existence. Lu's 64 placed him at 133, two shots in front of Park and Mijovic. They remained in close pursuit the rest of the way. The Chinese pro opened his lead to three Saturday with his 70 to Mijovic's 71 and Park's 72. The chasers had their chance Sunday when Lu slipped to the one-over 73, but the Canadian could manage only a 71 and the Korean forged the second-place tie with 70. Frankie Minoza closed with a 66, but started too far back and finished fifth at 280.

Daiichi Fudosan Cup—¥100,000,000
Winner: Brian Jones

Australia's Brian Jones, a regular on the Japan Tour with nine wins to his credit over the years, scored his 10th as that circuit launched its 1990 season the first week of March with the new Daiichi Fudosan Cup at the Miyazaki Kokusai Golf Club at Sadowaracho. Jones came from three strokes off the pace in the final round to score the victory, shooting a four-under-par 68 for 275.

The tournament, marking the earliest start ever for a large-purse event on the Japan Tour, got off to an unusual start as Hajime Meshiai, who opened in front with 65, and Norio Mikami, who was second at 66, both registered holes-in-one during the round. Hideki Kase took the lead Friday with 67 for 135, a shot better than the score of Ryoken Kawagishi, who chipped in at the 18th for an eagle and 66. Kase yielded first place to Kawagishi Saturday, the 24-year-old ex-college phenom edging a stroke ahead with his 68 for 204 as Kase shot 70. Jones rested at 207 with David Ishii before starting his winning surge Sunday with birdies on the first two holes. Kawagishi faltered with 76 and the Australian eased home with the two-stroke victory over Kase, who closed with a par round and edged Tomohiro Maruyama, Seiji Ebihara and Saburo Fujiki by a stroke.

Wills Indian Open—US$120,000
Winner: Andrew Debusk

The Indian Open has been a victory starting point for quite a few Western Hemisphere travelers over the years, most notably Payne Stewart, the highly successful U.S. star. Andrew Debusk became the latest to fit that pattern in the 1990 Wills Indian Open at Royal Calcutta Golf Club. The little-known, 29-year-old American put on a powerful finish and rolled to a six-stroke victory with 288, the only sub-par score at the finish at Royal Calcutta, a par-73 course of 7,721 yards that is one of the oldest in the world.

The Americans were at the top at the start, too. Gary Webb shot 69 and took a two-stroke lead over Debusk, Steve Flesch and Mark Aebli. Anthony Gilligan of Australia took over Friday with 72-71—143 as Calcutta pro Basad Ali carded a second 72 and moved into second place, delighting the home galleries who rarely have a local contender to support. Debusk, another shot back after 36 holes, stepped into first place with a 73 for 218 Saturday. Gilligan, with 76, slipped to 219 and Carlos Espinosa, the eventual runner-up, moved into third place at 220. At least a dozen players had a legitimate shot at the title Sunday until Debusk exploded in the stretch, holing putts in the 15-to-20-foot range on five of the last six holes, four for birdies, to post a 70 and run away from the field. Espinosa shot 69 for his 294.

Imperial—¥55,000,000
Winner: Toru Nakamura

Veteran Toru Nakamura ended a two-year victory drought when he landed the Imperial tournament title in early March at the Seve Ballesteros Golf Club at Sakuragawamura. Nakamura, the winner of 25 titles over the years on the Japan Tour and an occasional player on the international scene, came from two strokes off the pace with a final-round 71 and secured the victory on the fourth hole of a playoff.

Nakamura had taken the first-round lead Thursday with 69, but fell behind Friday when obscure pro Tisguaju Sudou added 68 to his opening 70 for a three-stroke lead over Nakamura and four over Masahiro Kuramoto and Naomichi Ozaki, the defending champion. Ozaki established a bid for a repeat Saturday when he posted a 70 for 212, jumping two shots ahead of Sudou and Nakamura. However, Naomichi began Sunday's final round with two bogeys and never completely recovered, ultimately missing the playoff by a stroke. Nakamura had four birdies and three bogeys in the 71 for his three-under-par 285, while Hideto Shigenobu forged the 72-hole tie with a four-birdie 68. Nakamura, 39, ended the playoff with a birdie at the fourth extra hole to put away his 26th title.

Epson Singapore Open—US$300,000
Winner: Antolin Fernando

Another Filipino was heard from at Singapore, the fifth stop on the Asia Circuit, resulting in an all-Philippine playoff and an initial Tour victory for Antolin Fernando in the Epson Singapore Open on the par-71 Bukit Course of Singapore Island Country Club. Fernando, the first-round leader and a contender throughout the tournament, delayed Frankie Minoza's big season when he defeated him on the second extra hole. His par was quite enough when Minoza double-bogeyed the par-three hole. In the early 1970s, Ben Arda and Eleuterio Nival of the Philippines had won the Singapore Open on consecutive years.

Fernando opened the tournament with 66, sharing the lead with Choi Sang Ho of Korea, then shot 71 to slip three behind Choi and veteran Kuo Chi Hsiung, a 12-tournament winner on the Asia and Japan circuits over the years. A 67 in Saturday's round moved Antolin within a stroke of first place, held then by Kuo and Park Nam Sin of Korea at 203. Stewart Ginn, a former Tour winner from Australia, and Jack Hay of Canada were at 204 with Fernando, but Minoza, after a 72, was four shots off the pace. However, Frankie vaulted into the first-place tie with a closing 66 for his 273 to match countryman Fernando's total after his final 69. Choi also shot 69, missing the playoff by a stroke.

Shizuoka Open—¥50,000,000
Winner: Ryoken Kawagishi

Ryoken Kawagishi did not take long to live up to his advance notices. A professional for less than six months after an excellent collegiate and international amateur career, the 22-year-old Kawagishi scored his first victory on the Japan Tour in mid-March when he posted a two-stroke victory in the Shizuoka Open, the long-time early fixture on the circuit.

Kawagishi, who won two important events on the U.S. amateur circuit in 1989 and attained fifth ranking in a major American magazine survey, proved his mettle in professional circuits on Shizuoka Country Club's Hamaoka Course after staking himself to a two-stroke lead with a third-round 66 for 212, four under par. Three established winners—Hiroshi Makino, Seiji Ebihara and especially the high-ranking star Tsuneyuki Nakajima—lurked at 214. Kawagishi was solid on Sunday, though. He turned in 34 after two front-nine birdies, added another at the 14th, bogeyed the 15th, but closed with a pair of birdies for 68 and 280. Makino mounted the only challenge, but he fell two short despite birdies on two of the last three holes. Saburo Fujiki and Kiyoshi Maita tied for third, three shots farther back at 285.

Indonesian Open—US$120,000
Winner: Frankie Minoza

Frankie Minoza displayed his resiliency and professional maturity in winning his second Indonesian Open championship at the Pondok Inden Golf Club at Jakarta. Quickly erasing memories of a playoff loss the week before in Singapore, the 30-year-old Minoza bounced back with a three-shot victory, his third on the Asia Circuit. His first was in the 1986 Indonesian Open.

Minoza bided his time at Pondok Inden, as American Chuck Moran took the first-round lead with 67, a shot in front of Brian Watts of the U.S. and Tony Malone of Australia. Two other American pros—Steve Flesch and Lee Porter—moved in front at 137 Friday as Minoza was shooting his second 69 to trail them by a stroke. Kuo Chi Hsiung also was at 138. Frankie made his move with a 66 Saturday, surging four shots ahead of runners-up Danny Mijovic (73-68-67) and Porter (71-66-71). A closing 71 enabled the Philippine pro to coast to the three-stroke victory at 275. Mijovic shot 70 and Rick Gibson 68 to tie for second at 278.

Taylor Made Setonaikai Open—¥60,000,000
Winner: Masahiro Kuramoto

Masahiro Kuramoto, who has 25 Japan Tour titles in his possession but none attained in 1989, made sure early on that it wouldn't happen again in 1990. He won the season's fourth 72-hole event—the Taylor Made Setonaikai Open—his first victory since his five-win 1988 year was completed in September, but it happened in rather unusual fashion. Kuramoto came from behind to win and did it with a three-over-par 75. He entered the final round in third place, four strokes behind Toru Nakamura and one in back of Ryoken Kawagishi, the winners of the two immediately preceding tournaments. The winds were strong and gusty, the greens difficult, but who would have expected Nakamura to shoot 81 and Kawagishi 77, opening the door for Kuramoto to win by a stroke with a seven-over-par 295, the season's highest winning total.

Masahiro was rather inconsistent through the week. He opened with 75 on a day of generally high scoring as Isamu Sugita led with 71, then jumped three strokes in front Friday with a 67 for 142, ringing up seven birdies during the round. It was one of only two scores in the 60s all week. Just as abruptly, Kuramoto plunged to a 78 and into a three-man tie at 220, as Nakamura, aided by an eagle chip-in at the ninth hole, shot 70 for 216 and Kawagishi 72 for 219, setting up the unexpected finish Sunday.

Benson & Hedges Malaysian Open—US$200,000
Winner: Glen Day

Malaysia has become a happy hunting ground for the American travelers on the Asia Circuit. With his four-stroke victory, Glen Day, a former All-America golfer at the University of Oklahoma, put a U.S. label on the Benson & Hedges Malaysian Open for a third consecutive year, following on the heels of Tray Tyner in 1988 and Jeff Maggert in 1989. Day's victory at the circuit's seventh stop was the third of 1990 for American pros. Ken Green won at Hong Kong, Andrew Debusk at Calcutta.

Actually, the tournament turned out to be a contest of Oklahoma-vs-the World. For the first two days, the leader was Todd Hamilton, like Day a 24-year-old former Sooner. Hamilton birdied his final three holes Thursday for 65—31 on the back nine—and took a three-stroke lead over Chen Liang Hsi of Taiwan and Suffian Tan of Malaysia. Todd shot 70 Friday and, at 135, remained two strokes in front but the runner-up then was Lu Wen Ter, the Thailand Open winner. Day and John O'Neill, yet another 24-year-old Oklahoma teammate, got into the act Saturday. Day carded a 68 despite two bogeys and O'Neill a sizzling 65 off six birdies and an eagle to move into joint shares of first place at 206. Hamilton was next at 207 after a 72, squandering a big lead with three bogeys and a double bogey on the back nine. Day fired a solid 67 Sunday in scoring his first victory with his 15-under-par 273. In the 277 runner-up slot were Chen and Danny Mijovic, who roared past much of the field with a closing 63 to finish second for the fourth time in the season.

Pocari Sweat Open—¥60,000,000
Winner: Nobumitsu Yuhara

Nobumitsu Yuhara snuffed out a seven-year winless streak on the Japan Tour in the Pocari Sweat Open just when it looked as though Masahiro Kuramoto had a lock on his second straight victory. Coming off his Setonaikai win, Kuramoto was rolling along with a four-stroke lead after 54 holes at Hakuryuko Country Club. But, the wheels came off and Masahiro stumbled to a 78 Sunday. The 33-year-old Yuhara took full advantage, shooting a four-under-par 67 for 277 and a two-shot victory, his first since the 1983 Fuji Sankei Classic and the fourth of his career.

After Koichi Suzuki held the first-round lead with 65, Kuramoto began his run at back-to-back victories with an eight-under-par 63 for a 133 that put him four strokes in front of Suzuki, who followed with a 72. Yuhara was then at 139 (69-70) and dropped seven strokes off the pace Saturday when he shot 71 for 210 while Kuramoto was adding 70 for 203. Yoshitaka Yamamoto, in second place after 54 holes at 207, did little better than Kuramoto, taking a 74. Yuhara's 67, the day's best and one of only two final rounds in the 60s, brought him home two ahead of Wayne Smith, who closed with 71 to edge four others, including Suzuki, for second place.

Sanyang Republic of China Open—US$200,000
Winner: Frankie Minoza

It wasn't that Frankie Minoza's victory was really surprising at all. It was his second of the season, he had lost in a playoff at another stop and was among the Asia Circuit point standings leaders when the pro tourists reached Taiwan for the Sanyang Republic of China Open. No, it was the unusual failure of the powerful group of home country players to be serious factors in the tournament, one that Taiwanese pros have won 17 times in its 26-year existence and have had somebody at least third every other time. In 1990, the top finishers among the native sons at Taiwan Golf and Country Club tied for fifth.

The only Taiwanese who seriously threatened was Kuo Chi Hsiung, a 12-tournament winner still playing well at age 51. He went into the final round at Tamsui in a three-way tie for the lead with Minoza and John Morse of the U.S. at 212, four under par, but couldn't hold up Sunday and shot 76, dropping into a fifth-place tie at 288 with Chen Tze Ming and John Jacobs, all former winners of the tournament. Minoza and Morse both scored 71s Sunday for 283s, putting Frankie in another playoff. He won this one when he birdied the first extra hole. The early leaders weren't around the top at the end. Mark Aebli, the American winner of the 1987 China Open, and Lin Chia were in front the first day with 70s, then yielded the lead to Canada's Jean-Louise Lamarre—142—Friday before Minoza, Morse and Kuo came to the fore.

Bridgestone Aso Open—¥37,500,000
Winner: Teruo Sugihara

The remarkable Teruo Sugihara is not yet ready to turn to senior golf on a full-time basis. He is still winning on the regular Japan Tour. The 52-year-old Sugihara notched his 55th career title, two of them senior events, when he captured the rain-shortened Bridgestone Aso Open at Aso Golf Club in Asomachi in mid-April. He led from start to finish, not fazed by the loss of Friday's round to wet weather.

Nobumitsu Yuhara, the Pocari Sweat winner the previous week, trailed the talented Sugihara closely all the way. Teruo opened with a four-under-par 68, Yuhara and Daisuke Serizawa followed with 69s. After Friday's heavy rains, both Sugihara and Yuhara shot 71s to remain one-two going into the final round. A 74 was sufficient for Sugihara in posting a three-under-par 213 for a two-stroke victory over Yuhara. Nobumitsu caught the older player at the fifth hole, but Teruo regained first place at the ninth and never trailed after that. He had two birdies and four bogeys while Yuhara had three birdies, four bogeys and a double bogey in his 75 for 215. Ryoken Kawagishi (71) and Terry Gale (72) made up ground Sunday and tied for third at 216.

Maekyung Korea Open—US$300,000
Winner: Lee Kang Sun

Home fans had their first countryman winner in eight years in the Maekyung Korea Open when Lee Kang Sun surged from behind in the final round at Nam Seoul Country Club and scored a three-stroke victory with his four-under-par 212. Heavy rains flooded out the scheduled opening round and the tournament was reduced to 54 holes.

Tatsuya Shiraishi, a little-known Japanese pro, took the lead when play got underway Friday and held first place until Sunday. Shiraishi opened with 67, shooting 31 on the back nine, to lead American Brian Watts by a stroke and the rest of the field by at least four. The Japanese pro slipped to a par-72 Saturday, but increased his lead to two strokes, then over Todd Hamilton (72-69). Watts, Tod Power of Australia and Hsieh Chin Sheng of Taiwan were at 142, Lee Kang Sun at 143 (72-71). Shiraishi's bubble burst Sunday. He was out of contention early on his way to an 80. Lee passed him going in the other direction on his way to a 69 and the three-shot triumph. He birdied four of the first 10 holes and took a meaningless bogey at the 17th hole in wrapping up his first Asia Circuit victory. Hsieh shot 73 and finished second at 215, Power 74 for 216.

Dunlop Open—¥100,000,000
Winner: Frankie Minoza

Frankie Minoza wrapped up his outstanding Asia Circuit season in brilliant fashion in the traditional concluding event in Japan—the Dunlop Open—which is also an important tournament in the early stretch of the Japan Tour. Minoza ran in a 35-foot birdie putt on the second hole of a playoff to defeat 53-year-old Teruo Sugihara and win his third title of the season. He was the first pro from the Philippines to win the Dunlop since Ben Arda's back-to-back victories in 1976-77. The victory also clinched the Asia Circuit title for the Mindano native.

In the early going, Canadian Rick Gibson and Taiwan's Lin Chie Hsiang led the first day with 67s, then yielded the top spot Friday to Hsieh Chin Sheng and Koichi Suzuki, who both posted pairs of 68s. Sitting close after the 36 holes were, among others, Sugihara and Graham Marsh at 137 and Minoza at 138. The weather knocked out the third round, the second successive week both the Japan and Asia Circuits lost a day to the elements. Sunday's finale refined itself into a three-way battle among Minoza, Sugihara and Tsukasa Watanabe and it went right to the final hole, where Minoza birdied for 67, Sugihara birdied for 68, both for 205, and Watanabe fell by the wayside after skulling a bunker shot over the green and taking a par to miss the playoff. Minoza made a great recovery from trees to keep the playoff alive at the first extra hole before holing the deciding 35-footer at the second one.

Chunichi Crowns—¥100,000,000
Winner: Noboru Sugai

As usual, the rich Chunichi Crowns tournament at Nagoya attracted a few successful players from the U.S. PGA Tour. Usually, at least one of them plays a decisive role in the outcome, either as a winner or near-miss loser. In 1990, that American was Steve Pate, a three-time winner in his six years on the U.S. circuit, and he was a victim rather than a victor. Pate fell to Japanese veteran Noboru Sugai on the first hole of a playoff after the two had dueled to a draw at 276 on the stormy final Sunday.

The two men led the field from the second round on after Yoshikazu Yokoshima opened in front Thursday with 65. The 29-year-old Pate, then just one back at 66, seized the lead Friday with 67—133, a shot ahead of Hiroshi Makino and Sugai, who mustered a 66 on the strength of two eagles. Noboru made another eagle Saturday, added three birdies and two bogeys for 67—201 and edged a stroke ahead of Pate, who had an uneventful 69. Masahiro Kuramoto was three strokes further back in third place and in Sunday's bad weather neither he nor anybody else was able to challenge Sugai and Pate. Sugai, 40, led by two until he bogeyed the last two holes for 75 to the American's 74. Pate lipped out a three-foot par putt at the 18th. Sugai parred the first extra hole to win his second Japan Tour title as Pate bogeyed again.

Fuji Sankei Classic—¥52,500,000
Winner: Masashi Ozaki

The way Masashi (Jumbo) Ozaki has dominated the Fuji Sankei Classic in recent years, the other members of the Japan Tour must feel they are playing for second place when they arrive at the Fuji course of the Kawana Hotel at Ito for the tournament. Three times in the previous four years and four times in all, Ozaki, the defending champion, left Fuji the winner. In 1990, though, it didn't seem likely to happen again as the field headed into the final round after a Saturday rainout.

Ozaki, Japan's premier player in 1988 and 1989, had stepped out in front in Thursday's opening round, sharing the first-day lead at 67 with Hawaiian David Ishii and Akiyoshi Omachi after bogeying the last hole. Omen or not, Jumbo tripped himself up badly Friday, plunging into a 28th-place tie at 144 when he shot 77. Akihito Yokoyama shot one of the day's two 67s for 136 and a one-stroke lead over Saburo Fujiki, who had the other 67. So, after the rainout with just 18 holes remaining, Ozaki trailed by eight strokes. Undaunted, Jumbo brewed a seven-under-par 64 and, aided by Yokoyama's 74 and Fujiki's 72, scored his first 1990 victory with his 208, nosing out Fujiki, Toru Nakamura, Yoshitaka Yamamoto, Masanobu Kimura and brother Naomichi, all at 209.

Japan Match Play Championship—¥50,000,000
Winner: Naomichi Ozaki

Masashi Ozaki chose not to defend his Japan Match Play Championship of 1989, so younger brother Naomichi kept the title in the family and scored his first 1990 victory in the event at Green Academy Country Club at Ishikawa. Naomichi (Joe in international circles) swept through his five matches, saving his strongest performances for the final two. After overwhelming Masahiro Kuramoto in the semi-finals, 9 and 8, Ozaki captured the title with a 6-and-5 triumph over Brian Jones, who reached the final with a 4-and-3 win over Yoshitaka Yamamoto. The field, also missing Isao Aoki and Teruo Sugihara, was comprised of 32 leading players on the Japan Tour.

The four semifinalists advanced thus: Ozaki—2 and 1 over Katsunari Takahashi, 5 and 4 over Akihito Yokoyama and 1 up over Masanobu Kimura; Jones—1 up over Noboru Sugai, 2 up over Katsuyoshi Tomori and 3 and 2 over Akiyoshi Omachi; Kuramoto—2 up over David Ishii, 1 up after 20 holes over Yoshikazu Yokoshima and 4 and 3 over Toshiaki Sudo; Yamamoto—3 and 2 over Nobumitsu Yuhara, 3 and 2 over Tsuneyuki Nakajima and 2 and 1 over Yoshinori Kaneko. Kuramoto defeated Yamamoto, 6 and 5, in the consolation 18-hole match.

Ozaki broke the championship match wide open in the afternoon after he and Jones broke for lunch all even. Naomichi won the first two holes after the break, then four in a row starting at the fifth. He was six up after 11 holes and halved the next two to secure the win.

Pepsi Ube—¥60,000,000
Winner: Tadao Nakamura

Another veteran was heard from on the Japan Tour when the pros teed it up in the Pepsi Ube at the Ube Country Club, Ajisucho, in mid-May. Playing some of the finest golf of his 17-year career, Tadao Nakamura, 44, rolled to a four-stroke victory in the Pepsi Ube. It was his fifth Tour win.

Nakamura never trailed in the tournament. His opening 67 put him in a first-place tie with Masaru Amano, who disappeared from view over the weekend. They led Katsuyoshi Tomori and Ikuo Shirahama by a shot. Rainy weather, which had washed out rounds in three of the previous five tournaments, continued to plague the circuit, forcing cancellation of Friday's round. Nakamura shot 70 when play resumed Saturday and took a one-stroke lead over Tadami Ueno (69-69—138). Tadao made it no contest Sunday when he racked up four birdies on a bogey-free front nine. He chopped another stroke off par coming in for 66 and a 10-under-par 203. Ueno held onto second place with 69 for 207, two in front of Yoshinori Kaneko, Katsunari Takahashi and Toshiaki Nakagawa.

Mitsubishi Galant—¥70,000,000
Winner: Isao Aoki

Isao Aoki etched a new tournament title to his long list of victories on the Japan Tour when he captured the Mitsubishi Galant crown at Nishiwaki. The Mitsubishi (with predecessor sponsors dating back to 1969) was one of very few long-standing tournaments not included on Aoki's record of 57 Japanese victories.

Golden Valley, a 7,014-yard course, was at its difficult best, yielding only four rounds in the 60s all week and scores in the 80s were fairly common. Aoki's best round was the first, when he shot 70 and trailed a pair of unknowns, Yukio Noguchi at 68 and Toshihiko Otsuko at 69. Although he slipped to 76 Friday, Isao remained in a tie for third place, three strokes behind Roger Mackay and one back of Otsuko. Masashi Ozaki, Katsunari Takahashi and Shigeru Kawamata shared the 146 slot with Aoki. A 71 enabled Aoki to move two strokes in front Saturday with 217, one over par. Teruo Sugihara shot 72 and tied Mackay for second at 219 and Ozaki kept his chances alive but fell back with 75 for 221. A steady par round—three birdies, three bogeys—carried Isao to victory Sunday. His 289 gave him a final three-stroke margin over Sugihara, Ozaki and Tsuyoshi Yoneyama, who jumped from 18th with the week's best score—66.

JCB Classic Sendai—¥60,000,000
Winner: Roger Mackay

You might say the Japan Tour went from the ridiculous to the sublime when it moved on from the Mitsubishi Galant's Golden Valley to Omote Zao Golf Club for the JCB Classic Sendai tournament at the end of May. Birdie production multiplied to the extent that Roger Mackay's winning score at Omote Zao was 20 strokes lower than Isao Aoki's victory total in the Mitsubishi Galant. In fact, the 269, one of two posted in 1990, was the lowest of the season.

Australian Mackay put together a sizzling 54-hole stretch of play after opening with a 73 that lodged him in a tie for 81st place, eight shots off the lead of Katsunari Takahashi. Roger made a huge jump Friday. He shot 64 for 137 and advanced into a tie for ninth, just three behind the leader, Satoshi Higashi—67-67—134. Mackay then followed with a five-under 66 Saturday and moved into a three-way tie for first at 203 with Higashi (69) and fellow Aussie Graham Marsh (67-69-67).

Mackay took sole possession of the lead with a birdie on the fourth hole Sunday and never relinquished it. He added six more birdies, took two bogeys, shot another 66 for the 269 that gave him a three-shot victory over Marsh and Tsuyoshi Yoneyama, who fired four straight 68s. Mackay, 34, who won the 1989 Bridgestone, his first in Japan, managed the final 54 holes in 196 strokes.

Sapporo Tokyu Open—¥60,000,000
Winner: Tadao Nakamura

An unlikely player became the season's first double winner in Japan when Tadao Nakamura captured the Sapporo Tokyo Open at the Sapporo International Golf Club. Holding or sharing the lead through the final three rounds, Nakamura finished a stroke in front of Brian Jones and Chen Tze Chung (T.C. Chen in overseas parlance) with a 10-under-par 278. Chen won the Sapporo Tokyu in 1981, early in his career.

Scoring his second Japan Tour victory in four weeks and sixth of his career, Nakamura shrugged off a weak third round, when he shot 75 and dropped into a five-way tie for the lead at 211 with Naomichi Ozaki, Toru Nakamura, Kiyoshi Muroda and Chen, whose 65 had given him first place Thursday. Tadao Nakamura had shot 69 that day, then shared the lead with Ozaki the second day at 136, a stroke ahead of Chen. Tadao came back with 67 Sunday to nose out Jones, who also carded a 67, and Chen, who came in with a 68 for his 279. Toru Nakamura was fourth with 281.

Yomiuri Sapporo Beer Open—¥80,000,000
Winner: Saburo Fujiki

Bad weather cost yet another Japan Tour tournament a day of play, but it inadvertently set up one of the more exciting finishes of the year. After a Friday rainout and Saturday's action, 11 men were bunched within two strokes of each other atop the standings of the Yomiuri Sapporo Beer Open at the Yomiuri Country Club near Osaka. Saburo Fujiki emerged from that pack to score a one-stroke victory with an 11-under-par 205.

The frenetic finish set up this way: After Katsuji Hasegawa and Yoshinori Kaneko led the first day with 68s and the second round was washed away, Taisei Inagaki, Tomohiro Maruyama and Nobuo Serizawa grabbed pieces of the lead at 138; Fujiki, Hasegawa and Katsunari Takahashi were at 139 and five others were at 140. Things thinned out during the final round, but the victor wasn't decided until the 72nd hole, where Fujiki sank a 20-foot birdie putt for 66. Inagaki had a chance from the same range at the final green, but missed and carded a 68 for 206. Maruyama and Serizawa tied for third at 207.

Mizuno Open—¥65,000,000
Winner: Brian Jones

Brian Jones shook off a feeble start, making up a seven-stroke deficit over the final 54 holes to win his second title of 1990 and, at the same time, frustrate Tsuneyuki Nakajima in the superstar's best effort of the year to end a victory drought approaching three years in length. The Australian followed a first-round 73 with scores of 66, 66 and 67 for a 16-under-par 272 in the Mizuno Open at Tokinodai Country Club.

Jones trailed Nakajima and Naomichi Ozaki by a stroke entering the final round and remained on his heels through the early going Sunday. Ozaki fell back. The turning point came at the 13th hole, where Jones made an eagle to seize command. He made two birdies in the closing stretch to open a four-stroke final margin as the inconsistent Nakajima headed for a 72, matching every birdie he made with a bogey. At 276, he claimed second place by two strokes over Roger Mackay, Nobuo Serizawa, Eduardo Herrera and Tateo Ozaki, who shot 63 Saturday. Naomichi Ozaki, the first-round leader with 66, finished at 279 with visitor Sandy Lyle. Naomichi remained on top—with Mackay and Nakajima—at 138 the second day and again with Nakajima after 54 holes Saturday before falling away to 75 Sunday. The victory was the 11th in Japan for Jones, who has lived in that country and played that circuit since 1971.

Kanto PGA Championship—¥50,000,000
Winner: Tsuneyuki Nakajima

Adversity usually has little effect in the subsequent play of the finest golfers. Tsuneyuki Nakajima proved that point most emphatically at the Kanto PGA Championship. He had just blown an excellent opportunity to end a long winless string the previous Sunday in the Mizuno Open by shooting a so-so par round. Nakajima shook it off immediately and finally got himself back into the win column at Royal Meadows Golf Club in the Kanto PGA.

Tsuneyuki hovered just off the pace for three days on the par-71 course at Haga. He shot 67 the first day as Koichi Suzuki led with 65, followed with another 67 Friday but dropped four behind as rookie Ryoken Kawagishi fired a 63 for 130, then narrowed the gap to one with a 68 Saturday when Kawagishi shot 71 for 201. Tsuyoshi Yoneyama also was at 202 with Nakajima.

Tsuneyuki was in and out of the lead on the front nine Sunday, then moved in front to stay with birdies at the 10th and 13th holes and pars the rest of the way. Kawagishi cracked on the back nine and bogeyed the last four holes to drop into a third-place tie with Yoneyama at 275, four behind Nakajima, who shot 69 for 271, 13 under par. Kiyoshi Muroda slipped into second place with 71—274. With the victory, his 42nd and third Kanto PGA, the 35-year-old Nakajima won for the first time since the 1987 Tokai Classic.

Kansai PGA Championship—¥40,000,000
Winner: Kouki Idoki

In the parallel Japan Tour event that same July week, the Kansai PGA Championship went to a player at the other end of the spectrum from Tsuneyuki Nakajima—Kouki Idoki, unheralded and winless before that Sunday at Daisen Heigen Golf Club in another part of the country. Idoki shot a third-round 67 and hung on Sunday to score a one-stroke victory. Seven under par at 279, Idoki edged veteran star Toru Nakamura, Yuzo Ohyama and Takeshi Shibata by a stroke.

Shinsaku Maeda was the first-round leader with 67. He yielded the top spot to 52-year-old Teruo Sugihara, who won his first of nine previous Kansai PGA Championships in 1964. Sugihara blazed a second-round 65 for

137, trailed Idoki by just a stroke after 54 holes, but dropped to sixth place when he took a final-round 74.

Yonex Open Hiroshima—¥60,000,000
Winner: Masashi Ozaki

The parallel was remarkable. Back in early May, Masashi (Jumbo) Ozaki was eight strokes behind entering the final round of the Fuji Sankei Classic, a tournament he had previously won four times, and pulled out a one-stroke victory. Now, in early July, he had fallen seven strokes behind after three rounds in the Yonex Open Hiroshima, an event he had captured five times since its inaugural in 1971 and again was defending champion. Surely he couldn't pull off another miracle? Surely he did! With a Jumbo rally, Ozaki pieced together a seven-under-par 65 at Hiroshima Country Club and nipped Tsuneyuki Nakajima by a stroke with his 278.

Brother Naomichi and Motomasa Aoki started the tournament in front with 67s. Five men were at 68 and six others, including Jumbo Ozaki, shot 69s. Things opened up the second day as Hiroshi Makino took first place with 68-67—135, followed by Aoki at 136, Katsuji Hasegawa at 137 and Masahiro Kuramoto at 138. Jumbo Ozaki was then seven back after a second-round 73 and he gained no ground Saturday. He was tied for 21st at 213 as Tsuyoshi Yoneyama, riding a month-long hot spell, shot 66 to lead at 206, one ahead of Aoki and two in front of Makino.

Ozaki started his Sunday charge with three birdies and a bogey on the first four holes, but did the real damage to the competition on the back nine, where he carved out an eagle and four birdies against a single bogey to nose out Nakajima, who was equally brilliant but one stroke shy with his flawless 66, the product of an eagle and four birdies.

Nikkei Cup Torakichi Nakamura Memorial—¥70,000,000
Winner: Satoshi Higashi

Satoshi Higashi, a two-time winner during his eight-season career on the Japan Tour, most recently in mid-1987, parlayed a blazing third round and an eagle on the final hole for a stirring victory in the Nikkei Cup Torakichi Nakamura Memorial at the Mitsui Kanko Tomakomai Golf Club in mid-July.

It was an adventurous trip for the 29-year-old Higashi the last two days. He had stayed within range with his 70-74 start as Akiyoshi Omachi and Seiichi Kanai led the first day with 69s and Eiichi Itai took a one-shot advantage at 140 midway through the tournament. Satoshi's eight-under-par 64 Saturday was a thing of beauty. After making two birdies on the front nine, he went wild coming in with four consecutive birdies from the 11th through the 14th and two more at the 16th and 17th. Eight birdies, no bogeys … and a five-stroke lead at 208 over Omachi, Toru Nakamura, Hiroshi Makino and Taisei Inagaki. It was a different story in the early going Sunday. Higashi double-bogeyed the second and sixth holes, obliterating his lead. He followed with two birdies and two bogeys and needed a birdie at the last hole to force a playoff. But he went one better with his sensational eagle to snatch victory away from Nobuo Serizawa, the 1987 Nikkei Cup winner, who shot 69 for 283. Higashi wound up with a 74 for the 282 and his third career win.

Yokohama Open—¥50,000,000
Winner: Noboru Sugai

For the second straight week on the Japan Tour, a scintillating third-round performance served as a victory springboard. Nearly duplicating the feat of Satoshi Higashi in the Nikkei Cup, Noboru Sugai fashioned a brilliant 63 in the Saturday round of the inaugural Yokohama Open and went on to victory in the final round.

The similarity ended with the third-round score, though. Sugai, winner of April's Chunichi Crowns, merely overtook Kiyoshi Maita with the course-record round. Unlike Higashi, Sugai was solid again on Sunday and sprinted away from the field with a one-bogey 68, winding up with a 272 and a seven-stroke victory. Even though shooting 75 Sunday, Maita finished second, a shot in front of Shigeru Kawamata.

Yoshinori Kaneko and Hiroshi Ueda were the first-round leaders with 66s before Maita squeezed into the picture with his 67-66—133 to take a three-stroke lead over Kaneko. Then came the masterpiece at Yokohama Country Club. Sugai caught fire on the back nine after going out in 36 with two birdies. He made two more birdies early on the incoming nine, then finished with five in a row for the 63, breaking Takaaki Kono's 1983 record by a stroke. He and Maita were then 12 under par at 204 before Noboru turned it into a rout Sunday.

NST Niigata Open—¥50,000,000
Winner: Seiichi Kanai

Not to be outdone by fellow senior Teruo Sugihara, Seiichi Kanai struck another blow for the older set with the 16th victory of his fine career, scoring a one-stroke triumph in the NST Niigata Open at the Forest Golf Club in Toyoura in northern Japan. Sugihara, 52, won the Bridgestone Aso tournament early in the season. Kanai, two years his junior, came from three strokes off the pace with a final-round 69 to eke out a one-stroke victory with his 10-under-par 278. It was his first win since the 1987 Tohoku Classic.

Kanai remained close during the early rounds. He was two behind the 68 of first-round leader Saburo Fujiki, then slipped five back Friday when he shot 72 for 142. Yoshinori Mizumaki and the winners of the two previous Tour tournaments, Noboru Sugai and Satoshi Higashi, led with 137. Kanai matched the 67 that carried Yoshinori Kaneko into first place at 206 and cut his deficit to the three strokes after 54 holes. Seiichi carded four birdies and a bogey in putting together his winning 69 Sunday. Yukio Noguchi shot 71 to claim second place at 279, Sugai finished at 280 and Higashi, Kaneko and Mizumaki posted 281s.

Japan PGA Championship—¥75,000,000
Winner: Hideki Kase

Hideki Kase picked a big one for his first Japan Tour victory—the Japan PGA Championship, a tournament that usually falls into the hands of one of the circuit's more prominent players. The 30-year-old Kase edged into the lead in the third round at Amanomiya Country Club and raced away to a five-stroke victory with a final-round 70 and a 14-under-par 274. Saburo Fujiki and Masahiro Kuramoto, the 1982 PGA champion, tied for second at 279.

Those two veterans had been Kase's most serious opposition through the final 54 holes after Tsukasa Watanabe stole first-day attention with a 64, then faded from contention. Fujiki, who opened with 71, came back Friday with 65 for 136 and a one-stroke lead over Kase and Colombian Eduardo Herrera as Watanabe fell to 138 with his 74. Kase made his move Saturday, following his second-round 66 with a five-birdie 67 and, at 204, headed Kuramoto (73-67-65) by one and Fujiki (70) by two going into the final round.

In the absence of a hot round by one of the close contenders, Kase found his 70 steadily widening his first-place lead to the final five-shot margin. Fujiki managed just a 73 and Kuramoto took a 74 as they tied for second.

Maruman Open—¥90,000,000
Winner: Masashi Ozaki

Once again Masashi (Jumbo) Ozaki flourished at a scene of former triumphs on the Japan Tour. The circuit's top player scored his third victory in five years in the Maruman Open at Hatoyama Country Club, but, unlike his other two earlier 1990 wins, Ozaki did not need an immense rally in the final round. Instead, he carried a three-stroke lead into play the last day and widened the final margin to five shots with a 68 for 273, 15 under par for the distance. The victory extended his all-time-high total in Japan to 67 wins over his 20-year career.

The tournament's healthy ¥90,000,000 purse attracted a strong field, including international star Ian Woosnam of Wales, leader of the European Tour's money list. Woosnam proved his mettle early when he shot 67 to share the first-round lead with Nobumitsu Yuhara, Tsukasa Watanabe and Taisei Inagaki. Chen Tze Chung (T.C. Chen) opened with 69, repeated Friday and took the second-round lead by a stroke over Ozaki and Saburo Fujiki. Woosnam shot 73 for 140, joined there by Shigeru Kawamata and Eduardo Herrera. Ozaki fired 66 Saturday as he stormed into the lead at 205, three strokes in front of Woosnam and Hideki Kase, the winner of the PGA Championship the previous week. Tsuneyuki Nakajima, who had been lurking close to the lead for two days, shot 67 Sunday to work into second place at 278, a stroke in front of Woosnam and two ahead of Kase.

Daiwa KBC Augusta—¥100,000,000
Winner: Masashi Ozaki

Masashi (Jumbo) Ozaki was in rare form when he arrived at Kyushu Shima Country Club for the Daiwa KBC Augusta tournament after his strong victory in the Maruman Open. He was so sharp, in fact, that he rolled up the biggest victory margin of the season as he made it two in a row on the Japan Tour and four for 1990. Even with his highest of four rounds Sunday—a 70—Jumbo won by 10 strokes over Chen Tze Chung with his 19-under-par 269.

Masahiro Kuramoto shared the first-round lead with Ozaki at 65, but was the last player to keep touch with the powerful Jumbo that week. Ozaki moved to a two-stroke lead over Katsunari Takahashi with a 66 Friday as Kuramoto shot 69 for 134. Katsuyoshi Tomori, in fourth place, was seven off Jumbo's pace. By the end of 54 holes, Ozaki had stretched his margin to five strokes with his 68 for 199. Takahashi shot 71 for 204 and the next men in the standings were Shigeru Kawamata and Tomohiro Maruyama at 207. Chen grabbed the runner-up slot with a 71 for 279 Sunday. Ian Baker-Finch, the Australian who was taking a break from the U.S. PGA Tour, climbed into a third-place tie with Takahashi with a final-round 69.

Kanto Open—¥30,000,000
Winner: Ryoken Kawagishi

Kansai Open—¥20,000,000
Winner: Teruo Sugihara

Kyushu Open—¥20,000,000
Winner: Katsuyoshi Tomori

Hokkaido Open—¥10,000,000
Winner: Katsuhige Takahashi

Chu-Shikoku Open—¥20,000,000
Winner: Seiki Okuda

Two of the Japan Tour's prominent players—the brilliant rookie and the astonishing senior—annexed victories when the circuit staged its five-tournament regional series of 72-hole events the first weekend of September.

Ryoken Kawagishi built a six-stroke lead with his 66-64 start in the Kanto (Eastern Japan) Open and held on for a two-stroke victory over Isao Aoki at Higashinomiya Country Club, posting a seven-under-par 273. In Western Japan, Teruo Sugihara won the Kansai Open for a ninth time, edging Yuzo Ohyama by a stroke with his six-under-par 282 at Pinlake Country Club. The 52-year-old Teruo took his first Kansai Open title in 1964.

In the other tournaments that week, Seiki Okuda defeated Masayuki Kawamura and Tsukasa Watanabe in a playoff for the Chu-Shikoku Open after the three tied at five-under-par 283, Katsuhige Takahashi won by five with his 278 in the Hokkaido Open and Katsuyoshi Tomori rolled to a six-stroke triumph in the Kyushu Open with his 277.

Suntory Open—¥100,000,000
Winner: Toru Nakamura

Toru Nakamura built a five-stroke lead over the first two rounds of the Suntory Open and carried it to a wire-to-wire victory despite the efforts of another Japan Tour veteran—Australian Graham Marsh—to overtake him. Marsh's bid came up a stroke shy of a tie as Nakamura posted a 17-under-par 271 for his second 1990 win and the 27th of his long career.

The 40-year-old Nakamura opened the Suntory at Narashino Country Club at Inzaimachi with a pair of seven-under 65s. He led by two over six other pros, including visiting American Larry Nelson, the defending champion, after the first 65 and widened the gap to five Friday with the second one. That's when Marsh took up the chase, shooting a matching 65 to go with his first-round 70 and moving into second place, two shots in front of fellow Aussie Anthony Gilligan, a first-year pro. Nakamura lost a shot of his margin Saturday when he shot 69 to a 68 by Marsh. Gilligan, with a 70, remained third but eight shots off the pace.

Toru's par-72 was just enough Sunday. At one point on the front nine, Marsh had whittled Nakamura's lead in half with a string of four birdies, but Toru reestablished his big edge with a birdie at the ninth hole as Marsh bogeyed. The finish turned exciting when Nakamura bogeyed the 15th and 17th holes and Marsh birdied the 17th to cut the deficit to one. Nakamura secured the triumph when Marsh missed a long birdie putt on the 18th green and parred for 69 and 272. Gilligan finished third at 276 and Nelson tied for fourth with Kiyoshi Maita at 279.

All Nippon Airways Open—¥90,000,000
Winner: Tsuneyuki Nakajima

More certainly, Tsuneyuki Nakajima was back. The major star of the Japan Tour in the middle 1980s had broken back into the win column after almost three years in early July but in the Kanto PGA when the circuit players were split between two events or even out of action. Nakajima beat the best, however, when he won the All Nippon Airways (ANA) Open in mid-September at Sapporo Golf Club in Hiroshimacho. He finished three strokes in front of Masashi (Jumbo) Ozaki, the dominant player in Japan since 1988, and further ahead of the rest of a strong field. It was his third victory in seven years in the ANA Open.

Masanobu Kimura forestalled Tsuneyuki for two rounds. He opened with 65 to lead Chen Tze Chung by three and Nakajima and four others, including prominent U.S. pro Mark O'Meara, by four. Kimura slipped to 73 Friday and still led by one, but over this group—Nakajima, O'Meara, Jumbo and Jet Ozaki and Pete Izumikawa. Tsuneyuki seized control Saturday when he shot 68 and moved into a four-stroke lead at 207 over the Ozakis and O'Meara, who all shot par rounds. Jumbo Ozaki, who had won in three of his last four starts in Japan, stirred up a move Sunday when he eagled the fifth hole, but could do no better than a one-under 35 on the back nine for 69 and 280. Nakajima fashioned a 70 with four birdies and two bogeys for the winning, 11-under-par 277. Jet Ozaki and O'Meara tied for third at 281.

Gene Sarazen Jun Classic—¥75,000,000
Winner: Naomichi Ozaki

Naomichi (Joe) Ozaki kept the Gene Sarazen Jun Classic in the family when the Japan Tour reached that stop at the Rope Club in late September. His older brothers had won that event three of the previous four years—Masashi (Jumbo) in 1986 and 1987 (also in 1983) and Tateo (Jet) in 1989. So, Naomichi's one-stroke victory was appropriate.

It was a struggle all the way for Naomichi before he recorded his second 1990 win and 13th of his career. Australians Anthony Gilligan and Wayne Smith opened with 66s on the par-71 Rope Club course at Shiotanimachi, two strokes ahead of Ozaki, eventual runner-up Yoshinori Kaneko and three others. Ozaki followed with a 66 Friday and acquired the lead at 134, one in front of Masanobu Kimura and two ahead of Shinsaku Maeda. Kimura shot 68 Saturday and advanced into a first-place tie with Ozaki at 203. Maeda and Chen Tze Ming were at 206 and Kaneko at 207 after 54 holes.

Kaneko made the only serious run at Ozaki Sunday. Naomichi was in and out with five birdies and four bogeys for 70 and 273, an 11-under-par score. Kaneko got started too late. He birdied the last four holes, but his 67 brought him home one stroke short of a tie at 274. Hajime Meshiai, Chen and Kimura deadlocked for third at 276.

Tokai Classic—¥70,000,000
Winner: Graham Marsh

Probably the only person in Japan who had a good word for Typhoon Gene was veteran golfer Graham Marsh. On Saturday, before the fierce storm blew in off the ocean, Marsh had come up with his finest round in many months—a 64—and vaulted into the lead in the Tokai Classic on the West course of Miyoshi Country Club. The downpours spawned by the typhoon inundated the course Sunday and forced cancellation of the final round. Marsh was declared the winner. It was the 25th in Japan for the 46-year-old Australian, who has campaigned extensively in the country for many years.

Marsh positioned himself close to the top the first two days with rounds of 70 and 72. Hiroshi Makino and little-known Shinji Ikeuchi shared the first-round lead at 68 in a field lacking the circuit's giants, then yielded to Saburo Fujiki and Noboru Sugai, both 1990 winners, who had identical 36-hole combinations of 69-70. They were most closely trailed by Tadami Ueno and Yutaka Hagawa at 140. Then came Marsh's own storm—of birdies. He had three on the front nine and went on to the 64 with five more coming in, four in a row from the 12th through 15th holes. His total was 10-under-par 206. Fujiki, with 69, and Ueno, with 68, tied for second at 208.

Japan Open Championship—¥100,000,000
Winner: Tsuneyuki Nakajima

It seemed as though the whole thing had been scripted. Japanese superstars Masashi (Jumbo) Ozaki, Tsuneyuki Nakajima and Isao Aoki and brilliant newcomer Ryoken Kawagishi battling it out over the final 36 holes for the national championship and occupying the four top positions when the Japan Open reached its conclusion at Otaru Country Club in Hokkaido.

Nakajima was the winner, shooting a comfortable 69 in the final round in coming from four strokes off the pace to win his third Open and prevent Ozaki from scoring an unprecedented third victory in a row in the country's most prestigious tournament. The finest players usually seem to come to the top in the Japan Open. Since 1983, Nakajima has won it three times and Ozaki and Aoki twice apiece, Koichi Uehara's victory in 1984 the only interruption.

Hajime Meshiai led the first day with 67 on the 7,119-yard Otaru course, but the impending battle for the championship had already taken form immediately behind him as Nakajima stood second at 68 and Ozaki third at 70. They both moved past Meshiai and his 78 Friday, Tsuneyuki taking the lead with 71—139, a stroke ahead of Ozaki. Kawagishi was next at 143 with two others and Aoki posted 144. Ozaki then charged ahead Saturday when Nakajima slipped to 73. Both Jumbo and Ryoken shot 68s and Isao a 69, setting up the final round with Ozaki at 208, Kawagishi at 211, Nakajima at 212 and Aoki at 213.

Nakajima pressured Ozaki with an outgoing 34 and caught him with his third birdie at No. 12. They were deadlocked again after the 16th, but Jumbo took his third bogey in a row at the 17th and Tsuneyuki made it a two-stroke victory with a birdie at the 72nd hole for 69 and 281, seven under par. Ozaki shot 75 for 283, Kawagishi 74 for 285 and Aoki 73 for 286. It was Nakajima's 44th career victory in Japan.

Asahi Beer Golf Digest—¥110,000,000
Winner: Noboru Sugai

Noboru Sugai added further luster and big money to the finest season of his long career when he won the rich Asahi Beer Golf Digest tournament and its ¥21,000,000 first prize. As had been the case in one of his two earlier 1990 victories, Sugai utilized a torrid individual round to produce the triumph at Tomei Country Club in Susuno. This time it was a nine-under-par 62 in the final round, carrying him from five strokes off the pace to a three-shot victory. This by a man who had won only once before 1990 and who was to finish sixth on the final Japan Tour money list.

Fotoshi Irino, who eventually finished 47th, led the first day with 66. The runners-up at 67—Hideki Kase, Yoshinori Mizumaki and Frankie Minoza, the Asia circuit champion from the Philippines—figured heavily in the next two rounds. Kase grabbed the lead Friday with another 67. Mizumaki shot 68 for second. Minoza shot Saturday's best round—67—and jumped into a three-way tie for the lead with Kase and Mizumaki at 207. Sugai was sitting at 212 after 72-72-68, then exploded Sunday. He had 10 birdies and a bogey in tying the course record en route to his 10-under-par winning score of 274. The three Saturday co-leaders all shot 71s Sunday and Masashi Ozaki and U.S. Tour star Larry Mize jumped past them into a second-place tie at 277 with closing 67s.

Bridgestone—¥120,000,000
Winner: Saburo Fujiki

A remarkable absence of playoffs on the Japan Tour ended at the Bridgestone tournament in mid-October when Saburo Fujiki went an extra hole to defeat Akihito Yokoyama at Chiba's Sodegaura Country Club. Not since the Chunichi Crowns in late April had a winner gone to overtime to secure his victory. Fujiki and Yokoyama had ended the 72 holes of the long-established tournament with identical 274s. Then Saburo claimed his second 1990 title when he birdied the par-five 18th, the designated first playoff hole, as Yokoyama managed only a par.

The two finalists almost duplicated each other's efforts throughout the tournament. Both opened with 67s, a stroke off the lead of 66 shared by Nobumitsu Yuhara and Shigeru Kawamata. It seemed as though everyone had a share of first place when the firing ended Friday. In front at 138 were Yokoyama, Hiroshi Makino, Kiyoshi Murota, Hiroshi Goda, Kazuhiro Takami and leading money winner Masashi Ozaki, the 1988 Bridgestone winner. Fujiki was then one back at 139. He produced a 66 Saturday, Yokoyama a 67 and the two entered the final round with 205s, two strokes ahead of Murota, three ahead of Ryoken Kawagishi and four on top of six others.

The carbon copy efforts of Fujiki and Yokoyama continued Sunday. They each made four birdies and took single bogeys as they posted 69s and forced the playoff. Nobuo Serizawa jumped into third place with a closing 67 for 276, a stroke in front of Tsukasa Watanabe.

Lark Cup—¥180,000,000
Winner: Ryoken Kawagishi

Ryoken Kawagishi ended his first year as a professional on the highest note of an outstanding season on the Japan Tour. His early-season victory in the Shizuoka Open and later win in the regional Kanto Open hardly compared to his late-October triumph in the Lark Cup, the second-richest event of the season with its ¥180,000,000 purse. Not only did he beat a much-stronger overall field, but Ryoken got the better of the country's best player of the time, Masashi (Jumbo) Ozaki, in a head-to-head finish at the ABC Golf Club course at Tojocho in Western Japan. The two went into the final round deadlocked at 209 and the 23-year-old prevailed by two strokes with his closing 68 for his 11-under-par final total.

Katsuji Hasegawa, a journeyman pro with a single victory in his 24 professional seasons, made an opening bid with 67 to lead by a stroke over Britain's Barry Lane and Shuichi Sano. The ultimate real contenders moved onto the scene Friday. Ozaki took a half-share of first place with Masahiro Kuramoto (both had 70-69) and Kawagishi was just a shot off the pace after a Friday 68. Ryoken's 69 Saturday boosted him into the leadership tie with Ozaki, who shot 70. Hasegawa bounced back from a second-round 74 with 69 and trailed by a stroke, one ahead of Kuramoto and two in front of Isao Aoki and Noboru Sugai.

One bad tee shot killed Ozaki Sunday. Kawagishi had four birdies on the last six holes, but might have faced a playoff if Jumbo had not driven out of bounds at the par-five 15th. Ozaki came back with birdies on the last two holes but fell two strokes short, though four in front of the next finishers—Aoki, Lane and David Ishii.

Asahi Glass Four Tours World Championship—US$1,150,000
Winner: Australia

An injury default in the first round came back to haunt the United States team in the Asahi Glass Four Tours World Championship, ultimately costing the Americans the title and ending their three-year winning streak in the international event.

In a peculiar turn of affairs, the Australian team won the championship without striking a blow in the scheduled final matches against the Americans when heavy Sunday rains prevented play and activated the retroactive alternative—total strokes over the first three rounds. Because Wayne Levi, the U.S. captain, had yielded to an aching back and forfeited his first-round match to Briton Mark James, the Americans did not have a complete score and the win automatically went to the Australian-filled Australasian squad.

The tournament format calls for a round-robin of stroke-play matches among the six-man teams from the world's four major tours with the top two point-makers meeting for the title. Europe upheld its favorites' role Thursday with an 8-4 victory over the United States while Japan and Australasia were battling to a 6-6 tie. The Americans bounced back Friday, winning four matches and halving the other two for a 10-2 triumph over Japan, and Australasia thumped the Europeans, 8-4, as Nick Faldo scored his team's only win. The U.S. and Australasia teams were then tied at 14 points apiece and it stayed that way at Yomiuri Country Club near Tokyo Saturday when the two teams met and played to a 6-6 deadlock. Craig Parry, Rodger Davis and Ian Baker-Finch won for Australasia, Tim Simpson, Mark Calcavecchia and Levi for the Americans.

Acom P.T.—¥75,320,000
Winner: Bob Gilder

Several other U.S. PGA Tour regulars, the American season over, came to Japan the same week as the six-man Four Tours Championship team, playing in the Acom P.T., an offbeat event somewhat similar to their own International held in August in Colorado. A scale awards points to each score on each hole and veteran Bob Gilder wound up with the highest total—115—to edge Bob Tway by a point at Japan Classic Country Club at Ayamacho. As happened to the Four Tours tournament, the final round of the Acom was rained out and cancelled. Gilder's daily point totals were 38-39-38, while

Tway had 37-38-39. The highest totals posted during the three days were 41s by Yoshinori Kaneko and Eduardo Herrera Saturday. Kaneko finished in a three-way tie for third at 113 with Jean van de Velde and Yoshiyuki Isomura.

Visa Taiheiyo Club Masters—¥130,000,000
Winner: Jose Maria Olazabal

The pro golf tourists from the other circuits of the world—in quantity and high quality—made their annual treks to Japan in November, presenting the fans of that country with by far the finest fields of the year for a stretch of three lucrative tournaments. First up—the Visa Taiheiyo Club Masters, which began the big-money-tournament era in Japan in the early 1970s.

In 1989, when Jose Maria Olazabal succeeded countryman Seve Ballesteros as the Taiheiyo Masters champion, his star was on the rise but he had not yet become a household name in the world of golf. By the time he returned to Gotemba to defend that title, he had clearly established himself as a player of top international rank—third in the year-end Sony Ranking—so a successful defense was no surprise.

The 24-year-old Spaniard had the tournament in his grip, in a manner of speaking, from start to finish. He launched his defense with a six-under-par 66, primarily because he took just 23 putts. He led four players, including Masashi and Naomichi Ozaki, by a stroke and eight others, including Nick Faldo, Curtis Strange and Wayne Grady, the U.S. PGA champion, by two. Grady eagled the par-five 18th for 66 Friday and took a half-share of the lead with Olazabal, who had a 68 for his 134. The Spaniard virtually clinched matters Saturday when he established a five-stroke lead with a three-under 69 as Ozaki dropped back into a second-place tie with Bernhard Langer at 208. Jose Maria was never threatened Sunday, at one point sailing along eight strokes ahead before giving back a couple to settle for 67 and 270, still a new tournament record at the Taiheiyo Club course, four better than the old mark set by Yasuhiro Funatogawa in 1986. Ozaki eagled the 18th and tied Langer for second at 275.

Dunlop Phoenix—¥200,000,000
Winner: Larry Mize

Larry Mize has discovered the solution to his victory void in America. Go to Japan. Without a win at home since the 1987 Masters, Mize has capitalized twice in the last two years on his brief late-season visits to Japan by winning the Dunlop Phoenix, the richest event on the Japan Tour at ¥200,000,000. Virtually duplicating Jose Maria Olazabal's successful defense the previous week in the Taiheiyo Club Masters, the slender Georgian registered a three-stroke victory at Phoenix Country Club in the southern resort area at Miyazaki.

The repetitions didn't end with Larry's twin victories. Naomichi Ozaki, the closest chaser in 1989, finished second again at Miyazaki, failing to end the American domination of the rich tournament. U.S. PGA Tour players have won the Dunlop the last five years and 11 times since 1974.

David Ishii, winless in Japan since 1988 but victor in the Hawaiian Open on the U.S. circuit in February, started the Dunlop with 65 and a two-stroke lead before yielding to hot-shooting Mize and Larry Nelson Friday. Mize had eight birdies and a bogey for 65—134, while Nelson matched that score with an eagle and seven birdies for a nine-under-par 63. A rules decision that went against Nelson Saturday helped Mize establish a three-stroke lead. He shot 69 for 203 and Naomichi Ozaki moved back into second place with 67 for 206. Had Nelson not taken a triple bogey at the 16th hole, where he imbedded a shot under a lip of a fairway bunker and was denied his appeal for a free lift under the embedded-ball rule, he would not have had to go into the final round four strokes off the pace.

Even though he took three bogeys on the back nine in shooting 71 Sunday for his 274 and the three-stroke victory, Mize was never in danger. The battle, instead, was for second place. Ozaki holed a 16-foot birdie putt on the last green for 71—277 and a one-shot margin over Nelson, Ishii, Seve Ballesteros and Tsuneyuki Nakajima, the last Japanese winner of the Dunlop in 1985.

Casio World Open—¥120,000,000
Winner: Mike Reid

Mike Reid played the U.S. PGA Tour for 10 years before landing his first victory. Ironically, the soft-spoken American had made his first visit and taken his first serious run at a title on the Japan Tour 10 years before scoring his initial victory by capturing the 1990 Casio World Open at Ibusuki in late November. It was a pleasant finish to a less-than-satisfactory American season for the Utah resident who had gone winless and placed 60th on the money list.

Reid first had to contend with the fast start of Larry Nelson, coming off a strong showing the previous week in the Dunlop Phoenix. Nelson didn't have a five on his card as he opened with a six-birdie 66 over the 7,014-yard Ibusuki Golf Club course in southern Kyushu and took a two-stroke lead over Naomichi Ozaki, Koki Idoki, Miguel Angel Martin and Robert Gamez, the U.S. circuit's Rookie of the Year. Nelson retained the lead with a 70 Friday, but by just a stroke over Craig Stadler. Ozaki, Seve Ballesteros and Mike Donald trailed by two and Reid was at 69-70—139.

Reid surged in front to stay Saturday. The 1988 World Series champion assembled a seven-under-par 65 to jump two strokes in front of Ballesteros and Ryoken Kawagishi. Then, on Sunday, his 70 was good enough to slough off several bidders. David Ishii and Yoshinori Kaneko started too far back to take full advantage of their 63 and 65, respectively. Ballesteros' run of back-nine birdies merely offset a poor start and, after holing out at the 14th for an eagle to close to within a stroke, Kawagishi double-bogeyed the par-three 17th and dropped back into a six-way tie for third behind runner-up Kaneko, whose 276 was two strokes short. Ishii, Donald, Ballesteros, Graham Marsh and Masahiro Kuramoto shared the 277 slot with Kawagishi.

Japan Series—¥60,000,000
Winner: Naomichi Ozaki

Twenty-three of the season's leading performers on the Japan Tour convened for the annual Japan Series tournament at Tokyo and Osaka at the end of November. All of the season's winners and the top 20 money winners were eligible and invited but not everyone appeared. The most notable absentee was Masashi (Jumbo) Ozaki, the No. 1 man in Japan for the third year in a row.

Brother Naomichi (Joe) Ozaki was there, though, and won the special tournament for the second time in three years, defeating Tsuneyuki (Tommy) Nakajima, the No. 2 money winner of the season, on the third hole of a playoff. Both had completed the split-scene 72 holes with 13-under-par scores of 275 in a virtual two-man show the last two days at Tokyo's Yomiuri Country Club.

David Ishii and Brian Jones, two of the three non-Japanese in the elite field, got off to the best starts at Osaka's Yomiuri Country Club, site of the first two rounds. Ishii led with 68, Jones had 69 and four others, including Nakajima, were at 70. Tsuneyuki vaulted into first place Friday with a birdie-birdie start to a 67. At 137, he led five players, among them Ishii and Jones, by two strokes. Ozaki, meanwhile, was nearby at 71-69—140. His turn came Saturday when the scene shifted to Tokyo. He and Nakajima put the rest of the field pretty much out of touch. Ozaki reeled off nine birdies, including four in a row at one point, for 64 while Nakajima was putting together a five-birdie 67 for his 204. They were then four shots ahead of the next man, Tsukasa Watanabe.

Naomichi moved three strokes ahead on the front nine Sunday with 34 to Tsuneyuki's 37, but Nakajima worked his way back into the 72-hole tie with a pair of birdies to Naomichi's bogey on the incoming nine. Both parred the first extra hole and bogeyed the second before Ozaki dropped a three-foot birdie putt to gain the victory, his third of the season and 14th of his career.

Daikyo Open—¥100,000,000
Winner: Teruo Sugihara

Teruo Sugihara polished off his truly remarkable 1990 campaign in impressive style in the season-ending Daikyo Open in Okinawa. The 52-year-old pro, already the winner of two tournaments earlier in the season, shot four consecutive rounds in the 60s and scored a one-stroke victory at Daikyo Country Club with his 15-under-par 273. The ¥18,000,000 prize boosted his 1990 Tour earnings to ¥64,245,358 (more than $450,000).

Sugihara began his march to career victory No. 57 with an opening-round 67 that lodged him in a four-way tie for first place with Hsieh Min Nan, Chen Tze Ming and Katsuji Hasegawa. Sugihara moved into the lead for good Friday when he shot 68 for 135 and a two-stroke lead over Hsieh and three over Tadao Nakamura, Seiki Okuda and Shinsaku Maeda. His margin slipped to one when he posted a 69 Saturday for 204. Hsieh remained on his heels at 205 with Okuda at 206 and Maeda and Masahiro Kuramoto at 207. Another 69 Sunday completed the victory run for the amazing Sugihara as he finished a stroke in front of Okuda and two ahead of Hsieh and Maeda.

Johnnie Walker Asian Classic—US$350,000
Winner: Nick Faldo

Things had not been going well at all for Nick Faldo on his last long trip of 1990 to Australia and Japan for the two Johnnie Walker tournaments. He had missed a plane connection and lost his luggage for a day, then aggravated a wrist injury and had to withdraw from the Australian Johnnie Walker event. Fortunately for him, Faldo put aside what thoughts he had about skipping the Johnnie Walker Asian Classic at Hong Kong the following week in mid-December. Instead, he played and capped his fine season with a four-stroke victory at Royal Hong Kong Golf Club to go with his earlier wins in the British Open and Masters.

After keeping himself within range the first two days with rounds of 72 and 68 and avoiding the practice tee to go easy on the wrist, Faldo took charge of the tournament Friday. Playing the sort of flawless golf that he exhibits so frequently these days, Nick lashed an eagle to seven birdies on the par-71, 6,732-yard course for a 62 and broke three strokes into the lead, supplanting Ireland's Ronan Rafferty, who had held the top spot through the first two rounds with his 67-69—136 start. Rafferty then trailed by three, Canada's Richard Zokol and Scotland's Colin Montgomerie by four with Ian Woosnam still a factor though five back at 207.

What chance Woosnam had disappeared with an early double bogey and Faldo kept the competition away with a typically solid, final-day performance Saturday—nine pars on the front nine, then birdies at the 10th, 13th and 18th for 68 and the four-shot margin with his 14-under-par 270. Woosnam shook off the early trouble to muster a 67 and finish second, a shot in front of Australia's Mike Clayton. Rafferty dropped to seventh place with a closing 72.

15. The Women's Tours

The story of the LPGA Tour in 1990 can be summed up in two words: Beth Daniel.

On an LPGA Tour that now has more depth, more good players and more money than ever in its history, the 34-year-old Daniel was the star of stars, Rolex Player of the Year, Vare Trophy winner and No. 1 money winner.

Daniel played in only 23 tournaments, but won seven, finished second in two others and had nine other top-10 finishes. Of the 78 rounds she played, she broke par in 49. Three times she won back-to-back. She won her first major, the Mazda LPGA Championship, and made a sweep of the LPGA's first million-dollar events, the LPGA Championship and Centel Classic.

Daniel amassed an LPGA record $863,578 and finished with a stroke average of 70.54, second only to her LPGA record of 70.38 set last year.

As Daniel streaked through the season, Patty Sheehan finished a scant nine points behind in Player of the Year points and produced a personal best $732,618. Betsy King won two majors, the Dinah Shore and U.S. Women's Open.

Cathy Gerring won the Hilton Bounceback Player of the Year Award in impressive fashion. In 1989, she won only $27,649, 90th on the money list, but rebounded in 1990 with the first three victories of her career, $487,326, and demonstrated that motherhood and golf do mix.

And once again, a foreign player was Rookie of the Year. Hiromi Kobayashi became the seventh foreigner and fourth straight, but the first from Japan, to earn the title, winning $66,325.

The most joyous event of 1990 was the first-ever Solheim Cup, the Ryder Cup of women's golf, if you will. The U.S. team of non-playing captain Kathy Whitworth—Pat Bradley, Nancy Lopez, Dottie Mochrie, Rosie Jones, Daniel, King, Sheehan and Gerring—defeated their European counterparts 11-1/2 to 4-1/2 at Lake Nona in Orlando, Florida.

And the least joyous, from a public relations standpoint, was the forced resignation of William Blue as Commissioner, only two years after he was hired. He was replaced by Charles Mechem.

The WPG European Tour had only two multiple winners. Trish Johnson had four victories, and Florence Descampe won three times. Such star attractions as Marie Laure de Lorenzi and Laura Davies had only one victory each.

Europe's major championship, the Weetabix Women's British Open, was won by Helen Alfredsson.

Jamaica Classic—$500,000
Winner: Patty Sheehan

There was a lot more at stake than merely getting off to a good start when Patty Sheehan teed it up in the season-opening Jamaica Classic. She needed a big paycheck pronto.

Sheehan's house in California's Santa Cruz mountains was destroyed in the earthquake of October, 1989. She had no insurance, and restoration was depleting her savings.

Sheehan shot rounds of 69-68-75—212, won the $75,000 winner's share of the $500,000 purse, plus another $80,000 from various Jamaica Series competitions, and breathed a very large sigh of relief.

"That's a big load off my mind," said Sheehan, who was the only player to break par over the par-71 Tryall Golf and Beach Club course, and who won by three over Pat Bradley, Lynn Connelly and Jane Geddes. "Winning the first time out is nice, but the money; oh, how I needed that paycheck."

Sheehan didn't lead wire-to-wire, trailing Sweden's Liselotte Neumann's opening 68 by a stroke in the first round. But when the winds became gale-force on Saturday, Sheehan rode them to a 68 and a five-stroke lead over Connelly. She needed such a margin after making three straight bogeys midway through Sunday's final round before righting herself with five pars coming in.

Sheehan could look far over her shoulder before finding some of the LPGA's biggest names. Betsy King, star of the 1989 season, started slow with 72-72 and finished with a 77 for 224, while Beth Daniel's final-round 65 wasn't enough to offset opening 78-76.

Oldsmobile Classic—$300,000
Winner: Pat Bradley

Yogi Berra's old baseball line that "it ain't over til it's over," spilled over into golf, making a firm believer out of Pat Bradley in the Oldsmobile Classic at Wycliffe Golf and Country Club in Lake Worth, Florida.

For 44 bogey-free holes, Bradley completely outclassed the rest of the field, rushing out to a 10-stroke lead. Then, without warning, she spent the next day and a half giving it all back before first sinking a 25-foot putt to get into a playoff with Dale Eggling, then making an 18-footer to win it on the first extra hole.

"Those last two days were hell," Bradley said of her 74-76 finish which followed a 66-65 start. "I have no idea how a person can go from making everything the first two days to making nothing the last two. The fans got their money's worth watching me. When was the last time you saw someone play the final 28 holes nine over par and win?"

Bradley was 12 under par after 36 holes and birdied three of the first eight in the third round before hitting the wall. She finished Saturday's round with five bogeys for 74 and opened Sunday's round with a bogey and double bogey. By the 17th, she was tied with Eggling, who had finished with 69, and playing partner Dottie Mochrie.

A three-way playoff seemed possible, then unlikely after Bradley had to lay up at No. 18 before hitting her third shot 25 feet above the hole. But she made it, Mochrie three-putted and Bradley then won it in the playoff.

Phar-Mor Inverrary Classic—$400,000
Winner: Jane Crafter

Nine years of pure frustration for Australian Jane Crafter were erased in one 40-foot electric moment.

That's how long the putt was that Crafter sank on the final hole to win the first phase of the Phar-Mor's Million Dollar Championship. When the putt rolled in, she leaped high into the air and then landed in the middle of a spotlight that wouldn't be turned off until midsummer.

As the tournament winner, she became the only player with a chance to earn $1 million by winning Phar-Mor's Youngstown Classic in July.

"I'm totally overwhelmed," Crafter said after surviving a five-player dogfight over the final nine holes. "It's a wonderful feeling. I just can't express it. When I came to the U.S., I didn't know if I would ever measure up, but for one week, at least, I beat the Lopezes and the Bradleys and the Whitworths and the Carners. It means all the hard work paid off."

When it was over, Crafter had beaten Lopez by one. At one point, it appeared that there would be a five-way playoff, but Crafter's birdie, and bogeys at No. 18 by Meg Mallon, Danielle Ammaccapane and Dale Eggling assured it wouldn't happen. They tied for third.

"I didn't think she would make it," Lopez said of Crafter's winning 40-footer. "But, I'm happy for her. That's the way you have to win sometimes."

Orix Hawaiian Open—$350,000
Winner: Beth Daniel

Beth Daniel believes in the numbers game. The way she figured it, a final-round 70 would be good enough to win the Hawaiian Ladies Open at Ko Olina Golf Club. She was off by two as 72 was good enough for her first victory of 1990.

Daniel opened with a 71, two off the lead shared by Cathy Gerring, Patty Sheehan and Elaine Crosby. She took a two-shot lead over Amy Benz with a second-round 67, then put the pencil to her chances of winning.

"I figured I'd have to shoot 70 to win. That would force Amy to shoot 68 and the others to shoot 67 or better," Daniel said. "But under the conditions (rain and wind), par was a good score."

It also was good for a three-shot victory over Benz and Patty Sheehan and the $52,500 winner's share of the $350,000 purse. The turning point came at the 13th, where Daniel reached the green in two and made birdie, while Benz three-putted for bogey on the way to 73.

Daniel's pursuers knew they'd have to charge, that Daniel would not make any mistakes. She didn't, hitting 17 greens and making only one bogey.

"You have to beat Beth. She's not going to beat herself," Benz said.

Women's Kemper Open—$500,000
Winner: Beth Daniel

Beth Daniel took care of a little unfinished business when she made it two in a row by winning the Women's Kemper Open at the Wailea Resort. For one thing, it was her 20th career victory, and for another, she added her name to the list of who's who in women's golf who had won this prestigious event.

Daniel overcame opening rounds of 73-75 to finish 66-69 for a one-under-par 283 and a one-stroke victory over Rosie Jones and Laura Davies and $75,000 to vault her into first place on the 1990 money list.

It also continued an amazing streak in which she had won six of her last 11 tournaments. "This is No. 20 and it feels unbelievable," Daniel said. "I especially enjoy winning this one because I've been so close to winning it the past two years. It's amazing how many people remember me for hitting it in the water at No. 18 to lose two years ago."

This time, she birdied the 18th, barely missing a 50-foot eagle putt. That put her two strokes in front of Jones and Davies, who later also birdied it.

The scores were unusually high for the tournament. Daniel's 283 was the highest winning score since the Kemper moved to Hawaii in 1982. Daniel had to come from way back to do it. She was five behind the 68s of Mitzi Edge and Patty Sheehan after the first round and nine back of Edge at the halfway point. But a third-round 66 moved her to within two of Edge after 54 holes.

"To barely make the cut (it was 150), then come back and win is especially satisfying," Daniel said.

Desert Inn International—$400,000
Winner: Maggie Will

Sometimes victory comes when you least expect it. Take Maggie Will, for instance. She opened the Desert Inn International in Las Vegas with a 73 and ended it with a 75. But in between, the 25-year-old North Carolinian shot 66 and that was the difference.

Will's 54-hole total of 214, two under par on the Desert Inn Country Club course, gave her a one-stroke victory over Ayako Okamoto, Val Skinner and Patti Rizzo.

"It's hard to describe how I feel," Will said. "I thought I had shot myself out of it in the first round, but I hit some solid shots down the stretch in the last round, and I guess that's what champions are made of."

It looked like Rizzo's tournament to win when she opened 66-70 for a three-stroke lead over Will entering the final round. But her fate was written on the wind, which sprang up Sunday and blew her to an embarrassing 79.

"I just had no energy down the stretch," Rizzo said. "I just didn't have the spark to fight back. I was guessing all day with the wind and never seemed to guess right."

Will won it with her putter. She made a par-saving 15-footer at No. 9, a 12-footer on No. 11 for another par and a knee-knocking six-footer on No. 17 for par.

The $60,000 winner's check was more than double what Will had earned since joining the Tour in October, 1988. More importantly, it gave her a five-year exemption.

Circle K Tucson Open—$300,000
Winner: Colleen Walker

To relax and work on her concentration, Colleen Walker listens to tapes that feature marine sounds, such as the beep of dolphins. But in the third round of the Circle K Tucson Open, she was hearing different sounds. Tweet-tweet, as in birdies.

Walker ran off six birdies in a seven-hole stretch on the way to a 65 and waltzed home on Sunday with a 72 for her first victory since 1988. Finishing second, five strokes behind, was the foursome of Pat Bradley, Betsy King, Kate Rogerson and Heather Drew.

Sporting a new streamlined look through diet and exercise, Walker was just one in the pack of six in pursuit of halfway leader Nancy Rubin as she made the turn on Saturday at Randolph Park Golf and Country Club. Then, she birdied No. 11 and, beginning at No. 13, ran off five straight birdies for an incoming five-under 32 and a stunning 65.

That gave her a five-stroke lead over Ayako Okamoto. For all practical purposes, the tournament was over. Just to make sure, however, Walker opened the final round with back-to-back birdies and said "catch-me-if-you-can." Nobody could.

Standard Register Turquoise Classic—$500,000
Winner: Pat Bradley

Give Pat Bradley a 10-shot lead after three rounds and she can turn the fourth into a suspenseful afternoon as she did in finally winning the Oldsmobile Classic early in the year.

But give her a one-shot lead and nobody grinds it better, as she did in winning the Standard Register Turquoise Classic at Moon Valley Country Club in Phoenix.

With her one-stroke victory over Ayako Okamoto, Bradley became the first two-time winner of this event. And a whole lot more.

The $75,000 first prize pushed her career earnings over $3 million, the first LPGA player to surpass that lofty milestone. The victory also moved her one step closer to her ultimate goal—the LPGA Hall of Fame. It was Bradley's 25th victory, including six majors, leaving her five short of induction.

"In my heart, I'm a Hall-of-Famer already," Bradley said. "But in my mind, it says five more. But I've got plenty of time. That last victory might be the killer, but I honestly think the next four are going to come along all right."

Bradley opened with rounds of 70-71 and trailed Rosie Jones by two strokes, but she started fast on Saturday—her 39th birthday—on the way to a 68 and the one-shot lead over Okamoto that she would guard throughout Sunday's final round.

"This represents 17 years of blood, sweat and tears," said Bradley, discussing her latest milestone, the $3 million mark. "It tells me all the determination and perseverance paid off. And it tells me the LPGA is getting stronger."

Nabisco Dinah Shore—$600,000
Winner: Betsy King

To all those who bugged Betsy King the first week of the season about her slow start, she finally came up with the right answer in the Nabisco Dinah Shore.

That answer was "nothing," as 1989's Player of the Year who took the tournament lead with a second-round 70, built it to five strokes after 54 holes and held on to win by two over Shirley Furlong and Kathy Postlewait despite a final-round 75.

It was her 21st LPGA victory, third major title and she became only the fourth player to have won the Dinah Shore event twice. It also hushed talk that she was in danger of joining Alice Miller (1985), Pat Bradley (1986) and Jane Geddes (1987) as disappearing acts following dominating seasons.

"I know I had a slow start," said King, who won six times and $600,000 in 1989. "But we're only talking about eight weeks. I wasn't worried. It wasn't time to change anything."

Almost as newsworthy as King's victory was Nancy Lopez's failure. Lopez shot an opening 80 and didn't make the cut, the first time that had happened in a major championship in her career.

King patiently shot an opening 69 to trail Lenore Rittenhouse by two shots, took the halfway lead by four over Rosie Jones and Laurie Rinker and strengthened her grip with another 69 on Saturday.

When play began Sunday, there was no sign of a King collapse. She still led Postlewait by five after 11 holes, but then began to stagger. She bunkered her approach at No. 12 and bogeyed; pushed drives at Nos. 13 and 15 for two more and then three-putted the 16th. But Postlewait was unable to take advantage.

"Sometimes when you're trying to make pars, that's the hardest score to make," King said. "You better believe I was concerned. Nobody had to tell me what was happening."

Frustrating was how Postlewait described her inability to make up ground. "She's making bogeys and I kept missing greens. I had a chance to put some heat on her and didn't."

As it turned out, King had just enough margin to play with and when it was gone, she played like the real Betsy King. She parred the final two holes, and while it wasn't pretty, it got the job done.

"I almost didn't make it," said King, who finished the 72 holes at five-under-par 283. "Playing with a big lead is tough. Make one mistake and things tend to snowball."

Red Robin Kyocera Inamori Classic—$300,000
Winner: Kris Monaghan

The old professional golf adage that you win when it's your turn to win finally fell into the slot belonging to 29-year-old Kris Monaghan, who came out of the pack with a final-round 67 to win the Red Robin Inamori Classic at StoneRidge Country Club in Poway, California.

Heading into the event, Monaghan had little to show for her five years on the LPGA Tour. She had never won more than $21,937 in a single season and had never finished higher than fourth anywhere. Whenever her name was mentioned, talk usually turned not to her game, but her health, physically and financially. Neither one were in very good shape. She had reconstructive knee surgery in 1987, which is bad for your game, and she sponsored herself, which is bad for your nerves.

Now, apparently the knee was fine and after collecting the $45,000 winner's share of the $300,000 purse, so was her bank account.

"No one will ever know how much this means to me," said Monaghan, her voice breaking with emotion. "I've struggled with money since I've been out here. All of a sudden, I won't have to be worrying about it."

Monaghan was four shots from the lead heading to the final round, which figured to be a battle between the leader Nancy Brown, Missie McGeorge, who was one back, and Cathy Gerring, also four behind. But Brown did another one of her disappearing acts (76) to tie for seventh, while Monaghan sped through the field with a front nine 31 and eventually finished two in front of Gerring.

Sara Lee Classic—$425,000
Winner: Ayako Okamoto

Welcome back, ladies. Those were the working words as the LPGA came to Nashville, Tennessee, for the Sara Lee Classic following a three-week vacation.

Only thing was, when the week was over Pat Bradley was left singing the blues. With victory in hand—a three-shot lead on the back nine—Bradley bogeyed three straight holes and opened the door for Ayako Okamoto to win her first event of 1990.

Okamoto, who started the final round five shots from Bradley's lead, finished with a 68 and 210 total, one in front of a handful of others: Bradley, Betsy King, Colleen Walker, JoAnne Carner and Dawn Coe.

It was payback time for Okamoto, who missed a short birdie putt in Phoenix that would have tied Bradley. This time, it was Bradley, whose birdie putt at No. 15 spun back in her face denying her a shot at a playoff.

"It never should have come down to that one putt," Bradley said. "But I made a couple of mistakes and couldn't get anything to fall. Just wasn't my day."

Coe, playing in the last group with Bradley, was the only other player with a chance to catch Okamoto, who posted her six-under-par 210 total an hour ahead of the leaders. A par at the final hole would have put her in a playoff, but she missed the green and finally a 10-footer.

"On this Tour, you never know what will happen from one day to the next," Okamoto said. "I thought Pat would win easily. It's a surprise that she didn't. But a happy surprise for me."

Crestar Classic—$350,000
Winner: Dottie Mochrie

With a little insistence from her friends, Dottie Mochrie entered the Crestar Classic for the first time in 1990. She'll need no such urging in the future after shooting rounds of 67-65-68—200 and a nine-stroke victory at Greenbrier Country Club in Chesapeake, Virginia.

Mochrie was having one of those blah years before hitting her stride in the Crestar—only $44,000 in earnings, one top-10 finish and a small torn rotator cuff in her left shoulder.

But she was on target from the get-go in the Crestar, becoming the LPGA's first wire-to-wire winner of the season. She led by two over Rosie Jones, Deedee Lasker and Kathy Guadagnino after one round and by seven over Jones after two.

The former Furman University All-American had only 27 putts in the first round, 23 in her course-record setting 65 second and left no doubt this one was her's with a birdie-par-birdie start in round three. Her 16-under total was a tournament record, her margin of victory four better than anyone in 1990 and five better than the previous Crestar record.

"I don't remember ever shooting under 70 in all three rounds of a tournament," Mochrie said. "I guess when it's going good even the bad shots come out good."

Planters Pat Bradley International—$400,000
Winner: Cindy Rarick

Another LPGA tournament bit the dust when the Planters Pat Bradley International lost its sponsor, RJR Nabisco, but not before Cindy Rarick put an exclamation point to this Stableford-format event.

Rarick did it the old-fashioned way, with patience, steadily climbing the leaderboard each day. She opened with three points on Thursday, eight behind Martha Nause; picked up four more on Friday, but was still eight behind second-round leader Deb Richard. She reached the top on Saturday, adding 12 points, then held on Sunday under the rush of Beth Daniel and Hollis Stacy and won by one point.

"I know a lot of the players don't like this format, but I love it; I hate to see it end," said Rarick, who won $60,000. "It's different, but you still have to play golf, still have to make the shots."

This was a more purposeful Rarick than the old version. During the LPGA's spring break, she visited sports psychologist Chuck Denton, who made Rarick realize she had no goals. "Before I was just out there playing and hoping," she said. "What Chuck wanted me to do was to think about coming up No. 18 with a lead, visualize accepting the trophy. Positive thoughts. They worked this week."

Rarick did have her anxious moments. At the turn on Sunday, Stacy had moved into a tie and Daniel was only one birdie away from making it a threesome. Then Rarick turned it on. She made an easy birdie at No. 13 before hitting what she called a "career shot" with a three wood from a bad lie to within five feet for another birdie at No. 14.

Both Stacy and Daniel had a shot at sending things into sudden death with birdies at No. 18, but neither reached the hole with their putts.

Corning Classic—$350,000
Winner: Pat Bradley

As she stood on the 18th green late Sunday afternoon with a check for $52,500 in one hand and the Corning (New York) Classic championship Steuben glass bowl glistening on a table before her Pat Bradley exclaimed joyously, "Who gives a damn about the Skins Game?"

She did initially, after being passed over as a participant. But another LPGA victory moved her one step, four tournament victories, closer to her ultimate goal, the LPGA Hall of Fame. "It's what motivates me," she said. "It's given me new desires and new excitement to reach the Hall of Fame."

By winning her third tournament of the year and becoming the leading money winner, Bradley had 26 victories in her 16-year career.

Bradley opened with solid rounds of 69-70 before storming into the lead Saturday with a five-under 66 that included seven birdies. That put her four in front of Patty Sheehan. It was Bradley all the way Sunday with five birdies more than off-setting her three bogeys.

When it was over, Bradley wouldn't say whether she would have skipped the Corning Classic to play in the Skins Game, had she been invited. "I wasn't asked to play, but my concern was that I was in the right place at the right time and that's all I care about," she said.

Lady Keystone Open—$300,000
Winner: Cathy Gerring

For once, it was Cathy Gerring's turn. When Gerring two-putted from 25 feet on the final hole to win the Lady Keystone Open at Hershey (Pennsylvania) Country Club, she exorcised some ghosts at the same time.

A loser three times previously in playoffs, Gerring picked up her first LPGA victory and $45,000 with a steady final-round 71, good for an eight-under-par 208 and a one-stroke victory over Pat Bradley and Elaine Crosby.

The victory made up for playoff losses to Jane Geddes in the 1987 Women's Kemper Open, to Betsy King in the 1986 Rail Charity and to Ai-Yu Tu in the 1986 Japan Mazda Classic.

After months of struggling with her game and coping with infant son Zachary's ear infection, the step into victory lane was very sweet indeed.

"I felt all week it was my tournament to win and I played like that all week," said Gerring, who is married to professional Jim Gerring of Muirfield Village Golf Club in Dublin, Ohio.

Gerring opened with a 70, took control with a middle-round 67 and led throughout her final round of 71. Bradley made a run with birdies at Nos. 13, 14, 16 and 17 to reach seven under par, but could only par the 18th.

"I didn't fall back enough today for anyone to catch me," Gerring said. "The times I've lost, I really never felt like I lost them, but I was beaten. Today, I felt like I finally found the heart to win."

Coming up short didn't bother Bradley, who saluted Gerring's victory. "It was Cathy's week and she handled it well," Bradley said. "She's put in her time."

McDonald's Championship—$650,000
Winner: Patty Sheehan

A funny thing happened to Patty Sheehan in last week's Lady Keystone Open. She didn't get to play. Seems she forgot to enter.

No big deal. Sheehan takes the week off, becomes an accidental tourist doing a little antique shopping and shows up in Wilmington, Delaware, at the McDonald's Championship rested and rarin' to go. Which she did. All the way to victory circle.

Against one of the best fields of the year—49 of the top 50 money winners—Sheehan shot rounds of 70-67-68-70—275 and won by a whopping four strokes over Kristi Abers, Betsy King, Keystone winner Cathy Gerring and Ayako Okamoto.

"I was disappointed with myself for forgetting to enter, but I think it made me more determined to play well this week because everyone was giving me the business," Sheehan said. "I just told myself, 'Go out and make yourself proud of yourself.'"

Which she did. Sheehan lingered just off the lead the first two rounds, then took a two-shot lead in round three with a 67 and fought off Okamoto over the final nine holes.

"It wasn't the most brilliant golf of my career, but I can't think of a tournament where I was so steady," she said of her four sub-par rounds that included 12 birdies and three bogeys. "It was a perseverance kind of tournament."

Though it was her first McDonald's victory at DuPont Country Club—she won in 1984 at White Manor—her scoring average coming in was 69.8 and she had finished among the top 10 three times. One of those was a bitter second place in 1988 when she shot a final-round 74 and lost in a playoff to Kathy Postlewait.

"This was payback time, not to the course, just to me," Sheehan said.

Atlantic City Classic—$300,000
Winner: Chris Johnson

Chris Johnson isn't one of the LPGA's marque names, but when she's on her game she can score with the best of them. Take the Atlantic City Classic, for instance, where she shot rounds of 69-67-69-70—275 and beat the likes of Nancy Lopez, Juli Inkster, Beth Daniel and Ayako Okamoto.

A four-time career winner, who finished eighth on the LPGA money list in both 1986 and 1987, the lanky and perpetually cheerful Johnson hadn't won in three years and admitted to battling personal problems, including a divorce, and shaky self-confidence. But she had worked all year on improving her attitude and came here—where she tied for second in 1989—ready to end her slump.

Johnson wasted little time in reasserting herself once the tournament began. A first-round 69 left her three behind Liselotte Neumann, a second-round 67 tied her with Sherri Steinhauer with Lopez, Daniel and Okamoto just three back, bringing predictions that Saturday would see a move by one of those big three.

Instead it was Pamela Wright who lit up the scoreboard. The LPGA's rookie of the year in 1989 shot a six-under-par 64 and moved into a tie with Johnson (69) and Dale Eggling (67). Lopez kept pace with 67, but Okamoto faded with a 70 and Daniel shot 75 to disappear altogether.

By the time the tournament headed to the back nine on Sunday, it was a two-player race, Johnson and Wright. Eggling missed 10 of the first 11 greens and was five over par. The turning point came at No. 11, where Johnson made birdie and Wright, a bogey. She then sealed the victory with a birdie at No. 17.

With the victory came the feeling that she was not a lucky player, rather a good one. "Now that I'm over the feeling that winning was an accident, the next step is believing this won't be the last time."

Rochester International—$400,000
Winner: Patty Sheehan

There are times when Patty Sheehan enters a tournament that she just knows she might win. The Rochester (New York) International was one of them, and never one to go against her feelings, Sheehan buried the field with rounds of 72-64-68-67 and won by four strokes over Amy Alcott with Nancy Lopez in third, five behind.

In winning, not only did Sheehan successfully defend her title, but returned a score of 271, 17 under par, shattering the tournament record by five shots.

"I felt all week I was going to be in the hunt," Sheehan said. "I've been playing so well that my confidence is soaring. I can't wait to get to the golf course every day."

This was a typical Sheehan victory. There was the ho-hum 72 start, then the course-record tying 64, which left her two shots behind Alcott, who had played the first 36 holes in a tournament record 10-under 134. Each shot 68 on Saturday, then after just hanging around on the front, Sheehan stormed Locust Hill's back nine in five-under 32 and left the rest of the field behind.

"All I can say is that I ran into a buzz-saw today," Alcott said. "I had a three-shot lead at the turn, then all of a sudden Patty kicked on the afterburner."

The mental turning point Sheehan needed came at No. 9 where a photographer distracted Sheehan and she made bogey. She got angry—"the kick in the butt I needed" is how she put it. From there, she birdied Nos. 10, 11 and took the lead for good at No. 13.

The physical turning point came at No. 15 where Sheehan made birdie and

Alcott bogey after she shanked one into the gallery and was lucky to make bogey.

"I felt bad for her," Sheehan said of Alcott. "But I wasn't about to let her back in the tournament."

du Maurier Ltd. Classic—$600,000
Winner: Cathy Johnson

Buzz-saws have no loyalty. A week ago, it was in the hands of Patty Sheehan as she left the field in her wake at the Rochester International. This week, Sheehan ran into one of her own, wielded by little-known Cathy Johnson, who is little-known no longer after making her first LPGA victory the major kind, the du Maurier Classic.

Entering the du Maurier, the 26-year-old Johnson stood 73rd on the money list, hadn't finished higher than eighth place and was in 62nd position the week before looking up at Sheehan's victory. All Johnson did in the season's second major was lead wire-to-wire and stare down Sheehan when things got a little sticky on the back side on Sunday afternoon.

Johnson was quick out of the starting gate with a 65, but excited few in the process. Unknowns do this all the time in majors. Wait until Sunday.

When Sunday came, Johnson was still there, with a pair of 70s leaving her four up on Sheehan and Patti Rizzo. Most experts figured she would crack going head-to-head with Sheehan, who had two victories and a second in her last three tournaments. It was Sheehan, however, who blinked first.

After falling one behind to Sheehan at No. 10, Johnson birdied No. 14, and Sheehan bogeyed. She birdied No. 15 for a three-stroke lead, gave one back to Sheehan's birdie at No. 17, then got up and down for par at No. 18.

"It was my turn to run into a buzz-saw," Sheehan said. "Cathy played brilliantly and won it. I didn't lose it. I can't complain."

The victory was worth $90,000 to Johnson, triple her 1990 earnings.

"Whew, that was hard work," Johnson said. "I just don't see how these people win 20 tournaments in a career. But I don't see myself as a one-time-only winner. I might have thought so last year, but now I'm playing too well."

Jamie Farr Toledo Classic—$325,000
Winner: Tina Purtzer

Last week it was non-winner Cathy Johnson getting the best of Patty Sheehan. It must be catching. A week later Tina Purtzer found herself sandwiched between Betsy King and JoAnne Carner going to the final round of the Jamie Farr Classic and slipped out a winner.

Purtzer, sister-in-law of the PGA Tour's Tom, was undaunted in such company, shooting a final-round 66 to beat Carner and Chris Johnson by four, while King slipped to 73 and tied for fourth.

She shot 67-72 before her career-best 66 and became the LPGA's sixth first-time winner in 1990. More importantly, she's no longer just Tom Purtzer's sister-in-law.

"I feel wonderful, ecstatic, elated, all those things and more," Purtzer said, holding the winner's check for $48,750, almost double her career earnings. "I still can't believe it happened."

Purtzer and Carner shared the first-round lead, but it was Carner who won the acclaim after posting her best opening round of the season and chasing her 43rd title. She had won more events than Purtzer had played in, the Jamie Farr being being's Purtzer's 39th LPGA event.

Besides the lead, the two shared the same birthday (April 4) and both attended Arizona State.

Purtzer started the final round the way first-time winners need to start, fast. She birdied the first two holes, then the fourth, fifth and sixth, the latter from 70 feet, to turn in 29 and never trailed as Carner and King fell six strokes back.

When it appeared her nerves were showing after a double bogey at No. 11, she birdied No. 12, then closed out her first victory with six straight pars.

U.S. Women's Open—$500,000
Winner: Betsy King

Just as Arnold Palmer hasn't won a PGA Championship and Sam Snead never won a U.S. Open, it seems as if fate has determined that Patty Sheehan will be denied a U.S. Women's Open title.

Consider that in the last three years, Sheehan was in position to win all of them and came up empty. In 1988, she finished second to Liselotte Neumann at Baltimore Country Club; in 1989, she tied for 17th after holding a share of the third-round lead with Betsy King, who did win.

And in 1990, the cruelest blow of all. Midway through her third round on a rain-forced 36-hole final, the 33-year-old Sheehan had nine shots on the field, 11 on King and showed no indication that she was about to lose the crown she covets the most. But she did, playing her final 27 holes in eight over par, and there to pick up the pieces of her broken heart was King.

King, on the other hand, got stronger as the day progressed and passed Sheehan with a birdie on No. 11, then held off Sheehan by grinding her way to the clubhouse with six straight pars.

King collected $85,000, the biggest paycheck of her career and became only the fifth player, the first since Hollis Stacy in 1977-78 to win back-to-back Women's Opens. But the outcome left her almost speechless.

"I'm surprised," King said. "I didn't think there was a chance Patty would lose."

The outcome left Sheehan in tears. That's what most of the television audience saw when ABC showed little feeling for someone's feelings and wanted to know what happened even before Sheehan had figured it out herself.

"It hurts a lot," Sheehan told ABC. And later, "I won't be able to forget this."

If you think the conclusion was weird, it was just the continuation of a weird week. The players, high profile and small, complained that the Atlanta Athletic Club Riverside course was not up to snuff as a U.S. Open course. The fairways too wide, the greens too slow. In a word, boring.

Then, there was the weather. Hot, humid and enough rain delays to keep away whatever fans might have shown up. The first round was completed on Friday with Sheehan and Jane Geddes tied at 66. The second round was a disaster. When it was finally halted at 8:30 p.m., 54 players had completed their rounds, 18 hadn't teed off and 84 were scattered about.

Out of such circumstances come Open champions. King was able to complete her round, while darkness caught Sheehan, who had moved to seven under par, and Colleen Walker, who birdied the first three to get to six under, at No. 4. The decision was made that the second round would be completed Saturday and a 36-hole finish for Sunday.

What that did was give King and others a day off, while Sheehan would play 14 holes on Saturday and 36 on Sunday. Fatigue more than pressure could have been Sheehan's undoing.

"Two rounds was too much for us," said Sheehan's caddy, John Killeen. "I was doing a rain dance, hoping we would go to Monday."

Sheehan completed the second round with 68 and was at 10 under par, the first time either man or woman had reached that figure in an Open. She led Geddes by six strokes and King by eight. She stretched those leads to eight and 10 by the turn, then like a long distance runner ran into a wall. She missed eight of her final 13 greens in the morning round, the killing one a fat four-iron shot into the lake at No. 18, which resulted in a double bogey and 75. Her lead was now four over Mary Murphy and five over King.

For all practical purposes, it was over at the ninth hole. King picked up three strokes with two birdies of her own at Nos. 3 and 4 and a Sheehan bogey on No. 2. It was even after Sheehan bogeyed Nos. 6 and 8 and King led by two when about the same moment she birdied No. 11, Sheehan three-putted No. 9. King had erased an 11-shot deficit.

"Playing 36 worked against her," King said.

"It hurts to know that all I had to do was play my game and I would have won," Sheehan said of her Sunday rounds of 75-76. Then quietly, she added, "I know I'm going to win a U.S. Open some day. It just isn't going to be this year."

Phar-Mor Youngstown Classic—$400,000
Winner: Beth Daniel

It is said that if you fall off a horse, the best thing to do is get up on another one. So Patty Sheehan dusted off her britches from her fall in Atlanta and headed to Vienna, Ohio for the Phar-Mor Youngstown Classic.

She fell again. And lost to Beth Daniel in a playoff in the $400,000 tournament that also offered $200,000 in bonus money from Phar-Mor as part of their package which included the Phar-Mor Classic in Florida.

And like Atlanta, Sheehan had an extra day to think about it as rain forced the tournament to a Monday conclusion. Daniel led the first round with a 65, two ahead of Danielle Ammaccapane and Dottie Mochrie. She was two up after two over Debbie Massey, Nancy Brown and Ammaccapane. Sheehan was three back.

Sheehan moved briefly ahead in the third round, but when she bogeyed the 17th and Daniel, playing two groups behind, birdied the 16th, they were tied. The playoff began at the 16th. Daniel birdied it again and Sheehan two-putted for par. End of game.

"I had my chances, but second is better than third," Sheehan said. "I'm proud of the way I played. After what happened in Atlanta, it was tough to come here and even tee it up."

With her victory, Daniel had won seven tournaments since August of 1989, plus one in Japan.

"The biggest thing is I'm putting better," said Daniel, who ended a four-year winless drought in the Greater Washington Open. "I'm making those 10-footers for par. And I'm not hitting as many bad shots."

The result is consistency. In 1988, Daniel finished in the top 10 in 20 of 25 tournaments. In 1990, she had 11 top tens in her first 15 events.

Mazda LPGA Championship—$1,000,000
Winner: Beth Daniel

For all her ability, tournament victories and money won, Beth Daniel still came up short in one category. Number of major championships won. That figure was none. Now it's one with her come-from-behind victory in the LPGA Championship at Bethesda (Maryland) Country Club.

"In order to be considered a great player, you have to win major championships," Daniel said. "It shows you can play your best golf under the most pressure. Winning a major was my No. 1 goal starting the year."

Daniel finally played her best golf under the most pressure, shooting a final-round 66 to beat Rosie Jones by one shot.

Daniel had been close before. She lost a final-round shootout to Pat Bradley in the 1981 Women's Open. Sandra Haynie made an 18-footer on the 72nd hole to beat her in the 1982 Peter Jackson and she blew 54-hole leads at both the 1982 Women's Open and 1983 Nabisco Dinah Shore.

"I've been second in all the majors," she said. "I can really appreciate this."

The performance of Jones also had to be appreciated. Winless since the 1988 Santa Barbara Open, the 30-year-old hung near the lead for most of the week, and if not for a disastrous quadruple bogey at her 34th hole, might have turned the tournament into a runaway.

She led by as many as three shots during the final round and nearly forced a playoff when her 40-foot try for a tying birdie on the final green hit the lip and spun out.

Chris Johnson was the early pacesetter with a 67, two ahead over five players. Sue Ertle came to the front on Saturday with a 67 of her own, giving her a two-stroke lead over Jones.

Jones was cruising with a five-shot lead when she reached the par-three, 195-yard 16th. She pushed a four-wood tee shot into the right bunker, skulled her second across the green into another bunker, where it nestled against the back lip. She thinned her third back across the green, flubbed her fourth, chipped seven feet short with her fifth and two-putted.

Jones took the third-round lead with another 70 and led Daniel by three. Her lead was two after seven before she began to stumble: A three-putt bogey at No. 8, shaky pars at Nos. 9 and 10, a missed four-footer for another bogey at No. 11. Ahead Daniel was making birdies at Nos. 12 and 13 to move two ahead, but gave one back with a bogey at No. 14, setting up the final hole dramatics of Jones.

Jones curled a 15-footer around the hole at No. 16 but it stayed on the lip, and her 40-footer at No. 18 looked good all the way. So good, in fact, she started a Hale Irwin-style jaunt around the green. But the ball hit the lip and spun out.

"I thought it was good all the way," Daniel said. "Even when they showed the replay, I thought it was going to be good."

Boston Five Classic—$350,000
Winner: Barb Mucha

There are times when the least expectations produce the greatest achievements. Just witness Barb Mucha, who, pleading exhaustion, had to be coaxed into entering the Boston Five Classic, then won it.

Mucha's steady rounds of 71-70-67-69—277 got her into a playoff with Lenore Rittenhouse, then her seven iron to within five feet of the hole for a resulting birdie earned the Ohioan her first LPGA victory.

After collecting her $52,500 winner's share of the purse, Mucha made good on a promise to jump into a lake if she won. She needed some prodding to make good on that promise and got a shove in the back from her scorekeeper.

"All in all, it's been a great week," said the 28-year-old Mucha. "At the beginning of the week, I just wanted to enjoy myself and when I went out with the lead on Sunday, I had the same thought. 'What a great position. Let's enjoy this.'"

If Mucha had her way she would have been miles away from the Tara Ferncroft Country Club on Sunday afternoon. She had played six straight weeks and had decided to withdraw. Friends she had planned to stay with talked her out of it, however.

After two rounds, Mucha was three behind Ellie Gibson, but she shot a bogey-free 67 on Saturday to move one in front of Laura Baugh. Only three behind were Amy Alcott and Pat Bradley. None of them were a factor on Sunday. Rittenhouse, with a finishing 65, caught Mucha on the final hole.

It was over quickly after Mucha's seven iron and dead-center putt.

"I guess this victory is going to make my years on tour more successful and that much more fun," Mucha said. "No matter what happens from here, I'll always know I won out here."

Stratton Mountain Classic—$450,000
Winner: Cathy Gerring

The Stratton Mountain Classic was Cathy Gerring's second victory of the year to go with the Lady Keystone in June. The $67,500 first-place check was nice, but it was the title that most interested the 29-year-old working mother of two-year-old Zachary. With it, she became the first player outside of the Big Four of Beth Daniel, Patty Sheehan, Pat Bradley and Betsy King to win twice this season.

Gerring proved to be just what the tournament needed. It was short on marque names and she helped give the event a most dramatic conclusion.

Entering the final round, Amy Benz and Karen Davies led at 211, but 10 others were within three shots, including Gerring, Rosie Jones and Donna White. When the field turned for home, it was a two-women race—Gerring and local favorite Caroline Keggi. Gerring led by one going to No. 18, but Keggi made a 20-footer there to send the tournament into a playoff.

They went back to the 18th tee and when Gerring drove into the right rough followed by Keggi's perfect drive, it appeared it was over. But Gerring hit a low-running hook that bounced up the hill and onto the green within three feet of the hole. Keggi missed right and chipped to a foot, but she never got a chance to putt. Gerring knocked her putt dead center.

JAL Big Apple Classic—$400,000
Winner: Betsy King

When Betsy King has her A-game going, it causes most players to roll their eyes back, sigh and wonder which of them is going to finish second. Because when King is on, nobody does it better.

Take the JAL Big Apple Classic at tough, old Wykagyl Country Club, for instance. After opening with a 75, seven behind Tammie Green, King played the next 54 holes in 18 under par and lapped the field, winning by three over Beth Daniel.

King started her run modestly with a second-round five-under-par 67, but was still five behind Green. Then came the field killer—a 63 that not only was the best round of her career, but broke Nancy Lopez's course record by two shots. That gave her a three-shot lead over Daniel and the rest of the field melted away.

During the week, King missed only one putt inside five feet and holed at least 18 beyond that distance. Then, as if to add insult to injury, she hit a metal wood down-wind second shot 250 yards to within eight feet on the par-five 18th, made her eagle three and left Daniel open-mouthed.

"I played one of the best tournaments of my life and got drilled," said Daniel, who shot rounds of 70-70-68-68. "Betsy was just outstanding."

King has had a 63 before, in the 1986 Rail Classic, but "there's no doubt this is the best round of my career," she said following her nine-birdie, no bogey round on Saturday. "And I don't think I've ever putted this well. This was one to remember."

Northgate Classic—$375,000
Winner: Beth Daniel

Figuring she had played well enough to win the week before when Betsy King did, Beth Daniel came to the Twin Cities of St. Paul-Minneapolis confident she could take the Northgate Classic. She did.

With rounds of 66-69-68—203, 13 under par around Edinburgh USA Golf Club, Daniel won for the fifth time in 1990 and for the third time in her last four tournaments.

And this might have been the easiest one. After trailing first-round leader Barb Bunkowsky by one, Daniel began to sprint away from the field in the second round and never looked back in the third round to win by six strokes over Chris Johnson and Penny Hammel.

This was like old home week for Daniel. She won her first LPGA event at St. Paul's Keller Golf Club in 1979 sitting in the clubhouse after the fourth round was rained out. In 1980, she won again on the way to Player of the Year honors.

"I've played awfully good golf for two years now," said Daniel, who won $56,250 in her 15th event and reached the $600,000 plateau faster than any player in LPGA history. "Last year was my best year (four victories in the last six tournaments) and this year has surpassed that. It's pretty remarkable."

Perhaps Bunkowsky said it best about Daniel: "She plays a totally different game than the rest of us. Think about it. If Betsy doesn't shoot 63 last week in New York, Beth probably wins that one, too. She's just amazing. I wouldn't be surprised if she won next week, too."

Rail Charity Classic—$300,000
Winner: Beth Daniel

Guess what? Beth Daniel won another one. Almost like she won the last one.

Riding her own personal rail, Daniel put together rounds of 67-69-67 for her second straight 13-under-par 203 and won her second consecutive Rail Classic, this time by three over Susan Sanders.

It was her sixth victory of the year, her fourth in the last five tournaments, and boosted her single season record earnings to $658,782, breaking Betsy King's mark of $654,132 set last year. Daniel's streak included shooting 38 under par for her last three tournaments.

Daniel trailed Judy Dickinson by one after the first round, was tied with Martha Nause after two, then put the field away early on the second nine in this only Monday finish on the LPGA Tour. Among those she left in her wake was King, who was only two strokes back with a round to go. But King quadrupled No. 7 in the final round and eventually finished nine shots back.

Unlike the previous tournaments, Daniel wasn't the only one making birdies by the bunches. There were 48 sub-70 scores in the three rounds. "I really didn't play that well this week," Daniel said. "But there's so much margin for error on this golf course. You can get away with murder. That's why the scores are always so low here. You don't have to hit it that well, just putt well."

Ping Cellular One Championship—$350,000
Winner: Patty Sheehan

With Beth Daniel taking the week off, the rest of the LPGA Tour breathed a sigh of relief. Especially Patty Sheehan, who, in winning the Ping Cellular

One Championship, ended almost two months of pain that came from losing the U.S. Open.

"Now, I don't have to think about the Open all winter," said Sheehan, who shot rounds of 70-71-67—208 for a one-stroke victory over Danielle Ammaccapane. "I can put it in the past."

It wasn't easy, however, not until she sank a 20-foot birdie putt on the final hole to break a deadlock with Ammaccapane, who finished earlier in the day with a course-record 64.

The victory was the 24th of Sheehan's career and her fourth this year, raising her season earnings to $595,751, just $63,031 behind Daniel.

Sheehan didn't take the lead until well into the third round. She trailed first-round leader Dottie Mochrie's 68 by three and entered the third round three behind Pat Bradley. But Bradley bogeyed the 17th on Sunday and Sheehan charged through the pack with a back-nine 31.

The victory was special in another way for Sheehan. It came on her father's 68th birthday. Before teeing off in the final round, she'd set a goal of shooting his age. "If I'd done that, I would have had to go into a playoff," Sheehan said. "I think he'll forgive me."

Safeco Classic—$350,000
Winner: Patty Sheehan

It just doesn't pay to take a week off on the LPGA Tour. Beth Daniel did after winning two straight and Patty Sheehan took advantage to win in Portland. Daniel was back for the Safeco Classic, but Sheehan picked up right where she left off the week before and ran away with the $350,000 tournament.

Sheehan was never out of the lead. She opened with a 69 to tie with Daniel and Dale Eggeling, shot 65 on Friday to lead by one stroke over Sherri Steinhauer, who had 64; shot 66 Saturday to increase her lead to 10 strokes, then closed with a 70 for a nine-stroke victory over Deb Richard.

With such a large lead going into the final round, Sheehan motivated herself in the chase for a couple of records—lowest-72-hole score of 268 and margin of victory, 14 strokes. She came up short but did throw the Player of the Year race into turmoil. Her $45,000 winner's share of the purse left Sheehan only $21,000 behind Daniel, who tied for 24th and won $2,796.

"Sure, I think I can catch Beth," said Sheehan, who then announced she was going to take a couple of weeks off.

MBS Classic—$325,000
Winner: Nancy Lopez

Just when it appeared 1990 would pass without the name of Nancy Lopez being engraved on some tournament's trophy, the full-time mother-wife and part-time golfer showed she still had the right stuff.

It came in the MBS Classic at Los Coyotes Country Club in Buena Park, California, where she put together rounds of 69-70-74-68—281 and a birdie-three on the first hole of a playoff to deny Cathy Gerring her third victory of the year.

It was the 43rd career victory for the Hall-of-Famer, but her first since she won this same event in 1989. She collected $48,750, but the money was secondary to the victory. "I'm sure Ray will find something to do with the money," she said of husband Ray Knight. "But winning. That's for me. I'd almost forgotten what this feels like."

It had been a long year for Lopez. She had finished second in the year's third event, but had only two top-10 finishes since and was 16th on the money list. Part of the problem was poor putting, unlike Lopez, and the remainder was a series of family-related problems. There was her miscarriage before the season began, followed by Knight's father having a stroke, then his mother suffering a broken hip in a fall.

"I just haven't been mentally here this year," Lopez said.

But she was all there this week. She trailed by one after the first round, shared the halfway lead with Caroline Keggi and Jill Briles, fell six behind Keggi after a third-round 74, then charged to the front with a final-round 68, while Keggi slumped to 75.

"I thought I could win after the first two rounds, then was kind of down going to the last round," Lopez said. "Winning? I'm ecstatic."

Centel Classic—$1,000,000
Winner: Beth Daniel

Put up a million dollar purse, throw in the best field of the year, add a generous helping of suspense and the result is a golf fan's delicacy. As in down-to-the-wire between Nancy Lopez, who has nothing else to prove, and Beth Daniel, who finally has played like the experts always thought she would, but seldom had.

And the winner is ... Beth Daniel. Again.

Victory No. 7 of 1990 came in the $1 million Centel Classic, once a nondescript PGA Tour stop in Florida's panhandle at Killearn Country Club in Tallahassee.

What's more, it gave her a sweep of the LPGA's million-dollar events. In July, she won the Mazda LPGA Championship, her first major title. The $150,000 winner's share of the Centel purse lifted Daniel's official earnings to an increasing record $811,578. More importantly, the victory increased her lead to seven points over Patty Sheehan in the LPGA Rolex Player of the Year standings.

Daniel shot rounds of 71-63-68-69—271, 17 under par. But her victory wasn't assured until Lopez uncharacteristically three-putted from 20 feet on the final hole.

Cathy Gerring led the first round with a 63, but played horribly in a second round of 78 and gave way to Sheehan's 65. She was at 132, two strokes ahead of Daniel, who rebounded from an opening 71 with a 63. The anticipated head-to-head duel between Daniel and Sheehan fizzled on Saturday, however, when Sheehan collapsed with 74.

It became a Daniel-Lopez sprint over the final three holes. Lopez cut it to two with a birdie at No. 16, drew even with another birdie at No. 17 after Daniel three-putted from 14 feet for bogey, then gave it back with the deciding bogey at No. 18.

"I think I was more surprised than Nancy when she missed that last putt," Daniel said. "It's been a phenomenal year, even if I don't win the Player of the Year. I have a lot of other things to draw from; my first major, seven victories."

Trophee Urban World Championship—$325,000
Winner: Cathy Gerring

All year Cathy Gerring had threatened to break through as one of the LPGA's brightest new stars. She did just that in Cely, France, with a wire-to-wire victory in the Trophee Urban World Championship of Women's Golf.

Gerring wasn't the only winner. By finishing second, Beth Daniel clinched at least a tie for Rolex Player of the Year, making a trip to Japan for the season finale unnecessary.

The victory was Gerring's third of the year and the $100,000 winner's share of the purse raised her season's earnings to $463,493, a solid fifth on the money list. It also helped erase the disappointment of wasting a big first-round lead in the Centel Classic.

Gerring and Cindy Rarick opened with 69s to lead Dottie Mochrie by one stroke. Gerring broke in front to stay on Friday with another 69, led Betsy King by three strokes after a third-round 69 and fought off Daniel down the stretch on Sunday with a closing 71.

"I'm really proud of myself," Gerring said. "To win a tournament like this, against the best players in the world, is special."

Gerring appeared to be on easy street when she opened the final round with birdies on four of the first five holes and headed into the final nine holes six in front of the field.

But Daniel wouldn't go away. After bogeying Nos. 14 and 15, Gerring looked at the leaderboard and saw Daniel had birdied a couple of holes and was within two shots. It could have been one a hole later, but Gerring saved her par from a tricky lie, which proved to be the winner when Daniel birdied the last hole.

Mazda Japan Classic—$550,000
Winner: Debbie Massey

The suspense of a Beth Daniel-Patty Sheehan battle was missing in the LPGA's final tournament. Instead, it was Debbie Massey who had to sweat this one out.

Daniel, having clinched a tie for Rolex Player of the Year honors, didn't play. And Sheehan, needing a victory for a share of the honor, finished tied for 17th.

Massey won it without having to tee it up in the final round, which was rained out. She did it with a second-round course-record-tying 64 that moved her three in front of Caroline Keggi.

It was Massey's third career victory, but only the first in 11 years. The $82,500 winner's share of the purse boosted her lifetime earnings past $1 million just a week after her 40th birthday.

"I can't think of a better birthday present," Massey said. "I wish we could have played all three rounds, but when you haven't won in such a long time, you take it any way you can."

Sheehan never was a factor. She opened with 72, six behind Nancy Brown, and a closing 69 left her eight off Massey's winning total of 133 and eventually nine points behind Daniel for Player of the Year.

"I can't be too disappointed," Sheehan said. "I had the best year of my career. With the kind of year Beth had, she deserved to win it."

Solheim Cup
Winner: United States

Where America's men have come up short lately in international competition, the women seem to be thriving.

They rode to the rescue this year after their male counterparts failed to win the Ryder Cup and Walker Cup in 1989 and the World Amateur Team championship this year.

First, there were the amateurs, led by 17-year-old Vicki Goetze, taking the Curtis Cup and Women's World Amateur Team championship. Then, late in the year, eight members of the LPGA added the first Solheim Cup to the U.S. trophy case, easily defeating a team of Europeans 11-1/2 to 4-1/2 at Lake Nona Country Club in Orlando, Florida.

With non-playing captain Kathy Whitworth warning her "girls" of overconfidence at every step, the U.S. led 3-1 after the first day, 6-2 after the second day, then won three of the first five matches and halved another in the final round to end this inaugural version of U.S. vs. Europe.

It never figured to be much of a contest, not with Betsy King and Beth Daniel anchoring a team that included Cathy Gerring, Pat Bradley, Nancy Lopez, Dottie Mochrie, Patty Sheehan and Rosie Jones, while the Europeans were short on depth, with only Laura Davies, Liselotte Neumann and Pam Wright having any extensive experience in the U.S.

As King said, "I know we had the best players in the world and we wanted to show it. 16-0 was my goal."

Davies and Alison Nichols shattered those U.S. hopes by winning the first match on opening day by 2 and 1 over Bradley and Lopez. It was a boost for the Europeans, but no momentum builder as the U.S. pairings of Gerring-Mochrie, Sheehan-Jones and Daniel-King dominated the rest of the day with routs of 6 and 5, 6 and 5, and 5 and 4. None of these twosomes made a bogey or lost a hole.

Itoman LPGA World Match Play—$450,000
Winner: Betsy King

There's something about the Princeville Makai Golf Club that brings out the best in Betsy King, as she won for the fourth time in her career there, this time in the $450,000 Itoman LPGA World Match Play.

King, who won the 1984, '88 and '89 Women's Kemper Open here, defeated Deb Richard 2-up in the final. It was the LPGA's first match-play event in 11 years and the list of no-shows might indicate it's hardly a popular format.

Missing were most of the U.S. Solheim Cup team—Beth Daniel, Patty Sheehan, Cathy Gerring, Pat Bradley, Nancy Lopez and Rosie Jones. Ayako Okamoto, one of the island's most popular players, also skipped it.

Maybe, the absentees share King's opinion of match-play events. "To be honest, I don't like match play," King said after each of her five victories. "You feel like people are either rooting for you or against you, the matches aren't always exciting and the best player doesn't always win."

In this case, the best player did win, and, as always at Makai, the 18th hole was King's best friend. In 1988, Daniel hit her approach into the lake fronting the green and King won. In 1989, Lopez did it and King won. And in the match play, King escaped her toughest match when Chris Johnson flew the green and King won 1-up. It happened again in the final as Richard, 1-down, came up 10 yards short of the lake's bank.

"It was anybody's match until Deb hit into the water," King said.

"The hardest thing about beating Betsy is that she has so many good memories of playing here," Richard said. "When you've won on a course as many times as she's won here, you tend to play fearlessly."

The Women's European Tour

Valextra Classic—£70,000
Winner: Florence Descampe

Belgium's Florence Descampe gave an impressive performance to collect the second title of her short career on the WPG European Tour. She finished six strokes ahead of her nearest rival, Scotland's Dale Reid, in the Valextra Classic in Rome.

Descampe opened with 71 to share the lead, and another 71 left her one shot behind America's Pearl Sinn. The winner of the 1988 Danish Ladies Open, Descampe made her move in the third round, when 69 gave her a two-stroke lead going into the final day. A 68 for a five-under-par total of 279 earned her a comfortable victory.

Ford Ladies Classic—£65,000
Winner: Marie Laure de Lorenzi

Marie Laure de Lorenzi shrugged off any thoughts of injury problems to retain her Ford Ladies Classic title at Woburn.

American Muffin Spencer-Devlin occupied much of the attention on opening day when she was disqualified for "unprofessional behavior" at the pro-am dinner the evening before. On the golf course Sweden's Helen Alfredsson led with 69, with de Lorenzi well down the field with 74.

De Lorenzi improved with a second-round 72, but was still five shots off the lead. A course-record 68 in the third round was the breakthrough she had been looking for, and took her into a share of the lead with South Africa's Laurette Maritz.

A final 70, including two closing birdies, gave the French player a 284 total, 12 under par, and a three-stroke victory.

Hennessy Ladies' Cup—£90,000
Winner: Trish Johnson

Glamor rather than golf was the first thing to hit the headlines in the Hennessy Ladies Cup in Paris. LPGA Tour players Deborah McHaffie and Tammie Green caused a sensation with their stylish appearance, along with the admission by promoters that they were invited over to add a little more glamor to the event. However, the Europeans began making the news on the golf course, and eventually Trish Johnson ended two years without a victory on the European circuit.

Valerie Michaud, a 20-year-old French amateur, upstaged the professionals on the opening day, shooting 70 to lead by a stroke. Johnson's 68 on the second day, added to her first-round 72, carried her into the halfway lead. A third-round 71 gave her a two-shot cushion over Tammie Green. No one challenged Johnson in the last round. She had 74 for a three-under-par 284 total, and won by three strokes over Marie Laure de Lorenzi and Green.

WPG European Tour Classic—£60,000
Winner: Tania Abitbol

Spain's Tania Abitbol won the second title of her career with a powerful finish in the WPG European Tour Classic in Cheshire, England.

Joanne Furby took the first-round lead with 69. Alison Shapcott led by three strokes after two rounds with 140, while Abitbol was five shots off the pace.

It was the first time Shapcott had been in contention and she played the first nine holes impeccably despite a challenge from Sweden's Anna Oxenstierna. Oxenstierna went out in 32 to draw even with Shapcott, while Abitbol, out in 33, was one shot off the lead.

A birdie at the 11th hole by the Spaniard and another at the 14th gave her a cushion. While the others dropped shots, Abitbol showed the maturity of a champion to hold off any charge, and birdied the last hole for 68 and a 213 total, three under par, to win by two strokes over Oxenstierna, with Shapcott one shot further back.

Bonmont Ladies Classic—£70,000
Winner: Evelyn Orley

Swiss professional Evelyn Orley had a fairytale debut in front of her home supporters to win the Bonmont Ladies Classic in Geneva. Orley beat Scotland's Gillian Stewart with a birdie at the first extra hole after they had tied at one-over-par 289.

Orley, a former winner of the French, Swiss and Italian amateur titles, had only turned professional a year earlier. An opening round of 71 left her two shots behind South Africa's Alison Sheard.

Diane Barnard took the lead on the second day with a 142 total. Heavy rains and strong winds made play difficult on the third day, but Orley kept her nerve to shoot 71 for a 214 total, and a two-stroke lead over Stewart.

She increased it to three with a birdie at the first hole of the final round, but then nerves got the better of her. She dropped three shots in the next six holes. Stewart had a two-stroke lead after 16 holes, but dropped a shot to lead by just one.

A birdie by Orley at the 18th hole, where she holed an impressive 10-footer, forced a playoff. At the first extra hole, she sank a putt from 35 feet to claim her first WPG European Tour title.

BMW European Masters—£120,000
Winner: Karen Lunn

Continuing her romance with the European Masters, Australia's Karen Lunn won for the second time in three years. The Sydney professional had an impressive performance, taking a share of the lead after two rounds, and never let go.

Corinne Soules took the first-round lead with a 69, and was the only person to break 70 during the tournament. After the second day, Soules and Lunn shared the lead at 143, then in the third round Lunn made her move. She had five birdies in six holes on the back nine for a 71 and 214 total, two shots ahead of Soules.

A seven at the third hole of the final round left Soules struggling, and Lunn was four shots clear at the turn, a lead she was never to relinquish. A 71 and 285 total earned her a check for £18,000, with Soules four shots back in second place.

BMW Ladies Classic—£70,000
Winner: Diane Barnard

England's Diane Barnard ended seven years on the WPG European Tour without a victory when she won the BMW Ladies Classic in Dusseldorf, Germany.

Corinne Dibnah set the early pace with 66, a course record, while Barnard shot 71. Karen Lunn took over at 136 after two rounds, while Barnard shot 68 for a 139 total. Dibnah's 69 in the third round earned her a two-shot lead over Barnard and Alison Nicholas.

Barnard made the turn in two under par to lead by one stroke over Dibnah, Nicholas and Lunn. She birdied the 11th and 13th holes to move three shots ahead, and not even a last-minute challenge from Dibnah unsettled her. A 69 for a 10-under-par total of 278 earned Barnard the victory by one shot.

Laing Ladies Charity Classic—£65,000
Winner: Laurette Maritz

Birdies and eagles abounded in the Laing Charity Classic at Stoke Poges, as South Africa's Laurette Maritz beat Alison Nicholas in a playoff.

Ireland's Maureen Garner was a leading figure, as she attempted to win her first tournament. She shot an opening 68 to lead by two strokes and added 67 in the second round for 135 to lead by three over Maritz. Garner still led by one over Maritz after 71 for a 206 total, with Nicholas in a pack of four players at 210.

The stage was set for a dramatic finish, as Garner and Maritz both opened with birdies. But Maritz struck a killer blow at the short third hole when she holed in one. Garner went out in 33 to lead Maritz by one. Nicholas was one shot behind on her way to a 65 to set the target at 275, 13 under par.

They arrived at the final green with Maritz one shot ahead at 14 under par, but both had to settle for fives, and the South African found herself in a playoff with Nicholas, while Garner had to make do with third place. The playoff hole was somewhat of an anticlimax, as Maritz won with a six to Nicholas' double-bogey seven.

Bloor Homes Eastleigh Classic—£66,000
Winner: Trish Johnson

England's Trish Johnson returned from a spell on the LPGA Tour in America to win the Bloor Homes Eastleigh Classic in Southampton for the second time, following her 1987 victory. Johnson went to the top of the Woolmark Order of Merit, a position she would not relinquish as she enjoyed her finest season on the WPG European Tour.

She joined Corinne Dibnah at the top of the leaderboard as both shot opening rounds of 61. Dale Reid, Kitrina Douglas and Dennise Hutton took the halfway lead at 124, with Johnson three strokes back.

A course-record equalling 58 put Johnson back on track in the third round. She moved into a four-stroke lead over Douglas with a 185 total. Her challengers had a brief glimmer of hope in the fourth round, as she dropped two shots in the opening holes. It was short-lived, and Johnson came home in 29 for a final-round 64 and an 11-under-par total of 249, while Dibnah placed second with 254.

Weetabix Women's British Open—£130,000
Winner: Helen Alfredsson

Chalking up her first professional victory, Sweden's Helen Alfredsson won the most sought-after of titles, the Weetabix Women's British Open. Her name joins those of Alison Nicholas, Laura Davies and Corinne Dibnah on the trophy. Alfredsson claimed the winner's £20,000 check when she beat Zimbabwe's Jane Hill in a playoff, but not before some of the most exciting golf Woburn had seen in a long time in sweltering conditions.

A record crowd followed the play as Kitrina Douglas set the pace with 69 on the opening day. She led by a stroke over Alfredsson, and was still that one shot ahead of the Swede after 71 in the second round. Meanwhile, Hill had to make a strong finish for 74 to make the halfway cut with just two shots to spare.

Marie Laure de Lorenzi came in with 72 to lead the third round at five under par, with Douglas and Alfredsson one shot behind. Hill had made her challenge with 69 to be five shots off the lead. She was even more impressive over the closing holes of her final round, when a hat-trick of birdies saw her finish with 68 to set the target at 288, four under par.

Alfredsson parred the final holes, as de Lorenzi slipped to a 79, and found herself facing Hill in a playoff. It went to four extra holes before Alfredsson holed a four-foot putt for "the title I have dreamed of, the most prestigious in Europe," she later exclaimed.

Lufthansa Ladies' German Open—£90,000
Winner: Ayako Okamoto

LPGA star Ayako Okamoto made a guest appearance on the WPG European Tour and travelled back to the United States with the trophy for the £90,000 Lufthansa Ladies German Open in Munich. The Japanese professional showed why she is rated as one of the best in the world when she made four birdies in the closing holes to force her way into a playoff with Cindy Rarick, another guest, and the Tour's own Laurette Maritz. The playoff threesome finished two shots ahead of Trish Johnson and Alison Nicholas with 14-under-par totals of 274.

Maritz made her move in the second round with 65, matched by Helen Alfredsson, and began the final round three shots ahead of Rarick. Maritz produced 14 straight pars and was two shots ahead after 15 holes. She then dropped only her third shot of the championship and Rarick's birdie meant the two were tied. Meanwhile, Okamoto had come home in 32 for 67 to set the pace and neither were able to produce a birdie to beat her.

Maritz made her exit at the first extra hole when she failed to match the two American birdies. Okamoto collected the title when Rarick three-putted the fourth extra hole. It was Okamoto's second victory in two visits to Europe, the first in 1984 when she won the Women's British Open.

Haninge Ladies' Open—£70,000
Winner: Dale Reid

Dale Reid won for the 19th time in her career when she finished one stroke clear of Alison Nicholas, Suzanne Strudwick and Maureen Garner in the Haninge Ladies' Open in Stockholm. It ended a two-year spell without a victory for the Scot, and saw her leap up the Woolmark Order of Merit so that she eventually claimed a place in the Solheim Cup team.

The stars were upstaged on the opening day when rookie Malin Burstrom shot 70 to be one stroke ahead of Gillian Stewart, with Reid four strokes off the lead. Swedish superstar Liselotte Neumann, making her first appearance in Europe, shot 70 on the second day for a 144 total and a one-stroke lead over Stewart and Reid.

Nicholas made her move on the third day when she chipped in on the final hole for a birdie and one-shot lead over Reid and Anna Oxenstierna, who had delighted the home crowd with 68. Tough, blustery conditions on the final day made good scores hard to come by, and only Nicholas and Reid were left to fight it out.

Nicholas led by two shots with nine holes to play, but three bogeys in the closing holes unsettled her and gave Reid the opening she needed. While Nicholas slipped to 76, Reid's 74 for a total of 291 was enough to earn the title and £10,500 winner's check by one shot.

Variety Club Celebrity Classic—£60,000
Winner: Alison Nicholas

Ending a frustrating time on the WPG European Tour, Alison Nicholas clinched her first victory of the season and ninth of her career in the Variety Club Celebrity Classic in Reading, England. The former British Open champion finished one shot ahead of Sofia Gronberg, and Trish Johnson grabbed third place to retain her spot at the top of the Woolmark Order of Merit.

Nicholas was not the only winner of the week, as the pro-celebrity event raised £50,000 for underprivileged children.

Kitrina Douglas took the first-round lead with 67, as Nicholas found herself one shot off the pace. She remained cautious, remembering her disappointment in Stockholm a week earlier when she had dropped three shots in four holes to lose the title. Douglas opened a three-shot lead over Nicholas with a second-round 66 and 136 total. Sofia Gronberg stole the third-round headlines with a course-record 65 for a 207 total.

Douglas began the final round one shot ahead of Nicholas at 203. It was to be a disappointing finale for the Bristol professional. She ran up 75 for a 278 total, while Nicholas arrived at the final hole needing a birdie to beat Gronberg, who was already in at 276. She holed a four-foot putt for 71 and an impressive 13-under-par 275 total to move into the second spot in the Woolmark Order of Merit.

TEC Players Championship—£80,000
Winner: Anne Jones

Australia's Anne Jones became the season's fourth first-time winner when she held off a challenge from Laurette Maritz to win the TEC Players Championship in Wolverhampton.

It was a popular victory made possible by a course-record 66 on the second day to put Jones at seven-under-par 139. Her round, which included eight birdies and an eagle, earned her a three-shot lead over Maritz, Alison Nicholas and Trish Johnson, and from then on it was just a matter of holding on.

If anyone doubted that Jones had the nerve to win they were eating their words after the third round, when the Sydney professional finished with five birdies in the final seven holes for 69 and an 11-under-par total of 208. She was now four strokes ahead of Maritz, with Helen Alfredsson one shot further back. She began the final round as her supporters hoped she would, with an eagle-three, but the drama was about to unfold.

Jones missed the first of three putts within three feet at the ninth hole, and Maritz was only two shots off the lead. She birdied the 16th to increase it to three, but four putts for a double-bogey five at the next had some in the crowd shaking their head.

Maritz was only one shot ahead, and when Jones pushed her drive at the 18th, a playoff seemed inevitable. She made a marvellous recovery, to the edge of the green, where a chip and a three-foot putt gave her a birdie and an 11-under-par aggregate of 281 to finish two shots clear.

Expedier Ladies European Open—£75,000
Winner: Trish Johnson

Trish Johnson completed her third victory of the season in the Expedier Ladies European Open at Kingswood in Surrey, and was almost unbeatable at the top of the Woolmark Order of Merit. She finished with 69 for a 12-under-par total of 276 for a two-shot victory in one of the closest-fought tournaments of the season.

Michele Estill, fresh from victory in the LPGA qualifying school, grabbed the headlines on the opening day with 67. She followed that with 70 to be one shot ahead of fellow American Pearl Sinn and Johnson.

Alison Nicholas made a move on the third day with 66 to tie Johnson at 207, but Estill held on with 68 to lead by two strokes going into the final round.

Johnson set the pace, as she stormed through the front nine in 32 and then eagled the 14th hole to be four shots ahead. It was looking almost over until Johnson suddenly dropped one shot after another over the final three holes for 69 and 12-under-par 276 total.

Estill, playing in the group behind, needed a par-four at the final hole to force a playoff, but dramatically hooked her drive out of bounds to finish with a double-bogey six for 73 and a 278 total.

Trophee International Coconut Skol—£70,000
Winner: Corinne Dibnah

Despite a heavy cold, Corinne Dibnah shot a last-round 66 to come from behind and win the Trophee International Coconut Skol in Paris.

Dibnah trailed Dennise Hutton and Helen Alfredsson by one shot after a 71 on opening day, and a second-round 75 saw her slip even further behind, as Anna Oxenstierna led with 141.

In the third round the event started to come alive. Anne Jones shot a course-record 66 to be at 219, but still trailed leaders Trish Johnson and Alison Nicholas by three strokes. Dibnah shot 72 and was four strokes behind.

Johnson was two shots ahead of Dibnah at the turn, but the Australian turned on the pressure and produced birdies galore in a closing 66 for an even-par 284 total. Johnson slipped to 71 for 285. It was Dibnah's eighth WPG European Tour win since turning professional in 1984.

Italian Ladies Open—£90,000
Winner: Florence Descampe

Belgium's Florence Descampe won the Italian Ladies Open in Gardagolf for her second victory of the year, but still was not given a place on the Solheim Cup team announced following the event. The final wild card went to Marie Laure de Lorenzi.

The Solheim Cup was uppermost in people's minds as the event got underway amid some spectacular scenery. Diane Barnard was trying to hold the fourth automatic spot, but was being chased by several players. Helen Alfredsson was virtually assured of a place, and allayed any doubts with an opening 67 to take the first-round lead.

Dale Reid shared the lead after two rounds at 142, with Descampe four strokes behind. Meanwhile, Barnard saw her chance of a Solheim Cup team place disappear and was nine shots off the lead.

Descampe hit the headlines in the third round, when she shot a course-record 66 for a 212 total and led Alfredsson and Nicholas by two strokes. She stormed home in 33 for a closing 70 and a 282 total for a three-shot victory over Alfredsson. A fourth place finish by Reid had earned her the final automatic Solheim Cup team spot, ahead of Barnard and de Lorenzi.

Woolmark Matchplay Championship—£80,000
Winner: Florence Descampe

Florence Descampe laid claim to her second successive title and third of the season when she won the Woolmark Matchplay Championship at Club de Campo in Spain. The young Belgian beat Dale Reid in the final by 2 and 1 to give her some satisfaction after losing out to Reid in the race for the final Solheim Cup team spot.

The experienced Reid took charge early on, winning the first two holes and remained two ahead until the 14th hole. Descampe hit back with three birdies in a row, including one at the 16th, where she chipped in from off the green and was one up with just two holes left. A safe par-three at the short 17th was enough to give her the title and £12,000 winner's check after Reid hit into a bunker.

Descampe began the week with an 8-and-6 win over Janet Soulsby while Reid went to the 19th hole to beat Maureen Garner, the losing finalist in last year's event. Descampe dispatched Diane Pavich and Helen Alfredsson in the second and third rounds to face a quarter-final battle with Tania Abitbol. Reid, meanwhile, had beaten Catrin Nilsmark and Suzanne Strudwick to find herself facing Alison Nicholas.

Both won their matches to find themselves playing Anne Jones and Xonia Wunsch-Ruiz in the semi-finals. Some astonishing scoring followed, as Descampe produced five birdies to beat Jones 5 and 4, while Wunsch-Ruiz could not match Reid and was convincingly beaten 8 and 6.

AGF Biarritz Ladies Open—£80,000
Winner: Laura Davies

The AGF Biarritz Ladies Open marked the first time in the WPG European Tour's history that two rounds were completely lost due to the bad weather, and Laura Davies was handed the trophy without having to hit a ball on the final day.

Davies, delighted at being awarded a wild card place in the Solheim Cup team, was brimming with confidence as she set out in the first round on one of her favorite courses, France's Golf de Biarritz. She had set all types of records while winning the event in 1988, and looked set to do so again when she shot an opening 63. She led by three shots over Helen Alfredsson, but then the rain began to play its part.

The second round was postponed until Saturday, when gales blew in across the Bay of Biscay. Alison Nicholas managed to shoot 66 for a 137 total, but Davies held the lead by one shot with a 73. Little did she know how vital that shot was going to be.

They woke up to torrential rain on the final day, and the tournament director had no choice but to cancel play. It was Davies' first win of the season.

Benson & Hedges Mixed Team Trophy—£182,000
Winner: Tania Abitbol and Jose Maria Canizares

Four low rounds, the highest being 68, were enough to enable Jose Maria Canizares and Tania Abitbol to become the second successive Spanish team to win the Benson & Hedges Mixed Team Trophy on home soil, at El Bosque in Valencia.

The pair, who succeeded Miguel Angel Jimenez and Xonia Wunsch-Ruiz, were in second place going to the final round. That 68 gave them a two-shot cushion over Ove Sellberg and Florence Descampe, who slipped to 74.

Mark Mouland and Alison Nicholas also shot four rounds in the 60s, but their closing 69 was not good enough to catch the Spanish duo, who finished at 21-under-par 267 for the mixed event. A further two strokes behind came

Brian Barnes and Laura Davies, whose 66 was the best round of the day.

The best round of the week over the superb Spanish course, hosting the event for the first time, was an eight-under-par 64 in the second round by Sellberg and Descampe, which was equalled in the third round by Juan Quiros Segura and Karen Lunn.

Longines Classic—£100,000
Winner: Trish Johnson

England's Trish Johnson claimed her fourth victory of the season in the Longines Classic in Nice, France, and became Europe's No. 1 player. She clinched the Woolmark Order of Merit and opened a £20,000 gap over second place Alison Nicholas.

Federica Dassu shot an opening 67 for a four-stroke lead. Johnson had 72, then 71 in the second round took her into a share of first place with Dassu at 143. Gillian Stewart made a big move on the third day with 69 for a total of 219, but Johnson held a one-stroke lead. She had a final round of 68 for a 286 total and a victory by six strokes over Stewart.

The win took her earnings to £83,043 and also earned her a £12,000 bonus for winning the Woolmark Order of Merit. Alison Nicholas finished in second place with £63,199 and collected an £8,000 bonus, while American Pearl Sinn won the Rookie of the Year award after finishing 18th spot on the merit table.

APPENDIXES

World Money List

This listing of the 200 leading money winners in the world of professional golf in 1990 was compiled from the results of all tournaments carried in the Appendixes of this edition, along with other non-tour and international events for which accurate figures could be obtained and in which the players competed for prize money provided by someone other than the players themselves. Skins games and shootouts are not included.

In the 25 years during which World Money Lists have been compiled, the earnings of the player in the 200th position have risen from a total of $3,326 in 1966 to $170,791 in 1990. The top 200 players in 1966 earned a total of $4,680,287. In 1990, the comparable total was $83,902,213.

Because of fluctuating values of money throughout the world, it was necessary to determine an average value of non-American currency to U.S. money to prepare this listing. The conversion rates used for 1990 were: British pound = US$1.85; 140 Japanese yen = US$1; South African rand = US40¢; US$1 = Australia/New Zealand 77¢.

POS.	PLAYER, COUNTRY	TOTAL MONEY
1	Jose Maria Olazabal, Spain	$1,633,640
2	Ian Woosnam, Wales	1,512,060
3	Greg Norman, Australia	1,457,378
4	David Frost, South Africa	1,456,393
5	Payne Stewart, U.S.	1,283,333
6	Wayne Levi, U.S.	1,151,306
7	Fred Couples, U.S.	1,145,669
8	Bernhard Langer, Germany	1,134,452
9	Paul Azinger, U.S.	1,106,009
10	Mark McNulty, Zimbabwe	1,084,326
11	Jodie Mudd, U.S.	1,055,746
12	Larry Mize, U.S.	1,051,672
13	Mark Calcavecchia, U.S.	1,042,097
14	Tim Simpson, U.S.	1,026,176
15	Hale Irwin, U.S.	964,890
16	Masashi Ozaki, Japan	956,726
17	Ian Baker-Finch, Australia	950,988
18	Ronan Rafferty, Northern Ireland	946,643
19	Nick Faldo, England	871,916
20	Mark O'Meara, U.S.	837,387
21	Lanny Wadkins, U.S.	820,307
22	Rodger Davis, Australia	808,877
23	Steve Elkington, Australia	804,896
24	Davis Love III, U.S.	745,071
25	Gil Morgan, U.S.	736,629
26	Billy Mayfair, U.S.	719,058
27	Wayne Grady, Australia	693,764
28	Tsuneyuki Nakajima, Japan	692,708
29	David Feherty, Northern Ireland	683,418
30	Naomichi Ozaki, Japan	682,708

POS.	PLAYER, COUNTRY	TOTAL MONEY
31	Robert Gamez, U.S.	679,413
32	Peter Jacobsen, U.S.	679,143
33	Ryoken Kawagishi, Japan	675,535
34	Tom Kite, U.S.	675,174
35	Mike Harwood, Australia	673,387
36	Chip Beck, U.S.	658,826
37	Saburo Fujiki, Japan	623,752
38	Nick Price, Zimbabwe	599,586
39	Mark James, England	572,193
40	Brian Jones, Australia	566,573
41	Curtis Strange, U.S.	565,840
42	Noboru Sugai, Japan	565,462
43	David Ishii, U.S.	564,124
44	Corey Pavin, U.S.	526,530
45	Craig Parry, Australia	521,379
46	Hideki Kase, Japan	517,649
47	Bob Tway, U.S.	513,088
48	Mike Donald, U.S.	510,268
49	Teruo Sugihara, Japan	504,966
50	Jim Gallagher, Jr., U.S.	498,456
51	John Cook, U.S.	494,112
52	Sam Torrance, Scotland	494,051
53	Loren Roberts, U.S.	492,572
54	Severiano Ballesteros, Spain	489,060
55	Masahiro Kuramoto, Japan	488,906
56	Craig Stadler, U.S.	484,783
57	Peter Senior, Australia	482,522
58	Tommy Armour, U.S.	471,649
59	Steve Pate, U.S.	469,151
60	Eduardo Romero, Argentina	461,906
61	John Huston, U.S	460,874
62	Raymond Floyd, U.S.	453,998
63	Brian Tennyson, U.S.	450,083
64	Mike Reid, U.S.	448,678
65	Ben Crenshaw, U.S.	446,549
66	Graham Marsh, Australia	442,583
67	Toru Nakamura, Japan	440,005
68	Ken Green, U.S.	436,390
69	David Peoples, U.S.	431,567
70	Yoshinori Kaneko, Japan	431,303
71	Steve Jones, U.S.	425,810
72	Brett Ogle, Australia	411,924
73	John Bland, South Africa	402,830
74	Nobuo Serizawa, Japan	402,521
75	Vijay Singh, Fiji	393,389
76	Gene Sauers, U.S.	387,485
77	John Mahaffey, U.S.	386,765
78	Bruce Lietzke, U.S.	377,794
79	Richard Boxall, England	377,278
80	Seiichi Kanai, Japan	373,731
81	Joey Sindelar, U.S.	373,646
82	Billy Ray Brown, U.S.	368,936
83	Scott Hoch, U.S.	363,996
84	Philip Walton, Ireland	362,893
85	Colin Montgomerie, Scotland	356,700
86	Fulton Allem, South Africa	352,480

POS.	PLAYER, COUNTRY	TOTAL MONEY
87	Mark Brooks, U.S.	348,859
88	Isao Aoki, Japan	346,775
89	Nolan Henke, U.S.	340,092
90	Jeff Sluman, U.S.	339,821
91	Dan Forsman, U.S.	325,070
92	Tom Purtzer, U.S.	314,414
93	Scott Verplank, U.S.	312,459
94	Kenny Perry, U.S.	312,306
95	Nobumitsu Yuhara, Japan	310,295
96	Satoshi Higashi, Japan	309,876
97	Sandy Lyle, Scotland	309,400
98	Hiroshi Makino, Japan	303,457
99	Tsukasa Watanabe, Japan	292,334
100	Tadao Nakamura, Japan	288,412
101	Kenny Knox, U.S.	287,822
102	Chris Perry, U.S.	287,733
103	Tony Johnstone, Zimbabwe	285,679
104	Bill Britton, U.S.	283,077
105	Peter Fowler, Australia	283,035
106	Mike Hulbert, U.S.	282,974
107	Jay Haas, U.S.	280,112
108	Stephen McAllister, Scotland	277,078
109	Jim Thorpe, U.S.	276,997
110	Scott Simpson, U.S.	276,685
111	Mike Clayton, Australia	273,440
112	Roger Mackay, Australia	270,960
113	Morris Hatalsky, U.S.	268,478
114	Bob Gilder, U.S.	266,547
115	Russ Cochran, U.S.	266,178
116	Frankie Minoza, Philippines	261,491
117	Frank Nobilo, New Zealand	260,476
118	Rocco Mediate, U.S.	260,000
119	Jeff Maggert, U.S.	258,456
120	Gordon Brand, Jr., Scotland	257,891
121	Eamonn Darcy, Ireland	256,679
122	Bob Lohr, U.S.	254,260
123	Chen Tze Chung, Taiwan	253,127
124	Jim Hallet, U.S.	251,559
125	Hal Sutton, U.S.	248,673
126	Tony Sills, U.S.	248,050
127	Miguel Angel Martin, Spain	247,858
128	Greg J. Turner, New Zealand	247,847
129	Donnie Hammond, U.S.	247,722
130	Billy Andrade, U.S.	246,637
131	Bobby Wadkins, U.S.	246,363
132	Blaine McCallister, U.S.	244,214
133	Mark Mouland, Wales	239,713
134	Larry Nelson, U.S.	238,554
135	Shigeru Kawamata, Japan	233,042
136	Jose Rivero, Spain	232,644
137	Malcolm Mackenzie, England	231,818
138	Jay Delsing, U.S.	231,740
139	Anders Sorensen, Denmark	227,578
140	Chen Tze Ming, Taiwan	226,228
141	Tomohiro Kanai, Japan	226,207
142	Ted Schulz, U.S.	225,927
143	Howard Clark, England	224,487

POS.	PLAYER, COUNTRY	TOTAL MONEY
144	Mark McCumber, U.S.	223,246
145	Peter Persons, U.S.	223,005
146	Andrew Magee, U.S.	222,107
147	Willie Wood, U.S.	221,722
148	Kirk Triplett, U.S.	221,389
149	Bob Estes, U.S.	220,858
150	Steven Richardson, England	220,488
151	Akihito Yokoyama, Japan	219,145
152	Katsunari Takahashi, Japan	219,081
153	Dave Barr, Canada	218,112
154	Kiyoshi Murota, Japan	217,822
155	Tom Watson, U.S.	215,007
156	Russell Claydon, England	214,597
157	Bill Glasson, U.S.	214,434
158	Richard Zokol, Canada	213,923
159	Roger Chapman, England	213,163
160	Fuzzy Zoeller, U.S.	211,629
161	Mark Wiebe, U.S.	210,435
162	Ove Sellberg, Sweden	207,609
163	Don Pooley, U.S.	206,496
164	Tom Byrum, U.S.	205,910
165	Peter O'Malley, Australia	204,908
166	Jose Maria Canizares, Spain	203,372
167	John Morse, Australia	203,318
168	Hajime Meshiai, Japan	202,861
169	Yoshitaka Yamamoto, Japan	202,221
170	Brad Faxon, U.S.	201,218
171	Mark Lye, U.S.	201,011
172	Phil Blackmar, U.S.	200,796
173	Masanobu Kimura, Japan	200,613
174	Buddy Gardner, U.S.	199,737
175	Katsuji Hasegawa, Japan	197,245
176	Peter McWhinney, Australia	196,083
177	Yoshinori Mizumaki, Japan	194,810
178	Brad Bryant, U.S.	192,670
179	Robert Wrenn, U.S.	192,058
180	Barry Lane, England	191,563
181	Mike Smith, U.S.	191,459
182	Des Smyth, Ireland	191,164
183	David Williams, England	190,804
184	Vicente Fernandez, Argentina	190,348
185	Katsuyoshi Tomori, Japan	184,513
186	Mats Lanner, Sweden	181,658
187	Anders Forsbrand, Sweden	180,027
188	Seiki Okuda, Japan	179,594
189	Fred Funk, U.S.	179,346
190	Rick Hartmann, U.S.	177,691
191	Brad Fabel, U.S.	177,376
192	David Edwards, U.S.	177,326
193	Andy Bean, U.S.	177,008
194	Gary Hallberg, U.S.	175,421
195	Tsuyoshi Yoneyama, Japan	174,897
196	Torsten Giedeon, Germany	174,508
197	Miguel Angel Jimenez, Spain	173,123
198	Bill Sander, U.S.	172,886
199	Grant Turner, England	171,498
200	Tadami Ueno, Japan	170,791

The Sony Ranking
(as of December 31, 1990)

Pos.	Player	Circuit	Points Average	Total Points	No. of Events	87/89 Total	87/89 Minus	1990 Plus
1 (1)	Greg Norman	ANZ 1	18.95	1402	74	1385	-771	788
2 (2)	Nick Faldo	Eur 1	18.54	1465	79	1365	-748	848
3 (7)	Jose Maria Olazabal	Eur 2	17.22	1343	78	864	-453	932
4 (9)	Ian Woosnam	Eur 3	15.47	1207	78	948	-557	816
5 (5)	Payne Stewart	USA 1	12.75	1109	87	1115	-618	612
6 (10)	Paul Azinger	USA 2	11.63	954	82	898	-524	580
7 (3)	Seve Ballesteros	Eur 4	10.15	751	74	1097	-634	288
8 (6)	Tom Kite	USA 3	10.10	788	78	993	-545	340
9 (31)	Mark McNulty	Afr 1	10.06	805	80	483	-302	624
10 (8)	Mark Calcavecchia	USA 4	9.96	976	98	1146	-626	456
11 (15)	Fred Couples	USA 5	9.69	862	89	814	-448	496
12 (4)	Curtis Strange	USA 6	9.58	757	79	1172	-663	248
13 (19)	Larry Mize	USA 7	8.86	735	83	595	-364	504
14 (16)	Bernhard Langer	Eur 5	8.78	746	85	720	-442	468
15 (11)	Chip Beck	USA 8	8.58	695	81	860	-469	304
16 (98)	Hale Irwin	USA 9	8.36	585	70	162	-89	512
17 (12)	Masashi Ozaki	Jpn 1	8.16	677	83	850	-473	300
18 (35)	Tim Simpson	USA 10	7.78	708	91	506	-266	468
19 (21)	Ronan Rafferty	Eur 6	7.71	732	95	666	-362	428
20 (67)	Wayne Levi	USA 11	7.69	569	74	266	-149	452
21 (25)	Lanny Wadkins	USA 12	7.49	569	76	489	-304	384
22 (27)	Mark O'Meara	USA 13	7.39	658	89	564	-318	412
23 (43)	Rodger Davis	ANZ 2	7.08	651	92	402	-251	500
24 (13)	David Frost	Afr 2	7.01	631	90	836	-473	268
25 (49)	Jodie Mudd	USA 14	6.64	571	86	375	-208	404
26 (61)	Gil Morgan	USA 15	6.35	457	72	252	-135	340
27 (42)	Wayne Grady	ANZ 3	6.32	588	93	434	-238	392
28 (17)	Ben Crenshaw	USA 16	6.32	493	78	673	-404	224
29 (46)	Peter Jacobsen	USA 17	6.27	483	77	338	-175	320
30 (28)	Steve Jones	USA 18	6.18	507	82	518	-271	260
31 (37)	Mark James	Eur 7	6.05	478	79	437	-227	268
32 (68)	Mike Harwood	ANZ 4	5.88	594	101	325	-171	440
33 (22)	Mike Reid	USA 19	5.81	447	77	565	-314	196
34 (30)	Craig Stadler	USA 20	5.74	436	76	460	-272	248
35 (53)	Eduardo Romero	SAm 1	5.68	420	74	265	-133	288
36 (59)	Ian Baker-Finch	ANZ 5	5.65	588	104	399	-227	416
37 (29)	Craig Parry	ANZ 6	5.30	535	101	531	-272	276
38 (38)	Nick Price	Afr 3	5.28	459	87	404	-233	288
39 (24)	Scott Hoch	USA 21	5.24	487	93	610	-351	228
40 (18)	Mark McCumber	USA 22	5.18	383	74	619	-340	104
41 (14)	Sandy Lyle	Eur 8	5.12	456	89	862	-506	100
42 (32)	Bruce Lietzke	USA 23	5.05	333	66	386	-209	156
43 (20)	Tom Watson	USA 24	5.03	307	61	429	-270	148
44 (65)	Davis Love III	USA 25	4.91	437	89	301	-180	316

( ) : Figures in brackets indicate 1987/89 positions.

THE SONY RANKING / 341

Pos.	Player	Circuit	Points Average	Total Points	No. of Events	87/89 Total	87/89 Minus	1990 Plus
45 (26)	Peter Senior	ANZ 7	4.67	495	106	641	-362	216
46 (79)	David Feherty	Eur 9	4.62	448	97	297	-161	312
47 (23)	Larry Nelson	USA 26	4.61	295	64	465	-294	124
48 (74)	Ray Floyd	USA 27	4.56	292	64	204	-120	208
49 (41)	Steve Pate	USA 28	4.53	453	100	467	-258	244
50 (60)	Sam Torrance	Eur 10	4.41	357	81	303	-186	240
51 (40)	Bob Tway	USA 29	4.33	411	95	441	-242	212
52 (69)	Brett Ogle	ANZ 8	4.27	384	90	264	-132	252
53 (741T)	Robert Gamez	USA 30	4.22	308	73	0	0	308
54 (84)	Corey Pavin	USA 31	4.09	364	89	242	-158	280
55 (36)	Scott Simpson	USA 32	4.07	342	84	474	-308	176
56 (33)	Ken Green	USA 33	4.04	384	95	509	-277	152
57 (113)	John Bland	Afr 4	4.04	343	85	180	-105	268
58 (48)	Naomichi Ozaki	Jpn 2	3.99	379	95	395	-212	196
59 (105)	Loren Roberts	USA 34	3.95	359	91	205	-106	260
60 (54)	Peter Fowler	ANZ 9	3.93	397	101	418	-221	200
61 (80)	Gene Sauers	USA 35	3.83	314	82	265	-155	204
62 (142)	Steve Elkington	ANZ 10	3.73	347	93	159	-84	272
63 (34)	Isao Aoki	Jpn 3	3.55	330	93	518	-300	112
64 (47)	Fuzzy Zoeller	USA 36	3.52	222	63	274	-160	108
65 (128)	John Huston	USA 37	3.51	312	89	144	-72	240
66 (66)	Tsuneyuki Nakajima	Jpn 4	3.49	314	90	320	-190	184
67 (231)	Billy Mayfair	USA 38	3.47	302	87	60	-30	272
68 (51)	Joey Sindelar	USA 39	3.41	307	90	391	-212	128
69 (55)	Jeff Sluman	USA 40	3.37	334	99	381	-215	168
70 (102)	Tom Purtzer	USA 41	3.32	262	79	181	-99	180
71 (82)	John Mahaffey	USA 42	3.32	305	92	271	-154	188
72 (493T)	John Morse	USA 43	3.27	196	60	8	-4	192
73 (56)	Graham Marsh	ANZ 11	3.26	248	76	298	-182	132
74 (158)	Jim Gallagher, Jr.	USA 44	3.24	295	91	135	-68	228
75 (39)	Don Pooley	USA 45	3.19	252	79	380	-232	104
76 (88)	Vijay Singh	Asa 1	3.18	302	95	204	-102	200
77 (62)	Jose Maria Canizares	Eur 11	3.18	197	62	222	-125	100
78 (52)	Gordon Brand, Jr.	Eur 12	3.16	294	93	395	-241	140
79 (71)	Jose Rivero	Eur 13	3.13	213	68	219	-134	128
80 (64)	Donnie Hammond	USA 46	3.12	268	86	307	-171	132
81 (162)	Colin Montgomerie	Eur 14	3.07	289	94	114	-57	232
82 (116T)	Eamonn Darcy	Eur 15	3.04	243	80	164	-97	176
83 (123)	Mike Donald	USA 47	2.98	331	111	203	-112	240
84 (45)	Blaine McCallister	USA 48	2.97	306	103	456	-234	84
85 (50)	Bill Glasson	USA 49	2.96	240	81	349	-181	72
86 (120)	Tony Johnstone	Afr 5	2.93	261	89	175	-102	188
87 (72)	Christy O'Connor, Jr.	Eur 16	2.84	199	70	232	-129	96
88 (107)	Philip Walton	Eur 17	2.81	233	83	182	-101	152
89 (75)	David Ishii	USA 50	2.79	262	94	288	-194	168
90 (119)	Kenny Perry	USA 51	2.73	224	82	164	-88	148
91 (137)	Peter O'Malley	ANZ 12	2.68	196	73	100	-52	148
92 (70)	Brian Jones	ANZ 13	2.66	255	96	327	-188	116
93T (226)	Billy Ray Brown	USA 52T	2.63	237	90	67	-34	204
93T (63)	Jay Haas	USA 52T	2.63	237	90	327	-190	100
95 (172)	Mark Brooks	USA 54	2.61	256	98	122	-62	196
96 (57)	Hal Sutton	USA 55	2.55	219	86	322	-203	100
97 (159)	John Cook	USA 56	2.54	203	80	127	-92	168

( ) : Figures in brackets indicate 1987/89 positions.

342 / THE SONY RANKING

Pos.	Player	Circuit	Points Average	Total Points	No. of Events	87/89 Total	87/89 Minus	1990 Plus
98 (58)	Howard Clark	Eur 18	2.52	209	83	318	-181	72
99 (181)	Brian Tennyson	USA 57	2.50	245	98	96	-55	204
100 (110)	Frank Nobilo	ANZ 14	2.43	233	96	203	-102	132
101 (165)	Tommy Armour III	USA 58	2.41	251	104	139	-72	184
102 (81)	Roger Mackay	ANZ 15	2.41	181	75	210	-117	88
103 (87)	Fulton Allem	Afr 6	2.39	213	89	207	-126	132
104 (156)	Dan Forsman	USA 59	2.37	220	93	148	-84	156
105 (77)	Des Smyth	Eur 19	2.35	186	79	238	-128	76
106 (160)	Scott Verplank	USA 60	2.34	211	90	135	-68	144
107 (90)	Mike Hulbert	USA 61	2.34	243	104	272	-149	120
108 (178)	Miguel Angel Martin	Eur 20	2.32	186	80	89	-47	144
109 (97)	Roger Chapman	Eur 21	2.30	207	90	206	-111	112
110 (193)	Richard Boxall	Eur 22	2.28	205	90	92	-47	160
111 (85)	David Edwards	USA 62	2.27	166	73	199	-113	80
112 (78)	Mark Wiebe	USA 63	2.25	216	96	301	-161	76
113 (76)	Andy Bean	USA 64	2.24	161	72	219	-126	68
114 (201)	Bill Britton	USA 65	2.18	198	91	94	-48	152
115 (104)	Ted Schulz	USA 66	2.17	195	90	190	-95	100
116 (432T)	Ryoken Kawagishi	Jpn 5	2.16	166	77	12	-6	160
117 (118)	Bob Gilder	USA 67	2.16	194	90	179	-93	108
118 (116T)	Ove Sellberg	Eur 23	2.12	163	77	152	-89	100
119 (187)	Mike Clayton	ANZ 16	2.11	228	108	111	-55	172
120 (285)	David Peoples	USA 68	2.10	187	89	47	-24	164
121 (106)	Brad Faxon	USA 69	2.09	188	90	200	-108	96
122 (182)	Russell Claydon	Eur 24	2.08	150	72	68	-34	116
123 (89)	Dave Barr	Can 1	2.06	167	81	216	-125	76
124 (94)	Mats Lanner	Eur 25	1.99	151	76	169	-98	80
125 (73)	David Rummells	USA 70	1.97	189	96	308	-163	44
126 (144)	Morris Hatalsky	USA 71	1.96	143	73	116	-69	96
127 (252)	Greg Turner	ANZ 17	1.94	134	69	42	-24	116
128 (109)	Masahiro Kuramoto	Jpn 6	1.94	184	95	189	-113	108
129 (388)	Stephen McAllister	Eur 26	1.89	153	81	19	-10	144
130 (741T)	Stephen Richardson	Eur 27	1.89	132	70	0	0	132
131 (138)	Mark Lye	USA 72	1.83	163	89	157	-82	88
132 (145)	Saburo Fujiki	Jpn 7	1.82	180	99	146	-82	116
133 (161)	Chris Perry	USA 73	1.82	178	98	140	-86	124
134 (92)	D.A. Weibring	USA 74	1.79	131	73	189	-126	68
135 (44)	Dan Pohl	USA 75	1.79	122	68	327	-205	0
136 (185)	Billy Andrade	USA 76	1.78	173	97	98	-49	124
137 (95)	Derrick Cooper	Eur 28	1.75	152	87	187	-95	60
138 (215T)	Rocco Mediate	USA 77	1.74	153	88	84	-47	116
139 (124)	Jack Nicklaus	USA 78	1.73	104	60	111	-63	56
140 (163)	Brian Claar	USA 79	1.71	120	70	116	-60	64
141 (204T)	Noboru Sugai	Jpn 8	1.71	164	96	86	-50	128
142 (108)	Tom Byrum	USA 80	1.70	167	98	220	-121	68
143 (323T)	Nolan Henke	USA 81	1.70	126	74	28	-14	112
144 (91)	Chen Tze Chung	Asa 2	1.70	134	79	204	-130	60
145 (99)	Barry Lane	Eur 29	1.69	159	94	199	-108	68
146 (260)	Malcolm Mackenzie	Eur 30	1.69	157	93	59	-30	128
147 (153)	Toru Nakamura	Jpn 9	1.69	167	99	144	-85	108
148 (86)	Michael Allen	USA 82	1.69	145	86	215	-110	40
149T (166)	Andrew Magee	USA 83	1.67	160	96	137	-73	96
149T (115)	Jeff Hawkes	Afr 7	1.67	125	75	163	-90	52

( ) : Figures in brackets indicate 1987/89 positions.

THE SONY RANKING / 343

Pos.	Player	Circuit	Points Average	Total Points	No. of Events	87/89 Total	87/89 Minus	1990 Plus
151 (191T)	Hideki Kase	Jpn 10	1.65	127	77	65	-34	96
152 (121)	Nobuo Serizawa	Jpn 11	1.64	161	98	174	-105	92
153 (258)	Frankie Minoza	Asa 3	1.63	98	60	38	-20	80
154 (83)	Tateo Ozaki	Jpn 12	1.62	152	94	263	-139	28
155 (227)	Yoshinori Kaneko	Jpn 13	1.61	137	85	60	-31	108
156 (136)	Kenny Knox	USA 84	1.61	164	102	181	-105	88
157 (203)	Teruo Sugihara	Jpn 14	1.60	133	83	71	-38	100
158 (157)	Mark Roe	Eur 31	1.60	141	88	134	-73	80
159 (325)	Vicente Fernandez	SAm 2	1.60	112	70	28	-16	100
160 (101)	Andrew Murray	Eur 32	1.59	121	76	175	-90	36
161 (152)	David Graham	ANZ 18	1.57	107	68	119	-68	56
162 (211)	Jeff Maggert	USA 85	1.57	94	60	56	-30	68
163 (114)	Gordon J. Brand	Eur 33	1.55	146	94	184	-102	64
164 (354)	Tony Sills	USA 86	1.55	130	84	33	-23	120
165 (112)	Robert Wrenn	USA 87	1.53	133	87	176	-103	60
166 (351T)	Kirk Triplett	USA 88	1.52	102	67	21	-11	92
167 (214)	Richard Zokol	Can 2	1.51	118	78	66	-40	92
168 (218T)	Peter McWhinney	ANZ 19	1.49	137	92	68	-35	104
169 (111)	Doug Tewell	USA 89	1.48	120	81	172	-100	48
170 (218T)	Russ Cochran	USA 90	1.46	137	94	85	-52	104
171 (194)	Phil Blackmar	USA 91	1.45	125	86	95	-54	84
172 (134)	Bob Lohr	USA 92	1.45	138	95	166	-92	64
173 (133)	Mark Mouland	Eur 34	1.45	139	96	161	-94	72
174 (212)	Paul Broadhurst	Eur 35	1.44	104	72	56	-28	76
175 (150)	Jay Don Blake	USA 93	1.43	129	90	142	-77	64
176 (127)	Bobby Wadkins	USA 94	1.41	134	95	178	-124	80
177 (188)	Tom Sieckmann	USA 95	1.41	121	86	102	-53	72
178 (307T)	Bob Estes	USA 96	1.40	108	77	32	-16	92
179 (278)	Jim Thorpe	USA 97	1.40	112	80	42	-26	96
180 (93)	Mike Sullivan	USA 98	1.35	112	83	193	-101	20
181 (103)	Gary Koch	USA 99	1.32	94	71	176	-90	8
182 (337)	Trevor Dodds	Afr 8	1.32	90	68	31	-13	72
183 (299T)	Ken Trimble	ANZ 20	1.30	78	60	30	-16	64
184 (132)	Hubert Green	USA 100	1.29	88	68	127	-67	28
185 (100)	Jim Carter	USA 101	1.29	126	98	228	-114	12
186 (220)	Bill Sander	USA 102	1.28	118	92	84	-50	84
187 (263)	Rick Hartmann	USA 103	1.28	110	86	53	-31	88
188 (213)	Brad Bryant	USA 104	1.26	110	87	70	-36	76
189 (471)	Anders Sorensen	Eur 36	1.25	90	72	12	-6	84
190 (233T)	Mike Smith	USA 105	1.24	88	71	56	-28	60
191 (459)	Jay Delsing	USA 106	1.23	101	82	17	-12	96
192 (741T)	Danny Mijovic	Can 3	1.23	80	65	0	0	80
193 (177)	Magnus Persson	Eur 37	1.23	86	70	81	-51	56
194 (125)	Jim Benepe	USA 107	1.22	106	87	141	-75	40
195 (122)	Denis Durnian	Eur 38	1.21	125	103	198	-105	32
196 (141)	Curt Byrum	USA 108	1.21	117	97	163	-102	56
197 (176)	Larry Rinker	USA 109	1.20	102	85	107	-57	52
198 (264)	David Williams	Eur 39	1.19	117	98	57	-32	92
199 (167)	Terry Gale	ANZ 21	1.18	99	84	116	-69	52
200 (180)	Carl Mason	Eur 40	1.17	98	84	96	-58	60

( ) : Figures in brackets indicate 1987/89 positions.

World's Winners of 1990

U.S. TOUR

MONY Tournament of Champions	Paul Azinger
Northern Telecom Tucson Open	Robert Gamez
Bob Hope Chrysler Classic	Peter Jacobsen
Phoenix Open	Tommy Armour III
AT&T Pebble Beach National Pro-Am	Mark O'Meara
Hawaiian Open	David Ishii
Shearson Lehman Hutton Open	Dan Forsman
Nissan Los Angeles Open	Fred Couples
Doral Ryder Open	Greg Norman (2)
Honda Classic	John Huston
The Players Championship	Jodie Mudd
The Nestle Invitational	Robert Gamez (2)
Independent Insurance Agent Open	Tony Sills
The Masters Tournament	Nick Faldo
Deposit Guaranty Classic	Gene Sauers
MCI Heritage Classic	Payne Stewart
K-mart Greater Greensboro Open	Steve Elkington
USF&G Classic	David Frost
GTE Byron Nelson Classic	Payne Stewart (2)
Memorial Tournament	Greg Norman (3)
Southwestern Bell Colonial	Ben Crenshaw
BellSouth Atlanta Classic	Wayne Levi
Kemper Open	Gil Morgan
Centel Western Open	Wayne Levi (2)
U.S. Open Championship	Hale Irwin
Buick Classic	Hale Irwin (2)
Canon Greater Hartford Open	Wayne Levi (3)
Westinghouse-Family House Invitational	Curtis Strange
Anheuser-Busch Classic	Lanny Wadkins
Bank of Boston Classic	Morris Hatalsky
Buick Open	Chip Beck
Federal Express St. Jude Classic	Tom Kite
PGA Championship	Wayne Grady
The International	Davis Love III
Fred Meyer Challenge	Bobby Wadkins/Lanny Wadkins (2)
NEC World Series of Golf	Jose Maria Olazabal (3)
Chattanooga Classic	Peter Persons
Greater Milwaukee Open	Jim Gallagher, Jr.
Hardee's Golf Classic	Joey Sindelar
Canadian Open	Wayne Levi (4)
B.C. Open	Nolan Henke
Buick Southern Open	Kenny Knox
H.E.B. Texas Open	Mark O'Meara (2)
Las Vegas Invitational	Bob Tway
Walt Disney World/Oldsmobile Classic	Tim Simpson
Nabisco Championship	Jodie Mudd (2)
Mexican Open	Bob Lohr
Isuzu Kapalua International	David Peoples
RMCC Invitational Hosted by Greg Norman	Raymond Floyd/Fred Couples (2)
World Cup	Germany/Payne Stewart (3)
J.C. Penney Classic	Davis Love III (2)/Beth Daniel (8)
Sazale Classic	Fred Couples (3)/Mike Donald
Spalding Invitational	Juli Inkster

U.S. SENIOR TOUR

MONY Senior Tournament of Champions	George Archer
Royal Caribbean Classic	Lee Trevino
GTE Suncoast Classic	Mike Hill
Aetna Challenge	Lee Trevino (2)
Chrysler Cup	United States
Vintage Chrysler Invitational	Lee Trevino (3)
Vantage at the Dominion	Jim Dent
Fuji Electric Grand Slam	Bob Charles
The Tradition at Desert Mountain	Jack Nicklaus
PGA Seniors Championship	Gary Player
Liberty Mutual Legends of Golf	Dale Douglass/Charles Coody
Murata Reunion Pro-Am	Frank Beard
Las Vegas Classic	Chi Chi Rodriguez
Southwestern Bell Classic	Jim Powell
Doug Sanders Kingwood Celebrity Classic	Lee Trevino (4)
Bell Atlantic Classic	Dale Douglass (2)
NYNEX Commemorative	Lee Trevino (5)
Mazda Senior TPC Championship	Jack Nicklaus (2)
MONY Syracuse Classic	Jim Dent (2)
Digital Classic	Bob Charles (2)
U.S. Senior Open	Lee Trevino (6)
Northville Long Island Classic	George Archer (2)
Kroger Classic	Jim Dent (3)
Ameritech Open	Chi Chi Rodriguez (2)
Newport Cup	Al Kelley
Volvo Seniors British Open	Gary Player (2)
PaineWebber Invitational	Bruce Crampton
Sunwest Bank/Charley Pride Classic	Chi Chi Rodriguez (3)
Showdown Classic	Rives McBee
GTE Northwest Classic	George Archer (3)
GTE North Classic	Mike Hill (2)
Vantage Bank One Classic	Rives McBee (2)
Greater Grand Rapids Open	Don Massengale
Crestar Classic	Jim Dent (4)
Fairfield Barnett Space Coast Classic	Mike Hill (3)
Vantage Championship	Charles Coody (2)
Gatlin Brothers Southwest Classic	Bruce Crampton (2)
Transamerica Championship	Lee Trevino (7)
Gold Rush at Rancho Murieta	George Archer (4)
Security Pacific Classic	Mike Hill (4)
Du Pont Cup	United States
Seniors Challenge	George Archer (5)
GTE Kaanapali Classic	Bob Charles (3)
New York Life Champions	Mike Hill (5)

EUROPEAN TOUR

Vinho Verde Atlantic Open	Stephen McAllister
Emirates Airline Desert Classic	Eamonn Darcy
American Express Mediterranean Open	Ian Woosnam
Open Renault de Baleares	Severiano Ballesteros
Tenerife Open	Vicente Fernandez
Volvo Open	Eduardo Romero
AGF Open	Brett Ogle
El Bosque Open	Vijay Singh
Credit Lyonnais Cannes Open	Mark McNulty
Cepsa Madrid Open	Bernhard Langer
Peugeot Spanish Open	Rodger Davis (2)
Benson and Hedges International Open	Jose Maria Olazabal
Peugeot-Trends Belgian Open	Ove Sellberg

Lancia-Martini Italian Open	Richard Boxall
Volvo PGA Championship	Mike Harwood
Dunhill British Masters	Mark James
Scandinavian Enterprise Open	Craig Stadler
Wang Four Stars National Pro-Celebrity	Rodger Davis (3)
Carrolls Irish Open	Jose Maria Olazabal (2)
Peugeot French Open	Philip Walton
Torras Monte Carlo Open	Ian Woosnam (2)
Bell's Scottish Open	Ian Woosnam (3)
British Open Championship	Nick Faldo (2)
KLM Dutch Open	Stephen McAllister (2)
PLM Open	Ronan Rafferty (2)
Murphy's Cup	Tony Johnstone
NM English Open	Mark James (2)
Volvo German Open	Mark McNulty (2)
Ebel European Masters-Swiss Open	Ronan Rafferty (3)
Panasonic European Open	Peter Senior
Lancome Trophy	Jose Maria Olazabal (4)
Motorola Classic	Paul Broadhurst
Suntory World Match Play Championship	Ian Woosnam (4)
BMW International Open	Paul Azinger (2)
Epson Grand Prix of Europe	Ian Woosnam (5)
Mercedes German Masters	Sam Torrance
Dunhill Cup	Ireland
Austrian Open	Bernhard Langer (2)
Portuguese Open-TPC	Michael McLean
Volvo Masters	Mike Harwood (2)

AFRICAN TOURS

Zimbabwe Open	Grant Turner
Zambia Open	Gordon J. Brand
Kenya Open	Christy O'Connor, Jr.
ICL International	Gavin Levenson
Lexington PGA Championship	Fulton Allem
Protea Assurance South African Open	Trevor Dodds
AECI Charity Classic	John Daly
Goodyear Classic	Phil Jonas
Hollard Royal Swazi Sun Classic	John Daly (2)
Palabora Classic	Tony Johnstone
Dewar's White Label Trophy	John Bland
Trustbank Tournament of Champions	Trevor Dodds (2)
Minolta Copiers Match Play	John Bland (2)
Twee Jongegzellen Masters	Fulton Allem (2)
Million Dollar Challenge	David Frost
Bloemfontein Spoornet Classic	John Bland (3)
Goodyear Classic	Fulton Allem (3)
Nigerian Open	Wayne Stephens
Ivory Coast Open	David Llewellyn

AUSTRALIAN TOUR

Daikyo Palm Meadows Cup	Rodger Davis
Coca Cola Classic	Ronan Rafferty
Vines Classic	Jeff Maggert
Mercedes-Benz Australian Match Play	David Smith
Australian Masters	Greg Norman
Monro Interiors Nedlands Masters	John Morse
New South Wales Open	Ken Trimble
Air New Zealand Shell Open	Wayne Riley
West End South Australian Open	Mike Harwood (3)
Australian PGA Championship	Brett Ogle (2)

Australian Open Championship	John Morse (2)
Johnnie Walker Classic	Greg Turner
Hyatt Regency Coolum Classic	Ian Baker-Finch

ASIA/JAPAN TOUR

San Miguel Beer/Coca Cola Philippine Open	Robert Pactolerin
Martell Hong Kong Open	Ken Green
Thai International Thailand Open	Wen-Ter Lu
Daiichi Fudosan Cup	Brian Jones
Wills Indian Open	Andrew Debusk
Imperial	Toru Nakamura
Epson Singapore Open	Antolin Fernando
Shizuoka Open	Ryoken Kawagishi
Indonesian Open	Frankie Minoza
Taylor Made Setonaikai Open	Masahiro Kuramoto
Benson & Hedges Malaysian Open	Glen Day
Pocari Sweat Open	Nobumitsu Yuhara
Sanyang Republic of China Open	Frankie Minoza (2)
Bridgestone Aso Open	Teruo Sugihara
Maekyung Korea Open	Kang-Sun Lee
Dunlop Open	Frankie Minoza (3)
Chunichi Crowns	Noboru Sugai
Fuji Sankei Classic	Masashi Ozaki
Japan Match Play Championship	Naomichi Ozaki
Pepsi Ube	Tadao Nakamura
Mitsubishi Galant	Isao Aoki
JCB Classic Sendai	Roger Mackay
Sapporo Tokyu Open	Tadao Nakamura (2)
Yomiuri Sapporo Beer Open	Saburo Fujiki
Mizuno Open	Brian Jones (2)
Kanta PGA Championship	Tsuneyuki Nakajima
Kansai PGA Championship	Kouki Idoki
Yonex Open Hiroshima	Masashi Ozaki (2)
Nikkei Cup Torakichi Nakamura Memorial	Satoshi Higashi
Yokohama Open	Noboru Sugai (2)
NST Nigata Open	Seiichi Kanai
Japan PGA Championship	Hideki Kase
Maruman Open	Masashi Ozaki (3)
Daiwa KBC Augusta	Masashi Ozaki (4)
Kanto Open	Ryoken Kawagishi (2)
Kansai Open	Teruo Sugihara (2)
Kyushu Open	Katsuyoshi Tomori
Hokkaido Open	Katsuhige Takahashi
Chu-Shikoku Open	Seiki Okuda
Suntory Open	Toru Nakamura
All Nippon Airways Open	Tsuneyuki Nakajima (2)
Gene Sarazen Jun Classic	Naomichi Ozaki (2)
Tokai Classic	Graham Marsh
Japan Open Championship	Tsuneyuki Nakajima (3)
Asahi Beer Golf Digest	Noboru Sugai (3)
Bridgestone	Saburo Fujiki (2)
Lark Cup	Ryoken Kawagishi (3)
Asahi Glass Four Tours World Championship	Australia/New Zealand
Acom P.T.	Bob Gilder
Visa Taiheiyo Club Masters	Jose Maria Olazabal (5)
Dunlop Phoenix	Larry Mize
Casio World Open	Mike Reid
Japan Series	Naomichi Ozaki (3)
Daikyo Open	Teruo Sugihara (3)
Johnnie Walker Asian Classic	Nick Faldo (3)

SOUTH AMERICAN TOUR

Los Leones Open	Angel Franco
Argentina Open	Vicente Fernandez (2)
Sao Pablo Open	Bruce Fleisher

THE LPGA TOUR

Jamaica Classic	Patty Sheehan
Oldsmobile Classic	Pat Bradley
Phar-Mor Inverrary Classic	Jane Crafter
Orix Hawaiian Open	Beth Daniel
Women's Kemper Open	Beth Daniel (2)
Desert Inn International	Maggie Hill
Circle K Tucson Open	Colleen Walker
Standard Register Turquoise Classic	Pat Bradley (2)
Nabisco Dinah Shore	Betsy King
Red Robin Kyocera Inamori Classic	Kris Monaghan
Sara Lee Classic	Ayako Okamoto
Crestar Classic	Dottie Mochrie
Planters Pat Bradley International	Cindy Rarick
Corning Classic	Pat Bradley (3)
Lady Keystone Open	Cathy Gerring
McDonald's Championship	Patty Sheehan (2)
Atlantic City Classic	Chris Johnson
Rochester International	Patty Sheehan (3)
du Maurier Ltd. Classic	Cathy Johnston
Jamie Farr Toledo Classic	Tina Purtzer
U.S. Women's Open	Betsy King (2)
Phar-Mor Youngstown Classic	Beth Daniel (3)
Mazda LPGA Championship	Beth Daniel (4)
Boston Five Classic	Barb Mucha
Stratton Mountain Classic	Cathy Gerring (2)
JAL Big Apple Classic	Betsy King (3)
Northgate Classic	Beth Daniel (5)
Rail Charity Classic	Beth Daniel (6)
Ping Cellular One Championship	Patty Sheehan (4)
Safeco Classic	Patty Sheehan (5)
MBS Classic	Nancy Lopez
Centel Classic	Beth Daniel (7)
Trophee Urban World Championship	Cathy Gerring (3)
Nichirei International	United States
Mazda Japan Classic	Debbie Massey
Solheim Cup	United States
Itoman LPGA World Match Play	Betsy King (4)

THE WOMEN'S EUROPEAN TOUR

Valextra Classic	Florence Descampe
Ford Ladies Classic	Marie Laure de Lorenzi
Hennessy Ladies' Cup	Trish Johnson
WPG European Tour Classic	Tania Abitbol
Bonmont Ladies Classic	Evelyn Orley
BMW European Masters	Karen Lunn
BMW Ladies Classic	Diane Barnard
Laing Ladies Charity Classic	Laurette Maritz
Bloor Homes Eastleigh Classic	Trish Johnson (2)
Weetabix Women's British Open	Helen Alfredsson
Lufthansa Ladies' German Open	Ayako Okamoto
Haninge Ladies' Open	Dale Reid
Variety Club Celebrity Classic	Alison Nicholas
TEC Players Championship	Anne Jones

Expedier Ladies European Open — Trish Johnson (3)
Trophee International Coconut Skol — Corinne Dibnah
Italian Ladies Open — Florence Descampe (2)
Woolmark Matchplay Championship — Florence Descampe (3)
AGF Biarritz Ladies Open — Laura Davies
Benson & Hedges Mixed Team Trophy — Tania Abitbol (2)/Jose Maria Canizares
Longines Classic — Trish Johnson (4)

Multiple Winners of 1990

PLAYER	WINS	PLAYER	WINS
Beth Daniel	8	Noboru Sugai	3
Lee Trevino	7	Teruo Sugihara	3
George Archer	5	Tania Abitbol	2
Mike Hill	5	Paul Azinger	2
Jose Maria Olazabal	5	Charles Coody	2
Patty Sheehan	5	Bruce Crampton	2
Ian Woosnam	5	John Daly	2
Jim Dent	4	Trevor Dodds	2
Trish Johnson	4	Dale Douglass	2
Betsy King	4	Vicente Fernandez	2
Wayne Levi	4	Saburo Fujiki	2
Masashi Ozaki	4	Robert Gamez	2
Fulton Allem	3	Hale Irwin	2
John Bland	3	Mark James	2
Pat Bradley	3	Brian Jones	2
Bob Charles	3	Bernhard Langer	2
Fred Couples	3	Davis Love III	2
Rodger Davis	3	Stephen McAllister	2
Florence Descampe	3	Rives McBee	2
Nick Faldo	3	Mark McNulty	2
Cathy Gerring	3	John Morse	2
Mike Harwood	3	Jodie Mudd	2
Ryoken Kawagishi	3	Tadao Nakamura	2
Frankie Minoza	3	Toru Nakamura	2
Tsuneyuki Nakajima	3	Jack Nicklaus	2
Greg Norman	3	Brett Ogle	2
Naomichi Ozaki	3	Mark O'Meara	2
Ronan Rafferty	3	Gary Player	2
Chi Chi Rodriguez	3	Lanny Wadkins	2
Payne Stewart	3		

Career World Money List

The following is a listing of the 50 leading money winners for their careers through the 1990 season. It includes active and inactive players. The World Money List from this and the 24 previous editions of this annual and a table prepared for a companion book, THE WONDERFUL WORLD OF PROFESSIONAL GOLF (Atheneum, 1973), form the basis for this compilation. Additional figures were taken from official records of major golf associations, although the shortcomings in records-keeping in professional golf outside the United States in the 1950s and 1960s and exclusions from U.S. records in a few cases during those years prevent these figures from being completely accurate. Conversions of foreign currency figures to U.S. dollars are based on average values during the particular years involved.

POS.	PLAYER, COUNTRY	TOTAL MONEY
1	Greg Norman, Australia	$8,015,366
2	Tom Kite, U.S.	7,258,027
3	Severiano Ballesteros, Spain	7,062,613
4	Curtis Strange, U.S.	7,059,948
5	Jack Nicklaus, U.S.	6,684,716
6	Tom Watson, U.S.	6,429,152
7	Lee Trevino, U.S.	6,306,785
8	Lanny Wadkins, U.S.	6,068,682
9	Payne Stewart, U.S.	5,895,856
10	Isao Aoki, Japan	5,721,427
11	Gary Player, South Africa	5,708,783
12	Masashi Ozaki, Japan	5,695,936
13	Ben Crenshaw, U.S.	5,678,768
14	Bernhard Langer, Germany	5,645,088
15	Ian Woosnam, Wales	5,520,082
16	Raymond Floyd, U.S.	5,417,623
17	Miller Barber, U.S.	5,387,811
18	Nick Faldo, England	5,125,180
19	David Frost, South Africa	5,099,999
20	Hale Irwin, U.S.	5,004,790
21	Bob Charles, New Zealand	4,764,966
22	Sandy Lyle, Scotland	4,705,144
23	Fred Couples, U.S.	4,658,285
24	Tsuneyuki Nakajima, Japan	4,652,888
25	Craig Stadler, U.S.	4,574,096
26	Gene Littler, U.S.	4,368,144
27	Billy Casper, U.S.	4,340,746
28	Graham Marsh, Australia	4,321,201
29	Paul Azinger, U.S.	4,318,455
30	Andy Bean, U.S.	4,298,470
31	Arnold Palmer, U.S.	4,275,977
32	Chip Beck, U.S.	4,185,040
33	Bruce Crampton, Australia	4,134,235
34	Mark Calcavecchia, U.S.	4,076,929
35	John Mahaffey, U.S.	3,984,104
36	Mark O'Meara, U.S.	3,965,793
37	Don January, U.S.	3,940,823
38	Chi Chi Rodriguez, U.S.	3,939,734
39	Scott Hoch, U.S.	3,905,169
40	Johnny Miller, U.S.	3,790,505

POS.	PLAYER, COUNTRY	TOTAL MONEY
41	Bruce Lietzke, U.S.	3,705,229
42	Larry Nelson, U.S.	3,702,234
43	Wayne Levi, U.S.	3,664,366
44	Jose Maria Olazabal, Spain	3,639,838
45	Larry Mize, U.S.	3,638,605
46	David Graham, Australia	3,607,664
47	Gil Morgan, U.S.	3,549,132
48	Peter Jacobsen, U.S.	3,495,832
49	Bob Tway, U.S.	3,444,032
50	Naomichi Ozaki, Japan	3,417,597

These 50 players have won $241,851,865 in their lifetimes playing professional tournament golf.

World Senior Money List

This list has been added for 1990, since it was deemed more logical to separate and therefore better reflect the earnings of the senior professionals in their own realm in a more relative and concise manner. Included are the official earnings on the Senior PGA and Japan Senior Tours, along with other winnings on the PGA and Japan Tours, in unofficial events on the U.S. Senior Tour and from non-circuit tournaments in the U.S. and abroad.

POS.	PLAYER	TOTAL MONEY
1	Lee Trevino	$1,311,031
2	Mike Hill	990,228
3	Charles Coody	917,901
4	George Archer	860,591
5	Chi Chi Rodriguez	848,658
6	Jim Dent	762,283
7	Bob Charles	719,153
8	Dale Douglass	707,531
9	Gary Player	589,786
10	Rives McBee	525,329
11	Bruce Crampton	524,000
12	Dave Hill	491,983
13	Harold Henning	491,872
14	Al Geiberger	463,624
15	Jack Nicklaus	452,431
16	Larry Mowry	367,272
17	Miller Barber	364,055
18	Frank Beard	359,896
19	Orville Moody	351,412

POS.	PLAYER	TOTAL MONEY
20	Don Bies	338,214
21	Rocky Thompson	312,248
22	Walter Zembriski	295,292
23	Terry Dill	278,372
24	Tom Shaw	252,999
25	Joe Jimenez	246,067
26	Don January	242,302
27	Don Massengale	229,531
28	Al Kelley	226,461
29	Shigeru Uchida, Japan	224,036
30	Arnold Palmer	219,369
31	John Paul Cain	213,544
32	Jimmy Powell	209,883
33	Ben Smith	201,223
34	Hsieh Min Nan, Taiwan	198,546
35	Hisashi Suzumura, Japan	190,897
36	Kesahiro Uchida, Japan	189,834
37	Larry Laoretti	165,339
38	Bobby Nichols	163,144
39	George Lanning	159,768
40	Lou Graham	159,300
41	Dick Hendrickson	159,070
42	Jim Ferree	158,614
43	Homero Blancas	157,075
44	Richard Rhyan	156,868
45	Butch Baird	155,313
46	Gay Brewer	134,310
47	Shozo Uchida, Japan	133,378
48	Ken Still	133,110
49	Teruo Suzumura, Japan	128,651
50	Phil Rodgers	127,339

LPGA Money List

This list includes official winnings from the U.S. LPGA Tour, along with earnings from the JC Penney, Nikkei Cup, Itoman LPGA World Match Play, Spalding and other unofficial events. Complete statistics could not be obtained to incorporate earnings from the women's tours in Japan and Europe into this listing.

POS.	PLAYER	TOTAL MONEY
1	Beth Daniel	$963,578
2	Patty Sheehan	746,618
3	Betsy King	649,294
4	Cathy Gerring	506,776
5	Pat Bradley	489,518

POS.	PLAYER	TOTAL MONEY
6	Rosie Jones	371,332
7	Nancy Lopez	360,262
8	Danielle Ammaccapane	332,731
9	Ayako Okamoto	316,885
10	Cindy Rarick	307,263
11	Deb Richard	275,936
12	Dawn Coe	250,653
13	Colleen Walker	247,018
14	Dottie Mochrie	243,460
15	Caroline Keggi	239,697
16	Jane Geddes	210,874
17	Chris Johnson	205,361
18	Barbara Mucha	198,972
19	Tammie Green	185,015
20	Cathy Johnston	184,565
21	Cindy Figg-Currier	184,401
22	Elaine Crosby	182,293
23	Debbie Massey	177,036
24	Dale Eggeling	171,090
25	Patti Rizzo	164,377
26	Nancy Brown	160,913
27	Penny Hammel	148,753
28	Sherri Turner	142,862
29	Meg Mallon	140,381
30	Amy Benz	137,316
31	Pam Wright	131,317
32	Kathy Postlewait	128,738
33	Missie McGeorge	128,221
34	Sue Ertl	121,422
35	Shirley Furlong	119,215
36	Juli Inkster	116,826
37	Jane Crafter	116,325
38	Maggie Will	115,038
39	Sherri Steinhauer	114,857
40	Kristi Albers	114,390
41	Alice Ritzman	112,840
42	Missie Berteotti	109,905
43	Susan Sanders	104,946
44	Vicki Fergon	103,924
45	Amy Alcott	102,325
46	Donna White	101,184
47	Lynn Connelly	94,031
48	Cathy Morse	91,778
49	JoAnne Carner	91,768
50	Martha Nause	88,833

The U.S. Tour

MONY Tournament of Champions

La Costa Country Club, Carlsbad, California
Par 36-36—72; 7,022 yards

January 4-7
purse, $750,000

	SCORES				TOTAL	MONEY
Paul Azinger	66	68	69	69	272	$135,000
Ian Baker-Finch	66	67	72	68	273	82,000
Mark O'Meara	69	73	65	69	276	52,000
Wayne Grady	69	68	72	69	278	36,800
Scott Hoch	69	68	71	71	279	29,750
Greg Norman	66	72	71	70	279	29,750
Mike Hulbert	72	68	73	68	281	24,666.67
Curtis Strange	71	73	70	67	281	24,666.67
Mark Calcavecchia	70	68	68	75	281	24,666.66
Mark McCumber	69	73	69	73	284	19,625
Tim Simpson	69	73	71	71	284	19,625
Payne Stewart	67	75	69	73	284	19,625
Bob Tway	71	73	68	72	284	19,625
John Mahaffey	74	69	73	69	285	16,500
Gene Sauers	74	70	71	70	285	16,500
Bill Britton	74	73	73	67	287	14,000
Bill Glasson	72	73	71	71	287	14,000
Ted Schulz	72	69	74	72	287	14,000
Mike Donald	71	72	74	71	288	12,000
David Frost	69	68	75	76	288	12,000
Donnie Hammond	72	73	75	68	288	12,000
Curt Byrum	71	74	76	69	290	11,100
Tom Kite	73	72	70	75	290	11,100
Mike Sullivan	75	71	71	74	291	10,700
Leonard Thompson	74	72	74	71	291	10,700
Jodie Mudd	74	73	74	71	292	10,400
Scott Simpson	72	73	71	77	293	10,200
Blaine McCallister	74	74	73	74	295	10,000
Stan Utley	71	78	73	74	296	9,800
Tom Byrum	78	75	70	74	297	9,600
Greg Twiggs	74	85	74	76	309	9,400

Northern Telecom Tucson Open

Tucson, Arizona
TPC at StarPass
Par 36-36—72; 7,010 yards

January 11-14
purse, $900,000

Randolph Park Golf Course
Par 36-36—72; 6,902 yards

	SCORES				TOTAL	MONEY
Robert Gamez	65	66	69	70	270	$162,000
Mark Calcavecchia	68	67	70	69	274	79,200
Jay Haas	66	64	72	72	274	79,200
Dan Forsman	70	67	69	69	275	35,437.50
Davis Love III	68	65	73	69	275	35,437.50
Corey Pavin	67	70	69	69	275	35,437.50

		SCORES			TOTAL	MONEY
Bill Sander	68	69	73	65	275	35,437.50
Joel Edwards	67	71	71	67	276	27,000
David Frost	70	60	71	75	276	27,000
Mike Reid	67	71	68	71	277	24,300
Bill Buttner	68	64	75	71	278	22,500
Paul Azinger	67	72	71	69	279	16,585.72
Steve Elkington	65	72	72	70	279	16,585.72
Loren Roberts	69	69	74	67	279	16,585.72
Buddy Gardner	71	69	68	71	279	16,585.71
Andrew Magee	65	70	72	72	279	16,585.71
David Peoples	72	65	69	73	279	16,585.71
Hal Sutton	72	69	67	71	279	16,585.71
Donnie Hammond	65	71	73	71	280	10,908
Mark Lye	72	66	71	71	280	10,908
Chris Perry	68	70	71	71	280	10,908
Tom Sieckmann	69	70	68	73	280	10,908
Robert Wrenn	66	70	75	69	280	10,908
*Phil Mickelson	71	66	71	72	280	
Bob Eastwood	70	64	75	72	281	7,470
Bob Gilder	71	68	71	71	281	7,470
Steve Jones	70	71	70	70	281	7,470
Brian Tennyson	69	68	74	70	281	7,470
Mark Wiebe	67	67	75	72	281	7,470
Keith Clearwater	70	72	72	68	282	6,390
Tommy Moore	69	73	69	72	283	5,348.58
Michael Allen	67	69	74	73	283	5,348.57
John Cook	70	72	71	70	283	5,348.57
Wayne Grady	73	69	69	72	283	5,348.57
Larry Silveira	70	67	72	74	283	5,348.57
Craig Stadler	69	69	72	73	283	5,348.57
Ray Stewart	69	66	74	74	283	5,348.57
Phil Blackmar	71	71	72	70	284	4,050
Jay Don Blake	74	68	68	74	284	4,050
Nolan Henke	71	66	75	72	284	4,050
Mike Hulbert	68	67	78	71	284	4,050
Jeff Sluman	68	68	71	77	284	4,050
John Adams	67	72	73	73	285	3,240
David Canipe	69	73	71	72	285	3,240
Rick Fehr	66	71	70	78	285	3,240
Kirk Triplett	66	70	73	76	285	3,240
Dave Barr	71	69	73	73	286	2,406.86
Lennie Clements	68	66	77	75	286	2,406.86
Morris Hatalsky	73	68	73	72	286	2,406.86
Pat McGowan	62	75	73	76	286	2,406.86
J.C. Snead	73	67	69	77	286	2,406.86
Bob Tway	70	71	74	71	286	2,406.85
Bobby Wadkins	71	69	75	71	286	2,406.85

Bob Hope Chrysler Classic

Bermuda Dunes Country Club, Bermuda Dunes, California
Par 36-36—72; 6,927 yards

January 17-21
purse, $1,000,000

Indian Wells Country Club, Indian Wells, California
Par 36-36—72; 6,478 yards

PGA West, Palmer Course, La Quinta, California
Par 36-36—72; 6,924 yards

Tamarisk Country Club, Palm Desert, California
Par 36-36—72; 6,869 yards

	SCORES					TOTAL	MONEY
Peter Jacobsen	67	66	69	66	71	339	$180,000
Scott Simpson	68	69	67	68	68	340	88,000
Brian Tennyson	73	68	66	67	66	340	88,000
Tim Simpson	70	70	67	68	66	341	41,333.34
Tom Kite	70	69	64	69	69	341	41,333.33
Ted Schulz	70	66	69	67	69	341	41,333.33
Davis Love III	67	72	67	69	67	342	32,250
Bob Tway	67	68	69	69	69	342	32,250
Bill Glasson	67	71	71	65	69	343	26,000
Scott Hoch	68	69	69	68	69	343	26,000
Andrew Magee	68	69	68	69	69	343	26,000
Bobby Wadkins	71	70	65	71	66	343	26,000
Steve Elkington	70	67	65	69	73	344	20,000
Jim Thorpe	68	68	71	70	67	344	20,000
Chip Beck	68	69	66	74	68	345	16,500
Jay Don Blake	69	70	71	67	68	345	16,500
Lennie Clements	69	67	70	70	69	345	16,500
Larry Mize	69	68	69	72	67	345	16,500
Robert Gamez	70	66	67	73	70	346	11,700
Steve Jones	75	69	68	68	66	346	11,700
Bob Lohr	73	70	68	66	69	346	11,700
Steve Pate	71	69	70	65	71	346	11,700
Don Pooley	65	70	66	73	72	346	11,700
Gene Sauers	71	67	67	70	71	346	11,700
Jim Gallagher, Jr.	69	70	69	72	67	347	7,975
Jodie Mudd	67	71	69	69	71	347	7,975
Mark O'Meara	73	68	68	69	69	347	7,975
Mike Reid	68	66	69	67	77	347	7,975
Brad Bryant	70	72	67	69	70	348	6,358.34
Peter Persons	67	72	68	70	71	348	6,358.34
John Inman	69	69	70	67	73	348	6,358.33
John Mahaffey	71	69	69	68	71	348	6,358.33
Gil Morgan	68	70	69	73	68	348	6,358.33
Stan Utley	68	73	70	69	68	348	6,358.33
Andy Bean	67	69	73	66	74	349	4,721.43
Mike Donald	68	72	67	68	74	349	4,721.43
Corey Pavin	71	69	69	68	72	349	4,721.43
David Peoples	71	69	70	69	70	349	4,721.43
Duffy Waldorf	71	69	70	70	69	349	4,721.43
Robert Wrenn	70	65	73	70	71	349	4,721.43
Don Shirey, Jr.	70	66	67	72	74	349	4,721.42
Billy Andrade	70	71	71	66	72	350	3,500
Mark Calcavecchia	67	74	69	70	70	350	3,500
Rick Fehr	68	70	71	71	70	350	3,500
Roger Maltbie	67	71	71	69	72	350	3,500

	SCORES					TOTAL	MONEY
Lee Trevino	69	72	68	72	69	350	3,500
Clark Burroughs	69	71	71	68	72	351	2,568.58
Tommy Armour III	68	67	71	71	74	351	2,568.57
Jim Booros	68	67	73	66	77	351	2,568.57
Brad Faxon	72	71	69	69	70	351	2,568.57
Hubert Green	70	71	69	70	71	351	2,568.57
Larry Rinker	70	68	71	72	70	351	2,568.57
Loren Roberts	72	68	69	71	71	351	2,568.57

Phoenix Open

TPC of Scottsdale, Scottsdale, Arizona
Par 35-36—71; 6,992 yards

January 25-28
purse, $900,000

	SCORES				TOTAL	MONEY
Tommy Armour III	65	67	67	68	267	$162,000
Jim Thorpe	69	69	66	68	272	97,200
Billy Ray Brown	69	66	70	69	274	52,200
Fred Couples	75	66	66	67	274	52,200
Billy Mayfair	73	66	70	66	275	32,850
Brian Tennyson	70	67	65	73	275	32,850
Bob Tway	71	67	71	66	275	32,850
Paul Azinger	69	67	71	70	277	27,000
Jay Delsing	69	67	68	73	277	27,000
Dave Barr	67	68	68	75	278	22,500
Clark Burroughs	68	67	70	73	278	22,500
Sandy Lyle	67	71	67	73	278	22,500
Scott Hoch	67	70	71	71	279	17,400
Gene Sauers	72	70	71	66	279	17,400
Lance Ten Broeck	65	73	71	70	279	17,400
Mark Lye	71	70	70	69	280	12,625.72
Tom Purtzer	65	68	77	70	280	12,625.72
Bill Sander	71	71	68	70	280	12,625.72
Andy Bean	69	71	68	72	280	12,625.71
Jay Don Blake	68	67	73	72	280	12,625.71
Bob Eastwood	69	70	71	70	280	12,625.71
Larry Rinker	70	71	71	68	280	12,625.71
Mike Hulbert	71	67	69	74	281	8,010
Peter Jacobsen	70	69	71	71	281	8,010
Pat McGowan	70	68	72	71	281	8,010
Jodie Mudd	69	66	71	75	281	8,010
Kenny Perry	71	70	70	70	281	8,010
Mark Calcavecchia	67	68	69	78	282	6,390
Ed Fiori	67	72	72	71	282	6,390
J.C. Snead	69	68	72	73	282	6,390
Ben Crenshaw	71	68	71	73	283	5,104.29
Lee Janzen	70	69	71	73	283	5,104.29
Kenny Knox	71	66	74	72	283	5,104.29
Chris Perry	71	72	69	71	283	5,104.29
Bobby Clampett	70	66	79	68	283	5,104.28
Corey Pavin	68	69	70	76	283	5,104.28
Lanny Wadkins	68	72	68	75	283	5,104.28
Ronnie Black	73	67	69	75	284	3,600
Jim Gallagher, Jr.	72	69	70	73	284	3,600
Robert Gamez	69	70	70	75	284	3,600
Steve Haskins	70	72	70	72	284	3,600
Davis Love III	72	70	68	74	284	3,600
Gil Morgan	69	74	73	68	284	3,600

	SCORES				TOTAL	MONEY
David Ogrin	70	73	68	73	284	3,600
Doug Tewell	69	71	69	75	284	3,600
Michael Allen	75	68	69	73	285	2,340
David Edwards	74	69	70	72	285	2,340
Rick Fehr	69	67	70	79	285	2,340
Buddy Gardner	68	69	74	74	285	2,340
Mark McCumber	67	73	71	74	285	2,340
Steve Pate	68	72	72	73	285	2,340
Ted Schulz	73	69	69	74	285	2,340
Jeff Sluman	72	70	69	74	285	2,340
Mike Sullivan	74	68	74	69	285	2,340

AT&T Pebble Beach National Pro-Am

Pebble Beach, California

February 1-4
purse, $1,000,000

Pebble Beach Golf Links
Par 36-36—72; 6,799 yards

Spyglass Hill Golf Club
Par 36-36—72; 6,810 yards

Cypress Point Golf Club
Par 36-36—72; 6,506 yards

	SCORES			TOTAL	MONEY
Mark O'Meara	67	73	69	72	281	$180,000
Kenny Perry	73	71	69	70	283	108,000
Tom Kite	69	69	75	71	284	58,000
Payne Stewart	66	71	74	73	284	58,000
David Frost	74	71	73	67	285	40,000
Mark Calcavecchia	69	71	74	72	286	34,750
Richard Zokol	75	71	71	69	286	34,750
Brad Faxon	75	69	74	69	287	29,000
Rick Fehr	70	72	73	72	287	29,000
Rocco Mediate	69	68	73	77	287	29,000
Mark Brooks	71	70	73	74	288	21,200
Bob Eastwood	69	72	77	70	288	21,200
Webb Heintzelman	73	67	76	72	288	21,200
Craig Stadler	72	73	72	71	288	21,200
Bobby Wadkins	70	68	78	72	288	21,200
Brian Claar	69	72	75	73	289	15,500
Ray Floyd	69	72	76	72	289	15,500
Loren Roberts	74	70	71	74	289	15,500
Willie Wood	73	72	71	73	289	15,500
Roger Maltbie	71	71	75	73	290	13,000
David Edwards	75	73	71	72	291	8,900
Dave Eichelberger	73	69	71	78	291	8,900
Steve Elkington	76	67	75	73	291	8,900
Nolan Henke	75	72	71	73	291	8,900
Peter Jacobsen	70	73	75	73	291	8,900
Andrew Magee	74	69	76	72	291	8,900
Johnny Miller	72	72	70	77	291	8,900
Jerry Pate	76	72	72	71	291	8,900
Nick Price	71	73	70	77	291	8,900
Larry Silveira	72	73	72	74	291	8,900
Mike Hulbert	72	70	76	74	292	6,350
Gene Sauers	73	68	76	75	292	6,350

	SCORES				TOTAL	MONEY
Billy Andrade	72	78	69	74	293	5,171.43
John Cook	70	68	78	77	293	5,171.43
Danny Edwards	75	70	76	72	293	5,171.43
Corey Pavin	74	68	78	73	293	5,171.43
Lanny Wadkins	72	71	78	72	293	5,171.43
Mark Wiebe	72	72	76	73	293	5,171.43
Dillard Pruitt	73	68	78	74	293	5,171.42
John Adams	74	74	72	74	294	3,800
Paul Azinger	78	70	73	73	294	3,800
Greg Bruckner	75	70	76	73	294	3,800
Sandy Lyle	74	70	74	76	294	3,800
Chris Perry	72	70	75	77	294	3,800
Robert Wrenn	73	72	76	73	294	3,800
Lennie Clements	74	69	77	75	295	2,772
Fred Couples	75	71	72	77	295	2,772
Hale Irwin	73	76	72	74	295	2,772
Hal Sutton	73	73	74	75	295	2,772
Stan Utley	68	73	78	76	295	2,772

Hawaiian Open

Waialae Country Club, Honolulu, Hawaii
Par 36-36—72; 6,975 yards

February 8-11
purse, $1,000,000

	SCORES				TOTAL	MONEY
David Ishii	72	67	68	72	279	$180,000
Paul Azinger	68	71	71	70	280	108,000
Clark Dennis	70	73	68	70	281	52,000
Jodie Mudd	72	72	68	69	281	52,000
Craig Stadler	71	67	72	71	281	52,000
Billy Ray Brown	72	71	69	70	282	30,250
Jim Hallet	69	73	70	70	282	30,250
Billy Mayfair	74	71	67	70	282	30,250
Peter Persons	72	68	73	69	282	30,250
Tim Simpson	72	69	71	70	282	30,250
Grant Waite	72	67	72	71	282	30,250
Hubert Green	73	67	66	77	283	19,000
Steve Lamontagne	73	73	65	72	283	19,000
Wayne Levi	71	74	69	69	283	19,000
Lanny Wadkins	74	66	73	70	283	19,000
Jim Woodward	73	69	69	72	283	19,000
Richard Zokol	73	72	69	69	283	19,000
Dave Barr	70	71	72	71	284	11,750
Bill Buttner	72	74	68	70	284	11,750
Mike Donald	74	69	72	69	284	11,750
Brad Fabel	70	74	70	70	284	11,750
Robert Gamez	74	72	67	71	284	11,750
Tom Kite	75	72	66	71	284	11,750
Gene Sauers	70	70	71	73	284	11,750
Bob Wolcott	72	72	71	69	284	11,750
Curt Byrum	77	67	70	71	285	7,100
Mark Lye	72	70	71	72	285	7,100
John Mahaffey	74	69	71	71	285	7,100
Larry Mize	72	75	68	70	285	7,100
Nick Price	74	71	71	69	285	7,100
Tony Sills	72	71	68	74	285	7,100
Ray Stewart	72	70	71	72	285	7,100
Clark Burroughs	76	72	68	70	286	5,171.43

	SCORES				TOTAL	MONEY
Brian Claar	76	71	69	70	286	5,171.43
Joel Edwards	76	69	70	71	286	5,171.43
Tomohiro Maruyama	77	71	68	70	286	5,171.43
Jack Renner	71	75	70	70	286	5,171.43
Mike Smith	68	78	70	70	286	5,171.43
Tommy Moore	70	77	72	67	286	5,171.42
Michael Allen	74	70	71	72	287	4,100
Steve Hart	75	68	68	76	287	4,100
Brian Tennyson	73	73	70	71	287	4,100
Jim Carter	74	72	70	72	288	2,784.62
Dave Eichelberger	69	73	72	74	288	2,784.62
Mark Hayes	71	73	73	71	288	2,784.62
John Inman	71	72	71	74	288	2,784.62
Bruce Lietzke	75	71	69	73	288	2,784.62
Davis Love III	72	73	71	72	288	2,784.62
David Peoples	75	70	72	71	288	2,784.62
Andy Bean	72	74	72	70	288	2,784.61
Mark Brooks	74	74	71	69	288	2,784.61
Ernie Gonzalez	72	69	77	70	288	2,784.61
Corey Pavin	72	76	69	71	288	2,784.61
Don Pooley	72	73	68	75	288	2,784.61
Robert Wrenn	74	74	69	71	288	2,784.61

Shearson Lehman Hutton Open

Torrey Pines Golf Club, La Jolla, California
North Course: Par 36-36—72; 7,021 yards
South Course: Par 36-36—72; 6,659 yards

February 15-18
purse, $900,000

	SCORES				TOTAL	MONEY
Dan Forsman	68	63	72	72	275	$162,000
Tommy Armour III	66	66	73	72	277	97,200
Tom Byrum	70	71	69	68	278	61,200
Fred Couples	68	68	74	69	279	32,625
Steve Elkington	72	69	70	68	279	32,625
Mark O'Meara	66	74	67	72	279	32,625
Tom Sieckmann	69	64	76	70	279	32,625
Craig Stadler	67	70	70	72	279	32,625
Kirk Triplett	71	66	72	70	279	32,625
Bob Estes	67	71	74	68	280	24,300
Bruce Lietzke	68	66	78	69	281	20,700
David Peoples	66	72	72	71	281	20,700
Scott Simpson	67	71	74	69	281	20,700
Michael Allen	68	69	78	67	282	15,300
Jim Booros	67	68	75	72	282	15,300
Jim Carter	69	68	74	71	282	15,300
Bob Eastwood	65	65	76	76	282	15,300
Loren Roberts	72	68	73	69	282	15,300
Phil Blackmar	72	69	72	70	283	10,908
Mark Brooks	75	61	75	72	283	10,908
Mark Lye	71	70	70	72	283	10,908
Nick Price	70	70	75	68	283	10,908
Jeff Wilson	72	70	75	66	283	10,908
Dave Barr	69	70	71	74	284	7,672.50
Jim Benepe	71	69	73	71	284	7,672.50
Jim Hallet	69	70	71	74	284	7,672.50
Mark Hayes	70	67	78	69	284	7,672.50
Lee Chill	69	72	73	71	285	5,610

	SCORES				TOTAL	MONEY
Brad Fabel	69	71	75	70	285	5,610
Rick Fehr	65	71	74	75	285	5,610
Bill Glasson	68	71	72	74	285	5,610
Kenny Knox	71	65	78	71	285	5,610
Wayne Levi	71	67	73	74	285	5,610
Bob Lohr	72	70	73	70	285	5,610
Gary McCord	73	67	74	71	285	5,610
Doug Tewell	66	76	75	68	285	5,610
Dewey Arnette	68	70	76	72	286	3,339.70
John Cook	71	67	76	72	286	3,339.70
Tom Purtzer	73	67	75	71	286	3,339.70
George Burns	71	69	74	72	286	3,339.69
Clark Dennis	67	74	75	70	286	3,339.69
Tom Eubank	72	68	73	73	286	3,339.69
Jodie Mudd	69	70	76	71	286	3,339.69
Tim Simpson	72	70	74	70	286	3,339.69
Payne Stewart	70	71	70	75	286	3,339.69
Ray Stewart	69	71	73	73	286	3,339.69
Paul Trittler	69	70	72	75	286	3,339.69
Willie Wood	69	73	76	68	286	3,339.69
Richard Zokol	69	68	78	71	286	3,339.69
Dave Eichelberger	70	66	72	79	287	2,154
Buddy Gardner	72	70	77	68	287	2,154
Lee Janzen	71	68	74	74	287	2,154
Jeff Sluman	69	73	74	71	287	2,154
Harry Taylor	70	70	72	75	287	2,154
Stan Utley	71	69	76	71	287	2,154

Nissan Los Angeles Open

Riviera Country Club, Pacific Palisades, California
Par 35-36—71; 6,946 yards

February 22-25
purse, $1,000,000

	SCORES			TOTAL	MONEY
Fred Couples	68	67	62	69	266	$180,000
Gil Morgan	67	67	65	70	269	108,000
Peter Jacobsen	65	69	70	66	270	58,000
Rocco Mediate	65	67	67	71	270	58,000
Tom Kite	67	70	69	65	271	38,000
Hal Sutton	68	67	67	69	271	38,000
Tony Sills	70	64	70	68	272	33,500
Mark Calcavecchia	71	68	69	65	273	28,000
John Mahaffey	69	69	67	68	273	28,000
Tom Sieckmann	68	68	68	69	273	28,000
Craig Stadler	68	66	72	67	273	28,000
Michael Allen	63	68	72	71	274	21,000
Jay Haas	70	72	63	69	274	21,000
Hale Irwin	71	67	64	72	274	21,000
Phil Blackmar	71	68	68	68	275	17,000
Jim Gallagher, Jr.	70	67	69	69	275	17,000
Larry Mize	70	71	66	68	275	17,000
Bill Buttner	69	69	70	68	276	12,171.43
Ed Dougherty	71	68	68	69	276	12,171.43
Rick Fehr	67	71	71	67	276	12,171.43
Bill Sander	72	67	71	66	276	12,171.43
Lanny Wadkins	69	68	72	67	276	12,171.43
Fuzzy Zoeller	71	66	69	70	276	12,171.43
Mike Reid	68	67	71	70	276	12,171.42

	SCORES				TOTAL	MONEY
Ian Baker-Finch	73	68	68	68	277	7,633.34
Lon Hinkle	69	72	67	69	277	7,633.34
Russ Cochran	69	72	66	70	277	7,633.33
Steve Elkington	68	70	69	70	277	7,633.33
John Inman	67	70	70	70	277	7,633.33
Corey Pavin	68	68	68	73	277	7,633.33
Larry Nelson	68	71	70	69	278	6,500
Andrew Magee	71	70	68	70	279	5,533.34
Billy Mayfair	72	70	67	70	279	5,533.34
Jay Delsing	72	68	71	68	279	5,533.33
Donnie Hammond	70	65	70	74	279	5,533.33
Mark Lye	69	72	70	68	279	5,533.33
Sam Randolph	70	69	68	72	279	5,533.33
Ronnie Black	73	68	64	75	280	4,000
Joel Edwards	68	69	70	73	280	4,000
Buddy Gardner	71	71	71	67	280	4,000
Jeff Hart	68	70	71	71	280	4,000
Jodie Mudd	71	70	67	72	280	4,000
Don Pooley	73	69	65	73	280	4,000
Scott Verplank	68	71	70	71	280	4,000
Bobby Wadkins	70	69	70	71	280	4,000
Scott Bentley	72	67	69	73	281	2,720
Jim Carter	69	71	71	70	281	2,720
Mike Donald	71	70	66	74	281	2,720
Steve Pate	69	69	72	71	281	2,720
Tom Purtzer	70	68	68	75	281	2,720
Ray Stewart	72	70	68	71	281	2,720

Doral Ryder Open

Doral Resort and Country Club, Miami, Florida
Par 36-36—72; 6,939 yards

March 1-4
purse, $1,400,000

	SCORES				TOTAL	MONEY
Greg Norman	68	73	70	62	273	$252,000
Mark Calcavecchia	68	67	73	65	273	104,533.34
Paul Azinger	68	66	70	69	273	104,533.33
Tim Simpson	70	71	66	66	273	104,533.33

(Norman defeated Calcavecchia, Azinger and Simpson on first hole of playoff.)

Tom Purtzer	67	70	70	68	275	53,200
Mike Reid	67	72	66	70	275	53,200
Fred Couples	67	67	70	72	276	46,900
David Edwards	69	75	68	65	277	39,200
Wayne Grady	69	71	71	66	277	39,200
Ken Green	68	71	70	68	277	39,200
Peter Jacobsen	68	72	72	65	277	39,200
John Adams	68	74	73	65	280	28,350
Ben Crenshaw	67	76	70	67	280	28,350
Bruce Lietzke	73	72	68	67	280	28,350
Gil Morgan	68	74	69	69	280	28,350
Gene Sauers	71	69	69	72	281	21,700
Ted Schulz	72	73	69	67	281	21,700
Brian Tennyson	71	72	70	68	281	21,700
Bob Tway	67	72	68	74	281	21,700
Calvin Peete	75	68	70	69	282	16,893.34
Fulton Allem	70	72	69	71	282	16,893.33
Bill Britton	68	73	72	69	282	16,893.33
Phil Blackmar	67	71	75	70	283	11,515

	SCORES				TOTAL	MONEY
Mark Brooks	74	70	69	70	283	11,515
Curt Byrum	70	70	72	71	283	11,515
Clark Dennis	67	73	75	68	283	11,515
Steve Pate	72	71	74	66	283	11,515
Peter Persons	71	71	68	73	283	11,515
Payne Stewart	70	73	72	68	283	11,515
Doug Tewell	70	69	72	72	283	11,515
Ian Baker-Finch	72	73	70	69	284	7,606.67
Jay Don Blake	72	73	71	68	284	7,606.67
Morris Hatalsky	72	70	73	69	284	7,606.67
David Ogrin	71	71	72	70	284	7,606.67
Don Shirey, Jr.	69	74	74	67	284	7,606.67
Bobby Wadkins	70	74	72	68	284	7,606.67
Hale Irwin	67	73	73	71	284	7,606.66
Andrew Magee	72	73	69	70	284	7,606.66
J.C. Snead	72	73	69	70	284	7,606.66
Billy Andrade	70	72	74	69	285	5,320
Ed Fiori	72	71	70	72	285	5,320
Gary Koch	67	77	69	72	285	5,320
Pat McGowan	69	75	69	72	285	5,320
Rocco Mediate	71	71	74	69	285	5,320
Duffy Waldorf	72	69	72	72	285	5,320
George Burns	71	73	75	67	286	3,598
Clark Burroughs	68	74	78	66	286	3,598
Bob Estes	71	74	72	69	286	3,598
Jim Gallagher, Jr.	65	74	72	75	286	3,598
Lon Hinkle	72	70	72	72	286	3,598
Mark O'Meara	73	70	74	69	286	3,598
Tom Sieckmann	73	67	75	71	286	3,598
Jeff Sluman	72	72	72	70	286	3,598
Craig Stadler	74	71	72	69	286	3,598
Tom Watson	70	73	71	72	286	3,598

Honda Classic

TPC at Eagle Trace, Coral Springs, Florida
Par 36-36—72; 7,037 yards

March 8-11
purse, $1,000,000

	SCORES			TOTAL	MONEY
John Huston	68	73	70	71	282	$180,000
Mark Calcavecchia	70	76	69	69	284	108,000
Mark Brooks	71	71	70	73	285	48,000
Billy Ray Brown	72	76	68	69	285	48,000
Ray Floyd	73	72	70	70	285	48,000
Bruce Lietzke	75	69	73	68	285	48,000
Dave Rummells	75	73	69	70	287	33,500
Brad Bryant	73	71	77	67	288	27,000
George Burns	75	71	71	71	288	27,000
Bob Eastwood	76	67	73	72	288	27,000
Ken Green	75	71	70	72	288	27,000
Tom Watson	73	69	73	73	288	27,000
Jay Don Blake	77	73	69	70	289	18,200
Joel Edwards	71	69	77	72	289	18,200
Bob Gilder	72	76	72	69	289	18,200
Hubert Green	75	69	73	72	289	18,200
Tim Simpson	71	75	70	73	289	18,200
David Canipe	77	70	72	71	290	11,750
Bob Estes	72	72	71	75	290	11,750

	SCORES				TOTAL	MONEY
Gary McCord	75	73	76	66	290	11,750
Gil Morgan	71	72	72	75	290	11,750
Steve Pate	73	71	73	73	290	11,750
Larry Rinker	76	69	71	74	290	11,750
Curtis Strange	74	71	74	71	290	11,750
Hal Sutton	74	74	71	71	290	11,750
Billy Andrade	77	71	68	75	291	7,400
David Peoples	75	74	72	70	291	7,400
Don Pooley	80	71	71	69	291	7,400
Scott Verplank	74	72	71	74	291	7,400
Mark Wiebe	73	74	75	69	291	7,400
Brian Claar	74	75	72	71	292	5,671.43
Gary Hallberg	76	74	70	72	292	5,671.43
Jim Hallet	75	75	73	69	292	5,671.43
Bob Lohr	77	71	74	70	292	5,671.43
Steve Lowery	73	74	71	74	292	5,671.43
Bill Sander	73	72	75	72	292	5,671.43
John Mahaffey	76	69	71	76	292	5,671.42
Emlyn Aubrey	77	71	72	73	293	3,800
Fred Couples	72	72	75	74	293	3,800
Brad Faxon	74	71	73	75	293	3,800
Ed Fiori	79	72	73	69	293	3,800
John Inman	76	73	72	72	293	3,800
Mark McCumber	76	74	70	73	293	3,800
Jodie Mudd	73	72	71	77	293	3,800
Mark O'Meara	75	71	71	76	293	3,800
Chris Perry	74	76	72	71	293	3,800
Gene Sauers	73	73	78	69	293	3,800
Tom Garner	75	76	71	72	294	2,485.72
Kenny Knox	73	74	77	70	294	2,485.72
Steve Lamontagne	77	73	72	72	294	2,485.72
Fulton Allem	74	72	73	75	294	2,485.71
Isao Aoki	75	70	73	76	294	2,485.71
Buddy Gardner	75	71	74	74	294	2,485.71
Loren Roberts	77	74	70	73	294	2,485.71

The Players Championship

TPC at Sawgrass, Ponte Vedra, Florida
Par 36-36—72; 6,881 yards

March 15-18
purse, $1,500,000

	SCORES				TOTAL	MONEY
Jodie Mudd	67	72	70	69	278	$270,000
Mark Calcavecchia	67	75	68	69	279	162,000
Steve Jones	75	71	69	69	284	87,000
Tom Purtzer	71	73	69	71	284	87,000
Billy Ray Brown	73	72	69	71	285	52,687.50
Ken Green	71	69	70	75	285	52,687.50
Hale Irwin	70	68	74	73	285	52,687.50
Tom Kite	72	70	70	73	285	52,687.50
Andy Bean	73	68	72	73	286	42,000
Mark McCumber	73	72	73	68	286	42,000
Fulton Allem	73	70	74	71	288	31,800
Bruce Lietzke	75	70	70	73	288	31,800
Rocco Mediate	72	67	76	73	288	31,800
Steve Pate	69	76	71	72	288	31,800
Payne Stewart	71	73	71	73	288	31,800
Clark Burroughs	69	71	72	77	289	20,362.50

	SCORES				TOTAL	MONEY
Steve Elkington	71	72	74	72	289	20,362.50
Larry Nelson	71	73	74	71	289	20,362.50
Greg Norman	71	76	74	68	289	20,362.50
David Ogrin	69	74	73	73	289	20,362.50
Chris Perry	73	74	72	70	289	20,362.50
Nick Price	69	75	77	68	289	20,362.50
Curtis Strange	72	71	73	73	289	20,362.50
Jim Booros	70	74	73	73	290	12,450
Bill Glasson	71	73	72	74	290	12,450
David Graham	68	75	74	73	290	12,450
Kenny Knox	73	73	75	69	290	12,450
Davis Love III	73	68	74	75	290	12,450
Mike Donald	76	71	72	72	291	9,332.15
Wayne Grady	72	72	74	73	291	9,332.15
Jim Gallagher, Jr.	76	71	72	72	291	9,332.14
Peter Jacobsen	74	67	75	75	291	9,332.14
Peter Persons	69	76	71	75	291	9,332.14
Gene Sauers	71	73	70	77	291	9,332.14
Tony Sills	72	74	76	69	291	9,332.14
Dave Barr	71	75	73	73	292	6,307.50
Mark Brooks	70	75	73	74	292	6,307.50
David Edwards	68	73	75	76	292	6,307.50
Dan Forsman	72	71	74	75	292	6,307.50
Jim Hallet	72	72	76	72	292	6,307.50
Andrew Magee	74	71	73	74	292	6,307.50
Kirk Triplett	72	74	74	72	292	6,307.50
Bobby Wadkins	77	70	72	73	292	6,307.50
Tom Watson	69	72	81	70	292	6,307.50
D.A. Weibring	72	72	73	75	292	6,307.50
Ian Baker-Finch	73	72	75	73	293	3,855
Robert Gamez	69	74	79	71	293	3,855
Hubert Green	72	74	75	72	293	3,855
Calvin Peete	73	72	72	76	293	3,855
Mike Reid	71	72	77	73	293	3,855
Loren Roberts	71	73	75	74	293	3,855
Joey Sindelar	74	73	74	72	293	3,855
J.C. Snead	73	72	76	72	293	3,855
Mike Sullivan	73	74	73	73	293	3,855
Robert Wrenn	71	75	74	73	293	3,855

The Nestle Invitational

Bay Hill Club and Lodge, Orlando, Florida
Par 36-36—72; 7,114 yards

March 22-25
purse, $900,000

	SCORES				TOTAL	MONEY
Robert Gamez	71	69	68	66	274	$162,000
Greg Norman	74	68	65	68	275	97,200
Larry Mize	71	70	67	68	276	61,200
Fulton Allem	74	69	65	69	277	37,200
Scott Hoch	69	68	70	70	277	37,200
Curtis Strange	69	70	68	70	277	37,200
Paul Azinger	70	70	70	68	278	30,150
Corey Pavin	69	69	72	70	280	27,000
Nick Price	72	68	72	68	280	27,000
Mark O'Meara	70	73	74	64	281	22,500
Jose Maria Olazabal	68	73	71	69	281	22,500
Tom Watson	71	68	72	70	281	22,500

	SCORES				TOTAL	MONEY
Nick Faldo	74	67	69	72	282	16,875
Jim Gallagher, Jr.	75	70	67	70	282	16,875
Larry Nelson	67	71	74	70	282	16,875
Tom Purtzer	72	73	68	69	282	16,875
Isao Aoki	70	73	70	70	283	11,777.15
Stan Utley	72	73	70	68	283	11,777.15
Mike Hulbert	72	71	68	72	283	11,777.14
Mark Lye	72	72	68	71	283	11,777.14
Billy Mayfair	71	68	73	71	283	11,777.14
Jodie Mudd	70	73	69	71	283	11,777.14
Craig Parry	72	67	69	75	283	11,777.14
Billy Andrade	68	70	73	73	284	7,470
Ian Baker-Finch	72	69	76	67	284	7,470
Bill Buttner	72	73	68	71	284	7,470
Andrew Magee	70	72	69	73	284	7,470
Mark McCumber	71	69	72	72	284	7,470
Dave Barr	71	72	72	70	285	5,599.29
John Huston	72	72	71	70	285	5,599.29
Kenny Knox	71	69	74	71	285	5,599.29
Chris Perry	73	71	72	69	285	5,599.29
Chip Beck	70	73	71	71	285	5,599.28
Ian Woosnam	68	75	71	71	285	5,599.28
Fuzzy Zoeller	69	72	73	71	285	5,599.28
Rick Fehr	73	68	71	74	286	4,522.50
Steve Pate	74	71	73	68	286	4,522.50
Tommy Armour III	69	73	74	71	287	4,050
Ray Floyd	73	72	70	72	287	4,050
Naomichi Ozaki	69	77	73	68	287	4,050
Michael Allen	72	74	72	70	288	3,150
David Graham	73	72	69	74	288	3,150
Jim Hallet	74	72	73	69	288	3,150
Masashi Ozaki	78	69	72	69	288	3,150
David Peoples	70	71	77	70	288	3,150
Jeff Sluman	70	73	72	73	288	3,150
Richard Zokol	71	74	73	70	288	3,150
Wayne Grady	69	74	76	70	289	2,237.15
Gary Koch	76	71	71	71	289	2,237.15
Peter Jacobsen	73	71	72	73	289	2,237.14
Kenny Perry	70	75	69	75	289	2237.14
Bill Sander	70	71	74	74	289	2,237.14
Tony Sills	74	68	73	74	289	2,237.14
Bob Tway	76	67	73	73	289	2,237.14

Independent Insurance Agent Open

TPC at The Woodlands, The Woodlands, Texas
Par 36-36—72; 7,042 yards
(Shortened to 54 holes - rain Thursday, Friday.)

March 29-April 1
purse, $1,000,000

	SCORES			TOTAL	MONEY
Tony Sills	67	72	65	204	$180,000
Gil Morgan	67	70	67	204	108,000
(Sills defeated Morgan on first extra hole.)					
Severiano Ballesteros	69	68	68	205	39,062.50
Brad Bryant	68	73	64	205	39,062.50
Fred Couples	67	69	69	205	39,062.50
Bruce Lietzke	67	70	68	205	39,062.50
Larry Mize	68	69	68	205	39,062.50

	SCORES			TOTAL	MONEY
David Peoples	67	66	72	205	39,062.50
Scott Simpson	68	68	69	205	39,062.50
Ian Woosnam	69	69	67	205	39,062.50
Brad Fabel	69	69	68	206	22,000
Bob Gilder	68	69	69	206	22,000
Andrew Magee	72	65	69	206	22,000
John Mahaffey	70	67	69	206	22,000
Ben Crenshaw	68	71	68	207	14,066.67
Nick Faldo	70	73	64	207	14,066.67
Brad Faxon	71	71	65	207	14,066.67
Steve Jones	68	71	68	207	14,066.67
Sandy Lyle	68	72	67	207	14,066.67
Craig Parry	70	67	70	207	14,066.67
Jay Haas	68	68	71	207	14,066.66
Corey Pavin	70	66	71	207	14,066.66
Hal Sutton	69	64	74	207	14,066.66
Tommy Armour III	68	69	71	208	8,525
Mark Brooks	71	68	69	208	8,525
Steve Elkington	67	73	68	208	8,525
Tim Simpson	70	67	71	208	8,525
Mark Hayes	71	70	68	209	6,950
Wayne Levi	68	71	70	209	6,950
Bob Lohr	69	70	70	209	6,950
Kirk Triplett	72	69	68	209	6,950
Emlyn Aubrey	69	70	71	210	5,660
Bob Estes	71	70	69	210	5,660
Fred Funk	71	69	70	210	5,660
Buddy Gardner	71	70	69	210	5,660
Mike Reid	71	69	70	210	5,660
Phil Blackmar	68	72	71	211	4,200
Clark Dennis	70	73	68	211	4,200
Gibby Gilbert	71	72	68	211	4,200
Jeff Hart	74	67	70	211	4,200
Lee Janzen	71	69	71	211	4,200
Billy Mayfair	70	72	69	211	4,200
Ray Stewart	70	71	70	211	4,200
Leonard Thompson	71	69	71	211	4,200
Billy Ray Brown	70	70	72	212	2,636.37
David Canipe	71	70	71	212	2,636.37
Ronan Rafferty	71	69	72	212	2,636.37
Lance Ten Broeck	72	68	72	212	2,636.37
Jim Booros	68	71	73	212	2,636.36
Bill Britton	69	74	69	212	2,636.36
George Burns	67	72	73	212	2,636.36
Steve Lamontagne	69	69	74	212	2,636.36
Larry Silveira	68	75	69	212	2,636.36
Curtis Strange	71	70	71	212	2,636.36
Harry Taylor	72	71	69	212	2,636.36

The Masters Tournament

Augusta National Golf Club, Augusta, Georgia
Par 36-36—72; 6,905 yards

April 5-8
purse, $1,189,500

	SCORES				TOTAL	MONEY
Nick Faldo	71	72	66	69	278	$225,000
Ray Floyd	70	68	68	72	278	135,000

(Faldo won playoff on second (No. 11) extra hole.)

	SCORES				TOTAL	MONEY
John Huston	66	74	68	75	283	72,500
Lanny Wadkins	72	73	70	68	283	72,500
Fred Couples	74	69	72	69	284	50,000
Jack Nicklaus	72	70	69	74	285	45,000
Severiano Ballesteros	74	73	68	71	286	35,150
Bill Britton	68	74	71	73	286	35,150
Bernhard Langer	70	73	69	74	286	35,150
Scott Simpson	74	71	68	73	286	35,150
Curtis Strange	70	73	71	72	286	35,150
Tom Watson	77	71	67	71	286	35,150
Jose Maria Olazabal	72	73	68	74	287	26,300
Ben Crenshaw	72	74	73	69	288	20,650
Scott Hoch	71	68	73	76	288	20,650
Tom Kite	75	73	66	74	288	20,650
Larry Mize	70	76	71	71	288	20,650
Ronan Rafferty	72	74	69	73	288	20,650
Craig Stadler	72	70	74	72	288	20,650
Mark Calcavecchia	74	73	73	69	289	15,100
Steve Jones	77	69	72	71	289	15,100
Fuzzy Zoeller	72	74	73	70	289	15,100
Masashi Ozaki	70	71	77	72	290	13,000
Lee Trevino	78	69	72	72	291	11,000
Donnie Hammond	71	74	75	71	291	11,000
Gary Player	73	74	68	76	291	11,000
Wayne Grady	72	75	72	73	292	9,267
Andy North	71	73	77	71	292	9,267
Jeff Sluman	78	68	75	71	292	9,267
Peter Jacobsen	67	75	76	75	293	8,133
Jodie Mudd	74	70	73	76	293	8,133
Ian Woosnam	72	75	70	76	293	8,133
Andy Bean	76	72	74	72	294	7,100
Bill Glasson	70	75	76	73	294	7,100
Naomichi Ozaki	75	73	74	72	294	7,100
Mark McCumber	74	74	76	71	295	6,133
Payne Stewart	71	73	77	74	295	6,133
Bob Tway	72	76	73	74	295	6,133
Chip Beck	72	74	75	75	296	5,500
Mark Lye	75	73	73	75	296	5,500
*Chris Patton	71	73	74	78	296	
John Mahaffey	72	74	75	76	297	4,867
Don Pooley	73	73	72	79	297	4,867
Peter Senior	72	75	73	77	297	4,867
Mike Hulbert	71	71	77	79	298	4,250
Tom Purtzer	71	77	76	74	298	4,250
Mike Donald	64	82	77	76	299	3,900
Larry Nelson	74	73	79	74	300	3,600
George Archer	70	74	82	75	301	3,400

Out of Final 36 Holes

Billy Casper	74	75	149
David Frost	74	75	149
Robert Gamez	73	76	149
Mark O'Meara	75	74	149
Mike Reid	76	73	149
Hubert Green	73	77	150
Blaine McCallister	73	77	150
Greg Norman	78	72	150
Tom Pernice, Jr.	74	76	150
Tommy Aaron	77	74	151

	SCORES	TOTAL
Ian Baker-Finch	77 74	151
Dan Forsman	79 72	151
Sandy Lyle	77 74	151
Dave Rummells	77 74	151
Ted Schulz	75 76	151
Tony Sills	77 74	151
Charles Coody	75 77	152
Tim Simpson	77 75	152
Hal Sutton	81 71	152
Tommy Armour III	75 78	153
Gay Brewer	76 77	153
Curt Byrum	76 77	153
Brian Claar	74 79	153
David Ishii	74 79	153
Tom Byrum	77 78	155
*Stephen Dodd	77 78	155
Leonard Thompson	80 75	155
Paul Azinger	80 76	156
Arnold Palmer	76 80	156
Craig Parry	80 76	156
Ken Green	78 80	158
*Timothy Hobby	76 82	158
Wayne Levi	77 81	158
*Danny Green	79 80	159
*James Taylor	83 78	161
Doug Ford	78 85	163

(Professionals who did not complete 72 holes received $1,500.)

Deposit Guaranty Classic

Hattiesburg Country Club, Hattiesburg, Mississippi
Par 35-35—70; 6,280 yards

April 5-8
purse, $300,000

	SCORES	TOTAL	MONEY
Gene Sauers	67 65 68 68	268	$54,000
Jack Ferenz	71 64 68 67	270	32,400
Mike McCullough	68 67 70 66	271	17,400
David Ogrin	67 70 69 65	271	17,400
Lee Janzen	69 64 71 68	272	12,000
Jim Booros	69 68 66 70	273	9,712.50
Nolan Henke	68 69 68 68	273	9,712.50
Tommy Moore	66 67 71 69	273	9,712.50
Ray Stewart	67 70 68 68	273	9,712.50
Neal Lancaster	72 68 68 66	274	7,500
Larry Silveira	68 69 69 68	274	7,500
Mike Smith	67 70 68 69	274	7,500
Mitch Adcock	67 67 70 71	275	5,460
David Canipe	65 71 68 71	275	5,460
Jay Delsing	67 68 68 72	275	5,460
Gibby Gilbert	68 66 71 70	275	5,460
Greg Hickman	68 65 72 70	275	5,460
Dick Mast	66 72 67 71	276	4,200
Mike Nicolette	68 67 71 70	276	4,200
Kirk Triplett	68 70 70 68	276	4,200
Perry Arthur	71 70 69 67	277	3,120
Lennie Clements	67 64 73 73	277	3,120
Carl Cooper	66 68 71 72	277	3,120

	SCORES				TOTAL	MONEY
Ron Streck	71	70	69	67	277	3,120
Lance Ten Broeck	69	65	69	74	277	3,120
Bob Estes	67	68	74	69	278	2,220
David Jackson	67	67	74	70	278	2,220
Sam Randolph	70	68	70	70	278	2,220
Robert Thompson	71	66	68	73	278	2,220
Jim Woodward	68	70	70	70	278	2,220
Bret Burroughs	70	71	71	67	279	1,818.75
Steve Lowery	69	70	71	69	279	1,818.75
Doug Martin	67	72	67	73	279	1,818.75
Don Reese	66	71	72	70	279	1,818.75
Russ Cochran	67	71	73	69	280	1,385.63
Brad Fabel	69	71	70	70	280	1,385.63
Richard Fulkerson	69	72	69	70	280	1,385.63
Brian Mogg	69	65	76	70	280	1,385.63
Jerry Anderson	70	68	69	73	280	1,385.62
Roy Biancalana	70	69	70	71	280	1,385.62
George Burns	72	65	71	72	280	1,385.62
Steve Hart	68	69	72	71	280	1,385.62
Tony Grimes	72	68	71	70	281	1,020
Barry Jaeckel	69	72	71	69	281	1,020
Jack Kay, Jr.	70	69	70	72	281	1,020
Doug Weaver	64	74	69	74	281	1,020
Billy Tuten	71	69	75	67	282	770.58
Greg Bruckner	71	69	73	69	282	770.57
Trevor Dodds	73	67	70	72	282	770.57
Dan Halldorson	70	69	72	71	282	770.57
Webb Heintzelman	71	66	73	72	282	770.57
Hicks Malonson	71	69	70	72	282	770.57
Sonny Skinner	67	70	72	73	282	770.57

MCI Heritage Classic

Harbour Town Golf Links, Hilton Head Island, South Carolina
Par 36-35—71; 6,657 yards

April 12-15
purse, $1,000,000

	SCORES				TOTAL	MONEY
Payne Stewart	70	69	66	71	276	$180,000
Steve Jones	68	73	66	69	276	88,000
Larry Mize	71	69	70	66	276	88,000

(Stewart won playoff, defeating Mize on second extra hole. Jones eliminated on first extra hole.)

Greg Norman	70	70	67	70	277	44,000
Steve Pate	67	69	73	68	277	44,000
Andy Bean	74	68	69	67	278	36,000
Loren Roberts	71	70	67	71	279	32,250
Gene Sauers	66	72	72	69	279	32,250
Chip Beck	74	70	68	68	280	23,142.86
David Edwards	71	73	71	65	280	23,142.86
Bob Estes	71	70	70	69	280	23,142.86
Hal Sutton	72	67	73	68	280	23,142.86
Lanny Wadkins	70	71	73	66	280	23,142.86
Tom Kite	68	70	72	70	280	23,142.85
Calvin Peete	70	66	72	72	280	23,142.85
Billy Andrade	68	73	70	70	281	13,575
Paul Azinger	72	68	73	68	281	13,575
Nick Faldo	68	69	70	74	281	13,575
Wayne Grady	71	69	73	68	281	13,575

	SCORES				TOTAL	MONEY
Scott Hoch	69	71	73	68	281	13,575
Davis Love III	72	67	69	73	281	13,575
Gil Morgan	70	71	71	69	281	13,575
Tim Simpson	75	70	69	67	281	13,575
Brad Faxon	72	72	70	68	282	9,600
Mike Hulbert	69	73	70	71	283	8,166.67
Ray Stewart	69	72	70	72	283	8,166.67
Jay Haas	68	72	70	73	283	8,166.66
Mark McCumber	70	76	71	67	284	7,100
Ted Schulz	76	68	72	68	284	7,100
Jeff Sluman	67	72	75	70	284	7,100
Billy Ray Brown	66	71	75	73	285	5,800
Clark Burroughs	74	71	71	69	285	5,800
Buddy Gardner	71	72	69	73	285	5,800
Donnie Hammond	69	71	74	71	285	5,800
Jerry Pate	73	70	69	73	285	5,800
Brian Tennyson	72	74	69	70	285	5,800
Jim Booros	73	70	75	68	286	4,500
Peter Jacobsen	74	68	71	73	286	4,500
Billy Mayfair	69	71	74	72	286	4,500
Jodie Mudd	70	73	71	72	286	4,500
Corey Pavin	71	73	69	73	286	4,500
Ronnie Black	71	73	69	74	287	3,600
Fred Couples	75	69	70	73	287	3,600
Ray Floyd	73	70	72	72	287	3,600
Larry Rinker	70	76	75	66	287	3,600
Dave Barr	68	72	73	75	288	2,772
Curt Byrum	69	75	73	71	288	2,772
John Mahaffey	74	71	72	71	288	2,772
Chris Perry	77	68	74	69	288	2,772
Clarence Rose	73	69	73	73	288	2,772

K-mart Greater Greensboro Open

Forest Oaks Country Club, Greensboro, North Carolina
Par 36-36—72; 6,958 yards

April 19-22
purse, $1,250,000

	SCORES				TOTAL	MONEY
Steve Elkington	74	71	71	66	282	$225,000
Mike Reid	72	70	67	75	284	110,000
Jeff Sluman	71	74	68	71	284	110,000
Paul Azinger	72	73	73	67	285	51,666.67
Mike Hulbert	73	70	73	69	285	51,666.67
Fred Couples	71	70	71	73	285	51,666.66
Joey Sindelar	70	73	75	68	286	38,958.34
Chip Beck	72	72	70	72	286	38,958.33
John Huston	74	69	71	72	286	38,958.33
Phil Blackmar	70	71	74	72	287	25,138.89
Lennie Clements	69	74	75	69	287	25,138.89
Jay Delsing	74	73	71	69	287	25,138.89
David Edwards	70	75	72	70	287	25,138.89
Jim Gallagher, Jr.	70	70	74	73	287	25,138.89
Bill Glasson	72	71	72	72	287	25,138.89
Donnie Hammond	71	71	76	69	287	25,138.89
Lanny Wadkins	71	73	73	70	287	25,138.89
Nick Price	71	71	71	74	287	25,138.88
John Cook	74	71	75	68	288	12,409.10
Tommy Armour III	71	70	76	71	288	12,409.09

	SCORES				TOTAL	MONEY
Bill Britton	74	72	72	70	288	12,409.09
George Burns	73	72	74	69	288	12,409.09
Brian Claar	73	71	71	73	288	12,409.09
Ed Fiori	71	71	75	71	288	12,409.09
Robert Gamez	70	73	72	73	288	12,409.09
Mark McCumber	71	71	75	71	288	12,409.09
Kenny Perry	72	72	72	72	288	12,409.09
Doug Tewell	71	71	74	72	288	12,409.09
Mark Wiebe	71	70	75	72	288	12,409.09
Loren Roberts	74	71	73	71	289	8,125
Bill Sander	73	72	74	70	289	8,125
Ted Schulz	70	73	75	71	289	8,125
Russ Cochran	74	73	74	69	290	6,604.17
Bob Gilder	73	69	76	72	290	6,604.17
Don Shirey, Jr.	74	69	78	69	290	6,604.17
J.C. Snead	74	73	72	71	290	6,604.17
Jay Don Blake	74	70	70	76	290	6,604.16
Mark Calcavecchia	74	70	71	75	290	6,604.16
Dave Eichelberger	73	72	73	73	291	5,125
Fred Funk	72	75	75	69	291	5,125
Steve Hart	75	71	73	72	291	5,125
Mark Lye	72	72	72	75	291	5,125
Ray Stewart	73	71	72	75	291	5,125
Bobby Clampett	70	76	73	73	292	4,125
Bobby Wadkins	75	71	74	72	292	4,125
Fuzzy Zoeller	71	72	74	75	292	4,125
Dave Barr	71	76	75	71	293	3,171.88
Jay Haas	73	73	76	71	293	3,171.88
Lee Janzen	70	73	80	70	293	3,171.88
Clarence Rose	74	73	76	70	293	3,171.88
Danny Edwards	73	72	76	72	293	3,171.87
Nolan Henke	75	71	75	72	293	3,171.87
Bob Lohr	72	74	75	72	293	3,171.87
Larry Nelson	73	74	74	72	293	3,171.87

USF&G Classic

English Turn Golf and Country Club, New Orleans, Louisiana
Par 36-36—72; 7,106 yards

April 26-29
purse, $1,000,000

	SCORES				TOTAL	MONEY
David Frost	71	70	66	69	276	$180,000
Greg Norman	73	68	71	65	277	108,000
Russ Cochran	72	69	71	67	279	68,000
Brian Tennyson	69	70	69	75	283	48,000
Jay Delsing	73	69	73	69	284	40,000
Tim Simpson	73	69	71	72	285	36,000
Brad Bryant	70	73	73	70	286	29,100
David Edwards	71	71	72	72	286	29,100
Tommy Moore	73	71	69	73	286	29,100
Mike Smith	73	72	69	72	286	29,100
Hal Sutton	74	69	74	69	286	29,100
Curt Byrum	76	66	69	76	287	23,000
Emlyn Aubrey	70	73	73	72	288	17,142.86
Fred Funk	69	71	72	76	288	17,142.86
Wayne Grady	73	74	71	70	288	17,142.86
David Peoples	72	74	71	71	288	17,142.86
Ted Schulz	70	72	72	74	288	17,142.86

	SCORES				TOTAL	MONEY
Mark O'Meara	69	69	71	79	288	17,142.85
Corey Pavin	72	67	70	79	288	17,142.85
Lee Janzen	72	72	72	73	289	13,000
Dave Barr	72	71	78	69	290	10,000
Phil Blackmar	74	70	72	74	290	10,000
George Burns	75	71	70	74	290	10,000
Steve Elkington	69	70	72	79	290	10,000
Brad Faxon	73	73	72	72	290	10,000
Gary Koch	70	67	75	78	290	10,000
Chip Beck	74	73	74	70	291	6,380
Ben Crenshaw	79	69	67	76	291	6,380
Bob Eastwood	74	70	71	76	291	6,380
Rick Fehr	73	69	70	79	291	6,380
Buddy Gardner	73	75	71	72	291	6,380
John Inman	74	70	71	76	291	6,380
Pat McGowan	70	71	73	77	291	6,380
Peter Persons	74	69	72	76	291	6,380
Tom Sieckmann	74	72	72	73	291	6,380
Paul Trittler	73	73	71	74	291	6,380
Bill Buttner	71	72	74	75	292	4,600
Mike Donald	76	70	78	68	292	4,600
Bill Sander	71	71	76	74	292	4,600
Kirk Triplett	74	71	73	74	292	4,600
Neal Lancaster	76	70	74	73	293	4,000
Tom Watson	75	73	71	74	293	4,000
Keith Clearwater	71	72	74	77	294	3,300
Mark Hayes	76	72	75	71	294	3,300
Mike Hulbert	74	73	73	74	294	3,300
Harry Taylor	76	71	75	72	294	3,300
Leonard Thompson	71	73	74	76	294	3,300
Lennie Clements	75	73	76	71	295	2,544
Jay Haas	75	73	74	73	295	2,544
Dan Halldorson	74	70	77	74	295	2,544
Jeff Hart	71	75	77	72	295	2,544
Brian Kamm	72	72	73	78	295	2,544

GTE Byron Nelson Classic

TPC at Las Colinas, Irving, Texas
Par 35-35—70; 6,767 yards
(First round cancelled - wet course unplayable.)

May 3-6
purse, $1,000,000

	SCORES			TOTAL	MONEY
Payne Stewart	67	68	67	202	$180,000
Lanny Wadkins	72	67	65	204	108,000
Mark Calcavecchia	69	69	69	207	58,000
Bruce Lietzke	71	68	68	207	58,000
Andrew Magee	69	68	71	208	38,000
Tim Simpson	72	66	70	208	38,000
Fred Funk	71	71	67	209	30,125
Greg Norman	73	67	69	209	30,125
Tom Purtzer	70	67	72	209	30,125
Tom Watson	71	69	69	209	30,125
Bob Estes	71	72	67	210	21,200
Mark Lye	68	69	73	210	21,200
Nick Price	74	67	69	210	21,200
Larry Rinker	74	68	68	210	21,200
Bobby Wadkins	74	69	67	210	21,200

374 / THE U.S. TOUR

	SCORES			TOTAL	MONEY
Curt Byrum	71	66	74	211	15,500
Davis Love III	75	69	67	211	15,500
Don Pooley	72	69	70	211	15,500
Dillard Pruitt	71	67	73	211	15,500
Brad Bryant	72	71	69	212	10,087.50
David Canipe	74	70	68	212	10,087.50
Ben Crenshaw	71	68	73	212	10,087.50
Ray Floyd	74	69	69	212	10,087.50
Wayne Grady	71	71	70	212	10,087.50
Gary Hallberg	75	68	69	212	10,087.50
Andy North	71	72	69	212	10,087.50
Dave Rummells	73	70	69	212	10,087.50
Bill Britton	68	73	72	213	5,850
Jay Delsing	75	67	71	213	5,850
Ed Dougherty	70	72	71	213	5,850
Rick Fehr	71	72	70	213	5,850
David Frost	74	71	68	213	5,850
P.H. Horgan III	71	72	70	213	5,850
Tom Kite	73	71	69	213	5,850
Bob Lohr	71	71	71	213	5,850
Mark O'Meara	74	71	68	213	5,850
Chris Perry	72	71	70	213	5,850
Jeff Sluman	74	66	73	213	5,850
Lance Ten Broeck	73	72	68	213	5,850
Fred Couples	76	67	71	214	3,332.73
Steve Elkington	73	69	72	214	3,332.73
Ed Fiori	71	72	71	214	3,332.73
Gary Koch	71	74	69	214	3,332.73
John Mahaffey	72	72	70	214	3,332.73
Loren Roberts	74	67	73	214	3,332.73
Duffy Waldorf	73	72	69	214	3,332.73
D.A. Weibring	69	75	70	214	3,332.73
Nolan Henke	70	68	76	214	3,332.72
Larry Nelson	67	73	74	214	3,332.72
Rocky Thompson	70	71	73	214	3,332.72

Memorial Tournament

Muirfield Village Golf Club, Dublin, Ohio
Par 36-36—72; 7,104 yards
(Final round cancelled - rain, unplayable course.)

May 10-13
purse, $1,000,000

	SCORES			TOTAL	MONEY
Greg Norman	73	74	69	216	$180,000
Payne Stewart	74	74	69	217	108,000
Mark Brooks	76	70	72	218	48,000
Fred Couples	69	74	75	218	48,000
Brad Faxon	77	69	72	218	48,000
Don Pooley	73	71	74	218	48,000
Peter Jacobsen	76	72	71	219	32,250
Bill Sander	75	72	72	219	32,250
Paul Azinger	74	73	73	220	26,000
Bill Glasson	78	71	71	220	26,000
Gil Morgan	79	72	69	220	26,000
Steve Pate	75	75	70	220	26,000
Mark Wiebe	79	70	72	221	19,333.34
Hale Irwin	73	74	74	221	19,333.33
Ricky Kawagishi	75	72	74	221	19,333.33

	SCORES	TOTAL	MONEY
John Cook	77 69 76	222	14,500
Dan Forsman	79 71 72	222	14,500
Davis Love III	77 74 71	222	14,500
Larry Mize	81 70 71	222	14,500
Lanny Wadkins	73 76 73	222	14,500
Tom Watson	77 74 71	222	14,500
Jay Delsing	73 72 78	223	10,000
Bob Eastwood	76 75 72	223	10,000
Ray Floyd	78 73 72	223	10,000
Curtis Strange	80 70 73	223	10,000
Tommy Armour III	76 78 70	224	7,550
Ian Baker-Finch	74 74 76	224	7,550
Jack Nicklaus	78 73 73	224	7,550
Corey Pavin	73 76 75	224	7,550
Mark Lye	78 78 69	225	6,650
Scott Verplank	77 77 71	225	6,650
Billy Andrade	79 73 74	226	5,533.34
Andy North	75 75 76	226	5,533.34
Billy Mayfair	78 77 71	226	5,533.33
Peter Persons	73 77 76	226	5,533.33
Scott Simpson	81 73 72	226	5,533.33
Craig Stadler	77 74 75	226	5,533.33
Bill Britton	81 74 72	227	4,300
Mike Hulbert	82 75 70	227	4,300
Wayne Levi	78 73 76	227	4,300
Bruce Lietzke	80 71 76	227	4,300
Mike Reid	82 72 73	227	4,300
Dave Barr	78 76 74	228	2,922
Billy Ray Brown	77 78 73	228	2,922
Mike Donald	81 72 75	228	2,922
Jim Gallagher, Jr.	77 77 74	228	2,922
Kenny Knox	76 78 74	228	2,922
Roger Maltbie	77 73 78	228	2,922
David Peoples	75 76 77	228	2,922
Kenny Perry	77 75 76	228	2,922
Hal Sutton	79 78 71	228	2,922
Jim Thorpe	79 78 71	228	2,922

Southwestern Bell Colonial

Colonial Country Club, Fort Worth, Texas
Par 35-35—70; 7,116 yards

May 17-20
purse, $1,000,000

	SCORES	TOTAL	MONEY
Ben Crenshaw	69 65 72 66	272	$180,000
John Mahaffey	67 72 70 66	275	74,666.67
Corey Pavin	66 71 70 68	275	74,666.67
Nick Price	72 68 67 68	275	74,666.66
Mike Hulbert	71 70 72 63	276	38,000
Curtis Strange	68 69 69 70	276	38,000
Andrew Magee	71 71 69 66	277	30,125
Gene Sauers	72 74 69 62	277	30,125
Payne Stewart	70 72 68 67	277	30,125
Brian Tennyson	73 68 70 66	277	30,125
Russ Cochran	65 69 73 71	278	22,000
John Huston	69 67 72 70	278	22,000
Rocco Mediate	73 72 68 65	278	22,000
Kenny Perry	69 71 71 67	278	22,000

	SCORES				TOTAL	MONEY
Ian Baker-Finch	73	71	71	64	279	16,000
Billy Mayfair	67	68	74	70	279	16,000
Tom Purtzer	67	70	73	69	279	16,000
Stan Utley	68	72	69	70	279	16,000
Scott Verplank	78	68	68	65	279	16,000
Billy Andrade	72	68	73	67	280	11,240
Tom Byrum	71	71	72	66	280	11,240
Gil Morgan	72	67	75	66	280	11,240
Loren Roberts	69	74	69	68	280	11,240
Tim Simpson	70	70	69	71	280	11,240
David Frost	72	70	68	71	281	7,975
Hale Irwin	73	71	69	68	281	7,975
Peter Jacobsen	70	72	70	69	281	7,975
Tom Watson	71	72	68	70	281	7,975
Dan Forsman	70	71	73	68	282	6,358.34
Scott Simpson	70	72	72	68	282	6,358.34
Curt Byrum	68	69	74	71	282	6,358.33
Mike Donald	70	73	68	71	282	6,358.33
Scott Hoch	67	73	68	74	282	6,358.33
Hal Sutton	71	72	70	69	282	6,358.33
Kenny Knox	70	74	71	68	283	4,930
Davis Love III	71	70	72	70	283	4,930
Larry Mize	73	70	68	72	283	4,930
David Peoples	74	73	68	68	283	4,930
Dave Rummells	71	76	71	65	283	4,930
Clark Dennis	69	70	72	73	284	4,100
Bruce Lietzke	70	73	69	72	284	4,100
Richard Zokol	67	71	76	70	284	4,100
Robert Gamez	70	74	72	69	285	3,300
Jay Haas	76	68	70	71	285	3,300
P.H. Horgan III	73	72	71	69	285	3,300
Blaine McCallister	69	76	72	68	285	3,300
Naomichi Ozaki	72	75	70	68	285	3,300
Jay Delsing	74	70	73	69	286	2,620
Bobby Wadkins	72	73	71	70	286	2,620
Robert Wrenn	73	69	69	75	286	2,620

BellSouth Atlanta Classic

Atlanta Country Club, Marietta, Georgia
Par 36-36—72; 7,018 yards

May 24-27
purse, $1,000,000

	SCORES				TOTAL	MONEY
Wayne Levi	72	66	68	69	275	$180,000
Keith Clearwater	70	68	66	72	276	74,666.67
Larry Mize	66	69	71	70	276	74,666.67
Nick Price	68	69	69	70	276	74,666.66
Mike Donald	68	72	68	70	278	38,000
Kenny Perry	69	70	70	69	278	38,000
Brian Claar	69	71	69	70	279	33,500
Tom Kite	72	69	68	71	280	28,000
Don Pooley	72	68	70	70	280	28,000
Howard Twitty	68	68	72	72	280	28,000
Scott Verplank	70	71	71	68	280	28,000
Russ Cochran	69	72	72	68	281	22,000
Fred Funk	68	72	72	69	281	22,000
Buddy Gardner	73	72	67	70	282	19,000
Michael Allen	75	67	71	70	283	15,000

	SCORES				TOTAL	MONEY
Jerry Anderson	74	71	72	66	283	15,000
Billy Andrade	69	70	73	71	283	15,000
Tommy Armour III	76	69	71	67	283	15,000
Bill Buttner	69	75	69	70	283	15,000
Billy Mayfair	72	69	73	69	283	15,000
Jim Thorpe	68	74	72	69	283	15,000
Chip Beck	69	74	70	71	284	9,014.29
Scott Hoch	68	72	74	70	284	9,014.29
Dave Rummells	74	66	74	70	284	9,014.29
Ted Schulz	71	74	69	70	284	9,014.29
Joel Edwards	71	73	69	71	284	9,014.28
Wayne Grady	66	72	72	74	284	9,014.28
Neal Lancaster	68	77	68	71	284	9,014.28
Bobby Clampett	74	67	73	71	285	6,500
Calvin Peete	68	72	72	73	285	6,500
Gene Sauers	73	71	72	69	285	6,500
Curtis Strange	73	67	76	69	285	6,500
Bob Tway	72	71	68	74	285	6,500
Ian Baker-Finch	70	69	78	69	286	4,942.86
Jeff Hart	71	74	69	72	286	4,942.86
Steve Lowery	66	74	73	73	286	4,942.86
Ray Stewart	69	75	72	70	286	4,942.86
Lanny Wadkins	72	72	72	70	286	4,942.86
Lee Janzen	69	71	72	74	286	4,942.85
Tim Simpson	75	70	65	76	286	4,942.85
Clark Dennis	73	71	72	71	287	3,800
Ed Fiori	75	70	69	73	287	3,800
Morris Hatalsky	73	65	79	70	287	3,800
Willie Wood	71	72	74	70	287	3,800
Brad Fabel	75	70	71	72	288	2,802.86
Andrew Magee	72	70	75	71	288	2,802.86
Jodie Mudd	75	69	72	72	288	2,802.86
Larry Rinker	73	70	75	70	288	2,802.86
Bobby Wadkins	73	70	73	72	288	2,802.86
P.H. Horgan III	71	74	74	69	288	2,802.85
Duffy Waldorf	69	75	69	75	288	2,802.85

Kemper Open

TPC at Avenel, Potomac, Maryland
Par 36-35—71; 6,917 yards

May 31-June 3
purse, $1,000,000

	SCORES				TOTAL	MONEY
Gil Morgan	68	67	70	69	274	$180,000
Ian Baker-Finch	67	72	70	66	275	108,000
Scott Hoch	68	68	69	71	276	58,000
Hale Irwin	69	73	65	69	276	58,000
Tom Kite	70	70	67	70	277	38,000
Denis Watson	67	72	70	68	277	38,000
Billy Ray Brown	68	70	72	70	280	28,083.34
Mark Hayes	72	70	70	68	280	28,083.34
Clark Burroughs	69	70	66	75	280	28,083.33
Joel Edwards	70	71	64	75	280	28,083.33
Steve Jones	69	68	65	78	280	28,083.33
Pat McGowan	65	72	70	73	280	28,083.33
Curt Byrum	72	71	69	69	281	17,666.67
Trevor Dodds	70	69	70	72	281	17,666.67
Billy Mayfair	72	69	70	70	281	17,666.67

	SCORES				TOTAL	MONEY
D.A. Weibring	73	70	69	69	281	17,666.67
Larry Rinker	72	68	69	72	281	17,666.66
Ted Schulz	65	72	71	73	281	17,666.66
Russ Cochran	70	70	71	71	282	13,000
Bob Gilder	69	72	70	71	282	13,000
Jim Thorpe	73	71	69	69	282	13,000
Jay Don Blake	70	67	70	76	283	10,400
George Burns	74	67	71	71	283	10,400
Doug Tewell	68	69	70	76	283	10,400
John Cook	72	70	72	70	284	7,633.34
Donnie Hammond	70	70	72	72	284	7,633.34
Dave Eichelberger	69	73	69	73	284	7,633.33
Jim Gallagher, Jr.	70	71	71	72	284	7,633.33
Jim Hallet	67	72	72	73	284	7,633.33
Bobby Wadkins	69	72	71	72	284	7,633.33
Clark Dennis	69	71	74	71	285	5,800
Mike Donald	71	71	71	72	285	5,800
Bill Glasson	72	70	76	67	285	5,800
Jay Haas	71	71	70	73	285	5,800
Gary Hallberg	73	67	75	70	285	5,800
Steve Lamontagne	76	68	70	71	285	5,800
Bob Eastwood	69	70	73	74	286	4,400
Buddy Gardner	69	69	70	78	286	4,400
Corey Pavin	68	75	72	71	286	4,400
Chris Perry	70	73	74	69	286	4,400
Jeff Sluman	69	73	68	76	286	4,400
Kirk Triplett	73	70	73	70	286	4,400
Tommy Armour III	69	71	72	75	287	3,300
Brian Claar	70	72	74	71	287	3,300
Ed Fiori	72	71	72	72	287	3,300
Mike Smith	75	64	74	74	287	3,300
Leonard Thompson	71	71	74	71	287	3,300
Phil Blackmar	71	73	74	70	288	2,620
Bob Lohr	72	70	72	74	288	2,620
Craig Stadler	73	71	68	76	288	2,620

Centel Western Open

Butler National Golf Club, Oak Brook, Illinois
Par 36-36—72; 7,097 yards

June 7-10
purse, $1,000,000

	SCORES				TOTAL	MONEY
Wayne Levi	70	66	70	69	275	$180,000
Payne Stewart	68	67	72	72	279	108,000
Peter Jacobsen	72	70	70	68	280	58,000
Loren Roberts	65	75	69	71	280	58,000
Mark Brooks	71	65	73	72	281	38,000
Greg Norman	71	69	71	70	281	38,000
Tom Watson	69	71	69	73	282	33,500
Jose Maria Olazabal	71	68	72	72	283	30,000
Curtis Strange	73	71	69	70	283	30,000
Wayne Grady	70	71	73	70	284	26,000
Steve Pate	71	68	73	72	284	26,000
Keith Clearwater	72	70	70	73	285	23,000
Tom Kite	74	73	72	67	286	19,333.34
Billy Andrade	75	69	71	71	286	19,333.33
Paul Azinger	72	69	69	76	286	19,333.33
Jay Don Blake	72	71	73	71	287	15,500

	SCORES				TOTAL	MONEY
Mark Calcavecchia	72	71	74	70	287	15,500
Tom Purtzer	73	71	71	72	287	15,500
Scott Verplank	77	68	72	70	287	15,500
Chip Beck	71	69	75	73	288	11,240
Fred Couples	71	76	70	71	288	11,240
John Inman	73	71	73	71	288	11,240
John Mahaffey	72	71	74	71	288	11,240
Ray Stewart	65	73	74	76	288	11,240
Ben Crenshaw	71	70	76	72	289	8,166.67
Dillard Pruitt	73	74	73	69	289	8,166.67
Scott Simpson	72	71	72	74	289	8,166.66
Jay Delsing	75	72	74	69	290	6,950
Bob Gilder	72	70	72	76	290	6,950
Gene Sauers	74	71	72	73	290	6,950
D.A. Weibring	72	73	74	71	290	6,950
Clark Burroughs	78	69	73	71	291	4,866.67
Ed Dougherty	75	72	70	74	291	4,866.67
Nick Faldo	72	75	70	74	291	4,866.67
Jim Gallagher, Jr.	72	73	74	72	291	4,866.67
Mike Hulbert	75	68	74	74	291	4,866.67
Roger Maltbie	68	74	74	75	291	4,866.67
Chris Perry	73	74	70	74	291	4,866.67
Kenny Perry	73	74	73	71	291	4,866.67
Isao Aoki	74	73	74	70	291	4,866.66
Russ Cochran	73	69	71	78	291	4,866.66
Corey Pavin	73	68	71	79	291	4,866.66
J.C. Snead	71	74	71	75	291	4,866.66
Curt Byrum	73	74	70	75	292	2,951.43
Tom Byrum	74	72	74	72	292	2,951.43
Hubert Green	72	75	73	72	292	2,951.43
Mark McCumber	70	73	74	75	292	2,951.43
Andy North	72	70	77	73	292	2,951.43
Greg Twiggs	73	73	70	76	292	2,951.43
Gary Hallberg	73	71	71	77	292	2,951.42

U.S. Open Championship

Medinah Country Club, Medinah, Illinois
Par 36-36—72; 7,195 yards

June 14-18
purse, $1,200,000

	SCORES				TOTAL	MONEY
Hale Irwin	69	70	74	67	280	$220,000
Mike Donald	67	70	72	71	280	110,000

(Irwin and Donald shot 74s in 18-hole playoff, Irwin won in sudden-death on 19th hole.)

Billy Ray Brown	69	71	69	72	281	56,878.50
Nick Faldo	72	72	68	69	281	56,878.50
Tim Simpson	66	69	75	73	283	33,271.34
Mark Brooks	68	70	72	73	283	33,271.33
Greg Norman	72	73	69	69	283	33,271.33
Scott Hoch	70	73	69	72	284	22,236.67
Tom Sieckmann	70	74	68	72	284	22,236.67
Craig Stadler	71	70	72	71	284	22,236.67
Fuzzy Zoeller	73	70	68	73	284	22,236.67
Steve Jones	67	76	74	67	284	22,236.66
Jose Maria Olazabal	73	69	69	73	284	22,236.66
Jim Benepe	72	70	73	70	285	15,712.43
John Huston	68	72	73	72	285	15,712.43

	SCORES				TOTAL	MONEY
Larry Mize	72	70	69	74	285	15,712.43
Larry Nelson	74	67	69	75	285	15,712.43
Scott Simpson	66	73	73	73	285	15,712.43
Jeff Sluman	66	70	74	75	285	15,712.43
John Inman	72	71	70	72	285	15,712.42
Steve Elkington	73	71	73	69	286	12,843.34
Curtis Strange	73	70	68	75	286	12,843.33
Ian Woosnam	70	70	74	72	286	12,843.33
Paul Azinger	72	72	69	74	287	11,308.80
Webb Heintzelman	70	75	74	68	287	11,308.80
Masashi Ozaki	73	72	74	68	287	11,308.80
Corey Pavin	74	70	73	70	287	11,308.80
Billy Tuten	74	70	72	71	287	11,308.80
Chip Beck	71	71	73	73	288	10,022
Brian Claar	70	71	71	76	288	10,022
Mike Hulbert	76	66	71	75	288	10,022
*Phil Mickelson	74	71	71	72	288	
Severiano Ballesteros	73	69	71	76	289	8,221.16
Jack Nicklaus	71	74	68	76	289	8,221.16
Steve Pate	75	68	72	74	289	8,221.16
Ted Schulz	73	70	69	77	289	8,221.16
Bob Tway	69	72	74	74	289	8,221.16
Isao Aoki	73	69	74	73	289	8,221.15
Tom Byrum	70	75	74	70	289	8,221.15
David Frost	72	72	72	73	289	8,221.15
Jim Gallagher, Jr.	71	69	72	77	289	8,221.15
Bob Lohr	71	74	72	72	289	8,221.15
Mike Reid	70	73	68	78	289	8,221.15
Kirk Triplett	72	70	75	72	289	8,221.15
Bobby Wadkins	71	73	71	74	289	8,221.15
Craig Parry	72	71	68	79	290	6,687
Dave Barr	74	71	75	71	291	6,140.50
Mark McCumber	76	68	74	73	291	6,140.50
Dave Rummells	73	71	70	77	291	6,140.50
Robert Thompson	71	73	72	75	291	6,140.50
Bill Glasson	71	73	72	76	292	5,184.40
Andy North	74	71	71	76	292	5,184.40
Ray Stewart	70	74	73	75	292	5,184.40
Greg Twiggs	72	70	73	77	292	5,184.40
Lanny Wadkins	72	72	70	78	292	5,184.40
Bob Gilder	71	70	74	78	293	4,694.25
Tom Kite	75	70	74	74	293	4,694.25
Blaine McCallister	71	72	75	75	293	4,694.25
Gil Morgan	70	72	73	78	293	4,694.25
*David Duval	72	72	72	77	293	
Robert Gamez	72	73	73	76	294	4,529.50
Scott Verplank	72	69	77	76	294	4,529.50
Ronan Rafferty	75	70	73	78	296	4,507
David Graham	72	73	74	79	298	4,507
Howard Twitty	73	72	77	77	299	4,507
Brad Faxon	70	74	76	81	301	4,507
Mike Smith	72	72	82	80	306	4,507
Randy Wylie	70	75	81	82	308	4,507

Out of Final 36 Holes

Phil Blackmar	75	71			146	
Fred Couples	74	72			146	
Trevor Dodds	75	71			146	
Donnie Hammond	71	75			146	

U.S. Tour

Rusty Jarrett

The Vardon Trophy and leading money winner, Greg Norman had two victories on the United States PGA Tour. He was No. 1 on the Sony Ranking.

Four wins pushed Wayne Levi to No. 2 on the money list.

Jodie Mudd had two significant victories—The Players and Nabisco Championship.

A winner in the Heritage and Byron Nelson events, Payne Stewart also was first in the World Cup.

Mark Calcavecchia (left) was a runner-up six times, while Mark O'Meara had two victories in the AT&T Pebble Beach Pro-Am and Texas Open.

Early U.S. winners included Paul Azinger (left) in the Tournament of Champions, and Fred Couples in the Nissan Los Angeles Open.

Lanny Wadkins took a Virginia duel for the Anheuser-Busch title.

Gil Morgan won the Kemper Open.

It was a great year for the Aussies, including Steve Elkington, who won the K-mart Greater Greensboro Open.

Larry Mize (left) won in Japan, and Peter Jacobsen took the Bob Hope title.

Memphis winner Tom Kite.

Robert Gamez holed a miracle shot to win at Bay Hill.

Ian Baker-Finch had a solid year.

Spain's Jose Maria Olazabal romped to a 12-shot margin in the World Series.

Chip Beck won the Buick Open.

Chris Patton (left) turned pro, but did not qualify for the Tour. Years of struggle paid off for Tommy Armour III (right), who won at Phoenix.

European Tour

The No. 1 European money winner, Ian Woosnam had five 1990 victories and was No. 4 on the Sony Ranking.

Mark McNulty had victories in France and Germany, and was second on the European money list.

Another five-time winner, Jose Maria Olazabal climbed to No. 3 on the Sony Ranking.

Two wins in Europe and one in Australia were highlights of Ronan Rafferty's year, as the Irishman further established himself as a world-class star.

Double Masters: Sam Torrance (left) won the German Masters and Mark James won the British Masters.

Rodger Davis (left) had three victories, and Bernhard Langer won twice.

Eduardo Romero of Argentina (left) and Vijay Singh of Fiji were among the European Tour winners.

John Bland (left) and Craig Parry both had steady years, but no European Tour victories. Bland won three times in South Africa.

Steven McAllister won twice.

Sandy Lyle had another poor year.

Only one win for Seve Ballesteros.

Richard Boxall won in Italy.

Senior Tour

Seven victories marked Lee Trevino's Senior Tour debut.

Charles Coody's top prize was the rich Vantage Championship.

Gary Player won the PGA Seniors and Seniors British Open.

Jim Dent posted four Senior victories.

Chi Chi Rodriguez won three times in another outstanding year.

Jack Nicklaus played infrequently, but won twice, including the Senior TPC Championship.

LPGA Tour

Beth Daniel led the LPGA with eight victories, including the LPGA Championship.

Patty Sheehan gave chase to Daniel with five triumphs.

Betsy King had four wins, including majors in the Dinah Shore and U.S. Women's Open.

Cathy Gerring won three.

Nancy Lopez won once.

Asia/Japan Tour

Masashi (Jumbo) Ozaki and his driver—J's Professional Weapon—again ruled the Japanese Tour with four victories.

David Ishii won the Hawaiian Open in his home state, but spent most of the year in Japan.

	SCORES		TOTAL
Peter Jacobsen	71	75	146
Thomas Lehman	75	71	146
Tommy Moore	72	74	146
*Chris Patton	74	72	146
Larry Rinker	70	76	146
Jay Don Blake	72	75	147
Jon Chaffee	76	71	147
Russ Cochran	75	72	147
Ben Crenshaw	75	72	147
Ed Dougherty	74	73	147
James Estes	74	73	147
Wayne Grady	74	73	147
Greg Ladehoff	73	74	147
Wayne Levi	71	76	147
Robert McNamara	72	75	147
Jeff Wilson	80	67	147
Emlyn Aubrey	69	79	148
Danny Edwards	74	74	148
Jaime Gomez	71	77	148
Hubert Green	71	77	148
Mark James	74	74	148
Bernhard Langer	78	70	148
Mike Lawrence	73	75	148
Billy Mayfair	73	75	148
Jodie Mudd	72	76	148
Don Pooley	76	72	148
Bill Sander	79	69	148
Ivan Smith	71	77	148
Payne Stewart	73	75	148
Mark Wiebe	73	75	148
R.W. Eaks	74	75	149
Brad Fabel	77	72	149
Greg Hickman	75	74	149
Gordon Johnson	75	74	149
Andrew Magee	79	70	149
Mark O'Meara	76	73	149
Mike Schuchart	75	74	149
Peter Senior	75	74	149
Hal Sutton	76	73	149
Tom Watson	74	75	149
Bob Boyd	76	74	150
Brad Bryant	75	75	150
Bill Buttner	76	74	150
Mark Calcavecchia	73	77	150
Kelly Gibson	72	78	150
Brandt Jobe	76	74	150
Mark Lye	74	76	150
Sandy Lyle	78	72	150
John Snyder	78	72	150
Bruce Vaughan	76	74	150
Jack Druga	76	75	151
Tom Garner	73	78	151
Joel Padfield	76	75	151
Tom Pernice, Jr.	76	75	151
Jay Townsend	76	75	151
Johnny Delong	77	75	152
Mark Hayes	73	79	152
Don Shirey, Jr.	74	78	152
Andy Bean	74	79	153
Kirk Hanefeld	80	73	153

	SCORES		TOTAL	
John Mahaffey	76	77	153	
Michael Bradley	73	81	154	
George Burns	74	80	154	
Ray Floyd	77	77	154	
Dan Forsman	77	77	154	
Richard Parker	78	76	154	
Larry Rinker	79	75	154	
Brad Sherfy	75	79	154	
Bruce Soulsby	81	73	154	
John Flannery	75	80	155	
Denny Hepler	74	81	155	
Ted Norby	78	77	155	
Chris Peddicord	76	79	155	
Jay Haas	78	78	156	
Fran Marrello	76	80	156	
Brian Kelly	81	76	157	
Robert Gaus	82	76	158	
Jeff Julian	79	79	158	
Steve Schroeder	87	71	158	
Ric Burgess	81	78	159	
Todd Erwin	80	81	161	
Britt Tuttle	78	84	162	
*Warren Pitman	83	81	164	
Bill King	79	86	165	

(All professionals who did not complete 72 holes received $1,000.)

Buick Classic

Westchester Country Club, Rye, New York
Par 36-35—71; 6,779 yards

June 21-24
purse, $1,000,000

	SCORES				TOTAL	MONEY
Hale Irwin	66	69	68	66	269	$180,000
Paul Azinger	67	70	69	65	271	108,000
Kirk Triplett	65	74	67	66	272	68,000
Ken Green	70	67	69	67	273	48,000
Jim Gallagher, Jr.	69	68	70	67	274	38,000
Blaine McCallister	66	67	70	71	274	38,000
Ray Floyd	70	73	65	68	276	30,125
Lee Janzen	69	70	69	68	276	30,125
Loren Roberts	71	67	69	69	276	30,125
Craig Stadler	67	71	68	70	276	30,125
Jay Haas	67	67	72	71	277	24,000
Gene Sauers	69	71	70	67	277	24,000
Bill Britton	66	70	72	70	278	21,000
Russ Cochran	71	71	69	68	279	16,500
Ben Crenshaw	75	63	72	69	279	16,500
Steve Elkington	70	71	71	67	279	16,500
Rick Fehr	71	70	71	67	279	16,500
David Peoples	68	67	71	73	279	16,500
Jeff Sluman	71	72	68	68	279	16,500
Fulton Allem	71	70	68	71	280	11,650
Buddy Gardner	66	71	71	72	280	11,650
P.H. Horgan III	71	72	69	68	280	11,650
Chris Perry	72	70	69	69	280	11,650
Billy Andrade	71	71	69	70	281	7,566.67
Isao Aoki	70	70	70	71	281	7,566.67

		SCORES			TOTAL	MONEY
Phil Blackmar	71	72	68	70	281	7,566.67
Kenny Knox	69	71	71	70	281	7,566.67
Peter Persons	69	70	71	71	281	7,566.67
Howard Twitty	72	69	71	69	281	7,566.67
Emlyn Aubrey	71	71	66	73	281	7,566.66
Jim Benepe	70	71	68	72	281	7,566.66
John Dowdall	68	74	68	71	281	7,566.66
Andy North	67	76	71	68	282	5,525
Don Pooley	69	73	67	73	282	5,525
Larry Rinker	67	70	72	73	282	5,525
Clarence Rose	68	72	73	69	282	5,525
Ian Baker-Finch	69	67	72	75	283	4,400
Greg Bruckner	68	71	72	72	283	4,400
Bob Gilder	70	69	72	72	283	4,400
Corey Pavin	73	70	70	70	283	4,400
Hal Sutton	69	74	70	70	283	4,400
Doug Tewell	68	70	74	71	283	4,400
Mark Brooks	70	66	72	76	284	3,120
Brad Faxon	71	70	72	71	284	3,120
Steve Hart	71	70	72	71	284	3,120
John Inman	73	69	73	69	284	3,120
Nick Price	72	70	69	73	284	3,120
Greg Twiggs	70	72	71	71	284	3,120
Bob Wolcott	68	74	71	71	284	3,120
Michael Allen	70	70	72	73	285	2,348.89
Tommy Armour III	70	69	74	72	285	2,348.89
Jim Booros	70	72	68	75	285	2,348.89
Mike Donald	70	68	74	73	285	2,348.89
Andrew Magee	70	70	71	74	285	2,348.89
Rocco Mediate	71	69	71	74	285	2,348.89
Tommy Moore	69	73	75	68	285	2,348.89
Leonard Thompson	71	72	72	70	285	2,348.89
Ted Schulz	71	68	70	76	285	2,348.88

Canon Greater Hartford Open

TPC of Connecticut, Cromwell, Connecticut
Par 36-35—71; 6,786 yards

June 28-July 1
purse, $1,000,000

		SCORES			TOTAL	MONEY
Wayne Levi	67	66	67	67	267	$180,000
Mark Calcavecchia	67	67	68	67	269	66,000
Brad Fabel	67	65	67	70	269	66,000
Rocco Mediate	65	69	70	65	269	66,000
Chris Perry	63	69	68	69	269	66,000
Nolan Henke	65	67	67	71	270	32,375
Bob Lohr	70	68	68	64	270	32,375
Loren Roberts	67	66	68	69	270	32,375
Brian Tennyson	69	69	65	67	270	32,375
David Canipe	67	68	72	64	271	25,000
John Cook	70	63	67	71	271	25,000
Robert Wrenn	70	66	70	65	271	25,000
Paul Azinger	68	68	68	68	272	16,625
Jim Booros	66	69	66	71	272	16,625
Brian Claar	66	69	67	70	272	16,625
John Huston	70	66	70	66	272	16,625
Tim Simpson	66	67	69	70	272	16,625
Kirk Triplett	69	66	68	69	272	16,625

	SCORES				TOTAL	MONEY
Paul Trittler	67	67	67	71	272	16,625
D.A. Weibring	69	64	70	69	272	16,625
Billy Andrade	69	70	69	65	273	10,000
Wayne Grady	66	68	71	68	273	10,000
Hubert Green	66	71	68	68	273	10,000
Steve Jones	64	68	69	72	273	10,000
Steve Pate	70	68	71	64	273	10,000
Hal Sutton	69	69	70	65	273	10,000
Mitch Adcock	68	68	70	68	274	6,516.67
Bill Britton	70	67	70	67	274	6,516.67
Dan Forsman	65	74	71	64	274	6,516.67
Ken Green	66	69	71	68	274	6,516.67
Kenny Perry	68	66	73	67	274	6,516.67
Bill Sander	73	66	67	68	274	6,516.67
Jim Gallagher, Jr.	71	66	68	69	274	6,516.66
P.H. Horgan III	68	71	67	68	274	6,516.66
Larry Mize	70	69	67	68	274	6,516.66
Phil Blackmar	67	69	71	68	275	4,406.25
Bob Eastwood	67	64	72	72	275	4,406.25
Steve Elkington	65	71	70	69	275	4,406.25
Billy Mayfair	66	66	73	70	275	4,406.25
Dillard Pruitt	68	69	74	64	275	4,406.25
Ray Stewart	68	68	66	73	275	4,406.25
Mark Wiebe	67	68	67	73	275	4,406.25
Bob Wolcott	67	67	71	70	275	4,406.25
Dave Barr	67	68	73	68	276	3,500
Lennie Clements	70	67	72	68	277	2,752.50
Buddy Gardner	67	72	68	70	277	2,752.50
Jay Haas	65	70	72	70	277	2,752.50
Peter Jacobsen	68	70	69	70	277	2,752.50
Blaine McCallister	68	67	71	71	277	2,752.50
Pat McGowan	72	65	68	72	277	2,752.50
Nick Price	66	69	71	71	277	2,752.50
Larry Silveira	68	70	70	69	277	2,752.50

Anheuser-Busch Classic

Kingsmill Golf Club, Williamsburg, Virginia
Par 36-35—71; 6,776 yards

July 5-8
purse, $1,000,000

	SCORES				TOTAL	MONEY
Lanny Wadkins	65	66	67	68	266	$180,000
Larry Mize	66	69	68	68	271	108,000
Scott Verplank	69	64	69	70	272	58,000
Bob Wolcott	69	65	68	70	272	58,000
Ian Baker-Finch	69	71	66	67	273	36,500
Russ Cochran	66	71	69	67	273	36,500
Chris Perry	67	67	68	71	273	36,500
Curtis Strange	67	66	68	73	274	30,000
D.A. Weibring	67	70	69	68	274	30,000
Jerry Haas	68	68	66	73	275	26,000
Tim Simpson	71	65	69	70	275	26,000
Mike Donald	68	72	70	66	276	19,000
Mark O'Meara	64	68	73	71	276	19,000
Larry Rinker	66	70	67	73	276	19,000
Jeff Sluman	70	70	72	64	276	19,000
Kirk Triplett	72	67	69	68	276	19,000
Robert Wrenn	69	71	71	65	276	19,000

	SCORES				TOTAL	MONEY
Bob Gilder	69	66	70	72	277	13,040
Peter Jacobsen	71	69	69	68	277	13,040
Barry Jaeckel	67	69	74	67	277	13,040
Steve Lamontagne	71	67	68	71	277	13,040
Bruce Lietzke	68	70	71	68	277	13,040
Bill Britton	69	70	73	66	278	7,672.73
David Canipe	70	68	71	69	278	7,672.73
Fred Funk	69	69	71	69	278	7,672.73
Tom Kite	70	70	69	69	278	7,672.73
Blaine McCallister	68	67	74	69	278	7,672.73
Greg Norman	66	69	75	68	278	7,672.73
Kenny Perry	67	69	73	69	278	7,672.73
Payne Stewart	70	67	72	69	278	7,672.73
Greg Bruckner	70	69	69	70	278	7,672.72
Neal Lancaster	66	70	72	70	278	7,672.72
Mark Wiebe	71	69	68	70	278	7,672.72
Jim Benepe	68	72	71	68	279	4,733.34
Jim Hallet	69	71	72	67	279	4,733.34
Greg Hickman	64	73	73	69	279	4,733.34
Brian Claar	65	69	72	73	279	4,733.33
Jim Gallagher, Jr.	66	68	70	75	279	4,733.33
Mark Hayes	67	68	70	74	279	4,733.33
P.H. Horgan III	70	67	72	70	279	4,733.33
Tom Sieckmann	68	70	70	71	279	4,733.33
Tom Watson	68	70	70	71	279	4,733.33
Mitch Adcock	69	68	69	74	280	3,045
John Cook	68	68	73	71	280	3,045
Rick Fehr	67	71	72	70	280	3,045
Gary Hallberg	67	72	74	67	280	3,045
Donnie Hammond	66	69	71	74	280	3,045
Gene Sauers	67	72	69	72	280	3,045
Mike Sullivan	79	62	69	70	280	3,045
Bob Tway	73	67	67	73	280	3,045

Bank of Boston Classic

Pleasant Valley Country Club, Sutton, Massachusetts
Par 36-35—71; 7,110 yards

July 12-15
purse, $900,000

	SCORES				TOTAL	MONEY
Morris Hatalsky	70	68	69	68	275	$162,000
Scott Verplank	67	68	68	73	276	97,200
Rick Fehr	68	71	68	70	277	46,800
Mike Smith	65	72	69	71	277	46,800
D.A. Weibring	68	69	72	68	277	46,800
Brad Bryant	69	69	70	70	278	27,225
Bill Glasson	67	70	70	71	278	27,225
Billy Mayfair	70	68	72	68	278	27,225
Steve Pate	72	65	70	71	278	27,225
Brian Tennyson	71	68	65	74	278	27,225
Willie Wood	69	71	66	72	278	27,225
Bill Buttner	74	69	65	71	279	15,600
Dave Eichelberger	75	64	70	70	279	15,600
P.H. Horgan III	70	69	69	71	279	15,600
Lee Janzen	72	71	66	70	279	15,600
Tommy Moore	72	68	67	72	279	15,600
Chris Perry	68	72	70	69	279	15,600
Francis Quinn	72	67	68	72	279	15,600

	SCORES				TOTAL	MONEY
Sam Randolph	69	71	66	73	279	15,600
Jim Thorpe	71	70	67	71	279	15,600
Jim Gallagher, Jr.	70	69	71	70	280	8,220
Buddy Gardner	71	71	68	70	280	8,220
Ernie Gonzalez	69	73	67	71	280	8,220
Jeff Hart	73	70	69	68	280	8,220
Neal Lancaster	72	67	68	73	280	8,220
Mark Lye	71	70	66	73	280	8,220
John Mahaffey	69	68	71	72	280	8,220
Brian Watts	69	68	70	73	280	8,220
Fuzzy Zoeller	72	68	67	73	280	8,220
Jim Hallet	74	66	67	74	281	5,120
Mark Hayes	74	68	66	73	281	5,120
Roger Maltbie	73	69	68	71	281	5,120
Blaine McCallister	70	73	71	67	281	5,120
Clarence Rose	69	69	68	75	281	5,120
Don Shirey, Jr.	74	70	70	67	281	5,120
Tom Sieckmann	72	68	70	71	281	5,120
Joey Sindelar	70	72	67	72	281	5,120
Curtis Strange	72	68	69	72	281	5,120
Ronnie Black	75	68	69	70	282	3,510
Mark Calcavecchia	72	69	71	70	282	3,510
Rocco Mediate	74	69	68	71	282	3,510
Ted Schulz	72	70	70	70	282	3,510
Larry Silveira	70	70	68	74	282	3,510
Ron Streck	72	72	70	68	282	3,510
Robert Wrenn	73	68	70	71	282	3,510
Dewey Arnette	69	75	71	68	283	2,551.50
Bill Kratzert	72	72	69	70	283	2,551.50
Larry Rinker	71	65	73	74	283	2,551.50
Stan Utley	72	69	70	72	283	2,551.50
Jim Carter	73	71	68	72	284	2,154
Keith Clearwater	72	70	71	71	284	2,154
Marco Dawson	69	71	69	75	284	2,154
Mike McCullough	73	70	67	74	284	2,154
Richard Parker	73	71	70	70	284	2,154
Howard Twitty	72	70	71	71	284	2,154

Buick Open

Warwick Hills Country Club, Grand Blanc, Michigan
Par 36-36—72; 7,014 yards

July 26-29
purse, $1,000,000

	SCORES				TOTAL	MONEY
Chip Beck	66	70	71	65	272	$180,000
Mike Donald	65	69	69	70	273	74,666.67
Fuzzy Zoeller	66	69	66	72	273	74,666.67
Hale Irwin	69	63	67	74	273	74,666.66
Fred Funk	69	71	69	65	274	40,000
Ken Green	71	63	71	70	275	36,000
Dave Barr	69	66	68	73	276	30,125
Doug Tewell	71	65	66	74	276	30,125
Leonard Thompson	66	72	67	71	276	30,125
Robert Wrenn	67	69	68	72	276	30,125
Billy Andrade	69	65	66	77	277	21,200
Peter Jacobsen	68	70	70	69	277	21,200
Don Pooley	67	65	72	73	277	21,200
Dave Rummells	67	71	71	68	277	21,200

		SCORES			TOTAL	MONEY
Mike Smith	71	68	69	69	277	21,200
John Cook	70	66	72	70	278	15,000
Kenny Perry	70	70	68	70	278	15,000
Payne Stewart	74	68	66	70	278	15,000
Mike Sullivan	67	67	70	74	278	15,000
Scott Verplank	67	72	71	68	278	15,000
Andrew Magee	73	68	68	70	279	11,600
Roger Maltbie	67	70	69	73	279	11,600
Buddy Gardner	65	72	72	71	280	8,428.58
Jerry Haas	67	69	69	75	280	8,428.57
Neal Lancaster	67	74	68	71	280	8,428.57
Mark O'Meara	68	69	72	71	280	8,428.57
Don Shirey, Jr.	69	72	67	72	280	8,428.57
Tom Sieckmann	71	67	71	71	280	8,428.57
Bobby Wadkins	70	67	71	72	280	8,428.57
Jim Carter	72	70	69	70	281	6,210
Dan Forsman	70	70	67	74	281	6,210
Steve Lamontagne	69	68	73	71	281	6,210
Mike Schuchart	69	72	70	70	281	6,210
D.A. Weibring	70	70	71	70	281	6,210
Russ Cochran	70	69	74	69	282	4,516.67
Greg Ladehoff	71	69	74	68	282	4,516.67
Wayne Levi	65	71	73	73	282	4,516.67
Billy Mayfair	67	71	73	71	282	4,516.67
Lance Ten Broeck	69	69	74	70	282	4,516.67
Brian Tennyson	68	72	70	72	282	4,516.67
Morris Hatalsky	71	68	70	73	282	4,516.66
Tom Purtzer	68	71	70	73	282	4,516.66
Lanny Wadkins	71	71	68	72	282	4,516.66
Ed Dougherty	69	69	73	72	283	2,951.43
Steve Elkington	68	73	69	73	283	2,951.43
Jim Hallet	70	71	70	72	283	2,951.43
Steve Hart	70	70	70	73	283	2,951.43
Mark Lye	69	72	71	71	283	2,951.43
Gary McCord	67	71	73	72	283	2,951.43
Sam Randolph	70	69	68	76	283	2,951.42

Federal Express St. Jude Classic

TPC at Southwind, Memphis, Tennessee
Par 36-35—71; 7,006 yards

August 2-5
purse, $1,000,000

		SCORES		TOTAL	MONEY
Tom Kite	72	68	62	67	269	$180,000
John Cook	69	67	66	67	269	108,000
(Kite defeated Cook on first extra hole.)						
David Canipe	66	73	64	69	272	68,000
David Frost	69	70	68	67	274	41,333.34
Bob Estes	67	69	69	69	274	41,333.33
Tim Simpson	69	68	67	70	274	41,333.33
Billy Andrade	68	70	70	67	275	31,166.67
Loren Roberts	66	68	73	68	275	31,166.67
Billy Mayfair	71	65	69	70	275	31,166.66
Brian Claar	72	65	68	71	276	26,000
Neal Lancaster	71	65	70	70	276	26,000
Carl Cooper	69	68	68	72	277	20,250
Larry Mize	69	71	66	71	277	20,250
Nick Price	65	70	71	71	277	20,250

388 / THE U.S. TOUR

	SCORES				TOTAL	MONEY
Larry Silveira	62	71	75	69	277	20,250
Brad Fabel	68	70	70	70	278	15,000
Steve Pate	71	70	68	69	278	15,000
Peter Persons	66	69	73	70	278	15,000
Greg Twiggs	68	69	70	71	278	15,000
Fuzzy Zoeller	69	68	70	71	278	15,000
Jay Don Blake	68	68	68	75	279	9,387.50
John Daly	69	70	70	70	279	9,387.50
Jerry Haas	70	66	69	74	279	9,387.50
Lee Janzen	67	71	67	74	279	9,387.50
Mark Lye	66	69	71	73	279	9,387.50
John Mahaffey	69	71	70	69	279	9,387.50
Paul Trittler	68	69	68	74	279	9,387.50
Willie Wood	69	69	67	74	279	9,387.50
Mark Brooks	66	70	68	76	280	6,650
Billy Ray Brown	70	68	73	69	280	6,650
Tom Byrum	66	75	69	70	280	6,650
Mike Smith	70	68	69	73	280	6,650
Lennie Clements	69	73	69	70	281	4,745.46
Dave Eichelberger	69	73	71	68	281	4,745.46
Jeff Hart	71	70	69	71	281	4,745.46
Gene Sauers	70	71	69	71	281	4,745.46
Ted Schulz	69	73	70	69	281	4,745.46
Chip Beck	65	71	70	75	281	4,745.45
Greg Bruckner	69	71	69	72	281	4,745.45
George Burns	67	72	71	71	281	4,745.45
Bob Eastwood	68	69	69	75	281	4,745.45
Joel Edwards	68	71	70	72	281	4,745.45
Andrew Magee	69	69	71	72	281	4,745.45
Don Shirey, Jr.	70	69	70	73	282	3,023.34
Howard Twitty	69	71	71	71	282	3,023.34
Russ Cochran	70	68	69	75	282	3,023.33
Rick Fehr	65	70	72	75	282	3,023.33
Dan Halldorson	73	68	67	74	282	3,023.33
Ted Tryba	68	71	70	73	282	3,023.33
Bill Buttner	72	68	71	72	283	2,412
Jim Carter	73	69	75	66	283	2,412
Ed Dougherty	75	67	70	71	283	2,412
Steve Lamontagne	68	72	73	70	283	2,412
Bill Sander	72	69	70	72	283	2,412

PGA Championship

Shoal Creek Country Club, Birmingham, Alabama
Par 36-36—72; 7,145 yards

August 9-12
purse, $1,200,000

	SCORES				TOTAL	MONEY
Wayne Grady	72	67	72	71	282	$225,000
Fred Couples	69	71	73	72	285	135,000
Gil Morgan	77	72	65	72	286	90,000
Bill Britton	72	74	72	71	289	73,500
Chip Beck	71	70	78	71	290	51,666.67
Billy Mayfair	70	71	75	74	290	51,666.67
Loren Roberts	73	71	70	76	290	51,666.66
Mark McNulty	74	72	75	71	292	34,375
Don Pooley	75	74	71	72	292	34,375
Tim Simpson	71	73	75	73	292	34,375
Payne Stewart	71	72	70	79	292	34,375

		SCORES			TOTAL	MONEY
Hale Irwin	77	72	70	74	293	27,000
Larry Mize	72	68	76	77	293	27,000
Billy Andrade	75	72	73	74	294	20,600
Morris Hatalsky	73	78	71	72	294	20,600
Jose Maria Olazabal	73	77	72	72	294	20,600
Corey Pavin	73	75	72	74	294	20,600
Fuzzy Zoeller	72	71	76	75	294	20,600
Bob Boyd	74	74	71	76	295	14,000
Nick Faldo	71	75	80	69	295	14,000
Blaine McCallister	75	73	74	73	295	14,000
Greg Norman	77	69	76	73	295	14,000
Mark O'Meara	69	76	79	71	295	14,000
Tom Watson	74	71	77	73	295	14,000
Mark Wiebe	74	73	75	73	295	14,000
Mark Brooks	78	69	76	73	296	8,650
Peter Jacobsen	74	75	71	76	296	8,650
Chris Perry	75	74	72	75	296	8,650
Ray Stewart	73	73	75	75	296	8,650
Brian Tennyson	71	77	71	77	296	8,650
Paul Azinger	76	70	74	77	297	6,500
Ben Crenshaw	74	70	78	75	297	6,500
David Frost	76	74	69	78	297	6,500
Steve Pate	71	75	71	80	297	6,500
Tom Purtzer	74	74	77	72	297	6,500
Dave Rummells	73	73	77	74	297	6,500
Jeff Sluman	74	74	73	76	297	6,500
Scott Verplank	70	76	73	78	297	6,500
Ian Woosnam	74	75	70	78	297	6,500
Isao Aoki	72	74	78	74	298	4,750
Tom Kite	79	71	74	74	298	4,750
Davis Love III	72	72	77	77	298	4,750
John Mahaffey	75	72	76	75	298	4,750
Craig Parry	74	72	75	77	298	4,750
Andrew Magee	75	74	73	77	299	3,700
Sammy Rachels	75	73	76	75	299	3,700
Mike Reid	71	78	78	72	299	3,700
Bob Tway	72	76	73	78	299	3,700
Scott Hoch	78	73	72	77	300	2,865.63
Mark McCumber	73	76	74	77	300	2,865.63
Kenny Perry	73	76	78	73	300	2,865.63
Hal Sutton	72	74	78	76	300	2,865.63
Ray Floyd	72	77	74	77	300	2,865.62
Robert Gamez	71	78	75	76	300	2,865.62
Mike Hulbert	71	75	79	75	300	2,865.62
Stan Utley	71	72	80	77	300	2,865.62
Ian Baker-Finch	74	71	78	78	301	2,525
Bob Gilder	73	78	73	77	301	2,525
John Huston	72	72	77	80	301	2,525
David Peoples	77	71	77	76	301	2,525
Craig Stadler	75	73	74	79	301	2,525
Peter Senior	74	75	72	81	302	2,450
Jay Delsing	75	73	73	82	303	2,400
Donnie Hammond	77	70	80	76	303	2,400
Nick Price	75	71	81	76	303	2,400
David Graham	75	75	75	79	304	2,325
Scott Simpson	76	75	72	81	304	2,325
Bobby Wadkins	68	75	80	81	304	2,325
James Blair	73	76	76	80	305	2,225
Ed Fiori	75	76	77	77	305	2,225
Cary Hungate	72	77	79	77	305	2,225

	SCORES				TOTAL	MONEY
Rocco Mediate	75	72	77	81	305	2,225
Masashi Ozaki	75	74	79	77	305	2,225
Bob Ford	75	75	79	77	306	2,150

Out of Final 36 Holes

Billy Ray Brown	75	77	152
Steve Elkington	75	77	152
Rick Fehr	77	75	152
Steve Jones	74	78	152
Bruce Lietzke	78	74	152
Bob Lohr	78	74	152
Larry Nelson	77	75	152
Jack Nicklaus	78	74	152
Rick Osberg	73	79	152
Jerry Pate	73	79	152
Ted Schulz	78	74	152
Mike Sullivan	75	77	152
Lee Trevino	77	75	152
Hubert Green	74	79	153
Kirk Hanefeld	76	77	153
Robert Hoyt	74	79	153
Mark James	77	76	153
Bernhard Langer	75	78	153
Lonnie Nielson	72	81	153
Jeff Thomsen	77	76	153
Mark Calcavecchia	77	77	154
Russ Cochran	74	80	154
Bob Estes	77	77	154
Bruce Fleisher	78	76	154
Kent Stauffer	78	76	154
Mike Donald	76	79	155
Brad Faxon	80	75	155
Bill Sander	80	75	155
Ken Schall	77	78	155
Curtis Strange	79	76	155
Lanny Wadkins	74	81	155
Larry Emery	79	77	156
Dan Forsman	76	80	156
Stu Ingraham	75	81	156
Jay Overton	77	79	156
Benny Passons	74	82	156
Ronan Rafferty	81	75	156
Gene Sauers	75	81	156
Kim Thompson	80	76	156
Kirk Triplett	74	82	156
Tommy Armour III	78	79	157
Pat Fitzsimons	78	79	157
Phil Hancock	82	75	157
Dana Quigley	77	80	157
Dave Stockton	80	77	157
Ray Freeman	79	79	158
Bob Makoski	82	76	158
Naomichi Ozaki	77	81	158
Mike San Filippo	81	77	158
Chris Tucker	76	82	158
Brad Bryant	80	79	159
Greg Cerulli	75	84	159
Rodger Davis	81	78	159
Eduardo Romero	84	75	159

	SCORES		TOTAL
Jim Sobb	76	83	159
Severiano Ballesteros	77	83	160
Jay Haas	82	78	160
Jim Thorpe	77	83	160
Ed Whitman	84	76	160
Steve Bowen	81	80	161
Larry Gilbert	83	79	162
Mike Gove	86	76	162
David Ishii	82	80	162
Arnold Palmer	81	81	162
Jim Gallagher, Jr.	82	81	163
Drue Johnson	79	84	163
Bob Borowicz	81	84	165
Chris Dachisen	84	81	165
Hunt Gilliland	82	83	165
Andy Bean	84	82	166
Curt Schnell	82	84	166
Ken Allard	81	86	167
Noel Caruso	84	83	167
Dale Fuller	82	87	169
Ted Goin	87	83	170
Jay Don Blake	77	WD	
Bill Glasson	WD		
Mark Lye	WD		

(All players who did not complete 72 holes received $1,500 each.)

The International

Castle Pines Golf Club, Castle Rock, Colorado
Par 36-36—72; 7,559 yards

August 16-19
purse, $1,000,000

	POINTS	MONEY
Davis Love III	+14	$180,000
Steve Pate	+11	74,666.67
Peter Senior	+11	74,666.67
Eduardo Romero	+11	74,666.66
Ben Crenshaw	+9	40,000
Stan Utley	+8	33,500
John Adams	+8	33,500
Jim Gallagher, Jr.	+8	33,500
Dillard Pruitt	+7	27,000
Mark McCumber	+7	27,000
Bob Lohr	+7	27,000
Chip Beck	+6	23,000
Kenny Perry	+5	18,200
Howard Twitty	+5	18,200
Jose Maria Olazabal	+5	18,200
Bruce Lietzke	+5	18,200
Mark Lye	+5	18,200
Ian Baker-Finch	+3	15,000
Bob Gilder	+1	14,000
Steve Elkington	0	13,000
Mark Calcavecchia	-1	12,000
Tom Purtzer	-2	11,200
Tom Watson	-5	10,400
John Huston	-6	9,600

NON-QUALIFIERS FOR FINAL ROUND

	POINTS			TOTAL	MONEY
D.A. Weibring	2	11	2	15	$8,800
Ken Green	6	2	6	14	7,250
Mike Sullivan	4	2	8	14	7,250
Tom Byrum	6	4	4	14	7,250
Chris Perry	4	2	8	14	7,250
Scott Verplank	1	3	10	14	7,250
Bob Tway	6	6	2	14	7,250
Hale Irwin	8	0	4	12	5,788
Curt Byrum	4	3	5	12	5,788
Jim Hallet	1	6	5	12	5,788
Corey Pavin	4	7	1	12	5,788
Bill Buttner	9	-1	3	11	4,916
Robert Wrenn	2	2	7	11	4,916
Mark O'Meara	8	7	-4	11	4,916
Ronan Rafferty	2	3	5	10	4,400
Paul Trittler	6	4	0	10	4,400
Rocco Mediate	1	8	0	9	4,000
Tom Eubank	0	6	3	9	4,000
Billy Ray Brown	-1	12	-3	8	3,600
Robert Gamez	4	7	-3	8	3,600
Bob Wolcott	4	5	-2	7	2,860
Peter Fowler	6	4	-3	7	2,860
Kenny Knox	3	2	2	7	2,860
Billy Andrade	4	7	-4	7	2,860
Naomichi Ozaki	5	-1	3	7	2,860
Craig Parry	0	4	3	7	2,860

Fred Meyer Challenge

Portland Golf Club, Portland, Oregon
Par 36-36—72; 6,612 yards

August 20-21
purse, $700,000

	SCORES		TOTAL	MONEY (Each)
Bobby Wadkins/Lanny Wadkins	60	62	122	$50,000
Fred Couples/Lee Trevino	65	60	125	37,500
Greg Norman/Curtis Strange	62	63	125	37,500
Hale Irwin/Mark McCumber	64	63	127	28,500
Paul Azinger/Ben Crenshaw	61	66	127	28,500
Arnold Palmer/Peter Jacobsen	63	65	128	25,500
Mark O'Meara/Payne Stewart	65	64	129	25,000
Craig Stadler/Joey Sindelar	66	66	132	24,500
John Mahaffey/Hubert Green	66	69	135	23,750
Tom Weiskopf/Hal Sutton	68	68	136	23,125
Bob Gilder/Mark Calcavecchia	67	69	136	23,125
Raymond Floyd/Chip Beck	68	71	139	22,500

NEC World Series of Golf

Firestone Country Club, Akron, Ohio
Par 35-35—70; 7,136 yards

August 23-26
purse, $1,100,000

	SCORES				TOTAL	MONEY
Jose Maria Olazabal	61	67	67	67	262	$198,000
Lanny Wadkins	70	68	70	66	274	118,600
Hale Irwin	70	67	66	74	277	74,600
Donnie Hammond	73	65	70	71	279	52,600
Larry Mize	66	71	73	70	280	44,000
Chip Beck	71	69	69	72	281	38,025
Greg Norman	71	73	69	68	281	38,025
Tom Kite	70	71	72	69	282	31,833.34
Paul Azinger	69	71	72	70	282	31,833.33
Trevor Dodds	72	71	68	71	282	31,833.33
Mark O'Meara	71	72	68	72	283	26,400
Payne Stewart	65	73	73	72	283	26,400
Fred Couples	71	68	68	77	284	20,020
Naomichi Ozaki	69	76	69	70	284	20,020
Tim Simpson	71	70	69	74	284	20,020
Craig Stadler	70	69	74	71	284	20,020
Stan Utley	74	71	70	69	284	20,020
Gil Morgan	71	72	75	67	285	13,378.58
Dan Forsman	75	67	72	71	285	13,378.57
David Frost	73	70	71	71	285	13,378.57
Mike Harwood	69	74	73	69	285	13,378.57
Morris Hatalsky	73	68	71	73	285	13,378.57
Peter Jacobsen	72	69	72	72	285	13,378.57
Ted Schulz	71	72	72	70	285	13,378.57
Isao Aoki	72	68	72	75	287	9,380
Ken Green	71	72	69	75	287	9,380
Davis Love III	74	71	74	68	287	9,380
Blaine McCallister	71	71	73	72	287	9,380
Peter Senior	72	70	72	73	287	9,380
Brian Jones	72	73	69	74	288	9,000
Bill Britton	74	68	76	71	289	8,800
Mike Hulbert	74	68	72	75	289	8,800
Andrew Murray	71	76	71	71	289	8,800
Fulton Allem	70	71	75	75	291	8,450
Steve Elkington	71	70	74	76	291	8,450
Wayne Grady	72	73	70	76	291	8,450
Jodie Mudd	71	71	78	71	291	8,450
Tommy Armour III	73	74	72	74	293	8,000
Ben Crenshaw	73	74	72	74	293	8,000
Bruce Fleisher	72	71	75	75	293	8,000
David Ishii	71	78	71	73	293	8,000
Wayne Levi	74	69	74	76	293	8,000
Robert Gamez	77	75	72	70	294	7,700
Aki Ohmachi	72	70	79	74	295	7,650
Peter Fowler	74	73	78	79	304	7,600
Tony Sills	80	76	73	76	305	7,550
John Huston	79	77	72	79	307	7,500

Chattanooga Classic

Valleybrook Golf & Country Club, Hixson, Tennessee
Par 35-35—70; 6,641 yards

August 23-26
purse, $600,000

	SCORES				TOTAL	MONEY
Peter Persons	64	64	65	67	260	$108,000
Richard Zokol	65	66	65	66	262	64,800
Fred Funk	65	67	66	66	264	34,800
Kenny Knox	68	70	61	65	264	34,800
Ray Pearce	70	66	64	66	266	21,900
David Peoples	67	66	67	66	266	21,900
Harry Taylor	66	66	67	67	266	21,900
John Adams	65	68	67	67	267	17,400
Dave Eichelberger	65	69	64	69	267	17,400
Steve Lowery	62	68	71	66	267	17,400
Russ Cochran	66	66	66	70	268	12,300
Bob Estes	67	68	65	68	268	12,300
Brad Faxon	65	69	65	69	268	12,300
Scott Hoch	68	69	66	65	268	12,300
Mike Holland	66	67	67	68	268	12,300
Billy Tuten	65	66	70	67	268	12,300
Mitch Adcock	64	66	69	70	269	7,590
Jim Benepe	70	64	67	68	269	7,590
Jim Booros	71	64	67	67	269	7,590
John Dowdall	63	70	69	67	269	7,590
Ed Fiori	71	66	64	68	269	7,590
Buddy Gardner	65	70	66	68	269	7,590
Bill Kratzert	68	65	65	71	269	7,590
Dave Rummells	68	68	72	61	269	7,590
Ed Dougherty	66	66	71	67	270	4,680
John Inman	65	67	67	71	270	4,680
Jack Larkin	71	65	68	66	270	4,680
Tom Pernice, Jr.	63	71	69	67	270	4,680
Sonny Skinner	66	67	68	69	270	4,680
Bobby Clampett	69	66	67	69	271	3,726
Brad Fabel	69	68	67	67	271	3,726
Kenny Perry	67	68	69	67	271	3,726
Ron Streck	68	70	62	71	271	3,726
Doug Tewell	70	64	68	69	271	3,726
Gibby Gilbert	66	69	65	72	272	2,958
Greg Ladehoff	72	66	68	66	272	2,958
Don Reese	69	66	68	69	272	2,958
Howard Twitty	68	69	68	67	272	2,958
Jeff Wilson	63	68	70	71	272	2,958
Lee Janzen	68	69	69	67	273	2,280
Gary Koch	69	67	67	70	273	2,280
Jack Renner	66	67	72	68	273	2,280
Bill Sander	67	70	65	71	273	2,280
Larry Silveira	65	71	67	70	273	2,280
Ted Tryba	73	65	69	66	273	2,280
Jim Carter	67	69	70	68	274	1,632
Jim Hallet	67	68	70	69	274	1,632
J.C. Snead	70	67	73	64	274	1,632
Mike Sullivan	71	66	69	68	274	1,632
Greg Twiggs	70	65	73	66	274	1,632
Robert Wrenn	68	64	72	70	274	1,632

Greater Milwaukee Open

Tuckaway Country Club, Franklin, Wisconsin
Par 36-36—72; 7,030 yards

August 30-September 1
purse, $900,000

	SCORES				TOTAL	MONEY
Jim Gallagher, Jr.	69	70	66	66	271	$162,000
Ed Dougherty	69	69	67	66	271	79,200
Billy Mayfair	66	69	68	68	271	79,200

(Gallagher defeated Dougherty and Mayfair on first extra hole.)

	SCORES				TOTAL	MONEY
Scott Hoch	70	66	69	67	272	37,200
Steve Lowery	69	67	71	65	272	37,200
Ray Stewart	63	70	67	72	272	37,200
Chris Perry	67	71	68	67	273	29,025
Hal Sutton	70	68	66	69	273	29,025
Corey Pavin	68	70	66	70	274	24,300
Gene Sauers	67	73	70	64	274	24,300
Scott Verplank	74	62	67	71	274	24,300
Brad Faxon	68	71	66	70	275	18,225
Ken Green	65	69	71	70	275	18,225
Morris Hatalsky	67	69	67	72	275	18,225
Bobby Wadkins	71	65	70	69	275	18,225
Billy Andrade	67	70	69	70	276	13,500
Bob Estes	70	68	68	70	276	13,500
Nolan Henke	66	73	69	68	276	13,500
Greg Norman	69	68	69	70	276	13,500
Joey Sindelar	68	68	72	68	276	13,500
Fulton Allem	70	67	68	72	277	9,000
Mark Brooks	69	70	70	68	277	9,000
Jay Delsing	70	69	70	68	277	9,000
Mark Lye	69	66	70	72	277	9,000
Jim Thorpe	63	73	71	70	277	9,000
Bob Wolcott	69	70	68	70	277	9,000
Jerry Anderson	70	67	70	71	278	5,990.63
Webb Heintzelman	71	68	70	69	278	5,990.63
Tom Pernice, Jr.	68	70	70	70	278	5,990.63
Curtis Strange	69	69	70	70	278	5,990.63
Brian Claar	68	67	69	74	278	5,990.62
David Edwards	69	69	68	72	278	5,990.62
Blaine McCallister	71	69	67	71	278	5,990.62
Sean Murphy	67	72	68	71	278	5,990.62
John Adams	72	64	69	74	279	3,973.50
Trevor Dodds	69	72	70	68	279	3,973.50
Dave Eichelberger	68	72	70	69	279	3,973.50
Bruce Lietzke	68	72	68	71	279	3,973.50
David Ogrin	64	74	67	74	279	3,973.50
Steve Pate	71	68	70	70	279	3,973.50
Mike Schuchart	69	71	69	70	279	3,973.50
Steve Stricker	69	71	69	70	279	3,973.50
Bob Tway	68	69	69	73	279	3,973.50
Mark Wiebe	70	71	65	73	279	3,973.50
Peter Senior	69	71	70	70	280	2,880
Jeff Sluman	68	71	70	71	280	2,880
Mitch Adcock	66	70	73	72	281	2,421
Dave Barr	72	68	70	71	281	2,421
Phil Blackmar	68	68	75	70	281	2,421
Carl Cooper	67	73	68	73	281	2,421

Hardee's Golf Classic

Oakwood Country Club, Coal Valley, Illinois
Par 35-35—70; 6,606 yards

September 6-9
purse, $1,000,000

	SCORES				TOTAL	MONEY
Joey Sindelar	70	65	67	66	268	$180,000
Willie Wood	68	63	68	69	268	108,000
(Sindelar defeated Wood on first extra hole.)						
Ian Baker-Finch	67	69	69	64	269	45,100
Dave Barr	67	70	65	67	269	45,100
Bill Britton	69	67	68	65	269	45,100
Jay Delsing	66	65	70	68	269	45,100
Jim Gallagher, Jr.	68	66	67	68	269	45,100
Emlyn Aubrey	66	68	69	67	270	28,000
Mark Lye	71	66	67	66	270	28,000
Jeff Sluman	64	72	65	69	270	28,000
Bob Tway	68	64	67	71	270	28,000
Bob Estes	66	70	68	67	271	22,000
Billy Mayfair	65	65	71	70	271	22,000
Larry Rinker	72	66	66	68	272	17,500
Loren Roberts	67	68	67	70	272	17,500
Jeff Wilson	66	69	70	67	272	17,500
Bob Wolcott	68	70	67	67	272	17,500
Ed Fiori	70	66	68	69	273	12,600
Larry Mize	69	69	67	68	273	12,600
Chris Perry	68	70	69	66	273	12,600
Bill Sander	69	67	67	70	273	12,600
Gene Sauers	67	66	70	70	273	12,600
Jim Thorpe	70	65	69	69	273	12,600
David Edwards	73	66	68	67	274	7,240.91
Steve Elkington	69	68	69	68	274	7,240.91
Jim Hallet	71	68	66	69	274	7,240.91
Gil Morgan	67	69	68	70	274	7,240.91
Andy North	69	68	71	66	274	7,240.91
David Peoples	66	68	72	68	274	7,240.91
Nick Price	68	68	70	68	274	7,240.91
J.C. Snead	68	66	70	70	274	7,240.91
D.A. Weibring	69	68	69	68	274	7,240.91
Robert Wrenn	69	68	68	69	274	7,240.91
Tom Purtzer	67	69	67	71	274	7,240.90
Mike Donald	68	70	67	70	275	4,721.43
Ed Dougherty	71	68	68	68	275	4,721.43
Gary Hallberg	68	71	67	69	275	4,721.43
Steve Hart	68	70	71	66	275	4,721.43
Gary Koch	66	68	70	71	275	4,721.43
Steve Pate	68	67	71	69	275	4,721.43
Keith Clearwater	67	66	70	72	275	4,721.42
Billy Ray Brown	71	68	68	69	276	3,217.50
Curt Byrum	70	69	71	66	276	3,217.50
Brian Claar	69	69	68	70	276	3,217.50
Dan Forsman	68	71	71	66	276	3,217.50
Ken Green	70	68	69	69	276	3,217.50
Donnie Hammond	70	67	71	68	276	3,217.50
Mike Schuchart	68	70	69	69	276	3,217.50
Ted Schulz	69	69	68	70	276	3,217.50
Mark Calcavecchia	68	70	69	70	277	2,377.15
Kenny Knox	69	69	68	71	277	2,377.15
David Frost	68	71	69	69	277	2,377.14
Dan Halldorson	66	72	70	69	277	2,377.14
Mike Smith	72	66	70	69	277	2,377.14

	SCORES	TOTAL	MONEY
Grant Waite	73 66 69 69	277	2,377.14
Jim Woodward	72 66 72 67	277	2,377.14

Canadian Open

Glen Abbey Golf Club, Oakville, Canada
Par 35-37—72; 7,102 yards

September 13-16
purse, $1,000,000

	SCORES	TOTAL	MONEY
Wayne Levi	68 68 72 70	278	$180,000
Ian Baker-Finch	68 70 73 68	279	88,000
Jim Woodward	68 71 74 66	279	88,000
Andy North	71 71 70 69	281	48,000
Paul Azinger	70 71 71 70	282	32,750
Brad Faxon	65 74 71 72	282	32,750
Buddy Gardner	72 68 67 75	282	32,750
Brian Tennyson	70 67 73 72	282	32,750
Bobby Wadkins	68 72 69 73	282	32,750
Mark Wiebe	69 73 68 72	282	32,750
Davis Love III	69 75 71 68	283	24,000
Nick Price	69 70 69 75	283	24,000
John Adams	68 72 75 69	284	20,000
Bruce Lietzke	71 73 70 70	284	20,000
John Cook	65 73 74 74	286	16,000
Jim Hallet	68 75 69 74	286	16,000
Steve Jones	70 75 74 67	286	16,000
Ray Stewart	72 71 74 69	286	16,000
Stan Utley	68 75 72 71	286	16,000
Scott Hoch	72 71 77 67	287	13,000
Dave Barr	66 72 72 78	288	10,000
Jay Don Blake	71 71 73 73	288	10,000
Mark Calcavecchia	71 72 73 72	288	10,000
Donnie Hammond	74 71 72 71	288	10,000
Jeff Sluman	70 70 76 72	288	10,000
Bob Wolcott	72 72 77 67	288	10,000
Emlyn Aubrey	69 72 74 74	289	7,250
Jim Benepe	70 73 73 73	289	7,250
Lee Janzen	71 71 74 73	289	7,250
Bob Lohr	73 72 76 68	289	7,250
Brian Claar	73 68 73 76	290	6,062.50
Wayne Grady	68 73 76 73	290	6,062.50
Jerry Haas	69 72 74 75	290	6,062.50
Blaine McCallister	73 71 76 70	290	6,062.50
Mark Brooks	69 71 74 77	291	5,037.50
Jeff Hart	71 71 73 76	291	5,037.50
Steve Pate	71 74 76 70	291	5,037.50
David Peoples	68 76 74 73	291	5,037.50
Ricky Kawagishi	69 73 74 76	292	4,300
Dillard Pruitt	70 71 78 73	292	4,300
Paul Trittler	70 75 71 76	292	4,300
Michael Allen	76 69 76 72	293	3,500
Mike Donald	72 72 75 74	293	3,500
P.H. Horgan III	71 73 77 72	293	3,500
Corey Pavin	71 74 72 76	293	3,500
Hal Sutton	72 73 75 73	293	3,500
Lance Ten Broeck	71 69 81 73	294	2,603.34
Grant Waite	74 68 77 75	294	2,603.34
Ed Fiori	72 72 74 76	294	2,603.33

	SCORES				TOTAL	MONEY
Mike Hulbert	72	72	74	76	294	2,603.33
Andrew Magee	68	75	76	75	294	2,603.33
Mark McCumber	70	75	73	76	294	2,603.33

B.C. Open

En-Joie Golf Club, Endicott, New York
Par 37-34—71; 6,966 yards

September 20-23
purse, $700,000

	SCORES				TOTAL	MONEY
Nolan Henke	66	64	70	68	268	$126,000
Mark Wiebe	70	69	68	64	271	75,600
Jim Benepe	68	69	67	68	272	33,600
Barry Jaeckel	70	68	65	69	272	33,600
Brian Tennyson	70	70	66	66	272	33,600
Doug Tewell	71	64	70	67	272	33,600
Blaine McCallister	71	66	69	68	274	23,450
Brad Bryant	74	65	68	68	275	21,700
Trevor Dodds	69	69	67	71	276	18,200
Jim Hallet	66	66	72	72	276	18,200
Mike Sullivan	69	68	69	70	276	18,200
Robert Wrenn	68	68	72	68	276	18,200
Howard Twitty	69	69	70	69	277	14,000
Fuzzy Zoeller	69	70	70	68	277	14,000
Michael Allen	71	72	67	68	278	11,550
Joey Sindelar	71	69	67	71	278	11,550
Mike Smith	70	68	71	69	278	11,550
Jim Thorpe	70	67	71	70	278	11,550
Billy Andrade	68	71	70	70	279	8,484
Lee Janzen	70	70	68	71	279	8,484
John McComish	70	69	69	71	279	8,484
David Peoples	70	67	70	72	279	8,484
Sonny Skinner	70	69	72	68	279	8,484
Jeff Hart	71	67	66	76	280	5,967.50
Billy Mayfair	69	71	71	69	280	5,967.50
Sean Murphy	74	66	70	70	280	5,967.50
Paul Trittler	71	70	67	72	280	5,967.50
Mark Brooks	71	71	68	71	281	4,655
Jerry Haas	73	69	72	67	281	4,655
David Ogrin	68	71	70	72	281	4,655
Don Shirey, Jr.	69	70	67	75	281	4,655
Jeff Sluman	69	69	71	72	281	4,655
Scott Verplank	72	70	68	71	281	4,655
Mitch Adcock	71	69	71	71	282	3,612
Jim Gallagher, Jr.	70	70	70	72	282	3,612
Buddy Gardner	71	71	72	68	282	3,612
Webb Heintzelman	71	71	72	68	282	3,612
John Inman	73	67	70	72	282	3,612
Mike Holland	70	72	68	73	283	2,940
Dillard Pruitt	70	70	72	71	283	2,940
Larry Rinker	69	73	70	71	283	2,940
Greg Twiggs	71	71	72	69	283	2,940
John Adams	71	71	73	69	284	2,045.40
Patrick Burke	71	72	70	71	284	2,045.40
Bobby Clampett	71	71	68	74	284	2,045.40
Bob Eastwood	73	67	73	71	284	2,045.40
Rick Fehr	72	68	72	72	284	2,045.40
Ed Fiori	71	68	72	73	284	2,045.40

	SCORES				TOTAL	MONEY
Ken Green	72	71	71	70	284	2,045.40
Steve Pate	76	64	77	67	284	2,045.40
Mike Schuchart	73	69	72	70	284	2,045.40
Brian Watts	71	69	71	73	284	2,045.40

Buick Southern Open

Green Island Country Club, Columbus, Georgia
Par 35-35—70; 6,775 yards

September 27-30
purse, $600,000

	SCORES				TOTAL	MONEY
Kenny Knox	69	62	68	66	265	$108,000
Jim Hallet	68	66	65	66	265	64,800
(Knox defeated Hallet on second extra hole.)
Jim Booros	67	67	68	66	268	40,800
Tommy Moore	69	68	65	67	269	23,625
Larry Nelson	70	67	68	64	269	23,625
David Peoples	67	62	70	70	269	23,625
Jeff Wilson	67	64	69	69	269	23,625
John Cook	70	69	67	64	270	18,000
Bob Estes	67	68	66	69	270	18,000
Andy Bean	70	67	65	69	271	12,450
Bill Britton	67	67	71	66	271	12,450
Tom Eubank	66	70	70	65	271	12,450
Dan Forsman	68	69	68	66	271	12,450
Nolan Henke	67	66	70	68	271	12,450
Mark Lye	66	70	65	70	271	12,450
Bill Sander	69	67	68	67	271	12,450
Howard Twitty	62	71	68	70	271	12,450
Jim Benepe	71	66	67	68	272	8,100
Greg Bruckner	66	68	68	70	272	8,100
Buddy Gardner	67	66	70	69	272	8,100
Willie Wood	69	67	66	70	272	8,100
Ronnie Black	69	69	65	70	273	5,760
Mike Donald	65	71	70	67	273	5,760
Webb Heintzelman	68	67	71	67	273	5,760
Larry Mize	64	71	69	69	273	5,760
Bob Tway	67	67	73	66	273	5,760
David Frost	69	66	67	72	274	4,260
Gary Hallberg	67	71	69	67	274	4,260
Dan Halldorson	65	70	70	69	274	4,260
Barry Jaeckel	69	65	68	72	274	4,260
Harry Taylor	69	69	71	65	274	4,260
Keith Clearwater	69	66	69	71	275	3,396
Mike Holland	68	69	68	70	275	3,396
John Inman	69	67	70	69	275	3,396
Peter Persons	69	70	67	69	275	3,396
Leonard Thompson	68	68	70	69	275	3,396
Joel Edwards	67	68	72	69	276	2,760
Jeff Hart	69	69	68	70	276	2,760
Lon Hinkle	70	69	67	70	276	2,760
Bill Kratzert	68	70	67	71	276	2,760
Mark Brooks	69	70	70	68	277	2,100
Trevor Dodds	70	69	67	71	277	2,100
Lee Janzen	69	69	68	71	277	2,100
David Ogrin	70	67	71	69	277	2,100
Ted Schulz	68	70	70	69	277	2,100
Tom Sieckmann	71	66	66	74	277	2,100

		SCORES			TOTAL	MONEY
Larry Silveira	73	66	68	70	277	2,100
Lennie Clements	69	69	70	70	278	1,508
Frank Conner	64	68	76	70	278	1,508
P.H. Horgan III	67	70	69	72	278	1,508
Jack Larkin	68	68	69	73	278	1,508
John McComish	67	67	70	74	278	1,508
Dillard Pruitt	65	71	72	70	278	1,508

H.E.B. Texas Open

Oak Hills Country Club, San Antonio, Texas
Par 35-35—70; 6,576 yards

October 4-7
purse, $700,000

		SCORES			TOTAL	MONEY
Mark O'Meara	64	68	66	63	261	$144,000
Gary Hallberg	63	69	64	66	262	86,400
Nick Price	65	66	63	69	263	54,400
Loren Roberts	70	65	64	65	264	38,400
Corey Pavin	67	68	62	68	265	32,000
Mark Brooks	69	64	65	68	266	28,800
Emlyn Aubrey	63	69	70	65	267	25,800
Steve Jones	65	63	70	69	267	25,800
Ed Fiori	69	67	65	67	268	20,000
Scott Hoch	68	67	66	67	268	20,000
Larry Mize	70	65	66	67	268	20,000
Jodie Mudd	68	65	67	68	268	20,000
Duffy Waldorf	67	63	68	70	268	20,000
Greg Bruckner	70	68	66	65	269	14,000
Lennie Clements	72	65	65	67	269	14,000
Lance Ten Broeck	67	64	71	67	269	14,000
Doug Tewell	69	68	66	66	269	14,000
Brad Bryant	65	69	67	69	270	10,432
Clark Dennis	70	65	66	69	270	10,432
Mike Donald	67	66	65	72	270	10,432
Billy Mayfair	69	67	67	67	270	10,432
Howard Twitty	64	69	69	68	270	10,432
Phil Blackmar	67	65	66	73	271	7,120
Billy Ray Brown	65	72	64	70	271	7,120
Dan Forsman	66	70	65	70	271	7,120
Bruce Lietzke	69	68	66	68	271	7,120
Mark McCumber	69	65	68	69	271	7,120
David Edwards	70	68	67	67	272	5,440
Jerry Haas	69	68	66	69	272	5,440
Blaine McCallister	69	69	66	68	272	5,440
Bill Sander	68	65	71	68	272	5,440
Leonard Thompson	68	70	66	68	272	5,440
Jay Haas	68	68	68	69	273	4,420
Webb Heintzelman	67	65	70	71	273	4,420
Tom Kite	66	66	72	69	273	4,420
Tommy Moore	69	66	69	69	273	4,420
Russ Cochran	70	66	71	67	274	3,680
Jay Delsing	67	67	66	74	274	3,680
Andrew Magee	71	67	67	69	274	3,680
Payne Stewart	68	69	66	71	274	3,680
Michael Allen	71	66	68	70	275	2,880
Dave Barr	65	70	72	68	275	2,880
Clark Burroughs	69	68	70	68	275	2,880
Steve Lamontagne	68	70	69	68	275	2,880

	SCORES				TOTAL	MONEY
Ted Schulz	70	68	71	66	275	2,880
Mike Sullivan	66	70	71	68	275	2,880
Jay Don Blake	68	67	67	74	276	2,152
Bob Estes	67	70	64	75	276	2,152
Harry Taylor	69	67	71	69	276	2,152
D.A. Weibring	67	69	70	70	276	2,152

Las Vegas Invitational

Las Vegas Country Club
Par 36-36—72; 7,162 yards

Spanish Trail Golf & Country Club
Par 36-36—72; 7,088 yards

Desert Inn Country Club
Par 36-36—72; 7,111 yards

Las Vegas, Nevada

October 10-14
purse, $1,300,000

	SCORES					TOTAL	MONEY
Bob Tway	67	67	65	65	70	334	$234,000
John Cook	64	70	66	67	67	334	140,400

(Tway defeated Cook on first extra hole.)

Phil Blackmar	67	69	68	66	67	337	75,400
Corey Pavin	72	68	66	68	63	337	75,400
Nolan Henke	69	69	70	66	64	338	49,400
Mark O'Meara	67	64	67	69	71	338	49,400
Paul Azinger	69	67	71	68	64	339	43,550
Steve Elkington	69	71	71	62	67	340	37,700
Joey Sindelar	72	68	70	66	64	340	37,700
Richard Zokol	69	68	66	67	70	340	37,700
Jay Don Blake	67	68	70	68	68	341	26,650
Davis Love III	70	71	69	65	66	341	26,650
Gene Sauers	74	67	69	63	68	341	26,650
Craig Stadler	70	68	69	65	69	341	26,650
Payne Stewart	71	73	66	66	65	341	26,650
Robert Wrenn	70	64	74	68	65	341	26,650
David Frost	64	72	69	66	71	342	19,500
Steve Jones	70	69	72	65	66	342	19,500
Mike Smith	70	69	68	69	66	342	19,500
Jim Carter	74	65	71	67	66	343	14,083.34
Tom Purtzer	69	69	72	67	66	343	14,083.34
Billy Mayfair	67	68	72	67	69	343	14,083.33
Tim Simpson	66	67	72	68	70	343	14,083.33
Howard Twitty	67	73	71	65	67	343	14,083.33
Duffy Waldorf	68	65	73	68	69	343	14,083.33
Dave Barr	68	70	70	66	70	344	9,425
P.H. Horgan III	69	68	73	66	68	344	9,425
Mark Lye	70	72	67	65	70	344	9,425
Gary McCord	67	68	76	65	68	344	9,425
Nick Price	69	69	71	66	69	344	9,425
Loren Roberts	66	68	70	69	71	344	9,425
Brad Fabel	69	68	72	68	68	345	7,193.34
Mike Reid	70	69	72	67	67	345	7,193.34
John Adams	69	74	68	64	70	345	7,193.33
Brad Bryant	71	65	72	70	67	345	7,193.33
Ed Fiori	74	65	72	68	66	345	7,193.33

	SCORES	TOTAL	MONEY
Kirk Triplett	67 69 68 69 72	345	7,193.33
Billy Andrade	69 74 69 68 66	346	5,200
Emlyn Aubrey	67 67 68 70 74	346	5,200
Andy Bean	69 72 71 67 67	346	5,200
Dan Forsman	68 69 71 71 67	346	5,200
Robert Gamez	72 68 72 66 68	346	5,200
Ken Green	66 70 73 67 70	346	5,200
Hal Sutton	71 70 70 68 67	346	5,200
Bob Wolcott	67 70 70 67 72	346	5,200
Blaine McCallister	68 70 70 69 70	347	3,476.58
Tommy Armour III	73 68 69 65 72	347	3,476.57
Tom Byrum	66 70 74 68 69	347	3,476.57
Jerry Haas	72 72 67 68 68	347	3,476.57
John Mahaffey	70 70 67 68 72	347	3,476.57
Mark McCumber	71 67 70 71 68	347	3,476.57
Fuzzy Zoeller	68 72 68 70 69	347	3,476.57

Walt Disney World/Oldsmobile Classic

Magnolia Golf Club
Par 36-36—72; 7,190 yards

Lake Buena Vista Golf Club
Par 36-36—72; 6,706 yards

Palm Golf Club
Par 36-36—72; 6,967 yards

Lake Buena Vista, Florida

October 17-20
purse, $1,000,000

	SCORES	TOTAL	MONEY
Tim Simpson	64 64 65 71	264	$180,000
John Mahaffey	67 66 68 64	265	108,000
Davis Love III	68 65 66 67	266	68,000
Gene Sauers	68 65 67 67	267	48,000
Paul Azinger	67 65 68 68	268	40,000
David Peoples	68 69 65 67	269	36,000
Bob Gilder	68 65 68 69	270	33,500
Chip Beck	70 67 65 69	271	28,000
Dan Forsman	70 68 65 68	271	28,000
Bruce Lietzke	68 68 68 67	271	28,000
Larry Nelson	72 66 66 67	271	28,000
Nolan Henke	68 67 68 69	272	21,000
Mark O'Meara	70 68 68 66	272	21,000
Kenny Perry	68 65 72 67	272	21,000
Tommy Armour III	71 67 67 68	273	16,000
Phil Blackmar	69 72 65 67	273	16,000
Tom Byrum	70 63 72 68	273	16,000
Brad Fabel	70 67 66 70	273	16,000
Loren Roberts	70 66 69 68	273	16,000
Richard Zokol	69 67 68 70	274	13,000
David Edwards	69 68 69 69	275	9,387.50
Fred Funk	69 70 71 65	275	9,387.50
Robert Gamez	69 68 73 65	275	9,387.50
Mark Hayes	71 67 69 68	275	9,387.50
Neal Lancaster	68 70 69 68	275	9,387.50
Corey Pavin	69 68 70 68	275	9,387.50
Payne Stewart	68 70 61 76	275	9,387.50

	SCORES				TOTAL	MONEY
Lance Ten Broeck	68	70	67	70	275	9,387.50
Mike Donald	69	67	69	71	276	6,358.34
Blaine McCallister	69	70	67	70	276	6,358.34
Billy Andrade	68	67	68	73	276	6,358.33
Jay Delsing	68	71	70	67	276	6,358.33
Joel Edwards	70	66	67	73	276	6,358.33
Bob Lohr	69	65	70	72	276	6,358.33
Dave Barr	67	69	69	72	277	4,415
Russ Cochran	68	73	68	68	277	4,415
Clark Dennis	69	66	71	71	277	4,415
Scott Hoch	70	67	71	69	277	4,415
Sandy Lyle	69	71	68	69	277	4,415
Rocco Mediate	68	68	72	69	277	4,415
Gil Morgan	68	70	68	71	277	4,415
Don Pooley	69	66	71	71	277	4,415
Mike Reid	69	68	69	71	277	4,415
Larry Rinker	71	65	66	75	277	4,415
Ben Crenshaw	72	64	69	73	278	2,752.50
Morris Hatalsky	72	70	68	68	278	2,752.50
Lon Hinkle	68	71	69	70	278	2,752.50
Kenny Knox	68	69	72	69	278	2,752.50
Tom Sieckmann	69	71	68	70	278	2,752.50
Curtis Strange	68	69	71	70	278	2,752.50
Hal Sutton	69	70	69	70	278	2,752.50
Stan Utley	70	69	70	69	278	2,752.50

Nabisco Championship

Champions Golf Club, Cypress Course, Houston, Texas
Par 36-35—71; 7,187 yards

October 25-28
purse, $2,500,000

	SCORES				TOTAL	MONEY
Jodie Mudd	68	69	68	68	273	$450,000
Billy Mayfair	69	66	70	68	273	270,000

(Mudd defeated Mayfair on first extra hole.)

Ian Baker-Finch	71	70	67	68	276	146,250
Wayne Levi	75	71	67	63	276	146,250
Nick Price	68	68	71	70	277	100,000
Chip Beck	69	68	71	70	278	90,000
Greg Norman	66	71	71	71	279	82,500
Tim Simpson	66	73	70	70	279	82,500
Wayne Grady	72	67	73	69	281	75,000
Steve Elkington	72	72	66	72	282	71,000
Paul Azinger	73	71	68	71	283	67,500
Davis Love III	70	72	72	70	284	62,500
Mark O'Meara	74	70	73	67	284	62,500
Mark Calcavecchia	71	75	73	66	285	54,250
Gil Morgan	73	70	69	73	285	54,250
Loren Roberts	73	70	71	71	285	54,250
Bob Tway	72	71	71	71	285	54,250
Tom Kite	73	71	70	72	286	50,000
Hale Irwin	75	70	70	72	287	48,500
Peter Jacobsen	70	70	73	74	287	48,500
Corey Pavin	74	71	72	71	288	47,000
John Cook	72	74	70	73	289	45,500
Fred Couples	73	75	70	71	289	45,500
Lanny Wadkins	73	71	74	72	290	44,000
Payne Stewart	77	71	73	70	291	42,500

404 / THE U.S. TOUR

	SCORES	TOTAL	MONEY
Brian Tennyson	75 72 71 73	291	42,500
Jim Gallagher, Jr.	73 74 76 69	292	41,500
John Huston	72 71 76 76	295	40,750
Larry Mize	75 76 69 75	295	40,750
Robert Gamez	76 73 81 70	300	40,000

Mexican Open

La Hacienda Golf Club, Mexico City, Mexico
Par 36-36—72

November 1-4
purse, $600,000

	SCORES	TOTAL	MONEY
Bob Lohr	69 66 67 67	269	$100,000
Carlos Espinoza	71 68 65 69	273	55,000
Kenny Knox	70 69 67 70	276	36,000
Andrew Magee	71 66 67 73	277	21,875
Steve Elkington	68 66 70 73	277	21,875
Rafael Alarcon	69 68 70 70	277	21,875
Gary Hallberg	69 68 71 69	277	21,875
Keith Clearwater	69 69 72 68	278	16,500
Jim Thorpe	68 71 70 69	278	16,500
Nolan Henke	68 68 70 72	278	16,500
Ed Fiori	70 71 67 72	280	13,000
John Cook	70 75 67 68	280	13,000
Tom Byrum	70 67 72 71	280	13,000
Juan Brito	71 70 69 71	281	11,400
Ernesto Perez	72 68 70 71	281	11,400
Joey Sindelar	70 72 68 71	281	11,400
Jim Colbert	70 69 70 72	281	11,400
Lon Hinkle	71 71 70 71	283	10,000
Calvin Peete	67 73 71 72	283	10,000
Blaine McCallister	66 74 71 72	283	10,000
George Burns	78 70 69 67	284	8,800
David Edwards	67 71 76 70	284	8,800
Billy Kratzert	69 72 72 71	284	8,800
Doug Tewell	74 72 69 70	285	7,600
Dave Eichelberger	73 70 71 71	285	7,600
Tommy Armour III	70 76 68 71	285	7,600

Isuzu Kapalua International

Kapalua Resort, Bay Course, Maui, Hawaii
Par 36-36—72; 6,671 yards

November 6-9
purse, $700,000

	SCORES	TOTAL	MONEY
David Peoples	63 69 66 66	264	$150,000
Davis Love III	69 69 63 68	269	87,000
Nick Price	69 67 66 68	270	55,000
Kenny Knox	69 72 67 64	272	28,700
Blaine McCallister	67 71 69 65	272	28,700
Steve Jones	68 69 67 68	272	28,700
Ted Schulz	66 72 67 67	272	28,700
Corey Pavin	67 71 69 67	274	17,000
Billy Andrade	66 74 69 66	275	12,875
Ben Crenshaw	64 73 70 68	275	12,875
Kirk Triplett	67 72 68 68	275	12,875

	SCORES				TOTAL	MONEY
Sam Torrance	69	68	68	70	275	12,875
Hale Irwin	67	70	68	71	276	10,033.34
Peter Jacobsen	68	69	69	70	276	10,033.33
Tom Purtzer	67	68	67	74	276	10,033.33
Bob Gilder	65	73	72	67	277	8,600
Eduardo Romero	69	72	69	67	277	8,600
Loren Roberts	73	69	67	68	277	8,600
Scott Simpson	70	71	67	69	277	8,600
Scott Verplank	68	72	67	70	277	8,600
Mike Reid	70	72	68	68	278	7,400
Steve Pate	70	72	66	70	278	7,400
Billy Mayfair	73	67	67	71	278	7,400
Brian Tennyson	74	72	65	68	279	6,575
Mark Wiebe	68	70	70	71	279	6,575
Chris Perry	73	70	66	70	279	6,575
Mark Brooks	72	69	67	71	279	6,575
Don Pooley	68	73	69	70	280	6,125
Bill Glasson	66	74	68	72	280	6,125
Jim Thorpe	68	71	71	71	281	5,750
Vijay Singh	72	69	69	71	281	5,750
Jim Gallagher	65	72	70	74	281	5,750
Mike Hulbert	74	71	67	71	283	5,450
Mike Donald	70	67	75	72	284	5,088.75
Morris Hatalsky	68	76	70	70	284	5,088.75
Andy Bean	67	72	71	74	284	5,088.75
Joey Sindelar	68	70	69	77	284	5,088.75
Tony Sills	73	69	70	73	285	4,700
Donnie Hammond	74	71	70	70	285	4,700
Russ Cochran	72	70	73	70	285	4,700
Peter Persons	72	74	70	70	286	4,500
John Mahaffey	69	76	72	70	287	4,400
Billy Ray Brown	73	73	68	74	288	4,300
Lance Suzuki	69	75	75	70	289	4,200
Robert Gamez	74	74	68	74	290	4,150
Andrew Magee	73	72	74	73	292	4,100
Dave Stockton	76	74	63	63	296	4,050
Mark Rolfing	74	76	72	81	303	4,000

RMCC Invitational Hosted by Greg Norman

Sherwood Country Club, Thousand, Oaks, California
Par 36-36—72; 7,025 yards
(Format: First round - better ball; second round - alternate shot; third round - scramble.)

November 16-18
purse, $1,000,000

	SCORES			TOTAL	MONEY (each)
Fred Couples/Raymond Floyd	64	57	61	182	$125,000
Peter Jacobsen/Arnold Palmer	61	66	60	187	70,000
Ben Crenshaw/Lanny Wadkins	63	69	58	190	44,500
Curtis Strange/Mark O'Meara	59	69	62	190	44,500
Mark Calcavecchia/Ian Baker-Finch	65	62	63	190	44,500
Wayne Levi/Hale Irwin	64	65	64	193	39,000
Andy Bean/Bruce Lietzke	66	70	58	194	36,500
Gil Morgan/Tom Weiskopf	69	63	64	196	34,000
Greg Norman/Jack Nicklaus	65	70	62	197	32,000
John Mahaffey/Chi Chi Rodriguez	67	68	66	201	30,000

World Cup

Grand Cypress Resort, Orlando, Florida
Par 36-36—71; 6,751 yards

November 22-25
purse, $1,100,000

	INDIVIDUAL SCORES				TOTAL
GERMANY (556)—$240,000					
Bernhard Langer	71	71	67	69	278
Torsten Giedeon	70	71	65	72	278
ENGLAND (559)—$104,000					
Mark James	68	71	68	72	279
Richard Boxall	68	69	70	73	280
IRELAND (559)—$104,000					
David Feherty	70	73	70	63	276
Ronan Rafferty	72	69	70	72	283
WALES (561)—$64,000					
Ian Woosnam	72	69	65	70	276
Mark Mouland	68	76	68	73	285
UNITED STATES (562)—$50,000					
Payne Stewart	69	68	68	66	271
Jodie Mudd	69	72	73	77	291
ARGENTINA (566)—$31,334					
Miguel Guzman	69	72	67	72	280
Luis Carbonetti	69	71	74	72	286
AUSTRALIA (566)—$31,334					
Peter Senior	68	71	70	71	280
Brian Jones	75	74	68	69	286
SPAIN (566)—$31,334					
Jose Rivero	68	67	73	74	282
Miguel Angel Jimenez	69	73	72	70	284
CANADA (570)—$18,000					
Dave Barr	69	70	70	73	282
Rick Gibson	73	69	74	72	288
TAIWAN (571)—$14,000					
Yuan Ching Chi	71	72	70	70	283
Chen Liang Hsi	74	75	70	69	288
MEXICO (571)—$14,000					
Carlos Espinoza	72	71	70	70	283
Carlos Pelaez	73	76	71	68	288
SCOTLAND (571)—$14,000					
Sam Torrance	69	75	66	72	282
Gordon Brand, Jr.	69	71	74	75	289
DENMARK (572)—$10,000					
Anders Sorensen	67	67	70	69	273
Steen Tinning	77	70	75	77	299

	INDIVIDUAL SCORES	TOTAL

NEW ZEALAND (575)—$7,500
Frank Nobilo   68   73   78   69   288
Greg Turner   74   73   69   71   287

KOREA (575)—$7,500
Sang Ho Choi   70   77   67   75   289
Nam Sin Park   71   73   72   70   286

SWITZERLAND (578)—$7,000
Paolo Quirici   72   71   73   75   291
Andre Bossert   73   72   71   71   287

SWEDEN (579)—$7,000
Mats Lanner   67   71   71   73   282
Magnus Persson   74   76   75   72   297

FRANCE (581)—$7,000
Emmanuel Dussart   74   72   71   73   290
Jean Van de Velde   71   76   72   72   291

HOLLAND (582)—$7,000
Ruud Bos   75   72   73   67   287
Chris Van Der Velde   75   77   72   71   295

ITALY (587)—$7,000
Costantino Rocca   74   69   72   74   289
Alberto Binaghi   74   74   79   71   298

THAILAND (588)—$7,000
Tawm Wiratchant   74   74   70   74   292
Saneh Sanqsui   65   76   74   81   296

JAPAN (590)—$7,000
Tadami Ueno   75   71   69   73   288
Katsuyoshi Tomori   78   74   73   77   302

COLOMBIA (594)—$7,000
Juan Pinzon   76   71   72   77   296
Ivan Renjifo   75   79   75   69   298

PHILIPPINES (597)—$7,000
Frankie Minoza   77   74   70   73   294
Robert Pactolerin   76   80   75   72   303

BRAZIL (603)—$7,000
Rafael Navarro   72   78   75   72   297
Acacio Jorge Pedro   78   77   72   79   306

ICELAND (603)
*Ulfar Jonsson   73   73   73   78   297
*Sigurjon Arnarsson   83   78   73   72   306

BERMUDA (620)—$7,000
Dwayne Pearman   73   80   72   72   297
Keith Smith   77   79   85   82   323

SINGAPORE (622)—$7,000
Samson Gimson   79   83   73   75   310
Bill Fung Hee Kwan   75   80   79   78   312

	INDIVIDUAL SCORES				TOTAL
JAMAICA (623)—$7,000					
Seymour Rose	72	78	88	74	312
Christian Bernard	76	76	79	80	311
PUERTO RICO (630)—$3,500					
Jesus Rodriguez	80	75	74	74	303
*Julio Martinez	81	76	84	86	327
FIJI (635)—$7,000					
Vilikesa Kalou	81	78	82	74	315
Manoa Rasigatale	79	80	84	77	320
CZECHOSLOVAKIA (667)—$7,000					
Jiri Zavazal	77	81	78	78	314
Miroslav Nemec	87	90	84	92	353

INTERNATIONAL TROPHY

WINNER: Stewart - 271 - $75,000. RUNNER-UP: Sorensen - 273 - $50,000. ORDER OF FINISH: Feherty, Woosnam - 276 - $35,000 each; Langer, Giedeon - 278 - $17,500 each; James - 279; Boxall, Guzman, Senior - 280; Rivero, Barr, Torrance, Lanner - 282; Rafferty, Ching, Espinoza - 283; Jimenez - 284; Mouland - 285; Carbonetti, Jones, Park - 286; Turner, Bossert, Bos - 287; Gibson, Liang, Pelaez, Nobilo, Ueno - 288; Brand, Choi, Rocca - 289; Dussart - 290; Mudd, Quirici, Van de Velde - 291; Wiratchant - 292; Minoza - 294; Van Der Velde - 295; Sanqsui, Pinzon - 296; Persson, Navarro, Jonsson, Pearman - 297; Binaghi, Renjifo - 298; Tinning - 299; Tomori - 302; Pactolerin, Rodriguez - 303; Pedro, Arnarsson - 306; Gimson - 310; Bernard - 311; Kwan, Rose - 312; Zavazal - 314; Kalou - 315; Rasigatale - 320; Smith - 323; Martinez - 327; Nemec - 353.

J.C. Penney Classic

Innisbrook Resort, Copperhead Course, Tarpon Springs, Florida
Par 71; 7,031 yards

November 29-December 2
purse, $1,000,000

	SCORES				TOTAL	MONEY (Each)
Davis Love III/Beth Daniel	67	70	62	67	266	$100,000
Jay Haas/Nancy Lopez	65	73	65	68	271	59,000
Jim Hallet/Pam Wright	71	70	70	63	274	34,500
Jim Thorpe/Missie McGeorge	70	69	68	67	274	34,500
Gary Hallberg/Shirley Furlong	63	72	72	68	275	20,000
Jay Delsing/Penny Hammel	68	67	69	71	275	20,000
David Peoples/Barb Mucha	65	70	71	69	275	20,000
Kenny Perry/Sherri Turner	67	76	65	68	276	12,425
Kenny Knox/Nancy Brown	68	74	66	68	276	12,425
Billy Mayfair/Caroline Keggi	71	70	70	67	278	9,500
Bill Glasson/Pat Bradley	68	71	71	68	278	9,500
Donnie Hammond/Tammie Green	68	70	72	69	279	7,750
Mike Smith/Elaine Crosby	69	73	68	69	279	7,750
Bob Estes/Cindy Figg-Currier	69	69	70	71	279	7,750
Tom Purtzer/Tina Purtzer	66	71	71	71	279	7,750
Doug Tewell/Betsy King	69	72	71	68	280	5,450
Andy North/Sherri Steinhauer	68	71	70	71	280	5,450
Willie Wood/Cathy Johnston	68	74	68	70	280	5,450

	SCORES				TOTAL	MONEY (Each)
Gary Koch/Deb Richard	69	71	69	71	280	5,450
Larry Mize/Martha Nause	68	71	69	72	280	5,450
Leonard Thompson/Cathy Gerring	67	72	68	73	280	5,450
Kirk Triplett/Maggie Will	74	70	66	71	281	4,550
Dan Forsman/Dottie Mochrie	67	71	74	69	281	4,550
Mike Hill/JoAnne Carner	65	77	68	71	281	4,550
Chi Chi Rodriguez/Laura Davies	71	71	68	71	281	4,550
Ted Schulz/Jane Crafter	70	74	68	70	282	4,100
Brad Faxon/Dale Eggeling	69	70	73	70	282	4,100
Bob Gilder/Cindy Rarick	69	75	68	70	282	4,100
John Huston/Amy Benz	70	74	70	68	282	4,100
Bill Britton/Donna White	72	73	69	68	282	4,100
Robert Gamez/Kris Tschetter	71	72	69	71	283	3,800
Loren Roberts/Danielle Ammaccapane	68	73	71	72	284	3,500
Chris Perry/Meg Mallon	69	74	71	70	284	3,500
Buddy Gardner/Lynn Connelly	66	77	72	69	284	3,500
John Mahaffey/Rosie Jones	73	74	69	68	284	3,500
Tom Byrum/Susan Sanders	73	76	68	67	284	3,500
Steve Pate/Amy Alcott	67	75	71	72	285	3,116.67
Larry Rinker/Laurie Rinker	68	72	69	76	285	3,116.67
Stan Utley/Cathy Morse	69	71	76	69	285	3,116.67
Brian Claar/Kristi Albers	69	72	72	73	286	2,875
Rocco Mediate/Missie Berteotti	76	73	65	72	286	2,875
Mark McCumber/Debbie Massey	70	76	69	71	286	2,875
Brad Bryant/Chris Johnson	68	74	74	70	286	2,875
Tommy Armour III/Lori Garbacz	74	73	70	69	286	2,875
Mike Hulbert/Vicki Fergon	71	74	73	68	286	2,875
Jim Dent/Kathy Postlewait	71	76	66	74	287	2,675
Dave Barr/Dawn Coe	70	74	74	69	287	2,675
Mike Sullivan/Juli Inkster	71	73	70	74	288	2,575
Paul Azinger/Susie Redman	70	72	74	72	288	2,575
Keith Clearwater/Colleen Walker	72	72	72	75	291	2,500
Joey Sindelar/Lauri Merten	71	76	76	70	293	2,450
Billy Andrade/Jan Stephenson	70	79	74	71	294	2,400

Sazale Classic

Binks Forest Golf Club
Par 72; 7,075 yards

December 6-9
purse, $1,000,000

Wellington Golf Club
Par 72; 6,850 yards

Wellington, Florida

	SCORES				TOTAL	MONEY (Each)
Fred Couples/Mike Donald	65	60	63	66	254	$90,000
Tom Byrum/Curt Byrum	63	65	64	66	258	52,500
Brian Claar/Bill Glasson	61	64	68	66	259	29,000
Joel Edwards/Nolan Henke	64	65	66	65	259	29,000
Mitch Adcock/Russ Cochran	65	63	66	64	259	29,000
Mark O'Meara/Denis Watson	63	63	69	66	261	20,000
Kenny Perry/Leonard Thompson	63	63	67	68	261	20,000
Greg Bruckner/Kirk Triplett	60	65	69	68	262	16,500
Buddy Gardner/Dave Eichelberger	66	60	70	66	262	16,500
Charles Epps/Blaine McCallister	64	64	66	69	263	13,000
Jim Hallet/P.H. Horgan	62	65	67	69	263	13,000
John Huston/Gene Sauers	66	63	67	67	263	13,000

410 / THE U.S. TOUR

	SCORES				TOTAL	MONEY (Each)
Mark McCumber/Dewey Arnette	65	63	69	66	263	13,000
Chris Perry/Bob Lohr	63	66	70	64	263	13,000
Morris Hatalsky/Mike Sullivan	62	66	68	68	264	9,750
Jay Haas/Jerry Haas	67	64	65	68	264	9,750
Billy Mayfair/Howard Twitty	65	65	70	65	265	8,500
Stan Utley/Bob Wolcott	61	64	71	69	265	8,500
Ernie Gonzales/Mike Smith	64	66	67	68	265	8,500
Bill Buttner/Pat McGowan	63	68	70	65	266	7,250
Isao Aoki/Tsukasa Watanabe	64	65	70	67	266	7,250
Joey Sindelar/Jim Thorpe	65	66	72	65	268	5,750
Steve Lamontagne/Larry Rinker	65	64	69	70	268	5,750
Bobby Wadkins/Robert Wrenn	65	63	69	71	268	5,750
Andy Bean/Peter Kostis	66	62	71	69	268	5,750
Jim Carter/Rocco Mediate	60	69	66	74	269	4,500

Spalding Invitational

Pebble Beach Golf Club, Par 72
Spyglass Hill Golf Club, Par 72
Poppy Hill Golf Club, Par 72
Pebble Beach, California

December 13-16
purse, $300,000

	SCORES				TOTAL	MONEY
Juli Inkster	69	73	71	71	284	$60,000
Mark Brooks	71	71	71	72	285	34,300
Keith Clearwater	75	75	70	67	287	13,156
Howard Twitty	69	71	71	76	287	13,156
Alan Tapie	73	67	73	74	287	13,156
Blaine McCallister	73	71	72	73	289	7,500
Bryan Gorman	70	71	75	74	290	6,500
Mark Wiebe	76	66	70	79	291	5,250
Mike Springer	72	73	75	71	291	5,250
Bob Gilder	77	75	67	72	291	5,250
Cathy Johnston	67	74	77	73	291	5,250
Brian Claar	81	75	69	67	292	3,875
Johnny Miller	74	76	70	72	292	3,875
Jim Thorpe	72	78	72	71	293	3,200
George Burns	75	73	72	73	293	3,200
Mike Reid	76	79	66	72	293	3,200
Marion Dantzler	76	73	72	72	293	3,200
Bobby Clampett	70	73	75	75	293	3,200
Barry Jaeckel	77	72	71	73	293	3,200
Jeff Wilson	73	73	72	75	293	3,200
Russ Cochran	77	68	74	75	294	2,200
Gary McCord	75	71	75	73	294	2,200
Dave Stockton	76	72	77	69	294	2,200
David Peoples	70	75	73	76	294	2,200
Bob Irving	74	72	77	71	294	2,200
Andy North	77	68	73	77	295	2,200
Charles Gibson	73	73	75	72	295	2,200
Kirk Triplett	75	73	71	76	295	2,200
Adam Armagost	76	77	70	74	296	1,950
Loren Roberts	74	75	72	75	296	1,950
John Adams	74	73	71	79	297	1,825
Danny Briggs	72	79	76	70	297	1,825
Tim Loustalot	70	75	73	80	298	1,700
Ray Stewart	73	74	77	74	298	1,700

	SCORES				TOTAL	MONEY
Eric Woods	73	77	73	75	298	1,700
Bruce Soulsby	75	76	71	77	299	1,575
Perry Parker	76	71	75	77	299	1,575
Rod Curl	79	73	72	76	300	1,450
Dale Riley	78	72	72	78	300	1,450
Jeff Brenaut	70	77	73	80	300	1,450
Brian Mogg	73	71	77	80	301	1,360
Ed Humenik	73	76	76	76	301	1,360
Dan Forsman	79	72	73	77	301	1,360

The U.S. Senior Tour

MONY Senior Tournament of Champions

La Costa Country Club, Carlsbad, California
Par 36-36—72; 6,815 yards

January 4-7
purse, $250,000

	SCORES				TOTAL	MONEY
George Archer	73	69	67	74	283	$37,500
Bruce Crampton	71	74	73	72	290	27,500
Bobby Nichols	71	74	74	71	290	27,500
Al Geiberger	74	71	71	76	292	19,500
Chi Chi Rodriguez	73	71	75	73	292	19,500
Don Bies	73	73	75	73	294	13,500
Dave Hill	77	72	73	72	294	13,500
Rives McBee	74	74	74	72	294	13,500
Butch Baird	72	74	74	75	295	10,000
Billy Casper	76	71	73	75	295	10,000
Jim Dent	74	73	73	75	295	10,000
Miller Barber	72	75	74	75	296	8,000
Charles Coody	74	74	77	73	298	7,000
Larry Mowry	74	76	73	77	300	6,000
Orville Moody	76	75	77	73	301	5,000
Gene Littler	73	74	80	75	302	4,700
Walter Zembriski	75	76	73	78	302	4,700
Homero Blancas	79	77	76	73	305	4,400
Tom Shaw	81	72	76	77	306	4,200
John Paul Cain	79	74	77	77	307	4,000

Royal Caribbean Classic

Key Biscayne Golf Club, Key Biscayne, Florida
Par 35-36—71; 6,715 yards

February 2-4
purse, $400,000

	SCORES			TOTAL	MONEY
Lee Trevino	71	67	68	206	$60,000
Butch Baird	70	70	67	207	32,000
Jim Dent	66	68	73	207	32,000
Jim Ferree	70	68	70	208	23,000
Frank Beard	69	68	72	209	16,150
Bruce Crampton	70	68	71	209	16,150
Walter Zembriski	73	69	68	210	13,600
George Archer	68	74	69	211	12,000
Al Geiberger	71	67	73	211	12,000
Larry Ziegler	73	71	68	212	9,633.34
Mike Hill	71	70	71	212	9,633.33
Babe Hiskey	75	69	68	212	9,633.33
Charles Coody	71	70	72	213	7,800
Chick Evans	74	67	72	213	7,800
Dewitt Weaver	76	70	67	213	7,800
Gay Brewer	71	68	75	214	6,400
Bob Brue	70	71	73	214	6,400
Tom Shaw	68	72	74	214	6,400
Rocky Thompson	69	73	72	214	6,400
Don Bies	70	73	72	215	4,714.29
Harold Henning	72	71	72	215	4,714.29
Gene Littler	74	72	69	215	4,714.29
Phil Rodgers	69	75	71	215	4,714.29
Dave Hill	68	73	74	215	4,714.28
Joe Jimenez	70	72	73	215	4,714.28
Orville Moody	74	68	73	215	4,714.28
Arnold Palmer	66	73	77	216	3,900
Bob Charles	74	69	74	217	3,400
Bruce Devlin	64	74	79	217	3,400
Larry Mowry	70	71	76	217	3,400
Gary Player	70	74	73	217	3,400
Terry Dill	74	73	71	218	2,825
Mike Fetchick	71	71	76	218	2,825
Charles Owens	71	74	73	218	2,825
Ken Still	73	74	71	218	2,825
Marion Heck	73	75	71	219	2,425
Don Massengale	73	72	74	219	2,425
Bobby Nichols	75	74	70	219	2,425
Chi Chi Rodriguez	72	75	72	219	2,425
J.C. Goosie	76	75	69	220	2,075
Larry Laoretti	74	75	71	220	2,075
Dan Morgan	72	75	73	220	2,075

GTE Suncoast Classic

Tampa Palms Golf and Country Club, Tampa, Florida
Par 36-36—72; 6,631 yards

February 9-11
purse, $450,000

	SCORES			TOTAL	MONEY
Mike Hill	68	69	70	207	$67,500
Lee Trevino	69	71	69	209	40,000
Larry Mowry	67	72	72	211	28,250

	SCORES	TOTAL	MONEY
Ben Smith	69 73 69	211	28,250
Orville Moody	68 77 67	212	19,000
George Archer	69 72 72	213	15,625
Bob Brue	72 71 70	213	15,625
Harold Henning	70 71 72	213	15,625
Larry Laoretti	70 76 67	213	15,625
Don Bies	74 69 71	214	9,912.50
Bob Charles	71 71 72	214	9,912.50
Bruce Crampton	72 73 69	214	9,912.50
Jim Dent	70 76 68	214	9,912.50
Dale Douglass	69 70 75	214	9,912.50
Dave Hill	69 74 71	214	9,912.50
Gary Player	70 70 74	214	9,912.50
Rocky Thompson	75 70 69	214	9,912.50
Dick Hendrickson	72 70 73	215	7,100
Paul Moran	72 72 71	215	7,100
Charles Coody	68 74 74	216	5,900
Bobby Nichols	73 72 71	216	5,900
Arnold Palmer	74 70 72	216	5,900
Richard Rhyan	73 70 73	216	5,900
Jack Fleck	76 72 69	217	4,375
Joe Jimenez	72 71 74	217	4,375
Chi Chi Rodriguez	73 70 74	217	4,375
Walter Zembriski	71 73 73	217	4,375
Quinton Gray	73 74 71	218	3,800
Frank Beard	69 75 75	219	3,220
Gay Brewer	73 73 73	219	3,220
John Paul Cain	76 69 74	219	3,220
Gene Littler	72 72 75	219	3,220
Charles Owens	74 71 74	219	3,220
Bruce Devlin	74 76 70	220	2,600
J.C. Goosie	67 77 76	220	2,600
George Lanning	73 74 73	220	2,600
Jim O'Hern	75 73 72	220	2,600
Doug Sanders	71 75 74	220	2,600
Jim Ferree	75 76 70	221	2,100
Don January	73 69 79	221	2,100
Rives McBee	72 75 74	221	2,100
Dan Morgan	72 75 74	221	2,100
Charles Sifford	70 75 76	221	2,100

Aetna Challenge

The Club at Pelican Bay, Naples, Florida
Par 36-36—72; 6,719 yards

February 16-18
purse, $400,000

	SCORES	TOTAL	MONEY
Lee Trevino	66 67 67	200	$60,000
Bruce Crampton	70 65 66	201	35,000
Charles Coody	69 69 67	205	29,000
Mike Hill	68 69 69	206	23,000
Butch Baird	70 71 66	207	16,150
Jim Dent	69 68 70	207	16,150
Jim Ferree	71 68 69	208	13,050
Larry Ziegler	74 64 70	208	13,050
Don January	73 67 70	210	11,500
Bob Charles	73 72 66	211	10,050
Gene Littler	71 72 68	211	10,050

	SCORES			TOTAL	MONEY
Agim Bardha	72	68	72	212	8,500
Richard Crawford	71	72	69	212	8,500
Dave Hill	72	72	69	213	7,200
Gary Player	73	70	70	213	7,200
Richard Rhyan	70	71	72	213	7,200
Chi Chi Rodriguez	71	69	73	213	7,200
Lee Elder	75	69	70	214	5,800
George Lanning	71	71	72	214	5,800
Rocky Thompson	72	71	71	214	5,800
Tommy Aaron	71	76	68	215	4,900
Lou Graham	72	71	72	215	4,900
Charles Owens	71	69	75	215	4,900
Gay Brewer	73	72	71	216	4,000
Bob Brue	70	71	75	216	4,000
Bruce Devlin	75	76	65	216	4,000
Fred Hawkins	73	71	72	216	4,000
Harold Henning	69	73	74	216	4,000
Joe Jimenez	72	72	72	216	4,000
Miller Barber	72	74	71	217	3,200
Rives McBee	74	72	71	217	3,200
Frank Beard	70	73	75	218	2,575
Billy Casper	72	71	75	218	2,575
Al Geiberger	75	70	73	218	2,575
Quinton Gray	74	69	75	218	2,575
Dick Hendrickson	73	73	72	218	2,575
Larry Laoretti	71	72	75	218	2,575
Carl Lohren	74	72	72	218	2,575
Arnold Palmer	75	69	74	218	2,575
Phil Rodgers	76	72	70	218	2,575

Chrysler Cup

TPC at Prestancia, Sarasota, Florida
Par 36-36—72; 6,763 yards

February 22-25
purse, $600,000

FINAL RESULT: United States 53.5, International 30.5.

FIRST ROUND
Four-Ball Team Match Play

Lee Trevino-Chi Chi Rodriguez (U.S.) defeated Bruce Crampton-Bob Charles, 4 and 2.
Arnold Palmer-Orville Moody (U.S.) defeated Roberto De Vicenzo-Peter Thomson, 1 up.
Al Geiberger-Dave Hill (U.S.) defeated Bruce Devlin-Billy Dunk, 4 and 3.
Gary Player-Harold Henning (Int.) defeated Miller Barber-Don Bies, 2 and 1.

STANDINGS: United States 12, International 4.

SECOND ROUND
Singles Match Play
(Round cancelled, heavy rains, course unplayable.)

THIRD ROUND
Four-Ball Team Stroke Play

Charles-Devlin (Int.) defeated Hill-Moody, 65-70.
Trevino-Rodriguez (U.S.) defeated Crampton-Player, 66-68.

De Vicenzo-Henning (Int.) defeated Palmer-Bies, 69-70.
Barber-Geiberger (U.S.) defeated Thomson-Dunk, 65-67.

STANDINGS: United States 26, International 18.

FOURTH ROUND
Singles Stroke Play

Bies (U.S.) defeated De Vicenzo, 69-72.
Hill (U.S.) defeated Charles, 70-72.
Barber (U.S.) halved with Player, 71-71.
Geiberger (U.S.) halved with Crampton, 73-73.
Henning (Int.) defeated Palmer, 70-74.
Devlin (Int.) halved with Moody, 73-73.
Rodriguez (U.S.) defeated Dunk, 73-77.
Trevino (U.S.) defeated Thomson, 69-83.

Each member of the United States team received $50,000; each member of the International team received $25,000.

Vintage Chrysler Invitational

The Vintage Club, Indian Wells, California
Par 36-36—72; 6,819 yards

March 2-4
purse, $400,000

	SCORES			TOTAL	MONEY
Lee Trevino	66	67	72	205	$60,000
Dale Douglass	70	69	67	206	30,050
Mike Hill	67	73	66	206	30,050
Don Massengale	67	69	70	206	30,050
Jim Dent	68	70	70	208	20,000
Bob Charles	72	69	68	209	13,973.34
Rives McBee	69	70	70	209	13,973.33
Gary Player	68	71	70	209	13,973.33
John Brodie	67	72	71	210	11,031.67
John Paul Cain	73	69	68	210	11,031.67
Ben Smith	70	68	72	210	11,031.66
Frank Beard	69	72	70	211	8,995
J.C. Goosie	73	67	71	211	8,995
Butch Baird	72	73	67	212	7,015.84
Charles Coody	71	72	69	212	7,015.84
Miller Barber	73	67	72	212	7,015.83
Don Bies	68	72	72	212	7,015.83
Dave Hill	69	72	71	212	7,015.83
Bobby Nichols	72	71	69	212	7,015.83
Gay Brewer	69	72	72	213	5,040
Bruce Crampton	69	70	74	213	5,040
Bruce Devlin	71	70	72	213	5,040
Jim Ferree	72	69	72	213	5,040
Al Geiberger	71	70	72	213	5,040
George Archer	72	71	71	214	4,000
Lou Graham	71	70	73	214	4,000
Larry Mowry	72	70	72	214	4,000
Tom Shaw	72	71	71	214	4,000
Ken Still	70	77	67	214	4,000
Art Wall	71	73	71	215	2,998.34
Walter Zembriski	71	73	71	215	2,998.34
Harold Henning	70	73	72	215	2,998.33
Don January	72	69	74	215	2,998.33

	SCORES	TOTAL	MONEY
Chi Chi Rodriguez	71 70 74	215	2,998.33
Larry Ziegler	68 74 73	215	2,998.33
Bob Brue	71 76 69	216	2,600
Kyle Burton	73 72 72	217	2,396.67
Gene Littler	73 71 73	217	2,396.67
Roberto De Vicenzo	71 71 75	217	2,396.66
Lee Elder	75 75 68	218	2,147.50
Charles Sifford	71 71 76	218	2,147.50

Vantage at the Dominion

The Dominion Country Club, San Antonio, Texas
Par 36-36—72; 6,814 yards

March 16-18
purse, $300,000

	SCORES	TOTAL	MONEY
Jim Dent	69 70 66	205	$45,000
Harold Henning	69 69 70	208	25,500
Lou Graham	73 68 69	210	18,500
Mike Hill	73 69 68	210	18,500
Dale Douglass	66 72 73	211	12,800
Dave Hill	68 73 70	211	12,800
Lee Elder	71 72 69	212	9,625
Ken Still	66 71 75	212	9,625
Don January	73 68 72	213	8,162.50
Rocky Thompson	72 68 73	213	8,162.50
Ben Smith	73 71 70	214	7,100
Bob Betley	70 69 76	215	6,025
Gay Brewer	70 71 74	215	6,025
Bruce Crampton	73 68 74	215	6,025
Larry Mowry	73 70 72	215	6,025
Robert Boldt	74 71 71	216	4,750
Billy Casper	75 71 70	216	4,750
Bob Erickson	74 70 72	216	4,750
Richard Rhyan	74 69 73	216	4,750
George Archer	70 72 75	217	3,431.25
Frank Beard	70 74 73	217	3,431.25
Charles Coody	71 68 78	217	3,431.25
George Lanning	72 76 69	217	3,431.25
Don Massengale	74 71 72	217	3,431.25
Rives McBee	72 72 73	217	3,431.25
Tom Shaw	73 71 73	217	3,431.25
Walter Zembriski	69 76 72	217	3,431.25
Richard Crawford	75 73 70	218	2,543.75
Doug Dalziel	70 72 76	218	2,543.75
Terry Dill	73 74 71	218	2,543.75
Larry Mancour	73 72 73	218	2,543.75
Mike Fetchick	75 71 73	219	2,125
Bob Goalby	71 73 75	219	2,125
Joe Jimenez	73 71 75	219	2,125
Miller Barber	73 75 72	220	1,775
John Brodie	74 73 73	220	1,775
Billy Maxwell	68 78 74	220	1,775
Bobby Nichols	73 73 74	220	1,775
Robert Rawlins	75 72 73	220	1,775
John Paul Cain	77 72 72	221	1,437.50
Quinton Gray	77 68 76	221	1,437.50
Carl Lohren	77 70 74	221	1,437.50
Phil Rodgers	76 75 70	221	1,437.50

Fuji Electric Grand Slam

Oak Hills Country Club, Kurimotomachi, Japan
Par 36-36—72; 6,599 yards

March 23-25
purse, $400,000

	SCORES			TOTAL	MONEY
Bob Charles	70	75	69	214	US$69,186
Hsu Chi San	67	76	73	216	30,749
Lee Trevino	69	76	74	219	17,937
Dave Hill	69	74	76	219	17,937
Miller Barber	71	74	74	219	17,937
Chi Chi Rodriguez	72	77	71	220	9,320
Harold Henning	72	76	72	220	9,320
Hsieh Min Nan	73	70	77	220	9,320
Larry Mowry	66	79	75	220	9,320
Orville Moody	72	80	69	221	6,688
Teruo Suzumura	73	75	73	221	6,688
Don January	69	77	76	222	6,226
Hsieh Yung Yo	72	75	76	223	5,832
Billy Casper	71	76	76	223	5,832
Gene Littler	75	72	76	223	5,832
Hideo Jibiki	69	76	78	223	5,832
Ryosuke Ohta	77	73	73	223	5,832
Tadashi Kitta	73	75	76	224	5,246
Mitsuo Hirukawa	74	74	76	224	5,246
Shozo Miyamoto	76	71	77	224	5,246
Kesahiko Uchida	72	73	79	224	5,246
John Paul Cain	72	77	76	225	4,785
Yutaka Asai	73	76	76	225	4,785
Hisashi Suzuki	77	72	76	225	4,785
Masao Hara	72	76	77	225	4,785
Seiichi Sato	75	74	77	226	4,497
Yukihiro Kudo	71	76	79	226	4,497
Rafe Botts	73	80	74	227	4,189
Tetsuo Ishii	78	75	74	227	4,189
Seiichi Kanai	76	76	75	227	4,189
Tetuhiro Ueda	71	77	79	227	4,189
Sadao Ogawa	75	75	77	227	4,189
Fujio Ishii	74	73	80	227	4,189
Tadashi Maejima	80	73	75	228	3,882
Ichio Sato	80	72	76	228	3,882
Kiyokuni Kimoto	76	77	76	229	3,689
Masayuki Imai	72	77	80	229	3,689
Yoshimasa Fujii	78	70	81	229	3,689
Shigeru Uchida	71	80	79	230	3,382
Minoru Nakamura	73	78	79	230	3,382
Tom Shaw	75	75	80	230	3,382
Hiroshi Gunji	77	72	81	230	3,382
Jim O'Hern	77	72	81	230	3,382

The Tradition at Desert Mountain

Desert Mountain, Cochise Course, Scottsdale, Arizona
Par 36-36—72; 6,837 yards
(Thursday round rained out; shortened to 54 holes.)

March 29-April 1
purse, $800,000

	SCORES			TOTAL	MONEY
Jack Nicklaus	71	67	68	206	$120,000
Gary Player	71	69	70	210	65,000
Charles Coody	73	71	68	212	48,500
Bruce Crampton	69	71	72	212	48,500
George Archer	70	72	71	213	35,550
Frank Beard	73	71	69	213	35,550
Miller Barber	72	74	69	215	26,333.34
Mike Hill	69	74	72	215	26,333.33
Al Kelley	71	73	71	215	26,333.33
Joe Jimenez	71	74	71	216	19,833.34
Terry Dill	71	70	75	216	19,833.33
Rives McBee	75	70	71	216	19,833.33
Butch Baird	74	73	70	217	13,500
Bob Charles	71	73	73	217	13,500
Dale Douglass	74	72	71	217	13,500
Harold Henning	71	74	72	217	13,500
Phil Rodgers	69	71	77	217	13,500
Rocky Thompson	70	72	75	217	13,500
Larry Ziegler	70	73	74	217	13,500
Doug Dalziel	72	73	73	218	9,250
Al Geiberger	69	73	76	218	9,250
Don Massengale	71	76	71	218	9,250
Jim O'Hern	73	72	73	218	9,250
Bob Brue	71	76	72	219	7,700
Billy Maxwell	73	77	69	219	7,700
Robert Rawlins	75	70	74	219	7,700
Lee Trevino	75	72	72	219	7,700
Don Bies	74	74	72	220	6,600
Homero Blancas	73	76	71	220	6,600
Lou Graham	76	74	70	220	6,600
Orville Moody	75	75	70	220	6,600
Paul Moran	72	72	76	220	6,600
Tom Shaw	72	74	74	220	6,600
Ben Smith	76	73	71	220	6,600
John Brodie	71	74	76	221	5,400
Bob Erickson	75	73	73	221	5,400
Mike Joyce	71	76	74	221	5,400
Bert Yancey	73	74	74	221	5,400
Walter Zembriski	76	71	74	221	5,400
Dave Hill	73	74	75	222	4,600
Charles Owens	72	80	70	222	4,600
Ken Still	73	74	75	222	4,600

PGA Seniors Championship

PGA National Golf Club, Palm Beach Gardens, Florida
Par 36-36—72; 6,530 yards

April 12-15
purse, $450,000

	SCORES				TOTAL	MONEY
Gary Player	74	69	65	73	281	$75,000
Chi Chi Rodriguez	74	70	73	66	283	45,000

	SCORES				TOTAL	MONEY
Jack Nicklaus	68	78	67	72	285	25,000
Lee Trevino	77	67	70	71	285	25,000
George Archer	72	72	73	72	289	16,000
Miller Barber	75	73	68	76	292	15,000
Dale Douglass	71	73	74	75	293	14,000
Al Kelley	71	77	74	73	295	13,000
Don Bies	74	75	73	74	296	10,500
Lou Graham	76	76	72	72	296	10,500
Harold Henning	74	69	81	72	296	10,500
Larry Ziegler	73	75	75	73	296	10,500
Bruce Crampton	76	73	71	77	297	8,000
Rives McBee	75	75	72	75	297	8,000
Arnold Palmer	80	73	73	71	297	8,000
Frank Beard	74	71	76	77	298	6,275
Terry Dill	75	77	72	74	298	6,275
Mike Hill	71	78	76	73	298	6,275
Richard Rhyan	77	76	74	71	298	6,275
Joe Carr	75	73	74	77	299	5,000
Don Massengale	72	76	73	78	299	5,000
Jim Ferree	71	77	77	75	300	4,066.67
Larry Mancour	76	73	77	74	300	4,066.67
Larry Laoretti	77	76	71	76	300	4,066.66
Jerry Barber	73	79	71	78	301	3,300
George Lanning	76	78	74	73	301	3,300
Charles Sifford	75	73	80	73	301	3,300
Ralph Terry	73	73	77	78	301	3,300
Bob Brue	76	72	79	75	302	2,400
John Paul Cain	74	80	76	72	302	2,400
Bob Charles	75	75	73	79	302	2,400
Al Geiberger	76	75	74	77	302	2,400
Mike Joyce	81	71	73	77	302	2,400
Orville Moody	76	73	75	78	302	2,400
Paul Moran	74	77	74	77	302	2,400
Dan Morgan	81	76	73	72	302	2,400
Gordon Waldespuhl	74	79	72	77	302	2,400
Butch Baird	74	76	76	77	303	1,750
Charles Coody	74	73	79	77	303	1,750
Jim Dent	78	72	74	79	303	1,750
Dewitt Weaver	73	82	78	70	303	1,750

Liberty Mutual Legends of Golf

Barton Creek Club, Austin, Texas
Par 36-36—72; 6,608 yards

April 19-22
purse, $750,000
(unofficial)

	SCORES				TOTAL	MONEY (Team)
Dale Douglass/Charles Coody	59	62	62	66	249	$140,000
Al Geiberger/Harold Henning	65	62	64	65	256	80,000
Larry Mowry/Frank Beard	65	63	67	63	258	65,000
Chi Chi Rodriguez/Dave Hill	64	66	61	68	259	50,000
Bruce Crampton/Orville Moody	65	68	67	60	260	43,000
Mike Hill/Walt Zembriski	66	66	63	66	261	38,000
Tommy Jacobs/Jim Ferree	68	68	63	63	262	27,666.66
Lee Trevino/Jim Dent	67	66	64	65	262	27,666.66
Tom Shaw/Miller Barber	64	67	71	70	262	27,666.66
George Archer/Don Bies	65	65	66	69	265	16,000

	SCORES				TOTAL	MONEY
Bob Charles/Bruce Devlin	67	68	67	64	266	11,666.66
Gene Littler/Don January	67	71	64	64	266	11,666.66
Billy Casper/Gay Brewer	69	65	66	66	266	11,666.66
Lee Elder/Ken Still	67	67	66	68	268	10,000
Bobby Nichols/Butch Baird	67	70	65	67	269	10,000
Tommy Aaron/Lou Graham	71	66	68	65	270	10,000
Doug Sanders/Peter Thomson	67	67	67	70	271	10,000
Homero Blancas/Don Massengale	DQ					

Murata Reunion Pro-Am

Stonebriar Country Club, Frisco, Texas
Par 36-36—72; 7,064 yards

April 27-29
purse, $400,000

	SCORES			TOTAL	MONEY
Frank Beard	66	67	74	207	$60,000
Walter Zembriski	68	73	68	209	35,000
Dale Douglass	69	70	71	210	29,000
Rocky Thompson	70	74	67	211	23,000
Phil Rodgers	70	73	69	212	17,600
Bob Wynn	69	71	73	213	14,700
George Archer	72	75	67	214	12,025
Bruce Crampton	69	73	72	214	12,025
Orville Moody	70	71	73	214	12,025
Tom Shaw	72	69	73	214	12,025
John Paul Cain	70	72	73	215	9,600
Don Massengale	74	72	70	216	8,800
Bruce Devlin	73	68	76	217	7,000
Terry Dill	72	78	67	217	7,000
Harold Henning	72	73	72	217	7,000
Dave Hill	74	75	68	217	7,000
Babe Hiskey	75	71	71	217	7,000
Larry Laoretti	69	71	77	217	7,000
Chi Chi Rodriguez	69	76	72	217	7,000
Butch Baird	74	72	72	218	5,025
Charles Coody	71	75	72	218	5,025
Rives McBee	75	71	72	218	5,025
Charles Owens	74	73	71	218	5,025
Dan Morgan	71	73	75	219	4,200
Jim O'Hern	73	73	73	219	4,200
Robert Rawlins	73	75	71	219	4,200
Richard Rhyan	73	73	73	219	4,200
J.C. Goosie	74	74	72	220	3,315
Mike Hill	71	76	73	220	3,315
Joe Jimenez	70	75	75	220	3,315
George Lanning	71	74	75	220	3,315
Bobby Nichols	68	75	77	220	3,315
Tommy Aaron	73	73	75	221	2,675
Miller Barber	72	73	76	221	2,675
Gay Brewer	74	72	75	221	2,675
Quinton Gray	72	69	80	221	2,675
Bert Yancey	76	71	74	221	2,675
Gene Littler	72	74	76	222	2,275
Ben Smith	74	75	73	222	2,275
Larry Ziegler	69	81	72	222	2,275

Las Vegas Classic

Desert Inn Country Club, Las Vegas, Nevada
Par 36-36—72; 6,810 yards

May 4-6
purse, $450,000

	SCORES			TOTAL	MONEY
Chi Chi Rodriguez	68	67	69	204	$67,500
George Archer	69	66	70	205	36,750
Charles Coody	67	71	67	205	36,750
Bob Charles	67	74	65	206	22,433.34
Al Geiberger	69	69	68	206	22,433.33
Lee Trevino	67	72	67	206	22,433.33
Jim Dent	72	67	70	209	15,180
Mike Hill	69	68	72	209	15,180
John Paul Cain	70	75	66	211	11,923.75
Harold Henning	73	70	68	211	11,923.75
Jimmy Powell	70	70	71	211	11,923.75
Tom Shaw	68	74	69	211	11,923.75
Walter Zembriski	69	70	73	212	9,785
Miller Barber	72	73	68	213	8,586.67
Don Bies	71	74	68	213	8,586.67
Larry Ziegler	71	72	70	213	8,586.66
Frank Beard	72	70	72	214	6,750
Gay Brewer	75	68	71	214	6,750
Dale Douglass	73	72	69	214	6,750
Jim Ferree	73	72	69	214	6,750
Martin Roesink	74	71	69	214	6,750
Dave Hill	71	74	70	215	5,287.50
Don January	73	70	72	215	5,287.50
Larry Mowry	73	72	70	215	5,287.50
Phil Rodgers	72	72	71	215	5,287.50
Bruce Devlin	73	69	74	216	4,725
Homero Blancas	74	72	71	217	4,387.50
Billy Maxwell	74	71	72	217	4,387.50
Tommy Aaron	70	73	75	218	3,712.50
Don Massengale	75	71	72	218	3,712.50
Orville Moody	75	69	74	218	3,712.50
Bobby Nichols	73	70	75	218	3,712.50
Lou Graham	76	73	70	219	3,205
Dick Hendrickson	73	76	70	219	3,205
Charles Owens	76	73	71	220	2,980
Dewitt Weaver	75	72	73	220	2,980
George Lanning	76	76	69	221	2,698.34
Joe Jimenez	78	71	72	221	2,698.33
Ken Still	72	75	74	221	2,698.33

Southwestern Bell Classic

Quail Creek Golf and Country Club, Oklahoma City, Oklahoma
Par 36-36—72; 6,708 yards

May 11-13
purse, $450,000

	SCORES			TOTAL	MONEY
Jimmy Powell	72	71	65	208	$67,500
Jim Dent	75	68	68	211	28,875
Terry Dill	70	69	72	211	28,875
Mike Hill	72	69	70	211	28,875
Rives McBee	71	73	67	211	28,875
Don January	71	72	70	213	17,500

422 / THE U.S. SENIOR TOUR

	SCORES			TOTAL	MONEY
Doug Dalziel	72	70	72	214	15,000
Lou Graham	73	71	70	214	15,000
Walter Zembriski	73	70	71	214	15,000
Miller Barber	75	71	69	215	11,000
Gay Brewer	79	67	69	215	11,000
Bob Brue	73	70	72	215	11,000
Dave Hill	75	70	70	215	11,000
Orville Moody	73	74	68	215	11,000
Joe Jimenez	71	71	74	216	8,100
Charles Owens	67	75	74	216	8,100
Rocky Thompson	73	72	71	216	8,100
George Archer	75	72	70	217	6,700
Jim Ferree	77	70	70	217	6,700
Dan Morgan	74	72	71	217	6,700
Dewitt Weaver	77	69	71	217	6,700
Bruce Devlin	79	72	67	218	4,900
Jack Fleck	77	68	73	218	4,900
Bobby Nichols	78	72	68	218	4,900
Tom Shaw	76	73	69	218	4,900
Ken Still	73	71	74	218	4,900
Al Geiberger	73	70	76	219	3,800
Gordon Jones	73	73	73	219	3,800
Don Massengale	73	72	74	219	3,800
Bob Betley	76	75	69	220	3,300
George Lanning	76	70	74	220	3,300
Ray Beallo	73	73	75	221	2,800
John Brodie	76	71	74	221	2,800
Dale Douglass	78	70	73	221	2,800
Phil Rodgers	73	74	74	221	2,800
Ben Smith	75	72	74	221	2,800
Agim Bardha	76	74	72	222	2,350
J.C. Goosie	76	71	75	222	2,350
Fred Hawkins	80	70	72	222	2,350
Howie Johnson	74	75	73	222	2,350

Doug Sanders Kingwood Celebrity Classic

Deerwood Club, Kingwood, Texas
Par 36-36—72; 6,564 yards

May 18-20
purse, $300,000

	SCORES			TOTAL	MONEY
Lee Trevino	67	67	69	203	$45,000
Gary Player	70	74	65	209	27,000
Bob Charles	70	68	72	210	22,500
Mike Hill	73	69	71	213	15,000
George Lanning	69	71	73	213	15,000
Orville Moody	74	66	73	213	15,000
Dave Hill	70	71	73	214	10,500
Charles Coody	74	74	67	215	9,375
Walter Zembriski	73	69	73	215	9,375
Miller Barber	74	71	71	216	7,600
Homero Blancas	73	74	69	216	7,600
Harold Henning	73	74	69	216	7,600
Babe Hiskey	71	74	72	217	6,525
Jim Dent	73	74	71	218	5,725
Ben Smith	72	74	72	218	5,725
Dewitt Weaver	71	74	73	218	5,725
John Paul Cain	75	74	70	219	4,800

	SCORES			TOTAL	MONEY
Dale Douglass	71	73	75	219	4,800
Al Kelley	75	74	70	219	4,800
Bobby Nichols	74	75	71	220	4,050
Rocky Thompson	72	74	74	220	4,050
Jimmy Powell	71	75	75	221	3,675
Tom Shaw	74	73	74	221	3,675
Bob Brue	75	71	76	222	3,300
Terry Dill	73	76	73	222	3,300
Charles Sifford	76	73	73	222	3,300
Jim Ferree	68	76	79	223	2,925
Rives McBee	72	75	76	223	2,925
Doug Dalziel	76	71	77	224	2,475
Lee Elder	77	73	74	224	2,475
Jack Fleck	80	73	71	224	2,475
Richard Rhyan	76	76	72	224	2,475
John Brodie	74	76	75	225	2,137.50
Jim O'Hern	74	78	73	225	2,137.50
Howie Johnson	76	79	72	227	2,025
Tommy Aaron	76	74	78	228	1,950
Bill Collins	75	75	79	229	1,725
Bruce Devlin	78	78	73	229	1,725
Bob Erickson	77	78	74	229	1,725
Chick Evans	79	73	77	229	1,725
Don Massengale	78	75	76	229	1,725

Bell Atlantic Classic

Chester Valley Golf Club, Malvern, Pennsylvania
Par 35-35—70; 6,406 yards

May 25-27
purse, $500,000

	SCORES			TOTAL	MONEY
Dale Douglass	70	66	70	206	$75,000
Gary Player	69	68	69	206	44,000

(Douglass defeated Player on second extra hole.)

Bob Charles	70	70	67	207	33,000
Charles Coody	69	68	70	207	33,000
George Archer	68	72	68	208	24,000
Lee Trevino	67	71	71	209	20,000
Jim Dent	69	70	71	210	15,175
Dave Hill	67	75	68	210	15,175
Orville Moody	70	74	66	210	15,175
Ken Still	71	67	72	210	15,175
Don Bies	70	71	70	211	11,500
Homero Blancas	69	70	72	211	11,500
Chi Chi Rodriguez	70	73	69	212	10,000
Mike Hill	67	76	70	213	9,500
Rocky Thompson	70	73	71	214	9,000
Don Massengale	72	71	72	215	8,500
Dick Hendrickson	70	73	73	216	7,200
Rives McBee	73	77	66	216	7,200
Richard Rhyan	72	75	69	216	7,200
Tom Shaw	69	71	76	216	7,200
Walter Zembriski	71	76	69	216	7,200
John Paul Cain	74	75	68	217	5,800
Larry Laoretti	72	76	69	217	5,800
Chuck Workman	70	75	72	217	5,800
Frank Beard	75	72	71	218	5,175
Terry Dill	68	75	75	218	5,175

	SCORES			TOTAL	MONEY
Joe Jimenez	72	73	74	219	4,600
Arnold Palmer	75	73	71	219	4,600
Jimmy Powell	73	75	71	219	4,600
Butch Baird	72	73	75	220	3,900
Bob Erickson	73	74	73	220	3,900
Babe Hiskey	75	73	72	220	3,900
Bobby Nichols	73	71	76	220	3,900
Tommy Aaron	75	72	74	221	3,125
Jim Ferree	74	75	72	221	3,125
Larry Mancour	71	78	72	221	3,125
Ben Smith	74	75	72	221	3,125
Lee Elder	73	78	71	222	2,700
Al Geiberger	81	70	71	222	2,700
Billy Maxwell	72	77	73	222	2,700

NYNEX Commemorative

Sleepy Hollow Country Club, Scarborough, New York June 1-3
Par 35-35—70; 6,545 yards purse, $350,000

	SCORES			TOTAL	MONEY
Lee Trevino	66	66	67	199	$52,500
Mike Fetchick	67	68	64	199	23,666.67
Jimmy Powell	64	69	66	199	23,666.67
Chi Chi Rodriguez	69	64	66	199	23,666.66

(Trevino defeated Fetchick on fifth extra hole. Powell and Rodriguez were eliminated on first extra hole.)

Gary Player	65	69	66	200	17,000
George Archer	70	65	66	201	13,000
Bob Charles	67	64	70	201	13,000
Richard Rhyan	63	71	69	203	10,500
Walter Zembriski	67	66	70	203	10,500
Gay Brewer	68	67	69	204	8,100
Al Kelley	68	70	66	204	8,100
Doug Sanders	71	65	68	204	8,100
Ken Still	72	67	65	204	8,100
Don Bies	70	67	69	206	6,550
Rocky Thompson	68	68	70	206	6,550
Bob Betley	67	69	71	207	5,300
Jim O'Hern	69	68	70	207	5,300
Ben Smith	69	66	72	207	5,300
Agim Bardha	70	70	68	208	4,116.67
Gene Borek	70	70	68	208	4,116.67
Al Geiberger	71	68	69	208	4,116.67
Dick Hendrickson	72	67	69	208	4,116.67
George Lanning	70	68	70	208	4,116.66
Larry Laoretti	71	67	70	208	4,116.66
Frank Beard	71	72	66	209	3,350
Lou Graham	68	69	72	209	3,350
Harold Henning	72	71	66	209	3,350
Mike Joyce	73	68	68	209	3,350
Larry Mancour	70	72	67	209	3,350
Robert Rawlins	73	68	68	209	3,350
Rafe Botts	71	71	68	210	2,900
John Brodie	71	70	69	210	2,900
Rives McBee	71	69	70	210	2,900
Jack Fleck	72	69	70	211	2,600
Fred Hawkins	72	71	68	211	2,600

	SCORES			TOTAL	MONEY
Joe Jimenez	70	71	70	211	2,600
Al Balding	72	71	69	212	2,250
Bob Brue	74	69	69	212	2,250
Bob Erickson	71	71	70	212	2,250
J.C. Goosie	69	70	73	212	2,250

Mazda Senior TPC Championship

Dearborn Country Club, Dearborn, Michigan
Par 36-36—72; 6,665 yards

June 7-10
purse, $1,000,000

	SCORES				TOTAL	MONEY
Jack Nicklaus	65	68	64	64	261	$150,000
Lee Trevino	66	68	66	67	267	88,000
Charles Coody	68	70	68	66	272	66,000
Jim Dent	71	70	66	65	272	66,000
Dave Hill	70	67	68	68	273	44,000
Chi Chi Rodriguez	70	67	68	68	273	44,000
Frank Beard	67	70	67	71	275	36,000
Orville Moody	70	69	68	69	276	28,466.67
Larry Mowry	69	67	71	69	276	28,466.67
Harold Henning	69	70	67	70	276	28,466.66
Dale Douglass	73	69	67	69	278	22,000
Mike Hill	68	72	67	71	278	22,000
Rocky Thompson	68	72	67	71	278	22,000
George Archer	71	71	65	72	279	17,500
Al Geiberger	68	68	72	71	279	17,500
Jimmy Powell	71	67	69	72	279	17,500
Larry Ziegler	68	72	64	75	279	17,500
Bob Charles	68	69	72	71	280	13,620
Rives McBee	67	72	71	70	280	13,620
Dan Morgan	69	71	70	70	280	13,620
Gary Player	67	68	76	69	280	13,620
Ben Smith	65	70	74	71	280	13,620
Terry Dill	67	67	71	76	281	11,350
Paul Moran	71	69	68	73	281	11,350
Walter Zembriski	70	72	70	70	282	10,600
Don Bies	71	70	72	70	283	9,016.67
Homero Blancas	71	68	75	69	283	9,016.67
John Paul Cain	69	68	74	72	283	9,016.67
Don Massengale	67	72	74	70	283	9,016.67
Miller Barber	69	67	71	76	283	9,016.66
Al Kelley	69	72	68	74	283	9,016.66
Ralph Terry	66	74	68	76	284	7,600
Tommy Aaron	73	71	69	72	285	7,000
Butch Baird	72	73	71	69	285	7,000
Bob Brue	71	73	70	72	286	5,525
Bill Collins	76	68	72	70	286	5,525
Chick Evans	70	70	71	75	286	5,525
Jim Ferree	67	73	75	71	286	5,525
Lou Graham	70	69	69	78	286	5,525
Dick Hendrickson	71	72	72	71	286	5,525
Bobby Nichols	71	73	72	70	286	5,525
Robert Rawlins	69	69	81	67	286	5,525

MONY Syracuse Classic

Lafayette Country Club, Jamesville, New York
Par 36-36—72; 6,540 yards

June 15-17
purse, $300,000

	SCORES			TOTAL	MONEY
Jim Dent	66	67	66	199	$60,000
George Archer	70	65	65	200	35,000
Mike Hill	66	67	69	202	26,000
Larry Mowry	66	68	68	202	26,000
Jack Kiefer	68	71	64	203	16,150
Robert Rawlins	70	68	65	203	16,150
John Paul Cain	70	68	66	204	13,050
Chi Chi Rodriguez	68	69	67	204	13,050
Harold Henning	71	66	68	205	11,500
Dick Hendrickson	65	71	70	206	8,716.67
George Lanning	70	68	68	206	8,716.67
Dan Morgan	68	68	70	206	8,716.67
Walter Zembriski	66	72	68	206	8,716.67
Charles Sifford	69	66	71	206	8,716.66
Art Wall	69	67	70	206	8,716.66
Don Massengale	69	68	70	207	7,000
J.C. Goosie	72	69	67	208	6,000
Lou Graham	68	69	71	208	6,000
Joe Jimenez	69	69	70	208	6,000
Phil Rodgers	70	69	69	208	6,000
Miller Barber	70	70	69	209	5,000
Richard Rhyan	69	73	67	209	5,000
Deray Simon	74	68	68	210	4,600
Dewitt Weaver	69	71	70	210	4,600
Al Kelley	74	68	69	211	3,900
Bobby Nichols	67	74	70	211	3,900
Jim O'Hern	70	72	69	211	3,900
Bob Rose	74	68	69	211	3,900
Ben Smith	75	67	69	211	3,900
Rives McBee	71	69	72	212	3,300
Bob Betley	72	71	70	213	2,983.34
Roland Stafford	71	73	69	213	2,983.33
Jimmy Wright	72	73	68	213	2,983.33
Agim Bardha	69	70	75	214	2,625
Bob Brue	73	71	70	214	2,625
Ken Still	71	69	74	214	2,625
Alexander Sutton	73	71	70	214	2,625
Terry Dill	74	68	73	215	2,125
Quinton Gray	73	73	69	215	2,125
Mike Kelly	74	73	68	215	2,125
Billy Maxwell	72	74	69	215	2,125
Paul Moran	74	70	71	215	2,125
Jimmy Powell	71	70	74	215	2,125

Digital Classic

Nashawtuc Country Club, Concord, Massachusetts
Par 36-36—72; 6,453 yards

June 22-24
purse, $350,000

	SCORES			TOTAL	MONEY
Bob Charles	69	67	67	203	$52,500
Lee Trevino	67	72	66	205	28,000

	SCORES	TOTAL	MONEY
Chi Chi Rodriguez	64 71 71	206	23,000
George Archer	67 70 70	207	18,500
Harold Henning	66 70 71	207	18,500
Tom Shaw	71 72 66	209	12,333.34
Frank Beard	69 69 71	209	12,333.33
Homero Blancas	70 70 69	209	12,333.33
Don Bies	70 68 72	210	8,775
Dick Hendrickson	67 71 72	210	8,775
Mike Hill	67 68 75	210	8,775
Orville Moody	70 73 67	210	8,775
Charles Coody	71 69 71	211	6,050
Robert Gaona	70 69 72	211	6,050
Larry Mancour	69 72 70	211	6,050
Rives McBee	75 69 67	211	6,050
Gary Player	73 72 66	211	6,050
Phil Rodgers	69 70 72	211	6,050
Jim Dent	70 70 72	212	4,400
Larry Laoretti	71 72 69	212	4,400
Don Massengale	70 71 71	212	4,400
Charles Sifford	71 72 70	213	3,900
Dewitt Weaver	70 73 70	213	3,900
Tommy Aaron	70 73 71	214	3,350
Robert Boldt	71 71 72	214	3,350
Roger Ginsberg	68 69 77	214	3,350
Lou Graham	72 71 71	214	3,350
Al Kelley	69 72 73	214	3,350
Jim O'Hern	75 72 67	214	3,350
Jimmy Powell	72 72 70	214	3,350
Deray Simon	70 72 72	214	3,350
Terry Dill	67 70 78	215	2,750
Joe Jimenez	69 74 72	215	2,750
Jim King	76 70 69	215	2,750
Larry Mowry	70 72 73	215	2,750
Gay Brewer	70 75 71	216	2,350
Doug Dalziel	71 72 73	216	2,350
Babe Hiskey	72 68 76	216	2,350
Robert Rawlins	71 69 76	216	2,350

U.S. Senior Open

Ridgewood Country Club, Paramus, New Jersey
Par 36-36—72; 6,697 yards

June 28-July 1
purse, $500,000

	SCORES	TOTAL	MONEY
Lee Trevino	67 68 73 67	275	$90,000
Jack Nicklaus	71 69 67 70	277	45,000
Chi Chi Rodriguez	73 74 68 66	281	20,881.34
Mike Hill	72 67 73 69	281	20,881.33
Gary Player	75 65 68 73	281	20,881.33
Charles Coody	68 73 72 69	282	12,828
Harold Henning	71 67 75 69	282	12,828
Miller Barber	75 68 67 73	283	10,550
Don Bies	75 69 67 72	283	10,550
Jim Dent	68 68 72 76	284	9,292
Terry Dill	71 73 73 68	285	8,480.50
Orville Moody	75 69 69 72	285	8,480.50
George Archer	70 72 72 72	286	7,623
Walter Zembriski	68 73 73 72	286	7,623

	SCORES				TOTAL	MONEY
John Paul Cain	68	71	76	72	287	6,614
Bob Charles	73	71	69	74	287	6,614
Dave Hill	73	69	73	72	287	6,614
Rocky Thompson	72	73	74	68	287	6,614
Jack Rule	74	71	69	74	288	5,899
Jim Ferree	74	70	74	71	289	5,492
Lou Graham	70	73	72	74	289	5,492
Joe Jimenez	74	74	69	72	289	5,492
Ken Still	68	75	75	72	290	4,964.34
Dick Hendrickson	73	71	74	72	290	4,964.33
Al Kelley	73	73	71	73	290	4,964.33
Larry Mowry	72	74	71	74	291	4,674
Jim Albus	70	72	76	75	293	4,333.25
John Brodie	73	73	74	73	293	4,333.25
Doug Sanders	74	74	77	68	293	4,333.25
Dewitt Weaver	72	75	74	72	293	4,333.25
Bob Betley	75	72	74	73	294	3,945
Rives McBee	73	74	74	73	294	3,945
Lynn Rosely	73	75	77	69	294	3,945
*Gary Cowan	73	71	74	76	294	
Frank Beard	77	70	74	74	295	3,716.50
Don Massengale	74	72	76	73	295	3,716.50
Al Geiberger	77	68	75	76	296	3,443.50
Babe Hiskey	69	75	73	79	296	3,443.50
Paul Moran	74	73	74	75	296	3,443.50
Art Wall	73	72	77	74	296	3,443.50

Northville Long Island Classic

Meadow Brook Club, Jericho, New York
Par 36-36—72; 6,595 yards

July 6-8
purse, $450,000

	SCORES			TOTAL	MONEY
George Archer	69	67	72	208	$67,500
Frank Beard	69	69	71	209	36,000
Charles Coody	68	70	71	209	36,000
Dave Hill	71	71	68	210	20,333.34
Homero Blancas	69	69	72	210	20,333.33
Jim Dent	68	71	71	210	20,333.33
Miller Barber	73	70	69	212	15,000
Joe Jimenez	68	71	73	212	15,000
Gary Player	67	74	71	212	15,000
Gay Brewer	74	71	68	213	13,000
Jim Albus	73	72	70	215	10,100
John Brodie	71	73	71	215	10,100
Mike Joyce	71	71	73	215	10,100
Chi Chi Rodriguez	72	73	70	215	10,100
Tom Shaw	73	70	72	215	10,100
Butch Baird	71	72	73	216	7,500
Don Bies	71	72	73	216	7,500
Don Massengale	69	73	74	216	7,500
Lee Trevino	72	70	74	216	7,500
Bob Charles	73	74	70	217	5,483.34
Richard Rhyan	72	74	71	217	5,483.34
Bob Brue	72	74	71	217	5,483.33
Al Kelley	73	74	70	217	5,483.33
Dan Morgan	71	73	73	217	5,483.33
Charles Sifford	73	71	73	217	5,483.33

	SCORES	TOTAL	MONEY
Dale Douglass	75 70 73	218	3,900
Jim O'Hern	70 76 72	218	3,900
Jimmy Powell	73 71 74	218	3,900
Dewitt Weaver	72 74 72	218	3,900
Billy Casper	74 75 70	219	2,942.86
Mike Hill	75 74 70	219	2,942.86
George Lanning	74 73 72	219	2,942.86
Rives McBee	71 75 73	219	2,942.86
Phil Rodgers	76 69 74	219	2,942.86
J.C. Goosie	71 70 78	219	2,942.85
Ken Still	70 74 75	219	2,942.85
Walter Zembriski	75 74 71	220	2,500
Robert Boldt	72 77 72	221	2,150
Chick Evans	76 73 72	221	2,150
Mike Fetchick	74 73 74	221	2,150
Jack Fleck	73 76 72	221	2,150
Harold Henning	72 77 72	221	2,150
Ben Smith	75 73 73	221	2,150

Kroger Classic

Jack Nicklaus Sports Center, Grizzly Course, Kings Island, Ohio
Par 36-35—71; 6,628 yards
(Second round cancelled - rain, unplayable course.)

July 13-15
purse, $600,000

	SCORES	TOTAL	MONEY
Jim Dent	67 66	133	$90,000
Harold Henning	70 64	134	53,500
Charles Coody	67 68	135	42,500
George Archer	67 69	136	24,600
Homero Blancas	67 69	136	24,600
Dave Hill	65 71	136	24,600
Lee Trevino	65 71	136	24,600
Walter Zembriski	66 70	136	24,600
Chi Chi Rodriguez	69 68	137	14,000
Miller Barber	70 68	138	10,342.86
Bob Charles	69 69	138	10,342.86
Orville Moody	68 70	138	10,342.86
Jimmy Powell	68 70	138	10,342.86
Ken Still	69 69	138	10,342.86
John Paul Cain	66 72	138	10,342.85
Rives McBee	67 71	138	10,342.85
Mike Hill	68 71	139	8,000
Joe Jimenez	66 73	139	8,000
Larry Mowry	68 71	139	8,000
Tom Shaw	69 70	139	8,000
Rocky Thompson	70 69	139	8,000
Frank Beard	71 69	140	6,900
Don Bies	68 72	140	6,900
Dale Douglass	70 70	140	6,900
Quinton Gray	70 70	140	6,900
Don January	69 71	140	6,900
Bobby Nichols	70 70	140	6,900
John Brodie	71 70	141	5,900
Bruce Devlin	71 70	141	5,900
Terry Dill	71 70	141	5,900
Jim Ferree	73 68	141	5,900
Jack Fleck	71 71	142	5,200

	SCORES		TOTAL	MONEY
Al Geiberger	73	69	142	5,200
Richard Rhyan	69	73	142	5,200
Butch Baird	71	72	143	4,100
Bob Brue	71	72	143	4,100
Mike Fetchick	71	72	143	4,100
Lou Graham	73	70	143	4,100
George Johnson	73	70	143	4,100
Robert Rawlins	70	73	143	4,100
Charles Sifford	72	71	143	4,100
Bob Wynn	70	73	143	4,100

Ameritech Open

Grand Traverse Resort, Bear Course, Grand Traverse Village, Michigan — July 20-22
Par 36-36—72; 6,754 yards — purse, $500,000

	SCORES			TOTAL	MONEY
Chi Chi Rodriguez	67	70	66	203	$75,000
George Archer	69	70	71	210	40,000
Al Kelley	69	71	70	210	40,000
Dave Hill	68	71	72	211	23,000
Mike Hill	70	71	70	211	23,000
Gordon Jones	68	71	72	211	23,000
Phil Rodgers	70	74	67	211	23,000
Don January	67	69	76	212	14,850
Don Massengale	74	68	70	212	14,850
Paul Moran	71	70	72	213	12,500
Walter Zembriski	71	73	69	213	12,500
Quinton Gray	73	75	67	215	10,166.67
Bob Rose	73	74	68	215	10,166.67
Lou Graham	74	71	70	215	10,166.66
Don Bies	72	76	68	216	8,060
Jim Ferree	72	74	70	216	8,060
Al Geiberger	70	71	75	216	8,060
Harold Henning	69	71	76	216	8,060
Rives McBee	74	69	73	216	8,060
Charles Coody	69	75	73	217	6,600
Joe Jimenez	72	77	68	217	6,600
Bruce Devlin	75	74	69	218	5,307.15
Charles Mehok	75	75	68	218	5,307.15
Tommy Aaron	68	74	76	218	5,307.14
Gay Brewer	76	70	72	218	5,307.14
Billy Casper	75	74	69	218	5,307.14
Jim Dent	68	77	73	218	5,307.14
Jimmy Powell	72	74	72	218	5,307.14
John Paul Cain	76	73	70	219	4,100
Dick Hendrickson	68	75	76	219	4,100
Tom Shaw	76	70	73	219	4,100
Ken Still	73	73	73	219	4,100
Bob Brue	75	74	71	220	3,300
Terry Dill	72	72	76	220	3,300
Mike Fetchick	74	79	67	220	3,300
Richard Rhyan	73	73	74	220	3,300
Doug Dalziel	70	79	72	221	2,750
Chick Evans	74	73	74	221	2,750
J.C. Goosie	73	70	78	221	2,750
Alexander Sutton	76	73	72	221	2,750

Newport Cup

Newport Country Club, Newport, Rhode Island
Par 36-36—72; 6,566 yards
(Friday round cancelled - rain.)

July 27-29
purse, $300,000

	SCORES		TOTAL	MONEY
Al Kelley	66	68	134	$45,000
John Paul Cain	71	65	136	24,750
Jim Dent	69	67	136	24,750
Joe Jimenez	68	69	137	15,000
Rives McBee	70	67	137	15,000
Lee Trevino	65	72	137	15,000
Ben Smith	71	67	138	10,500
George Lanning	69	70	139	9,750
Dale Douglass	69	71	140	7,665
Lee Elder	69	71	140	7,665
Lou Graham	71	69	140	7,665
Quinton Gray	68	72	140	7,665
Jim O'Hern	70	70	140	7,665
Richard Rhyan	70	71	141	5,887.50
Bert Yancey	72	69	141	5,887.50
Chick Evans	71	71	142	4,950
Babe Hiskey	72	70	142	4,950
Robert Rawlins	72	70	142	4,950
Rocky Thompson	70	72	142	4,950
Dick Hendrickson	70	74	144	3,950
Paul Moran	72	72	144	3,950
Walter Zembriski	70	74	144	3,950
Gay Brewer	73	72	145	3,375
Doug Dalziel	72	73	145	3,375
Doug Sanders	71	74	145	3,375
Charles Sifford	70	75	145	3,375
Robert Boldt	75	71	146	2,775
Bruce Crampton	74	72	146	2,775
Mike Fetchick	77	69	146	2,775
Dewitt Weaver	71	75	146	2,775
Paul Barkhouse	71	76	147	2,150
Terry Dill	66	81	147	2,150
J.C. Goosie	75	72	147	2,150
Larry Laoretti	74	73	147	2,150
Dan Morgan	73	74	147	2,150
Tom Shaw	73	74	147	2,150
Miller Barber	69	79	148	1,800
Bob Erickson	75	73	148	1,800
Ralph Terry	73	75	148	1,800
John Brodie	76	73	149	1,612.50
Fred Hawkins	75	74	149	1,612.50

Volvo Seniors British Open

Turnberry Hotel, Ailsa Course, Ayrshire, Scotland
Par 35-35—70; 6,486 yards

July 26-29
purse, £150,000

	SCORES				TOTAL	MONEY
Gary Player	69	65	71	75	280	£25,000
Deane Beman	67	66	67	81	281	12,775
Brian Waites	66	70	69	76	281	12,775

	SCORES				TOTAL	MONEY
Arnold Palmer	66	68	69	79	282	7,350
Simon Hobday	67	70	67	79	283	6,150
Billy Casper	70	70	70	74	284	4,720
Bob Charles	68	67	73	76	284	4,720
Deray Simon	71	68	66	80	285	3,422.50
Harold Henning	72	75	62	76	285	3,422.50
Larry Mowry	70	66	71	79	286	2,795
John Fourie	68	72	69	77	286	2,795
Neil Coles	69	71	67	80	287	2,560
Charles Mehok	70	68	72	80	290	2,430
David Butler	70	77	68	76	291	2,310
Austin Skerritt	71	71	70	80	292	2,200
Anthony Grubb	76	74	67	76	293	2,040
Christy O'Connor	72	71	74	76	293	2,040
Bernard Hunt	73	69	73	79	294	1,870
Peter Butler	73	72	73	76	294	1,870
*Charles Green	71	69	72	83	295	
Hugh Boyle	71	71	70	84	296	1,682.50
Arthur Proctor	74	70	71	81	296	1,682.50
David Snell	71	75	70	80	296	1,682.50
Jack O'Keefe	71	70	71	84	296	1,682.50
*Gordon Murray	72	69	76	79	296	
Roger Fidler	71	72	74	80	297	1,520
Allen Balding	69	73	71	84	297	1,520
David Jimenez	73	70	71	83	297	1,520
Jimmy Kinsella	74	73	71	79	297	1,520
Norman Drew	78	71	69	80	298	1,420
Frank Rennie	77	71	73	78	299	1,340
Ramon Sota	75	71	72	81	299	1,340
Alec Bickerdike	72	69	74	84	299	1,340
Roland C. Stafford	73	74	73	80	300	1,200
Hugh Jackson	70	74	73	83	300	1,200
Joe Carr	69	80	75	76	300	1,200
Jack Wilkshire	70	75	73	82	300	1,200
Stan Dudas	74	76	74	77	301	1,060
Ron Nicol	70	74	72	85	301	1,060
William Hector	70	77	76	78	301	1,060
Peter Gill	75	76	72	79	302	980
Craig Shankland	74	72	71	86	303	905
David Talbot	72	74	74	83	303	905
Ross Whitehead	73	77	75	78	303	905

PaineWebber Invitational

TPC at Piper Glen, Charlotte, North Carolina
Par 36-36—72; 6,774 yards

August 3-5
purse, $450,000

	SCORES			TOTAL	MONEY
Bruce Crampton	68	69	68	205	$67,500
Tom Shaw	72	65	69	206	40,000
Bob Charles	66	70	71	207	28,300
Larry Mowry	71	71	65	207	28,300
Rives McBee	69	71	68	208	18,300
Richard Rhyan	71	69	68	208	18,300
Don Bies	70	69	70	209	15,500
Joe Jimenez	68	69	72	209	15,500
Chi Chi Rodriguez	71	69	70	210	13,500
Lee Trevino	70	69	71	210	13,500

	SCORES			TOTAL	MONEY
Dave Hill	70	68	73	211	11,500
Orville Moody	71	68	72	211	11,500
Harold Henning	67	72	73	212	9,500
Mike Joyce	70	74	68	212	9,500
Bobby Nichols	75	71	67	213	8,500
Jim Dent	69	72	73	214	7,300
Jim Ferree	75	70	69	214	7,300
Robert Gaona	71	71	72	214	7,300
Mike Hill	68	72	74	214	7,300
Charles Owens	73	70	71	214	7,300
Miller Barber	73	72	70	215	5,700
Gay Brewer	70	74	71	215	5,700
Dan Morgan	74	72	69	215	5,700
John Paul Cain	69	71	76	216	4,566.67
Charles Coody	75	69	72	216	4,566.67
Bob Erickson	72	68	76	216	4,566.66
Doug Dalziel	75	72	70	217	4,100
Robert Boldt	73	72	73	218	3,600
Chick Evans	73	70	75	218	3,600
Paul Moran	74	72	72	218	3,600
Rocky Thompson	71	70	77	218	3,600
Jack Fleck	73	70	76	219	2,950
Al Kelley	71	72	76	219	2,950
Larry Laoretti	73	72	74	219	2,950
Larry Mancour	76	71	72	219	2,950
Lee Elder	74	73	73	220	2,400
J.C. Goosie	70	75	75	220	2,400
Lou Graham	73	73	74	220	2,400
Quinton Gray	72	73	75	220	2,400
Arnold Palmer	70	79	71	220	2,400
Alexander Sutton	76	70	74	220	2,400
Bob Wynn	74	70	76	220	2,400

Sunwest Bank/Charley Pride Classic

Four Hills Country Club, Albuquerque, New Mexico
Par 36-36—72; 6,722 yards

August 10-12
purse, $350,000

	SCORES			TOTAL	MONEY
Chi Chi Rodriguez	66	71	68	205	$52,500
Jim Dent	67	72	68	207	23,666.67
Jim Ferree	73	66	68	207	23,666.67
Charles Coody	70	66	71	207	23,666.66
George Archer	74	67	68	209	14,333.34
Bob Betley	72	68	69	209	14,333.33
Larry Mowry	71	68	70	209	14,333.33
Mike Hill	71	73	66	210	10,000
Don January	72	72	66	210	10,000
Tom Shaw	71	68	71	210	10,000
Billy Casper	69	71	71	211	8,050
Joe Jimenez	69	67	75	211	8,050
Dale Douglass	73	69	70	212	6,300
Babe Hiskey	70	71	71	212	6,300
Bobby Nichols	72	68	72	212	6,300
Richard Rhyan	73	70	69	212	6,300
Ben Smith	71	68	73	212	6,300
Don Bies	72	70	71	213	4,700

	SCORES			TOTAL	MONEY
Terry Dill	77	68	68	213	4,700
Bob Charles	72	73	69	214	3,950
Doug Dalziel	74	71	69	214	3,950
Dick Hendrickson	72	70	72	214	3,950
Don Massengale	70	68	76	214	3,950
Jim O'Hern	71	73	70	214	3,950
Robert Rawlins	76	69	69	214	3,950
Gay Brewer	69	74	72	215	3,150
John Paul Cain	73	72	70	215	3,150
Bruce Devlin	71	71	73	215	3,150
Bob Erickson	75	71	69	215	3,150
J.C. Goosie	73	71	71	215	3,150
George Lanning	71	72	72	215	3,150
Rives McBee	70	70	75	215	3,150
Dan Morgan	76	70	69	215	3,150
Al Geiberger	77	69	70	216	2,650
Larry Mancour	72	70	74	216	2,650
Butch Baird	71	72	74	217	2,300
Agim Bardha	72	73	72	217	2,300
Homero Blancas	72	70	75	217	2,300
Chick Evans	70	74	73	217	2,300
Phil Rodgers	74	77	66	217	2,300

Showdown Classic

Jeremy Ranch Golf Club, Park City, Utah
Par 36-36—72; 7,103 yards

August 17-19
purse, $350,000

	SCORES			TOTAL	MONEY
Rives McBee	64	70	68	202	$52,500
Don Bies	66	66	71	203	25,500
Lee Trevino	67	68	68	203	25,500
George Archer	67	68	71	206	17,000
Dale Douglass	70	69	67	206	17,000
Mike Hill	66	68	72	206	17,000
Richard Rhyan	69	68	70	207	11,500
Rocky Thompson	70	69	68	207	11,500
Chi Chi Rodriguez	73	67	69	209	10,000
Bob Betley	68	72	70	210	9,000
John Paul Cain	68	71	72	211	8,300
Charles Coody	72	69	71	212	7,550
Tom Shaw	73	69	70	212	7,550
Bruce Crampton	74	72	67	213	6,300
Orville Moody	69	72	72	213	6,300
Phil Rodgers	67	75	71	213	6,300
Butch Baird	74	71	69	214	4,660
Bob Brue	73	75	66	214	4,660
Al Geiberger	71	74	69	214	4,660
Babe Hiskey	74	70	70	214	4,660
Don January	73	72	69	214	4,660
Charles Owens	75	70	70	215	3,900
Ken Still	73	73	69	215	3,900
Robert Gaona	74	70	72	216	3,600
Dick Hendrickson	74	72	70	216	3,600
Al Kelley	70	75	71	216	3,600
Frank Beard	75	74	68	217	3,300
Bob Charles	74	73	70	217	3,300
Walter Zembriski	70	69	78	217	3,300

	SCORES			TOTAL	MONEY
Tommy Aaron	71	72	75	218	2,750
Homero Blancas	74	75	69	218	2,750
Billy Casper	69	72	77	218	2,750
Terry Dill	73	71	74	218	2,750
Quinton Gray	74	74	70	218	2,750
Fred Hawkins	76	73	69	218	2,750
Bobby Nichols	70	74	74	218	2,750
Alexander Sutton	70	73	75	218	2,750
Robert Boldt	73	73	73	219	2,100
Roberto De Vicenzo	73	76	70	219	2,100
Lou Graham	69	73	77	219	2,100
Larry Mancour	71	74	74	219	2,100
Charles Mehok	76	75	68	219	2,100

GTE Northwest Classic

Inglewood Country Club, Wenmore, Washington
Par 37-35—72; 6,501 yards

August 24-26
purse, $350,000

	SCORES			TOTAL	MONEY
George Archer	69	66	70	205	$52,500
Bruce Crampton	70	70	67	207	28,000
Don Bies	67	67	74	208	23,000
Al Geiberger	71	69	69	209	18,500
Don January	71	68	70	209	18,500
Chi Chi Rodriguez	68	70	72	210	14,000
Tommy Aaron	71	70	70	211	11,500
George Lanning	72	70	69	211	11,500
Frank Beard	73	70	69	212	8,775
Larry Laoretti	71	68	73	212	8,775
Lee Trevino	75	71	66	212	8,775
Walter Zembriski	69	74	69	212	8,775
Charles Coody	71	69	73	213	7,050
Larry Mowry	75	67	71	213	7,050
Terry Dill	72	69	73	214	6,050
Tom Shaw	68	71	75	214	6,050
Gene Littler	71	73	71	215	5,050
Don Massengale	73	70	72	215	5,050
Bob Brue	66	76	74	216	4,500
Rives McBee	72	72	72	216	4,500
Dale Douglass	73	71	73	217	3,860
Harold Henning	68	74	75	217	3,860
Joe Jimenez	71	74	72	217	3,860
Orville Moody	74	71	72	217	3,860
Bob Wynn	77	72	68	217	3,860
Miller Barber	75	71	72	218	3,250
Homero Blancas	72	72	74	218	3,250
Bruce Devlin	73	69	76	218	3,250
Robert Gaona	72	71	75	218	3,250
Jim O'Hern	72	72	74	218	3,250
Rocky Thompson	73	71	74	218	3,250
Doug Dalziel	74	73	72	219	2,700
Charles Mehok	73	73	73	219	2,700
Richard Rhyan	73	73	73	219	2,700
Ben Smith	76	71	72	219	2,700
Ken Still	72	76	71	219	2,700
J.C. Goosie	73	77	70	220	2,400
Butch Baird	75	73	73	221	1,900

	SCORES	TOTAL	MONEY
Agim Bardha	73 75 73	221	1,900
John Paul Cain	71 78 72	221	1,900
Roberto De Vicenzo	75 75 71	221	1,900
Bob Erickson	76 74 71	221	1,900
Larry Mancour	73 73 75	221	1,900
Ted Naff	72 69 80	221	1,900
Phil Rodgers	71 75 75	221	1,900
Charles Sifford	73 75 73	221	1,900

GTE North Classic

Broadmoor Country Club, Indianapolis, Indiana
Par 35-37—72; 6,670 yards

August 31-September 2
purse, $450,000

	SCORES	TOTAL	MONEY
Mike Hill	66 67 68	201	$67,500
Bruce Crampton	68 67 66	201	40,000
(Hill defeated Crampton on first extra hole.)			
Dale Douglass	65 67 71	203	32,000
Harold Henning	66 70 69	205	24,500
George Archer	68 71 67	206	18,250
Rocky Thompson	65 74 67	206	18,250
Bobby Nichols	69 68 70	207	16,000
Terry Dill	65 72 71	208	15,000
Don Bies	74 65 70	209	12,500
John Paul Cain	71 66 72	209	12,500
Charles Coody	70 73 66	209	12,500
Dave Hill	69 67 73	209	12,500
Dan Morgan	69 70 71	210	10,000
Gary Player	70 70 71	211	8,533.34
Homero Blancas	67 71 73	211	8,533.33
George Lanning	72 68 71	211	8,533.33
Rives McBee	66 71 75	212	7,500
Ben Smith	72 68 72	212	7,500
Charles Owens	70 67 76	213	6,900
Tommy Aaron	70 73 71	214	5,900
Joe Jimenez	68 70 76	214	5,900
Orville Moody	71 72 71	214	5,900
Walter Zembriski	72 69 73	214	5,900
Gay Brewer	68 75 72	215	4,260
Don January	71 73 71	215	4,260
Arnold Palmer	68 72 75	215	4,260
Phil Rodgers	73 73 69	215	4,260
Ken Still	72 74 69	215	4,260
Miller Barber	72 74 70	216	3,025
Doug Dalziel	71 73 72	216	3,025
Bob Erickson	72 75 69	216	3,025
Dick Hendrickson	72 68 76	216	3,025
Gordon Jones	71 70 75	216	3,025
Gene Littler	72 72 72	216	3,025
Charles Sifford	68 79 69	216	3,025
Deray Simon	70 74 72	216	3,025
Agim Bardha	66 71 80	217	2,450
Babe Hiskey	76 72 69	217	2,450
Mike Fetchick	72 72 74	218	2,150
Al Kelley	75 73 70	218	2,150
Jim O'Hern	71 72 75	218	2,150
Dewitt Weaver	71 72 75	218	2,150

Vantage Bank One Classic

Kearney Hill Links, Lexington, Kentucky
Par 36-36—72; 6,744 yards

September 7-9
purse, $300,000

	SCORES			TOTAL	MONEY
Rives McBee	66	67	68	201	$45,000
Mike Hill	70	71	64	205	25,500
Tommy Aaron	76	65	66	207	17,166.67
George Archer	73	66	68	207	17,166.67
Harold Henning	69	68	70	207	17,166.66
Miller Barber	71	67	71	209	9,335
Jim Dent	73	72	64	209	9,335
Dave Hill	68	73	68	209	9,335
Rocky Thompson	70	68	71	209	9,335
Lee Trevino	71	66	72	209	9,335
Quinton Gray	68	67	75	210	6,425
Larry Laoretti	74	68	68	210	6,425
Orville Moody	68	71	71	210	6,425
Dewitt Weaver	69	69	72	210	6,425
Bruce Crampton	71	70	70	211	5,350
Jim O'Hern	75	67	69	211	5,350
Agim Bardha	69	73	70	212	4,450
Bob Erickson	72	69	71	212	4,450
Ted Naff	71	71	70	212	4,450
Gary Player	74	70	68	212	4,450
John Paul Cain	69	72	72	213	3,350
Terry Dill	68	70	75	213	3,350
Mike Joyce	72	68	73	213	3,350
Larry Mancour	73	68	72	213	3,350
Richard Rhyan	71	69	73	213	3,350
Deray Simon	72	70	71	213	3,350
Ben Smith	72	71	70	213	3,350
Lou Graham	73	69	72	214	2,608.34
Bob Betley	72	68	74	214	2,608.33
Walter Zembriski	69	69	76	214	2,608.33
Bob Brue	73	71	71	215	1,996.88
Robert Gaona	69	73	73	215	1,996.88
Dan Morgan	71	71	73	215	1,996.88
Bobby Nichols	70	74	71	215	1,996.88
Alton Duhon	71	71	73	215	1,996.87
Mike Fetchick	72	70	73	215	1,996.87
George Lanning	71	69	75	215	1,996.87
Phil Rodgers	73	73	69	215	1,996.87
Gay Brewer	75	67	74	216	1,550
George Johnson	74	69	73	216	1,550
Charles Sifford	74	70	72	216	1,550

Greater Grand Rapids Open

The Highlands, Grand Rapids, Michigan
Par 36-35—71; 6,453 yards
(Tournament shortened to 36 holes - rain.)

September 14-16
purse, $300,000

	SCORES		TOTAL	MONEY
Don Massengale	69	65	134	$45,000
Terry Dill	69	66	135	20,833.34
Dave Hill	64	71	135	20,833.33

	SCORES		TOTAL	MONEY
Larry Laoretti	68	67	135	20,833.33
Orville Moody	67	69	136	14,500
Rocky Thompson	69	68	137	11,100
Ken Still	70	68	138	9,258.34
Jack Fleck	65	73	138	9,258.33
Lee Trevino	69	69	138	9,258.33
Jim Dent	73	66	139	6,925
Jim O'Hern	69	70	139	6,925
Charles Owens	70	69	139	6,925
Walter Zembriski	70	69	139	6,925
Lou Graham	67	73	140	5,050
Mike Hill	71	69	140	5,050
Joe Jimenez	71	69	140	5,050
Gary Player	69	71	140	5,050
Phil Rodgers	70	70	140	5,050
Tom Shaw	70	70	140	5,050
Roger Ginsberg	70	71	141	3,816.67
Chi Chi Rodriguez	72	69	141	3,816.67
Agim Bardha	69	72	141	3,816.66
Tommy Aaron	69	73	142	3,050
Butch Baird	71	71	142	3,050
Frank Beard	70	72	142	3,050
Billy Casper	71	71	142	3,050
Al Kelley	69	73	142	3,050
Rives McBee	71	71	142	3,050
Larry Ziegler	71	71	142	3,050
Al Balding	74	69	143	2,350
Deray Simon	72	71	143	2,350
Dewitt Weaver	71	72	143	2,350
Miller Barber	70	74	144	1,745
Homero Blancas	71	73	144	1,745
Bobby Breen	70	74	144	1,745
Al Geiberger	69	75	144	1,745
Harold Henning	70	74	144	1,745
Howie Johnson	71	73	144	1,745
Dan Morgan	73	71	144	1,745
Bobby Nichols	72	72	144	1,745
Jimmy Powell	72	72	144	1,745
Richard Rhyan	72	72	144	1,745

Crestar Classic

Hermitage Country Club, Manakin-Sabot, Virginia
Par 36-36—72; 6,644 yards

September 21-23
purse, $350,000

	SCORES			TOTAL	MONEY
Jim Dent	73	64	65	202	$52,500
Lee Trevino	68	68	67	203	28,000
Gary Player	67	64	73	204	23,000
Larry Laoretti	69	69	68	206	20,000
George Lanning	68	70	69	207	17,000
George Archer	70	69	69	208	12,333.34
Rives McBee	66	67	75	208	12,333.33
Chi Chi Rodriguez	69	67	72	208	12,333.33
Frank Beard	70	67	72	209	9,500
Dale Douglass	68	72	69	209	9,500
Terry Dill	70	67	73	210	8,300
Rocky Thompson	69	70	72	211	7,800

	SCORES	TOTAL	MONEY
Bob Charles	68 72 72	212	6,550
Mike Joyce	69 75 68	212	6,550
Larry Mowry	68 72 72	212	6,550
Dewitt Weaver	70 70 72	212	6,550
Jim Ferree	74 71 68	213	4,900
Dan Morgan	72 72 69	213	4,900
Bobby Nichols	69 68 76	213	4,900
Homero Blancas	71 68 75	214	3,950
J.C. Goosie	69 71 74	214	3,950
George Johnson	74 70 70	214	3,950
Richard Rhyan	72 73 69	214	3,950
Jesus Rodriguez	68 73 73	214	3,950
Bob Wynn	70 70 74	214	3,950
John Paul Cain	71 69 75	215	3,200
Charles Coody	75 71 69	215	3,200
Alton Duhon	73 70 72	215	3,200
Larry Mancour	73 69 73	215	3,200
Ted Naff	69 71 75	215	3,200
David Philo	72 72 71	215	3,200
Ben Smith	73 69 73	215	3,200
John Brodie	72 68 76	216	2,500
Chick Evans	73 71 72	216	2,500
Robert Gaona	69 70 77	216	2,500
Lou Graham	70 73 73	216	2,500
Ted Hayes	74 70 72	216	2,500
Marion Heck	72 73 71	216	2,500
Jack Kiefer	71 72 73	216	2,500
Tommy Aaron	73 68 76	217	1,800
Bruce Devlin	74 71 72	217	1,800
David Jimenez	73 70 74	217	1,800
Gordon Jones	69 74 74	217	1,800
Robert Rawlins	73 73 71	217	1,800
Deray Simon	72 73 72	217	1,800
Walter Zembriski	75 71 71	217	1,800

Fairfield Barnett Space Coast Classic

Suntree Country Club, Melbourne, Florida
Par 36-36—72; 6,590 yards

September 28-30
purse, $300,000

	SCORES	TOTAL	MONEY
Mike Hill	66 70 64	200	$45,000
Dale Douglass	66 67 67	200	25,500
(Hill defeated Douglass on first extra hole.)			
Bob Charles	65 66 70	201	20,000
Gary Player	68 69 66	203	17,000
Dave Hill	69 68 67	204	12,800
Robert Rawlins	66 71 67	204	12,800
Bruce Crampton	69 70 66	205	9,625
Chi Chi Rodriguez	68 71 66	205	9,625
Harold Henning	69 68 69	206	8,525
Homero Blancas	68 67 72	207	7,450
Jack Fleck	70 68 69	207	7,450
Miller Barber	71 68 69	208	6,200
Al Geiberger	70 71 67	208	6,200
Larry Laoretti	72 67 69	208	6,200
Jim Dent	72 71 66	209	4,900
Bruce Devlin	72 69 68	209	4,900

	SCORES			TOTAL	MONEY
Joe Jimenez	71	69	69	209	4,900
Phil Rodgers	69	69	71	209	4,900
Bob Wynn	76	66	67	209	4,900
Bob Betley	73	70	67	210	3,583.34
Charles Coody	70	73	67	210	3,583.34
Larry Mowry	71	68	71	210	3,583.33
Bob Rose	71	69	70	210	3,583.33
Ken Still	72	67	71	210	3,583.33
Larry Ziegler	71	70	69	210	3,583.33
Agim Bardha	70	73	68	211	2,559.38
Babe Hiskey	70	72	69	211	2,559.38
Gordon Jones	74	69	68	211	2,559.38
Tom Shaw	70	72	69	211	2,559.38
Mike Fetchick	71	71	69	211	2,559.37
Charles Owens	72	72	67	211	2,559.37
Jimmy Powell	74	68	69	211	2,559.37
Walter Zembriski	72	70	69	211	2,559.37
Don January	71	71	70	212	1,933.34
Bobby Nichols	70	71	71	212	1,933.33
Deray Simon	68	69	75	212	1,933.33
Don Bies	75	70	68	213	1,625
Dick Hendrickson	73	71	69	213	1,625
George Lanning	74	68	71	213	1,625
Rives McBee	72	70	71	213	1,625
Jim O'Hern	71	71	71	213	1,625

Vantage Championship

Tanglewood Park, Clemmons, North Carolina
Par 36-36—72; 6,680 yards

October 5-7
purse, $1,500,000

	SCORES			TOTAL	MONEY
Charles Coody	67	65	70	202	$202,500
Bob Charles	72	69	64	205	126,000
Al Geiberger	69	64	72	205	126,000
Larry Mowry	68	70	68	206	81,750
Lee Trevino	68	68	70	206	81,750
Rives McBee	66	73	68	207	56,666.67
Chi Chi Rodriguez	71	68	68	207	56,666.67
Gary Player	70	69	68	207	56,666.66
Dale Douglass	68	69	71	208	45,000
Bruce Crampton	71	67	71	209	32,500
Dick Hendrickson	70	71	68	209	32,500
Al Kelley	67	72	70	209	32,500
Dewitt Weaver	71	69	69	209	32,500
Rocky Thompson	69	71	70	210	20,000
Chick Evans	70	74	67	211	18,250
Harold Henning	74	68	69	211	18,250
Mike Hill	74	67	71	212	15,750
Don January	70	71	71	212	15,750
Larry Laoretti	69	73	70	212	15,750
Bob Betley	73	69	71	213	11,850
Don Bies	73	70	70	213	11,850
John Brodie	72	70	71	213	11,850
Jim Dent	72	69	72	213	11,850
Joe Jimenez	71	71	71	213	11,850
Frank Beard	71	72	71	214	9,750
George Archer	72	75	68	215	9,350

	SCORES			TOTAL	MONEY
Dave Hill	72	68	75	215	9,350
Dan Morgan	73	73	69	215	9,350
Butch Baird	71	73	72	216	8,350
Doug Dalziel	72	72	72	216	8,350
Roberto De Vicenzo	74	72	70	216	8,350
Terry Dill	76	67	73	216	8,350
Bobby Nichols	73	71	72	216	8,350
Jimmy Powell	70	75	71	216	8,350
Larry Ziegler	69	70	77	216	8,350
Jim O'Hern	69	75	73	217	7,350
Ben Smith	75	75	67	217	7,350
Ken Still	73	72	72	217	7,350
Tommy Aaron	76	72	70	218	6,350
Mike Fetchick	69	74	75	218	6,350
J.C. Goosie	75	72	71	218	6,350
Mike Joyce	74	71	73	218	6,350
Paul Moran	73	72	73	218	6,350
Arnold Palmer	71	77	70	218	6,350
Robert Rawlins	74	72	72	218	6,350

Gatlin Brothers Southwest Classic

Fairway Oaks Country Club, Abilene, Texas
Par 36-36—72; 6,843 yards

October 12-14
purse, $300,000

	SCORES			TOTAL	MONEY
Bruce Crampton	67	68	69	204	$45,000
Lee Trevino	71	70	67	208	25,500
Terry Dill	68	72	70	210	18,500
Chi Chi Rodriguez	70	72	68	210	18,500
Richard Rhyan	71	74	66	211	11,866.67
Rocky Thompson	71	70	70	211	11,866.67
Robert Gaona	67	71	73	211	11,866.66
Don January	69	70	73	212	9,250
John Paul Cain	69	71	73	213	8,162.50
Rives McBee	69	73	71	213	8,162.50
Miller Barber	71	74	69	214	6,633.34
George Archer	71	72	71	214	6,633.33
J.C. Goosie	68	72	74	214	6,633.33
Quinton Gray	73	71	71	215	5,200
Joe Jimenez	71	72	72	215	5,200
Jim O'Hern	74	71	70	215	5,200
Ben Smith	69	70	76	215	5,200
Bob Wynn	70	69	76	215	5,200
Charles Coody	70	75	71	216	3,937.50
Chick Evans	73	71	72	216	3,937.50
Don Massengale	72	74	70	216	3,937.50
Orville Moody	71	78	67	216	3,937.50
Al Balding	78	71	68	217	3,275
Bob Betley	67	72	78	217	3,275
Doug Dalziel	70	71	76	217	3,275
Larry Laoretti	72	71	74	217	3,275
Butch Baird	73	73	72	218	2,615
Al Kelley	68	74	76	218	2,615
Robert Rawlins	73	74	71	218	2,615
Deray Simon	70	72	76	218	2,615
Dewitt Weaver	71	75	72	218	2,615
Agim Bardha	75	75	69	219	1,946.43

442 / THE U.S. SENIOR TOUR

	SCORES			TOTAL	MONEY
Billy Casper	75	74	70	219	1,946.43
Doug Ford	73	74	72	219	1,946.43
Ted Naff	75	74	70	219	1,946.43
Tom Shaw	72	76	71	219	1,946.43
Larry Ziegler	76	72	71	219	1,946.43
John Brodie	70	76	73	219	1,946.42
Tommy Aaron	74	76	70	220	1,550
Bruce Devlin	73	78	69	220	1,550
George Lanning	74	72	74	220	1,550

Transamerica Championship

Silverado Country Club, Napa, California
Par 35-37—72; 6,632 yards

October 19-21
purse, $500,000

	SCORES			TOTAL	MONEY
Lee Trevino	73	67	65	205	$75,000
Mike Hill	70	72	65	207	44,000
Miller Barber	72	72	64	208	36,000
Rives McBee	71	69	69	209	30,000
Terry Dill	76	66	68	210	20,666.67
Harold Henning	74	67	69	210	20,666.67
Don January	69	72	69	210	20,666.66
Jim Dent	67	73	71	211	14,850
Orville Moody	72	68	71	211	14,850
Al Geiberger	71	72	69	212	12,000
Lou Graham	71	69	72	212	12,000
Dick Hendrickson	72	71	69	212	12,000
Tom Shaw	71	71	71	213	10,000
Gay Brewer	74	67	73	214	9,250
Billy Casper	75	70	69	214	9,250
George Archer	74	72	69	215	7,620
George Lanning	72	70	73	215	7,620
Don Massengale	72	71	72	215	7,620
Rocky Thompson	70	73	72	215	7,620
Walter Zembriski	72	71	72	215	7,620
Don Bies	75	70	71	216	5,443.75
Dale Douglass	75	73	68	216	5,443.75
Chick Evans	71	74	71	216	5,443.75
Robert Gaona	72	70	74	216	5,443.75
Al Kelley	73	72	71	216	5,443.75
Gary Player	70	70	76	216	5,443.75
Ben Smith	72	70	74	216	5,443.75
J.C. Snead	70	75	71	216	5,443.75
Frank Beard	74	72	71	217	3,900
Charles Coody	74	69	74	217	3,900
Bruce Crampton	74	73	70	217	3,900
Bruce Devlin	75	72	70	217	3,900
Bill Garrett	76	71	70	217	3,900
Jimmy Powell	75	68	74	217	3,900
Robert Boldt	74	72	72	218	2,866.67
Gene Littler	76	68	74	218	2,866.67
Arnold Palmer	76	71	71	218	2,866.67
Bob Toski	76	70	72	218	2,866.67
Jerry Barber	70	73	75	218	2,866.66
Bob Charles	74	69	75	218	2,866.66

Gold Rush at Rancho Murieta

Rancho Murieta Golf Club, Rancho Murieta, California
Par 36-36—72; 6,674 yards

October 26-28
purse, $350,000

	SCORES			TOTAL	MONEY
George Archer	70	68	66	204	$60,000
Dale Douglass	71	66	68	205	35,000
Charles Coody	71	69	69	209	29,000
Bob Charles	68	70	72	210	23,000
Bob Betley	72	66	73	211	16,150
Dick Hendrickson	69	72	70	211	16,150
Chi Chi Rodriguez	72	70	70	212	13,050
J.C. Snead	70	72	70	212	13,050
Agim Bardha	76	69	68	213	10,100
Bruce Crampton	71	73	69	213	10,100
Joe Jimenez	71	71	71	213	10,100
Walter Zembriski	73	73	67	213	10,100
Orville Moody	77	70	67	214	7,800
Tom Shaw	72	72	70	214	7,800
Rocky Thompson	72	70	72	214	7,800
Tommy Aaron	76	69	70	215	6,200
Miller Barber	71	69	75	215	6,200
Al Geiberger	73	70	72	215	6,200
Gordon Jones	76	68	71	215	6,200
Ben Smith	74	72	69	215	6,200
Terry Dill	75	69	72	216	5,000
Lou Graham	73	74	69	216	5,000
Lee Elder	77	72	68	217	4,600
Richard Rhyan	73	73	71	217	4,600
Bob Brue	75	72	71	218	4,000
Mike Hill	73	73	72	218	4,000
George Lanning	75	74	69	218	4,000
Larry Laoretti	73	75	70	218	4,000
Homero Blancas	71	73	75	219	3,087.50
Gay Brewer	74	73	72	219	3,087.50
Jim Dent	76	71	72	219	3,087.50
Jack Fleck	73	73	73	219	3,087.50
Gene Littler	74	77	68	219	3,087.50
Gary Player	72	73	74	219	3,087.50
John Brodie	76	71	73	220	2,475
Dave Hill	76	71	73	220	2,475
Bobby Nichols	71	75	74	220	2,475
Ken Still	74	75	71	220	2,475
Art Wall	73	75	72	220	2,475
Butch Baird	73	73	76	222	2,125
Jim O'Hern	74	72	76	222	2,125

Security Pacific Classic

Rancho Park Golf Course, Rancho Park, California
Par 36-35—71; 6,307 yards

November 2-4
purse, $500,000

	SCORES			TOTAL	MONEY
Mike Hill	70	68	63	201	$75,000
Gary Player	66	68	68	202	44,000
Chi Chi Rodriguez	69	66	68	203	36,000
Dale Douglass	68	70	67	205	24,666.67

	SCORES	TOTAL	MONEY
Joe Jimenez	67 68 70	205	24,666.67
Lee Trevino	72 64 69	205	24,666.66
Jim Dent	70 71 65	206	16,850
Al Geiberger	72 64 70	206	16,850
Dave Hill	67 71 69	207	13,000
Rives McBee	73 69 65	207	13,000
J.C. Snead	72 66 69	207	13,000
Homero Blancas	72 68 68	208	8,622.23
Tom Shaw	72 68 68	208	8,622.23
Miller Barber	70 69 69	208	8,622.22
Bob Charles	68 71 69	208	8,622.22
Charles Coody	71 67 70	208	8,622.22
Bruce Devlin	72 67 69	208	8,622.22
George Lanning	67 70 71	208	8,622.22
Orville Moody	69 66 73	208	8,622.22
Arnold Palmer	68 71 69	208	8,622.22
Gay Brewer	70 70 69	209	5,564.29
Roberto De Vicenzo	69 71 69	209	5,564.29
Al Kelley	70 71 68	209	5,564.29
Dan Morgan	69 71 69	209	5,564.29
Terry Dill	69 67 73	209	5,564.28
Lee Elder	71 67 71	209	5,564.28
Jim O'Hern	71 68 70	209	5,564.28
Bob Betley	74 64 72	210	3,800
Robert Gaona	70 70 70	210	3,800
Quinton Gray	69 72 69	210	3,800
Don January	68 72 70	210	3,800
Howie Johnson	72 70 68	210	3,800
Gene Littler	71 67 72	210	3,800
Ken Still	70 70 70	210	3,800
Dewitt Weaver	70 69 71	210	3,800
Bob Wynn	71 71 68	210	3,800
Tommy Aaron	70 70 71	211	2,600
Don Bies	70 70 71	211	2,600
Bruce Crampton	71 69 71	211	2,600
Jack Fleck	69 70 72	211	2,600
Dick Hendrickson	69 71 71	211	2,600
Larry Laoretti	71 69 71	211	2,600
Rocky Thompson	73 69 69	211	2,600

Du Pont Cup

TPC at Batoh, Bato-machi, Japan
Par 36-36—72; 6,545 yards

November 9-11
purse, $550,000

FINAL RESULT: United States 20, Japan 12.

FIRST ROUND
Alternate Shot

Tetsuhiro Ueda and Yoshimasa Fujii halved with George Archer and Gene Littler, 70-70.
Teruo Suzumura and Shigeru Uchida defeated Mike Hill and Dave Hill, 71-72.
Kesahiko Uchida and Seiichi Kanai defeated Jim Dent and Rives McBee, 66-73.
Hisashi Suzumura and Shozo Miyamoto defeated Dale Douglass and Charles Coody, 70-72.

Japan 7, United States 1.

SECOND ROUND
Better Ball

Douglass and Coody defeated Hisashi Suzumura and Miyamoto, 61-66.
Hill and Hill defeated Teruo Suzumura and Shigeru Uchida, 64-67.
Archer and Littler defeated Ueda and Fujii, 65-70.
Dent and McBee defeated Kanai and Kesahiko Uchida, 66-67.

United States 9, Japan 7.

THIRD ROUND
Singles

Mike Hill defeated Kesahiko Uchida, 68-72.
Dent defeated Hisashi Suzumura, 72-77.
Dave Hill defeated Miyamoto, 70-73.
Archer defeated Ueda, 71-78.
Coody defeated Shigeru Uchida, 73-74.
Fujii defeated Littler, 69-71.
Kanai defeated Douglass, 69-74.
McBee halved with Teruo Suzumura, 74-74.

(Each U.S. player received $45,000; each Japanese player $23,750.)

Seniors Challenge

Princeville Golf Club, Prince Course, Princeville, Kauai November 30-December 2
Par 36-36—72; 6,826 yards purse, $300,000

	SCORES			TOTAL	MONEY
George Archer	70	69	72	211	$45,000
Bob Brue	71	70	71	212	20,000
Dale Douglass	70	70	76	216	10,000
Lee Elder	72	73	72	217	8,500
Don January	74	71	73	218	6,000
Harold Henning	73	73	74	220	4,250
Tommy Aaron	70	73	77	220	4,250
Billy Casper	71	73	77	221	3,450
Al Kelley	72	77	72	221	3,450
Bob Erickson	71	75	76	222	3,000
Howie Johnson	72	75	76	223	2,800
Jerry Barber	75	74	76	225	2,600
Mike Fetchick	74	78	77	229	2,300
Dow Finsterwald	77	77	75	229	2,300
Seymour Rose	71	81	80	232	2,000
Don Schuppert	79	76	84	239	1,850
Bill Johnston	77	82	80	239	1,850
Jimmy Powell	81	77	84	242	1,700
Lanny Nielsen	77	86	82	245	1,550
Bob Harrison	79	84	82	245	1,550

GTE Kaanapali Classic

Royal Kaanapali Golf Club, North Course, Kaanapali, Maui, Hawaii December 7-9
Par 35-35—70; 6,479 yards purse, $450,000

	SCORES			TOTAL	MONEY
Bob Charles	65	71	70	206	$67,500
George Archer	67	70	73	210	36,000
Lee Trevino	69	67	74	210	36,000
Don January	68	70	73	211	21,750
Harold Henning	67	68	76	211	21,750
Terry Dill	74	66	73	213	16,750
Jim O'Hern	69	71	73	213	16,750
J.C. Snead	69	71	74	214	15,000
Gene Littler	72	70	73	215	14,000
John Brodie	71	69	76	216	12,500
Billy Casper	70	69	77	216	12,500
Chick Evans	70	72	75	217	8,800
Frank Beard	71	71	75	217	8,800
Bob Betley	67	74	76	217	8,800
Larry Mowry	70	70	77	217	8,800
George Lanning	72	66	79	217	8,800
Bob Wynn	68	69	80	217	8,800
Larry Laoretti	71	67	79	217	8,800
Orville Moody	68	73	77	218	6,500
Bobby Nichols	69	72	77	218	6,500
Arnold Palmer	66	73	79	218	6,500
Don Massengale	69	74	76	219	5,300
Al Geiberger	73	70	76	219	5,300
Charles Coody	70	72	77	219	5,300
Mike Fetchick	70	75	75	220	4,200
Rives McBee	68	73	79	220	4,200
Dick Hendrickson	67	71	82	220	4,200
Tom Shaw	71	74	76	221	3,316.67
Jerry Barber	72	72	77	221	3,316.67
Alan Yamamoto	71	71	79	221	3,316.67
Rocky Thompson	68	72	81	221	3,316.67
Mike Hill	72	67	82	221	3,316.66
Dick Rhyan	67	70	84	221	3,316.66
DeWitt Weaver	69	76	77	222	2,750
Homero Blancas	69	71	82	222	2,750
Joe Jimenez	72	73	78	223	2,500
Dale Douglass	68	77	78	223	2,500
Don Bies	75	72	76	223	2,500
Bob Brue	71	72	81	224	2,200
Miller Barber	74	71	79	224	2,200
Tommy Aaron	77	72	75	224	2,200

New York Life Champions

Hyatt Dorado Beach Club, Dorado, Puerto Rico December 13-16
Par 72; 6,740 yards purse, $1,000,000

	SCORES			TOTAL	MONEY
Mike Hill	69	64	68	201	$150,000
Lee Trevino	68	68	65	201	95,000
Dale Douglass	65	68	68	201	95,000

(Hill defeated Trevino and Douglass on first extra hole.)

	SCORES			TOTAL	MONEY
Chi Chi Rodriguez	67	67	70	204	60,000
Rocky Thompson	69	69	67	205	40,500
Al Geiberger	65	71	69	205	40,500
Bob Charles	68	68	70	206	33,000
Charles Coody	68	68	70	206	33,000
George Archer	70	70	67	207	29,200
Ben Smith	70	66	71	207	29,200
Miller Barber	73	68	68	209	26,300
Jim Dent	70	69	70	209	26,300
Harold Henning	69	72	69	210	22,700
Rives McBee	70	71	69	210	22,700
Bruce Crampton	68	71	71	210	22,700
Don January	70	68	72	210	22,700
Frank Beard	69	71	71	211	20,400
Al Kelley	73	71	68	212	19,600
Orville Moody	76	66	70	212	19,600
Walter Zembriski	70	68	74	212	19,600
Dave Hill	72	70	71	213	18,600
Don Massengale	67	70	76	213	18,600
John Paul Cain	77	70	68	215	18,000
Terry Dill	71	72	73	216	17,600
Don Bies	72	75	70	217	17,000
Larry Mowry	76	68	73	217	17,000
Jimmy Powell	71	76	73	220	16,500
Tom Shaw	74	72	74	220	16,500
Joe Jimenez	75	72	74	221	16,200

The European Tour

Vinho Verde Atlantic Open

Camp Golfe, Estela, Oporto, Portugal
Par 36-36—72; 6,703 yards

February 15-18
purse, £200,000

	SCORES				TOTAL	MONEY
Stephen McCallister	71	71	72	74	288	£33,330
Ronan Rafferty	72	70	74	72	288	12,038
David Williams	70	71	73	74	288	12,038
Stephen Hamill	71	67	74	76	288	12,038
Richard Boxall	71	73	73	71	288	12,038
Anders Sorensen	68	73	70	77	288	12,038

(McCallister defeated Rafferty, Williams, Hamill, Boxall and Sorensen on first playoff hole.)

Steven Bowman	71	73	73	72	289	4,632
Ronald Stelten	70	69	70	80	289	4,632
Steven Richardson	72	70	71	76	289	4,632
Ross Drummond	70	73	70	76	289	4,632

448 / THE EUROPEAN TOUR

	SCORES				TOTAL	MONEY
Miguel Angel Jimenez	73	68	72	76	289	4,632
Santiago Luna	72	72	70	76	290	3,330
Des Smyth	69	73	70	78	290	3,330
Paul Carrigill	73	71	73	74	291	2,880
Manuel Moreno	75	72	70	74	291	2,880
Miguel Angel Martin	71	71	74	75	291	2,880
Peter Baker	72	71	74	74	291	2,880
Steven Bottomley	69	72	75	76	292	2,351.43
Daniel Silva	70	76	71	75	292	2,351.43
Peter Smith	70	69	73	80	292	2,351.43
Mariano Aparicio	72	72	74	74	292	2,351.43
Emmanuel Dussart	71	73	74	74	292	2,351.43
Denis Durnian	74	71	71	76	292	2,351.43
Roger Chapman	71	70	75	76	292	2,351.43
Malcolm Mackenzie	73	73	71	76	293	1,890
Paolo Quirici	70	74	72	77	293	1,890
Chris Cookson	72	69	77	75	293	1,890
Brian Marchbank	76	71	73	73	293	1,890
Ken Brown	72	73	76	72	293	1,890
Neal Briggs	71	72	74	76	293	1,890
Eamonn Darcy	66	76	74	77	293	1,890
Joakim Haeggman	72	68	77	76	293	1,890
Mark Roe	73	69	75	77	294	1,560
Paul Broadhurst	74	71	73	76	294	1,560
Mark Davis	74	70	79	71	294	1,560
Antonio Garrido	72	72	71	79	294	1,560
Jimmy Heggarty	72	73	74	75	294	1,560
Juan Quiros	74	73	68	80	295	1,420
Patrick Hall	74	73	70	78	295	1,420
Magnus Jonsson	72	75	75	74	296	1,220
Grant Turner	73	72	72	79	296	1,220
Neil Hansen	70	70	79	77	296	1,220
Gordon Brand, Jr.	71	74	74	77	296	1,220
Sam Torrance	73	69	71	83	296	1,220
Martin Poxon	72	73	74	77	296	1,220
David A. Russell	73	70	71	82	296	1,220
Marc Farry	72	72	75	77	296	1,220
Martin Sludds	72	74	76	75	297	900
Rob Huff	73	71	76	77	297	900
Andrew Sherborne	72	71	73	81	297	900
Alberto Binaghi	72	70	72	83	297	900
Craig Maltman	71	70	76	80	297	900
Bill Longmuir	70	72	79	76	297	900
David Ray	73	72	76	76	297	900
Mike Miller	75	71	75	76	297	900

Emirates Airline Desert Classic

Emirates Golf Club, Dubai
Par 35-37—72; 7,100 yards

February 22-25
purse, £275,000

	SCORES				TOTAL	MONEY
Eamonn Darcy	64	68	75	69	276	£45,825
David Feherty	73	69	70	68	280	30,530
Severiano Ballesteros	72	69	71	70	282	15,482.50
Des Smyth	68	71	74	69	282	15,482.50
David Gilford	70	73	69	72	284	11,655
Peter Fowler	72	70	73	70	285	8,250

	SCORES				TOTAL	MONEY
Steven Richardson	72	70	72	71	285	8,250
Denis Durnian	72	67	73	73	285	8,250
Brett Ogle	71	73	75	67	286	5,175
Nick Faldo	72	73	72	69	286	5,175
Mark McNulty	69	74	71	72	286	5,175
Peter O'Malley	68	70	77	71	286	5,175
Bill Longmuir	70	69	74	73	286	5,175
Ronan Rafferty	73	70	75	69	287	4,122.50
Anders Sorensen	73	70	75	69	287	4,122.50
Mark James	67	75	75	71	288	3,637.50
Malcolm Mackenzie	71	73	73	71	288	3,637.50
Vijay Singh	72	70	75	71	288	3,637.50
Martin Poxon	76	68	71	73	288	3,637.50
Peter Smith	69	73	74	73	289	3,257.50
Wraith Grant	75	70	73	71	289	3,257.50
Costantino Rocca	72	73	73	72	290	3,092.50
Jean Van de Velde	72	74	74	70	290	3,092.50
David R. Jones	73	72	75	71	291	2,640
Bernard Gallacher	73	73	76	69	291	2,640
Michael McLean	72	71	74	74	291	2,640
Ken Brown	70	74	74	73	291	2,640
Miguel Angel Martin	72	74	75	70	291	2,640
Russell Claydon	73	73	75	70	291	2,640
Sam Torrance	74	71	73	73	291	2,640
Magnus Sunesson	73	73	72	73	291	2,640
Wayne Riley	72	73	76	70	291	2,640
Emmanuel Dussart	72	74	70	76	292	2,172.50
Brian Barnes	73	73	76	70	292	2,172.50
Mats Lanner	75	66	77	74	292	2,172.50
David Ecob	72	70	80	70	292	2,172.50
Peter Teravainen	72	75	72	74	293	1,760
Andrew Sherborne	72	71	80	70	293	1,760
Glyn Krause	73	74	71	75	293	1,760
Craig Maltman	74	70	77	72	293	1,760
Bill Malley	72	72	78	71	293	1,760
Johan Tumba	72	74	72	75	293	1,760
Philip Parkin	70	76	75	72	293	1,760
John Morgan	76	68	78	71	293	1,760
James Spence	74	72	74	73	293	1,760
Derrick Cooper	74	72	71	76	293	1,760
Jimmy Heggarty	68	75	79	71	293	1,760
Carl Mason	75	70	75	74	294	1,347.50
John Hawksworth	76	70	75	73	294	1,347.50
Chris Moody	72	75	71	76	294	1,347.50
Jeffrey Pinsent	73	74	76	71	294	1,347.50

American Express Mediterranean Open

Las Brisas, Marbella, Spain
Par 37-35—72; 6,664 yards
(Third round cancelled - rain.)

March 1-4
purse, £400,000

	SCORES			TOTAL	MONEY
Ian Woosnam	68	68	74	210	£66,660
Eduardo Romero	70	71	71	212	34,720
Miguel Angel Martin	69	69	74	212	34,720
Christy O'Connor, Jr.	71	71	71	213	20,000
Mark James	67	71	76	214	16,940

	SCORES			TOTAL	MONEY
Peter Smith	72	72	72	216	13,000
Andrew Murray	74	70	72	216	13,000
John Morgan	74	75	68	217	8,580
Peter Fowler	71	72	74	217	8,580
Mark McNulty	72	69	76	217	8,580
Mats Lanner	70	71	76	217	8,580
Bernhard Langer	70	76	72	218	6,660
Steen Tinning	69	77	72	218	6,660
Manuel Pinero	72	73	74	219	5,760
Ross Drummond	72	73	74	219	5,760
Severiano Ballesteros	70	74	75	219	5,760
Richard Boxall	69	74	76	219	5,760
Antonio Garrido	76	72	72	220	4,702.86
Mark Davis	70	75	75	220	4,702.86
Des Smyth	69	75	76	220	4,702.86
Brett Ogle	71	72	77	220	4,702.86
Antonio Postiglione	71	72	77	220	4,702.86
Juan Quiros	69	73	78	220	4,702.86
Neal Briggs	72	69	79	220	4,702.86
Jim Rutledge	75	72	74	221	3,960
Paul Curry	76	72	73	221	3,960
Peter Senior	73	76	72	221	3,960
Grant Turner	73	73	75	221	3,960
Philip Walton	71	73	77	221	3,960
David Williams	71	75	76	222	3,172
Vicente Fernandez	72	75	75	222	3,172
Ken Brown	71	76	75	222	3,172
David Feherty	75	72	75	222	3,172
Peter Teravainen	75	72	75	222	3,172
Ove Sellberg	71	77	74	222	3,172
Jose Rivero	72	76	74	222	3,172
Gordon Brand, Jr.	73	73	76	222	3,172
Jose Maria Canizares	69	76	77	222	3,172
David Ecob	75	74	73	222	3,172
Rick Hartmann	74	73	76	223	2,600
Neil Hansen	72	76	75	223	2,600
Magnus Persson	74	75	74	223	2,600
Howard Clark	74	68	81	223	2,600
Jose Rozadilla	76	73	75	224	2,320
Anders Forsbrand	72	73	79	224	2,320
Wayne Riley	75	68	81	224	2,320
Malcolm Mackenzie	73	74	78	225	1,880
Peter Mitchell	72	75	78	225	1,880
David A. Russell	77	72	76	225	1,880
Jimmy Heggarty	74	75	76	225	1,880
Marc Farry	77	72	76	225	1,880
Eamonn Darcy	75	74	76	225	1,880
Keith Waters	69	76	80	225	1,880
Jean Van de Velde	69	74	82	225	1,880

Open Renault de Baleares

Son Vida, Palma, Majorca
Par 35-37—72; 6,239 yards

March 8-11
purse, £275,000

	SCORES				TOTAL	MONEY
Severiano Ballesteros	66	65	70	68	269	£45,825
Magnus Persson	65	65	66	73	269	30,530
(Ballesteros defeated Persson on first extra hole.)						
Juan Quiros	68	64	71	68	271	17,215
Mark McNulty	67	70	69	66	272	13,750
Jean Van de Velde	71	66	69	67	273	10,640
Rodger Davis	70	64	70	69	273	10,640
Armando Saavedra	67	68	70	70	275	8,250
Bernhard Langer	66	70	70	70	276	6,875
Christy O'Connor, Jr.	68	68	70	71	277	6,160
Peter Mitchell	70	65	73	70	278	4,784
Peter O'Malley	70	68	69	71	278	4,784
Ronan Rafferty	69	69	67	73	278	4,784
Eamonn Darcy	69	68	71	70	278	4,784
Bill Malley	63	72	73	70	278	4,784
Miguel Angel Martin	67	70	70	72	279	3,718
Richard Boxall	70	72	70	67	279	3,718
Jose Maria Canizares	70	67	69	73	279	3,718
Jose Rivero	69	68	73	69	279	3,718
Johan Rystrom	70	68	71	70	279	3,718
Torsten Giedeon	71	69	72	68	280	2,970
Ossie Moore	68	72	71	69	280	2,970
Antonio Garrido	73	68	67	72	280	2,970
Manuel Moreno	67	71	70	72	280	2,970
Eduardo Romero	70	71	72	67	280	2,970
Andrew Murray	68	68	71	73	280	2,970
Juan Anglada	71	70	69	70	280	2,970
Bradley Hughes	68	73	73	66	280	2,970
Mike Clayton	68	68	71	73	280	2,970
Paul Curry	69	69	70	73	281	2,214.55
Costantino Rocca	68	73	71	69	281	2,214.55
Emmanuel Dussart	69	72	73	67	281	2,214.55
Jose Davila	69	68	74	70	281	2,214.55
Peter Senior	71	68	70	72	281	2,214.55
Alfonso Pinero	69	72	70	70	281	2,214.55
Vicente Fernandez	67	72	71	71	281	2,214.55
Miguel Angel Jimenez	72	68	69	72	281	2,214.55
Jim Rutledge	68	74	72	67	281	2,214.55
Joakim Haeggman	69	68	74	70	281	2,214.55
Keith Waters	72	70	70	69	281	2,214.55
Andrew Oldcorn	72	70	69	71	282	1,677.50
Grant Turner	72	68	72	70	282	1,677.50
Jesper Parnevik	66	68	78	70	282	1,677.50
Magnus Sunesson	69	70	74	69	282	1,677.50
Tony Charnley	75	66	69	72	282	1,677.50
Stephen Hamill	68	70	71	73	282	1,677.50
Ron Commans	74	68	70	70	282	1,677.50
Gordon J. Brand	68	70	72	72	282	1,677.50
Paul Hoad	69	73	69	72	283	1,320
Peter Teravainen	67	74	73	69	283	1,320
Fernando Roca	72	70	71	70	283	1,320
Manuel Calero	72	70	68	73	283	1,320
Ross McFarlane	73	66	70	74	283	1,320

Tenerife Open

Amarilla Golf Club, Tenerife, Canary Islands
Par 36-36—72; 6,590 yards

March 15-18
purse, £200,000

	SCORES				TOTAL	MONEY
Vicente Fernandez	67	74	72	69	282	£33,330
Mark Mouland	70	73	71	68	282	22,200

(Fernandez defeated Mouland on third extra hole.)

Christy O'Connor, Jr.	74	71	66	73	284	10,330
Emmanuel Dussart	71	74	69	70	284	10,330
Tony Charnley	71	74	66	73	284	10,330
Miguel Angel Jimenez	68	72	75	70	285	7,000
Grant Turner	70	76	69	71	286	5,160
Manuel Pinero	68	73	73	72	286	5,160
Bradley Hughes	71	71	74	70	286	5,160
David R. Jones	72	71	71	74	288	3,308.57
Jesper Parnevik	70	71	71	76	288	3,308.57
Steven Bottomley	73	71	67	77	288	3,308.57
Paul Carrigill	71	74	70	73	288	3,308.57
Jose Rivero	71	73	72	72	288	3,308.57
Peter O'Malley	71	74	72	71	288	3,308.57
Jim Rutledge	70	72	72	74	288	3,308.57
Miguel Angel Martin	71	74	78	66	289	2,298.18
Luis Carbonetti	74	73	71	71	289	2,298.18
Russell Claydon	71	73	71	74	289	2,298.18
Magnus Persson	69	76	68	76	289	2,298.18
Mike Miller	73	71	74	71	289	2,298.18
Michael McLean	73	70	73	73	289	2,298.18
Des Smyth	72	73	72	72	289	2,298.18
Andrew Sherborne	72	74	72	71	289	2,298.18
Juan Anglada	71	70	75	73	289	2,298.18
Craig Maltman	70	72	71	76	289	2,298.18
Eamonn Darcy	72	73	69	75	289	2,298.18
Malcolm Mackenzie	74	71	73	72	290	1,800
Armando Saavedra	78	70	73	69	290	1,800
Bill Malley	72	70	72	76	290	1,800
Paul Kent	73	75	72	70	290	1,800
Antonio Garrido	73	74	72	71	290	1,800
Marc Farry	67	79	73	72	291	1,580
Bryan Norton	76	72	70	73	291	1,580
Santiago Luna	71	76	72	72	291	1,580
Denis Durnian	71	76	73	71	291	1,580
Paul Hurring	73	70	77	72	292	1,340
Thomas Nilsson	75	72	67	78	292	1,340
Colin Montgomerie	70	76	74	72	292	1,340
Jorge Berendt	75	73	66	78	292	1,340
Brendan McGovern	67	78	80	67	292	1,340
Eduardo Romero	72	74	75	71	292	1,340
Paul Mayo	72	73	73	74	292	1,340
John Price	68	75	77	72	292	1,340
Roger Chapman	75	70	75	73	293	1,060
Patrick Ball	73	72	71	77	293	1,060
Bob E. Smith	73	74	70	76	293	1,060
Jose Maria Canizares	67	69	78	79	293	1,060
Yago Beamonte	75	73	71	74	293	1,060
Steen Tinning	73	72	74	74	293	1,060

Volvo Open

Ugolino Golf Club, Florence, Italy
Par 36-36—72; 6,280 yards

March 22-25
purse, £200,000

	SCORES				TOTAL	MONEY
Eduardo Romero	68	66	64	67	265	£33,330
Colin Montgomerie	65	64	67	70	266	17,360
Russell Claydon	63	68	66	69	266	17,360
Rodger Davis	69	63	71	66	269	9,235
Mats Hallberg	71	63	67	68	269	9,235
Peter O'Malley	67	64	68	71	270	7,000
Roger Chapman	65	66	70	71	272	5,160
Peter Senior	69	67	68	68	272	5,160
Jim Rutledge	72	65	64	71	272	5,160
Stephen Hamill	66	69	67	71	273	3,840
Mark Mouland	68	71	67	67	273	3,840
Ossie Moore	66	68	69	71	274	3,330
David Williams	69	67	68	70	274	3,330
Steven Bowman	69	63	71	72	275	2,940
Vijay Singh	70	72	68	65	275	2,940
Baldovino Dassu	72	68	68	67	275	2,940
Mike Harwood	69	72	67	68	276	2,586.67
Andrew Sherborne	69	72	67	68	276	2,586.67
Brett Ogle	66	70	70	70	276	2,586.67
Luis Carbonetti	68	70	68	71	277	2,280
Gavin Levenson	69	71	68	69	277	2,280
Mike Clayton	71	71	68	67	277	2,280
David Feherty	70	69	73	65	277	2,280
Richard Boxall	68	69	72	68	277	2,280
Mikael Hoegberg	67	72	71	68	278	1,980
Johan Tumba	73	68	69	68	278	1,980
Jean Van de Velde	71	70	72	65	278	1,980
Jorge Berendt	74	66	70	68	278	1,980
Ruud Bos	71	71	67	69	278	1,980
Gordon Brand, Jr.	71	67	73	68	279	1,606.67
Paul Hoad	71	70	69	69	279	1,606.67
James Spence	72	70	70	67	279	1,606.67
Wraith Grant	68	70	71	70	279	1,606.67
Barry Lane	68	71	69	71	279	1,606.67
Peter Mitchell	69	69	72	69	279	1,606.67
David Llewellyn	69	71	65	74	279	1,606.67
David R. Jones	73	67	67	72	279	1,606.67
Denis Durnian	69	68	72	70	279	1,606.67
Bill Malley	74	64	72	70	280	1,280
Joakim Haeggman	68	73	70	69	280	1,280
Rick Hartmann	70	72	68	70	280	1,280
Alessandro Rogato	65	70	70	75	280	1,280
John McHenry	67	74	74	65	280	1,280
Ignacio Gervas	67	70	73	70	280	1,280
Leif Hederstrom	65	75	68	72	280	1,280
Silvio Grappasonni	69	70	73	69	281	1,080
Silvano Locatelli	70	67	72	72	281	1,080
David Ecob	70	71	72	68	281	1,080
Kevin Dickens	74	68	71	69	282	960
Paul Kent	71	70	69	72	282	960
Wayne Stephens	69	72	70	71	282	960

AGF Open

La Grande Motte, Montpellier, France
Par 36-36—72; 6,704 yards

March 29-April 1
purse, £200,000

	SCORES				TOTAL	MONEY
Brett Ogle	72	66	70	70	278	£33,330
Paul Curry	70	71	69	71	281	17,360
Bill Longmuir	71	72	69	69	281	17,360
Denis Durnian	71	71	71	69	282	9,235
Mark McNulty	72	71	68	71	282	9,235
Mark James	77	68	67	71	283	7,000
Peter McWhinney	73	69	70	72	284	6,000
Miguel Angel Martin	68	74	72	71	285	4,493.33
Russell Claydon	73	71	70	71	285	4,493.33
Michael McLean	69	73	71	72	285	4,493.33
Jim Rutledge	70	74	72	70	286	3,268
Wayne Riley	74	72	68	72	286	3,268
Sandy Stephen	74	70	68	74	286	3,268
Paul Broadhurst	75	71	68	72	286	3,268
Des Smyth	72	69	70	75	286	3,268
Derrick Cooper	72	72	70	73	287	2,645
Alberto Binaghi	75	71	71	70	287	2,645
Sam Torrance	72	74	71	70	287	2,645
Joakim Haeggman	72	72	70	73	287	2,645
Tony Charnley	72	71	75	70	288	2,250
Mats Lanner	73	71	70	74	288	2,250
Glyn Krause	74	72	69	73	288	2,250
Anders Sorensen	73	70	72	73	288	2,250
David Ray	77	66	72	73	288	2,250
Torsten Giedeon	77	71	72	68	288	2,250
Manuel Moreno	75	71	73	70	289	1,920
Richard Boxall	72	72	71	74	289	1,920
Darren Prosser	73	75	71	70	289	1,920
Wraith Grant	72	72	74	71	289	1,920
David Whelan	74	70	68	77	289	1,920
Steven Bowman	70	77	73	70	290	1,623.33
Vijay Singh	73	71	73	73	290	1,623.33
Philip Parkin	72	75	69	74	290	1,623.33
Carl Mason	75	70	75	70	290	1,623.33
Ken Brown	71	72	76	71	290	1,623.33
Neal Briggs	73	72	75	70	290	1,623.33
Eric Giraud	72	73	75	71	291	1,340
Jose Davila	77	67	72	75	291	1,340
Stephen Bennett	74	69	74	74	291	1,340
Peter Mitchell	72	73	74	72	291	1,340
Neil Hansen	76	71	68	76	291	1,340
Mark Roe	73	73	71	74	291	1,340
James Spence	75	71	71	74	291	1,340
Bradley Hughes	75	70	75	71	291	1,340
Jose Rivero	73	73	69	77	292	1,060
Paul Way	72	73	73	74	292	1,060
Grant Turner	72	75	70	75	292	1,060
Brian Marchbank	71	74	71	76	292	1,060
Hugh Baiocchi	73	73	74	72	292	1,060
Ron Commans	76	69	72	75	292	1,060

El Bosque Open

El Bosque Golf and Country Club, Valencia, Spain
Par 36-36—72; 6,955 yards

April 5-8
purse, £200,000

	SCORES				TOTAL	MONEY
Vijay Singh	66	69	74	69	278	£33,330
Chris Williams	68	71	70	71	280	17,360
Richard Boxall	70	69	70	71	280	17,360
Johan Rystrom	72	72	69	68	281	9,235
Brian Marchbank	69	69	75	68	281	9,235
Philip Parkin	68	72	71	71	282	5,620
Tony Charnley	72	72	67	71	282	5,620
Miguel Angel Jimenez	74	70	66	72	282	5,620
John Hawksworth	73	72	68	69	282	5,620
Jose Rivero	73	70	68	72	283	3,840
Mike Clayton	71	69	70	73	283	3,840
Santiago Luna	70	71	75	68	284	3,240
Sam Torrance	69	68	75	72	284	3,240
Miguel Angel Martin	70	68	78	68	284	3,240
Mark Mouland	67	71	80	67	285	2,567.50
Ross McFarlane	74	71	70	70	285	2,567.50
Paul Carrigill	67	69	73	76	285	2,567.50
Grant Turner	72	72	71	70	285	2,567.50
Mike Harwood	74	66	76	69	285	2,567.50
Mikael Krantz	76	69	73	67	285	2,567.50
Jeffrey Pinsent	75	68	72	70	285	2,567.50
Peter McWhinney	67	72	75	71	285	2,567.50
Paul Broadhurst	73	70	74	69	286	2,070
Denis Durnian	68	74	76	68	286	2,070
Chris Cookson	70	73	73	70	286	2,070
Greg J. Turner	70	71	76	69	286	2,070
Manuel Pinero	73	72	72	69	286	2,070
Mats Hallberg	75	70	73	68	286	2,070
Peter Fowler	71	71	75	70	287	1,770
Jose Davila	74	68	75	70	287	1,770
Steven Bowman	76	68	73	70	287	1,770
Mariano Aparicio	68	71	76	72	287	1,770
John Slaughter	70	72	72	74	288	1,520
Darren Prosser	72	70	77	69	288	1,520
Magnus Persson	74	69	73	72	288	1,520
Paul Mayo	72	73	75	68	288	1,520
Marc Pendaries	69	71	76	72	288	1,520
Jose Maria Canizares	67	74	76	71	288	1,520
Des Smyth	70	70	74	74	288	1,520
Adam Hunter	72	73	72	72	289	1,360
Peter Teravainen	69	76	72	73	290	1,200
Chris Platts	73	70	70	77	290	1,200
Roger Chapman	70	69	75	76	290	1,200
Keith Jones	70	70	78	72	290	1,200
James Spence	74	71	75	70	290	1,200
Hugh Baiocchi	70	70	75	75	290	1,200
David J. Russell	74	70	75	71	290	1,200
Juan Anglada	69	71	79	72	291	940
Ruud Bos	69	71	74	77	291	940
Ossie Moore	73	68	76	74	291	940
Chris Moody	74	71	78	68	291	940
Andrew Sherborne	72	69	72	78	291	940
Jose Carriles	73	72	73	73	291	940

Credit Lyonnais Cannes Open

Cannes Mougins Country Club, Cannes
Par 36-36—72; 6,786 yards

April 13-16
purse, £300,000

	SCORES				TOTAL	MONEY
Mark McNulty	69	71	69	71	280	£50,000
Ronan Rafferty	73	67	72	69	281	33,300
Mark Roe	72	71	66	73	282	18,780
Vijay Singh	69	72	74	69	284	11,800
Mark O'Meara	70	70	75	69	284	11,800
Jesper Parnevik	69	68	73	74	284	11,800
Anders Sorensen	68	68	75	73	284	11,800
Magnus Persson	70	74	68	73	285	6,740
Ian Woosnam	69	72	67	77	285	6,740
Howard Clark	72	68	73	72	285	6,740
David Williams	73	71	75	67	286	5,170
Antonio Garrido	71	70	73	72	286	5,170
James Spence	70	69	76	71	286	5,170
Peter Mitchell	71	72	71	73	287	4,410
Hugh Baiocchi	71	73	73	70	287	4,410
Grant Turner	70	69	74	74	287	4,410
Jean Van de Velde	74	69	73	72	288	3,750
Andrew Murray	72	72	72	72	288	3,750
Bryan Norton	72	70	78	68	288	3,750
Emmanuel Dussart	72	70	72	74	288	3,750
Peter Teravainen	68	71	75	74	288	3,750
Joakim Haeggman	75	71	69	74	289	3,330
Steven Bowman	71	71	75	72	289	3,330
Ross Drummond	67	72	72	78	289	3,330
Mats Lanner	76	67	74	73	290	2,793.33
Jose Davila	73	71	76	70	290	2,793.33
Gavin Levenson	73	73	75	69	290	2,793.33
Jim Rutledge	73	73	69	75	290	2,793.33
Russell Claydon	71	71	73	75	290	2,793.33
Des Smyth	70	71	79	70	290	2,793.33
David Feherty	70	71	75	74	290	2,793.33
Mike Harwood	67	73	72	78	290	2,793.33
Colin Montgomerie	72	63	76	79	290	2,793.33
Malcolm Mackenzie	71	73	75	72	291	2,220
Jorge Berendt	71	73	74	73	291	2,220
Steven Richardson	73	71	69	78	291	2,220
Christy O'Connor, Jr.	73	72	72	74	291	2,220
Mark Mouland	76	70	76	69	291	2,220
Stephen Bennett	73	73	69	76	291	2,220
Chris Moody	74	66	78	73	291	2,220
Mike Miller	69	75	76	72	292	1,860
Paul Carrigill	73	73	68	78	292	1,860
Peter Hedblom	71	75	71	75	292	1,860
Neal Briggs	70	72	76	74	292	1,860
Philip Walton	73	68	74	77	292	1,860
Manuel Pinero	72	71	69	81	293	1,560
Costantino Rocca	71	72	76	74	293	1,560
Sam Torrance	70	73	73	77	293	1,560
Marc Pendaries	71	74	72	76	293	1,560
Michael McLean	71	70	76	76	293	1,560

Cepsa Madrid Open

Real Club de la Puerta de Hierro, Madrid, Spain
Par 36-36—72; 6,941 yards

April 19-22
purse, £275,000

	SCORES				TOTAL	MONEY
Bernhard Langer	70	67	66	67	270	£45,825
Rodger Davis	67	70	68	66	271	30,530
Brett Ogle	72	66	73	61	272	17,215
Magnus Sunesson	72	65	66	70	273	13,750
Ronald Stelten	73	68	67	68	276	11,655
Philip Walton	70	69	71	67	277	8,937.50
Jose Rivero	67	71	70	69	277	8,937.50
John Hawksworth	69	68	72	69	278	6,517.50
Gordon Brand, Jr.	68	70	72	68	278	6,517.50
Greg J. Turner	70	70	70	69	279	5,280
Jim Rutledge	71	69	69	70	279	5,280
Peter Fowler	68	72	67	73	280	4,255
Mariano Aparicio	68	72	66	74	280	4,255
Jose Maria Canizares	70	72	68	70	280	4,255
Carl Mason	74	70	68	68	280	4,255
Mike Clayton	69	75	66	70	280	4,255
Mike Harwood	67	76	66	72	281	3,386.67
David Feherty	69	72	69	71	281	3,386.67
Roger Chapman	73	67	69	72	281	3,386.67
Anders Sorensen	68	73	71	69	281	3,386.67
Rick Hartmann	67	71	72	71	281	3,386.67
Costantino Rocca	72	69	72	68	281	3,386.67
Miguel Angel Martin	70	73	69	70	282	3,055
Paul Carrigill	69	71	73	70	283	2,764.17
Jesper Parnevik	69	70	71	73	283	2,764.17
Magnus Persson	74	68	71	70	283	2,764.17
Mark McNulty	68	73	69	73	283	2,764.17
Eamonn Darcy	71	70	71	71	283	2,764.17
Chris Moody	74	68	70	71	283	2,764.17
Peter Mitchell	71	72	68	73	284	2,357.50
Howard Clark	71	72	68	73	284	2,357.50
Mark Davis	72	67	75	70	284	2,357.50
Vijay Singh	73	71	70	70	284	2,357.50
Wayne Stephens	71	71	74	69	285	2,035
Emmanuel Dussart	70	73	72	70	285	2,035
Malcolm Mackenzie	69	72	72	72	285	2,035
Ian Woosnam	71	71	72	71	285	2,035
Sam Torrance	71	71	71	72	285	2,035
Richard Boxall	71	68	73	73	285	2,035
Jimmy Heggarty	71	73	72	69	285	2,035
Miguel Angel Jimenez	67	74	70	75	286	1,732
David Ray	69	71	74	72	286	1,732
Armando Saavedra	71	72	74	69	286	1,732
Mike Miller	73	70	71	72	286	1,732
David A. Russell	71	73	71	72	287	1,595
Santiago Luna	72	71	72	73	288	1,485
Mark Mouland	70	73	73	72	288	1,485
Ross McFarlane	72	70	76	70	288	1,485
Jamie Howell	73	69	75	72	289	1,320
Mark James	72	69	72	76	289	1,320
Tony Charnley	74	70	74	71	289	1,320

Peugeot Spanish Open

Club de Campo, Madrid, Spain
Par 36-36—72; 6,966 yards

April 26-29
purse, £300,000

	SCORES				TOTAL	MONEY
Rodger Davis	74	69	68	66	277	£50,000
Nick Faldo	70	71	72	65	278	22,360
Bernhard Langer	70	71	69	68	278	22,360
Peter Fowler	72	68	69	69	278	22,360
Stephen McAllister	74	71	65	70	280	12,700
Yago Beamonte	71	75	67	68	281	8,430
Severiano Ballesteros	74	70	68	69	281	8,430
Jose Maria Olazabal	71	67	71	72	281	8,430
Steven Bowman	71	70	68	72	281	8,430
Jesper Parnevik	70	72	72	68	282	5,560
Mark McNulty	69	70	72	71	282	5,560
Miguel Angel Martin	68	70	72	72	282	5,560
Neil Hansen	73	69	74	67	283	4,515
David Williams	76	67	75	65	283	4,515
Jean Van De Velde	69	77	69	68	283	4,515
David Feherty	68	78	68	69	283	4,515
Neal Briggs	75	71	73	65	284	3,880
Manuel Calero	70	70	74	70	284	3,880
Roger Chapman	69	67	74	74	284	3,880
Anders Sorensen	70	73	72	70	285	3,375
Carl Mason	68	75	72	70	285	3,375
Johan Rystrom	72	71	72	70	285	3,375
Vicente Fernandez	72	72	71	70	285	3,375
Colin Montgomerie	67	71	75	72	285	3,375
Eduardo Romero	70	70	72	73	285	3,375
Jim Rutledge	72	73	71	70	286	2,925
Manuel Moreno	75	69	73	69	286	2,925
Greg J. Turner	70	71	73	72	286	2,925
David J. Russell	68	77	69	72	286	2,925
Costantino Rocca	69	72	75	71	287	2,505
Mariano Aparicio	74	72	71	70	287	2,505
Armando Saavedra	72	71	74	70	287	2,505
Alberto Binaghi	74	71	73	69	287	2,505
Joakim Haeggman	72	70	76	69	287	2,505
Michael McLean	72	71	72	72	287	2,505
Bill Longmuir	72	74	70	72	288	2,130
Vijay Singh	68	71	77	72	288	2,130
Gordon Brand, Jr.	76	70	71	71	288	2,130
John Hawksworth	72	74	71	71	288	2,130
Mark James	69	75	74	70	288	2,130
Paul Way	73	72	70	73	288	2,130
Mark Davis	69	73	76	71	289	1,800
Martin Poxon	70	74	75	70	289	1,800
Bill Malley	70	71	74	74	289	1,800
Ross McFarlane	69	74	71	75	289	1,800
Derrick Cooper	72	70	71	76	289	1,800
Andrew Sherborne	72	73	71	74	290	1,470
Steven Bottomley	75	69	72	74	290	1,470
Paolo Quirici	72	71	72	75	290	1,470
Santiago Luna	72	72	71	75	290	1,470
Mike Harwood	72	73	70	75	290	1,470
Sandy Stephen	69	69	74	78	290	1,470

Benson and Hedges International Open

St. Mellion Golf & Country Club, St. Mellion, Cornwall, England May 4-7
Par 36-36—72; 7,054 yards purse, £350,000

	SCORES				TOTAL	MONEY
Jose Maria Olazabal	69	68	69	73	279	£58,330
Ian Woosnam	69	69	69	73	280	38,860
Bernhard Langer	72	72	68	70	282	21,910
Mark McNulty	68	68	73	74	283	17,500
John Bland	68	71	75	72	286	12,526.67
Mike Harwood	71	68	75	72	286	12,526.67
Philip Walton	70	71	75	70	286	12,526.67
Ronan Rafferty	67	72	74	74	287	7,507.50
Colin Montgomerie	69	72	70	76	287	7,507.50
Gordon Brand, Jr.	72	71	71	73	287	7,507.50
Andrew Oldcorn	75	65	72	75	287	7,507.50
Richard Boxall	67	70	77	74	288	5,414
Nick Faldo	78	70	71	69	288	5,414
Kenneth Trimble	74	75	65	74	288	5,414
Johan Rystrom	71	68	74	75	288	5,414
Peter Fowler	73	73	74	68	288	5,414
Eamonn Darcy	71	77	68	73	289	4,375
David Feherty	73	70	72	74	289	4,375
Roger Chapman	74	68	76	71	289	4,375
Howard Clark	70	69	76	74	289	4,375
Ross McFarlane	74	69	72	74	289	4,375
Philip Parkin	75	70	71	74	290	3,885
Peter Senior	73	70	80	67	290	3,885
Paul Hoad	72	74	71	73	290	3,885
Tony Johnstone	71	70	75	75	291	3,570
Jim Rutledge	73	73	74	71	291	3,570
Eduardo Romero	74	74	71	72	291	3,570
Tony Charnley	76	72	68	76	292	3,103.33
Mark Mouland	69	76	74	73	292	3,103.33
Bryan Norton	75	74	74	69	292	3,103.33
Christy O'Connor, Jr.	71	70	75	76	292	3,103.33
Michael McLean	73	71	71	77	292	3,103.33
Greg J. Turner	74	73	72	73	292	3,103.33
Emmanuel Dussart	74	73	72	74	293	2,590
Grant Turner	76	69	79	69	293	2,590
Anders Sorensen	78	71	73	71	293	2,590
Manuel Pinero	75	72	73	73	293	2,590
Brian Barnes	76	71	74	72	293	2,590
Luis Carbonetti	75	69	76	73	293	2,590
Glenn Ralph	75	73	74	71	293	2,590
Steven Bowman	71	75	76	72	294	2,135
David Ray	76	72	70	76	294	2,135
Severiano Ballesteros	68	77	73	76	294	2,135
Vicente Fernandez	73	71	76	74	294	2,135
Gordon J. Brand	72	76	74	72	294	2,135
Mike Clayton	72	74	78	70	294	2,135
David Williams	72	75	75	73	295	1,715
Bradley Hughes	73	73	73	76	295	1,715
Bernard Gallacher	74	71	74	76	295	1,715
Andrew Sherborne	77	69	75	74	295	1,715
Carl Mason	80	69	71	75	295	1,715
Brian Marchbank	81	66	74	74	295	1,715

Peugeot-Trends Belgian Open

Royal Waterloo Golf Club, Brussels, Belgium
Par 36-36—72; 6,813 yards

May 10-13
purse, £250,000

	SCORES				TOTAL	MONEY
Ove Sellberg	68	66	67	71	272	£41,660
Ian Woosnam	66	70	70	70	276	27,760
Eduardo Romero	69	72	69	68	278	15,650
Grant Turner	68	74	68	70	280	11,550
Jose Maria Olazabal	69	71	71	69	280	11,550
Ronan Rafferty	70	70	74	68	282	7,500
Colin Montgomerie	69	73	72	68	282	7,500
Mike Miller	68	72	74	68	282	7,500
James Spence	68	76	68	71	283	5,600
Paul Carman	69	70	71	74	284	4,633.33
Glenn Ralph	71	73	73	67	284	4,633.33
Bill Malley	74	70	69	71	284	4,633.33
Jeff Pinsent	71	74	71	69	285	3,920
David J. Russell	74	67	78	66	285	3,920
Leif Hederstrom	75	70	72	69	286	3,447.50
Jose Rivero	72	71	72	71	286	3,447.50
David Williams	74	69	73	70	286	3,447.50
Gordon J. Brand	74	71	69	72	286	3,447.50
Manuel Calero	69	68	75	75	287	2,853.57
Andrew Murray	72	72	75	68	287	2,853.57
Tony Johnstone	72	71	77	67	287	2,853.57
Steven Bowman	71	72	71	73	287	2,853.57
Wayne Riley	69	73	75	70	287	2,853.57
Peter Smith	73	73	71	70	287	2,853.57
Ruud Bos	70	73	74	70	287	2,853.57
Joe Higgins	70	72	71	75	288	2,550
Michael McLean	73	72	75	69	289	2,134.09
Gordon Brand, Jr.	70	73	75	71	289	2,134.09
Vijay Singh	73	71	74	71	289	2,134.09
Mats Lanner	72	72	73	72	289	2,134.09
Neil Hansen	74	69	78	68	289	2,134.09
John Slaughter	70	73	76	70	289	2,134.09
Mikael Krantz	70	74	75	70	289	2,134.09
Wayne Henry	70	70	73	76	289	2,134.09
Richard Boxall	72	70	74	73	289	2,134.09
Ken Brown	72	72	74	71	289	2,134.09
Patrick Hall	75	71	76	67	289	2,134.09
Barry Lane	71	73	79	67	290	1,775
Sandy Stephen	74	70	72	74	290	1,775
Paul Way	73	70	72	76	291	1,500
John Morgan	73	73	76	69	291	1,500
Mark Davis	73	72	71	75	291	1,500
Roger Chapman	72	74	73	72	291	1,500
Johan Rystrom	71	71	75	74	291	1,500
Roy Mackenzie	72	72	71	76	291	1,500
Malcolm Mackenzie	75	68	77	71	291	1,500
Paul Kent	72	71	76	72	291	1,500
Philip Harrison	73	73	73	72	291	1,500
Steven Richardson	69	75	76	72	292	1,175
Craig Maltman	71	72	76	73	292	1,175
Tony Charnley	73	73	75	71	292	1,175
Peter Hedblom	71	70	75	76	292	1,175

Lancia-Martini Italian Open

Milano Golf Club, Milan, Italy
Par 36-36—72; 7,043 yards

May 17-20
purse, £300,000

	SCORES				TOTAL	MONEY
Richard Boxall	65	64	70	68	267	£50,000
Jose Maria Olazabal	67	69	68	68	272	33,330
Eduardo Romero	72	69	66	68	275	18,780
John Bland	67	74	68	68	277	15,000
Severiano Ballesteros	75	68	66	69	278	12,700
Giusseppe Cali	71	71	67	70	279	8,430
Keith Waters	70	70	71	68	279	8,430
Anders Sorensen	66	72	71	70	279	8,430
Craig Stadler	68	68	71	72	279	8,430
Jose Maria Canizares	73	72	66	69	280	5,560
Jim Rutledge	68	71	71	70	280	5,560
Steven Richardson	71	68	72	69	280	5,560
Malcolm Mackenzie	71	72	68	70	281	4,515
David Feherty	70	71	70	70	281	4,515
Peter Fowler	71	70	68	72	281	4,515
Bill Malley	71	69	71	70	281	4,515
Grant Turner	70	73	70	70	283	3,750
Greg J. Turner	69	74	68	72	283	3,750
Marc Pendaries	73	71	73	66	283	3,750
Peter O'Malley	73	67	70	73	283	3,750
Miguel Angel Martin	68	70	73	72	283	3,750
Mats Lanner	72	72	70	70	284	3,240
Sam Torrance	70	71	69	74	284	3,240
Miguel Angel Jimenez	72	69	73	70	284	3,240
Rodger Davis	69	71	72	72	284	3,240
Steven Bottomley	70	67	73	74	284	3,240
Hugh Baiocchi	72	71	70	72	285	2,835
Denis Durnian	71	72	72	70	285	2,835
Jose Rivero	73	69	72	71	285	2,835
James Spence	73	69	70	73	285	2,835
Carl Mason	70	73	73	70	286	2,497.50
David Williams	72	72	71	71	286	2,497.50
Neil Hansen	72	72	71	71	286	2,497.50
Michael McLean	68	74	72	72	286	2,497.50
Alberto Binaghi	71	72	73	71	287	2,070
Vijay Singh	72	71	71	73	287	2,070
Keith Jones	75	68	72	72	287	2,070
Juan Anglada	70	73	73	71	287	2,070
Martin Sludds	70	74	70	73	287	2,070
Wayne Riley	73	71	74	69	287	2,070
Vicente Fernandez	73	72	74	68	287	2,070
Costantino Rocca	71	70	71	75	287	2,070
Jorge Berendt	73	68	75	71	287	2,070
Baldovino Dassu	67	72	76	72	287	2,070
Andrew Sherborne	69	74	73	72	288	1,650
Mike Miller	70	74	71	73	288	1,650
Wraith Grant	69	76	71	72	288	1,650
Jacob Rasmussen	73	69	74	72	288	1,650
Chris Cookson	72	71	75	71	289	1,380
Glenn Ralph	70	73	74	72	289	1,380
Daniel Silva	70	74	74	71	289	1,380
Bernard Gallacher	72	72	71	74	289	1,380
Paolo Quirici	71	71	73	74	289	1,380

Volvo PGA Championship

Wentworth Club, West Course, Virginia Water, England
Par 35-37—72; 6,945 yards

May 25-28
purse, £400,000

	SCORES				TOTAL	MONEY
Mike Harwood	69	68	67	67	271	£66,660
Nick Faldo	67	71	69	65	272	34,720
John Bland	67	67	71	67	272	34,720
Jose Maria Olazabal	66	68	69	70	273	18,470
Rodger Davis	68	68	71	66	273	18,470
Eduardo Romero	66	71	69	68	274	14,000
Paul Curry	66	70	72	68	276	11,000
Tony Johnstone	66	72	67	71	276	11,000
Colin Montgomerie	70	70	68	69	277	8,960
Marc Farry	68	71	71	68	278	7,170
Jeff Hawkes	70	69	72	67	278	7,170
Philip Walton	70	67	71	70	278	7,170
David Williams	70	70	70	68	278	7,170
Jose Rivero	72	67	67	73	279	5,760
Mark James	75	66	68	70	279	5,760
Eamonn Darcy	70	71	68	70	279	5,760
Gordon Brand, Jr.	75	67	71	66	279	5,760
Wraith Grant	73	68	69	70	280	4,900
Mark McNulty	73	69	69	69	280	4,900
Jimmy Heggarty	68	70	73	69	280	4,900
Christy O'Connor, Jr.	76	68	70	66	280	4,900
Vicente Fernandez	69	69	74	69	281	4,200
Vijay Singh	71	71	72	67	281	4,200
Andrew Murray	70	72	72	67	281	4,200
Craig Parry	68	69	74	70	281	4,200
Manuel Moreno	68	75	68	70	281	4,200
Mats Lanner	74	68	67	72	281	4,200
Mike Miller	72	70	71	68	281	4,200
Mark Roe	70	75	68	69	282	3,540
Sandy Lyle	74	70	70	68	282	3,540
Ian Woosnam	70	72	72	68	282	3,540
Neil Hansen	70	69	70	73	282	3,540
Brett Ogle	74	69	69	71	283	3,160
Barry Lane	68	71	75	69	283	3,160
Emmanuel Dussart	71	69	72	71	283	3,160
Anders Sorensen	72	69	70	72	283	3,160
Ronan Rafferty	73	71	71	69	284	2,760
Mike Clayton	71	71	72	70	284	2,760
Martin Poxon	71	68	72	73	284	2,760
Peter O'Malley	69	74	69	72	284	2,760
Sam Torrance	69	73	67	75	284	2,760
Gavin Levenson	69	76	70	69	284	2,760
Des Smyth	73	72	70	70	285	2,200
Howard Clark	74	68	70	73	285	2,200
Wayne Riley	74	71	73	67	285	2,200
Armando Saavedra	69	73	71	72	285	2,200
Bill Malley	74	70	69	72	285	2,200
Mark Mouland	70	73	71	71	285	2,200
Brian Barnes	70	74	69	72	285	2,200
Peter Fowler	73	69	71	72	285	2,200

Dunhill British Masters

Woburn Golf & Country Club, Bucks, England
Par 34-38—72; 6,940 yards

May 31-June 3
purse, £300,000

	SCORES			TOTAL	MONEY
Mark James	70 67 66 67			270	£50,000
David Feherty	65 70 68 69			272	33,300
Carl Mason	69 70 68 67			274	18,780
Brett Ogle	70 65 68 73			276	12,733
Mark McNulty	68 70 72 66			276	12,733
Jeff Hawkes	69 69 72 66			276	12,733
Vijay Singh	72 67 71 68			278	9,000
Vicente Fernandez	69 71 69 70			279	5,760
Craig Parry	71 69 69 70			279	5,760
Barry Lane	70 69 75 65			279	5,760
Bill Longmuir	67 67 73 72			279	5,760
Tony Johnstone	71 68 72 68			279	5,760
Peter Senior	68 69 75 67			279	5,760
Roger Chapman	67 70 75 67			279	5,760
Mike Harwood	69 75 69 67			280	4,230
Colin Montgomerie	68 67 71 74			280	4,230
Jose Maria Canizares	74 69 70 67			280	4,230
John Bland	68 69 74 70			281	3,730
Andrew Sherborne	70 72 69 70			281	3,730
Andrew Murray	71 64 72 74			281	3,730
Sam Torrance	68 66 76 72			282	3,465
Paul Broadhurst	72 70 70 70			282	3,465
Richard Boxall	69 68 72 74			283	3,105
Miguel Angel Martin	68 71 71 73			283	3,105
Philip Parkin	71 73 69 70			283	3,105
Johan Rystrom	68 71 74 70			283	3,105
Howard Clark	70 69 76 68			283	3,105
David Llewellyn	71 71 70 71			283	3,105
Mark Davis	66 71 74 73			284	2,580
Tony Charnley	67 74 73 70			284	2,580
Ken Brown	67 72 71 74			284	2,580
Martin Poxon	73 68 71 72			284	2,580
Malcolm Mackenzie	68 72 72 72			284	2,580
Peter Fowler	68 74 71 71			284	2,580
Ian Woosnam	69 73 69 74			285	2,220
Keith Waters	70 72 71 72			285	2,220
Manuel Moreno	73 71 71 70			285	2,220
Paul Hoad	73 71 69 72			285	2,220
Bryan Norton	71 72 69 73			285	2,220
Peter O'Malley	65 79 73 69			286	1,920
Marc Farry	71 70 75 70			286	1,920
Eamonn Darcy	69 72 71 74			286	1,920
Derrick Cooper	72 67 73 74			286	1,920
Des Smyth	69 72 74 71			286	1,920
Greg J. Turner	72 72 72 71			287	1,650
Mats Lanner	69 70 70 78			287	1,650
Jesper Parnevik	73 69 71 74			287	1,650
Gordon Brand, Jr.	70 70 74 73			287	1,650
David Williams	72 68 74 74			288	1,380
David R. Jones	72 69 71 76			288	1,380
Jean Van de Velde	71 73 71 73			288	1,380
Costantino Rocca	73 71 72 72			288	1,380
Russell Claydon	69 75 75 69			288	1,380

Scandinavian Enterprise Open

Drottningholm Golf Club, Stockholm, Sweden
Par 36-36—72; 6,747 yards

June 7-10
purse, £400,000

	SCORES				TOTAL	MONEY
Craig Stadler	68	72	67	71	268	£66,660
Craig Parry	66	70	69	67	272	44,400
Ronan Rafferty	70	71	65	67	273	25,040
Mats Lanner	69	71	70	64	274	20,000
Miguel Angel Jimenez	67	69	72	67	275	15,470
Mike Harwood	68	69	69	69	275	15,470
Peter McWhinney	67	68	71	70	276	10,320
Gordon Brand, Jr.	69	66	68	73	276	10,320
Roger Chapman	72	68	65	71	276	10,320
John Morgan	67	70	71	69	277	6,780
Paul Curry	66	72	71	68	277	6,780
Peter Senior	67	67	72	71	277	6,780
Ian Woosnam	70	69	71	67	277	6,780
Grant Turner	70	68	68	71	277	6,780
Malcolm Mackenzie	73	68	66	70	277	6,780
Howard Clark	65	71	71	71	278	5,400
Magnus Sunesson	71	66	71	70	278	5,400
Jose Maria Canizares	71	67	72	68	278	5,400
Glenn Ralph	73	67	69	70	279	4,813.33
Robert Karlsson	66	71	69	73	279	4,813.33
Paul Carrigill	67	71	70	71	279	4,813.33
Bob Shearer	69	72	69	70	280	4,320
Mark McNulty	72	69	69	70	280	4,320
Leif Hederstrom	68	73	67	72	280	4,320
Mike Clayton	74	70	69	67	280	4,320
Anders Gillner	73	67	70	70	280	4,320
Anders Forsbrand	68	73	70	70	281	3,720
Joakim Haeggman	72	70	73	66	281	3,720
Barry Lane	73	67	72	69	281	3,720
Brian Marchbank	72	68	65	76	281	3,720
Miguel Angel Martin	71	69	75	66	281	3,720
David J. Russell	69	75	70	68	282	3,080
John Slaughter	71	71	67	73	282	3,080
Joe Higgins	73	71	67	71	282	3,080
Ove Sellberg	71	71	70	70	282	3,080
Jim Rutledge	70	66	70	76	282	3,080
Steven Bottomley	67	71	78	66	282	3,080
Mark Mouland	76	67	73	66	282	3,080
Paul Broadhurst	77	67	70	68	282	3,080
Sandy Stephen	69	71	70	73	283	2,680
Vijay Singh	70	73	67	73	283	2,680
Colin Montgomerie	69	73	75	67	284	2,480
Philip Parkin	69	72	68	75	284	2,480
Stephen Bennett	73	70	68	73	284	2,480
Rodger Davis	75	68	71	71	285	2,120
Mike Miller	72	72	73	68	285	2,120
Juan Quiros Segura	67	72	75	71	285	2,120
Brett Ogle	70	69	70	76	285	2,120
Jose Davila	69	74	73	69	285	2,120
Greg J. Turner	73	70	71	71	285	2,120

Wang Four Stars National Pro-Celebrity

Moor Park Golf Club, Rickmansworth, England
Par 37-35—72; 6,855 yards

June 14-17
purse, £225,000

	SCORES				TOTAL	MONEY
Rodger Davis	67	72	65	67	271	£36,500
Mark McNulty	68	69	69	65	271	16,716.67
Mike Clayton	68	70	66	67	271	16,716.67
Bill Malley	68	66	67	70	271	16,716.67

(Davis defeated Clayton on seventh extra hole. McNulty and Malley eliminated on first extra hole.)

Peter Mitchell	66	66	69	71	272	9,500
Paul Hoad	69	69	67	69	274	8,000
Rick Hartmann	66	66	73	70	275	6,050
Paul Way	69	67	67	72	275	6,050
David J. Russell	71	66	71	68	276	4,350
Ken Brown	69	68	72	67	276	4,350
Jeremy Bennett	71	66	67	72	276	4,350
Frank Nobilo	71	68	70	68	277	3,266.67
Colin Montgomerie	67	67	73	70	277	3,266.67
Ronald Stelten	70	69	65	73	277	3,266.67
Jim Rutledge	72	71	67	68	278	2,732
Michael McLean	70	70	68	70	278	2,732
Gordon Brand, Jr.	69	68	70	71	278	2,732
Michael King	69	71	67	71	278	2,732
Sam Torrance	66	69	71	72	278	2,732
Tony Charnley	70	73	70	66	279	2,222.50
David Williams	70	66	72	71	279	2,222.50
Gavin Levenson	71	65	72	71	279	2,222.50
Peter Teravainen	69	66	73	71	279	2,222.50
Costantino Rocca	70	69	70	70	279	2,222.50
Barry Lane	70	69	69	71	279	2,222.50
Andrew Chandler	72	68	66	73	279	2,222.50
Peter McWhinney	67	70	67	75	279	2,222.50
Paul Broadhurst	72	69	72	67	280	1,802.50
Denis Durnian	71	69	71	69	280	1,802.50
Richard Boxall	67	72	72	69	280	1,802.50
Chris Moody	68	71	70	71	280	1,802.50
Ross McFarlane	74	68	73	66	281	1,542
Stephen Bennett	72	66	70	73	281	1,542
Greg J. Turner	71	70	68	72	281	1,542
Jeff Hawkes	69	70	70	72	281	1,542
Bob Shearer	70	71	69	71	281	1,542
Ossie Moore	72	71	72	67	282	1,281.67
Martin Poxon	73	67	72	70	282	1,281.67
Mike Harwood	71	70	70	71	282	1,281.67
Peter Baker	71	71	69	71	282	1,281.67
Andrew Sherborne	66	73	70	73	282	1,281.67
Russell Claydon	72	68	70	72	282	1,281.67
Hugh Baiocchi	74	67	72	70	283	1,040
Keith Waters	71	69	71	72	283	1,040
Brian Barnes	71	69	69	74	283	1,040
Paul Carrigill	72	70	69	72	283	1,040
Stephen Hamill	68	70	69	76	283	1,040
Wayne Riley	72	70	65	76	283	1,040
Silvio Grappasonni	73	69	72	70	284	855
Christy O'Connor, Jr.	69	74	72	69	284	855
Gordon J. Brand	71	71	68	74	284	855
Chris Williams	72	66	72	74	284	855

Carrolls Irish Open

Portmarnock Golf Club, Dublin, Ireland
Par 36-36—72; 7,102 yards

June 21-24
purse, £347,390

		SCORES			TOTAL	MONEY
Jose Maria Olazabal	67	72	71	72	282	£57,833.28
Mark Calcavecchia	66	75	72	72	285	30,155.17
Frank Nobilo	73	70	69	73	285	30,155.17
Rick Hartmann	72	74	71	69	286	17,369.15
John Bland	71	69	73	74	287	13,441.41
Russell Claydon	71	71	72	73	287	13,441.41
Eamonn Darcy	70	70	74	74	288	9,553.04
Brian Marchbank	71	73	71	73	288	9,553.04
David Ray	71	73	72	73	289	7,364.52
Martin Sludds	72	72	76	69	289	7,364.52
Peter Mitchell	76	71	75	68	290	5,985.80
Stephen Bennett	72	73	74	71	290	5,985.80
Marc Farry	67	73	70	80	290	5,985.80
Ian Woosnam	69	75	70	77	291	5,000.58
Steven Richardson	73	71	70	77	291	5,000.58
Brett Ogle	72	73	75	71	291	5,000.58
Ronan Rafferty	70	74	70	77	291	5,000.58
Robert Lee	71	76	69	76	292	4,029.64
David J. Russell	71	76	73	72	292	4,029.64
Hugh Baiocchi	74	71	73	74	292	4,029.64
Philip Walton	70	78	71	73	292	4,029.64
Kenneth Trimble	71	77	72	72	292	4,029.64
Malcolm Mackenzie	70	73	74	75	292	4,029.64
Mike Miller	71	75	73	73	292	4,029.64
Sam Torrance	74	74	72	72	292	4,029.64
Richard Boxall	70	77	70	76	293	3,230.66
Peter Smith	72	74	75	72	293	3,230.66
Bill Longmuir	72	75	74	72	293	3,230.66
Mark James	70	75	75	73	293	3,230.66
Glenn Ralph	70	75	69	79	293	3,230.66
Christy O'Connor, Jr.	72	72	73	76	293	3,230.66
Mark McCumber	75	72	71	75	293	3,230.66
Patrick Hall	72	74	75	73	294	2,744.33
Rodger Davis	72	75	73	74	294	2,744.33
Derrick Cooper	71	74	76	73	294	2,744.33
Mark Davis	69	78	69	78	294	2,744.33
David Williams	73	74	73	75	295	2,501.16
Mark Roe	73	74	72	76	295	2,501.16
Gordon Brand, Jr.	71	74	76	74	295	2,501.16
Philip Harrison	71	77	73	75	296	2,327.47
Steven Bottomley	70	76	74	76	296	2,327.47
John Morgan	70	76	75	76	297	2,119.04
Ronald Stelten	69	73	76	79	297	2,119.04
Noel Ratcliffe	78	70	73	76	297	2,119.04
Keith Waters	73	73	75	76	297	2,119.04
John Hawksworth	74	74	76	74	298	1,910.61
Ossie Moore	73	73	76	76	298	1,910.61
Johan Tumba	71	73	72	83	299	1,771.66
Tony Charnley	72	75	75	77	299	1,771.66
Wayne Stephens	74	73	73	80	300	1,632.70
Bill Malley	73	75	74	78	300	1,632.70
*Darren Clarke	72	76	75	77	300	

Peugeot French Open

Chantilly Golf Club, Chantilly, Paris, France
Par 35-35—70; 6,983 yards

June 28-July 1
purse, £350,000

	SCORES				TOTAL	MONEY
Philip Walton	73	66	67	69	275	£58,330
Bernhard Langer	71	65	72	67	275	38,860
(Walton defeated Langer on second extra hole.)						
Eduardo Romero	68	69	69	70	276	21,910
Nick Faldo	68	69	68	72	277	16,165
Rick Hartmann	68	65	73	71	277	16,165
Ronan Rafferty	70	70	66	72	278	9,268
Mark McNulty	71	65	69	73	278	9,268
Richard Boxall	70	69	66	73	278	9,268
Bernard Gallacher	70	65	72	71	278	9,268
Malcolm Mackenzie	70	70	70	68	278	9,268
Stephen McAllister	70	70	70	70	280	6,230
Peter Fowler	72	65	69	74	280	6,230
Alberto Binaghi	72	67	71	71	281	5,262.50
Roger Chapman	69	68	70	74	281	5,262.50
John Bland	70	67	72	72	281	5,262.50
Anders Sorensen	68	68	72	73	281	5,262.50
Jose Rivero	70	70	69	73	282	4,445
Quentin Dabson	67	72	70	73	282	4,445
Martin Poxon	69	70	69	74	282	4,445
Mark Davis	71	66	74	71	282	4,445
Steven Richardson	70	71	73	69	283	3,832.50
Bradley Hughes	69	69	70	75	283	3,832.50
Peter Teravainen	67	68	70	78	283	3,832.50
Gavin Levenson	70	70	74	69	283	3,832.50
Howard Clark	68	72	73	70	283	3,832.50
Paul Broadhurst	74	68	72	69	283	3,832.50
Steven Bowman	66	70	70	78	284	3,110.63
Wayne Riley	71	69	70	74	284	3,110.63
Ross Drummond	70	68	72	74	284	3,110.63
Chris Moody	68	69	73	74	284	3,110.63
Mark James	69	68	72	75	284	3,110.63
Mike Harwood	73	67	72	72	284	3,110.63
Gordon Brand, Jr.	74	65	72	73	284	3,110.63
Gery Watine	71	66	73	74	284	3,110.63
*Christian Cevaer	70	67	72	75	284	
Brian Marchbank	71	70	71	73	285	2,590
Peter Smith	69	69	72	75	285	2,590
Peter McWhinney	70	72	70	73	285	2,590
Juan Quiros Segura	71	70	73	71	285	2,590
Mike Clayton	70	71	72	72	285	2,590
Keith Waters	72	69	72	73	286	2,100
Miguel Angel Martin	69	70	71	76	286	2,100
Paul Way	68	72	72	74	286	2,100
Emmanuel Dussart	69	72	71	74	286	2,100
Armando Saavedra	70	72	70	74	286	2,100
Paul Carrigill	70	70	74	72	286	2,100
Manuel Pinero	68	74	71	73	286	2,100
Magnus Persson	74	68	70	74	286	2,100
Peter Baker	71	71	72	72	286	2,100
Miguel Angel Jimenez	70	72	68	77	287	1,403.18
Marc Farry	74	68	71	74	287	1,403.18
Tony Charnley	68	72	73	74	287	1,403.18
Stephen Bennett	72	70	72	73	287	1,403.18

	SCORES				TOTAL	MONEY
Michael McLean	71	71	72	73	287	1,403.18
Paul Curry	69	71	70	77	287	1,403.18
Peter O'Malley	73	66	75	73	287	1,403.18
Grant Turner	72	70	70	75	287	1,403.18
Derrick Cooper	71	67	73	76	287	1,403.18
Manuel Moreno	68	69	75	75	287	1,403.18
Ken Brown	67	72	70	78	287	1,403.18

Torras Monte Carlo Open

Mont Agel Golf Club, La Turbie, Monte Carlo
Par 34-35—69; 6,198 yards

July 4-7
purse, £354,970

	SCORES				TOTAL	MONEY
Ian Woosnam	66	67	65	60	258	£59,158.22
Costantino Rocca	67	66	67	63	263	39,411.76
Mark McNulty	67	66	66	65	264	19,984.79
Mark Mouland	63	67	65	69	264	19,984.79
Mats Lanner	68	66	72	63	269	13,732.26
Jeff Hawkes	70	66	67	66	269	13,732.26
Chris Williams	70	70	66	64	270	9,158.22
Juan Anglada	70	64	69	67	270	9,158.22
Severiano Ballesteros	72	66	63	69	270	9,158.22
David Williams	69	71	66	65	271	6,815.42
Hugh Baiocchi	64	69	70	68	271	6,815.42
Paul Mayo	70	70	64	68	272	5,613.59
Miguel Angel Jimenez	68	65	69	70	272	5,613.59
Peter Smith	67	67	67	71	272	5,613.59
Anders Sorensen	70	64	65	73	272	5,613.59
Philip Price	73	64	71	65	273	4,896.05
Wraith Grant	71	67	69	66	273	4,896.05
Peter Teravainen	70	72	68	64	274	4,117.65
Jose Rozadilla	67	72	71	64	274	4,117.65
Bill Malley	69	71	68	66	274	4,117.65
Frank Nobilo	70	67	70	67	274	4,117.65
Jose Maria Canizares	65	71	70	68	274	4,117.65
Stephen Bennett	69	68	68	69	274	4,117.65
Ignacio Gervas	71	69	65	69	274	4,117.65
Rodger Davis	67	69	68	70	274	4,117.65
Peter McWhinney	72	70	67	66	275	3,301.22
Paul Hoad	74	67	69	65	275	3,301.22
Malcolm Mackenzie	72	69	69	65	275	3,301.22
John Hawksworth	70	72	69	64	275	3,301.22
Silvio Grappasonni	70	71	67	67	275	3,301.22
Michael McLean	72	67	67	69	275	3,301.22
Bryan Norton	70	66	69	70	275	3,301.22
Antonio Garrido	72	65	72	67	276	2,804.26
Craig Parry	70	69	69	68	276	2,804.26
Jose Rivero	72	63	72	69	276	2,804.26
Santiago Luna	72	67	67	70	276	2,804.26
David Llewellyn	68	70	72	67	277	2,413.79
Ronald Stelten	74	66	71	66	277	2,413.79
Eduardo Romero	70	70	72	65	277	2,413.79
Mike Harwood	73	69	66	69	277	2,413.79
Jose Davila	70	70	68	69	277	2,413.79
Magnus Sunesson	72	63	72	70	277	2,413.79
Bradley Hughes	69	70	68	70	277	2,413.79
Peter Mitchell	71	69	69	69	278	1,952.33

	SCORES				TOTAL	MONEY
Alberto Binaghi	72	67	70	69	278	1,952.33
Wayne Henry	70	72	68	68	278	1,952.33
Justin Hobday	73	69	69	67	278	1,952.33
Wayne Riley	68	64	76	70	278	1,952.33
Luis Carbonetti	69	69	70	70	278	1,952.33
Grant Turner	68	71	72	68	279	1,632.86
Manuel Moreno	70	71	71	67	279	1,632.86
Jose Coceres	69	71	73	66	279	1,632.86

Bell's Scottish Open

Gleneagles Hotel, King's Course, Gleneagles, Scotland
Par 35-36—71; 6,789 yards

July 11-14
purse, £400,000

	SCORES				TOTAL	MONEY
Ian Woosnam	72	62	67	68	269	£66,660
Mark McNulty	73	67	64	69	273	44,400
Gordon Brand, Jr.	65	67	72	71	275	22,520
Malcolm Mackenzie	71	72	65	67	275	22,520
Nick Faldo	72	73	67	65	277	14,313.33
David Feherty	69	72	68	68	277	14,313.33
Derrick Cooper	68	69	68	72	277	14,313.33
Peter Fowler	74	70	65	69	278	10,000
Craig Parry	67	74	71	67	279	8,106.67
Ross Drummond	71	69	68	71	279	8,106.67
Mark Roe	74	68	66	71	279	8,106.67
Paul Curry	77	65	68	70	280	6,192
Fred Couples	75	69	69	67	280	6,192
Jose Rivero	72	69	69	70	280	6,192
Roger Chapman	72	71	70	67	280	6,192
Richard Boxall	73	67	69	71	280	6,192
Stephen Bennett	76	70	67	68	281	5,173.33
Johan Rystrom	72	70	71	68	281	5,173.33
Sam Torrance	69	72	72	68	281	5,173.33
Denis Durnian	75	68	69	70	282	4,680
Andrew Sherborne	69	73	74	66	282	4,680
Eduardo Romero	75	69	71	67	282	4,680
Colin Montgomerie	75	69	73	66	283	4,260
Davis Love III	73	70	68	72	283	4,260
Mike Clayton	74	69	70	70	283	4,260
Rodger Davis	71	70	72	70	283	4,260
Barry Lane	76	69	70	69	284	3,720
Brett Ogle	73	72	70	69	284	3,720
Russell Weir	73	71	68	72	284	3,720
Payne Stewart	70	72	68	74	284	3,720
Silvio Grappasonni	73	73	71	67	284	3,720
Andrew Oldcorn	75	68	73	69	285	3,160
Mike Harwood	70	74	75	66	285	3,160
Ronan Rafferty	75	69	73	68	285	3,160
Michael Allen	71	71	72	71	285	3,160
Mike Hulbert	73	73	71	68	285	3,160
Vijay Singh	74	72	72	67	285	3,160
Gordon J. Brand	74	69	71	72	286	2,880
Isao Aoki	71	72	75	69	287	2,680
John Bland	76	70	71	70	287	2,680
Carl Mason	73	72	69	73	287	2,680
Hugh Baiocchi	73	72	74	68	287	2,680
Howard Clark	73	70	74	71	288	2,200

	SCORES				TOTAL	MONEY
Jean Van De Velde	76	70	70	72	288	2,200
Kenny Walker	73	70	72	73	288	2,200
Emmanuel Dussart	74	71	73	70	288	2,200
Brian Marchbank	74	69	72	73	288	2,200
Stephen McAllister	74	70	73	71	288	2,200
Paul Broadhurst	77	65	74	72	288	2,200
Richard Zokol	72	70	69	77	288	2,200

British Open Championship

St. Andrews Old Course, St. Andrews, Scotland
Par 36-36—72; 6,933 yards

July 19-22
purse, £827,700

	SCORES				TOTAL	MONEY
Nick Faldo	67	65	67	71	270	£85,000
Mark McNulty	74	68	68	65	275	60,000
Payne Stewart	68	68	68	71	275	60,000
Ian Woosnam	68	69	70	69	276	40,000
Jodie Mudd	72	66	72	66	276	40,000
Ian Baker-Finch	68	72	64	73	277	28,500
Greg Norman	66	66	76	69	277	28,500
Steve Pate	70	68	72	69	279	22,000
Corey Pavin	71	69	68	71	279	22,000
Donnie Hammond	70	71	68	70	279	22,000
David Graham	72	71	70	66	279	22,000
Vijay Singh	70	69	72	69	280	16,375
Tim Simpson	70	69	69	72	280	16,375
Robert Gamez	70	72	67	71	280	16,375
Paul Broadhurst	74	69	63	74	280	16,375
Mark Roe	71	70	72	68	281	11,150
Steve Jones	72	67	72	70	281	11,150
Sandy Lyle	72	70	67	72	281	11,150
Jose Maria Olazabal	71	67	71	72	281	11,150
Peter Jacobsen	68	70	70	73	281	11,150
Frank Nobilo	72	67	68	74	281	11,150
Eamonn Darcy	71	71	72	68	282	7,933.33
Craig Parry	68	68	69	77	282	7,933.33
James Spence	72	65	73	72	282	7,933.33
Nick Price	70	67	71	75	283	6,383.33
Fred Couples	71	70	70	72	283	6,383.33
Christy O'Connor, Jr.	68	72	71	72	283	6,383.33
Lee Trevino	69	70	73	71	283	6,383.33
Jose Rivero	70	70	70	73	283	6,383.33
Jeffrey Sluman	72	70	70	71	283	6,383.33
Bryan Norton	71	72	68	73	284	5,125
Larry Mize	71	72	70	71	284	5,125
Ronan Rafferty	70	71	73	70	284	5,125
Ben Crenshaw	74	69	68	73	284	5,125
Mark McCumber	69	74	69	72	284	5,125
Mark James	73	69	70	72	284	5,125
Vicente Fernandez	72	67	69	76	284	5,125
Greg Powers	74	69	69	72	284	5,125
Derrick Cooper	72	71	69	73	285	4,216.67
Naomichi Ozaki	71	71	74	69	285	4,216.67
Don Pooley	70	73	71	71	285	4,216.67
Mike Hulbert	70	70	70	75	285	4,216.67
Mike Reid	70	67	73	75	285	4,216.67
Andy North	71	71	72	71	285	4,216.67

	SCORES				TOTAL	MONEY
Scott Simpson	73	70	69	73	285	4,216.67
Raymond Floyd	72	71	71	71	285	4,216.67
Sam Torrance	68	70	75	72	285	4,216.67
Mark O'Meara	70	69	73	74	286	3,720
Colin Montgomerie	72	69	74	71	286	3,720
Bernhard Langer	74	69	75	68	286	3,720
Peter Fowler	73	68	71	74	286	3,720
Paul Azinger	73	68	68	77	286	3,720
Hale Irwin	72	68	75	72	287	3,475
Eduardo Romero	69	71	74	73	287	3,475
John Bland	71	72	72	72	287	3,475
Michael Allen	66	75	73	73	287	3,475
David Ray	71	69	73	75	288	3,225
Anders Sorensen	70	68	71	79	288	3,225
Blaine McCallister	71	68	75	74	288	3,225
Jim Rutledge	71	69	76	72	288	3,225
Danny Mijovic	69	74	71	74	288	3,225
Mike Clayton	72	71	72	73	288	3,225
Martin Poxon	68	72	74	75	289	2,950
Peter Baker	73	68	75	73	289	2,950
Jack Nicklaus	71	70	77	71	289	2,950
Roger Chapman	72	70	74	73	289	2,950
David Canipe	72	70	69	78	289	2,950
Jorge Berendt	75	66	72	77	290	2,775
David Feherty	74	69	71	76	290	2,775
Armando Saavedra	72	69	75	75	291	2,700
Malcolm Mackenzie	70	71	76	75	292	2,700
Jose Maria Canizares	72	70	78	76	296	2,700

Out of Final 36 Holes

			TOTAL
Jeff Woodland	73	71	144
Tom Kite	71	73	144
Greg J. Turner	69	75	144
Rick Hartmann	73	71	144
Juan Quiros Segura	73	71	144
Brian Barnes	73	71	144
Wayne Westner	72	72	144
Mike Harwood	72	72	144
Arnold Palmer	73	71	144
John Morgan	74	70	144
Andrew Oldcorn	74	71	145
Lanny Wadkins	71	74	145
Severiano Ballesteros	71	74	145
Tom Watson	72	73	145
Howard Clark	73	72	145
Curtis Strange	74	71	145
Andrew Hare	73	72	145
Mikael Krantz	72	73	145
David Williams	74	71	145
Chris Moody	71	74	145
David Frost	72	73	145
Steve Elkington	74	71	145
Gary Player	72	73	145
Bill Glasson	72	73	145
Stephen Bennett	74	71	145
Patrick Hall	74	71	145
Paul Mayo	73	72	145
Bob Estes	73	72	145
*A.C. Nash	73	72	145

	SCORES		TOTAL
Mark Calcavecchia	71	75	146
Bob Tway	73	73	146
Paul Curry	72	74	146
Kenny Knox	74	72	146
Peter Hedblom	75	71	146
Miguel Angel Martin	74	72	146
Wayne Player	76	70	146
Ross Drummond	75	71	146
Philip Harrison	72	75	147
Tom Weiskopf	73	74	147
Gordon Brand, Jr.	77	70	147
Wayne Grady	73	74	147
Tommy Armour III	74	73	147
Scott Hoch	71	76	147
Peter Mitchell	72	75	147
Ignacio Gervas	78	69	147
Des Smyth	73	74	147
John Huston	77	70	147
Peter Senior	72	75	147
Masashi Ozaki	72	75	147
Denis Durnian	73	74	147
David A. Russell	75	73	148
David R. Jones	74	74	148
Brian Jones	72	76	148
Stewart Ginn	73	75	148
Paul J. Archbold	78	70	148
Richard Boxall	78	70	148
Brett Ogle	78	70	148
Jeff Hawkes	75	73	148
Ken Green	73	75	148
Davis Love III	73	75	148
Kenneth Trimble	75	73	148
Philip Walton	74	75	149
Mark Mouland	76	73	149
Jose Davila	74	75	149
Yutaka Hagawa	78	71	149
Ossie Moore	74	75	149
Gavin Levenson	75	74	149
*Chris Patton	74	75	149
*Yasunobo Kuramoto	77	72	149
Andrew Murray	74	76	150
Russell Weir	77	73	150
Keith Waters	76	74	150
Bob Charles	76	75	151
Isao Aoki	73	78	151
Joe Higgins	78	73	151
Chip Beck	76	75	151
Paul Hoad	75	76	151
Graham Farr	82	70	152
Paul Way	75	77	152
*Rolf Muntz	78	74	152
Paul Lyons	77	76	153
Ricardo Gonzalez	75	78	153
Craig Stadler	82	71	153
Rodger Davis	82	71	153

(Each professional who completed 36 holes received £550.)

KLM Dutch Open

Kennemer Golf & Country Club, Haarlem, The Netherlands
Par 36-34—70; 6,597 yards

July 26-29
purse, £350,000

	SCORES				TOTAL	MONEY
Stephen McAllister	69	67	68	70	274	£58,330
Roger Chapman	73	68	66	71	278	38,860
Jose Maria Olazabal	73	70	65	71	279	21,910
Colin Montgomerie	71	68	73	68	280	16,165
Danny Mijovic	71	70	71	68	280	16,165
Peter Baker	69	73	71	68	281	9,268
Vicente Fernandez	72	69	69	71	281	9,268
Peter McWhinney	76	69	67	69	281	9,268
Martin Poxon	71	69	68	73	281	9,268
James Spence	71	72	69	69	281	9,268
Andrew Hare	69	71	68	74	282	6,230
Barry Lane	77	67	68	70	282	6,230
Bryan Norton	73	73	65	72	283	5,490
Derrick Cooper	77	67	69	70	283	5,490
John Huston	72	71	74	67	284	4,360
Vijay Singh	72	74	67	71	284	4,360
Gordon J. Brand	74	70	67	73	284	4,360
Michael McLean	74	70	70	70	284	4,360
Marc Farry	71	71	71	71	284	4,360
Anders Forsbrand	69	71	74	70	284	4,360
Tony Johnstone	76	69	68	71	284	4,360
Miguel Angel Martin	72	70	73	69	284	4,360
Patrick Hall	72	70	68	74	284	4,360
Torsten Giedeon	69	74	72	69	284	4,360
Philip Walton	71	76	72	66	285	3,412.50
Manuel Moreno	74	70	70	71	285	3,412.50
Stephen Hamill	74	73	69	69	285	3,412.50
Wraith Grant	73	68	73	71	285	3,412.50
Magnus Persson	70	71	71	73	285	3,412.50
Chris Platts	74	70	69	72	285	3,412.50
Grant Turner	76	72	70	68	286	2,913.75
Keith Waters	73	68	70	75	286	2,913.75
Mark Roe	73	71	70	72	286	2,913.75
David R. Jones	81	67	70	68	286	2,913.75
Steven Richardson	72	72	73	70	287	2,555
Paul Way	73	75	70	69	287	2,555
Mike Miller	74	73	72	68	287	2,555
David A. Russell	75	70	71	71	287	2,555
John Hawksworth	77	69	68	73	287	2,555
Chris Moody	70	72	71	74	287	2,555
Andrew Murray	69	75	71	73	288	2,275
Noel Ratcliffe	73	75	70	70	288	2,275
Ian Mosey	74	73	68	74	289	2,065
Andre Bossert	74	69	73	73	289	2,065
Craig Parry	76	72	71	70	289	2,065
David Feherty	77	68	70	74	289	2,065
Juan Anglada	75	72	74	69	290	1,750
Antonio Garrido	69	73	74	74	290	1,750
Tony Charnley	70	78	72	70	290	1,750
Jorge Berendt	76	69	74	71	290	1,750
Chris Van Der Velde	71	71	72	76	290	1,750

PLM Open

Bokskogen Golf Club, Malmo, Sweden
Par 36-36—72; 6,889 yards

August 2-5
purse, £350,000

	SCORES				TOTAL	MONEY
Ronan Rafferty	64	67	70	69	270	£58,330
Vijay Singh	69	71	69	65	274	38,860
Bernhard Langer	72	68	67	68	275	21,910
Ove Sellberg	68	66	72	70	276	16,165
Fred Couples	70	72	69	65	276	16,165
Chris Cookson	68	71	72	67	278	10,500
Rodger Davis	70	70	73	65	278	10,500
Jeff Pinsent	71	69	71	67	278	10,500
Frank Nobilo	67	70	72	71	280	7,093.33
Mike Clayton	73	70	65	72	280	7,093.33
Jean Van de Velde	68	70	68	74	280	7,093.33
David Williams	69	71	73	68	281	5,535
Roger Chapman	73	69	71	68	281	5,535
Stephen Hamill	69	73	70	69	281	5,535
Ross Drummond	69	71	70	71	281	5,535
Peter Dahlberg	70	71	76	65	282	4,542
Sam Torrance	69	71	72	70	282	4,542
Paul Carman	72	70	70	70	282	4,542
Santiago Luna	71	70	70	71	282	4,542
Philip Walton	72	70	69	71	282	4,542
Mark Davis	70	71	74	68	283	3,990
Paul Broadhurst	71	71	70	71	283	3,990
Howard Clark	70	69	70	74	283	3,990
Jimmy Heggarty	69	75	74	66	284	3,570
Wraith Grant	71	71	72	70	284	3,570
Anders Gillner	71	73	70	70	284	3,570
Glenn Ralph	73	71	69	71	284	3,570
Derrick Cooper	72	71	68	73	284	3,570
Fredrik Lindgren	68	69	79	69	285	2,819.09
Mike Miller	72	72	72	69	285	2,819.09
Barry Lane	69	74	72	70	285	2,819.09
Miguel Angel Jimenez	75	69	71	70	285	2,819.09
Jose Rozadilla	70	69	75	71	285	2,819.09
Steven Bottomley	71	73	70	71	285	2,819.09
John Morgan	73	69	71	72	285	2,819.09
Alberto Binaghi	72	70	69	74	285	2,819.09
Colin Montgomerie	72	71	67	75	285	2,819.09
Wayne Henry	69	72	69	75	285	2,819.09
Patrick Hall	70	71	68	76	285	2,819.09
Grant Turner	72	71	73	70	286	2,170
Philip Price	71	73	71	71	286	2,170
Jorge Berendt	72	66	75	73	286	2,170
Mikael Hoegberg	68	70	75	73	286	2,170
John Hawksworth	71	70	72	73	286	2,170
David Gilford	73	68	70	75	286	2,170
Torsten Giedeon	72	72	67	75	286	2,170
David Ray	72	72	75	68	287	1,575
Vicente Fernandez	69	72	77	69	287	1,575
Philip Parkin	72	72	74	69	287	1,575
Marc Farry	71	69	77	70	287	1,575
Brett Ogle	72	68	77	70	287	1,575
Gordon J. Brand	71	70	74	72	287	1,575
Ian Mosey	67	77	70	73	287	1,575
Greg J. Turner	69	72	72	74	287	1,575
Ruud Bos	70	71	72	74	287	1,575
Anders Haglund	72	71	70	74	287	1,575

Murphy's Cup

Fulford Golf Club, York, England
Par 36-36—72; 6,807 yards

August 9-12
purse, £250,000

	SCORES				TOTAL	MONEY
Tony Johnstone	6	23	6	15	50	£41,660
Malcolm Mackenzie	8	13	16	11	48	27,760
Russell Claydon	10	15	7	12	44	15,650
Sandy Lyle	9	10	8	13	40	12,750
Martin Poxon	7	7	9	16	39	10,800
Barry Lane	5	13	10	9	37	8,900
Glyn Krause	7	17	9	3	36	6,525
Christy O'Connor, Jr.	8	8	11	9	36	6,525
Paul Way	4	9	10	13	36	6,525
Peter Baker	2	11	9	12	34	5,050
Mike Harwood	8	4	13	7	32	4,500
Ross Drummond	11	11	12	-2	32	4,500
Sam Torrance	9	7	4	11	31	3,970
Des Smyth	6	7	9	9	31	3,970
Patrick Hall	2	9	7	12	30	3,645
Jeff Hawkes	3	9	7	11	30	3,645
Paul Broadhurst	5	14	2	8	29	3,350
Tony Charnley	7	12	-1	11	29	3,350
Howard Clark	1	11	7	9	28	3,018.75
Chris Moody	-3	12	12	7	28	3,018.75
Mark Mouland	2	13	5	8	28	3,018.75
Jeff Pinsent	1	11	9	7	28	3,018.75
Martin Sludds	2	11	6	8	27	2,825
Bill Longmuir	4	12	7	3	26	2,637.50
Hugh Baiocchi	8	3	5	10	26	2,637.50
Richard Boxall	6	3	11	6	26	2,637.50
Eamonn Darcy	4	9	7	6	26	2,637.50
Jimmy Heggarty	6	7	2	10	25	2,450
Derrick Cooper	8	8	2	6	24	2,337.50
Mike Clayton	7	6	8	3	24	2,337.50
Ken Brown	5	6	6	6	23	2,158.33
Mark Roe	3	9	4	7	23	2,158.33
Mark Davis	7	5	5	6	23	2,158.33
James Spence	5	8	4	5	22	2,000
Gordon J. Brand	9	3	-1	11	22	2,000
Gavin Levenson	0	10	11	1	22	2,000
Stephen Hamill	6	12	-1	4	21	1,875
Bob E. Smith	9	0	11	1	21	1,875
Paul Carrigill	0	10	3	7	20	1,775
David A. Russell	8	3	4	5	20	1,775
Wayne Player	10	2	-1	8	19	1,675
David Feherty	7	5	4	3	19	1,675
Steven Richardson	9	2	6	1	18	1,475
Colin Montgomerie	4	6	2	6	18	1,475
Gordon Brand, Jr.	9	4	2	3	18	1,475
Simon Hobday	0	9	-1	10	18	1,475
Rick Hartmann	9	6	-1	4	18	1,475
Anders Forsbrand	7	8	3	0	18	1,475
Greg J. Turner	1	9	1	6	17	1,275
Johan Rystrom	1	8	8	0	17	1,275

NM English Open

The Belfry Golf and Country Club, Brabazon Course, Sutton, England August 16-19
Par 36-36—72; 7,202 yards purse, £400,000

	SCORES				TOTAL	MONEY
Mark James	76	68	65	75	284	£66,660
Sam Torrance	75	67	69	73	284	44,400
(James defeated Torrance on first extra hole.)						
David Feherty	73	75	69	68	285	25,040
Severiano Ballesteros	72	72	68	75	287	20,000
Derrick Cooper	77	73	71	67	288	13,235
Stephen McAllister	74	74	72	68	288	13,235
Howard Clark	76	73	69	70	288	13,235
Mike Harwood	74	73	69	72	288	13,235
Gordon Brand, Jr.	71	75	72	71	289	8,480
Steven Richardson	71	76	67	75	289	8,480
Sandy Stephen	71	74	75	70	290	7,120
Peter McWhinney	76	74	68	72	290	7,120
Russell Claydon	78	72	72	69	291	6,146.67
Brett Ogle	73	74	69	75	291	6,146.67
Vijay Singh	77	72	67	75	291	6,146.67
Eoghan O'Connell	76	75	73	68	292	5,192
Frank Nobilo	75	74	72	71	292	5,192
Gordon J. Brand	76	72	72	72	292	5,192
Sandy Lyle	77	74	68	73	292	5,192
Carl Mason	75	72	71	74	292	5,192
Graham Farr	75	73	74	71	293	4,380
Johan Rystrom	73	74	74	72	293	4,380
Jose Rivero	78	72	71	72	293	4,380
Jim Rutledge	72	78	71	72	293	4,380
Malcolm Mackenzie	74	76	69	74	293	4,380
Des Smyth	75	72	68	78	293	4,380
Jeff Hawkes	75	76	73	70	294	3,900
John Bland	74	75	77	68	294	3,900
Tony Johnstone	74	74	74	73	295	3,600
Antonio Garrido	76	67	77	75	295	3,600
Stephen Bennett	75	73	72	75	295	3,600
Anders Sorensen	75	77	73	71	296	3,160
Peter O'Malley	77	73	75	71	296	3,160
Brian Waites	76	74	71	75	296	3,160
Peter Mitchell	75	73	71	77	296	3,160
Philip Parkin	76	72	71	77	296	3,160
Brian Marchbank	76	75	67	78	296	3,160
David Williams	76	75	72	74	297	2,520
Mike Clayton	73	75	71	78	297	2,520
Barry Lane	78	72	73	74	297	2,520
Brian Barnes	77	74	73	73	297	2,520
Jose Davila	75	75	74	73	297	2,520
Roger Chapman	76	76	73	72	297	2,520
Paul Curry	77	72	73	75	297	2,520
Keith Waters	72	77	72	76	297	2,520
Wayne Riley	73	75	71	78	297	2,520
Rodger Davis	78	72	73	74	297	2,520
David A. Russell	73	73	76	76	298	2,000
Michael McLean	74	76	75	73	298	2,000
Jean Van de Velde	76	73	72	77	298	2,000

Volvo German Open

Hubbelrath Golf Club, Dusseldorf, Germany
Par 36-36—72; 6,756 yards

August 23-26
purse, £467,445

	SCORES				TOTAL	MONEY
Mark McNulty	67	68	70	65	270	£77,896.49
Craig Parry	66	65	72	70	273	51,953.26
Eamonn Darcy	66	70	68	70	274	26,310.52
Anders Forsbrand	64	66	73	71	274	26,310.52
Jose Rivero	70	71	70	64	275	16,727.88
Philip Walton	69	67	69	70	275	16,727.88
Des Smyth	68	66	73	68	275	16,727.88
Mark James	67	73	66	71	277	9,662.77
Tony Johnstone	70	70	66	71	277	9,662.77
Sam Torrance	70	70	70	67	277	9,662.77
Peter O'Malley	68	73	71	65	277	9,662.77
Carl Mason	69	68	71	69	277	9,662.77
Anders Sorensen	67	73	71	67	278	6,800.22
Stephen McAllister	70	70	70	68	278	6,800.22
Peter Smith	69	69	69	71	278	6,800.22
Jean Van de Velde	67	69	71	71	278	6,800.22
Vicente Fernandez	70	71	68	69	278	6,800.22
Ken Brown	69	72	70	67	278	6,800.22
Rick Hartmann	66	68	70	75	279	5,420.15
Derrick Cooper	69	70	70	70	279	5,420.15
Kevin Dickens	71	70	70	68	279	5,420.15
John Bland	70	72	68	69	279	5,420.15
Bernhard Langer	70	70	68	71	279	5,420.15
Chris Moody	69	67	73	70	279	5,420.15
Howard Clark	71	66	74	69	280	4,474.12
Chris Platts	69	70	74	67	280	4,474.12
Hugh Baiocchi	70	72	68	70	280	4,474.12
Costantino Rocca	69	69	72	70	280	4,474.12
Mike Clayton	68	71	71	70	280	4,474.12
Miguel Angel Jimenez	73	69	71	67	280	4,474.12
Brett Ogle	71	70	71	68	280	4,474.12
Frank Nobilo	71	68	69	72	280	4,474.12
Joakim Haeggman	67	70	73	71	281	3,606.01
Steven Richardson	69	72	73	67	281	3,606.01
Michael McLean	69	71	71	70	281	3,606.01
Peter Baker	69	72	69	71	281	3,606.01
Tony Charnley	67	72	70	72	281	3,606.01
Rodger Davis	71	68	71	72	282	3,013.36
Peter Mitchell	70	68	72	72	282	3,013.36
Vijay Singh	69	70	71	72	282	3,013.36
Stephen Bennett	73	67	73	69	282	3,013.36
Jim Rutledge	71	67	72	73	283	2,671.12
Manuel Calero	70	70	73	70	283	2,671.12
Johan Rystrom	66	75	69	73	283	2,671.12
Manuel Moreno	67	71	70	76	284	2,370.62
David Gilford	70	72	72	70	284	2,370.62
Stephen Hamill	70	72	71	71	284	2,370.62
Torsten Giedeon	71	67	69	77	284	2,370.62
Gordon Brand, Jr.	69	72	72	71	284	2,370.62
Miguel Angel Martin	71	70	69	74	284	2,370.62

Ebel European Masters-Swiss Open

Crans-Sur-Sierre, Montana, Switzerland
Par 36-36—72; 6,745 yards

August 30-September 2
purse, £460,000

	SCORES				TOTAL	MONEY
Ronan Rafferty	70	65	66	66	267	£76,636
John Bland	70	66	66	67	269	51,060
James Spence	66	67	68	69	270	28,796
Craig Parry	72	65	66	68	271	21,252
Howard Clark	64	66	72	69	271	21,252
Mark McNulty	65	72	68	67	272	14,950
Jose Maria Canizares	69	67	65	71	272	14,950
Mark Mouland	68	72	66	68	274	8,832
Mats Lanner	73	67	66	68	274	8,832
David Gilford	70	71	64	69	274	8,832
Keith Waters	68	68	69	69	274	8,832
Anders Forsbrand	68	67	71	68	274	8,832
David Williams	69	66	71	68	274	8,832
Sandy Lyle	67	66	71	70	274	8,832
Marc Farry	68	72	67	68	275	6,486
Peter McWhinney	68	71	68	68	275	6,486
Miguel Angel Martin	69	69	67	70	275	6,486
Philip Parkin	71	69	70	66	276	5,719.33
Hugh Baiocchi	67	73	69	67	276	5,719.33
Peter Teravainen	70	69	66	71	276	5,719.33
Bernhard Langer	68	71	70	68	277	5,106
Jimmy Heggarty	71	69	67	70	277	5,106
Severiano Ballesteros	73	66	69	69	277	5,106
Miguel Angel Jimenez	66	69	74	68	277	5,106
Ove Sellberg	66	67	67	77	277	5,106
Jim Rutledge	71	70	66	71	278	4,623
David J. Russell	68	71	69	70	278	4,623
Stephen Bennett	72	68	72	67	279	3,915.11
Jose Rivero	69	72	69	69	279	3,915.11
Gordon J. Brand	70	71	71	67	279	3,915.11
Jesper Parnevik	68	71	71	69	279	3,915.11
Jean Van de Velde	68	71	70	70	279	3,915.11
Des Smyth	70	69	70	70	279	3,915.11
Costantino Rocca	69	70	73	67	279	3,915.11
Rick Hartmann	70	67	68	74	279	3,915.11
Gordon Brand, Jr.	68	69	69	73	279	3,915.11
Wayne Riley	66	74	69	71	280	3,312
Wraith Grant	72	69	70	69	280	3,312
Frank Nobilo	69	69	72	70	280	3,312
Paul Hoad	69	71	72	69	281	2,944
Jamie Howell	72	69	68	72	281	2,944
Philip Walton	71	70	71	69	281	2,944
David A. Russell	69	70	71	71	281	2,944
Bill Longmuir	69	67	73	72	281	2,944
Paul Curry	72	69	70	71	282	2,576
Ronald Stelten	71	70	71	70	282	2,576
Stephen McAllister	72	66	73	71	282	2,576
Brian Marchbank	67	74	73	69	283	2,208
Chris Moody	68	73	70	72	283	2,208
Colin Montgomerie	73	68	76	66	283	2,208
Ian Mosey	72	69	71	71	283	2,208
Derrick Cooper	71	68	70	74	283	2,208

Panasonic European Open

Sunningdale Golf Club, Old Course, Sunningdale, England
Par 35-35—70; 6,607 yards

September 6-9
purse, £400,000

	SCORES				TOTAL	MONEY
Peter Senior	67	68	66	66	267	£66,660
Ian Woosnam	65	68	68	67	268	44,400
Jose Maria Canizares	69	69	63	68	269	25,040
Tim Simpson	67	72	64	67	270	15,735
Jose Maria Olazabal	65	69	70	66	270	15,735
Nick Faldo	68	70	64	68	270	15,735
Gordon J. Brand	70	65	65	70	270	15,735
Eduardo Romero	70	65	69	67	271	10,000
David Feherty	73	65	66	68	272	8,480
Jimmy Heggarty	72	70	66	64	272	8,480
Brett Ogle	69	73	68	63	273	7,120
Jose Rivero	70	66	69	68	273	7,120
Paul Broadhurst	71	71	67	65	274	5,550
Richard Boxall	66	74	68	66	274	5,550
Steven Richardson	68	66	70	70	274	5,550
Mark Roe	71	68	68	67	274	5,550
Frank Nobilo	72	70	65	67	274	5,550
Sam Torrance	68	71	67	68	274	5,550
Mike Clayton	68	71	64	71	274	5,550
Magnus Sunesson	67	67	72	68	274	5,550
Miguel Angel Jimenez	67	71	70	67	275	4,560
Sandy Lyle	69	73	65	68	275	4,560
Russell Claydon	69	69	68	69	275	4,560
Antonio Garrido	70	68	68	70	276	4,200
Colin Montgomerie	69	70	68	69	276	4,200
Bill Malley	71	69	68	68	276	4,200
Hugh Baiocchi	64	76	70	67	277	3,660
Paul Curry	69	71	65	72	277	3,660
Barry Lane	68	69	69	71	277	3,660
Tony Johnstone	68	72	69	68	277	3,660
Ove Sellberg	70	72	66	69	277	3,660
Jose Davila	69	71	69	68	277	3,660
Miguel Angel Martin	69	71	69	69	278	3,000
Anders Sorensen	70	72	68	68	278	3,000
Martin Sludds	74	65	68	71	278	3,000
Malcolm Mackenzie	66	74	67	71	278	3,000
Robert Gamez	69	73	66	70	278	3,000
Andrew Sherborne	73	69	66	70	278	3,000
Mark James	67	71	68	72	278	3,000
Silvio Grappasonni	72	68	70	68	278	3,000
Ross Drummond	68	70	73	68	279	2,280
Jim Rutledge	69	72	70	68	279	2,280
Michael King	70	71	68	70	279	2,280
Stephen Bennett	69	72	73	65	279	2,280
Wayne Riley	70	72	66	71	279	2,280
John Bland	73	68	67	71	279	2,280
Anders Forsbrand	69	72	69	69	279	2,280
Des Smyth	70	71	69	69	279	2,280
Andrew Murray	72	70	72	65	279	2,280
Ross McFarlane	65	75	69	70	279	2,280

Lancome Trophy

St. Nom-la-Breteche, Versailles, France
Par 35-35—70; 6,756 yards

September 13-16
purse, £420,000

	SCORES	TOTAL	MONEY
Jose Maria Olazabal	68 66 70 65	269	£69,970
Colin Montgomerie	69 63 71 67	270	46,620
Tony Johnstone	68 69 70 64	271	26,290
Rodger Davis	69 66 71 69	275	17,833.33
Craig Parry	69 70 66 70	275	17,833.33
Mark James	72 64 68 71	275	17,833.33
Eamonn Darcy	70 70 67 69	276	10,846.67
Severiano Ballesteros	70 69 70 67	276	10,846.67
Eduardo Romero	71 67 71 67	276	10,846.67
Mike Clayton	71 67 73 66	277	8,025
Jose Rivero	68 70 70 69	277	8,025
Malcolm Mackenzie	75 68 67 68	278	6,396
Russell Claydon	71 71 69 67	278	6,396
Rick Hartmann	70 69 71 68	278	6,396
John Bland	69 72 70 67	278	6,396
Bernhard Langer	70 68 67 73	278	6,396
Robert Gamez	74 70 69 66	279	5,520
Sam Torrance	71 71 67 71	280	5,190
Ronan Rafferty	73 68 68 71	280	5,190
Peter Fowler	70 68 73 70	281	4,930
Hale Irwin	68 72 71 71	282	4,570
Frank Nobilo	71 70 69 72	282	4,570
Peter Senior	67 71 72 72	282	4,570
Tom Kite	70 69 70 73	282	4,570
David Feherty	73 70 70 69	282	4,570
Mark Mouland	74 69 71 69	283	3,850
Gordon Brand, Jr.	71 69 72 71	283	3,850
Jose Maria Canizares	68 72 73 70	283	3,850
David Williams	72 70 71 70	283	3,850
Ove Sellberg	73 71 70 69	283	3,850
Peter McWhinney	74 73 70 66	283	3,850
Mark Roe	74 69 72 68	283	3,850
Mark Davis	71 72 71 70	284	3,370
Costantino Rocca	68 69 73 74	284	3,370
Des Smyth	72 68 73 72	285	3,130
Stephen McAllister	71 70 71 73	285	3,130
Ian Woosnam	67 75 69 74	285	3,130
Brett Ogle	70 70 73 72	285	3,130
Roger Chapman	68 73 72 73	286	2,850
Mark McNulty	71 72 72 71	286	2,850
Anders Sorensen	73 70 71 72	286	2,850
Magnus Persson	71 70 72 74	287	2,690
Bill Malley	72 74 74 68	288	2,530
Mats Lanner	71 74 72 71	288	2,530
Miguel Angel Jimenez	71 67 75 75	288	2,530
Jim Rutledge	73 73 73 70	289	2,330
James Spence	76 69 72 72	289	2,330
Vicente Fernandez	71 73 70 76	290	2,050
Miguel Angel Martin	75 69 74 72	290	2,050
Grant Turner	71 67 78 74	290	2,050
Philip Walton	73 69 72 76	290	2,050
Marc Farry	73 72 71 74	290	2,050

Motorola Classic

East Sussex National Golf Club, Little Horsted, England
Par 36-36—72; 7,172 yards

September 13-16
purse, £69,000

	SCORES				TOTAL	MONEY
Paul Broadhurst	68	73	67	69	277	£10,500
Wayne Henry	73	75	66	66	280	7,100
Sandy Stephen	74	72	66	69	281	5,100
David J. Russell	73	68	71	74	286	3,237
Stephen Bennett	73	70	72	71	286	3,237
Philip Parkin	72	72	70	72	286	3,237
Robert Lee	69	69	74	74	286	3,237
Jorge Berendt	73	69	71	74	287	1,950
Ross McFarlane	71	70	76	70	287	1,950
Peter Mitchell	72	75	68	73	288	1,550
Armando Saavedra	70	73	73	72	288	1,550
David A. Russell	71	77	74	69	291	1,425
Philip Price	74	72	72	73	291	1,425
Paul Mayo	74	72	73	74	293	1,325
Paul Hoad	77	75	71	70	293	1,325
Paul Kent	75	72	70	77	294	1,200
David Llewellyn	75	74	71	74	294	1,200
Paul Carrigill	77	73	71	73	294	1,200
Charles Cox	80	71	75	68	294	1,200
Neil Wichelow	69	78	71	77	295	1,100
Tony Stevens	71	75	79	71	296	1,000
Jonathan Sewell	76	76	73	71	296	1,000
John Hay	73	70	77	76	296	1,000
Steven Bowman	72	72	74	78	296	1,000
Tony Ashton	75	75	68	79	297	860
Neil Hansen	74	74	78	71	297	860
Jeremy Robinson	77	71	75	74	297	860
Glenn Ralph	76	75	71	76	298	760
Wraith Grant	77	72	76	73	298	760
Jeremy Bennett	75	77	73	74	299	700
Chris Moody	74	75	77	74	300	640
Mark Nichols	77	73	76	74	300	640
Rob Huff	72	73	76	79	300	640
Keith Jones	80	71	80	70	301	580
Peter Teravainen	74	73	75	80	302	535
Brendan McGovern	76	71	79	76	302	535
Brian Barnes	71	78	79	75	303	475
Martin Sludds	75	75	79	74	303	475
Paul Hurring	76	75	76	77	304	430
Neil Coles	74	75	78	78	305	400
Ossie Moore	74	77	75	81	307	400
Chris De Bruin	77	75	78	78	308	400

Suntory World Match Play Championship

Wentworth Club, West Course, Virginia Water, England
Par 434 534 444—35; 345 434 455—37—72; 6,945 yards

September 20-23
purse, £350,000

FIRST ROUND

Chip Beck defeated Ryoken Kawagishi, 4 and 3
| Beck | 434 | 624 | 454 | 36 | 234 | 434 | 445 | 33 | 69 |
| Kawagishi | 534 | 335 | 444 | 35 | 344 | 434 | 554 | 36 | 71 |

Beck leads, 4 up
| Beck | 434 | 445 | 445 | 37 | 354 | 433 |
| Kawagishi | 434 | 353 | 443 | 33 | 435 | 434 |

Ronan Rafferty defeated Seve Ballesteros, 8 and 6
| Ballesteros | 456 | 434 | 445 | 39 | 235 | 534 | 433 | 32 | 71 |
| Rafferty | 534 | 333 | 344 | 32 | 334 | 334 | 334 | 30 | 62 |

Rafferty leads, 6 up
| Ballesteros | 335 | 434 | 554 | 36 | 334 |
| Rafferty | 535 | 433 | 444 | 35 | 343 |

Wayne Grady defeated Bernhard Langer, 4 and 2
| Grady | 434 | 424 | 445 | 34 | 345 | 434 | 353 | 34 | 68 |
| Langer | 424 | 324 | 343 | 29 | 444 | 434 | 554 | 37 | 66 |

Langer leads, 2 up
| Grady | 434 | 443 | 434 | 33 | 244 | 433 | 3 |
| Langer | 345 | 445 | 454 | 38 | 344 | 434 | 4 |

Mark McNulty defeated Billy Ray Brown, 4 and 2
| McNulty | 435 | 434 | 444 | 35 | 344 | 424 | 445 | 34 | 69 |
| Brown | 445 | 325 | 544 | 36 | 344 | 334 | 354 | 33 | 69 |

Match all-square
| McNulty | 455 | 433 | 43 | 35 | C35 | 333 | 3 |
| Brown | 435 | 534 | 444 | 33 | 244 | 344 |

SECOND ROUND

Chip Beck defeated Nick Faldo, 2 and 1
| Faldo | 334 | 434 | 545 | 35 | 446 | 535 | 445 | 40 | 75 |
| Beck | 444 | 424 | 444 | 34 | 344 | 534 | 453 | 35 | 69 |

Beck leads, 4 up
| Faldo | 534 | 434 | 344 | 34 | 445 | 334 | 45 |
| Beck | 435 | 544 | 435 | 37 | 534 | 434 | 44 |

Ian Woosnam defeated Ronan Rafferty, 5 and 4
| Woosnam | 444 | 524 | 454 | 36 | 343 | 434 | 444 | 33 | 69 |
| Rafferty | 435 | 424 | 445 | 35 | 455 | 444 | 455 | 40 | 75 |

Woosnam leads, 5 up
| Woosnam | 445 | 524 | 445 | 37 | 343 | 42 |
| Rafferty | 534 | 534 | 444 | 36 | 344 | 33 |

Greg Norman defeated Wayne Grady at 38th hole
| Norman | 544 | 434 | C54 | X | 243 | 435 | 454 | 34 | X |
| Grady | 544 | 434 | W44 | X | 453 | 434 | 444 | 35 | X |

Grady leads, 2 up
| Norman | 435 | 434 | 444 | 35 | 345 | 544 | 444 | 37 | 72 |
| Grady | 524 | 435 | 555 | 38 | 345 | 434 | 544 | 36 | 74 |

Match all-square
| Norman | 42 |
| Grady | 43 |

Mark McNulty defeated Hale Irwin, 6 and 4
Irwin	444	424	434	33	443	435	455	37	70
McNulty	433	434	444	33	334	434	345	33	66

McNulty leads, 4 up
Irwin	536	524	344	36	344	4C
McNulty	434	534	434	34	334	53

SEMI-FINALS

Ian Woosnam defeated Chip Beck, 5 and 3
Beck	435	424	444	34	43C	434	445	XX
Woosnam	434	434	444	34	24W	434	344	XX

Woosnam leads, 3 up
Beck	324	434	545	34	245	444
Woosnam	434	424	444	33	354	433

Mark McNulty defeated Greg Norman, 3 and 2
Norman	424	534	544	35	334	434	444	33	68
McNulty	433	434	444	33	445	533	444	36	69

Norman leads, 1 up
Norman	434	533	444	34	444	324	5
McNulty	434	423	444	32	343	334	4

FINAL

Ian Woosnam defeated Mark McNulty, 4 and 2
Woosnam	344	333	444	32	344	443	343	32	64
McNulty	433	434	544	34	334	433	454	33	67

Woosnam leads, 3 up
Woosnam	434	434	445	35	244	433	3
McNulty	434	434	334	32	445	434	4

THIRD PLACE

Greg Norman tied with Chip Beck
Beck	435	434	444	35	344	434	443	33	68
Norman	424	434	445	34	344	434	44C	XX

PRIZE MONEY: Woosnam £100,000; McNulty £60,000; Beck, Norman £30,000 each; Faldo, Rafferty, Grady, Irwin £18,500 each; Kawagishi, Ballesteros, Langer, Brown £14,000 each.

LEGEND: C—conceded hole to opponent; W—won hole by concession without holing out; X—no total score.

BMW International Open

Golfplatz Munchen Nordekhenried, Munich, Germany
Par 36-36—72; 6,910 yards

September 20-23
purse, £400,000

	SCORES				TOTAL	MONEY
Paul Azinger	63	73	73	68	277	£66,660
David Feherty	62	72	71	72	277	44,400
(Azinger defeated Feherty on first extra hole.)						
Peter O'Malley	70	71	71	66	278	25,040
Russell Claydon	66	76	67	70	279	20,000
Jay Haas	73	70	68	69	280	16,940
David A. Russell	66	79	69	67	281	13,000

	SCORES				TOTAL	MONEY
Jose Maria Olazabal	70	73	69	69	281	13,000
Vijay Singh	66	81	69	66	282	8,580
Mike Clayton	69	75	69	69	282	8,580
Philip Walton	71	73	71	67	282	8,580
Jesper Parnevik	71	71	70	70	282	8,580
David J. Russell	73	75	72	63	283	6,192
Ove Sellberg	71	74	69	69	283	6,192
Jose Coceres	69	75	70	69	283	6,192
Anders Forsbrand	68	74	73	68	283	6,192
Tom Purtzer	71	71	72	69	283	6,192
Jeff Pinsent	73	74	69	68	284	5,280
David Frost	71	74	70	69	284	5,280
Steven Richardson	71	74	68	72	285	4,750
Steven Bowman	70	75	70	70	285	4,750
Bill Longmuir	69	74	70	72	285	4,750
Ian Mosey	70	72	70	73	285	4,750
Noel Ratcliffe	71	75	69	71	286	4,020
Ross McFarlane	72	75	70	69	286	4,020
Armando Saavedra	71	76	71	68	286	4,020
Mark Mouland	73	75	71	67	286	4,020
Sven Struver	69	79	69	69	286	4,020
Neal Briggs	68	77	72	69	286	4,020
Manuel Moreno	68	77	70	71	286	4,020
Kevin Dickens	68	76	72	70	286	4,020
Rob Huff	71	76	73	67	287	3,373.33
Joakim Haeggman	71	73	73	70	287	3,373.33
Rick Hartmann	66	77	74	70	287	3,373.33
Manuel Calero	66	75	71	76	288	3,200
Johan Rystrom	71	76	70	72	289	3,040
Grant Turner	71	77	69	72	289	3,040
Vicente Fernandez	69	72	77	71	289	3,040
Juan Quiros Segura	69	77	72	72	290	2,600
Jose Rozadilla	73	73	70	74	290	2,600
Paul Kent	72	74	72	72	290	2,600
David R. Jones	72	75	71	72	290	2,600
Chris Cookson	72	76	69	73	290	2,600
Heinz P. Thuel	68	77	74	71	290	2,600
Paul Curry	71	74	71	74	290	2,600
Torsten Giedeon	69	74	74	73	290	2,600
Brian Marchbank	72	74	71	74	291	2,040
Martin Sludds	69	77	73	72	291	2,040
Stephen Hamill	70	77	75	69	291	2,040
Paul Carrigill	70	75	75	71	291	2,040
Wraith Grant	69	76	72	74	291	2,040
Payne Stewart	70	73	76	72	291	2,040

Epson Grand Prix of Europe

St. Pierre Golf and Country Club, Chepstow, Wales
Par 36-35—71; 6,883 yards

September 27-30
purse, £400,000

	SCORES				TOTAL	MONEY
Ian Woosnam	65	67	67	72	271	£66,660
Jose Maria Olazabal	71	67	67	69	274	34,720
Mark McNulty	67	67	68	72	274	34,720
Miguel Angel Martin	75	72	63	65	275	16,780
Ronan Rafferty	72	71	65	67	275	16,780
Brett Ogle	66	70	71	68	275	16,780

	SCORES	TOTAL	MONEY
Johan Rystrom	73 69 68 66	276	8,720
Bernhard Langer	71 68 70 67	276	8,720
Mark James	67 71 70 68	276	8,720
Peter Fowler	70 69 69 68	276	8,720
Colin Montgomerie	65 72 70 69	276	8,720
Severiano Ballesteros	67 71 68 70	276	8,720
Mats Lanner	72 69 70 66	277	6,190
Frank Nobilo	69 67 71 70	277	6,190
David Williams	69 70 73 66	278	5,680
Des Smyth	69 69 71 69	278	5,680
Ross Drummond	71 70 72 67	280	4,920
Peter O'Malley	68 72 72 68	280	4,920
Vicente Fernandez	70 72 70 68	280	4,920
Malcolm Mackenzie	74 71 67 68	280	4,920
Sandy Lyle	70 71 69 70	280	4,920
Anders Forsbrand	71 74 70 66	281	4,480
Howard Clark	72 69 72 69	282	4,180
Vijay Singh	73 68 71 70	282	4,180
Rodger Davis	71 70 69 72	282	4,180
Mike Clayton	69 72 69 72	282	4,180
Tony Johnstone	72 71 72 68	283	3,640
Barry Lane	73 72 68 70	283	3,640
Magnus Persson	75 71 67 70	283	3,640
Carl Mason	71 71 69 72	283	3,640
David Feherty	71 73 67 72	283	3,640
Jim Rutledge	70 72 72 70	284	3,160
Russell Claydon	73 69 72 70	284	3,160
Sam Torrance	72 69 71 72	284	3,160
Steven Richardson	69 73 70 72	284	3,160
Mark Roe	70 75 69 71	285	2,800
Stephen McAllister	70 75 69 71	285	2,800
Gordon J. Brand	69 73 72 71	285	2,800
Gordon Brand, Jr.	74 69 72 70	285	2,800
Craig Parry	71 70 68 76	285	2,800
Anders Sorensen	74 71 73 68	286	2,400
Miguel Angel Jimenez	73 66 74 73	286	2,400
Rick Hartmann	72 67 73 74	286	2,400
Eamonn Darcy	70 71 71 74	286	2,400
Daniel Silva	72 70 70 74	286	2,400
Paul Broadhurst	71 73 70 73	287	2,000
Jose Maria Canizares	66 75 73 73	287	2,000
James Spence	73 70 72 72	287	2,000
Costantino Rocca	70 73 72 72	287	2,000
Richard Boxall	72 72 76 67	287	2,000

Mercedes German Masters

Stuttgarter Golf Club, Stuttgart, Germany
Par 36-36—72; 6,839 yards

October 4-7
purse, £450,000

	SCORES	TOTAL	MONEY
Sam Torrance	70 65 64 73	272	£75,000
Bernhard Langer	66 67 74 68	275	39,065
Ian Woosnam	75 69 69 62	275	39,065
Jose Maria Olazabal	69 70 69 69	277	20,780
Mike Harwood	71 67 70 69	277	20,780
David Feherty	69 68 74 67	278	15,750
Scott Simpson	72 67 71 70	280	13,500

	SCORES				TOTAL	MONEY
Mark McNulty	71	68	72	70	281	10,110
Sandy Lyle	69	72	71	69	281	10,110
Paul Broadhurst	67	73	69	72	281	10,110
Derrick Cooper	71	72	71	68	282	8,010
Johan Rystrom	72	73	68	69	282	8,010
Russell Claydon	72	73	69	69	283	7,060
Peter O'Malley	76	71	67	69	283	7,060
Grant Turner	68	71	71	74	284	6,082
Peter Fowler	70	73	71	70	284	6,082
Gordon Brand, Jr.	76	68	69	71	284	6,082
Ronan Rafferty	71	74	71	68	284	6,082
Jose Rivero	69	76	71	68	284	6,082
Craig Stadler	73	73	70	69	285	5,265
Frank Nobilo	68	72	72	73	285	5,265
Mike Clayton	72	71	73	69	285	5,265
Mark Roe	71	70	72	73	286	4,995
David Williams	72	72	72	71	287	4,320
Richard Boxall	69	77	69	72	287	4,320
Eduardo Romero	73	70	73	71	287	4,320
Luis Carbonetti	74	71	71	71	287	4,320
Anders Forsbrand	70	77	69	71	287	4,320
Ross Drummond	76	70	72	69	287	4,320
Chip Beck	72	73	71	71	287	4,320
Miguel Angel Martin	75	72	73	67	287	4,320
David J. Russell	76	71	70	70	287	4,320
Manuel Calero	73	71	74	70	288	3,510
Gordon J. Brand	72	75	70	71	288	3,510
Vijay Singh	74	71	75	68	288	3,510
Peter Teravainen	72	74	72	70	288	3,510
David A. Russell	73	74	68	73	288	3,510
Carl Mason	75	71	72	71	289	3,150
Severiano Ballesteros	70	72	75	72	289	3,150
Eric Giraud	72	75	72	70	289	3,150
Jesper Parnevik	73	70	75	72	290	2,700
Robert Lee	70	76	71	73	290	2,700
Tony Charnley	73	74	74	69	290	2,700
Antonio Garrido	69	73	72	76	290	2,700
Barry Lane	72	70	74	74	290	2,700
Bill Malley	69	76	74	71	290	2,700
Chris Moody	72	74	70	74	290	2,700
Magnus Persson	72	74	73	72	291	2,160
Andrew Sherborne	70	75	76	70	291	2,160
Colin Montgomerie	72	75	72	72	291	2,160
Thomas Goegele	70	73	74	74	291	2,160
Martin Poxon	75	69	73	74	291	2,160

Dunhill Cup

Old Course, St. Andrews, Scotland
Par 36-36—72; 6,933 yards

October 11-14

FIRST ROUND

JAPAN DEFEATED ARGENTINA, 2-1
Satoshi Higashi (J) defeated Miguel Guzman, 68-70; Yoshinori Kaneko (J) defeated Vicente Fernandez, 72-73; Eduardo Romero (A) defeated Hajime Meshiai, 73-76.

FRANCE DEFEATED UNITED STATES, 2-1/2—1/2
Marc Farry (F) defeated Mark Calcavecchia, 70-73; Jean Van de Velde (F) halved with Curtis Strange, 69-69; Emmanuel Dussart (F) defeated Tom Kite, 73-74.

SPAIN DEFEATED SWEDEN, 2-1
Miguel Angel Jimenez (Sp) defeated Ove Sellberg, 67-72; Jose Rivero (Sp) defeated Magnus Persson, 69-77; Mats Lanner (Sw) defeated Jose Maria Canizares, 68-71.

ENGLAND DEFEATED THAILAND, 3-0
Richard Boxall (E) defeated Sukree Onsham, 74-77; Howard Clark (E) defeated Suthep Messawat, 68-78; Mark James (E) defeated Boonchu Ruengkit, 70-79.

SCOTLAND DEFEATED MEXICO, 2-1/2—1/2
Sandy Lyle (S) defeated Rafael Alarcon, 68-73; Stephen McAllister (S) defeated Enrique Serna, 73-77; Sam Torrance (S) halved with Carlos Espinosa, 69-69.

IRELAND DEFEATED KOREA, 3-0
Ronan Rafferty (I) defeated Choi Sang Ho, 70-73; Philip Walton (I) defeated Park Nam Shin, 71-74; David Feherty (I) defeated Choi Yoon Soo, 69-81.

WALES DEFEATED TAIPEI, 2-1
Ian Woosnam (W) defeated Hsieh Yu Shu, 71-78; Chen Liang Hsi (T) defeated Mark Mouland, 72-73; Philip Parkin (W) defeated Kuo Chi Hsiung, 77-78.

NEW ZEALAND DEFEATED AUSTRALIA, 2-1
Frank Nobilo (NZ) defeated Greg Norman, 67-76; Simon Owen (NZ) defeated Wayne Grady, 74-78; Rodger Davis (A) defeated Greg Turner, 66-75.

(Each player on each losing team received US$7,500.)

SECOND ROUND

JAPAN DEFEATED FRANCE, 3-0
Higashi (J) defeated Farry, 71-80; Kaneko (J) defeated Dussart, 71-75; Meshiai (J) defeated Van de Velde, 70-72.

IRELAND DEFEATED SPAIN, 2-1
Feherty (I) defeated Jimenez, 76-77; Canizares (S) defeated Rafferty, 70-71; Walton (I) defeated Rivero, 70-82.

NEW ZEALAND DEFEATED WALES, 2-1
Woosnam (W) defeated Nobilo, 67-70; Owen (NZ) defeated Mouland, 72-83; Turner (NZ) defeated Parkin, 72-76.

ENGLAND DEFEATED SCOTLAND, 2-1
Boxall (E) defeated McAllister, 73-75; Lyle (S) defeated Clark, 75-77; James (E) defeated Torrance, 72-73.

(Each player on each losing team received US$15,000.)

SEMI-FINALS

IRELAND DEFEATED NEW ZEALAND, 2-1/2—1/2
Walton (I) defeated Owen, 70-71; Rafferty (I) halved with Nobilo, 68-68; Feherty (I) defeated Turner, 68-69.

ENGLAND DEFEATED JAPAN, 2-1
Clark (E) defeated Higashi, 70-70, on first playoff hole; Kaneko (J) defeated Boxall, 69-70; James (E) defeated Meshiai, 70-70, on first playoff hole.

PLAYOFF FOR THIRD-FOURTH PLACES

NEW ZEALAND DEFEATED JAPAN, 2-1
Turner (NZ) defeated Higashi, 72-75; Kaneko (J) defeated Owen, 74-77; Nobilo (NZ) defeated Meshiai, 73-77.

(Each New Zealand player received US$36,666; each Japanese player received US$26,666.)

488 / THE EUROPEAN TOUR

FINAL

IRELAND DEFEATED ENGLAND, 3-1/2—2-1/2
Morning—James (E) halved with Walton, 72-72; Rafferty (I) defeated Boxall, 71-73; Clark (E) defeated Feherty, 73-74. Afternoon—James (E) defeated Walton, 76-77; Rafferty (I) defeated Boxall, 71-77; Feherty (I) tied with Clark, won playoff on third extra hole.

(Each Irish player received US$100,000; each English player received US$50,000.)

Austrian Open

Gut Altenann Golf and Country Club, Salzburg, Austria
Par 36-36—72; 6,806 yards

October 11-14
purse, £250,000

	SCORES				TOTAL	MONEY
Bernhard Langer	65	66	72	68	271	£41,660
Lanny Wadkins	67	68	68	68	271	27,760
(Langer defeated Wadkins on third extra hole.)						
Des Smyth	70	69	72	62	273	15,650
Manuel Moreno	74	67	67	67	275	11,550
Miguel Angel Martin	68	69	70	68	275	11,550
Gordon Manson	72	67	72	65	276	8,750
Chris Moody	70	69	70	69	278	7,500
David J. Russell	70	74	66	69	279	5,925
Rick Hartmann	70	70	66	73	279	5,925
Ross Drummond	72	70	71	67	280	4,800
Sandy Stephen	70	77	66	67	280	4,800
Grant Turner	71	72	68	70	281	4,160
Juan Quiros Segura	67	72	70	72	281	4,160
Jack Nicklaus	71	72	70	69	282	3,745
David Gilford	68	70	71	73	282	3,745
David R. Jones	69	70	75	69	283	3,373.33
David Whelan	71	75	70	67	283	3,373.33
Johan Rystrom	72	75	67	69	283	3,373.33
Joakim Haeggman	71	71	72	70	284	3,100
Anders Sorensen	69	72	78	66	285	2,812.50
Anders Forsbrand	72	72	70	71	285	2,812.50
Paul Carrigill	70	73	70	72	285	2,812.50
Ignacio Gervas	75	68	69	73	285	2,812.50
Alberto Binaghi	70	67	73	75	285	2,812.50
Mike Clayton	67	68	74	76	285	2,812.50
Gordon J. Brand	69	76	70	71	286	2,325
Alexander Cejka	73	74	71	68	286	2,325
David Williams	71	70	73	72	286	2,325
Stephen Hamill	70	73	71	72	286	2,325
Tony Charnley	73	71	70	72	286	2,325
Brian Marchbank	71	72	70	73	286	2,325
Peter Fowler	70	75	68	73	286	2,325
Bryan Norton	70	74	71	72	287	2,025
Peter Teravainen	73	69	73	72	287	2,025
Jeff Pinsent	69	73	73	73	288	1,675
Ken Brown	72	68	75	73	288	1,675
Jesper Parnevik	73	71	72	72	288	1,675
Paul Broadhurst	70	76	71	71	288	1,675
Paul Curry	73	71	74	70	288	1,675
Ronald Stelten	72	72	76	68	288	1,675
Costantino Rocca	68	74	72	74	288	1,675
Jose Davila	73	69	72	74	288	1,675
John Hawksworth	71	71	72	74	288	1,675

	SCORES				TOTAL	MONEY
Denis Durnian	71	75	67	75	288	1,675
Bill Longmuir	69	72	70	77	288	1,675
Bradley Hughes	67	76	68	77	288	1,675
Noel Ratcliffe	71	74	74	70	289	1,325
Torsten Giedeon	68	74	72	75	289	1,325
Andrew Murray	73	72	71	74	290	1,175
Paul Hoad	74	69	74	73	290	1,175
David A. Russell	74	70	74	72	290	1,175
Robert Lee	75	72	76	67	290	1,175

Portuguese Open-TPC

Quinta do Lago, Algarve, Portugal
Par 36-36—72; 7,095 yards

October 18-21
purse, £275,000

	SCORES				TOTAL	MONEY
Michael McLean	69	69	65	71	274	£45,825
Gordon Brand, Jr.	68	70	68	69	275	23,872.50
Mike Harwood	70	68	71	66	275	23,872.50
Mark James	68	69	70	69	276	12,702.50
Paul Broadhurst	70	69	68	69	276	12,702.50
Rick Hartmann	68	68	73	68	277	8,937.50
Ove Sellberg	67	68	70	72	277	8,937.50
Martin Poxon	73	68	69	68	278	6,517.50
David Williams	72	69	69	68	278	6,517.50
Juan Quiros Segura	72	68	68	71	279	5,280
Stephen Bennett	73	69	70	67	279	5,280
Steven Richardson	67	74	72	67	280	4,165
Colin Montgomerie	70	68	74	68	280	4,165
Mark McNulty	72	68	69	71	280	4,165
Grant Turner	67	73	69	71	280	4,165
Peter McWhinney	70	71	71	68	280	4,165
Magnus Persson	64	67	75	74	280	4,165
Mats Lanner	72	72	68	69	281	3,232.86
Peter Teravainen	71	69	70	71	281	3,232.86
Peter Mitchell	72	70	70	69	281	3,232.86
James Spence	71	68	72	70	281	3,232.86
Eamonn Darcy	72	68	72	69	281	3,232.86
Brian Barnes	75	65	71	70	281	3,232.86
Carl Mason	68	69	73	71	281	3,232.86
Ian Mosey	69	75	70	68	282	2,681.67
Mark Roe	70	68	70	74	282	2,681.67
Joakim Haeggman	69	66	73	74	282	2,681.67
Anders Forsbrand	72	72	67	71	282	2,681.67
Manuel Moreno	71	74	69	68	282	2,681.67
Gavin Levenson	71	71	70	70	282	2,681.67
Kevin Dickens	73	68	71	71	283	2,254
Roger Chapman	74	71	68	70	283	2,254
Des Smyth	70	71	71	71	283	2,254
Eduardo Romero	73	72	68	70	283	2,254
Sandy Stephen	71	73	67	72	283	2,254
Mikael Krantz	72	70	71	71	284	2,035
Mark Mouland	73	68	73	70	284	2,035
Christy O'Connor, Jr.	71	74	66	73	284	2,035
Ross McFarlane	71	74	70	70	285	1,732.50
Brian Marchbank	73	70	71	71	285	1,732.50
Brett Ogle	70	71	73	71	285	1,732.50
Alberto Binaghi	68	76	67	74	285	1,732.50

	SCORES				TOTAL	MONEY
Vijay Singh	75	70	73	67	285	1,732.50
John Bland	73	70	70	72	285	1,732.50
Ronald Stelten	69	71	71	74	285	1,732.50
Jim Rutledge	72	70	72	71	285	1,732.50
David R. Jones	70	72	69	75	286	1,347.50
Antonio Garrido	77	67	74	68	286	1,347.50
Derrick Cooper	73	72	70	71	286	1,347.50
Frank Nobilo	69	72	70	75	286	1,347.50
Denis Durnian	74	67	73	72	286	1,347.50
Russell Claydon	71	70	72	73	286	1,347.50

Volvo Masters

Valderrama Golf Club, Sotogrande, Spain
Par 35-36—71; 6,951 yards

October 25-28
purse, £450,000

	SCORES				TOTAL	MONEY
Mike Harwood	70	72	73	71	286	£75,000
Sam Torrance	69	73	72	73	287	39,065
Steven Richardson	71	73	70	73	287	39,065
Bernhard Langer	72	71	72	73	288	17,962.50
Anders Forsbrand	75	69	71	73	288	17,962.50
Jose Maria Olazabal	72	69	74	73	288	17,962.50
Mark McNulty	73	73	71	71	288	17,962.50
Colin Montgomerie	71	72	71	75	289	10,955
David Feherty	70	77	67	75	289	10,955
Rodger Davis	74	71	74	72	291	9,300
Tony Johnstone	74	74	74	70	292	7,650
Howard Clark	73	73	70	76	292	7,650
Gordon Brand, Jr.	79	68	71	74	292	7,650
Vicente Fernandez	76	73	73	70	292	7,650
Rick Hartmann	74	71	75	72	292	7,650
Christy O'Connor, Jr.	72	74	71	76	293	6,140
Jose Rivero	76	65	75	77	293	6,140
Grant Turner	71	77	73	72	293	6,140
Miguel Angel Martin	72	73	76	72	293	6,140
Vijay Singh	74	74	73	72	293	6,140
Sandy Lyle	73	74	75	72	294	5,497.50
Ian Woosnam	74	72	76	72	294	5,497.50
Ove Sellberg	78	72	73	72	295	5,227.50
Ronan Rafferty	71	74	76	74	295	5,227.50
Mark Mouland	72	76	74	74	296	4,890
Des Smyth	74	72	75	75	296	4,890
Anders Sorensen	75	79	69	73	296	4,890
Mark Roe	75	74	76	72	297	4,485
Paul Broadhurst	78	77	72	70	297	4,485
Jose Maria Canizares	73	72	77	75	297	4,485
Frank Nobilo	78	74	73	73	298	4,147.50
David Williams	72	73	79	74	298	4,147.50
James Spence	77	72	75	75	299	3,900
Michael McLean	74	79	73	73	299	3,900
Mike Clayton	73	73	80	73	299	3,900
Jim Rutledge	72	78	73	77	300	3,675
Mats Lanner	73	76	74	77	300	3,675
Magnus Persson	70	80	75	77	302	3,495
Miguel Angel Jimenez	75	74	76	77	302	3,495
Malcolm Mackenzie	77	73	73	80	303	3,270
Peter Fowler	74	75	79	75	303	3,270

	SCORES			TOTAL	MONEY
Eduardo Romero	78	73	74	78	303	3,270
John Bland	73	76	76	79	304	3,090
Stephen McAllister	79	74	76	76	305	3,000
Mark James	78	74	77	77	306	2,910
Richard Boxall	75	82	72	78	307	2,820
Costantino Rocca	75	77	77	79	308	2,730
Paul Way	79	76	75	84	314	2,640
Philip Walton	78	81	75	82	316	2,550
Eamonn Darcy	72	84				2,280
Russell Claydon	75	75				2,280
Brett Ogle	74	72				2,280
Roger Chapman	74	72				2,280
Derrick Cooper	81	76	72			2,280

The African Tours

Zimbabwe Open

Chapman Golf Club, Harare, Zimbabwe
Par 36-36—72; 7,151 yards

January 11-14
purse, £46,431.86

	SCORES			TOTAL	MONEY
Grant Turner	68	71	71	71	281	£7,634.79
Lee Jones	69	72	71	70	282	5,066.38
Steven Richardson	73	73	66	74	286	2,871.85
Stephen McAllister	74	73	68	72	287	2,113.25
Gordon J. Brand	75	69	71	72	287	2,113.25
Brian Barnes	74	73	68	73	288	1,598.48
Paul Affleck	70	74	71	74	289	1,381.74
Charles Giddins	75	73	73	69	290	1,034.05
Craig Maltman	71	71	78	70	290	1,034.05
Brendan McGovern	71	71	75	73	290	1,034.05
Bill McColl	73	71	75	72	291	740.99
Mark Litton	74	75	71	71	291	740.99
David Blakeman	72	71	75	73	291	740.99
John Vingoe	78	74	66	73	291	740.99
David Wood	74	74	69	74	291	740.99
John McHenry	68	79	69	75	291	740.99
Paul Hurring	74	76	73	69	292	589.27
*Craig Singleton	78	70	73	71	292	
William Koen	69	73	76	74	292	589.27
Jonathan Lomas	75	70	73	74	292	589.27
Andrew Clapp	69	77	71	75	292	589.27
Andrew Stubbs	73	76	70	74	293	549.99
Brian Waites	78	73	71	72	294	512.73
James Lebbie	77	74	71	72	294	512.73

	SCORES				TOTAL	MONEY
Joe Higgins	74	73	75	72	294	512.73
Wayne Stephens	73	73	78	70	294	512.73
Glenn Ralph	78	73	74	70	295	445.68
David Jones	75	74	75	71	295	445.68
Paul Carman	74	69	77	75	295	445.68
Simon Townend	73	71	76	75	295	445.68
Wayne Henry	75	75	69	76	295	445.68

Zambia Open

Lusaka Golf Club, Lusaka, Zambia
Par 35-38—73; 7,216 yards

January 18-21
purse, £75,000

	SCORES				TOTAL	MONEY
Gordon J. Brand	70	74	68	72	284	£12,500
Phil Golding	71	73	70	74	288	6,505
Craig Maltman	71	74	75	68	288	6,505
Paul Carrigill	75	72	72	70	289	3,180
Steven Richardson	75	67	75	72	289	3,180
Paul Carman	78	72	72	67	289	3,180
Jeremy Robinson	72	72	77	69	290	1,935
Mark Litton	74	73	72	71	290	1,935
Lee Jones	73	77	72	68	290	1,935
Wayne Stephens	74	72	72	73	291	1,390
Adam Hunter	73	71	72	75	291	1,390
David Jones	75	73	74	69	291	1,390
Brian Barnes	73	75	72	72	292	1,153.33
Jonathan Lomas	73	72	72	75	292	1,153.33
Michael Ingham	74	73	74	71	292	1,153.33
Andrew Clapp	73	71	73	76	293	1,060
Grant Turner	72	75	75	72	294	1,010
Andrew Hare	77	73	73	72	295	907
Paul Affleck	74	77	73	71	295	907
Joe Higgins	71	76	74	74	295	907
John Vingoe	73	74	75	73	295	907
David Wood	74	72	78	71	295	907
Wayne Henry	73	74	75	74	296	820
Brian Waites	73	74	72	77	296	820
Jeremy Bennett	73	74	73	77	297	765
William Koen	71	75	73	78	297	765
Nick Godin	73	78	74	72	297	765
Peter Harrison	75	72	78	73	298	710
Tim Price	74	76	76	72	298	710
John McHenry	72	75	81	71	299	610
Michael Brunton	76	76	74	73	299	610
Robert Purdie	75	74	75	75	299	610
John Price	70	80	73	76	299	610
James Lebbie	77	74	73	75	299	610
Richard Fish	77	77	73	72	299	610
Brendan McGovern	73	79	74	73	299	610
Ian Campbell	77	72	78	72	299	610

Kenya Open

Muthaiga Golf Club, Nairobi, Kenya
Par 36-35—71; 6,765 yards

January 24-27
purse, £75,205

	SCORES				TOTAL	MONEY
Christy O'Connor, Jr.	66	67	67	71	271	£12,500.70
Chris Platts	67	68	67	71	273	8,329.03
Paul Eales	69	72	66	67	274	4,697.19
Steven Richardson	68	73	68	66	275	3,186.49
Paul Affleck	69	70	69	67	275	3,186.49
Mark Litton	66	71	70	68	275	3,186.49
Wayne Henry	70	70	71	65	276	2,251.05
David Jones	67	71	70	69	277	1,875.88
Jeremy Robinson	70	70	74	64	278	1,590.75
Mark Mouland	69	70	66	73	278	1,590.75
Adam Hunter	68	70	74	67	279	1,293.08
David Wood	69	73	70	67	279	1,293.08
Andrew Hare	66	72	70	71	279	1,293.08
Jeremy Bennett	71	72	72	65	280	1,058.01
Graham Griffiths	74	70	71	65	280	1,058.01
Craig Maltman	67	71	73	69	280	1,058.01
Stephen Hamill	71	67	72	70	280	1,058.01
Grant Turner	73	65	72	70	280	1,058.01
Paul Carrigill	70	70	68	73	281	930.43
Alan Saddington	72	68	73	69	282	877.93
Donald Stirling	70	70	72	70	282	877.93
James Spence	67	71	71	73	282	877.93
Richard Fish	70	71	71	71	283	821.60
Peter Harrison	72	70	69	72	283	821.60
James Lebbie	69	72	75	68	284	754.14
Joe Higgins	74	69	73	68	284	754.14
Andrew Clapp	71	75	68	70	284	754.14
Bill McColl	70	72	71	71	284	754.14
Ian Spencer	74	69	72	70	285	675.27
Charles Farrar	72	69	71	73	285	675.27
Michael Ingham	72	72	67	74	285	675.27

ICL International

Zwartkop Country Club, Verwoerdburg, South Africa
Par 36-36—72; 7,125 yards

January 10-13
purse, R250,000

	SCORES				TOTAL	MONEY
Gavin Levenson	67	68	66	68	269	R40,000
Wayne Westner	66	69	69	67	271	28,750
Jimmy Johnson	69	67	68	68	272	17,500
Justin Hobday	68	71	70	64	273	12,500
Fulton Allem	73	67	65	69	274	9,750
Simon Hobday	68	69	68	69	274	9,750
Allan Henning	68	69	70	68	275	6,062.50
Trevor Dodds	70	73	63	69	275	6,062.50
Hugh Baiocchi	65	67	72	71	275	6,062.50
Jeff Hawkes	70	67	65	73	275	6,062.50
David Feherty	65	73	67	71	276	4,500
Desmond Terblanche	72	70	70	65	277	4,000
Phil Simmons	67	71	70	69	277	4,000
John Bland	68	70	70	69	277	4,000

		SCORES			TOTAL	MONEY
John Fourie	71	74	68	65	278	3,562.50
Wayne Player	70	71	69	68	278	3,562.50
Kevin Stone	72	68	71	68	279	3,250
Brian Evans	72	71	69	67	279	3,250
Bobby Lincoln	73	69	68	69	279	3,250
John Daly	70	70	72	68	280	2,868.75
Thomas Tolles, Jr.	71	67	73	69	280	2,868.75
Chip Sullivan	72	71	68	69	280	2,868.75
Steve van Vuuren	66	72	71	71	280	2,868.75
Tom Lehman	71	73	69	69	282	2,450
Wayne Bradley	72	70	70	70	282	2,450
Schalk van der Merwe	70	71	71	70	282	2,450
Tony Johnstone	70	67	73	72	282	2,450
Scott Dunlap	71	67	72	72	282	2,450
Chris Williams	68	71	70	73	282	2,450
James Kingston	68	73	67	74	282	2,450

Lexington PGA Championship

Wanderers Golf Club, Johannesburg, South Africa
Par 35-35—70; 6,960 yards

January 17-20
purse, R250,000

		SCORES			TOTAL	MONEY
Fulton Allem	61	71	67	67	266	R40,000
Chris Davison	65	71	65	67	268	28,750
Richard Kaplan	67	70	67	65	269	17,500
Trevor Dodds	68	69	68	66	271	9,150
Tony Johnstone	63	69	70	69	271	9,150
Wayne Westner	67	70	67	67	271	9,150
Robin Freeman	72	65	63	71	271	9,150
Wayne Bradley	64	65	71	71	271	9,150
Justin Hobday	64	69	69	70	272	5,500
Stuart Smith	71	68	68	66	273	4,750
Kevin Stone	69	66	67	71	273	4,750
Sean Pappas	70	66	74	64	274	4,250
Mark Wiltshire	71	70	66	68	275	3,791.67
Gavin Levenson	69	64	71	71	275	3,791.67
Hugh Baiocchi	66	71	68	70	275	3,791.67
Simon Hobday	68	72	68	68	276	3,250
Andre Bossert	67	70	70	69	276	3,250
David Feherty	68	69	70	69	276	3,250
Wayne Player	68	67	71	70	276	3,250
Ashley Roestoff	67	68	70	71	276	3,250
Phil Simmons	67	71	72	68	278	2,675
Desmond Terblanche	70	69	70	69	278	2,675
Mark James	72	70	67	69	278	2,675
Allan Henning	66	68	73	71	278	2,675
Glenn James	70	68	69	71	278	2,675
Hugh Royer	73	68	66	71	278	2,675
Roger Wessels	67	69	69	73	278	2,675
Steve van Vuuren	73	66	71	69	279	2,230
Bruce Vaughan	70	68	70	71	279	2,230
John Daly	71	66	71	71	279	2,230
Tom Lehman	67	69	72	71	279	2,230
Teddy Webber	71	69	67	72	279	2,230

Protea Assurance South African Open

Royal Cape Golf Club, Cape Town, South Africa
Par 36-36—72

January 24-27
purse, R325,000

	SCORES				TOTAL	MONEY
Trevor Dodds	72	71	72	70	285	R52,000
Hugh Royer	75	71	69	71	286	37,375
Mark James	79	72	66	71	288	22,750
Robbie Stewart	75	71	73	70	289	12,837.50
Simon Hobday	74	73	69	73	289	12,837.50
Desmond Terblanche	75	66	74	74	289	12,837.50
Ian Palmer	70	74	70	75	289	12,837.50
Tom Lehman	77	71	70	73	291	7,258.33
Thomas Tolles, Jr.	72	74	71	74	291	7,258.33
Jeff Hawkes	74	72	70	75	291	7,258.33
Roger Wessels	75	72	78	67	292	5,525
David Feherty	74	71	70	77	292	5,525
Wayne Player	75	68	70	79	292	5,525
John Bland	80	70	67	76	293	4,875
John Daly	76	67	81	70	294	4,229.64
Wayne Bradley	77	74	71	72	294	4,229.64
Allan Henning	77	72	72	73	294	4,229.64
Wilhelm Winsnes	73	75	74	72	294	4,229.64
Kevin Johnson	76	73	71	74	294	4,229.64
Ron McCann	75	70	73	76	294	4,229.64
Gavin Levenson	72	71	74	77	294	4,229.64
Ashley Roestoff	75	75	74	71	295	3,477.50
Steve Wilson	77	73	74	71	295	3,477.50
Hugh Baiocchi	75	74	73	73	295	3,477.50
Sean Pappas	78	72	70	75	295	3,477.50
Richard Kaplan	76	74	68	77	295	3,477.50
Hendrik Buhrmann	75	75	74	72	296	3,136.25
Phil Jonas	81	69	72	74	296	3,136.25
Noel Maart	74	74	76	73	297	2,743.93
De Wet Basson	76	73	73	75	297	2,743.93
Brian Mahon	76	73	73	75	297	2,743.93
Phillip Hatchett	80	71	70	76	297	2,743.93
Wayne Westner	74	75	71	77	297	2,743.93
Nico van Rensburg	77	74	68	78	297	2,743.93
Marty Schiene	76	74	69	78	297	2,743.93

AECI Charity Classic

Rand Park Golf Club, Johannesburg, South Africa
Par 36-36—72; 7,320 yards

January 31 - February 3
purse, R250,000

	SCORES				TOTAL	MONEY
John Daly	70	67	62	65	264	R40,000
David Feherty	62	70	66	67	265	23,750
Chris Williams	65	65	72	68	270	17,500
John Bland	67	68	70	69	274	11,500
Andre Cruce	66	69	67	72	274	11,500
Charlie Whittington	68	71	69	67	275	6,650
Bob McDonnell	67	69	70	69	275	6,650
Alan Pate	70	69	68	68	275	6,650
Tom Lehman	70	68	68	69	275	6,650

		SCORES			TOTAL	MONEY
Mark Carnevale	71	69	75	70	275	6,650
Hendrik Buhrmann	69	67	70	70	276	4,250
Steve van Vuuren	67	70	68	71	276	4,250
Chris Davison	67	70	67	72	276	4,250
Richard Kaplan	70	73	67	67	277	3,562.50
Phil Jonas	70	72	65	70	277	3,562.50
Hugh Biaocchi	70	72	64	71	277	3,562.50
Desmond Terblanche	71	69	74	73	277	3,562.50
Wayne Westner	70	72	69	67	278	2,975
Sean Pappas	70	72	68	68	278	2,975
Allan Henning	69	70	70	69	278	2,975
Teddy Webber	69	71	69	69	278	2,975
John Fourie	67	69	70	72	278	2,975
Gavin Levenson	69	71	66	72	278	2,975
Stuart Smith	70	72	71	66	279	2,450
Justin Hobday	70	68	72	69	279	2,450
Ashley Roestoff	72	67	71	69	279	2,450
Roger Wessels	69	73	68	69	279	2,450
Craigen Pappas	69	68	70	72	279	2,450
Ernie Els	68	69	70	72	279	2,450
Phil Simmons	69	69	69	72	279	2,450

Goodyear Classic

Humewood Golf Club, Port Elizabeth, South Africa
Par 35-37—72; 6,454 yards

February 7-10
purse, R250,000

		SCORES			TOTAL	MONEY
Phil Jonas	72	71	70	74	287	R40,000
Steve van Vuuren	79	69	70	70	288	28,700
Tony Johnstone	78	67	71	73	289	17,500
Hugh Baiocchi	76	73	71	70	290	12,500
Trevor Dodds	76	72	74	70	292	9,000
William Kane	76	75	60	71	292	9,000
John Mashego	77	70	69	76	292	9,000
Wayne Westner	77	74	74	68	293	5,875
Wayne Bradley	71	76	72	74	293	5,875
Gavin Levenson	73	78	73	70	294	4,437.50
Tom Lehman	72	81	71	70	294	4,437.50
Tony Louw	80	72	72	70	294	4,437.50
Marty Schiene	78	73	72	71	294	4,437.50
Craigen Pappas	73	76	74	72	295	3,625
Wayne Player	78	71	73	73	295	3,625
Chris Davison	78	71	71	75	295	3,625
Ron McCann	78	73	75	70	296	2,987.50
De Wet Basson	80	74	71	71	296	2,987.50
Bill McDonald	72	77	75	72	296	2,987.50
Bobby Lincoln	76	72	76	72	296	2,987.50
Marty Caifano	76	74	73	73	296	2,987.50
Schalk van der Merwe	74	73	75	74	296	2,987.50
Ian Palmer	77	74	72	73	296	2,987.50
Teddy Webber	73	79	70	74	296	2,987.50
Chip Sullivan	77	76	73	71	297	2,525
Alan Pate	78	76	70	73	297	2,525
John Fourie	79	71	73	74	297	2,525
John Bland	73	72	74	79	298	2,230
Glenn James	76	79	74	69	298	2,230
Graeme Watson	75	75	76	72	298	2,230

	SCORES	TOTAL	MONEY
Bob Byman	75 73 77 73	298	2,230
Peter van der Riet	75 72 75 76	298	2,230

Hollard Royal Swazi Sun Classic

Royal Swazi Spa and Country Club, Swaziland
Par 36-36—72; 6,708 yards

February 15-18
purse, R250,000

	SCORES	TOTAL	MONEY
John Daly	66 71 64 66	267	R40,000
John Bland	67 66 65 71	269	28,750
Tony Johnstone	68 68 68 69	273	17,500
Hugh Baiocchi	65 68 69 72	274	11,500
Allan Henning	67 68 67 72	274	11,500
Wayne Westner	70 65 70 70	275	8,250
De Wet Basson	67 70 67 71	275	8,250
Phil Jonas	69 70 70 67	276	5,875
Teddy Webber	67 69 69 71	276	5,875
Wayne Bradley	71 66 73 67	277	4,187.50
Richard Kaplan	72 71 67 67	277	4,187.50
Hugh Royer	70 69 70 68	277	4,187.50
Gary Gilchrist	71 72 66 68	277	4,187.50
Jim Becker	69 69 70 69	277	4,187.50
Mark Carnevale	69 68 70 70	277	4,187.50
Stuart Smith	70 73 69 66	278	3,090.63
Michael Green	72 72 68 66	278	3,090.63
Steve van Vuuren	69 70 72 67	278	3,090.63
Desmond Terblanche	73 71 67 67	278	3,090.63
Schalk van der Merwe	67 70 71 70	278	3,090.63
Jeff Hawkes	70 67 70 71	278	3,090.63
William Kane	72 67 68 71	278	3,090.63
Trevor Dodds	70 64 71 73	278	3,090.63
Graeme Watson	67 72 72 68	279	2,525
Wayne Player	67 69 74 69	279	2,525
Bobby Lincoln	72 72 66 69	279	2,525
Andre Cruse	70 68 71 70	279	2,525
Justin Hobday	71 69 69 70	279	2,525
Bobby Verwey, Jr.	69 71 75 65	280	2,058.33
Peter van der Riet	75 69 70 66	280	2,058.33
Phil Simmons	71 68 73 68	280	2,058.33
Kevin Stone	70 71 70 69	280	2,058.33
Sam Stein	69 71 70 70	280	2,058.33
Francis Quinn	74 68 68 70	280	2,058.33
Brian Mahon	70 68 71 71	280	2,058.33
Gavin Levenson	66 70 72 72	280	2,058.33
Thomas Tolles, Jr.	68 67 72 73	280	2,058.33

Palabora Classic

Hans Merensky Golf Club, Phalaborwa, South Africa
Par 36-36—72; 6,727 yards

February 21-24
purse, R250,000

	SCORES	TOTAL	MONEY
Tony Johnstone	73 70 65 66	274	R40,000
Wayne Westner	67 71 69 70	277	23,125
John Bland	67 71 68 71	277	23,125

	SCORES				TOTAL	MONEY
Justin Hobday	70	70	74	66	280	11,500
Jim Johnson	72	73	67	68	280	11,500
Scott Dunlap	71	73	68	69	281	8,250
Gavin Levenson	72	70	69	70	281	8,250
Mervyn Galant	69	74	72	67	282	5,875
Sean Collard	69	71	72	70	282	5,875
Trevor Dodds	70	76	69	68	283	4,437.50
Jeff Hawkes	69	72	73	69	283	4,437.50
Ernie Els	69	73	71	70	283	4,437.50
Stuart Smith	70	71	71	71	283	4,437.50
Wilhelm Winsnes	71	72	69	72	284	3,562.50
Wayne Player	70	69	72	73	284	3,562.50
Allan Henning	70	72	67	75	284	3,562.50
Ian Palmer	67	72	71	74	284	3,562.50
Marty Schiene	73	72	71	69	285	3,187.50
Roger Wessels	75	70	70	70	285	3,187.50
Desmond Terblanche	71	67	74	74	286	2,908.33
James Kingston	72	73	69	72	286	2,908.33
Bobby Lincoln	71	69	72	74	286	2,908.33
Steven Burnett	74	73	71	69	287	2,637.50
Robbie Stewart	73	69	73	72	287	2,637.50
Jim Becker	74	69	73	71	287	2,637.50
Teddy Webber	68	75	71	73	287	2,637.50
Bruce Vaughan	71	70	75	72	288	2,375
Phillip Hatchett	74	74	69	71	288	2,375
Tom Lehman	70	72	72	74	288	2,375
Bob McDonnell	73	70	74	72	289	2,187.50
Bob Byman	72	70	74	73	289	2,187.50

Dewar's White Label Trophy

Durban Country Club, Durban, South Africa
Par 36-36—72; 6,558 yards

February 28 - March 3
purse, R250,000

	SCORES				TOTAL	MONEY
John Bland	64	70	71	69	274	R40,000
Ray Townsend	70	70	67	68	275	28,750
John Daly	71	70	68	67	276	15,000
Thomas Tolles, Jr.	68	71	68	69	276	15,000
Roger Wessels	72	69	70	66	277	9,750
Bruce Vaughan	65	69	74	69	277	9,750
Tony Johnstone	71	69	69	69	278	7,500
Mark Wiltshire	72	69	69	69	279	6,250
Wayne Westner	71	72	67	70	280	5,500
Wilhelm Winsnes	70	70	69	72	281	5,000
Steven Burnett	70	71	75	66	282	4,250
Wayne Player	67	75	72	68	282	4,250
Irving Reid	70	69	73	70	282	4,250
Gavin Levenson	73	74	67	69	283	3,315.63
Derek James	73	71	69	70	283	3,315.63
Hendrik Buhrmann	71	67	75	70	283	3,315.63
Hugh Baiocchi	74	71	68	70	283	3,315.63
Justin Hobday	76	69	68	70	283	3,315.63
Simon Hobday	70	70	72	71	283	3,315.63
Trevor Dodds	73	68	70	72	283	3,315.63
Craigen Pappas	74	69	67	73	283	3,315.63
Kevin Johnson	73	73	70	68	284	2,637.50
Allan Henning	75	67	72	70	284	2,637.50

	SCORES				TOTAL	MONEY
Wayne Bradley	75	70	68	71	284	2,637.50
Jeff Klein	72	72	68	72	284	2,637.50
Tad Holloway	71	70	70	73	284	2,637.50
Robin Freeman	67	71	73	73	284	2,637.50
Andre Cruse	67	72	71	75	285	2,375
Michael Green	73	71	69	73	286	2,300
Ashley Roestoff	74	72	73	68	287	2,028.13
Teddy Webber	72	72	73	70	287	2,028.13
Ben Fouchee	73	70	73	71	287	2,028.13
Brian Mahon	73	67	74	73	287	2,028.13
David Armor	68	71	75	73	287	2,028.13
Hugh Royer	74	72	68	73	287	2,028.13
Marty Schiene	72	72	68	75	287	2,028.13
Desmond Terblanche	71	72	69	75	287	2,028.13

Trustbank Tournament of Champions

Kensington Golf Club, Johannesburg, South Africa
Par 35-37—72; 6,716 yards

March 7-10
purse, R250,000

	SCORES				TOTAL	MONEY
Trevor Dodds	70	65	68	69	272	R40,000
Francis Quinn	66	70	70	67	273	28,750
John Daly	67	71	67	69	274	17,500
Wayne Westner	67	68	65	75	275	12,500
Ernie Els	71	69	69	67	276	9,750
Wayne Player	72	63	71	70	276	9,750
Jeff Hawkes	69	74	66	68	277	6,875
Allan Henning	69	69	67	72	277	6,875
Mark Carnevale	68	74	66	70	278	5,500
Desmond Terblanche	71	71	69	68	279	5,000
Kevin Johnson	72	71	71	66	280	4,250
James Kingston	67	69	75	69	280	4,250
Wilhelm Winsnes	70	67	70	73	280	4,250
Bob McDonnell	71	73	69	68	281	3,562.50
Hugh Baiocchi	70	70	72	69	281	3,562.50
John Bland	72	68	72	69	281	3,562.50
Andre Cruse	71	69	71	70	281	3,562.50
Hendrik Buhrmann	71	72	72	67	282	3,068.75
Phil Jonas	71	73	70	68	282	3,068.75
Thomas Tolles, Jr.	69	72	72	69	282	3,068.75
Richard Kaplan	71	64	73	74	282	3,068.75
Gavin Levenson	71	70	74	68	283	2,712.50
Bruce Vaughan	70	72	72	69	283	2,712.50
Phillip Hatchett	72	69	70	72	283	2,712.50
Jay Townsend	70	73	68	72	283	2,712.50
Don Robertson	73	71	70	70	284	2,525
Bobby Lincoln	73	73	70	69	285	2,375
Hugh Royer	75	69	71	70	285	2,375
Justin Hobday	70	71	73	71	285	2,375
Kevin Stone	73	70	76	67	286	2,158.33
Mervyn Galant	72	70	73	71	286	2,158.33
Mark Wiltshire	76	69	70	71	286	2,158.33

Twee Jongegzellen Masters

Stellenbosch Golf Club, Stellenbosch
Par 37-35—72

November 21-24
purse, R350,000

	SCORES				TOTAL	MONEY
Fulton Allem	69	69	68	70	276	R55,200
Ian Palmer	69	71	70	68	278	39,675
John Bland	71	70	68	70	279	24,150
Roger Wessels	69	70	70	71	280	17,250
Tony Johnstone	71	70	68	72	281	14,490
Wayne Westner	71	72	71	70	284	12,420
Bobby Lincoln	69	68	71	77	285	10,350
Hugh Baiocchi	69	70	71	76	286	7,585
Andre Cruse	74	69	68	75	286	7,585
Justin Hobday	68	69	72	77	286	7,585
Retief Goosen	68	76	71	72	287	5,710
Allan Henning	74	70	73	70	287	5,710
Ian Hutchings	68	71	71	77	287	5,710
Chris Williams	70	74	72	71	287	5,710
David Frost	70	73	71	74	288	5,005
John Fourie	72	71	77	69	289	4,486
Rick Hartmann	74	69	70	76	289	4,486
Richard Kaplan	72	70	72	75	289	4,486
John Mashego	73	69	72	75	289	4,486
Steve van Vuuren	70	69	76	74	289	4,486
Wayne Bradley	75	70	71	74	290	3,797
Steven Burnett	73	70	71	76	290	3,797
Jannie Le Grange	67	74	76	73	290	3,797
Marty Schiene	72	70	71	77	290	3,797
Murray Supple	67	75	76	72	290	3,797
De Wet Basson	70	73	72	76	291	3,435
Schalk van der Merwe	71	72	76	72	291	3,435
Hendrik Buhrmann	73	72	69	78	292	2,998.57
Chris Davison	73	74	73	72	292	2,998.57
Derek James	73	74	75	70	292	2,998.57
Jimmy Johnson	75	69	74	74	292	2,998.57
Noel Maart	73	76	76	67	292	2,998.57
Sean Pappas	74	71	75	72	292	2,998.57
Desmond Terblanche	69	72	73	78	292	2,998.57

Million Dollar Challenge

Gary Player Country Club, Sun City, Bophuthatswana
Par 36-36—72; 7,665 yards

December 6-9
purse, US$2,500,000

	SCORES				TOTAL	MONEY
David Frost	71	71	71	71	284	$1,000,000
Jose Maria Olazabal	73	70	73	69	285	300,000
Bernhard Langer	69	74	70	75	288	225,000
Steve Elkington	77	68	68	75	288	225,000
Fulton Allem	73	72	74	71	290	150,000
Robert Gamez	79	76	69	69	293	135,000
Ken Green	75	72	70	76	293	135,000
Sandy Lyle	80	67	74	78	299	120,000
Tommy Armour III	81	71	71	77	300	110,000
Tim Simpson	75	74	73	81	303	100,000

Bloemfontein Spoornet Classic

Schoeman Park Golf Club, Bloemfontein
Par 36-36—72

December 12-15
purse, R280,000

	SCORES				TOTAL	MONEY
John Bland	65	67	73	68	273	R44,800
Hugh Baiocchi	67	69	72	71	279	32,200
Ernie Els	74	71	68	67	280	19,600
Wayne Westner	69	71	70	71	281	12,880
Fulton Allem	68	67	72	74	281	12,880
Trevor Dodds	71	70	70	71	282	9,240
Ian Palmer	73	71	65	73	282	9,240
Bobby Lincoln	75	72	69	67	283	6,580
Steve van Vuuren	70	68	72	73	283	6,580
Chris Williams	78	69	68	69	284	5,320
Rick Hartmann	70	73	71	70	284	5,320
De Wet Basson	74	70	74	67	285	4,620
Wayne Player	72	67	78	68	285	4,620
Justin Hobday	73	73	72	68	286	3,920
Chris Davison	69	69	78	70	286	3,920
Samuel Daniels	72	70	73	71	286	3,920
Roger Wessels	74	68	72	72	286	3,920
Joe Dlamini	70	73	71	72	286	3,920
Tony Johnstone	72	71	74	70	287	3,430
Schalk van der Merwe	76	66	74	71	287	3,430
Teddy Webber	72	75	72	69	288	2,912
Gary Gilchrist	72	75	72	69	288	2,912
Wilhelm Winsnes	70	74	74	70	288	2,912
Andre Cruse	70	72	76	70	288	2,912
Retief Goosen	70	71	76	71	288	2,912
Lance du Toit	72	73	70	73	288	2,912
Desmond Terblanche	75	69	71	73	288	2,912
Allan Henning	74	67	72	75	288	2,912
Thomas Tolles, Jr.	68	70	74	76	288	2,912
James Kingston	71	73	74	71	289	2,387
Michael Green	75	72	71	71	289	2,387
Derek James	72	75	69	73	289	2,387
Greg Reid	73	71	70	75	289	2,387

Goodyear Classic

Humewood Golf Club, Port Elizabeth, South Africa
Par 35-37—72; 6,454 yards

December 19-22
purse, R280,000

	SCORES				TOTAL	MONEY
Fulton Allem	72	69	68	68	277	R43,988
John Bland	70	74	69	66	279	31,612
Hendrik Buhrmann	69	69	73	69	280	19,264
Gavin Levenson	72	72	70	68	282	12,656
Justin Hobday	70	75	68	69	282	12,656
Ian Palmer	69	70	72	72	283	9,912
Hugh Baiocchi	70	72	75	69	286	7,065.33
Wilhelm Winsnes	73	71	70	72	286	7,065.33
Roger Wessels	74	75	65	72	286	7,065.33
Phillip Hatchett	73	74	69	71	287	5,058.67
Stuart Smith	73	70	73	71	287	5,058.67
Simon Hobday	72	71	73	71	287	5,058.67

	SCORES				TOTAL	MONEY
Steve van Vuuren	76	72	69	71	288	4,236
Andre Cruse	73	72	70	73	288	4,236
Steven Burnett	70	75	74	70	289	3,920
Ernie Els	77	68	70	74	289	3,920
Joe Dlamini	74	75	72	69	290	3,392.67
Jimmy Johnson	74	75	72	69	290	3,392.67
Wayne Westner	77	73	70	70	290	3,392.67
Wayne Player	75	69	73	73	290	3,392.67
Trevor Dodds	76	75	65	74	290	3,392.67
Marty Schiene	70	74	71	75	290	3,392.67
Derek James	75	75	72	69	291	2,856
Jannie Le Grange	79	72	70	70	291	2,856
Teddy Webber	75	70	75	71	291	2,856
Schalk van der Merwe	75	74	70	72	291	2,856
Tony Johnstone	73	74	70	74	291	2,856
Tony Louw	73	73	74	72	292	2,478
Bobby Lincoln	73	73	71	75	292	2,478
Chris Williams	70	73	74	75	292	2,478
Gary Gilchrist	74	74	71	73	292	2,478

Nigerian Open

Ikoyi Golf Club, Lagos, Nigeria
Par 36-35—71; 6,389 yards

December 6-9
purse, £78,862.63

	SCORES			TOTAL	MONEY
Wayne Stephens	68	64	66	198	£12,953.37
Chris Platts	66	70	68	204	8,632.12
Sunday Okpe	73	67	66	206	4,015.54
Roger Winchester	67	71	68	206	4,015.54
David R. Jones	67	69	70	206	4,015.54
Glyn Krause	68	70	69	207	2,720.21
Jeremy Robinson	69	73	67	209	2,137.31
Jeff Pinsent	69	70	70	209	2,137.31
Nigel Graves	71	71	68	210	1,515.54
John Morgan	71	70	69	210	1,515.54
Bello Seibidor	69	68	73	210	1,515.54
Paul Lyons	70	66	74	210	1,515.54
Marcel Soumahoro	71	71	69	211	1,143.52
Larry Batchelor	73	69	69	211	1,143.52
David Llewellyn	68	72	71	211	1,143.52
Tunde Raime	72	68	71	211	1,143.52
Garry Harvey	70	68	73	211	1,143.52
Philip Harrison	73	70	69	212	938.86
L. Lasisi	69	73	70	212	938.86
Ian Spencer	70	72	70	212	938.86
Andrew Hare	71	69	72	212	938.86
Mathias Gronberg	72	67	73	212	938.86
James Lebbie	71	77	65	213	862.69
Gordon J. Brand	71	75	68	214	769.43
Jonathan Sewell	71	73	70	214	769.43
David Jones	73	70	71	214	769.43
Yakuba Chollom	71	72	71	214	769.43
Tony Uduimoh	73	70	71	214	769.43
Glenn Ralph	68	73	73	214	769.43
Stephen Keenan	68	70	76	214	769.43

Ivory Coast Open

President Golf Club, Yamoussoukro, Ivory Coast
Par 36-36—72; 6,516 yards

December 13-16
purse, £82,547.80

	SCORES				TOTAL	MONEY
David Llewellyn	67	66	71	71	275	£13,643.90
Jeff Pinsent	69	70	68	70	277	9,095.90
Adam Hunter	72	67	71	69	279	4,613.50
Gordon J. Brand	65	73	69	72	279	4,613.50
Glenn Ralph	71	71	67	71	280	3,470.40
Mike Miller	72	74	68	67	281	2,860.10
Ian Spencer	70	71	74	69	284	1,897.90
Roger Winchester	72	75	67	70	284	1,897.90
Siaka Kone	72	69	73	70	284	1,897.90
Stephan Halee	68	73	71	72	284	1,897.90
Jonathan Cheltham	72	69	68	75	284	1,897.90
David Wood	71	71	73	70	285	1,327.50
John Morgan	71	72	71	71	285	1,327.50
Salim Hwanyenza	72	70	67	76	285	1,327.50
Jerome Cantagrel	75	72	70	69	286	1,130.80
Paul Le Chevalier	72	72	73	69	286	1,130.80
Philip Talbot	73	73	70	70	286	1,130.80
Craig Cassells	75	73	67	71	286	1,130.80
Jeremy Robinson	71	77	72	67	287	973.10
Richard Fish	72	71	75	69	287	973.10
Marcel Soumaboro	69	72	75	71	287	973.10
Peter Akakasiaka	71	72	71	73	287	973.10
Fabrice Honnorat De Mal	75	69	71	73	288	909.60
Simon Hurley	69	78	70	72	289	823.60
Garry Harvey	74	71	72	72	289	823.60
Paul Kent	72	71	74	72	289	823.60
John Vingoe	71	77	67	74	289	823.60
Stephen Keenan	68	75	71	75	289	823.60
Richard Foreman	72	71	69	77	289	823.60
Blaise Adje	76	71	71	72	290	725.20
David R. Jones	69	75	73	73	290	725.20

The Australasian Tour

Daikyo Palm Meadows Cup

Palm Meadows Golf Club, Gold Coast, Queensland
Par 36-36—72; 6,973 yards
January 11-14
purse, A$800,000

	SCORES				TOTAL	MONEY
Rodger Davis	64	67	71	69	271	A$144,000
Curtis Strange	66	64	69	72	271	86,400
(Davis defeated Strange on second hole of playoff.)						
Mike Harwood	67	66	69	71	273	55,200
Terry Gale	72	68	69	66	275	32,760
Ryoken Kawagishi	68	67	73	67	275	32,760
Jon Evans	75	64	66	70	275	32,760
Brad Hughes	66	67	71	71	275	32,760
Peter Lonard	69	73	63	71	276	23,840
Brett Ogle	74	68	68	67	277	18,933.33
Nobumitsu Yuhara	70	71	68	68	277	18,933.33
Isao Aoki	65	67	73	72	277	18,933.33
Simon Owen	71	69	69	69	278	13,120
Ossie Moore	68	68	72	70	278	13,120
Frank Nobilo	65	70	73	70	278	13,120
Graham Marsh	74	66	72	67	279	9,893.33
Roger Mackay	69	68	71	71	279	9,893.33
Paul Foley	69	66	72	72	279	9,893.33
Peter McWhinney	71	66	70	72	279	9,893.33
Ian Baker-Finch	68	71	67	73	279	9,893.33
Ronan Rafferty	70	71	64	74	279	9,893.33
Eitaro Deguchi	70	71	69	70	280	8,320
John Wilson	68	73	65	74	280	8,320
Kyi Hla Han	70	69	73	69	281	7,040
Michael Bradley	72	69	71	69	281	7,040
John Clifford	71	71	69	70	281	7,040
David Smith	71	67	72	71	281	7,040
Steve Bann	69	71	70	71	281	7,040
Jeff Maggert	71	69	69	72	281	7,040
Bob Shearer	65	70	78	69	282	5,302.85
Shizuo Mori	73	69	69	71	282	5,302.85
Danny Mijovic	71	68	71	72	282	5,302.85
Russell Swanson	70	72	68	72	282	5,302.85
Stuart Hendley	69	72	68	73	282	5,302.85
Glenn Joyner	68	67	72	75	282	5,302.85
Anthony Gilligan	69	69	69	75	282	5,302.85

Coca Cola Classic

Royal Melbourne Golf Club, Composite Course, Melbourne, Victoria
Par 35-37—72; 6,944 yards
January 18-21
purse, A$700,000

	SCORES				TOTAL	MONEY
Ronan Rafferty	72	69	68	69	278	A$126,000
Bryan Watts	69	72	69	70	280	75,600
Donnie Hammond	69	69	74	69	281	34,755

	SCORES				TOTAL	MONEY
Vijay Singh	65	74	69	73	281	34,755
Peter Senior	70	70	70	71	281	34,755
Peter Fowler	71	70	67	73	281	34,755
Craig Warren	70	71	73	68	282	22,400
Peter Lonard	71	68	70	73	282	22,400
Mike Harwood	71	72	73	67	283	14,756
Jack Kay, Jr.	71	71	73	68	283	14,756
Masahiro Kuramoto	71	71	73	68	283	14,756
Rodger Davis	72	65	76	70	283	14,756
Brian Jones	68	70	72	73	283	14,756
Kiyoshi Muroda	72	72	68	72	284	10,080
Peter McWhinney	75	67	69	73	284	10,080
Brad Hughes	71	71	75	68	285	8,820
Mike Clayton	69	72	76	68	285	8,820
Isao Aoki	68	72	72	73	285	8,820
John O'Neill	68	71	79	68	286	7,140
John Clifford	71	74	73	68	286	7,140
Wayne Riley	73	72	71	70	286	7,140
Garry Merrick	71	71	73	71	286	7,140
Peter O'Malley	70	72	72	72	286	7,140
Tsuyoshi Yoneyama	72	72	70	72	286	7,140
Roger Mackay	69	71	71	75	286	7,140
Grant Waite	71	71	75	70	287	5,460
Terry Gale	68	77	71	71	287	5,460
Jeff Maggert	75	66	73	73	287	5,460
Stewart Ginn	73	68	71	75	287	5,460
David Ishii	71	69	71	76	287	5,460
Graham Marsh	72	71	75	70	288	4,410
Anthony Gilligan	73	70	74	71	288	4,410
Payne Stewart	69	71	75	73	288	4,410
Craig Parry	71	73	73	71	288	4,410
Brad King	76	69	72	71	288	4,410
Frank Nobilo	70	72	72	74	288	4,410

Vines Classic

The Vines Golf Club, Perth, Western Australia
Par 36-36—72; 7,067 yards

January 25-28
purse, A$700,000

	SCORES				TOTAL	MONEY
Jeff Maggert	64	71	73	73	281	A$126,000
Brett Ogle	70	69	69	74	282	75,600
John Morse	70	69	68	77	284	48,300
Mike Harwood	70	67	76	72	285	31,990
Ed Pfister	70	71	68	76	285	31,990
Peter O'Malley	69	73	69	75	286	26,740
Craig Stadler	73	71	74	70	288	22,400
John Wilson	74	71	70	73	288	22,400
Stuart Hendley	77	71	67	74	289	18,900
David Ecob	71	71	76	72	290	16,520
David De Long	70	74	75	72	291	12,180
Bob Shearer	70	75	73	73	291	12,180
Graham Marsh	72	71	74	74	291	12,180
Peter Senior	73	71	68	79	291	12,180
Peter Jones	73	73	72	74	292	7,994
Daisuke Serizawa	70	77	72	73	292	7,994
Terry Gale	74	74	71	73	292	7,994
Michael Bradley	71	71	78	72	292	7,994

	SCORES				TOTAL	MONEY
Ossie Moore	71	71	75	75	292	7,994
Stewart Ginn	69	75	73	75	292	7,994
Danny Mijovic	72	73	72	75	292	7,994
Bryan Watts	67	70	79	76	292	7,994
Craig Parry	72	70	73	77	292	7,994
Eduardo Herrera	70	72	72	78	292	7,994
Anthony Edwards	73	74	72	74	293	5,880
Doug Martin	72	75	73	73	293	5,880
Carlos Espinosa	73	73	72	75	293	5,880
Ronan Rafferty	71	73	73	76	293	5,880
Terry Price	71	76	72	75	294	4,946.66
Brian Jones	75	70	73	76	294	4,946.66
Simon Owen	72	71	74	77	294	4,946.66

Mercedes-Benz Australian Match Play Championship

Kingston Heath Golf Club, Melbourne, Victoria
Par 36-36—72; 6,814 yards

February 8-11
purse, A$200,000

FIRST ROUND

Peter Senior defeated Peter Jones, 7 and 6.
Ken Trimble defeated George Serhan, 1 up, 19 holes.
*Steve Conran defeated Greg Hohnen, 1 up, 19 holes.
Brad Hughes defeated Peter Lonard, 3 and 2.
Roger Mackay defeated Tony Wolsey, 6 and 5.
Craig Warren defeated Ian Stanley, 2 and 1.
Mike Clayton defeated Graeme Trew, 4 and 3.
Lyndsay Stephen defeated John Wilson, 3 and 1.
Bob Shearer defeated Doug Martin, 1 up, 19 holes.
Michael Bradley defeated Paul Foley, 1 up.
Brad Andrews defeated Terry Price, 2 up.
Louis Brown defeated Zoran Zorkic, 1 up, 19 holes.
Mike Harwood defeated Andrew La'Brooy, 4 and 3.
David Smith defeated Tim Elliott, 7 and 6.
John Clifford defeated Mark K. Nash, 4 and 2.
Hank Baran defeated David De Long, 2 up.
Peter Fowler defeated Ray Picker, 5 and 4.
Cameron Howell defeated Richard Gilkey, WD.
Ian Baker-Finch defeated Anthony Gilligan, 1 up.
Steve Rintoul defeated Wayne Smith, 2 up.
Peter O'Malley defeated Noel Ratcliffe, 5 and 3.
Lucien Tinkler defeated David Ecob, 1 up, 19 holes.
Craig Parry defeated Wayne Case, 3 and 2.
Brad King defeated Ken Dukes, 2 and 1.
Brett Ogle defeated Jeff Wagner, 1 up, 23 holes.
Wayne Riley defeated Glenn Joyner, 6 and 5.
Ossie Moore defeated Jon Evans, 1 up.
Anthony Painter defeated Peter McWhinney, 2 and 1.
Russell Claydon defeated Russell Swanson, 3 and 1.
*Stuart Bouvier defeated Jeff Maggert, 4 and 2.
Jeff Woodland defeated Garry Merrick, 5 and 3.
Mike Colandro defeated Stewart Ginn, 2 and 1.
(Each losing player received A$755.)

SECOND ROUND

Peter Senior defeated Ken Trimble, 2 and 1.
*Steve Conran defeated Brad Hughes, 1 up.
Roger Mackay defeated Craig Warren, 1 up.
Mike Clayton defeated Lyndsay Stephen, 1 up.
Bob Shearer defeated Michael Bradley, 4 and 3.
Louis Brown defeated Brad Andrews, 1 up, 19 holes.
David Smith defeated Mike Harwood, 2 and 1.
John Clifford defeated Hank Baran, 4 and 3.
Peter Fowler defeated Cameron Howell, 4 and 3.
Ian Baker-Finch defeated Steve Rintoul, 4 and 3.
Lucien Tinkler defeated Peter O'Malley, 2 and 1.
Craig Parry defeated Brad King, 1 up, 19 holes.
Brett Ogle defeated Wayne Riley, 3 and 2.
Ossie Moore defeated Anthony Painter, 1 up.
*Stuart Bouvier defeated Russell Claydon, 1 up, 19 holes.
Jeff Woodland defeated Mike Colandro, 5 and 4.
(Each losing player received A$2,028.)

THIRD ROUND

*Steve Conran defeated Peter Senior, 3 and 2.
Mike Clayton defeated Roger Mackay, 1 up.
Bob Shearer defeated Louis Brown, 5 and 4.
David Smith defeated John Clifford, 6 and 5.
Peter Fowler defeated Ian Baker-Finch, 3 and 1.
Craig Parry defeated Lucien Tinkler, 6 and 5.
Brett Ogle defeated Ossie Moore, 5 and 4.
Jeff Woodland defeated *Stuart Bouvier, 4 and 3.
(Each losing professional received A$4,286.)

QUARTER-FINALS

Mike Clayton defeated *Steve Conran, 2 up.
David Smith defeated Bob Shearer, 1 up, 20 holes.
Peter Fowler defeated Craig Parry, 3 and 1.
Jeff Woodland defeated Brett Ogle, 4 and 3.
(Each losing professional received A$7,600.)

SEMI-FINALS

David Smith defeated Mike Clayton, 1 up.
Peter Fowler defeated Jeff Woodland, 4 and 3.

THIRD-FOURTH PLACE PLAYOFF

Mike Clayton defeated Jeff Woodland, 4 and 2.

FINAL

David Smith defeated Peter Fowler, 4 and 2.
(Smith received A$36,000, Fowler A$21,600, Clayton A$13,800, Woodland A$9,960.)

Australian Masters

Huntingdale Golf Club, Melbourne, Victoria
Par 37-36—73; 6,955 yards

February 15-18
purse, A$500,000

	SCORES				TOTAL	MONEY
Greg Norman	68	67	70	68	273	A$90,000
John Morse	71	69	68	67	275	37,800
Mike Clayton	64	74	69	68	275	37,800
Nick Faldo	68	67	68	72	275	37,800
Rodger Davis	69	71	68	69	277	19,950
David De Long	68	71	68	70	277	19,950
Peter O'Malley	69	71	70	68	278	16,000
Jeff Woodland	70	67	71	70	278	16,000
Craig Parry	68	71	69	71	279	11,833.33
Roger Mackay	70	68	69	72	279	11,833.33
Brad King	71	67	68	73	279	11,833.33
Curtis Strange	69	73	71	67	280	8,600
David Feherty	68	73	71	68	280	8,600
Terry Gale	72	69	70	70	281	7,400
Ian Baker-Finch	66	71	69	76	282	7,000
Russell Swanson	70	71	70	72	283	6,300
Ken Trimble	70	71	70	72	283	6,300
Steve Bann	69	68	72	74	283	6,300
Richard Gilkey	69	71	72	72	284	5,600
Ken Dukes	68	70	73	73	284	5,600
Brett Ogle	73	70	70	72	285	5,300
Brad Hughes	72	73	73	68	286	4,900
Wayne Grady	69	74	74	69	286	4,900
Kyi Hla Han	73	70	74	69	286	4,900
Frank Nobilo	69	73	74	71	287	4,200
Peter Fowler	69	72	73	73	287	4,200
Jeff Maggert	73	71	69	74	287	4,200
Bryan Watts	73	71	68	75	287	4,200
Peter Senior	70	75	75	68	288	3,600
Stewart Ginn	71	72	71	74	288	3,600

Monro Interiors Nedlands Masters

Nedlands Golf Club, Perth, Western Australia
Par 36-36—72; 6,289 yards

March 8-11
purse, A$150,000

	SCORES				TOTAL	MONEY
John Morse	67	69	70	69	275	A$27,000
Terry Price	69	71	65	71	276	16,200
Ray Picker	69	69	67	72	277	10,350
Peter Lonard	74	67	71	67	279	6,855
Danny Mijovic	69	71	71	68	279	6,855
Terry Gale	73	69	69	69	280	5,430
Lyndsay Stephen	66	70	72	72	280	5,430
Graham Marsh	68	74	70	69	281	4,470
Paul Foley	70	69	75	68	282	3,795
Garry Merrick	68	68	75	71	282	3,795
Tod Power	68	70	76	69	283	2,740
George Serhan	69	71	72	71	283	2,740
Ken Dukes	74	69	69	71	283	2,740
Wayne Smith	68	76	68	72	284	2,220
Craig Mann	70	72	71	72	285	1,990

	SCORES				TOTAL	MONEY
Jeff Wagner	71	71	69	74	285	1,990
Jeff Woodland	70	69	71	75	285	1,990
Roger Mackay	68	78	69	71	286	1,755
Magnus Grankvist	70	72	67	77	286	1,755
Brad King	72	75	69	72	288	1,620
Tony Mahoney	73	71	71	73	288	1,620
Mark Spencer	72	75	73	69	289	1,470
John Clifford	72	78	67	72	289	1,470
Jonas Reffborn	69	72	71	77	289	1,470
Anthony Edwards	73	72	75	70	290	1,320
Craig Warren	75	71	71	73	290	1,320
*Glenn Carbon	72	75	73	70	290	
Glenn Joyner	74	67	77	73	291	1,170
David Smith	71	78	70	72	291	1,170
Louis Brown	71	75	72	73	291	1,170

Air New Zealand Shell Open

Titirangi Golf Club, Auckland
Par 35-35—70; 6,311 yards

November 8-11
purse, NZ$250,000

	SCORES				TOTAL	MONEY
Wayne Riley	67	65	66	70	268	NZ$45,000
Frank Nobilo	69	64	69	73	275	27,000
Bob Charles	67	71	72	69	279	14,850
Craig Warren	67	66	71	75	279	14,850
Greg Turner	70	67	70	73	280	9,500
Ian Stanley	69	70	68	73	280	9,500
David Iwasaki-Smith	69	70	67	74	280	9,500
George Serhan	71	69	71	70	281	5,940
Mark Allen	68	72	70	71	281	5,940
Gabriel Hjertstedt	73	71	67	70	281	5,940
Bruce Crampton	72	68	68	73	281	5,940
Jeff Wagner	71	70	65	75	281	5,940
Peter Fowler	70	72	70	70	282	3,458.33
Paul Powell	72	72	68	70	282	3,458.33
Mike Ferguson	71	68	72	71	282	3,458.33
Bruce Soland	70	68	72	72	282	3,458.33
Bill Dunk	68	74	69	71	282	3,458.33
Robin Smalley	68	71	70	73	282	3,458.33
Bob Lendzion	71	73	69	70	283	2,600
Bob Shearer	69	67	75	72	283	2,600
Ben Jackson	73	70	67	73	283	2,600
Simon Owen	74	67	68	74	283	2,600
Tony Maloney	72	66	70	75	283	2,600
Guy Boros	69	69	69	76	283	2,600
Chris Gray	72	69	72	71	284	1,957.14
John Clifford	69	75	69	71	284	1,957.14
Wayne Smith	65	75	72	72	284	1,957.14
Lyndsay Stephen	75	68	68	73	284	1,957.14
Leith Wastle	72	71	68	73	284	1,957.14
Garry Merrick	68	70	72	74	284	1,957.14
Grant Kenny	70	74	67	73	284	1,957.14

West End South Australian Open

Royal Adelaide Golf Club, Adelaide, South Australia
Par 37-36—73; 6,985 yards

November 15-18
purse, A$150,000

	SCORES				TOTAL	MONEY
Mike Harwood	66	71	73	68	278	A$27,000
Paul Maloney	70	72	72	69	283	13,275
Simon Owen	68	73	69	73	283	13,275
Craig Mann	75	71	74	66	286	6,855
Wayne Smith	73	70	73	70	286	6,855
Matthew Lane	72	70	76	69	287	4,845
Rodger Davis	73	69	75	70	287	4,845
Tod Power	76	70	72	69	287	4,845
Peter O'Malley	68	72	71	76	287	4,845
Craig Warren	71	74	75	68	288	3,540
John Clifford	72	74	73	70	289	2,610
Peter Jones	74	74	69	72	289	2,610
Greg Hohnen	71	75	67	76	289	2,610
Stephen Bennett	75	73	67	74	289	2,610
Chris Gray	76	69	73	72	290	1,896
George Serhan	75	72	72	71	290	1,896
Ken Tanigawa	75	70	74	71	290	1,896
Mike Clayton	74	73	69	74	290	1,896
Shane Robinson	75	72	72	71	290	1,896
Anthony Painter	71	71	76	73	291	1,530
John Morse	75	70	71	75	291	1,530
Lyndsay Stephen	72	78	73	68	291	1,530
Mike Ferguson	72	74	75	70	291	1,530
Paul Foley	77	67	74	73	291	1,530
*Neil Crafter	72	72	72	75	291	
*Robert Allenby	69	77	70	75	291	
Ben Jackson	70	75	70	77	292	1,320
Louis Brown	74	71	73	74	292	1,320
*John Wade	75	71	74	72	292	
Brett Griffiths	73	76	75	69	293	1,057.50
Richard Gilkey	72	73	77	71	293	1,057.50
Grant Kenny	77	70	75	71	293	1,057.50
Trevor McDonald	74	74	74	71	293	1,057.50
Garry Merrick	73	75	72	73	293	1,057.50
Neil Kerry	75	74	79	75	293	1,057.50
Stephen Hutchison	72	75	71	75	293	1,057.50
Paul Powell	75	74	69	75	293	1,057.50

Australian PGA Championship

PGA National Riverside Oaks, Cattai, New South Wales
Par 36-35—71; 6,946 yards

November 22-25
purse, A$500,000

	SCORES				TOTAL	MONEY
Brett Ogle	65	70	69	69	273	A$90,000
Wayne Grady	65	71	75	67	278	44,250
Rodger Davis	75	68	65	70	278	44,250
Lee Carter	69	74	64	72	279	24,900
Lyndsay Stephen	69	73	69	69	280	19,950
David Graham	70	71	70	69	280	19,950
Wayne Riley	71	73	68	69	281	16,000
Wayne Smith	72	69	69	71	281	16,000

	SCORES				TOTAL	MONEY
Noel Ratcliffe	67	71	72	72	282	11,833.33
Peter Fowler	68	72	70	72	282	11,833.33
Ken Trimble	72	70	68	72	282	11,833.33
Terry Price	73	72	71	67	283	7,900
Simon Owen	72	68	72	71	283	7,900
Craig Mann	72	72	68	71	283	7,900
Mike Harwood	69	69	71	74	283	7,900
John Morse	71	71	74	68	284	6,150
Stuart Hendley	71	73	71	69	284	6,150
Jeff Maggert	69	72	71	72	284	6,150
Tod Power	72	68	69	75	284	6,150
Ian Stanley	74	69	71	71	285	5,400
Hank Baran	74	68	70	73	285	5,400
Chris Gray	73	68	76	69	286	4,500
Mike Ferguson	71	73	73	69	286	4,500
Brad Wright	71	70	74	71	286	4,500
Mike Clayton	70	75	70	71	286	4,500
Tony Maloney	68	74	72	72	286	4,500
Mark K. Nash	72	70	70	74	286	4,500
Peter O'Malley	71	73	66	76	286	4,500
Grant Kenny	70	73	72	72	287	3,420
Ken Dukes	67	74	73	73	287	3,420
Peter Lonard	71	70	73	73	287	3,420
Danny Mijovic	73	71	70	73	287	3,420
John Clifford	72	68	73	74	287	3,420

Australian Open Championship

The Australian Golf Club, Sydney, New South Wales
Par 36-36—72; 7,045 yards

November 29-December 2
purse, A$600,000

	SCORES				TOTAL	MONEY
John Morse	72	70	73	68	283	A$108,000
Craig Parry	72	70	69	72	283	64,800
(Morse defeated Parry on first hole of playoff.)						
Greg Norman	70	68	76	72	286	35,640
Wayne Riley	70	72	75	69	286	35,640
Rodger Davis	70	71	75	71	287	22,800
Ian Baker-Finch	71	71	71	74	287	22,800
Jeff Maggert	71	69	75	72	287	22,800
Brett Ogle	71	69	74	76	290	16,080
Peter Fowler	76	72	73	69	290	16,080
Colin Montgomerie	75	71	73	71	290	16,080
Peter McWhinney	74	71	71	75	291	10,960
Steve Elkington	75	69	71	76	291	10,960
Nick Faldo	74	70	74	73	291	10,960
Brad King	72	73	79	68	292	8,400
Peter Lonard	70	70	75	77	292	8,400
Greg Turner	75	67	73	77	292	8,400
John Clifford	74	73	74	72	293	7,200
Mike Harwood	73	73	74	73	293	7,200
Vijay Singh	69	72	80	72	293	7,200
Louis Brown	72	78	71	73	294	6,600
David Iwasaki-Smith	77	72	72	74	295	5,520
Guy Boros	74	74	73	74	295	5,520
Chris Gray	69	78	70	78	295	5,520
Ian Stanley	73	72	74	76	295	5,520
Leith Wastle	76	69	80	70	295	5,520

	SCORES				TOTAL	MONEY
Michael Bradley	77	67	75	76	295	5,520
Peter Senior	76	74	75	70	295	5,520
Simon Owen	71	75	75	74	295	5,520
Frank Nobilo	76	71	78	71	296	4,170
Max Stevens	74	74	78	70	296	4,170
Richard Zokol	71	78	76	71	296	4,170
Tod Power	72	74	75	75	296	4,170
Wayne Smith	74	75	75	73	297	3,840
Wayne Grady	71	76	74	77	298	3,480
Danny Mijovic	78	72	76	72	298	3,480
David Graham	73	78	76	71	298	3,480
Glen Day	73	73	76	76	298	3,480
Greg Hohnen	71	75	76	76	298	3,480
Sandy Armour	76	73	75	75	299	2,940
Chris Patton	71	78	74	76	299	2,940
Don Fardon	80	65	79	75	299	2,940
Matthew Lane	74	75	75	75	299	2,940
Bob Shearer	73	77	70	80	300	2,340
Gabriel Hjerstedt	75	76	76	73	300	2,340
Hank Baran	76	70	79	75	300	2,340
Kyi Hla Han	75	73	75	77	300	2,340
Mark K. Nash	74	75	76	75	300	2,340
Mike Ferguson	72	74	73	81	300	2,340
*Stephen Leaney	73	77	74	76	300	
Michael Barry	73	77	75	76	301	1,860
Roger Mackay	75	72	78	76	301	1,860

Johnnie Walker Classic

Royal Melbourne Composite Course, Melbourne, Victoria
Par 35-36—71; 6,936 yards

December 6-9
purse, A$1,000,000

	SCORES				TOTAL	MONEY
Greg Turner	69	68	70	69	276	A$180,000
Rodger Davis	70	69	71	70	280	108,000
Peter McWhinney	70	70	70	71	281	59,400
Ian Baker-Finch	72	70	63	76	281	59,400
Raymond Floyd	70	69	71	74	284	41,600
Mike Harwood	70	72	72	71	285	36,200
Danny Mijovic	69	71	70	75	285	36,200
John Morse	70	70	73	73	286	26,800
Gabriel Hjerstedt	70	68	74	74	286	26,800
Ken Trimble	71	69	72	74	286	26,800
Simon Owen	67	75	72	73	287	20,400
Barry Lane	70	71	72	75	288	15,800
Michael Bradley	73	71	73	71	288	15,800
Tod Power	71	77	71	69	288	15,800
Stephen Bennett	72	72	73	71	288	15,800
Greg Norman	71	73	73	72	289	12,900
Terry Price	70	75	71	73	289	12,900
Graham Marsh	72	73	72	73	290	10,833.33
Colin Montgomerie	71	73	79	67	290	10,833.33
Ossie Moore	72	73	74	71	290	10,833.33
Roger Mackay	71	71	76	72	290	10,833.33
Stewart Ginn	72	73	68	77	290	10,833.33
Richard Zokol	68	73	71	78	290	10,833.33
David De Long	71	72	73	75	291	9,000
John Clifford	70	71	74	76	291	9,000

	SCORES				TOTAL	MONEY
Vijay Singh	69	73	71	78	291	9,000
David Iwasaki-Smith	78	71	72	71	292	7,171.42
Peter Fowler	71	72	72	77	292	7,171.42
Mike Clayton	71	73	71	77	292	7,171.42
Stuart Hendley	73	69	74	76	292	7,171.42
Guy Boros	73	70	73	76	292	7,171.42
Vaughan Somers	74	71	73	74	292	7,171.42
Brad King	70	75	72	75	292	7,171.42

Hyatt Regency Coolum Classic

Hyatt Regency Coolum, Coolum Beach, Queensland
Par 36-36—72; 6,918 yards

December 13-16
purse, A$150,000

	SCORES				TOTAL	MONEY
Ian Baker-Finch	66	67	67	71	271	A$27,000
Rodger Davis	68	69	70	69	276	13,275
Stephen Bennett	69	66	69	72	276	13,275
Craig Parry	70	67	68	72	277	6,855
David De Long	68	70	69	70	277	6,855
Peter Lonard	67	70	72	70	279	5,730
Peter McWhinney	74	69	68	69	280	5,130
Jim Empey	71	71	69	70	281	4,470
Glenn Joyner	66	69	75	75	285	3,162
John Morse	70	68	71	76	285	3,162
Brad Hughes	77	67	73	68	285	3,162
Ken Trimble	73	74	70	68	285	3,162
Tim Elliott	69	72	74	70	285	3,162
Lucien Tinkler	73	68	68	77	286	2,047.50
Mike Colandro	72	70	68	76	286	2,047.50
Zoran Zorkic	74	69	70	73	286	2,047.50
Brad Andrews	76	70	71	69	286	2,047.50
John Clifford	69	71	74	73	287	1,755
Jack Kay, Jr.	70	72	69	76	287	1,755
David Iwasaki-Smith	73	70	73	72	288	1,650
Anthony Gilligan	70	72	75	72	289	1,530
Paul Moloney	74	73	73	69	289	1,530
Ian Stanley	72	68	74	75	289	1,530
Darrell Kestner	76	70	73	71	290	1,380
Terry Price	74	69	72	75	290	1,380
Barry Fabyan	65	75	78	73	291	1,200
Jeff Senior	71	76	73	71	291	1,200
John O'Neill	75	72	72	72	291	1,200
Ossie Moore	74	73	68	76	291	1,200
Craig Warren	77	67	75	73	292	1,035
Greg Hohnen	76	70	71	75	292	1,035
*Lester Peterson	76	75	68	73	292	

The Asia/Japan Tour

San Miguel Beer/Coca Cola Philippine Open

Wack Wack Golf and Country Club, Manila
Par 36-36—72; 7,009 yards

February 15-18
purse, US$140,000

	SCORES				TOTAL	MONEY
Robert Pactolerin	68	75	72	72	287	US$23,324
Lee Porter	72	71	72	74	289	10,439
Lai Chung Jen	73	70	71	75	289	10,439
Chen Liang Hsi	74	69	72	74	289	10,439
Antolin Fernando	70	71	77	73	291	5,012
Glen Day	75	71	72	73	291	5,012
Choi Sang Ho	75	70	71	75	291	5,012
Frankie Minoza	70	70	79	74	293	3,500
Michael Blewett	71	74	74	75	294	2,744
Mark Aebli	71	77	72	74	294	2,744
Bill Israelson	74	78	72	70	294	2,744
Tsao Chien Teng	81	68	72	73	294	2,744
Todd Hamilton	73	74	70	78	295	2,261
Tim Fleming	79	68	72	76	295	2,261
Chen Yung Mao	73	75	72	76	296	1,890
Mario Siodina	74	71	76	75	296	1,890
Mark Trauner	72	73	76	75	296	1,890
Jean-Louis LaMarre	72	75	69	80	296	1,890
Russell Biersdorf	67	78	74	77	296	1,890
Gary Rusnak	75	75	74	73	297	1,617
Carlos Espinosa	71	77	75	74	297	1,617
Lin Chi Chen	80	73	72	72	297	1,617
Gary Webb	72	74	75	76	297	1,617
Rick Gibson	78	73	71	76	298	1,360
Chung Chun Hsing	78	71	75	74	298	1,360
Kwun Oh Shiu	72	77	71	78	298	1,360
Gohhie Sato	69	76	76	77	298	1,360
Howie Johnson	75	73	76	74	298	1,360
Kazunari Matsunaga	77	74	72	75	298	1,360
Lu Hsi Chuen	75	73	73	77	298	1,360
Li Wen Sheng	79	74	71	74	298	1,360
Ireneo Legaspi	74	77	73	74	298	1,360

Martell Hong Kong Open

Royal Hong Kong Golf Club, Fanling Course, Hong Kong
Par 35-36—71; 6,760 yards
(Third round cancelled - rain, course unplayable.)

February 22-25
purse, US$200,000

	SCORES			TOTAL	MONEY
Ken Green	66	67	72	205	US$33,320
Brian Watts	71	71	67	209	17,370
Danny Mijovic	70	72	67	209	17,370
Brett Franklin	72	68	70	210	10,000
Thomas Levet	70	72	69	211	7,160

	SCORES	TOTAL	MONEY
Kyi Hla Han	69 73 69	211	7,160
Choi Kwang Soo	66 71 74	211	7,160
Mark Aebli	70 71 71	212	4,493
Ian Doig	70 69 73	212	4,493
Yau Sui Ming	67 69 76	212	4,494
Bill Israelson	72 72 69	213	3,085
Lim Jin Han	74 68 71	213	3,085
Michael Blewett	70 71 72	213	3,085
Stuart Hendley	68 73 72	213	3,085
Bob Lendzion	70 70 73	213	3,085
Kuo Chi Hsiung	68 72 73	213	3,085
Robert Farley	70 69 74	213	3,085
Lee Porter	69 69 75	213	3,085
Dominique Boulet	68 75 71	214	2,375
Glen Day	71 69 74	214	2,375
Bernhard Langer	71 68 75	214	2,375
Chen Tze Ming	68 71 75	214	2,375
Barry Conser	75 69 71	215	2,173
Gary Rusnak	70 73 72	215	2,173
Stewart Ginn	73 69 73	215	2,174
Harumitsu Hamano	70 75 71	216	1,827
Chen Tze Chung	69 76 71	216	1,827
Magnus Rosenback	73 71 72	216	1,827
Mark Diamond	72 72 72	216	1,827
Wayne Smith	71 72 73	216	1,827
Carlos Espinosa	71 71 74	216	1,827
Archin Sophon	70 72 74	216	1,826
Tim Fleming	69 73 74	216	1,826
Eric Meeks	69 70 77	216	1,826

Thai International Thailand Open

Royal Thai Army Golf Club, Bangkok, Thailand
Par 36-36—72; 6,865 yards

March 1-4
purse, US$150,000

	SCORES	TOTAL	MONEY
Lu Wen Ter	69 64 70 73	276	US$25,000
Park Nam Sin	68 67 72 70	277	13,027.50
Danny Mijovic	66 69 71 71	277	13,027.50
Lin Chi Chen	68 69 72 70	279	7,300
Frankie Minoza	68 73 73 66	280	5,370
Lu Hsi Chuen	72 68 70 70	280	5,370
Todd Hamilton	70 71 70 69	280	5,370
Choi Sang Ho	70 72 72 67	281	3,555
Bob Lendzion	71 69 72 69	281	3,555
Jean-Louis LaMarre	71 74 66 71	282	2,895
Robert Martin	71 72 70 69	282	2,895
Chuck Moran	72 69 73 69	283	2,297.50
Rick Gibson	72 69 72 70	283	2,297.50
Choi Kwang Soo	71 71 70 71	283	2,297.50
Hsieh Chin Sheng	69 72 71 71	283	2,297.50
Remi Bouchard	71 72 68 72	283	2,297.50
Hsieh Yu Shu	71 69 71 72	283	2,297.50
Michael Blewett	67 74 73 70	284	1,837.50
Brian Watts	73 72 68 71	284	1,837.50
Boonchu Ruangkit	69 72 72 71	284	1,837.50
Lin Chi Hsiung	73 70 69 72	284	1,837.50
Kyi Hla Han	71 69 75 70	285	1,670

	SCORES				TOTAL	MONEY
Ian Doig	71	72	73	69	285	1,670
Kyle Coody	68	70	72	75	285	1,670
David Wettlaufer	71	73	72	70	286	1,477.50
Kim Jong Duk	71	72	72	71	286	1,477.50
Lim Jin Han	73	72	72	69	286	1,477.50
Carlos Espinosa	73	70	72	71	286	1,477.50
Bryan Wagner	73	69	74	70	286	1,477.50
Santi Sopron	71	70	72	73	286	1,477.50

Daiichi Fudosan Cup

Miyazaki Kokusai Golf Club, Miyazaki
Par 72; 6,430 yards

March 1-4
purse, ¥100,000,000

	SCORES				TOTAL	MONEY
Brian Jones	71	66	70	68	275	¥18,000,000
Hideki Kase	68	67	70	72	277	10,000,000
Tomohiro Maruyama	73	68	70	67	278	5,200,000
Seiji Ebihara	74	70	64	70	278	5,200,000
Saburo Fujiki	68	72	68	70	278	5,200,000
Katsuyoshi Tomori	67	75	69	68	279	3,400,000
Masahiro Kuramoto	68	73	67	71	279	3,400,000
Eitaro Deguchi	72	69	68	71	280	2,600,000
Eiichi Itai	72	71	66	71	280	2,600,000
Ryoken Kawagishi	70	66	68	76	280	2,600,000
Kinpachi Yoshimura	73	71	69	68	281	1,577,000
Kiyoshi Muroda	71	66	71	73	281	1,577,000
Toshihiko Otsuka	68	72	72	69	281	1,577,000
Pete Izumikawa	68	74	68	71	281	1,577,000
Takeru Shibata	73	71	67	70	281	1,577,000
David Ishii	69	69	69	74	281	1,577,000
Yutaka Hagawa	71	72	67	71	281	1,577,000
Tsuyoshi Yoneyama	70	71	70	71	282	1,053,000
Hiroaki Uenishi	68	70	73	71	282	1,053,000
Yoshitaka Yamamoto	76	69	66	71	282	1,053,000
Yoichi Yamamoto	70	69	73	71	283	892,000
Hideto Shigenobu	71	68	72	72	283	892,000
Teruo Sugihara	72	72	73	66	283	892,000
Hajime Meshiai	65	72	75	71	283	892,000
Yoshimi Niizeki	70	70	71	72	283	892,000
Noboru Sugai	71	72	70	71	284	770,000
Chen Tze Ming	67	71	72	74	284	770,000
Kiyoshi Maita	71	73	71	69	284	770,000
Naomichi Ozaki	72	69	76	67	284	770,000
Masanobu Kimura	68	75	69	72	284	770,000
Toru Nakamura	73	71	68	72	284	770,000

Wills Indian Open

Royal Calcutta Golf Club, Calcutta, India
Par 36-37—73; 7,271 yards

March 8-11
purse, US$120,000

	SCORES				TOTAL	MONEY
Andrew Debusk	71	74	73	70	288	US$19,992
Carlos Espinosa	77	72	76	69	294	13,332
Aaron Meeks	75	73	73	74	295	6,756

	SCORES				TOTAL	MONEY
Basad Ali	72	72	78	73	295	6,756
Stewart Ginn	73	72	78	73	296	3,672
Li Wen Sheng	76	74	76	70	296	3,672
Mark Trauner	73	76	75	72	296	3,672
Anthony Gilligan	72	71	76	77	296	3,672
Jean-Louis LaMarre	72	72	76	77	297	2,352
Firoz Ali	73	74	74	76	297	2,352
Tim Fleming	74	76	71	76	297	2,352
Mark Aebli	71	78	72	76	297	2,352
Lee Porter	72	77	75	74	298	1,992
Robert Martin	78	71	79	71	299	1,737
Craig McClellan	73	76	73	77	299	1,737
Lin Keng Chi	77	69	73	80	299	1,737
Asgar Ali	76	75	77	71	299	1,737
Remi Bouchard	74	73	76	77	300	1,430
Gary Webb	69	79	74	78	300	1,430
John O'Neill	77	72	79	72	300	1,430
Greg Peterson	74	75	75	76	300	1,430
Bryan Wagner	74	73	82	71	300	1,430
Wang Ter Chang	77	71	79	73	300	1,430
*V. Bhandari	77	75	74	74	300	
Gary Rusnak	77	75	75	74	301	1,254
Ho Ming Chung	75	73	74	79	301	1,254
Harumitsu Hamano	76	75	75	75	301	1,254
Hsieh Yu Shu	73	74	75	79	301	1,254
Yu Chin Han	72	74	80	76	302	1,094
Susumu Kikuichi	78	75	74	75	302	1,094
Rob Lae Singh	75	76	74	77	302	1,094
Howie Johnson	74	72	80	76	302	1,094
Richard Greenwood	76	72	75	79	302	1,094

Imperial

Seve Ballesteros Golf Club, Sakuragawamura
Par 72; 6,901 yards

March 8-11
purse, ¥55,000,000

	SCORES				TOTAL	MONEY
Toru Nakamura	69	72	73	71	285	¥9,900,000
Hideto Shigenobu	71	73	73	68	285	5,500,000
(Nakamura defeated Shigenobu on fourth extra hole.)						
Naomichi Ozaki	75	67	70	74	286	3,740,000
Hajime Meshiai	78	69	74	66	287	2,640,000
Tisguaju Sudou	70	68	76	74	288	2,200,000
Tomohiro Maruyama	75	71	72	71	289	1,778,000
Katsuji Hasegawa	72	73	71	73	289	1,778,000
Yoshinori Mizumaki	77	69	69	74	289	1,778,000
Tsukasa Watanabe	76	73	73	70	292	1,201,000
Motoharu Aoki	78	71	71	72	292	1,201,000
Satoshi Higashi	76	73	73	70	292	1,201,000
Yoshinori Kaneko	73	71	77	71	292	1,201,000
Kiyoshi Maita	74	71	79	69	293	834,000
Chen Tze Ming	81	72	70	70	293	834,000
Ikuo Shirahama	75	76	71	71	293	834,000
Koichi Suzuki	74	71	72	76	293	834,000
Saburo Fujiki	74	74	71	75	294	599,000
Shizuo Mori	75	77	73	69	294	599,000
Yoshikazu Yokoshima	73	71	77	73	294	599,000
Koji Kobayashi	74	75	72	73	294	599,000

	SCORES				TOTAL	MONEY
Masahiro Kuramoto	74	68	81	72	295	490,000
Yutaka Hagawa	75	75	70	75	295	490,000
Yoshimi Niizeki	74	73	71	77	295	490,000
Tateo Ozaki	80	68	73	74	295	490,000
Yukio Noguchi	74	71	75	75	295	490,000
Hideki Kase	81	71	76	68	296	440,000
Eitaro Deguchi	77	74	74	71	296	440,000
Masanobu Kimura	74	76	72	74	296	440,000
David Ishii	75	73	75	74	297	391,000
Yoshitaka Yamamoto	77	73	75	72	297	391,000
Hiroya Kamide	77	76	74	70	297	391,000
Yuzo Oyama	75	72	75	75	297	391,000
Toshiaki Nakagawa	76	76	74	71	297	391,000
Futoshi Irino	80	72	71	74	297	391,000

Epson Singapore Open

Singapore Island Country Club, Bukit Course, Singapore
Par 35-36—71; 6,651 yards

March 15-18
purse, US$300,000

	SCORES				TOTAL	MONEY
Antolin Fernando	66	71	67	69	273	US$49,980
Frankie Minoza	70	65	72	66	273	33,330

(Fernando defeated Minoza on second extra hole.)

Choi Sang Ho	66	68	71	69	274	18,780
Jack Kay	71	66	67	72	276	13,860
Park Nam Sin	69	66	68	73	276	13,860
Stewart Ginn	69	69	66	73	277	9,000
Kuo Chi Hsiung	68	66	69	74	277	9,000
John Morse	71	67	70	69	277	9,000
Robert Pactolerin	68	69	69	72	278	6,100
Howie Johnson	68	72	73	65	278	6,100
Scott Taylor	69	69	74	66	278	6,100
Lucien Tinkler	68	67	71	73	279	5,100
Brett Franklin	69	69	72	69	279	5,100
Lu Wen Ter	72	69	71	68	280	4,710
Danny Mijovic	71	69	73	68	281	4,220
Chen Liang Hsi	74	69	69	69	281	4,220
Ho Ming Chung	68	72	70	71	281	4,220
Rick Gibson	72	68	72	70	282	3,531
Jean-Louis LaMarre	72	70	74	66	282	3,531
David Wettlaufer	71	72	71	68	282	3,531
Jacob Rusmussen	70	71	69	72	282	3,531
Yau Sui Ming	69	73	69	71	282	3,531
Lee Porter	70	70	69	73	282	3,531
Gary Webb	70	71	70	71	282	3,531
Poh Bing Chong	71	72	70	70	283	3,045
Tsao Chien Teng	72	72	73	66	283	3,045
Santi Sophon	72	69	72	70	283	3,045
Chuck Moran	71	70	73	69	283	3,045
Wayne Smith	69	71	70	74	284	2,567
Dan Cruz	70	70	73	71	284	2,567
Bill Fung	71	71	67	75	284	2,567
Li Wen Sheng	69	74	72	69	284	2,567
Lu Hsi Chuen	72	72	71	69	284	2,567
Wang Ter Chang	72	68	71	73	284	2,567
Glen Day	73	71	70	70	284	2,567

Shizuoka Open

Shizuoka Country Club, Hamaoka Course, Hamaoka
Par 72; 6,921 yards

March 15-18
purse, ¥50,000,000

		SCORES			TOTAL	MONEY
Ryoken Kawagishi	73	73	66	68	280	¥9,000,000
Hiroshi Makino	73	68	73	68	282	5,000,000
Saburo Fujiki	71	72	72	70	285	2,900,000
Kiyoshi Maita	80	66	72	67	285	2,900,000
Yoshimi Niizeki	74	70	71	71	286	1,900,000
Nobuo Serizawa	72	72	73	69	286	1,900,000
Kiyoshi Muroda	75	73	72	67	287	1,300,000
Motomasa Aoki	69	71	76	71	287	1,300,000
Ikuo Shirahama	74	69	73	71	287	1,300,000
Tsuneyuki Nakajima	72	69	73	73	287	1,300,000
Seiichi Kanai	74	72	69	72	287	1,300,000
Tadao Nakamura	75	72	72	69	288	815,000
Hisao Inoue	71	79	70	68	288	815,000
Shinsaku Maeda	74	76	72	66	288	815,000
Tatsuo Fujima	78	71	69	70	288	815,000
Seiji Ebihara	72	69	73	75	289	585,000
David Ishii	75	71	72	71	289	585,000
Yoshiyuki Isomura	76	74	72	67	289	585,000
Futoshi Irino	69	75	72	73	289	585,000
Katsuyoshi Tomori	73	71	72	74	290	442,000
Katsuji Hasegawa	76	71	74	69	290	442,000
Yoshitaka Yamamoto	78	71	67	74	290	442,000
Masanobu Kimura	75	71	74	70	290	442,000
Sadao Sakashita	75	73	72	70	290	442,000
Yukio Noguchi	75	70	71	74	290	442,000
Seiki Okuda	73	71	72	74	290	442,000
Yasuhiro Funatogawa	71	72	75	72	290	442,000
Tomohiro Maruyama	74	74	72	71	291	380,000
Nobumitsu Yuhara	68	75	74	74	291	380,000
Hatsutoshi Sakai	76	72	72	71	291	380,000

Indonesian Open

Pondok Inden Golf Club, Jakarta, Indonesia

March 22-25
purse, US$120,000

		SCORES			TOTAL	MONEY
Frankie Minoza	69	69	66	71	275	US$19,992
Danny Mijovic	73	68	67	70	278	10,422
Rick Gibson	72	71	67	68	278	10,422
Robert Pactolerin	72	70	67	70	279	6,000
Marimuthu Ramayah	73	69	70	68	280	5,088
Mike Cunning	71	69	71	70	281	3,372
Lee Porter	71	66	71	73	281	3,372
Chen Liang Hsi	70	74	67	70	281	3,372
Anthony Gilligan	70	71	70	70	281	3,372
Tony Maloney	68	72	70	72	282	2,316
Glen Day	69	71	73	69	282	2,316
Lin Chie Chen	76	69	68	70	283	2,040
Allen Saddington	71	69	71	72	283	2,040
Steve Flesch	69	68	73	74	284	1,836
Lin Chie Hsiang	71	70	74	69	284	1,836

	SCORES				TOTAL	MONEY
John Morse	74	69	73	69	285	1,680
Susumu Kikuichi	73	74	71	68	286	1,495
Chuck Moran	67	75	76	68	286	1,495
Wang Ter Chang	74	70	73	69	286	1,495
Tim Fleming	74	68	71	73	286	1,495
Gary Webb	73	72	70	71	286	1,495
Chen Tze Ming	76	68	72	71	287	1,336
Kuo Chi Hsiung	70	68	72	77	287	1,336
Buari	75	70	70	72	287	1,336
Sumarno	71	73	71	73	288	1,254
Greg Peterson	71	72	73	72	288	1,254
E.J. Pfister	73	73	73	70	289	1,145
Brian Watts	68	71	74	76	289	1,145
Bill Israelson	73	71	70	75	289	1,145
Mark Aebli	74	71	74	70	289	1,145

Taylor Made Setonaikai Open

Sanyo Golf Club, Yoshii Course, Yoshiicho
Par 72; 7,304 yards

March 22-25
purse, ¥60,000,000

	SCORES				TOTAL	MONEY
Masahiro Kuramoto	75	67	78	75	295	¥10,800,000
Ryoken Kawagishi	73	74	72	77	296	5,040,000
Noboru Sugai	75	76	75	70	296	5,040,000
Toru Nakamura	72	74	70	81	297	2,340,000
Hideto Shigenobu	74	74	73	76	297	2,340,000
Yoshitaka Yamamoto	74	75	73	75	297	2,340,000
Shigeru Kawamata	75	77	72	73	297	2,340,000
Tsukasa Watanabe	79	74	73	72	298	1,740,000
Kiyoshi Muroda	77	75	71	76	299	1,470,000
Koki Idoki	77	73	74	75	299	1,470,000
Seiji Ebihara	77	71	74	78	300	1,022,000
Eitaro Deguchi	76	72	75	77	300	1,022,000
Yutaka Hagawa	75	76	74	75	300	1,022,000
Teruo Sugihara	76	69	80	75	300	1,022,000
Toshiaki Nakagawa	74	72	77	77	300	1,022,000
Teruo Nakamura	75	71	79	76	301	756,000
Shoichi Yamamoto	76	75	76	74	301	756,000
Brian Jones	73	74	75	80	302	604,000
Katsuyoshi Tomori	77	78	74	73	302	604,000
Toshihiko Otsuka	76	74	74	78	302	604,000
Nobuo Serizawa	79	72	73	78	302	604,000
Masanobu Kimura	74	78	71	79	302	604,000
Hiroshi Makino	74	72	76	81	303	510,000
Hajime Meshiai	78	76	73	76	303	510,000
Eiichi Itai	73	80	73	77	303	510,000
Akihito Yokoyama	82	71	72	78	303	510,000
Hideki Kase	72	76	79	78	305	450,000
Kiyoshi Maita	77	71	78	79	305	450,000
Ikuo Shirahama	83	71	73	78	305	450,000
Hiroaki Uenishi	79	76	72	78	305	450,000
Hiroshi Ueda	77	71	72	85	305	450,000
Eduardo Herrera	75	71	81	78	305	450,000

Benson & Hedges Malaysian Open

Royal Perak Golf Club, Ipoh, Malaysia
Par 36-36—72; 6,796 yards

March 29-April 1
purse, US$200,000

	SCORES				TOTAL	MONEY
Glen Day	69	69	68	67	273	US$33,320
Danny Mijovic	70	72	72	63	277	17,370
Chen Liang Hsi	68	70	72	67	277	17,370
Todd Hamilton	65	70	72	71	278	10,000
Rick Gibson	71	68	71	69	279	8,480
Mike Cunning	71	70	69	71	281	6,000
Tim Fleming	72	67	69	73	281	6,000
Tod Power	73	68	69	71	281	6,000
Brian Watts	74	67	69	72	282	4,240
Suffian Tan	68	73	67	74	282	4,240
Remi Bouchard	69	72	68	74	283	3,328
Jean-Louis LaMarre	71	69	72	71	283	3,328
Howie Johnson	70	68	74	71	283	3,328
Aaron Meeks	75	69	67	72	283	3,328
John O'Neill	71	70	65	77	283	3,328
Frankie Minoza	74	70	68	72	284	2,730
Chris Endres	69	72	73	70	284	2,730
Stewart Ginn	71	67	72	75	285	2,530
Takenori Hiraishi	70	69	72	74	285	2,530
Kuo Chi Hsiung	72	71	72	71	286	2,310
Lu Wen Ter	70	67	74	75	286	2,310
Wang Ter Chang	74	72	68	72	286	2,310
John Morse	69	72	73	72	286	2,310
George Serhan	76	69	67	75	287	2,090
Liao Kuo Chie	70	73	70	74	287	2,090
Neil Hickerson	72	70	70	75	287	2,090
Lee Porter	72	72	72	71	287	2,090
John Clifford	70	76	71	71	288	1,627
Steven Rintoul	73	72	68	75	288	1,627
Steve Chapman	72	71	70	75	288	1,627
Kiyoto Kimura	71	70	74	73	288	1,627
Mitsuhiro Okunaka	76	68	71	73	288	1,627
Carlos Espinosa	72	71	71	74	288	1,627
Lin Chei Hsiang	71	70	70	77	288	1,627
Santi Sophon	73	70	73	72	288	1,627
Michael Blewett	70	71	72	75	288	1,627
Stuart Hendley	72	72	72	72	288	1,627
John Jacobs	72	68	74	74	288	1,627
Tony Maloney	70	68	74	76	288	1,627

Pocari Sweat Open

Hakuryuko Country Club, Daiwacho
Par 71; 6,780 yards

April 5-8
purse, ¥60,000,000

	SCORES			TOTAL	MONEY
Nobumitsu Yuhara	69	70	71	67	277	¥10,800,000
Wayne Smith	71	67	70	71	279	6,000,000
Kiyoshi Maita	70	71	68	71	280	2,880,000
Pete Izumikawa	70	69	69	72	280	2,880,000
Koichi Suzuki	65	72	72	71	280	2,880,000
Tadami Ueno	68	70	70	72	280	2,880,000

	SCORES				TOTAL	MONEY
Masahiro Kuramoto	70	63	70	78	281	1,650,000
Yoshitaka Yamamoto	69	71	67	74	281	1,650,000
Seiichi Kanai	69	70	72	70	281	1,650,000
Toru Nakamura	70	72	70	70	282	1,062,000
Tsukasa Watanabe	69	71	70	72	282	1,062,000
Kinpachi Yoshimura	70	71	68	73	282	1,062,000
Nichito Hashimoto	72	68	71	71	282	1,062,000
Masanobu Kimura	70	74	68	71	283	864,000
Tatsuo Fujima	69	68	75	72	284	792,000
Hideki Kase	74	69	72	70	285	654,000
Shigeru Kawamata	75	76	70	75	285	654,000
Teruo Nakamura	73	70	70	72	285	654,000
Seiichi Koizumi	72	71	67	75	285	654,000
Masahiro Shiota	71	73	70	72	286	576,000
Kiyoshi Muroda	74	70	74	69	287	518,000
Hiroya Kamide	74	69	71	73	287	518,000
Seiki Okuda	72	68	73	74	287	518,000
Tatsuo Nakagami	73	69	74	71	287	518,000
Masayuki Kawamura	72	71	67	77	287	518,000
Hiroshi Makino	71	73	70	74	288	462,000
Katsunari Takahashi	72	72	72	72	288	462,000
Terry Gale	70	70	71	77	288	462,000
Nobuhiro Yoshino	75	70	70	73	288	462,000

Sanyang Republic of China Open

Taiwan Golf and Country Club, Tamsui, Taiwan
Par 36-36—72; 7,161 yards

April 5-8
purse, US$200,000

	SCORES				TOTAL	MONEY
Frankie Minoza	75	69	68	71	283	US$33,320
John Morse	71	72	69	71	283	22,220
(Minoza defeated Morse on first extra hole.)
Lucien Tinkler	78	70	66	71	285	12,520
Todd Hamilton	75	72	67	72	286	10,000
Kuo Chi Hsiung	72	71	69	76	288	7,160
Chen Tze Ming	75	71	70	72	288	7,160
John Jacobs	75	72	68	73	288	7,160
Tung Ching Chi	72	75	72	70	289	4,740
Hsieh Chin Sheng	76	72	69	72	289	4,740
Carlos Espinosa	79	69	69	73	290	4,000
Rick Gibson	71	74	72	74	291	3,600
Tod Power	72	71	73	75	291	3,600
E.J. Pfister	74	76	69	73	292	3,320
Mike Cunning	75	71	69	78	293	2,973
Liao Kuo Chie	74	76	71	72	293	2,973
Taso Chien Teng	76	72	71	74	293	2,973
Chen Tze Chung	75	75	71	73	294	2,573
Lai Chung Jen	74	74	72	74	294	2,573
Rigoborto Velasguez	76	73	72	73	294	2,573
Gary Webb	73	73	75	74	295	2,284
Lin Chie Hsiang	77	71	67	80	295	2,284
Chen Chien Chung	76	71	72	76	295	2,284
John Clifford	74	71	75	75	295	2,284
Hsu Chi San	76	75	71	73	295	2,284
Michael Blewett	77	72	74	73	296	2,030
Remi Bouchard	73	75	73	75	296	2,030

	SCORES				TOTAL	MONEY
Yu Chin Han	72	77	73	74	296	2,030
Lin Chie Chen	78	72	72	74	296	2,030
Scott Taylor	75	74	76	72	297	1,683
George Serhan	73	74	73	77	297	1,683
Hsieh Yu Shu	73	74	70	80	297	1,683
Chen Liang Hsi	73	72	75	77	297	1,683
Bob Laskens	74	74	77	72	297	1,683
Hiroshi Yamada	73	73	73	78	297	1,683
Don Robertson	76	74	72	75	297	1,683
Chris Endres	77	74	72	74	297	1,683

Bridgestone Aso Open

Aso Golf Club, Asomachi
Par 72; 7,0937 yards
(First round cancelled - rain, course unplayable.)

April 13-15
purse, ¥37,500,000

	SCORES			TOTAL	MONEY
Teruo Sugihara	68	71	74	213	¥6,750,000
Nobumitsu Yuhara	69	71	75	215	3,750,000
Ryoken Kawagishi	72	73	71	216	2,175,000
Terry Gale	73	71	72	216	2,175,000
Saburo Fujiki	73	71	73	217	1,284,000
Shigeru Kawamata	70	75	72	217	1,284,000
Yoshimi Niizeki	73	72	72	217	1,284,000
Tatsuo Takasaki	73	75	69	217	1,284,000
Katsunari Takahashi	71	74	73	218	819,000
Toshimitsu Kai	76	68	74	218	819,000
Yusuke Yoda	71	75	72	218	819,000
Takashi Kurihara	74	72	72	218	819,000
Eiichi Itai	73	72	74	219	585,000
Yutaka Hagawa	74	73	72	219	585,000
Eduardo Herrera	71	72	76	219	585,000
Hideki Kase	74	74	72	220	395,000
Noboru Sugai	75	71	74	220	395,000
Yoshinori Mizumaki	75	74	71	220	395,000
Satoshi Higashi	74	72	74	220	395,000
Yoshinori Kaneko	73	69	78	220	395,000
Yukio Noguchi	76	74	70	220	395,000
Tsutomu Irie	74	74	72	220	395,000
Kikuo Arai	75	71	74	220	395,000
Kiyoshi Muroda	75	75	71	221	288,000
Toshihiko Otsuka	78	70	73	221	288,000
Takeru Shibata	73	70	78	221	288,000
Yoshikazu Yokoshima	73	75	73	221	288,000
Teruo Nakamura	74	76	71	221	288,000
Toshiaki Nakagawa	73	73	75	221	288,000
Yuzo Oyama	71	76	74	221	288,000
Shizuo Mori	70	75	76	221	288,000
Kazuhiro Takami	74	73	74	221	288,000
Daisuke Serizawa	69	76	76	221	288,000

Maekyung Korea Open

Nam Seoul Country Club, Seoul, South Korea April 12-15
Par 36-36—72; 6,862 yards purse, US$300,000
(First round cancelled - rain, unplayable course.)

	SCORES			TOTAL	MONEY
Kang-Sun Lee	72	71	69	212	US$49,980
Hsieh Chin Sheng	73	69	73	215	33,330
Tod Power	72	70	74	216	18,780
Lucien Tinkler	76	71	70	217	15,000
Tadao Nakamura	74	72	72	218	10,740
Brian Watts	68	74	76	218	10,740
Brett Franklin	72	79	67	218	10,740
Harumitsu Hamano	73	75	71	219	6,450
Cho Ho Sang	74	74	71	219	6,450
Chen Liang Hsi	71	74	74	219	6,450
Tatsuya Shiraishi	67	72	80	219	6,450
Kyl Hla Han	71	74	75	220	4,845
Park Nam Sin	74	76	70	220	4,845
Todd Hamilton	72	69	79	220	4,845
Mark Trauner	75	75	70	220	4,845
John Morse	76	73	72	221	3,656
Tony Maloney	74	74	73	221	3,656
Yan Youn Nam	73	75	73	221	3,656
Jean-Louis LaMarre	73	74	74	221	3,656
Lee Myoung Ha	73	73	75	221	3,656
E.J. Pfister	73	77	71	221	3,656
Li Won Sheng	76	72	73	221	3,656
Chen Tze Chung	72	77	72	221	3,656
Kuo Chi Hsiung	73	74	74	221	3,656
*Min Hye Sik	75	75	71	221	
Choi Kwang Soo	73	74	75	222	3,135
Aaron Meeks	74	78	70	222	3,135
Yu Chin Han	74	74	75	223	2,780
Takashi Hishinunma	74	76	73	223	2,780
Akihito Yokoyama	76	75	72	223	2,780
Don Robertson	74	76	73	223	2,780
Stuart Hendley	75	73	75	223	2,780
Bryan Wagner	75	70	78	223	2,780
*Kim Chang Min	77	72	74	223	

Dunlop Open

Ibaraki Golf Club, East Course, Imamachi April 19-22
Par 36-36—72; 7,163 yards purse, ¥100,000,000
(Third round cancelled - rain, course unplayable.)

	SCORES			TOTAL	MONEY
Frankie Minoza	70	68	67	205	¥13,500,000
Teruo Sugihara	69	68	68	205	7,500,000
(Minoza defeated Sugihara on second extra hole.)					
Tsukasa Watanabe	71	67	68	206	5,100,000
Terry Gale	68	70	71	209	3,600,000
Rick Gibson	67	73	70	210	2,325,000
Chen Tze Chung	69	70	71	210	2,325,000
Graham Marsh	68	69	73	210	2,325,000
Tod Power	70	68	72	210	2,325,000

	SCORES			TOTAL	MONEY
Saburo Fujiki	68	71	71	210	2,325,000
Hsieh Chin Sheng	68	68	74	210	2,325,000
David Ishii	71	69	71	211	1,500,000
Peter Senior	72	72	68	212	1,050,000
Ryoken Kawagishi	73	68	71	212	1,050,000
Brian Jones	72	70	70	212	1,050,000
Yoshitaka Yamamoto	70	72	70	212	1,050,000
Kiyoshi Murota	71	72	69	212	1,050,000
Akiyoshi Omachi	68	73	71	212	1,050,000
Yoshinori Kaneko	71	69	72	212	1,050,000
Shigeru Kawamata	69	71	72	212	1,050,000
Seiki Okuda	70	72	71	213	705,000
Akihito Yokoyama	72	68	73	213	705,000
Hajime Meshiai	69	71	73	213	705,000
Toshiaki Sudo	68	76	69	213	705,000
Nobumitsu Yuhara	71	74	69	214	615,000
Yutaka Hagawa	70	74	70	214	615,000
Satoshi Higashi	74	69	71	214	615,000
Billy Ray Brown	69	74	71	214	615,000
Brian Watts	75	68	71	214	615,000
Masahiro Kuramoto	71	74	70	215	496,000
Hideto Shigenobu	70	72	73	215	496,000
Katsuyoshi Tomori	73	68	74	215	496,000
Tsuyoshi Yoneyama	75	70	70	215	496,000
Toshimitsu Kai	74	70	71	215	496,000
Yoshiyuki Isomura	70	72	73	215	496,000
Eduardo Herrera	73	71	71	215	496,000
Todd Hamilton	73	69	73	215	496,000
Brian Tennyson	75	68	72	215	496,000
Lu Chien Soon	70	73	72	215	496,000
Masashi Ozaki	70	75	70	215	496,000
Lin Chie Hsiang	67	74	74	215	496,000

Chunichi Crowns

Nagoya Golf Club, Wago Course, Togocho
Par 70; 6,473 yards

April 26-29
purse, ¥100,000,000

	SCORES				TOTAL	MONEY
Noboru Sugai	68	66	67	75	276	¥18,000,000
Steve Pate	66	67	69	74	276	10,000,000
(Sugai defeated Pate on first extra hole.)						
Hiroshi Makino	68	66	71	73	278	4,480,000
Chen Tze Chung	72	69	71	66	278	4,480,000
Masashi Ozaki	66	70	70	72	278	4,480,000
Davis Love III	70	72	66	70	278	4,480,000
Jeff Sluman	71	75	67	65	278	4,480,000
Masahiro Kuramoto	67	70	68	74	279	2,600,000
Kouichi Suzuki	69	69	72	69	279	2,600,000
Chen Tze Ming	69	73	67	70	279	2,600,000
Teruo Sugihara	70	70	72	68	280	1,920,000
Yoshikazu Yokoshima	65	73	71	71	280	1,920,000
Nobumitsu Yuhara	69	68	70	74	281	1,500,000
Toru Nakamura	72	73	69	67	281	1,500,000
Shigeru Kawamata	71	73	68	69	281	1,500,000
Graham Marsh	69	66	73	73	281	1,500,000
Naomichi Ozaki	73	70	68	71	282	1,090,000
David Ishii	68	74	70	70	282	1,090,000

	SCORES				TOTAL	MONEY
Nobuo Serizawa	69	72	70	71	282	1,090,000
Roger Mackay	77	68	68	69	282	1,090,000
Brian Jones	68	68	73	75	284	892,000
Ikuo Shirahama	71	72	71	70	284	892,000
Toshimitsu Kai	77	69	71	67	284	892,000
Akihito Yokoyama	75	72	68	69	284	892,000
Eduardo Herrera	69	71	70	74	284	892,000
Hideki Kase	72	65	74	74	285	790,000
Yoshitaka Yamamoto	68	69	74	74	285	790,000
Peter Senior	73	72	72	68	285	790,000
Namio Takasu	70	69	69	77	285	790,000
Saburo Fujiki	73	74	68	71	286	669,000
Hideto Shigenobu	68	70	72	76	286	669,000
Yoshimi Niizeki	74	70	71	71	286	669,000
Yutaka Hagawa	70	71	74	71	286	669,000
Yoshinori Kaneko	70	77	70	69	286	669,000
Tateo Ozaki	70	73	72	71	286	669,000
Tsuyoshi Yoneyama	71	75	68	72	286	669,000
Hsieh Min Nan	72	72	71	71	286	669,000
Shigeru Uchida	69	77	68	72	286	669,000

Fuji Sankei Classic

Kawana Hotel, Fuji Course, Ito
Par 71; 6,694 yards
(Third round cancelled - rain, course unplayable.)

May 3-6
purse, ¥52,500,000

	SCORES			TOTAL	MONEY
Masashi Ozaki	67	77	64	208	¥9,450,000
Toru Nakamura	70	70	69	209	3,066,000
Saburo Fujiki	70	67	72	209	3,066,000
Yoshitaka Yamamoto	70	71	68	209	3,066,000
Naomichi Ozaki	70	70	69	209	3,066,000
Masanobu Kimura	70	70	69	209	3,066,000
Noboro Sugai	73	70	67	210	1,522,000
Chen Tze Chung	70	70	70	210	1,522,000
Akihito Yokoyama	69	67	74	210	1,522,000
Tsukasa Watanabe	70	72	69	211	1,026,000
Toshiaki Sudo	71	71	69	211	1,026,000
Shizuo Mori	75	69	67	211	1,026,000
Tsutomu Irie	73	71	67	211	1,026,000
Ryoken Kawagishi	69	73	70	212	697,000
Koichi Suzuki	70	73	69	212	697,000
Yutaka Hagawa	71	70	71	212	697,000
David Ishii	67	73	72	212	697,000
Graham Marsh	73	70	69	212	697,000
Chen Tze Ming	73	68	72	213	525,000
Tsuneyuki Nakajima	68	75	70	213	525,000
Ted Schulz	69	73	71	213	525,000
Brian Jones	72	71	71	214	472,000
Tadao Nakamura	70	73	71	214	472,000
Eduardo Herrera	71	71	73	215	435,000
Akiyoshi Omachi	67	72	76	215	435,000
Isamu Sugita	73	73	69	215	435,000
Masakatsu Sano	71	74	70	215	435,000
Teruo Sugihara	69	75	72	216	369,000
Hideki Kase	75	71	70	216	369,000
Hideto Shigenobu	75	72	69	216	369,000

		SCORES		TOTAL	MONEY
Kiyoshi Maita	72	73	71	216	369,000
Seiji Ebihara	75	69	72	216	369,000
Yoshikazu Yokoshima	72	71	73	216	369,000
Eiichi Itai	73	72	71	216	369,000
Tateo Ozaki	72	71	73	216	369,000
Kinpachi Yoshimura	73	73	70	216	369,000

Japan Match Play Championship

Green Academy Country Club, Ishikawa
Par 72; 7,083 yards

May 10-13
purse, ¥50,000,000

FIRST ROUND

Naomichi Ozaki defeated Katsunari Takahashi, 2 and 1.
Akihito Yokoyama defeated Hajime Meshiai, 1 up.
Saburo Fujiki defeated Tsukasa Watanabe, 3 and 2.
Masanobu Kimura defeated Kouichi Suzuki, 1 up, 21 holes.
Tateo Ozaki defeated Chen Tze Ming, 6 and 5.
Toshiaki Sudo defeated Toru Nakamura, 1 up.
Yoshikazu Yokoshima defeated Kiyoshi Muroda, 1 up, 21 holes.
Masahiro Kuramoto defeated David Ishii, 2 up.
Brian Jones defeated Noboru Sugai, 1 up.
Katsuyoshi Tomori defeated Katsuji Hasegawa, 1 up.
Akiyoshi Omachi defeated Chen Tze Chung, 1 up.
Seiichi Kanai defeated Yoshimi Niizeki, 2 and 1.
Yoshinori Kaneko defeated Nobuo Serizawa, 1 up.
Hiroshi Makino defeated Tadao Nakamura, 5 and 4.
Tsuneyuki Nakajima defeated Tadami Ueno, 4 and 3.
Yoshitaka Yamamoto defeated Nobumitsu Yuhara, 3 and 2.
(Each defeated player received ¥250,000.)

SECOND ROUND

Naomichi Ozaki defeated Yokoyama, 5 and 4.
Kimura defeated Fujiki, 6 and 4.
Sudo defeated Tateo Ozaki, 1 up, 20 holes.
Kuramoto defeated Yokoshima, 1 up, 20 holes.
Jones defeated Tomori, 2 up.
Omachi won by default over Kanai.
Kaneko defeated Makino, 1 up.
Yamamoto defeated Nakajima, 3 and 2.
(Each defeated player received ¥500,000.)

THIRD ROUND

Naomichi Ozaki defeated Kimura, 1 up.
Kuramoto defeated Sudo, 4 and 3.
Jones defeated Omachi, 3 and 2.
Yamamoto defeated Kaneko, 2 and 1.
(Each defeated player received ¥1,000,000.)

SEMI-FINALS

Naomichi Ozaki defeated Kuramoto, 9 and 8.
Jones defeated Yamamoto, 4 and 3.

PLAYOFF FOR THIRD-FOURTH

Kuramoto defeated Yamamoto, 6 and 5.
(Kuramoto received ¥3,500,000; Yamamoto ¥2,500,000.)

FINAL

Naomichi Ozaki defeated Jones, 6 and 5.
(Ozaki received ¥14,000,000; Jones ¥7,000,000.)

Pepsi Ube

Ube Country Club, Ajisucho
Par 71; 6,853 yards
(Second round cancelled - rain, course unplayable.)

May 17-20
purse, ¥60,000,000

	SCORES			TOTAL	MONEY
Tadao Nakamura	67	70	66	203	¥8,100,000
Tadami Ueno	69	69	69	207	4,500,000
Yoshinori Kaneko	69	71	69	209	2,340,000
Katsunari Takahashi	73	66	70	209	2,340,000
Toshiaki Nakagawa	69	71	69	209	2,340,000
Kiyoshi Muroda	69	71	70	210	1,530,000
Nozomu Kamatsu	75	68	67	210	1,530,000
Teruo Sugihara	69	71	71	211	1,170,000
Ikuo Shirahama	68	71	72	211	1,170,000
Seiki Okuda	72	68	71	211	1,170,000
Hideki Kase	69	74	69	212	766,000
Tsukasa Watanabe	73	71	68	212	766,000
Seiji Ebihara	70	72	70	212	766,000
Yutaka Hagawa	70	69	73	212	766,000
Katsuji Hasegawa	71	73	68	212	766,000
Kiyoshi Maita	72	71	70	213	511,000
Eiichi Itai	74	69	70	213	511,000
Eduardo Herrera	72	72	69	213	511,000
Takeshi Shibata	69	70	74	213	511,000
Namio Takasu	71	71	71	213	511,000
Hideto Shigenobu	70	73	71	214	390,000
Shigeru Kawamata	69	72	73	214	390,000
Wayne Smith	71	68	75	214	390,000
Motomasa Aoki	71	72	71	214	390,000
Yurio Akitomi	70	73	71	214	390,000
Shinji Kuraoka	73	70	71	214	390,000
Tomio Uno	73	71	70	214	390,000
Saburo Fujiki	72	70	73	215	342,000
Tateo Ozaki	71	72	72	215	342,000
Nobuo Serizawa	72	73	70	215	342,000

Mitsubishi Galant

Golden Valley Golf Club, Nishiwaki
Par 72; 7,014 yards

May 24-27
purse, ¥70,000,000

	SCORES				TOTAL	MONEY
Isao Aoki	70	76	71	72	289	¥12,600,000
Teruo Sugihara	75	72	72	73	292	5,040,000
Masashi Ozaki	73	73	75	71	292	5,040,000

	SCORES				TOTAL	MONEY
Tsuyoshi Yoneyama	73	78	75	66	292	5,040,000
Noboru Sugai	75	75	75	68	293	2,660,000
Katsunari Takahashi	74	72	77	70	293	2,660,000
Eduardo Herrera	72	76	76	70	294	2,240,000
David Ishii	73	74	78	70	295	1,820,000
Graham Marsh	78	73	71	73	295	1,820,000
Roger Mackay	73	70	76	76	295	1,820,000
Akiyoshi Omachi	73	76	76	71	296	1,344,000
Shinsaku Maeda	74	73	77	72	296	1,344,000
Seiichi Koizumi	75	76	73	73	297	1,176,000
Nobumitsu Yuhara	76	77	73	72	298	966,000
Shigeru Kawamata	72	74	81	71	298	966,000
Akihito Yokoyama	74	76	76	72	298	966,000
Hideyuki Satoh	76	73	76	73	298	966,000
Eiichi Itai	71	81	72	75	299	737,000
Katsuji Hasegawa	75	73	74	77	299	737,000
Takeshi Shibata	71	79	77	72	299	737,000
Seiichi Kanai	75	79	74	72	300	658,000
Yoshiyuki Isomura	76	77	75	72	300	658,000
Ryoken Kawagishi	76	73	79	73	301	595,000
Toshihiko Otsuka	69	76	80	76	301	595,000
Yukio Noguchi	68	81	80	72	301	595,000
Yoshinori Ichioka	73	77	79	72	301	595,000
Chen Tze Chung	75	75	78	74	302	539,000
Yoshikazu Yokoshima	75	78	78	71	302	539,000
Pete Izumikawa	77	74	77	74	302	539,000
Junji Matsuzawa	75	75	82	70	302	539,000

JCB Classic Sendai

Omote Zao Kokusai Golf Club, Shibatamachi
Par 71; 6,622 yards

May 31-June 3
purse, ¥60,000,000

	SCORES			TOTAL	MONEY
Roger Mackay	73	64	66	66	269	¥10,800,000
Tsuyoshi Yoneyama	68	68	68	68	272	5,040,000
Graham Marsh	67	69	67	69	272	5,040,000
Hiroshi Makino	69	72	65	67	273	2,480,000
Tomohiro Maruyama	69	70	66	68	273	2,480,000
Satoshi Higashi	67	67	69	70	273	2,480,000
Brian Jones	72	66	66	70	274	1,650,000
Teruo Sugihara	70	68	68	68	274	1,650,000
Masashi Ozaki	71	70	65	68	274	1,650,000
Masanobu Kimura	70	70	68	66	274	1,650,000
Norikazu Kawakami	72	67	67	69	275	1,200,000
Seiki Okuda	71	70	67	69	277	1,016,000
Shinsaku Maeda	70	73	67	67	277	1,016,000
Hiroshi Ueda	68	70	69	70	277	1,016,000
Katsunari Takahashi	65	70	72	71	278	828,000
Eiichi Itai	67	70	72	69	278	828,000
Masahiro Kuramoto	73	67	71	68	279	638,000
Tsukasa Watanabe	69	67	73	70	279	638,000
Tadao Nakamura	74	69	67	69	279	638,000
David Ishii	70	71	72	66	279	638,000
Taisei Inagaki	71	72	65	71	279	638,000
Ryoken Kawagishi	73	67	70	70	280	512,000
Saburo Fujiki	72	68	70	70	280	512,000
Kiyoshi Maita	71	67	70	72	280	512,000

	SCORES				TOTAL	MONEY
Hideyuki Satoh	67	70	69	74	280	512,000
Joji Furuki	69	69	70	72	280	512,000
Yoshio Fumiyama	72	71	65	72	280	512,000
Yoshitaka Yamamoto	68	72	67	74	281	450,000
Yoshimi Nizeki	68	68	71	74	281	450,000
Hikaru Emoto	70	68	70	73	281	450,000
Taijiro Tana	74	67	71	69	281	450,000

Sapporo Tokyu Open

Sapporo Kokusai Country Club, Sapporo
Par 72; 6,948 yards

June 7-10
purse, ¥60,000,000

	SCORES				TOTAL	MONEY
Tadao Nakamura	69	67	75	67	278	¥10,800,000
Brian Jones	74	71	67	67	279	5,040,000
Chen Tze Chung	65	72	74	68	279	5,040,000
Toru Nakamura	71	69	71	70	281	2,880,000
Tsukasa Watanabe	70	71	72	69	282	2,280,000
Kiyoshi Muroda	67	71	73	71	282	2,280,000
Katsunari Takahashi	70	69	74	70	283	1,830,000
Seiichi Kanai	68	71	74	70	283	1,830,000
Naomichi Ozaki	68	68	75	74	285	1,380,000
Ryoken Kawagishi	72	71	73	69	285	1,380,000
Hideki Kase	71	75	70	69	285	1,380,000
Roger Mackay	72	73	72	69	286	1,016,000
Hajime Meshiai	68	72	73	73	286	1,016,000
Takeshi Kitashiro	69	72	72	73	286	1,016,000
Graham Marsh	75	71	70	71	287	864,000
Teruo Sugihara	74	73	74	67	288	702,000
Masahiro Kuramoto	72	73	72	71	288	702,000
Tomohiro Maruyama	73	74	76	65	288	702,000
David Ishii	68	71	77	72	288	702,000
Koichi Suzuki	70	76	75	68	289	564,000
Chen Tze Ming	72	74	75	68	289	564,000
Takeshi Shibata	72	73	72	72	289	564,000
Toshihiko Otsuka	70	74	72	73	289	564,000
Tadami Ueno	73	73	72	72	290	510,000
Kouki Idoki	72	72	74	72	290	510,000
Katsuji Hasegawa	72	72	71	76	291	486,000
Nobuo Serizawa	74	72	71	74	291	486,000
Yoshitaka Yamamoto	71	74	77	70	292	444,000
Terry Gale	72	74	74	72	292	444,000
Futoshi Irino	72	74	74	72	292	444,000
Seiichi Sato	74	69	80	69	292	444,000
Masami Aihara	73	72	73	74	292	444,000

Yomiuri Sapporo Beer Open

Yomiuri Country Club, Nishinomiya
Par 72; 7,023 yards
(Second round cancelled - rain, course unplayable.)

June 14-17
purse, ¥80,000,000

	SCORES			TOTAL	MONEY
Saburo Fujiki	71	68	66	205	¥10,800,000
Taisei Inagaki	71	67	68	206	6,000,000

	SCORES	TOTAL	MONEY
Tomohiro Maruyama	71 67 69	207	3,480,000
Nobuo Serizawa	69 69 69	207	3,480,000
Katsunari Takahashi	69 70 69	208	2,400,000
Seiichi Kanai	70 70 69	209	2,040,000
Katsuji Hasegawa	68 71 70	209	2,040,000
Ryoken Kawagishi	71 69 70	210	1,560,000
Tsukasa Watanabe	72 69 69	210	1,560,000
Hajime Meshiai	71 70 69	210	1,560,000
Teruo Sugihara	69 71 71	211	1,104,000
Shigeru Kawamata	73 69 69	211	1,104,000
Yoshinori Kaneko	68 72 71	211	1,104,000
Toru Nakamura	69 73 70	212	796,000
David Ishii	69 72 71	212	796,000
Eiichi Itai	71 71 70	212	796,000
Wayne Smith	69 72 71	212	796,000
Hideyuki Satoh	73 72 67	212	796,000
Naomichi Ozaki	70 72 71	213	557,000
Tadao Nakamura	69 72 72	213	557,000
Roger Mackay	72 70 71	213	557,000
Graham Marsh	72 69 72	213	557,000
Masanobu Kimura	71 72 70	213	557,000
Seiki Okuda	70 73 70	213	557,000
Shinsaku Maeda	73 70 70	213	557,000
Hideki Kase	72 73 69	214	456,000
Koichi Suzuki	71 74 69	214	456,000
Chen Tze Chung	74 71 69	214	456,000
Tateo Ozaki	69 74 71	214	456,000
Tsuneyuki Nakajima	73 69 72	214	456,000
Hiroya Kamide	70 70 74	214	456,000
Nobuhiro Yoshino	72 73 69	214	456,000

Mizuno Open

Tokinodai Country Club, Bijodai Course, Hakui
Par 72; 6,796 yards

June 21-24
purse, ¥65,000,000

	SCORES	TOTAL	MONEY
Brian Jones	73 66 66 67	272	¥11,700,000
Tsuneyuki Nakajima	68 70 66 72	276	6,500,000
Roger Mackay	70 68 70 70	278	3,120,000
Nobuo Serizawa	68 71 69 70	278	3,120,000
Eduardo Herrera	70 72 67 69	278	3,120,000
Tateo Ozaki	73 72 63 70	278	3,120,000
Naomichi Ozaki	66 72 66 75	279	1,982,000
Sandy Lyle	74 67 71 67	279	1,982,000
Yuzo Ohyama	71 74 66 69	280	1,690,000
Hideki Kase	69 73 70 69	281	1,495,000
Katsuyoshi Tomori	71 69 67 75	282	1,248,000
Keith Clearwater	73 70 68 71	282	1,248,000
Masahiro Kuramoto	70 70 71 72	283	936,000
Ryoken Kawagishi	70 70 69 74	283	936,000
Chen Tze Chung	75 69 68 71	283	936,000
David Ishii	72 71 68 72	283	936,000
Masahiko Akazawa	71 71 70 71	283	936,000
Nobumitsu Yuhara	74 69 67 74	284	619,000
Tsuyoshi Yoneyama	71 73 67 73	284	619,000
Shigeru Kawamata	70 73 72 69	284	619,000
Katsuji Hasegawa	72 71 72 69	284	619,000

	SCORES				TOTAL	MONEY
Yoshiyuki Isomura	70	70	70	74	284	619,000
Brian Tennyson	70	71	70	73	284	619,000
Chen Liang Hsi	70	69	77	68	284	619,000
Keiji Tejima	70	69	70	75	284	619,000
Kiyoshi Muroda	71	70	72	72	285	520,000
Seiichi Kanai	72	70	73	70	285	520,000
Shinsaku Maeda	70	74	68	73	285	520,000
Satoshi Higashi	75	66	72	73	286	481,000
Toshimitsu Kai	75	65	72	74	286	481,000
Hideyuki Sato	74	72	72	68	286	481,000

Kanto PGA Championship

Royal Meadows Golf Club, Haga
Par 71; 6,830 yards

June 28-July 1
purse, ¥50,000,000

	SCORES				TOTAL	MONEY
Tsuneyuki Nakajima	67	67	68	69	271	¥9,000,000
Kiyoshi Muroda	66	67	70	71	274	5,000,000
Ryoken Kawagishi	67	63	71	74	275	2,900,000
Tsuyoshi Yoneyama	66	68	68	73	275	2,900,000
Saburo Fujiki	71	67	69	69	276	1,900,000
Haruo Yasuda	68	68	69	71	276	1,900,000
Seiichi Kanai	68	70	71	68	277	1,520,000
Katsuji Hasegawa	69	70	69	69	277	1,520,000
Yoshinori Kaneko	73	67	69	69	278	1,225,000
Masahiko Akazawa	68	70	69	71	278	1,225,000
Katsunari Takahashi	68	71	71	69	279	885,000
Shigeru Kawamata	71	69	71	68	279	885,000
Koichi Suzuki	65	72	71	71	279	885,000
Hiroshi Ueda	66	70	75	68	279	885,000
Nobumitsu Yuhara	69	70	73	68	280	635,000
Hideki Kase	72	67	70	71	280	635,000
Taisei Inagaki	67	74	70	69	280	635,000
Harumitsu Hamano	72	69	71	68	280	635,000
Kiyoshi Maita	73	68	69	71	281	500,000
Chen Tze Ming	71	68	71	71	281	500,000
Yoshinori Mizumaki	67	74	72	68	281	500,000
Yukio Noguchi	72	71	69	70	282	437,000
Hiroshi Tominaga	72	70	70	70	282	437,000
Haruhito Yamamoto	72	69	71	70	282	437,000
Takao Komizo	72	72	69	69	282	437,000
Hiroshi Makino	71	70	70	72	283	385,000
Nobuo Serizawa	73	71	71	68	283	385,000
Satoshi Higashi	71	67	74	71	283	385,000
Akiyoshi Ōmachi	70	69	71	73	283	385,000
Kikuo Arai	71	68	73	71	283	385,000
Fumio Tanaka	67	70	74	72	283	385,000

THE ASIA/JAPAN TOUR / 533

Kansai PGA Championship

Daisen Heigen Golf Club, Kishimoto
Par 72; 7,068 yards

June 28-July 1
purse, ¥40,000,000

	SCORES				TOTAL	MONEY
Kouki Idoki	69	71	67	72	279	¥7,200,000
Toru Nakamura	71	70	68	71	280	2,880,000
Takeshi Shibata	73	67	70	70	280	2,880,000
Yuzo Ohyama	75	70	67	68	280	2,880,000
Shinsaku Maeda	67	73	70	71	281	1,600,000
Teruo Sugihara	72	65	71	74	282	1,440,000
Hiroshi Ishii	72	70	71	70	283	1,280,000
Isamu Sugita	74	68	70	72	284	1,160,000
Katsutoshi Tomori	68	71	74	72	285	1,040,000
Toshimitsu Kai	68	71	74	73	286	782,000
Teruo Nakamura	73	69	73	71	286	782,000
Hiroya Kamide	68	77	70	71	286	782,000
Takenori Hiraishi	73	71	69	73	286	782,000
Yuji Takagi	71	70	73	73	287	600,000
Norihiko Matsumoto	75	72	68	72	287	600,000
Eitaro Deguchi	75	73	71	69	288	454,000
Toyotake Nakao	71	76	69	72	288	454,000
Yukihiro Yamamoto	75	68	77	68	288	454,000
Tomonori Takamura	73	70	77	68	288	454,000
Kazuki Nagao	74	69	71	74	288	454,000
Tadao Nakamura	74	70	73	72	289	368,000
Kenji Sogame	75	71	71	72	289	368,000
Takamasa Miyata	75	71	72	71	289	368,000
Yoshitaka Yamamoto	68	73	72	77	290	328,000
Tadami Ueno	70	77	72	71	290	328,000
Toshiaki Nakagawa	69	74	74	73	290	328,000
Shoichi Yamamoto	70	72	75	73	290	328,000
Toshiharu Kusaka	76	69	73	72	290	328,000
Hisashi Nakase	74	74	71	72	291	288,000
Noboru Fujiike	75	71	72	73	291	288,000
Mitsuo Harada	71	73	73	74	291	288,000
Kiminori Kato	68	73	77	73	291	288,000
Takamasa Sakai	75	71	73	72	291	288,000

Yonex Open Hiroshima

Hiroshima Country Club, Hiroshima
Par 72; 6,830 yards

July 5-8
purse, ¥60,000,000

	SCORES				TOTAL	MONEY
Masashi Ozaki	69	73	71	65	278	¥10,800,000
Tsuneyuki Nakajima	71	72	70	66	279	6,000,000
Hiroshi Makino	68	67	73	72	280	3,480,000
Shinji Ikeuchi	73	70	69	68	280	3,480,000
Naomichi Ozaki	67	72	70	72	281	2,055,000
Kiyoshi Muroda	71	70	68	72	281	2,055,000
Tsuyoshi Yoneyama	70	70	66	75	281	2,055,000
Yoshinori Kaneko	75	69	70	67	281	2,055,000
Hideki Kase	68	72	71	71	282	1,250,000
Tsukasa Watanabe	73	70	73	66	282	1,250,000
Nobuo Serizawa	75	69	65	73	282	1,250,000
Akihito Yokayama	70	71	70	71	282	1,250,000

	SCORES				TOTAL	MONEY
Motomasa Aoki	67	69	71	75	282	1,250,000
Masahiro Kuramoto	71	67	73	72	283	864,000
Shigeru Kawamata	71	70	71	71	283	864,000
Yoshihisa Kawashita	71	72	69	71	283	864,000
Noboru Sugai	70	73	66	75	284	638,000
Tadami Ueno	69	74	66	75	284	638,000
Katsuji Hasegawa	69	68	74	73	284	638,000
Masayuki Kawamura	68	76	67	73	284	638,000
Hiromichi Namiki	74	70	69	71	284	638,000
Toru Nakamura	70	70	72	73	285	518,000
Masanobu Kimura	69	72	72	72	285	518,000
Shinsaku Maeda	71	70	70	74	285	518,000
Minoru Hatsumi	71	71	73	70	285	518,000
Kenji Ikeda	74	67	70	74	285	518,000
Satoshi Higashi	69	73	72	72	286	468,000
Gregory Mayor	73	68	74	71	286	468,000
Gohei Satoh	70	73	72	71	286	468,000
Teruo Sugihara	73	68	76	70	287	421,000
Yoshinori Mizumaki	72	68	74	73	287	421,000
Hiroya Kamide	72	72	72	71	287	421,000
Nobuhiro Yoshino	74	72	70	71	287	421,000
Yoshikazu Sakamoto	70	74	73	70	287	421,000

Nikkei Cup Torakichi Nakamura Memorial

Mitsui Kanko Tomakomai Golf Club, Tomakomai
Par 72; 7,027 yards

July 12-15
purse, ¥70,000,000

	SCORES				TOTAL	MONEY
Satoshi Higashi	70	74	64	74	282	¥12,600,000
Nobuo Serizawa	73	70	71	69	283	7,000,000
Shigeru Kawamata	70	76	69	69	284	4,760,000
Akiyoshi Omachi	69	72	72	72	285	2,893,333
David Ishii	70	71	73	71	285	2,893,333
Toru Nakamura	70	72	71	72	285	2,893,333
Noboru Sugai	70	76	69	71	286	1,925,000
Hiroshi Makino	71	75	67	73	286	1,925,000
Saburo Fujiki	72	72	70	72	286	1,925,000
Nobumitsu Fukuhara	74	68	73	71	286	1,925,000
Taisei Inagaki	71	71	71	74	287	1,239,000
Yoshinori Kaneko	70	71	73	73	287	1,239,000
Hideki Kase	72	75	70	70	287	1,239,000
Toshimitsu Kai	73	72	72	70	287	1,239,000
Liwen Sheng	75	69	71	73	288	856,800
Teruo Sugihara	74	72	74	68	288	856,800
Yishinori Mizumaki	74	71	76	67	288	856,800
Katsuyoshi Tomori	73	73	71	71	288	856,800
Anthony Gilligan	74	73	70	71	288	856,800
Toshiaki Sudo	72	73	70	74	289	700,000
Toyotake Nakao	74	72	71	73	290	608,000
Ryoichi Takamoto	72	74	72	72	290	608,000
Kinpachi Yoshimura	70	74	75	71	290	608,000
Motomasa Aoki	75	70	74	71	290	608,000
Kazuhiro Takami	72	74	75	69	290	608,000
Hideto Shigenori	75	73	71	71	290	608,000
Shigenori Mori	73	71	73	73	290	608,000
Kouichi Uehara	74	73	71	73	291	511,466
Shinsaku Maeda	75	71	73	72	291	511,466

	SCORES				TOTAL	MONEY
Seiichi Kanai	69	74	76	72	291	511,466
Tomohiro Maruyama	73	71	73	74	291	511,466
Hikaru Emoto	74	69	72	76	291	511,466
Seiji Ebihara	71	77	73	70	291	511,466

Yokohama Open

Yokohama Country Club, Yokohama
Par 72; 6,560 yards

July 19-22
purse, ¥50,000,000

	SCORES				TOTAL	MONEY
Noboru Sugai	70	71	73	68	272	¥9,000,000
Kiyoshi Maita	67	66	71	75	279	5,000,000
Shigeru Kawamata	72	67	71	70	280	3,400,000
Yoshinori Kaneko	66	70	72	73	281	2,400,000
Hiromichi Namiki	69	69	70	74	282	1,712,500
Tatsuo Fujima	67	73	69	73	282	1,712,500
Misao Yamamoto	73	70	68	71	282	1,712,500
Yasuo Sone	70	70	76	66	282	1,712,500
Haruo Yasuda	70	67	74	72	283	998,333
Hiroshi Ueda	66	72	75	70	283	998,333
Nobuo Serizawa	71	69	74	69	283	998,333
Gregory Mayor	68	73	74	68	283	998,333
Yoshinori Mizumaki	72	68	72	71	283	998,333
Mitsunobu Hatsumi	69	68	72	74	283	998,333
Pete Izumikawa	69	68	72	75	284	660,000
Akiyoshi Omachi	72	72	71	69	284	660,000
Naoki Morita	71	70	72	71	284	660,000
Tsuyoshi Yoneyama	73	72	68	72	285	540,000
Fujio Kobayashi	70	74	70	71	285	540,000
Hideki Kase	70	71	74	71	286	470,000
Satoshi Ogawa	70	71	73	72	286	470,000
Hiroshi Takada	68	72	74	72	286	470,000
Kouji Morisaki	72	72	71	71	286	470,000
Yoshihisa Iwahsita	68	72	75	72	287	410,000
Miyuki Omori	69	72	74	72	287	410,000
Tetsuya Tsuda	70	73	74	70	287	410,000
Takaaki Fukusawa	74	68	73	72	287	410,000
Futoshi Irino	72	75	69	71	287	410,000
Kouji Nishiwaki	70	71	74	73	288	370,000
Tetsuhiko Murayama	72	75	70	71	288	370,000
Shigenori Mori	71	74	69	74	288	370,000

NST Niigata Open

Forest Golf Club, Toyoura
Par 72; 6,726 yards

July 26-29
purse, ¥50,000,000

	SCORES				TOTAL	MONEY
Seiichi Kanai	70	72	67	69	278	¥9,000,000
Yukio Noguchi	71	69	68	71	279	5,000,000
Noboru Sugai	70	67	70	73	280	3,400,000
Yoshinori Mizumaki	69	68	76	68	281	2,066,000
Satoshi Higashi	70	67	70	74	281	2,066,000
Yoshinori Kaneko	70	69	67	75	281	2,066,000
Shinsaku Maeda	74	69	67	72	282	1,525,000

536 / THE ASIA/JAPAN TOUR

	SCORES				TOTAL	MONEY
Hideki Kase	70	68	70	74	282	1,525,000
Masanobu Kimura	74	72	68	69	283	1,225,000
Futoshi Irino	72	70	70	71	283	1,225,000
Shinji Ikeuchi	72	73	69	70	284	960,000
Ikuo Shirahama	71	71	69	73	284	960,000
Pete Izumikawa	75	70	69	71	285	780,000
Kiminori Kato	72	71	71	71	285	780,000
Akihito Yokoyama	73	68	71	73	285	780,000
Yoshinori Ichioka	74	71	69	72	286	630,000
Takeshi Shibata	74	69	70	73	286	630,000
Harumitsu Hamano	74	72	73	68	287	515,000
Tomohiro Maruyama	72	71	73	71	287	515,000
Kazuhiro Takami	73	72	70	72	287	515,000
Nobuo Serizawa	71	73	69	74	287	515,000
Katsuyoshi Tomori	75	72	68	73	288	460,000
Hiroshi Tominaga	70	72	74	73	289	440,000
Toshiya Shibutani	71	74	77	68	290	405,000
Shigeru Kawamata	69	75	74	72	290	405,000
Takaaki Fukuzawa	71	75	72	72	290	405,000
Tateo Ozaki	74	73	70	73	290	405,000
Yoshikazu Sakamoto	71	74	72	73	290	405,000
Taisei Inagaki	71	72	70	77	290	405,000
Kikuo Arai	70	72	77	72	291	360,000
Namio Takasu	70	75	74	72	291	360,000
Gregory Mayor	72	74	70	75	291	360,000

Japan PGA Championship

Amanomiya Country Club, Kawachinagano
Par 72; 6,880 yards

August 2-5
purse, ¥75,000,000

	SCORES				TOTAL	MONEY
Hideki Kase	71	66	67	70	274	¥13,500,000
Saburo Fujiki	71	65	70	73	279	6,300,000
Masahiro Kuramoto	73	67	65	74	279	6,300,000
Yoshinori Mizumaki	71	70	66	73	280	3,600,000
Yoshinori Ichioka	71	70	69	72	282	3,000,000
Yoshinori Kaneko	75	68	71	69	283	2,306,000
Hiroshi Makino	71	69	71	72	283	2,306,000
Toshiaki Sudo	77	70	65	71	283	2,306,000
David Ishii	70	69	70	74	283	2,306,000
Toshimitsu Kai	70	77	69	68	284	1,250,000
Fujio Kobayashi	71	75	70	68	284	1,250,000
Yuzo Ohyama	73	73	68	70	284	1,250,000
Haruo Yasuda	74	68	71	71	284	1,250,000
Graham Marsh	73	69	70	72	284	1,250,000
Tadami Ueno	73	69	70	72	284	1,250,000
Futoshi Irino	69	73	70	72	284	1,250,000
Takeru Shibata	71	69	69	75	284	1,250,000
Jun Hattori	75	71	71	68	285	790,000
Yoshihisa Kohsaka	76	70	69	70	285	790,000
Kinpachi Yoshimura	72	70	68	75	285	790,000
Pete Izumikawa	76	70	72	68	286	651,000
Teruo Sugihara	72	74	69	71	286	651,000
Taisei Inagaki	70	76	69	71	286	651,000
Kazuhiro Takami	71	69	74	72	286	651,000
Kiminori Kato	67	74	73	72	286	651,000
Seiji Ebihara	71	74	68	73	286	651,000

	SCORES	TOTAL	MONEY
Noboru Sugai	69 72 71 74	286	651,000
Tsukasa Watanabe	64 74 79 70	287	548,000
Akihito Yokoyama	72 75 69 71	287	548,000
Akiyoshi Omachi	77 69 69 72	287	548,000
Toshio Ozaki	73 70 70 72	287	548,000
Hajime Meshiai	67 71 76 73	287	548,000
Hideyuki Sato	74 70 70 73	287	548,000

Maruman Open

Hatoyama Country Club, Hatoyama
Par 72; 7,062 yards

August 16-19
purse, ¥90,000,000

	SCORES	TOTAL	MONEY
Masashi Ozaki	69 70 66 68	273	¥16,200,000
Tsuneyuki Nakajima	71 70 70 67	278	9,000,000
Ian Woosnam	67 73 68 71	279	6,120,000
Hideki Kase	69 72 67 72	280	4,320,000
Shigeru Kawamata	71 69 71 71	282	3,600,000
Eduardo Herrera	71 69 74 69	283	2,767,000
Yutaka Hagawa	72 73 68 70	283	2,767,000
Masanobu Kimura	70 71 70 72	283	2,767,000
Chen Tze Chung	69 69 71 74	283	2,767,000
Satoshi Higashi	70 74 71 69	284	1,842,000
Hajime Meshiai	72 70 71 71	284	1,842,000
Tomohiro Maruyama	69 73 70 72	284	1,842,000
Kiyoshi Maita	73 69 74 69	285	1,512,000
Futoshi Irino	74 69 74 69	286	1,296,000
Nobumitsu Yuhara	67 76 71 72	286	1,296,000
Toru Nakayama	71 73 70 72	286	1,296,000
Masakazu Noritake	69 75 76 67	287	957,000
Motomasa Aoki	71 76 70 70	287	957,000
Terry Gale	74 71 71 71	287	957,000
Hideyuki Satoh	75 71 70 71	287	957,000
Toyotake Nakao	68 73 73 73	287	957,000
Yoshinori Ichioka	74 68 76 70	288	730,000
Noboru Sugai	69 75 73 71	288	730,000
Tadao Nakamura	71 74 72 71	288	730,000
Ikuo Shirahama	68 74 74 72	288	730,000
Eitaro Deguchi	73 73 70 72	288	730,000
Gohei Satoh	70 75 71 72	288	730,000
Yukio Noguchi	72 72 71 73	288	730,000
Chen Tze Ming	72 72 71 73	288	730,000
Fujio Kobayashi	75 68 71 74	288	730,000
Tsukasa Watanabe	67 74 71 76	288	730,000

Daiwa KBC Augusta

Kyushu Shima Country Club, Shimamachi
Par 72; 7,125 yards

August 23-26
purse, ¥100,000,000

	SCORES	TOTAL	MONEY
Masashi Ozaki	65 66 68 70	269	¥18,000,000
Chen Tze Chung	71 69 68 71	279	10,000,000
Ian Baker-Finch	72 71 68 69	280	5,800,000
Katsunari Takahashi	68 65 71 76	280	5,800,000

	SCORES				TOTAL	MONEY
Shigeru Kawamata	70	69	68	74	281	3,800,000
Tomohiro Maruyama	70	69	68	74	281	3,800,000
Toshimitsu Kai	70	70	73	69	282	2,750,000
Tsuneyuki Nakajima	72	68	69	73	282	2,750,000
Katsuyoshi Tomori	70	68	71	73	282	2,750,000
Masahiro Kuramoto	65	69	74	74	282	2,750,000
Masanobu Kimura	69	74	71	69	283	2,000,000
Hsieh Min Nan	72	73	70	69	284	1,840,000
Yoshinori Mizumaki	67	72	74	72	285	1,500,000
Yoshitaka Yamamoto	70	70	72	73	285	1,500,000
Tateo Ozaki	71	72	69	73	285	1,500,000
Nobumitsu Yuhara	68	72	71	74	285	1,500,000
Taisei Inagaki	72	69	75	70	286	1,200,000
Yuji Takagi	68	72	76	71	287	1,030,000
Yoshiyuki Isomura	73	70	72	72	287	1,030,000
Ikuo Shirahama	71	70	70	76	287	1,030,000
Masayuki Kawamura	69	72	69	77	287	1,030,000
Satoshi Higashi	75	70	72	71	288	886,000
Hideki Kase	72	71	73	72	288	886,000
Chen Tze Ming	68	72	75	73	288	886,000
Eduardo Herrera	71	75	75	68	289	790,000
Yutaka Hagawa	73	71	74	71	289	790,000
Seiji Ebihara	73	71	73	72	289	790,000
Terry Gale	72	74	71	72	289	790,000
Hikaru Emoto	72	75	70	72	289	790,000
Graham Marsh	67	72	73	77	289	790,000

Kanto Open

Higashinomiya Country Club, Higashinomiya
Par 70; 6,774 yards

August 30-September 2
purse, ¥30,000,000

	SCORES				TOTAL	MONEY
Ryoken Kawagishi	66	64	73	70	273	¥6,000,000
Isao Aoki	69	68	68	70	275	3,000,000
Yutaka Hagawa	68	68	70	70	276	1,800,000
Taisei Inagaki	75	70	67	67	279	1,200,000
Hideki Kase	70	70	71	69	280	900,000
Pete Izumikawa	71	70	69	70	280	900,000
Sugai Noboru	70	71	70	69	280	900,000
Seiji Ebihara	69	71	70	71	281	725,000
Anthony Gilligan	68	74	68	71	281	725,000
Tsukasa Watanabe	72	70	67	73	282	590,000
Yoshinori Mizumaki	73	73	70	66	282	590,000
Kiyoshi Maita	72	68	71	71	282	590,000
Takaaki Fukuzawa	73	72	69	68	282	590,000
Nobuo Serizawa	72	69	68	74	283	480,000
Akiyoshi Omachi	71	67	74	71	283	480,000
Nobumitsu Yuhara	71	74	69	69	283	480,000
Satoshi Higashi	73	70	69	74	286	420,000
Shigeru Kawamata	74	67	71	74	286	420,000
Masahiko Akazawa	68	74	73	72	287	380,000
Shigenori Mori	72	70	70	75	287	380,000
Harumitsu Hamano	71	69	73	74	287	380,000
Chen Tze Ming	70	76	72	70	288	340,000
Ikuo Shirahama	73	70	72	73	288	340,000
Hiroshi Ueda	76	71	68	73	288	340,000
Hideyuki Sato	69	73	73	73	288	340,000

	SCORES	TOTAL	MONEY
Hiroshi Makino	74 66 76 72	288	340,000
Nichito Hashimoto	72 72 72 73	289	305,000
Yukio Noguchi	72 73 71 73	289	305,000
Shigeru Kubota	77 70 73 70	290	285,000
Haruo Yasuda	69 71 74 76	290	285,000

Kansai Open

Pinlake Golf Club
Par 72; 7,034 yards

August 30-September 2
purse, ¥20,000,000

	SCORES	TOTAL	MONEY
Teruo Sugihara	71 67 71 73	282	¥5,000,000
Yuzo Ohyama	68 73 69 73	283	2,500,000
Takumi Horiuchi	69 71 71 73	284	1,300,000
Toru Nakamura	70 71 73 73	287	1,100,000
Yukihiro Yamamoto	69 70 74 75	288	900,000
Toyotake Nakao	72 70 72 76	290	800,000
Yoahiyuki Isomura	71 73 71 76	291	700,000
Toshimutsu Kai	73 74 72 74	293	575,000
Toshiaki Nakagawa	72 76 71 74	293	575,000
Yoshitaka Yamamoto	72 76 69 77	294	475,000
Toshiharu Kusaka	73 76 68 77	294	475,000
Yuji Takagi	71 76 73 75	295	375,000
Koki Idoki	75 70 74 76	295	375,000
Toshiharu Morimoto	76 77 71 72	296	250,000
Masanobu Kimura	71 81 76 68	296	250,000
Takeshi Matsukawa	75 76 72 73	296	250,000
Toshiya Shibutani	74 76 75 72	297	200,000
Masashi Shimoi	70 78 74 75	297	200,000
Shinsaku Maeda	72 73 75 77	297	200,000
Hiroya Kamide	73 78 77 70	298	180,000
Yoshinori Ichioka	71 78 72 77	298	180,000
Keiichi Nagata	75 74 73 77	299	160,000
Kenji Ikeda	78 74 74 73	299	160,000
Hajime Matsui	72 79 69 79	299	160,000
Wataru Kaji	83 70 76 71	300	140,000
Takenori Hiraishi	74 72 76 78	300	140,000
Oasamu Watanabe	76 75 77 72	300	140,000

Kyushu Open

Dazaifu Golf Club
Par 72; 6,824 yards

August 30-September 2
purse, ¥20,000,000

	SCORES	TOTAL	MONEY
Katsuyoshi Tomori	69 69 67 72	277	¥5,000,000
Keiji Tejima	68 69 70 76	283	2,000,000
Kinpachi Yoshimura	75 73 66 69	283	2,000,000
Tsunehisa Yamamoto	73 72 70 72	287	1,100,000
Ryoji Honda	71 69 73 76	289	766,666
Yoshihiro Hori	68 76 70 75	289	766,666
Misao Yamamoto	73 73 73 70	289	766,666
Toshiomi Inaba	71 75 70 74	290	550,000
Makoto Nanbu	72 68 76 74	290	550,000
Reiji Bando	74 76 68 72	290	550,000

Hokkaido Open

Noboribetsu Country Club
Par 72; 7,035 yards

August 30-September 2
purse, ¥10,000,000

	SCORES				TOTAL	MONEY
Katsuhige Takahashi	69	68	73	68	278	3,000,000
Mamoru Takahashi	69	71	71	72	283	1,500,000
Koichi Uehara	71	73	70	71	285	800,000
Kazuhiro Takami	72	72	70	71	285	800,000
Toshiaki Nakamura	75	72	71	68	286	450,000
Mitsuyoshi Goto	75	72	71	69	287	400,000
Fukuji Kikuchi	72	74	70	72	288	235,000
Toshinori Horiki	71	71	72	74	288	235,000
Takamoto Ryoichi	72	70	75	73	290	200,000

Chu-Shikoku Open

Syunan Country Club
Par 72; 7,027 yards

August 30-September 2
purse, ¥20,000,000

	SCORES				TOTAL	MONEY
Seiki Okuda	71	70	71	71	283	¥5,000,000
Masayuki Kawamura	69	69	77	68	283	2,000,000
Tsukasa Watanabe	70	72	70	71	283	2,000,000
Tadami Ueno	70	71	69	74	284	1,000,000
Yoshikazu Sakamoto	70	71	70	74	285	900,000
Kiminori Kato	73	71	70	74	288	800,000
Nobuhiro Yoshino	71	77	73	69	290	700,000
Atsuo Suemura	73	71	74	73	291	550,000
Kazuki Nagao	77	69	71	74	291	550,000
Hideto Shigenobu	73	73	72	74	292	400,000

Suntory Open

Narashino Country Club, Inzaimachi
Par 72; 7,056 yards

September 6-9
purse, ¥100,000,000

	SCORES				TOTAL	MONEY
Toru Nakamura	65	65	69	72	271	¥18,000,000
Graham Marsh	70	65	68	69	272	10,000,000
Anthony Gilligan	68	69	70	69	276	6,800,000
Kiyoshi Maita	70	69	72	68	279	4,400,000
Larry Nelson	67	72	72	68	279	4,400,000
Hiroshi Makino	69	73	71	68	281	3,233,000
Masanobu Kimura	67	73	73	68	281	3,233,000
Nobuo Serizawa	68	72	70	71	281	2,527,000
Akiyoshi Omachi	69	74	72	67	282	2,300,000
Nobumitsu Yuhara	70	70	73	69	282	2,300,000
Yoshinori Kaneko	68	71	73	70	282	2,300,000
Motomasa Aoki	69	71	71	72	283	1,840,000
Masahiro Kuramoto	72	72	69	71	284	1,440,000
Seiichi Kanai	70	71	72	71	284	1,440,000
Akihito Yokoyama	68	76	68	72	284	1,440,000
Takenori Hiraishi	72	70	70	72	284	1,440,000
Ikuo Shirahama	68	71	72	73	284	1,440,000

	SCORES				TOTAL	MONEY
Futoshi Irino	73	72	71	69	285	1,030,000
Naomichi Ozaki	70	73	72	70	285	1,030,000
Harumitsu Hamano	68	75	70	72	285	1,030,000
Koichi Suzuki	67	73	70	75	285	1,030,000
Yoshinori Mizumaki	70	73	74	69	286	864,000
Tsuneyuki Nakajima	71	71	74	70	286	864,000
Kiyoshi Muroda	67	77	72	70	286	864,000
Saburo Fujiki	72	72	71	71	286	864,000
Yoshinori Ichioka	70	71	74	71	286	864,000
Toyotake Nakao	74	71	73	69	287	760,000
Hikaru Emoto	71	72	73	71	287	760,000
Kazuhiro Takami	72	72	72	71	287	760,000
Tomori Katsuyoshi	69	74	71	73	287	760,000
Haruo Yasuda	69	70	75	73	287	760,000

All Nippon Airways Open

Sapporo Golf Club, Hiroshimacho
Par 72; 7,063 yards

September 13-16
purse, ¥90,000,000

	SCORES				TOTAL	MONEY
Tsuneyuki Nakajima	69	70	68	70	277	¥16,200,000
Masashi Ozaki	70	69	72	69	280	9,000,000
Tateo Ozaki	71	68	72	70	281	5,220,000
Mark O'Meara	69	70	72	70	281	5,220,000
Hideki Kase	70	72	71	69	282	3,600,000
Satoshi Higashi	72	73	69	70	284	3,240,000
Chen Tze Ming	68	75	71	72	286	2,800,000
Nobumitsu Yuhara	74	73	70	70	287	2,475,000
Pete Izumikawa	71	68	75	73	287	2,475,000
Koichi Suzuki	74	71	73	70	288	1,935,000
Eiichi Itai	70	72	76	70	288	1,935,000
Roger Mackay	73	74	73	69	289	1,356,000
Nobuo Serizawa	72	73	73	71	289	1,356,000
David Ishii	73	72	73	71	289	1,356,000
Yoshinori Kaneko	75	72	69	73	289	1,356,000
Kan Takahashi	71	72	72	74	289	1,356,000
Masahiro Kuramoto	72	70	72	75	289	1,356,000
Sandy Lyle	72	73	77	68	290	857,000
Hiroshi Makino	74	71	73	72	290	857,000
Seiichi Kanai	73	73	72	72	290	857,000
Kinpachi Yoshimura	75	69	73	73	290	857,000
Hiroshi Goda	73	70	74	73	290	857,000
Hisayuki Sasaki	74	69	74	73	290	857,000
Masanobu Kimura	65	73	78	74	290	857,000
Katsunari Takahashi	73	70	72	75	290	857,000
Yoshinori Mizumaki	73	73	75	70	291	711,000
Kiyoshi Muroda	71	71	77	72	291	711,000
Akiyoshi Omachi	71	72	75	73	291	711,000
Yoshihisa Kosaka	71	75	69	76	291	711,000
Hajime Meshiai	72	75	75	70	292	624,000
Naomichi Ozaki	72	70	78	72	292	624,000
Chen Tze Chung	70	75	75	72	292	624,000
Gohei Satoh	73	72	75	72	292	624,000
Seiji Ebihara	72	72	74	74	292	624,000
Terry Gale	71	73	72	76	292	624,000

Gene Sarazen Jun Classic

Rope Club, Shiotanimachi
Par 71; 6,917 yards

September 20-23
purse, ¥75,000,000

	SCORES				TOTAL	MONEY
Naomichi Ozaki	68	66	69	70	273	¥13,500,000
Yoshinori Kaneko	68	69	70	67	274	7,500,000
Hajime Meshiai	71	71	66	68	276	3,900,000
Chen Tze Ming	70	68	68	70	276	3,900,000
Masanobu Kimura	69	66	68	73	276	3,900,000
Anthony Gilligan	66	75	67	70	278	2,700,000
Chen Tze Chung	71	69	68	71	279	2,400,000
Tsuneyuki Nakajima	74	70	69	67	280	2,062,000
Shinsaku Maeda	68	68	70	74	280	2,062,000
Wayne Smith	66	77	72	66	281	1,535,000
Yoshitaka Yamamoto	70	71	70	70	281	1,535,000
Katsuji Hasegawa	71	71	69	70	281	1,535,000
Satoshi Higashi	74	69	71	68	282	1,080,000
Hideki Kase	73	67	70	72	282	1,080,000
Tadao Nakamura	69	71	70	72	282	1,080,000
Yoshinori Mizumaki	69	72	69	72	282	1,080,000
Yutaka Hagawa	71	68	71	72	282	1,080,000
Yuzo Oyama	70	72	72	69	283	772,000
Brian Jones	73	69	70	71	283	772,000
Masahiro Kuramoto	69	71	72	71	283	772,000
Taisei Inagaki	70	70	72	71	283	772,000
Nobumitsu Yuhara	70	71	71	72	284	665,000
Koichi Suzuki	75	70	67	72	284	665,000
Futoshi Irino	71	70	70	73	284	665,000
Hiroshi Makino	72	73	70	70	285	615,000
Shigeru Kawamata	71	70	72	72	285	615,000
Katsuyoshi Tomori	72	68	72	73	285	615,000
Seiji Ebihara	71	73	73	69	286	541,000
Yoshinori Ichioka	71	72	72	71	286	541,000
Saburo Fujiki	71	74	69	72	286	541,000
Tsuyoshi Yoneyama	73	70	71	72	286	541,000
Akiyoshi Omachi	73	70	71	72	286	541,000
Yukio Noguchi	72	70	72	72	286	541,000
Harumitsu Hamano	71	72	70	73	286	541,000

Tokai Classic

Miyoshi Country Club, West Course, Miyoshicho
Par 72; 7,089 yards
(Final round cancelled - rain, course unplayable.)

September 27-30
purse, ¥70,000,000

	SCORES			TOTAL	MONEY
Graham Marsh	70	72	64	206	¥10,800,000
Tadami Ueno	69	71	68	208	5,040,000
Saburo Fujiki	69	70	69	208	5,040,000
Katsunari Takahashi	71	71	69	211	2,640,000
Hiroshi Makino	68	73	70	211	2,640,000
David Ishii	69	73	70	212	2,040,000
Noboru Sugai	69	70	73	212	2,040,000
Yoshinori Kaneko	72	73	68	213	1,740,000
Masahiro Shioda	75	70	69	214	1,311,000
Chen Tze Ming	71	71	72	214	1,311,000

	SCORES			TOTAL	MONEY
Taisei Inagaki	71	71	72	214	1,311,000
Teruo Sugihara	70	71	73	214	1,311,000
Tom Kite	73	71	71	215	972,000
Yutaka Hagawa	69	71	75	215	972,000
Eitarao Deguchi	72	75	69	216	712,000
Toyotake Nakao	77	70	69	216	712,000
Akihito Yokoyama	74	72	70	216	712,000
Kouki Idoki	73	72	71	216	712,000
Motomasa Aoki	75	69	72	216	712,000
Toshio Ozaki	70	71	75	216	712,000
Kinpachi Yoshimura	76	70	71	217	564,000
Toru Nakamura	72	73	72	217	564,000
Yoshitaka Yamamoto	73	74	71	218	498,000
Anthony Gilligan	73	72	73	218	498,000
Masahiko Akazawa	74	71	73	218	498,000
Shinsaku Maeda	70	74	74	218	498,000
Yoshinori Mizumaki	72	71	75	218	498,000
Yukio Nokuchi	72	71	75	218	498,000
Nobumitsu Yuhara	78	69	72	219	412,000
Eduardo Herrera	74	73	72	219	412,000
Eiichi Itai	72	74	73	219	412,000
Yoshikazu Yokoshima	70	76	73	219	412,000
Pete Izumikawa	74	71	74	219	412,000
Toshiaki Sudo	75	69	75	219	412,000
Seiji Ebihara	72	71	76	219	412,000

Japan Open Championship

Otaru Country Club, Otaru
Par 72; 7,119 yards

October 4-7
purse, ¥100,000,000

	SCORES				TOTAL	MONEY
Tsuneyuki Nakajima	68	71	73	69	281	¥18,000,000
Masashi Ozaki	70	70	68	75	283	10,000,000
Ryoken Kawagishi	73	70	68	74	285	6,800,000
Isao Aoki	73	71	69	73	286	4,800,000
Kiyoshi Kanai	72	75	69	74	290	4,000,000
Koichi Suzuki	74	73	76	68	291	3,230,000
Hideki Kase	74	69	73	75	291	3,230,000
Kouki Idoki	73	70	73	75	291	3,230,000
Chen Tze Ming	77	74	67	74	292	2,600,000
Eiichi Itai	76	69	73	75	293	2,046,000
Haruo Yasuda	75	70	73	75	293	2,046,000
Hajime Meshiai	67	78	71	77	293	2,046,000
David Ishii	73	76	70	75	294	1,500,000
Shigenori Mori	74	74	71	75	294	1,500,000
Tateo Ozaki	73	72	73	76	294	1,500,000
Kinpachi Yoshimura	74	70	72	78	294	1,500,000
Frankie Minoza	71	78	74	72	295	1,120,000
Yoshinori Kaneko	72	77	73	73	295	1,120,000
Shoichi Yamamoto	75	75	72	73	295	1,120,000
Nobumitsu Yuhara	76	74	72	74	296	960,000
Tsukasa Watanabe	72	76	72	76	296	960,000
Masahiro Kuramoto	76	75	68	77	296	960,000
*Takahiro Nakagawa	71	78	75	73	297	
Ikuo Shirahama	75	73	74	75	297	870,000
Katsuji Hasegawa	76	72	73	76	297	870,000
Hiroshi Makino	78	73	71	76	298	820,000

	SCORES				TOTAL	MONEY
Katsuyoshi Tomori	72	75	73	78	298	820,000
Yoshiyuki Isomura	73	72	75	78	298	820,000
Graham Marsh	75	72	78	74	299	713,000
Yoshikazu Yokoshima	74	75	75	75	299	713,000
Brian Jones	77	70	76	76	299	713,000
Nobuo Serizawa	75	71	77	76	299	713,000
Yukio Noguchi	71	78	74	76	299	713,000
Kikuo Arai	74	73	76	76	299	713,000
Satoshi Higashi	71	76	73	79	299	713,000
Yoshihisa Kosaka	75	71	74	79	299	713,000
Tomohiro Murayama	76	73	76	75	300	604,000
*Shigeki Maruyama	77	71	77	75	300	
Noboru Sugai	75	72	77	76	300	604,000
Yutaka Hagawa	74	76	74	76	300	604,000
*Yasunobu Kuramoto	76	71	76	77	300	
Pete Izumikawa	74	76	72	78	300	604,000
Yoshitaka Yamamoto	75	75	69	81	300	604,000
Kiyoshi Muroda	77	74	76	74	301	532,000
Tatsuo Nakagami	72	76	77	76	301	532,000
Toru Nakamura	76	73	75	77	301	532,000
Eitaro Deguchi	72	74	78	77	301	532,000
Masanobu Kimura	72	78	77	75	302	470,000
Tsuyoshi Yoneyama	78	71	77	76	302	470,000
Toru Nakayama	72	76	76	78	302	470,000
Kazuhiro Takami	75	73	73	81	302	470,000

Asahi Beer Golf Digest

Tomei Country Club, Susuno
Par 71; 6,782 yards

October 11-14
purse, ¥110,000,000

	SCORES				TOTAL	MONEY
Noboru Sugai	72	72	68	62	274	¥21,000,000
Masashi Ozaki	68	72	70	67	277	10,080,000
Larry Mize	70	70	70	67	277	10,080,000
Hideki Kase	67	67	73	71	278	4,960,000
Yoshinori Mizumaki	67	68	72	71	278	4,960,000
Frankie Minoza	67	73	67	71	278	4,960,000
Scott Simpson	73	68	70	68	279	3,300,000
Katsuji Hasegawa	71	70	69	69	279	3,300,000
Hiroshi Makino	71	68	70	70	279	3,300,000
Harumitsu Hamano	68	69	71	71	279	3,300,000
Tateo Ozaki	71	70	70	69	280	2,304,000
Seiki Okuda	68	70	72	70	280	2,304,000
Terry Gale	68	70	72	71	281	2,016,000
Graham Marsh	67	73	74	68	282	1,656,000
Toru Nakamura	73	69	70	70	282	1,656,000
Seiji Ebihara	70	70	71	71	282	1,656,000
Toyotake Nakao	67	71	71	73	282	1,656,000
Hiroshi Goda	72	71	73	67	283	1,264,000
Akiyoshi Omachi	71	72	69	71	283	1,264,000
Hiromichi Namiki	72	69	71	71	283	1,264,000
Hideto Shigenobu	74	71	72	67	284	1,056,000
Yoshitaka Yamamoto	71	71	74	68	284	1,056,000
Eiichi Itai	69	72	74	69	284	1,056,000
Daisuke Serizawa	72	68	74	70	284	1,056,000
Nobumitsu Yuhara	72	69	70	73	284	1,056,000
Toshimitsu Kai	70	70	71	73	284	1,056,000

	SCORES				TOTAL	MONEY
David Ishii	71	72	73	69	285	900,000
Yoshikazu Yokoshima	68	74	74	69	285	900,000
Ryoken Kawagishi	68	74	73	70	285	900,000
Teruo Sugihara	70	70	75	70	285	900,000
Masanobu Kimura	71	69	75	70	285	900,000
Hale Irwin	70	70	72	73	285	900,000

Bridgestone

Sodegaura Country Club, Chiba
Par 72; 7,120 yards

October 18-21
purse, ¥120,000,000

	SCORES				TOTAL	MONEY
Saburo Fujiki	67	72	66	69	274	¥21,600,000
Akihito Yokoyama	67	71	67	69	274	12,000,000

(Fujiki defeated Yokoyama on first extra hole.)

Nobuo Serizawa	68	71	70	67	276	8,160,000
Tsukasa Watanabe	72	69	69	67	277	5,760,000
Tadao Nakamura	74	66	69	69	278	4,800,000
Eduardo Herrera	70	69	73	68	280	3,504,000
Masashi Ozaki	68	70	72	70	280	3,504,000
Nobumitsu Yuhara	66	76	68	70	280	3,504,000
Fujio Kobayashi	67	72	70	71	280	3,504,000
Kyoshi Muroda	67	71	69	73	280	3,504,000
David Ishii	72	69	71	69	281	2,208,000
Brian Jones	71	68	70	72	281	2,208,000
Ryoken Kawagishi	70	70	68	73	281	2,208,000
Eiichi Itai	72	70	70	70	282	1,593,000
Yukio Noguchi	70	71	70	71	282	1,593,000
Isamu Noguchi	71	68	72	71	282	1,593,000
Hideki Kase	69	73	68	72	282	1,593,000
Shigeru Kawamata	66	73	70	73	282	1,593,000
Chen Tze Ming	69	73	72	69	283	1,200,000
Raymond Floyd	73	71	70	69	283	1,200,000
Katsuyoshi Tomori	71	72	67	73	283	1,200,000
Seiichi Kanai	68	73	74	69	284	1,036,000
Yoshitaka Yamamoto	70	73	71	70	284	1,036,000
Katsunari Takahashi	70	73	70	71	284	1,036,000
Hiroshi Makino	70	68	73	73	284	1,036,000
Isao Aoki	75	66	70	73	284	1,036,000
Tsuneyuki Nakajima	78	66	72	69	285	867,000
Motomasa Aoki	69	74	73	69	285	867,000
Teruo Sugihara	70	73	70	72	285	867,000
Kazuhiro Takami	68	70	75	72	285	867,000
Satoshi Ogawa	70	73	70	72	285	867,000
Noboru Sugai	68	73	71	73	285	867,000
Akiyoshi Omachi	73	68	71	73	285	867,000
Hiroshi Goda	67	71	74	73	285	867,000
Katsuji Hasegawa	72	69	69	76	285	867,000

/ THE ASIA/JAPAN TOUR

Lark Cup

ABC Golf Club, Tojocho
Par 72; 7,176 yards

October 25-28
purse, ¥180,000,000

	SCORES				TOTAL	MONEY
Ryoken Kawagishi	72	68	69	68	277	¥32,400,000
Masashi Ozaki	70	69	70	70	279	18,000,000
David Ishii	70	72	71	70	283	9,360,000
Barry Lane	68	75	70	70	283	9,360,000
Isao Aoki	71	73	68	71	283	9,360,000
Nobuo Serizawa	72	71	76	65	284	5,820,000
Peter Senior	71	72	70	71	284	5,820,000
Katsuji Hasegawa	67	74	69	74	284	5,820,000
Roger Mackay	71	73	71	70	285	4,680,000
Tomohiro Maruyama	71	71	79	65	286	3,870,000
Koichi Suzuki	71	71	73	71	286	3,870,000
Tsuneyuki Nakajima	73	72	72	70	287	2,712,000
Terry Gale	73	72	71	71	287	2,712,000
Tateo Ozaki	71	75	69	72	287	2,712,000
Satoshi Higashi	70	74	69	74	287	2,712,000
Kouki Idoki	69	75	69	74	287	2,712,000
Noboru Sugai	74	67	71	75	287	2,712,000
Hideki Kase	69	76	73	70	288	1,854,000
Yoshinori Kaneko	70	70	76	72	288	1,854,000
Eiichi Itai	69	72	74	73	288	1,854,000
Masahiro Kuramoto	70	69	72	77	288	1,854,000
Kiyoshi Muroda	72	73	74	70	289	1,555,000
Futoshi Irino	74	73	71	71	289	1,555,000
Graham Marsh	69	76	71	73	289	1,555,000
Yoshinori Mizumaki	71	70	75	73	289	1,555,000
Naomichi Ozaki	72	71	72	74	289	1,555,000
Saburo Fujiki	74	71	73	72	290	1,350,000
Norikazu Kawakami	69	77	72	72	290	1,350,000
D.A. Weibring	71	71	76	72	290	1,350,000
Pete Izumikawa	69	74	74	73	290	1,350,000
Tsukasa Watanabe	70	73	73	74	290	1,350,000
Yoshinori Ichioka	71	72	71	76	290	1,350,000

Asahi Glass Four Tours World Championship

Yomiuri Country Club, Inagi
Par 72; 7,017 yards

November 1-4
purse, US$1,150,000

FIRST ROUND

POINTS: EUROPE 8, UNITED STATES 4.
Ronan Rafferty (E) defeated Mark Calcavecchia (US), 71-73.
David Feherty (E) defeated Payne Stewart (US), 71-72.
Fred Couples (US) defeated Nick Faldo (E), 65-69.
Mark James (E) defeated Wayne Levi (US), default (injury).
Ian Woosnam (E) defeated Tim Simpson (US), 68-71.
Jodie Mudd (US) defeated Bernhard Langer (E), 69-70.

POINTS: AUSTRALASIA 6, JAPAN 6.
Nobuo Serizawa (J) defeated Peter Senior (A), 69-70.
Saburo Fujiki (J) defeated Rodger Davis (A), 68-71.
Craig Parry (A) defeated Hideki Kase (J), 71-75.

Naomichi Ozaki (J) defeated Brian Jones (A), 71-73.
Wayne Grady (A) defeated Masahiro Kuramoto (J), 71-72.
Ian Baker-Finch (A) defeated Noboru Sugai (J), 67-68.

SECOND ROUND

POINTS: AUSTRALASIA 8, EUROPE 4.
Davis (A) halved with Rafferty (E), 69-69.
Jones (A) defeated Feherty (E), 72-74.
Parry (A) halved with James (E), 71-71.
Baker-Finch (A) defeated Woosnam (E), 68-69.
Faldo (E) defeated Grady (A), 67-69.
Senior (A) defeated Langer (E), 71-75.

POINTS: UNITED STATES 10, JAPAN 2.
Simpson (US) defeated Serizawa (J), 69-71.
Couples (US) defeated Fujiki (J), 66-69.
Stewart (US) halved with Kase (J), 68-68.
Calcavecchia (US) defeated Sugai (J), 68-73.
Mudd (US) halved with Ozaki (J), 71-71.
Levi (US) defeated Kuramoto (J), 69-74.

STANDINGS AFTER 36 HOLES:
United States and Australasia 14, Europe 12, Japan 8.

THIRD ROUND

POINTS: UNITED STATES 6, AUSTRALASIA 6.
Simpson (US) defeated Grady (A), 69-71.
Calcavecchia (US) defeated Senior (A), 70-74.
Parry (A) defeated Stewart (US), 68-70.
Davis (A) defeated Couples (US), 67-69.
Baker-Finch (A) defeated Mudd (US), 68-76.
Levi (US) defeated Jones (A), 66-70.

POINTS: EUROPE 6, JAPAN 6.
Kuramoto (J) defeated Rafferty (E), 68-72.
Sugai (J) defeated James (E), 70-73.
Woosnam (E) defeated Ozaki (J), 69-71.
Langer (E) defeated Serizawa (J), 68-70.
Kase (J) defeated Feherty (E), 70-74.
Faldo (E) defeated Fujiki (J), 69-71.

STANDINGS AFTER 54 HOLES:
United States and Australasia 20, Europe 18, Japan 14.

Australasia declared winner based on total-strokes tie-breaker when final round was cancelled because of rain, which made course unplayable. United States had no stroke total because of Levi withdrawal in first round.

MONEY BREAKDOWN:
Each Australasian player received $80,000 each; U.S. player $45,000; each European player $35,000; each Japanese player $30,000.

Acom P.T.

Japan Classic Country Club, Ayamacho
Par 72; 6,796 yards
(Final round cancelled - rain, course unplayable.)

November 1-4
purse, ¥75,320,000

	POINTS			TOTAL	MONEY
Bob Gilder	38	39	38	115	¥10,220,000
Bob Tway	37	38	39	114	
Yoshinori Kaneko	36	36	41	113	
Jean Van De Velde	39	37	37	113	
Yoshiyuki Isomura	39	37	37	113	
Hideyuki Sato	38	36	37	111	
Hiroshi Makino	39	37	35	111	
Toyotake Nakao	36	39	36	111	
Akihito Yokoyama	39	37	35	111	
Ken Green	35	36	39	110	
Hiroshi Ueda	37	38	35	110	
Seiki Okuda	39	37	34	110	
Ikuo Shirahama	39	32	38	109	
Yoshinori Mizumaki	35	36	38	109	
Hideto Shigenobu	39	33	37	109	
Motomasa Aoki	37	36	36	109	
Katsushige Takahashi	37	37	35	109	
Eduardo Herrera	35	33	41	109	
Anthony Gilligan	35	39	35	109	
Masanobu Kimura	38	38	33	109	
Teruo Nakamura	38	33	37	108	
Toshiaki Sudo	35	37	36	108	
Frankie Minoza	35	37	36	108	
Tomohiro Maruyama	37	37	34	108	

Visa Taiheiyo Club Masters

Taiheiyo Golf Course, Gotemba
Par 72; 7,027 yards

November 8-11
purse, ¥130,000,000

	SCORES				TOTAL	MONEY
Jose Maria Olazabal	66	68	69	67	270	¥23,400,000
Masashi Ozaki	67	69	72	67	275	10,920,000
Bernhard Langer	71	68	69	67	275	10,920,000
Nobuo Serizawa	67	71	74	64	276	6,240,000
Yoshiyuki Isomura	68	70	71	70	279	5,200,000
Fred Couples	70	69	72	69	280	4,420,000
Miguel Angel Martin	67	73	69	71	280	4,420,000
Graham Marsh	72	68	72	69	281	3,575,000
Wayne Grady	68	66	75	72	281	3,575,000
*Shigeki Maruyama	68	70	70	73	281	
Steve Elkington	70	71	72	69	282	2,795,000
Ikuo Shirahama	69	71	71	71	282	2,795,000
Saburo Fujiki	69	68	78	68	283	2,038,000
Brian Jones	72	70	73	68	283	2,038,000
David Ishii	72	72	70	69	283	2,038,000
Yoshinori Mizumaki	72	69	72	70	283	2,038,000
Roger Mackay	69	71	71	72	283	2,038,000
Yoshitaka Yamamoto	71	71	71	71	284	1,560,000
Shigeru Kawamata	72	72	69	72	285	1,404,000
Jeff Sluman	73	67	72	73	285	1,404,000

	SCORES				TOTAL	MONEY
Ronan Rafferty	74	68	77	67	286	1,183,000
Masahiro Kuramoto	71	68	76	71	286	1,183,000
Naomichi Ozaki	67	73	74	72	286	1,183,000
Kinpachi Yoshimura	69	73	72	72	286	1,183,000
Pete Izumikawa	70	73	70	73	286	1,183,000
Ian Baker-Finch	68	72	73	73	286	1,183,000
Ryoken Kawagishi	74	68	73	72	287	1,066,000
Kiyoshi Muroda	71	73	74	70	288	988,000
Yoshinori Kaneko	70	75	71	72	288	988,000
Shinsaku Maeda	68	75	73	72	288	988,000
Yoshikazu Yokoshima	72	70	73	73	288	988,000
Katsuji Hasegawa	74	67	73	74	288	988,000

Dunlop Phoenix

Phoenix Country Club, Miyazaki
Par 72; 6,993 yards

November 15-18
purse, ¥200,000,000

	SCORES				TOTAL	MONEY
Larry Mize	69	65	69	71	274	¥36,000,000
Naomichi Ozaki	67	72	67	71	277	20,000,000
Tsuneyuki Nakajima	69	73	70	66	278	9,600,000
David Ishii	65	74	71	68	278	9,600,000
Severiano Ballesteros	71	68	70	69	278	9,600,000
Larry Nelson	71	68	73	71	278	9,600,000
Graham Marsh	69	71	69	70	279	6,100,000
Tom Watson	69	71	69	70	279	6,100,000
Roger Mackay	72	71	69	68	280	4,900,000
Tsukasa Watanabe	67	70	72	71	280	4,900,000
Masahiro Kuramoto	74	73	68	66	281	3,408,000
Jose Maria Olazabal	71	72	71	67	281	3,408,000
Yoshiyuki Isomura	69	75	67	70	281	3,408,000
Steve Jones	71	71	67	72	281	3,408,000
Mike Reid	70	69	69	73	281	3,408,000
Brian Jones	69	72	71	70	282	2,426,000
Scott Hoch	68	74	70	70	282	2,426,000
Jim Gallagher, Jr.	72	69	71	70	282	2,426,000
Craig Parry	70	74	70	69	283	2,000,000
Eduardo Romero	71	71	72	69	283	2,000,000
Craig Stadler	68	71	71	73	283	2,000,000
Teruo Sugihara	70	73	69	72	284	1,800,000
Ken Green	68	73	69	74	284	1,800,000
Hajime Meshiai	68	73	75	69	285	1,620,000
Ikuo Shirahama	69	72	73	71	285	1,620,000
Nobuo Serizawa	72	72	69	72	285	1,620,000
Brian Tennyson	72	69	72	72	285	1,620,000
Davis Love	70	71	70	74	285	1,620,000
Jeff Sluman	67	68	73	77	285	1,620,000
Masashi Ozaki	68	73	76	69	286	1,440,000
Chen Tze Ming	75	68	71	72	286	1,440,000
Seiichi Kanai	73	70	69	74	286	1,440,000

Casio World Open

Ibusiki Golf Club, Ibusiki
Par 72; 7,014 yards

November 22-25
purse, ¥120,000,000

	SCORES				TOTAL	MONEY
Mike Reid	69	70	65	70	274	¥21,600,000
Yoshinori Kaneko	70	71	70	65	276	12,000,000
David Ishii	71	71	72	63	277	5,060,000
Graham Marsh	72	70	68	67	277	5,060,000
Masahiro Kuramoto	74	68	66	69	277	5,060,000
Mike Donald	70	68	69	70	277	5,060,000
Ryoken Kawagishi	71	69	66	71	277	5,060,000
Severiano Ballesteros	71	67	68	71	277	5,060,000
Tsukasa Watanabe	70	71	69	68	278	2,760,000
Naomichi Ozaki	68	70	70	70	278	2,760,000
Yukio Noguchi	71	71	66	70	278	2,760,000
Eduardo Romero	75	67	71	66	279	1,956,000
Craig Stadler	70	67	73	69	279	1,956,000
Chen Tze Ming	71	69	69	70	279	1,956,000
Larry Nelson	66	70	72	71	279	1,956,000
Larry Mize	74	67	72	67	280	1,456,000
Jeff Sluman	73	69	71	67	280	1,456,000
Teruo Nakamura	69	70	73	68	280	1,456,000
Miguel Angel Martin	68	74	70	69	281	1,176,000
Isao Aoki	71	69	70	71	281	1,176,000
Hale Irwin	72	73	65	71	281	1,176,000
Robert Gamez	68	72	69	72	281	1,176,000
Noboru Sugai	72	68	75	67	282	1,080,000
Nobumitsu Yuhara	70	71	71	70	282	1,080,000
Eduardo Herrera	76	68	68	70	282	1,080,000
Tsuneyuki Nakajima	69	71	71	71	282	1,080,000
Chen Tze Chung	71	71	69	71	282	1,080,000
Yoshinori Ichioka	74	70	71	68	283	888,000
Brian Tennyson	73	69	71	70	283	888,000
Yoshiyuki Isomura	71	71	70	71	283	888,000
Kouki Idoki	68	72	72	71	283	888,000
Hideki Kase	70	74	65	74	283	888,000

Japan Series

Yomiuri Country Club, Osaka
Par 72; 7,039 yards

November 29-30

Yomiuri Country Club, Tokyo
Par 72; 7,017 yards

December 1-2
purse, ¥60,000,000

	SCORES				TOTAL	MONEY
Naomichi Ozaki	71	69	64	71	275	¥15,000,000
Tsuneyuki Nakajima	70	67	67	71	275	8,200,000

(Ozaki defeated Nakajima on third extra hole.)

Toru Nakamura	73	71	65	69	278	5,500,000
Brian Jones	69	70	71	69	279	4,000,000
Hideki Kase	70	73	70	68	281	3,000,000
Tsukasa Watanabe	74	65	69	73	281	3,000,000
Teruo Sugihara	72	69	71	70	282	2,250,000
Kouki Idoki	73	69	68	72	282	2,250,000
Masahiro Kuramoto	74	70	70	69	283	1,825,000

	SCORES				TOTAL	MONEY
Ryoken Kawagishi	70	69	71	73	283	1,825,000
David Ishii	68	71	70	75	284	1,600,000
Graham Marsh	71	71	70	73	285	1,500,000
Hiroshi Makino	71	68	74	73	286	1,400,000
Yoshinori Kaneko	73	75	71	68	287	1,200,000
Seiichi Kanai	76	67	69	75	287	1,200,000
Nobuo Serizawa	71	69	71	76	287	1,200,000
Isao Aoki	72	72	72	72	288	1,000,000
Saburo Fujiki	73	67	73	67	289	900,000
Noboru Sugai	74	70	73	73	290	750,000
Nobumitsu Yuhara	75	73	68	74	290	750,000
Tadao Nakamura	74	70	74	75	293	600,000
Satoshi Higashi	70	76	75	73	294	550,000
Katsuyoshi Tomori	78	74	73	72	297	500,000

Daikyo Open

Daikyo Country Club, Onnason, Okinawa
Par 72; 6,273 yards

December 6-9
purse, ¥100,000,000

	SCORES				TOTAL	MONEY
Teruo Sugihara	67	68	69	69	273	¥18,000,000
Seiki Okuda	68	70	68	68	274	10,000,000
Shinsaku Maeda	68	70	69	69	276	5,800,000
Hsieh Min Nan	67	70	68	71	276	5,800,000
Yoshitaka Yamamoto	71	73	70	67	281	3,425,000
Chen Tze Ming	67	75	69	70	281	3,425,000
Tadao Nakamura	71	67	71	72	281	3,425,000
Masahiro Kuramoto	70	69	68	74	281	3,425,000
Futoshi Irino	73	73	70	67	283	2,084,000
Hiroya Kamide	72	74	69	68	283	2,084,000
Takaaki Fukuzawa	71	73	71	68	283	2,084,000
Saburo Fujiki	70	69	74	70	283	2,084,000
Kiyoshi Maita	70	72	71	70	283	2,084,000
Kinpachi Yoshimura	75	71	68	70	284	1,440,000
Norikazu Kawakami	70	71	72	71	284	1,440,000
Tadami Ueno	68	71	72	73	284	1,440,000
Tatsuo Fujima	72	71	72	70	285	1,120,000
Yoshikazu Yokoshima	71	72	71	71	285	1,120,000
Katsuji Hasegawa	67	73	73	72	285	1,120,000
Tsuyoshi Yoneyama	75	73	71	67	286	960,000
Noboru Sugai	76	71	69	70	286	960,000
Shigeru Kawamata	70	75	69	72	286	960,000
Toshiaki Sudo	70	74	74	69	287	840,000
Akiyoshi Omachi	76	68	70	73	287	840,000
Toru Nakamura	73	70	70	74	287	840,000
Kazujiro Takami	71	75	67	74	287	840,000
Yoshimi Nizeki	70	71	69	77	287	840,000
Ryoken Kawagishi	75	68	76	69	288	750,000
Brian Jones	75	73	71	69	288	750,000
Hideto Shigenobu	72	75	69	72	288	750,000
Kouki Idoki	79	67	69	73	288	750,000

Johnnie Walker Asian Classic

Royal Hong Kong Golf Club, Hong Kong
Par 35-36—71; 6,732 yards

December 12-15
purse, US$350,000

	SCORES				TOTAL	MONEY
Nick Faldo	72	68	62	68	270	$50,000
Ian Woosnam	69	68	70	67	274	32,000
Mike Clayton	72	70	66	67	275	18,500
Colin Montgomerie	68	70	68	70	276	12,500
Lee Porter	69	70	70	67	276	12,500
Todd Hamilton	69	68	69	70	276	12,500
Ronan Rafferty	67	69	69	72	277	9,000
Richard Zokol	70	68	66	73	279	6,666.67
Rick Gibson	69	69	70	71	279	6,666.67
Kyi Hla Han	73	74	66	66	279	6,666.67
Mats Lanner	71	70	71	69	281	5,850
Marimuthu Ramayah	72	70	68	71	281	5,850
Chris Perry	69	73	68	72	282	5,550
Barry Lane	75	68	70	69	282	5,550
Peter Teravainen	71	69	70	72	282	5,550
Frank Nobilo	72	71	70	69	282	5,550
Alberto Binaghi	68	70	75	70	283	5,250
Joey Sindelar	69	72	72	70	283	5,250
Chris Dimarco	70	70	71	73	284	5,100
Vijay Singh	71	72	71	71	285	4,900
Ove Sellberg	77	67	71	70	285	4,900
Mario Siodina	79	70	67	69	285	4,900
Greg Turner	72	72	72	70	286	4,600
Hsieh Chin Sheng	72	73	69	72	286	4,600
Dominique Boulet	74	72	70	70	286	4,600
Mark Aebli	71	73	69	74	287	4,350
Anders Forsbrand	76	66	72	73	287	4,350
Lu Wen Ter	74	71	73	70	288	4,150
Yu Chin Han	71	70	77	70	288	4,150
Robert Pactolerin	75	70	71	73	289	3,850
Peter Baker	76	69	72	72	289	3,850
Thaworn Wiratchant	77	70	72	70	289	3,850
Lim Wee Chew	76	76	68	69	289	3,850

The Women's Tours

Jamaica Classic

The Tryall Club, Montego Bay, Jamaica
Par 34-37—71; 6,191 yards

January 19-21
purse, $500,000

	SCORES			TOTAL	MONEY
Patty Sheehan	69	68	75	212	$75,000
Pat Bradley	74	74	67	215	35,417
Jane Geddes	73	73	69	215	35,417
Lynn Connelly	74	68	73	215	35,416
Muffin Spencer-Devlin	76	72	68	216	19,375
Patti Rizzo	72	75	69	216	19,375
Maggie Will	79	70	68	217	13,167
Alice Ritzman	76	68	73	217	13,167
Missie Berteotti	69	75	73	217	13,166
Jody Anschutz	76	73	69	218	9,251
Deb Richard	72	76	70	218	9,250
Jan Stephenson	72	76	70	218	9,250
Robin Walton	74	71	73	218	9,250
Beth Daniel	78	76	65	219	6,750
Penny Hammel	75	77	67	219	6,750
Marta Figueras-Dotti	74	74	71	219	6,750
Jenny Lidback	73	74	72	219	6,750
Dale Eggeling	71	76	72	219	6,750
JoAnne Carner	75	69	75	219	6,750
Allison Finney	78	71	71	220	5,382
Danielle Ammaccapane	75	73	72	220	5,381
Cindy Rarick	71	76	73	220	5,381
Cathy Morse	70	73	77	220	5,381
Sherri Steinhauer	75	74	72	221	4,775
Susan Sanders	74	74	73	221	4,775
Lauri Merten	74	74	74	222	4,250
Sue Ertl	75	72	75	222	4,250
Laurie Rinker	74	73	75	222	4,250
Myra Blackwelder	71	76	75	222	4,250
Cathy Marino	75	70	77	222	4,250

Oldsmobile Classic

Wycliffe Golf and Country Club, Lake Worth, Florida
Par 36-36—72; 6,275 yards

February 1-4
purse, $300,000

	SCORES				TOTAL	MONEY
Pat Bradley	66	65	74	76	281	$45,000
Dale Eggeling	72	73	67	69	281	27,750

(Bradley defeated Eggeling on first extra hole.)

Dottie Mochrie	72	71	67	72	282	20,250
Myra Blackwelder	73	73	70	68	284	10,450
Beth Daniel	72	71	72	69	284	10,450
Deborah McHaffie	71	69	74	70	284	10,450
Elaine Crosby	70	69	73	72	284	10,450
Sue Thomas	71	70	70	73	284	10,450

	SCORES				TOTAL	MONEY
Laurel Kean	71	68	72	73	284	10,450
Colleen Walker	71	72	68	74	285	6,300
Missie Berteotti	72	74	72	68	286	4,996
Deb Richard	75	70	70	71	286	4,996
Tina Barrett	71	73	70	72	286	4,996
JoAnne Carner	70	71	72	73	286	4,996
Jane Geddes	72	67	74	73	286	4,996
Gina Hull	71	73	72	71	287	3,766
Jane Crafter	75	71	69	72	287	3,766
Laura Davies	71	73	70	73	287	3,766
Carolyn Hill	72	70	72	73	287	3,766
Dawn Coe	71	68	73	75	287	3,766
Amy Benz	69	72	75	72	288	3,110
Jenny Lidback	70	73	72	73	288	3,110
Meg Mallon	69	73	73	73	288	3,110
Barb Thomas	71	70	74	73	288	3,109
Cathy Morse	73	74	71	71	289	2,746
Patty Jordan	68	73	74	74	289	2,745
Nicky LeRoux	66	76	72	75	289	2,745
Kim Shipman	72	73	73	72	290	2,388
Cindy Mackey	71	75	71	73	290	2,388
Judy Dickinson	71	71	75	73	290	2,388
Cathy Johnston	74	73	69	74	290	2,388
Cindy Figg-Currier	72	74	69	75	290	2,388

Phar-Mor Inverrary Classic

Inverrary Country Club and Resort, Fort Lauderdale, Florida
Par 36-36—72; 6,248 yards
February 16-18
purse, $400 000

	SCORES			TOTAL	MONEY
Jane Crafter	70	67	72	209	$60,000
Nancy Lopez	73	67	70	210	37,000
Meg Mallon	72	68	71	211	21,667
Danielle Ammaccapane	72	68	71	211	21,667
Dale Eggeling	69	68	74	211	21,666
Patty Sheehan	72	70	70	212	12,900
Elaine Crosby	68	71	73	212	12,900
Beth Daniel	71	73	69	213	9,400
Susan Sanders	70	73	70	213	9,400
Pat Bradley	74	67	72	213	9,400
Laurel Kean	74	69	71	214	7,067
Betsy King	72	71	71	214	7,067
Missie Berteotti	71	69	74	214	7,066
Jane Geddes	70	76	69	215	5,520
Cathy Morse	72	73	70	215	5,520
Donna Wilkins	75	69	71	215	5,520
Alison Nicholas	73	70	72	215	5,520
Jill Briles	72	71	72	215	5,520
Sherri Turner	74	72	70	216	4,238
Deb Richard	74	71	71	216	4,237
Rosie Jones	74	71	71	216	4,237
Laura Baugh	74	71	71	216	4,237
Deedee Lasker	73	71	72	216	4,237
Sandra Palmer	73	71	72	216	4,237
Gina Hull	71	73	72	216	4,237
Debbie Massey	73	73	71	217	3,400
Amy Alcott	76	70	71	217	3,400

	SCORES			TOTAL	MONEY
Donna White	71	74	72	217	3,400
Nancy Brown	72	71	74	217	3,400
Tammie Green	70	67	80	217	3,400

Orix Hawaiian Open

Ko Olina Golf Club, Ewa Beach, Hawaii
Par 36-36—72; 6,204 yards

February 22-24
purse, $350,000

	SCORES			TOTAL	MONEY
Beth Daniel	71	67	72	210	$52,500
Patty Sheehan	69	73	71	213	28,000
Amy Benz	70	70	73	213	28,000
Myra Blackwelder	71	74	70	215	12,985
Missie Berteotti	73	70	72	215	12,985
Patti Rizzo	73	70	72	215	12,985
Lori Poling	70	72	73	215	12,985
Sherri Turner	70	71	74	215	12,985
Michelle McGann	71	74	71	216	6,826
Rosie Jones	72	72	72	216	6,826
Amy Alcott	72	71	73	216	6,826
Deedee Lasker	72	70	74	216	6,825
Judy Dickinson	72	69	75	216	6,825
Jill Briles	74	73	70	217	4,945
Jane Geddes	73	71	73	217	4,945
Cathy Gerring	69	75	73	217	4,945
Lynn Connelly	71	72	74	217	4,944
Laurie Rinker	76	73	69	218	4,114
Dawn Coe	73	74	71	218	4,114
Sue Ertl	71	72	75	218	4,113
Nancy Ramsbottom	71	72	75	218	4,113
Gail Anderson-Graham	71	74	74	219	3,596
Elaine Crosby	69	72	78	219	3,596
Jane Crafter	74	73	73	220	3,185
Penny Hammel	73	72	75	220	3,185
Marci Bozarth	71	74	75	220	3,185
Miki Oda	71	74	75	220	3,185
Vicki Fergon	72	72	76	220	3,185
Caroline Keggi	76	74	71	221	2,358
Mayumi Hirase	73	77	71	221	2,358
Sherri Steinhauer	76	72	73	221	2,358
Allison Finney	75	73	73	221	2,358
Mitzi Edge	74	74	73	221	2,358
Shirley Furlong	75	72	74	221	2,358
Becky Pearson	75	72	74	221	2,358
Kim Bauer	75	71	75	221	2,358
Hollis Stacy	74	72	75	221	2,358
Sally Little	72	74	75	221	2,358
Cindy Rarick	74	71	76	221	2,358
Hiromi Kobayashi	72	70	79	221	2,357

Women's Kemper Open

Wailea Resort, Maui, Hawaii
Par 35-36—71; 6,139 yards

March 1-4
purse, $500,000

	SCORES				TOTAL	MONEY
Beth Daniel	73	75	66	69	283	$75,000
Rosie Jones	71	73	69	71	284	40,000
Laura Davies	70	71	72	71	284	40,000
Cathy Gerring	71	71	73	70	285	23,750
Mitzi Edge	68	71	73	73	285	23,750
Deb Richard	73	74	70	69	286	17,500
Liselotte Neumann	74	72	71	70	287	12,500
Caroline Keggi	73	72	72	70	287	12,500
Vicki Fergon	71	74	71	71	287	12,500
Cindy Figg-Currier	70	73	73	71	287	12,500
Sally Little	76	73	70	69	288	9,219
Marci Bozarth	74	73	72	69	288	9,219
Val Skinner	73	75	73	68	289	7,594
Sue Ertl	76	71	71	71	289	7,594
Myra Blackwelder	71	74	73	71	289	7,594
Trish Johnson	72	74	71	72	289	7,594
Jane Crafter	74	74	72	70	290	6,094
Nancy Lopez	72	74	73	71	290	6,094
Penny Hammel	73	72	74	71	290	6,094
Pat Bradley	71	74	72	73	290	6,094
Patty Sheehan	68	76	72	74	290	6,094
Barb Bunkowsky	73	72	76	70	291	5,136
Jenny Lidback	70	74	77	70	291	5,136
Danielle Ammaccapane	74	74	72	71	291	5,135
Michelle McGann	75	71	74	72	292	4,719
Shirley Furlong	73	73	74	72	292	4,719
Becky Pearson	73	76	75	69	293	3,988
Lisa Walters	74	73	76	70	293	3,988
Chihiro Nakajima	77	73	71	72	293	3,988
Cathy Reynolds	70	78	73	72	293	3,988
Carolyn Hill	75	71	75	72	293	3,988
Miki Oda	77	71	72	73	293	3,988
Cathy Morse	72	74	73	74	293	3,987
Lenore Rittenhouse	73	74	71	75	293	3,987

Desert Inn International

Desert Inn Country Club, Las Vegas, Nevada
Par 36-36—72; 6,285 yards

March 9-11
purse, $400,000

	SCORES			TOTAL	MONEY
Maggie Will	73	66	75	214	$60,000
Ayako Okamoto	73	69	73	215	28,334
Val Skinner	71	70	74	215	28,333
Patti Rizzo	66	70	79	215	28,333
Sherri Steinhauer	74	69	73	216	14,267
Cathy Morse	73	70	73	216	14,267
Cathy Gerring	71	70	75	216	14,266
Deborah McHaffie	73	71	73	217	9,900
Beth Daniel	72	70	75	217	9,900
Nancy Lopez	72	70	76	218	8,400
Trish Johnson	70	73	76	219	7,067

	SCORES	TOTAL	MONEY
Patty Sheehan	70 72 77	219	7,067
Liselotte Neumann	69 73 77	219	7,066
Vicki Fergon	72 75 73	220	5,800
Sherri Turner	72 72 76	220	5,800
Danielle Ammaccapane	68 72 80	220	5,800
Deb Richard	73 74 74	221	4,700
Rosie Jones	72 74 75	221	4,700
Myra Blackwelder	72 74 75	221	4,700
Colleen Walker	72 72 77	221	4,700
Betsy King	70 74 77	221	4,700
Robin Walton	72 71 78	221	4,700
Kathy Guadagnino	74 74 74	222	3,704
Susie Redman	76 71 75	222	3,704
Pat Bradley	72 74 76	222	3,703
Kay Cockerill	73 71 78	222	3,703
Dottie Mochrie	72 72 78	222	3,703
Marta Figueras-Dotti	68 74 80	222	3,703
Laurie Rinker	74 75 74	223	3,000
Kate Rogerson	68 78 77	223	3,000
Kim Shipman	72 73 78	223	3,000
Lauri Merten	73 70 80	223	3,000
Jane Geddes	72 71 80	223	3,000
Tina Barrett	70 72 81	223	3,000

Circle K Tucson Open

Randolph North Golf Course, Tucson, Arizona
Par 35-37—72; 6,243 yards

March 15-18
purse, $300,000

	SCORES	TOTAL	MONEY
Colleen Walker	71 68 65 72	276	$45,000
Pat Bradley	70 74 71 66	281	19,125
Kate Rogerson	69 71 74 67	281	19,125
Heather Drew	73 68 69 71	281	19,125
Betsy King	71 70 69 71	281	19,125
Jane Geddes	76 70 68 69	283	10,500
Cindy Figg-Currier	76 70 71 67	284	7,500
Susie Redman	74 72 70 68	284	7,500
Ok Hee Ku	70 72 71 71	284	7,500
Marta Figueras-Dotti	67 74 72 71	284	7,500
Nancy Brown	78 68 68 71	285	5,305
Alice Ritzman	73 70 70 72	285	5,305
Missie McGeorge	71 71 69 74	285	5,305
Amy Benz	68 72 73 73	286	4,505
Trish Johnson	71 72 69 74	286	4,505
Kristi Albers	74 72 74 67	287	3,605
Kay Cockerill	73 74 72 68	287	3,605
Jill Briles	71 76 71 69	287	3,605
Dottie Mochrie	73 71 72 71	287	3,605
Cathy Reynolds	73 70 70 74	287	3,605
Lisa Walters	71 72 70 74	287	3,605
Nancy Rubin	67 70 74 76	287	3,605
Caroline Keggi	71 75 73 69	288	2,647
Barb Mucha	73 74 71 70	288	2,647
Gina Hull	72 74 72 70	288	2,647
Kathy Guadagnino	73 73 71 71	288	2,647
Sue Ertl	75 69 73 71	288	2,647
Laurel Kean	70 74 73 71	288	2,647

	SCORES				TOTAL	MONEY
Becky Pearson	69	74	72	73	288	2,646
Nancy Lopez	75	71	67	75	288	2,646
Ayako Okamoto	71	67	71	79	288	2,646

Standard Register Turquoise Classic

Moon Valley Country Club, Phoenix, Arizona
Par 36-37—73; 6,514 yards
March 22-25
purse, $500,000

	SCORES				TOTAL	MONEY
Pat Bradley	70	71	68	71	280	$75,000
Ayako Okamoto	72	69	69	71	281	46,250
Betsy King	69	72	70	71	282	33,750
Beth Daniel	72	71	71	71	285	21,667
Cindy Figg-Currier	68	74	72	71	285	21,667
Kristi Albers	70	70	71	74	285	21,666
Elaine Crosby	69	75	68	74	286	14,750
Marta Figueras-Dotti	73	72	74	69	288	11,750
Rosie Jones	69	70	75	74	288	11,750
Donna White	69	71	73	75	288	11,750
Danielle Ammaccapane	69	74	76	70	289	7,822
Cindy Mackey	75	72	71	71	289	7,822
Cindy Rarick	71	74	72	72	289	7,822
Janet Coles	73	69	75	72	289	7,822
Martha Nause	71	72	73	73	289	7,821
Judy Dickinson	73	71	70	75	289	7,821
Vicki Fergon	68	76	70	75	289	7,821
Patty Sheehan	72	73	74	71	290	6,250
Kris Tschetter	71	77	72	71	291	5,505
Susie Redman	70	73	76	72	291	5,505
Sally Little	73	74	71	73	291	5,505
Shirley Furlong	72	69	77	73	291	5,505
Colleen Walker	72	71	73	75	291	5,505
Patti Rizzo	75	71	74	72	292	4,700
Mitzi Edge	75	71	73	73	292	4,700
Jane Geddes	72	72	69	79	292	4,700
Debbie Massey	74	72	75	72	293	4,100
Nancy Lopez	72	75	73	73	293	4,100
Laura Davies	77	72	70	74	293	4,100
Sherri Turner	75	72	70	76	293	4,100
Penny Hammel	73	71	70	79	293	4,100

Nabisco Dinah Shore

Mission Hills Country Club, Rancho Mirage, California
Par 36-36—72; 6,441 yards
March 29-April 1
purse, $600,000

	SCORES				TOTAL	MONEY
Betsy King	69	70	69	75	283	$90,000
Shirley Furlong	74	73	70	68	285	42,000
Kathy Postlewait	73	72	68	72	285	42,000
Cindy Rarick	72	72	72	70	286	28,000
Colleen Walker	74	72	67	74	287	24,000
Ayako Okamoto	73	72	72	71	288	17,217
Beth Daniel	71	73	72	72	288	17,217
Rosie Jones	72	71	71	74	288	17,216

	SCORES				TOTAL	MONEY
Pat Bradley	74	73	69	73	289	12,699
Meg Mallon	74	72	70	73	289	12,698
Dottie Mochrie	71	76	72	71	290	9,209
Deb Richard	74	71	74	71	290	9,209
Juli Inkster	70	75	74	71	290	9,209
Jill Briles	73	72	73	72	290	9,209
Patty Sheehan	76	73	68	73	290	9,208
Elaine Crosby	73	71	73	73	290	9,208
Donna White	75	70	73	73	291	7,021
Amy Benz	71	73	74	73	291	7,021
Dale Eggeling	72	75	69	75	291	7,021
Margaret Ward	72	72	71	76	291	7,021
Val Skinner	74	74	76	68	292	6,165
Patti Rizzo	72	76	72	72	292	6,165
Janet Anderson	72	77	71	73	293	5,487
Cathy Marino	73	75	72	73	293	5,487
Missie Berteotti	71	74	72	76	293	5,487
Lynn Adams	77	67	72	77	293	5,487
Cathy Morse	76	71	75	72	294	4,796
Danielle Ammaccapane	79	70	71	74	294	4,795
Lori Garbacz	72	74	74	74	294	4,795
Pamela Wright	74	71	74	75	294	4,795
Debbie Massey	72	78	73	72	295	4,225
JoAnne Carner	75	72	70	78	295	4,224
Cathy Reynolds	72	74	70	79	295	4,224
Mitzi Edge	78	69	78	71	296	3,306
Chris Johnson	77	72	74	73	296	3,306
Dawn Coe	76	73	74	73	296	3,306
Jane Crafter	72	76	75	73	296	3,306
Shelley Hamlin	74	73	75	74	296	3,306
Janet Coles	73	73	75	75	296	3,305
Jane Geddes	77	73	70	76	296	3,305
Amy Alcott	72	73	75	76	296	3,305
Lenore Rittenhouse	67	78	74	77	296	3,305
Penny Hammel	73	76	67	80	296	3,305
Jody Anschutz	73	75	77	72	297	2,255
Laura Davies	74	72	79	72	297	2,255
Sally Little	76	74	72	75	297	2,255
Judy Dickinson	74	75	73	75	297	2,255
Missie McGeorge	76	70	76	75	297	2,255
Martha Foyer	72	76	73	76	297	2,255
Anne-Marie Palli	75	74	71	77	297	2,254

Red Robin Kyocera Inamori Classic

Stoneridge Country Club, Poway, California
Par 35-36—71; 6,042 yards

April 5-8
purse, $300,000

	SCORES				TOTAL	MONEY
Kris Monaghan	72	67	70	67	276	$45,000
Cathy Gerring	70	72	67	69	278	27,750
Rosie Jones	70	74	67	68	279	18,000
Ayako Okamoto	71	70	69	69	279	18,000
Kris Tschetter	69	72	72	67	280	11,625
Patti Rizzo	72	68	70	70	280	11,625
Laurel Kean	70	72	70	69	281	7,500
Cindy Figg-Currier	69	72	71	69	281	7,500
Juli Inkster	72	69	70	70	281	7,500

	SCORES				TOTAL	MONEY
Nancy Brown	67	69	69	76	281	7,500
Colleen Walker	73	68	72	69	282	4,981
Betsy King	69	70	72	71	282	4,980
Janice Gibson	70	73	67	72	282	4,980
Cathy Morse	70	71	69	72	282	4,980
Missie McGeorge	70	68	68	76	282	4,980
Amy Benz	74	72	71	66	283	3,900
Liselotte Neumann	74	70	69	70	283	3,900
Dawn Coe	73	69	70	71	283	3,900
Vicki Fergon	69	74	73	68	284	3,450
Melissa McNamara	71	70	72	71	284	3,450
Nina Foust	72	68	73	71	284	3,450
Sue Thomas	74	72	72	67	285	3,083
Jane Crafter	73	71	72	69	285	3,082
Kathryn Young	72	75	72	67	286	2,775
Val Skinner	71	76	70	69	286	2,775
Cindy Mackey	70	74	72	70	286	2,775
Susan Sanders	70	71	72	73	286	2,775
Sue Ertl	74	72	71	70	287	2,373
Pamela Wright	72	73	72	70	287	2,373
Barb Mucha	72	71	74	70	287	2,373
Mitzi Edge	72	70	73	72	287	2,373
Lauren Howe	71	69	73	74	287	2,373

Sara Lee Classic

Hermitage Golf Course, Old Hickory, Tennessee
Par 36-36—72; 6,242 yards

May 3-6
purse, $425,000

	SCORES			TOTAL	MONEY
Ayako Okamoto	71	71	68	210	$63,750
Betsy King	72	71	68	211	24,650
Colleen Walker	71	70	70	211	24,650
JoAnne Carner	73	67	71	211	24,650
Dawn Coe	70	69	72	211	24,649
Pat Bradley	70	68	73	211	24,649
Carolyn Hill	74	68	70	212	12,537
Cathy Johnston	73	73	67	213	8,749
Nancy Lopez	72	72	69	213	8,748
Tammie Green	72	71	70	213	8,748
Patti Rizzo	67	76	70	213	8,748
Nancy Brown	70	72	71	213	8,748
Rosie Jones	75	65	73	213	8,748
Danielle Ammaccapane	74	73	67	214	5,866
Sherri Turner	73	73	68	214	5,866
Alice Ritzman	72	73	69	214	5,866
Stephanie Farwig	73	69	72	214	5,865
Jane Geddes	69	73	72	214	5,865
Barb Mucha	73	73	69	215	4,588
Allison Finney	76	69	70	215	4,587
Marci Bozarth	74	71	70	215	4,587
Cindy Mackey	73	70	72	215	4,587
Margaret Ward	73	70	72	215	4,587
Patty Sheehan	71	72	72	215	4,587
Lauri Merten	75	71	70	216	3,805
Kathy Postlewait	71	75	70	216	3,805
Shirley Furlong	72	73	71	216	3,804
Janet Anderson	71	74	71	216	3,804

	SCORES	TOTAL	MONEY
Donna White	79 69 69	217	3,026
Cindy Rarick	72 75 70	217	3,026
Michelle Dobek	72 74 71	217	3,025
Kate Rogerson	71 75 71	217	3,025
Caroline Keggi	73 72 72	217	3,025
Laurie Rinker	72 72 73	217	3,025
Pamela Wright	70 72 75	217	3,025
Sandra Palmer	69 73 75	217	3,025
Kris Tschetter	69 73 75	217	3,025

Crestar Classic

Greenbrier Country Club, Chesapeake, Virginia
Par 36-36—72; 6,275 yards

May 11-13
purse, $350,000

	SCORES	TOTAL	MONEY
Dottie Mochrie	67 65 68	200	$52,500
Chris Johnson	73 67 69	209	32,375
Meg Mallon	70 72 68	210	23,625
Judy Dickinson	71 71 69	211	16,625
Patty Sheehan	70 71 70	211	16,625
Carolyn Hill	70 72 70	212	12,250
Margaret Ward	74 70 69	213	9,217
Donna White	72 70 71	213	9,217
Rosie Jones	69 70 74	213	9,216
Melissa McNamara	72 73 69	214	7,350
Cathy Johnston	73 74 68	215	5,631
Cathy Morse	75 71 69	215	5,630
Betsy King	74 71 70	215	5,630
Janet Anderson	71 74 70	215	5,630
Cathy Marino	73 71 71	215	5,630
Kristi Albers	72 72 71	215	5,630
Michelle McGann	71 77 68	216	4,114
Kris Monaghan	74 71 71	216	4,114
Cindy Figg-Currier	75 69 72	216	4,113
Jane Geddes	75 68 73	216	4,113
Deedee Lasker	69 73 74	216	4,113
Deb Richard	72 69 75	216	4,113
Sherri Steinhauer	73 74 70	217	3,188
Susan Sanders	75 71 71	217	3,188
Cindy Schreyer	74 72 71	217	3,188
Joan Delk	73 73 71	217	3,187
Penny Hammel	71 75 71	217	3,187
Mitzi Edge	75 70 72	217	3,187
Tracy Kerdyk	71 72 74	217	3,187
Beth Daniel	76 71 71	218	2,444
Gina Hull	74 73 71	218	2,444
Danielle Ammaccapane	74 73 71	218	2,443
Sue Thomas	76 69 73	218	2,443
Val Skinner	72 73 73	218	2,443
Cathy Reynolds	72 71 75	218	2,443
Kathy Guadagnino	69 73 76	218	2,443
Vicki Fergon	70 71 77	218	2,443

Planters Pat Bradley International

Willow Creek Golf Course, High Point, North Carolina
Par 36-36—72; 6,260 yards

May 17-20
purse, $400,000

	SCORES				TOTAL	MONEY
Cindy Rarick	3	4	12	6	25	$60,000
Beth Daniel	8	1	5	10	24	37,000
Hollis Stacy	5	3	5	10	23	27,000
Sherri Steinhauer	4	7	5	6	22	21,000
Juli Inkster	9	-4	7	9	21	17,000
Deb Richard	10	5	0	5	20	12,900
Danielle Ammaccapane	1	5	3	11	20	12,900
Rosie Jones	-2	3	12	6	19	10,400
Nancy Brown	-4	9	6	7	18	9,400
Mitzi Edge	4	0	6	5	15	8,014
Debbie Massey	-1	5	4	7	15	8,014
Jane Geddes	4	4	-2	8	14	7,028
Allison Finney	4	6	-2	5	13	6,228
Val Skinner	4	-3	4	8	13	6,228
Laurel Kean	5	-2	2	8	13	6,228
Elaine Crosby	7	2	-1	4	12	5,328
Dawn Coe	4	-3	4	7	12	5,328
Barb Mucha	7	5	-5	4	11	4,531
Jill Briles	0	8	-2	5	11	4,531
Dale Eggeling	-2	2	5	6	11	4,531
JoAnne Carner	-1	1	4	7	11	4,532
Trish Johnson	-3	2	4	8	11	4,532
Cathy Gerring	6	0	4	1	11	4,531
Marta Figueras-Dotti	9	-2	3	0	10	3,608
Barb Thomas	2	2	-3	9	10	3,608
Penny Hammel	0	1	0	9	10	3,608
Sandra Palmer	0	-1	0	11	10	3,608
Cindy Figg-Currier	-2	5	2	5	10	3,608
Cathy Johnston	0	-1	9	2	10	3,608
Nina Foust	-2	5	-1	7	9	3,023
Vicki Fergon	2	0	-2	9	9	3,023
Martha Nause	11	-10	1	7	9	3,023
Dottie Mochrie	-2	1	3	7	9	3,023

Corning Classic

Corning Country Club, Corning, New York
Par 35-36—71; 6,006 yards

May 24-27
purse, $350,000

	SCORES				TOTAL	MONEY
Pat Bradley	69	70	66	69	274	$52,500
Patty Sheehan	71	69	69	68	277	32,375
Alice Ritzman	68	68	74	68	278	23,625
Rosie Jones	72	68	73	66	279	16,625
Dawn Coe	72	68	70	69	279	16,625
Ayako Okamoto	70	72	68	70	280	12,250
Trish Johnson	68	70	72	71	281	10,325
Hiromi Kobayashi	71	71	70	70	282	8,663
Tammie Green	68	74	69	71	282	8,662
Donna White	70	73	71	69	283	6,709
Kathy Postlewait	72	70	71	70	283	6,709
Cindy Rarick	71	73	66	73	283	6,709

	SCORES				TOTAL	MONEY
Jane Geddes	70	68	76	70	284	5,601
Meg Mallon	70	70	71	73	284	5,601
Colleen Walker	75	69	73	68	285	4,683
Robin Walton	74	74	68	69	285	4,682
Joan Pitcock	70	73	73	69	285	4,682
Martha Foyer	73	70	71	71	285	4,682
Nancy Rubin	72	76	72	66	286	4,201
Jane Crafter	76	71	71	69	287	3,851
Lisa Walters	68	77	72	70	287	3,851
Kay Cockerill	74	72	70	71	287	3,850
Barb Bunkowsky	73	71	74	70	288	3,241
Kathryn Young	73	70	74	71	288	3,241
Adele Lukken	75	68	71	74	288	3,240
Marianne Morris	69	72	73	74	288	3,240
Kris Monaghan	69	70	74	75	288	3,240
Sherri Turner	71	67	74	76	288	3,240
Janet Anderson	75	70	74	70	289	2,536
Shelley Hamlin	77	70	71	71	289	2,535
Robin Hood	69	75	74	71	289	2,535
Cathy Reynolds	72	72	73	72	289	2,535
Barb Mucha	71	74	71	73	289	2,535
Allison Finney	75	69	72	73	289	2,535
Janice Gibson	73	73	69	74	289	2,535
Cathy Johnston	68	73	72	76	289	2,535

Lady Keystone Open

Hershey Country Club, Hershey, Pennsylvania
Par 36-36—72; 6,348 yards

June 1-3
purse, $300,000

	SCORES			TOTAL	MONEY
Cathy Gerring	70	67	71	208	$45,000
Pat Bradley	72	69	68	209	24,000
Elaine Crosby	70	69	70	209	24,000
Kathy Postlewait	70	71	69	210	14,250
Barb Mucha	71	69	70	210	14,250
Jill Briles	70	73	68	211	9,675
Kate Rogerson	67	76	68	211	9,675
Betsy King	69	73	70	212	7,800
Danielle Ammaccapane	69	75	69	213	6,357
Dale Eggeling	71	71	71	213	6,357
Lisa Walters	70	71	72	213	6,357
Michelle McGann	74	72	68	214	4,334
Patti Rizzo	74	71	69	214	4,334
Laurel Kean	69	75	70	214	4,334
Marianne Morris	69	75	70	214	4,334
Donna White	72	71	71	214	4,333
Trish Johnson	72	71	71	214	4,333
Barb Thomas	73	69	72	214	4,333
Mary Beth Zimmerman	67	72	75	214	4,333
Myra Blackwelder	74	71	70	215	3,471
Deb Richard	74	73	69	216	3,009
Tina Purtzer	73	72	71	216	3,009
Marta Figueras-Dotti	73	71	72	216	3,009
Barb Bunkowsky	72	72	72	216	3,008
Caroline Pierce	68	73	75	216	3,008
Cathy Marino	68	72	76	216	3,008
Lynn Connelly	73	74	70	217	2,318

	SCORES			TOTAL	MONEY
Terry-Jo Myers	72	75	70	217	2,318
Cathy Johnston	72	75	70	217	2,318
Pam Allen	77	69	71	217	2,318
Janet Anderson	75	70	72	217	2,318
Kris Tschetter	75	70	72	217	2,318
Laura Davies	73	71	73	217	2,317
Sherri Steinhauer	72	72	73	217	2,317
Amy Alcott	70	73	74	217	2,317

McDonald's Championship

Du Pont Country Club, Wilmington, Delaware
Par 35-36—71; 6,366 yards

June 7-10
purse, $650,000

	SCORES				TOTAL	MONEY
Patty Sheehan	70	67	68	70	275	$97,500
Kristi Albers	69	73	69	68	279	41,438
Betsy King	70	70	70	69	279	41,438
Cathy Gerring	69	72	67	71	279	41,437
Ayako Okamoto	70	69	69	71	279	41,437
Colleen Walker	69	71	71	69	280	19,609
Jane Geddes	68	68	74	70	280	19,608
Barb Mucha	68	72	67	73	280	19,608
Pat Bradley	70	73	71	67	281	14,463
Deb Richard	68	71	73	69	281	14,462
Debbie Massey	75	71	66	70	282	11,885
Carolyn Hill	72	69	71	70	282	11,884
Nancy Lopez	70	72	73	68	283	9,772
Rosie Jones	74	69	71	69	283	9,772
Beth Daniel	74	72	66	71	283	9,772
Tammie Green	71	71	70	71	283	9,772
Dottie Mochrie	74	69	72	69	284	8,147
Deedee Lasker	72	74	67	71	284	8,147
Laurie Rinker	67	71	72	74	284	8,147
Shirley Furlong	72	74	70	69	285	6,880
Alice Ritzman	72	71	73	69	285	6,880
Patti Rizzo	73	71	71	70	285	6,879
Dale Eggeling	74	72	68	71	285	6,879
Sherri Turner	69	74	71	71	285	6,879
Cathy Morse	74	71	73	68	286	5,645
JoAnne Carner	71	74	71	70	286	5,645
Chris Johnson	75	70	69	72	286	5,645
Martha Nause	70	74	70	72	286	5,644
Missie McGeorge	71	70	72	73	286	5,644
Allison Finney	73	71	68	74	286	5,644

Atlantic City Classic

Sands Country Club, Somers Point, New Jersey
Par 35-35—70; 6,015 yards

June 14-17
purse, $300,000

	SCORES				TOTAL	MONEY
Chris Johnson	69	67	69	70	275	$45,000
Pamela Wright	72	69	64	72	277	27,750
Nancy Lopez	67	72	68	71	278	20,250
Dale Eggeling	67	71	67	74	279	15,750

	SCORES				TOTAL	MONEY
Lenore Rittenhouse	70	68	71	71	280	12,750
Mitzi Edge	68	72	72	70	282	10,500
Jennifer Wyatt	76	67	69	71	283	8,325
Robin Walton	70	71	68	74	283	8,325
Beth Daniel	70	69	76	69	284	5,468
Laura Baugh	72	73	69	70	284	5,468
Terry-Jo Myers	71	74	68	71	284	5,468
Alice Ritzman	72	72	69	71	284	5,468
Rosie Jones	70	71	72	71	284	5,468
Juli Inkster	70	71	69	74	284	5,468
Nancy Brown	71	69	69	75	284	5,467
Patty Jordan	74	72	69	70	285	3,755
Donna White	73	69	71	72	285	3,755
Liselotte Neumann	66	75	71	73	285	3,755
Tracy Kerdyk	70	71	70	74	285	3,755
Ayako Okamoto	69	71	70	75	285	3,755
Martha Foyer	72	74	72	68	286	3,230
Sherri Steinhauer	68	68	75	75	286	3,230
Amy Benz	71	74	74	68	287	2,692
Adele Lukken	72	73	73	69	287	2,692
Susie McAllister	73	73	71	70	287	2,692
Michelle Dobek	72	73	71	71	287	2,692
Nancy Ramsbottom	71	74	71	71	287	2,692
Kris Tschetter	71	72	71	73	287	2,692
Barb Bunkowsky	72	70	71	74	287	2,692
Loretta Alderete	75	68	69	75	287	2,691

Rochester International

Locust Hill Country Club, Pittsford, New York
Par 36-36—72; 6,162 yards

June 21-24
purse, $400,000

	SCORES				TOTAL	MONEY
Patty Sheehan	72	64	68	67	271	$60,000
Amy Alcott	69	65	68	73	275	37,000
Nancy Lopez	68	70	70	68	276	27,000
Tammie Green	76	67	68	69	280	21,000
Kathy Postlewait	68	68	68	77	281	17,000
Jane Geddes	72	72	67	71	282	14,000
Missie McGeorge	73	66	71	73	283	11,800
Joan Pitcock	69	73	75	67	284	9,900
Shirley Furlong	72	72	70	70	284	9,900
Martha Foyer	72	70	74	69	285	7,400
Pamela Wright	73	70	72	70	285	7,400
Caroline Keggi	70	71	72	72	285	7,400
Alice Ritzman	73	68	67	77	285	7,400
Danielle Ammaccapane	74	71	71	70	286	5,520
Jenny Lidback	73	72	70	71	286	5,520
Dawn Coe	72	71	71	72	286	5,520
Jane Crafter	72	69	73	72	286	5,520
Elaine Crosby	73	71	69	73	286	5,520
Betsy King	73	69	74	71	287	4,800
Jill Briles	75	68	74	71	288	4,305
Ok Hee Ku	74	68	74	72	288	4,305
Cindy Rarick	71	73	70	74	288	4,305
Ayako Okamoto	72	71	71	74	288	4,305
Sally Little	71	72	76	70	289	3,760
Kristi Albers	76	68	74	71	289	3,760

	SCORES				TOTAL	MONEY
Allison Finney	72	72	72	73	289	3,760
Adele Lukken	74	70	77	69	290	3,280
Deedee Lasker	73	70	73	74	290	3,280
Colleen Walker	75	71	69	75	290	3,280
Dottie Mochrie	71	72	72	75	290	3,280
Amy Benz	72	70	73	75	290	3,280

du Maurier Ltd. Classic

Westmount Golf & Country Club, Kitchener, Canada
Par 37-36—73; 6,420 yards

June 28-July 1
purse, $600,000

	SCORES				TOTAL	MONEY
Cathy Johnston	65	70	70	71	276	$90,000
Patty Sheehan	69	70	70	69	278	55,500
Beth Daniel	74	66	71	70	281	40,500
Liselotte Neumann	68	72	70	72	282	31,500
Missie Berteotti	74	68	69	72	283	25,500
Gina Hull	70	68	76	70	284	19,350
Jody Anschutz	70	72	70	72	284	19,350
Pat Bradley	73	69	70	73	285	14,850
Patti Rizzo	67	69	73	76	285	14,850
Jane Geddes	72	67	74	73	286	12,000
Betsy King	70	72	70	74	286	12,000
Janet Anderson	70	75	73	69	287	9,300
Donna White	72	73	71	71	287	9,300
Tammie Green	73	70	73	71	287	9,300
Vicki Fergon	69	73	73	72	287	9,300
Amy Benz	73	70	71	73	287	9,300
Sherri Turner	74	70	72	72	288	7,650
Deb Richard	69	71	74	74	288	7,650
Caroline Keggi	74	70	75	70	289	6,750
Dawn Coe	72	70	76	71	289	6,750
Sherri Steinhauer	71	72	72	74	289	6,750
Missie McGeorge	74	70	67	78	289	6,750
Cindy Rarick	73	73	72	72	290	5,738
Danielle Ammaccapane	75	69	74	72	290	5,738
Laurel Kean	72	72	74	72	290	5,737
Nina Foust	70	75	72	73	290	5,737
Terri Lyn Carter	69	74	73	75	291	5,010
Dottie Mochrie	72	71	72	76	291	5,010
Susan Sanders	70	70	75	76	291	5,010
Laura Baugh	71	75	68	77	291	5,010
Ayako Okamoto	74	73	75	70	292	3,885
Hiromi Kobayashi	73	73	75	71	292	3,885
Debbie Massey	76	71	73	72	292	3,885
Kim Shipman	73	67	80	72	292	3,885
Cindy Figg-Currier	75	72	72	73	292	3,885
Val Skinner	76	72	70	74	292	3,885
Jill Briles	72	74	72	74	292	3,885
Sandra Palmer	73	71	73	75	292	3,885
Lenore Rittenhouse	71	76	68	77	292	3,885
Jerilyn Britz	71	70	74	77	292	3,885
Margaret Ward	76	72	72	73	293	2,640
Ok Hee Ku	74	74	72	73	293	2,640
Alice Ritzman	75	71	74	73	293	2,640
Carolyn Hill	72	76	71	74	293	2,640
Kris Tschetter	73	74	72	74	293	2,640

	SCORES				TOTAL	MONEY
Chris Johnson	73	72	74	74	293	2,640
Sue Ertl	74	71	72	76	293	2,640
Tina Purtzer	75	71	70	77	293	2,640
Penny Hammel	71	77	74	72	294	1,759
Kay Cockerill	73	74	75	72	294	1,759
Cathy Sherk	74	73	72	75	294	1,759
Kate Rogerson	69	77	73	75	294	1,759
Kathy Postlewait	73	70	76	75	294	1,759
Deedee Lasker	74	68	77	75	294	1,759
Heather Drew	73	72	73	76	294	1,758
Jane Crafter	70	72	76	76	294	1,758

Jamie Farr Toledo Classic

Highland Meadows Golf Club, Sylvania, Ohio
Par 34-37—71; 6,270 yards

July 6-8
purse, $325,000

	SCORES			TOTAL	MONEY
Tina Purtzer	67	72	66	205	$48,750
JoAnne Carner	67	73	69	209	26,000
Chris Johnson	68	71	70	209	25,999
Cathy Gerring	72	72	67	211	12,058
Sue Ertl	73	69	69	211	12,057
Robin Walton	74	67	70	211	12,057
Patti Rizzo	70	70	71	211	12,057
Betsy King	68	70	73	211	12,057
Dale Eggeling	70	71	71	212	7,637
Elaine Crosby	73	71	69	213	6,249
Jennifer Wyatt	72	71	70	213	6,249
Penny Hammel	70	71	72	213	6,249
Diana Heinicke-Rauch	73	72	69	214	4,775
Joan Pitcock	70	73	71	214	4,775
Missie Berteotti	72	70	72	214	4,775
Laura Baugh	72	69	73	214	4,774
Martha Foyer	71	70	73	214	4,774
Sarah McGuire	73	74	68	215	3,768
Mei Chi Cheng	76	69	70	215	3,767
Lauri Merten	71	73	71	215	3,767
Anne-Marie Palli	75	68	72	215	3,767
Nancy Lopez	72	69	74	215	3,767
Lori West	74	71	71	216	3,138
Laurel Kean	74	70	72	216	3,138
Kay Cockerill	74	70	72	216	3,137
Michelle Dobek	71	72	73	216	3,137
Susan Sanders	75	73	69	217	2,518
Tracy Kerdyk	73	73	71	217	2,518
Sue Thomas	74	71	72	217	2,518
Martha Nause	72	73	72	217	2,518
Marianne Morris	71	74	72	217	2,518
Barb Mucha	71	72	74	217	2,518
Cindy Mackey	69	74	74	217	2,518
Becky Pearson	72	70	75	217	2,517
Nancy Rubin	69	73	75	217	2,517

U.S. Women's Open

Atlanta Athletic Club, Duluth, Georgia
Par 36-36—72; 6,298 yards

July 12-15
purse, $500,000

	SCORES				TOTAL	MONEY
Betsy King	72	71	71	70	284	$85,000
Patty Sheehan	66	68	75	76	285	42,500
Dottie Mochrie	74	74	72	66	286	23,956
Danielle Ammaccapane	72	73	70	71	286	23,956
Mary Murphy	70	74	69	74	287	15,904
Elaine Crosby	71	74	73	70	288	12,464
Tammie Green	70	74	73	71	288	12,464
Beth Daniel	71	71	74	72	288	12,464
Hollis Stacy	71	72	77	69	289	8,533
Meg Mallon	71	71	77	70	289	8,533
Cathy Gerring	70	78	70	71	289	8,533
Sherri Turner	74	72	71	72	289	8,533
Colleen Walker	69	75	73	72	289	8,533
Amy Alcott	72	72	72	73	289	8,533
Caroline Keggi	67	75	73	74	289	8,533
Missie McGeorge	72	74	72	72	290	6,727
Rosie Jones	72	70	74	74	290	6,727
JoAnne Carner	73	71	70	77	291	6,287
Alice Ritzman	77	70	73	72	292	5,424
Donna Andrews	75	72	73	72	292	5,424
Jody Anschutz	72	73	74	73	292	5,424
Pat Bradley	74	70	75	73	292	5,424
Nancy Lopez	68	76	75	73	292	5,424
Jane Geddes	66	74	79	73	292	5,424
Cindy Rarick	73	74	70	75	292	5,424
Cindy Figg-Currier	76	72	73	72	293	4,623
Barb Mucha	74	72	75	72	293	4,623
Laura Davies	73	73	74	73	293	4,623
Kathy Postlewait	75	74	75	70	294	4,221
Debbie Massey	70	73	75	76	294	4,221
Allison Finney	73	73	71	77	294	4,221
Cathy Morse	73	75	74	73	295	3,694
Martha Nause	75	71	76	73	295	3,694
Ayako Okamoto	74	74	73	74	295	3,694
Hiromi Kobayashi	75	72	73	75	295	3,694
Deb Richard	74	72	74	75	295	3,694
Pamela Wright	72	74	74	75	295	3,694
Nancy Rubin	71	72	76	76	295	3,694
Shirley Furlong	71	71	77	76	295	3,694
Janet Anderson	70	72	80	74	296	3,185
Nancy Brown	72	75	74	75	296	3,185
Susan Sanders	70	77	72	77	296	3,185
Cathy Marino	71	77	78	71	297	2,817
Heather Drew	75	74	74	74	297	2,817
Gina Hull	73	72	78	74	297	2,817
Alison Nicholas	75	73	74	75	297	2,817
Jackie Gallagher	74	73	74	76	297	2,817
Jan Stephenson	75	72	73	78	298	2,540
Amy Benz	74	75	76	74	299	2,264
Myra Blackwelder	75	71	78	75	299	2,264
Kris Tschetter	70	75	79	75	299	2,264
Jerilyn Britz	69	74	78	78	299	2,264
Joan Delk	74	73	73	79	299	2,264

Phar-Mor Youngstown Classic

Squaw Creek Country Club, Youngstown, Ohio
Par 36-36—72; 6,297 yards
(Tournament extended through Monday - rain delays.)

July 20-23
purse, $400,000

	SCORES			TOTAL	MONEY
Beth Daniel	65	69	73	207	$60,000
Patty Sheehan	70	68	69	207	37,000
Danielle Ammaccapane	69	67	72	208	27,000
Ayako Okamoto	70	68	71	209	19,000
Debbie Massey	71	65	73	209	19,000
Rosie Jones	72	68	70	210	12,900
Dottie Mochrie	67	71	72	210	12,900
Penny Hammel	70	72	69	211	9,400
Donna Andrews	72	69	70	211	9,400
Pat Bradley	71	69	71	211	9,400
Marta Figueras-Dotti	70	74	68	212	6,640
Lori West	70	71	71	212	6,640
Colleen Walker	68	73	71	212	6,640
Cindy Rarick	72	67	73	212	6,640
Nancy Brown	69	67	76	212	6,640
Gina Hull	74	72	67	213	5,300
Dawn Coe	75	69	69	213	5,300
Nina Foust	71	73	70	214	4,182
Lenore Rittenhouse	69	75	70	214	4,182
Tammie Green	73	70	71	214	4,182
Robin Hood	70	73	71	214	4,182
Jill Briles	68	75	71	214	4,182
Nancy Lopez	71	71	72	214	4,182
Janet Anderson	71	71	72	214	4,182
Becky Pearson	69	72	73	214	4,182
Myra Blackwelder	67	74	73	214	4,182
Martha Foyer	69	71	74	214	4,182
Cindy Mackey	75	71	69	215	2,851
Cathy Gerring	73	72	70	215	2,851
Jerilyn Britz	70	75	70	215	2,851
Janice Gibson	73	71	71	215	2,851
Robin Walton	72	72	71	215	2,851
Chris Johnson	72	72	71	215	2,851
Martha Nause	76	66	73	215	2,851
Judy Dickinson	73	69	73	215	2,851
Janet Coles	71	70	74	215	2,851
Shirley Furlong	70	71	74	215	2,851
Anne-Marie Palli	69	71	75	215	2,850

Mazda LPGA Championship

Bethesda Country Club, Bethesda, Maryland
Par 35-36—71; 6,246 yards

July 26-29
purse, $1,000,000

	SCORES				TOTAL	MONEY
Beth Daniel	71	73	70	66	280	$150,000
Rosie Jones	69	70	70	72	281	92,500
Dawn Coe	73	71	68	72	284	67,500
Sue Ertl	70	67	79	69	285	52,500
Betsy King	72	73	72	69	286	33,250
Patty Sheehan	75	71	70	70	286	33,250

	SCORES				TOTAL	MONEY
Tammie Green	72	72	70	72	286	33,250
Cindy Figg-Currier	72	68	73	73	286	33,250
Anne-Marie Palli	75	72	70	70	287	19,500
Pat Bradley	73	71	71	72	287	19,500
Ayako Okamoto	75	69	70	73	287	19,500
Deb Richard	71	72	70	74	287	19,500
Cathy Johnston	70	70	71	76	287	19,500
Martha Nause	73	73	75	67	288	13,500
Amy Benz	69	75	76	68	288	13,500
Nancy Lopez	78	70	70	70	288	13,500
Cindy Rarick	74	71	72	71	288	13,500
Danielle Ammaccapane	73	73	68	74	288	13,500
Susan Sanders	73	73	68	74	288	13,500
Laura Hurlbut	73	75	72	69	289	10,179
Margaret Ward	76	73	71	69	289	10,179
Meg Mallon	72	71	75	71	289	10,179
Judy Dickinson	71	75	71	72	289	10,179
Jill Briles	72	72	71	74	289	10,178
Penny Hammel	71	74	70	74	289	10,178
Chris Johnson	67	77	68	77	289	10,178
Pamela Wright	71	76	73	70	290	8,200
Nancy Brown	70	74	73	73	290	8,200
Gina Hull	70	76	71	73	290	8,200
Liselotte Neumann	75	71	71	73	290	8,200
Trish Johnson	73	71	71	75	290	8,200
Cathy Gerring	75	73	72	71	291	6,975
Jane Crafter	77	68	74	72	291	6,975
Laura Baugh	75	70	73	73	291	6,975
Tracy Kerdyk	72	75	69	75	291	6,975
Jane Geddes	75	75	72	70	292	5,608
Shirley Furlong	71	74	76	71	292	5,607
Sara Anne McGetrick	73	73	75	71	292	5,607
Terry-Jo Myers	74	74	73	71	292	5,607
Barb Mucha	74	72	73	73	292	5,607
Sherri Steinhauer	75	75	68	74	292	5,607
Jennifer Wyatt	72	74	72	74	292	5,607
Becky Pearson	73	75	74	71	293	4,500
Lauri Merten	72	75	73	73	293	4,500
Donna White	73	77	70	73	293	4,500
Missie Berteotti	75	73	73	73	294	3,900
Amy Alcott	76	70	74	74	294	3,900
Jan Stephenson	71	74	72	77	294	3,900
Kathy Postlewait	76	74	77	68	295	3,238
Vicki Fergon	76	73	75	71	295	3,238
Elaine Crosby	72	73	74	76	295	3,237
Marta Figueras-Dotti	72	69	78	76	295	3,237

Boston Five Classic

Tara Ferncroft Country Club, Danvers, Massachusetts
Par 35-37—72; 6,008 yards

August 2-5
purse, $350 000

	SCORES				TOTAL	MONEY
Barb Mucha	71	70	67	69	277	$52,500
Lenore Rittenhouse	72	69	71	65	277	32,375
(Mucha defeated Rittenhouse on second extra hole.)
Cindy Rarick	69	74	69	66	278	23,625
Amy Alcott	73	72	66	69	280	16,625

	SCORES				TOTAL	MONEY
Ok Hee Ku	64	77	69	70	280	16,625
Nancy Brown	72	69	70	70	281	11,288
Laura Baugh	71	70	68	72	281	11,287
Colleen Walker	71	72	69	71	283	9,100
Dale Eggeling	71	68	74	71	284	7,788
Pat Bradley	75	67	69	73	284	7,787
Jan Stephenson	71	72	71	71	285	6,400
Ayako Okamoto	72	69	73	71	285	6,399
Kim Shipman	76	72	74	64	286	5,612
Laurie Rinker	70	73	75	68	286	5,612
Sarah McGuire	72	74	67	74	287	5,087
Joan Pitcock	75	72	70	71	288	4,650
Martha Nause	70	70	77	71	288	4,649
Kay Cockerill	72	76	74	67	289	3,953
Karen Davies	71	72	75	71	289	3,953
Tracy Kerdyk	74	71	71	73	289	3,952
Missie McGeorge	70	74	70	75	289	3,952
Dottie Mochrie	69	73	72	75	289	3,952
Sandra Palmer	72	68	72	77	289	3,952
Marga Stubblefield	75	73	71	71	290	3,145
Marta Figueras-Dotti	77	70	71	72	290	3,145
Barb Bunkowsky	72	71	75	72	290	3,145
Lori West	74	73	70	73	290	3,144
Becky Pearson	73	71	73	73	290	3,144
Heather Drew	73	70	73	74	290	3,144
Caroline Pierce	75	72	71	73	291	2,725
Donna Andrews	73	72	69	77	291	2,724

Stratton Mountain Classic

Stratton Mountain Country Club, Stratton Mountain, Vermont
Par 36-36—72; 6,219 yards

August 9-12
purse, $450,000

	SCORES				TOTAL	MONEY
Cathy Gerring	71	70	72	68	281	$67,500
Caroline Keggi	71	72	70	68	281	41,625
(Gerring defeated Keggi on first extra hole.)						
Lynn Connelly	70	71	71	71	283	27,000
Cindy Figg-Currier	68	72	72	71	283	27,000
Amy Benz	69	72	70	73	284	19,125
Maggie Will	74	70	73	68	285	14,513
Nancy Harvey	68	78	67	72	285	14,512
Rosie Jones	70	73	71	72	286	11,700
Pat Bradley	72	77	69	69	287	8,241
Terry-Jo Myers	73	71	72	71	287	8,241
Missie McGeorge	71	73	71	72	287	8,241
Deb Richard	70	73	72	72	287	8,240
Lauri Merten	72	72	69	73	287	8,240
Nancy Brown	73	69	72	73	287	8,240
Karen Davies	69	72	70	76	287	8,240
Donna White	70	72	72	74	288	6,024
Laura Hurlbut	70	68	74	76	288	6,023
Patty Sheehan	73	75	74	67	289	5,461
Susie McAllister	72	77	71	69	289	5,461
Elaine Crosby	74	71	73	71	289	5,461
Martha Foyer	74	75	73	68	290	4,543
Kate Rogerson	79	69	72	70	290	4,542
Barb Bunkowsky	73	74	73	70	290	4,542

	SCORES				TOTAL	MONEY
Sherri Turner	71	78	69	72	290	4,542
Tammie Green	73	73	72	72	290	4,542
Hiromi Kobayashi	75	70	73	72	290	4,542
Julie Hennessy	75	74	72	70	291	3,819
Alice Ritzman	74	74	71	72	291	3,819
Cathy Morse	72	72	74	73	291	3,818
Sue Ertl	72	73	72	74	291	3,818

JAL Big Apple Classic

Wykagyl Country Club, New Rochelle, New York
Par 36-36—72; 6,209 yards

August 16-19
purse, $400,000

	SCORES				TOTAL	MONEY
Betsy King	75	67	63	68	273	$60,000
Beth Daniel	70	70	68	68	276	37,000
Rosie Jones	69	69	71	70	279	27,000
Tammie Green	68	69	74	70	281	21,000
Dawn Coe	70	70	72	70	282	17,000
Kristi Albers	72	70	73	69	284	12,067
Pat Bradley	73	71	69	71	284	12,067
Patty Sheehan	70	73	70	71	284	12,066
Penny Hammel	72	72	70	72	286	8,900
Kay Cockerill	74	70	69	73	286	8,900
Colleen Walker	72	72	75	68	287	6,661
Cindy Rarick	76	71	71	69	287	6,661
Cindy Schreyer	70	72	75	70	287	6,661
Nancy Lopez	75	71	70	71	287	6,661
Cathy Morse	70	72	72	73	287	6,661
Dottie Mochrie	72	69	77	70	288	5,321
Meg Mallon	77	73	67	71	288	5,321
Laura Baugh	73	70	76	70	289	4,821
Anne-Marie Palli	75	71	70	73	289	4,821
Jan Stephenson	72	70	72	75	289	4,821
Vicki Fergon	75	70	76	69	290	4,146
Dale Eggeling	70	76	73	71	290	4,146
Susan Sanders	74	71	74	71	290	4,146
Kris Monaghan	69	73	74	74	290	4,146
Tracy Kerdyk	71	78	74	68	291	3,481
Sherri Steinhauer	75	73	73	70	291	3,481
Maggie Will	75	73	72	71	291	3,481
Sherri Turner	75	72	71	73	291	3,481
Kate Rogerson	72	72	74	73	291	3,481
Marci Bozarth	69	71	75	76	291	3,481

Northgate Classic

Edinburgh USA Golf Course, Brooklyn Park, Minnesota
Par 36-36—72; 6,149 yards

August 23-26
purse, $375,000

	SCORES			TOTAL	MONEY
Beth Daniel	66	69	68	203	$56,250
Chris Johnson	66	75	68	209	30,000
Penny Hammel	69	71	69	209	29,999
Barb Bunkowsky	65	75	71	211	16,250
Caroline Keggi	71	68	72	211	16,250

	SCORES			TOTAL	MONEY
Cindy Rarick	66	71	74	211	16,249
Pamela Wright	72	71	69	212	10,406
Elaine Crosby	72	69	71	212	10,406
Debbie Massey	73	71	69	213	7,594
Barb Mucha	69	72	72	213	7,594
Deb Richard	69	72	72	213	7,594
Myra Blackwelder	71	69	73	213	7,594
Janice Gibson	69	75	70	214	5,476
Donna Andrews	74	69	71	214	5,476
Margaret Ward	72	71	71	214	5,476
Cathy Morse	72	69	73	214	5,475
Nina Foust	68	71	75	214	5,475
Becky Pearson	72	72	71	215	4,501
Meg Mallon	73	69	73	215	4,501
Danielle Ammaccapane	72	70	73	215	4,500
Terry-Jo Myers	70	77	69	216	3,673
Rosie Jones	72	73	71	216	3,673
Dottie Mochrie	73	70	73	216	3,673
Ann Walsh	72	71	73	216	3,673
Nancy Rubin	71	71	74	216	3,673
Betsy King	73	68	75	216	3,673
Laurel Kean	71	69	76	216	3,673
Dale Eggeling	74	73	70	217	2,917
Cindy Figg-Currier	71	76	70	217	2,917
Kim Shipman	75	71	71	217	2,916
Amy Benz	72	74	71	217	2,916
Mitzi Edge	73	72	72	217	2,916
Tracy Kerdyk	73	69	75	217	2,916

Rail Charity Classic

Rail Golf Club, Springfield, Illinois
Par 36-36—72; 6,403 yards

September 1-3
purse, $300,000

	SCORES			TOTAL	MONEY
Beth Daniel	67	69	67	203	$45,000
Susan Sanders	71	69	66	206	27,750
Nancy Brown	69	71	67	207	18,000
Alice Ritzman	69	70	68	207	18,000
Donna Andrews	70	68	70	208	12,750
Kate Rogerson	72	68	69	209	10,500
Michelle McGann	72	71	67	210	7,900
Pat Bradley	74	67	69	210	7,900
Sherri Turner	68	72	70	210	7,900
Cathy Gerring	70	71	70	211	5,551
Judy Dickinson	66	75	70	211	5,550
Sue Ertl	71	69	71	211	5,550
Sarah McGuire	69	71	71	211	5,550
Hiromi Kobayashi	73	70	69	212	3,965
Nicky LeRoux	70	73	69	212	3,965
Pamela Wright	73	69	70	212	3,964
Kristi Albers	70	71	71	212	3,964
Dale Eggeling	70	70	72	212	3,964
Betsy King	68	70	74	212	3,964
Martha Nause	69	67	76	212	3,964
Lenore Rittenhouse	75	68	70	213	3,039
Cindy Rarick	72	71	70	213	3,039
Gail Graham	71	72	70	213	3,039

	SCORES	TOTAL	MONEY
Myra Blackwelder	73 69 71	213	3,039
Laura Baugh	73 69 71	213	3,039
Caroline Pierce	74 70 70	214	2,463
Deedee Lasker	71 73 70	214	2,462
Jill Briles	70 72 72	214	2,462
Shirley Furlong	72 69 73	214	2,462
Elaine Crosby	72 69 73	214	2,462
Ellie Gibson	69 72 73	214	2,462
Nina Foust	70 69 75	214	2,462

Ping Cellular One Championship

Columbia Edgewater Country Club, Portland, Oregon
Par 36-36—72; 6,261 yards

September 7-9
purse, $350,000

	SCORES	TOTAL	MONEY
Patty Sheehan	70 71 67	208	$52,500
Danielle Ammaccapane	72 73 64	209	32,375
Pat Bradley	70 68 72	210	23,625
Sherri Turner	69 70 74	213	16,625
Dottie Mochrie	68 71 74	213	16,625
Donna White	71 72 71	214	12,250
Hiromi Kobayashi	72 72 71	215	7,651
Dawn Coe	71 72 72	215	7,651
Donna Andrews	70 73 72	215	7,651
Betsy King	69 74 72	215	7,650
Sherri Steinhauer	71 71 73	215	7,650
Kay Cockerill	73 68 74	215	7,650
Cindy Rarick	70 70 75	215	7,650
Colleen Walker	73 75 68	216	4,626
Martha Nause	74 72 70	216	4,626
Cathy Gerring	73 70 73	216	4,626
Deb Richard	71 71 74	216	4,626
Pamela Wright	72 69 75	216	4,626
Cindy Mackey	71 70 75	216	4,626
Nancy Brown	69 71 76	216	4,626
Kathy Postlewait	71 73 73	217	3,681
Amy Alcott	70 74 73	217	3,681
Vicki Fergon	70 72 75	217	3,681
Cindy Figg-Currier	70 78 70	218	3,343
Meg Mallon	73 72 73	218	3,342
Penny Hammel	74 71 74	219	2,975
Barb Mucha	71 74 74	219	2,975
Jane Geddes	72 71 76	219	2,975
Elaine Crosby	72 71 76	219	2,975
Ok Hee Ku	70 72 77	219	2,975

Safeco Classic

Meridian Valley Country Club, Kent, Washington
Par 36-36—72; 6,222 yards

September 13-16
purse, $300,000

	SCORES	TOTAL	MONEY
Patty Sheehan	69 65 66 70	270	$45,000
Deb Richard	75 67 71 66	279	27,750
Martha Foyer	74 70 68 68	280	20,250

	SCORES				TOTAL	MONEY
Vicki Fergon	71	74	68	69	282	13,000
Tammie Green	76	67	68	71	282	13,000
Dawn Coe	74	68	68	72	282	13,000
Dottie Mochrie	70	77	70	66	283	7,900
Dale Eggeling	69	72	71	71	283	7,900
Nancy Rubin	70	70	70	73	283	7,900
Pat Bradley	72	71	73	68	284	5,764
Colleen Walker	71	73	70	70	284	5,764
Sherri Steinhauer	71	64	77	72	284	5,764
Judy Dickinson	71	73	71	70	285	4,671
Ok Hee Ku	76	69	68	72	285	4,671
Danielle Ammaccapane	72	68	71	74	285	4,671
Kathryn Young	72	74	70	70	286	3,921
Kathy Postlewait	72	72	72	70	286	3,921
Cindy Figg-Currier	72	68	70	76	286	3,921
Nancy Ramsbottom	71	75	69	72	287	3,324
Mary Beth Zimmerman	74	71	70	72	287	3,324
Terry-Jo Myers	72	73	70	72	287	3,324
Pamela Wright	73	70	72	72	287	3,324
Juli Inkster	70	70	72	75	287	3,324
Cindy Mackey	70	76	72	70	288	2,796
Beth Daniel	69	72	77	70	288	2,796
Janet Anderson	74	73	70	71	288	2,796
Lynn Connelly	71	73	72	72	288	2,796
Debbie Massey	77	67	77	68	289	2,354
Shirley Furlong	75	66	78	70	289	2,354
Meg Mallon	77	70	71	71	289	2,354
Becky Pearson	75	71	72	71	289	2,353
Sarah McGuire	75	70	72	72	289	2,353
Barb Mucha	72	71	71	75	289	2,353

MBS Classic

Los Coyotes Country Club, Buena Park, California
Par 36-36—72; 6,351 yards

September 20-23
purse, $325,000

	SCORES				TOTAL	MONEY
Nancy Lopez	69	70	74	68	281	$48,750
Cathy Gerring	71	70	68	72	281	30,062

(Lopez defeated Gerring on first extra hole.)

Caroline Keggi	70	69	68	75	282	21,937
Kim Shipman	70	71	74	69	284	15,437
Nancy Brown	69	72	71	72	284	15,437
Danielle Ammaccapane	74	71	68	72	285	11,375
Dottie Mochrie	72	74	71	69	286	8,125
Sherri Steinhauer	74	71	69	72	286	8,125
Martha Foyer	70	72	72	72	286	8,125
Chris Johnson	72	69	73	72	286	8,124
Hollis Stacy	76	72	71	68	287	5,596
Missie McGeorge	70	72	76	69	287	5,595
Missie Berteotti	72	71	74	70	287	5,595
Meg Mallon	73	70	73	71	287	5,595
Janice Gibson	74	74	70	70	288	4,472
Barb Bunkowsky	71	75	70	72	288	4,471
Cindy Rarick	70	70	73	75	288	4,471
Sherri Turner	73	74	72	70	289	3,930
Martha Nause	74	74	70	71	289	3,930
Colleen Walker	74	70	73	72	289	3,929

	SCORES	TOTAL	MONEY
Margaret Ward	74 74 71 71	290	3,160
Vicki Fergon	72 74 71 73	290	3,160
Allison Finney	72 73 72 73	290	3,160
Lauri Merten	72 72 72 74	290	3,160
Anne-Marie Palli	71 71 74 74	290	3,160
Deb Richard	73 73 69 75	290	3,160
Cathy Morse	68 77 70 75	290	3,160
Sarah McGuire	69 74 72 75	290	3,159
Judy Dickinson	74 74 75 68	291	2,343
Janet Anderson	68 75 79 69	291	2,343
Robin Hood	75 72 74 70	291	2,343
Dale Eggeling	75 71 75 70	291	2,343
Pamela Wright	73 73 75 70	291	2,343
Penny Hammel	73 72 73 73	291	2,342
Jenny Lidback	71 74 73 73	291	2,342
Diana Heinicke-Rauch	71 75 71 74	291	2,342
Maggie Will	74 69 73 75	291	2,342

Centel Classic

Killearn Country Club, Tallahassee, Florida
Par 36-36—72; 6,269 yards

October 4-7
purse, $1,000,000

	SCORES	TOTAL	MONEY
Beth Daniel	71 63 68 69	271	$150,000
Nancy Lopez	70 67 69 66	272	92,500
Patty Sheehan	67 65 74 72	278	67,500
Cathy Gerring	63 78 67 71	279	52,500
Dawn Coe	69 73 70 68	280	42,500
Danielle Ammaccapane	71 71 69 70	281	32,250
Sue Thomas	70 72 69 70	281	32,250
Terry-Jo Myers	71 70 71 70	282	23,500
Colleen Walker	71 70 71 70	282	23,500
Pat Bradley	74 70 66 72	282	23,500
Robin Walton	73 73 69 68	283	18,250
Betsy King	72 73 67 71	283	18,250
Cindy Rarick	70 76 70 68	284	13,929
Hiromi Kobayashi	72 72 71 69	284	13,929
Martha Nause	70 73 71 70	284	13,929
Rosie Jones	69 74 71 70	284	13,929
Cathy Marino	70 73 70 71	284	13,928
Nancy Ramsbottom	69 73 71 71	284	13,928
Missie McGeorge	69 68 72 75	284	13,928
Sherri Turner	71 74 70 70	285	10,359
Kristi Albers	71 70 74 70	285	10,359
Dottie Mochrie	72 71 71 71	285	10,358
Susan Sanders	72 69 73 71	285	10,358
Amy Read	72 68 73 72	285	10,358
Judy Dickinson	72 70 68 75	285	10,358
Nancy Rubin	71 74 71 70	286	8,500
Lenore Rittenhouse	70 74 72 70	286	8,500
Amy Benz	72 70 74 70	286	8,500
Elaine Crosby	72 74 69 71	286	8,500
Laurie Rinker	73 73 67 73	286	8,500

Trophee Urban World Championship

Cely Golf Club, Paris, France
Par 36-36—72; 6,155 yards

October 11-14
purse, $325,000

	SCORES				TOTAL	MONEY
Cathy Gerring	69	69	69	71	278	$100,000
Beth Daniel	71	74	66	68	279	52,000
Betsy King	72	69	69	72	282	31,000
Patty Sheehan	73	74	69	68	284	17,167
Cindy Rarick	69	74	71	70	284	17,167
Dottie Mochrie	70	72	72	70	284	17,166
Chris Johnson	72	73	70	71	286	11,000
Cathy Johnston	72	76	67	76	291	10,000
Marie Laure de Lorenzi	71	75	75	71	292	7,167
Danielle Ammaccapane	71	70	74	77	292	7,167
Pat Bradley	74	71	73	74	292	7,166
Ayako Okamoto	73	66	80	75	294	6,000
Dawn Coe	74	74	76	71	295	5,250
Rosie Jones	77	73	73	72	295	5,250
Colleen Walker	78	74	70	74	296	4,500
Trish Johnson	72	78	71	76	297	4,250

Nichirei International

Tsukuka Country Club, Ina, Japan
Par 36-36—72; 6,268 yards

October 26-28
purse, $350,000

FIRST ROUND
Better Ball

Huang Yueh Chun and Huang Bie Shyun defeated Patty Sheehan and Danielle Ammaccapane, 70-71.
Hisako Higuchi and Fukumi Tani defeated Colleen Walker and Deb Richard, 66-71.
Tu Ai Yu and Chikayo Yamazaki defeated Rosie Jones and Dale Eggeling, 65-66.
Tammie Green and Patti Rizzo defeated Junko Yasui and Ikuyo Shiotani, 64-70.
Dottie Mochrie and Cathy Johnston defeated Yuko Moriguchi and Fusako Nagata, 68-69.
Ayako Okamoto and Cindy Figg-Currier halved with Hiromi Takamura and Aiko Takasu, 68-68.
Jane Geddes and Barb Mucha halved with Mayumi Hirase and Mitsuko Hamada, 67-67.
Cathy Gerring and Cindy Rarick halved with Norimi Terasawa and Nayoko Yoshikawa, 68-68.

Japan 4-1/2, United States 3-1/2.

SECOND ROUND
Better Ball

Gerring/Rarick defeated Moriguchi/Nagata, 68-69.
Geddes/Mucha defeated Huang/Huang, 66-67.
Walker/Richard defeated Hirase/Hamada, 65-74.
Jones/Eggeling defeated Terasawa/Yoshikawa, 69-72.
Mochrie/Johnston defeated Takamura/Takasu, 69-73.
Okamoto/Figg-Currier defeated Yamazaki/Tu, 65-66.
Higuchi/Tani defeated Sheehan/Ammaccapane, 63-64.
Yasui/Shiotani defeated Green/Rizzo, 68-69.

United States 9-1/2, Japan 6-1/2.

THIRD ROUND
Singles

Mochrie defeated Yasui, 68-72.
Sheehan defeated Higuchi, 68-71.
Jones defeated Nagata, 68-74.
Rizzo defeated Hamada, 71-73.
Rarick defeated Huang Bie Shyun, 71-73.
Green defeated Huang Yueh Chun, 70-72.
Ammaccapane defeated Hirase, 70-76.
Walker defeated Shiotani, 71-77.
Richard defeated Takamura, 76-78.
Eggeling defeated Takasu, 73-75.
Johnston defeated Tu, 75-78.
Gerring defeated Tani, 74-75.
Okamoto defeated Yamazaki, 69-78.
Terasawa defeated Mucha, 72-73.
Yoshikawa defeated Geddes, 73-74.
Moriguchi defeated Figg-Currier, 74-75.

United States 22-1/2, Japan 9-1/2.

(Each member of U.S. team received $14,000; each member of Japanese team received $7,875.)

Mazda Japan Classic

Musashigaoka Golf Club, Hanno, Japan
Par 36-36—72; 6,376 yards
(Final round cancelled - rain.)

November 2-3
purse, $550,000

	SCORES		TOTAL	MONEY
Debbie Massey	69	64	133	$82,500
Danielle Ammaccapane	69	67	136	44,000
Caroline Keggi	68	68	136	44,000
Betsy King	72	65	137	23,834
Elaine Crosby	69	68	137	23,833
Cathy Gerring	69	68	137	23,833
Fusako Nagata	71	67	138	15,263
Rosie Jones	68	70	138	15,262
Sherri Steinhauer	70	69	139	11,659
Jane Geddes	69	70	139	11,658
Vicki Fergon	68	71	139	11,658
Sue Ertl	72	68	140	8,575
Amy Benz	71	69	140	8,575
Barb Mucha	71	69	140	8,575
Pat Bradley	70	70	140	8,575
Nancy Brown	66	74	140	8,575
Patty Sheehan	72	69	141	7,200
Missie McGeorge	74	68	142	6,375
Deb Richard	73	69	142	6,375
Cindy Rarick	72	70	142	6,375
Hiromi Kobayashi	70	72	142	6,375
Nayoko Yoshikawa	69	73	142	6,375
Junko Yasaui	74	69	143	4,813
Lynn Connelly	73	70	143	4,813
Cathy Johnston	73	70	143	4,813
Yuko Moriguchi	73	70	143	4,813
Meg Mallon	72	71	143	4,813

	SCORES	TOTAL	MONEY
Dale Eggeling	71 72	143	4,813
Yueh Chyn Huang	71 72	143	4,813
Aiko Takasu	71 72	143	4,813
Donna White	71 72	143	4,813
Ayako Okamoto	70 73	143	4,812

Solheim Cup

Lake Nona Golf Club, Orlando, Florida
Par 36-36—72; 6,338 yards

November 16-18

FINAL RESULT: United States, 11-1/2; Europe 4-1/2.

FIRST ROUND
Foursomes

Laura Davies and Alison Nicholas (Europe) defeated Pat Bradley and Nancy Lopez, 2 and 1.
Cathy Gerring and Dottie Mochrie (U.S.) defeated Pamela Wright and Liselotte Neumann, 6 and 5.
Patty Sheehan and Rosie Jones (U.S.) defeated Dale Reid and Helen Alfredsson, 6 and 5.
Beth Daniel and Betsy King (U.S.) defeated Trish Johnson and Marie Laure de Lorenzi, 5 and 4.

United States 3, Europe 1.

SECOND ROUND
Four-Ball

Daniel and King (U.S.) defeated Davies and Nicholas, 4 and 3.
Neumann and Wright (Europe) defeated Gerring and Mochrie, 4 and 2.
Sheehan and Jones (U.S.) defeated Johnson and de Lorenzi, 2 and 1.
Bradley and Lopez (U.S.) defeated Reid and Alfredsson, 2 and 1.

United States 6, Europe 2.

THIRD ROUND
Singles

Bradley (U.S.) defeated Johnson, 8 and 7.
Daniel (U.S.) defeated Neumann, 7 and 6.
Lopez (U.S.) defeated Nicholas, 6 and 4.
Gerring (U.S.) defeated Alfredsson, 4 and 3.
Mochrie (U.S.) defeated de Lorenzi, 4 and 2.
Davies (Europe) defeated Jones, 3 and 2.
Reid (Europe) defeated Sheehan, 2 and 1.
King (U.S.) halved with Wright.

Itoman LPGA World Match Play Championship

Princeville Makai Golf Club, Princeville, Kauai, Hawaii
Par 72; 6,478 yards

December 6-9
purse, $450,000

FIRST ROUND

Betsy King defeated Ikuyo Shiotani, 3 and 2.
Fukumi Tani defeated Cindy Figg-Currier, 3 and 2.
Nancy Brown defeated Junko Yasui, 1 up, 22 holes.
Chris Johnson defeated Ok Hee Ku, 4 and 3.
Sherri Turner defeated Hiromi Takamura, 7 and 5.
Caroline Keggi defeated Yuko Moriguchi, 4 and 3.
Dawn Coe defeated Hiromi Kobayashi, 1 up, 22 holes.
Barb Mucha defeated Aiko Takusu, 5 and 4.
Danielle Ammaccapane defeated Sue Ertl, 1 up.
Debbie Massey defeated Cathy Johnston, 5 and 4.
Meg Mallon defeated Colleen Walker, 3 and 2.
Deb Richard defeated Patty Rizzo, 1 up.
Cindy Rarick defeated Kathy Postlewait, 3 and 2.
Tammie Green defeated Elaine Crosby, 1 up, 22 holes.
Dottie Mochrie defeated Amy Benz, 2 up.
Jane Geddes defeated Dale Eggeling, 1 up.
(Each losing player received $5,000.)

SECOND ROUND

King defeated Tani, 3 and 2.
Keggi defeated Turner, 1 up, 19 holes.
Mucha defeated Coe, 3 and 2.
Johnson defeated Brown, 4 and 2.
Ammaccapane defeated Massey, 5 and 3.
Richard defeated Mallon, 4 and 2.
Rarick defeated Green, 1 up.
Geddes defeated Mochrie, 1 up, 19 holes.
(Each losing player received $7,500.)

QUARTER-FINALS

King defeated Johnson, 1 up.
Keggi defeated Mucha, 2 up.
Richard defeated Ammaccapane, 1 up.
Rarick defeated Geddes, 2 and 1.
(Each losing player received $15,000.)

SEMI-FINALS

King defeated Keggi, 2 up.
Richard defeated Rarick, 3 and 2.

PLAYOFF FOR THIRD-FOURTH PLACE

Keggi defeated Rarick, 3 and 2.
(Keggi received $50,000; Rarick $30,000.)

FINAL

King defeated Richard, 2 up.
(King received $100,000; Richard $70,000.)

The Women's European Tour

Valextra Classic

Olgiata Golf Club, Rome, Italy
Par 35-36—71; 5,917 yards

April 19-22
purse, £70,000

	SCORES				TOTAL	MONEY
Florence Descampe	71	71	69	68	279	£10,500
Dale Reid	75	68	70	72	285	7,105
Laura Davies	74	73	69	70	286	4,900
Dennise Hutton	73	74	69	72	288	3,374
Pearl Sinn	73	68	73	74	288	3,374
Kitrina Douglas	72	71	75	71	289	2,458
Alison Nicholas	75	72	72	71	290	1,925
Xonia Wunsch-Ruiz	74	74	72	70	290	1,925
Karen Lunn	75	73	74	69	291	1,568
Trish Johnson	72	77	71	72	292	1,400
Alison Sheard	75	72	73	73	293	1,176
Corinne Soules	77	74	73	69	293	1,176
Gillian Stewart	75	71	76	71	293	1,176
Helen Alfredsson	76	73	71	73	293	1,176
Diane Barnard	77	74	70	73	294	1,050
Maureen Garner	74	69	73	79	295	1,022
Janet Soulsby	78	74	72	72	296	994
Tania Abitbol	71	73	75	78	297	938
Debbie Dowling	76	73	72	76	297	938
Sofia Gronberg	73	76	76	72	297	938
Marie Laure de Lorenzi	73	77	76	72	298	878.50
Corinne Dibnah	77	75	74	72	298	878.50
Karine Espinasse	79	76	71	73	299	826
Stefania Croce	76	75	74	74	299	826
Evelyn Orley	79	73	75	72	299	826
Jane Connachan	78	73	75	74	300	752.50
Catherine Panton	78	76	74	72	300	752.50
Susan Shapcott	73	76	76	75	300	752.50
Michelle Estill	76	76	76	72	300	752.50
Suzanne Strudwick	75	79	72	75	301	689.50
Anne Jones	79	74	75	73	301	689.50

Ford Ladies Classic

Woburn Golf Club, Duchess Course, Woburn, England
Par 37-37—74; 6,079 yards

April 25-28
purse, £65,000

	SCORES				TOTAL	MONEY
Marie Laure de Lorenzi	74	72	68	70	284	£9,750
Laurette Maritz	70	73	71	73	287	6,600
Trish Johnson	73	72	72	73	290	4,550
Rae Hast	72	78	73	68	291	3,133
Alison Nicholas	71	75	70	75	291	3,133
Diane Barnard	70	71	74	78	293	2,112.50
Sofia Gronberg	73	73	74	73	293	2,112.50

582 / THE WOMEN'S TOURS

	SCORES	TOTAL	MONEY
Maria Navarro Corbachio	74 78 71 71	294	1,540.50
Evelyn Orley	72 75 71 76	294	1,540.50
Federica Dassu	73 72 77 73	295	1,300
Kitrina Douglas	75 74 70 77	296	1,091.75
Debbie Dowling	76 74 72 74	296	1,091.75
Suzanne Strudwick	72 76 75 73	296	1,091.75
Helen Alfredsson	69 80 74 73	296	1,091.75
Laura Davies	70 72 78 78	298	949
Gillian Stewart	73 75 75 75	298	949
Xonia Wunsch-Ruiz	77 75 75 71	298	949
Tania Abitbol	73 80 72 74	299	884
Tracey Craik	78 73 74 74	299	884
Maureen Garner	76 73 79 72	300	835
Anne Jones	75 74 75 76	300	835
Janice Arnold	75 77 73 76	301	755
Jane Hill	73 76 77 75	301	755
Alison Sheard	70 75 76 80	301	755
Judy Statham	74 73 78 76	301	755
Kim Lasken	73 74 73 81	301	755
Pearl Sinn	74 76 75 76	301	755
Joanne Furby	77 75 75 75	302	685
Sonja Van Wyk	73 73 73 84	303	645
Alicia Dibos	73 77 75 78	303	645
Karen Davies	77 74 76 76	303	645

Hennessy Ladies' Cup

Golf de St. Germain, Paris, France
Par 37-35—72; 6,004 yards

May 10-13
purse, £90,000

	SCORES	TOTAL	MONEY
Trish Johnson	72 68 71 74	285	£13,500
Marie Laure de Lorenzi	75 71 69 73	288	7,717.50
Tammie Green	72 75 66 75	288	7,717.50
Sofia Gronberg	72 69 73 75	289	4,860
Tania Abitbol	77 69 72 72	290	3,222
Diane Barnard	71 74 71 74	290	3,222
Catherine Panton	74 72 72 72	290	3,222
Beverley New	73 73 74 71	291	2,250
Janice Arnold	73 75 73 72	293	2,016
Corinne Soules	76 73 71 75	295	1,728
Xonia Wunsch-Ruiz	78 74 74 69	295	1,728
Jane Connachan	73 76 70 77	296	1,435.50
Debbie Dowling	73 73 71 79	296	1,435.50
Laurette Maritz	81 73 73 69	296	1,435.50
Alison Nicholas	73 75 75 73	296	1,435.50
*Valerie Michaud	70 76 74 76	296	
Susan Moon	74 77 72 74	297	1,278
Tracey Craik	79 73 72 73	297	1,278
Sally Prosser	75 75 72 75	297	1,278
Federica Dassu	72 76 69 81	298	1,158.75
Elisabeth Quelhas	76 67 76 79	298	1,158.75
Catrin Nilsmark	75 74 77 72	298	1,158.75
*Caroline Bourtayre	80 72 73 73	298	
Evelyn Orley	76 74 74 74	298	1,158.75
Claire Duffy	72 76 72 79	299	1,089
*Sophie Louapre-Pfeiffer	71 79 73 76	299	
Karine Espinasse	76 79 75 70	300	1,048.50

	SCORES			TOTAL	MONEY
Karyn Dallas	74	75	72 79	300	1,048.50
Maureen Garner	75	74	73 79	301	951
Regine Lautens	74	76	76 75	301	951
Michelle Estill	77	74	71 79	301	951

WPG European Tour Classic

The Tytherington Club, Cheshire, England
Par 36-36—72; 5,812 yards

May 23-26
purse, £60,000

	SCORES			TOTAL	MONEY
Tania Abitbol	76	69	68	213	£9,000
Anna Oxenstierna	72	73	70	215	6,090
Susan Shapcott	70	70	76	216	4,200
Diane Barnard	73	72	72	217	2,892
Sofia Gronberg	71	75	71	217	2,892
Debbie Dowling	72	74	72	218	1,950
Corinne Soules	75	74	69	218	1,950
Federica Dassu	74	72	73	219	1,348
Kitrina Douglas	72	71	76	219	1,348
Xonia Wunsch-Ruiz	74	74	71	219	1,348
Jane Connachan	76	69	75	220	968
Beverley New	71	75	74	220	968
Sonja Van Wyk	72	71	77	220	968
Joanne Furby	69	77	74	220	968
Maria Navarro Corbachio	74	71	75	220	968
Pearl Sinn	73	75	72	220	968
Maxine Burton	73	74	75	222	816
Karine Espinasse	81	72	69	222	816
Laurette Maritz	75	70	77	222	816
Catrin Nilsmark	76	74	72	222	816
Margaret Kelt	72	77	74	223	762
Maureen Garner	77	74	73	224	744
Peggy Conley	75	72	79	225	672
Judy Greco	75	73	77	225	672
Tracy Hammond	76	74	75	225	672
Catherine Panton	73	75	77	225	672
Anne Jones	70	78	77	225	672
Michelle De Vries	79	71	75	225	672
Frances Martin	80	73	72	225	672
Claire Duffy	74	75	77	226	573
Jo Rumsey	75	75	76	226	573
Gillian Stewart	77	75	74	226	573
Kiernan Prechtl	75	78	73	226	573

Bonmont Ladies Classic

Club de Bonmont, Geneva, Switzerland
Par 37-35—72; 6,007 yards

June 7-10
purse, £70,000

	SCORES				TOTAL	MONEY
Evelyn Orley	71	72	71	75	289	£10,500
Gillian Stewart	74	72	70	73	289	7,105
(Orley defeated Stewart on first extra hole.)						
Tania Abitbol	72	71	76	71	290	4,340
Dale Reid	70	74	75	71	290	4,340

	SCORES				TOTAL	MONEY
Florence Descampe	72	72	73	74	291	2,968
Federica Dassu	77	69	71	75	292	2,275
Sofia Gronberg	77	74	68	72	292	2,275
Kitrina Douglas	75	74	75	70	294	1,501.50
Laurette Maritz	76	71	77	70	294	1,501.50
Alison Sheard	69	74	78	73	294	1,501.50
Xonia Wunsch-Ruiz	72	74	74	74	294	1,501.50
Debbie Dowling	75	71	74	76	296	1,138.66
Sabine Etchevers	78	77	70	71	296	1,138.66
Pearl Sinn	73	76	76	71	296	1,138.66
Marie Laure de Lorenzi	74	72	76	75	297	994
Beverley New	70	78	74	75	297	994
Sonja Van Wyk	74	75	76	72	297	994
Alicia Dibos	72	73	80	72	297	994
Stefania Croce	74	73	76	74	297	994
Diane Barnard	72	70	79	77	298	889
Barbara Helbig	74	74	75	75	298	889
Anna Oxenstierna	72	80	71	75	298	889
Rica Comstock	72	75	74	78	299	836.50
Michelle Estill	70	73	79	77	299	836.50
Jane Connachan	70	74	80	76	300	752.50
Patricia Gonzalez	75	76	77	72	300	752.50
Regine Lautens	72	78	77	73	300	752.50
Karen Lunn	75	76	81	68	300	752.50
Jo Rumsey	76	74	76	74	300	752.50
Helen Alfredsson	75	75	76	74	300	752.50

BMW European Masters

Golf du Bercuit, Brussels, Belgium
Par 35-37—72; 6,010 yards

June 21-24
purse, £120,000

	SCORES				TOTAL	MONEY
Karen Lunn	72	71	71	71	285	£18,000
Corinne Soules	69	74	73	73	289	12,180
Gillian Stewart	70	76	73	72	291	8,400
Pearl Sinn	72	77	73	71	293	6,480
Corinne Dibnah	76	74	71	73	294	4,644
Jane Hill	74	75	72	73	294	4,644
Jane Connachan	77	71	73	74	295	3,300
Sofia Gronberg	77	74	72	72	295	3,300
Laurette Maritz	75	76	72	73	296	2,544
Tracey Craik	78	74	73	71	296	2,544
Marie Laure de Lorenzi	73	74	71	79	297	1,972.80
Kitrina Douglas	72	77	77	71	297	1,972.80
Alison Sheard	72	75	76	74	297	1,972.80
Xonia Wunsch-Ruiz	74	74	75	74	297	1,972.80
Helen Alfredsson	71	79	71	76	297	1,972.80
Debbie Dowling	75	75	76	73	299	1,704
Rae Hast	74	76	76	73	299	1,704
Anna Oxenstierna	74	73	74	78	299	1,704
Tania Abitbol	75	78	70	77	300	1,584
Diane Barnard	76	77	75	72	300	1,584
Regine Lautens	79	72	75	75	301	1,434
Alison Nicholas	70	78	76	77	301	1,434
Marie From	76	79	74	72	301	1,434
Marie Navarro Corbachio	74	78	74	75	301	1,434
Sharon Smith Cranmer	75	79	77	70	301	1,434

	SCORES				TOTAL	MONEY
Michelle Estill	78	75	76	72	301	1,434
Claire Duffy	77	75	77	73	302	1,200
Alison Munt	79	75	72	76	302	1,200
Catherine Panton	72	77	77	76	302	1,200
Diane Pavich	78	75	73	76	302	1,200
Dale Reid	80	74	72	76	302	1,200
Suzanne Strudwick	73	77	79	73	302	1,200
Elisabeth Quelhas	75	77	78	72	302	1,200

BMW Ladies Classic

Hubbelrath Golf Club, Dusseldorf, Germany
Par 36-36—72; 5,896 yards

June 28-July 1
purse, £70,000

	SCORES				TOTAL	MONEY
Diane Barnard	71	68	70	69	278	£10,500
Corinne Dibnah	66	71	69	73	279	7,105
Alison Nicholas	71	67	70	72	280	4,900
Karen Lunn	67	69	73	72	281	3,780
Marie Laure de Lorenzi	69	72	70	71	282	2,968
Peggy Conley	69	69	73	72	283	2,450
Debbie Dowling	74	72	73	68	287	2,100
Jane Connachan	68	69	74	78	289	1,442
Laurette Maritz	74	70	69	76	289	1,442
Gillian Stewart	72	73	72	72	289	1,442
Dana Lofland	73	70	71	75	289	1,442
Nadene Hall	76	69	73	71	289	1,442
Elisabeth Quelhas	73	77	69	71	290	1,106
Rebecca Gasthrop	68	73	75	74	290	1,106
Federica Dassu	71	72	73	75	291	1,022
Beverley New	72	72	72	75	291	1,022
Corinne Soules	74	70	73	74	291	1,022
Claire Duffy	74	70	74	74	292	925.75
Patricia Gonzalez	72	71	74	75	292	925.75
Jane Hill	75	71	71	75	292	925.75
Michelle Estill	73	71	70	78	292	925.75
Alison Munt	70	73	76	74	293	867.50
Alicia Dibos	71	71	75	76	293	867.50
Alison Sheard	76	70	71	77	294	805
Florence Descampe	77	66	77	74	294	805
Debbie Hanna	75	72	71	76	294	805
Kitrina Douglas	73	73	75	74	295	763
Susan Moorcraft	70	73	75	78	296	742
Maureen Garner	79	73	70	75	297	668.50
Dale Reid	79	70	75	73	297	668.50
Janet Soulsby	73	72	72	80	297	668.50
Suzanne Strudwick	75	72	76	74	297	668.50
Xonia Wunsch-Ruiz	74	74	73	76	297	668.50
Maria Navarro Corbachio	77	72	74	74	297	668.50

Laing Ladies Charity Classic

Stoke Poges Golf Club, London, England
Par 36-36—72; 5,776 yards

July 5-8
purse, £65,000

	SCORES				TOTAL	MONEY
Laurette Maritz	71	67	69	68	275	£9,750
Alison Nicholas	71	70	69	65	275	6,600
(Maritz defeated Nicholas on first extra hole.)						
Maureen Garner	68	67	71	70	276	4,550
Corinne Soules	70	71	69	67	277	3,510
Patricia Gonzalez	71	69	70	73	283	2,756
Diane Barnard	75	68	71	70	284	1,950
Karen Lunn	74	74	63	67	284	1,950
Florence Descampe	73	65	72	74	284	1,950
Jo Rumsey	74	71	69	73	287	1,378
Helen Alfredsson	72	70	71	74	287	1,378
Debbie Dowling	73	73	68	74	288	1,091.75
Gillian Stewart	74	71	69	74	288	1,091.75
Catrin Nilsmark	71	70	75	72	288	1,091.75
Michelle Estill	71	71	76	70	288	1,091.75
Kitrina Douglas	75	71	65	78	289	962
Claire Duffy	74	72	72	71	289	962
Federica Dassu	74	69	72	75	290	910
Beverley New	76	72	73	69	290	910
Janice Arnold	70	76	72	73	291	795.75
Jane Connachan	74	72	77	68	291	795.75
Karine Espinasse	77	72	72	70	291	795.75
Penny Grice-Whittaker	76	71	71	73	291	795.75
Alison Munt	76	72	69	74	291	795.75
Dana Lofland	74	74	69	74	291	795.75
Mardi Lunn	78	69	73	71	291	795.75
Sharon Smith Cranmer	79	70	71	71	291	795.75
Cindy Mah-Lyford	76	74	75	68	293	675
Nicola McCormack	75	77	72	69	293	675
Suzanne Strudwick	73	73	74	73	293	675
Cindy Scholefield	75	75	72	71	293	675

Bloor Homes Eastleigh Classic

Fleming Park, Southhampton, England
Par 34-31—65; 4,231 yards

July 12-15
purse, £66,000

	SCORES				TOTAL	MONEY
Trish Johnson	61	66	58	64	249	£9,765
Corinne Dibnah	61	69	64	60	254	6,615
Debbie Dowling	65	62	66	62	255	4,565
Kitrina Douglas	62	62	65	67	256	3,148
Dale Reid	62	62	67	65	256	3,148
Florence Descampe	66	66	64	62	258	2,127.50
Tina Yarwood	61	67	65	65	258	2,127.50
Dennise Hutton	63	61	69	66	259	1,555.50
Karen Lunn	64	69	61	65	259	1,555.50
Diane Barnard	68	60	68	64	260	1,219.66
Penny Grice-Whittaker	68	62	64	66	260	1,219.66
Alison Sheard	66	68	62	64	260	1,219.66
Laurette Maritz	68	66	63	64	261	1,061
Marion Burton	68	65	61	68	262	978.50

	SCORES				TOTAL	MONEY
Regine Lautens	67	67	61	67	262	978.50
Alicia Dibos	64	64	68	66	262	978.50
Sharon Smith Cranmer	69	65	64	64	262	978.50
Nadene Hall	69	62	67	65	263	912
Maureen Garner	65	66	67	66	264	831
Rae Hast	69	62	67	66	264	831
Cindy Mah-Lyford	70	64	70	60	264	831
Suzanne Strudwick	66	65	66	67	264	831
Debbie Petrizzi	70	61	65	68	264	831
Helen Alfredsson	71	66	65	62	264	831
Connie Baker	66	67	67	65	265	670.60
Sue Nyhus	68	66	67	64	265	670.60
Debbie Clum	67	68	61	69	265	670.60
Tiru Fernando	62	69	69	65	265	670.60
Sofia Gronberg	66	62	70	67	265	670.60
Beverly Huke	64	66	69	66	265	670.60
Jo Rumsey	67	63	69	66	265	670.60
Dana Lofland	64	69	69	63	265	670.60
Mardi Lunn	71	65	67	62	265	670.60
Cindy Scholefield	66	64	70	65	265	670.60

Weetabix Women's British Open

Woburn Golf Club, Duke's Course, Woburn, England
Par 37-36—73; 6,224 yards

August 2-5
purse, £130,000

	SCORES				TOTAL	MONEY
Helen Alfredsson	70	71	74	73	288	£20,000
Jane Hill	77	74	69	68	288	13,200

(Alfredsson defeated Hill on fourth extra hole.)

Laura Davies	75	73	73	70	291	7,353.33
Kitrina Douglas	69	71	75	76	291	7,353.33
Dana Lofland	73	70	75	73	291	7,353.33
Marie Laure de Lorenzi	72	70	72	79	293	4,130
Trish Johnson	71	74	73	75	293	4,130
Myra Blackwelder	73	70	78	72	293	4,130
Diane Barnard	75	70	73	76	294	2,750
Alison Nicholas	75	75	68	76	294	2,750
Pearl Sinn	70	74	77	74	295	2,390
Allison Shapcott	73	74	76	73	296	2,230
Claire Duffy	76	74	74	73	297	2,013.33
Li Wen-Lin	73	69	76	79	297	2,013.33
Michelle Estill	77	70	76	74	297	2,013.33
Tiru Fernando	74	73	74	77	298	1,855
Alicia Dibos	76	73	72	77	298	1,855
Janice Arnold	79	73	74	73	299	1,712.50
Corinne Dibnah	71	81	74	73	299	1,712.50
Beverly Huke	76	76	74	73	299	1,712.50
Suzanne Strudwick	79	71	71	78	299	1,712.50
Jane Connachan	74	75	76	75	300	1,570
Dennise Hutton	77	76	74	73	300	1,570
Terri Luckhurst	74	72	76	78	300	1,570
Tania Abitbol	74	75	75	77	301	1,430
Dale Reid	76	70	77	78	301	1,430
Maoi Sugimoto	76	74	79	72	301	1,430
Tracey Craik	76	76	75	74	301	1,430
Alison Sheard	72	80	77	73	302	1,270
Gillian Stewart	74	73	77	78	302	1,270

	SCORES	TOTAL	MONEY
Xonia Wunsch-Ruiz	72 78 75 77	302	1,270
Susan Shapcott	72 75 76 79	302	1,270
*Sarah Bennett	75 77 78 72	302	

Lufthansa Ladies' German Open

Worthsee Golf Club, Munich, Germany
Par 36-36—72; 6,108 yards

August 9-12
purse, £90,000

	SCORES	TOTAL	MONEY
Ayako Okamoto	68 70 69 67	274	£13,500
Laurette Maritz	70 65 67 72	274	7,717.50
Cindy Rarick	70 68 67 69	274	7,717.50

(Okamoto defeated Maritz on first, Rarick on fourth extra hole.)

	SCORES	TOTAL	MONEY
Trish Johnson	67 67 72 70	276	4,860
Alison Nicholas	71 70 71 66	278	3,483
Helen Alfredsson	71 65 71 71	278	3,483
Laura Davies	70 69 70 70	279	2,700
Diane Barnard	70 69 69 72	280	2,250
Ray Bell	71 72 70 68	281	1,908
Liselotte Neumann	70 69 70 72	281	1,908
Patti Rizzo	73 71 70 69	283	1,656
Dale Reid	72 71 70 71	284	1,464
Corinne Soules	70 70 71 73	284	1,464
Suzanne Strudwick	73 72 69 70	284	1,464
Janice Arnold	74 69 70 72	285	1,296
Jane Connachan	70 76 72 67	285	1,296
Marie Laure de Lorenzi	72 72 71 70	285	1,296
Pearl Sinn	73 73 71 68	285	1,296
Alison Sheard	73 73 72 68	286	1,206
Sonja Van Wyk	70 70 75 72	287	1,170
Federica Dassu	76 68 73 71	288	1,129.50
Marci Lunn	73 73 72 70	288	1,129.50
Tania Abitbol	74 71 70 74	289	967.50
Patricia Gonzalez	70 74 77 68	289	967.50
Judy Greco	72 70 74 73	289	967.50
Dennise Hutton	72 72 73 72	289	967.50
Elisabeth Quelhas	69 75 78 67	289	967.50
Catrin Nilsmark	73 70 72 74	289	967.50
Alicia Dibos	70 70 76 73	289	967.50
Helene Andersson	76 72 71 70	289	967.50
Nadene Hall	74 71 73 71	289	967.50
Terri Luckhurst	75 70 73 71	289	967.50

Haninge Ladies' Open

Haninge Golf Club, Stockholm, Sweden
Par 36-37—73; 6,097 yards

August 23-26
purse, £70,000

	SCORES	TOTAL	MONEY
Dale Reid	74 71 72 74	291	£10,500
Maureen Garner	75 75 70 72	292	5,261.66
Alison Nicholas	72 73 71 76	292	5,261.66
Suzanne Strudwick	73 72 73 74	292	5,261.66
Gillian Stewart	71 74 74 74	293	2,968
Federica Dassu	72 76 72 74	294	2,450

	SCORES				TOTAL	MONEY
Liselotte Neumann	74	70	76	76	296	1,704.50
Anna Oxenstierna	78	71	68	79	296	1,704.50
Tracey Craik	76	76	72	72	296	1,704.50
Allison Shapcott	72	75	73	76	296	1,704.50
Kitrina Douglas	77	75	76	69	297	1,288
*Maria Bertilskold	78	75	71	73	297	
Trish Johnson	75	72	75	76	298	1,165.50
Helen Alfredsson	74	77	73	74	298	1,165.50
Diane Barnard	76	73	71	79	299	1,037.75
Jane Connachan	72	73	78	76	299	1,037.75
Catherine Panton	75	74	74	76	299	1,037.75
Malin Burstrom	70	76	78	75	299	1,037.75
Laura Davies	72	75	73	80	300	952
Corinne Dibnah	72	77	74	77	300	952
Janice Arnold	75	72	76	78	301	889
Alison Munt	74	77	74	76	301	889
Jo Rumsey	78	72	77	74	301	889
*Carin Hjalmarsson	78	71	76	76	301	
Tania Abitbol	75	72	75	81	303	815.50
Sofia Gronberg	75	74	77	77	303	815.50
Anne Jones	72	78	77	76	303	815.50
Florence Descampe	76	73	75	79	303	815.50
*Asa Gottno	78	75	73	77	303	815.50
Tiru Fernando	73	77	73	81	304	710.50
Dennise Hutton	75	76	75	78	304	710.50
Corinne Soules	78	74	75	77	304	710.50
Janet Soulsby	73	72	80	79	304	710.50
Xonia Wunsch-Ruiz	76	72	78	78	304	710.50
Kathryn Imrie	73	78	71	82	304	710.50

Variety Club Celebrity Classic

Calcot Park Golf Club, Reading, England
Par 36-36—72; 5,780 yards

August 30-September 2
purse, £60,000

	SCORES			TOTAL	MONEY
Alison Nicholas	68	68	68	71	275	£7,800
Sofia Gronberg	72	70	65	69	276	5,280
Trish Johnson	69	73	67	68	277	4,080
Kitrina Douglas	67	66	70	75	278	3,240
Catherine Panton	72	70	67	71	280	2,520
Gillian Stewart	70	72	68	71	281	2,040
Jane Connachan	74	66	71	71	282	1,620
Laurette Maritz	70	72	71	70	283	1,320
Diane Barnard	69	78	67	70	284	1,110
Louise Mullard	71	73	70	71	285	990
Janice Arnold	69	69	73	75	286	900
Laura Davies	69	68	74	75	286	900
Dennise Hutton	72	67	75	72	286	900
Regine Lautens	72	69	73	73	287	810
Anne Jones	73	69	75	70	287	810
Kim Lasken	70	72	70	75	287	810
Jane Hill	75	68	73	72	288	744
Dale Reid	71	72	76	69	288	744
Karen Lunn	73	72	74	71	290	696
Diane Pavich	70	73	74	73	290	696
Corinne Dibnah	78	69	72	72	291	624
Maureen Garner	68	74	72	77	291	624

	SCORES	TOTAL	MONEY
Penny Grice-Whittaker	73 73 74 71	291	624
Susan Moon	77 70 73 71	291	624
Pat Smillie	73 72 74 72	291	624
Susan Moorcraft	74 74 74 70	292	552
Nadene Hall	72 73 72 75	292	552
Sharon Smith Cranmer	72 76 73 71	292	552
Julie Brown	74 75 72 72	293	498
Debbie Petrizzi	74 73 72 74	293	498
Li Wen-Lin	71 79 68 75	293	498

TEC Players Championship

Patshull Park Golf Club, Wolverhampton, England
Par 37-36—73; 5,941 yards

September 6-9
purse, £80,000

	SCORES	TOTAL	MONEY
Anne Jones	73 66 69 73	281	£12,000
Laurette Maritz	72 70 70 71	283	8,120
Sofia Gronberg	74 69 72 70	285	4,960
Helen Alfredsson	75 70 68 72	285	4,960
Trish Johnson	71 71 72 72	286	3,392
Tania Abitbol	70 80 69 70	289	2,118.40
Diane Barnard	78 71 70 70	289	2,118.40
Jane Connachan	76 74 70 69	289	2,118.40
Corinne Soules	68 75 72 74	289	2,118.40
Catrin Nilsmark	72 74 71 72	289	2,118.40
Marie Laure de Lorenzi	74 74 70 72	290	1,472
Dennise Hutton	71 75 74 71	291	1,301.33
Alison Nicholas	68 74 77 72	291	1,301.33
Suzanne Strudwick	76 71 73 71	291	1,301.33
Alison Munt	76 70 73 73	292	1,152
Sabine Etchevers	74 72 74 72	292	1,152
Nadene Hall	74 70 75 73	292	1,152
Pearl Sinn	73 73 71 75	292	1,152
Federica Dassu	74 76 71 72	293	1,017.60
Laura Davies	73 74 73 73	293	1,017.60
Tracy Hammond	68 75 75 75	293	1,017.60
Alicia Dibos	74 77 71 71	293	1,017.60
Cindy Scholefield	70 77 74 72	293	1,017.60
Debbie Dowling	76 77 71 70	294	932
Anna Oxenstierna	70 73 72 79	294	932
Peggy Conley	75 73 71 76	295	848
Kitrina Douglas	76 71 79 69	295	848
Diane Pavich	72 78 71 74	295	848
Mardi Lunn	78 75 71 71	295	848
Li Wen-Lin	76 74 74 71	295	848

Expedier Ladies European Open

Kingswood Golf Club, Surrey, England
Par 36-36—72; 5,919 yards

September 13-16
purse, £75,000

	SCORES	TOTAL	MONEY
Trish Johnson	71 67 69 69	276	£11,250
Michelle Estill	67 70 68 73	278	6,430
Pearl Sinn	70 68 72 68	278	6,430

	SCORES			TOTAL	MONEY
Alison Nicholas	69	72 66	74	281	4,050
Laura Davies	69	70 73	70	282	2,902.50
Stefania Croce	73	66 72	71	282	2,902.50
Beverly Huke	75	69 73	67	284	1,935
Alison Sheard	73	72 70	69	284	1,935
Nadene Hall	74	70 72	68	284	1,935
Janice Arnold	76	68 72	69	285	1,390
Debbie Dowling	68	72 71	74	285	1,390
Penny Grice-Whittaker	69	71 73	72	285	1,390
Janet Soulsby	73	71 71	71	286	1,184.50
Allison Shapcott	71	73 75	67	286	1,184.50
Anne Jones	71	69 75	72	287	1,125
Regine Lautens	71	73 72	72	288	1,050
Gillian Stewart	73	73 75	67	288	1,050
Alicia Dibos	72	70 74	72	288	1,050
Helen Alfredsson	71	71 74	72	288	1,050
Kitrina Douglas	71	74 70	74	289	952
Dale Reid	73	70 74	72	289	952
Tina Yarwood	72	71 72	74	289	952
Diane Barnard	71	73 74	72	290	837
Anna Oxenstierna	74	75 73	68	290	837
Florence Descampe	71	73 74	72	290	837
Lynne Chesterton	73	75 75	67	290	837
Tracey Craik	70	72 72	76	290	837
Maria Navarro Corbachio	72	67 79	72	290	837
Nicola Way	74	74 72	70	290	837
*Helen Wadsworth	74	69 74	73	290	

Trophee International Coconut Skol

Golf de Fourqueux, Paris, France
Par 37-34—71; 5,739 yards

September 20-23
purse, £70,000

	SCORES			TOTAL	MONEY
Corinne Dibnah	71	75 72	66	284	£10,500
Trish Johnson	71	73 70	71	285	6,002.50
Helen Alfredsson	70	73 71	71	285	6,002.50
Alison Nicholas	72	73 69	74	288	3,780
Marie Laure de Lorenzi	72	75 72	71	290	2,709
Kitrina Douglas	74	70 74	72	290	2,709
Anne Jones	72	81 66	73	292	2,100
Corinne Soules	71	71 75	76	293	1,572.66
Florence Descampe	72	75 70	76	293	1,572.66
Pearl Sinn	72	73 75	73	293	1,572.66
Regine Lautens	75	77 71	71	294	1,288
Federica Dassu	79	72 74	71	296	1,165.50
Claire Duffy	72	71 75	78	296	1,165.50
Karine Espinasse	75	78 74	70	297	1,037.75
Maureen Garner	72	76 74	75	297	1,037.75
Dennise Hutton	70	76 73	78	297	1,037.75
Caryn Louw	75	73 72	77	297	1,037.75
Debbie Dowling	77	73 74	74	298	914.20
Dale Reid	78	70 77	73	298	914.20
Janet Soulsby	74	74 73	77	298	914.20
Leigh Mills	82	73 74	69	298	914.20
Li Wen-Lin	74	73 77	74	298	914.20
Sue Nyhus	74	76 75	74	299	836.50
Louise Mullard	74	74 75	76	299	836.50

	SCORES				TOTAL	MONEY
Alicia Dibos	72	77	75	76	300	805
Jane Connachan	78	71	75	77	301	763
Stefania Croce	77	75	78	71	301	763
Kathryn Imrie	78	76	73	74	301	763
Debbie Clum	76	76	76	74	302	689.50
Laurette Maritz-Atkins	77	77	72	76	302	689.50
Sabine Etchevers	73	76	77	76	302	689.50
Tracey Craik	76	76	75	75	302	689.50

Italian Ladies Open

Gardagolf Golf Club, Gardagolf, Italy
Par 36-36—72; 6,061 yards

October 4-7
purse, £90,000

	SCORES				TOTAL	MONEY
Florence Descampe	72	74	66	70	282	£13,500
Helen Alfredsson	67	75	72	71	285	9,135
Karine Espinasse	72	73	72	70	287	6,300
Dale Reid	69	73	74	72	288	4,860
Marie Laure de Lorenzi	72	73	71	73	289	3,816
Federica Dassu	72	75	72	71	290	3,150
Claire Duffy	73	75	71	72	291	2,191.50
Laurette Maritz-Atkins	75	75	72	69	291	2,191.50
Alison Nicholas	69	74	71	77	291	2,191.50
Stefania Croce	73	74	74	70	291	2,191.50
Tania Abitbol	75	73	76	69	293	1,602
Caryn Louw	74	74	71	74	293	1,602
Sofia Gronberg	70	73	74	77	294	1,449
Diane Barnard	75	76	74	70	295	1,395
Catrin Nilsmark	76	76	72	72	296	1,350
Kitrina Douglas	74	79	72	72	297	1,314
Jane Connachan	75	75	71	77	298	1,207.80
Jo Rumsey	72	75	75	76	298	1,207.80
Suzanne Strudwick	75	76	75	72	298	1,207.80
Xonia Wunsch-Ruiz	74	70	77	77	298	1,207.80
Helen Andersson	78	75	75	70	298	1,207.80
Debbie Dowling	72	76	75	76	299	1,008
Maureen Garner	75	77	75	72	299	1,008
Anna Oxenstierna	75	76	75	73	299	1,008
Corinne Soules	77	73	78	71	299	1,008
Gillian Stewart	73	76	75	75	299	1,008
Debbie Petrizzi	74	74	80	71	299	1,008
Elisabeth Quelhas	74	72	75	78	299	1,008
Maria Navarro Corbachio	76	75	74	74	299	1,008
Kathryn Imrie	76	79	73	71	299	1,008

Woolmark Matchplay Championship

Club de Campo, Madrid, Spain
Par 36-37—73; 5,865 yards

October 18-21
purse, £80,000

SECOND ROUND

Trish Johnson defeated Karine Espinasse, 5 and 4.
Anne Jones defeated Vanessa Marvin, 2 and 1.
Gillian Stewart defeated Janice Arnold, 5 and 3.

Kitrina Douglas defeated Nadene Hall, 1 up, 19 holes.
Corinne Dibnah defeated Catherine Panton, 5 and 4.
Tania Abitbol defeated Susan Moon, 4 and 2.
Florence Descampe defeated Diane Pavich, 4 and 3.
Helen Alfredsson defeated Beverley New, 3 and 2.
Laurette Maritz-Atkins defeated Sonja Van Wyk, 4 and 2.
Xonia Wunsch-Ruiz defeated Jane Hill, 5 and 4.
Dennise Hutton defeated Corinne Soules, 2 and 1.
Susan Moorcraft defeated Maxine Burton, 1 up.
Dale Reid defeated Catrin Nilsmark, 7 and 6.
Suzanne Strudwick defeated Allison Shapcott, 6 and 4.
Laura Davies defeated Anna Oxenstierna, 4 and 3.
Alison Nicholas defeated Caryn Louw, 5 and 3.

THIRD ROUND

Jones defeated Johnson, 1 up, 19 holes.
Douglas defeated Stewart, 1 up.
Abitbol defeated Dibnah, 5 and 4.
Descampe defeated Alfredsson, 5 and 4.
Wunsch-Ruiz defeated Maritz-Atkins, 1 up, 19 holes.
Moorcraft defeated Hutton, 5 and 4.
Reid defeated Strudwick, 6 and 4.
Nicholas defeated Davies, 1 up.

QUARTER-FINALS

Jones defeated Douglas, 4 and 2.
Descampe defeated Abitbol, 2 and 1.
Wunsch-Ruiz defeated Moorcraft, 4 and 2.
Reid defeated Nicholas, 5 and 4.

SEMI-FINALS

Descampe defeated Jones, 5 and 4.
Reid defeated Wunsch-Ruiz, 8 and 6.

FINALS

Descampe defeated Reid, 2 and 1.
(Descampe received £12,000.)

AGF Biarritz Ladies Open

Golf de Biarritz, Biarritz, France
Par 35-34—69; 5,505 yards

October 25-28
purse, £80,000

	SCORES		TOTAL	MONEY
Laura Davies	63	73	136	£12,000
Alison Nicholas	71	66	137	8,120
Kelly Leadbetter	68	70	138	4,960
Laurette Maritz-Atkins	69	69	138	4,960
Marie Laure de Lorenzi	69	70	139	2,648
Trish Johnson	69	70	139	2,648
Beverley New	69	70	139	2,648
Helen Alfredsson	66	73	139	2,648
Janice Arnold	69	71	140	1,696
Florence Descampe	71	69	140	1,696
Maureen Garner	73	68	141	1,344

594 / THE WOMEN'S TOURS

	SCORES		TOTAL	MONEY
Corinne Soules	72	69	141	1,344
Stefania Croce	70	71	141	1,344
Kathryn Imrie	69	72	141	1,344
Allison Shapcott	72	70	142	1,200
Barbara Helbig	71	72	143	1,136
Alison Munt	72	71	143	1,136
Nadene Hall	71	72	143	1,136
Sofia Gronberg	73	71	144	1,005.33
Dale Reid	70	74	144	1,005.33
Gillian Stewart	72	72	144	1,005.33
Xonia Wunsch-Ruiz	72	72	144	1,005.33
Frances Martin	71	73	144	1,005.33
Julie Forbes	73	71	144	1,005.33
Karine Espinasse	69	76	145	908
Alicia Dibos	69	76	145	908
Corinne Dibnah	71	75	146	800
Jane Hill	71	75	146	800
Alison Sheard	75	71	146	800
Janet Soulsby	70	76	146	800
Tracey Craik	73	73	146	800
Kim Lasken	70	76	146	800
Jean Bartholomew	73	73	146	800

Benson & Hedges Mixed Team Trophy

El Bosque Golf and Country Club, Valencia, Spain
Par 36-36—72; Men - 6,898 yards, Women - 6,118 yards

November 1-4
purse, £182,870

	SCORES				TOTAL	MONEY (Team)
Jose Maria Canizares/Tania Abitbol	66	67	66	68	267	£30,500
Mark Mouland/Alison Nicholas	65	66	69	69	269	22,500
Brian Barnes/Laura Davies	67	67	71	66	271	17,250
Gordon J. Brand/Jane Hill	68	67	66	71	272	12,020
Ove Sellberg/Florence Descampe	69	64	65	74	272	12,020
Anders Forsbrand/Corinne Soules	66	71	67	69	273	9,000
Manuel Pinero/Marta Figueras-Dotti	65	72	67	70	274	7,720
Juan Quiros Segura/Karen Lunn	71	71	64	71	277	6,270
Tony Charnley/Dale Reid	66	70	69	72	277	6,270
John Hawksworth/Anna Oxenstierna	68	72	66	72	278	5,140
David J. Russell/Maureen Garner	68	68	71	72	279	4,340
John Morgan/Anne Jones	73	67	67	72	279	4,340
Keith Waters/Maria Navarro Corbachio	68	70	72	70	280	3,880
Bryan Norton/Pearl Sinn	70	73	69	69	281	3,386.66
Derrick Cooper/Laurette Maritz-Atkins	72	69	70	70	281	3,386.66
Torsten Giedeon/Barbara Helbig	71	67	69	74	281	3,386.66
Manuel Moreno/Karine Espinasse	67	72	71	73	283	2,920
Magnus Persson/Helen Alfredsson	72	76	69	67	284	2,600
Giuseppe Cali/Stefania Croce	69	73	73	69	284	2,600
Vicente Fernandez/Patricia Gonzalez	72	63	73	72	285	2,305
Roger Chapman/Diane Barnard	71	69	72	73	285	2,305
Miguel Angel Jimenez/ Xonia Wunsch-Ruiz	73	71	66	76	286	2,140
Andre Bossert/Evelyn Orley	69	71	72	75	287	2,040
Andrew Sherborne/Kitrina Douglas	73	72	74	69	288	1,890
Peter Smith/Gillian Stewart	71	74	72	71	288	1,890
Antonio Garrido/Corinne Dibnah	71	71	74	73	289	1,740
Mike Miller/Jane Connachan	75	71	74	70	290	1,600
Jeff Pinsent/Suzanne Strudwick	73	72	74	71	290	1,600

	SCORES				TOTAL	MONEY
Steen Tinning/Sofia Gronberg	70	75	75	71	291	1,500
James Lebbie/Regine Lautens	71	73	73	75	292	1,460
Ross McFarlane/Federica Dassu	78	72	71	72	293	1,440
Carl Mason/Trish Johnson	71	68	WD			1,430

Longines Classic

Golf Esterel, Nice, France
Par 36-35—71, 6,009 yards

November 8-11
purse, £100,000

	SCORES				TOTAL	MONEY
Trish Johnson	72	71	75	68	286	£15,000
Gillian Stewart	71	79	69	73	292	10,150
Karen Lunn	80	71	72	70	293	7,000
Helen Hopkins	74	76	73	71	294	4,820
Helen Alfredsson	72	77	71	74	294	4,820
Kitrina Douglas	77	72	75	71	295	3,500
Federica Dassu	67	76	78	77	298	2,435
Laurette Maritz-Atkins	75	79	69	75	298	2,435
Alison Nicholas	74	75	73	76	298	2,435
Dale Reid	76	73	77	72	298	2,435
Joanne Furby	77	78	73	71	299	1,840
Rae Hast	76	76	74	74	300	1,665
Pearl Sinn	77	72	76	75	300	1,665
Sofia Gronberg	75	75	72	80	302	1,462
Suzanne Strudwick	75	74	78	75	302	1,462
Anne Jones	75	81	70	76	302	1,462
Alicia Dibos	74	72	79	77	302	1,462
Maria Navarro Corbachio	78	75	77	72	302	1,462
Jane Connachan	71	74	77	81	303	1,303.33
Laura Davies	72	78	71	82	303	1,303.33
Debbie Dowling	76	80	76	71	303	1,303.33
Diane Barnard	72	78	74	80	304	1,240
Patricia Gonzalez	80	69	78	78	305	1,180
Regine Lautens	80	76	75	74	305	1,180
Li Wen-Lin	79	77	72	77	305	1,180
Julie Forbes	74	78	78	76	306	1,120
Janice Arnold	78	79	75	75	307	1,030
Peggy Conley	78	74	79	76	307	1,030
Karine Espinasse	75	76	80	76	307	1,030
Dennise Hutton	77	75	79	76	307	1,030
Stefania Croce	78	75	76	78	307	1,030